# Dictionary
# of
# Midwestern
# Literature

# Dictionary of Midwestern Literature

## Volume One: The Authors

Philip A. Greasley, GENERAL EDITOR

*Indiana*
*University*
*Press*

BLOOMINGTON AND INDIANAPOLIS

This book is a publication of
*Indiana University Press*
601 North Morton Street
Bloomington, Indiana 47404–3797 USA

http://www.indiana.edu/~iupress

*Telephone orders* 800–842–6796
*Fax orders* 812–855–7931
*Orders by e-mail* iuporder@indiana.edu

MANUFACTURED IN THE UNITED STATES OF AMERICA

**Library of Congress Cataloging-in-Publication Data**

Dictionary of Midwestern literature / Philip A.
Greasley, general editor.
  p.  cm.
  Entries created by the members of the Society
for the Study of Midwestern Literature.
  Includes bibliographical references and index.
  Contents: v. 1. The authors
  ISBN 0-253-33609-0 (alk. paper)
  1. American literature—Middle West—
Dictionaries. 2. American literature—
Middle West—Bio-bibliography—Dictionaries.
3. Authors, American—Middle West—
Biography—Dictionaries. 4. Middle West—
In literature—Dictionaries. I. Greasley, Philip A.
II. Society for the Study of Midwestern
Literature (U.S.)

PS273 .D53 2001
810.9'977'03—dc21    00-040753

1 2 3 4 5 06 05 04 03 02 01

# Contents

# The Editorial Board

The *Dictionary of Midwestern Literature* Editorial Board consists of the following individuals:

GENERAL EDITOR:

PHILIP A. GREASLEY, Associate Professor of English and Dean, University Extension, University of Kentucky

SENIOR EDITORS:

DAVID D. ANDERSON, University Distinguished Professor Emeritus, Department of American Thought and Language, Michigan State University

PATRICIA A. ANDERSON, Retired Librarian, Lansing Public Schools

MARILYN J. ATLAS, Associate Professor of English, Ohio University

MARY JEAN DeMARR, Professor Emerita, English and Women's Studies, Indiana State University

ROBERT DUNNE, Associate Professor of English, Central Connecticut State University

MARY JOAN MILLER, Retired Reference Librarian, Springfield, Ohio

PAUL W. MILLER, Professor Emeritus, English, Wittenberg University

MARCIA NOE, Professor of English, The University of Tennessee at Chattanooga

MARY DeJONG OBUCHOWSKI, Professor of English, Central Michigan University

DAVID PICHASKE, Professor of English, Southwest State University

THOMAS R. PRIBEK, Associate Professor of English, University of Wisconsin–La Crosse

ARTHUR W. SHUMAKER, Professor Emeritus, English, DePauw University

GUY SZUBERLA, Professor of English, University of Toledo

ASSISTANT EDITORS:

TRACEY A. HOLMES, University of Kentucky

STEVEN F. HOPKINS, University of Kentucky

ROBIN L. KIDD, University of Kentucky

# Acknowledgments

Many individual contributions, each unique and important, underlie this work. Among the debts incurred in producing this volume were these to:

The Society for the Study of Midwestern Literature and its members, who gave their ideas, effort, and time to make this book a reality;

Henry L. Kenney, a University of Kentucky student who provided assistance in the final stages of this project;

Marsha O. Greasley, who sought pictures for the volume and provided innumerable services to the editorial board;

Matthew J. Darling and Scott W. Gordon, University of Kentucky students who researched the format for the *Dictionary of Midwestern Literature;*

Jane S. Bakerman, who helped give direction to the project at its inception;

Robin L. Kidd, Tracey A. Holmes, and Steven F. Hopkins, University of Kentucky students whose work as assistant editors was invaluable and whose intelligence, good humor, and consummate organization kept the *DML* moving forward;

LaVerne C. Ballard, staff assistant extraordinaire, for organizing, typing, proofreading, and fostering Midwestern literature in more ways than any Texas woman should ever be called upon to do;

David Durant and the University of Kentucky English department, whose interest and encouragement for this project were consistent;

Elisabeth Zinser, Jack C. Blanton, James A. Boling, Louis J. Swift, James P. Chapman, and David S. Watt, who modeled the University of Kentucky Lexington Campus's commitment to scholarly research at the undergraduate and graduate level and who provided support and encouragement to the *Dictionary of Midwestern Literature;*

Roger J. Jiang Bresnahan, secretary-treasurer of the Society for the Study of Midwestern Literature and professor, Department of American Thought and Language, Michigan State University, whose assistance, ideas, and encouragement were never ending; though not officially a member of the editorial board, Roger participated as fully and as selflessly as any, always merging roles as scholar, corporate officer to the society, and good friend;

David D. Anderson, the "creator" of Midwestern literature, founder and guiding father of the Society for the Study of Midwestern Literature, exemplar of the best in unselfish scholarship, mentor, friend, and inspiration; and

Marsha, Mark, and Karen Greasley, who forbore their many legitimate claims on husband and father through eight long years as this labor of love slowly came to fruition.

Philip A. Greasley, General Editor
University of Kentucky

## ACKNOWLEDGMENTS FOR PUBLIC DOMAIN AUTHOR PHOTOS

Carleton, Will. *Rhymes of Our Planet.* New York: Harper and Brothers, 1895.

Field, Eugene. *Second Book of Tales.* New York: Scribner, 1896.

Kittredge, Herman E. *Ingersoll: A Biographical Appreciation.* New York: Dresden Publishing Co., 1911.

Kirkland, Joseph. *The Captain of Company K.* Chicago: Donohue, Henneberry and Co., 1891.

Moody, William Vaughn. *The Poems and Plays of William Vaughn Moody,* vol. 1. Boston: Houghton Mifflin Company, 1912.

Phillips, David Graham. *Susan Lenox: Her Fall and Rise,* vol. 1. New York: D. Appleton and Co., 1917.

Riley, James Whitcomb. *Afterwhiles.* Indianapolis: Bobbs-Merrill, 1898.

Wilcox, Ella Wheeler. *The Worlds and I.* New York: George H. Doran Co., 1918.

# Dictionary
## of
# Midwestern
# Literature

# Introduction

## Purpose

Volume 1, *The Authors,* is the first of a projected series of the *Dictionary of Midwestern Literature.* This volume surveys the lives and writings of approximately four hundred Midwestern authors as well as some of the most important criticism of their writings. In aggregate, volume 1 presents individual lives and literary orientations while simultaneously reflecting a much broader long-term sense of the Midwestern experience for its many, diverse peoples.

## Background

The Society for the Study of Midwestern Literature, a national scholarly society with offices at Michigan State University and more than five hundred members across the United States and abroad, has undertaken this project. The society is dedicated to illuminating and fostering the literature of America's Midwest—that of the states of Michigan, Ohio, Indiana, Illinois, Wisconsin, Minnesota, Iowa, Missouri, Kansas, Nebraska, and North and South Dakota.

Members of the Society for the Study of Midwestern Literature conceived this project as a means of giving focus and prominence to Midwestern literature. The society considered the concept, developed a proposal, and orga-

nized an editorial board. This board then began the lengthy tasks of identifying authors for inclusion, designing the format, and assigning, writing, and reviewing entries. Now, eight years later, over one hundred members have provided author entries. The *Dictionary of Midwestern Literature* would not have been possible were it not for the auspices of the Society for the Study of Midwestern Literature and the selfless participation of its members.

## Philosophy

Underpinning this work is the belief that the literature of any region simultaneously captures the experience and influences the worldview of its people; literature reflects as well as shapes the evolving sense of individual and collective identity, meaning, and values. Individual worldview and collective experience evolve out of multiple long-term relationships between the individual, family, immediate and larger communities, and natural and man-made environments. These interactions occur in all areas of human experience, including the social, economic, aesthetic, intellectual, political, and religious realms. They arise from work and play, worship, and civic involvement. They develop everywhere, on isolated farmsteads and in big-city steel mills, factories, corporate offices, stores, apartment houses, and churches. At times these experiences are positive, strengthening and reinforcing connections between the individual, the community, and the geographic locale. At other times they are negative, inducing alienation and hostility. Often, the nature of these interactions is mixed, producing complex and even conflicting responses. Whatever their character, experiences rise over time to philosophy, to a view of self, place, society, life, and God.

## What Is the Midwest?

All or parts of twelve states comprise the Midwest. They include the states emerging from the old Northwest Territory—Ohio, Michigan, Indiana, Illinois, Wisconsin, and Minnesota—as well as the Trans-Mississippi River states of the Louisiana Purchase—Iowa, Missouri, Kansas, Nebraska, and North and South Dakota. Midwestern landforms and settlement patterns are varied, giving rise to diverse economic opportunities, career types, and lifestyles. Huge cities such as Chicago and Detroit are present, as are large expanses of sparsely populated land given over to agriculture or livestock pasturing. Climatic and rainfall patterns also vary markedly, from the lush green grasslands and forests of the region's more easterly states to the dry prairies farther west. Shifting land use and decreasing population density follow annual climatic and rainfall patterns. The 100th Meridian bisects the Midwest's westernmost states and marks the region's western terminus; this meridian heralds the advent of a treeless arid plain marked by sparse rainfall, vegetation, and population and, with it, the American West.

Midwestern people and culture are equally diverse. Beyond the early over-mountain and up-river routes used by the earliest settlers, two major East-West migration routes, one through Ellis Island and New York, the other via Canada, opened the Midwest to people of many nations. Even after early European settlement was complete, waves of subsequent immigration and intraregional migration began and still continue, bringing new populations to the Midwest, changing ethnic and racial balances, and introducing new social customs and cultural orientations. With the twentieth century and the Great Depression, south to north population shifts developed, providing Midwestern homes and jobs for African Americans and Appalachian whites. Even more recently the Midwest has witnessed the influx of significant Southeast Asian and Latino populations.

But who are Midwesterners and what are their values? Negative characterizations of the Midwest and its people have been frequent. The Midwest has been viewed as a cultural backwater with stolid, excessively conservative, unsophisticated people intellectually and culturally dwarfed early on by the dominant East or left behind by the more recent emergence of the New South, the Southwest, or the ultimate multicultural, polyglot, change-oriented American subculture, that of California.

The Midwest has also received its share of accolades. In his 1989 study *The Middle West: Its Meaning in American Culture*, cultural geographer James R. Shortridge indicates that in the early twentieth century, Midwesterners were commonly perceived as sturdy, dependable yeoman farmers—strong, independent, and confident in their ability, realistic in nature, and possessed of the best in youthful vigor along with the insight, experience, and dependability of maturity (8). This view considered Midwesterners neither brashly impulsive nor excessively conservative, neither in their cultural dotage nor foolishly impulsive. They were seen as solid citizens who could be counted on. And positive portrayal of the Midwest has become even more dominant in recent decades. Shortridge cites a strong contemporary view of the Midwest as the "keeper of the nation's values" (143). Implicit in this view is the sense that the Midwest has remained true to America's core values—honesty, hard work, openness, and belief in the spirituality of life—values that people across America consider increasingly central and important to America's meaning and its prospects for the future. Shortridge describes "an increased realization that the positive values that grow out of a rootedness in place are needed to give meaning to life and that the Middle West provides the nation with a needed touchstone for such values" (143). Implicit in this conception is a sense of the Midwest's balancing of the claims of past and present, thought and action. A future orientation coexists with reverence for the past; aspiration to the ideal is complemented by pragmatism born of experience. Recognition of limits coexists with commitment to dreams and determination to mold a positive, value-based future.

Contemporary conceptions of the Midwest almost certainly include a component of romantic escapism, of nostalgic longing for an imagined idyllic past, but they also make clear Americans' strong sense that contemporary life has lost something valuable and that return to values associated with the Midwest can guide America to a positive, human-centered future. Literary theory growing out of colonial domination also provides a basis for understanding the Midwest, its peoples, and its values. This theory recognizes societal perceptions of culturally central or "elite" areas and people as well as of culturally peripheral, or "provincial," people and places. For much of America's existence, the Midwest and its people have been viewed and characterized primarily from the outside as being distant, peripheral, and unattuned to sophisticated life and culture. These outsiders from areas traditionally considered elite have regularly seen the Midwest as a "hinterland," an unsophisticated, provincial locale remote from America's intellectual capital, centers of government, and culture. Even sympathetic external portrayals over the Midwest's first hundred years, such as HAMLIN GARLAND's *Main-Travelled Roads* (1891), have regularly represented Midwesterners as heroic victims caught in lives of unavailing suffering, deficient in beauty, culture, recognition, and remuneration.

From the "inside," however, through an extended time period Midwesterners have consistently viewed their lives with strong and rising pride and satisfaction. Early on, they perceived themselves as advancing American civilization through backbreaking labor, taming and transforming the wilderness of the Northwest Territory and beyond into productive landholdings while providing the bulwark of American democracy. The Midwest was proud of sending the largest number of soldiers to the Northern Civil War effort, of successfully preserving the Union, and of extending American democracy. In that same spirit, Midwesterners from the time of the Civil War forward have accorded the central position in their pantheon of democratic American heroes to President ABRAHAM LINCOLN, Kentuckian turned Illinoisan, the leader of the Republic, and a martyr to democracy and social justice.

The spread of railroads during and after the Civil War further opened America's interior for settlement, allowing unprecedented access to the heartland's agricultural produce, industrial products, and natural resources. Chicago was deservedly America's "second city" in the late 1800s. Chicago's population was second only to New York City's, and Chicagoans were fiercely proud of their success in overcoming the ravages of the 1871 Chicago fire. This burgeoning inland metropolis was determined to achieve agricultural, industrial, mercantile, and cultural leadership. Chicago's location at the focal point of American railroad routes, the aggregating point for Midwestern agricultural and industrial products, and the processing and transshipment center for Southwestern cattle provided a strong economic basis for rising Midwestern pride. The city's motto, "I will," reflected its determination to overcome all obstacles.

In the 1880s the world's first skyscrapers rose along Lake Michigan's shores. They provided new perspectives on wealth and progress in the American interior and employed technological advances that made huge cities possible. The technology behind these skyscrapers and the communication and transportation networks supporting them were the sine qua non of modern technological society and supported unprecedented agricultural, industrial, and mercantile empires. Midwestern artisans and day laborers who built these world-changing monuments identified as fully and unreservedly with them as did the architects who designed them and the corporate leaders whose purposes these skyscrapers were created to serve.

And as America transformed itself from an inward-looking agricultural nation to an outward-looking international industrial power, Midwestern iron and copper, factories, and advances in technology and production systems, epitomized by Henry Ford's assembly line, propelled America forward. World's fairs held in the Midwest—such as Chicago's 1893 Columbian Exposition, St. Louis's 1904 Louisiana Purchase Exposition, and Chicago's 1933 Century of Progress Exposition—reflected the acknowledged political and economic power of America's rich interior. These expressions of Midwestern pride, strength, and cultural determination appeared at the very time when antiquated Eastern factories and industries were increasingly declining into uncompetitiveness.

During and after the first and second world wars, the Midwest fed America and the world. The output of the world's best soil and most productive agriculture were mighty weapons, and the Midwest's auto and steel industries transformed themselves to create the arsenal of democracy, producing planes, tanks, vehicles, and munitions that were the keys to victory.

With rising self-confidence came increasing distaste in the Midwest for elitist concepts of personal and regional superiority not based on individual effort and achievement. The assertion of the strength, ability, and nobility of common people was a natural complement of Midwestern egalitarianism, born of its frontier heritage.

## *What Is Midwestern Literature?*

Midwestern geography, history, economy, and philosophy provide significant experiential touchstones influencing Midwestern thought and literature. Diversity in the human and natural environments is reflected in Midwestern lives and writings that are diverse, dynamic, and often characterized by values held in common with groups of people associated with other regions. Let us consider each of these points.

First, Midwestern thought and literature are not monolithic. Individual perceptions and literary styles vary markedly in the Midwest as elsewhere. As a philosophical starting point, the region encompasses widely divergent Native American orientations. Cultural separatist views of indigenous leaders such as BLACK ELK or BLACK HAWK are offset by the mediated orientations such as those of ANDREW BLACKBIRD, who, a Native American himself, presents indigenous culture from a position between the two cultures. At the other end of the spectrum, contemporary writers, such as LOUISE ERDRICH, brought up more fully immersed in Caucasian culture, seek to reclaim earlier Native American culture and values.

Midwestern African American thought and expression are equally diverse in their celebrations of black culture, in the philosophical positions they maintain, and in their degree of involvement with or rejection of white culture. The lives and writings of PAUL LAURENCE DUNBAR, GWENDOLYN BROOKS, MALCOLM X, LORRAINE HANSBERRY, VIRGINIA HAMILTON, TONI MORRISON, and RITA DOVE exemplify this rich multiplicity of African American attitudes and approaches toward the African American community and more broadly toward all elements of American society. These views are expressed in vibrant and divergent literary forms and styles.

Midwestern thought is broad and inclusive, bridging divisions of race, ethnicity, and gender. Its literary figures include staunch intellectual conservatives such as RUSSELL KIRK and socialist thinkers such as JACK CONROY and ROBERT INGERSOLL as well as more aggressive rebels including NELSON ALGREN and WILLIAM S. BURROUGHS. Similarly, the Midwest is home to the social-activist pragmatism of JANE ADDAMS and SOJOURNER TRUTH as well as the intellectual populism of CARL SANDBURG and STUDS TERKEL. The region reflects the values of Mid-America's most representative figure—Abraham Lincoln. Midwestern thought encompasses the two antagonists of the Scopes "Monkey Trial," WILLIAM JENNINGS BRYAN and CLARENCE DARROW. Many, like Carl Sandburg, find home, identity, and meaning in the rich cultural diversity of the Midwest while others like SINCLAIR LEWIS rebel against its perceived narrowness and cultural desiccation. T. S. ELIOT attempts to transcend his Midwestern upbringing and immerse himself in European antecedents and culture while a broad range of writers, including OLE RØLVAAG, BHARATI MUKHERJEE, and BIENVENIDO SANTOS, reverse this movement, retaining diverse international roots while immersing themselves in Midwestern life and thought.

The Midwest also encompasses the diametrically opposed views of writers like Hamlin Garland, whose life orientations center on urban culture, and ecological writers like JOHN MUIR and ALDO LEOPOLD. Garland reflects late-nineteenth-century views that life on the frontier and in rural areas is inhumanly demanding while ecowriters of that period and later consider wilderness a palliative to urban-based social ills and human depredation of the land. Between these two camps stands WILLA CATHER, the cultured Midwestern pioneer able to see both sides.

Midwestern thought and literature are also highly dynamic. Though sometimes portrayed as frozen in the past, no region or people can remain static or isolated. Midwestern social and economic lives and social orientations are inextricably tied to world ideas and markets. Midwestern thought is equally attuned to world experience and to the expression of universal human values and societal truths.

The earliest Midwestern writings in English tend to merge literature and life in accounts of exploration and settlement. As time passes, these narratives increasingly give way to belles lettres. The earliest imaginative writings typically transport into Midwestern and American settings literary traditions associated with European homelands. As such, in the Midwest, as in the American East earlier, early Midwestern writers regularly adopt Neoclassic or Romantic worldview, themes, techniques, and commonplaces. Many tell stories of idealized life far away and long ago. Characters are polarized into extreme heroes and villains, and outcomes have little to do with Midwestern frontier and early settlement life. These stories could have just as easily been written anywhere. While not directly expressing Midwestern locales or experience, these early writings do fulfill one important local function: they provide idealized, romanticized relief from all-too-real experiences of rugged early Midwestern farm or small-town life.

Because of the Midwest's great east-to-west breadth and the east-to-west migration pattern, early-settled eastern portions of the Midwest advance to later economic and social patterns while those farther west still remain frontier. The writings of MARK TWAIN, Willa Cather, Hamlin Garland, and the mother and daughter "Little House" series collaboration between LAURA INGALLS WILDER and ROSE WILDER LANE exemplify Mid-America's social and literary transformation in mid course.

In time, Midwestern literature comes to reflect life in Mid-American small towns, as exemplified by SHERWOOD ANDERSON, VACHEL LINDSAY, and SINCLAIR LEWIS. Later still, Midwestern cities become the norm, as witnessed by writers like THEODORE DREISER, UPTON SINCLAIR, JAMES T. FARRELL, and many others.

Midwestern literature embodies all aspects of the movement from dominant mid-nineteenth-century romanticism to highly developed realistic prose fiction and poetry. It is distinguished in its journalism, fiction, poetry, and drama.

## Journalism

Growing literacy and population expansion in the mid-1800s produced an important venue for aspiring Midwestern writers. Small-town and big-city newspapers provided incipient Midwestern writers with income, training, and audiences. Newspapers, with their obligatory centering on the local, freed journalists to write about familiar people and places and permitted inclusion of regional dialects. As such, writers including SAMUEL LANGHORNE CLEMENS, WILLIAM DEAN HOWELLS, GEORGE ADE, Willa Cather, Sherwood Anderson, ERNEST HEMINGWAY, and many others benefited from journalistic internships. For some, journalism was an end in itself; for others, local events were primarily important in providing Midwestern authors convenient, widely known touchstones for considering timeless, universal issues.

## Fiction

Many Midwestern writers have consistently been important innovators in the short story and novel. Mark Twain led the way with his experiments in subject, character, dialect, thematic use of humor, and realism. William Dean Howells provided theory and exemplars that developed literary realism's ability to treat serious subjects and everyday life. Sherwood Anderson offered new directions in short story structuring and em-

phasis. A series of Midwestern writers led by individuals like Theodore Dreiser significantly advanced naturalistic portrayal of individuals and urban settings. JOHN DOS PASSOS conducted important experiments with multiple points of view and narrative perspectives.

Many Midwestern fiction writers have gained international recognition for their fiction. These include Nobel Prize laureates—SAUL BELLOW, Ernest Hemingway, Sinclair Lewis, and Toni Morrison—as well as other acknowledged masters including Mark Twain, Sherwood Anderson, and F. SCOTT FITZGERALD.

## Poetry

Midwestern poets and poetic theoreticians have played perhaps an even more important role. Nineteenth-century romantic poets such as ALICE CARY and PHOEBE CARY were nationally recognized. Later in the century, Midwestern critics and poets led the rejection of nineteenth-century romantic form, content, and worldview in poetry. WILLIAM MARION REEDY, a St. Louis–based publisher and critic, used the literary page of his *St. Louis Mirror* to begin building sentiment for changes in American poetry and prose near the end of the nineteenth century. Later, Chicago-based HARRIET MONROE and Alice Corbin Henderson created a critically important early-twentieth-century context in 1912 with *Poetry: A Magazine of Verse,* and MARGARET ANDERSON did the same in 1914 with the *Little Review.* All espoused new poetic norms, provided venues for hitherto unpublished poets, and offered a rallying point for avant-garde writers as well as radical literary and social orientations. This nurturing environment spawned poetic experimentation and revival beginning with the Chicago Renaissance poets, including Carl Sandburg, EDGAR LEE MASTERS, and Vachel Lindsay. But the contributions of *Poetry: A Magazine of Verse* did not end with the century's second decade. The list of poets given their start on the pages of *Poetry* reads like the Who's Who of twentieth-century American poetry. T. S. Eliot, the 1948 Nobel Prize winner, had ties to *Poetry: A Magazine of Verse,* St. Louis, and the Midwest, although his primary allegiances and sources of inspiration lay elsewhere. Later in the twentieth century, practicing poets and advocates of African American poetry such as DUDLEY RANDALL and HERBERT WOODWARD MARTIN have widened the available range of Midwestern poetic publication. Throughout the twentieth century great American poets like ARCHIBALD MACLEISH, Gwendolyn Brooks, THEODORE ROETHKE, JAMES WRIGHT, THOMAS MCGRATH, Rita Dove, and many others have expressed Midwestern language, experience, and values in distinguished, internationally recognized poetry.

## Drama

Although Midwestern writers have not been as crucial to national and international developments in drama as to those in poetry and fiction, Midwestern playwrights and producers have been and remain important in socially based and arts theater. Laura Dainty Pelham and her Hull-House Players provided strong early drama centering on social issues. Maurice Browne and his wife, Ellen Van Volkenburg, founded the Chicago Little Theater in 1912 and were significant in the Little Theater movement as well as in development of serious American drama. Chicagoan ALICE GERSTENBERG left her mark on experimental and children's theater. GEORGE CRAM COOK, SUSAN GLASPELL, and FLOYD DELL were significant in their involvement with the Provincetown Players. The Midwest has produced LANFORD WILSON and WILLIAM INGE, with their strong dramatic consideration of small towns, shifting environments, and the lives and problems of people living there. Lorraine Hansberry achieved significant national recognition for her socially oriented drama, with the stream of first-produced plays extending well beyond her death in 1965; her reputation continues to build. Now, at the advent of the new millennium DAVID MAMET is a highly productive nationally recognized dramatist focusing on contemporary urban society.

## Literary Images of the Midwest

Perhaps the best way of documenting the continuing strength as well as the ongoing shifts in Midwestern thought and literature is to consider the memorable Midwestern images these authors have provided. The starting point must be the inclusive democratic vision of Abraham Lincoln expressed throughout his public writings and speeches as well as his private correspondence. If any one person embodies quintessential American democratic values and expresses them memorably, it is Lincoln.

Later, Mark Twain's fiction provides two contrasting images: the first is of Midwestern innocence and joy, with Hannibal children paying to whitewash Tom Sawyer's fence; the second that of Huck and Jim standing together, naked, on the raft, affirming nature and fleeing American civilization.

Willa Cather's *O Pioneers!* (1913) offers memorable images of Midwestern wilderness, tamed productive farmland, and society. She presents Ivor's pristine prairieland and duck pond and later opposes them with the stark Lincoln, Nebraska, prison. She gives us the initial desolate winter image of Alexandra and Emil crying over his escaped kitten in the frozen Nebraska frontier town and later complements it with the Edenic summer picture of prosperous, productive, well-to-do Nebraska farms divided into neat rectangles bordered with roads and telephone lines.

Ole Rølvaag's *Giants in the Earth* (English translation 1927) captures the precarious immigrant experience of the upper Midwest with the final image of Per Hansa found by young boys on a warm May afternoon, still sitting ashenfaced where he died of exposure at the height of a blizzard months before, a heavy stocking cap still pulled low on his forehead, large mittens still shielding his hands, his back to a moldering pile of hay, one pair of skis at his feet, another strapped to his back, his eyes permanently fixed on the distant west.

And who can forget L. FRANK BAUM's opposition of the rural Kansas landscape with Dorothy and Toto's tornado and delirium-assisted journey to Oz. Sherwood Anderson captures Mid-America poignantly at the crossroads in *Winesburg, Ohio* (1919) with multiple opposed pictures, perhaps most notably Reverend Curtis Hartman viewing the naked body of Kate Swift through the stained-glass window of Christ calling the children to come to him.

Upton Sinclair portrays horrifying stockyards sights, sounds, and smells experienced by Jurgis Rudkus in *The Jungle* (1906), while Sinclair Lewis portrays Zenith realtor and local booster George Babbitt's intellectual chameleonism, his rationalized unethical business practices, and his sexual fantasies in *Babbitt* (1922).

In the 1980s and 1990s, GARRISON KEILLOR's wounded yet loving narratives of self-doubt and purgatorial experience in Lake Wobegon, Minnesota, depict people and lifestyles that time has left behind. He allows us the easy pleasure of felt-superiority while simultaneously selecting images of permanency amid change, simplicity in a distressingly complex world, and innocence in a society increasingly subjected to negative experience. Keillor brings us Mid-

America. Thus, these mythic portrayals, as in the literature of the Midwest more generally, take us full circle—from small towns to big cities and back to small-town roots.

## Contents

The *Dictionary of Midwestern Literature: Volume 1: The Authors* recounts the lives, literary significance, major works, and critical appraisal of the literary production of approximately four hundred authors and critics whose writings reflect significant continuing connection with the American Midwest. The volume presents representative Midwestern authors writing in, or transcribed into, English over this two-century period. In doing so, a conscious effort has been made to include not only Midwestern writers with established national and international reputations but also a range of emerging and lesser-known authors. This broad inclusiveness allows the volume to reflect the widest possible range of Midwestern literary experience and response over two centuries. Recognized giants of Midwestern literature—figures including Samuel Langhorne Clemens, Willa Cather, Carl Sandburg, Sinclair Lewis, Ernest Hemingway, Edna Ferber, Toni Morrison, and Gwendolyn Brooks—have exerted and will continue to exert a major influence on Midwestern and American literature and worldview. Yet other Midwestern writers of the past and present also provide valid perspectives on the Midwest and offer views and works which, while not considered mainstream today, may well be attuned to important movements and modes which contemporary orientations have overlooked. All play an important role in shaping future Midwestern literature and worldview.

One major contribution of this volume will be the early notice provided to emerging as well as less recognized Midwestern writers. The *Dictionary of Midwestern Literature* hopes to continue the tradition of early notice set in 1981 by the publication of Society for the Study of Midwestern Literature member Gerald Nemanic's *A Bibliographical Guide to Midwestern Literature*. There, Nemanic recognized many emerging authors, among them Toni Morrison. Since that time, Morrison's talent has been recognized with awards and prizes culminating in the 1993 Nobel Prize for literature. The *Dictionary of Midwestern Literature* hopes also that the current volume will provide a venue for reconsideration of Midwestern writers past and present.

## Criteria for Inclusion

Authors were selected for inclusion in the *Dictionary of Midwestern Literature* by the editorial board in consultation with the state librarians of Midwestern states and with members of the Society for the Study of Midwestern Literature and other professional literary societies.

Criteria for authorial inclusion included:

• significant extended connection between the author and the Midwest, as reflected in the author's writings. Accidents of birth or residence were considered insufficient in and of themselves to warrant inclusion;

• a body of writings dealing significantly with the Midwest, its life, its people, their speech, experience, and values;

• literary products of quality and importance sufficient to warrant recognition for contributions to Midwestern literature of the author's time or for influence on subsequent literature.

Finally, the *Dictionary of Midwestern Literature* consciously presents diverse Midwestern perceptions and voices. In doing so, this volume records the richness and cultural variety of past and present Midwestern literature and life and provides an inclusive range of thought and expression for contemporary and future Midwestern writers and thinkers.

## Using the Dictionary of Midwestern Literature

The *Dictionary of Midwestern Literature* is designed for readability and ease of use. It is valuable for those seeking answers to narrow questions of biography, bibliography, or criticism about individual authors as well as for those pursuing broader und :rstanding of Midwestern literature, history, and society. Intended readers include literary scholars, librarians, high school and college students, and the general public.

## Entry Format

Each *Dictionary of Midwestern Literature* entry includes the author's name; birth and death date, if available; major pseudonyms; biographical information; literary significance; and major works along with references to the most significant critical commentaries on the author. Each author entry is signed by the writer and accompanied by the writer's institutional affiliation or geographical location.

Author entries are listed alphabetically by

last name, with cross-referencing for pseudonyms of major writers. First lines of each entry provide the author's name with any elements of the author's real name not included in the widely known pen name included in parentheses. Thus, for example, Carl Sandburg appears as Carl (August) Sandburg. The second line provides the author's birth date as well as the date of death for deceased authors. The third line of many entries lists in parentheses major pseudonyms used by the author. Thus, the third line of the Samuel Langhorne Clemens entry reads (Mark Twain). As an additional aid to readers, first references in each entry to names of Midwestern writers included in the *Dictionary of Midwestern Literature* are written in small capital letters to identify additional easily located sources of information.

The Biography section of each entry provides the author's place of birth, parents' names, including mother's maiden name in parentheses, major jobs and life experiences, spouses and children, honors and awards, and, where possible, the location and cause of death.

The Significance section describes the author's literary significance with particular emphasis on works dealing with Midwestern settings, characters, experiences, or values as well as the author's influence on subsequent literature. To assist readers, the first reference to each book-length literary work mentioned is followed immediately in parentheses by the date of its first publication.

The Selected Works section presents the author's most significant works, particularly as viewed from a Midwestern perspective. The first dates of publication of these works follow in parenthesis along with brief statements regarding them.

The Further Reading section provides a starting point for readers seeking critical commentary on the author's works. The amount of readily available literary criticism on Midwestern authors and their works is extremely variable. Thousands of critical commentaries cover the lives and works of major Midwestern writers. At the other end of the spectrum, few readily available critical sources exist for many Midwestern writers, particularly those of earlier periods and those whose worldviews and literary orientations are at odds with contemporary literary norms. The same is true for emerging authors, especially those with few volumes to their credit, those with especially strong regional orientations, and those published by very small presses. Students seeking avenues for primary literary research and publication should consider the opportunity afforded by these less-canonical authors. The Society for the Study for Midwestern Literature and its members can be counted on to assist in this endeavor.

The author-title index is the volume's final organizational and integrative tool. Listings of pages containing references to each author assist readers in placing individual writers in their broadest literary and societal contexts. These page references tie together strands of biographical data, bibliographic reference, and critical commentary spread across four hundred author entries. They reveal associations and suggest influences. Title indexing complements author indexing, allowing readers to move from a known title to the author's name, biography, literary significance, major writings, and the critical commentary the author's writings have elicited.

## Coverage

Careful review of the authors selected for inclusion in this volume makes clear the higher incidence of writers associated with the eastern half of the Midwest—the states formed from the Northwest Territory. While this representation at first appears to skew the literary expression of the Midwest, it accurately reflects both Midwestern population centering and the earlier dates of settlement there.

Choices to include authors in the *Dictionary of Midwestern Literature* are professional decisions based upon the fullest possible marshaling of information and the widest possible scholarly input. Inevitably, in such an enterprise some worthy authors may be omitted. The Editorial Board sees this volume as the beginning of an extended conversation regarding the nature of Midwestern life and literature, not the end. We hope that this work will provoke response and raise consciousness about the literature of this dynamic and ever-changing region.

Scholarly quibbles aside, ultimately, Midwestern life and literature transcend stereotypes and rapid overviews. DAVID D. ANDERSON's lead essay provides an extended introduction to Midwestern history, life, and literature. Beyond that, the diverse experiences and expressions of authors reflected in this volume allow readers to draw their own conclusions on the nature of Midwestern life and literature in its first two hundred years. We invite all readers to explore and enjoy!

Philip A. Greasley, General Editor
University of Kentucky

# The Origins and Development of the Literature of the Midwest

The literature of the American Midwest, the region that SHERWOOD ANDERSON called his "Mid-America," "the place between mountain and mountain" (*Letters* 43) out of which his works came, is, like all literature, the result of the complex relationship among place, people, and the writer who attempts to construct a literary reality out of the raw material of that relationship. Whether literature is characterized as regional, national, or international, its function is to describe, define, and, if possible, interpret that relationship. As JOHN T. FREDERICK (1893–1975), Midwestern novelist, teacher, critic, and founder of the *Midland* (1915–33), wrote half a century ago, the regional writer—and, by implication, every writer—"uses the literary substance which he knows best . . . the material about which he is most likely to be able to write with meaning" (*Out of the Midwest* xv). Frederick maintained that in so doing the writer interprets his people to others and perhaps even to themselves.

As Frederick made clear, Midwestern writers, like all writers, fuse time and place and people, the local of human experience, whether it be in the little patch of Mississippi about which Sherwood Anderson told William Faulkner he should write, or in An-

derson's own Ohio, SINCLAIR LEWIS's Minnesota, ERNEST HEMINGWAY's northern Michigan, or the countless other literary places of Sherwood Anderson's Mid-America. Then, out of that fusion, writers attempt to extract not the meaning of place or natural or social environment, but the meaning of human experience as it is manifested in that place, which is often the place out of which the writer has come and to which he returns in his work, if not in his life.

Never has the Mississippi Valley been more real, the lives of its people more vividly portrayed than when MARK TWAIN wrote about them in his study in Hartford, Connecticut. Sherwood Anderson did the same for the Ohio town and its people when he wrote about them in a Chicago boardinghouse. CARL SANDBURG eloquently expressed the anguish of the urban industrial Chicagoan in his homespun—but not homely—verse, and VACHEL LINDSAY magically projected the urban-rural vision. In a later Midwestern America, two competing and contrasting interpretations of Midwestern life were eloquently and universally portrayed in the works of two recent Midwestern Nobel laureates in literature, SAUL BELLOW and TONI MORRISON. Bellow writes of the ethnic-intellectual-social morass of Chicago, while Toni Morrison depicts the Midwestern African American experience in a gritty Midwestern steel town, Lorain, Ohio.

Each of these writers and hundreds more, whether noted, celebrated, anthologized, and remembered or preserved only in increasingly musty journals, esoteric critical studies, or fading memories, is part of a literary tradition that is at once the oldest and the youngest of American literary traditions, as is the cultural landscape out of which it comes.

Midwestern literature is not, however, a literature that reflects, as Alfred Kazin and other Eastern critics have insisted, "the ideas of unlimited space and the sense of place [both of which] were identical" (*A Writer's America* 105). Rather, it is the attempt to interpret the unknowable in terms of the known human experience. The orally transmitted tales of the *Algic Researches* (1839) gathered by HENRY ROWE SCHOOLCRAFT (1793–1864) defined the attempts of a primitive people in an inhospitable land to explain the unknown within the context of their own experience. These were the earliest attempts to find meaning in the relationship between a place that was not yet the Midwest and the people who lived there.

The inevitable conflicts of post-Renaissance European discovery, exploration, and exploitation resulted in cultural and literary discontinuity. They introduced an alien perspective and a literature that attempted to interpret place, people, and experience in an alien language and with a radically different worldview. This is the record of a century of French experience and exploration that is the *Jesuit Relations*, published originally in annual volumes in Paris in the seventeenth century and translated and edited by R. G. Thwaites, in seventy-three volumes between 1896 and 1901. The *Relations*, like *The Memoir of La Mothe Cadillac* (ca. 1720), by the founder of the city of Detroit (ca. 1658–1730), and Father Louis Hennepin's (1640–1701) *Description of Louisiana* (1682), describing the Great Lakes country and what is now Minnesota, are ignored in the history of the literature of the region. As such, they are like the comic verse and the recorded and versified Indian and English speeches published as *Miscellaneous by an Officer* (1813) by Arent Schuyler de Peyster

(1736–1822), commander of the English garrisons at Mackinac and Detroit as the Great Lakes country was about to become American.

Both the forgotten and the equally ignored oral tales and legends of Native Americans who for millennia had inhabited the Midwest and attempted to find and convey meaning in the oral transmission of their interpreted experience, and the equally ignored or forgotten works of those who would supplant aboriginal culture with that of post-Renaissance Europe, attempt to define and interpret human experience in an area older than any recorded experience. And yet, in terms of literary continuity and homogeneity, the literature of that region, that is, the literature that begins with the Anglo-American people in the Ohio and Upper Mississippi Valleys, is comparatively young.

Its origins were in the late eighteenth century as a new nation emerged on the North American continent and began to move inexorably from the Eastern seaboard across the Appalachian mountains to replicate itself—with inevitable differences—in what was then the West or the wilderness. That literature, which we have come to call Midwestern literature, is fused to the place and its people and their experience over more than two centuries of increasingly complex history.

The Midwest is at once the oldest and the youngest region in the contiguous forty-eight United States. As Burke Aaron Hinsdale (1837–1900), professor of the science and art of teaching at the University of Michigan, pointed out in his centennial history of the Northwest Territory, *The Old Northwest* (1888): "save New England alone, there is no section of the United States embracing several states that is so distinct an historical unit, and that so readily yields to historical treatment as the Old Northwest" (iii).

Yet the Old Northwest, from which the modern Midwest has evolved, its beginning marked by the passage by Congress of the successive Ordinances of 1784, 1785, and finally of 1787, to govern and provide for the orderly transition of "the Territories North and West of the River, Ohio," passed quickly into history, becoming, in turn, the West, the Old West, and, in ABRAHAM LINCOLN's Annual Message to Congress on December 1, 1862, together with its adjacent states and territories, "the great interior region" of the nation (*Collected Works of Abraham Lincoln* 528). By century's end, it had become the Middle West, synonymous with the later "Midwest," defined by FREDERICK JACKSON TURNER (1861–1932) as "the States of Ohio, Indiana, Illinois, Michigan and Wisconsin ('the old Territory Northwest of the River, Ohio'), and the trans-Mississippi states of the Louisiana Purchase—Missouri, Iowa, Minnesota, Kansas, Nebraska, North Dakota, and South Dakota," bound together by the "vast water system" of the Mississippi, the Missouri, the Ohio, and the Great Lakes (*The Frontier in American History* 126–27).

For Turner, as for Lincoln, the unity of the geographical region was clear, as it has been for more recent scholars and political observers. That historical unit, defined in the works of Hinsdale and his successors, including HARLAN HATCHER, WALTER HAVIGHURST, RUSSEL NYE, and others, has remained in an equally clear perspective that begins with the Mound Builder cultures of prehistory in the Upper Mississippi and Ohio River Valleys. However, some scholars and critics have limited the Western boundary to the 100th meridian of longitude; that is, the demarcation line between the long-grass prairies dominated by a farming economy and the short-grass prairies of the grazing economy of the West. In doing so, they have divided the Western-most states of Kansas, Nebraska, North Dakota, and South Dakota between the Midwest and the West. Others would relegate much of northern Michigan, Wisconsin, and Minnesota, together with much of southern Ontario to a Northland region. But for practical as well as historical reasons, Turner's definition continues to prevail in many cultural and historical, if not in economic and geographical, studies.[1]

Yet, Hinsdale and other Midwestern historians notwithstanding, the history of the Midwest has been disjointed. The region has been marked by the domination, successively, of Native American Indian cultures from prehistory to the seventeenth century; by French commercial and military cultures for a century, from the late seventeenth to the late eighteenth century; by British military power for a generation in the late eighteenth century; and then by the United States to the Mississippi. After the Louisiana Purchase two decades later, it extended its domain to the trans-Mississippi West. Unlike the other major regions of the country, it is clearly, through the Ordinance of 1787—which included a philosophy of government, a process for political development, and a definition of governmental responsibility—a creation not of colonial and pre-colonial myth and history but of the United States federal government.

Its origins are equally clear. Unlike the other major regions—the South, the West, New England—it has been said to have neither an enduring myth nor a regional metaphor, and some historians and social critics, recognizing its short history and denying that it has regional characteristics, a regional culture, or a regional psyche, insist that it no longer exists if, indeed, it ever had existed. They relegate any concept of a Midwest to an unfolding national history or myth, or even make it synonymous with an abstraction called "Middle America," a characteristic perceived by some in late-twentieth-century American culture.

Nevertheless, three factual observations are fundamental to a discussion of the Midwest as an authentic American region with a history, a myth, a psyche, and a culture that produces and, in turn, is shaped by its literature. First, unlike the other continental regions, it is an American, rather than a European or an aboriginal creation. Second, it is a creation of eighteenth-century rational philosophy. Third, it occupies, as Abraham Lincoln recognized, a unique geographical position as the American Heartland, astride the main path of American destiny, the land route to the Pacific and beyond. These controlling factors give it an identity, a reality, and a psyche which combine to produce the substance of a literature that is at once regional, national, and universal.

The Midwestern identity and its concomitant reality and psyche are composed of a number of characteristics that have their origins in Midwestern history and evolution, as well as change. Fundamental to the Midwest and the states of which it is composed is the fact that from the beginning, unlike other re-

1. See, for example, the definitions included by Gerald Nemanic, ed., in "Introduction," *A Bibliographical Guide to Midwestern Literature* (Iowa City: University of Iowa Press, 1981): xi–xii.

gions of the country, the Midwest has been characterized by a national, rather than a colonial or regional, tradition and identity, and it has been dominated by the practical consequences of its conception in eighteenth-century philosophy.

From the beginning, evolution of the Midwest has been marked by a faith in progress, an acceptance of change, a willingness—perhaps even an eagerness—to move on, and by a search for success and for order and a confidence in human ability. All of these have marked its political history from the beginning. Consequently, the Midwest has been in the forefront of political and moral movements ranging from Jacksonian democracy through abolition to populism and prohibition and beyond.

These traits directed its economic history from the work of practical tinkerers such as Thomas Edison and Henry Ford to the rise of great cities and industrial empires. At the same time these traits contributed to an increasing social and economic rift between country and city, an increasingly diverse population in both, and an increasingly negative image. Within as well as outside the Midwest, too often, from both Eastern and Western perspectives, its people are seen as provincial, its institutions second-rate, and its culture naive.

From its beginnings as the Northwest Territory the Midwest developed in unique ways. The Northwest Ordinance called for establishment of free public education and the prohibition of slavery. It provided for the easy transfer of public lands to private individuals who would make them their homes. It encouraged development of a free, open society in new states with rational boundaries, and it asserted the equality of these emergent states in all respects to the original thirteen. The Northwest would not be an Eastern colony, and its statutory rights included many not yet open to the original thirteen states. Rather, it was a part of a united democratic whole, and for most of its history it would lead the nation in progressive social change.

After the Revolutionary War, people came to the Midwest in staggering numbers. In 1800 one-twentieth of the American population lived in "the West"; by 1820 one-third of them had crossed the mountains, gone up and down the rivers and begun a process that be-

fore the century's end would see the territory and its trans-Mississippi extensions the site of twelve states and a substantial part of the national whole. Ohio was the first part of the territory to become a state and was admitted as the seventeenth state in 1803. North and South Dakota, the thirty-ninth and fortieth, were admitted in 1889.

As the people came, the mythical, metaphorical, social, political, and literary patterns began their evolution. The people, coming largely from New England and the Central and Southern states, were at first a homogenous Anglo-American group with occasional Anglo-Dutch and Anglo-French characteristics. But before midcentury, these "old" Americans were joined by an increasingly complex array of "new" Americans. In the 1830s Irish, Germans, Dutch, and Scandinavians began their influx. Many of them went immediately to the West to work on the construction of canals, the first of the government-sponsored "internal improvements"—a key phrase in political debates in the territories and new states. Many others cleared the forest, broke the prairie sod, and founded countless towns, many of which enjoy ethnic flavors even yet.

With post–Civil War industrial expansion and a growing need for labor, they were joined by Eastern and Southern Europeans. The twentieth century saw the influx of Southerners, black and white, to the industrial centers of Detroit, Chicago, Cleveland, and others. Even more recently Latin Americans and a wide variety of other immigrants have followed. All of these have combined to produce what is perhaps the most dramatic evolutionary change in American history. Today, in flat northwest Ohio, from I-75, the freeway that ties the Midwest to the South, one can ponder the sudden appearance of a magnificent mosque in what had a decade earlier been a fertile cornfield. This is only one of the many manifestations of a dramatic—and orderly—evolution dictated by the region's eighteenth-century foundations.

From its earliest days onward, the Midwest's diverse, dynamic population has almost universally accepted two related articles of faith—a belief in progress and in the search for success. These values have been inherent in the region from its statutory definition, and they have influenced regional change even as they formed the myths and metaphors that would give the region its cultural identity and literature. The eighteenth-century belief in progress and its nineteenth-century counterpart, the search for success, had brought a diverse population across mountains, up and down rivers, through unmarked forests and across prairies, even across oceans and forbidding political barriers. To Midwesterners, adopted or native-born, the forces that created the Midwest are still operating. Most Midwesterners believe fulfillment is within reach, and the pursuit of happiness is often a literal movement. Both are measurable in money, in status, and in respect.

Many of the myths created by an evolving Midwest contributed to a growing American myth. These have their foundations in complementary faiths. The open society has made possible the most durable Midwestern myth, that of the possibility of change, at the center of which is the brooding image of Abraham Lincoln. In Jeffersonian terms, there is no artificial aristocracy in the Midwest, and one may succeed, as did Lincoln, in one generation. The "log cabin to White House" journey is an achievable reality, the "self-made man" is an object of respect, and humble origins are virtually mandatory to a successful political career. One *can* go "from rags to riches," and the pantheon of Midwestern folk heroes is replete with such imagery. Tinkerers become industrialists, as personified by Edison, Ford, and the Wright brothers. Practical merchants become financial barons—perhaps even robber barons—as did Rockefeller, McCormick, and Marshall Field; the military heroes become political leaders—Jackson, Taylor, Grant, Eisenhower, even the astronaut John Glenn.

But counter to these articles of faith and the myths they create emerges another myth, unspoken but widely held in late-nineteenth-century Midwestern rural areas and urban industrial centers. This is the principle of social Darwinism. Following Darwin, the principle of "survival of the fittest" was extended from the natural world to the social. It threatened—or promised—a new aristocracy, an aristocracy of money, status, and power.

In spite of the growth of a diverse people of complex origins marked by a lack of homogeneity in ideology, religion, and politics as well as in ethnic, geographical, and social origins, certain often paradoxical patterns emerged. Their emergence was largely a result of Midwestern faith in progress and the search for success. Before 1850 the principles of Jacksonian democracy were widespread, often held even by those who faithfully voted Whig. In the post–Civil War Midwest the principles of an increasingly militant populism and later resurgent democracy were subscribed to by a people overwhelmingly Republican. Made forever free by its empowering legislation, the Midwest was strongly anti-slavery if not downright abolitionist in spite of "black laws" in Illinois, Indiana, and Ohio. It was marked by advocates-become-martyrs. Elijah Lovejoy (1802–37) was killed in Alton, Illinois, while defending his presses and his principles. John Brown (1800–1859), of Connecticut's Western Reserve in Ohio and freedom fighter in Kansas and Virginia, went to the gallows at Charles Town, Virginia, under the watchful eye of Colonel Robert E. Lee.

The Midwest was marked, too, by an active underground railroad, and places such as Oberlin College, founded in 1833, were staunchly abolitionist, even to the extent of defying federal authority; in 1834 Oberlin became the first institution in the nation to admit women and blacks on an equal basis with its white male students. In Jackson, Michigan, on July 6, 1854, the first major party devoted to an anti-slavery philosophy was established. In 1861 it sent Abraham Lincoln, a sectional, if not a regional, candidate, to the White House. The Republican Party, without a faith in the post–Civil War years, became increasingly dominated by business interests, and, even as the region maintained its sentimental attachments to the party, it sent a series of Midwestern Republican Civil War generals—Grant, Hayes, Garfield, Benjamin Harrison, and a lone major, McKinley—to the White House.

The conviction that education is the surest means by which the individual can rise was and remains important to the open society and the faith in progress and the attainability of success in the evolving Midwest. This faith is reflected in the clause in the Ordinance of 1787 that states that "Religion, morality, and knowledge being necessary to good government and the happiness of mankind, schools and the means of education shall be forever encouraged" (*The Old Northwest* 271).

Even earlier, the allocation in the Land Ordinance of 1785 states that "there shall be reserved from sale the lot No. 16 of every township for the maintenance of common schools within the said township" (401). Education has been and remains a paramount governmental responsibility in the territories and the states that followed them. This is perhaps best typified by these words from the Constitution of the state of Indiana, adopted in 1816: "It shall be the duty of the general assembly to provide by law for a general system of education, ascending in regular gradation from township schools to a State University, wherein tuition shall be gratis and equally open to all" (*Indiana: A History* 95).

The fading remains of one-room township schools, marking the progress of education to the West, regularly dot the Midwestern landscape even yet, but equally evident are the institutions of higher learning that began almost immediately to mark the path of progress. Ohio University was founded in 1804, Miami in 1809, Kenyon in 1824, Denison in 1831, Oberlin in 1833, all in Ohio. Out to the west, Illinois College was founded in 1829, and Franklin in Indiana followed in 1837. Knox in Illinois began in 1837, Kalamazoo in Michigan in 1833, and Olivet, also in Michigan, in 1844. Grinnell in Iowa and Beloit in Wisconsin were established in 1846. And the pattern continued on to the North and West.

Beside these private institutions grew what were to become the state universities. Many of them antedated the Morrill Act of 1862, which allotted public lands to the support of higher education in the mechanical, agricultural, and military arts. Indiana was founded in 1824, Missouri in 1839, Michigan in 1841, Iowa in 1847, Minnesota in 1851, Michigan State, the first of the land-grant colleges, in 1855, Illinois in 1867, Ohio State in 1870, and on again to the North and West. So ubiquitous were institutions of higher learning in the Midwest before century's end that President Frederick Barnard of Columbia University wondered how England, a nation of twenty-three million, could function with only four degree-granting colleges, whereas Ohio, a state of three million, had thirty-seven.

In 1697 nearly two hundred years before President Barnard's observation, Father Louis Hennepin, in his *A New Discovery of a Vast Country in America*, described a country on the shores of the Great Lakes so rich and suitable for human habitation that it challenged his own powers of description. He maintained:

The country . . . is very well situated, and the soil very fertile. [There] are vast meadows, and the prospect is terminated by some hills covered with vineyards. Trees bearing good fruit, groves and forests so well disposed that one would think nature alone would not have made, without the help of art, so charming a prospect. That country is stocked with stags, wild goats, and bears, which are good for food, and not fierce as in other countries: some think they are better than our pork. Turkey cocks and swans are there also very common; and our men brought several other beasts and birds, whose names are unknown to us, but they are extraordinary relishing.

The forests are chiefly made up of walnut trees, chestnut trees, plum trees, and pear trees, loaded with their own fruit and vines. There is also abundance of timber fit for building; so that those who shall be so happy as to inhabit that noble country, cannot but remember with gratitude those who have discovered the way. . . . (109)

A century later, Hennepin's rich land had not yet been settled, but Thomas Jefferson, in his inaugural address at the dawn of a new century, was visionary as he saw the land beyond the mountains as part of "a rising nation, spread over a wide and fruitful land, traversing all the seas with the rich productions of their industry, . . . advancing rapidly to destinies beyond the reach of mortal eye" (*Writings of Thomas Jefferson* 2).

Perhaps Hennepin was, as his critics then and now insist, the first writer of Midwestern fiction, but Jefferson, knowing the nature of the statutory foundations in which he was intimately involved, saw clearly the orderly transition that would lead to the vision becoming real in the lifetimes of people then alive. The region beyond the mountains would become one, part of the whole and yet uniquely identifiable, seeking and welcoming change as it pursued an eighteenth-century vision through the nineteenth and twentieth centuries and into the twenty-first. It would become a region unique in its past, its identity, its faith, its myth, and its literature. It was so uniquely placed in time and space as the American Heartland that Abraham Lincoln saw it to be in the midst of a deadly war that threatened the national existence.

As the Midwest constructed an identity, a reality, and an enduring myth out of the elements of its complex origins and development, so it constructed a literature that at once explains and interprets that development and the many dimensions out of which it came. What is identifiably Midwestern, or more properly Western, in the earliest literary attempts to define the Anglo-American experience paralleled that of the years of discovery and initial settlement by Europeans. It can best be classified as travel literature. At first it consisted of personal journals or diaries, often later transcribed as descriptive and interpretive documents. The volumes of the *Jesuit Relations* were the first and remain very important. Together, they constituted a collaborative work that transmuted transcriptions of the notes of explorer-missionaries into important historical, geographic, and social history. They offered description and insight into the place and people seen by Europeans in the sixteenth and seventeenth centuries in what was called French North America, French Canada, or French Louisiana.

Such literature describing ventures into what was the West or the Ohio Country by the Anglo-English who were becoming Americans is rare. The earliest was a brief, factual diary by Christopher Gist (ca. 1706–17), a frontiersman who explored the Ohio Valley for the Ohio Company in 1750, explored the Appalachians from eastern Kentucky to North Carolina, and in 1753–54 accompanied and guided George Washington to the Ohio country to warn the French to depart. This journey was the subject of his brief journal of incidents, weather, and encounters. It was followed by others, including Edward Braddock's expedition against Fort Duquesne in 1755. Gist died of smallpox in Cherokee country in 1759, and his journal was forgotten until it fell into the hands of the Massachusetts Historical Society, when it was published in the Society's *Collections* (1835). Later, with others of his journals, it was edited by W. M. Darlington and published in 1893.

Another eighteenth-century journal, more properly American, is that of General Benjamin Lincoln (1733–1810), Revolutionary War veteran, suppresser of Shay's Rebellion in 1787, a long-time confidant of George Washington, and, on several occasions his emissary to Western Indians, including to the Creek Indians. Later, in the spring and summer of 1793, General Lincoln was to treat with the assembled tribes of the Indians of the Ohio Country, by then legally but ambiguously the Northwest Territory. Unlike Gist's sparse frontiersman's account, Lincoln's journal, published in the same issue of the Massachusetts Historical Society's *Collections*, is a remarkable document. Lincoln was a keen observer and an eloquent recorder. He had a clear understanding of the forces and philosophy that were to send generations of Americans and others to the West and to accomplish in a generation one of the most complete transformations of a land in recorded history.

General Lincoln's journal covers the period from April 27, 1793, when he left Philadelphia with Washington's commission, to July 14, 1793, when he departed from Fort Erie en route to Philadelphia to report his failure. It is replete with observations on the rich soil, magnificent sweet-water lakes, productive and promising forests, and the able, intelligent, colorful, and eloquent indigenous people who inhabited them, and whose speeches, more than his own, he recorded in detail. He also recorded the stalemate between competing populations. The Americans wanted what is now about three-quarters of the state of Ohio; the Indians insisted that the settlers retreat beyond the Ohio and stay there. The Americans offered the largest sum of money ever offered to Indians; the Indians replied simply and bluntly that "money to us is of no value" (*Journal* 165). Even while they spoke, General "Mad Anthony" Wayne was assembling twenty-five hundred volunteers at Pittsburgh. He transported them to Cincinnati, they marched north, and on August 20, 1794, they met the assembled Indians, many of whom had treated with Lincoln the year before, at a place called Fallen Timbers on the Maumee. In an hour the Indians were in flight and the course of history in the West, now clearly the Northwest Territory, was forever altered. The Treaty of Greenville, signed in August 1795 was an anticlimax, as a young Indian named Tecumseh stood by and brooded.

A third diary of this transitional period, that of a young woman named Margaret Van Horn Dwight (1790–1834), is the record of a journey to Ohio by wagon in 1810. The journal, unlike those of Gist and Lincoln, is intensely personal, written only for the eyes of her cousin and confidante, Elizabeth Woolsey. Miss Dwight, a niece of the poet Timothy Dwight, accompanied a clergyman, a deacon, and his family West. Her journey was ostensibly to visit cousins in Warren, Ohio, an emerging town in the first of the states to have been carved from the Northwest Territory, only seven years before Miss Dwight's journey. The journal is the record of Miss Dwight's education. In it, she learns about the West, about deacons, about men, about taverns—of which she becomes a connoisseur—and she learns, too, about the epic movement of which she is a part.

About the new Western American language, she writes: "They say there has been a *heap* of people moving this fall; I don't know exactly how many a heap is, or a *sight* either, which is another way of measuring people—I would be *apt* to think it was a terrible *parcel*, to use the language of the people around me" (*A Journey to Ohio in 1810* 39).

As the party pauses at the foot of the Allegheny Mountains, Miss Dwight records the passage of empire, of which she is a perceptive part: "From what I have seen and heard, I think the State of Ohio will be well-filled before winter—Wagons without number, everyday go on" (47). Miss Dwight, like many of the others, remained in the West, perhaps giving the lie to the ostensible purpose of the journey. She married a young man she met in the West, William Bell Jr. He became a wholesale merchant in Pittsburgh, where she gave birth to thirteen children and lived out her days. The manuscript remained in the family until a granddaughter brought it to the attention of Yale University Press and it was published in 1912 as *A Journey to Ohio in 1810*.

Other personal recollections of the region's transition are virtually unknown, lost, filed away and forgotten, or more likely, never written, and much of the personal history of an epic period in American history is beyond recall. But these three documents not only preserve insights, observations, and facts that might otherwise have been lost, they also provide insight into the remarkable people who reconnoitered the country, who made it American, and who came to stay and make it their home.

Even as Miss Dwight was compiling a record of her remarkable journey, in the southeastern corner of the new state of Ohio, a new community around Fort Washington had become Cincinnati, named after the Order of the Cincinnati, an organization of Revolutionary War officers. A village in 1802, it was to become a city in 1819 and the first Western town to lay claim to cultural and literary dimensions. Already, on November 9, 1793, William Maxwell had printed the first issue of the *Sentinel of the North-Western Territory*. In the process he began a tradition that not only flourished but ultimately led to a great Midwestern journalism tradition that produced political leaders and laid the foundation for the region's literary tradition. Maxwell's paper still exists after two centuries and a number of changes. Moved to Chillicothe, the new territorial capital, in 1800, it survives moves and mergers as today's *Chillicothe Gazette*.

In that first issue, perhaps to fill space, but perhaps also as a mark of literary pretensions, Maxwell published a pirated chapter from Laurence Sterne's novel *Sentimental Journey*, a three-and-a-half column excerpt entitled "The Monk-Calais." The inauspicious beginning marked the foundation of a publishing industry that ultimately sent McGUFFEY readers and other educational and literary works to the nation. It marked, also, the beginning of a literary movement that contributed substantially to Cincinnati's claim to be the "Queen City of the West," rather than "Porkopolis," as some of its critics designated it.

This was the beginning, too, of the publication of a series of literary magazines in Cincinnati that provided a place for Western writers to be heard. Some of the journals flourished, but most did not. The array is impressive. The new publications included the *Literary Cadet* (1819), *Ohio* (1821), *Literary Gazette* (1824), *Western Review* (1827–30), *Cincinnati Mirror* (1831–36), *Western Messenger* (1827–30), *Western Monthly Magazine* (1833–37), and the most durable, the *Ladies Repository and Gatherings of the West* (1841–76), extending its influences even to the East. The first volume of poetry published in the West was *American Bards: A Modern Poem*, in three parts. It was published in Cincinnati in 1849; its author was anonymous but believed to be a Cincinnati banker, Gorham A. Worth.

By the late 1820s, Cincinnati had a resident philosopher, intellectual, and educator, Daniel Drake, M.D. (1785–1852). It also had seven colleges, seminaries, or institutes, libraries with more than forty thousand books, and a flourishing publishing industry that included the works of poets who, from their homes in the West, had begun to reach out to the rest of the nation. By 1860 Cincinnati's role as focal point—a cultural and financial center of a developing region unique in the nation—was beginning to be challenged by Chicago, a younger upstart at the foot of Lake Michigan.

In that year, William T. Coggeshall's (1824–67) *The Poets and Poetry of the West* was published in Columbus, Ohio, by Follett, Foster and Company. It was a substantial literary achievement that contains the works of 142 poets, eighty-seven men and fifty-five women, together with a preface that enumerates the origins and residences of the poets and provides an historical sketch of the development of poetry in the West. Most of those poets experienced what fame they would know in the pages of provincial journals or papers usually associated with Cincinnati, but a few of the poets in the volume, most notably WILLIAM DEAN HOWELLS (1837–1900) and the CARY sisters, PHOEBE (1824–71) and ALICE (1820–70), went East to seek their literary futures. A number of the poets who remained in the West, notably Otway Curry (1804–55), Coates Kinney (1826–1904), Charles A. Jones (1815–51), John James Piatt (1835–1917), Sarah M. B. Piatt (1836–1919), and William Davis Gallagher (1808–94), enjoyed reputations that gave them national recognition as well as regional prominence. None of the poets earned their livings through the practice of their art, although most were editors of Western newspapers and periodicals at one time or another. Some, particularly William D. Gallagher, were important editors.

Most of the poets in the volume, including all of those listed here and those in Emerson Venable's *Poets of Ohio* (1909), are products of the literary fashions that dominated Eastern America and particularly New England. Their verse is usually sentimental and romantic, its prosody conventional and regular, sometimes to the point of contrivance, and one detects at times a determined imitation or, at best, a clear echo of such prominent Eastern poets as Longfellow, Lowell, Poe, and Emerson.

And yet, if the celebration of place and the interpretation of human experiences in that place are acceptable criteria for ascribing geographical and cultural significance to individual works and their writers, most of the poets selected by Coggeshall are poets of the Old West in transition. Their writings are marked by the sense of discovery in their depiction of place. At the same time they reflect a recognition that the old is passing and the new is on the horizon. Clearly these poets are romantic and avowedly American, as were their Eastern counterparts, yet each is confidently and committedly of the West. Their West is one that would maintain its separable identity despite massive ongoing change.

Particularly illustrative of poetry that is at once American and clearly Western are Curry's "The Eternal River" and "Autumn Mornings," as well as his "Buckeye Cabin," Gallagher's "Miami Woods," and Jones's "The Old Mound." Each of them, with the exception of Curry's "Buckeye Cabin," which became a famous Whig campaign song in 1840, is consciously literary in the tradition that was coming West with the course of settlement. At the same time, however, each is determinedly of the time and place from which it came. Curry's river is clearly the Ohio as well as the river of destiny, of hope, of eternal promise: "The silvery tide will bear thee / Amid the sand and bloom / Of many a green and blessed isle / Whose shining banks illume / Each wandering bank and pathway dim / along the passing billow's brim" (*Poets and Poetry of the West* 99–100).

Curry's "Autumn Mornings" is not a celebration of fall color amid the glory of hardwood forests of the West; it is instead the portrayal of an autumn that foreshadows a mid-continental winter: "The spectrum is sombre, on conveying the vision that vestal Truth leads on the silent hours / of autumn's lonely reign. The weary gales / Creep over the waters, and the sun-browned plains / Off whispering as they pass a long farewell / To the frail emblems of the waning year, / the drooping foliage, and the dying years" (*Poets and Poetry of the West* 98–99).

Unlike his perceptions of seasonal transience as they relate to the poet as well as his place, Curry's "Buckeye Cabin" is a rollicking song that ultimately makes William Henry Harrison, "Old Tippecanoe," and the dynamic West one in spirit with the nation. He ends: "Oh, who fell before him in battle, tell me who? / Oh, who fell before him in battle, tell me who? / He drove the savage legions, and British armies, too. / At the Rapids, and the Thames, and old Tippecanoe. // By whom, tell me whom, will the battle next be won? / By whom, tell me whom, will the battle next be won? / The spoilsmen and leg treasurers will soon begin to run! / And the 'Log Cabin Candidate' will march to Washington" (50).

Gallagher's "Miami Woods" is a major pastoral work examining the magnificent hardwood forests of southwestern Ohio and southeastern Indiana as they had stood for a millennium to shelter the aboriginal inhabitants and remained to challenge the newcomer. In it, permanence is found with transience, that of time as well as the natural cycles of an as-yet-uncorrupted nature. Particularly clear in its depiction of place and time is the passage describing the forest as the poet sees it in all its permanence:

> Around me here rise up majestic trees
> That centuries have nurtured: graceful elms,
> Which interlock their limbs among the
>     clouds;
> Dark-columned walnuts, from whose
>     liberal store
> The nut-brown Indian maids their baskets
>     fill'd
> Ere the first pilgrims knelt on Plymouth
>     Rock;
> Giant sycamores, whose mighty arms
> Sheltered the Redman in his wigwam
>     prone, . . .
> And towering oaks . . .
> Tracing the plain, but shrouded in the gloom
> Of dark, impenetrable shades, that fall
> From the dark centuries . . . . (*Poets and
>     Poetry of the West* 17–18)

In this introductory passage, Gallagher includes all the elements of early-nineteenth-century romanticism: reverence for nature and the past, perception of the Indians as nature's noblemen, fascination with the implications of natural mysteries. But here, and in the remainder of the poem, as Gallagher examines and celebrates the natural cycle of the year, particularly that Western phenomenon known as "Indian Summer," he demonstrates a deep knowledge of, and keen insight into, the facts of nature as the poet knows them to be.

Here, indeed, is the beginning of a literature of place as well as of experience. In his sequel to "Miami Woods," "The Song of the Pioneers," he records the coming of the settler into that natural world. But that coming is neither an intrusion nor a corruption. Gallagher's recreation of the life of the pioneer is reality rather than romance; and the wilderness, as a result, is not destroyed but transformed into something that simultaneously celebrates what it was and what it has become as it records what Gallagher sees as the unfolding of God's plan in the working out of human destiny.

Unlike Gallagher, however, Charles A. Jones sees the transformation of the natural setting of the West as intrusion and desecration rather than divine plan or human destiny. In "The Old Mound," his reverence for what was, and his regret for what is, are clear: "Lonely and sad it stands / The trace of ruthless hands / Is on its sides and summit, and, around / the dwellings of the white man pile the ground; / And, curling in the air, / the smoke of thrice a thousand hearths is there: . . . // Upon its top I tread, / And see around me spread / Temples and mansions, and the hoary hills, / Bleak with the labor that the coffer fills, . . . //" (*Poets and Poetry of the West* 205).

Jones's mound had already had its top removed when he saw the city encroaching upon it. Today its only remnant lies in the name of a Cincinnati city street. Mound Street is its epitaph and memorial, a result that Jones could not foresee as he portrayed the incongruousness of the city surrounding a vanishing and forgotten remnant of the past.

As Coggeshall's anthology indicates, the West had a thriving poetic literature by 1860, when his anthology was published. Yet even then the region was continuing to change internally through continuing westward migration as well as with the evolution within a continental nation. These poets and dozens of others provide clear images of what was, even as they see what it will become. Their works remain as testaments to the beginning of a new voice in a new place that demanded its own.

As the Northwest Territory became the

West, and by the outbreak of the Civil War, something quite different, something that Lincoln saw as "the great interior region of the country" (*Works of Abraham Lincoln* 528), it became the subject of Eastern and European curiosity and of curiosity gratified. Countless visits to the region by the curious of both places made it the subject of dozens of travelers' reports in essays, news items, letters, and their inevitable transformation into books. Charles Dickens visited the West in 1842 and produced *American Notes* (1842) and a novel, *Martin Chuzzlewit* (1843), both sharply critical of what he saw. Mrs. Frances Trollope came to Cincinnati to make her fortune, failed, and wrote *The Domestic Manners of the Americans* (1832); Margaret Fuller visited the Great Lakes and Mackinac Island in 1843 and wrote her transcendental feminist *A Summer on the Lakes in 1843* (1844).

A flourishing guidebook industry developed for the curious as well as the potential emigrant. "Western fever" struck, and in parts of New England entire villages lost their young men if not their entire population. Works such as *Western Emigration: The Journal of Doctor Jeremiah Simpleton's Tour to Ohio* appeared. Published in Boston (ca. 1810) by one H. Trumbull, the title page contains a caricature of two horsemen meeting. One, splendidly dressed, well-fed, mounted on a fine horse, says, "I am going to Ohio"; the other, in rags, emaciated, mounted on a nag, says, "I have been." Further, according to the title page, the work contains "An account of the numerous difficulties, Hair-breadth Escapes, Mortifications and Privations which the Doctor and his family experienced on their Journey from Maine to the 'Land of Promise,' and during a residence of three years in that highly extolled country." That Doctor Simpleton's trials and tribulations were but little exaggerated is clear in the absence of prose works refuting Trumbull by those who had come to the West to stay.

James Hall (1793–1868) provided insights into the factual and legendary West in *Legends of the West* (1832) and later in his *Sketches of History, Life, and Manners in the West* (1834, 1835). The West's shortcoming are dramatized as well in *Tales of the Northwest* (1830) by William Joseph Snelling (1804–48).

But the best writing of this type appears in a series of books written by a young wife who came with her husband to Michigan in 1835 to stay and remained for eight years, during which time she became famous in the East. The woman was CAROLINE MATILDA STANSBURY KIRKLAND (1801–64). She was the wife of William Kirkland, who came to Detroit in 1835 as principal of the Detroit Female Seminary and later, in 1837, was a founder of Pinckney, Michigan. Her son, JOSEPH KIRKLAND (1830–94), was later to become a pioneer Midwestern realist, but Mrs. Kirkland's literary works and a reputation that still endures are her own. Her works include *A New Home—Who'll Follow* (1839); her best work, published under the pseudonym Mrs. Mary Clavers, *Forest Life* (1842); and *Western Clearings* (1846).

All of her works are compounded of reality and humor. In them she recreates the life of movement and settlement, and she depicts the search for an elusive stability that marks the transition from wilderness to order. Her people are not those of Western romance, then or later, but the housewives, farmers, hunters, and speculators who had come to make the West their own. She writes, also, of a rustic democracy that ignored theory for practice. The best of her generation, she influenced the work of her son Joseph and in turn of HAMLIN GARLAND (1860–1940), EDWARD EGGLESTON (1837–1902), and dozens of other new realistic writers emerging from the West. That influence is still evident.

HENRY HOWE (1816–93) is another writer of prose, the author of works quite unlike those of Mrs. Kirkland. Howe came from the East in 1846 to compile a social, historical, geographical, and cultural examination of the forty-three-year-old state of Ohio. He spent nearly a year visiting every section of the state, interviewing pioneers and other residents, and recording what he found. The result, *The Historical Collections of Ohio* (1847), is a remarkable assembly of fact, observation, opinion, and statistics making up the history of the state. He stayed in Ohio as a publisher, editor, and compiler in Cincinnati and later in Columbus. In his last years he retraced his steps, recording a new reality in a new version, published in two volumes in 1888–89. His works, illustrated by his own drawings, may be naive, biased, and unreliable, but they are real. Both the commentary Howe provides and his realistic orientation give a clear indication of what had transpired in the West in half a century by 1847. The later volumes further depict the changes that two additional generations had made in the Midwest.

The post–Civil War years saw the emergence of two important literary movements. The first of these was a home-grown, local-color, realistic movement that was to have a profound influence on Midwestern and other American writers in the next century. The second was a group of young writers who came out of the Midwest to take over the literary leadership of both the East and the Far West. Among the former are Edward Eggleston, Joseph Kirkland, Edgar Watson Howe (1853–1937), and Hamlin Garland (1860–1940). The latter include AMBROSE BIERCE (1842–1914?), Mark Twain (Samuel Langhorne Clemens, 1835–1910), and William Dean Howells (1837–1920). In the works of these writers, not only was a new, recognizably Midwestern literature coming of age, but Midwestern writing had clearly become a significant part of the national whole.

Eggleston and Kirkland were among the first to attempt to transmute into literature the experience of the small-town and rural Midwest that had attained a measure of post–Civil War stability. Eggleston in Indiana and Kirkland in Illinois attempted, with limited success, to reproduce the dialect of the region as well as the character types and situations encountered in the Midwestern countryside. Both blended romance and sentimentality with a realism often harsh and unpleasant in its implications.

Eggleston wrote seven novels set in Indiana, of which *The Hoosier Schoolmaster* (1871) has proved the most lasting. The thinness of plot in this and in his other novels indicates that Eggleston saw plot structure as an expedient means of presenting his people, often caricatured but most frequently vivid and real, as are the incidents of their lives. His realism, even at its best in his reproduction of social conditions, is too frequently distorted by his conviction that the novel must ultimately be moral.

Kirkland's works of fiction are three, of which *Zury: The Meanest Man in Spring County* (1887) is the most durable. Like Eggleston, his strengths lie in his reproduction of Midwestern dialect, his realistic incidents, and his often effective characterization. Unfortunately,

weaknesses in structure and romantic and sentimental intrusions often mar what would otherwise be graphically realistic portraits of a time and place in pursuit of an elusive rural fulfillment.

Edgar Watson Howe and Hamlin Garland are the first of their generation of Midwestern writers to move beyond realism in their depictions of small-town and rural Midwestern life and to approach the helplessness and hopelessness of naturalism in defining the course of their people's lives. Howe's *The Story of a Country Town* (1883) is a powerful and bitter indictment of small-town life in the Midwest after the Civil War. His fictional towns of Fairview and Twin Mounds anticipate the portrayal of later fictional towns by Sherwood Anderson (1876–1941) and Sinclair Lewis (1885–1951). His other three novels are weak, but *The Story of a Country Town* is a significant contribution to Midwestern literature.

Hamlin Garland's literary career was certainly the most prolific of his generation and perhaps the most prolific in all of Midwestern literature. It spanned fifty years and produced thirty-eight volumes of fiction, biography, autobiography, and verse. Garland's first work, *Main-Travelled Roads* (1891), and his later Middle Border series of fiction and autobiography remain the best known and the most frequently discussed, reprinted, and anthologized. His works range from the rural Midwestern realism of *Main-Travelled Roads* through the historical romance of such novels as *Rose of Dutcher's Coolly* (1895) to the near-sentimental reminiscences of his autobiographical works. Like the other nineteenth-century realists, Garland is important in the evolution of Midwestern literature both because of his interpretations of the region and its people and because his work foreshadows the great literature that was to come out of the Midwest in the next century in the works of THEODORE DREISER, Sherwood Anderson, EDGAR LEE MASTERS, and the others who moved the literary center of the United States west of the Appalachians.

AMBROSE BIERCE took his youthful rural Ohio and Indiana background, his grim Civil War service, and his brief newspaper experience to San Francisco and to London and back. He produced such bitter and biting works as the sketches in *The Fiend's Delight*

(1892), the grim stories in *Tales of Soldiers and Civilians* (1891, retitled *In the Midst of Life*, 1892), the bitter epigrams in *Black Beetles in Amber* (1892), and the satirical definitions in *The Cynic's Word Book* (1906, retitled *The Devil's Dictionary*, 1911). He had become the literary dictator of the West Coast before disappearing into the Mexican dust in 1913. Both Mark Twain and William Dean Howells took their youthful small-town Midwestern backgrounds and their intensive small-town newspaper experiences to the East. By century's end, each had earned a major place in American literature, Mark Twain as America's foremost literary humorist and William Dean Howells as the Dean of American Letters, but both carried with them to the end the Midwestern countryside out of which they came and to which they returned again and again in their work.

Mark Twain, born Samuel Langhorne Clemens in Florida, Missouri, took his newspaper apprenticeship, his Mississippi River steamboat experience, and his brief Confederate Army service to Nevada and then to San Francisco. There he began his reputation as a rustic but barbed humorist. Twain traveled from San Francisco to the East, where he wrote his major works, *Life on the Mississippi* (1883), *The Adventures of Tom Sawyer* (1876), and his masterpiece, *Adventures of Huckleberry Finn* (1884, 1885), the most important novel written in nineteenth-century America, influencing such later major writers as Sherwood Anderson (1876–1941), Ernest Hemingway (1898–1961), and William Faulkner (1897–1962). Because Twain's best work was set in the middle Mississippi Valley and his influence has been as pervasive in the works of Western and Southern as well as Midwestern writers, all three regions claim him, but it was through Sherwood Anderson that his influence spread to the writers who came of age in the 1920s in all three regions. Mark Twain has shaped the realistic language of modern literature, its characters, and its loose structure. Of most importance to the evolution of Midwestern literature, he added the dimension of movement. It is in movement that the people of Midwestern modernism, like Huckleberry Finn, seek their elusive destinies down the river or in what have become the mythical American territories beyond the horizon, the city, the West, and increasingly, like Mark

Twain and Howells, the world of the East, where the ultimate reward appears to be within reach, however elusive it may prove to be.

William Dean Howells was perhaps the most prolific and versatile Midwestern writer to influence the course of American writing in his time and ours. Poet, essayist, dramatist, critic, editor, and above all novelist, he was most influential in defining and practicing realism as a literary technique in which the mirror image of human life and experience becomes the substance of literature. His realism is most evident in *The Rise of Silas Lapham* (1885), *A Hazard of New Fortunes* (1890), and his later works in which he returns to the Ohio country, *The Kentons* (1902), *New Leaf Mills* (1913), and *The Leatherwood God* (1916).

With the appearance of major works by Mark Twain and William Dean Howells, together with those of Henry James (1843–1916), Easterner and expatriate, it is evident that, as the beginning of a new century appeared on the horizon, American literature was becoming a significant part of the literature of a new age. The literature by Midwesterners, using the place and people of their Midwestern origins as the substance of their work, had become a significant part of the American whole.

This new maturity in American literature and that of the Midwest, its most important component, carried on into the new century and influenced a new generation of young writers. WILLA CATHER (1873–1947) exemplified the workers of that generation, many of whom were to become known and read throughout the country and beyond. By 1920 it was becoming evident in the United States and particularly in Europe that the new American literature and the new Midwestern literature had become virtually synonymous. The English *Nation*, that country's leading literary and intellectual journal, published a major supplement, the "American Literature Supplement," in its issue of Saturday, April 17, 1920. The supplement consists of four essays by four distinguished Irish, Irish American, and American critics. Each of these essays is a survey of one of the three major genres—recent American poetry, recent American criticism, recent American fiction—and the fourth assesses the major literary centers. Three of the four essays, poetry, fiction, and the American literary place, demonstrate clearly—and each of the critics comments on it—that modern Midwestern writing by far dominates new writing in the new American century.

The essay on recent American poetry, by Padraic Colum (1881–1972), a major poet of the Irish Renaissance, discusses five American poets, Vachel Lindsay (1879–1931), EDGAR LEE MASTERS (1869–1950), Carl Sandburg (1878–1967), Edwin Arlington Robinson (1869–1995), and Amy Lowell (1874–1925). Three of the five poets are Midwestern in origins, subject matter, and inspiration, and in their clear attempts to make the local the poetic universal. Colum also comments that these three, unlike their Eastern counterparts, are the poets of "new beginnings," of a "freshness and abundance of vocabulary" (*Nation* 80); they are truly the "poets of the Great Valley" (80).

The section on recent American novels by Irish American FRANCIS HACKETT (1885–1962) is even more completely dominated by writers who "defy the views of respectability" (*Nation* 83) and who reject the genteel tradition still dominant in the East. Bred in the "newspaper offices of the Middle West" (83), Hackett asserts that these writers "face the raw United States with a desperate resolution to subdue it to the novel . . ." (83). Hackett's list is impressive: "the most titanic Theodore Dreiser" (83) (1871–1945), DAVID GRAHAM PHILLIPS (1867–1911), BRAND WHITLOCK (1864–1934), and "a late comer . . . Sherwood Anderson . . . a naturalist with a spirit of music haunting him" (83). Hackett also asserts that HENRY BLAKE FULLER (1857–1927) and Hamlin Garland or Willa Cather (1873–1947)—and James Branch Cabell (1879–1958)—are said to have "an art all their own, but I have not read them" (83). Hackett recognizes that "the possibilities of the American novel are still practically untouched" but from the works of Dreiser and the other Midwesterners "may yet come a much deeper and more beautiful expression" (83).

The last word and the most unqualified assessment of the situation in the supplement is left to H. L. Mencken (1880–1956), already a critical curmudgeon. His essay is entitled "The Literary Capital of the United States" and that, he asserts, is Chicago. New York he dismisses at once: "There is no longer a New York school of writers . . . the play of ideas is not there . . . . It produces nothing" (*Nation* 83–84). But Chicago is alive:

In Chicago there is the mysterious something that makes for individuality, personality, charm; in Chicago a spirit broods upon the face of the waters. Find a writer who is indubitably an American in every pulse-beat, snort and adenoid, an American who has something new and peculiarly American to say and who says it in an unmistakably American way, and nine times out of ten you will find that he has some sort of connection with the gargantuan and inordinate abattoir by Lake Michigan—that he was bred there, or got his start there, or passed through there when he was young and tender.

. . . With two exceptions there is not a single American novelist of the younger generation—that is, a serious novelist, a novelist deserving a civilized reader's attention—who has not sprung from the Middle Empire that has Chicago as his capital . . . Dreiser, Anderson, Miss Cather, Mrs. Watts, [BOOTH] TARKINGTON, Wilson, [ROBERT] HERRICK, Patterson, even Churchill. It was Chicago that produced Henry B. Fuller, the father of the modern American novel. It was Chicago that developed FRANK NORRIS, its final practitioner of genius. And it was Chicago that produced Dreiser, undoubtedly the greatest artist of them all. (84)

The Chicago that Mencken and the others cite as the well-head of American literature in the first two decades of the twentieth century is, of course, the Chicago of what has come to be called the Chicago Renaissance, an in-gathering of young people from all over the Midwest who had come to Chicago to found a new art, a new literature, and a new sense of self. It sponsored an active Chicago Little Theater, and it produced two major and influential literary journals: *Poetry*, founded by poet HARRIET MONROE (1860–1936) in 1912 and still in existence; and the *Little Review* (1914–29), founded by MARGARET ANDERSON (1886?–1973). Both provided outlets for the impressive literary energy of the new younger writers, whether they had come to Chicago or not.

The Chicago Renaissance gave many important writers to the American literary mainstream. These included Sherwood Anderson, MAXWELL BODENHEIM (1893–1954), and FLOYD DELL (1887–1969), poets Edgar Lee Masters and Carl Sandburg (1878–1967), playwright SUSAN GLASPELL (1882–1948), and dozens of others. Ironically, even as Mencken wrote, the Chicago Renaissance had largely run its course, its participants going off to New York or joining the exodus of young writers to Paris. Even in leaving Chicago, however, many of them took with them the Chicago and the Midwest they had known and that was to continue to be the substance of their works. By 1922 the Chicago Renaissance was a memory.

The primacy gained in American literature by those who came out of the Midwest and the Chicago Renaissance in the second decade of the twentieth century was not fleeting. Rather, they were joined by other young writers who came out of World War I, the Great War in the language of the day. They became a new generation of American writers, continuing the domination of American letters by Midwestern writers, and founding a new but not homogeneous group called by Gertrude Stein (1874–1946) a lost generation. Among them were Ernest Hemingway, F. SCOTT FITZGERALD (1896–1940), LOUIS BROMFIELD (1896–1956), HART CRANE (1899–1932), and dozens of others. They were joined in the next decade by NELSON ALGREN (1909–81), JAMES T. FARRELL (1904–79), JACK CONROY (1899–1990), RICHARD WRIGHT (1908–60), RUTH SUCKOW (1892–1960), and many more. By midcentury Midwestern literature continued its central role in the unfolding literary interpretation of the nation. Names appeared like SAUL BELLOW (b. 1915), JAMES JONES (1921–77), JESSAMYN WEST (1902–84), JAMES PURDY (b. 1914), WRIGHT MORRIS (b. 1910), ROSS LOCKRIDGE JR. (1914–48), and dozens of others who came to the forefront. All of them use the Midwest and its people as the substance of their works.

As the twentieth century, the century in which the Midwest and its literature have come to dominate American life and letters, becomes the twenty-first, the array of contemporary writers who have come out of the Midwest to become productive and prominent writers is impressive. Among them are North Dakota's novelists LARRY WOIWODE (b. 1941) and LOUISE ERDRICH (b. 1954), Iowa's R. V. CASSILL (b. 1919), Indiana's WILLIAM GASS

(b. 1924), Nebraska's TILLIE OLSEN (b. 1913), Michigan's poet-novelist JIM HARRISON (b. 1937), Nebraskan and Minnesotan JONIS AGEE (b. 1943), Iowa's Robert Coover (b. 1932), and Minnesota's JON HASSLER (b. 1933).

Equally impressive is the array of contemporary poets, including Ohio's RITA DOVE (b. 1952), Illinois' JOHN KNOEPFLE (b. 1923), Iowa and Missouri's MONA VAN DUYN (b. 1921), Chicago's GWENDOLYN BROOKS (b. 1917), and Minnesota's ROBERT BLY (b. 1926). Chicago's DAVID MAMET (b. 1947) has become a major playwright, and Minnesota's CAROL BLY (b. 1930) is a leader in the short story and the essay. The Midwest has also produced the most prolific of modern novelists, Chicago's ANDREW GREELEY (b. 1928), and the author of the runaway best-seller *The Bridges of Madison County* (1992), Iowa's ROBERT JAMES WALLER (b. 1939).

Perhaps the most telling of any statistic in assessing the significance of the Midwest and its literature at the end of the twentieth century is the fact that since the inception of the Nobel Prize in literature in 1901, it has been awarded to eight American writers. Four of these eight have been Midwesterners whose origins are integral to their work. The first American and the first Midwestern writer to win the award was Sinclair Lewis (1930). He had contributed the terms "Main Street" and "Babbitt" to the American language. He was followed in 1954 by Ernest Hemingway, whose Nick Adams in all his various guises had traveled in sensitive disbelief from northern Michigan across Europe and Africa. In 1976 Saul Bellow, whose Chicago is at once a microcosm of and a point of departure for a broader, larger world of the spirit, received the prize. In 1993 Toni Morrison (b. 1931) became the newest Nobel laureate. She has come out of Lorain, Ohio, to define the African American experience of that place and her time in terms that are intimate, compassionate, and universal.

David D. Anderson
Michigan State University

WORKS CITED

Anderson, Sherwood. *Letters*, edited by Howard Mumford Jones, with Walter B. Rideout. Boston: Little Brown, 1953.

Colum, Padraic. "Recent American Poetry," in

the *Nation* (London), "American Literature Supplement," April 17, 1920.

Curry, Otway. "The Eternal River," "Autumn Mornings," "Buckeye Cabin," in William T. Coggeshall, *The Poets and Poetry of the West*. Columbus: Follett, Foster, 1860.

Dwight, Margaret Van Horn. *A Journey to Ohio in 1810*. New Haven: Yale University Press, 1912.

Frederick, John T., ed. *Out of the Midwest*. New York: Whittlesey House, 1944.

Gallagher, William Davis. "Miami Woods," in William T. Coggeshall, *The Poets and Poetry of the West*. Columbus: Follett, Foster, 1860.

Hackett, Francis. "The American Novel," in the *Nation* (London), April 17, 1920.

Hinsdale, Burke Aaron. *The Old Northwest*. New York: Townsend MacCoun, 1888.

Jefferson, Thomas. *The Writings of Thomas Jefferson*, edited by Paul Leicester Ford. New York: G. P. Putnam's Sons, 1897.

Jones, Charles A. "The Old Mound," in William T. Coggeshall, *The Poets and Poetry of the West*. Columbus: Follett, Foster, 1860.

Kazin, Alfred. *A Writer's America: Landscape in Literature*. New York: Knopf, 1988.

Lincoln, Abraham. "Annual Message to Congress." *The Collected Works of Abraham Lincoln*, edited by Roy P. Basler. New Brunswick, N.J.: Rutgers University Press, 1953.

Lincoln, Benjamin. *Journal*. Massachusetts Historical Society *Collections* (3 ser. V, 1836), 109–73.

Mencken, H. L. "The Literary Capital of the United States," in the *Nation* (London), April 17, 1920.

Turner, Frederick Jackson. "The Middle West," in *The Frontier in American History*. New York: Henry Holt, 1948.

Wilson, William E. *Indiana: A History*. Bloomington: Indiana University Press, 1996.

## FRANKLIN (PIERCE) ADAMS

November 15, 1881–March 23, 1960
(F. P. A., Franklin Leopold Adams)

**BIOGRAPHY:** Born in Chicago of business-class parents, Moses and Clara (Schlossman) Adams, Franklin attended the modern Armour Institute during his adolescent years. His subsequent attendance at the University of Michigan ended after one year with the death of his mother. Returning to Chicago, Adams sold insurance, which led to a meeting with his hero, GEORGE ADE of the *Chicago Record*, who encouraged Adams to submit humorous verse to Bert Leston Taylor's (BLT's) column, "Poets' Corner." In 1903, while writing a weather column for the *Chicago Journal*, he volunteered articles for the theater section, which resulted in a regular column, "A Little about Everything."

Once Adams met Minna Schwartz, a touring Florodora showgirl, his literary sights and love interests moved to New York. Relocating to New York in 1904, he married Minna and started a regular feature, "Snide Lights on Literature," for the *New York Evening Mail*. He adopted an eclectic format similar to BLT's. "Always in Good Humor" became a daily column. As he made his way into literary circles, he became well known among an influential group of wits who produced sophisticated, intellectual humor. In 1909 Harry Askin, a Chicago theatrical manager, urged Adams to collaborate with O. Henry on the lyrics for a musical comedy entitled *Lo*, which was neither a critical nor a commercial success. In 1911 Adams began a personal memoir, "The Diary of Our Own Samuel Pepys," a Saturday feature written in seventeenth-century style.

His most famous literary venue, "The Conning Tower," appeared in the *New York Tribune* in 1914. World War I found him in Paris where he met Harold Ross, working on *Stars and Stripes*, an overseas news service. His postwar popularity soared as he recorded the witticisms of the Algonquin group, of which he was a member. After appearing in the *New York World* and the *New York Herald Tribune*, "The Conning Tower" ended in 1941 in the *New York Evening Post*. In 1938 he appeared as a regular panelist on "Information Please," a popular radio show that ended in 1947. Freelance work included seasonal work for the *New Yorker*.

**SIGNIFICANCE:** Franklin P. Adams's influence on Midwestern and American culture came more through his tastemaking and mentorship than through his literary contributions. Adams encouraged many budding authors, giving them a popular forum to display their talents. JAMES THURBER, it is reputed, might have returned to Columbus had it not been for recognition in "The Conning Tower." Adams also featured some early work by Robert Benchley, John O'Hara, and George S. Kaufman. He fostered the careers of RING LARDNER, Louis Untermeyer, Edna St. Vincent Millay, E. B. White, Phyllis McGinley, Dorothy Parker, and others.

Adams's column and weekly diary were widely imitated throughout the country. His poetry, which has been collected in many volumes, reflects America of the early twentieth century. His style is the result of fastidious care and devotion to classical tradition, clean rhythm and rhyme, and disdain for modernist blank or free verse. His subjects were the daily concerns of his personal life. He wrote about the books he read, the people he met, and the theater.

**SELECTED WORKS:** Adams's collected works include compilations with some of his column contributors, some exclusively prose work, some volumes of his own poetry, and some mixed genres. His *The Conning Tower Book* (1926) and *The Second Conning Tower Book* (1927) include his collected works and, like *The Diary of Our Own Samuel Pepys* (1935), record New York's contemporary life. Volumes of collected works include *Tobogganing on Parnassus* (1911), *Christopher Columbus and Other Patriotic Verses* (1931), *The Melancholy Lute: Selected Songs of Thirty Years* (1936), and *Nods and Becks* (1944). Adams wrote forewords and introductions for works by William Congreve, Berenice Dewey, FINLEY PETER DUNNE, and William Ely Hill. He also wrote articles collected in tribute of Heywood Broun as well as Percy Hammond.

**FURTHER READING:** Sally Ashley's *FPA: The Life and Times of Franklin Pierce Adams* (1986) is the major biography. Adams's manuscripts can be found at the University of Chicago, Harvard University, and the New York Public Library. Viking Press in New York is the primary repository for Adams's correspondence.

RUSSELL J. BODI                OWENS COLLEGE

# JANE ADDAMS

September 6, 1860–May 21, 1935

**BIOGRAPHY:** Jane Addams was born in Cedarville, Illinois, to John Huy Addams, owner of a sawmill and a gristmill and president of a bank, and his first wife, Sarah (Weber), who died carrying her ninth child when Jane was two. A state senator and friend of ABRAHAM LINCOLN, John Addams schooled his daughter in Midwestern politics and egalitarian ideology, sending her to Rockford Female Seminary, later known as Rockford College, from which she graduated in 1882. After her father's death, she attended Women's Medical College of Philadelphia but broke down in the spring of 1882, suffering from "hysteria," now called depression.

In 1889 Addams, together with Ellen Gates Starr, founded Hull House, a social settlement on Chicago's Halsted Street, a working-class neighborhood of European immigrants. Her brilliance came from her ability to synthesize European social ideas, including those of Ruskin, Morris, and Tolstoy, and American notions of organic unity and democratic spirit, expressed by Emerson, Lincoln, and Whitman, to define and reform the Midwestern city. William James in a February 12, 1907, letter to her characterized her writing as "revolutionary in the extreme."

Hull House provided impoverished members of the community with a wide array of community services ranging from the most basic to the most elevated. These included infant and child care, an employment bureau, a juvenile court, and an ambitious array of educational facilities and advanced social and cultural activities. Hull House's cultural activities and aspirations led to its becoming a Midwestern salon that attracted intellectuals and writers, among them William Butler Yeats, William James, John Dewey, FRANK LLOYD WRIGHT, Richard T. Ely, Florence Kelley, Henry Demarest Lloyd, Ida B. Wells, and Charlotte Perkins Gilman.

Addams, the leading female Midwestern progressive, became the first female recipient of the Nobel Peace Prize in 1931. She and Mary Rozet Smith, a wealthy Chicagoan, enjoyed a forty-year homosocial companionship known in the East as a "Boston marriage." She died in Chicago of intestinal cancer.

**SIGNIFICANCE:** "I have not written as a philanthropist merely," Addams explained in the *New York Sun* (April 30, 1910). Throughout her career as a reformer, she wrote essays and speeches, collecting them into books, eleven in all. Her writing on the nature of Midwestern American culture and the development of middle-class ethics continues to draw readers because of the gracefulness of her style and the power of her literary imagination.

At the time the naturalist writers THEODORE DREISER, UPTON SINCLAIR, and FRANK NORRIS were using science to give credibility to realist portraits of Midwestern urban life, Addams did the reverse, using narratives, real and fictionalized accounts of life in Chicago, to give credibility to social science. As she put it in *Democracy and Social Ethics* (1902), "ideas only operate upon the popular mind through will and character, and must be dramatized before they reach the mass of men" (227).

The themes in her books are those of contemporary Midwestern writers of fiction. Her characters, like those of HAMLIN GARLAND and SHERWOOD ANDERSON, sense the isolation of rural and small-town Midwestern life and yearn to move to Chicago, the vital, enticingly flawed place she describes in *The Spirit of Youth and the City Streets* (1909). Her portraits of urban industrial labor look much like Sinclair's. *A New Conscience and an Ancient Evil* (1912) explores, as do Dreiser's portraits of his sister, sexual slavery and the risks for working women who dare to venture alone into the city. Addams's *The Long Road of Woman's Memory* (1916) is a modern—even modernist—exploration of female mythology and psychology, themes that WILLA CATHER worked out in novels. In this her most literary book, Addams portrays herself and immigrant women in Chicago as part of a collective maternal memory, one she imagines as thrusting its "ghostly fingers into the delicate fabric of human experience" (Introduction x). The book begins with several local accounts of a "Devil baby," an urban myth about a child of sin, and weaves together threads of gossip and folklore that conclude with a trip Addams took to Egypt, where the pyramids overlap with images of the Cedarville landscape of her youth.

The book most often read today is *Twenty Years at Hull House*, an autobiography that expresses her Midwestern view, pragmatic and realistic yet hopeful, a useful contrast to the mournful Eastern view of Henry Adams.

**SELECTED WORKS:** Jane Addams, together with Florence Kelley, wrote *Hull-House Maps and Papers* (1895), a sociological study of the Halsted Street neighborhood. She experimented with a more literary style of writing in *Democracy and Social Ethics* (1902). Her three most enduring books followed: *The Newer Ideals of Peace* (1907), *The Spirit of Youth and the City Streets* (1909), and *Twenty Years at Hull-House* (1910). During the decade of World War I, Addams wrote two books about women, *A New Conscience and an Ancient Evil* (1912) and *The Long Road of Woman's Memory* (1916). Following the war she wrote a female response, *Peace and Bread in Time of War* (1922). Before she died in 1935, she wrote three last books: *The Second Twenty Years at Hull-House* (1930), *The Excellent Becomes the Permanent* (1932), and *My Friend, Julia Lathrop* (1935).

**FURTHER READING:** Allen Davis's *American Heroine: The Life and Legend of Jane Addams* (1973) is a detailed and useful biography. The family account of her life, *Jane Addams: A Biography* (1935), was written by her nephew James Weber Linn. Christopher Lasch admires her politics in *New Radicalism in America* (1965) and *The Social Thought of Jane Addams* (1965), a selection of her essays. In "Women Reformers and American Culture, 1870–1930," in *Journal of Social History* 5.1 (Winter 1971): 164–77, Jill Conway criticizes Addams for adopting a literary style of writing.

Several recent articles consider Addams as a writer. These include Lois Rudnick's "A Feminist American Success Myth: Jane Addams's *Twenty Years at Hull-House*," in *Tradition and the Talents of Women*, edited by Florence Howe (1991): 145–67; Marianne DeKoven's "Excellent Not a Hull House: Gertrude Stein, Jane Addams, and Feminist-Modernist Political Culture," in *Rereading Modernism*, edited by Lisa Rado (1994): 321–50; Francesca Sawaya's "Domesticity, Cultivation, and Vocation in Jane Addams and Sarah Orne Jewett," in *Nineteenth-Century Literature* 48.4 (1994): 507–28; and Katherine Joslin's "Literary Cross-Dressing: Jane Addams Finds Her Voice in *Democracy and Social Ethics*," in *Femmes de conscience: aspects du féminisme américain, 1848–1875*, edited by Susan Goodman and Daniel Royot (1994).

The Swarthmore College Peace Collection and the Jane Addams Memorial Collection at the University of Illinois, Chicago, are the primary repositories of her papers. Most material is also available on microfilm. The Hull

House Museum on Halsted Street in Chicago exhibits maps, pictures, books, art, and crafts projects from the period.

KATHERINE JOSLIN   WESTERN MICHIGAN UNIVERSITY

## GEORGE ADE
February 9, 1866–May 16, 1944

**BIOGRAPHY:** John Ade was brought as a boy from England to Cheviot, Ohio, where he met and married Adaline Adair. Their son George was born in Kent, later known as Kentland, Indiana, with a population of less than six hundred. As the fifth of six children, he became known as something of an impractical dreamer. He attended Purdue University. George was a hard-working student who did nothing sensational but who was capable of uttering amusing witticisms. He formed a lasting friendship with another student, John T. McCutcheon. After graduation George drifted about for a time, tried to study law, then joyfully worked on Lafayette newspapers.

Ade accepted the invitation of Mc-Cutcheon, an artist on the *Morning News*, later the *Chicago Record,* to join him. Soon Ade was a reporter on the *Record* at a salary of twelve dollars a week and immersed himself in the study of Chicago. He got his chance when the managing editor sent him to cover an explosion on a freighter in the Chicago River; his accurate, dramatic lead story on the first page attracted great attention. Soon he was regarded as the star reporter.

With McCutcheon supplying the sketches, Ade established the column "Stories of the Streets and of the Town," which covered many subjects, inconsequential but interesting, and rose to the rank of popular literature. The paper published selections from the column in paperback from 1894 to 1900. After a time the column was succeeded by the "Doc' Horne" series, based on an odd old gentleman liar and introducing Pink Marsh, a lovable black bootblack of questionable ethics. These stories impressed many readers, including MARK TWAIN, WILLIAM DEAN HOWELLS,and HAMLIN GARLAND. Ade and McCutcheon, however, developed a yearning to travel. They went to Europe, sending colorful reports about European life back to the newspaper twice a month.

Other types of writing, such as fables, were yet to come, but soon Ade's fables had become so popular that *Fables in Slang* was published in 1900. These fables appeared to say that an individual should use common sense, mind his or her own affairs, and make no other pretense. Ade's unusual figures of speech and capitalization, slang, and compressed thought produced an amusing effect. In 1900 he left the *Record* to devote his time to authorship. He issued many collections of the *Fables*, which became so popular that motion pictures were made from them. Ade also interested himself in the stage. A trip to the Far East in 1900 led to the successful musical comedy, *The Sultan of Sulu* (1903).

The latter part of his bachelor life was filled with civic duties, philanthropy, great friendships, and honors. He and David Ross contributed heavily and secured the erection of the great Ross-Ade stadium at Purdue. He was director of publicity for the Indiana Council of Defense during World War I and was an intimate friend of Theodore Roosevelt, BOOTH TARKINGTON, JAMES WHITCOMB RILEY, and others. Honorary degrees from Purdue and Indiana Universities and Wabash College came his way. He was a moralist, a social historian, a short story writer and playwright, an entertainer, a shrewd satirical observer, and a commentator on life. He died at Brook, Indiana, on May 16, 1944.

**SIGNIFICANCE:** George Ade's writings are consistently Midwestern in wit and point of view. His characters are steadily suspicious of poets, saints, reformers, eccentricity, snobbishness, and affectation; like Ade, they are amused by tales of townspeople who do not distinguish themselves, of rough Westerners who compare favorably with Easterners of greater polish. They laugh at long-winded statesmen. Usually they talk about work, and love, and play, but they do not take any of these very seriously. They feel that love must be considered an aspect of comedy and that aristocracy merits contempt mixed with curiosity. Native-born and largely untraveled, they do not pretend to understand newcomers and foreigners, yet they delight in jokes at their own expense or at their neighbors' as long as the jibes are in their vernacular and are constructed by someone who has a reputation.

Ade presented himself as guilty of these same errors, and he laughed at himself. Because of his own background he knew well the beliefs of ordinary people, the types of human folly that he censured, and how far he could go without dissenting from popular ideas. His wit was essentially urban. In that he demolished greed, pretense, selfishness, bohemians, and climbers, he was a moralist. One finds in his fables no deep philosophy but rather a social record of how ridiculous some people make themselves; his liberties with language both delighted and astonished. Ade was regarded as a great humorist and satirist, as a person who observed particularly well, and as a moralist. He was personally popular with nearly everyone and was considered one of the greatest writers in his time.

**SELECTED WORKS:** Individuals wanting to learn much about Ade would do well to read some of the "Stories of the Streets and of the Town" until they feel that they understand Ade's purpose and method. After that could come several of the plays, such as *The Sultan of Sulu* (1903), *The County Chairman* (1924), *The Shogun* (1904), *The College Widow* (1924), *Just Out of College* (1924), and *The Old Town* (1909). In drama, Ade serves as a corrective wit.

**FURTHER READING:** Major sources on George Ade's life and writings include Lee Coyle's *George Ade* (1964); Thomas Dickinson's *Playwrights of the New American Theater* (1925); Fred Kelly's *George Ade, Warmhearted Satirist* (1947), and *The Permanent Ade: The Living Writings of George Ade* (1947); Julia Levering's *Historic Indiana* (1909); Fred Pattee's *The New American Literature, 1890–1930* (1930); Dorothy Russo's *A Biography of George Ade, 1866–1944* (1947); CARL VAN DOREN's "Old Wisdom in a New Tongue," in *Many Minds* (1924); and James DeMuth's *Small Town Chicago: The Comic Perspectives of Finley Peter Dunne, George Ade, and Ring Lardner* (1980).

ARTHUR SHUMAKER          DePAUW UNIVERSITY

# JONIS AGEE
May 31, 1943

**BIOGRAPHY:** Jonis Agee, from her earliest beginnings, was marked with the prairie dust of the Midwest that has settled into most of her adult work. Born in Omaha, Nebraska, and raised by parents Lauranel (Willson) and Eugene Agee Jr., Jonis Agee descends from a long line of explorers, visionaries, and outlaws that includes Lewis and Clark, the Younger brothers, and Jesse James. She and her five siblings all left home relatively early.

Agee earned her BA at the University of Iowa and her MA and PhD at the State University of New York at Binghamton, now Binghamton University, focusing on classical poetry and American literature. Her dissertation was her first book, *Houses* (1976), a long poem exploring family history and landscape, published subsequently by Truck Press as their first book. A daughter named Brenda Bobbitt, her only child, was born in 1964. After teaching for two decades at the College of St. Catherine, Agee was appointed professor of English and creative writing at the University of Michigan in 1995.

Her years in Nebraska, Iowa, and Minnesota gave her a deep reservoir of geography and landscape which functions significantly in her fiction. *Sweet Eyes* (1991), a complicated book about small-town life in the middle of Iowa, took her ten years to write. *Strange Angels* (1993) was composed in two years, during which time she made monthly forays into the sandhills of Nebraska to soak up atmosphere and memories from her native state. Although her solid credentials and book-lined office walls may imply the life of a genteel scholar, Agee has a passionate fascination for Elvis Presley and is commonly seen wearing handmade cowboy boots and a cowboy hat festooned with porcupine quills. She avidly studies the culture and ritual of the vanishing Lakota people and believes in a reality that includes ghosts and gods in disguise.

**SIGNIFICANCE:** Agee's best fiction illustrates how the physical geography of rural Iowa, in particular, not only impinges upon but actually demarcates the moral geography of her fictional characters. Her work has been compared to that of the more mature and prolific CAROL BLY, who uses the landscape of central Minnesota in a similar way.

The fictional Divinity, Iowa, is the setting for *Sweet Eyes*, where the main character works out an acceptance of self which is at the same time a resigned acceptance of an unremarkable place. There is debris and desolation in Agee's rural landscape, and its ugly, hard-edged particulars bespeak the suffering and aberrations of its inhabitants. Her characters are shown in a jangled harmony with the seasons, as an April snowstorm opens the novel and a summer parade a year later closes it. Her subjects are largely farmers and ranchers who live in nature, their shoes more often than not thick with mud and manure. Physical bonding with the natural world is underscored, and animals function in her best imagery. A dramatic account of the death of a mare following the birth of her foal is in many ways more moving than the parallel human episode later in the novel.

*Strange Angels*, too, is an urgent book with the Dreiserian sense of a primitive life force that is unbridled, unexplored, and unencumbered with intellect. Set in the Nebraska sandhills and the contemporary West, the novel weaves a powerful tale of familial and cultural myth centering on the three adult children of Heywood Bennett, recently deceased rancher. These three—Arthur, the family's sole legitimate heir, Cody, who has cowboyed on the ranch since he was fourteen, and Kya, the free-spirited sister with Lakota blood whom both brothers adore—battle with one another and with the ghost of their father, who controls them even from the grave. While some critics praise Agee's fictions and others are more qualified in their assessments, her ability to capture small-town life with precise details of place has earned her respect as an emerging novelist to watch.

**SELECTED WORKS:** Agee's entrée into the publishing world was as an editor, first of *Border Crossings* (1984), a Minnesota Voices project reader, and then of *Stiller's Pond* (1988, expanded in 1991), a collection of fiction from the upper Midwest. She has published three collections of short stories: *Bend This Heart* (1989); *Pretend We've Never Met* (1989); and *A .38 Special and a Broken Heart* (1995); and two novels: *Sweet Eyes* (1991) and *Strange Angels* (1993). Both novels and *Bend This Heart* have been selected as *New York Times* Notable Books. Another novel, *South of Resurrection*, was published in 1997.

**FURTHER READING:** No book-length study of Jonis Agee has been published. An essay, "The Cutting Art: Sharpness of Image in the Fiction of Jonis Agee," by Jill B. Gidmark, appeared in *Exploring the Midwestern Literary Imagination* (1993): 130–41. Book reviews that are particularly informative are those of *Bend This Heart* (July 16, 1989): 22, and *Sweet Eyes* (March 3, 1991): 12–13, both in the *New York Times Book Review;* and of *Pretend We've Never Met* in the *Review of Contemporary Fiction* 10

(1990): 211–13. A longer article that is primarily biographical appeared in the *Minneapolis Star Tribune* (September 23, 1993): 1E, 3E, under the title "Writing the Range: 'Angels' Author Loves Literature and the Rodeo."

JILL B. GIDMARK          UNIVERSITY OF MINNESOTA

# Zoë Akins
October 30, 1886–October 29, 1958

**BIOGRAPHY:** Best known as a playwright and screenwriter, Zoë Akins also wrote poetry, fiction, and critical essays. She was born into a prosperous Republican family in Humansville, Missouri, the second child of Thomas and Sarah Elizabeth (Green) Akins. After her father was named Republican State Chairman in 1898, the family moved to St. Louis, where Akins attended school across the river in Godfrey, Illinois, and then at Hosmer Hall in St. Louis, graduating in 1903.

Her interest in the theater developed early as she attended traveling shows at the opera house in Humansville and produced her own little plays with her dolls. In St. Louis, she began to write seriously, publishing poetry and drama reviews.

When she was seventeen, Akins was briefly engaged to the forty-two-year-old William Marion Reedy, editor of the weekly *Mirror* and a central figure in the St. Louis literary life of the period. When the engagement was broken, Akins's parents sent her to New York City to attend college. From then on Akins divided her life between St. Louis and New York City, finally moving to New York after the success of her play *Déclassée* in 1919. Her plays appeared steadily until 1936. For health reasons she moved to California in 1928 and wrote screenplays and adaptations. In 1932 she married Hugo Rumbold, a British set designer, who died in that same year. Akins was working on her memoirs when she died of cancer in Los Angeles in 1958.

**SIGNIFICANCE:** Although Akins was born and grew up in the Midwest, she did not use that area as a setting for her plays, which were primarily drawing room dramas or comedies that might be compared to the plays of George Bernard Shaw or Somerset Maugham. They were definitely not Midwestern in tone or subject matter. The Midwest, however, provided Akins with friends and mentors who contributed to her desire to write and to succeed. Some of these people were WILLIAM MARION REEDY, ORRICK JOHNS, SARA TEASDALE, and WILLA CATHER. The latter befriended Akins in New York City.

Her plays, romantic in nature, included dramas, comedies, and farces, some original and some adaptations, some well received and some failures. Some were presented at regional theaters. Her play *The Magical City* opened at the Pabst Theatre in Milwaukee, on June 3, 1918, followed by a play by G. B. Shaw.

It was Broadway, however, and later Hollywood, where Akins found success. Year after year her plays appeared, most starring the leading actors and actresses of the period, including Ethel Barrymore and Judith Anderson on the stage and Katharine Hepburn, Greta Garbo, and Robert Taylor in film. Akins received the 1935 Pulitzer Prize for her play *The Old Maid*, an adaptation of Edith Wharton's story. Some of her best-known plays which later became films were *Déclassée* (1919), *Daddy's Gone A-Hunting* (1921), *The Moon-Flower* (1924), *The Furies* (1928), and *The Greeks Had a Word for It* (1930). Her play *Morning Glory* became the film starring Katharine Hepburn portraying a young actress from Kansas, a role which won an Academy Award for Hepburn as Best Actress, 1932–33.

**SELECTED WORKS:** As a highly successful playwright, Akins had more than thirty plays produced on the stage or on film. In 1915, however, she wrote a series of twenty-three weekly articles on poetry for Reedy's *Mirror*. These have been gathered, edited, and introduced by Catherine N. Parke in *In the Shadow of Parnassus, Zoë Akins's Essays on American Poetry* (1994). In her introductions, both to the book and to individual articles, Parke gives much information about Akins, some of the early influences on her writing, and the background of the poets she writes about. Parke's notes are especially valuable. Some of Akins's other published writings are: *Interpretations: A Book of First Poems* (1912); *Cake upon the Waters*, a novel (1919); *Déclassée, Daddy's Gone A-Hunting*, and *Greatness*, plays (1923); *The Hills Grow Smaller*, poems (1937); and *Forever Young*, a novel (1941).

**FURTHER READING:** No biography of Zoë Akins has yet appeared. Useful sources are the introduction and notes by Catherine N. Parke in *In the Shadow of Parnassus* (1994):

15–39, 250–56; "Zoë Akins," by Felicia Hardison Londre, in *Notable Women in the American Theatre* (1989): 11–13; "Zoë Akins," by Anthony Slide, in *Dictionary of Literary Biography*, Screenwriters 26 (1984): 9–13; "Zoë Akins," by Barry B. Witham, in *Dictionary of American Biography*, Supplement 6, 1956–60 (1980): 10–11; and "Zoë Akins," by Patricia Yongue, in *American Women Writers* (1979): 15–17. An unpublished dissertation at Ohio State University entitled "The Plays of Zoe Akins Rumbold" (1974), by Ronald Albert Mielech, provides good critical insights into Akins's plays.

There are collections of Akins's papers at the Henry E. Huntington Library, San Marino, California, and the Research Library (Special Collections) at the University of California, Los Angeles. The Missouri Historical Society in St. Louis, Missouri, also has a collection of memorabilia, diaries, letters, and manuscripts. The St. Louis Public Library has supplementary information on Akins's life.

PATRICIA A. ANDERSON       DIMONDALE, MICHIGAN

# BESS STREETER ALDRICH
February 17, 1881–August 3, 1954
(Margaret Dean Stevens)

**BIOGRAPHY:** The daughter of Mary (Anderson) and James Wareham Streeter, pioneers in Iowa, Aldrich was born in Cedar Falls, where she grew up and graduated from Iowa State Teachers' College in 1901. She taught school in Iowa and Salt Lake City, returned to Iowa State to supervise prospective teachers, and married Charles S. Aldrich in Iowa in 1907. They eventually settled in Elmwood, Nebraska, and brought up four children. Aldrich wrote her first stories under the name Margaret Dean Stevens until 1918, then under the name Bess Streeter Aldrich. After her husband's death in 1925, she supported her family by writing short stories for periodicals, novels, and collections of short fiction. Her son James illustrated some of her books. She died in Lincoln in 1954.

**SIGNIFICANCE:** Aldrich used the reminiscences and history of her family and others in such books as *A Lantern in Her Hand* (1928), which, with its sequel, *A White Bird Flying* (1931), chronicles the generations of those who homesteaded in Iowa and Nebraska and settled down to middle-class lives. She portrayed aspects of pioneer opportunity,

**Bess Streeter Aldrich.**
Courtesy of the Nebraska State Historical Society

hardship, sorrow, and courage which are tempered by compassion and humor. The pioneer novels capture the labor, everyday happenings, and character of those who settled the prairie. Aldrich also produced several volumes of short stories. *Journey into Christmas* (1949) and *A Bess Streeter Aldrich Treasury* (1959) include many of Aldrich's best-known short stories and novels as well as a retrospective essay that reveals how much Aldrich used her experiences and relatives' recollections.

Aldrich maintains a balance between the regional and the universal. On one hand, she expresses rural and small-town attitudes through her characters, describes the landscape, and conveys the history of Iowa, Nebraska, and Illinois settlers and their descendants. On the other, she proposes that each small town is a microcosm, with joy and sorrow, crime and virtue, simplicity and complexity. She also treads a line between realism, with harsh weather and farming conditions, deaths by farm accident and in childbirth, and failure; and optimism, showing courage, en-

terprise, perseverance, humor, and charity. However, she leans inevitably toward the romantic, the strong of heart, the community supporters, and the generous of spirit.

**SELECTED WORKS:** Aldrich's novels about Midwestern pioneers include *A Lantern in Her Hand* (1928), *A White Bird Flying* (1931), *Spring Came on Forever* (1935), *A Song of Years* (1939), and *The Lieutenant's Lady* (1942). *The Rim of the Prairie* (1925) and *Miss Bishop* (1933) take place somewhat later. *Mother Mason* (1924) and *The Cutters* (1926) consist of stories about particular families in the Midwest, set in the first part of the century. *The Man Who Caught the Weather* (1936), *The Drum Goes Dead* (1941), *Journey into Christmas* (1949), *The Bess Streeter Aldrich Reader* (1950), and *A Bess Streeter Aldrich Treasury*, edited by Robert S. Aldrich (1959), are collections of stories, novels, and essays.

**FURTHER READING:** Aldrich's reminiscence "I Remember" appears in *Journey into Christmas* and in *A Bess Streeter Aldrich Treasury* (1959), which also includes a short biographical sketch by her son Robert. Essays, "Bess Streeter Aldrich," by CLARENCE ANDREWS, in *A Bibliographical Guide to Midwestern Literature*, edited by Gerald Nemanic (1981): 133–34; and by Helen Stauffer in *American Women Writers*, vol. 1, edited by Lina Mainiero (1979): 35–36, are useful summaries. A. Mabel Meier's master's thesis, "Bess Streeter Aldrich: Her Life and Works" (1968), from Kearney State College, remains the only book-length study. The Nebraska State Historical Library in Lincoln houses the primary collection of Aldrich's papers.

MARY DEJONG OBUCHOWSKI

CENTRAL MICHIGAN UNIVERSITY

## NELSON ALGREN
March 28, 1909–May 9, 1981
**BIOGRAPHY:** Born Nelson Ahlgren Abraham, he was named after his paternal grandfather, Nels Ahlgren, a Swede who converted first to Judaism and then simultaneously to all religions and to none. Algren explicitly identified with this convert-for-hire, whom he never met, wondering aloud, in an interview in Martha Heasley Cox and Wayne Chatterton's *Nelson Algren* (1975), if "pseudo-intellectualism [can] be inherited" (18). His parents, Gerson and Goldie (Kalisher) Abraham, were both from second-generation im-

migrant families. During his first years, the family lived in Detroit, where his father worked for the Packard Motor Company, but Algren grew up and went to school in Chicago. With his older sister's encouragement, he received a bachelor of science degree in journalism from the University of Illinois at Urbana-Champaign in 1931.

Unable to find regular employment, he worked odd jobs and hoboed around the country collecting experiences including some time in a Texas county jail. He worked as a writer and editor for the WPA Illinois Writers' Project and for the Venereal Disease Control Program of the Chicago Board of Health and served as a private in the U.S. Army Field Artillery and Medical Corps during World War II. He legally changed his name to Nelson Algren in 1942.

His masterpiece *The Man with the Golden Arm* (1949) won the first National Book Award in 1950. He went to Hollywood briefly to work on the movie version, which he considered a mockery of his efforts. Producer Otto Preminger claimed all the credit for breaking the taboo against movies about drug addiction and made millions on the film, which starred Frank Sinatra, while Algren received a total of fifteen thousand dollars in royalties. Adding heartbreak to Algren's humiliation, French feminist Simone de Beauvoir expounded her theory of "contingent loves" to rationalize a long-distance affair with Algren, despite her lifetime commitment to Jean-Paul Sartre. De Beauvoir published two excerpts from her autobiography *Force of Circumstances* in articles titled "A Question of Fidelity" and "An American Rendezvous" in the November and December 1964 *Harper's*. Algren published his wild and bitterly sarcastic riposte "The Question of Simone de Beauvoir" in the May 1965 issue of the same magazine.

Finally, after critics slashed *A Walk on the Wild Side* (1956), Algren made a conscious decision to renounce literature except as a protest against the powers that be, a stance expressed primarily by indulging his predilection for betting on horse races. In *Nelson Algren: A Life on the Wild Side* (1989), his biographer, Bettina Drew, notes that just before his death of a heart attack in Sag Harbor, New York, Algren was voted into the American

Nelson Algren.
Photo © Nancy Crampton

Academy and Institute of Arts and Letters (373).

**SIGNIFICANCE:** Nelson Algren has been ignored by academia, with very few exceptions. Although his short stories were widely anthologized while he was alive, Algren's outspoken defiance has never been fashionable. His Midwestern nonconformity does not fit into the preconceived categories of the literary canon. Algren identified himself within a radical American tradition including ABRAHAM LINCOLN, Walt Whitman, THEODORE DREISER, and Eugene V. Debs. For the time being, he seems to have been forgotten except by a small coterie of enthusiastic readers, many of whom read him in translation. His books have been far better received in Europe than in America.

As quoted by Cox and Chatterton in *Nelson Algren*, he offers fellow authors the hard advice: "The role of the writer is always to stand against the culture he is in . . . . [T]he writer's place today is with the accused, guilty or not guilty, with the accused" (132). Despite progressive trends of multiculturalism, Algren is even more of an outsider now than when he lived and wrote. His fatal flaw was to find humanity in members of the social underclass who live on the dark side of the American Dream. He has never been forgiven for having had compassion for the losers and misfits of society. As exemplified in *The Man with the Golden Arm*, Algren speaks in the enduring urban wise-guy voice of both his best fiction and nonfiction for those burdened by that "great, secret and special American guilt of owning nothing, nothing at all, in the one land where ownership and virtue are one" (7). In another passage, Algren reminds us, through a nameless, defrocked priest in one of the endless police lineups which he specialized in describing, that "we are all members of one another" (198).

**SELECTED WORKS:** Algren is best known for *The Man with the Golden Arm* (1949) and *A Walk on the Wild Side* (1956), along with his collection of short stories *The Neon Wilderness* (1947). His first novel was *Somebody in Boots* (1935), followed by *Never Come Morning* (1942). He also wrote nonfiction including a book-length prose poem, *Chicago: City on the Make* (1951); travel books mixed with literary criticism such as *Who Lost an American?* (1963) and *Notes from a Sea Diary: Hemingway All the Way* (1965); and *The Last Carousel* (1973), a gallimaufry collection of fiction and nonfiction. His last novel, *The Devil's Stocking* (1983), was published posthumously.

**FURTHER READING:** The best place to begin is the Twayne series *Nelson Algren* (1975), by Martha Heasley Cox and Wayne Chatterton, and *Conversations with Nelson Algren* (1964), by H. E. F. Donohue. The other indispensable volume is the biography by Bettina Drew, *Nelson Algren: A Life on the Wild Side* (1989). Significant recent contributions on Algren include *Confronting the Horror: The Novels of Nelson Algren* (1989), by James Giles, who defines Algren as an existentialist, and *Writing Chicago: Modernism, Ethnography, and the Novel* (1993), by Carla Cappetti, who places Algren in the tradition of Chicago writers and sociologists. The best essays on Algren include George Bluestone's "Nelson Algren," in *Western Review* 22 (Autumn 1957): 27–44, which analyzes Algren's portrayal of "the living death that follows love's destruction" (39). Also, Maxwell Geismar's "Nelson Algren: The Iron Sanctuary," in *American Moderns: From Rebellion to Conformity* (1958), analyzes the inner soul of Algren's realism. Lawrence Lipton's "A Voyeur's View of the Wild Side: Nelson Al-

gren and His Reviewers," in *Chicago Review Anthology* (Winter 1957): 31–41, defends the author from his harsher critics. *Nonconformity: Writing on Writing* (1996), an essay suppressed during the McCarthy era, was found forty years later in Algren's papers located in the library of Ohio State University.

JAMES A. LEWIN                    SHEPHERD COLLEGE

# MICHAEL ANANIA
August 5, 1939

**BIOGRAPHY:** Michael Anania, son of Angelo and Dora (Van Der Berg) Anania, was born in Omaha, Nebraska, and grew up there during the turbulent decade of the 1950s, a time and place lovingly evoked in his highly autobiographical novel *The Red Menace* (1984). Anania's father supported the family with a series of odd jobs, which he performed in spite of his tuberculosis. Michael attended the University of Nebraska at Lincoln from 1957 to 1958, then transferred to the University of Nebraska at Omaha. He married Joanne Oliver on December 22, 1960, and they later had a daughter (Francesca). In 1961 Anania graduated with a BA from the University of Nebraska at Omaha. Moving east, Anania worked as a bibliographer and poetry editor at the State University of New York at Buffalo from 1963 to 1967, and as an instructor of English at the State University of New York at Fredonia from 1964 to 1965. Then he returned to the Midwest, settling in Chicago, the city that was to figure most prominently in his literary and professional life, working as an instructor of English at Northwestern University until 1968, when he was hired by the University of Illinois at Chicago, a position he has maintained ever since. In 1968 he also became poetry editor of Swallow Press, then located in downtown Chicago, a position he held until 1974 and one that afforded him considerable power and visibility, as did his work as poetry advisor to *Partisan Review* and his subsequent book reviewing for the *Chicago Tribune*. Michael Anania received his PhD in 1969 from the State University of New York at Buffalo. In the same year, his poetry career began in earnest when he edited the *New Poetry Anthology* for Swallow Press. Anania remained in the Chicago area, although he moved from the city proper to the nearby suburb of LaGrange, Illinois.

**SIGNIFICANCE:** Besides his graphic novel of life in Omaha, with its replication of Midwestern speech and its vivid depiction of Midwestern climate, Michael Anania has been *par excellence* the poet of Midwestern rivers, especially the Missouri, which he examines meticulously in two significant sequences of poetry: "Stops along the Western Bank of the Missouri River" (nine poems) and "The Riversongs [*sic*] of Arion" (ten poems). In addition, Anania often describes generic scenes of Midwestern rural and urban life, as in such poems as "Interstate 80," "After Milking," "News Notes, 1970," and "Nights at the Bon Ton." Besides these documentary treatments of rivers, roadhouses, highways, and dairy barns, Michael Anania celebrates an uncluttered apprehension of nature on the Midwestern prairie, a kind of Oriental meditative process that produces such poems as "The Edge of Autumn" and "April Snow: An Improvisation." Like the poetry of fellow Midwesterner ROBERT BLY, these poems by Anania are inseparable from the Midwestern landscape that generated them.

Michael Anania's poetics, then, proceed from a highly original mixture of personal voice, historical fact, journalistic observation, and a haiku-like format that pares lines down to the bare bones and pushes language to its limit. In this respect, his tightly compressed verse, as printed on the page, closely resembles the poetic formats of contemporary poets such as Robert Creeley and A. R. Ammons. There is also a strong family resemblance between the verse of Anania and that of two other important Illinois poets—JOHN KNOEPFLE and LUCIEN STRYK. As editor, book reviewer, and chairman and originator of the Program for Writers at the University of Illinois, Chicago, Michael Anania has had a profound influence, not merely on the writing of the Windy City but on that of the whole Midwestern region and beyond.

**SELECTED WORKS:** Anania's three best-known books of poetry are *The Color of Dust* (1970), *Riversongs* (1978), and *The Sky at Ashland* (1986). Most of these poems also appear in *Selected Poems* (1994). He has also published two chapbooks: *Set / Sorts* (1974) and *Construction / Variations* (1985). Anania's book reviews and his essays on literature and pop culture can be found in the collection *In Plain Sight: Obsessions, Morals, and Domestic Laughter* (1991).

**FURTHER READING:** No biography of Michael Anania exists, but his autobiographical novel, *The Red Menace* (1984), fills in many of the gaps of his life, as do some of the essays in *In Plain Sight*. Anania's place in the complex history of Illinois poetry is discussed in Daniel L. Guillory's "Tradition and Innovation in Illinois Poetry," *Studies in Illinois Poetry*, edited by JOHN E. HALLWAS (1989): 43–61. Leslie Fiedler's introduction to *In Plain Sight* is also helpful in this regard. A good videotape of Michael Anania discussing his work is *Rainbow Bridges: An Illinois Walk-about, No. 4, Michael Anania* (Library Cable Network, 1988). Anania's poetry and a brief biography are also included in *Heartland II: Poets of the Midwest*, edited by Lucien Stryk (1975).

DANIEL L. GUILLORY                    MILLIKIN UNIVERSITY

## DAVID D(ANIEL) ANDERSON
June 8, 1924

**BIOGRAPHY:** Born in Lorain, Ohio, of David and Nora Marie (Foster) Anderson, David Anderson grew up hearing the stories and chanties of his maternal grandfather, who had captained a Lake Erie schooner in the early years of the century. After graduating from St. Mary's High School in Lorain, he served in the amphibious forces of the U.S. Navy from 1942 through 1945, participating in the Anzio landing and earning a silver star, a purple heart, and five battle stars, and in the U.S. Army Artillery from 1952 through 1953, part of that time as paymaster at Camp Atterbury in Indiana. He met Patricia Ann Rittenhour while at Bowling Green State University in 1950, and they married in the chapel at Fort Sill, Oklahoma, in 1953.

Anderson received a BS in English and geology in 1951 and an MA in English the following year, both from Bowling Green State University. He received his PhD from Michigan State University in 1960, having written his dissertation, "Sherwood Anderson and the Meaning of the American Experience," under the direction of RUSSEL B. NYE. He taught English at the General Motors Institute in Flint from 1953 through 1956 and then at Michigan State University in the Department of English (1956–57) and the Department of American Thought and Language from

**David D. Anderson.**
Courtesy of David D. Anderson

1957 until his retirement in 1994. During 1963 and 1964 he served as a Fulbright lecturer in American literature at the University of Karachi. From 1975 until 1980 he served as assistant dean of University College at Michigan State University. He edited the *University College Quarterly* from 1971 until its demise in 1980.

David D. Anderson has received much recognition for his scholarship and service to the profession. He has chaired the American Literature Section of the Modern Language Association and the Modern American Literature Section of the Midwest Modern Language Association. He has been a U.S. delegate to the International Federation for Modern Languages and Literatures and the International Congress of Orientalists. He is a founding member of both the Association of Literary Scholars and Critics and the American Literature Association. Since the mid-1970s he has been invited by the Swedish Academy to submit nominations for the Nobel Prize in literature. He received Michigan State University's Distinguished Faculty Award in 1974, Bowling Green State University's Distinguished Alumnus Award in 1976,

and the Society for the Study of Midwestern Literature's Distinguished Service Award in 1982. In 1986 he received the doctorate of letters, *honoris causa,* from Wittenberg University in Springfield, Ohio; and in 1988 the Michigan Association of Governing Boards awarded him its Distinguished Faculty Award. In the same year he was advanced to the newly created rank of university distinguished professor, a title he now holds as emeritus.

**SIGNIFICANCE:** Anderson's principal scholarly interest is Midwestern literature. Together with BERNARD DUFFEY, Merton Babcock, Russel B. Nye, William B. Thomas, William McCann, and Robert Hubach, he founded the Society for the Study of Midwestern Literature in 1971, which has held a conference every year since. He has edited *MidAmerica, Midwestern Miscellany,* and the *Society for the Study of Midwestern Literature Newsletter* continuously since their inception. The dedication page of the *Bibliographical Guide to Midwestern Literature* (1981), compiled by Gerald Nemanic, reads as follows: "For David Anderson, who helped invent the Midwest." Anderson is the author or editor of at least thirty-five books and hundreds of published articles, essays, and poems, besides a collection of his short fiction and a novel. He has lectured throughout Europe, Asia, Africa, and the Americas and has presented more than a hundred papers to scholarly societies.

**SELECTED WORKS:** David Anderson considers his critical biography *Sherwood Anderson: An Introduction and Interpretation* (1967), which received the Michigan State University Book Manuscript Award, his most important work because it reawakened interest in that author. He has published biographies of numerous American historical figures in the Twayne series: *LOUIS BROMFIELD* (1964), *BRAND WHITLOCK* (1968), *ABRAHAM LINCOLN* (1970), *ROBERT INGERSOLL* (1972), *Woodrow Wilson* (1978), *IGNATIUS DONNELLY* (1980), and *WILLIAM JENNINGS BRYAN* (1982). His treatment of them is literary as well as historical in that he sees them primarily as writers and thinkers. Not incidentally, all of them are men of the people, as well.

Anderson's scholarship breaks down into a number of categories, reflecting areas of interest over a long, productive, and ongoing literary career. There are a number of articles on Pakistani literature originating from his Fulbright year at Karachi. Several works reflect his continuing fascination with both Lincoln and the Lincoln myth. Numerous essays seek to define and delineate the Midwest, Midwestern culture, the myth of the Midwest, the dimensions of the Midwest, characteristics of Midwestern towns, and the notion of Midwestern modernism. Five books and at least twenty essays reflect an abiding interest in SHERWOOD ANDERSON, to whom David D. Anderson is not related, with a work-in-progress to be titled *The Four Stages of a Man's Life: A Photo Biography of Sherwood Anderson*. And there is a more recent interest in SAUL BELLOW, with several articles published and another book-in-progress, tentatively titled *Saul Bellow and the Midwestern Tradition*. There are comparative studies, such as his essay on Cincinnati, "The Queen City and a New Literature," in *MidAmerica* 4 (1977): 7–17; and "Chicago Cityscapes by Theodore Dreiser, Sherwood Anderson, and Saul Bellow," in *Midwestern Miscellany* 13 (1985): 43–49; and the work-in-progress, *Makers of a Midwestern Dream: A Cultural History*. There are books and essays on individual writers too numerous to list.

Of Anderson's edited volumes, several might be mentioned, including *Critical Studies in American Literature* (1964), *The Literary Works of Abraham Lincoln* (1970), *The Dark and Tangled Path: Race in America*, coedited with Robert L. Wright (1971), *Sunshine and Smoke: American Writers and the American Environment* (1971), *Critical Essays on Sherwood Anderson* (1981), and *Michigan: A State Anthology* (1983). Anderson has published a collection of short stories titled *The Path in the Shadow: Stories of World War II and Korea* (1998). In 1993 he published his novel, *Route 2, Titus, Ohio*.

**FURTHER READING:** Anderson is the subject of an extensive feature story published in the *Detroit Free Press* (April 30, 1989). Two Festschrift collections dedicated to him have been published by colleagues and protégés involved with the Society for the Study of Midwestern Literature, both edited by Marcia Noe. One, *Celebrate the Midwest! Poems and Stories for David D. Anderson* (1991), contains creative tributes, including a poem written expressly for that volume by GWENDOLYN BROOKS. The second, *Exploring the Midwestern Literary Imagination: Essays in Honor of David*

*D. Anderson* (1993), contains papers reflecting the breadth of Anderson's interests in Midwestern literary studies, as well as a chronological listing of his published writings through 1992 compiled by Ronald M. Grosh. That volume begins with Ronald Primeau's essay, "Dave Anderson as Audience: An Essay on Reception Aesthetics," and ends with "Midwestern Muckrakers," by James Seaton, an essay that builds to an appreciation of David Anderson's accomplishments.

ROGER JIANG BRESNAHAN
MICHIGAN STATE UNIVERSITY

## MARGARET C. ANDERSON
November 26, 1886–October 19, 1973

**BIOGRAPHY:** Margaret Anderson, American magazine journalist, founder of the *Little Review*, published between 1914 and 1919, and the author of three autobiographies, participant in the Chicago Renaissance, feminist, romantic, and rebel, was born in Indianapolis, Indiana, to Arthur Aubrey Anderson and Jessie (Shortridge) Anderson. Her father, of Scottish and Dutch descent, was manager of the combined utilities and street railway system in Youngstown, Ohio. Her mother, Jessie Shortridge of Kokomo, Indiana, came from a distinguished family and was proud to be related to a Civil War governor. She was musically ambitious and extremely frustrated to be away from an urban setting. Margaret had two sisters, Lois and Jean, and the five of them moved from house to house. Margaret's life was marked by discomfort and discontent.

Margaret spent her youth in Youngstown, Ohio, and Columbus, Indiana. During the summers, the family congregated at Lake Wawasee in Indiana, the setting of Margaret's early romantic yearnings. At sixteen, she entered the Western College for Women in Oxford, Ohio, where she studied piano from 1903 through 1906 but left before graduating.

In 1908 Margaret Anderson with her sister Lois escaped to Chicago, a center of artistic rebellion. Her first job was as a book reviewer for the *Interior*, later renamed the *Continent*, edited by CLARA LAUGHLIN. During these first Chicago years, Anderson reviewed books for the *Chicago Evening Post*'s *Friday Literary Review*, then edited by FRANCIS HACKETT and FLOYD DELL. She also worked in Frances Browne's bookstore in the Fine Arts Building and served on the staff of the *Dial*, where she learned how to print, publish, and edit a journal. She founded and edited the *Little Review* in 1914 for the purpose of creating stimulating "conversation" among writers, artists, and anarchists. The journal became a forum for critical exchange. In 1915 she met and fell in love with Jane Heap, a talented woman who studied painting and jewelry design at Chicago's Art and Lewis Institute, acted with the Chicago Little Theatre, and designed sets for ALICE GERSTENBERG's innovative experimental mask play *Overtones*. With the help of Jane Heap, who quickly became a coeditor and then, in 1923, took over the journal, the *Little Review* took on a new look: the covers went from brown to brilliantly colored and used a bolder type. Jane's interest in the plastic arts also influenced the selection of published material.

The two women worked together in Chicago, California, and New York. They published SHERWOOD ANDERSON, EUNICE TIETJENS, EDGAR LEE MASTERS, VACHEL LINDSAY, ARTHUR DAVISON FICKE, Mary Aldis, and Margery Currey, as well as other Midwestern writers such as ERNEST HEMINGWAY. With Ezra Pound as its foreign editor from 1917 through 1919, the magazine became increasingly international, publishing W. B. Yeats, T. S. ELIOT, H. D., and James Joyce. Yet, even before Pound took on his duties, writers such as Amy Lowell and Emma Goldman were strong, radical voices in the journal. Sherwood Anderson's "The New Note" appeared in the first issue calling for truth and honesty rather than merely adapting the effects of the new in fiction. The journal also became the central place where Imagist theory could be discussed and Imagist poetry appear.

Margaret Anderson, happy when she was making political gestures, disrupted the conspiracy trials of Emma Goldman and Alexander Berkman in mid-1917. She and Jane Heap serialized James Joyce's *Ulysses* between 1916 and 1920. The magazine was often confiscated by the U.S. Postal Service and was burned three times for episodes of *Ulysses*. In 1921 Anderson was declared guilty of publishing obscene literature. No New York paper supported her cause, and it was not until 1933 that *Ulysses* passed America's censors.

Anderson's personal relationships were troubled. By the time Jane Heap and Margaret Anderson traveled to California, there was disharmony between the two. In 1918 Margaret Anderson began an affair with Gladys Tilden, the young niece of Chicago friend Harriet Vaughn Moody. Gladys Tilden's aunt, Josephine Plows Day, Aunt Tippy, was another source of romantic feelings for Anderson. This woman, seventeen years her senior, was recreated as Audrey Leigh, a character in her lesbian novel, *Forbidden Fires*. Written in France, completed in 1958, *Forbidden Fires* remained unpublished until 1996.

Relationships were central to Anderson's life and philosophy as were direct-action politics. In 1921 she met the actress and singer Georgette Leblanc and formed a relationship that lasted Leblanc's lifetime. In 1927 she met another important friend after moving to Paris, Solita Solano Wilkinson, Janet Flanner's companion. Solita Wilkinson edited the first of Anderson's three autobiographies, *My Thirty Years' War* (1930), which concentrates on Chicago's role in the Modernist movement. For Anderson, the 1930s were filled with inner struggles and the teachings of Georges Gurdjieff, French psychologist, philosopher, and mystic, which marked Anderson's move away from literature as an avenue toward the spiritual, and her embrace of spirituality itself.

After Leblanc died of breast cancer in 1941, Anderson formed a thirteen-year relationship with Dorothy Caruso, who died of the same disease. During her time with Caruso, Anderson wrote her second autobiography, *The Fiery Fountains* (1951), which explored her story of a transcendent love for Georgette Leblanc. By 1942 she was back in America but living in New York, not Chicago. Margaret Anderson died of emphysema and is buried beside Georgette Leblanc in the village of Le Cannet, France.

**SIGNIFICANCE:** Chicago was important to Margaret Anderson and she to Chicago. She loved the arts that were blossoming there during the 1910s and helped quicken the experimental course of poetry and fiction in post–World War I America. The *Little Review*, from its very first issue, represents bohemian Chicago and the international Modern literary movement. Mathilda M. Hills in *Notable American Women: The Modern Period* (1980) calls it a "salon in print" (149). Anderson introduced the world to the creative writers of the 1920s. Jayne Marek in *Women Editing Modernism: "Little" Magazines and Literary History* (1995) calls it "the premier forum for avant garde literary and artistic activity" during that era (60). Anderson gave works like *Ulysses* a much needed home and introduced readers to Imagism and Modernism. The journal specialized in "call to action" editorials addressing the need for personal freedom. Its tone was conversational and irreverent. Anderson's editorials and memoirs were important mirrors of the early period of Modernism and its Midwestern flavor.

Anderson moved from city to city, but it was new people, new conversations for which she searched and not new scenes or landscapes. Place was only a means toward an end. Anderson, because of her interest in mysticism, helped to make Modernism a more spiritually centered art movement than it would have been otherwise.

After 1923 the *Little Review* became Jane Heap's journal. New York and Paris disappointed Anderson, and she remarked in her first autobiography that her favorite conversations had taken place in Chicago (149). Probably this was because she was young in Chicago, and there, more than in any other place, she believed in the healing power of literature.

Anderson's leaving Chicago in 1916 reflected both personal and historical mood, a beginning of the end of the Chicago Renaissance. One of her most famous issues was that of September 1916 (Volume III, 6), edited from San Francisco shortly after leaving Chicago. In it she offered twelve blank pages as a "Want Ad" for worthy art. In her memoir *My Thirty Years' War*, she talks about leaving Chicago: "I loved Chicago forever, I could never forget it, I would come back to it . . . but I must go on" (136).

Besides her lesbian novel, written during an era when few such texts ever became public, her journal, her three autobiographies, and her presentation of self in this important genre are also of historical, artistic, and theoretical importance. One turns to the first autobiography in order to understand the Midwestern childhood and young womanhood of an editor whose journal rocked the early

part of our century. One turns to the second and third to see how one radical journalist and writer perceived and refigured her personal relationships, sense of time and place, and journey toward and away from art and artifact.

**SELECTED WORKS:** Most relevant to Midwestern studies is Margaret Anderson's *My Thirty Years' War* (1930) and the early issues of the *Little Review*, 1914–16. To get a full view of Anderson's prose one should read *The Fiery Fountains* (1951), *The Little Review Anthology* (1953), *The Unknowable Gurdjieff* (1962), *The Strange Necessity* (1969), and Anderson's only novel, *Forbidden Fires* (1996).

**FURTHER READING:** Mathilda M. Hills's introduction to *Forbidden Fires* (1996) offers an excellent biography of Margaret Anderson. Jackson R. Bryer's dissertation, "A Trial-Track for Racers: Margaret Anderson and 'The Little Review'" (1965), written at the University of Wisconsin, is an invaluable resource. In 1961 Kenneth A. Lohf and Eugene P. Sheehy compiled an index to the *Little Review*, published at the New York Public Library, which helps locate articles and authors. BERNARD DUFFEY's *The Chicago Renaissance in American Letters* (1954); Dale Kramer's *Chicago Renaissance* (1966); Mathilda Hills's "Margaret Anderson," in *Notable American Women: The Modern Period,* edited by Barbara Sicherman et al. (1980); and Hugh Hill's *Four Lives in Paris* (1987) are also helpful in understanding Margaret Anderson's contribution to Modernism. There is some recent work on Anderson that should not be missed: Susan Noyes Platt's article "The *Little Review*: Early Years and Avant-Garde Ideas" (139–55) can be found in Sue Ann Prince's *The Old Guard and the Avant-Garde, Modernism in Chicago, 1910–1940* (1990). J. Gerald Kennedy's *Imagining Paris: Exile, Writing and American Identity* (1993) and Jayne E. Marek's *Women Editing Modernism: "Little" Magazines and Literary History* (1995) are both important if one wants to understand Anderson's life and career. For a Midwestern perspective, one might look at Marilyn J. Atlas's "Harriet Monroe, Margaret Anderson, and the Spirit of the Chicago Renaissance," *Midwestern Miscellany* 9 (1981): 43–53.

Margaret Anderson's papers can be found in various places, including the Janet Flanner holdings in the Berg Collection at the

**Sherwood Anderson, ca. 1939.**
Courtesy of David D. Anderson

New York Public Library; the Flanner-Solano collection of letters and scrapbooks at the Library of Congress; Jane Heap's *Little Review* papers at the Golda Meir Library of the University of Wisconsin–Milwaukee; the Van Volkenburg–Browne collection at the University of Michigan; the Alice Gerstenberg collection at the Newberry Library; and the Florence E. Reynolds collection related to Jane Heap and the *Little Review* at the University of Delaware Library, Newark, Delaware. The Harry Ransom Humanities Research Center at the University of Texas at Austin and the Beinecke Library at Yale also hold some of her papers.

MARILYN J. ATLAS                  OHIO UNIVERSITY

## SHERWOOD ANDERSON
September 13, 1876–March 8, 1941

**BIOGRAPHY:** The facts and fictions surrounding Sherwood Anderson's life have had almost as much staying power in American literary history as have his writings. For much of his early life before he dedicated himself to a writing career, Anderson was a faithful subscriber to the American Dream of Horatio Alger and the Gilded Age. Most of his childhood years were spent in Clyde, Ohio, where from an early age he had to resort to taking whatever odd jobs he could to help support his family, because of his father, Irwin's, penchant for storytelling and drinking rather than working. Anderson's hustle as a boy earned him the nickname Jobby and also prevented him from graduating from high school. In 1895, upon the death of his mother, Emma (Smith) Anderson, he left small-town life and began an odyssey that took him to Chicago for the first time, where he worked as a common laborer; then to Cuba at the close of the Spanish-American War; and eventually back to Chicago after he finished his secondary education at the Wittenberg Academy in 1900. It is from this time that he began to write and attain some success as a businessman.

In Chicago, Anderson was an advertising copywriter, and he published short pieces in his company's in-house magazine. Four years later, in 1904, he married Cornelia Lane, the first of his four wives, with whom he had three children. In 1906, at just thirty years of age, he served a brief stint as president of a mail-order company in Cleveland, and in the following year he moved to Elyria, Ohio, to become head of another company, which he later expanded into a full-scale roofing and painting business. As a release from financial pressures and marital problems, Anderson began to write fiction, but in 1912 he suffered a mental breakdown, an incident which he would later turn into the stuff of legend. Although he would not make a final break from the business world for another ten years, Anderson regarded his breakdown as the moment he decided to become an artist. He was then thirty-six years of age.

During this decade, his efforts to become an author benefited from the encouragement of a coterie of writers and artists who comprised the Chicago Renaissance. Estranged from Cornelia since his breakdown, Anderson divorced her in 1916 and married Tennessee Mitchell, an artist and teacher who socialized in the same circles. The Chicago experience paid off, for he rapidly published his first two novels, *Windy McPherson's Son* (1916) and *Marching Men* (1917), and a collection of poetry, *Mid-American Chants* (1918). In 1915 he also began writing tales gleaned from his childhood life in Clyde which he would later include in *Winesburg, Ohio* (1919).

Anderson's experiences in Chicago made him more confident that he could make a career as a creative writer. After 1917 he gravitated to artistic circles in New York, in New Orleans, and briefly in Paris, and thereafter returned to the Midwest only on short visits. During this period he encouraged ERNEST HEMINGWAY, in Chicago, and William Faulkner, in New Orleans, while both were just starting their writing careers. Meanwhile, Anderson himself was buoyed by the critical—though not the commercial—reception of *Winesburg*, the novel *Poor White* (1920), and a collection of tales, *The Triumph of the Egg* (1921). Anderson was at the height of his career in 1922, when he was named the first recipient of *The Dial*'s award given to "a young American writer" (Townsend 184). He was forty-five years old at this time. By the end of the decade, however, many critics considered him a writer past his prime.

The novel *Many Marriages* (1923) and the short story collection *Horses and Men* (1923) precipitated this decline, although some of Anderson's best tales appear in the latter work. During this time Anderson was involved in lengthy divorce proceedings with his wife, Tennessee, which culminated in 1924, after which he was married for the third time, to Elizabeth Prall, a bookstore manager in New York. In the same year, he returned to his Midwestern roots in *A Story-Teller's Story*, a semi-autobiographical book that helped mythologize Anderson's transition from stifled businessman to successful artist. Two years later, in 1926, he again foraged material from his childhood and from his life as a writer in *Tar: A Midwest Childhood* and *Sherwood Anderson's Notebook*, respectively. The following year he published his second collection of verse, *A New Testament*.

Aware of his own decline in reputation, Anderson settled back into small-town life after he built a home near Troutdale, Virginia, with the proceeds of his only popular success, *Dark Laughter* (1925). In nearby Marion, Virginia, he purchased two newspapers and wrote regular columns under the pen name Buck Fever; in 1929 he collected some of his newspaper writings in *Hello Towns!* When he separated from his wife in 1929 and gave over the editorship of his newspapers to his son Robert, Anderson began visiting factory towns in the Midwest and the South with Eleanor Copenhaver, who worked in the Industrial Program of the YWCA. Upon divorcing Elizabeth Prall in 1932, Anderson married Eleanor, with whom he remained until his death. With encouragement from Eleanor, Anderson began writing about the struggles of working-class citizens in Depression-era America, publishing the novels *Beyond Desire* (1932) and *Kit Brandon* (1936), the short story collection *Death in the Woods and Other Stories* (1933), and two collections of nonfiction prose, *Perhaps Women* (1931) and *Puzzled America* (1935).

Further encouraged by his wife, Anderson in 1933 started compiling notes for what would become his unfinished *Memoirs*, which were edited by Paul Rosenfeld and published posthumously in 1942. In 1937 he tried his hand at playwriting and published *Plays, Winesburg and Others*, which included an unsuccessful adaptation of his most famous book. In the last work published during his lifetime, the photo-essay *Home Town* (1940), Anderson returned to his small-town roots, attempting again to counter the pressures of modernity with the values of preindustrial America. In 1941, during a trip to South America with his wife, Anderson developed peritonitis from swallowing a toothpick, and died in Colón.

**SIGNIFICANCE:** Writing during a period in American history when rampant industrialism and urbanization were expanding outward from the cities and into small towns and rural areas, Sherwood Anderson often looked to his Midwestern small-town past in order to articulate the means whereby Americans could confront and endure the pressures of modern society. The timing of his emergence as a writer proved fortuitous. In literary circles in Chicago and New York especially, where literary modernism was taking shape in the United States, Anderson found a nurturing audience of literary peers who, like himself, rejected the fashion of plot-driven stories whose purpose, as he said in *A Story-Teller's Story*, "must point a moral, uplift the people, [and] make better citizens" (352). Anderson's character-driven psychological portraits helped to revolutionize the short story form, and his preoccupation in many of his nonfiction works with his own struggle to become a creative artist provided inspiration to a younger generation of aspiring writers.

But it was in the Midwest that his contributions to artistic innovation and social concerns found their most enduring expression. From Midwestern landscapes came his experimentation with the short story form, his grappling with the diminution of the individual in the midst of both technological progress and society's inhibitive norms, his rebellion against what he called New England's puritanical influence on American culture, his love-hate relationship with machines, and his attempts to probe Americans' obsession with "getting up" in the world.

From the publication in 1916 of his first novel, *Windy McPherson's Son*, Anderson spent the next ten years exploring how the Midwest evolved from the rural, complacent home of his youth into the amorphous industrialized center of the nation. His first novel is a flawed work that explores the disappointment Sam McPherson discovers after he rises from rags to riches in the arms industry and finds himself torn between materialistic rewards of success and neglected values gleaned from his childhood. Again, in *Marching Men*, Anderson focuses on the clash of modern industrial society and the plight of the individual by having his protagonist, Beaut McGregor, strive to give downtrodden laborers meaning in their lives by organizing them into marching units, the purpose of which is never made clear in the book. Both novels received mixed, although encouraging, reviews, and if they are remembered at all today it is primarily because they address issues that Anderson would explore with more depth and maturity in subsequent works.

This waiting period would not be long. Anderson achieved his greatest critical success with *Winesburg, Ohio*. A collection of interrelated tales, the book allowed Anderson to showcase his talent for describing luminous moments and guiding truths in the lives of individual people in isolated settings. In tracing the gradual maturing of young George Willard in the preindustrial Ohio town, he provides glimpses of characters whose frustrated lives revolve around incidents of their past when they perceived themselves to be on the brink of fulfilling their dreams. In the aftermath, however, these individuals regularly end up disappointed and often disillusioned. In a manner more sophisticated and suggestive than in his previous works, Anderson fleshes out the dilemma of a nation reared on the prescriptive formulas of success and yet incapable of persevering when such formulas prove false.

In the opening story Anderson calls such characters grotesques, but his portraits do not dwell on defeat or despair, as did those of other Midwestern authors, such as SINCLAIR LEWIS, who championed the flight from the village. Instead, the reader, with George Willard, is delicately shown by the end of the book, in "Sophistication," that despite all the pressures inherent in modern American culture, genuine human understanding may very well be "the thing that makes the mature life of men and women in the modern world possible" (243, Penguin ed.). George Willard leaves Winesburg at the end of the book headed for life in the city, but he goes equipped with the values and experiences acquired in his small Ohio town.

From the publication of *Winesburg, Ohio*, Anderson's reputation was made. In his first two novels he felt compelled to spell out specific solutions to the problems of coping with modern life, with the unsatisfactory result that neither Sam McPherson nor Beaut McGregor could resolve their conflicts. But with his *Winesburg* tales, he was able to flesh out the personal dilemmas of his characters without substituting one formulaic solution for another. Disdaining the moralistic and structural conventions of popular fiction, Anderson elevated his work to a complex art form while situating his tales geographically and thematically in the Midwest. He would continue to build upon his reputation as a short story writer with such tales as "The Egg" and "I Want to Know Why," from *The Triumph of the Egg*; "I'm a Fool" and "The Man Who Became a Woman," from *Horses and Men*; and "Death in the Woods," from *Death in the Woods and Other Stories*. All of these stories appear regularly in American literature anthologies.

Anderson has never been recognized as an accomplished novelist, although *Poor White* is commonly acknowledged to be his best novel. In this work he tackles head-on the transformation of a small Midwestern town into an alienated industrial capital as the result of Hugh McVey's invention of labor-saving machines. In chronicling the development of Bidwell, Ohio, he explores with mixed results his most important themes: the temptations and pitfalls of material success, the dehumanization of factory work, the breakdown of small-town life, the consequent alienation of human beings, and the groping need for interpersonal understanding.

From the 1920s until his death, Anderson was a visitor to rather than a resident of the Midwest, with one result that his fiction, nonfiction, and poetry portrayed the lives of men and women from across the country. Nevertheless, the critical awareness of social and psychological issues that he developed in his specifically Midwestern locales was successfully carried over to other regions, particularly in the South. His focus on other regions in later works did not result in significant contributions to American literary history, but it does demonstrate a keen perception in finding common bonds between Midwesterners and Americans nationwide.

A writer who served to bridge the small-town society and the modern industrialized nation, Anderson spent his most productive years as a writer chronicling this transformation in the Midwest. During his lifetime he was celebrated and later rejected by many of his literary peers, while genteel society labeled him a writer preoccupied with sex. But he is best remembered today as a Midwestern writer and innovator of the short story form. Although he is often overshadowed in this period of American literary history by peers such as Hemingway and Faulkner, the profound record he left of life in Middle America has placed Sherwood Anderson among the leading writers who emerged from that region.

**SELECTED WORKS:** Midwestern locales and themes figure prominently in Anderson's early fiction: *Windy McPherson's Son* (1916); *Marching Men* (1917); *Winesburg, Ohio* (1919); *Poor White* (1920); *The Triumph of the Egg* (1921); and several stories in *Horses and Men* (1923). *A Story-Teller's Story* (1924), *Sherwood Anderson's Notebook* (1926), and *Tar: A Midwest Childhood* (1926) are each semi-au-tobiographical accounts that touch variously on Anderson's childhood in Ohio or on his later thoughts and experiences as a writer. Anderson's closest attempt at straightforward autobiography is *Sherwood Anderson's Memoirs* (1942; critical edition edited by RAY LEWIS WHITE, 1969). Also notable for their treatment of factory workers during the Depression are the impressionistic essays *Perhaps Women* (1931) and *Puzzled America* (1935). Since his death, many editions have been published of Anderson's previously uncollected prose. One work focused on his years in the Midwest is *Sherwood Anderson: Early Writings*, edited by Ray Lewis White (1989), which contains some fiction and numerous writings from Anderson's years as a copywriter. A similar work that includes magazine and newspaper articles from throughout his career is *Sherwood Anderson: The Writer at His Craft*, edited by Jack Salzman, DAVID D. ANDERSON, and Kichinosuke Ohashi (1979). Several editions of Anderson's letters have been published, each reflecting the range and abundance of his correspondences. Those containing material on the Midwest include *Letters of Sherwood Anderson*, edited by Howard Mumford Jones and WALTER RIDEOUT (1953); *Sherwood Anderson: Selected Letters*, edited by Charles E. Modlin (1984); and *Letters to Bab: Sherwood Anderson to Marietta D. Finley, 1916–33*, edited by William A. Sutton (1985).

**FURTHER READING:** Irving Howe's *Sherwood Anderson* (1951), James Schevill's *Sherwood Anderson: His Life and Work* (1951), and Kim Townsend's *Sherwood Anderson* (1987) are major book-length studies of Anderson's life and work. William A. Sutton's loosely organized *The Road to Winesburg: A Mosaic of the Imaginative Life of Sherwood Anderson* (1972) provides a close examination of Anderson's early life up to his Chicago years. Douglas G. Rogers's *Sherwood Anderson: A Selective, Annotated Bibliography* (1976) and Eugene P. Sheehy and Kenneth A. Lohf's *Sherwood Anderson: A Bibliography* (1960) are the standard, though at times inaccurate, bibliographies. Also see Ray Lewis White's *Sherwood Anderson: A Reference Guide* (1977). The most reliable bibliographies of Anderson materials published since 1975 are the annual summer issues of *Sherwood Anderson Review*, formerly the *Winesburg Eagle*. Judy Jo Small's *A Reader's Guide to the Short Stories of Sherwood Anderson* (1994) provides detailed treatment of the composition, influences, publication history, and selected bibliography of Anderson's tales. See also David D. Anderson's *Sherwood Anderson: An Introduction and Interpretation* (1967) and *The Achievement of Sherwood Anderson: Essays in Criticism*, edited by Ray Lewis White (1966). Other notable collections of essays that touch on a variety of Anderson's works include *Sherwood Anderson: A Collection of Critical Essays*, edited by Walter Rideout (1974); *Sherwood Anderson: Centennial Studies*, edited by Hilbert H. Campbell and Charles E. Modlin (1976); and *Critical Essays on Sherwood Anderson*, edited by David D. Anderson (1982). BERNARD DUFFEY's seminal *The Chicago Renaissance in American Letters: A Critical History* (1954), KENNY J. WILLIAMS's *A Storyteller and a City: Sherwood Anderson's Chicago* (1988), and Ronald Weber's *The Midwestern Ascendancy in American Writing* (1992) study Anderson's significance in the Chicago Renaissance. The primary repository of Anderson's papers is the Newberry Library, Chicago.

ROBERT DUNNE

CENTRAL CONNECTICUT STATE UNIVERSITY

## CLARENCE ANDREWS.

*See* appendix (1982)

## HARRIETTE SIMPSON ARNOW

July 7, 1908–March 22, 1986

**BIOGRAPHY:** Born in Wayne County, Kentucky, to Elias and Mollie (Denney) Simpson and a family rich in oral tradition, Harriette Louisa Simpson spent her childhood in Burnside near the Cumberland River. Young Harriette would often change the endings of the stories she heard to her liking if they were sad, and she referred to this practice as the beginning of her writing. Her mother, however, encouraged her to teach rather than to write, and reluctantly, she took teaching jobs. In 1926, at the end of her sophomore year at Berea College, she taught in a one-room schoolhouse in Pulaski County, which provided the substance for her first novel, *Mountain Path* (1936). She earned a bachelor of science degree from the University of Louisville in 1931.

Harriette Simpson Arnow.
Courtesy of University of Kentucky Special Collections.
Used by permission of Tom Arnow

A turning point came in the summer of 1934 at the Conway Inn in Petoskey, Michigan. In a lakeside cottage, she began her first book and renewed her commitment to writing. That fall, she went to Cincinnati determined to pursue a writing career and lived alternately in Cincinnati and in Covington, Kentucky, just across the Ohio River. Working odd jobs at first, she managed to have short stories and her first novel published. Later, in Cincinnati, while writing and doing historical research for the Federal Writers Project, she met Harold Arnow from Chicago. They married in 1939 and departed to live as subsistence farmers and writers in Keno, Kentucky. Their daughter, Marcella, was born there in 1941.

It was in Michigan that Harriette Simpson Arnow became most productive. In 1945, after Harold Arnow obtained employment with the *Detroit Times*, the family moved to a wartime housing project in Detroit. Their son, Thomas, was born in 1946, and in 1949 her second novel, *Hunter's Horn*, was published. In 1950, seeking a country life, the Arnows bought a modest farmhouse and forty acres of land in Ann Arbor. There, she would rise at three or four in the morning to write while her young family slept. Sitting on a milk crate and typing on a portable Olivetti-Underwood, she wrote essays, book reviews, three novels, and three nonfiction books, including her best-known novel, *The Dollmaker* (1954). During the 1960s, Arnow befriended activists who were involved in addressing various social injustices. She was a lifelong Democrat and a member of the ACLU and of the Women's International League for Peace and Freedom. In 1983 she was inducted into the Michigan Women's Hall of Fame. She was the recipient of the Society for the Study of Midwestern Literature's 1984 Mark Twain Award for distinguished contributions to Midwestern literature.

The Arnows wished to move south to get away from the "outlandish" Michigan winters, but they never did. Arnow died in Ann Arbor in March 1986, a year after her husband's death.

**SIGNIFICANCE:** An essayist, short story writer, novelist, and social historian, Harriette Simpson Arnow has made significant contributions to the meaning of the American experience. Her work has received critical attention from various perspectives, including regionalism, feminism, Marxism, and even Transcendentalism.

Arnow's early fiction from the Cincinnati period shows an emerging social realist with a passion for history. *Mountain Path* and five published short stories "recapture" fast disappearing Kentucky hill communities. In particular, they give voice to the hill women silently suffering under the yoke of patriarchal hill culture and fundamentalist religion. Some of her unpublished short stories from this period deal with the urban dispossessed and clearly demonstrate her social conscience which was sharpened during the Depression era. Arnow maintained her artistic independence from the literary tendencies of her time and region. A self-proclaimed realist, Arnow subscribed neither to the idealism of the Southern Renaissance nor to proletarian naturalism. She was faithful to none other than the enduring characters of her imagination.

Arnow's later work in Michigan embodies the depth of her artistry and her commitment to a democratic vision of America. *Hunter's Horn*, set in the south-central Kentucky hills, exemplifies Arnow's narrative craftsmanship with its compelling characterization and unflinching realism. Arnow's artistic vision further expands with *The Dollmaker*, runner-up to Faulkner's *A Fable* for the 1955 National Book Award. In this novel, Arnow intersects agrarian values and urban realities, themes that she explored separately in her earlier short stories. Against the pastoral system of life in the Kentucky hills, industrialized Detroit during World War II is depicted as a hostile place plagued by regional prejudice, religious intolerance, and capitalistic exploitation. Arnow's Detroit is a modern day Babel that tempts and tests, but fails to defeat, the innermost human spirit. Arnow's ideological orientation becomes even more apparent in *The Weedkiller's Daughter* (1970). Set in a Detroit suburb in the mid-1960s, this novel delivers a scathing indictment of a fragmented society, in which environmentally destructive weed killing symbolizes the political, religious, and racial persecution of the unwanted and the outcast. This is Arnow's exposition on "the hypocritical North" of the 1950s and 1960s. Her growing disillusionment with the erosion of civil liberties during the McCarthy era is well documented in her unpublished letters and short stories written in Ann Arbor.

Arnow did not see these social ills as inherent aspects of the Midwest, but rather as indicative of the overall decay of American culture that accompanied the "progress" of technology and industrialization. Thus, she wistfully recalled an American past when the pioneer communities had "faith in democracy" and existed in racial and ethnic harmony. In her two social history books about the Cumberland basin around 1800 and in her last novel, *The Kentucky Trace: A Novel of the American Revolution* (1974), Arnow explores themes of a more perfect egalitarian society, even as she reclaims kinship with Kentucky.

**SELECTED WORKS:** Arnow's major novels include *Mountain Path* (1936), *Hunter's Horn* (1949), *The Dollmaker* (1954), *The Weedkiller's Daughter* (1970), and *The Kentucky Trace: A Novel of the American Revolution* (1974). The social history books in which she reconstructs pioneer settlements in the Cumberland River country are *Seedtime on the Cumberland* (1960) and *Flowering of the Cumberland* (1963); *Old Burnside* (1977) is a semi-autobiography about her hometown. Her craftsmanship is most clearly seen in her short stories such as "Marigolds and Mules," in *Kosmos: Dynamic Stories of Today* 3 (February–March 1935): 3–6; "A Mess of Pork," in *New Talent* 10 (October–December 1935): 4–11; "Washerwoman's Day," in *Southern Review* 1 (Winter 1936): 522–27; "The Two Hunters," in *Esquire* 18 (July 1942): 74–75, 96; and "The Hunter," in *Atlantic Monthly* 174 (November 1944): 79–84. Arnow's manuscript "Between the Flowers," an intriguing link between her first and second published novels, was published in 1999.

**FURTHER READING:** *Harriette Simpson Arnow: 1908–1986* (1988) is an excellent documentary on Arnow directed by Herb E. Smith, Appalshop Inc. in Whitesburg, Kentucky. Two book-length critical studies exist on Arnow: Wilton Eckley's *Harriette Arnow* (1974) focuses on Arnow's first four novels, four published short stories, and two social history books; and Haeja K. Chung's *Harriette Simpson Arnow: Critical Essays on Her Work* (1995) attempts a comprehensive look at Arnow scholarship which examines nearly all of Arnow's major writings. Two bibliographical studies are Sandra L. Ballard's "Harriette Simpson Arnow," *Appalachian Journal* 14.4 (Summer 1987): 360–72, and Mary Anne Brennan's "Harriette Simpson Arnow: Checklist," *Bulletin of Bibliography and Magazine Notes* 46.1 (March 1989): 46–52. The Arnow Special Collection in the Margaret I. King Library at the University of Kentucky is the main repository of Arnow's manuscripts and letters. Although most of Arnow's voluminous personal letters remain in the possession of her friends, some letters from the 1960s are available from the Michigan Historical Collections in the Bentley Historical Library at the University of Michigan.

HAEJA K. CHUNG        MICHIGAN STATE UNIVERSITY

## JAMES C. AUSTIN.
*See* appendix (1989)

## MARY (HUNTER) AUSTIN
September 9, 1868–August 13, 1934

**BIOGRAPHY:** Mary Austin was born and lived her first twenty years in Carlinville, Illinois. Her mother, Susannah Savilla (Graham) Hunter, was an advocate of women's suffrage and temperance. Her father, Captain George Hunter, a lawyer, died before his daughter was ten. Austin's early feelings of rejection by her mother were intensified after her father's death. Her independent nature as well as her determination to get an education and to become a writer made her the black sheep of her family. She attended Normal School in Bloomington, Indiana (1885), then graduated from Blackburn College in Carlinville in 1888.

Immediately following graduation, Hunter homesteaded in southern California with her mother and brother. Her alumni magazine description of their trip west, later published as *One Hundred Miles on Horseback*, marked the beginning of her writings about the Southwest. In May 1891 she married Stafford Wallace Austin and lived with him in the Owen Valley, teaching and homesteading. Their daughter Ruth was born October 30, 1892, the same year Austin's first story was accepted in *Overland Monthly*.

In 1899, while teaching at the Normal School in Los Angeles (later UCLA), Austin met writers, including Charlotte Perkins Gilman, who like herself were publishing in Charles Lummis's *Out West* magazine. Austin's publication of *The Land of Little Rain* (1903) established her as a nationally known writer. By 1906 she settled in Carmel among a community of writers that included George Sterling, Jack London, and Lincoln Steffens. She traveled to Europe from 1907 to 1910, where she met and was admired by colleagues including Shaw, Wells, and Conrad. Returning to New York City in 1910, she wrote and published prolifically, while dividing her time for the next fourteen years between New York and Carmel. In 1914 she divorced Wallace Austin, and her daughter, severely retarded and institutionalized, died in 1918. In New York Austin became an active feminist, making friends with Emma Goldman, Margaret Sanger, and Elizabeth Gurley Flynn. She returned to England in 1921–22, renewing old literary acquaintances and making new. During this period her friendship with Mabel Dodge Luhan, who shared her interest in the Southwest, led to meeting D. H. Lawrence.

In 1925 Austin settled permanently in Santa Fe, New Mexico. There she continued writing, collaborating on a book with Ansel Adams and loaning her house to WILLA

CATHER, so she could complete *Death Comes for the Archbishop*. Austin died in Santa Fe in 1934.

**SIGNIFICANCE:** Although cited most often for her sketches and novels of the Southwest, two of Austin's major works are significant to Midwestern literary studies: her novel, *A Woman of Genius* (1912), and her autobiography, *Earth Horizon* (1932). Both explore the struggle of a woman artist to balance creativity with socially prescribed roles as wife and mother, and both present that struggle in small Midwestern towns whose social pressures and values are the villains of the stories.

Olivia Lattimore Bettersworth, a talented actress, is the title character in *A Woman of Genius*. But her achievements have a high cost: she fights a lifelong battle against the social and religious strictures of Taylorville, Ohiana, a marvelous amalgam of Ohio and Indiana. Like hundreds of other towns in the Midwest, Taylorville has rigidly maintained social distinctions and a narrow Protestant moral code. Austin's critique of the hypocrisy and shallowness of Taylorville is as scathing as that of SINCLAIR LEWIS in *Main Street* and predates it by eight years. Indeed, Lewis and Austin knew each other in New York City during the years surrounding both publications. The conflict is clear in the novel's structure as well as content. Olivia is addressing the story to her hometown friend and Chicago society matron, Pauline Allingham Mills, who epitomizes and enacts the double standards, hypocritical class consciousness, and rigid gender roles that have proved so stifling to Olivia. Olivia's rebellion is starkly contrasted to Pauline's growth along the lines that small-town Ohiana demanded. Olivia's descriptions of living in both a small Midwestern town and the working-class section of Chicago are important depictions of Midwestern life at the turn of the twentieth century.

Austin's autobiography, *Earth Horizon*, provides the nonfiction version of this same feminist struggle for self-expression. Small-town Carlinville, Illinois, was as class bound and stifling to the young Austin as Taylorville was to Olivia. Her childhood history in particular is closely paralleled in the two books. But in *Earth Horizon* a positive element of Midwestern life appears in Austin's use of landscape to denote spirituality. Her pivotal experience of unity with nature, in what she called her childhood and small-town social activities, including church and group picnics, was also very regional in details and emphases. Although Austin went on to discover a strong affinity for the Southwest and its landscape, the small-town Midwest shaped her initial understanding of her spirituality, her struggle to be an artist, and her gender issues. Her work on these themes influenced other Midwestern writers, including Willa Cather and Sinclair Lewis, whom she knew personally. Austin's finely drawn depictions of Midwestern small towns and her ironic tone are rarely surpassed.

In her career, Austin wrote and published more than thirty-one books, including novels, an autobiography, sketches, children's literature, drama, and nonfiction. She also wrote more than two hundred short stories and articles which appeared in more than sixty-five periodicals.

**SELECTED WORKS:** For the student of Midwestern literature, the primary texts remain *A Woman of Genius* (1912) and *Earth Horizon* (1932). Another novel that looks at gender expectations and issues without so strong a regional background is *No. 26 Jayne Street* (1920). Her best-known Southwestern works include *The Land of Little Rain* (1903), *Isidro* (1905), and *Starry Adventure* (1931). A good collection of sketches and excerpts is available in Esther F. Lanigan's *A Mary Austin Reader* (1996). Her children's books are best represented by *The Basket-Woman: A Book of Fanciful Tales for Children* (1904). Austin's nonfiction includes not only her autobiography but a book on Indian chants and poetry, *The American Rhythm* (1923), and a book on spirituality, *Everyman's Genius* (1925).

**FURTHER READING:** The most helpful of the four biographies of Austin is the most recent, Esther F. Lanigan's *Mary Austin: Song of a Maverick* (1989), although all offer interesting anecdotes and interpretations. Peggy Pond Church focuses on Austin's early life in *Wind's Trail* (1990). Helen MacKnight Doyle offers a contemporary friend's view in *Mary Austin, Woman of Genius* (1939), while Augusta Fink's *I-Mary* (1983) is the first to relate closely the psychological and literary development of Austin. Critical books that are particularly useful include T. M. Pearce's *Mary Hunter Austin* (1965) and a section in Elizabeth Ammons's *Conflicting Stories: American Women Writers at the Turn into the Twentieth Century* (1991). Scholars and readers should also consult *Literary America, 1903–1934: The Mary Austin Letters*, selected and edited by T. M. Pearce (1979). The largest and most complete primary collection on Austin is housed at the Henry E. Huntington Library in San Marino, California. It includes manuscripts, letters, and photographs. Some additional materials are housed at the Coronado Room in the main library of the University of New Mexico.

MELODY M. ZAJDEL

MONTANA STATE UNIVERSITY

# B

## RAY STANNARD BAKER
April 17, 1870–July 12, 1946
(David Grayson)

**BIOGRAPHY:** Born in Lansing, Michigan, the oldest of six sons of Joseph and Alice (Potter) Baker, Ray Stannard Baker spent his youth in the prairie town of St. Croix Falls, Wisconsin. After graduating from what was then Michigan Agricultural College in 1889, later Michigan State University, he married Jessie I. Beal, the daughter of one of his professors, and joined the reporting staff of the *Chicago Record*. There, during the 1890s, he chronicled the social and economic problems facing the country in an age of rapid industrialization and urbanization. At the same time, he authored adventure tales for boys published in the *Youth's Companion* and *Century Magazine*.

His reputation as a crusading writer established, Baker moved to *McClure's* in New York in 1898 and expressed its progressive philosophy in articles on the labor movement, the corporate world, race relations, technological advance, and other pressing issues. In 1905, along with fellow "muckrakers" Ida Tarbell and Lincoln Steffens, he bought the *American Magazine* and continued as a spokesman for the social gospel in his role as writer and editor for ten years. Under the pen name "David Grayson," he also produced a series of familiar essays collected in nine volumes between 1907 and 1942, beginning with *Adventures in Contentment* (1907), which won him a wide audience. Baker made the acquaintance of Woodrow Wilson during these years; eventually, he became an important advocate of the president, championing his policies in writings such as *What Wilson Did at Paris* (1919), an apologia for the Versailles Treaty. Baker was designated by Wilson himself as his official biographer. The eight-volume *Woodrow Wilson: Life and Letters* (1927–39) won a Pulitzer Prize in 1940.

After leaving the *American Magazine*, Baker devoted himself to writing at his Amherst, Massachusetts, home. His major opus—though not his most enduring work—was the Wilson biography. He also penned two autobiographies before his 1946 death in Amherst, Massachusetts, of heart disease.

**SIGNIFICANCE:** During his lifetime, Baker was well known as a commentator, the author of numerous articles addressing American socioeconomic situations and espousing progressivist ideals. Respected as one of America's finest reporters, he served his writing apprenticeship in Chicago during a time of change and upheaval, recording Midwestern events such as the agricultural depression of the 1890s, the march of Coxey's Army, and the Pullman strike, all of which helped to shape the reform agenda he brought to his career as a muckraking journalist in the East.

As Woodrow Wilson's defender and biographer, Baker's heartland values were manifest. His admiration for the president's resourcefulness, independence, and commitment to a global commonwealth grew out of Baker's own abiding faith in his frontier legacy of individualism, democratic communalism, and personal integrity. Also, as David Grayson, he articulated that heritage, offering homey wisdom, philosophical optimism, and celebration of rural life. His autobiographical works were written to eulogize the pastoral world of his youth. *Native American* (1941) in particular extols the humane pragmatism at the heart of the Midwestern ethos as epitomized in Baker's portrait of his father, who dominates the memoir. Always a man of affirmative vision, at his death, Baker was at work on a book about the delights of everyday life.

**SELECTED WORKS:** Baker's journalistic commentary was collected into a number of volumes. Especially important are *Our New Prosperity* (1900), *Following the Color Line* (1908), and *The Spiritual Unrest* (1910). As a popularizer of science and technology, he wrote *The Boys' Book of Inventions* (1899) and its sequel, *The Boys' Second Book of Inventions* (1903). In addition to his eight-volume biography of Wilson, *Woodrow Wilson: Life and Letters* (1927–39), he edited, with William E. Dodd, Wilson's correspondence in *The Public Papers of Woodrow Wilson*, in six volumes (1927–39), and produced several books of commentary on the president's leadership, including *What Wilson Did at Paris* (1919) and the three-volume *Woodrow Wilson and World Settlement* (1922). The best-known David Grayson books include *Adventures in Contentment* (1907), *Adventures in Friendship* (1910), *The Friendly Road* (1913), *Adventures in Solitude* (1931), and *The Countryman's Year* (1936). Baker's two autobiographies preserve his best writing: *Native American: The Book of My Youth* (1941) and *American Chronicle* (1945).

**FURTHER READING:** Two monographs on Baker exist: John E. Semonche's *Ray Stannard Baker: A Quest for Democracy in Modern America*

(1969), an examination of Baker's career up to its midpoint in 1918; and Robert C. Bannister Jr.'s *Ray Stannard Baker: The Mind and Thought of a Progressive*, an intellectual biography. Frank P. Rand's *The Story of David Grayson* (1963) is a fanciful recollection of the world of the Grayson stories. The author's papers are housed in the Library of Congress, the Jones Library at Amherst, and the Princeton University Library.

LIAHNA BABENER

CENTRAL WASHINGTON UNIVERSITY

## JANE S. BAKERMAN.
*See* appendix (1993)

## PAMILLA W. BALL
ca. 1790–1838

**BIOGRAPHY:** Pamilla W. Ball, or Mrs. Phillippa W. Ball, was a pioneer short story writer, journalist, and newspaper editor. She claims in "Home Again" (*Evening Visiter,* August 2, 1837: 130), to be the daughter of an aristocratic, slave-owning Virginia family whose plantation went into decline (130). Ball's fiction provides a few glimpses of Eastern seacoast life, as in her story "The Wrecker's Daughter." By 1831 she had emigrated to Cincinnati, Ohio, and was publishing regional fiction about the area. In 1837, a widow with two children, Ball launched an early regional newspaper, the *Zanesville Evening Visiter*. After its failure, Ball ceased publishing and vanished from the public record.

**SIGNIFICANCE:** Ball's fiction is firmly rooted in her Ohio experiences on the frontier. Mentored by the friendly and influential pioneer editor W. D. Gallagher, she published many stories about pioneer women's hardships in such publications as his prestigious *Cincinnati Mirror*. Her sympathies reflect the concerns and preoccupations of the early Midwestern, or at the time "Western," setting; for example, temperance is the theme in her story "Woman's Destiny," which shows a frontier family imperiled by a husband's alcoholism. Other depictions of frontier life are humorous: "A Tale of Early Times" specifically rebuts Frances Trollope's 1834 complaint about Ohio pioneers, defending Ohio's egalitarian conventions such as "help" being treated like friends. Ball's Virginia emigrants in this story aspire to become "real Buckeyes" in the classless wilderness (174). Other stories demonstrate her interest in local Indians, whom she saw as prospective objects of racial genocide. In "The Maid of the Muskingum," the first story in her April 1837 edition of the *Evening Visiter*, Ball rejects Virginia's corruption and counterbalances it with a vision of Ohio's edenic Western setting. Here she romantically reconciles East and West, white and red. The first woman editor of a weekly newspaper in Ohio, Pamilla W. Ball bravely attempted to support her family in Zanesville, a frontier town of four thousand, by her fiction and editorial work, but after 1838 her refreshing observations, sentimental idealism, and trenchant wit were silenced.

**SELECTED WORKS:** Pamilla Ball published primarily in newspapers. Citations for some of her major stories are as follows: "Woman's Destiny" was published in the *Cincinnati Mirror* and *Ladies' Parterre* 2.23 (August 3, 1833): 175–79; "A Tale of Early Times" appeared in the *Cincinnati Mirror*, and *Western Gazette of Literature and Science* 4.22 (March 23, 1835): 173–74; and "The Maid of the Muskingum" saw publication in the *Evening Visiter* 1.1 (April 1, 1837): 1–4. Her personal essay "Home Again" appeared in the *Evening Visiter* 1.6 (August 2, 1837): 129–30.

**FURTHER READING:** Lucille B. Emch, in her "Ohio in Short Stories, 1824–1839," in the *Ohio State Archeological and Historical Society Quarterly* 53 (July–September 1944): 233–34, calls this author a "feminine writer of the thirties." Ball's fiction is available in collections of early Ohio publications, such as in the Rare Books and Special Collections of Cincinnati's Public Library and Ohio University's Archives located in its library. Two of her stories, "A Tale of Early Times" and "Maid of the Muskingum," have recently been reprinted by Sandra Parker in *Home Material, Ohio's Nineteenth Century Regional Fiction*.

SANDRA PARKER                    HIRAM COLLEGE

# EDWIN BALMER
July 26, 1883–March 21, 1959
**BIOGRAPHY:** Edwin Balmer, born in Chicago to Helen Clark (Pratt) and Thomas Balmer, received an AB from Northwestern in 1902 and an MA from Harvard in 1903. In 1909 he married Katharine MacHarg, sister of WILLIAM MACHARG, one of his collaborators. They had three children, and after her death

he married Grace A. Kee in 1927. He began his career as a reporter for the *Chicago Tribune* and then turned to magazine work and books. He became editor of *Redbook* in 1927 and later was associate publisher. His best-known works were joint efforts. With William MacHarg, he wrote a collection of short mysteries, *The Achievements of Luther Trant* (1910), which was regarded as innovative because of its psychological and scientific approaches to crime detection. A novel written with MacHarg, *The Indian Drum* (1917), has become a collectors' item for those interested in Michigan fiction. Balmer collaborated on six books with Philip Wylie, including two works of science fiction, *When Worlds Collide* (1933) and *After Worlds Collide* (1934). The former became one of several of his works which were made into films. In addition, Balmer wrote a number of mysteries, romances, and adventure stories and novels.

**SIGNIFICANCE:** Many of Balmer's books have Chicago as their primary setting. They explore a variety of aspects of the city, including its history and geography, social strata, ethnic diversity, police activity, shipping industry, business world, and underworld. His fiction, *That Royle Girl* (1925) in particular, emphasizes the vigor that ethnic diversity has brought to the Midwest. His work also records noteworthy events such as a fire at the Chicago World's Fair of 1893 in *Dragons Drive You* (1934).

Some of the novels also take place, at least in part, in Michigan. *The Indian Drum*, an adventure about shipping on the Great Lakes and in Chicago, features crime, power, greed, romance, concealed identities, and a purported Indian legend. The story reaches its climax in a great storm and shipwreck on Lake Michigan, where those on the shore can hear a mysterious Manitou drum beat for each of those drowned. The book has proved sufficiently popular that, once the copyright expired, it was reprinted in nearly identical form under a different title and author. The fictional location of *Resurrection Rock* (1920) lies off the coast of the Upper Peninsula in Lake Huron, and the story involves struggles over logging in Michigan and the control of the finances of the Cullen family in Chicago. In *Dangerous Business* (1927), which features rivalry among Chicago businessmen, two of the key characters come from Emmet County,

Michigan; another sails in the Chicago-Mack-inac Race; and another character saves sailors from a wreck in a Lake Michigan storm.

The conflicts in the novels clearly distinguish between good and evil, with good prevailing at the end. The protagonists, mainly male, but sometimes female, usually exhibit intelligence, compassion, patience, resourcefulness, and courage, with a strong emphasis on integrity.

**SELECTED WORKS:** Alone and with Mac-Harg and Wylie, Balmer wrote more than twenty novels. Many have Midwestern settings. They include *The Indian Drum* (1917) with MacHarg, and *Resurrection Rock* (1920), which take place in Chicago and Michigan. Among those set partly or entirely in Chicago are *Blind Man's Eyes* (1916) and the volume of short stories, *The Achievements of Luther Trant* (1910), both with MacHarg; *Keeban* (1923); *Fidelia* (1924); *That Royle Girl* (1925); *Dangerous Business* (1927); *Dragons Drive You* (1934); and *The Shield of Silence* (1936). Balmer wrote a pair of science fiction thrillers with Philip Wylie, *When Worlds Collide* (1933) and *After Worlds Collide* (1934); a crucial series of episodes in the former occurs in Michigan's Upper Peninsula. *The Candle of the Wicked* (1956) starts and finishes in a small town in Iowa; and *With All the World Away* (1958) begins in Indiana and ends in Michigan.

**FURTHER READING:** Short biographical and bibliographical entries on Balmer appear in such reference works as Chris Steinbrunner and Otto Penzler's *Encyclopedia of Mystery and Detection* (1976), John M. Reilly's *Twentieth Century Crime and Mystery Writers* (1980), and ROBERT BEASECKER'S *Michigan in the Novel, 1816–1996* (1998). In *Michigan in Literature* (1992), CLARENCE ANDREWS discusses the Michigan aspects of the novels, particularly in *The Indian Drum* and *Resurrection Rock*.

MARY DEJONG OBUCHOWSKI

CENTRAL MICHIGAN UNIVERSITY

# MARGARET AYER BARNES
April 8, 1886–October 25, 1967

**BIOGRAPHY:** Margaret Ayer was born to Benjamin and Janet (Hopkins) Ayer in Chicago, the city that would provide the setting for her best-selling novels. In 1904 she was graduated from the University School for Girls and in 1907 she earned a BA in English and philosophy from Bryn Mawr College. Af-ter college she returned to Chicago, married attorney Cecil Barnes in 1910, and spent the next two decades raising their three sons. Always active in the Bryn Mawr Alumnae Association, Barnes served as its vice-president and as alumna director, helping to found the Bryn Mawr Working Woman's College in 1921. She also appeared in amateur theatricals with the Aldis Players in Lake Forest and the North Shore Theater in Winnetka, Illinois. This interest in the theater came to fruition in her dramatization of Edith Wharton's *The Age of Innocence* (1928), and in her collaboration with lifelong friend Edward Sheldon on two plays: *Jenny* (1929) and *Dishonored Lady* (1930).

While recovering from a 1925 auto accident, Barnes began writing fiction, following in the footsteps of her sister, JANET AYER FAIRBANK. After publishing a collection of short stories, *Prevailing Winds* (1928), she produced five novels during the 1930s, all employing Chicagoland settings and characters. In 1931 her first novel, *Years of Grace*, was awarded the Pulitzer Prize.

Barnes retired from writing in 1945; she died at age eighty-one of a pulmonary embolism at her home in Cambridge, Massachusetts.

**SIGNIFICANCE:** Barnes's stories and novels reflect not only her upper-middle-class upbringing in late-nineteenth- and early-twentieth-century Chicago but also her Bryn Mawr years, where she was very much influenced by its feminist president, M. Carey Thomas. Although Barnes's main focus is the female experience, her work is also valuable for its delineation of Chicago history, particularly the social history of its upper middle class, during the first three decades of the twentieth century. Her characters are the well-provided-for wives of bankers, lawyers, and businessmen who work on La Salle Street. These women spend their days in North Shore suburbs, planning elegant dinner parties, supervising servants, and agonizing over issues that their mothers' generation never had to deal with: careers, love affairs, divorces, remarriages, blended families. Several of Barnes's novels are family sagas seen from the perspective of a central female character. *Years of Grace* (1930) employs this narrative technique, rendering historical events, as well as domestic occurrences, from the perspective of Jane Ward Carver. As we

see Jane develop from a girl of fourteen to a middle-aged mother and grandmother, we also see Chicago evolve in a similar way, from its debut as a major American city at the time of the World Columbian Exposition to its transformation into a metropolis of smoke-stained skyscrapers by the 1930s.

**SELECTED WORKS:** Margaret Ayer Barnes published one collection of short fiction, *Prevailing Winds* (1928), and five novels: *Years of Grace* (1930), *Westward Passage* (1931), *Within This Present* (1933), *Edna His Wife* (1935), and *Wisdom's Gate* (1938).

**FURTHER READING:** Lloyd C. Taylor's *Margaret Ayer Barnes* (1974) is the only book-length study. Her papers are held by Harvard University and the New York Public Library.

MARCIA NOE

THE UNIVERSITY OF TENNESSEE AT CHATTANOOGA

## L(YMAN) FRANK BAUM

May 15, 1856–May 6, 1919

(Floyd Akers, Laura Bancroft, Louis F. Baum, George Brooks, John Estes Cooke, Captain Hugh Fitzgerald, Suzanne Metcalf, Schuyler Staunton, Edith Van Dyne)

**BIOGRAPHY:** Son of Benjamin Ward and Cynthia (Stanton) Baum, L. Frank Baum was born in Chittenango, New York. He was educated through home tutoring and private schools. On November 9, 1882, he married women's activist Maude Gage, with whom he had four sons. Baum had a checkered career, working in his family oil business, operating an opera house, and raising fancy poultry in New York from 1881 to 1888; operating a variety store and editing a newspaper in South Dakota from 1888 to 1891; and holding positions as newspaper and magazine editor, traveling salesman, and crockery buyer in Chicago from 1897 to 1901. He settled in Hollywood, California, in 1901 to devote himself full-time to writing. Best known for his Oz series, Baum also wrote a number of other children's series, adult novels, and plays and musicals. He operated the Oz Film Company from 1914 to 1915. After experiencing chronic heart trouble, he died in Hollywood in 1919 following a gallbladder operation.

**SIGNIFICANCE:** L. Frank Baum is best remembered for his Oz books, which are significantly informed by Midwestern experience. Baum's opening description in *The Wonderful Wizard of Oz* (1900) portrays Dorothy's

Kansas farm life and landscape gloomy, and flat, and the plains are by good but dour hard-working pe is a characteristic passage of turn-o tury naturalistic writing as well as a of national assumptions about the The dismal portrait of plains life is provide relief for the fantastic an Land of Oz, and it is so striking that ily translated to the screen in the fa MGM film starring Judy Garla many people's conceptions of K the Midwest have been formed by toned, barren landscape and viole of the film, the moviemakers bor scene directly from Baum's book. N sumptions about Midwestern valu ing on home and family are also Dorothy's central purpose in her j of the fantastic Land of Oz. These form the film as well, although th sented more sentimentally than in In the novel, the Wizard himself of Dorothy's return to her Midwes is revealed to have humble O braska, origins.

Baum's impressions of the Mi no doubt shaped by his years in South Dakota. After years of fin ble, Baum's wife, Maude Gage, u relocate the family to the Dakota relatives told stereotypical stories spaces and vast financial possibil prairies. Their general store, Bau failed as Aberdeen entered a Baum then took over the *Dakota P* paper, changing the name to the *urday Pioneer*. His penchant for and his perceptive observance of foibles led to a successful column, lady." This feature is presented a among residents of a boarding humorous local gossip, satire, u tasy, and local portraiture, inclu ing anxiety over and disturbingl tudes toward the Ghost Dance w whites and Lakota Sioux. The pa well, however, and in 1891 the B to Chicago.

Baum's Oz stories have bee their "Americanness," that is, fo components of their fairy-tale la out of distinctly American mate his collection entitled *American*

a deliberate attempt to create a uniquely American form, with settings in the Midwest and other American locations. Often the Scarecrow and the Tin Woodman of the Oz stories are cited as some of the best examples of fantasy characters derived from an American agricultural and industrial sensibility, and many of Baum's other stories are populated by farm animals and mechanical creatures. While not necessarily distinctly Midwestern, the agricultural and industrial landscapes of South Dakota and Chicago no doubt influenced Baum's imaginative vision.

**SELECTED WORKS:** Baum's most famous work, of course, is his Oz series, which includes *The Wonderful Wizard of Oz* (1900), *The Marvelous Land of Oz* (1904), *Ozma of Oz* (1907), *Dorothy and the Wizard in Oz* (1908), *The Road to Oz* (1909), *The Emerald City of Oz* (1910), *The Patchwork Girl of Oz* (1913), *Tik-Tok of Oz* (1914), *The Little Wizard Stories of Oz* (1914), *The Scarecrow of Oz* (1915), *Rinkitink in Oz* (1916), *The Lost Princess of Oz* (1917), *The Tin Woodman of Oz* (1918), *The Magic of Oz* (1919), and *Glinda of Oz* (1920).

Baum also wrote numerous other children's fantasy books, including *American Fairy Tales* (1901), *Dot and Tot of Merryland* (1901), *The Life and Adventures of Santa Claus* (1902), and *The Sea Fairies* (1911). Under a number of pseudonyms, Baum wrote several children's series, such as "Boy Fortune Hunters" as Floyd Akers and "Aunt Jane's Nieces" as Edith Van Dyne. He also wrote a number of adult novels under his own name and pseudonyms, including *The Fate of a Crown* (1905) and *The Last Egyptian: A Romance of the Nile* (1908). Baum's "Our Landlady" columns from the *Aberdeen Saturday Post* have recently been reprinted (1995).

**FURTHER READING:** Frank J. Baum and Russell P. MacFall's *To Please a Child* (1961) remains the standard Baum biography, though a more recent juvenile biography is Angelica S. Carpenter and Jean L. Shirley's *L. Frank Baum: Royal Historian of Oz* (1991). The only full-length critical study of Baum's work is Raylyn Moore's *Wonderful Wizard, Marvelous Land* (1974), though numerous critical essays have been written for and reprinted in *The Wizard of Oz and Who He Was*, edited by Martin Gardner and Russel B. Nye (1957), and *The Wizard of Oz*, edited by Michael Patrick Hearn (1983). Hearn has also edited *The Annotated Wizard of Oz* (1973). Less scholarly but useful book-length accounts of Baum and Oz include *The Oz Scrapbook*, by David L. Greene and Dick Martin (1977), and *The World of Oz*, by Allen Eyles (1985). Bibliographic information can be found in *Bibliographia Oziana: A Concise Bibliographical Checklist of the Oz Books by L. Frank Baum and His Successors* (International Wizard of Oz Club, 1975, revised and expanded 1988). Further bibliographic and critical pieces continue to be published in *The Baum Bugle*, the publication of the International Wizard of Oz Club. Baum manuscripts can be found in the libraries of Yale University, Columbia University, and the University of Texas, as well as the New York Public Library.

THOMAS K. DEAN                          UNIVERSITY OF IOWA

# CHARLES BAXTER
May 13, 1947

**BIOGRAPHY:** Born in Minneapolis to an insurance salesman and his wife, John and Mary Barbara (Eaton) Baxter, Charles Baxter and his two older brothers were raised on a lavish forty-acre estate in Excelsior, Minnesota, with a large library and house servants. Though childhood privilege included private secondary schooling, Baxter fought convention and parental expectation with his subsequent choice of Macalester College, where the political activism and liberality of campus life nurtured his independent spirit. Gentility, rebellion, and his native state all find their way into Baxter's fiction. He sets "Cataract," for example, in rural and urban Minnesota, notably along Minnehaha Creek, which a retired real estate developer decides to paint one afternoon. Later, over martinis, the protagonist is surprised when his wife points out that he has inserted a screaming, Edvard Munch-like face under the water.

Following a year of high school teaching in Pinconning, Michigan, Baxter earned his PhD at the State University of New York at Buffalo. He taught at Wayne State University for fifteen years and has been professor of English at the University of Michigan since 1989. He lives in Ann Arbor with his wife and son. In addition to his stories appearing in *Pushcart Prize* and *Best American Short Stories*, Baxter has received the prestigious Lila Wallace–Reader's Digest Foundation's Award for Writers.

**SIGNIFICANCE:** "Home" is a major theme in Baxter's work, and his adopted state of Michi-

gan is the setting for many of his best stories. Specifically, he uses the mythical town of Five Oaks in central Michigan in both of his novels; for "Gryphon," perhaps his best-known and most anthologized short story; and for other fiction such as "Created Things," "Scissors," "A Late Sunday Afternoon by the Huron," and "Saul and Patsy Are Getting Comfortable in Michigan." Other Michigan towns and neighborhoods appear as well, one of the most intriguing of which is Detroit in "The Disappeared." Here the big city appears disorienting and frightening as it is eerily perceived through the eyes of an outsider.

But any specific neighborhood in the Midwest is perhaps less important in itself for Baxter than is his unusual treatment of it. He uses the *idea* of that place as a backdrop for his characters' camouflages, counterfeit identities, and expressions of need. Baxter says of his method: "I tend to use banal and realistic imagery from small-town America to describe . . . conscious and unconscious states. The mind, in other words, is as remote and strange as South Dakota" (*Contemporary Authors* 57–60 [1976]: 50). In "Saul and Patsy Are Pregnant," he refers to Midwesterners as "connoisseurs of violence and piety" (*A Relative Stranger* 194).

Baxter's use of the Midwest signifies neither conventional nostalgia nor rootedness. It becomes a place of pregnant and sometimes threatening potential. Forces that seem illogical put normal lives into disarray. The reader is never certain just where the center lies. In Baxter's second novel, for example, Five Oaks is rife with unemployment and For Sale signs. The very culture of the place, as Bettina Drew points out, seems toxic. As Baxter himself has said, his Midwestern characters wrestle not with the infinite, but with the finite.

Critics have compared Baxter's prose with that of John Cheever, Raymond Carver, and even James Joyce. It has a chill yet domestic quality that hints of both beauty and danger.
**SELECTED WORKS:** Baxter moves eloquently and comfortably between four genres. The novels he has published are *First Light* (1987) and *Shadow Play* (1993). He has three volumes of poetry: *Chameleon* (1970), *The South Dakota Guidebook* (1974), and *Imaginary Paintings and Other Poems* (1989). His short story collections are titled *Harmony of the*

*World* (1984), *Through the Safety Net* (1985), *A Relative Stranger* (1990), and *Believers: A Novella and Stories* (1997). He has one book of nonfiction, *Burning Down the House: Essays on Fiction* (1997). The frequently anthologized short story "Gryphon" has been adapted for film.
**FURTHER READING:** Several interviews with Charles Baxter have been published; perhaps the most useful appears in Kevin Breen's September–October 1994 "An Interview with Charles Baxter" in *Poets and Writers* (60–69). Another, Elizabeth Devereaux's December 7, 1993, article in *Publishers Weekly*, "Charles Baxter" (45–46), discusses Baxter's invention of Five Oaks and his perception of his characters. Bettina Drew's Summer 1993 article "Midwestern Landscapes" (*Michigan Quarterly Review* 32.3: 491–97) examines the geographical implications in *Shadow Play*. Perhaps the most comprehensive article to date is "Knowledge, Home and Gender in Charles Baxter's Short Fiction" (1994), by Terry Caesar, published in *Revista UNIMAR* (16.1 [1994]: 217–28).

JILL B. GIDMARK                    UNIVERSITY OF MINNESOTA

## ROBERT BEASECKER.
*See* appendix (1984)

## THOMAS BEER
November 22, 1889–April 18, 1940
**BIOGRAPHY:** Thomas Beer was born to William C. and Martha Ann (Baldwin) Beer in Council Bluffs, Iowa, but moved to Yonkers, New York, before age two. He graduated from Yale in 1911 and spent a short time in the U.S. Army in France during World War I; he then returned to New York and began a writing career that gained him a large popular audience for his magazine short stories and a respectful literary audience for his novels and cultural histories. These two very different kinds of writing were indicative of Beer's dual nature as both a witty and despairing skeptic, and one who had a nostalgic admiration for a simple and virtuous life. While Beer's popularity has waned, after his sudden fatal heart attack, the *New York Times* devoted twenty-four column inches to commemorate a significant American life of letters.
**SIGNIFICANCE:** Beer's short stories, published in the *Saturday Evening Post* and other magazines and collected in *Mrs. Egg and Other Barbarians* (1933) and *Mrs. Egg and Other Amer-*

*icans* (1947), constitute Beer's contribution to Midwestern literature. Unlike his cosmopolitan and very Eastern novels, these stories were drawn from Beer's Midwestern roots and his visits to the home of his paternal grandfather, Justice Thomas Beer, in Bucyrus, Ohio, nearly every summer until 1910. Beer's fictional hometown of the Egg family in Zerbetta, Ohio, is based on his experiences in Bucyrus and his acquaintance with his Midwestern relatives. Although Alfred Kazin and other prominent Eastern critics dismissed Beer's popular short fiction in favor of his more literary novels, Beer was clearly as interested in the life of the small towns and farm communities of Ohio as in that of the literary elite of New York.

**SELECTED WORKS:** Beer's novels include *The Fair Rewards* (1922), *Sandoval: A Romance of Bad Manners* (1924), and *The Road to Heaven: A Romance of Morals* (1928). He is also the author of *The Mauve Decade: American Life at the End of the Nineteenth Century* (1926) and two biographies: *Stephen Crane: A Study in American Letters* (1923), and [Mark] *Hanna* (1929). Beer has two published collections of short stories, *Mrs. Egg and Other Barbarians* (1933) and *Mrs. Egg and Other Americans* (1947).

**FURTHER READING:** The only full-length studies of Beer are Evans Harrington's PhD thesis, "The Work of Thomas Beer: An Appraisal and Bibliography" (1968); William Daniel Coyle's PhD thesis, "The Short Stories of Thomas Beer" (1977); and August Michael Alfieri's PhD thesis, "Thomas Beer, Freelance Writer and the Changes in the Literary Marketplace, 1920–1940" (1994). Wilson Follett's introduction to the 1947 Knopf edition of *Mrs. Egg and Other Americans* is also very useful. Recent studies include DAVID D. ANDERSON's "Thomas Beer," in the *Society for the Study of Midwestern Literature Newsletter* 14.2 (Summer 1989): 2–10.

KEITH FYNAARDT          NORTHWESTERN COLLEGE

## HENRY BELLAMANN
April 28, 1882–June 16, 1945
(Heinrich Hauer Bellamann)

**BIOGRAPHY:** Henry Bellamann—novelist, poet, educator, and musician—was born in Fulton, Missouri, to George and Caroline (Krahenbuhle) Bellamann. He was educated in Fulton at Westminster College and attended the University of Denver before studying music in New York, London, and Paris. In 1907 he married Katherine Jones and became dean of fine arts at Chicora College for Woman in Columbia, South Carolina, a post he held for seventeen years. Subsequently he held positions at Julliard, Vassar, the Rockefeller Foundation, and the Curtis Institute of Music, where he edited the music magazine *Overtones*. He received an honorary doctor of music degree from DePauw University in 1926 and published three books of verse and two novels during the 1920s. In 1931 France named Bellamann a Chevalier of the Legion of Honor, and he retired from music education to devote himself to writing. At age sixty-three he was at work on a new novel when he died of a heart attack at his New York City home.

**SIGNIFICANCE:** Although he had begun his writing career as a poet, Henry Bellamann's biggest success was his fifth novel, *Kings Row* (1940), which was adapted as a film starring Ronald Reagan. Bellamann's treatment of the Midwestern small town in *Kings Row* and in its sequel, *Parris Mitchell of Kings Row* (1948), is in the tradition of SHERWOOD ANDERSON, EDGAR LEE MASTERS, SINCLAIR LEWIS, and other early-twentieth-century Midwestern writers who debunk the myth of the Midwestern small town as a place that fosters goodness, peace, and harmony in its residents. Like his predecessors, Bellamann demonstrates that a veneer of gentility and middle-class morality disguises the bigotry, greed, lust, and psychological abnormalities of many of the town's citizens. In *Kings Row* the prettiest girl in town is the victim of her father's incestuous compulsions, the town's leading doctor is a sadist who performs unnecessary operations, and a scion of the town's first family has an illegitimate daughter with his mulatto housekeeper. In his portrait of Kings Row, Bellamann also emphasizes the Midwestern small town's tendency to trap and stifle its residents and its intolerance of individuals who fail to conform to its norms.

**SELECTED WORKS:** Bellamann published three volumes of verse: *A Music Teacher's Notebook* (1920), *Cups of Illusion* (1923), and *The Upward Pass* (1928). He also published eight novels: *Petenera's Daughter* (1926), *Crescendo* (1928), *The Richest Woman in Town* (1932), *The Gray Man Walks* (1936), *Kings Row* (1940), *Floods of*

*Spring* (1942), *Victoria Grandolet* (1943), and *Parris Mitchell of Kings Row,* with Katherine Bellamann (1948).

**FURTHER READING:** Harry M. Bayne's dissertation, "A Critical Study of Henry Bellamann's Life and Works" (University of Mississippi, 1990), is the only book-length source on Bellamann.

MARCIA NOE
THE UNIVERSITY OF TENNESSEE AT CHATTANOOGA

## SAUL (C.) BELLOW
June 10, 1915

**BIOGRAPHY:** Saul Bellow was born in Lachine, Quebec. Because his name, life, and fiction are so closely identified with Chicago, it comes as something of a surprise to recall that Bellow, the city's preeminent novelist, lived his first nine years in a small Canadian town just outside Montreal. His parents, Abraham and Liza (Gordon) Bellows, were Russian Jewish immigrants who had come to Canada from St. Petersburg, Russia, two years before his birth. Solomon Bellows, as he was named, was their fourth and last child. His father had been an onion importer before fleeing Russia; in Lachine, he was, among other things, a small-time bootlegger. Growing up in Lachine, Saul Bellow learned to speak English, French, and Yiddish; in response to his mother's wish that he become a rabbi, he also learned to read Hebrew. Bellow sketched these hard, early Lachine years in his abandoned novel *Memoirs of a Bootlegger's Son* (excerpted in *Granta* 41 [1992]: 9–35).

In 1924, when he was nine years old, the Bellows moved to Chicago, settling in Humboldt Park on the city's near northwest side. Their neighborhood, in the years before and after World War I, was a melting pot for Eastern Europeans: Polish and Russian Jews, Poles, Slovaks, Ukrainians, Lithuanians, and Italians, immigrant communities that Bellow was to invoke in his Chicago novels. Young Saul, his two brothers, Maurice and Samuel, and his sister, Zelda, grew up in the neighborhood's brick two-flats and six-flats, the last on LeMoyne Avenue. In 1933, shortly after his mother's death, Bellow graduated from Tuley High School and after a time at Crane College moved on to the University of Chicago, where he studied literature. In 1935 he transferred to Northwestern University, completing a degree in anthropology under

Saul Bellow.
Photo © Nancy Crampton

the famed anthropologist Melville J. Herskovits. Discouraged by the chairman of Northwestern's Department of English from pursuing a PhD in English—told that he would never, as a Jew and a son of Russian Jews, have the right "feel" for Anglo-Saxon traditions and the English language—Bellow began graduate study in anthropology at the University of Wisconsin (Miller, *Saul Bellow: A Biography of the Imagination* 9).

In December 1937 he married Anita Goshkin, a Chicago social worker, and gave up graduate studies. Within a few months, the young couple moved in with Anita's parents in Ravenswood, on Chicago's north side. Bellow has said that the Depression freed him and his generation from the obligation to find regular employment or to seek a profession (*It All Adds Up* 20). Freed from the routines of employment, he began his long apprenticeship as a writer, teaching himself to write fiction in his in-laws' small back bedroom.

Toward the end of the 1930s, he worked on the Chicago Works Progress Administration Writers Project where he sometimes encountered JACK CONROY and NELSON AL-GREN. In *Illinois: A Descriptive Guide*, he wrote items on JOHN DOS PASSOS, SHERWOOD ANDERSON, and JAMES T. FARRELL, among others (*It All Adds Up* 102; Atlas, "The Shadows in the Garden" 84). Between 1938 and 1942, he taught composition courses at Chicago's Pestalozzi Froebel Teacher's College. During these years he was writing fiction. His first short story, "Two Morning Monologues," appeared in the *Partisan Review* (May–June 1941). Just before being inducted in 1944, he rushed to finish his first novel, "The Very Dark Trees"; this tale of transformed racial identity was not to be published, and Bellow has said he destroyed the manuscript (Atlas, *Granta* 41 (1992): 46–48).

His first published novel, *Dangling Man* (1944), took him close to seven years to complete and place. Drafted and then deferred, he voluntarily enlisted in the Merchant Marines in April 1945. Until his release to inactive service in September 1945, he was stationed at Sheepshead Bay in Brooklyn. Over the next winter, he rented a farmhouse in upstate New York, supporting his family by reviewing books and freelancing. His first son, Gregory, was born in 1944. Between the fall of 1946 and 1948, and intermittently through 1959, Bellow taught English at the University of Minnesota. There he met Robert Penn Warren who, over some long lunches, read and approved drafts of Bellow's second novel, *The Victim* (1947). Winning a Guggenheim Fellowship in 1948, Bellow traveled to Paris and other parts of Europe, where he wrote *The Adventures of Augie March* (1953). He set the novel in a Depression-era Chicago that from Paris cafés and Roman hotels "had grown exotic" ("How I Wrote Augie March's Story" 3). The novel won the National Book Award, was selected as a Book-of-the-Month Club alternate, and secured Bellow his first large measure of popular recognition.

From the time of his merchant marine service until 1962, when he joined the University of Chicago's Committee on Social Thought, Bellow lived and traveled largely outside Chicago. Returning to the United States in 1950, he taught for a time at New York University and then at Bard College, the period during which his marriage to Anita Goshkin broke up. He held several other teaching positions in the 1950s, including a

Creative Writing Fellowship at Princeton, where in 1952 he worked with his friend, the poet Delmore Schwartz. Schwartz and JOHN BERRYMAN, whom he knew at Minnesota, have often been cited as models for the fictional poet Humboldt in Bellow's novel *Humboldt's Gift* (1975).

Through his new publisher, Viking Press, Bellow met Alexandra Tschacbasov, whom he married in 1956; in 1957 she bore his second son, Adam. Bellow left Alexandra in 1959, and some of the bitter memories of the marriage and divorce filtered into his 1965 novel, *Herzog* (Miller 137; Atlas, "The Uses of Misery" 100–102, 104–105). In 1961 he married Susan Glassman, the daughter of a prominent Chicago doctor. The marriage, which lasted but three years, heralded his return to Chicago in 1962.

Though *The Noble Savage*, the literary magazine he launched in 1959, fizzled after five issues, and his play *The Last Analysis* closed after a short run on Broadway in 1964, Bellow had, with the publication of *Herzog*, found himself on "a road of prizes and awards and medals and enormous sales" (Miller 212). *Herzog* won the National Book Award in 1964; *Mr. Sammler's Planet* (1970) brought him that award for an unprecedented third time in 1971. *Humboldt's Gift* won the Pulitzer Prize in 1976, and, in the same year, he was awarded the Nobel Prize for literature.

In 1975, having divorced Susan Glassman, the mother of his third son, Daniel, he married Alexandra Ionescu Tulcea, a mathematician and daughter of a Romanian minister of health. Their trip to Bucharest in 1976, taken so that Alexandra might be with her dying mother, led some six years later to his ninth novel, *The Dean's December* (1982). Bellow framed this novel as a tale of two cities, comparing communist Bucharest, in its totalitarian grayness and bone-chilling cold, to Chicago, a city he now called "the contempt center of the USA" (42).

*More Die of Heartbreak* (1987), his next novel, meditates on love, sex, and marriage in a postmodern age and asks, along the way, why anyone would return to Chicago and the Midwest. Bellow married his fifth wife, Janis Friedman, in 1989. In 1993 he left Chicago to live and teach in Boston. When he and his wife moved to New England, they converted his summer home near Bennington, Vermont, into a permanent residence. Freedman gave birth to their daughter, Naomi Rose, on December 23, 1999.

*It All Adds Up: From the Dim Past to the Uncertain Future* (1994), his gathering of previously published essays and memoirs, may not add up to his final statement about Chicago or the Midwest. And yet, in essays like "In the Days of Mr. Roosevelt," "Chicago: The City That Was, the City That Is," and in his "Farewells" to Isaac Rosenfeld, Allan Bloom, and other dead friends, he speaks in elegiac tones about Chicago as it was in the 1930s and 1940s. He laments the disappearance of "ethnic neighborhoods" and lambastes the "depressing odors of cultural mildew rising from the giant suburbs" (145).

His recent short novel, *The Actual* (1997), reiterates such complaints about Chicago, notes the degradation of mass democracy, and derides the spectacle of money-getting and the spending it spawns. The story is told by Henry Trellman, a brooding and aging narrator who at times seems to speak for Bellow. Pressed to say why, after so many years and travels, he has returned to Chicago, Trellman replies cryptically, "I have a connection here" (76). Bellow, though he has moved out of Chicago and away from the Midwest, holds on to his own connections there, to family, to bonds of memory and desire that his novel exhumes and consecrates.

**SIGNIFICANCE:** However local or peculiar the struggles of Bellow's heroes and anti-heroes, their actions have illuminated universal themes and posed unanswered eternal questions. Readers interpret his city-bred, anxiety-ridden figures, his comic sufferers, schlemiels, and con-men as projections of the human spirit at large in the contemporary world. Awarding Bellow the Nobel Prize for literature in 1976, the Swedish Academy praised him for creating characters who "in a tottering world . . . never relinquish [their] faith that the value of life depends on dignity, not its success, and that truth must triumph at last." He has been called "our most accomplished American writer" (Bach, *Critical Responses to Saul Bellow* 295).

Bellow characterizes himself as "a Midwesterner, the son of immigrant parents" and also as "a young man from Chicago, the center of brutal materialism" (Preface to Allan Bloom's *Closing of the American Mind* 13). Dur-

ing the 1930s, he has said, he went to the Chicago Public Library not to read the Talmud but "F. SCOTT FITZGERALD, SINCLAIR LEWIS's *Babbitt*, THEODORE DREISER's *The Titan*, SHERWOOD ANDERSON's *Mid-American Chants*," and other standards of modern Midwestern literature (*It All Adds Up* 110). He admires Dreiser for his "power of lament," for the bitter, grudging art he "insisted upon under the severest discouragements" ("Dreiser and the Triumph of Art" 503).

This tribute to Dreiser's art and the hard conditions he met in achieving it, with some qualifications, describes Bellow's own struggles with the "brutal materialism" of Chicago and the Midwest. As a result, perhaps, Bellow has shaped stubborn, bitter, and often unyielding characters who resist pressures to perform and conform, who defy forces that would magnify and distort their sense of integrity and self. Such willful resistance can make Joseph of the *Dangling Man*, Herzog, Augie March, and the young man in "Something to Remember Me By" into figures, by turns comic and heroic, spiritual and brutish. The typical Bellow hero, as many have noted, is a "dangling man," dangled and jerked between two worlds.

Acknowledging a point the late columnist MIKE ROYKO once made, Bellow said that "no novelist can be Chicago's representative man" (*It All Adds Up* 131). And yet in his seven Chicago novels, from the *Dangling Man* through *The Adventures of Augie March* and to *The Actual*, Bellow has, rather faithfully and fully, represented Chicago and its polyglot and multiethnic neighborhoods. His novels, exercising a reverence for the smallest of facts and the crudest of details, have mapped the city's landscape and weather, chronicled its history and culture, and dissected its prejudices and most sacred and enduring values.

Bellow has, perhaps just as importantly, captured the babel and sounds of its speech. *The Adventures of Augie March* (1953), with its youthful hero and episodic structure, can be and has been justly compared to the *Adventures of Huckleberry Finn*. The Chicago novel opened the way to a playful, energetic use of language, to runs and riffs on the city's street slang and his own second-generation Yiddish. Bellow found he could deploy, with grace and humor, Jewish jokes, racial epithets, and the learned diction of philosophical discourse.

The story first traces an immigrant family's struggles during the Depression and moves on to witness Augie's picaresque adventures. Short stories, like the much admired "A Silver Dish," dramatize, in the conflict of an old-world father and an Americanized son, themes and plot lines that Bellow took up recurringly in his work. At a critical point in the story, Woody Selbst's father, an immigrant and Jew, taunts his Christianized son: "You worried because I speak bad English? Embarrassed? I have a mockie accent?" (*Him with His Foot in His Mouth* 206).

Given his focus on family and ethnic identity, given his intense awareness of immigrant experiences and speech, Bellow has often been categorized as a "Jewish writer." He has, just as often, protested the categorization. Yet many see his work paving the way for Philip Roth, Norman Mailer, and other post–World War II Jewish writers (Miller 43–44).

His sense of the Midwest and his own Midwesternness has been complex, shifting, and sometimes contradictory. The first-person narrator in *More Die of Heartbreak* characterizes the Midwest as "a cultural throwback, unconscious of its philistinism" (30). If in the closing pages of *The Actual*, Bellow notes that "big trees don't thrive in [the] sandy soil" of the Midwest as they do in the East, it is not to decry the deficiencies of the prairies and plains or to stipulate again the flatland's cultural inferiority (79). Those who, like the Zetlands, find Chicago boring, see it as a city where "shadows of loveliness were lacking," who contend "everything was better" in the East, inevitably become the butt of Bellow's sharp satire (*Him with His Foot in His Mouth* 173, 181). In the travel sketch "Illinois Journey," Bellow contended that from the flat, monotonous line of the prairies an idea of both uniformity and democracy might be derived (*It All Adds Up* 197). Critics, Alfred Kazin and Richard Chase prominent among them, have placed him within a broadly defined American tradition of spiritual beliefs, individualism, and self-liberation that stretches back to Emerson and Whitman, a tradition that has found many adherents in the Midwest. Stanley Crouch, discussing the transcendent in Bellow, speaks of the "humanity" of his vision and his unwavering acceptance of "humbling truths" in a chaotic world (103).

Many have derisively tagged his novels as novels of ideas; such readers have balked at the wide-ranging historical and cultural knowledge that his writing seems to demand. His intellectuals, characters like Herzog and Charlie Citrine of *Humboldt's Gift*, engage in monologues that are, for some readers, forbiddingly long and erudite. Bellow, who was a Trotskyite in his twenties, now regularly criticizes what he terms the "crisis-chatter" of the "cultural-intelligentsia" and "puffy-headed academics" (*Conversations* 117; Bach 4). His politics and his ideology have, not surprisingly, changed over the past fifty years, but he remains a politically engaged and socially conscious writer. The ruminations on Chicago politics and Communism, the disquisitions on the city's racial dilemmas and conflicts Albert Corde delivers in *The Dean's December* (1982), illustrate the depth of his concerns and the sharp specificity of his probings. Bellow's views on Chicago politics and its racial dilemma, as DAVID D. ANDERSON has noted, have been "distorted, misunderstood" much as the Dean's are in the novel ("The Dean's Chicago" 146).

Bellow seems at times to court and deliberately provoke his academic critics. For his friend Allan Bloom, he wrote the introduction to *The Closing of the American Mind* (1987), a criticism of higher education with a neoconservative cast that many academics resented and dismissed. In some academic circles his fiction has lost favor, and, as a result, stories like "Looking for Mr. Green" have disappeared from the reigning introductory literary anthologies. Still, the number of national and international awards, degrees, prizes, and honors celebrating Bellow's achievements mounts steadily. Their collective assessment of his work defies simple reckoning and summary. These recognitions include France's *Croix de Chevalier des Arts et Lettres* and the Jewish Heritage Award (1968), the Pulitzer Prize for *Humboldt's Gift* (1975), the Nobel Prize (1976), an unprecedented three National Book Awards, and the National Medal of Arts (1988). In his eighties Bellow remains an active writer and astute critic of American politics and culture.

**SELECTED WORKS:** Bellow has published twelve novels, eight of which, in significant part or entirely, are set in Chicago: *Dangling Man* (1944); *The Adventures of Augie March* (1953); *Herzog* (1964); *Humboldt's Gift* (1975); *The*

*Dean's December* (1982); *More Die of Heartbreak* (1987); *The Actual* (1997); and *Ravelstein* (2000). *The Victim* (1947), *Seize the Day* (1956), and *Mr. Sammler's Planet* (1970) are placed in New York, while *Henderson the Rain King* (1959) uses a half-mythic, half-realistic African setting. Bellow's novellas and short stories are too numerous to offer a comprehensive listing. Notable, however, for their Midwestern or Chicago story lines are: "Two Morning Monologues," appearing in the *Partisan Review* 8 (May–June 1941): 230–36; "A Sermon by Dr. Pep," in the *Partisan Review* 16 (May–June 1949): 455–62; "Looking for Mr. Green," collected in *Mosby's Memoirs* (1968); "Zetland: By a Character Witness," "Cousins," and "A Silver Dish," collected in *Him with His Foot in His Mouth and Other Stories* (1984). "Something to Remember Me By," the serio-comic story of Depression-era Chicago, appears in *Something to Remember Me By: Three Tales* (1991). Bellow has written several plays, including *The Last Analysis* (staged in New York in 1964). Though readers inevitably disagree over the ranking of his individual works and their merits, many contend that *Herzog* is the best, most representative novel.

Useful for an understanding of Bellow's early years and his sense of his immigrant parents are the excerpts from his abandoned, unfinished novel *Memoirs of a Bootlegger's Son*, published in *Granta* 41 (1992): 9–35. Bellow supplies a brief introduction, noting that fragments of the novel were used in *Herzog*. His essay, "Starting Out in Chicago," *American Scholar* 44 (Winter 1974–75): 71–77, outlines his reading and writing efforts in the 1930s. "Dreiser and the Triumph of Art," published in *Commentary* 11 (May 1951): 502–503, expresses his appreciation for his fellow Midwesterner's art. For a view of Bellow the writer in the 1950s, see "How I Wrote Augie March's Story," *New York Times Book Review* (January 1954): 3, 17. *To Jerusalem and Back: A Personal Account* (1976) is at once travel literature, political reporting, and autobiography, all of a high order. Other important autobiographical essays are collected in *It All Adds Up: From the Dim Past to the Uncertain Future* (1994); the volume includes "Writers, Intellectuals, Politics: Mainly Reminiscence," "Illinois Journey," and "Chicago: The City That Was, the City That Is." Bellow's foreword to his friend Allan Bloom's *The Closing of the American Mind*

(1987) restates his own criticisms of American culture and redefines his "resistance to [Chicago's] material weight" (13).

**FURTHER READING:** No definitive biography exists. Ruth Miller's *Saul Bellow: A Biography of the Imagination* (1991) draws astutely on Bellow's papers and on a friendship with the writer that goes back to 1938. James Atlas's biography of Bellow exists as a work in progress but may be glimpsed in recent articles: "Starting Out in Chicago," *Granta* 41 (1992): 9–35; "The Shadow in the Garden," *New Yorker* (June 26 and July 3, 1995): 74–85; and "The Uses of Misery," *New Yorker* (August 24 and 31, 1998): 97–109. Though not a full-fledged or formal biography, Mark Harris's *Saul Bellow: Drumlin Woodchuck* (1980), in recounting a failed effort to write a biography, yields an illuminating character sketch of Bellow in the 1970s. *Conversations with Saul Bellow*, edited by Gloria L. Cronin and Ben Siegel (1994), offers insights into Bellow's life, work, and contemporary writing.

*The Critical Responses to Saul Bellow*, edited by Gerhard Bach (1995), supplies a generous sampling of criticism and reviews and adds, in an appendix, a brief but valuable bibliographical guide. The *Saul Bellow Journal*, begun in 1982, publishes critical articles, interviews, and an annual bibliography of Bellow studies. B. A. Sokoloff and Mark E. Posner's *Saul Bellow: A Comprehensive Bibliography* (1985) and Marianne Nault's *Saul Bellow: His Work and His Critics: An Annotated International Bibliography* (1978) are two reference tools indispensable for most studies of Bellow.

Among the many book-length critical assessments of Bellow, Irving Malin's *Saul Bellow's Fiction* (1969) and Tony Tanner's *Saul Bellow* (1965) remain important and suggestive. Marianne M. Friedrich's *Character and Narration in the Short Fiction of Saul Bellow* (1995) addresses a once neglected area of scholarly inquiry. David D. Anderson, in two articles, emphasizes the Midwestern Bellow: "The Dean's Chicago," *MidAmerica* 12 (1985): 136–47, and "Saul Bellow and the Midwestern Myth of the Search," *Midwestern Miscellany* 22 (1994): 46–53. Stanley Crouch's "Barbarous on Either Side: The New York Blues of *Mr. Sammler's Planet*," in *Philosophy and Literature* 20 (April 1996): 89–103, explores race and the vision of "humanity" in Bellow's writing. For another view of Bellow and the city, see Steven Marcus's "Reading the Illegible: Modern Representations of Urban Experience," *Southern Review* 22 (1986): 443–64. Robin Williams played Tommy Wilhelm in a 1987 adaptation of *Seize the Day*, filmed for Public Broadcasting on site in New York, the videotape is widely available. The bulk of Bellow's papers, including the manuscript of his unfinished novel, *Memoirs of a Bootlegger's Son,* are held in the Regenstein Library at the University of Chicago.

GUY SZUBERLA                    UNIVERSITY OF TOLEDO

## JOHN BERRYMAN

October 25, 1914–January 7, 1972

**BIOGRAPHY:** John Berryman was born John Allyn Smith Jr. in McAlester, Oklahoma. His father was born and raised in Stillwater, Minnesota, and later settled in Oklahoma. The family moved to Florida in 1925, and a year later, after suffering financial and marital troubles, John Allyn Smith Sr. shot himself. His father's suicide haunted John Berryman for the rest of his life. After moving the family to New York City, his mother remarried and young John took his stepfather's name. In 1932 Berryman entered Columbia College. After receiving an AB from Columbia in 1936, he spent two years at Clare College, Cambridge University, where he was awarded a BA in 1938.

In 1939 Berryman took his first teaching position at Wayne State University, Detroit, beginning a teaching career that would take him to many different schools. Berryman's literary fame grew during the following decades, particularly with the publication of the long poem *Homage to Mistress Bradstreet* (1956).

In 1954 Berryman taught at the Writers' Workshop at the University of Iowa, where his students included W. D. Snodgrass and Donald Justice. After being dismissed for drunken behavior, he obtained a teaching position the following year in the humanities program at the University of Minnesota in Minneapolis, where he joined friends Allen Tate and SAUL BELLOW. He made Minneapolis his home for the rest of his life and eventually became Regents' Professor of the Humanities at the University of Minnesota. In the 1960s Berryman published *The Dream Songs*, a long autobiographical poem of 385 parts, the first volume of which won the Pulitzer Prize in 1965.

Berryman was a charismatic teacher, insightful scholar and critic, friend of many leading writers, and successful poet, but these successes did not bring him personal happiness. He struggled with depression, his father's suicide, and, from the late 1940s on, alcoholism. He married three times—to Eileen Mulligan in 1942, Ann Levine in 1956, and Kate Donahue in 1961—and had three children. He was the recipient of numerous prizes and honors, including honorary degrees from Cambridge University and Drake University. On January 7, 1972, Berryman leaped to his death from the Washington Avenue Bridge, which crosses the Mississippi River in Minneapolis near the University of Minnesota. He is buried in Resurrection Cemetery, Mendota Heights, Minnesota.

**SIGNIFICANCE:** Although the Midwest was not a central subject for Berryman, his long residence in the region means that it figures in the background of much of his work. Thus his stay in Detroit led to the early poem "Thanksgiving: Detroit," which deals with labor unrest. The *Dream Songs* contain many references to places in Minnesota.

The much-traveled Berryman alternately saw Minnesota as a forgiving refuge and a provincial backwater. In the late poem "Mpls, Mother," he harshly characterizes Minneapolis as a "site without history," an "essential nonentity," and "Place of great winds and higher and higher drifts / far into March" (*Henry's Fate* 59, 61). He also describes its features: "Vast eyesore granaries, pathetic monopoly newspapers, / a pretty little Mall we're so vain of, / the redman in the gutter, a University / only by the voters of our own State hated" (60). In "Roots" he proclaims, "I'd rather live in Venice or Kyoto, / but / O really I don't care where I live or have lived" (*Henry's Fate* 58). The autobiographical novel *Recovery* (1973) is set in Minnesota and deals with Berryman's experiences in alcohol treatment centers. The story "Wash Far Away" contains a scene set near Lake Superior.

**SELECTED WORKS:** Berryman's earliest books of poetry include his appearance in *Five Young American Poets* (1940); his first volume, *Poems* (1942); and *The Dispossessed* (1948)—all of which show the influence of Yeats and Auden. He achieved great critical success in *Homage to Mistress Bradstreet* (1956), which most critics group with the *Dream Songs* as his most successful poetry. The latter first appeared in *77 Dream Songs* (1964) and *His Toy, His Dream, His Rest* (1968), winner of the 1969 Bollingen Prize and National Book Award. These two volumes were combined in *The Dream Songs* (1969). Berryman's other books include *Stephen Crane* (1950, rev. 1962); *His Thought Made Pockets and the Plane Buckt* (1958); *Berryman's Sonnets* (1967); *Short Poems* (1967); *Love and Fame* (1970); *Delusions, Etc.* (1972); an unfinished, autobiographical novel *Recovery* (1973), with a foreword by Saul Bellow commenting on their time together in Minnesota; *The Freedom of the Poet* (1976), stories and essays, including essays on THEODORE DREISER, ERNEST HEMINGWAY, F. SCOTT FITZGERALD, RING LARDNER, and Bellow; *Henry's Fate and Other Poems 1967–72* (1977); and *Collected Poems: 1937–1971* (1989). See also *We Dream of Honour: John Berryman's Letters to His Mother*, edited by Richard Kelly (1988).

**FURTHER READING:** Berryman's interesting and varied life has been the subject of two full-length biographies, *The Life of John Berryman* (1982), by John Haffenden, and *Dream Song: The Life of John Berryman* (1990), by Paul Mariani; and of a book by his ex-wife, Eileen Simpson, *Poets in Their Youth* (1982). Bibliographical information can be found in *John Berryman: A Check-list* (1972), by Richard Kelly, and *John Berryman: A Descriptive Bibliography* (1974), by Ernest C. Stefanik Jr. For criticism of his work see Joel Conarroe's *John Berryman: An Introduction to the Poetry* (1977); Gary Q. Arpin's *The Poetry of John Berryman* (1978); John Haffenden's *John Berryman: A Critical Commentary* (1980); *Berryman's Understanding: Reflections on the Poetry of John Berryman*, edited by Harry Thomas (1988); *Modern Critical Views: John Berryman*, edited by Harold Bloom (1989); and *Recovering Berryman: Essays on a Poet*, edited by Richard Kelly and Alan Lathrop (1993). Berryman's papers are at the University of Minnesota Library.

WILLIAM OSTREM          PRINCETON, NEW JERSEY

## AMBROSE (GWINETT) BIERCE
June 24, 1842–January 1914?
(Dod Grile, Mrs. J. Milton Bowers, William Herman)

**BIOGRAPHY:** Born in Meigs County, Ohio, Ambrose Gwinett Bierce was the tenth of thirteen children born to Marcus Aurelius Bierce and Laura (Sherwood) Bierce. The Bierces were farmers with little formal schooling but a large library of classical works. Ambrose Bierce used this library during his early years but later spoke disparagingly about his parents' lack of education and meager background.

The Bierce family settled near Warsaw, Indiana, in 1846, where Bierce spent his formative years. At age fifteen, he worked for the *Northern Indianan* newspaper, before attending the Kentucky Military Institute for a year, where he studied primarily surveying and drafting. Bierce used these skills as a Union soldier in the Civil War and afterward, when he assisted an expedition to map the area between Omaha, Nebraska, and San Francisco, California. Upon reaching San Francisco, Bierce resigned from the army and found work at the U.S. Mint. He also began working as a freelance writer for various newspapers.

Bierce had his first short story, "The Haunted Valley," published in 1871 in the *Overland Monthly* journal. Also in 1871, he married Mary Ellen ("Mollie") Day, on December 25; they separated in 1889 and divorced in 1905. They had three children: two sons, Day (1872) and Leigh (1874), and a daughter, Helen (1875).

In 1913 Bierce toured many of the Civil War battlefields where he had fought in his youth. Later in the year, he was granted permission to travel with Pancho Villa and chronicle the Mexican Civil War. Bierce's last correspondence to his daughter was dated December 26, 1913, but nothing else was heard from him. Bierce is presumed to have died in a battle in January 1914, his "disappearance" adding greatly to his mystique.

**SIGNIFICANCE:** Born in Ohio and raised in Indiana, Bierce was first exposed to journalism in this Midwestern milieu. His disdain for his upbringing after moving to San Francisco is a somewhat typical rejection of Midwestern values, including ruralism, and emphasizes the perceived intellectual inferiority of the region.

In his fiction, Bierce rejected realism as inadequate and corresponded with WILLIAM DEAN HOWELLS over its merit. While Howells was a leading proponent of realism, Bierce thought it too limited because it did not include the strange or unusual. Bierce is regarded as an impressionist, in part due to his characters' psychological interpretations of situations they cannot control, which lead to their alternate perceptions of reality.

Bierce is also remembered for *The Devil's Dictionary*, originally published as *The Cynic's Word Book* in 1906, which contains sardonically humorous definitions of words delineating the human condition.

**SELECTED WORKS:** Bierce's first books were collections of work that first appeared in various outlets, mainly newspapers. They were printed under the pseudonym Dod Grile and include *Nuggets and Dust Panned Out in California* (1872), *The Fiend's Delight* (1873), and *Cobwebs from an Empty Skull* (1874).

His satire is evident in the 1877 novel *The Dance of Death*, written with T. A. Harcourt under the joint pseudonym William Herman. It purported to be a denunciation of the waltz but actually was a jibe at those who condemned the dance. It is also seen in *The Devil's Dictionary* (1906), which was republished as *The Enlarged Devil's Dictionary, with 851 Newly Discovered Words and Definitions* in 1967.

Bierce's impressionism is seen in many of his short stories. Perhaps the most famous of these is "An Occurrence at Owl Creek Bridge," included in *Tales of Soldiers and Civilians* (1891). This short story was made into a film which won an award at the 1962 Cannes Film Festival and was later adapted as an episode of *The Twilight Zone* in 1963.

*The Collected Works of Ambrose Bierce* (1909–12) is a twelve-volume set of Bierce's various columns, short stories, and satire. It was published prior to his disappearance in 1914.

**FURTHER READING:** Major biographies of Bierce are Carey McWilliams's *Ambrose Bierce, A Biography* (1929), the first biography written after Bierce's disappearance; Paul Fatout's *Ambrose Bierce, the Devil's Lexicographer* (1951); and Richard O'Connor's *Ambrose Bierce, A Biography* (1967). One of the most interesting sources of information is *Ambrose Gwinett Bierce: Bibliography and Biographical Data*, edited by Joseph Gaer (1935). It provides a chronological bibliography and offers some critical insight into Bierce's work. Some of his correspondence was collected in two volumes, *Twenty-One Letters of Ambrose Bierce*, edited by Samuel Loveman (1922), and *The Letters of Ambrose Bierce*, edited by Barbara Clark Pope (1922).

There is no single, definitive collection of Bierce's papers; instead, several significant collections exist around the country. Major repositories include the Huntington Library in San Marino, California; the Clifton Waller Barrett Collection at the University of Virginia; the American Literature Collection of the University of Southern California; the Division of Special Collections at Stanford University; and the Library of Congress.

SCOTT GORDON          UNIVERSITY OF KENTUCKY

## RICHARD PIKE BISSELL
June 27, 1913–May 4, 1977

**BIOGRAPHY:** Richard Bissell was born in Dubuque, Iowa, to industrialist Frederick Ezekiel and Edith Mary Bissell. Although his father was general manager and his grandfather president of H. B. Glover Company, a Dubuque garment manufacturer "of awesome longevity, sublime virtue, and declining sales" (*Life* 47), Bissell spent a Huck Finn boyhood rafting on the Mississippi and bumming freights on the Milwaukee Road. He attended Phillips Exeter Academy in New Hampshire, and Harvard College, receiving a BS in anthropology in 1936. After sailing the Mediterranean briefly as an ordinary seaman with the American Export Line, Bissell worked as a deckhand on the Upper Mississippi on the stern wheel steamer *James W. Good*. In 1938 he joined his father and grandfather at Glover, and married Marian van Patten Grilk when his salary reached $22.50 a week. The couple lived on a refurbished houseboat, the *Prairie Belle*, and ultimately had four children. Rejected by the navy because of poor eyesight, Bissell returned to steamboating during World War II, working as a deckhand and mate on the Mississippi and Illinois Rivers, and later as a pilot on the Ohio and Monongahela. After his wartime service, Bissell bought another houseboat, the *Floating Cave*.

Bissell was a writer as well as a businessman and pilot. In 1949 he published his first story, "Prairie Belle," in the *Atlantic*. In 1950 he published his first book, a fictional reminiscence of riverboat life titled *A Stretch on the River*. His factory experience became the novel *7 1/2 Cents* (1953). *The Pajama Game*, a musical comedy made from *7 1/2 Cents* in 1954, ran 1,063 performances at the St. James Theater and won both the Antoinette Perry

Award and the Donaldson Award. The musical became a movie with Doris Day and John Raitt and was revived for the stage in 1975 and 1989. *Say, Darling* (1957) recounts Bissell's adventures in New Yorkland while working on *The Pajama Game*. The book opens with the line, "I don't think I ever was cut out for it in the first place," and closes with the line, "Let's get out of here, kiddo." *Say, Darling* too became a stage drama.

His reputation as a literary man made, Bissell settled the family into southern Connecticut. Throughout the 1950s he published frequently in the *Atlantic* and other popular magazines. While Bissell the writer divorced himself from the Mississippi, Bissell the businessman became in the late 1950s absentee president of the Bissell Towing and Transport Company, in reality a sixty-thousand-dollar switch boat tug *Coal Queen*, operating out of Dubuque. For this and other reasons he returned frequently to Iowa, to which he had moved permanently two years before his death in 1977 of a brain tumor.

SIGNIFICANCE: Bissell's early books paint a vivid picture of Midwestern America before, during, and immediately after World War II. They are filled with snappy dialogue, wry humor, and subtle jokes involving the Midwestern quotidian: Grain Belt Beer, Peoria, Frankie Yankovic. His depictions of life in the factory and on the river are bittersweet reminiscences. They recall the days of cigar-chomping businessmen (*7 1/2 Cents*), deckhands named "Swede" and "Kid" and "Grease Cup" (*High Water*), and river towns like East Dubuque described in *My Life on the Mississippi* as, "a ripsnorter in those days" with slots, craps, and "Bonbon McClure's place, a first class whorehouse with girls from Chicago" (35).

*A Stretch on the River* (1950) recounts the initiation of its narrator into life as a Mississippi deckhand during a 1943 voyage up-river toward Merle, the girl he left behind in St. Paul. *High Water* (1954) traces another voyage up the flooded Mississippi, this of Duke Snyder (the ship's first mate, not the Brooklyn Dodgers' center fielder). When the *Royal Prince* wrecks at Quincy, Illinois, thirty-three-year-old Duke decides to abandon river life to marry sixteen-year-old Marie Chouteau. The novel *7 1/2 Cents* is about an office romance between twenty-eight-year-old Chi-cagoan Sid Sorokin, superintendent of the Sleep Tite pajama plant, and twenty-year-old Catherine "Babe" Williams, who organizes a plant-wide slowdown in support of the union's demand for a seven-and-a-half-cent raise.

Subsequent books included *Good Bye, Ava* (1961), the story of a Mississippi River houseboat owner who refuses to make way for a fertilizer plant; *Still Circling Moose Jaw* (1965), the story of an aging millionaire's last fling; the trans-America travelogue *How Many Miles to Galena?* (1968); and an irreverent history of the American Revolution, *New Light on 1776 and All That* (1975).

Bissell had a fine ear for dialogue, a head full of good yarns, and an eye for Midwestern character types. He was, however, a writer of his times, the 1950s. His males are hard-boiled and speak in Mickey Spillane slang: "swell," "dolls," "terrific," "Do It." Plots tend toward cliches: boy-meets-girl, girl-wins-boy's-heart, boy-abandons-promising-career-to-wed-girl. Bissell favors happy endings, especially for the protagonist. His stylistic debts to ERNEST HEMINGWAY, SHERWOOD ANDERSON, and MARK TWAIN are sometimes too clear.

As the 1950s turned to the 1960s and American culture turned its attention to more somber truths, Bissell became less popular. His influence is felt in the work of Midwest poets such as DAVE ETTER and JOHN KNOEPFLE, but today his work is attractive mainly for its nostalgia.

SELECTED WORKS: Bissell's Mississippi River books rank just below *Huck Finn* and *Life on the Mississippi* as American river-adventure stories: *A Stretch on the River* (1950), *High Water* (1954), and *My Life on the Mississippi; or, Why I Am Not Mark Twain* (1973), which also contains a running commentary on Mark Twain, pilot and Mississippi River author. Bissell's *Monongahela River* (1952), for the Rivers of America series, is also good. *7 1/2 Cents* compares favorably with SINCLAIR LEWIS's *Main Street* and *Babbitt* as a gentler satire of small-town life and American business practices. *Say, Darling* (1957) and *How Many Miles to Galena?* (1968) are witty satires of East and West Coast absurdities observed by a commonsensical Midwesterner.

FURTHER READING: Bissell is a project in literary archaeology waiting to happen. Obituaries in the *New York Times* (May 5, 1977) and *Newsweek* and *Time* (May 16, 1977) were brief. Serious articles are limited to Frank J. Anderson's essay "The View from the River," in *Midwest Quarterly* (1964): 311–22, and Joe Bellamy's "Two Eras, Two Epitaphs: Steamboating Life in the Works of Mark Twain and Richard Bissell," in *Ball State University Forum* (1972): 48–52.

DAVID PICHASKE        SOUTHWEST STATE UNIVERSITY

## ANDREW J. BLACKBIRD
ca. 1814–September 8, 1908

**BIOGRAPHY:** In his book *History of the Ottawa and Chippewa Indians of Michigan* (1887), Andrew J. Blackbird has included an account of his own life. Identifying himself as an Ottawa, the English spelling of the Indian word "Odawa," he believed himself to be descended from Plains Indians who were captured by Ottawas. His Indian name, Mack-a-te-be-nessy, was translated "Blackbird." Raised south of the straits between Michigan's two peninsulas, he learned the blacksmith trade, studied four years at the Twinsburg Institute in Ohio, and studied over two years at Ypsilanti State Normal School. Back in his own region of Michigan, in the vicinity of Harbor Springs, Blackbird was appointed U.S. Interpreter, an official position he held many years. As a youth he had seen delegates leave to attend the meetings of the 1836 Treaty of Washington, and he himself participated in the councils for the Treaty of Detroit in 1855. Along with converting tribal control of their remaining land to individual ownership, this treaty gave the Ottawas lasting protection against removal to the West.

Blackbird married Elizabeth Martha Fish in 1858, and they had four children. In the final phase of his career, he was appointed postmaster in Harbor Springs, a position he held for eleven years. In poor circumstances toward the end of his long life, Blackbird passed away at Brutus, Michigan. Elizabeth lived on until 1920.

**SIGNIFICANCE:** In addition to covering significant events such as his tribe's lack of support for Pontiac's 1763 rebellion, Blackbird's *History* (1887) contains personal history. It also includes a grammar of the Indian language; it remains significant in that variants of the Algonquin language are spoken over a larger area of North America than any other native tongue, from Michigan to Manitoba. The book also provides a few legends from the rich canon of such stories, for which we must usually rely on non-native writers such as HENRY SCHOOLCRAFT. One wishes Blackbird had written more.

Blackbird's account shows the last days of a primordial way of life that had endured along Lake Michigan for perhaps a thousand years. Starting from the area of the straits in the autumn, the people traveled down the lakeshore in large canoes to winter camps in the river valleys of the south. Blackbird remembered the trips as a boy, and thus he provides a rare, firsthand account of aboriginal life. It is a state of harmony with nature. Although hunting involves dominance over the game, in a larger sense the Indians were not interested in heaping up large amounts of possessions. Blackbird shows that the patterns of human interaction reflected a similar personal modesty and appreciation of everyone's needs.

In spite of periodic native as well as European warfare, Andrew Blackbird presents the L'Arbre Croche country as a kind of paradise: " . . . such an abundance of wild strawberries, raspberries and blackberries that they fairly perfumed the air of the whole coast with fragrant scent of ripe fruit. The wild pigeons and every variety of feathered songsters filled all the groves, warbling their songs joyfully and feasting upon these wild fruits of nature . . ." (11). During the author's lifetime the Indians struggled with alcohol, sank further into poverty and dependence, continued to lose their domain, and were threatened with removal from their homeland and forced migrations to the West. Blackbird laments his people's misfortune and narrates several personal tragedies. The aboriginal state must have seemed like a paradise in comparison to the conditions developing, but the author's theme may have a larger relevance. Instead of a blind force to be conquered, nature is coming to be valued more positively. Voices like Blackbird's are also to be valued for their testimony about being at home in the natural world.

**SELECTED WORKS:** A reprint of Andrew J. Blackbird's 1887 *History of the Ottawa and Chippewa Indians of Michigan* is currently available from the Little Traverse Historical Society, Petoskey, Michigan. Michigan State University, with assistance from the Little Traverse Bay Band of Odawa Indians, plans to issue a new edition of Blackbird's *History*. The annotated edition will incorporate biographical and historical information along with a selection of Blackbird's letters and some additions which the author prepared through 1897. Another work, *The Indian Problem from the Indian's Standpoint* (1900), circulated by the National Indian Association of Philadelphia, Pennsylvania, remains out of print.

**FURTHER READING:** In *Gah-Baeh-Jhagway-Buk: The Way It Happened: A Visual Culture History of the Little Traverse Bay Band of Odawa* (1991), James McClurken presents Blackbird's specific cultural environment. A wider background view is found in Clifton, Cornell, and McClurken's *People of the Three Fires: The Ottawa, Potawatomi, and Ojibway of Michigan* (1986) and also in Helen Hornback Tanner's *Atlas of Great Lakes Indian History* (1987).

Reissued in 1965 as *Savagism and Civilization: A Study of the Indian and the American Mind*, Roy H. Pearce's *The Savages of America: A Study of the Indian and the Idea of Civilization* (1953) details the American obsession with transforming the Indian, including discussion of Henry Rowe Schoolcraft's collecting of Indian legends. A Michigan Indian agent, Schoolcraft was the primary writer and editor of the six-volume *Historical and Statistical Information Respecting the History, Condition, and Prospects of the Indian Tribes of the United States* (1851–57). Schoolcraft had much contact with the "Anishinabeg," the Algonquin tribes; his work epitomizes civilization's disapproving attitude toward Indians and defines the reasons Blackbird wrote in defense of the native humanity of his people.

JEFFREY A. JUSTIN                    MUSKEGON, MICHIGAN

## BLACK ELK

December 1863–August 1950
(Hehake Sapa, Nicholas Black Elk)

**BIOGRAPHY:** A Teton Lakota (Western Sioux) of the Oglala subband, Black Elk was the fourth person in his familial line of descent to bear the Black Elk name, which designates a holy man of unusual healing powers. He was born to Black Elk (third generation) and White Cow Sees on the Little Powder River in the Devils Tower area of Wyoming and was raised along with five sisters and one brother in the traditional bison-centered culture of the northern plains Indians. At nine, during a serious illness, he obtained a prophetic vision which is recounted in his collaborative book with JOHN G. NEIHARDT, *Black Elk Speaks* (1932).

His family was encamped with Crazy Horse on the Little Big Horn and participated in the battle against Custer's forces. Later, when Black Elk was fourteen, his family joined Sitting Bull's and Gall's bands in Canada. After returning to Pine Ridge and beginning his career as a medicine man, Black Elk joined Buffalo Bill's Wild West Show in 1886 and toured Europe. For two years, from his return until the Wounded Knee Massacre in 1890, he became involved in the Ghost Dance. In 1893 he married Katie War Bonnet with whom he had three sons, one of whom, Ben, survived childhood.

Shortly after the turn of the century, Black Elk became a Roman Catholic and relinquished his shamanic services in favor of being a catechist for the Jesuit missionaries. His wife, Katie, died in 1903, and three years later he married Anna Brings White, a widow with a daughter. They had a daughter, Lucy, and two sons, Henry and Nicholas. Black Elk provided his account of his life and Lakota ways to John Neihardt in 1930 and, at Black Elk's own insistence, to Joseph Epes Brown from 1947 to 1949, which resulted in the book *The Sacred Pipe* (1953) three years after Black Elk's death. According to his son, Ben Black Elk, he returned to the Lakota way of religious life and observance in his later years.

**SIGNIFICANCE:** Despite controversy over whether *Black Elk Speaks* is an appropriation of Lakota materials for the transcendentalist designs of his collaborator John Neihardt and whether Black Elk's theological authenticity is compromised by Roman Catholic catechism, the book is the most widely recognized and influential account by a Native American author throughout the world. Its power is in portrayals of lifestyles and events of significance to the Lakota people and in the coherent presentation of Lakota theology. The explanations of the imagery of story and ritual are supported and further explained in *The Sacred Pipe*. Subsequent scholarship and commentary, particularly by Black Elk's family, establishes that the aesthetic power and incisive spirituality in the books are Black Elk's. His accounts made

Lakota life and thought an accepted part of the American literary experience of the northern Midwest.

**SELECTED WORKS:** The two books which record Black Elk's accounts are *Black Elk Speaks: Being the Life Story of a Holy Man of the Oglala Sioux* (1931, reprinted 1961, 1984), as told to John G. Neihardt, and *The Sacred Pipe: Black Elk's Account of the Seven Rites of the Oglala Sioux*, recorded and edited by Joseph Epes Brown (1953).

**FURTHER READING:** An explanation of the circumstances and processes of the production of *Black Elk Speaks* appears in *The Sixth Grandfather: Black Elk's Teachings Given to John G. Neihardt*, edited by Raymond J. DeMaillie (1984). The book contains materials and accounts not included in *Black Elk Speaks* by Neihardt; it also includes a foreword by his daughter, Hilda Neihardt Petri. A recent biographical study is Michael F. Steltenkamp's *Black Elk: Holy Man of the Oglala* (1993). Two articles by Clyde Holler are exceptionally illuminating: "Black Elk's Relationship to Christianity," in *American Indian Quarterly* 8.1 (1984): 37–49; and "Lakota Religion and Tragedy: The Theology of *Black Elk Speaks*," in *Journal of the American Academy of Religion* 52.1 (1984): 19–43. Elizabeth Cook-Lynn, a contemporary poet of the Crow Creek Sioux, makes a valuable appraisal in "Black Elk: The Sacred Ways of a Lakota," in *Wicaza Sa Review* 7.2 (Fall 1995): 90–94.

DAVID L. NEWQUIST    NORTHERN STATE UNIVERSITY

## BLACK HAWK
1767–October 3, 1838

**BIOGRAPHY:** Black Hawk, Sauk warrior and autobiographer, was born at Saukenuk, a large tribal village located above the mouth of the Rock River, where Rock Island, Illinois, is today. His parents were Pyesa and Kneebingkemewoin, and his Indian name was Ma-ka-tai-me-she-kia-kiak (Black Sparrow Hawk). In his youth and early manhood he participated in tribal warfare against the Osages and Cherokees, eventually becoming a respected military leader, the war chief of his people. He had a wife, Asshewequa, two sons, and a daughter.

The war that made him famous had its roots in the Treaty of 1804 (reaffirmed in 1816), which ceded more than fifty million acres of land in what eventually became southwestern Wisconsin, western Illinois, and north-eastern Missouri to the United States government in return for a small annuity to the Sauk and Fox (Mesquakie) tribes. Those closely allied Indian groups were apparently deceived and coerced by American officials. Small wonder that in the War of 1812 Black Hawk and other Sauks fought under Tecumseh on the British side. During the 1820s Americans started to settle on the ceded land, and Saukenuk itself was bought in 1829, necessitating Indian removal. Black Hawk became the leader of those Sauks who refused to relinquish their claim to the village, and he hoped to lead an Indian confederacy to resist the whites. The Black Hawk War, in the summer of 1832, was essentially a pursuit of his band by frontier militia, who eventually caught up with them and slaughtered Indian men, women, and children near Bad Axe River in Wisconsin. Black Hawk was captured and then imprisoned at Fort Armstrong, where he dictated his life story. In 1833 he was taken to see President Jackson in Washington, then placed in the custody of Chief Keokuk, his hated rival. But by then Black Hawk had become famous, and many Americans regarded him as a hero. He was eventually released, to live in Iowa Territory until his death five years later.

**SIGNIFICANCE:** Several of Black Hawk's speeches have been preserved. One of them, delivered to General Joseph M. Street at the close of the war, is a powerful condemnation of the whites and assertion of his identity as an Indian. But his major achievement is his autobiography, told to criticize American actions, justify his response, and assert his identity. Interpreter Antoine LeClaire translated his words, and Oquawka newspaperman J. B. Patterson edited the work and published it. *Life of Ma-ka-tai-me-she-kia-kiak, or Black Hawk* (Cincinnati, 1833) was the first "as-told-to" Indian autobiography in America and the first "best-seller" from the Midwest. It chronicled the end of Indian culture east of the Mississippi and made the Indian perspective a part of the national consciousness. It remains a classic of Native American literature.

**SELECTED WORKS:** The standard edition of Black Hawk's life story is *Black Hawk: An Autobiography*, edited by Donald Jackson (1955). His finest speech is available in *Illinois Literature: The Nineteenth Century*, edited by John E. Hallwas (1986): 35–36. Some others are included in Frank E. Stevens's *The Black Hawk War* (1903): 35, 36, 261, 264, 265, 271. The speeches have never been collected.

**FURTHER READING:** The most recent study of Black Hawk is Roger L. Nichols's *Black Hawk and the Warrior's Path* (1992), which has a useful bibliographical essay. Literary studies have focused primarily on the autobiography: John E. Hallwas's "Black Hawk: A Reassessment," in *Annals of Iowa* 45 (1981): 599–619; Arnold Krupat's "Indian Autobiography: Origins, Type, and Function," in *For Those Who Come After: A Study of Native American Autobiography* (1985): 28–53; William Boelhower's "Saving Saukenuk: How Black Hawk Won the War and Opened the Way to Ethnic Semiotics," in *Journal of American Studies* 25 (1991): 333–61; Neil Schmitz's "Captive Utterance: Black Hawk and Indian Irony," in *Arizona Quarterly* 48 (Winter 1992): 1–18; Timothy Sweet's "Masculinity and Self-Performance in the *Life of Black Hawk*," in *American Literature* 65 (September 1993): 475–99.

JOHN E. HALLWAS      WESTERN ILLINOIS UNIVERSITY

## NORBERT BLEI
August 23, 1939

**BIOGRAPHY:** Norbert Blei was born in Cicero, Illinois, to Bohemian parents George and Emily (Papp) Blei. He graduated from Illinois State University in 1957 and took advanced work at the University of Chicago. Blei worked as a reporter with the City News Bureau of Chicago from 1958 to 1959, then taught English at Lyon Township High School from 1960 to 1968. Beginning in 1969, he committed himself to working full time as a freelance reporter in Chicago, and to the life of a man of letters in pastoral Ellison Bay, Door County, Wisconsin. He married Barbara in 1959 and fathered two children, Christopher and Bridget.

A frequent visitor to Santa Fe, Blei has also traveled extensively abroad: Europe (1962), Greece (1974), San Salvador (1989), and Central Europe (1990). Blei is a frequent guest on Wisconsin Public Radio, a prolific writer of columns, reviews, stories and essays, and a workshop instructor in writing at The Clearing in Ellison Bay, Wisconsin. Although perpetually penniless, from 1994 to 1997 Blei operated Cross Roads Press, publishing chapbooks by his numerous friends and disciples.

**SIGNIFICANCE:** A wildly exaggerated and enormously entertaining version of Blei's Illinois high school teaching career may be found in his 1982 *Adventures in an American's Literature*, described by *Choice* review service as "a valuable perspective to any undergraduate considering teaching," and the possible source of some material in the film *Dead Poet's Society*, particularly the scenes in which an iconoclastic instructor has students destroy pedantic texts inherited from a predecessor (119–26). An equally entertaining record in letters, rejection forms, diary entries, and other fragments of Blei's development as a writer may be found in *The Second Novel* (1979). Blei's love-hate relationship with both ends of a life divided between rural Wisconsin and urban Chicago is chronicled in his Door trilogy: *Door Way* (1981), *Door Steps* (1983), and *Door to Door* (1985). Of the three, *Door Way* has proved most popular. A series of character studies, the book offers a sensitive and moving photograph of one rural Midwestern landscape in transition from a fishing and agricultural community to an arts- and tourism-based economy. Blei's portraits of fishermen and used car salesmen, restaurateurs and town drunks, aging farmers, orchardmen, auto mechanics, poets, and painters suggest his environmentalism and reverence for endangered species, for the spirit of the landscape and its people.

A companion to *Door Way*, *Chi Town* (1990) reprints portraits and interviews from Blei's days as a freelance journalist in Big Windy. *Door Steps* (1983), a day book of rural meditations, is fresh material, Blei's most personal and calmest meditation. *Neighborhood* (1987) gathers memories of Blei's boyhood in Bohemian Cicero, although the book transcends time and place to become a celebration of all urban ethnic communities of the post–World War II period. A more recent record of Blei's increasingly precarious life as a straight-shooting rural journalist hired, fired, rehired, refired by the local advertising weekly is to be found in the reprinted columns, editorials, letters to the editor, and replies to letters to the editor of *Chronicles of a Rural Journalist* (1990). A multi-talented author, Blei is a masterful storyteller. His best work grows mysteriously out of archetypal, almost mythological characters rooted in the old Bohemian neighborhoods in Cicero and Cermak, Illinois, the dark Wisconsin woods, or the American Southwest. Blei has also experimented in paste-pot, cut-up, and concrete poems which combine words with photos, drawings, images, and other graphic elements. He paints in the Kenneth Patchen–Henry Miller mode. A number of his books have been published in special editions containing original Blei art, and a series of watercolor paintings based visually and conceptually on the Berlin Wall was exhibited at the LewAllen Gallery in Santa Fe in April 1993.

**SELECTED WORKS:** Paste-pot and concrete poems are reproduced in *The Watercolored Word* (1969) and *Paint Me a Picture/Make Me a Poem* (1987), short fiction in *The Hour of the Sunshine Now* (1978) and *The Ghost of Sandburg's Phizzog* (1986), journalistic sketches and profiles in *Door Way* (1981), *Door to Door* (1985), *Neighborhood* (1987), and *Chi Town* (1990). Blei's two novels are *The Second Novel* (1978) and *Adventures in an American's Literature* (1982).

**FURTHER READING:** David Pichaske discusses Blei's art and concrete poems in "Kenneth Patchen, Norbert Blei: The Literary Text as Graphic Form," in *Crossing Borders: American Literature and Other Artistic Media*, edited by Jadwiga Maszewska (1992). Blei's small book *Meditations on a Small Lake* (1987) contains essays, interviews, and appreciations. Paul Schroeder's introduction to *Paint Me a Picture/Make Me a Poem* (1987) offers an historical context for Blei's paintings and paste-pot poems.

DAVID PICHASKE    SOUTHWEST STATE UNIVERSITY

## JOAN W(INSOR) BLOS
December 9, 1928

**BIOGRAPHY:** Born in New York to Max and Charlotte (Biber) Winsor, a psychiatrist and a teacher, respectively, Joan Blos received a BA from Vassar College (1949) and an MA from City College of New York (1956). In 1953 she married a physician, Peter Blos Jr., and they had two children. Trained in psychology, she found that her interest in child development fulfilled itself in teaching children's literature, notably at Bank Street College of Education in New York and the University of Michigan, and in writing books for children, including picture books and novels for young people. She won the 1980 Newbery Medal and the National Book Award for *A Gathering of Days: A New England Girl's Journal, 1830–32* (1979). She

has also written on children and reading, has reviewed books, and has been the U.S. editor of *Children's Literature in Education*.

**SIGNIFICANCE:** Many of Blos's books, such as *Martin's Hats* (1984), could take place anywhere in the western world, or at least in the United States, but others, such as *A Gathering of Days*, have very specific locations. In *Brothers of the Heart: A Story of the Old Northwest, 1837–1838* (1985), she tells the story of a late-nineteenth-century boy of fourteen, Shem Perkins, a recent immigrant to Michigan. It describes the hardships of homesteading in the Midwest and traces Shem's flight from supposed disgrace as he travels around the state. This portion of the book sketches portraits of trappers and traders and records the sagas of the development of the early lumbering and shipping industries in the Great Lakes states. Stranded in the wilderness, Shem survives by sharing winter shelter with an elderly Native American woman who has left her family and gone off to die. She saves his life, and he comforts her during her final days, while she teaches him her customs and other lessons about living in the world.

**SELECTED WORKS:** Blos wrote the primers *People Read* (1964) and *In the City* (1964), the former in collaboration with Betty Miles and both illustrated by Dan Dickas. Her early picture books include *"It's Spring," She Said*, illustrated by Julie Maas (1968), *Just Think!* illustrated by Pat Grant Porter (1971), and *Joe Finds a Way*, illustrated by Lee Ames (1967). For young adults, she wrote *A Gathering of Days: A New England Girl's Journal 1830–32* (1979) and *Brothers of the Heart: A Story of the Old Northwest, 1837–1838* (1985), which has also been produced as a play (1999). More recently she has published the picture books *Old Henry*, illustrated by Stephen Gammell (1987), which received the Boston Globe Horn Book Award for illustration; *Lottie's Circus*, illustrated by Irene Trivas (1989); *The Grandpa Days*, illustrated by Emily Arnold McCully (1989); in verse, *The Heroine of the Titanic: A Tale Both True and Otherwise of the Life of Molly Brown*, illustrated by Tennessee Dixon (1991); *A Seed, a Flower, a Minute, an Hour*, illustrated by Hans Poppel (1992); *Brooklyn Doesn't Rhyme*, illustrated by Paul Birling (1994); *The Hungry Little Boy*, illustrated by Dana Schutzer (1995);

*Nellie Bly's Monkey: His Remarkable Story in His Own Words*, illustrated by Catherine Stock (1996); *Bedtime!* illustrated by Stephen Lambert (1998); *One Very Best Valentine's Day*, illustrated by Emily Arnold McCully (1998); and *Hello, Shoes!* illustrated by Ann Boyajian (1999).

**FURTHER READING:** No full-length work on Blos has yet appeared. Two useful articles are Blos's "Newbery Medal Acceptance," *Horn Book Magazine* (August 1980): 369–73, and Betty Miles, "Joan W. Blos," *Horn Book Magazine* (August 1980): 374–77. Her papers are in the Kerlan Collection at the University of Minnesota.

MARY DEJONG OBUCHOWSKI
CENTRAL MICHIGAN UNIVERSITY

## CAROL BLY
April 16, 1930

**BIOGRAPHY:** Born in Duluth to Charles Russell and Mildred (Washburn) McLean, Carol Bly graduated from Wellesley in 1951, then pursued graduate studies at the University of Minnesota in 1954–55. In 1955 she married ROBERT BLY, with whom she lived in Madison, Minnesota, while editing *Fifties* and *Sixties* magazine, raising four children, doing writing of her own, and participating in the social and political events of the town and the nation. The essays of *Letters from the Country* (1981), first published in *Minnesota Monthly* between 1973 and 1978, are the fruits of those years. They are pithy meditations on what has gone wrong in the Minnesotan countryside and the American soul and what might be done to repair the damage.

In 1979 she and her husband divorced and moved diagonally across the state, Robert to Moose Lake, Carol to Sturgeon Lake. In 1986 Carol Bly bought a house in St. Paul, but she still spends as much time as possible in Sturgeon Lake. Bly has been indefatigable as a writer, a teacher of writing, and a social critic. From 1978 to 1981 she did pioneering work for the American Farm Project. In 1984 she founded and became the first editor of "Literary Post," a very successful correspondence writing program for Minnesotans over the age of sixty. She has earned her living mainly as a speaker and as a teacher of courses and workshops at the Loft, an independent Minneapolis "Place for Writers," and at Split Rock Summer Arts Program, the University of Minnesota, Hamline, Carleton, Ashland (Wisconsin), and Moorhead State. Her recent teaching has been an ethics-in-literature course for the University of Minnesota's master's in liberal studies program.

**SIGNIFICANCE:** Carol Bly's undergraduate studies in history and English combine with a characteristically Minnesotan concern for ethics and the work ethic to imbue her writing with a stern moralism. Both her nonfiction and "ethical fiction" (*Bad Government and Silly Literature* 1986) may be described, depending upon a reader's proclivities, as abrasive or bracing. The cardinal sins as presented in *Letters from the Country* and Bly's short stories are sloth, mediocrity, meanness, and complacency. While portraying Midwest villagers as emotionally and intellectually crippled, Bly views her criticism as constructive. "When you take a rotten potato out of the barrel, in good time, you save the barrel," she notes (*Letters* 52). Her depiction of Midwest life is thus more balanced and her view of the Midwestern village more affectionate than they might at first appear.

Bly has a good ear for dialect and a wonderful sense of motivation, conscious and unconscious. Her fictional Minnesotans in spiritual crisis speak with the tongues and act with the minds of true natives. With her move to St. Paul and her turn from fiction to ethics, Bly's writing has lost some of its sense of rural Minnesota place, but it retains that Midwestern insistence on doing the right thing.

**SELECTED WORKS:** Bly works in several genres, including creative nonfiction in *Letters from the Country* (1981), writing theory in *The Passionate, Accurate Story: Making Your Heart's Truth into Literature* (1990), and short fiction in *Backbone* (1985) and *The Tomcat's Wife and Other Stories* (1991), which won a Friends of American Writers Award. *Bad Government and Silly Literature*, a long essay published as a chapbook by Milkweed Editions in 1986, is as relevant today as then. The film *Rachel Rive*—shot in Hudson, Wisconsin, and Afton, Lindstrom, Sandstone, and Scandia, Minnesota—is based on three Carol Bly stories from *Backbone*. *Changing the Bully Who Rules the World* was published in 1996. Bly reports a novel and another collection of essays in process.

FURTHER READING: Secondary sources on Bly include "Carol Bly," in *A Guide to Minnesota Writers* (1993); Noel Perrin's "Rural Time Bomb," in the *New York Times Book Review* (May 24, 1981); Dave Wood's "Stiff Breeze from Main Street," in *Minneapolis Star Tribune* (July 30, 1991).

DAVID PICHASKE        SOUTHWEST STATE UNIVERSITY

## ROBERT (ELWOOD) BLY
December 23, 1926

BIOGRAPHY: Robert Bly, one of America's most influential living poets, was born on a farm near Madison, Minnesota, to Norwegian American Lutheran parents Jacob and Alice (Aws) Bly. After education in a one-room country schoolhouse, he spent two years in the U.S. Navy and a year at St. Olaf College. Bly transferred to Harvard, where he studied English with poet ARCHIBALD MACLEISH and critic F. O. Matthiessen, served as literary editor for the *Harvard Advocate*, and began his life-long friendship with DONALD HALL. After graduating *magna cum laude* in 1950, Bly spent three lonely years in New York, reading and writing. From 1954 to 1956 he studied at the Iowa Writers' Workshop. In 1955 he married Carolyn McLean. The couple divorced in 1979, and in 1980 he married Ruth Ray.

During the 1956–57 academic year, while on a research Fulbright scholarship in Norway, Bly discovered European and Latin American surrealist poets. He found them an attractive alternative to his disengaged Minnesota Lutheran heritage, to American "confessional" poets with their sensational explorations of their own egos, and to cool, apolitical "academics" with their emphasis on form and rhetoric. In 1958 Bly moved onto his father's farm to raise his children and get on with the business of being a man of letters: writing his own poems; publishing a magazine called *The Fifties* (later *The Sixties* and *The Seventies*); and translating foreign poets such as Trakl (1961), Neruda (1968), Vallejo (1971), Kabir (1977), Tranströmer (1980), and Machado (1983).

A private and introspective poet, Bly nevertheless became a public figure. His magazine was obstreperous and iconoclastic. *Silence in the Snowy Fields* (1962) received very good reviews; *The Light around the Body* (1967) won a National Book Award. After he and David Ray organized American Writers against the Vietnam War in 1966, Bly crisscrossed the country for readings and teach-ins. In 1967 he declined a five-thousand-dollar National Endowment for the Arts grant to his Sixties Press as a protest against the war. He donated his one-thousand-dollar National Book Award stipend to the War Resisters League. The Amy Lowell (1964–65), Guggenheim (1965–66), and Rockefeller (1967) fellowships he accepted.

During the 1970s, Bly devoted increased attention to Jungian psychology and mythology. In 1974 he organized the first Great Mother Conference. By the 1977 Conference on the Great Mother and the New Father, he was focusing primarily on male issues. A mesmerizing and indefatigable performer who combines poetry, music, dance, and theater, Bly became a leader of the so-called mythopoetic men's movement of the 1980s. Bill Moyers's television special "A Gathering of Men" aired in 1990; and *Iron John: A Book about Men* spent sixty-two weeks on the *New York Times* best-sellers list in 1990–91. "No discipline is immune to his poking about," observed Louis Camp in 1992 (Smith 156).

SIGNIFICANCE: The various facets of Robert Bly's complex personality appear to compartmentalize nicely within successive publications: literary politics in *The Fifties* and *The Sixties* magazine, rural contemplation in *Silence in the Snowy Fields* (1962), political engagement in *The Light around the Body* (1967), Jungian psychology in *Sleepers Joining Hands* (1973), and personal reflection in *The Man in the Black Coat Turns* (1981). Compartmentalization is superficial, however, as all five concerns can be found throughout Bly's writing. So also can such characteristically Midwestern traits as moral indignation, the Protestant work ethic, an eye for rural image, and an ear for the music of spoken Midwestern English.

The Minnesota landscape of *Silence in the Snowy Fields* (1962) established Bly's reputation as a regional pastoral poet of solitude and self-awareness. Wayne Dodd suggests that Bly returned to American letters nothing less than "the spirit of the American (prairie) landscape" (Peseroff 223). From the picked corn fields, lighted barns, and pale Minnesota lakes of Lac Qui Parle County, Bly constructs a poetic universe that reaches through Illinois and Wisconsin to Chesapeake Bay, Brooklyn Heights, and the American republic. Features of the physical landscape, however, are but markers on a spiritual journey to a personal interior, and what Bly really gives America is an appreciation of the symbolic richness of his austere rural Minnesota geography.

Bly's rural imagery is not, then, mere local color. His term "grounding" has both geographical and psychological meaning: we grow rooted in place and in a ripening, expanding personality. The poet, Bly suggests, grows psychologically by absorbing the "grief" of history and the "otherness" of nature, a process he sometimes calls "eating one's shadow." In Bly's poetry that shadow side can appear as a feminine Other in "A Man Writes to Part of Himself" (*Silence* 36), as "those roads in South Dakota that feel around in the darkness" in "Come with Me" (*Light* 13), as "Those great sweeps of snow that stop suddenly six feet from the house" in "Snowbanks North of the House" (*Man in the Black Coat* 3).

Because he associates the shadow side with nature, the "leaping images" of which Bly constructs his poems are drawn from his rural landscape. They are clustered associatively, not logically or rhetorically, to give the poetry a surrealistic quality. "The white flake of snow / That has just fallen on the horse's mane" (*Silence* 46) radiates spiritual significances. It is, however, neither metaphor nor symbol. Like a Transcendentalist, Bly senses an actual presence, or being, in the landscape, which he associates with subconsciousness, and thus with night or shadow. In a television interview with Bill Moyers, Bly noted that most poems in *Silence in the Snowy Fields* were written at dusk, a time of solitude and contemplation, "when the unconscious opens up."

Other aspects of Bly's career—his conjunction of poetry, music, and other forms of art; his prophetic reading of the American Jeremiad; his surrealism; his mysticism—invite comparison with fellow Midwesterner VACHEL LINDSAY and fellow Minnesotan Bob Dylan, but whether these are similarities of geography, temperament, or genius is difficult to say.

**SELECTED WORKS:** Important collections of poetry include *Silence in the Snowy Fields* (1962), *The Light around the Body* (1967), *Sleepers Joining Hands* (1973), *This Body Is Made of Camphor and Gopherwood* (1977), *The Man in the Black Coat Turns* (1981), *Meditations on the Insatiable Soul* (1995), and of course *Selected Poems* (1986). Bly is an important editor of anthologies, including *News of the Universe: Poems of Twofold Consciousness* (1980) and, with James Hillman and Michael Meade, *The Rag and Bone Shop of the Heart: Poems for Men* (1992). *Iron John: A Book about Men* (1990) is essential reading, as much for the light it sheds on Bly's thought and poetry as for its commentary on stages of male (and female) growth. *The Fifties* and *The Sixties*, reprinted in 1984, offer a theoretical context for Bly's poetry. Useful interviews, criticisms, and essays can be found in *Leaping Poetry: An Idea and Translation* (1975) and *Talking All Morning* (1980). Chester G. Anderson's *Growing Up in Minnesota* (1976) contains Bly's reminiscence "Being a Lutheran Boy-God."

**FURTHER READING:** The entries on Robert Bly in *Contemporary Literary Criticism* 5: 61–65 and 38: 49–60 (1976 and 1986) are expansive proportional to Bly's achievement. Useful books include *Of Solitude and Silence: Writings on Robert Bly*, edited by Richard Jones and Kate Daniels (1981); *Robert Bly: An Introduction to the Poetry*, edited by Howard Nelson (1984); *When Sleepers Awake*, edited by Joyce Peseroff (1984); William Roberson, *Robert Bly: A Primary and Secondary Bibliography* (1986). Richard P. Sugg's *Robert Bly* (1986) is intelligent and intelligible. *Walking Swiftly: Writings and Images on the Occasion of Robert Bly's 65th Birthday*, edited by Thomas Smith (1992), contains a useful selected bibliography and reprints the text of Bly's March 6, 1969, National Book Award speech. Two Bill Moyers videotapes ("Robert Bly: Poet at Large," 1979, and "A Gathering of Men," 1990) circulate, as do dozens of audiocassettes. Alley Press Center (St. Paul, Minnesota) functions as a clearinghouse for Robert Bly materials.

DAVID R. PICHASKE     SOUTHWEST STATE UNIVERSITY

# MAXWELL BODENHEIM
May 26, 1892–February 7, 1954

**BIOGRAPHY:** When Maxwell Bodenheim is remembered, it is almost inevitably as one of the most rakish if not notorious writers of his age, memorialized in scandalous, often apocryphal anecdotes, particularly of his early years in Chicago and his last years in Greenwich Village. His murder, together with that of his third wife, at the hands of an emotionally disturbed young man, was seen by some as an inevitable and perhaps fitting conclusion to the fact that in his last years he was reduced to selling his poems for change or drinks in Greenwich Village bars.

In spite of the persistent anecdotes about Bodenheim's life and death, he was not only a member of two of the most productive literary groups early in this century, those of the Chicago Renaissance and Greenwich Village, but one of the most productive poets and novelists of his generation.

Born in Hermanville, Mississippi, to Jewish parents Solomon W. and Catherine (Herman) Bodenheim, he was brought to Chicago at eight years of age. He attended school sporadically, ran away, enlisted in and deserted from the army, and then wandered around the country for several years.

When he returned to Chicago in 1912, he found the Chicago Renaissance; *Poetry*, the avant-garde magazine founded by HARRIET MONROE that year; a new vocation; and a growing reputation as a poet. He contributed to both *Poetry* and the *Little Review*, founded by MARGARET ANDERSON in 1914. He became part of the group that gathered at Schlogl's Tavern, at the soirees held by FLOYD DELL and Margery Currey, and became especially close to BEN HECHT, with whom he worked on various newspapers. He married his first wife, Minna Schein, in 1918, edited the *Chicago Literary Times* with Hecht, and also with Hecht wrote *Cutie: A Warm Mama* (1924, 1952), a brief, barbed satire on conventional manners, mores, and censorship. He also collaborated with Hecht on several plays. As the Chicago Renaissance ran its course by the early 1920s, Bodenheim drifted to New York and began his career as a novelist.

In 1935, having been reduced by the Depression to living on relief, he marched with other writers on the New York City Hall to demand support for writers. He worked briefly in the Federal Writers' Project and was fired for his alleged Communist Party membership. In 1938 Minna divorced him, and in 1939 he married Grace Finan, who died in 1950. Increasingly eccentric, he began what was apparently a common-law relationship with a young woman, Ruth Fagan, in 1951. On February 7, 1954, he and Ruth were murdered by Harold Weinberg, who declared at his trial that he had killed two Communists.

**SIGNIFICANCE:** Bodenheim's novels are as much of the times as they are of place. He discovered his major themes as a member of the Chicago Renaissance. In both prose and poetry he was strongly critical of conventional sexual mores of Midwestern America in the early twentieth century, expressing the theme of the movement, as did SHERWOOD ANDERSON, FLOYD DELL, BEN HECHT, and others, as a search for both personal and artistic liberation. His novels, like those of Anderson, Dell, and Hecht that had their inspiration in Chicago, deal with the young person who seeks identity, freedom, and meaning in the city.

Bodenheim's first serious novel, *Blackguard* (1923), is also his most autobiographical, reflecting his recurring interest in satire and humor. Set in Chicago, it follows Bodenheim's life, his rebellion from his family, and his discovery of poetry and the life of the artist even in the harshness of dynamic, impersonal Chicago. The novel carries him through love affairs, emotional turmoil, and finally an honest, sexless relationship with Georgie May, a young prostitute who would be the subject of a later novel.

As in *Blackguard*, *Crazy Man* (1924) explores the search of two young people as they struggle against Chicago and its social and moral values for a place and an identity. Selma Thallinger, a dance-hall girl, resembles THEODORE DREISER'S *Sister Carrie* in her search. John Carley, a self-educated thief, saves her from the mindlessness of her parents' values and those of the dance hall. Even as he continues to steal, however, he knows that he will ultimately pay society's price for his crimes.

Others of Bodenheim's Chicago novels are *Sixty Seconds* (1929) and *A Virtuous Girl* (1930). His New York novels, *Replenishing Jessica* (1925), later the subject of a trial alleging pornography, and *Ninth Avenue* (1926), carry on the quest of the young for a place in which they can live and a code they can accept. Later works, such as *Naked on Roller Skates* (1930) and *Duke Herring* (1931), satirize his contemporaries, CARL VAN VECHTEN and Ben Hecht. Finally, his last novel, *Slow Vision* (1934), reflects the final defeat of his people, the artists, writers, and bohemians of Chicago and New York who were the subjects of his fiction.

Bodenheim's notoriety has outlived that of his works. His literary flaws—looseness of structure, lack of control, and repetitiousness—make a resurgence of his literary reputation unlikely. But each of his novels is a clear portrayal as well as an indictment of a newly urban America.

**SELECTED WORKS:** Bodenheim's early poems appear in *Minna and Myself* (1918); his best are collected in *Selected Poems* (1946). His later novels, *6 A.M.* (1932), *Run, Sheep, Run* (1932), and *Slow Vision* (1934), reflect the deterioration of his own life. *My Life and Loves in Greenwich Village* (1954), attributed to Bodenheim, was ghost-written. Most of Bodenheim's novels, including *Blackguard* (1923), *Crazy Man* (1924), *Sixty Seconds* (1929), *A Virtuous Girl* (1930), *Replenishing Jessica* (1925), *Ninth Avenue* (1926), *Naked on Roller Skates* (1930), *Duke Herring* (1931), and *Slow Vision* (1934), are readable, although their attempts to use daring material make them sometimes seem dated.

**FURTHER READING:** Allen Churchill's *The Improper Bohemians* (1959) and Ben Hecht's *A Child of the Century* (1954) deal with aspects of Bodenheim's life. Jack B. Moore's *Maxwell Bodenheim* (1970) is a critical biography. Bodenheim's papers are scattered, with concentrations in the Charles Patterson Van Pelt Library of the University of Pennsylvania, the Virginia State Library, the University of Wisconsin Library, and the Theatre Collection of the New York Public Library, now housed at Lincoln Center. He recorded a number of his poems for the Library of Congress, tape LWO 2529.

DAVID D. ANDERSON     MICHIGAN STATE UNIVERSITY

# SARAH T(ITTLE BARRETT) BOLTON

December 18, 1814–August 4, 1893

**BIOGRAPHY:** Born in Newport, Kentucky, to Jonathan Belcher and Esther (Pendleton) Barrett, a first cousin to President James Madison, Sarah was brought overland under difficult conditions to southern Indiana while a small child. She had dramatic and frightening memories of the frontier wilderness which the family traversed on its way to the farm northeast of Vernon where they settled. Her childhood inculcated a romantic love of nature which later characterized her verse. In 1823 her father moved the family to Madison, Indiana, to make it possible for the children to be educated.

On October 15, 1831, at the age of sixteen, Sarah married Nathaniel Bolton, the founder and publisher of a Madison newspaper and a man well known in Indiana journalistic circles; the couple settled in Indianapolis. Over the years, while Nathaniel was active in politics, Sarah bore a daughter, Sarah Adah, and a son, James, and for several difficult years ran a country inn on their farm. Eventually Nathaniel became state librarian (1847–53), clerk to a U.S. Senate committee, and, under President Pierce, consul at Geneva, Switzerland, in 1855; he died in 1858.

During her husband's consular appointment, Sarah traveled widely in Europe, accompanied by her daughter. After his death, she returned to Indianapolis, although she later resumed her European travels, even living for a time in Dresden, Germany, to enable her young grandson to receive a European education. She was also actively involved in rearing her granddaughter. A second marriage, to Judge Addison Reese of Missouri, entered on September 15, 1863, was not particularly happy and did not affect her literary work or reputation.

In her later years in Indianapolis, she was an honored literary figure and friend to such other leading personages of the day as LEW WALLACE, JAMES WHITCOMB RILEY, and Robert Dale Owen. She has sometimes been considered an unofficial "Pioneer Poet Laureate of Indiana" (Downing 92). A bronze plaque honoring her was placed in the rotunda of the Indiana state capitol building on October 18, 1941.

**SIGNIFICANCE:** Although Bolton is completely forgotten today outside Indiana—and almost forgotten there—one or two of her poems have made a lasting impression. Both a daughter of the Midwestern frontier and a world traveler, Bolton holds a slim but secure place in the literary history of her state. Her life spanned the period of change from frontier to settled urban culture and her poetry mirrors that change. The slang phrase "Paddle your own canoe" is the title and tag line of one of her best-known poems, and her "Indiana," from *The Life and Poems of Sarah T. Bolton* (1880), was for many years a kind of unofficial state poem, read and even memorized by generations of Hoosier young people. Rhythmic and sentimental, this poem lauds the landscape, history, and people of the state, closing with an apostrophe to the God "whose love and bounteous grace / Gave to the people of our race / A freehold, an abiding place, / In glorious Indiana" (383).

Her poetry frequently is both trite and

sentimental, and the linguistic facility that enabled her to use fluently the meters of "The Raven" in paying tribute to its author in "Edgar A. Poe" often causes her verse to degenerate into doggerel. However, her romantic love of nature and her ready sympathy for the downtrodden sometimes give an unexpected distinction to her creativity in such poems as "Ye Sons of Toil" and "The Miner's Story." A supporter of women's rights and sometimes a sympathizer with proponents of other radical causes, she adopted tones of indignation in poems of protest, as in her denunciation of the execution of the Haymarket rioters in "The Doomed Anarchists," and of sentimentality in the narrative verse and poems of praise of nature which make up the greatest part of her work. While the Europe of her travels gave her many of her materials, she always returned to Indiana— its landscapes and its people, especially its pioneers—for her most deeply felt poetry.

**SELECTED WORKS:** Four collections of her poetry exist: *Poems* (1865), *The Life and Poems of Sarah T. Bolton* (1880), *Songs of a Life-time* (1892), and *Paddle Your Own Canoe and Other Poems* (1897).

**FURTHER READING:** For biographical information, see the anonymous and laudatory "Life" in *The Life and Poems of Sarah T. Bolton* and Olive Inez Downing's uncritical and fulsome *Indiana's Poet of the Wildwood* (1941). For a later attempt to survey Bolton's career, see Mary Jean DeMarr's "Sarah T. Barrett Bolton: Nineteenth-Century Hoosier Poet," *Midwestern Miscellany* 17 (1990).

MARY JEAN DEMARR　　INDIANA STATE UNIVERSITY

## GERTRUDE BONNIN.
*See* Zitkala-Ša.

## VANCE (NYE) BOURJAILY
September 17, 1922

**BIOGRAPHY:** Born in Cleveland, Ohio, Vance Bourjaily is the second of three sons of Monte Ferris Bourjaily, a Lebanese-born journalist and publisher, and Barbara (Webb) Bourjaily, a journalist and writer of popular romance fiction. Raised in Connecticut, New York City, and, after his parents' divorce, on a dairy farm in Virginia, he became acquainted with the writers of the Lost Generation through his prep-schooling, his mother,

and her agent, Maxwell Perkins, the editor for many Lost Generation writers. Perkins read and made suggestions for Bourjaily's early literary efforts.

Bourjaily interrupted his undergraduate work at Bowdoin College to join the American Field Service as an ambulance driver from 1942 to 1944. He served in the U.S. Army from 1944 to 1946 after which he completed his AB at Bowdoin in 1947. He worked as a journalist in San Francisco until 1951 when he co-founded and edited *Discovery*. He married Bettina Yensen in 1946, with whom he had three children, Anna (deceased), Philip, and Robin. In 1985 he married Yasmin Mogul, with whom he had one child, Omar. From 1958 to 1980, Bourjaily was on the faculty of the Writers' Workshop at the University of Iowa. In 1980 he joined the writing faculty at the University of Arizona, and from 1985 until 1992 he was director of the creative writing program at Louisiana State University. In addition to fifteen prose books, Bourjaily has written television drama, numerous works for periodicals, and the libretto for an opera.

**SIGNIFICANCE:** The common critical appraisal of Vance Bourjaily is that he has fallen short of the prediction that he would become a dominant post–World War II literary figure in the tradition established by Lost Generation writers. An equally insistent view is that Bourjaily is a major talent with a virtuoso's command of narrative forms, but not content to replicate past work, he pushes them beyond conventional artistic boundaries in trying to shape his works as expressions of the times. His literary influence, however, is more strongly identified with the legends he inspired during his twenty-two years on the faculty of the University of Iowa Writers' Workshop. An outdoorsman who revels in all kinds of settings, Bourjaily's closeness to the land is apparent in all his works, three of which have specifically Midwestern settings. *Brill among the Ruins* (1971), nominated for the National Book Award, is a novel about a lawyer in an Illinois river town who drinks, womanizes, and does archaeology in Mexico when his marriage fails to work. *Now Playing in Canterbury* (1976) is a set of tales told by the cast of an opera under production at a Midwestern university, suggested by the production of his own opera, *$4,000. The Great Fake*

*Book* (1987) is the story of an Iowa congressman's aide who uses the forms of jazz themes and improvisation to construct the fragmented story of his father, who died when he was a child. Bourjaily does not portray the Midwest as a discrete cultural province but as a connecting point where values deeply rooted in the land's ability to meet essential human needs confront characters for whom postwar society contains few values. Bourjaily's accurate rendering of Midwestern dialogue, his precise evocation of the landscape, and his exuberant sense of how story and song emanate from the relationships people establish with the land capture the Midwest both as setting and as the repository of values which are elusive or lost.

**SELECTED WORKS:** *The End of My Life* (1947), *The Hound of Earth* (1955), *The Violated* (1958), *Confessions of a Spent Youth* (1960), and *The Man Who Knew Kennedy* (1967) have various settings and provide demonstrations of Bourjaily's talent for capturing regional flavors and ambiance. They provide acute points of comparison which define his success in capturing the essence of the Midwest in *Brill among the Ruins* (1970), *Now Playing at Canterbury* (1976), and *The Great Fake Book* (1987). Other recent novels of critical note are *A Game Men Play* (1980) and *Old Soldier* (1993). His nonfiction *Country Matters* (1973) and a book of letters about outdoor experiences exchanged with his son Philip, *Fishing by Mail: The Outdoor Life of a Father and Son* (1993), deal with Midwestern materials.

**FURTHER READING:** John Aldridge's *After the Lost Generation* (1951) explains why so much was expected of Bourjaily. He has not received much attention from the critical establishment, so most of the commentary on his work is in book reviews. One book-length study of his work is a doctoral dissertation by William Albert Cyril Francis, "The Novels of Vance Bourjaily: A Critical Analysis" (1976), listed in *Dissertation Abstracts*. Francis has also published "The Motif of Names of Bourjaily's *The Hound of Earth*," in *Critique: Studies in Modern Fiction* 17.3 (1976): 64–72; "A Conversation about Names with Novelist Vance Bourjaily," in *Names: A Journal of Onomastics* 34.4 (December 1986): 355–63; "Vance Bourjaily's *The Man Who Knew Kennedy:* A Novel of Camelot Lost," in *Literary Onomastics Studies* 14 (1987):

199–211; and "From Jazz to Joyce: A Conversation with Vance Bourjaily," in *Literary Review: An International Journal of Contemporary Writing* 31.4 (Summer 1988): 403–14. Bourjaily has been much sought after for his professor-writer perspectives on contemporary fiction, as evidenced by the number of published interviews with him and commentaries by him. They include William Parill's "The Art of the Novel: An Interview with Vance Bourjaily," in *Louisiana Literature: A Review of Literature and Humanities* 5.2 (Fall 1988): 3–20; his "After the Lost Generation: A Conversation with Vance Bourjaily," in *The Long Haul: Conversations with Southern Writers* (1994); and Matthew J. Bruccoli's "Vance Bourjaily," in *Conversations with Writers* (1977). John M. Muste covers four of Bourjaily's early novels in his essay "The Second Major Subwar: Four Novels by Vance Bourjaily," in *The Shaken Realist: Essays in Modern Literature in Honor of Frederick J. Hoffman* (1970). John Aldridge updates his original assessment of Bourjaily in his article "Vance Bourjaily's *The End of My Life,*" in *Centennial Review* 28.2 (Spring 1984): 100–105. Manuscripts and correspondence of Bourjaily's are undergoing assembly at Bowdoin College in a notable alumni project and at the University of North Carolina in the Louis Decimus Rubin Papers.

DAVID L. NEWQUIST    NORTHERN STATE UNIVERSITY

# RAY (DOUGLAS) BRADBURY
August 22, 1920

**BIOGRAPHY:** Ray Bradbury, widely recognized and respected as a major science fiction writer, was born in Waukegan, Illinois. His father, Leonard Spaulding Bradbury, was descended from an English family that came to America in the seventeenth century. Ray Bradbury's mother, Edith Marie (Moberg) Bradbury, was born in Stockholm, Sweden, and came to America in 1890, moving with her family to Waukegan when she was eight. Bradbury claimed that he was aware at birth and that he could remember several experiences from his first year of life, notably his first snowfall in the winter of 1921. In 1926 the family moved to New Mexico, then to Arizona, and back to Waukegan in 1927. The family moved permanently to California in 1934, and Bradbury graduated from high school in Los Angeles. As a young child, he was fond of movies, reading, carnivals, circuses, and comic strips. His imagination was captured especially by *The Phantom of the Opera*. After attending a performance by the famous magician Blackstone in 1931, Bradbury decided that he would become the world's greatest magician. As a youth in California, he was divided by his love for acting and for writing. Finally he chose writing and spent hours in libraries typing his stories. He married Marguerite "Maggie" McClure in 1947, and the Bradburys have four daughters. Although he had been publishing short stories in various magazines in the 1940s, Bradbury experienced a major breakthrough in 1950, when Doubleday published *The Martian Chronicles*. In 1953 John Huston asked Bradbury to write the film script for the movie *Moby Dick*. Bradbury accepted, and, since the movie was filmed in Ireland, Bradbury and his family spent six months there, giving them a vacation and him the material for several Irish stories which he would write later. In 1954 *Playboy* magazine published *Fahrenheit 451* serially.

More recently, Bradbury has done important work in television, hosting *The Ray Bradbury Theater* in the 1980s. Always generous with his support of libraries, Bradbury has made frequent appearances to open or dedicate a library or to give the keynote speech at a professional meeting of librarians. He is currently in great demand as a lecturer. When he is not writing, dedicating libraries, giving lectures, or visiting Paris in the summer, Bradbury is at home in Los Angeles with his wife, caring for their cats and entertaining grandchildren.

**SIGNIFICANCE:** Although Bradbury's reputation is international and his works are avidly read and enjoyed by people all across America, his roots are distinctively Midwestern. Walt Whitman's poem "There Was a Child Went Forth" provides the insight to enable one to understand the powerful influence of Waukegan on Bradbury's life and work. Indeed, Bradbury has admitted that he kept the early loves of his life, such as dinosaurs, Buck Rogers comic strips, and Walt Disney's *Fantasia*, and used them for inspiration for his life and his creative writing. Perhaps the most important event of his childhood occurred on Labor Day weekend in 1932, when Timothy Perrin reports Bradbury was literally touched at the carnival by Mr. Electrico and told to

"Live forever!" ("Ray Bradbury's Nostalgia for the Future," *Writer's Digest,* February 1986: 26). A conversation the following day with Mr. Electrico inspired Bradbury to become a writer, and he read widely in Jules Verne, H. G. Wells, and Edgar Allan Poe, as well as short story writers throughout the world.

Although many of his stories are set in such remote places as Mars and Venus, Bradbury's idea of home—his locus amoenus—is essentially defined by his early childhood in Waukegan, which is called Greentown, Illinois, in his novel *Dandelion Wine* (1957). The values and meaning of home are so strong that in *The Martian Chronicles* the settlers return to earth even though it is being destroyed by an atomic war. Home is so important in Bradbury's vision because it is there that we begin life and acquire those important values that will enable us to live fully. *Fahrenheit 451* is not set in any specific locale, but what is clearly missing are those positive, dynamic values of home that Bradbury gained from his childhood in the Midwest in the 1920s and early 1930s.

The publication of *The Martian Chronicles* in 1950 was an important literary event in America. The success of that book caused the big publishing houses to accept the work of science fiction writers as they had not done before. Thus Bradbury opened the door for other science fiction writers, who could now reach larger audiences than previously.

Bradbury does not like to be categorized as a science fiction writer, nor does he accept the label of prophet that some people impose on authors who write about the future. Rather, Bradbury describes himself as a "preventor of futures, not a predictor of them" ("Ray Bradbury: An Interview," *SunRise* 3.8 [1975]: 28). Bradbury's objection is understandable because he moves freely in several genres: fantasy, film, drama, science fiction, detective fiction, children's literature, television, and poetry. Bradbury has acknowledged that he has been influenced by SHERWOOD ANDERSON, and Bradbury can be compared with Nathaniel Hawthorne in terms of the moral concerns that are so powerful and central in their works. However, Bradbury's work defies any precise or narrow classification in a literary movement. He is a romantic in terms of his treatment of the sadness of bad timing in life. Some of his finest love stories are based on the idea of bad timing and the human impulse to correct the errors of time. But he is also a realist in his awareness of the flaws in human beings and the mistaken values in American society.

Bradbury's importance to the Midwest is highlighted by his receiving the Mark Twain Award in 1992 from the Society for the Study of Midwestern Literature. The city of Waukegan named a public park for him in 1990. **SELECTED WORKS:** From 1938 until 1947, Bradbury published several short stories in a variety of magazines. His first book was *Dark Carnival* in 1947. *The Martian Chronicles* (1950), *The Illustrated Man* (1951), *The Golden Apples of the Sun* (1953), *Fahrenheit 451* (1954), and *Dandelion Wine* (1957) are examples of Bradbury's early major works. *The October Country* (1955) is a collection of fantasy stories, many of which were published separately earlier. *Something Wicked This Way Comes*, a major fantasy novel, was published in 1962, and *R Is for Rocket*, a collection of science fiction tales for young adults, appeared in the same year. In January 1965, *Life* magazine published "The Kilimanjaro Machine," which is Bradbury's tribute to ERNEST HEMINGWAY. *S Is for Space*, a companion piece to *R Is for Rocket*, was published in 1966. A collection of new stories, *I Sing the Body Electric!* appeared in 1969. In 1980 the major stories were collected and published under the title *The Stories of Ray Bradbury*. More recently, *The Toynbee Convector* (1988) is a collection of new stories, followed in 1990 by the novel *A Graveyard for Lunatics*. *Green Shadows, White Whale*, a novel set in Ireland, was published in 1992. Then in 1996, *Quicker Than the Eye*, a collection of new short stories, appeared. Bradbury has also written several plays, beginning with *The Meadow* (1960) and followed in 1963 by a book of plays entitled *The Authentic Sprinter*. His dramatic musical *The Wonderful Ice Cream Suit* was published in 1965, and *Dandelion Wine* was staged as a musical in 1967. *Fahrenheit 451* was made into a film and released in 1966, as was *The Illustrated Man* in 1969. Many of Bradbury's short stories as well as *The Martian Chronicles* were dramatized for television. Bradbury's books for children include *The Halloween Tree* (1972) and *Dogs Think That Every Day Is Christmas* (1997). *When Elephants Last in the Dooryard Bloomed* is a book of poetry published in 1973. Bradbury has published two recent collec-

tions of essays: *Zen in the Art of Writing* (1990) and *Yestermorrow* (1991).

**FURTHER READING:** Since Bradbury has been generous in giving interviews over the years, no single source provides an inclusive bibliography of them. However, the best single source for information about Bradbury's life and for his early interviews as well as his articles in newspapers and magazines is William F. Nolan's *The Bradbury Companion* (1975), which also lists the movies on which Bradbury worked, the television shows that dramatized his stories, and facsimiles from Bradbury's unpublished and uncollected work. Two important book-length studies of Bradbury's fiction are George Slusser's *The Bradbury Chronicles* (1977) and William F. Touponce's *Ray Bradbury and the Poetics of Reverie* (1984). Martin Greenberg and Joseph Olander have collected several fine critical essays on Bradbury's work in their *Writers of the 21st Century: Ray Bradbury* (1980), which includes a bibliography compiled by Marshall B. Tymn (227–41).

LOREN LOGSDON                              EUREKA COLLEGE

## EDGAR M. BRANCH.

*See* appendix (1994)

## CAROL RYRIE BRINK

December 28, 1895–August 15, 1981

**BIOGRAPHY:** A popular author of more than thirty juvenile and adult books, Carol Ryrie Brink was an only child, born and raised in Moscow, Idaho. Since her parents, Alexander and Henrietta (Watkins) Ryrie, died by the time she was eight, she moved in with her maternal grandmother and aunt, both superb storytellers. Her grandmother's vivid accounts of her pioneer childhood in Wisconsin captivated Brink's imagination, giving her a rich, vicarious experience of Midwestern farm life during the Civil War. Thirty years later her grandmother's story came to life in Brink's exuberant portrayal of Caddie Woodlawn and her family on the Wisconsin frontier.

Brink attended the University of Idaho, transferring to the University of California at Berkeley for her senior year. After graduating Phi Beta Kappa in 1918, she moved to the Midwest to marry University of Minnesota instructor Raymond W. Brink. Making their home in St. Paul for forty-two years, the Brinks enjoyed family life with their son and daughter, traveled abroad, and spent carefree summers in backwoods Wisconsin. Brink drew heavily on these family experiences for the themes and settings of many of her twenty children's books and several adult books published between 1934 and 1978. She retired to La Jolla, California, where she died of heart failure at age eighty-five.

**SIGNIFICANCE:** Brink is important today for her 1936 Newbery Medal winner, *Caddie Woodlawn: A Frontier Story* (1935), a landmark of Midwestern realism for children. Brink's visit to her ancestors' homestead and extensive research proved her grandmother's stories to be accurate, trustworthy accounts of the places, people, and historical framework of Wisconsin in the 1860s. Brink provides lyrical descriptions of the untamed natural world as well as grim accounts of the settlers' slaughter of the beautiful passenger pigeons for sport. The Woodlawns, although usually portrayed as "ordinary" frontier folks, kill only the birds they need for food; they also try to diffuse the pioneer community's hatred and fear of the local Indian tribe.

The three daring adventurers, eleven-year-old Caddie and her brothers, run wild and free on the open land, hunting, fishing, and exploring the wilderness on horseback. Tomboy Caddie's dangerous escapades along with prairie fires and threats of "Indian massacrees" provide dramatic action and suspense.

The Woodlawns are staunch patriots, believing in democracy and in the worth of the common people. Like the pioneer family in LAURA INGALLS WILDER'S "Little House" books, they face their future with courage, optimism, self-reliance, and a willingness to work together to ensure their place in the fulfillment of the American dream.

A best-seller for fifty years, *Caddie Woodlawn* is still widely read today. Each year throngs of visitors tour the restored Woodlawn farmhouse in Caddie Woodlawn Memorial Park, twelve miles south of Menomonie, Wisconsin.

Brink's other books continue to reflect her zest for life and her deep commitment to family, to the natural world, and to the old-fashioned American values of the pioneers. Her settings range from the Midwest to Idaho, Europe, and fantasy islands. Although her preferred genre is realistic fiction, she moves easily to fantasy, biography, local history, and drama. Her literary awards include the Lewis Carroll Shelf Award, the Kerlan Award, and an honorary degree from the University of Idaho in 1965.

**SELECTED WORKS:** *Caddie Woodlawn: A Frontier Story* (1935) was so enthusiastically received by both children and critics that Brink rewrote it as a drama, *Caddie Woodlawn: A Play* (1945), that is frequently performed. A sequel, *Magical Melons: More Stories about Caddie Woodlawn* (1944), never became as popular as the original work. Brink wrote two other richly humorous, realistic novels set in the Midwest: *Family Grandstand* (1952), the story of an academic family at "Midwestern University"; and *Winter Cottage* (1968), the poignant yet amusing tale of a penniless, eccentric father and his resourceful children wintering in the beautiful Wisconsin wilderness during the Depression.

Although Brink was established first as a Midwestern children's author, she also secured her place in Western American literature with four juvenile and four adult works. Her semi-autobiographical children's novels set in small-town Idaho include *All Over Town* (1939), *Two Are Better Than One* (1968), and *Louly* (1974). Her Western novels for adults, reprinted in 1993, combine stories of her family with the local history of the Moscow area: *Buffalo Coat* (1944), *Strangers in the Forest* (1959), and the autobiographical *Snow in the River* (1964), winner of the McKnight Family Foundation Medal and the American Pen Women's Award. The posthumous publication *A Chain of Hands* (1993) is a collection of Brink's reminiscences of the "ordinary" people who influenced her early life in Idaho, many of whom are fictionalized in her works. An informative foreword written by Mary E. Reed and a useful bibliography are also included.

**FURTHER READING:** Alethea K. Helbig's "Carol Ryrie Brink," in *Writers for Children*, edited by Jane S. Bingham (1988), is a perceptive biographical and critical study of Brink's children's books. A monograph, Mary E. Reed's *Carol Ryrie Brink* (1991), is part of the Western Writers series. Four of Brink's manuscripts belong to the University of Idaho Library in Moscow. All of her working materials for *Caddie Woodlawn*, her correspondence with her grandmother, and eighteen book manuscripts are held in the Kerlan Collection at the University of Minnesota in Minneapolis.

MARY JOAN MILLER                    SPRINGFIELD, OHIO

## LOUIS BROMFIELD
December 27, 1896–March 18, 1956

**BIOGRAPHY:** Louis Bromfield was born in Mansfield, Ohio, the son and grandson of farmers. As a young man he aspired to the same vocation, hoping to bring the ancestral farm back to its earlier prosperity. His father, Charles, but not his mother, Annette Maria (Coulter) Bromfield, encouraged his agricultural ambition, but after a year at Cornell University studying agriculture, he switched to journalism at Columbia. After service in World War I, he made writing his career, working as a journalist, arts critic, and novelist.

Following a literary apprenticeship of several years, Bromfield published the highly regarded novel *The Green Bay Tree* in 1924; not long after, he moved to France with his wife, Mary Appleton (Wood) Bromfield, and oldest daughter and devoted himself to writing. There, he produced his major fiction, beginning with a series of interrelated novels: *Possession* (1925); *Early Autumn* (1926), which won a Pulitzer Prize; and *The Good Woman* (1927). These and *The Green Bay Tree* set forth the theme that would dominate Bromfield's art, the plight of the heroic individual caught in the conflict between the old agrarian order and the materialism of the new age.

There followed another decade of important fiction, most notably *The Strange Case of Miss Annie Spragg* (1928), *The Farm* (1933), and *The Rains Came* (1937). In 1938 Bromfield returned to the Ohio of his youth, purchased a thousand-acre plot near his birthplace, and turned it into a working farm, where he practiced new scientific and conservation-oriented techniques for which he gained much public notice.

Though Bromfield continued to write novels, his major literary energy now went to a series of nonfiction accounts of life at Malabar Farm, widely read and admired. Of note were *Pleasant Valley* (1945); *Malabar Farm* (1948); and *From My Experience* (1955). Until his death in 1956, he sought to live out the harmonious natural life he had always championed.

**SIGNIFICANCE:** Bromfield's creative output

**Louis Bromfield, ca. 1955.**
Courtesy of David D. Anderson

was abundant: he published more than thirty books and numerous other writings. His work is made cohesive by its rootedness in the agrarian ethos of his Midwestern upbringing, reflecting a sustained belief in the consolations of the natural world, in the worth of individual character as the proper underpinning of society, and in an abiding skepticism about the damages—both ecological and spiritual—inflicted by industrialism and materialism.

His earlier novels, especially the tetralogy begun with *The Green Bay Tree* and culminating in *A Good Woman*, chronicle the trials endured by a series of strong individualists whose resourcefulness and vitality are thwarted by modern cultural and economic forces that have driven people from the land and into a social structure that suppresses human creativity. Bromfield drew inspiration from his personal history. His progenitors had pioneered in rural Ohio in the nineteenth century, cultivating the family farm for nearly a century until the area was transformed into an industrial community, imposing a sense of dislocation upon its inhabitants that Bromfield dramatized.

In the middle phase of his career, he produced important fiction that continued to reflect his lingering pastoral ideals. *The Farm*, which most critics consider his best novel, is a fictionalized lament for the decline of the family farm. Other novels from the 1930s extend the rural philosophy to the international landscape, including *The Strange Case of Annie Spragg*, set in Italy, and *The Rains Came*, set in India. Despite his continued viability as a novelist, Bromfield's reputation deteriorated, in part due to the disparagement he had received from leftist critics at journals such as the *Nation* and the *New Republic*, who found his Jeffersonian bent and his credo of hardy individualism politically unpalatable.

In his later years, Bromfield was known for his celebratory narratives of country life. In these nonfiction works, particularly in *Pleasant Valley*—described by DAVID D. ANDERSON in the *Dictionary of Literary Biography* 9 (1981) as "Bromfield's Walden" (97)—he traced his return to the Midwestern wellspring that had spawned his vision. Bromfield is best remembered for the forcefully articulated agrarian idealism at the heart of that vision.

**SELECTED WORKS:** A prolific author, Bromfield's most important novels include *The Green Bay Tree* (1924), *Possession* (1925), *Early Autumn* (1926), *A Good Woman* (1927), *The Strange Case of Miss Annie Spragg* (1928), *Twenty-Four Hours* (1930), *A Modern Hero* (1932), *The Farm* (1933), *The Man Who Had Everything* (1935), *The Rains Came* (1937), *Night in Bombay* (1940), *Mrs. Parkington* (1943), and *The Wild Country* (1948). *Awake and Rehearse* (1929), *Here Today and Gone Tomorrow* (1934), and *The World We Live In* (1944) are collections of short stories. Bromfield also wrote plays, including *The House of Women* (1927), adapted from *The Green Bay Tree*, and *Times Have Changed* (1935). His best nonfiction writings about farm life and rural lore include *Pleasant Valley* (1945), *Malabar Farm* (1948), *Out of the Earth* (1950), *From My Experience* (1955), and *Animals and Other People* (1955). More polemical and less satisfying writings are *A Few Brass Tacks* (1946), which advocates a return to Jeffersonian economic principles, and *A New Plan for a Tired World* (1954), which offers ideas for global economic development in the postwar era.

**FURTHER READING:** Two lengthy studies are David D. Anderson's *Louis Bromfield* (1964) and Morrison Brown's *Louis Bromfield and His Books* (1957). Ellen Bromfield Geld has re-membered her father in *The Heritage: A Daughter's Memories of Louis Bromfield* (1962). Most of Bromfield's papers are held at the Munroe Archives of the Ohio Historical Society and at Malabar Farm State Park in Lucas, Ohio.

LIAHNA BABENER CENTRAL WASHINGTON UNIVERSITY

## GWENDOLYN BROOKS
June 7, 1917–December 3, 2000

**BIOGRAPHY:** Gwendolyn Brooks was born in Topeka, Kansas, where her mother, Keziah (Wims) Brooks, had gone to visit her parents during pregnancy. Soon after her birth, the family returned to Chicago. Her father, David Brooks, had earlier spent a year at Fisk University with aspirations of becoming a doctor. Circumstances had not allowed that, however, and he had migrated to Chicago and taken a job as a porter in a music publishing company. Her mother was also educated. She had attended Emporia Normal School in Kansas, taking music courses and dreaming of becoming a concert pianist. After the birth of Gwendolyn and her brother, Raymond, the family moved to a single-family home in a middle-class neighborhood on Chicago's south side.

As a child, Gwendolyn Brooks internalized many middle-class values and orientations, particularly family, individual and community responsibility, and faith in God. She maintained a positive, nonfatalistic worldview and an optimistic faith in the goodness of all human beings under God. She believed in the strength of logic and graphic presentation to expose and eliminate abuses and enhance human sympathy and harmony. George Kent in his *Life of Gwendolyn Brooks* (1990) cites Brooks's youthful list of resolutions, a list as infused with youthful optimism and faith in the American Dream as that of F. SCOTT FITZGERALD's fictional James Gatz as he endeavored to transform himself imaginatively into Jay Gatsby (27–28).

Ironically, Brooks's earliest consciousness of racial prejudice came from the African American community. She became aware that her relatively dark skin decreased her status, popularity, and attractiveness in the black community.

Brooks attended several Chicago south side high schools, with her parents always attempting to secure the best possible edu-

**Gwendolyn Brooks.**
Courtesy of Gwendolyn Brooks

cation for her. She then attended Chicago's Wilson Junior College, graduating in 1937. Throughout high school, college, and beyond, her early sense of physical inferiority and low status reinforced her innate shyness and reclusiveness, tendencies that success and recognition limited but never fully erased. Brooks recognized very early that intellect and artistry were her avenues to recognition and success. She found her place in active participation in the NAACP Youth Council, providing intellectual leadership to Chicago's African American youth. There she met Henry Blakely, an intelligent, aspiring writer, who, like her father, remained employed beneath his ability because of the Depression and the continuing color line, which barred African Americans from professional and managerial positions in white-owned businesses. The marriage of Gwendolyn and Henry saw competition and tension. It also celebrated the birth of two children, Henry Lowington Blakely III in 1940 and Nora Brooks Blakely in 1951.

Brooks's poetic internship began early. While in high school, she regularly published in the *Chicago Defender* and in time placed poems in more and more prestigious venues. Increasing publication brought greater recognition and income. Her first volume of poetry, *A Street in Bronzeville*, appeared in 1945.

Brooks's pre-1967 poetry followed white European–based poetic models. Philosophically the poet subscribed to the then-dominant assimilationist-integrationist view of African American upward movement. Time and events in Chicago and across America increasingly challenged this view and led Brooks to revise her intellectual and poetic orientations.

Brooks won most major awards available to poets, including the Pulitzer Prize for poetry in 1950 for *Annie Allen* (1949) and two Guggenheim Fellowships. She received the Society for the Study of Midwestern Literature's Mark Twain Award in 1985 and was recognized as poet laureate of Illinois (1969–present) and poet laureate of the United States under the earlier name, consultant-in-poetry to the Library of Congress (1985–86). She received honorary doctorates from more than seventy prestigious American universities. For distinguished intellectual achievement in the humanities, the National Endowment for the Humanities awarded her its "Highest Honor for Achievement in the Humanities," the position as 1994 Jefferson lecturer. In 1995 she was honored with the Medal for Distinguished Contribution to American Letters by the National Book Foundation.

She lived and worked near the University of Chicago campus on Chicago's south side until her death of cancer at her home.

**SIGNIFICANCE:** Poet, novelist, autobiographer, children's writer, book reviewer, editor, publisher, teacher, benefactor, literary and social mentor—Gwendolyn Brooks did it all with great distinction. In all of these roles she worked consistently and tirelessly, delineating the life of Chicago's African American community and presenting the Chicago black experience as an exemplar of the American black life in the mid- and late-twentieth century.

Her work centers on Chicago and is unfailingly Midwestern in subject matter, setting, situation, character, and values. Her writings are permeated with references to Chicago streets, neighborhoods, working-class life in once-proud buildings like the

Mecca at 34th Street between State Street and Dearborn, Black Pride murals like the wall at 43rd and Langley, civic art like Chicago's Picasso, newspapers like the *Chicago Defender* and the *Tribune*, real and fictional characters like De Witt Williams and Satin Legs Smith, and the minutiae of life in Chicago's predominantly African American south side community. The totality of Brooks's work provides a picture of Mid-American black life so comprehensive that no aspect is omitted. War, economic struggle, childhood aspirations and heartbreaks, racial, ethnic, class, and gender bias, motherhood, abortion, gangs, pool halls, manicures, theaters, night clubs, Saturday night joys, and untimely death provide the context and content of life.

Brooks's work focuses on those on the bottom, the struggling, the less privileged and prestigious, the African American poor for whom she asserts upper-middle-class white women love to provide grudging assistance as a means of gratuitously asserting their racial and cultural superiority. Despite daily pain, loss, and struggle, this poetry asserts human dignity and determination to struggle for the good. It takes local Chicago surroundings, situations, and characters and molds them into art that speaks to people everywhere.

Brooks shared the Midwestern philosophical and literary urge to assert the worth and dignity of the disenfranchised, the marginalized, the otherwise invisible men and women of our society. Her experience as African American woman and Midwesterner provided multiple perspectives from which she based her readiness to affirm the downtrodden and be wary of the elite. Egalitarianism is always present in her writing. It is expressed in poems as diverse in time and subject as "Negro Hero," "the children of the poor," "A Bronzeville Mother Loiters in Mississippi. Meanwhile, a Mississippi Mother Burns Bacon," "The Lovers of the Poor," and "Music for Martyrs." While egalitarianism is not the exclusive province of African Americans or Midwesterners, it recurs regularly in both.

In more than fifty years of book-length publishing, some important changes occurred in her writing. Most significant was the change from her pre-1967 European-based traditional elite poetic language, technique, and orientation aimed at more experienced poetry readers of all races to her later more oral and popular literary styles directed toward reaching the largest African American audience.

While faithfully describing the particulars of life of Chicago's black community on every page of works such as *A Street in Bronzeville* (1945), *Annie Allen* (1949), and *The Bean Eaters* (1960), Brooks's pre-1967 poetic orientation was dominantly intellectual and aesthetic, not immediately or exclusively propagandistic. This poetry was complex, making multiple appeals, some logical, some linguistic, some image-based, some lodged in the technical artistic craft of poetic construction, including the possibilities of the poetic line and phrase. In adopting an intellectual-aesthetic orientation, Brooks's carefully crafted form, language, and images captured African American experiences of immense inequity, horror, and brutality, but these potentially visceral experiences were aesthetically framed, distancing them from immediate rage or physical response.

An intellectual-aesthetic craft orientation was Brooks's instinctive approach as well as the most effective vehicle for an African American poet in the 1940s, 1950s, and early 1960s. Even beyond the aesthetic advantages, it allowed more effective presentation of Gwendolyn Brooks's social message to non–African American audiences. By focusing on the intellectual and aesthetic, the craft element in literature, her poetry could present significant issues for consideration without being too directly and immediately confrontational for elite white readers. The underlying philosophy of her writings was clear: the poet, like her readers, believed in God, in the dominance of the forces of good, in self-reliance, and social responsibility. Together, her pre-1967 poems suggested that with God's help, thoughtful, caring people of all races could work together.

The increasingly volatile and divisive American civil rights movement, the tide of assassination of black and white leaders, the polarization of the nation in the late 1960s, and the ferment associated with the Vietnam war played out partially in Chicago with the

1968 Democratic Party convention and led Brooks to reconsider her philosophical and literary orientations.

Black writers at this time were increasingly demanding new literary orientations and focus on African Americans. George Kent's *A Life of Gwendolyn Brooks* cites Lerone Bennett reiterating calls to black writers at the Fisk University conference "The Black Writer and Human Rights," attended by Gwendolyn Brooks, "to come home to the black community," finding it exceedingly odd "that a man or an oppressed person would choose to address his oppressors, primarily," and calling instead for a "literature of transformation" (198, 197).

Brooks's poetic and philosophical sea change came with that of Chicago's black community and of the nation as a whole. In addition to the societal forces producing restiveness in the black community, black artists and leaders presented compelling evidence of continuing conscious efforts by whites in power to maintain black subjugation. These black activist leaders also provided a viable though painful strategy for redressing wrongs. Their increasingly strong and ever more frequent calls for black writers to write directly to black people, returning to them their history, pride, and sense of direction, exerted a strong effect on Gwendolyn Brooks. In response to this call, in the years following 1967 her skills as an elite poet schooled primarily in European-based poetic traditions merged consciously with her determination to support, affirm, and address the African American community, seeking to reconnect them with their history and to instill pride and direction for the future. In 1969 she left her publisher, Harper & Row, for Detroit-based DUDLEY RANDALL's Broadside Press, which published and fostered emerging African American writers. By 1972 Brooks asserted in her *Report from Part One*, "My aim, in my next future, is to write poems that will somehow successfully call . . . all black people: black people in taverns, black people in alleys, black people in gutters, schools, offices, factories, prisons, the consulate; I wish to reach black people in pulpits, black people in mines, on farms, on thrones; *not* always to teach—*I* shall wish often to entertain, to illumine. My newish voice will not

be an imitation of the contemporary young black voice, which I do so admire, but an extending adaptation of today's G. B. voice" (183).

In making this conscious choice, Gwendolyn Brooks never renounced her faith in common humanity. Rather, she refocused her audience and began writing more directly and exclusively to African Americans. In doing so, Brooks modified her literary approaches, techniques, and styles to achieve her revised goals. Her post-1967 poetry makes greater use of the repetitive oral line, very much like Whitman's, to enhance rhythm, order, and ease of understanding. Brooks used her post-1967 poetry to mentor the African American community while remaining true to her poetic craft as well as to the transmutation necessary to raise individual experience to general truth and art.

Gwendolyn Brooks was a woman of principle. Throughout her life she remained dedicated to community involvement and service. Poetry was her vehicle for leading, teaching, and inspiring. Her increasing personal fame, poetic recognition, and income allowed her to add direct personal appeal, recognition, and financial incentives in fostering poetry and its leadership possibilities. Over several decades she visited many schools each year and consistently offered literary prizes to children and adults alike. She embodied the best of Midwestern literary and humanitarian impulses, using art to teach, inspirit, and make lives richer and fuller.

**SELECTED WORKS:** The best-known volumes of poetry by Brooks include *A Street in Bronzeville* (1945), *Annie Allen* (1949), *The Bean Eaters* (1960), *In the Mecca* (1968), *Beckonings* (1975), *To Disembark* (1981), *The Near-Johannesburg Boy and Other Poems* (1986), and *Gottschalk and the Grande Tarantelle* (1988). In addition to these, *Selected Poems* (1963), *The World of Gwendolyn Brooks* (1971), and *Blacks* (1987) offer the best of her previous poetry but also include new poems. *Family Pictures* (1970) and *Black Steel: Joe Frazier and Muhammad Ali* (1971) exemplify her efforts to portray African American role models. *Maud Martha* (1953) is her only novel. *Report from Part One* (1972) and *Report from Part Two* (1996) provide book-length autobiographical statements and intellectual memoirs. *A Primer for Blacks* (1980) is a strong philosophical statement on the role of African American poets and poetry. Gwendolyn Brooks edited several volumes containing the work of emerging African American writers. She also published poetry for children.

**FURTHER READING:** Many recent book-length biographical and critical works exist on Gwendolyn Brooks. These include Harold Bloom's *Gwendolyn Brooks* (2000), Stephen C. Wright's *On Gwendolyn Brooks: Reliant Contemplation* (1996), George E. Kent's *A Life of Gwendolyn Brooks* (1990), D. H. Melhem's *Gwendolyn Brooks: Poetry and the Heroic Voice* (1987), Maria Mootry and Gary Smith's *A Life Distilled: Gwendolyn Brooks, Her Poetry and Fiction* (1987), Harry B. Shaw's *Gwendolyn Brooks* (1980), and Bernard DeFilippo's *Gwendolyn Brooks: A Consideration* (1973). The December 5, 2000, *New York Times* contains an extended appreciation and obituary, "Gwendolyn Brooks, 83, Passionate Poet, Dies" (c22), by Mel Watkins.

PHILIP A. GREASLEY     UNIVERSITY OF KENTUCKY

Charles Farrar Browne.
Courtesy of the Ohio Historical Society

## CHARLES FARRAR BROWNE
April 26, 1834–March 6, 1867
(Artemus Ward)

**BIOGRAPHY:** Charles Farrar Brown was born in Waterford, Maine, to Levi and Caroline (Farrar) Brown. At age thirteen, after his father's death, Browne (he added the "e" to his surname) was a journeyman printer at various places, from New England to Ohio, and contributed to country newspapers before acquiring a national audience as "A. Ward" for his widely reprinted column begun in the pages of the *Cleveland Plain Dealer* in 1858. Two years later he joined *Vanity Fair* in New York and further developed his comic persona, and in 1861 he began several immensely successful lecture tours in New England and the Midwest.

Browne's newspaper columns and lectures were published in several volumes, all huge sellers, beginning in 1862. In 1863 he lectured across the country to the Far West, continuing for two years. By 1866 he was drawing immense lecture audiences in England as well, the first American humorist to acquire popularity there. His death from tuberculosis, while on a lecture tour in Southampton, England, came at the height of his international fame. Browne was unmarried.

**SIGNIFICANCE:** "Artemus Ward" was created in the pages of the *Cleveland Plain-Dealer* and became so popular that Browne began to impersonate him on stage, acquiring popularity as a comic lecturer that only MARK TWAIN later surpassed. Browne had worked itinerantly, moving westward, and his literary persona was likewise a traveler. Artemus Ward, an itinerant showman, was originally modeled on P. T. Barnum's formula of sober solemnity and humbug. As Browne developed his persona, it became the model for a generation of popular Western and Midwestern humorists who acted awkwardly and absurdly on stage, exaggerated with poker-faced sincerity, and digressed aimlessly in a quiet and apparently unself-conscious manner. Himself often a target of self-satire, on stage and in essay, Artemus Ward gibed at authority figures and frauds, pomposity and pretentiousness, and sentimentality—the familiar targets of popular, rustic humor. As a lecturer, Artemus Ward was a notable contrast to other popular speakers like the erudite and solemn Ralph Waldo Emerson and the romantic and sentimental J. G. Holland and John G. Saxe. While the character was created in print, with misspelling to suggest dialect, "accidental" puns, and malapropisms, the Artemus Ward persona was essentially a live personality that required an apparent lack of self-consciousness, physical humor, and perfect comic timing. Artemus Ward was the acknowledged model for Mark Twain's stage persona and, by Twain's influence, since Browne died young, the indirect source for other comic performers, including EDGAR WILSON "BILL" NYE, ROBERT BURDETTE, GEORGE WILBUR PECK, and Will Rogers.

**SELECTED WORKS:** Collections of newspaper columns and lectures are *Artemus Ward, His Book* (1862), *Artemus Ward, His Travels* (1865), *Artemus Ward in London* (1867), and *Artemus Ward's Lecture, as Delivered at the Egyptian Hall* (1869).

**FURTHER READING:** Walter Blair and Hamlin Hill's *America's Humor* (1978) and Brom Weber's chapter in *The Comic Imagination in American Literature*, edited by Louis Rubin Jr. (1973), discuss Browne's literary craft. Don Carlos Seitz's *Artemus Ward* (1919) and JAMES AUSTIN's *Artemus Ward* (1964) are critical biographies with bibliographies; and John Pullen's *Comic Relief* (1983) contains the most material about Artemus Ward as a lecturer. Papers and manuscripts have been lost.

THOMAS PRIBEK
UNIVERSITY OF WISCONSIN–LACROSSE

# WILLIAM JENNINGS BRYAN
March 19, 1860–July 26, 1925

**BIOGRAPHY:** Born in Salem, Illinois, to Silas Bryan, a lawyer and state politician, and Mariah (Jennings) Bryan, William drew much from his rural Illinois upbringing. He was valedictorian at Illinois College and later took a master's degree there and a degree in law from Union College of Chicago. Bryan married Mary Baird, also a lawyer, in 1884, and they moved to Nebraska in 1887. Bryan and his wife had two sons and a daughter. In Nebraska, Bryan served in Congress from 1891 to 1895 but achieved national fame as a three-time Democratic nominee for president and the most popular political speaker on the Chautauqua circuit. He also wrote for newspapers and founded his own, *The Commoner*, in 1901. The "Cross of Gold" speech was delivered to the Democratic convention on July 8, 1896, and secured his first nomination for president when he was only thirty-six.

His themes for oratory were those of his politics: Bryan advocated agrarian interests,

inflationary monetary policy, bank security and lending reform, income tax, women's suffrage, civil rights, and prohibition, and he opposed tariffs, monopoly, and imperialism. With values like those of the Midwestern Populists and Progressives, though he remained a Democrat all his life, his political base was always the Midwest, West, and South.

Bryan moved to Florida in 1921 and became wealthy through real estate investments. He died in Dayton, Tennessee, of diabetes and fatigue only days after the conclusion of the John Scopes trial, in which he assisted the prosecution.

**SIGNIFICANCE:** In the Lyceum, Midwestern Chautauqua gatherings, and national political campaigns, Bryan spoke directly to masses of people more prominently and frequently than any other politician of his day, a model followed later by Progressive Robert La Follette.

The Great Commoner, as he was often called, Bryan was the epitome of an ironic Midwestern character: he was socially tolerant and politically liberal while personally and religiously conservative. His voice was clear and powerful, but his personal stage presence was even more impressive: sincere and unpretentious, interesting and informed, passionate and sober, humorous and friendly. Bryan seemed a natural; he was what the common man could be through energy and personal application. To the Midwestern audience, he was the antithesis of the presumably artificial, studied Eastern aristocrat. On the Lyceum and Chautauqua circuits, he spoke eloquently for Christian dogma, agrarian values, and world peace, often advertised as "The Political and Economic Questions of the Day." His unrivaled popularity at Midwestern Chautauqua gatherings reflects their roots as a forum of intellectual culture and religious enthusiasm. Bryan's advocacy made the election of 1896 probably the most direct electoral confrontation of agrarian and industrial America. The Boy Orator of the Platte, as he first became nationally known, Bryan himself has become a character of fiction, poetry, and movies, a mythic figure arguing to exhaustion the virtues of naive, rural simplicity. His *Memoirs* (1925) contains fond reminiscences of farming, hunting, and small-town schooling during his youth in Illinois.

**SELECTED WORKS:** Collections compiled in

**William Jennings Bryan.**
Courtesy of the Nebraska State Historical Society

Bryan's lifetime include *Life and Speeches of William J. Bryan* (1896), *Speeches of William Jennings Bryan* (1909 and 1913), and *Heart to Heart Appeals* (1917). *The First Battle* (1896) and *The Second Battle* (1900) contain writings and speeches from presidential campaigns. *William Jennings Bryan: Selections*, edited by Ray Ginger (1967), is a sampling of many issues. *The Memoirs of William Jennings Bryan* (1925), incomplete at his death and finished by his wife, is principally the story of Bryan as a national political figure. *The Commoner* (1901–23) is available in many library archives. Film and sound recordings of Bryan exist.

**FURTHER READING:** Bryan's appeal to Midwestern audiences is studied in Donald Springen's *William Jennings Bryan: Orator of Small Town America* (1991). Biography and bibliography are presented in Robert Cherny's revised *A Righteous Crusade* (1994), LeRoy Ashby's *William Jennings Bryan* (1987), Kendrick Clements's *William Jennings Bryan: Missionary Isolationist* (1982), and Paolo Colleta's *William Jennings Bryan* (1969). DAVID D. ANDERSON provides a critical biography in *William Jennings Bryan* (1981).

Bryan's papers are collected at the Li-

brary of Congress, the State Historical Society of Nebraska, and Occidental College. Because Bryan was a personality who attracted notice, there are many local newspaper reports of his speeches and public appearances.
THOMAS PRIBEK

UNIVERSITY OF WISCONSIN–LACROSSE

## ROBERT JONES BURDETTE
July 30, 1844–November 19, 1914

**BIOGRAPHY:** Robert Burdette, sentimental humorist and minister, was born in Greensboro, Pennsylvania, to Frederick and Sophia (Jones) Burdette and spent his boyhood in Peoria, Illinois. Burdette served with the Illinois Volunteers in the Civil War, taught briefly, then wrote for Peoria newspapers but failed to start his own. In 1874 he began writing for the Burlington, Iowa, *Hawk-eye* and earned popularity as "The Burlington *Hawk-eye* Man," one of several small-town editors and newspaper writers to achieve fame as a humorist. His work was collected in seven volumes and sold more than a million copies. As comic lecturer, he spent eight to ten months a year on the lecture circuit, and his "Rise and Fall of the Moustache" was reputedly performed more than five thousand times. He moved to New York to become a full-time lecturer, was licensed as a Baptist minister in 1887, and eventually settled in California as a preacher although he continued his comic lecturing. Some of his books are products of his ministry. Although he was a social activist, in general he did not mix his humor with strong didacticism. He was married twice, to Carrie Garrett (1870), and after her death to Clara Wheeler-Baker (1899); he had one son, Robert J. Burdette.

**SIGNIFICANCE:** In print and on stage, Burdette possessed the familiar Midwestern style of poker-faced exaggeration with a touch of the absurd, but he lacked the iconoclastic tone and rural setting; his was a civilized persona, with only moderate use of dialect and the comic misspelling popularized by ARTEMUS WARD. Burdette's column, "Hawk-eyetems," contained anecdotes of small-town life in a tone that was satiric, sentimental, and commonsensical but rarely expressed the rough-and-tumble of frontier life. His literary creation, "Tom," was a sweet kid, not a prankster, and for women characters too he used the sentimental tone. Burdette's fictional setting could be any actual Midwestern locale: the same small-town characters appeared by name in columns written in Peoria, Burlington, and elsewhere. His "eyetems," brief news-column fillers, featured conventional poetry as well. He was a good friend of JAMES WHITCOMB RILEY and admired Henry Ward Beecher, both fellows on the lecture circuit. Burdette often preached on his lecture tours.

**SELECTED WORKS:** Collections of lectures and various newspaper pieces include *The Rise and Fall of the Mustache and Other Hawk-Eyetems* (1877), *Hawk-Eyes* (1879), *Innach Garden* (1886), *Schooners That Pass in the Dark* (1894), *Chimes from a Jester's Bells* (1897), *Smiles Yoked with Sighs* (1900), *Old Time and Young Tom* (1912), and *The Silver Trumpets* (1912). Some modern reprints are available.

**FURTHER READING:** JACK CONROY's *Midland Humor* (1947) provides an introduction and selected writing. A useful contemporary resource is A. Augustus Wright's *Who's Who in the Lyceum* (1906). Burdette is featured prominently by selections in MARK TWAIN's *Library of American Humor* (1906). Burdette's wife, Clara, published a biography, *Robert J. Burdette: His Message* (1922). Burdette is covered briefly by CLARENCE ANDREWS's *A Literary History of Iowa* (1972). Gary Engle's unpublished essay for the Society for the Study of Midwestern Literature, "Robert J. Burdette and Midwestern Humor," is useful for comparisons to contemporary humorists.

THOMAS PRIBEK UNIVERSITY OF WISCONSIN–LACROSSE

# WILLIAM S(EWARD) BURROUGHS (II)

February 5, 1914–August 2, 1997

**BIOGRAPHY:** Novelist William Burroughs was born in St. Louis, Missouri, to middle-class parents, Mortimer and Laura (Lee) Burroughs. He attended the John Burroughs School in St. Louis and Los Alamos Ranch (Secondary) School in New Mexico. Thought to be a misfit at Los Alamos, Burroughs left for home two months before graduation. Through the aid of a private tutor, he entered Harvard in 1932; following graduation in 1936, he studied medicine in Vienna. Returning to Harvard in 1937, he studied archaeology for a year and shared a small house with his friend from St. Louis, Kells Elvins. In 1939 Burroughs left Harvard, and after brief interludes in New York, Chicago, and back home in St. Louis,

he followed two friends, Lucien Carr and David Kammerer, to New York in 1943.

Burroughs met Herbert Huncke, a Times Square hustler, and through Huncke's influence, engaged in petty crime and became addicted to heroin. In the environs of Columbia University, he met Allen Ginsberg, Jack Kerouac, and John Clellon Holmes. Older than they, he took the role of mentor and teacher, encouraging the others in their writing efforts. With his friends Ginsberg and Kerouac, Burroughs later became one of the leading writers of the Beat generation of poets and novelists who, in the aftermath of World War II, protested against the atomic bomb and what they saw as a mindless, suburban, consumer society. During this period he lived with Joan Vollmer and later moved with her, via Texas and New Orleans, to Mexico City. Burroughs had a son with Joan: Billy Jr. Wanted by the Mexican police for the death of Joan, whom he accidentally shot while playing a William Tell game, he returned to the United States in 1952. By 1954 he was in Tangier, where he could live comfortably on the two hundred dollars a month he received from his parents, who took Billy Jr. to raise. Burroughs later moved on to Paris and London and did not return to the United States to live until 1974.

With the help of Allen Ginsberg, *Junkie* (1953) was published as a trade paperback by Ace Books under the pseudonym "William Lee." In 1959, *Naked Lunch* was published in Paris by the Olympia Press. Other books followed, and by the end of the 1960s, Burroughs had a worldwide audience for his work. He was a member of the American Academy and Institute of Arts and Letters and a *Commandeur de l'Ordre des Arts et des Lettres* of France. Burroughs died of a heart attack in Lawrence, Kansas.

**SIGNIFICANCE:** William S. Burroughs was a postmodern experimentalist and a black humorist. His Midwestern humoristic storyteller's approach was reflected in his themes and characters, especially in his later writings. While *Junkie* was written as a flat, realistic narrative, with *Naked Lunch* and *Nova Express* (1964) Burroughs the humorist found his voice. Burroughs said he was ridding himself of his "educated Middlewest background" in the writing of *Naked Lunch* (Charters, *The Portable Beat Reader* 103), but his humor structured the style of the novel, as did a futuristic surrealism. This tendency is fully developed in his trilogy, *Cities of the Red Night* (1981), *The Place of Dead Roads* (1984), and *The Western Lands* (1987). In collaboration with Brion Gysin, Burroughs worked on "cut ups" and other forms of automatic writing in the late 1950s and early 1960s (Miles, *William Burroughs*, 111–28).

Burroughs was a strong influence on other members of the Beat generation, especially on Allen Ginsberg and Jack Kerouac, and the details of his life are part of the folklore of the Beat movement. He appears as Old Bull Lee in Kerouac's *On the Road* (1957) and is present under other pseudonyms in Kerouac's *The Subterraneans* (1958), *The Town and the City* (1950), and *The Vanity of Duluoz* (1967). He is mentioned in Ginsberg's poem *Howl*. Several cult filmmakers have noted his influence on their work, and in the 1970s and 1980s he was an icon of the punk movement. He has been the subject of much critical attention in Europe, where he is considered a leading literary postmodernist.

**SELECTED WORKS:** Burroughs's works include a memoir of his days as a petty thief and addict, *Junkie* (1953). *Naked Lunch*, a fable of a futuristic world of bureaucratic mind control, caused a sensation when it was first published in the United States (1959). It was followed by *The Soft Machine* (1961), *The Ticket That Exploded* (1962), and *Nova Express* (1964). *Exterminator* (1973) chronicles his experience in Chicago during World War II. *Cities of the Red Night* (1981), *The Place of Dead Roads* (1983), and *The Western Lands* (1987) are a futuristic trilogy. *Queer* (1985) is a story of unrequited homosexual love. *The Yage Letters* (1963) includes correspondence between Burroughs and Allen Ginsberg. Many of his shorter writings are collected in *The Burroughs File* (1984) and *The Adding Machine* (1985).

**FURTHER READING:** *Literary Outlaw: The Life and Times of William S. Burroughs*, by Ted Morgan (1988), is a detailed biography and a chronicle of Burroughs's relationship to the Beat generation. *William Burroughs: El Hombre Invisible*, by Barry Miles (1992), is an introduction to his work and contains a useful bibliography of first editions of his publications. *The Portable Beat Reader*, edited by Ann Charters (1992), includes four selections from his works. *The Birth of the Beat Generation:*

*Visionaries, Rebels, and Hipsters, 1944–1960*, by Steven Watson (1995), is an informative introduction to the Beats and their early writings. Arizona State University at Tempe holds a collection of Burroughs manuscripts, and the Ginsberg repository at Columbia University contains important Burroughs materials.

TOM L. PAGE              WICHITA STATE UNIVERSITY

## ELLIS PARKER BUTLER
December 5, 1869–September 13, 1937

**BIOGRAPHY:** Humorist Ellis Parker Butler was born in Muscatine, Iowa, the eldest of Audley and Adelia (Vesey) Butler's eight children. Butler's formal education ended when he left high school after his freshman year to help support his siblings. However, he began to write verses and humor pieces at this time and was an early contributor to JOHN T. FREDERICK's *Midland Monthly*. In 1897 Butler moved to New York where he wrote for several trade papers while continuing to publish humor pieces until the phenomenal success of *Pigs Is Pigs* (1906) allowed him to sustain a career as a full-time humorist. He married Ida Zipser in 1899; the couple moved to Flushing, New York. There they raised four children and Butler continued to gain fame as a writer and speaker, serving as president of the Authors League of America and the Flushing Federated Savings and Loan. In 1935 Butler retired, moving to Williamsville, Massachusetts, where he died at the age of sixty-seven.

**SIGNIFICANCE:** Of Butler's thirty-two books, those that most engagingly evoke a Midwestern ambiance are his boys' books. Butler's fond memories of his own boyhood on the Mississippi, fishing in sloughs and inlets with his ragtag gang in a beat-up motorboat, hunting for buried treasure, and solving mysteries are amusingly recalled in *Swatty* (1920), *Jibby Jones* (1923), and *Jibby Jones and the Alligator* (1924), all set in Riverbank, Iowa, a fictionalized Muscatine. Butler's novel *Dominie Dean* (1917), also set in Riverbank, is interesting as a social history of mid-nineteenth-century life in a Mississippi River town, emphasizing the dominance of crass commercial interests in the vicissitudes of small-town life. Butler treats this theme satirically in an earlier novel set in central Iowa, *Kilo* (1907), a humorous account of book agent

Eliph' Hewlitt's successful but convoluted efforts to win the heart of the town's most desirable maiden. However, Butler is at his best in portraying Midwestern values and character in "Bread," published in *Prairie Gold by Iowa Authors and Artists* (1917). In this well-crafted short story, wheat bread functions metonymically to suggest the life-sustaining gifts of the heartland to several generations of an Iowa pioneer family.

**SELECTED WORKS:** Butler's best-known works include *Pigs Is Pigs* (1906), *The Great American Pie Company* (1907), *Kilo* (1907), *That Pup* (1908), *Mike Flannery, On Duty and Off* (1909), *Dominie Dean* (1917), *Goat-Feathers* (1919), *Swatty* (1920), *Ghosts What Ain't* (1923), *Jibby Jones* (1923), *Jibby Jones and the Alligator* (1924), *The Behind Legs of the 'orse* (1927), and *Pups and Pies* (1927).

**FURTHER READING:** There are no book-length studies or scholarly articles on Butler or his works. Frank Luther Mott's amusing essay "Ellis Parker Butler," in *A Book of Iowa Authors by Iowa Authors*, edited by Johnson Brigham (1930): 31–42, is a good place to start reading about Butler. A brief biographical entry and an exhaustive bibliography are found in Frank Pakula's *Iowa Authors* (1967), and CLARENCE ANDREWS devotes several pages to Butler in *A Literary History of Iowa* (1972). Butler's papers are held by the New York Public Library.

MARCIA NOE

THE UNIVERSITY OF TENNESSEE AT CHATTANOOGA

# C

## MARCUS CAFAGÑA
December 12, 1956

**BIOGRAPHY:** Marcus Cafagña, poet, was born in Ann Arbor, Michigan, to Albert Carl and Dora (Favale) Cafagña, then University of Michigan graduate students active in the Congress of Racial Equality (CORE). They divorced in 1963, and the future poet soon moved with his mother to East Lansing, Michigan, where he would attend school and later earn degrees in English at Michigan State University (BA 1986, MA 1989). He married Dianne Kitsmiller, also a poet and graduate student, in 1987; she died in 1993. Already well-published in major literary journals, Cafagña was selected for the 1995 National Poetry Series for his first book, *The Broken World* (1996). He currently lives in Philadelphia, Pennsylvania.

**SIGNIFICANCE:** Marcus Cafagña's poetry emerges from Midwestern cities, particularly in Michigan, though his sympathies range from the postwar New York of his Jewish relatives, Holocaust survivors, to the desert Southwest. In selecting *The Broken World* for the National Poetry Series, Pulitzer Prize–winning poet Yusef Komunyakaa praised Cafagña's "beguiling clarity that distills fragmented moments and attempts to connect them" (*The Broken World* xv). While this concern with psychic and social fragmentation recalls the modernism of Williams and Crane, Cafagña's Midwestern locus connects him to a long-standing urban tradition that includes CARL SANDBURG, GWENDOLYN BROOKS, and JIM DANIELS. Like his predecessors, Cafagña tends toward portraiture, seeing himself in others and bearing witness to the pain meted out by malevolence, fate, or chance. *The Broken World* begins with narratives of individuals caught up in circumstance—a distressed girl on a Detroit overpass, for example, and a boy shooting baskets at a crisis center. But as suggested by the book's epigraph, a foreboding passage from Raymond Carver's story "A Small, Good Thing," fate can turn against the observer. The book's last section focuses on the poet's marriage, lived out in Michigan, which tragically ended in his wife's suicide, a death which comes to symbolize the confusion, cruelty, and madness of the twentieth century.

**SELECTED WORKS:** Cafagña's poems have appeared in *Poetry, Iowa Review, Kenyon Review, Quarterly, Harvard Review, Ploughshares*, and many other journals. His books of poetry are *The Broken World* (1996) and *Roman Fever* (2000).

Marcus Cafagña.
Photo by Cherelyn Bush. Courtesy of Marcus Cafagña

**FURTHER READING:** A consideration of Cafagña's interest in the World War II era appears in "'Bandages Finally Lifted from My Eyes': A Poet's Sense of History," *Muses* (Michigan State University College of Arts and Letters, 1992–93): 24. Keith Taylor's "Marcus Cafagña: No Easy Answers," *Ann Arbor Observer* (October 1996): 27, compares Cafagña's poetry to that of Sylvia Plath, noting "one big difference. Where Plath wrote to save herself, Cafagña writes out of compassion for those he loves, and the knowledge he gains is perhaps a more painful one." Reviews of *The Broken World* include Jane McCafferty's "Zeroing in on Emotional Truths," *Pittsburgh Post-Gazette* (August 18, 1996): G11–12; William Barillas's *Harvard Review* 11 (Fall 1996): 174–75; Frank Allen's "Dilemmas of Communication," *Poet Lore* 91.4 (Winter 1996–97): 56–57; and Joyce Peseroff's *Ploughshares* 23.1 (Spring 1997): 209–10.

WILLIAM BARILLAS

UNIVERSITY OF WISCONSIN–LA CROSSE

## LOUIS J. CANTONI
May 22, 1919

**BIOGRAPHY:** Louis Cantoni, a poet and sculptor as well as a professional psychologist, was born in Detroit, Michigan, where he has lived much of his life. He is the son of Pietro and Stella (Puricelli) Cantoni. The recipient of the AB from the University of California at Berkeley in 1946, and the MSW in 1949 and the PhD in 1959 from the University of Michigan, he married Lucile Eudora Moses in 1948 and is the father of two children.

Professionally affiliated with Wayne State University for much of his career, where he was professor of psychology and director of the Graduate Program in Rehabilitation Counseling, he has published widely in his professional field at the same time that he has published many poems in a wide variety of journals. He has received much professional recognition including the Award for Meritorious Service from Wayne State University, and he has also been recognized for his poetry, including the Edwin A. Falkowski Memorial Award from the World Poetry Society in 1990. He served in the U.S. Army during World War II and was released as a second lieutenant.

**SIGNIFICANCE:** Cantoni draws heavily on his own experiences as a psychologist, his family relationships, his close observations of life in Detroit, and his clear eye for and wonder at the natural world as the basis of much of his poetry. Also clearly evident are his love of music, his close attention to details, and his eagerness to experiment with the forms as well as the sounds and rhythms of his verse. His poems are at once wide-ranging and carefully focused as they reflect a life well lived in the urban Midwest in the second half of the twentieth century as a manifestation of the human condition.

**SELECTED WORKS:** Cantoni has published three collections of poetry, *With Joy I Called to You* (1969), *Gradually the Dreams Change* (1979), and *A Festival of Lanternes* (1994). He also edited *Golden Song: The Fiftieth Anniversary Anthology of the Poetry Society of Michigan 1935–1985* (1985) and has published more than a hundred poems in periodicals as well as essays in the *Society for the Study of Midwestern Literature Newsletter*.

**FURTHER READING:** Cantoni is listed in *Who's Who in America*, and his works are widely reviewed.

DAVID D. ANDERSON     MICHIGAN STATE UNIVERSITY

## WILL(IAM McKENDREE) CARLETON
October 21, 1845–December 18, 1912

**BIOGRAPHY:** Growing up on the farm where

**Will Carleton.**
Courtesy of the University of Kentucky Libraries

he was born near Hudson, Michigan, Will Carleton was a dreamy boy whose father, John H. Carleton, was mildly disapproving of his ambition to be a poet. His mother, Celestia (Smith) Carleton, was supportive. Rejected for service in the Union Army, Carleton entered Hillsdale College in September 1865. The need to work prolonged his college years, but he graduated in 1869. He made his living by writing, principally verse, though he also sold articles and fiction, lectured on literature, and gave readings of his poetry. To be close to editors, he moved to Boston in 1878 and then in 1882 to Brooklyn. On March 2, 1882, he married Adora Niles Goodell. The couple had no children. Adora died on November 9, 1909. Will died of pneumonia in Brooklyn on December 18, 1912.

**SIGNIFICANCE:** Carleton's verse expresses the nostalgia Americans felt in the decades when they were moving from the farm to the city. Some poems also suggest sociological significances he may not have been aware of. Amos Elwood Corning, his friend and author of the brief book *Will Carleton* (1917), aptly terms his subject the "heart-element" in daily life. Readers in less moralistic years recognize that Carleton's poems reflect the weakening in Midwestern rural domestic life of the strong family ties that had been characteristic of the agricultural age.

His two best-known poems draw on observations he made while working on a newspaper, the *Hillsdale Standard*. Both were first published in 1871 in the Toledo *Blade*. "Betsey and I Are Out," printed on March 17, gives the story of a divorce which a Hillsdale lawyer had told Carleton about. Like many realistic novelists, Carleton loaded a heavy freight of moralizing pathos onto his narrative. The poem shows the slow accretion of minor arguments that brings an apparently good marriage to an end. Appearing at a time when divorce, once rare, was becoming common, the poem impressed readers with its recognition that routine frictions may kill a marriage.

The famous "Over the Hill to the Poor-House," printed on June 17, is based on Carleton's awareness that the majority of those sent to the county poorhouse near Hillsdale were elderly women. The speaker, a widow, tries living with each of her five surviving children but finds it impossible to win acceptance. Readers of that day saw the poem as an account of familiar experiences; perhaps few then realized that the institution of the extended family was beginning to disappear.

Poems on urban life that Carleton published after moving to the city lack the strong feeling of many of his pieces on Midwestern rural life. It is fair to say that his later poems show him trying to repeat the success of his early career.

**SELECTED WORKS:** Carleton wrote verse all his life, but the poems in *Farm Ballads* (1873) remain his best known. The book includes both pieces that brought him early fame, "Betsey and I Are Out" and "Over the Hill to the Poor-House." This collection has frequently been reprinted, sometimes in editions with bucolic rural scenes and gold stampings on the covers. Carleton later designated it as the first of three volumes in his Farm series; the others are *Farm Legends* (1875) and *Farm Festivals* (1881). Also among works of his prime are the three volumes in the City series, including *City Ballads* (1885), *City Legends* (1889), and *City Festivals* (1892). Carleton also published short stories and children's verse. He wrote five plays, two of them labeled dramas and three designated as one-act farces. Altogether, his books sold more than six hundred thousand copies. His fame, however, comes principally from "Over the Hill to the Poor-House." In 1920 William Knox produced a film version of the poem. This ran for more than a year in New York and was then shown throughout the country. Edward Albee in his play "Quotations from Chairman Mao Tse-Tung" (1968) parallels lines from the poem with sayings by the dictator to suggest that banality is universal. The building that served as the Hillsdale County Poorhouse burned down in 1867 but was restored and used as a farmhouse; in 1989 it was refurbished for the county historical society. A plaque honoring Carleton is mounted on a boulder in front of the building. A law making Carleton's birthday a school holiday in Michigan is still on the books, although it is no longer observed.

**FURTHER READING:** No major biographies have appeared. Carleton's papers and memorabilia are in the Carr Library at Hillsdale College. His friend and schoolmate Byron A. Finney set down his reminiscences in the essay "Will Carleton, Michigan's Poet." This appeared in *Michigan Historical Collections* 39 (1915): 30–42. Amos Elwood Corning's brief book *Will Carleton* (1917) is more useful, giving a sketch of Carleton's life and several pages of critical comment. Corning approves of Carleton's moralizing but finds flaws in his diction and versification. Jerome A. Fallon's *The Will Carleton Poorhouse* (1989) recognizes that his "poetic gifts were hardly Wordsworthian" but maintains that he was able to "ignite" the moral convictions of his readers (23). It is unlikely that the future will see Carleton's work as having aesthetic importance. However, the sociological significance of his best-known poems may keep his name alive. Additionally, the title "Over the Hill to the Poor-House" has become a stock expression everywhere English is spoken.

BERNARD F. ENGEL    MICHIGAN STATE UNIVERSITY

# ALICE CARY
April 26, 1820–February 12, 1871

# PHOEBE CARY
September 4, 1824–July 31, 1871

**BIOGRAPHY:** Alice and Phoebe Cary were among the first well-known poets of the Midwest. With seven brothers and sisters, they were born and grew up on the farm known as Clovernook, eight miles north of Cincinnati. Their parents, Robert Cary and Elizabeth

Alice and Phoebe Cary.
Courtesy of David D. Anderson

(Jessup) Cary, were both fond of reading. The sisters continued to write of Ohio fields and forests and of rural life even though they moved to New York, Alice in 1850 and Phoebe early in 1851. They made their home in the city

a literary salon, having such guests as Rufus Griswold, John Greenleaf Whittier, Horace Greeley, and Bayard Taylor.

SIGNIFICANCE: Country life in the Midwest gave the Cary sisters a stock of topics and metaphors, imagery, and analogies. Didactic to the core, they wrote poems of devotion, love, nature, moral assertion, and social comment. Both women were fond of graveyard scenes, penitent sinners, dying prisoners, examples of fortitude, and triumphs of good over evil. They sometimes published their poems in the same volume, and they both took as models Tennyson, Longfellow, Whittier, and, above all, their hymn books.

Though better known for verse, Alice also published four novels and numerous "sketches," much of this output dealing with people and situations seen, or purportedly seen, at Clovernook. Her prose often has the same overburden of religiosity and the funereal that thickens her verse. The Dickensian story "Eliza Anderson" in *Clovernook Sketches*, second series (1853), telling of a failed rural romance, has characters who in the end have physical or emotional troubles paralleling their moral condition. Eliza herself does not smile, George is lame and has lost one arm, and Casper goes late at night to Eliza's gate to mourn what might have been. Alice, indeed, was moving toward the study of Midwestern village characters, a practice later to be exploited by EDGAR LEE MASTERS and SHERWOOD ANDERSON among others.

Seeing her as an early literary Realist, Henry Nash Smith, in his 1950 book *Virgin Land*, wrote that she could observe closely because she disregarded demands that Midwestern writers contrast their region with the East. Certainly Alice presented emotions and circumstances of the domestic life that mid-century people saw as the center of existence. Her ties to the domestic, however, caused Alice to judge her characters by the standards of sentimental moralism.

Most readers think Alice's best verse is that which draws on observation. Her poem "The Spinster's Stint" shows effectively the eagerness of a young woman to finish work at the spinning wheel in order to make ready for a visit from a young man. "Summer Storm" records a close look at the behavior of farm animals as heavy weather approaches. The lines note what only one who pays careful attention would see—that sheep, though considered the consummate herd animals, abandon their formation to seek shelter individually.

In religious poems, Alice usually followed the convention of finding a heartening spiritual message in an object or circumstance of nature or in some bit of human behavior. Rarely, however, she could avoid easy consolations. In the poem "Contradictory," her speaker recites a roster of glooms and ends with what is in popular verse the decidedly unconventional realization that in maturity we lose youthful ardors "Until we stand against the last black truth / Naked and cold, and desolate enough" (*Poetical Works* 156–57).

Phoebe Cary seems always to have played the role of little sister, leaving responsibilities to Alice. Phoebe, however, was more interested in the men and women of her world, including other literary figures, and the social codes they followed. This interest led her to produce parodies and satires on the work of even so famous a contemporary as Longfellow. In her poem "A Psalm of Life: What the Heart of the Young Woman Said to the Old Man," anthologized in William Coggeshall's *The Poets and Poetry of the West* (1860), the speaker aptly sends up Longfellow by applying the urgings of his "A Psalm of Life" to society's insistence that the only success for a woman is getting married. Phoebe declares: "Tell me not, in idle jingle, / Marriage is an empty dream, / For the girl is dead that's single, / And things are not what they seem" (361). Phoebe could also perceive the cruelty in the century's requirements for "old maids." The poem "The Christian Woman" recognizes that the unmarried woman is supposed to lead a self-sacrificing life as comforter of the prisoner and the dying, must never know passionate love, and is expected to reinforce moral precepts. This and a handful of other poems by Phoebe expresses the restlessness that was increasing among women who could cast a cold eye on their society.

Phoebe's abilities sometimes appear even in routine work. "Light in Darkness" is an exhortation to recognize that comfort may be found on even the darkest day. But the reader willing to tolerate blatant cheerfulness, and to dispense with irony, will recognize Phoebe's skill in use of one-syllable words and of sound repetitions. Phoebe could also write spirited dialogue. The poem "Was He Henpecked?", appearing in Roman Clemmer's *A Memorial of Alice and Phoebe Cary* (1874), shows a man and wife talking past each other. The woman frets under the restrictions placed on members of her gender; the man, unable to understand her objections, is the most stuffed of shirts.

Both Cary sisters usually accepted the ways of their time. But Alice's ability to present observations, and Phoebe's knack for perceiving realities often obscured by social pretense, can still please. The Cary sisters show that Midwestern writers were not wholly in the grip of the staid.

**SELECTED WORKS:** The principal source for poems by the sisters is *The Poetical Works of Alice and Phoebe Cary*, edited by Mary Clemmer (1881).

**FURTHER READING:** Judith Fetterley has edited a collection of Alice's prose entitled *Clovernook Sketches and Other Stories* (1987). Though the focus is on Alice, Fetterley often compares her with Phoebe. Fetterley writes as a moderate feminist. She perhaps overemphasizes the significance of Alice's funereal tone. This tone was much in vogue in the midcentury decades, and does not necessarily imply that an author's own experiences were unbearably sad. An important early source is W. H. Venable's *The Beginnings of Literary Culture in the Ohio Valley* (1891).

BERNARD F. ENGEL    MICHIGAN STATE UNIVERSITY

## VERA CASPARY

November 13, 1904–June 13, 1987

**BIOGRAPHY:** Born and educated in Chicago, to Paul and Julia (Cohen) Caspary, Vera Caspary departed from her conservative Jewish upbringing to enter the professional world as a writer. In her early twenties, she had already worked as a stenographer, editor, and composer of advertising copy. From 1925 to 1927 she served as editor of *Dance* magazine, then struck out on her own as a freelance writer. Caspary's recognition as an author of novels, dramas, and screenplays grew steadily, but the publication of *Laura* in 1943 and Otto Preminger's highly memorable 1944 film version elevated her to national stature.

She married Isadore G. Goldsmith, a film producer, in 1949, and remained his partner until his death in 1964. During these years, her writing career flourished. She published a series of best-selling novels, and several of her plays were produced successfully on Broadway, including her own adaptation of *Laura*. Of the seventeen screenplays that she wrote or coauthored, many were critical and commercial hits. She was honored by the Screen Writers Guild for two significant films: *A Letter to Three Wives* (1949) and *Les Girls* (1957). Caspary continued to write well into the 1970s; her final book, an autobiography published in 1979, marked the consummation of a productive career that spanned over fifty years.

**SIGNIFICANCE:** As she demonstrates in her autobiography, *The Secrets of Grown-Ups* (1979), Caspary's formative years in Chicago had a shaping influence on her fiction. Her early efforts to launch a career as a writer and her experiences as an independent woman in an urban culture not yet prepared for female professionals stayed with her and became recurrent subjects in her fiction.

Though her output was substantial and diverse, Caspary is best known for her mystery novel *Laura*, a classic that remains an American favorite. Here, she set forth a number of the fictional techniques and themes that govern her best work. *Laura* presents the story of a police detective who falls in love with a murdered woman during the investigation of her apparent death. When the victim turns up alive, the detective must sort through a complex knot of deceptions to uncover the identity of the dead woman and her killer. Using the device of multiple narration, Caspary enhances suspense and fosters psychological disclosure that leads to the solution of the crime.

Recent feminist commentary on *Laura* demonstrates the way Caspary probes, if not necessarily resolves, important questions about women's vulnerability to emotional and sexual exploitation in a patriarchal society. She addresses the pitfalls for women in the professional world as well as those embedded in the misleading promises of romantic courtship and marriage. Such questions are treated as well in many of Caspary's other novels, particularly in *Stranger Than Truth* (1946), *False Face* (1954), *The Husband* (1957), *Evvie* (1960), and *The Man Who Loved His Wife* (1966). Caspary confronts her Jewish heritage in *A Chosen Sparrow* (1964), the story of a woman who survives the Nazi death camps only to relive psychically the holocaust in her marriage to a brutal man. Her eventual liberation from his influence reprises the pattern evident in most of Caspary's novels, that of women achieving a measure of self-possession after personal struggle.

Though her later life was spent in New York and Hollywood, Caspary was haunted by her Midwestern roots. Her autobiography begins and ends with the poignant memory of herself as a young working woman waiting for the train at a south side Chicago el station, dreaming of the better life that can be hers only after strife and with great determination. For Caspary, Chicago was a symbol of the promise—and elusiveness—of the American Dream.

**SELECTED WORKS:** Caspary's output was considerable, but her best-known works are novels written during the three decades from the 1940s through the 1960s. These include *Laura* (1943), *Bedelia* (1945), *The Murder in the Stork Club* (1946), *Stranger Than Truth* (1946), *Thelma* (1952), *False Face* (1954), *The Husband* (1957), *Evvie* (1960), *A Chosen Sparrow* (1964), and *The Man Who Loved His Wife* (1966), along with her autobiography, *The Secrets of Grown-Ups* (1979).

**FURTHER READING:** There is surprisingly little critical treatment of Caspary's work. JANE BAKERMAN's two essays, "Vera Caspary's Chicago, Symbol and Setting," in *MidAmerica* 11 (1984): 81–89, and "Vera Caspary's Fascinating Females: Laura, Evvie, and Bedelia," in *Clues* 1.1 (1980): 46–52, are especially valuable, as is Eugene McNamara's book *Laura as Novel, Film, and Myth* (1992). For feminist interpretations of Caspary's work, see Gary Storhoff's "Vera Caspary," in *Great Women Mystery Writers: Classic to Contemporary*, edited by Kathleen Klein (1994), and Liahna Babener's "De-feminizing *Laura*: Novel to Film," in *It's a Print!: Detective Fiction from Page to Screen*, edited by William Reynolds and Elizabeth Trembley (1994).

LIAHNA BABENER CENTRAL WASHINGTON UNIVERSITY

# R(ONALD) V(ERLIN) CASSILL
May 17, 1919

**BIOGRAPHY:** Born in Cedar Falls, Iowa, the son of Howard Earl and Mary (Glosser) Cassill, while his parents were attending Iowa State Teachers College, R. V. Cassill was reared in several Iowa towns and graduated from Blakesburg High School. Reading Zane Grey's *Desert Gold* as a boy provided him with a glimpse not of escape but of the far horizons of the imagination, and he became and remained a voracious reader. Cassill hitchhiked around the country after graduation and then enrolled in the Iowa State Teachers College. In college he was inspired to paint and to write. He remained a competent painter, with a number of exhibits and prizes to his credit, but he was to become a prolific, respected writer. He graduated from the University of Iowa in 1939 and married Kathleen Rosecrans in 1941. Cassill served in the Far East as a first lieutenant in the U.S. Army Medical Corps in World War II, traveled and studied in Europe, and then began a varied career as an academic, editor, and writer in Illinois and Iowa, receiving an MA from the University of Iowa in 1949.

Cassill and Kathleen Rosecrans were divorced in 1952, and the next year he moved East to write and edit. In 1956 he married Karilyn Kay Adams, with whom he had three children, Orin, Erica, and Jesse. In 1966 he settled at Brown University to teach and write. In 1968–69 he received a Guggenheim Fellowship, and he remained at Brown until 1983, when he became professor emeritus. He lives in Providence, Rhode Island, where he continues to write.

**SIGNIFICANCE:** As Cassill made clear in an essay entitled "Why I Left the Midwest," in his collection *In an Iron Time: Statements and Reiterations* (1969), his relationship with the Midwest, as a human being as well as a writer, has been ambiguous, as places of origin have been with so many other writers. For Cassill the ambiguity has been both an asset, providing background, setting, characters, and values to much of his best fiction, and a detriment, limiting his perception of the larger world beyond the Midwest. This dichotomy also provides a significant motif in much of his fiction, that of the Midwesterner who is also an artist and who, like Cassill, finds himself in exile from the place that has given him form and direction.

This motif provides the substance of Cassill's first novel, *The Eagle on the Coin* (1950), as it does in his comic satire *La Vie Passionnée of Rodney Buckthorne* (1968). It is reversed in his best novel, *Clem Anderson* (1961). Based loosely on the life of Dylan Thomas, *Clem Anderson* is the story of the success and decline of a distinguished American poet, as seen by his narrator-friend. As the novel nears its denouement, the poet has an unsettling vision in a Kansas game preserve which gives him, however momentarily, a sense of the myth of the poet. *Clem Anderson* is a substantial, innovative novel that has been too little appreciated. *Labors of Love* (1980) is, like the earlier novels, somewhat autobiographical as it examines the conditions of the novelist's life and the obligations that limit him. Like much of Cassill's work, including *Dr. Cobb's Game* (1970), based on the Profumo scandal in England in the early 1960s, *Labors of Love* is shadowed by a strongly psychosexual mood.

**SELECTED WORKS:** Cassill's original paperback novels, such as *The Wound of Love* (1956), *My Sister's Keeper* (1961), and *Night School* (1961), are superior examples of popular erotic fiction. Other novels, including *The President* (1964), *The Goss Women* (1974), *Flame* (1980), and the novella *Unknown Soldier* (1990), are well worth reading, as are his collections of short stories, including *The Father, and Other Stories* (1965), *Patrimonies* (1987), *Collected Stories of R. V. Cassill* (1989), and *Late Stories* (1993). *The Eagle on the Coin* (1950) and *La Vie Passionnée of Rodney Buckthorne* (1968) are also interesting novels, but *Clem Anderson* (1961) remains his best work. *In an Iron Time* (1969), *Doctor Cobb's Game* (1970), *Hoyt's Child* (1976), *Labors of Love* (1980), and *After Goliath* (1985) are among his other works. He has also edited *The Norton Anthology of Short Fiction* (1977, 1981, 1986, 1990, 1995) and *The Anthology of Contemporary Fiction* (1987, 1997).

**FURTHER READING:** No book has yet appeared on Cassill's life and work, but he is treated in detail in CLARENCE A. ANDREWS's *A Literary History of Iowa* (1972). His works have been extensively reviewed, and he is considered in *Contemporary Literary Criticism* 4 (1975): 94–95, *Contemporary Novelists* (1986): 177–79, and *Dictionary of Literary Biography* 6 (1980): 33–36.

DAVID D. ANDERSON   MICHIGAN STATE UNIVERSITY

## WILLA CATHER
December 7, 1873–April 24, 1947

**BIOGRAPHY:** Willa Cather was not a native of the Nebraska that she made famous in her novels and stories; she was born in Back Creek Valley, Virginia, the eldest of Charles and Mary Virginia (Boak) Cather's seven children. When nine-year-old Willa moved with her family to a ranch outside Red Cloud, Nebraska, she felt as if she had come to the end of everything. But Nebraska would prove to be a beginning, not an end, for the land that at first seemed to her so empty was full of stories, stories which would help a young writer find her own voice and establish herself as a major American novelist.

The young Willa was strongly influenced by her grandmother, Rachel Boak, who fostered an early love of reading and introduced her to such works as the Bible and *Pilgrim's Progress*. After graduating from Red Cloud High School in 1890, Cather entered the University of Nebraska at Lincoln, where she majored in classics and English, reviewing plays and concerts for the *Nebraska State Journal* during her junior year. Her university years also brought emotional involvements with college friends Dorothy Canfield and Louise Pound, initiating a pattern of close female friendships that would continue throughout her life.

Cather earned her BA in 1895 and left Nebraska a year later for Pittsburgh, where she worked as managing editor of the *Home Monthly*. For the next ten years she would live in Pittsburgh, writing, editing, and teaching high school English. In 1899 she began a four-decade friendship with Isabelle McClung, moving into Isabelle's family home in Pittsburgh and traveling to Europe with her in 1902. She published a volume of poems, *April Twilights*, in 1903, and her first short story collection, *The Troll Garden*, appeared in 1905.

The following year Cather moved to New York after S. S. McClure hired her as associate editor for his muckraking magazine. There she met Edith Lewis, a young copyreader at *McClure's*, with whom she would share her life for nearly forty years. The *McClure's* job also introduced Cather to a second woman who would change her life; when in Boston researching a series of articles on Mary Baker Eddy, she met Sarah Orne Jewett, who advised Cather to leave journalism and concentrate on fiction writing. Taking her advice, Cather gave notice to McClure in 1912, the year her first novel, *Alexander's Bridge*, was published.

In 1913 *O Pioneers!* appeared, the inaugural volume of Cather's chronicle of the Garden of the West. She continued to trace its transformation from wilderness to commodity in *The*

Song of the Lark (1915), My Ántonia (1918), and the Pulitzer Prize–winning One of Ours (1922). During this decade Isabelle McClung's marriage to Jan Hambourg was a terrible shock to Cather; this event, coupled with the trauma of World War I, may have motivated Cather to write that around 1922, the world broke in two. A Lost Lady (1923), The Professor's House (1925), and My Mortal Enemy (1926) were written out of this sense of loss and disillusionment.

Cather found inspiration in the historical past for Death Comes for the Archbishop (1927) and Shadows on the Rock (1931), turning again to her Nebraska roots for Lucy Gayheart (1935), and then to Virginia family history for Sapphira and the Slave Girl (1940). The last two decades of her life brought many honors: the Howells Medal for fiction in 1930, the Prix Femina Americaine in 1932 for Shadows on the Rock, a National Institute of Arts and Letters gold medal in 1944, numerous honorary degrees, and a Time cover story. She died of a cerebral hemorrhage in New York City at age 73.

**SIGNIFICANCE:** Though Cather would set novels in the American Southwest, in Quebec, and in Avignon, France, Nebraska would provide the inspiration for her best work. O Pioneers!, My Ántonia, and A Lost Lady, written over a period of ten years, can be viewed as three parts of Cather's great pastoral trilogy that enact the promise, fruition, and decline of the Garden of the West.

As Alexandra Bergson, the heroine of O Pioneers!, grows to maturity, she participates in the transformation of the wilderness of the Nebraska Divide into fields of grain, gardens, and orchards. Alexandra's love of the land and of living things is reflected in her love for old Ivar, who lives in a sod house, doctors sick animals, and lives alongside the wild ones as a brother. Her refusal to allow her brothers to hunt on old Ivar's property and her tender protection of him from those who want him declared insane demonstrate that her ethic centers on a respect for nature that prohibits the wanton destruction of nature's creatures. By closely linking Alexandra with nature in this novel, Cather parallels Alexandra's maturation into a strong, self-reliant woman with the development of the region.

In My Ántonia Cather represents the Midwest at its peak, with its vast fertile farmlands offering a new chance to everyone who is willing to work hard. The title character,

Willa Cather.
Courtesy of the Nebraska State Historical Society

Ántonia Shimerda Cuzak, symbolizes the fecundity of the region and the fruition of its early promise; after much struggle and suffering, she achieves the good life on the prairie with her farmer husband and many children. Cather also stresses the democratic possibilities of the Garden of the West by including a multitude of other immigrant characters: Russian Peter, who cherishes the cow he could never have owned in Russia, the Italians who establish the dancing school, and the Scandinavian and Bohemian hired girls who achieve dignity and self-sufficiency as farm wives. The central symbol of the novel, a plow silhouetted and magnified against the setting sun, suggests Cather's belief in the power and beauty of the agrarian dream.

A Lost Lady chronicles the decline of Captain Daniel Forrester, one of the giants of the pioneer era, who helped to build the railroads and develop the Midwest, but whose strong ethic of honesty and reverence for the environment leaves him vulnerable to the next generation, opportunists like lawyer Ivy Peters who are interested only in profit and plunder. Forrester's defeat is echoed in the moral and social degeneration of the title character, his wife, Marian. Once a paragon of beauty and social graces, Marian becomes an aging and impoverished widow who, out of expediency, succumbs to Peters's advances. The couple's loss of fortune and social standing can be read as an analog of the region's loss of innocence and of the failure of the Jeffersonian dream, as the prairie paradise so carefully cultivated by their generation is destroyed by the predatory Peters and his contemporaries.

But if the novels in Cather's pastoral trilogy represent the Midwest as an abundant garden, many of her other works portray it as a cultural desert. Cather exposes the meager cultural resources of the region in *One of Ours*, particularly in the first half of the novel, which offers a detailed account of the daily life of the Nat Wheelers, a typical well-to-do Nebraska farm family in the early twentieth century. Cather focuses on two major regional attitudes that frustrate those seeking a rich life of the mind and spirit: an obsession with money and material goods and an enslavement to religious fundamentalism.

The master trope of this novel is the machine, which in its many manifestations represents the materialistic values of the Wheelers and most of their neighbors. Enid Royce, who marries the protagonist, owns an electric car and is a skilled and enthusiastic driver. The Royces' mill, once powered by water, is now run by a gasoline engine while the old waterwheel lies choked with weeds. Mahailey, the Wheelers' hired girl, is continually confused by labor-saving devices, such as the dishwasher, that are introduced into her kitchen.

The Wheelers always have money for more land, more automobiles, more farm machinery, and more household appliances but none for university tuition for their son Claude, the novel's central figure. His attempts to broaden his cultural and intellectual horizons are thwarted by his philistine father and brothers and his Bible-quoting mother. The cultural sterility of their home life is set in relief against the Erlich household in Lincoln, which Claude loves to visit because it is filled with books, music, and conversation. Ironically, in his native state of Nebraska, Claude is never able to fit in; it is only after he is shipped overseas to fight the Kaiser that he is able to develop fully as a person and achieve a sense of belonging shortly before he dies in World War I.

Like *One of Ours*, many of Cather's short stories emphasize the cultural limitations of her region. Some stories focus on the inability of Midwesterners obsessed with getting and spending to appreciate those with artistic sensibilities or nonconformist views. Cather handles this theme with skillful irony in "The Sculptor's Funeral," using a third-person observer to note the contrast between the subtleties of deceased sculptor Harvey Merrick's talent and the crude Nebraska environment that produced him, as well as the inhabitants' inability to recognize his achievements. Similarly, "The Treasure of Far Island" brings playwright Douglass Burnham back to his Nebraska hometown, whose citizens still view him as the mischievous lad he was when he left twelve years earlier.

Often music suggests the cultural resources lacking on the prairie. In "The Bohemian Girl" the music-loving Bohemian household of the Vavrikas is contrasted with the Ericsons' vast farmstead with its automobile and modern conveniences. "A Wagner Matinee" brings Nebraska farmwife Georgiana Carpenter back to Boston, where she had taught music before she married and moved west; a symphony playing Wagner reawakens the spirit that had long lain dormant within her, deadened by the harshness of Midwestern farm life. The title character of "Eric Hermannson's Soul," having destroyed his violin after his religious conversion, is moved to eloquence in response to the organ playing of a beautiful, sophisticated visitor from back East. Another violinist, the title character of "Peter," destroys his violin to keep it out of the hands of his money-grubbing brother, who has threatened to sell it. The title character of "The Joy of Nellie Deane" becomes engaged to a traveling salesman who can take her away from her native Midwestern town to live in Chicago, where she can take singing lessons and go to the opera. When he disappears, her horizons narrow: she soon gives up singing, becomes a school teacher, and marries a penny-pinching merchant. By contrast Eden Bower in "Coming, Aphrodite" succeeds in escaping her stultifying prairie village and prospers as an opera singer in New York City and abroad.

Willa Cather's treatment of the Midwest is subtly nuanced and skillfully developed in a later story, "Neighbour Rosicky" (1932). For the story's central character, Bohemian immigrant Anton Rosicky, the Midwest is a dream-fulfilling region that fosters freedom, the dignity and independence that come from earning a good livelihood on one's own land, and the serenity of living close to nature. As he nears the end of his life, Rosicky reflects on the contrast between his younger days as a tailor in New York City and London, where he felt alienated from nature, and his later life on his own farm in Nebraska where, with his family, his neighbors, and his farm animals, he has found his happiest home. He does not fear his imminent death because he knows he will be buried on his own land under his own wide sky, in death becoming an inextricable part of the natural world that has grounded and centered him throughout his life.

Like many of her Midwestern contemporaries, Willa Cather was ambivalent about her native region. The poetry of her prairie descriptions is a testament to her love of the land where she grew up; however, many of the same stories and novels which stress the beauty of the region also emphasize its lack of cultural opportunities and its people's obsession with money, material things, conventionality, and conformity. Willa Cather, both a pioneer and a backtrailer, viewed the Midwest from a dual perspective; perhaps this unique point of view is what enabled her to illuminate its complexities so perceptively and memorably.

**SELECTED WORKS:** Cather published twelve novels: *Alexander's Bridge* (1912), *O Pioneers!* (1913), *The Song of the Lark* (1915), *My Ántonia* (1918), *One of Ours* (1922), *A Lost Lady* (1923), *The Professor's House* (1925), *My Mortal Enemy* (1926), *Death Comes for the Archbishop* (1927), *Shadows on the Rock* (1931), *Lucy Gayheart* (1935), and *Sapphira and the Slave Girl* (1940). She is the author of six short story collections: *The Troll Garden* (1905), *Youth and the Bright Medusa* (1920), *Obscure Destinies* (1932), *The Old Beauty and Others* (1948), *Early Stories of Willa Cather* (1957), and *Uncle Valentine and Other Stories* (1973), as well as two collections of essays, *Not Under Forty* (1936) and *Willa Cather on Writing* (1949), and one book of poems, *April Twilights* (1903).

**FURTHER READING:** Three recent biographies are Hermione Lee's *Willa Cather: Double Lives* (1989), James Woodress's *Willa Cather: A Literary Life* (1987), and Sharon O'Brien's *Willa Cather: The Emerging Voice* (1987). See also O'Brien's *Willa Cather* (1994) and Marilee Lindemann's *Willa Cather: Queering America* (1999) for a discussion of Cather's lesbianism. Susan Rosowski's *The Voyage Perilous: Willa Cather's Romanticism* (1986) discusses Cather's work as a continuation of the Romantic tradition.

Recent critical analyses of Cather's regionalism and pastoralism are Guy Reynolds's *Willa Cather in Context: Progress, Race, Empire* (1996), Joseph Urgo's *Willa Cather and the Myth of American Migration* (1995), Sally Peltier Harvey's *Redefining the American Dream: The Novels of Willa Cather* (1995), Laura Winters's *Willa Cather: Landscape and Exile* (1994), and Jamie Ambrose's *Willa Cather: Writing at the Frontier* (1988).

The Nebraska State Historical Society, the Willa Cather Pioneer Memorial at Red Cloud, and the University of Nebraska are major manuscript repositories.

MARCIA NOE
THE UNIVERSITY OF TENNESSEE AT CHATTANOOGA

## MARY HARTWELL CATHERWOOD
December 16, 1847–December 26, 1902

**BIOGRAPHY:** Mary Hartwell Catherwood was born in the small settlement of Luray, in Licking County, Ohio. She was the daughter of Dr. Marcus Hartwell, who had attended Marietta College and studied medicine in Columbus, and Phoebe (Thompson) Hartwell. When Mary was ten, the family joined the current of western migration, settling at Milford, Illinois, where the parents soon died, leaving their three children to be brought up by their maternal grandparents in Hebron, Ohio. At fourteen Mary Hartwell began to teach country schools, and two years later she began publishing her poetry and fiction in the *North American* of Newark. She worked her way through the Granville Female Seminary by teaching, and from 1868 to 1874 she taught in schools in Ohio and Danville, Illinois, and continued her writing.

Encouraged by the favorable reception of her work, in 1874 she gave up teaching for freelance writing, first in Newburgh, New York, then in Cincinnati, producing her first novel, *A Woman in Armor* (1875). After a brief period of dependence on others, she married James Steele Catherwood, and the couple lived in Oakford, Indiana. Being no longer forced to support herself, Mrs. Catherwood began reporting on the ugliness of Western towns and narrowness of Western minds. Several stories of this nature were finally included in *The Queen of the Swamp, and Other Plain Americans* (1899).

In Kokomo she met JAMES WHITCOMB RILEY, whose poetry had not yet been recognized and who was discouraged. Their ripening friendship and mutual literary inspiration resulted in collaboration on several projects, such as "The Whittleford Letters," a romantic story of the lives of two writers, which strongly resembled theirs, and consequently was soon abandoned.

In 1879 the Catherwoods moved to Indianapolis, where Mr. Catherwood operated a confectionery, and immediately his wife was swept into the city's literary life. She enjoyed her experience there, and she contributed to the *Saturday Review* and published stories and novels. Then for some reason she slowly left realism and turned to romanticism. The family lived next in Hoopeston, Illinois, from 1882 to 1899, where Mr. Catherwood was postmaster, and here Mary Hartwell Catherwood awoke to her best subject, the early history of the French in North America. This topic inspired her to write romantically, so much so that at the World's Columbian Exposition in 1893 she defended her romantic point of view effectively in a debate with the young realist HAMLIN GARLAND.

From 1889 until 1901 nearly everything she wrote was romantic, and most of it dealt with the French. Gladly she accepted the invitation of Benjamin S. Parker, an Indiana poet, to visit him at his work as American Consul in Sherbrooke, Canada, where she happened to see in a procession celebrating St. John's Day a float representing Dollard des Ormeaux and his sixteen men who were killed in 1660 trying to check the attack of the Iroquois on Montreal, then a small French outpost. She did much research on the story and published *The Romance of Dollard* in the *Century* magazine in 1888; as a book it appeared in 1889 with a preface by historian Francis Parkman commending her historical accuracy. Similar romances of New France followed, including *The Lady of Fort St. John* (1891), *Old Kaskaskia* (1893), and *The White Islander* (1893). In 1899 she separated from her husband. Her greatest success was *Lazarre* (1901), an historical romance. Mrs. Catherwood died in Chicago on December 26, 1902.

**SIGNIFICANCE:** Mary Hartwell Catherwood was a realist in the first part of her career and then a romanticist, and her life touched the careers of many other writers. Some of her stories are important in that they precede novels which often have been thought to be the first in their fields. For example, one of her novels, *Craque-O'Doom* (1881), first published as a story, traces her unhappy girlhood in Hebron, which she calls Barnet, telling in bitter words of the respectable but decadent life there and anticipating SHERWOOD ANDERSON'S *Winesburg, Ohio* (1919) and EDGAR WATSON HOWE'S *The Story of a Country Town* (1883). A second story, *A Little God,* published in a newspaper in 1878–1879, provides a realistic picture of the boom-town development of Hoopeston, Illinois, disguised somewhat as Whoopertown. This work portrays the developing town's squabbles, its squalor, and the rush for nearby salable lands. Eighteen years later she reworked the story as a novelette, *The Spirit of an Illinois Town* (1897). Her first writings, including her first novel, *A Woman in Armor,* were mediocre. Catherwood also wrote several juvenile pieces of the same type. However, her change in point of view from realistic to romantic brought her best novels, including *The Romance of Dollard*, which, in spite of her inventing a few new characters for the story, was fundamentally historical and interesting. Her *Lazarre* (1901) was based on the story of Eleazar Williams, whose claim to be the lost dauphin of France provided an intriguing theme, and a play was produced based on it. She was at her best in treatments of French history; and her poor plotting, over-sentimentalized characters, and over-documentation are more than offset by her careful research and her ability to vitalize the past and convey a strong feeling for the wilderness. Catherwood's romances had a certain flimsy quality that has made them less likely to endure; however, because she wrote mostly when romance was suddenly flowing, perhaps she could not be expected to produce the sort of thing that would be most welcome today. She was an intriguing person and might well have become more of a leader in realism.

**SELECTED WORKS:** Critics agree that

Catherwood's best novels are *The Romance of Dollard* (1889) and *Lazarre* (1901), though many readers may wish to sample other novels, particularly those dealing with French-American history.

**FURTHER READING:** Mary Hartwell Catherwood has attracted several critics, including Milton Wilson's *Biography of Mary Hartwell Catherwood* (1904); Robert Price's *A Critical Biography of Mrs. Mary Hartwell Catherwood: A Study in Middle Western Regional Authorship* (1943); Dorothy Dondore's *The Prairie and the Making of Middle America: Four Centuries of Description* (1926); and Eileen Cunningham's *Lower Illinois Valley: Local Sketches of Long Ago of Mrs. Mary Hartwell Catherwood* (1975). The Newberry Library holds a collection of her papers.

ARTHUR W. SHUMAKER          DePAUW UNIVERSITY

## (CHARLES) BRUCE CATTON

October 9, 1899–August 28, 1978

**BIOGRAPHY:** Born to George R. Catton and Adela M. (Patten) Catton in Petoskey, a city on Little Traverse Bay in northwestern lower Michigan, Bruce Catton was raised in nearby Benzonia, a crossroads college town settled after lumbering days. His father was principal of the academy which was the successor to the college. In this optimistic, earnest village shaped by evangelical Christianity, Catton played baseball, took part in other sports on and around Crystal Lake, played in the local orchestra, went to Christian Endeavor, heard veterans' reminiscences, and played Civil War games near the cemetery which they likened to Gettysburg.

He interrupted studies at Oberlin College to serve in the navy during World War I. He returned to Oberlin but left without graduating in 1920 to take up journalism. He married Hazel H. Cherry on August 16, 1925; they had one son, William Bruce, who would collaborate with his father in writing some of the latter's works. A reporter in Cleveland and Boston until 1926, Catton then became a correspondent and columnist for the Newspaper Enterprise Association, moving to Washington in 1939. During and after World War II he was director of information, successively, for two government agencies. He left government service in 1948 to write his first book, *The War Lords of Washington* (1949), about War Production Board activities.

Civil War regimental histories acquired in the 1930s led to his first Civil War history, *Mr. Lincoln's Army* (1951). Eleven books on the Civil War followed. The third of these, *A Stillness at Appomattox* (1953), received the Pulitzer Prize for history writing and also the National Book Award in 1954. That year he joined associates to publish *American Heritage* magazine, for which he served as editor until 1959. The Ohioana Library Association gave him its nonfiction award for *The Coming Fury* (1962), and in 1977 he received the Presidential Freedom Award. In semi-retirement, summering in Benzonia, as senior editor of *American Heritage* he continued to contribute articles and reviews until his death at his home in Frankfort, Michigan, after a respiratory illness.

**SIGNIFICANCE:** A Civil War historian of national importance, Catton is credited with accuracy, fairness and balance, a keen sense of anecdote, a skill at storytelling, deep compassion for his subjects, and a vision of the grand movements of history. Arguably, his stripping away romantic glamour from the actions of war places Catton in continuity with the Midwestern realists in their disdain for Southern laments for a lost cause. He attributes Midwesterners' Union loyalty to a sense that the national government opened territory for settlement through the victories of General Wayne and Commodore Perry. He finds in the rural Midwestern backgrounds of ABRAHAM LINCOLN and Ulysses S. Grant traits of simplicity, hardihood, empathy with suffering, concern for common soldiers, and eagerness to end the war in a conciliatory and forgiving way.

Sometimes faulted for seeing history as a crusade rather than considering economics and power struggles, he stresses both in Michigan's history, claiming an inevitably developing technology exhausted one natural resource after another, forever changing the region. Crediting Union victory partly to Michigan's iron mining, he says Michigan's history reflected insatiable desires and an illusion of inexhaustible resources. That illusion was present in Benzonia, evangelically confident that society was perfectible through education and failing to acknowledge more sinister forces in successive exploitations of land and human resources. He portrays successive historical conflicts, with such protagonists as fur traders, woods-runners, missionaries, Indians, French and British authorities, colonists, Michigan territorial and Ohio state officials, private citizens along unfenced railroad lines, and Mayor and then Governor Pingree and major corporations. Catton stresses the temporariness of each phase of frontier life. His knowledge of lake boats, railroads, and automobiles provides a wide range of transportation metaphors to sum up the region's history.

**SELECTED WORKS:** *A Stillness at Appomattox* (1953), his third volume of Civil War history, describes the war's last year. Written for a popular audience, its careful detail and vigorous style appeal to professional historians as well. *U. S. Grant and the American Military Tradition* (1954) locates roots in Grant's Ohio childhood for military decisiveness, a democratic sense of the national will represented in Congress, a conciliatory attitude toward the Confederacy, and the political naivete which doomed his efforts toward reconstruction. *Michigan's Past and the Nation's Future* (1960) and *Michigan: A Bicentennial History* (1976) reflect a wide knowledge of Michigan's economic role in manufacturing and trade but note the state's failure to overcome illusions of inexhaustible resources. *Waiting for the Morning Train: An American Boyhood* (1972) places Catton's own life in a context of regional prehistory, including vivid descriptions of lumbering camp life, and stresses the tension between hope and despair in the region's decline. His essays and reviews in *American Heritage* from 1954 to 1978 deal not only with the Civil War but with World War I and the issues of appropriate historical commemoration.

**FURTHER READING:** Oliver Jensen's "Working with Bruce Catton," in *American Heritage* 30:2 (February–March 1979): 44–50, and Roy William Norris's unpublished 1977 doctoral dissertation "The Rhetoric of Bruce Catton: History as Literature" (Ann Arbor: University Microfilms, 1977) provide useful material on Catton. Manuscripts including those of seven of his Civil War books plus notes from 1951 to 1961 are at the Citadel Archives-Museum in Charleston, South Carolina.

EUGENE H. PATTISON                    ALMA COLLEGE

## JOAN CHASE
Unknown
**BIOGRAPHY:** Joan Chase was born in Ohio and received her BA from the University of Maryland, but little more of her personal information is available. She served as assistant director of the Ragdale Foundation in Lake Forest, Illinois, from 1980 to 1984. She taught at the Iowa Writers' Workshop in 1988 and at Princeton University in 1990. In 1983, with the publication of her first novel, *During the Reign of the Queen of Persia*, Chase became a celebrated voice of the Midwest, garnering the Best Midwest Fiction Award from the Friends of American Writers, the Best Fiction in the Middle States Award from the Society of Midland Authors, the ERNEST HEMINGWAY Foundation Award, the Janet Heidinger Kafka Prize, and a nomination for the National Book Critics Circle Award. Her second novel, *The Evening Wolves* (1989), and a collection of short fiction, *Bonneville Blue* (1991), have continued to demonstrate her talent and have been praised by reviewers for their strong characters and candid observations, particularly those of women's lives.

**SIGNIFICANCE:** In a review of *During the Reign of the Queen of Persia* in the June 12, 1983, issue of the *New York Times Book Review*, Douglas Bauer, another Midwestern writer, points out that the characters in Chase's fiction, particularly the adolescent girl narrators in *During the Reign of the Queen of Persia*, are largely defined on the basis of their relationship to their place (10). The girls' place is a northern Ohio farm of the 1950s. Chase masterfully evokes the rural Ohio setting through the girls' observations of the adult world they see around them. The story is told through the communal "we," and Chase has said that this aggregate point of view provides a kind of family consciousness or "royal we" behind individual points of view. The family perspective is centered around their home, "Gram's," or the "Queen of Persia's" Ohio farm, and although it is clear that the girls will have to find their own identities as they grow up and move away from the farm, which Gram sells at the end of the novel, it is the farm home, the character of the place, and the socialization and developmental qualities that that place provides that form the basis of the girls' adult lives. The Midwestern character of Chase's first novel is a careful balance between the cavorting freedom and stifling deprivation of childhood lived in small towns and on the farm.

**SELECTED WORKS:** Chase's works include

her celebrated first novel *During the Reign of the Queen of Persia* (1983), her second novel, *The Evening Wolves* (1989), and a collection of short fiction, *Bonneville Blue* (1991). An interview with Chase appears in *Contemporary Authors* 134 (1992): 107–10. A third novel is in progress.

**FURTHER READING:** Criticism on Joan Chase's work is limited. Among the available sources are: Katherine B. Payant's "Female Friendship in Contemporary Bildungsroman," in *Communication and Woman's Friendship: Parallels and Intersections in Literature and Life*, edited by Janet Daubler Ward (1993); Adalaide Morris's "First Persons Plural in Contemporary Feminist Fiction," in *Tulsa Studies in Woman's Literature* 11.1 (Spring 1992): 11–29; and Mary S. Velasquez's "Prisoners and Refugees: Language and Violence in *The House of Bernarda Alba* and *During the Reign of the Queen of Persia*," in *Women and Violence in Literature: An Essay Collection*, edited by Katherine Ann Ackley (1990): 221–36.

KEITH FYNAARDT    NORTHWESTERN COLLEGE

## HOBART (CHATFIELD) CHATFIELD-TAYLOR

March 24, 1865–January 15, 1945

**BIOGRAPHY:** Though he prided himself on his New England ancestry, Hobart Chatfield-Taylor was born in Chicago. The son of Henry Hobart Taylor, a wealthy manufacturer, and Adelaide (Chatfield) Taylor, he grew up comfortably on "Old Washington Street" in the once-elegant heart of Chicago's near west side. He recalled this neighborhood as a prim New England village of "dignified mansions" where people observed the Sabbath with Puritan strictness (*Chicago* 64). After his father's death in 1875, he began in earnest his lifelong habit of extended European travel. Most of his early education, including a lengthy period in England, came under private tutors. In 1886 he graduated from Cornell University, returning to Chicago to work briefly as a reporter for the *Chicago Record*. Between 1890 and 1892 he served as European correspondent for the *Chicago Daily News*.

From his uncle, Wayne Chatfield, he inherited a large fortune and his redundant surname, the hyphenated name, a condition of his uncle's bequest. He spent with an open hand in establishing the weekly *America: A Journal for Americans: Devoted to Honest Politics and Good Literature*. With the veteran Chicago newsman Slason Thompson, Chatfield-Taylor edited the journal, contributing numerous articles on the perils of unrestricted immigration, the sacredness of the New England tradition, and the necessity of preserving the Anglo-Saxon race. He also sought to promote Chicago as a literary center and, in general, the cause of "Western" literature. During its short-lived existence—between 1888 and 1891—*America* published such writers as Kate Chopin, EUGENE FIELD, HAMLIN GARLAND, JOSEPH KIRKLAND, HARRIET MONROE, ELIA W. PEATTIE, and JAMES WHITCOMB RILEY. In 1890 Chatfield-Taylor married Rose Farwell, the daughter of Charles Farwell, a U.S. senator; they had four children, three sons and a daughter. Two years after Rose's death in 1918, he married Estelle Barbour Stillman of Detroit.

Throughout the 1890s and 1900s, Chatfield-Taylor participated in and gave financial support to the "Upward Movement" in Chicago arts and letters. He belonged to the Whitechapel Club, the Little Room, the Society of Midland Authors, and the Cliff-Dwellers Club. He played "angel" to Chicago's Little Theater movement and later, in 1912, helped his friend HARRIET MONROE create the subscription plan that financed *Poetry*. He wrote six novels between 1891 and 1902; four— *With Edge Tools* (1891), *An American Peeress* (1894), *Two Women and a Fool* (1895), *The Vice of Fools* (1897)—used Chicago as a subject or transient setting. These novels delivered social satire both genteel and world-weary; in them, he occasionally envisioned a mythic Midwest, unsullied by cities, the "new immigration," or industrial decay. As the heroine in *With Edge Tools* proclaims, "toward the West they are still kept green and vigorous by the pure, native breezes" (106–107). Two scholarly studies, *Moliere, A Biography* (1906) and *Fame's Pathway* (1909), established him as an authority on the French playwright.

In 1913 he received an honorary doctorate from Lake Forest University. Elected to the National Institute of Arts and Letters, he served as its vice-president in 1914–15. He died at his retirement home in Santa Barbara, California.

**SIGNIFICANCE:** When Chatfield-Taylor congratulated his friend novelist HENRY BLAKE

FULLER for *With the Procession* (1895), he readily acknowledged the limits of his own literary talents and the difficulties of writing about Chicago from suburban Lake Forest. Critics and literary historians, mostly by their silence, have endorsed this self-appraisal. BERNARD DUFFEY characterized him not as a novelist but as a patron of the arts. Popular historians, including Finis Farr, have drawn freely on *Chicago* (1917) and *Cities of Many Men* (1925) for the nostalgic reminiscences of dinner-dances, the 1893 World's Columbian Exposition, and the privileged life of postbellum Chicago. *Tawny Spain* (1927) and his other travel writings, though they once commanded respect, have passed from favor. *America*, the nativist journal he edited and bankrolled, remains an underused resource for the study of the first Chicago Renaissance and the cause of Midwestern literature in the 1880s and 1890s.

**SELECTED WORKS:** For a glimpse of Chatfield-Taylor boosting Chicago as a literary center, see the article attributed to him, "The Profession of Letters in Chicago. By a Man of Letters," in the journal he founded and edited, *America* 5 (December 11, 1890): 309–12. None of his novels remain in print, and but one holds a claim on the interest of contemporary readers: *Two Women and a Fool* (1895), a satire of Hull House uplifters and literary poseurs. His other novels include *With Edge Tools* (1891), *An American Peeress* (1894), and *The Vice of Fools* (1897). *Chicago* (1917) and *Cities of Many Men* (1925) are Chatfield-Taylor's bittersweet recollections of Chicago in the late nineteenth century, tales of the city's elegant social life and cultural aspirations with snarling comments about the non-English-speaking immigrants. He was also the author of two works of literary criticism on Moliere: *Moliere, A Biography* (1906) and *Fame's Pathway* (1909).

**FURTHER READING:** Guy Szuberla considers Chatfield-Taylor's role and editorial policies at *America* in "The Making and Breaking of Chicago's *America*," in *American Periodicals* 2 (Fall 1992): 100–12. Bernard Duffey's *The Chicago Renaissance in American Letters: A Critical History* (1954) mentions Chatfield-Taylor in several listings of groups involved in the city's turn-of-the-century renaissance.

Chatfield-Taylor's letters and extant manuscripts are scattered: the Newberry Library, the American Academy of Arts and Letters, Butler Library, and Columbia University hold the largest collections.

GUY SZUBERLA                                       UNIVERSITY OF TOLEDO

## MAXINE CHERNOFF
February 24, 1962

**BIOGRAPHY:** Maxine Chernoff, daughter of Philip B. and Idell (Lubove) Hahn, was born and educated in Chicago. In 1971 she married Arnold Chernoff but divorced him the following year, a year in which she also received her BA from the University of Illinois at Chicago, then known as the University of Illinois at Chicago Circle. In 1974 she earned her MA from the same institution, thus launching an intense period of teaching, public reading, and publication, all of which defined her reputation as a formidable young poet and fiction writer on the Chicago literary scene. From 1977 to 1980 she taught at the University of Illinois at Chicago, on a part-time basis, combining classes there with work at Truman College from 1978 to 1980. From 1980 to 1984 she served as an associate professor of English at Truman College. She also managed to work as a visiting lecturer at the prestigious School of the Art Institute of Chicago from 1988 to 1991. She thus established herself as a highly visible and influential teacher of other young Chicago writers. In 1995, however, she made a dramatic move, leaving her home base of Chicago for northern California and taking a position as a professor of creative writing at San Francisco State University. But the subject matter of her fiction continued to be the same voices and venues of Chicago Jewish and Gentile speech, the West and the south sides of this sprawling urban landscape.

Chernoff practiced what she preached, and her ideal of craftsmanship, in both poetry and prose, is clear in her own numerous publications. During this period she was contributing regularly to such nationally known publications as *New Directions*, *Paris Review*, and *Tri-Quarterly*. Her books also reflected the same preoccupations and themes as her periodical publications: intricate relationships and the language of the city. In effect, CARL SANDBURG's "City of the Big Shoulders" had become domesticated by a street-smart young author, as shown in such poetry collections as *A Vegetable Emergency* (1977), *Utopia TV Store* (1979), *New Faces of 1952* (1985), *Japan* (1988), and *Leap Year Day: New and Selected Poems* (1990).

Even more important than the poetry, perhaps—excepting the important volume, *New Faces of 1952*, with its self-referential biographical quality and unfailingly accurate transcription of urban voices—are the works of fiction: *Bop* (1987), a brilliant collection of short stories; the novel *Plain Grief* (1991); *Signs of Devotion* (1993), another short story collection; and the novel *American Heaven* (1996).

**SIGNIFICANCE:** In both her poetry and her fiction, including the novel *American Heaven*, which is set in typical Chicago neighborhoods, Chernoff evokes the dialects of the largest Midwestern city, Chicago. She specializes in the minutiae of individual relationships, the ambiguous moments and situations when the future hangs in perpetual doubt, as in "Signs of Devotion" or "Baudelaire's Drainpipe" from *Signs of Devotion*. Chernoff's characters somehow survive in an uncertain and topsy-turvy world, empowered and defined by particular communities, including artists, ethnic groups, young professionals, and the elderly. As SCOTT RUSSELL SANDERS has noted in *Writing from the Center* (1995), a preoccupation with community is one of the enduring hallmarks of Midwestern literature.

The literary terrain that Chernoff creates is uniquely personal, depicting communities not found in the work of Sandburg, JAMES T. FARRELL, LORRAINE HANSBERRY, or GWENDOLYN BROOKS. In his critically important study, *Writing Illinois* (1992), James Hurt lauds her in a chapter that includes the likes of NELSON ALGREN, STUDS TERKEL, and SAUL BELLOW. Hurt is particularly drawn to the title story of *Bop*, in which a young baby is abandoned in the big city but miraculously rescued and adopted by an ethnic community, even if no one understands the strange monosyllabic utterances ("bop") of the lost child. In Chernoff's world, the lost and the marginalized can somehow be found and redeemed, even in the postmodern era. Like James Joyce, Maxine Chernoff may have physically departed from her native land, but she cannot abandon it in the pages of her fictive and poetic imagination.

**SELECTED WORKS:** Chernoff's work was originally published, in many instances, by small presses; some of those titles were then reprinted by larger commercial houses in relatively small numbers, so some of her most important work remains out of print. Nevertheless, her most important poetry collections are *New Faces of 1952* (1985) and *Leap Year Day: New and Selected Poems* (1990). Her best short stories can be found in *Bop* (1987) and *Signs of Devotion* (1993). Her major fiction includes *Plain Grief* (1991) and the widely praised *American Heaven* (1996).

**FURTHER READING:** Although trade publications such as *Booklist* and *Publishers Weekly* have reviewed most of Chernoff's titles since 1990, there is no major scholarly treatment of her work. Fernanda Eberstadt provides a fairly detailed overview of her work in a review of *American Heaven* that appeared in the *New York Times Book Review* (June 9, 1996): 14. No biography of Maxine Chernoff has yet appeared. Good contexts for her work exist in Scott Russell Sanders's *Writing from the Center* (1995), especially his chapter entitled "The Common Life." Most helpful of all the sources is *Writing Illinois* (1992), by James Hurt. His chapter on "Writing Chicago," with its discussion of "alternative" Chicagos is most revealing.

DANIEL L. GUILLORY     MILLIKIN UNIVERSITY

## CHARLES WADDELL CHESNUTT
June 20, 1858–November 15, 1932

**BIOGRAPHY:** Born in Cleveland, Ohio, to Anne Maria (Sampson) and Andrew Jackson Chesnutt, who were "half-Negro" on both sides and had the status of "free Negroes," Charles Waddell Chesnutt quickly developed a passion for reading. His parents moved to Cleveland from Fayetteville, North Carolina, before Chesnutt's birth to escape growing intolerance in the South toward free Negroes. After the Civil War, they moved back to Fayetteville when Charles was nine years old. By the time he turned thirteen, he had become a pupil-teacher at the Howard School. In 1878 he married Susan Perry and began a family. In 1880, when Chesnutt was only twenty-two, he became the principal of the Normal School for Colored Teachers.

From the time he was sixteen, Chesnutt kept a journal in which he documented the obstacles he needed to overcome in order to succeed. He decided his best chance for success was a literary career. In *Cultures of Letters* (1993), Richard Brodhead asserts, "The journal Chesnutt kept at this time is one of the great private records of the growth of the self-made man" (190). In 1883 Chesnutt moved to New York and then on to Cleveland, Ohio, where he became part of the African American professional class which had migrated to the North after the war. Chesnutt studied law and passed the Ohio bar with the highest marks of 1887. His career as a legal stenographer earned him a national reputation. However, he gave up the practice in 1899 to pursue writing full time.

Chesnutt began his literary career as a reporter for Dow, Jones, and Company in New York in 1883. His first short story, "Uncle Peter's House," appeared in 1885. This was followed by his best-known story, "The Goophered Grapevine," published in 1888. Early supporters of Chesnutt included Thomas Bailey Aldrich and WILLIAM DEAN HOWELLS. Howells compared Chesnutt with Henry James. In a review, "Mr. Charles W. Chesnutt's Stories," which appeared in the *Atlantic Monthly*, Howells proclaimed, "one of the places at the top is open to him" (May 1900): 699–700. Chesnutt also corresponded frequently with George Washington Cable. In his early dialect stories, Chesnutt self-consciously emulated the form of other regionalist writers, most notably Joel Chandler Harris and Thomas Nelson Page.

**SIGNIFICANCE:** While Chesnutt is best known for his Southern fiction, he had a wide impact. His use of African American cultural expression and folk material is credited with paving the way for both the Harlem Renaissance and the protest fiction of RICHARD WRIGHT. Chesnutt's writing also reflects middle-class values which he associated with his home in Ohio. Throughout his career, Cleveland embraced him as one of its own.

Frequently called a social historian, Chesnutt often described the conditions endured by African Americans who had migrated to progressive Midwestern urban centers. His stories portrayed the lives of both the professional and lower classes. Chesnutt's Ohio stories emphasize the new color line that had emerged in the Midwest after the Civil War. The Groveland (Cleveland, Ohio) stories illustrate the prejudice arising among African Americans because of differences in skin color. The best-known Groveland stories are "Uncle Wellington's Wives," "A Matter of Principle," and the popular "The Wife of His Youth."

In "The Wife of His Youth," Chesnutt tells the story of Mr. Ryder, "the dean of the Blue Veins" (1). The Blue Veins were the light-skinned professional class of the North. The Blue Veins in Groveland sought "to establish and maintain correct social standards among people of color" (1). However, when the uneducated and dark-skinned 'Liza Jane comes looking for her "slave husband," Mr. Ryder acknowledges her as "the wife of his youth" (24). In "A Matter of Principle," another story featured in *The Wife of His Youth, and Other Stories of the Color Line*, Cicero Clayton, "a prominent member" of the Blue Veins, claims that he is not a Negro (94). While he espouses the brotherhood of man, he is upset when his daughter is courted by a "darkey" (118). In "Uncle Wellington's Wives," racial envy leads Wellington Braboy to abandon his wife and marry a white woman in Groveland. By the end of this tragicomedy, Wellington realizes his mistake and returns to his former wife. Other Groveland stories include "Her Virginia Mammy," and "Jim's Romance." Chesnutt uses objectivity and irony as he confronts the problems of color-conscious society. Considered by many as his best short story, "Baxter's Procrustes" takes a different tack. Chesnutt satirizes the elite literary establishment, the Cleveland Rowfant Club, which excluded women and minorities. Later, in 1910, Chesnutt was inducted as its first minority member.

In addition to the Rowfant Club, Chesnutt broke other racial barriers in Cleveland through his work as a legal stenographer and by his participation in such groups as the Cleveland Chamber of Commerce, the Cleveland Bar Association, and the Cleveland Council of Sociology.

Chesnutt is often referred to as the first great African American novelist. This is startling because he was all but forgotten before a resurgence of interest in his works in the 1970s. Several of his short stories have recently been added to various anthologies. His novel *The Marrow of Tradition* (1901) was included in Henry Louis Gates's 1990 collection *Three Classic African-American Novels*. Chesnutt's most famous works include *House behind the Cedars* (1900) and *Conjure Woman* (1899), a collection of seven tales focusing on "conjure," the folk religion practiced by some slaves in the South.

In 1906 he retired from fiction writing because he felt it did not bring in enough income to support his family. However, he continued writing articles on race relations for the rest of his life. Chesnutt became a recognized spokesman for African Americans. He was a friend of Booker T. Washington but disagreed with Washington's arguments over the position of African Americans in society. Chesnutt believed in the necessity of equality and nonseparation for all people in society. In his 1933 "Postscript: Chesnutt" appearing in *Crisis* 40 (January 1933), W. E. B. DuBois praised him posthumously: "Merit and friendship in his broad and tolerant mind knew no lines of color or race, and all men, good, bad and indifferent, were simply men" (20). In 1928 Chesnutt was awarded the Spingarn Gold Medal from the National Association for the Advancement of Colored People for his "pioneer work as a literary artist depicting the life and struggles of Americans of Negro descent" ("Postscript: The Fourteenth Spingarn Medal," W. E. B. DuBois, *Crisis* 35 [August 1928]: 276). Chesnutt died in Cleveland in 1932.

**SELECTED WORKS:** Chesnutt's works include *Conjure Woman* (1899), *The Wife of His Youth and Other Stories of the Color Line* (1899), the biography *Frederick Douglass* (1899), *House behind the Cedars* (1900), *The Marrow of Tradition* (1901), and *The Colonel's Dream* (1905). Collected stories can be found in *The Short Fiction of Charles W. Chesnutt*, edited by Sylvia Lyon Render (1974). *The Journals of Charles W. Chesnutt Collection*, edited by Richard Brodhead (1993), also provide significant insight into this important literary figure.

**FURTHER READING:** Richard H. Brodhead's *Scenes of Reading and Writing in Nineteenth-Century America* (1993), especially chapter 6: "'Why Not a Colored Man?': Chesnutt and the Transaction of Authorship" (177–210), offers an acute analysis of how Chesnutt positioned himself as a writer. Chesnutt's first biographer was his daughter, Helen. Helen C. Chesnutt's *Charles W. Chesnutt: A Pioneer of the Color Line* (1952) and Frances Richardson Keller's *An American Crusade: The Life of Charles Waddell Chesnutt* (1978) provide a social context for Chesnutt's writing. Much Chesnutt scholarship is in the form of critical biography including William Andrews's *The Literary Career of Charles W. Chesnutt* (1980), J. Noel Heermance's *Charles W. Chesnutt: America's First Great Black Novelist* (1974), and Sylvia Lyons Render's *Charles W. Chesnutt* (1980). Three essays in *The Columbia Literary History of the United States*, edited by Emory Elliott (1988), provide interesting analysis and contextualization of Chesnutt's work, including Richard H. Brodhead's "Literature and Culture," Werner Sollors's "Immigrants and Other Americans," and Eric J. Sundquist's "Regionalism and Realism." Curtis Ellison's *Charles W. Chesnutt: A Reference Guide* (1977) is a useful source guide for Chesnutt scholarship. Another important tool is Olivia J. Martin's *Guide to the Microfilm Edition of the Charles Waddell Chesnutt Papers in the Library of the Western Reserve Historical Society* (1972). Chesnutt's papers are located in the Chesnutt Collection at the Fisk University Library.

JOHN L. SUTTON NEW YORK UNIVERSITY

## SANDRA CISNEROS
December 20, 1954

**BIOGRAPHY:** Born in Chicago, Illinois, Sandra Cisneros is the only daughter among the seven children of Mexican-born Alfredo Cisneros Del Moral and Mexican American Elvira (Cordero Anguiano) Cisneros. During her early childhood, the family divided its time between the United States and Mexico, where her father cared for his mother. Each return to Chicago meant moving to a different house and attending a different school. With neither an established set of friends nor a sister, Cisneros turned to books, an interest her mother encouraged by getting her daughter a library card and excusing her from household chores.

When Sandra was eleven years old, the family was able to buy the home on the north side of Chicago that served as a model for the fictional house on Mango Street. Sandra Cisneros earned a BA degree at Loyola University in 1976 and a Master of Fine Arts from the University of Iowa Writers' Workshop in 1978. A seminar discussion on houses as metaphors at Iowa led Cisneros to a major breakthrough. The differences between her classmates' experiences and her own no longer intimidated her. Rather, she began to realize these differences gave her not only unique material for her work, but a unique voice.

Sandra Cisneros.
Photo © Nancy Crampton

Though the idea for *The House on Mango Street* (1984) may have been born at this time, the book itself required almost five more years to finish. During this time, Cisneros also worked in educational programs geared for Latino youth within the Chicago public schools and at Loyola University. She won her first fellowship from the National Endowment for the Arts in 1982 and a second in 1987. *The House on Mango Street* won the American Book Award from the Before Columbus Foundation in 1985. Cisneros then taught as a writer in residence at several universities. In 1991 she won the Lannan Foundation Literacy Award, and in 1995 she was named a MacArthur Fellow, an honor that also brought her financial security. She lives in San Antonio, Texas.

**SIGNIFICANCE:** Both Cisneros's style and thematic concerns make her work significant. The brief vignettes of *The House on Mango Street* build dramatic intensity and have the cumulative effect of a novel because of Cisneros's careful attention to significant detail and skillful handling of pace. Like GWENDOLYN BROOKS, Cisneros renders vividly the surge of street life in her Chicago neighborhood. She depicts as well the reflective inner life of her main character, Esperanza. A touch of the Chicago of THEODORE DREISER'S *Sister Carrie*

lingers in the episode of Esperanza's sexual harassment at her job and in the portrayal of Marin's loitering in the doorway of her house, longing for an escape from her assigned role.

In such images, Cisneros brings a Midwestern Latina perspective to feminism. Esperanza in *The House on Mango Street* seeks not just a room of her own, as did Virginia Woolf, but a house of her own, space to realize her potential and to write. Until that time, she finds with her mother the comfort she seeks "when she makes room for you on her side of the bed still warm with her skin" (7). Cisneros's emphasis on the mother as source of strength and creativity is underscored by her choosing to give Esperanza her own mother's birth name, Cordero. Similarly Lucy in "My Friend Lucy Who Smells Like Corn" from *Woman Hollering Creek* (1991) is given the name Anguiano, also from the lineage of Cisneros's mother.

**SELECTED WORKS:** With its Chicago setting, *The House on Mango Street* (1984) is both Cisneros's most Midwestern and her most acclaimed work. In her poetry chapbook *Bad Boys* (1980), Cisneros presents images drawn from her experience in the Mexican inner city of Chicago. Images of Chicago also emerge in a few of the poems in *My Wicked, Wicked Ways* (1987) and in stories such as "Barbie Q," from *Woman Hollering Creek* (1991). The majority of these later stories, however, are set in Texas and depict more southwestern or borderland themes. Another collection of poems, *Loose Woman* (1994), features themes of love and longing, sometimes in frankly erotic terms, without a particularly regional flavor.

**FURTHER READING:** Robin Ganz provides an overview of Cisneros's work and life in "Sandra Cisneros: Border Crossing and Beyond," *MELUS* 19.1 (Spring 1994): 19–29. Martha Satz's wide-ranging interview with Cisneros, "Returning to One's House," appeared in *Southwest Review* 82.2 (Spring 1997): 166–85. An analysis of *The House on Mango Street* as the story of Esperanza's self-invention is found in Maria Elena Valdes's "In Search of Identity in Cisneros's *The House on Mango Street,"* in *Canadian Review of American Studies* 23.1 (Fall 1992): 55–72. Ilan Stavans argues that Cisneros's work is "overly accessible" in "Sandra Cisneros: Form over Content," *Academic Questions* 9.4 (Fall 1996): 29–34. For an extended, well-argued discussion of the ways Cisneros extends the legacy of Virginia Woolf's *A Room of One's Own*, see Jacqueline Doyle, "More Room of Her Own: Sandra Cisneros's *The House on Mango Street*," *MELUS* 19.4 (Winter 1994): 5–35. A helpful bibliography accompanies this article. Emphasis on the Chicago setting of *The House on Mango Street* is found in Cordelia Chavez Candelaria's "Latina Women Writers: Chicana, Cuban American and Puerto Rican Voices," in *Handbook of Hispanic Cultures in the United States: Literature and Art* (1993).

MARGARET ROZGA

UNIVERSITY OF WISCONSIN–WAUKESHA

## DAVID CITINO
March 13, 1947

BIOGRAPHY: A widely published and anthologized Ohio poet, David Citino was born in Cleveland to John D. and Mildred Rita (Bunasky) Citino. Educated in Cleveland schools, he graduated from St. Ignatius High School in 1965. In 1969 he received the BA in English from Ohio University, the MA in English in 1974, and the PhD in English in 1977, both from Ohio State University in Columbus.

He was assistant professor of English at Ohio State University in Marion from 1974 to 1980, associate professor of English at Marion and Columbus from 1980 to 1988, and since 1988 he has been professor of English and creative writing at Ohio State University in Columbus. He is currently poetry editor of Ohio State University Press. On July 26, 1969, he married Mary Helen Hicks, and they have three children.

He has received numerous awards, including the first annual Poetry Award from the Ohioana Library Association, the Alumni Distinguished Teaching Award from Ohio State University, and a fellowship in poetry from the National Endowment for the Arts.

SIGNIFICANCE: Citino's poetry draws heavily on his Ohio background and experiences and his family relationships. In subject matter his poems reflect his wide-ranging interests in myth, history, modern life in Cleveland and Columbus, and the smooth-flowing, life-sustaining rivers of Ohio. In the collection *The House of Memory* (1990) he explores the significance of urban Midwestern life in the second half of the twentieth century; *The Discipline: New and Selected Poems, 1980–1992* (1992) reflects the life of the mind and emotions of the poet as clear reflections of the human condition. In all his work he exhibits a keen ear, a close attention to details, a willingness to reach for effect, and a strong sense of the importance of time and place. From *Last Rites and Other Poems* (1980) to the poems in *Broken Symmetry* (1977, 1997), Citino exhibits a deep appreciation of and respect for the Ohio relationships out of which he came and those that he continues to celebrate. His works are firmly rooted in Ohio.

SELECTED WORKS: Citino's volumes of poetry include *Broken Symmetry* (1977, 1997), *Last Rites and Other Poems* (1980), *The Appassionata Poems* (1983), *The Appassionata Doctrines* (1986), *The Gift of Fire* (1986), *The House of Memory* (1990), *A Letter of Columbus* (1990), *The Discipline: New and Selected Poems, 1980–1992* (1992), *The World Without* (1993), *The Weight of the Heart* (1996), and *The Book of Appassionata: Collected Poems* (1998). He has edited two anthologies, *Poetry Ohio, Art of the State: An Anthology of Ohio Poems* (1984) and *73 Ohio Poets* (1978).

FURTHER READING: Citino is listed in *Contemporary Authors* 104 (1982): 82 and other directories of writers and poets. His verse is widely reviewed.

DAVID D. ANDERSON     MICHIGAN STATE UNIVERSITY

## SAMUEL LANGHORNE CLEMENS
November 30, 1835–April 21, 1910
(Mark Twain)

BIOGRAPHY: Mark Twain, one of the few American writers whose pen name has almost completely obscured that of his birth, Samuel L. Clemens, was born in Florida, Missouri, to John Marshall Clemens, a lawyer of Virginia origins, and Jane (Lampton) Clemens, from Daniel Boone–era Kentucky. When he was five, the family moved to Hannibal, Missouri, where they lived until his father's death in 1847. Thus, at twelve, young Sam found his formal education and his boyhood ended, at the same time bringing to a close the experience that was to provide much of the substance of his best-known works. He was then apprenticed to his older brother Orion, who edited and published the *Missouri Courier*. Six years later young Sam set out for the East as a tramp journeyman printer, then returning to Keokuk, Iowa, where Orion edited another paper. However, in 1857, he became an apprentice pilot on the Mississippi River, an experience that ended with the Civil War but which furnished much more of the substance of his best works.

After a two-week lark in the Confederate Army, Clemens went west to Carson City, Nevada Territory, where Orion, a Unionist and ABRAHAM LINCOLN supporter, had been appointed secretary to the governor of the territory. He served briefly as his brother's secretary, prospected, and then turned again to journalism. He became city editor of the *Virginia City Territorial Enterprise*, where he first used the pen name "Mark Twain," meaning a measured depth of two fathoms, an echo of his river boat days. In Virginia City he met Artemus Ward (CHARLES FARRAR BROWNE) and produced his first crude literary works. A quarrel and a nonsensical duel, which resulted from the no-holds-barred journalism of the time and place, caused him to go to San Francisco in 1864. There he joined the staff of the *San Francisco Morning Call* and also wrote for the *Golden Era* and the *Alta California*. He met and was influenced by Bret Harte. Shortly thereafter, he wrote "The Celebrated Jumping Frog of Calaveras County," which was published in the *New York Saturday Press* on November 18, 1865. Although Twain later pointed out the story's flaws, it nevertheless made him a celebrated humorist with a variety of options available. The *Sacramento Union* contracted with him for a series of travel sketches from the Sandwich Islands (Hawaii) and, after the success of the sketches and the beginning of his lecturing career, contracted with him to travel around the world, then itself a major feat, and to describe his adventures by letter.

However, the direction of his life and career changed when, in New York, he decided to sail on the steamer *Quaker City* on an excursion to the Holy Land. The result was his travel record, *Innocents Abroad* (1869), which established him as a significant writer and at the same time led him to turn his back on the West in his works for nearly a decade, until his return to the West of his boyhood in *The Adventures of Tom Sawyer* (1876).

The publication of *The Celebrated Jumping Frog of Calaveras County and Other Sketches* in 1867 and a series of successful lectures led to his meeting with Olivia Langdon of Elmira, New York. They were married in 1870, while Clemens was editing the *Buffalo Express*, of

**Samuel Clemens.**
Photo © fotofolio

which he had become part owner in 1869. In 1870 his son Langdon, who was to die at two, was born. In 1871 the family moved to Hartford, Connecticut, where Twain was to make his home until 1891, when he moved to Europe for four years.

The Hartford years were among Twain's happiest and most successful. He traveled and lectured extensively, beginning a lifelong affection for England. His family life, marked by the births of Olivia Susan in 1872, Clara in 1874, and Jean in 1880, was secure and fulfilling. In this period also Twain published his most successful works: *Roughing It* (1872), *The Gilded Age* (1873), *The Prince and the Pauper* (1881), and the work upon which his reputation rests most solidly, *Adventures of Huckleberry Finn* (1884). His lecture tours, both in the United States and in Europe, were immensely successful, and Clemens—known universally and almost exclusively as Mark Twain—was considered the great American humorist.

The decade of the 1890s saw Clemens almost constantly in motion, much of the time abroad. From 1891 to 1895 he lived in England, Germany, and Italy. In 1895 he made his celebrated trip around the world, which resulted in *Following the Equator* (1897); he remained in Europe except for brief periods until 1900. His life and his spirits, which had survived the failure of his publishing house in 1894, began to turn gloomy with the death of Olivia Susan in 1896, leading simultaneously to the most honored and most somber period of his life as he began to receive the academic recognition that had previously eluded him.

In 1901 Yale University, which had awarded

him an MA in 1888, made him an LLD, as did the University of Missouri in 1902. But the award that he was proudest to receive was the LLD presented by Oxford University in 1907, and he wore the red robes of the award at every later occasion. During the first decade of the new century, the last of Mark Twain's life, his misfortune continued and his pessimism grew, yet he produced such works as *The Man That Corrupted Hadleyburg* (1900), *What Is Man?* (1906) and *The Mysterious Stranger* (1916). He lived in Italy in 1903–1904. There his beloved wife Livy died in June 1904. His daughter Jean died in 1909. In 1908 he had built a house called "Stormfield" at Redding, Connecticut, and there he died, as he once predicted he would, in 1910. He had come into the world with Halley's Comet when it approached the earth in 1835, and he departed with its return seventy-five years later at the end of a career as spectacular in its way as the astronomical events that framed his life. He died of heart disease, survived only by his daughter Clara.

SIGNIFICANCE: The popular view of Mark Twain continues that which prevailed in his lifetime. He is seen as a humorous writer and lecturer as well as a writer of children's stories. Such interpretations overlook not only the profound pessimism of his later works and the skepticism in much of the earlier work but also the great influence his work, particularly *Adventures of Huckleberry Finn*, has had upon twentieth-century American writing.

No other writer has been more respected by his contemporaries than Mark Twain. WILLIAM DEAN HOWELLS wrote to him in 1899 that "You have pervaded your century almost more than any other man of letters, if not more" (Paine, *Mark Twain* 3, 1912, 1079); SHERWOOD ANDERSON wrote that he was "among the two or three really great American artists" (Anderson, *Letters*, 1953, 3); ERNEST HEMINGWAY wrote in *Green Hills of Africa* (1935) that "All modern American literature comes from one book by Mark Twain called *Huckleberry Finn*" (22); William Faulkner, responding to a question about Anderson's role in modern American literature in an interview later published as "The Art of Fiction" in the *Paris Review* 4, replied, "He [Anderson] was the father of my generation of American writers . . . . [THEODORE] DREISER is his older brother and Mark Twain the father of them both . . ." (40).

Yet the major influence of Mark Twain's work upon American literature for more than a century, essentially the creation of a uniquely American literature in style, structure, substance, and attitude, has not been without its critics. Upon the publication of *Adventures of Huckleberry Finn* in 1884, the Concord, Massachusetts, library committee declared it to be "rough, coarse, inelegant, more suitable to the slums than to intelligent, respectable people" and dismissed it as "veritable trash" (from the *Springfield* [Massachusetts] *Republican*, quoted in the *Critic* 6, March 28, 1885, 155). In succeeding years it has regularly been denounced by well-meaning parents and removed from high school reading lists. In its centennial year a symposium of distinguished African American Americanists unanimously declared that the novel made them uneasy at best.

These deeply felt responses to the novel make one fact clear: Mark Twain's critical reputation and his effect on later writers would be much less had he not written *Adventures of Huckleberry Finn*. As important as are *The Adventures of Tom Sawyer* (1876), *Life on the Mississippi* (1883), and other works, *Adventures of Huckleberry Finn* is the one work that came out of nineteenth-century America whose influence is as strong in the second century of its existence as it was in the first.

Like all of Mark Twain's works, *Adventures of Huckleberry Finn* is firmly rooted in his own experience. The product of a keen ear for the spoken language and its innate rhythms, a clear memory, a sharp eye for detail, and a vivid imagination, it transmutes Mark Twain's boyhood experiences and memories of the Old Southwest of pre–Civil War Missouri as it was beginning its transformation into a more stable Midwest and into a durable statement on the nature of American society and the character of its people.

Mark Twain's major influences on Midwestern American writing and the American modernism that it came to dominate lie in the characters, the language, and the plot structure that are so vivid in *Adventures of Huckleberry Finn*. Huck's people, including Pap Finn, Miss Watson, the King and the Duke, the Grangerfords, and others, are the original American grotesques, those that came to dominate the fiction of Anderson, Hemingway, Faulkner, and through them later generations of American writers, including Flannery O'Connor, Carson McCullers, SAUL BELLOW, William Saroyan, TONI MORRISON, and dozens of other writers who make up the mosaic of American fiction today. Mark Twain's people, like those of his successors, are those who have been psychologically distorted by circumstances, by the values that they accept—or reject—without either questioning or understanding them, into a caricature of what they might have been had they been able to see through or beyond them, as Huck and later George Willard, Augie March, and others learn to do.

Had this uniquely American character type been all that Mark Twain contributed to his successors, it would have been formidable. But he contributed, too, a uniquely American literary language, that of the living language of his youth, of the American vernacular, a rhythm, a syntax, and a vocabulary that had come across an ocean, over the mountains, and up and down the rivers of an expanding continent, remote from the literary centers of Boston and Concord but close to the lives of a people in transition geographically and socially.

Further, Mark Twain has contributed an important part of his experience to the plot structure of *Adventures of Huckleberry Finn*, to the consciousness of the Midwestern writers who followed him, and to the mainstream of American writing today. This is the recognition that the American experience and the writing that defines it is as much compounded of movement as it is of place, that this movement, a search like that of Huckleberry Finn and his companion Jim, is as much toward something—freedom, fulfillment, accomplishment, success, or material accumulation—as it is of escape from that which denies whatever it is Americans value and seek. And Twain makes clear, too, as do Anderson, Hemingway, and their successors, that that search, compounded of innocence and determination, is ultimately futile as rivers end and innocence is lost to experience.

To Mark Twain and his successors it is clear that whatever meaning of fulfillment their people find is not at the end of the search but in the search itself, the only reality achievable in a society that continues to pursue a future that continues to recede even as America and its people move into their third century.

**SELECTED WORKS:** Mark Twain's works are as effective today as they were a century ago, and each of the following is important in its place in Twain's canon: *The Celebrated Jumping Frog of Calaveras County and Other Sketches* (1867); *Innocents Abroad* (1869); *Roughing It* (1872); *The Gilded Age*, with Charles Dudley Warner (1873); *The Adventures of Tom Sawyer* (1876); *A Tramp Abroad* (1880); *The Prince and the Pauper* (1881); *Life on the Mississippi* (1883); *Adventures of Huckleberry Finn* (1884); *A Connecticut Yankee at King Arthur's Court* (1889); *Following the Equator* (1897); *The Man That Corrupted Hadleyburg* (1900); *What Is Man?* (1906); and posthumously, *The Mysterious Stranger* (1916), *Letters* (1917), and *Autobiography* (1924).

**FURTHER READING:** Many biographical and critical studies of Mark Twain have been published. Important biographies are Albert Bigelow Paine's three-volume *Mark Twain: A Biography* (1912), Dixon Wecter's *Sam Clemens of Hannibal* (1952), Justin Kaplan's *Mr. Clemens and Mark Twain* (1966), and Hamlin Hill's *Mark Twain: God's Fool* (1973). Important critical studies are Edgar M. Branch's *The Literary Apprenticeship of Mark Twain* (1950), Walter Blair's *Mark Twain and Huck Finn* (1960), James M. Cox's *Mark Twain: The Fate of Humor* (1966), and Henry Nash Smith's *Mark Twain: The Development of a Writer* (1962). A controversial study is Shelley Fisher Fishkin's *Was Huck Black?* (1993). The Bancroft Library of the University of California at Berkeley is the primary repository of Twain's papers.

DAVID D. ANDERSON    MICHIGAN STATE UNIVERSITY

## CYRUS COLTER
January 8, 1910

**BIOGRAPHY:** Cyrus Colter was born in Noblesville, Indiana, one of two children of James Alexander Colter, an early NAACP organizer, and Ethel Marietta (Bassett) Colter. In an interview presented in *Callaloo* 14.4, Colter commented on his origins: "I was born down in the cornfields of central Indiana, where my people have lived since the 1830s. How are you going to get any more Midwestern than that?" ("Fought for It and Paid Taxes Too" 892). He attended Youngstown College, now Youngstown University, and Ohio State University and received a law degree from Chicago–Kent College of Law. Appointed to the Illinois Commerce Commission in 1951, he served as a commissioner until 1973. Colter was Tripp Professor of Humanities at Northwestern University from 1973 to 1978. His first book, *The Beach Umbrella* (1970), won the Iowa School of Letters Award for Short Fiction, and his novel *Night Studies* (1979) was awarded the 1980 CARL SANDBURG Prize for fiction. In 1977 Cyrus Colter received an honorary doctor of letters from the University of Illinois, Chicago.

**SIGNIFICANCE:** Colter's importance as a Midwestern writer rests largely on the short stories collected in *The Beach Umbrella*. Stories like "Black for Dinner" and "An Untold Story" reveal Colter's ability to render with equal persuasiveness a catered dinner party in Hyde Park, as presented in "Black for Dinner," and a fight in a south side bar, as in "An Untold Story." Although Colter captures each milieu in authentic detail, his characterizations are never mere case studies; he evokes the intensity of Mildred's envy of the party-goers in "The Lookout," Essie's desperation in "The Rescue," and the urgency of Elijah's desire for "A Beach Umbrella" with sympathetic yet critical imagination. In Colter's stories the south side of Chicago becomes a setting for the full variety of human feeling and aspiration.

Colter's novels, the first three of which are set in the Midwest, have not received the nearly unanimous acclaim accorded his short stories. Reginald Gibbons argues that "in his novels Colter's ambitions are greater" as the writer extends and deepens "his structural, thematic and stylistic explorations of the open-endedness of life" (898). Gibbons considers *The Hippodrome* (1973) and *A Chocolate Soldier* (1988) especially remarkable for their "complexities and prizes and depths" and their ability to "stir such intensities of thought and emotion" (905). Robert Bender feels that "By comparison with the short stories, however, the first two novels, *The Rivers of Eros* (1972) and *The Hippodrome* are somewhat limited" (95). For Bender, *Night Studies* (1979) is the novel in which "Colter has brought to bear the skills at characterization so evident in his short stories within the framework of a major exploration of life in our society" (103).

**SELECTED WORKS:** Cyrus Colter remains best known for his short stories, published in *The Beach Umbrella* (1970) and *The Amoralists*

*and Other Tales: Collected Stories* (1988). Colter's five novels are *The River of Eros* (1972), *The Hippodrome* (1973), *Night Studies* (1979), *A Chocolate Soldier* (1988), and *City of Light* (1993).

**FURTHER READING:** *Callaloo* 14.4 (Fall 1991): 831–906 has a special section dedicated to Cyrus Colter, including four interviews with Colter in a section entitled "Fought for It and Paid Taxes Too" (855–97) and Reginald Gibbon's essay "Colter's Novelistic Contradictions" (898–905). Robert M. Bender discusses "The Fiction of Cyrus Colter," focusing on *The Hippodrome, Night Studies*, and *The Rivers of Eros*, in *New Letters* 48.1 (Fall 1981): 93–103.

SANDRA SEATON    CENTRAL MICHIGAN UNIVERSITY

# EVAN S(HELBY) CONNELL
August 17, 1924

**BIOGRAPHY:** Evan Shelby Connell Jr., novelist, short story writer, essayist, dramatist, and poet, was born in Kansas City, Missouri. He is the son of Evan S. Connell Sr. a surgeon, and Elton (Williamson) Connell. Connell grew up in Kansas City. Some of his early education occurred at Southwest High School, followed by Dartmouth College (1941–43), and the University of Kansas (1946–47), where he received his AB. His graduate studies have taken him to the following universities: Stanford (1947–48), Columbia (1948–49), and San Francisco State College. He has worked as a writer as well as serving in the U.S. Navy as a pilot and a flight instructor from 1943 through 1945.

Connell's most productive years resulted in a substantial body of work produced from 1957 to the present. During this period he wrote or edited books in each of the recognized literary genres. He has been the recipient of numerous honors and awards, including the Eugene F. Saxton Fellowship (1953), Guggenheim Fellowship (1963), Rockefeller Grant (1967), California Literature Silver Medal (1974), National Book Critics Circle Award nomination (1984), *Los Angeles Times* Book Award for History (1985), and American Academy and Institute of Arts and Letters Award (1987).

**SIGNIFICANCE:** When Evan S. Connell began his publishing career, he was greeted by a distinguished group of critics and reviewers: Anne Chamberlain, Ralph E. Sipper, William H. Nolte, Siegfried Mandell, and the late Hollis Summers, who praised his style

Evan S. Connell.
Photo © Nancy Crampton

and use of language as well as his approach to developing characters.

Connell's vision of landscape and community has always led him to explore the Midwest and West. *Mrs. Bridge* (1959) is representative of his ability to show a character with all of the flaws and foibles one might exhibit. Mrs. Bridge is upper-middle class, is married, has three children, and still finds her environment tedious and dull. Connell looks at the Midwest with careful dissecting eyes; we see the West and Midwest with all of their possibilities and failings. Connell's use of irony and juxtaposition comes into play in *The Connoisseur* and *Double Honeymoon,* where the character's name, Muhlbach, is drawn from the name of a hotel in his hometown. In New York, Muhlbach is the epitome of innocence out of place and surrounded by corrupt sophistication.

In a number of short stories set in the Midwest, Connell features Midwestern protagonists or juxtaposes Midwestern culture with that of another region. These include "Nan Madol," "The Condor and the Guests," "The Beau Monde of Mrs. Bridge," "Mademoiselle from Kansas City," "Bowen," "The Short

Happy Life of Henrietta," "Mrs. Proctor Bemis," "The Walls of Avila," "The Color of the World," and "The Anatomy Lesson." This is Connell's special talent; he did not need to travel to New York or the international capitals to explore the theme of place; he found it in the region of his birth.

In the years following the publication of *The Anatomy Lesson and Other Stories* (1957), he has lived up to the first praise he garnered and has been extraordinarily productive as well. Connell has at one time or other served as a contributor or editor to the following periodicals or journals: *New York Times, Washington Post, Chicago Sun-Times, San Francisco Chronicle, Carolina Quarterly, Paris Review, Esquire,* and *Contact.* His novels *Mrs. Bridge* (1959) and *Mr. Bridge* (1969) brought him considerably more acclaim when they were adapted for film under the inclusive title *Mr. and Mrs. Bridge.* This work was produced by Merchant Ivory Productions in 1990 and starred Paul Newman and Joanne Woodward.

**SELECTED WORKS:** A brief list of Connell's published works includes *The Anatomy Lesson and Other Stories* (1957), *Mrs. Bridge* (1959), *The Patriot* (1960), *Notes from a Bottle Found on the Beach at Carmel* (1963), *At the Crossroads* (1965), *The Diary of a Rapist* (1966), and *Mr. Bridge* (1969). In 1961 and 1969, respectively, he edited *I Am the Lover,* by Jerry Stoll, and *Woman by Three,* by Joanne Leonard. In the 1970s he turned again to his own work and wrote *Points for a Compass Rose* (1973), *The Connoisseur* (1973), *Double Honeymoon* (1976), *A Long Desire* (1979), *The White Lantern* (1980), *St. Augustine's Pigeon* (1980), *Son of the Morning Star: Custer and the Little Bighorn* (1984), *The Alchymist's Journal* (1991), and *Collected Stories* (1995).

For the past three years Connell has been working on a book about the crusades. Publication of that book, *Deus Lo Volt!,* is expected soon.

**FURTHER READING:** No major biography or critical dissertation exists, but a number of critical essays have been written about Connell. Among them are: Brooke Allen's "Introverts and Emigres," in *New Criterion* 14.2 (1995): 58–63; Bruce Bawer's "The Luther of Science," in *New Criterion* 9.10 (1991): 30–35; Sven Birkerts's "A World Ripe with Magic," in *New York Times Book Review* 16.2 (1991): 7; Gus Blaisdell's "After Ground Zero: The Writings of Evan S. Connell, Jr.," in *New Mexico Quarterly* 36 (1966): 181–207; Graham Fuller's "Joanne Woodward/Evan S. Connell/ . . . Margaret Walsh/Robert Sean Leonard," in *Interviews* 20.11 (1990): 128–35; Marie Lather's "Mr. and Mrs. Bridge in the Louvre," in *Centennial Review* 36.3 (1992): 607–17; John Pym's "Evan S. Connell," in *Sight and Sound* 59.1 (1989): 20–21; Gerald Shapiro's "Evan S. Connell: A Profile," in *Ploughshares* 13.2–3 (1987); Allen Shepherd's "Mr. Bridge in Mrs. Bridge," in *Notes on Contemporary Literature* 3.3 (1973): 7–11; Joyce Wadler's "The Creator of Mr. and Mrs. Bridge Goes Home Again," in *People Weekly* 34.23 (1990): 65–66; and RAY LEWIS WHITE's "Evan S. Connell Jr.'s Mrs. Bridge and Mr. Bridge: A Critical Documentary," in *MidAmerica* 6 (1979): 141–59.

Boston University has several of Connell's manuscripts, but the major portion of his uncollected materials is still in his possession.

HERBERT WOODWARD MARTIN

UNIVERSITY OF DAYTON

# (JOHN WESLEY) "JACK" CONROY
December 5, 1898–February 28, 1990

**BIOGRAPHY:** The second-born from the marriage of an Irish immigrant miner, Thomas Conroy, and Eliza Jane (McCullough) McKiernan, whose first husband was killed in the mines, John Wesley "Jack" Conroy was named in honor of the founder of Methodism, a faith to which Thomas had converted after studying to become a Jesuit priest.

Monkey Nest, the coal mining camp in northern Missouri where Jack was born and raised, left a deep, lasting impression on him, with its communal and oral traditions and frequent strikes and workplace accidents. Conroy lost his father, two uncles, his brother, and two half-brothers in workplace accidents.

At age thirteen, he entered an apprenticeship in the Wabash Railroad shops in Moberly, Missouri. Recording secretary of his union local at age fifteen, Jack, a tireless reader, published his earliest writings in the union's journal. Married on June 30, 1922, to Gladys Kelly, Conroy joined fellow members of the Brotherhood Railway Carmen in the Great Railroad Strike. When the strike was broken some six months later, Jack, along with thousands of other dispossessed workers, sought work in factory cities, where he wrote of his experiences at night between exhausting shifts in steel mills and shoe factories and on automobile assembly lines. Jack and Gladys were parents to three children: Margaret Jean, born in 1923; Tom, born in 1925; and Jack Jr., born in 1928.

Conroy's earliest publications appeared in obscure little magazines like Ben Hagglund's *Northern Light* during this time. In 1929 he helped found the Rebel Poets organization which connected isolated worker-writers and radical poets through its publication *Rebel Poet* (1931–32). Conroy's stories appeared in H. L. Mencken's *American Mercury*, *Pagany*, and other prominent literary magazines in the early 1930s. As editor of the *Anvil* (1933–35), Conroy sought out and published young, untried writers—RICHARD WRIGHT, NELSON ALGREN, Erskine Caldwell, MERIDEL LE SUEUR, Sanora Babb, and others—who later achieved literary renown.

His first novel, *The Disinherited*, was published in 1933, followed by *A World to Win* in 1935. Awarded a Guggenheim grant in 1935, Conroy studied the migration of workers to Northern factory cities. He joined the Missouri Writers' Project in 1936, working on the state guidebook, and the Illinois Writers' Project in 1938, where he made important contributions to the new field of occupational folklore. His collaborations with black novelist Arna Bontemps, whom he met on the Illinois Writers' Project, produced three children's books, including the best-selling *The Fast Sooner Hound* (1942) based on folktales Conroy had collected, and two black history studies, *They Seek a City* (1944) and *Anyplace but Here* (1965).

Beginning in 1944, Conroy reviewed for Chicago newspapers, worked as an encyclopedia editor, and, following his retirement in 1966, returned to Moberly, Missouri, where he continued to write short stories and essays well into his eighties. Like many others of his generation, Conroy suffered neglect and calumny during the McCarthy era. Critical efforts to recover and reevaluate the long-obscured cultural achievements of the 1930s, however, are resulting in more balanced assessments of his literary contributions. He was the recipient of the Society for the Study of Midwestern Literature's 1980 Mark Twain Award for distinguished contributions to Midwestern literature. During the last seven years of his life Conroy suffered from diabetes and strokes. He died of heart failure in Moberly, Missouri, at age ninety-one.

**SIGNIFICANCE:** Conroy, along with other Midwestern literary radicals such as Meridel Le Sueur, Joseph Kalar, Sanora Babb, H. H. Lewis, PAUL COREY, and Nelson Algren, addressed the lives and experiences of working-class people in the Great Depression. Drawing upon the resources of oral expression characteristic of work communities he had known first-hand, Conroy refashioned genres of everyday speech to represent the events and lives of ordinary people within a social context. His sympathies lay with the working-class people he had known in Midwestern mining towns and factory cities; he wrote from within their experience, which was also his experience. Often labeled "proletarian," his writing is sharply distinguished from proletarian literature that reduces "the worker" and "the people" to undifferentiated stereotypes. Perceiving the continuity of vernacular traditions in industrial settings, Conroy fused humor, orality, and folk perspectives to expressions of worker protest. In addition, an important part of his legacy to American literature was, as editor, to provide the means for the voices of working-class people, those who do not write, to be heard. In doing so he revived earlier nonhierarchical methods of literary production that substituted "horizontal" peer circuits of communication for more hierarchical modes and "crude vigor," as he called it in the *Anvil* (March 1933), for "polished urbanity" (1). Conroy's unorthodoxy and independent judgments linked him to earlier Midwestern radical labor and populist traditions. Few writers of such talent and imagination have known as much about the worker's world within which Conroy forged the material of literary narrative and folktale, a legacy that remains vital today wherever "men live by truth and stand in need of expression" (Ralph Waldo Emerson, "The Poet").

**SELECTED WORKS:** The most recent edition of Conroy's best-known novel, *The Disinherited* (1933), was published in 1991, edited by Douglas Wixson. Translated into German, Russian, French, and Japanese, it has become a literary classic in its depiction of working-class life and expression between the world wars. *A World to Win* (1935), Conroy's other novel, is of uneven quality, reflecting unsure aims and the trying circumstances of its composition. Stories that Conroy edited and published in the *Anvil* and the *New Anvil* appear in *Writers in Revolt: The Anvil Anthology, 1933–1940*, edited by Conroy and Curt Johnson (1973). Conroy's short stories, sketches, and folktales are gathered in *The Weed King and Other Stories*, edited by Douglas Wixson (1985). His three children's books, coauthored by Arna Bontemps, are *The Fast Sooner Hound* (1942), *Slappy Hooper, the Wonderful Sign Painter* (1946), and *Sam Patch, the High, Wide and Handsome Jumper* (1951). Conroy also collaborated with Bontemps in writing two pioneering studies of black migration, *They Seek a City* (1945) and *Anyplace but Here* (1966; 1997). Conroy edited a collection of Midwestern humor entitled *Midland Humor* (1947). A number of Conroy's stories and essays are collected in *The Jack Conroy Reader*, edited by Jack Salzman and David Ray (1979).

**FURTHER READING:** Conroy's life and work are viewed in their social, historical, and literary contexts in *Worker-Writer in America: Jack Conroy and the Tradition of Midwestern Literary Radicalism, 1898–1990* (1994), by Douglas Wixson. Daniel Aaron's introduction to the 1963 edition of *The Disinherited* holds up well. Two groundbreaking studies, Aaron's *Writers on the Left* (1961) and WALTER RIDEOUT's *The Radical Novel in the United States, 1900–1954*, were early attempts to view the work of Conroy and other radical writers of his generation objectively. An early study of Conroy's work as editor, Michel Fabre's "Jack Conroy as Editor," appears in *New Letters* (Winter 1972): 115–37. Also see two issues of *New Letters* devoted to Conroy (Fall 1972 and Summer 1991). Robert Thompson interviewed Conroy for the *Missouri Review* (Fall 1983): 149–73. A brief but revealing personal recollection of Conroy appears in Stuart Brent's *The Seven Stairs* (1962): 43–46. For short overviews, see Wixson's essays in *Book Forum* 6 (1982): 201–206, and *Against the Current* (January–February 1991): 44–47, as well as *American Literary Magazines: The Twentieth Century* (1992): 281–88, *Encyclopedia of American Humorists* (1988): 98–104, and *American Folklore: an Encyclopedia* (1996): 156–57. The Newberry Library (Chicago) has an important collection of Conroy's papers. Some five thousand books from his personal library, as well as his book reviews and literary effects, are housed in a special room at the Moberly Area Community College (Missouri). The Jack Conroy Memorial Literary Society at MACC sponsors annual lectures and readings.

DOUGLAS WIXSON  UNIVERSITY OF MISSOURI–ROLLA

## GEORGE CRAM COOK

October 7, 1873–January 14, 1924
(Jig Cook)

**BIOGRAPHY:** Born in Davenport, Iowa, to Edward E. and Ellen (Dodge) Cook, Jig Cook was educated in that city before moving on to the University of Iowa, Harvard, and Heidelberg. He taught English at the University of Iowa from 1896 to 1898, served briefly in the army during the Spanish-American War, and took a teaching post at Stanford for the 1902–1903 academic year. He then returned to his family's country estate near Buffalo, Iowa, to raise vegetables and write fiction and poetry. His 1902 marriage to Sara Swain had ended by the time he met journalist Mollie Price. Cook and Price married in 1908; two children, Nilla and Harl, resulted from their union.

Cook had been introduced to socialism a few years earlier by the young writer FLOYD DELL, and their friendship solidified his commitment to socialist goals. He joined the Socialist Party in 1907 and in 1910 became that party's candidate for Congress from Iowa's Second Congressional District. Through his involvement in Davenport intellectual and political circles, he met novelist SUSAN GLASPELL, who soon became his new romantic interest. Public disapproval of his relationship with Glaspell prompted Cook to move to Chicago, where he served as associate literary editor of the *Chicago Evening Post's Friday Review*, working under editor Floyd Dell. Glaspell and Cook married in 1913 and began spending winters in Greenwich Village and summers in Provincetown, Massachusetts. There, in 1915, they founded the Provincetown Players and devoted themselves to this amateur theater group until 1922. Through the Provincetown Players, Cook hoped to recreate the true communal spirit of drama that originally grew out of the Dionysian rituals of ancient Greece. When the group failed to live up to Cook's vision, he and Glaspell emigrated to Delphi, Greece, where he died of glanders in 1924, after contracting the disease from the couple's pet dog.

**SIGNIFICANCE:** Jig Cook was the great-grandson of pioneer settler Ira Cook, grandson of congressman and banker John P. Cook, and son of attorney Edward E. Cook, one of Davenport's most wealthy and respected citizens. Although his pedigree suggests he would be an unlikely candidate for the radical life, much of his work is informed by the Midwestern tradition of protest, reform, and resistance that reflected the reaction of Midwestern intellectuals and artists to the region's tendency toward strangling convention. His second novel, *The Chasm* (1911), traces the conversion of Marion Moulton, daughter of a wealthy Moline plow manufacturer, from upper-middle-class elitism to socialism. Her arguments with Socialist gardener Walt Bradfield suggest those in which Cook and Dell would have engaged. They also suggest the soul-searching Cook would have undergone before he embraced socialism.

His first full-length play, *The Athenian Women*, portrays Pericles' companion Aspasia leading a strike for peace. Produced in 1918, the play had special resonance when experienced against the controversy surrounding America's entrance into World War I. Cook's second full-length play, *The Spring* (1921), set in Illinois on land where Chief BLACK HAWK'S village, Saukenuk, once stood, pits a young psychologist who aspires to investigate psychic phenomena against authority figures representing the forces of Midwestern oppression and convention.

Cook's three comedies are also shaped by his political leanings; however, these plays spoof the radical chic of intellectuals or artists whose trendiness brings unforescen consequences. Henrietta Brewster of *Suppressed Desires* becomes less enthusiastic about psychoanalysis when it threatens her marriage; Ian Joyce of *Tickless Time* (1918) changes his mind about burying the household clocks when his obsession with his sundial alienates everyone around him, and *Change Your Style*'s (1915) Marmaduke Marvin finds post-Impressionism less appealing when it begins to have commercial potential.

Jig Cook was typical of those early-twentieth-century Midwesterners who rebelled against the forces of convention and conservatism in their native towns and moved eastward to sample bohemian life in Chicago, Greenwich Village, and Europe. His work reflects his commitment to social change, at the same time acknowledging the sometimes ironic ramifications of extremism.

**SELECTED WORKS:** Cook collaborated with Charles Eugene Banks on *In Hampton Roads: A Dramatic Romance* (1899) and also published *Company B of Davenport* that year. His two published novels are *Roderick Taliaferro: A Story of Maximillian's Empire* (1903) and *The Chasm* (1911). He also wrote three one-act plays: *Change Your Style* (1915), and, with Susan Glaspell, *Suppressed Desires* (1915) and *Tickless Time* (1918). His longer plays are *The Athenian Women* (1918) and *The Spring* (1921). With Frank Shay he edited *The Provincetown Plays* (1921). *Greek Coins*, a book of his poems, was published posthumously in 1925.

**FURTHER READING:** In 1927 Susan Glaspell published *The Road to the Temple*, the only biography of Cook to date. Robert Sarlos's *Jig Cook and the Provincetown Players: Theatre in Ferment* (1982) treats Cook's influence on American theater. Thomas Tanselle's "George Cram Cook and the Poetry of Living, with a Checklist," in *Books at Iowa* 24 (1976): 3–25, provides a complete bibliography of Cook's works. Most of Cook's papers are held in the Berg Collection of the New York Public Library.

MARCIA NOE
THE UNIVERSITY OF TENNESSEE AT CHATTANOOGA

## PAUL (FREDERICK) COREY
July 8, 1903–December 17, 1992

**BIOGRAPHY:** Paul Frederick Corey was the last of seven children born to Edwin Olney and Margaret Morgan (Brown) Corey on a 160–acre farm in Shelby County, Iowa. Paul Corey's father died when Paul was not yet two years old, leaving the farm in the hands of his mother and four older brothers. In 1909 the oldest daughter, Elizabeth (Bess), homesteaded in South Dakota, an experience recorded in letters published in 1990 under the title *Bachelor Bess* by the University of Iowa Press with Paul Corey's introduction.

Paul's formal education, begun in a one-room schoolhouse, was continued in Atlantic, Iowa, where the family moved in 1918. In the fall of 1921, he matriculated at the University of Iowa, where as a student of Edwin Ford Piper, noted ballad collector, Corey excelled in writing. Through JOHN T. FREDERICK's *The Midland* in Iowa City, Corey met poet Ruth Lechlitner. Graduating in 1925,

Corey left for Chicago and subsequently New York City, taking various jobs while getting his start as a writer. After marrying on February 1, 1928, followed by a nine-month sojourn in Europe, Paul and Ruth built a native-stone house in Putnam County, New York, where they pursued their literary careers.

A frequent contributor to little magazines in the 1930s, including the *Anvil*, *Story*, and *Scribner's*, Paul chose Midwestern farm life as his subject. The Coreys' daughter Anne was born in 1941.

With the decline of interest in critical realism following World War II, Paul wrote nonfiction articles and books on home construction and furniture design. In 1947 the Coreys moved to Sonoma, California, across the valley from Jack London's final home. Corey continued to write until he died of a cerebral hemorrhage on December 17, 1992, leaving a distinguished and varied legacy of literary contributions to Midwestern literature.

**SIGNIFICANCE:** Eschewing the dreary fatalism of naturalism, Corey's work belongs to the tradition of Midwestern literary radicalism expressing thematically democratic values and social responsibility in conflict with the destructive forces of rapacious institutional and business practices. Corey's literary work carries forth the spirit of early settlers in the Midwest: self-sufficiency; non-ideological independence of thought; a sense of community; cooperative practices; and an inventive artisan's approach to work, including writing.

Corey's trilogy of Midwestern farm life, beginning with *Three Miles Square* (1939), followed by *The Road Returns* (1940) and *County Seat* (1941), dramatizes the joys and hardships of the Mantzes, an Iowa farm family struggling to maintain a rapidly disappearing way of life during the early decades of the twentieth century. In that era of rapid technological innovation and tumultuous economic upheaval, the effect of machine values, rationalized farming methods, and a growing attitude that land is simply another form of capital investment undermined the community-mindedness and economic independence so prized by farmers.

In *Acres of Antaeus* (1946), Corey's method of critical realism focuses on the rise of corporate farming and the response of independent farmers, largely ineffective, to resist proletarianization. The value of Corey's writing lies in its literary documentation, through finely drawn human portrayals, of these social forces and their consequences rendered in vigorous, accurate prose, reflecting his first-hand knowledge of Midwestern farm life and intellectual grasp of complex historical issues.

**SELECTED WORKS:** Corey's most significant literary work includes the Mantz family trilogy—*Three Miles Square* (1939), *The Road Returns* (1940), and *County Seat* (1941)—and *Acres of Antaeus* (1946). In addition, Corey wrote a science fiction novel entitled *The Planet of the Blind* (1968), translated as *Die Raderwelt* in a German edition appearing in 1972. A novella, *Bushel of Wheat, Bushel of Barley*, was printed in the prestigious *The New Caravan* anthology in 1936.

Beginning in the early 1930s, more than forty of Corey's short stories and essays appeared in magazines including *Scribner's, 1933: A Year Magazine, 1934, Anvil, Esquire, Hinterland, Story, Farm Journal, Look*, and others. Like a number of other writers associated with the left in the 1930s who experienced a decline in interest in critical realism after World War II, Corey turned to juvenile and young adult fiction. These include *The Red Tractor* (1944), *Five Acre Hill* (1946), *The Little Jeep* (1946), *Shad Haul* (1947), *Corn Gold Farm* (1948), and *Milk Flood* (1956). Corey also drew upon his skills as a builder and designer to publish articles and books on furniture and home construction, including *Buy an Acre* (1944), *Build a Home* (1946), *Homemade Homes* (1950), *Furniture Projects* (1957), *Holiday Homes* (1966), and *How to Build Country Homes on a Budget* (1975).

His lifelong interest in individual rights extended to animal rights. His two books on animal behavior, *Do Cats Think?* (1977, 1991) and *Are Cats People?* (1979), were, ironically, Corey's best-sellers.

In addition to his introduction to Elizabeth Corey's homesteading letters, *Bachelor Bess* (1990), Corey's autobiographical memoir, "Lurching toward Liberalism: Political and Literary Reminiscences," *Books at Iowa* 49 (November 1988): 35–71, offers the most complete personal account of his early life, college years, lifelong devotion to letters, and humane values. The short story "The Hunt," set in Corey's native Shelby County, appears in CLARENCE A. ANDREWS's anthology of Iowa writing, *Growing Up in Iowa* (1978).

**FURTHER READING:** Robert A. McCown's article "Paul Corey's Mantz Trilogy," in *Books*

at *Iowa* 17 (November 1972): 15–26, is an important discussion of Corey's work. Also, Roy Meyers in *The Middlewestern Farm Novel in the Twentieth Century* (1965) provides an introduction to Corey's novels, classifying them rather narrowly as "farm fiction."

Douglas Wixson's *Worker-Writer in America: Jack Conroy and the Tradition of Midwestern Literary Radicalism, 1898–1990* (1994) describes the traditions and literary milieus to which Corey belonged, furnishing biographical information based upon extensive interviews with Corey and Ruth Lechlitner. Lechlitner's brief but valuable memoir of the 1930s, ". . . anti-war and anti-fascism . . . ," appears in *Carleton Miscellany* 6 (Winter 1965): 77–82; indeed the entire magazine issue establishes a context for understanding and interpreting Corey's work. Loosely associated with progressive cultural movements in the 1930s, Corey nonetheless rejected orthodox "party line" ideology in his writing.

Corey's papers are gathered in Special Collections at the University of Iowa Library. Arranged by Robert A. McCown, the papers contain important correspondence, drafts, galley proofs, editorial notes, and drawings. Corey's daughter Anne wisely has preserved a number of rare books from the Coreys's personal library.

DOUGLAS C. WIXSON

UNIVERSITY OF MISSOURI–ROLLA

# (HAROLD) HART CRANE
July 21, 1899–April 27, 1932

**BIOGRAPHY:** Harold Hart Crane was born in Garrettsville in northeast Ohio. His father, Clarence Arthur Crane, known as C. A., was a vigorous, no-nonsense, successful businessman who opened his own maple sugar refinery in Warren, Ohio, when his son was four. C. A. Crane's most romantic act was the flamboyant wooing of Grace Hart, a delicate, beautiful, artistically ambitious girl from Chicago. Whether caused by C. A.'s obsessive working or Grace's distaste for physical love, the marriage was marked by long separations, violent quarrels, Grace's depressions, and frequent psychological collapses. During these unhappy years Grace entered into an emotionally intense relationship with her son, making him her confidant and companion. Her demands on his love were to become a significant psychological burden for Hart and possibly contributed to his own desperate need for love.

After his parents separated in 1908, Hart was sent to live in the house recently bought by his maternal grandparents at 1709 East 115 Street in Cleveland, Ohio, where he was to live for the next eight years. In his tower bedroom, the possible source of tower imagery in his poetry, he began in his teens to write and to think of himself as a poet. An indifferent student at Cleveland's East High, Hart Crane still showed remarkable precocity. Harriet Moody, the widow of University of Chicago professor and poet WILLIAM VAUGHN MOODY, became an early critic and supporter. Perhaps even more important to the young poet's education was Richard Laukhuff's Cleveland bookstore, opened in 1916. There Crane listened to local writers and artists such as George Henry Keller, Charles Burchfield, and William Sommer. There he read the little magazines so important to his career, among them *Bruno's Weekly*, where he published his first poem, "C 33," the number of Oscar Wilde's cell. In 1917, following his parents' final separation, the seventeen-year-old Crane escaped to New York, where in a year's time he published seven poems, one of them in the *Little Review*, and attracted the favorable attention of William Carlos Williams. After a brief return to Cleveland, where he worked for a short time as a reporter on the *Cleveland Plain Dealer*, Crane left again for New York. There he continued to write and make new friends, among them SHERWOOD ANDERSON, who recommended to him the strong masculine virtues of the American businessman. Anderson introduced Crane to Waldo Frank's *Our America,* which argued that only through involvement with an industrial society can the artist overcome its barbarisms. Impoverished and unable to write, Crane once again returned to Cleveland in November 1919 and stayed until March 1923. While there he conceived the general structure of *The Bridge*, his epic-scale poem about America that he worked on for seven years. The last eight years of his life blended literary success and personal misery. Waldo Frank praised *White Buildings* (1926) and linked Crane with Walt Whitman. Crane broke with his mother in 1928 after she had threatened to tell C. A. about his homosexuality. He never saw her again. In late 1929, after a trip to Paris, Crane

spent some time with his father in Chagrin Falls, Ohio, where C. A. had opened a restaurant. While there Crane successfully applied for a Guggenheim Fellowship to be spent in Mexico. His final year was filled with the drunkenness, debauchery, and hysterical quarrels for which Crane was by then famous. On the trip home from Mexico, Hart Crane climbed to the stern of the SS *Orizaba* and jumped to his death.

SIGNIFICANCE: Hart Crane's life appears fashioned from the fictions of some of his Midwestern contemporaries. His family life dramatizes the tensions between the world of the imaginative spirit and the pragmatic, harsh world of business. Like Sherwood Anderson, Hart Crane has become a symbol of the difficulties faced by the artist in a materialistic culture. His need to escape the Midwest, where he felt that poetry was "a bedroom occupation" ("Porphyro in Akron"), and his desperate and self-destructive search for love make him an icon of both the Midwest and of America itself.

Marked by the repeated destruction of his extraordinary sense of hope and promise, Hart Crane's life belongs to the dark tradition of Herman Melville, Nathaniel Hawthorne, Anderson, and F. SCOTT FITZGERALD. His poetry, however, belongs to America's transcendent Romantic tradition of Henry David Thoreau and Walt Whitman. In his art Crane evinced a Midwestern innocence untainted by irony and skepticism. He sought the reconciliation of the very worlds that seemed irreconcilable in his life. He intended *The Bridge* to be a symbol of the connection of the dimensional world and the world of the imagination, of past and present—in fact, a synthesis of all the significant oppositions in the American experience. Crane had hoped to create a myth of America that would counteract the bleak modernism of T. S. ELIOT's "The Wasteland." *The Bridge* was met mainly, however, by critics more receptive to irony than to rhapsody. Final estimations of this poem and of Crane divide generally along the lines of critics' attitudes toward the transcendental tradition. New Critic giants such as Yvor Winters and Alan Tate were suspicious of the poem's excessive feeling and lack of organic form. Later critics such as L. S. Dembo, Glauco Cambon, and M. L. Rosenthal applauded the very qualities that earlier critics had lamented. All have agreed, however, that *The Bridge* is, along with T. S. Eliot's *The Waste Land* and William Carlos Williams's *Paterson*, one of the century's major poetic statements. **SELECTED WORKS:** Crane published only two volumes during his lifetime: *White Buildings* (1926) and *The Bridge* (1930). *White Buildings* expresses Crane's enduring interest in the quest for the ideal and the relationship of the ideal to the real. Clearly the work of a major poet, this volume contains the especially noteworthy "For the Marriage of Faustus and Helen" and "Voyages," a sequence of six poems that concludes the volume. Critics have rightly complained that *The Bridge* has dominated criticism. "Voyages" alone establishes Crane as a major American poet. *The Bridge* was published first in Paris by the Black Sun Press (1930) three months before H. Liveright published it in America (1930). Brom Weber's *Letters of Hart Crane* (1965) is an important source for those interested in Crane's intellectual and aesthetic development, but those interested in Crane's relationship to both the Midwest and to his Midwestern family will want to look at Thomas Lewis's *Letters of Hart Crane and His Family* (1974). There are several editions of Crane's collected poetry. The latest edition, *The Poems of Hart Crane*, edited by Marc Simon (1986), has grouped thirteen of Crane's unpublished poems under the title *Key West: An Island Sheaf* because Crane clearly intended them to be a separate volume. Some of Crane's early poems are especially interesting because they are rooted in his Midwest experience. In a very few we see uncomplicated images of a joyful Midwestern boyhood. In "Sunday Morning Apples," dedicated to his friend William Sommer, a "boy runs with a dog before the sun." But mainly these poems dramatize the alienation Crane felt toward his Midwestern home. Even in the fine, gentle "My Grandmother's Love Letters," in which Crane desires to "lead my grandmother by the hand / Through much of what she would not understand," there is the sense of the impossibility of the connection. The poem ends with the "gentle pitying laughter" of the rain. It is "Porphyro in Akron," however, that succinctly states Crane's artistic alienation: "O City, your axles need not the oil of song. / I will whisper words to myself . . . ." **FURTHER READING:** Among several good biographies of Crane, John Unterecker's *Voy-*

*ager: A Life of Hart Crane* (1969), the latest full-length study, connects images from the poems to specific childhood experiences. Those interested in the influence of Crane's family and the Midwest, especially in respect to his development as an artist, will want to look at Vivian Pemberton's "Hart Crane's Heritage," in *Artful Thunder: Versions of the Romantic Tradition* (1975): 221–40. Among many good, full-length general studies of Crane are the especially useful *The Broken Arc* (1969), by R. W. Butterfield, and *Hart Crane: An Introduction and Interpretation* (1963), by Samuel Hazo. Paul Giles's *Hart Crane: The Contexts of "The Bridge"* (1986) examines the significance of such issues as homosexuality and capitalism to a reading of the poem. Although Crane's papers are fairly scattered, significant collections exist at Columbia, Yale, Ohio State University, the University of Pennsylvania, and the University of Texas libraries.

CLARENCE LINDSAY                    UNIVERSITY OF TOLEDO

## HOMER CROY
March 11, 1883–May 24, 1965

**BIOGRAPHY:** One of the many young Midwesterners who came out of the small towns of the region in the late nineteenth and early twentieth centuries to seek his fame and fortune in the city and the East, Homer Croy was born on a farm near Maryville, Missouri, the son of Amos J. and Susan (Sewell) Croy. He rode a horse to high school and then studied journalism at the University of Missouri but left without a degree to work on small-town newspapers.

Early in the new century he went to New York, where he worked for THEODORE DREISER, who was then editing three women's magazines, including the *Delineator*. For Dreiser he began to write the articles and stories that started his writing career. In the next forty years he wrote literally hundreds of articles and stories, including a number about and for the moving picture business, with which he became fascinated, and eight novels based on his youthful experiences in Missouri. In the last years he wrote several biographies of Westerners as well as popular histories.

Croy married Mae Belle Savell in February 1915 and was the father of a daughter, Carol. His best-known and most profitable novel was *They Had to See Paris* (1926), which was one of his favorites. The novel, the story of a rural Missouri couple in Europe, became Will Roger's first talking picture; it was re-written as a stage play by his wife and became a musical comedy. Croy died of heart disease in New York and was cremated.

**SIGNIFICANCE:** If the film industry became one of Croy's major interests, the other re-mained the Missouri farm and small town of his youth, the substance of his best fiction. Of his more than twenty books, most of them humorous, his two best novels, *West of the Water Tower* (1922) and *R. F. D. #3* (1924), both of them realistic, are set in Junction City, Mis-souri, a fictional representation of his native Maryville. Both are in the tradition of the small town defined by MARK TWAIN and im-mortalized by SHERWOOD ANDERSON. In both novels the story focuses upon young people who attempt to transcend what they see as the town's restrictive mores, and each young person fails, thereby learning an important lesson. Both novels are rooted in the tradition defined by CARL VAN DOREN in his 1921 essay "The Revolt from the Village," and Croy, aware of home-town criticism received by Anderson and others, published *West of the Water Tower* anonymously in 1923. Both nov-els and much of his other fiction are deeply rooted in the late-nineteenth- and early-twentieth-century Midwest.

**SELECTED WORKS:** Croy's first works, *Boone Stop* (1918) and *How Motion Pictures Are Made* (1918) are journalistic. His next three novels, *West of the Water Tower* (1923), *R. F. D. #3* (1924), and *They Had to See Paris* (1926), portray the Midwest and its people as he knew them. *Fancy Lady* (1927), *Caught* (1928), *Sixteen Hands* (1938), *Country Cured* (1943), *Corn Country* (1948), and *Wheels West* (1955) are somewhat conde-scending in their humor.

**FURTHER READING:** DAVID D. ANDERSON'S "Three Generations of Missouri Fiction," in *Midwestern Miscellany* 9 (1981): 7–20, examines Croy's major works as representative of Mis-souri writing. Most of his papers are in the Uni-versity of Missouri Library and the Missouri Historical Society Library.

DAVID D. ANDERSON    MICHIGAN STATE UNIVERSITY

# DANIEL CURLEY
October 4, 1918–December 30, 1988
**BIOGRAPHY:** Daniel Curley, short story writer, novelist, teacher, and editor, was born in East Bridgewater, Massachusetts, received an MA from the University of Alabama, and taught at Syracuse and Plattsburgh, New York. Much of his career, however, is associ-ated with the University of Illinois, where he held appointments from 1955 until 1988. He served on the editorial board of *Accent* from 1955 to 1960, coediting with Kirker Quinn *Ac-cent, an Anthology* in 1960. He established *As-cent* in 1975, serving as its editor until his death. Under Curley's editorship, the maga-zine garnered a reputation for publishing high-quality fiction oftentimes by writers who had received little previous recognition.

Curley's collection *Living with Snakes* (1985) won the Flannery O'Connor Award for Short Fiction for 1985. He also received a Guggenheim Fellowship in fiction, an O. Henry Award, a National Council of the Arts Award, and sev-eral Illinois Arts Council awards. His stories have been frequently anthologized.

Curley died after being struck by a car in Tallahassee, Florida.

**SIGNIFICANCE:** Curley's association with the Midwest, more than thirty years of it in Illinois, is primary in his lifetime of work. His ninety stories and three novels may be set in locations from East to South, from England to Mexico, but there is a Midwestern famili-arity. They are the sometimes humorous, sometimes sardonic accounts of a lone man, or a lone man and a lone woman, often en-cumbered by a mother or spouse and man-aging to make sense of a preposterous condi-tion. One character transports his mummified mother on the top of a car, another is charged with murdering himself, another assists in a hunt in which he may be the one hunted. Other characters find the unusual in the or-dinary while visiting a cemetery or watching birds. They are most often characters who come to peace with themselves in spite of seemingly disorderly surroundings. Curley's stories have held a special appeal in the Mid-west. Dan Jaffe describes Curley in an intro-duction to *The Curandero* (1991) as much val-ued by Chicago readers. His stories appeared in Chicago magazines including *Playboy*, *Chicago*, and the quarterly *ACM*. He published reviews and essays in the *Chicago Sun Times*. His plays were produced in Urbana, Illinois, and his books were published by the Univer-sity of Illinois Press and the BkMk Press of Kansas City as well as by Boston and New York houses.

**SELECTED WORKS:** Curley's stories are collected in five separate volumes: *The Marriage Bed of Procrustes* (1957), *In the Hands of Our Enemies* (1970), *Love in the Winter* (1976), *Living with Snakes* (1985), and *The Curandero* (1991). There are three novels: *How Many Angels?* (1958), *A Stone Man, Yes* (1964), and *Mummy* (1987). There is also a travel book, *The Perfect London Walk* (1986), written with Roger Ebert, that has been continuously in print. As well, there are three children's books: *Ann's Spring* (1976), *Billy Beg and the Bull* (1977), and *Hilarion* (1979).

**FURTHER READING:** Curley's books have been widely reviewed, including a June 22, 1964, *New Leader* piece in which he was described by Stanley Edgar Hyman as "one of the most gifted writers of my generation" (22). Recent and useful are a thoughtful review by Robert W. Lewis in the *North Dakota Quarterly* entitled "Daniel Curley, *The Curandero*" (Summer 1992): 241–42, and the Dan Curley Memorial Issue of *Accent* 15.1 (1990), including a previously unpublished story and poem of Curley's as well as remarks by his wife, Audrey, who continued the publication of *Accent* in Urbana through 1996. Dan Curley's papers are held in the library at the University of Illinois.

WILLIAM POWERS

MICHIGAN TECHNOLOGICAL UNIVERSITY

## JAMES OLIVER CURWOOD
June 12, 1878–August 13, 1927

**BIOGRAPHY:** James Oliver Curwood, adventure writer, naturalist, and historical novelist, boasts in his autobiography, *Son of the Forests* (1930), of a Mohawk Indian as his great-grandmother and of the British adventure writer, Frederick Marryat, as a great-uncle. His parents were Abigail (Griffin) Curwood and James Moran Curwood; and in actuality they had to move the family in 1885 to a farm near the small town of Ceylon in Erie County, Ohio, because of his father's failure as a cobbler. Curwood's autobiography narrates vividly this early move as well as his continuing emotional ties to his birthplace of Owosso, Michigan, fifteen miles due west of Flint. In fact, young Curwood was sent back to Owosso in 1892 at the urging of an older sister, Amy, who had not left. From that point on in his autobiography it is clear that he considers his youthful adventures along the river

in Owosso, which he calls "his river," the modest Shiawassee, were a seedbed for his later real life adventures along the massive Mackenzie River in northwest Canada and in the Hudson Bay area (*Son of the Forests* 70). Continually in this autobiography, Curwood relates his experiences around Owosso as a boy to his eventual writings about nature and about adventure. Later he did some writing in a log cabin in the Huron Mountains on the edge of Baraga and Marquette Counties in Michigan's Upper Peninsula near the location now called Mount Curwood in his honor, which Michigan Department of National Resources maps identify as the highest point in the state. A city park in the nearby town of L'Anse is also named in honor of Curwood, and his log cabin has been brought down from the woods and reassembled in the park.

With strong family support of his early ambition to write, Curwood studied at the University of Michigan and then began newspaper work in Detroit. He sold articles to *Munsey's Magazine* about Lake Michigan and western Canada and credited the Sunday editor of the *News-Tribune*, Annesley Burrowes, with teaching him to write about his love of adventure. By 1905 Curwood had placed an article in *Cosmopolitan* and after that sold much of his early fiction, notably his dog stories, which he later collected for *Kazan, The Wolf Dog* (1914), to International Magazine Company editor Ray Long. Curwood's first novel, *The Courage of Captain Plum* (1908), a tale about the Mormon settlements on Beaver Island in Lake Michigan, is his only story set in Michigan. When this novel was promoted well by Bobbs-Merrill, he was able to quit newspaper work. Curwood received grants from the Canadian government to travel and write about the Northwest; his second wife, Ethel Greenwood, whom he married on September 27, 1909, accompanied him on many of these adventures. Curwood had earlier married Cora Leon Johnson on January 21, 1900; they divorced in 1908. Finally, though Curwood claimed in his autobiography that his continual conditioning and a diet of "largely vegetables and meat once a week" (212–13) would give him a long life, he died in Owosso at the relative young age of forty-nine from blood poisoning. At the time of his death, Curwood was at the peak of his career and had a large readership for his twenty-six novels.

**SIGNIFICANCE:** Curwood created classic fiction in the modes of romance adventure and the particularly American version of nature romanticism. Though it is true that some of his tales, most notably the dog stories, are still marketed as adolescent literature, even those express his mature ideas about nature. For example, in one of the stories near the end of *Kazan*, Curwood notes that the "little professor had written a number of articles on dog intellect which had attracted wide attention among naturalists" (227–28). Despite his science and nature reporting, however, a continual romantic flight from progress pervades Curwood's fictions with the image of a Midwest frontier fading farther west and north. This may be one reason why he set most of his adventure stories outside Michigan and the Midwest. It would be a sad and ironic fulfillment of these primitivist fears if Curwood were able to see his beloved Owosso today as an industrial suburb of Flint as well as his mountain cabin in the Upper Peninsula moved to a city park. In nearly all of his Northwest fictions that culminate in *The Alaskan* (1923), one can find eloquent passages of an American version of Matthew Arnold's warning to the Scholar Gypsy, "Fly hence, our contact fear!" Thus Curwood continually writes in these novels of what he labels later in his autobiography as "far frontiers" (201), and he mixes nicely with this theme of pastoral escape the equally ancient tradition of convoluted and mistaken-identity romance plots. For example, his most successful book in terms of sales in the 1920s, *The Valley of Silent Men* (1920), concludes with nearly as much improbability and rapid unravelings of "family plots" as Horace Walpole's early gothic tale *The Castle of Otranto*.

Toward the end of his career, Curwood was working successfully away from romance and fantasy toward historical fictions set in Quebec and linked to Michigan through the French *voyageurs*. One transitional link between the two sorts of fiction might be seen in his hero "Jeems," the French way of pronouncing James, in *The Plains of Abraham* (1928) and his heroine, Marette Radisson, in the earlier romance, *The Valley of Silent Men* (1920). Marette loves Jeems and had been sent from the Yukon to school in Montreal. The French had left solid traces around L'Anse in the Upper Peninsula, where Curwood would often retreat to do his writing at this time. Thus we can trace a fictional self-consciousness of a "Jimmy Curwood" writing both romantic fictions about Mounties and escape and historical fictions about *voyageurs*, and the blending of the names James and Jimmy suggests what an artist he was becoming. In other words, his career was showing promise for new directions at the end.

**SELECTED WORKS:** *Kazan* (1914) and the trilogy set around the Three Rivers region of northwest Canada show Curwood at his peak, with the second and third of the trilogy, *The Valley of Silent Men* (1920) and *The Flaming Forest* (1921), as the best. Two other successful and representative books are *The Alaskan* (1923) and his posthumous autobiography *Son of the Forests* (1930), which treats Michigan and Ohio.

**FURTHER READING:** The collection edited by Ray Long, *My Story That I Like Best* (1925), shows how important Curwood was as a popular writer, and Edward Wagenknecht's *Cavalcade of the American Novel* (1952) acknowledges Curwood. Two biographies, one by Hobart Donald Swiggett (1943) and one by Judith A. Eldridge (1993), bear one title—*James Oliver Curwood*—as the main title. See also Grace Lee Nute's *Lake Superior* (1944) for some useful comments on Curwood and on those who enjoyed the adventure fiction that he wrote. The most complete collection of books and papers related to Curwood is at the Owosso Public Library. There has also been an annual Curwood Festival in the town since 1978. Some of Curwood's papers are in the Bentley Historical Library at the University of Michigan in Ann Arbor.

DONALD M. HASSLER          KENT STATE UNIVERSITY

# BRUCE CUTLER
October 8, 1930

**BIOGRAPHY:** Bruce Cutler, poet, essayist, playwright, and educator, was born in Evanston, Illinois, to Richard S. and Dorothea (Wales) Cutler. He attended Northwestern University and graduated from the University of Iowa with honors in 1951. He earned his MS at Kansas State College (now Kansas State University) in 1957, with further graduate study at the Universita degli Studi, Naples, from 1957 to 1958. A music major at Northwestern, he was a jazz musician in the Chicago area. Cutler is a member of the Society of Friends and was a social worker for the American Friends Service Committee from 1951 to 1955. He worked with migrants in a United Nations Demonstration Area for Health and Education in El Salvador from 1952 to 1953, and again with migrants in Texas from 1953 to 1955. He was married to Tina Cirelli from 1954 until her death on April 6, 1993. There are three children by their marriage.

Cutler was an instructor in English at Kansas State University from 1958 to 1960 and then became an instructor at the University of Wichita (later Wichita State University), Wichita, Kansas, in 1960. He was appointed Distinguished Professor of Humanities in 1973 and Adele M. Davis Distinguished Professor of Humanities in 1978. At Wichita State, he was coordinator of the creative writing program from 1967 until he retired from teaching in 1987. His first book of poetry, *The Year of the Green Wave*, was published in 1960. In all, Cutler has published ten books of poetry and has contributed to several collections including *Midland*, edited by PAUL ENGLE and others (1961), and *Heartland: Poets of the Midwest*, edited by LUCIEN STRYK (1967). *Seeing the Darkness* (1998) is a series of poems concerning Naples, Italy, in World War II, from the time Allied troops entered the city in 1943 until 1945. Cutler also has written essays and plays. He has taught in Latin America and Europe under the Fulbright Exchange Program and on grants from the U.S. Department of State. He lives in Saint Paul, Minnesota.

**SIGNIFICANCE:** KARL SHAPIRO, in his introduction to *The Year of the Green Wave*, wrote that Cutler "has his own style, a rare thing in the poetry of our time. He tries to make his language approach the strange, still-unwritten language of America . . ." (vii). Cutler draws upon a rich historical knowledge and creative imagination in his poetry to bring the reader into Midwestern situations, past and present, which have shaped the culture of the region. The narrative poems in *A West Wind Rises* recount the massacre of Free State settlers at Trading Post, Kansas Territory, in 1858, by slaveowners and their sympathizers. In the long poem in ten parts, *The Doctrine of Selective Depravity* (1980), he tells the story of criminals, victims, and courts in a Midwestern urban setting. Cutler writes of international themes as well, and many of his poems are influenced by his travels in Latin America and Europe.

**SELECTED WORKS:** Cutler's volumes of poetry include *The Year of the Green Wave* (1960), *A West Wind Rises* (1962), *Sun City* (1964), *A Voyage to America* (1967), *The Maker's Name* (1980), *The Doctrine of Selective Depravity* (1980), *Dark Fire* (1985), *The Massacre at Sand Creek* (1995), *Afterlife* (1997), and *Seeing the Darkness* (1998). A collection of essays, *Nectar in a Sieve* (1983), offers several examples of his prose.

**FURTHER READING:** Little has been written about Bruce Cutler, one of the Midwest's finest poets. See the selections in *Heartland: Poets of the Midwest* (1967), and *Pioneer Press* (St. Paul, Minn.), February 12, 1989.

TOM L. PAGE          WICHITA STATE UNIVERSITY

# D

## EDWARD DAHLBERG
July 22, 1900–February 27, 1977

**BIOGRAPHY:** Edward Dahlberg, one of the foremost exponents of the baroque style in modern American literature, was born in Boston, to Elizabeth Dalberg and Sol Gottdank. Edward would later change the spelling to Dahlberg. The insecurity caused by his family circumstances and poverty led to Dahlberg's being placed in an orphanage from 1907 until 1908 and from 1912 until 1917. He often returned to his experiences in orphanages in his writings. His mother had fled Boston and New York via Dallas, Memphis, New Orleans, and Louisville, finally arriving in 1905 in Kansas City. Elizabeth Dalberg was a barber at the Star Lady Barbershop, located first on Walnut Street and later at 16 East Eighth Street.

Dahlberg's contacts with early Kansas City "characters" and orphans in the institutions where he spent portions of his childhood provided the basis for some of his best literary creations. After his graduation from an orphanage school in Cleveland, he briefly returned to Kansas City and then set out on a cross-country tour. Dahlberg attended the University of California at Berkeley from 1922 until 1923. He then attended Columbia University, receiving a bachelor of science in philosophy in 1925. From 1926 until 1929, he lived abroad, gaining much from his associations with ROBERT MCALMON, Ethel Moorhead, Winifred Eaton Webb, Carnevali, and HART CRANE, among others. In 1929 *Bottom Dogs* was published with an introduction by D. H. Lawrence.

Dahlberg returned to the United States in 1929 and joined the MacDowell Colony in New Hampshire. With the publication of *Bottom Dogs*, he gained a reputation as an exponent of American realism and naturalism. His literary associations with Edmond Wilson, Kenneth Burke, and JAMES T. FARRELL illustrate his involvement with the rising new group of literary figures. His second book, *From Flushing to Calvary,* was published in 1932. The critical reaction was at best lukewarm. In 1933 he made a trip to Germany during the Hitler era, which resulted in *Those Who Perish* (1934). From 1936 through 1950, Dahlberg generally retreated from the literary world. During this period, he immersed himself in the study of literary style, moving from the realistic and naturalistic prose of *Bottom Dogs* to a more complicated prose style that has much in common with that of Sir Thomas Browne. He also taught at New York University and lived in New York and Cape Cod. In addition to participating in the New York Writers' Project, he developed new literary associations with SHERWOOD ANDERSON, THEODORE DREISER, and Charles Olson. The death of his mother in 1945 was a severe blow.

Publication of *The Flea of Sodom* in 1950 moved Dahlberg once again into the literary limelight. His political ideals had shifted dramatically, moving from the left of the political spectrum toward the right. His marriage to R'Lene Howell on October 14, 1950, coincided with a renewal of public attention. His wife was part of a critical collaboration during the most fruitful period of his life. Holding a variety of part-time jobs to supplement publishers' advances, Dahlberg traveled extensively for the balance of his life. He then viewed New York as his home but spent a great deal of time in Majorca, Kansas City, and California. Perhaps the culmination of his career was the recognition accorded *Because I Was Flesh* (1964), which was nominated for a National Book Award. This work focused public attention on Dahlberg's "new voice." He was elected to the National Institute of Arts and Letters and received prestigious grants to enable him to continue writing. He died of lung congestion in New York City.

**SIGNIFICANCE:** Dahlberg's masterpiece, *Because I Was Flesh*, is set in Kansas City, Missouri. Much of it is a retelling of his childhood, which he had fictionalized in *Bottom Dogs*. His characterization of stockmen, "chippies," and other brawling characters out of early Kansas City has lasting value. His portrayal of Lizzie Dalberg has gained special attention for its honesty and incisiveness. In similar fashion, other works, especially *From Flushing to Calvary*, reflect the growth of his artistry from Midwestern roots. Dahlberg's best works relate to his life in Kansas City. As he observed in *Because I Was Flesh*, he drew his artistic strength from the city and his experiences there. In his depiction of Midwestern characters shortly after the turn of the century, he captured essential human truths. However, Dahlberg also played a broader role in English and American literature. Operating on the assumption that "truth is more sacred than friendship," he often alienated influential critics and editors with no regard for the consequences. His decision to explore the full range of language led him to stylistic preferences quite different from those of some famous friends. Yet his Midwestern roots continued to emerge. It was perhaps a common interest in Midwestern character traits and settings which brought Dahlberg and his friends together.

**SELECTED WORKS:** Dahlberg's best and most widely known work is *Because I Was Flesh* (1964). The volume was nominated for a National Book Award. It epitomizes his strengths as a writer of the Midwest and the nation. The early fictionalized version of his life, *Bottom Dogs* (1929), spans much of the same time period and has become a minor classic of American literature. *The Confessions of Edward Dahlberg* (1971) is a sequel to the events in the two earlier works. A fine selection of his exists in *Cipango's Hinder Door* (1965). Dahlberg's criticism, often blunt and even brutal, is perhaps best exemplified by *Truth Is More Sacred* (1961), a volume of letters he exchanged with Sir Herbert Read.

**FURTHER READING:** Despite Dahlberg's own complaints that he was neglected during his lifetime, he has been the subject of numerous critical studies. Harold Billings's *Edward Dahlberg: American Ishmael of Letters* (1968) contains a wide variety of original essays and appreciations by friends and colleagues such as Sir Herbert Read, Alan Tate, Alfred Kazin, Frank MacShane, and Kay Boyle. A special issue of *TriQuarterly*, edited by Jonathan Williams (1970), similarly contains appraisals by Anthony Burgess, William M. Ryan, Josephine Herbst, KARL SHAPIRO, Norman Holmes Pearson, Thomas Merton, and others. The only book-length critical study of Dahlberg's work is *Edward Dahlberg* (1972) by Fred Moramarco in the Twayne U.S. Authors series. The volume provides an excellent overview of critical approaches to Dahlberg's work. A biography, *The Wages of Expectation*, written by Charles DeFanti, appeared in 1978. It is the only complete study of Dahlberg's life. For further critical study, Harold Billings's *A Bibliography of Edward Dahlberg* (1971) is essential. While it does not cover all of Dahlberg's career, it gives thorough and meticulous attention to his publications and criticism prior to 1970. Numerous shorter critical studies have appeared. The best collection of his papers and works is at the University of Texas at Austin.

ROBERT L. KINDRICK        UNIVERSITY OF MONTANA

## LEO DANGEL
August 7, 1941

**BIOGRAPHY:** Leo Dangel was born on a farm near Freeman, South Dakota, to John and Sylvia (Andersen) Dangel. He received his elementary education in a one-room schoolhouse. After receiving a BA degree in social science from Emporia State University (1966) and an MA in English from the same institution (1968), Dangel taught until his retirement at Southwest State University in Marshall, Minnesota. Surrounded by writer colleagues including HOWARD MOHR, Phil Dacey, and BILL HOLM, Dangel came late in life to writing poetry. His work appeared first in the chapbook *Keeping between the Fences* (1981), then two small paperbacks: *Old Man Brunner Country* (1987) *and Hogs and Personals* (1992). His collected poems, *Home from the Field* (1997), was nominated for a Minnesota State Book Award and adapted for a reader's theater production by the Lyric Theatre of Minneapolis, Minnesota (1998).

**SIGNIFICANCE:** Dangel's models include writers of fiction in the regional-realist tradition such as SHERWOOD ANDERSON, WILLA CATHER, and SINCLAIR LEWIS, and contemporary Midwestern poets such as BILL KLOEFKORN and Ted Kooser. While his poetry invites comparison with that of Kloefkorn and DAVE ETTER especially, his work is clearly his own in its wry and characteristically rural Minnesotan understatement, its vivid scenes and characters drawn mostly from boyhood memories, and its sympathy with the conditions of rural Midwestern life: restrained feeling, Protestant work ethic, fond tolerance of eccentricity, and vestigial prairie populism. Among his fictional poetic creations, Old Man Brunner and Arlo loom especially large as archetypal curmudgeonous bachelor farmer and callow farm lad, respectively. Dangel's poems first attract a reader with their Midwestern characters and speech, but beneath the surface lies a subtle understanding of human nature. The best of his poem-stories verge on fables, little lessons on the danger of fitting in too easily (disguising a rural walk as a hunting trip to avoid suspicion), on the necessity of controlled license (keeping a car between the fences while driving home drunk to a failing farm), or the necessity of controlled revenge (praying for the death of that "bandit John Deere dealer" who sold the tractor with a cracked block).

**SELECTED WORKS:** Dangel's collected poems, *Home from the Field* (1997), contains all work published in the earlier collections, *Old Man Brunner Country* (1987) and *Hogs and Personals* (1992), both of which are now out of print, and additional recent work.

**FURTHER READING:** Ronald Barron has a brief essay on Leo Dangel in *A Guide to Minnesota Writers* (1993): 35–36. A helpful newspaper appreciation is Lee Eggerstrom's review "Books Share Quiet Joys of Farming," in the *St. Paul Pioneer Dispatch* (March 7, 1987): 3B. Dangel was the featured poet in *Great River Review* 22 (April 1994).

DAVID PICHASKE      SOUTHWEST STATE UNIVERSITY

## JIM (JAMES RAYMOND) DANIELS
June 6, 1956

**BIOGRAPHY:** Jim Ray Daniels, poet and screenwriter, was born James Raymond Daniels in Detroit and raised in Warren, Michigan. His father, Raymond J. Daniels, worked at a Ford Motor Company axle housing plant. His mother, Mary (Rivard) Daniels, is a nurse. After working at Ford and at other jobs, he earned degrees at Alma College (BA 1978) and Bowling Green State University (MFA 1980), while refining a colloquial style of poetic narrative in which Midwestern factory workers are portrayed with dignity and humanity.

In 1981 Daniels accepted a position as writer-in-residence at Carnegie Mellon University in Pittsburgh, Pennsylvania, where he is now professor of English. Because of a dedicated grassroots interest in his poetry, he has published limited edition chapbooks as often as full-length volumes of poetry. His poems also appear in many anthologies and national journals, such as *Paris Review* and *New England Review*, though primarily in Midwestern venues such as *Michigan Quarterly Review*, *Iowa Review*, *Witness*, and *Ohio Review*. He has been interviewed and has frequently read his poems on National Public Radio. In 1985 he married author and editor Kristin Kovacic, with whom he has two children, Ramsay and Rosalie.

**SIGNIFICANCE:** Daniels's poetry, like his prose and screenwriting, is rooted in the urban Midwest, in Detroit, in the auto plants of Warren, in the cars themselves, in baseball stadiums, bowling alleys, fast-food restaurants, department stores, living rooms, backyards, and out in the street. His tightly wrought po-

**Jim Daniels.**
Photo by Andrea Stephany. Courtesy of Jim Daniels

ems are peopled with colorful narrators who reveal the devastating effects upon workers of a society so stratified by class structure and racial prejudice that it threatens to erupt into violence at any time. In his poem "Time/Temperature," for example, Daniels takes on the 1943 and 1967 Detroit riots and the pervasiveness of racism even within his own family. Writing in the February 6, 1994, *New York Times Book Review*, Carol Muske notes that "unlike most contemporary poems" on racism, "Time/Temperature" is "unsparing in its self-indictment" (33).

In 1985 Daniels was awarded the annual Brittingham Prize in Poetry from the University of Wisconsin Press in a competition judged that year by poet C. K. Williams. In his preface to the book, *Places/Everyone*, Williams quotes French author Simone Weil: "Many indispensable truths, which could save men, go unspoken for reasons of this kind: those who could utter them cannot formulate them and those who could formulate them cannot utter them" (ix). Daniels, like Weil, worked on the assembly line, and like his father and his grandfather worked blue-collar jobs and lived in Detroit. He lived in the neighborhoods of Eight Mile Road, which he describes in the poem "Trouble at the Drive-In" as "the border between Detroit and Warren . . . [where] the / anger / is stewing

just like always, every day / guns pointed at our own dumb heads" (*M-80* 83).

Daniels writes from a working-class perspective uncommon in American poetry. That his first three books form a trilogy of industrial America and the city of Detroit is partly due to the appearance in each of Digger, a persona for Daniels, Daniels's father, and every factory worker. The humor and empathy with which Daniels characterizes Digger affirms the dignity of working-class people. As a writer of proletarian experience, Daniels contributes to a Midwestern tradition that includes JOHN CONROY, HARRIETTE ARNOW, Philip Levine, and JAMES WRIGHT.

Daniels's most recent book, *Blessing the House* (1997), integrates Detroit poems with others set in Pittsburgh and Italy. While developing themes from the previous books, such as social class, urban violence, and family life, *Blessing the House* emphasizes spiritual concerns, from the poet's Catholic upbringing to a meditation on his loss of faith, inspired by an examination of Italian medieval art. Such an integration of themes also occurs in Daniels's longest poem to date, "Niagara Falls," which appears in a chapbook by the same title. In it, Daniels connects his youthful experience as a Catholic altar boy to religious iconography in small Italian villages, and to the Falls, where water flowing from Detroit and the entire Great Lakes watershed churns on its way to the ocean—an apt metaphor for the expanding of the Midwest itself into the world.

**SELECTED WORKS:** Daniels's books of poetry are *Places/Everyone* (1985), *Punching Out* (1990), *M-80* (1993), *Blessing the House* (1997), and *No Pets* (1999). His chapbooks, which largely consist of poems unavailable in the full-length collections, are *Factory Poems* (1979), *On the Line* (1981), *The Long Ball* (1988), *Digger's Territory* (1989), and *Niagara Falls* (1994). Daniels wrote the screenplay for the Tony Buba film *No Pets* (1994), based on one of his short stories about factory work. "Troubleshooting: Poetry, the Factory, and the University," an autobiographical essay illustrated with photographs, appears in *Liberating Memory: Our Work and Our Working-Class Consciousness,* edited by Janet Zandy (1995): 86–96. Literary anthologies that Daniels has edited include *Ten Years with the Mill Hunk Herald* (1990), *The Carnegie Mellon Anthology* (with Gerald Costanzo, 1993), and *Letters to America: Contemporary American Poetry on Race* (1995).

**FURTHER READING:** Though no book-length studies of his work have yet been published, Daniels's books have been widely reviewed. "Landscapes and Still Lives," Peter Stitt's influential notice of *Places/Everyone,* appeared in the *New York Times Book Review* (May 4, 1986): 22. In "The Wilderness Surrounds the World," appearing in *Hudson Review* 43 (Winter 1991): 669–78, Robert McDowell notes that Daniels depicts management as well as labor with fairness and honesty in *Punching Out.* "His most useful implied criticism," McDowell argues, "is reserved for the system itself, a system that codifies human behavior and bludgeons the individual into ever more impossible roles and situations" (678). Criticism of *M-80* includes Carol Muske's "Outside the Fence, Three Renegade Stylists," in *New York Times Book Review* (February 6, 1994): 32–33, and an untitled, uncredited essay in *Virginia Quarterly Review* 70.1 (Winter 1994): 31. Daniels engages in an extended conversation about his early life, literary influences, and ambitions as a writer in "An Interview with Jim Daniels" by William Barillas, with MARCUS CAFAGÑA, in *Passages North* 17.1 (Summer 1996): 36–58. His papers are housed in Special Collections, Michigan State University Library.

MARCUS CAFAGÑA
SOUTHWEST MISSOURI STATE UNIVERSITY

# CLARENCE DARROW
April 18, 1857–March 13, 1938

**BIOGRAPHY:** Born in Farmdale, Ohio, in Ohio's Western Reserve, to Amirus and Emily (Eddy) Darrow and raised in nearby Kinsman, Clarence Darrow became and remains legendary as an American criminal lawyer, socio-legal and autobiographical writer, and humanitarian. Although he attended the local district school and academy and attended Allegheny College in Pennsylvania for a year, his real early education came in his father's eclectic but humble library as well as in factory work, store clerking, and country school teaching. These occupied the three years between Allegheny College and his first and only year of law school at the University of Michigan, which he completed at nineteen. He spent a second year reading law in an attorney's office and was admitted to the Ohio bar in 1878 at age twenty-one.

He married Jessie Ohl in 1880, began to practice in nearby Andover, Ohio, and then moved on to Ashtabula, where he was modestly successful. However, in 1888 he moved to Chicago, where he fell under the influence of John P. Altgeld and became friends with BRAND WHITLOCK. There he formulated his legal principles: that poverty is the cause of crime and that people are helpless organisms controlled by forces beyond their control. He became a Darwinian and an agnostic and quickly became successful as a criminal lawyer. Among his most successful and notorious cases were acquittals for Eugene V. Debs and "Big Bill" Hayward and his saving the notorious Leopold and Loeb from the death penalty by his innovative plea of mitigating circumstances. Darrow became famous as the lawyer for the defense in the 1925 Scopes trial in Dayton, Tennessee.

He and Jessie had one son, Paul; they were divorced in 1897, and he later married Ruby Hamerstrom, who survived him. He died of heart disease, was cremated, and as he requested, his ashes were strewn over Chicago's Jackson Park lagoon.

**SIGNIFICANCE:** Although Darrow wrote hundred of legal briefs, many of them published, as well as other legal studies, his literary reputation is based on three works, *A Persian Pearl and Other Essays* (1899), which he edited and to which he contributed; *Farmington* (1904), a fictional memoir; and *The Story of My Life* (1932), an autobiography. All three reflect both Darrow's lifelong interest in literature and his early recognition of the ties between the profession he selected and that of letters, which he often regretted not pursuing.

*A Persian Pearl* is an early attempt to define and support the realistic literary naturalism that was beginning to make its influence felt in Chicago writing, but both *Farmington* and *The Story of My Life* are autobiography of a very high standard. The former is the story of Darrow's boyhood in Kinsman, of a boy growing up in a small Ohio town a generation after the frontier has passed. In its clear focus on place as the source of experience, it bears favorable comparison to two other stories of Ohio boyhoods, WILLIAM DEAN HOWELLS's *A Boy's Town* (1890) and SHERWOOD ANDERSON's

*Tar: A Midwest Childhood* (1926). Of the three, Darrow's, depicting a period of relative tranquility in the Midwestern past, is the most idyllic.

*The Story of My Life* takes the boy to Chicago, to the practice of law, and to the discovery of the city, the modern age, and social Darwinism, the three elements that produced his legal theories and success. He remained a Midwestern modern to the end.

**SELECTED WORKS:** Darrow's chief legal publications are *Resist Not Evil* (1903), *An Eye for an Eye* (1905), *Crime: Its Causes and Treatment* (1922), and *The Prohibition Mania* (1927), with Victor S. Yarros. He also wrote *Infidels and Heretics* (1929), with Wallace Rice.

**FURTHER READING:** There has been a sustained interest in Darrow. Useful biographies include Allen Crandall's *The Man from Kinsman* (1932); Abe Ravitz's *Clarence Darrow and the American Literary Tradition* (1962); Richard J. Jensen's *Clarence Darrow: The Creation of an American Myth* (1972); James Edward Sayer's *Clarence Darrow: Public Advocate* (1978); Kevin Tierney's *Darrow: A Biography* (1979); and Arthur Weinberg's *Clarence Darrow: A Sentimental Rebel* (1988). For an interesting comparison, see DAVID D. ANDERSON's "From Memory to Meaning: The Boys' Stories of William Dean Howells, Clarence Darrow, and Sherwood Anderson," in *MidAmerica* 10 (1983): 69–84.

A useful bibliography is Willard D. Hunsberger's *Clarence Darrow: A Bibliography* (1972). His papers are scattered, with a concentration at the State Historical Society of Wisconsin.

DAVID D. ANDERSON     MICHIGAN STATE UNIVERSITY

## CLYDE BRION DAVIS

May 22, 1894–July 19, 1962

**BIOGRAPHY:** The son of Charles N. Davis and Isabel (Brion) Davis, Clyde Brion Davis, journalist and prolific novelist, was born in Unadilla, Otoe County, Nebraska. He grew up in Chillicothe, Missouri; there and later in Kansas City he attended public schools. At fourteen he dropped out of school to become, in turn, a printer's devil, pressman, commercial artist, and salesman; he was also, at one time or another, a private detective and a ranch hand, and he worked at a variety of other temporary jobs.

When the United States entered World War I, he enlisted in the Regular Army, serv-ing in France. After the Armistice he found himself a journalist when he worked on *Pontanezen Duckboard*, an army newspaper in Brest in 1919. After his discharge he worked in turn at the *Denver Post*, 1919–20, *Denver Rocky Mountain News*, 1920–21, *San Francisco Examiner*, 1921–22, *Denver News*, 1922–29, *Seattle Post Intelligencer*, 1930, and *Buffalo Times*, 1930–37. He served as a European correspondent for *New York PM* in 1941. He received Huntington Hartford Fellowships in 1956–57 and 1959–60. On April 20, 1926, he married Martha Wirt of Denver. They had one son, David Brion Davis. His wife died on January 14, 1932. He continued to write until his death of heart disease.

**SIGNIFICANCE:** Davis wrote twenty books, including novels, autobiographical memoirs, a volume in the Rivers of America series, and novels for young people dealing with adolescent initiation. He edited a collection of stories for boys, and he published a number of essays on the art and craft of writing. In all of these works Davis drew heavily on his own experiences: his boyhood years in Chillicothe, his army experience, and his years as a wandering newspaperman. His first novel, *The Anointed* (1937), the story of a vagabond sailor-adventurer from Tennessee whose eventual love for a San Francisco librarian turns him into a grocery clerk, was a selection of the Book-of-the-Month Club, and it became the basis for a film, *The Adventurer* (1945), starring Clark Gable and Greer Garson. It was followed by *"The Great American Novel—"* (1938), also a Book-of-the-Month Club selection. The first of Davis's newspaper stories, in the form of a first-person journal written over a period of thirty years, it takes Homer Zigler from Buffalo to Cleveland to Kansas City to San Francisco to Denver as a newspaperman in pursuit of his dream—to write the Great American Novel. Finally, at the end, sufficient leisure presents itself; but first he must endure major surgery, and we never learn whether the novel is written, or whether, indeed, he survives the surgery.

The first two novels were Davis's most successful. The first is firmly rooted in his imagination and the second in his journalistic career, but both have their origins in small-town Chillicothe, Missouri, and the trek to the city and beyond, where his protagonists seek the success and fulfillment that have eluded them in the small town. In both there are echoes of THEODORE DREISER, SHERWOOD ANDERSON, and FLOYD DELL.

In other novels, including *Jeremy Bell* (1947) and *The Big Pink Kite* (1960), he focuses on life in the town, Down's Mill, Illinois, in the former and Calhoun, Missouri, in the latter. Neither novel revolts from nor rejects the village: life is rewarding in each, but each is, like *Winesburg, Ohio*, intrinsically tied to the larger world beyond, and inevitably the protagonists seek their future in the city, by choice in the former and through economic necessity in the latter. As each novel ends, fulfillment remains elusive, and a future looms that is far more uncertain than it had been in the towns.

Davis's autobiographical memoir, *The Age of Indiscretion* (1950), examines life in Chillicothe, Missouri, in the late nineteenth century and early twentieth in great detail, both from his experiences as he remembered them and from the perspective of maturity a half-century later. As a memoir it is superb, and Davis makes his premise clear: that life was neither richer nor happier in what were clearly not the good old days. But it remains a fine re-creation of the Midwestern town at its zenith just before the outbreak of World War I.

**SELECTED WORKS:** Davis's books for boys, including *North End Wildcats* (1938) and *North Woods Whammy* (1951), are reminiscent of MARK TWAIN. *Thudbury* (1952) is an attempted epic of an American family, and *The Rebellion of Leo McGuire* (1944) and *Playtime Is Over* (1949) are picaresque fictional biographies. *Nebraska Coast* (1939) is his only fictional portrayal of the nineteenth-century Midwestern frontier. His other novels, including *The Anointed* (1937), "*The Great American Novel—*" (1938), *Jeremy Bell* (1947), and *The Big Pink Kite* (1960), remain readable and interesting in their view of the past. *The Age of Indiscretion* (1950) is an accurate portrayal of the Midwest of his youth. He also wrote *The Arkansas* (1940) in the Rivers of America series.

**FURTHER READING:** No biography of Davis has been written, but his works were widely reviewed by such prominent critics as Harrison Smith and DAWN POWELL; critical assessments appear in *Dictionary of Literary Biography* 9 (1981): 184–87; and in Steven G. Kellerman's "The Self-Begetting Great American Novel: Clyde Brion Davis's Melding of Traditions," in *Southwest Review* 62 (Winter 1977): 65–72. His own comments appear in *Twentieth Century Authors* (1942, 1951): 352 and *First Supplement* (1955, 1963): 265. Rinehart published a pamphlet on Davis, "Man with the Seeing Eye," in 1946 as one of a series, Profiles of Well-Known Rinehart and Company Authors.

DAVID D. ANDERSON    MICHIGAN STATE UNIVERSITY

# FRANK MARSHALL DAVIS
December 31, 1905–August 9, 1987

**BIOGRAPHY:** Frank Marshall Davis, poet and journalist, was born in Arkansas City, Kansas, where he attended public schools and graduated from high school. Although he attended integrated schools in a locality and a state known for liberality in civil rights, it was clear to him, from childhood on, that he would be treated differently because he was African American. After attending Friends University in Wichita for a year, he transferred to Kansas State College in Manhattan, Kansas, to major in journalism. There he was introduced to free verse by one of his teachers, published poems in the student newspaper, and developed a life-long interest in poetry.

Davis left without taking his degree and, after a short period in Chicago, took a job editing a semiweekly newspaper in Atlanta, Georgia. Under his direction the paper became the successful *Atlanta Daily World*. He joined the staff of the Associated Negro Press (ANP), a news service, in Chicago in 1935, where he worked until 1948. That year he and his wife left Chicago for Hawaii, where he made a living running a wholesale paper company and lived in relative obscurity. He was invited to the mainland in 1973 to give lectures at Howard and several other universities. Davis died in Honolulu in 1987.

**SIGNIFICANCE:** Davis published several collections of poems during his Chicago years, including *Black Man's Verse* (1935), *I Am the American Negro* (1937), *Through Sepia Eyes* (1938), and *47th Street Poems* (1948). His poetry was well received; in 1937 he was awarded a Julius Rosenwald Foundation grant. Interested in jazz and in its history, he had a radio program on WJJD in Chicago, where he produced a series of fifteen-minute jazz shows. Much of his poetry is influenced by jazz, and in 1985 a collection of jazz poems taken from his earlier work was published as *Jazz Interlude* (1985). After his death, his autobiography, *Livin' the Blues* (1993), was published.

Davis was an important figure in the group of artists that included GORDON PARKS and GWENDOLYN BROOKS in Chicago in the 1930s and 1940s. He was well known in black newspaper circles of the day and was regarded as a unique voice among black poets. Active in the civil rights movement as well, he was a member of the national board of the Civil Rights Congress in 1947–48.

His autobiography, an important document in Midwestern African American literary history, details his childhood and youth in Kansas and provides valuable information concerning the Chicago African American artists' movement and groups of the 1930s and 1940s. As John Edgar Tidwell notes in his introduction to *Livin' the Blues*, Davis felt that "the establishment of several writers' groups in Chicago during the 1920s and 1930s was no mere effort to emulate Harlem but, instead, was motivated by these Midwestern writers' sense that the East was effete, its literature inadequate" (xvii).

Davis's poetry, as well as his other writings, reflects his worldview and his social concerns. He wrote of black history, of racism as he experienced it, and of black liberation. His poetry is included in many anthologies.

**SELECTED WORKS:** Davis's poetry includes *Black Man's Verse* (1935), *I Am the American Negro* (1937), *Through Sepia Eyes* (1938), *47th Street Poems* (1948), and *Jazz Interlude* (1985). His autobiography, *Livin' the Blues*, edited by John Edgar Tidwell, (1993), includes a section from his unpublished manuscript, "That Incredible Waikiki Jungle," as an appendix.

**FURTHER READING:** HARRIET MONROE, "A New Negro Poet," *Poetry* 48.5 (1936): 295, and John Edgar Tidwell, "An Interview with Frank Marshall Davis," *Black American Literature Forum* 19 (1985): 107, are useful sources, as is Tidwell's introduction to *Livin' the Blues*.

TOM L. PAGE          WICHITA STATE UNIVERSITY

# MARGUERITE (LOFFT) DE ANGELI
March 14, 1889–June 16, 1987

**BIOGRAPHY:** Marguerite Lofft was born to Shadrach George Lofft, who worked for Eastman Kodak, and Ruby (Tuttle) Lofft in Lapeer, Michigan, where she lived most of the time until the Lofft family moved to Philadelphia in 1902. She dropped out of high school and began a career as a contralto soloist until her marriage to John Dailey de Angeli in 1910. She began writing and illustrating children's books in 1935, drawing on her experiences and people she knew, as well as research. A work of historical fiction, *The Door in the Wall* (1949) received the 1950 John Newbery Medal, one of her many awards. She died in Philadelphia, having continued her writing career into the 1980s.

**SIGNIFICANCE:** Marguerite de Angeli wrote in a variety of modes for a broad range of age groups. She created illustrated editions of such traditional matter as Bible stories, nursery rhymes, and fairy tales. She wrote the *Ted and Nina* readers for the very young. She may be best known for stories employing a variety of religious and ethnic materials, such as the Pennsylvania Dutch (*Skippack School,* 1939, and *Yonie Wondernose,* 1944), Quakers (*Thee, Hannah!* 1940), and Swedish immigrants (*Elin's Amerika,* 1941); and for historical fiction such as *Black Fox of Lorne* (1956). *Bright April* (1946) was ahead of its time in presenting a young African American girl's growing awareness of racial prejudice. The *New York Herald Tribune* named it an Honor Book.

Memories of her childhood in Lapeer and family reminiscences went into *Copper-Toed Boots* (1938), a story based on her father, his parents and other relatives, and her father's boyhood friend. His mischief, work in a general store, school experiences, watering the animals at a circus, desire for a puppy and copper-toed boots, and other aspects of the life of a child in a nineteenth-century small town in Michigan make a lively and vivid story.

The move of her daughter's family from Pennsylvania to Ohio inspired *Just Like David* (1951), which records the journey, complete with map on the endpapers, and gives some history of the region and scenes along the route. *Butter at the Old Price* (1971), de Angeli's autobiography, recalls her family history and her childhood in Chicago and Lapeer and explains the relationship between her life and her work. Some of the poems in *Friendship and Other Poems* (1981) refer to her childhood in Michigan.

**SELECTED WORKS:** The books by Marguerite de Angeli which are most notable for their Midwestern content are *Copper-Toed Boots* (1938); *Turkey for Christmas* (1944), which was drawn from her family's move from Michigan to Philadelphia; *Just Like David* (1971); and her autobiography, *Butter at the Old Price* (1971). *Skippack School* (1939), *Yonie Wondernose* (1944), *Thee, Hannah!* (1940), *Elin's Amerika* (1941), and *Bright April* (1946) explore religious and ethnic aspects of society. *The Door in the Wall* (1949) and *The Black Fox of Lorne* (1956) represent her historical fiction. A further sampling of de Angeli's books might include *The Ted and Nina Story Book* (1965), which contains all of the Ted and Nina books; *Henner's Lydia* (1936); *Petite Suzanne* (1937), about a French-Canadian girl; *Book of Nursery and Mother Goose Rhymes* (1954); *The Old Testament* (1960, 1967); and *The Goose Girl* (1964).

**FURTHER READING:** William Anderson wrote *Michigan's Marguerite de Angeli* (1987) for the Marguerite de Angeli Library in Lapeer. The *Dictionary of Literary Biography*, vol. 22, provides one of the many good discussions of de Angeli and her books to be found in reference works; shorter treatments appear in such resources as ROBERT BEASECKER'S *Michigan in the Novel, 1816–1996* (1998) and Carol Smallwood's *Michigan Authors* (1993). Her manuscripts may be found in the Philadelphia Free Library, the Kerlan Collection at the University of Minnesota, the Marguerite de Angeli Library, and the Lapeer Historical Society.

MARY DEJONG OBUCHOWSKI

CENTRAL MICHIGAN UNIVERSITY

## DAVID CORNEL DEJONG

June 6, 1901–September 5, 1967

(Tjalmar Breda)

**BIOGRAPHY:** David Cornel DeJong, a Dutch-American man of letters, was born in Blija, Friesland, the northwestern province of the Netherlands. Memories of his childhood in the fishing village of Wierum on the North Sea provided him with a rich provincial background, setting, and characters for some of his best fiction. His parents, Remmeren R. and Jantje (DeJong-Cornel) DeJong, indoctrinated their sons into the strict Calvinistic beliefs of the Reformed Church, both in their native Friesland and in the United States. When David was almost thirteen, the DeJong family immigrated to the religious Dutch community in Grand Rapids, Michigan, where they were treated with contempt and hostility. He learned English at the local parochial school where he was so humiliated by being

placed with younger children that he changed his age to match that of his classmates.

After helping to support his family for several years, DeJong was determined to work his way through school. While studying for his AB at Calvin College, he and his young brother MEINDERT DEJONG, a fellow student and aspiring writer, turned out stories, poetry, and plays in a futile attempt to earn a living by writing. David Cornel graduated in 1929, taught high school for a year, then left the Midwest to accept a fellowship at Duke University, where he received his MA in 1932. He began work toward a doctorate at Brown University, in Providence, Rhode Island, but when his first novel was published in 1934 he became a dedicated full-time writer. He married Helen Elizabeth Moffitt on June 29, 1949. He continued to live in Rhode Island until his death from cancer at age sixty-six.

**SIGNIFICANCE:** DeJong's unique contribution to Midwestern literature is found in his trio of books set in urban Michigan, portraying in illuminating detail the plight of penniless Dutch immigrants settling into a small, conformist, religious neighborhood. Based on his bitter memories of the DeJongs' reception by the Dutch Calvinist community in Grand Rapids, he chronicles the suffering and disharmony of an immigrant family in his first novel, *Belly Fulla Straw* (1934). In the second ethnic novel, *Two Sofas in the Parlor* (1952), his view of the religious community is more sanguine and he includes some delightful, uproariously comic family scenes. His use of the Dutch-English patois adds authenticity and humor to his immigrant portraits. He is particularly successful in depicting the intense generational conflicts between the parents who cherish their traditional Dutch values and the children who are influenced by the culture of their new land. In his autobiography, *With a Dutch Accent: How a Hollander Became an American* (1944), he gives a poignant, deeply felt account of his early years in Friesland and of his difficulties in America as a young immigrant tormented by neighborhood bullies. Unleashing his rage toward the Grand Rapids "Christian" community, he rebels against his Dutch Calvinist heritage to embrace the unlimited freedom of opportunity promised in a secular America. His view of human nature, however, remains grim. His American fictional characters, though honest and forthright, suffer from loneliness, yearning for the warmth of loving human relationships. Like his contemporary PETER DE VRIES, who is similarly removed from his Dutch ethnic-religious roots, DeJong searches for a balance between his protagonists' need for both freedom and community.

CLARENCE ANDREWS in *Michigan in Literature* (1992) ranks DeJong as "the most significant Michigan writer who used Dutch themes" as well as "an important author on the American scene" (66). DeJong's "non-Dutch" American novels received generally favorable reviews, particularly in the 1940s. They were praised for their characterization, clarity of style, and craftsmanship. His short stories, articles, and poems appeared frequently in almost all the little magazines and in periodicals of national importance, including *Scribner's, Esquire, Atlantic Monthly, Harper's Magazine*, and the *Saturday Review*. He also ventured into the children's book field, but without the success of his brother Meindert. Highly respected in the Eastern literary community, he was in demand as an editor, translator of Dutch fiction, teacher of university writing courses and workshops, lecturer, and speaker on radio and television.

**SELECTED WORKS:** Urged by his editors to use Dutch themes and settings, DeJong wrote his memoir of Holland, *Old Haven* (1938), funded by a fellowship from Houghton Mifflin. The book is considered his most successful work and was translated into six languages. In *Day of the Trumpet* (1941), he relates the dramatic story of a small Dutch city being invaded and occupied by Nazi troops in 1939 and 1940. His immigrant experience in Michigan informs his novels *Belly Fulla Straw* (1934) and *Two Sofas in the Parlor* (1952) as well as his autobiography, *With a Dutch Accent: How a Hollander Became an American* (1944). In *Light Sons and Dark* (1940), his only rural Midwestern novel, he gives a realistic portrayal of a divided American family who live on a dilapidated Michigan farm. *Somewhat Angels* (1945), a novel set in an industrial town in Michigan during World War II, gives an account of the lives of the women left on the homefront. *Benefit Street* (1942), his best novel with an East Coast setting, is an entertaining story of the bohemian lives of fourteen residents of a boardinghouse in Providence,

Rhode Island. His first poetry collection, *Across the Board* (1943), and the volumes that followed were not as well received as his fiction. His collections of short stories that were already published, *Snow-on-the-Mountain* (1946) and the *Unfairness of Easter* (1959), are well worth reading. His amusing, illustrated books for young children include *The Happy Birthday Umbrella* (1959), *Looking for Alexander* (1963), and *The Squirrel and the Harp* (1966).

**FURTHER READING:** DeJong's life and works are treated in *American Novelists of Today* (1951) and the *National Cyclopedia of American Biography* 53 (1971): 404. Cornelius John Ter Maat, born into the Dutch Calvinist community, gives an insider's evaluation of DeJong's fiction in his University of Michigan doctoral dissertation, "Three Novelists and a Community: A Study of American Novelists with Dutch Calvinist Origins" (1963). James D. Bratt analyzes DeJong's writing along with that of other Midwestern "renegade novelists" in his 1984 *Dutch Calvinism in Modern America: A History of a Conservative Subculture* (159). DeJong's papers can be found in the John Hay Library of Brown University, the Beinecke Library of Yale University, the Archives of the University of Illinois, the Lilly Library of Indiana University, and the Archives of the Hekman Library of Calvin College and Theological Seminary, Grand Rapids, Michigan.

MARY JOAN MILLER                    SPRINGFIELD, OHIO

## MEINDERT DEJONG
March 4, 1906–July 16, 1991

**BIOGRAPHY:** Celebrated children's author Meindert DeJong was born in Wierum, a fishing village along the North Sea in the Netherlands province of Friesland. He was the youngest son of Remmeren R. and Jantje (DeJong-Cornel) DeJong. Because he was born with a membrane over his head, the fishwives of the town predicted he was destined for great woe in the beginning and great fame later in life. In fact, he was near death from pneumonia three times before he was five and by age seventy he had received almost every major award in children's literature.

When he was a frail four-year-old, his doting, devout grandfather taught him to read the poetry and heroic stories of the Old Testament. DeJong attributes his love of words, his delight in rhythm and repetition, and the development of his unique writing style to his early immersion in biblical literature.

In 1914, when Meindert was eight, his Calvinist parents left the middle-class comforts of their Frisian family and village to immigrate with their sons to the Dutch Reformed community in Grand Rapids, Michigan. Here they lived in poverty and were treated like outcasts, an experience that fueled Meindert's profound empathy with rejected, defenseless creatures. He attended the Christian Reformed denominational schools and along with his older brother DAVID CORNEL DEJONG worked his way through Calvin College, receiving his AB in 1928. In 1932 he married Hattie Overeinter, whom he divorced many years later. Failing to find gainful employment during the Depression, he worked for three years on his father's failing forty-acre Michigan farm, where he made the significant discovery of his great love of animals and the land. While peddling eggs at the Grand Rapids Public Library, he was urged by the children's librarians to write about his eccentric pet goose. This little story, published by Harper's as *The Big Goose and the Little White Duck* in 1938, launched DeJong on his life work of writing for children.

In 1962 he married Beatrice DeClaire McElwee, an astute, valued critic of his work. They lived in Mexico and North Carolina but eventually moved back to Michigan, settling in Allegan, where Beatrice died in 1978. He married his lifelong friend Gwendolyn Jonkman two years before his death from emphysema at age eighty-five.

**SIGNIFICANCE:** DeJong draws largely on two wellsprings of his past to create his fictional worlds. More than half of his twenty-seven books are firmly rooted in his father's failing Midwestern farm; seven come from his childhood memories of Friesland. Always the realist, DeJong recreates the vast cornfields, droughts, sudden thunderstorms, and tornadoes of Michigan, providing a dramatic background for his small, lonely protagonists. The farm environment contributes to his characters' feelings of isolation and helplessness, but it also provides the animals that can transform their lives. In *The Singing Hill* (1962), for example, a young boy's devotion to an aged, neglected horse empowers him to act with great daring and courage to save the animal in a storm. The book's title, taken

**David and Meindert DeJong, April 1988.**
Photo courtesy of Archives, Calvin College

from the poetry of the Old Testament, suggests the deep spiritual dimensions in DeJong's writing. The old-fashioned values of strong family relationships and a concern for others in the community are also present, along with a deep respect for the earth. His realistic portrayals of ordinary yet unconventional characters, including the disabled, the infirm, and the aged, affirm his belief in the importance of every living creature, an egalitarian stance shared by many Midwestern authors.

DeJong's books are praised by critics for their originality, humor, eloquence, psychological depth, and powerful emotional impact. One of the most honored children's writers of the mid-twentieth century, he is the first American author to receive the Hans Christian Andersen International Medal, which is awarded for the entire body of a writer's work. His books have been translated into twenty-two languages.

**SELECTED WORKS:** DeJong's Midwestern farm books include his first publication, *The Big Goose and the Little White Duck* (1938), continuing with *The Little Cow and the Turtle* (1955), followed by two Newbery Honor Books, *Hurry Home Candy* (1953) and *Along Came a Dog* (1958), and *The Singing Hill* (1962).

His Netherlands books give a rare glimpse into the lives of the people, the dynamics of village life, the dramatic seaquakes and floods, and the power of the ancient traditions and religious practices of Friesland, the ancestral land of many Midwesterners. A selection of his Frisian novels must include the darkly realistic *Tower by the Sea* (1950), the Newbery Medal winner *The Wheel on the School* (1954), and the winner of the first National Book Award for Children's Literature in 1969, *Journey from Peppermint Street* (1968). The landscape changes to the interior of China in *The House of Sixty Fathers* (1956), the terrifying story of a small Chinese refugee DeJong befriended while serving as historian for the U.S. Air Corps during World War II. From among his many award acceptance speeches reprinted in *Horn Book*, two are especially revealing of his inner life, his enormous debt to librarians and books, and his odyssey as a writer: "The Cry and the Creation" 39 (April 1963): 197–206; and his eloquent swan song, "For the Love of the Word" 60 (September 1984): 569–77.

**FURTHER READING:** The *Dictionary of Literary Biography* 52 gives a comprehensive treatment of DeJong's life and work (115–32). For an understanding of the DeJong family, see DAVID CORNEL DEJONG's fascinating autobiography, *With a Dutch Accent* (1944). David Cornel also gives an entertaining and informative portrait of Meindert in "My Brother Meindert," in *Newbery Medal Books, 1922–1955,* edited by Bertha M. Miller and Elinor W. Field (1955): 427–33. An audiocassette, "A Conversation with Meindert DeJong," conducted by Clarence Hogeterp at Calvin College in the mid-1980s, gives a strong sense of DeJong's lively, robust personality and his total commitment to the art of writing for children. To conclude the conversation, DeJong reads from his last public speech, "For the Love of the Word" (1983). Richard H. Harm's brief article in *Michigan History 77* (September 1993): 46–47, "Michigan Profiles: Meindert and David Cornel DeJong," highlights both brothers' lives and work. Meindert DeJong's manuscripts are in the Kerlan Collection in the University of Minnesota Library. The Clarke Library of Central Michigan University in Mount Pleasant holds a collection of his books. DeJong donated his letters and personal papers, his award medals and other memorabilia, and more than eighty separate foreign language editions of his books to the Archives of the Hekman Library of Calvin College and Theological Seminary in Grand Rapids, Michigan.

MARY JOAN MILLER                    SPRINGFIELD, OHIO

## PAUL (HENRY) DE KRUIF
March 2, 1890–February 28, 1971

**BIOGRAPHY:** Born in Zeeland, Michigan, the son of Hendrik, a farm implement dealer, and Hendrika J. (Kremer) de Kruif, Paul de Kruif attended the University of Michigan, where he received a BS in 1912 and a PhD in 1916. He went on to do research and teach pathology there, served in the U.S. Army during World War I, and continued in research at the Pasteur Institute in Paris and the Rockefeller Institute for Medical Research. In 1922 de Kruif turned to writing on medical science and scientists for magazines and in books. He also served as a consultant and on city, state, and national organizations on health and research. In 1922 he married Rhea Elizabeth Barbarin, who died in 1957, and in 1959 he married Eleanor Lappage. He had two sons, Hendrik and David, by an earlier marriage, which ended in divorce. He maintained a residence on Lake Michigan near Holland and died in Holland of a heart attack.

**SIGNIFICANCE:** Paul de Kruif's articles and books largely took the form of biographical and scientific portraits of physicians and scientists engaged in medical research. His enthusiastic tone and down-to-earth vocabulary popularized the topic and educated his readers. *Microbe Hunters* (1926) and *Hunger Fighters* (1928) became best-sellers; the former, as *Dr. Erlich's Magic Bullet* (1940), was one of several movies made from his books.

Paul de Kruif's best-known contribution to Midwestern literature involved his collaboration with SINCLAIR LEWIS on *Arrowsmith* (1925). Dr. Frederick Novy, de Kruif's own mentor at the University of Michigan, provided part of the model for Max Gottlieb, Martin Arrowsmith's teacher. Winnemac is Michigan, Zenith represents Detroit, and Mohalis looks like Ann Arbor. De Kruif also contributed much of the scientific material for the book. *A Man against Insanity* (1957) treats the life and work of Jack Ferguson, M.D., of the Traverse City (Michigan) State Hospital. Paul de Kruif described his own career in *The*

*Sweeping Wind: A Memoir* (1962). In many of his works, he referred to his house on the sand dunes of Lake Michigan.

**SELECTED WORKS:** Paul de Kruif also wrote for the U.S. government and national organizations to inform the public on health matters, but his most notable works, more than a dozen books, were made up of lively biographies of scientists. *Microbe Hunters* (1926), *Men against Death* (1932), and *Hunger Fighters* (1928) remain among the best known of those, and in *Arrowsmith* (1925), he contributed realistic detail to the fictionalization of the life of such a man.

**FURTHER READING:** No book has appeared on de Kruif. Two articles on his contributions to *Arrowsmith* are N. Richardson Lyon's "*Arrowsmith*: Genesis, Development, Versions," in *American Literature* 27 (May 1955): 225–44, and Charles E. Rosenberg's "Martin Arrowsmith: The Scientist as Hero," in *American Quarterly* 15 (1963): 447–58, both of which appear in Robert J. Griffin's *Twentieth Century Interpretations of Arrowsmith* (1968) with most footnotes deleted. His memoir *The Sweeping Wind* (1962) remains the primary source of information about de Kruif.

MARY DEJONG OBUCHOWSKI

CENTRAL MICHIGAN UNIVERSITY

## FLOYD DELL
June 28, 1887–July 23, 1969

**BIOGRAPHY:** Floyd Dell, born in Barry, Illinois, established a formidable reputation as a novelist, critic, editor, poet, playwright, bohemian, socialist, critic of patriarchy, proponent of free love, and champion of feminism, progressive education, and Freudianism. His father, Anthony, a Civil War veteran, worked as a butcher; his mother, Kate (Crone), taught school. Spending most of his childhood and adolescence in Quincy, Illinois, Dell settled eventually in Davenport, Iowa, where he embraced his life-long interest in socialism and pursued a budding career as a poet and journalist. In 1903 Dell moved to Chicago, where he wrote for the *Chicago Evening Post's Friday Literary Review*, and then in 1913 to New York City, where he lived the bohemian life in Greenwich Village.

Dell's New York years were his most productive. He was editor of the *Masses* and its successor the *Liberator*, two socialist magazines of the era. He wrote a critically suc-cessful novel, *Moon-Calf* (1920), and a collection of essays, *Intellectual Vagabondage* (1926), in which he espoused Marxist literary theory. He commented on love and marriage in *Love in the Machine Age* (1930) and penned an autobiography, *Homecoming* (1933). Also, he wrote a successful Broadway comedy, *Little Accident* (1928). In all of these efforts, Dell struggled to reconcile art and politics into a viable aesthetic.

Dell counted among his friends and colleagues many of the great figures of the times: radical Socialists John Reed and Max Eastman; feminist Charlotte Perkins Gilman; Christian Socialist Dorothy Day; novelists THEODORE DREISER, UPTON SINCLAIR, and SHERWOOD ANDERSON; and poet Edna St. Vincent Millay.

During the Depression, Dell wrote for the WPA's Writers' Project while continuing his life as a man of letters. After the war and until his death, Dell remained a chronicler of his age and found solace with his wife of fifty years Marie, their two sons, Anthony and Christopher, and their grandchildren.

**SIGNIFICANCE:** Dell's connections with the Midwest and its literary traditions began during his boyhood when his family lived in Barry and Quincy, Illinois. In Davenport, Iowa, Dell was introduced to Marxism and began a career in journalism. In Chicago, however, he figured prominently in that city's literary renaissance. As editor of the *Friday Literary Review*, he introduced Midwesterners to the early major figures of literary modernism: T. S. ELIOT, Ezra Pound, HARRIET MONROE, Upton Sinclair, Sherwood Anderson, and Theodore Dreiser. He also reviewed poetry by CARL SANDBURG and VACHEL LINDSAY, two Midwestern poets whose careers were just beginning. Dell also drew upon Midwestern characters and themes in his fiction, most notably *Moon-Calf*, an autobiographical novel.

As editor of the *Friday Literary Review*, Dell also established himself as one of the most powerful figures on Chicago's cultural scene. His book reviews and essays offered Midwesterners serious praise, lighthearted approval, and devastating critiques. Dell helped make this literary supplement a significant defense of modern ideas and of society's influence upon literary works. During these Chicago years, Dell's critical judgments offered his Midwestern audiences refined, balanced, modern, and learned analyses of both classical and modern literature.

**SELECTED WORKS:** Dell's best fiction, which typifies his Midwestern background, is the trilogy *Moon-Calf* (1920), *Briary-Bush* (1921), and *Souvenir* (1930). *Intellectual Vagabondage* (1926), a collection of essays, is significant for Dell's developing understanding of Marxist literary theory. *Love in the Machine Age* (1930) represents Dell's concept of love and marriage, further refined in his autobiography *Homecoming* (1933). *Little Accident* (1927), a successful Broadway comedy, ran for 289 performances. As a proto-feminist text, Dell's *Women as World Builders* (1913) has been examined for its contributions to gender and women's studies.

**FURTHER READING:** A number of general studies have situated Dell in the intellectual community that emerged before World War I. Steven Biel's *Independent Intellectuals in the United States, 1910–1945* (1992) recounts how Dell, Max Eastman, and Randolph Bourne rivaled university scholars during the early years of modernism. WALTER RIDEOUT's *The Radical Novel in the United States* (1992) and Daniel Aaron's *Writers on the Left* (1992) credit Dell as an influential Marxist theorist of the 1920s and 1930s. Barbara Foley's *Radical Representations* (1993) positions him as a major literary theorist of the Depression era. Douglas Clayton's biography *Floyd Dell: The Life and Times of an American Rebel* (1994) reassesses Dell's contributions to American literary history during one of its most critical times. A compilation of Dell's *Friday Literary Review* essays is available in *Floyd Dell: Essays from the Friday Literary Review, 1909–1913* (1995). Dell's papers and manuscripts are reposited in the Beinecke Library at Yale University, the Lilly Library at Indiana University, and the Newberry Library in Chicago.

JAMES M. BOEHNLEIN    UNIVERSITY OF DAYTON

# GENE H. DENT.
*See* appendix (1986)

# AUGUST (WILLIAM) DERLETH
February 24, 1909–July 4, 1971
(Stephen Grendon, Tally Mason)
**BIOGRAPHY:** August Derleth was born and died in Sauk City, Wisconsin, the "Sac Prairie" of his novels, short stories, essays, poetry, and plays. His parents, Julius and Rose Louise

(Volk), both of German ancestry, operated a blacksmith's shop in the predominantly German Catholic Sauk City, which borders the English Protestant Prairie du Sac. Derleth grew up along the Wisconsin River and developed an enduring relationship with the area residents, land, river, plants, and animals—a relationship which informs virtually all of the 150 books he produced during his lifetime. In 1938 Derleth won a Guggenheim Fellowship with the support of SINCLAIR LEWIS and EDGAR LEE MASTERS. In his application, he proposed to create a Sac Prairie Saga, a series of at least twenty-five volumes of poems, novels, essays, and short stories tracing the history of the area from the early 1800s through the 1950s. A youthful correspondent with H. P. Lovecraft, Derleth founded Arkham House in 1939 in order to publish Lovecraft's tales posthumously in book format. Derleth wrote popular detective fiction, weird tales, and juvenile novels as a way of financing Arkham House and the serious regional fiction and poetry he produced. In addition to writing and publishing, he served as literary editor of the Madison *Capital Times* for almost thirty years and wrote a regular column, "Wisconsin Diary," for the same newspaper for more than a decade. In 1953 he married Sandra Winters, but the relationship was not a happy one, and in their 1959 divorce, Derleth gained custody of their two children, April Rose and Walden. Derleth died of a heart attack suffered at Place of Hawks, his Sauk City home, on July 4, 1971.

**SIGNIFICANCE:** Shortly after graduating from the University of Wisconsin–Madison in 1930, Derleth accepted a job editing a magazine for Fawcett Publishing in Minneapolis. Six months later, he returned to Wisconsin, declaring in his introduction to *Walden West* (1961) that he would make his Sac Prairie home "a base of operations into a life more full in the knowledge of what went on in the woods as well as in the houses along the streets of Sac Prairie and in the human heart" (xvii). For the next forty years, Derleth set about to do exactly that, tracing the history of the development of Sac Prairie and Wisconsin, as well as observing the natural world and the people who lived along the Wisconsin River. In many of his works, Derleth investigates the responses of individuals to loss in their changing environments. His works frequently focus on memory and time contrasted with the timelessness of the natural world. In addition, many of the novels in the saga link major events in Wisconsin history to the lives of Sac Prairie residents, often pointing up conflicts over religious or cultural values that develop over time or because of social and economic forces. A number of his earlier novels were published by Scribner's under the editorship of Maxwell Perkins, editor of F. SCOTT FITZGERALD, William Faulkner, and ERNEST HEMINGWAY. *Evening in Spring* (1941), an early semi-autobiographical novel, traces a doomed first love between a Catholic boy and Protestant girl in the Sac Prairie of the 1920s. Among Derleth's later works, *Walden West* (1961) and *Return to Walden West* (1970), each a series of alternating essays on village life and the natural world, achieved general critical appreciation but not the national readership Sinclair Lewis had earlier predicted for him. Derleth actively promoted regional writing in his edited anthologies of poetry and fiction, such as *Poetry Out of Wisconsin* (1937) and *Wisconsin Harvest* (1966), and in his biography *Still Small Voice* (1940), which records the life of ZONA GALE, another Midwestern regional writer living along the Wisconsin River in Portage, Wisconsin. In many of his Sac Prairie novels and poems Derleth focuses on a universal pattern of growth and decay played out against the Midwestern landscape of his home, including the rise and fall of Native American settlements, the fur trade, the family farm, and the family itself.

**SELECTED WORKS:** Among the most widely read works in Derleth's Sac Prairie Saga are the novels *Wind over Wisconsin* (1938), *Evening in Spring* (1941), *Shadow of Night* (1943), and *Shield of the Valiant* (1945); among the journals and essays, *Atmosphere of Houses* (1939), *Village Year: A Sac Prairie Journal* (1941), *Walden West* (1961), *Return to Walden West* (1970); and the poetry in *Collected Poems 1937–1967* (1967). The Wisconsin Saga, comprising five novels, presents events from the period of the Wisconsin fur trade through the early years of statehood; these include *Bright Journey* (1955), *The Hills Stand Watch* (1960), *The House on the Mound* (1958), *The Shadow in the Glass* (1963), and *The Wind Leans West* (1969). Derleth's popular detective, horror, and juvenile fiction are still widely read by devoted fans; among them are *The Solar Pons Omnibus* (1982); the "posthu-

mous" collaboration with H. P. Lovecraft, *The Watcher Out of Time and Others* (1974); and *The Moon Tenders* (1958).

**FURTHER READING:** An annotated list of Derleth's periodical and book-length publications, as well as a thumbnail biography, is presented in Alison M. Wilson's *August Derleth: A Bibliography* (1983). Derleth's regional writings are discussed in Evelyn M. Schroth's *The Derleth Saga* (1979). *August Harvest*, edited by Ely M. Liebow (1994), offers a series of essays assessing Derleth's contributions to the full range of genres in which he wrote.

KENNETH B. GRANT

UNIVERSITY OF WISCONSIN CENTER–
BARABOO/SAUK COUNTY

## PETER DE VRIES

February 27, 1910–September 28, 1993

**BIOGRAPHY:** Best known for his irreverent comic novels, Peter De Vries was born in a Chicago Dutch Calvinist community to Joost and Henrietta (Eldersveld) De Vries, who intended that he enter the ministry. Peter received a rigorous Calvinist education at Englewood Christian School, Chicago Christian High School, and Calvin College in Grand Rapids, Michigan. At Calvin he stood out as a basketball player, debater, wit, and dandy. Graduating with a BA in English in 1931, De Vries returned to Chicago as an aspiring journalist, poet, and fiction writer. Working at jobs including moving, radio acting, and delivering taffy apples, he also engaged in Chicago reform politics. He began publishing stories and poems in little magazines, then in *Esquire* and in *Poetry,* whose staff he joined in 1938. By 1944 he had published three novels. In 1943 he married the writer Katinka Loeser, with whom he would raise four children.

A 1943 De Vries essay about JAMES THURBER led to Thurber's coming to Chicago to give a benefit reading for *Poetry.* Thurber promptly recruited De Vries for the staff of the *New Yorker.* The De Vrieses moved to Greenwich Village in 1944 and to Westport, Connecticut, in 1948.

De Vries's first best-selling novel, *The Tunnel of Love* (1954), brought him prominence in the Eastern literary establishment. As his books won reviewers' acclaim and a wide audience, De Vries himself was celebrated in popular national magazines. He was elected to the National Institute of Arts and Letters in 1969 and to the American Academy of Arts and Letters in 1983. Peter De Vries died of pneumonia at the age of eighty-three in Norwalk, Connecticut.

**SIGNIFICANCE:** De Vries's first three novels exploit their Chicago settings for social comedy, psychological drama, and political satire, respectively. His later novels often juxtapose Midwestern scenes and attitudes with those of the East, as in *The Blood of the Lamb* (1962), *I Hear America Swinging* (1976), and *Peckham's Marbles* (1986); he carries Babbitry to Connecticut in *The Mackerel Plaza* (1958), updates *The Scarlet Letter* Midwestern-style in *Slouching Towards Kalamazoo* (1983), and sends up the classic Midwesterner-goes-East tragedy, *The Great Gatsby*, in *The Prick of Noon* (1985). With deadpan humor and tall-tale imagination, De Vries sustains in these works provocative meditations on region, class, culture, and conscience.

De Vries has fun inflating and puncturing cliches about Midwestern life through incongruous characters like a farmhand art critic and a matronly avant-garde filmmaker, settings real (Cedar Rapids) and fanciful (Slow Rapids), and dialogue reflecting his keen ear for dialect and his deadly skill at parody. Absurd disasters of human intention are preeminent, as when a couple build a house like FRANK LLOYD WRIGHT's "Fallingwater" and their child drowns in the living room.

De Vries has been said to bring the moral instincts of a Midwestern Dutch Calvinist to bear on suburban life in the secular East. Yet even in high school he gravitated to SHERWOOD ANDERSON, THEODORE DREISER, BEN HECHT, EDGAR LEE MASTERS, and CARL SANDBURG, and his favorite book in his teens was Thomas De Quincey's *Confessions of an English Opium-Eater*. All the diverse influences De Vries received in Chicago, from aesthetes, Modernists, proletarians, sophisticates, and even radio scriptwriters, to the bohemians and surrealists he encountered through *Poetry*, contributed to his outlook.

**SELECTED WORKS:** Author of twenty-six books, De Vries came to regard his first three novels, *But Who Wakes the Bugler?* (1940), *The Handsome Heart* (1943), and *Angels Can't Do Better* (1944), as apprentice work, but they presage, indeed often achieve, his pyrotechnic later style. His first five novels after moving East are set in Connecticut or Massachusetts, but he returned to a Chicago setting in

**Peter De Vries, 1931.**
Photo courtesy of Archives, Calvin College

*The Blood of the Lamb* (1962) and often thereafter reexplores the Midwest: Indiana in *Let Me Count the Ways* (1965), *Mrs. Wallop* (1970), and *The Glory of the Hummingbird* (1974); Iowa in *I Hear America Swinging* (1976) and *Peckham's Marbles* (1986); Michigan in *Slouching Towards Kalamazoo* (1983); and Chicago again in *The Vale of Laughter* (1967), *Into Your Tent I'll Creep* (1971), and *Consenting Adults, or The Duchess Will Be Furious* (1980). De Vries often alludes to other native Midwestern writers, as when *The Mackerel Plaza* (1958) plays variations on SINCLAIR LEWIS and *The Prick of Noon* (1985) takes a cue from F. SCOTT FITZGERALD. De Vries's two collections of short stories, *No But I Saw the Movie* (1952) and *Without a Stitch in Time* (1972), contain fiction that draws on his Midwestern youth. His many poems, reviews, and occasional pieces are uncollected. Several De Vries novels, including *The Tunnel of Love* (1954) and *Reuben, Reuben* (1964), have served as the basis for plays and motion pictures, and the film *Pete 'n' Tillie* (1972) was based on De Vries's novella *Witch's Milk* (1968).

**FURTHER READING:** Edwin T. Bowden provides an authoritative description of De Vries's publications in *Peter De Vries: A Bibliography 1934–1977* (1978), and T. A. Straayer an indispensable annotated guide to secondary sources in "Peter De Vries: A Bibliography of Secondary Sources, 1940–1981," in *Bulletin of Bibliography* 39.3 (1982): 146–69. Roderick Jellema's *Peter De Vries: A Critical Essay* (1966) and J. H. Bowden's *Peter De Vries* (1983) are useful studies. Dan Campion's *Peter De Vries and Surrealism* (1995) includes biographical material about De Vries in Chicago, at Calvin College, and as coeditor of *Poetry* magazine, and its list of works cited supplements the earlier published bibliographies. Among the best interviews are Douglas M. Davis's "An Interview with Peter De Vries," in *College English* 28.7 (1967): 524–28; Roy Newquist's "Peter De Vries," in *Counterpoint* (1964); and Ben Yagoda's "Peter De Vries: Being Seriously Funny," in *New York Times Magazine* (June 12, 1983): 42–56. Valuable discussions of De Vries are included in Richard Boston's *Anatomy of Laughter* (1974), James D. Bratt's *Dutch Calvinism in Modern America* (1984), Wilbur Merrill Frohock's *Strangers to This Ground* (1961), and Ralph C. Wood's *The Comedy of Redemption: Christian Faith and Comic Vision in Four American Novelists* (1988). Boston University Library holds a selection of De Vries's manuscripts, and an extensive collection of materials, including manuscripts, is lodged in the archives of Calvin College.

DAN CAMPION                                    IOWA CITY, IOWA

## SCOTT DONALDSON.
*See* appendix (1996)

## MARY FRANCES DONER
July 29, 1893–April 1, 1985
(Julia Ward, Hope Darrow, Virginia Chilvers, Mary Doner Moore, Mrs. Claude Louis Payzant, and others)

**BIOGRAPHY:** Mary Frances Doner, born in Port Huron, Michigan, to Mary (O'Rourke) and James Doner, captain of Lake Michigan freighters and later manager of the Reiss Coal Company fleet, watched ships ply the St. Clair River and accompanied her father, when possible, on voyages. She attended high school in Detroit and in St. Clair, Michigan, both of which provided the settings for many of her novels. She studied music in Detroit and New York and attended City College of the City University of New York and Columbia University. Pulp magazines began taking her short stories in 1921, and she became a staff writer for Dell Publishing Company. In

1930 her first three novels were published, and she married a Boston physician, Claude Louis Payzant. In Boston she reviewed music and books for the *Post-Herald* and other newspapers and taught creative writing at the Boston Center for Adult Education. She spent summers with her family in St. Clair, sometimes doing research for her novels, and in 1949 returned there to live. In 1964 she moved to Ludington, Michigan, where she wrote and sometimes set more novels as well as biography and local history. She also taught creative writing in Ludington, where she remained to the end of her life.

**SIGNIFICANCE:** Doner's early books take place mostly on the East Coast, but the dairy farm set in St. Gabriel, really St. Clair, in *Gallant Traitor* (1938) marks the move to Michigan as the location for most of her succeeding novels. *Some Fell among Thorns* (1939) is the first of many of her books to focus on the lives of those who work on Great Lakes ships. *Chalice* (1940), rich in autobiography, begins and ends with men whose love for life on the water dominates their lives and those of the women who love them. The chronology follows that of Doner's life to some extent, with settings on a St. Clair farm, in Detroit, and in New York, where Doner pursued her career for a time, and again in St. Clair, to which Doner also returned. *Not by Bread Alone* (1941) features Maggie and Jim Murphy, who run the kitchen on a ship until the great storm of 1913 disables Jim. Doner modeled these characters on friends of her mother in St. Clair. *Glass Mountain* (1942) records the failure of a ship captain too reckless to sail in safety. Doner departed from these subjects somewhat to explore the mining industry in Michigan's Upper Peninsula in the nineteenth century in *O Distant Star* (1944); the automobile industry in *Blue River* (1946); salt mining and refining in *Ravenswood* (1948); issues surrounding migrant workers in *Cloud of Arrows* (1950); and uranium mining, in this case in Ontario, in *The Host Rock* (1952). Ecological themes having to do with the Great Lakes and nearby areas dominate *The Shores of Home* (1961), *While the River Flows* (1962), *Return a Stranger* (1970), and *Thine Is the Power* (1972). Other novels involving sailing matters are *The Wind and the Fog* (1963) and *Not by Appointment* (1972). In between, Doner produced two books of nonfiction, *The Salvager: The Life* *of Captain Tom Reid on the Great Lakes* (1958), the chronicle of a man who raised shipwrecks; and *Cleavenger vs. Castle: A Case of Breach of Promise and Seduction* (1968), based on a famous trial in Detroit. Her late works included *The Darker Star* (1974), set near Ludington, as well as a life of Père Marquette and histories of places in Michigan.

This remarkable collection of books illustrates the richness of Michigan's resources, the rise and fall of some of its industries, farm life, and the changes of the seasons, often in counterpoint to the comings and goings of those who worked on the water. Occupations on commercial sailing vessels; methods of raising sugar beets, strawberries, asparagus, and dairy cattle; the influence of salt refineries; the complexities of developing a community around an automobile factory; and the workings of iron, copper, and uranium mines all became topics on which Doner informed herself. She explored related issues: the effects that shipping had on communities, such as the long absences of husbands and fathers, and the rise and fall of lake levels set in motion by the Soo Locks; migrant workers' living and working conditions and their far-reaching reverberations; the reactions of communities to the encroachment of industry and to its departure as well as to urban renewal and development of power sources. These matters are not unique to Michigan, but all of the locations in which Doner explores them exist in that state and reflect the landscapes, the changes that evolved in these areas, and the residents' reactions to those changes.

**SELECTED WORKS:** Doner's early romances set on the East Coast include *The Dancer in the Shadow* (1930), *The Dark Garden* (1930), *The Lonely Heart* (1930), *Broken Melody* (1932), *Let's Burn Our Bridges* (1935), which she regarded as her first "serious" novel, and *Child of Conflict* (1936). Two more romances, *Fool's Heaven* (1932) and *Forever More* (1934), take place in Michigan and touch on farming and salt refining. In a brochure, the Penn Publishing Company advertised Doner's next three novels, *Gallant Traitor* (1938), *Some Fell among Thorns* (1939), and *Chalice* (1940), as "Romances of the Great Lakes." Shipping themes occur in *Not by Bread Alone* (1941), *The Glass Mountain* (1942), *The Wind and the Fog* (1963), and *Not by Appointment* (1973). Further Michi-

gan novels include *O Distant Star* (1944), *Blue River* (1946), *Cloud of Arrows* (1950), *While the River Flows* (1962), *Return a Stranger* (1970), *Thine Is the Power* (1972), and *The Darker Star* (1974). Her nonfiction includes *The Salvager* (1958), *Cleavenger vs. Castle* (1968), *Père Marquette* (a pamphlet), *Soldier of the Cross* (1969), and some local history.

**FURTHER READING:** Little critical work has been done on Doner aside from reviews and notices in reference works such as Carol Smallwood's *Michigan Authors* (1993) and ROBERT BEASECKER's *Michigan in the Novel 1816–1996* (1998). She distributed manuscripts of her books and other materials to several libraries, including the Boston Public; Boston University; Albion College; Sault Ste. Marie, Ontario; Peter White in Marquette, Michigan; Port Huron, Michigan; and the Burton Historical. She gave most of her papers to the Bentley Library at the University of Michigan.

MARY DEJONG OBUCHOWSKI

CENTRAL MICHIGAN UNIVERSITY

## IGNATIUS LOYOLA DONNELLY
November 3, 1831–January 1, 1901

**BIOGRAPHY:** Politician, social reformer, popular lecturer, and novelist, Ignatius Donnelly was born in Philadelphia, to Philip Donnelly, a physician, and Catharine (Gavin) Donnelly. He attended high school in Philadelphia, where he also read law and was admitted to the bar. In 1855 he married Katharine McCaffrey and moved to Minnesota the next year, where he practiced law, farmed, and lived the rest of his life. His promotion of Nininger City, a utopian community, was unsuccessful. Donnelly wrote for various newspapers and lectured throughout his career.

He served as Minnesota lieutenant governor and U.S. congressman during the Civil War and Reconstruction years. Later, finding that the major political parties ignored institutional racism in the South and failed to represent agrarian interests while favoring banks, railroads, and milling companies, Donnelly joined the Grange and assisted in forming the Greenback, People's, and Populist parties and the Farmers Alliance in Minnesota. Donnelly served in the state legislature but failed to win reelection to national office. He championed education, land-use reform, currency reform, income tax, labor law, and civil rights while opposing laissez-faire capitalism, social Darwinism, racism, and anti-Semitism. Donnelly predicted class warfare would result without reform of capitalism and social inequality. Donnelly had two sons and a daughter; after the death of his first wife, he married Marian Hansen in 1898. He died of heart failure at home in Hastings, Minnesota, near the site of the proposed Nininger City.

**SIGNIFICANCE:** Donnelly was a major player in the most significant political movements to come from the Midwest in the later half of the nineteenth century, and his career often paralleled that of WILLIAM JENNINGS BRYAN. Both had journalistic and legal backgrounds, were known as spellbinding speakers and commanded national attention without political office, and endured unfair criticism as radicals who would provoke class warfare. In his dystopian novel *Caesar's Column* (1890), Donnelly claimed that revolution could come only from inattention to social and economic reform. Donnelly lacked Bryan's optimism for democratic values and confidence in common people, but he asserted that people would not be complacent in the face of injustice. Although he was a partisan of rural interests, Donnelly's Nininger City was not planned as an agrarian utopia; rather it was to be a cultured and technological metropolis, the Athens of the Midwest.

Moreover, as a literary man, Donnelly was also a novelist and stage performer in the Midwestern/Western humor tradition. Neither *Doctor Huguet* (1891) nor *The Golden Bottle* (1892), set in Kansas, is realistic, though both accurately depict rural economic plights with a sentimental portrayal of poor farmers. In *Doctor Huguet*, a Southern aristocrat is turned by an act of God into a black man, to portray the nightmares of life for freed slaves. In *The Golden Bottle*, a poor farm boy is given the power to create gold, by which he attempts to pay off mortgages. Donnelly's foreword to *The Golden Bottle* called it a dramatization of the Populist platform of 1892; it was his version of the "Cross of Gold" speech which Bryan would deliver four years later to secure the presidential nomination. As both social reformer and scientist, Donnelly was often regarded as a faker and sometimes even advertised as a comic lecturer for his theories about the mythical Atlantis and the hidden author-

Ignatius Donnelly.
Photo courtesy of David D. Anderson. Used by permission of the Minnesota Historical Society

ship of Shakespeare's works. Later published as *Atlantis: The Antediluvian World* (1882), *The Great Cryptogram* (1887), and *The Cipher in the Plays* (1899), these essays possess a scholarly tone but include outrageous claims and dubious evidence, very much like the ironic, poker-faced stage personae of ARTEMUS WARD and MARK TWAIN. Donnelly brought the sincerity and exaggeration of Western humor to science and literature, with serious intent to take a populist stand against conventional wisdom. His choice to argue such dubious theories may well express his frustrated, political positions outside the mainstream.

Donnelly's literary imagination, like his politics, was deliberately provocative. He was, nonetheless, quite serious about his lifelong ideal of a classless Midwestern community, as evidenced by his youthful belief in Manifest Destiny, his failed land development, and finally in his creation of *Caesar's Column* as cautionary tale. Donnelly responded to the approaching millennium with some disillusionment expressed in an anti-utopian novel, which should be considered alongside WILLIAM DEAN HOWELLS's *A Traveler from Altruria* (1894) and Twain's *A Connecticut Yankee in King Arthur's Court* (1889). Ironically, Donnelly died at a New Year's party for the new century; he was, at that time, the vice-presidential candidate for the Populists.

**SELECTED WORKS:** Donnelly's scientific theories are contained in *Atlantis: The Antediluvian World* (1882) and *Ragnarok: The Age of Fire and Gravel* (1883). His theories concerning Shakespeare's authorship are published in *The Great Cryptogram* (1887) and *The Cipher in the Plays* (1899). Novels are *Caesar's Column* (1890), *Doctor Huguet* (1891), and *The Golden Bottle* (1892).

**FURTHER READING:** Biography, literary study, and bibliography are contained in DAVID ANDERSON's *Ignatius Donnelly* (1980) and Martin Ridge's *Ignatius Donnelly* (1962). Jay Martin's *Harvests of Change* (1967) and Michael Fellman's *The Unbounded Frame* (1973) contain chapters on Donnelly's utopian themes. Donnelly's manuscripts, papers, and pamphlets are collected in the Minnesota Historical Society.

THOMAS PRIBEK

UNIVERSITY OF WISCONSIN–LACROSSE

# RICHARD M(ERCER) DORSON
March 12, 1916–September 11, 1981

**BIOGRAPHY:** Richard M. Dorson was born in New York City to Louis Jasper Dorson, a businessman, and Gertrude (Lester) Dorson. He received three degrees from Harvard, including an AB in 1937, an MA in 1940, and a PhD in 1943. In 1940 he married Dorothy Diamond. They had one son, Ronald, and were divorced in 1948. He married Gloria Irene Gluski, an actress, on August 8, 1953, and had three children, Roland, Jeffrey, and Linda.

Dorson began his teaching career at Harvard in 1943 as an instructor in history. In 1944 he moved to Michigan State University, where he published his first book in 1946, a collection of New England folktales, and undertook research in the Upper Peninsula of Michigan, resulting in *Bloodstoppers and Bearwalkers* in 1952. This work was formative in the development of Dorson's theories and protocols for handling folk materials. His methods became the standard for the study of folklore in America. After a Fulbright year at the University of Tokyo in 1956–57, Dorson moved to Indiana University, where he was professor of history and folklore from 1957 to 1971, distin-

guished professor from 1971 to 1981, and director of the Folklore Institute from 1963 to 1981.

Dorson was author of twelve books, editor of fourteen, editor of three series of books on international folklore, contributor to numerous anthologies and periodicals, and recipient of major awards and honors. He died in Bloomington, Indiana, after a three-month coma following his collapse while playing tennis.

**SIGNIFICANCE:** Dorson is called the father of American folklore because of the formative influence he exerts on its study. He is credited with having brought a scientific and independent methodology to the study of American folklore. This methodology brought international acknowledgment and established folk literature as an essential part of a region's and a nation's literature. In his book *American Folklore* (1959), Dorson defined folklore according to its regional characteristics, stating that each regional complex of materials demonstrates "its own genius" in the mix of historical, ethnic, and geographical elements which shape it (75). In *Bloodstoppers and Bearwalkers* (1952), Dorson identified the elements of Native American and European folklore in Michigan's Upper Peninsula and examined how they combine to form what he called a native folklore of self-conscious explanations and stories of the people living in a region.

Although he applied his theories to international folklore, he developed them largely through his work in research and writing on Midwestern materials. He analyzed how those materials are distinguished as Midwestern as well as the influences they exert. In *American Folklore*, for example, he explains how ABRAHAM LINCOLN drew upon Midwestern folk sayings and stories for use in his political rhetoric and moral suasion. In framing regional identities for folk literature, Dorson criticized regionalism based upon convenience and emotional ties to a locality and emphasized that geography and history interrelate to form distinctive motifs and forms.

Other works he wrote or edited with a Midwestern emphasis include *Buying the Wind: Regional Folklore in the United States* (1964), *Negro Folktales in Michigan* (1956), and *The Land of the Millrats* (1981), a collection of folktales about the steel-making industry from Calumet City, Indiana.

**SELECTED WORKS:** Works significant for the development of the American perspective Dorson developed and refined in the Midwest are *Jonathan Draws the Long Bow: New England Popular Tales and Legends* (1946, reprinted 1970); *Bloodstoppers and Bearwalkers: Folk Traditions of the Upper Peninsula* (1952, reprinted 1972); and *American Folklore* (1959, revised 1977). A work which shows how Dorson applied his approach to international materials is *Folk Legends of Japan* (1961). Works which study the role of folk materials in the development of American history are *American Folklore and the Historian* (1971); *Folklore: Selected Essays* (1972); and *America in Legend: Folklore from the Colonial Period to the Present* (1973). A seminal study on the criticism of folk materials is *Folklore and Fakelore: Essays toward a Discipline of Folk Studies* (1976), which examines the history of the Paul Bunyan legends as the work of an advertising copywriter for a lumber company. **FURTHER READING:** Dorson edited a number of works which contain collections of Midwestern folklore and further develop the theories and techniques which grew out of his Midwestern researches. These include *Davy Crockett, American Comic Legend* (1939, reprinted 1980); *Negro Folktales in Michigan* (1956, reprinted 1974); *Negro Tales from Pine Bluff, Arkansas, and Calvin, Michigan* (1958); and *Folklore in the Modern World* (1978). Some instructive essays regarding Dorson's technique and influence are Jan Harold Brunvand's "Dorson and the Urban Legend," in the *Journal of the Folklore and History Section of the American Folklore Society* (1990): 16–22, and the January–April 1989 issue of the *Journal of Folklore Research*, which is devoted to essays on Dorson.

DAVID L. NEWQUIST     NORTHERN STATE UNIVERSITY

## JOHN DOS PASSOS

January 14, 1896–September 28, 1970

**BIOGRAPHY:** John Dos Passos was born in Chicago, the son of John Randolph Dos Passos and Lucy Addison Sprigg Madison. Significantly, he was born in a hotel and spent much of his childhood in hotels in America and Europe. He never really outgrew his wanderlust, even after he acquired his first home in middle age. Upon graduation from Harvard in 1916, Dos Passos served in France in the ambulance corps, where he met and befriended ERNEST HEMINGWAY. As

with Hemingway and so many others of their generation, World War I served as an inspiration for much of Dos Passos's best writing. During his most productive years, the 1920s and 1930s, he traveled the world, seldom stopping for more than a few weeks at a time. During these years his friends and acquaintances included the most important figures of the literary and art worlds: F. SCOTT FITZGERALD, THEODORE DREISER, Hemingway, E. E. Cummings, Malcolm Cowley, and Edmund Wilson were among his intimates. At the same time, Dos Passos became a forceful critic of American society and was, by the mid-1930s, the most eloquent practitioner of the politically engaged collectivist novel. Upon the completion of his *U.S.A.* trilogy in 1936, he was regarded by many as one of the world's greatest writers. In 1938, in his essay "John Dos Passos and *1919*," Jean-Paul Sartre called him "the greatest writer of our time" (published in English in 1955 in *Literary and Philosophical Essays* 103).

During the late 1930s, however, he began to be soured by the internecine struggles of the American left and the increasing Stalinization of the international left. These trends sparked his long, unwavering migration to the political right, ultimately alienating him from many of his oldest literary friends and sapping much of his creative energy. As productive as ever in his later years, the fiction, journalism, and popular history which he published in the decades after World War II proved to be of only marginal interest to the critics and a dwindling readership. But Dos Passos did find in these years a personal contentment to balance the restlessness of his early years. After the tragic 1947 death of his first wife, the writer Katherine Foster Smith Dos Passos, in an automobile accident, Dos Passos moved into the first real home he had ever known, a family farm at Spence's Point, Virginia. In 1949 he married Elizabeth Holdridge and, in the following year, they celebrated the birth of Dos Passos's only child, Lucy. Appropriately, the chronicler of twentieth-century American life was nearing completion of a novel called *Century's Ebb* when he died of congestive heart failure at the age of seventy-four.

**SIGNIFICANCE:** Like the man himself, Dos Passos's writing ranged over a wide geography, and most of his best writing made use of Midwestern settings and characters. Significantly, his great panoramic trilogy, *U.S.A.*, begins and ends in the Midwest. In fact, the Midwest always seemed to function for him as a touchstone of the American culture. In his early writing, such as *Three Soldiers* (1921), it tended to be an Edenic world, though one often treated ironically. During the Depression, Dos Passos saw in the devastated cities of the industrial Midwest a harbinger of the collapse of capitalism. During the 1950s and early 1960s, in works such as the novel *Chosen Country* (1951) and the essay collection *The Prospect before Us* (1950), he portrayed the post-war transformation of Midwestern agriculture as a hopeful fusion of the values of Jefferson's yeoman farmer and the can-do spirit of earlier American technocrats such as Edison.

**SELECTED WORKS:** Dos Passos was a tremendously prolific and versatile writer. Best known for his fiction, he also published poetry, popular history, drama, film criticism, journalism, and travel writing. Among his many novels, unquestionably his greatest achievement is the trilogy *U.S.A.* comprising *The 42nd Parallel* (1930), *1919* (1932), and *The Big Money* (1936). His *Three Soldiers* (1921) was one of the first and most influential American novels of World War I; *Manhattan Transfer* (1925) is important both as a chronicle of the modern metropolis and as a modernist experimental narrative.

**FURTHER READING:** Townsend Ludington's *John Dos Passos: A Twentieth Century Odyssey* (1980) and Virginia Spencer Carr's *Dos Passos: A Life* (1984) are fine, detailed biographies which complement each other nicely. Linda W. Wagner's *Dos Passos: Artist as American* (1979) is a good overview of his career and canon. There are two book-length secondary bibliographies, John Rohrkemper's *John Dos Passos: A Reference Guide* (1980) and David Sanders's *John Dos Passos: A Comprehensive Bibliography* (1987). The Aldeman Library of the University of Virginia houses most of Dos Passos's papers and manuscripts.

JOHN ROHRKEMPER        ELIZABETHTOWN COLLEGE

# LLOYD C(ASSEL) DOUGLAS
August 27, 1877–February 13, 1951

**BIOGRAPHY:** Lloyd C. Douglas, addressed with customary courtesy as Dr. Douglas by his Protestant congregations, was born in Columbia City, Indiana, on August 27, 1877, to Alexander Jackson Douglas, a minister, and his wife, Sarah Jane (Cassel). He earned an AB in 1900 and an AM in 1903 from Wittenberg, a Lutheran college in Springfield, Ohio. He also was awarded a BD at the Hamma Divinity School in Springfield in 1903, where he trained for the ministry. He began preaching in Indiana before moving on to become pastor of a church in Washington, D.C. His calling led him to direct religion programs at the University of Illinois and serve as pastor of the First Congregational Church in Ann Arbor, Michigan. After tiring of living in college towns, he became pastor of churches in Akron, Ohio; Montreal; and Los Angeles. He was also awarded the DD in 1920 by Fargo College in North Dakota; the University of Southern California, 1928; the University of Vermont, 1931; an LLD from Gettysburg College in Pennsylvania, 1935; and Litt D degrees from Northeastern University, 1936, and Wittenberg College, 1945.

His first novel, *Magnificent Obsession* (1929), rose slowly to best-seller status. In 1933 he retired from the ministry to write more novels. Several of Douglas's novels were made into successful movies. He and his wife, Bessie Porch, a minister's daughter, had two children who wrote a candid, moving, and humorous biography of their parents' lives, *The Shape of Sunday* (1952). Douglas died of a heart ailment in a Los Angeles hospital at the age of seventy-three. His daughters were with him at the hospital and heard the beloved Christian author's last words, "I'm happy," as they held his hands. He is buried in the Sanctuary of the Good Shepherd at Forest Lawn Memorial Park in Glendale, California. A chapel honoring Douglas and his wife was built alongside the First Congregational Church in Ann Arbor, Michigan.

**SIGNIFICANCE:** Douglas's novels are an extension of his work as a minister and reflect the remarkable understanding of medicine he absorbed while conducting pastoral care visits to patients at Midwestern teaching hospitals. His first novel, *Magnificent Obsession*, was published by a religious press but slowly gained a secular audience. While his themes are inspirational and uplifting, they appeal to the general population because his plots, which sometimes develop using too many coincidences, are not didactic. Characterization, particularly when portraying persons with strong Midwestern values, shows readers how to live according to the Golden Rule. In his novels, good triumphs over evil, true love overcomes all obstacles, common sense speaks louder than education or wealth, and people change for the better when they live according to biblical principles. His Midwestern characters are generous, are devoted to their families and employers, meet obligations, and judge others by who they are rather than by what they do or own. Douglas's settings span the globe, yet it is in the rural Midwest where his characters find comfort, simplicity, and acceptance. At a time when his contemporaries were writing about the poor and downtrodden in society, Douglas chose to minister to the rich professionals whose spiritual poverty was, in his opinion, as troublesome and painful as the monetary poverty suffered by farmers in the Dust Bowl or laborers in the factory. Many of his characters are doctors and academics whose values are molded by controversial scientific theories rather than by religious principles.

**SELECTED WORKS:** Douglas's novels using Midwestern or rural settings include *Magnificent Obsession* (1929), *White Banners* (1936), *Disputed Passage* (1939), and *Invitation to Live* (1940). Other novels by Douglas include his famous religious works, *The Robe* (1942) about the life of Christ, and *The Big Fisherman* (1948) about the life of the Apostle Peter; *Doctor Hudson's Secret Journal* (1939), a book requested by readers of *Magnificent Obsession* (1929); *Forgive Us Our Trespasses* (1932); *Green Light* (1935); and *Precious Jeopardy* (1933). The most popular works were adapted into screenplays and became film classics. Douglas also wrote several volumes of nonfiction, including sermons and other inspirational works. *Time to Remember* (1951) was written by Douglas for those readers who wanted to know more about him. This autobiography is reflective and incomplete.

**FURTHER READING:** Douglas's autobiography was followed by his daughters' biography of their parents, *The Shape of Sunday* (1952), written by Virginia Douglas Dawson and Betty Douglas Wilson. The Douglas daughters share their travels through the territory where their father and mother had lived as well as the correspondence they had written to family, friends, and publishers. The Lloyd C. Douglas Collection at the University of Michigan's Bentley Historical Library contains letters to Douglas from many contemporaries including Pearl Buck and William Saroyan, notebooks, speeches, sermons, scrapbooks, photographs, and original manuscripts donated by his daughters. Additional secondary sources about Douglas include Edmund Wilson's "'You Can't Do This to Me!' Shrilled Celia," in *Classics and Commercials: A Literary Chronicle of the Forties* (1950): 204–208; and Carl Bode's "Lloyd Douglas and America's Largest Parish" and "Lloyd Douglas: Loud Voice in the Wilderness," in *The Half-World of American Culture* (1965): 175–83 and 141–57 respectively.

SUSAN BOURRIE          EASTERN MICHIGAN UNIVERSITY

# RITA DOVE
August 28, 1952

**BIOGRAPHY:** Rita Dove—poet, dramatist, novelist, short story writer, and college professor—was born to Ray and Elvira (Hord) Dove and raised in Akron, Ohio. Ray, a chemist, and Elvira, a housewife, encouraged young Rita, her older brother, and her two younger sisters to educate themselves by reading from the family's relatively large collection of books. Yet it wasn't until high school that Dove became interested in becoming a writer. Dove credits her high school English teacher, who took her to her first book signing, with showing her that it was possible to write poetry and give it to the world.

Nonetheless, Dove attended college thinking she was going to be a lawyer, believing that was what a second-generation middle-class child was supposed to do. At Miami University (Ohio) she majored in what she told her parents was pre-law but was actually English. Gradually she became more seriously interested in writing and the study of literature. Upon receiving a BA from Miami in 1973, Dove attended the University of Tübingen in Germany on a Fulbright Fellowship, where she studied modern European literature. She returned to the United States to earn an MFA from the Iowa Writers' Workshop in 1977.

Three years later she published her first book of poems, *The Yellow House on the Corner* (1980), which, while dealing with the problems of racism, expressed her reaction to the black nationalist literary aesthetic that had prevailed since the late 1960s by refusing to allow indignation, anger, or protest to control her verse. Her next book of poems, *Mu-*

*seum* (1983), further developed this expression while exploring the vicissitudes of multiculturalism from the vantage point of her experiences in the United States and abroad.

In 1987 Dove was awarded the Pulitzer Prize for poetry for *Thomas and Beulah* (1986), a sequence of poems which told the story of Dove's grandparents who moved from the Tennessee ridge to Ohio's iron and steel region during the Great Migration. In 1993, following the success of her fourth book of poems, *Grace Notes* (1989), and her first novel, *Through the Ivory Gate* (1991), Dove was named poet laureate of the United States, making her to date not only the youngest person but also the only African American to have achieved this honor. Marking the end of her tenure as poet laureate, Dove's most recent book of poems, *Mother Love* (1995), examined how the Demeter/Persephone cycle of betrayal and regeneration has relevance to her own and today's mother-daughter relationships. Although she continues to travel widely in America, Europe, and the Middle East, Dove lives with her husband, writer Fred Viebahn, and her daughter, Aviva, near the University of Virginia, where she is Commonwealth Professor of English.

Rita Dove.
Photo by Fred Viebahn. Courtesy of Fred Viebahn

**SIGNIFICANCE:** Some of the poems in *The Yellow House on the Corner* and *Museum* narrate Dove's memory of her childhood in the Midwest. In *Thomas and Beulah*, Dove more closely examines her relationship with the Midwest by pursuing her abiding interest in her heritage, specifically her Akron grandparents. Often praised for its lyrical depth and attention to historical detail, this book of poems established Dove as a poet with unique concerns about not only the contemporary lyric poem but also the cultural history of the American Midwest. Much of Dove's poetry published after 1986 continues to develop these concerns, but mostly in light of her European experiences.

Dove is fascinated with questioning the idea of individual destiny and its relationship to time and place. How does where an individual comes from determine where he or she ends up? Where does an individual reside most completely? These questions constantly emerge in Dove's poems as well as in her fiction. Whether imaginatively describing a bag lady's journey through an arcade in rainy Cleveland or lyrically telling the story

of a woman artist who returns to her hometown in the Midwest to teach at a local public school, Dove attempts in her fiction to answer those possibly unanswerable questions about individual destiny and often does so in terms of her Midwestern experience.

**SELECTED WORKS:** Dove's poems which perhaps best typify her interests in Midwest culture, tradition, and history are: "Small Town" from *The Yellow House on the Corner* (1980); "A Father Out Walking on the Lawn" from *Museum* (1983); "Jiving," "The Zeppelin Factory," "One Volume Missing," "Wingfoot Lake," and "Company" from *Thomas and Beulah* (1986); "Silos" and "The Buckeye" from *Grace Notes* (1989); and "In the Old Neighborhood" from *Selected Poems* (1993). Many of the short stories collected in *Fifth Sunday* (1985) address the problem of surviving in the contemporary Midwest with its landlocked dreams. Dove's novel *Through the Ivory Gate* (1991), in a strikingly TONI MORRISON–like fashion, describes a middle-aged Midwestern woman's search for spiritual healing. In addition, Dove has written a play entitled *The Darker Face of the Earth* (1994).

**FURTHER READING:** A number of good interviews with Dove are available. In these she discusses her childhood, education, travels, and past and present influences and interests. Both Steven Schneider's "Coming Home: An Interview with Rita Dove," in *Iowa Review* 19.3

(Fall 1989): 112–23, and Emily Lloyd's "Navigating the Personal: An Interview with Poet Laureate Rita Dove," in *Off-Our-Backs: A Woman's News Journal* 24.4 (April 1994): 1, 4, 22, touch upon some Midwestern aspects of Dove's poetry, but William Walsh's "Isn't Reality Magic? An Interview with Rita Dove," in *Kenyon Review* 16.3 (Summer 1994): 142–54, is most central to understanding some of the intellectual and emotional concerns lying beneath the surface of her writing. Bill Moyers's book *The Language of Life* (1995) offers a straightforward interview with Dove. The literary journal *Callaloo: A Journal of African American Arts and Letters* has published several noteworthy articles on Dove. These include Bonnie Costello's "Scars and Wings: Rita Dove's *Grace Notes*" (Spring 1991): 438–44; Ekaterini Georgoudaki's "Rita Dove: Crossing Boundaries" (Spring 1991): 419–33; and Arnold Rampersad's "The Poems of Rita Dove" (Winter 1986): 52–60. Kirkland C. Jones's "Folk Idiom in the Literary Expression of Two African American Authors: Rita Dove and Yusef Komunyakaa," in *Language and Literature in the African American Imagination*, edited by Carol Aisha Blackshire Belay (1992): 149–65, is an interesting comparison of Dove's and Komunyakaa's literary visions. "Ohio-Born Poet's Dedication to Motherly Love," a short review of Dove's *Mother Love*, can be found in the Spring 1996 issue of *Nexus* (136–37), Wright State University's journal of literature and art.

WILL M. CLEMENS        UNIVERSITY OF CINCINNATI

**Theodore Dreiser.**
Courtesy of Theodore Dreiser Papers, Rare Book & Manuscript Library, University of Pennsylvania

## (HERMAN) THEODORE DREISER
August 27, 1871–December 28, 1945

**BIOGRAPHY:** Born in Terre Haute, Indiana, of working-class immigrant parents, John Paul and Sarah (Schanab) Dreiser, Theodore Dreiser became one of the most admired and representative Midwestern writers of the twentieth century. The family was large. Theodore, the next-to-youngest child, had five sisters and four brothers, the oldest and most successful being John Paul Jr., known as Paul Dresser, the musical-comedy star and songwriter. The various experiences of his siblings, especially those of his sisters, helped shape Dreiser's attitudes toward life and provided him with much of his material for fiction.

His earliest years were inauspicious. Severe financial difficulties plagued his family, who were forced to move repeatedly from one Indiana town to another. The most significant of the family wanderings brought Dreiser in his mid-teens to Chicago, then burgeoning into a great metropolis, the railroading, meatpacking, and manufacturing hub of Mid-America. Even though Dreiser lived in Chicago for less than a decade, those years were formative, and Chicago remained the quintessential city of his fiction, one that he often revisited and which he compared with Florence in its early days, youthful and blithe, not content to borrow traditions but busily making its own. Dreiser was happy to be in on the making of a great city.

Working at a succession of menial jobs during his teen years in Chicago was discouraging to this ambitious young man who felt that he had considerable potential, but the work familiarized him with the rapidly developing city and its immigrant population. Dreiser spent one unsatisfactory year, 1889–1890, at Indiana University in Bloomington and then returned to Chicago, locating work as a newspaperman, his first step toward a literary career.

His assignments as a reporter sent him to all parts of the city and opened doors into social, business, and political circles. He was inquisitive, wondering about the way society was organizing itself in Chicago, and he was continually learning more about it—often to his consternation. Possessing a facility for words, Dreiser located older, more experienced newspapermen willing to serve as mentors and generally employed journalism as a self-teaching device for becoming an effective writer.

Chicago in the late 1880s was growing at a phenomenal rate and the construction boom appeared to be without limit. Its most imposing features were the impressive new skyscrapers that were beginning to crowd streets within the downtown streetcar Loop established by traction magnate Charles T. Yerkes. Dreiser walked these streets in a continual state of amazement at the great buildings, the immense crowds, the incessant clangor of steel girders being riveted. Further stints on newspapers in St. Louis, Cleveland, Pittsburgh, and eventually New York completed Dreiser's education regarding the industrial city of his day, confirming every trend he had first witnessed in Chicago and helping eventually to make him into the preeminent novelist of the American urban landscape. In one manner or another, every Dreiser novel uses his Chicago experiences.

In 1898 Dreiser married Sara Osborne White (1869–1942), a Missouri schoolteacher he had met during an assignment to cover Chicago's great World's Fair, the World's Columbian Exposition of 1893. Theirs was not a happy marriage; for three decades after 1910 the couple was estranged but remained undivorced. At the time of his marriage, Dreiser was living in New York, where he had moved in 1894 and where his brother Paul was well established in the Broadway theatrical world. Dreiser continued his newspaper career, gradually branching out into magazine articles and then fiction. After writing a number of short stories, he produced his first novel, *Sister Carrie* (1900). Its failure to succeed commercially was an element in the author's subsequent emotional breakdown, and Dreiser did not publish another novel until *Jennie Gerhardt* appeared in 1911. The latter initiated Dreiser's most prolific period. In 1912 he published the first novel of a projected trilogy,

*The Financier,* covering the life and career of Charles T. Yerkes. That was followed by a second volume, *The Titan* (1914), and then by a heavily autobiographical novel with a Midwestern artist as its hero, *The "Genius"* (1915).

From the onset of his career, conservative critics and publishers had frowned upon Dreiser's bold, naturalistic subject matter and his frank treatment of themes. In 1914, after printing *The Titan,* Harper and Brothers declined to be its publisher. Censorship loomed on other fronts as well, and cumulatively this opposition became instrumental in Dreiser's temporary retirement from fiction. But he did not stop writing; far from it. He had published in other genres and hoped to continue doing so. In 1913 his *A Traveler at Forty* had recorded his European adventures ostensibly in search of data for later parts of his trilogy about Yerkes. He was interested in the drama and produced a series of one-act plays as well as a longer tragedy, *The Hand of the Potter* (1918). A volume of biographical profiles, *Twelve Men,* appeared in 1919 and a collection of essays, *Hey, Rub-a-Dub-Dub,* in 1920. These were followed by a portion of his autobiography dealing with his newspaper days in Chicago and elsewhere and entitled *A Book about Myself* (1922). Dreiser was a very busy writer, and his reputation was steadily growing.

Dreiser always intended to return to fiction, and by mid-1925, when the publishing world was less conservative, due in part to Dreiser's efforts, and the official censors on the defensive, he was ready to publish *An American Tragedy.* This immense novel is widely regarded as his masterpiece, and its great commercial success made Dreiser rich for a time. Kansas City and Chicago provided the setting for Dreiser's story, before the action moved east to New York state. By 1929 Dreiser had published *Chains* (1927), a collection of stories, a revised version of *The Financier,* and a two-volume edition of biographical sketches in which he did for women what he had done for his own sex in *Twelve Men,* giving it the title *A Gallery of Women* (1929). But while he planned and worked at several other full-length fictions, no new novel appeared during his lifetime.

By 1930 Dreiser was considered sufficiently illustrious to be nominated for the Nobel Prize in literature, which no American had yet won. His name was forwarded to the

Swedish committee along with that of SIN-CLAIR LEWIS, his fellow Midwesterner and author of a string of extremely popular satirical novels that poked fun at the same targets that Dreiser approached in a somber tone. In the final balloting, Lewis was chosen over Dreiser and became the first American writer honored with the Nobel Prize. With these two authors, Midwestern fiction had become dominant in American literature.

In 1938 Dreiser moved to Hollywood, California, where he hoped to arrange for motion-picture versions of his novels. In 1944—his estranged wife having died in 1942—he married Helen Richardson, with whom he had lived off and on since the early 1920s. In 1944 also, he received the Award of Merit Medal for "extraordinary achievement" from the American Academy of Arts and Letters. Dreiser died in Hollywood, of a heart attack, on December 28, 1945.

**SIGNIFICANCE:** By 1912 Dreiser was established as the de facto leader of those American prose writers who employed the methods of literary naturalism in depicting the typically baneful effects of American industrialization. Many new young writers were beginning to emerge from the Midwest, and Dreiser was recognized by them as a leader also. Increasingly, today, he is recognized as being the indispensable novelist of the period from 1900 through 1920. A good deal of credit is owed to his friend, critic H. L. Mencken, who backed Dreiser in his conflicts with timid publishers and aggressive censors. Mencken encouraged Dreiser to persevere in bucking the genteel trends of his day, turning American literary taste from head-in-the-sand romanticism toward a braver facing of the here-and-now realities of life. He was a trailblazer for other literary naturalists, including Eugene O'Neill and Tennessee Williams in drama; SHERWOOD ANDERSON, JOHN DOS PASSOS, and John Steinbeck in the novel; and EDGAR LEE MASTERS and Robinson Jeffers in verse. It is difficult to imagine any of these writers developing as they did without Dreiser's pioneering of the realistic approach. So undeniable was Dreiser's impact upon his generation and that which followed that Sinclair Lewis, accepting the Nobel Prize for himself, was impelled to turn the spotlight from his own considerable accomplishment and onto Dreiser's brave persistence, usually

alone, often against great odds, in leading the way for American fiction.

Dreiser's great theme concerned the constant and usually unsuccessful struggle of the individual to survive in contention with the powerful socioeconomic forces unleashed by the machine age. All of his other works are peripheral to the important writings that center upon the effects of the great change that transformed Americans from farmers to factory workers and effected a social stratification that separated owners from employees, placed barriers between the wealthy and the destitute, and exalted the strong over the weak. Unlike writers such as Sherwood Anderson and Erskine Caldwell, whose center was small-town and rural America, Dreiser from his beginnings focused on the metropolis, a phenomenon which he rightly saw as representing the American future. This urban focus sets him apart from most of his contemporaries and is responsible to a large degree for the enduring significance of his work in American letters.

The difference between Dreiser's approach to industrialization and those of his contemporaries is striking. In *Winesburg, Ohio* (1919), Sherwood Anderson depicts the turn-of-the-century small Midwestern town as a place rooted in the past, a locale that his young hero must break from in order to realize his potential. But only in the final pages of the novel, in which George Willard catches the train for Chicago, is there any suggestion of the context which awaits him, the city where George must strive to make his way in a new and brutal world. By way of contrast, the opening pages of Dreiser's greatest works tend to depict his protagonists in the act of abandoning their early environments, his novels then being devoted to portraying what truly excites their author: the plight of the individual caught among the welter of unfriendly urban forces newly unleashed. What the heroine of *Sister Carrie* learns, at age eighteen, as she pounds the teeming sidewalks of Chicago in a desperate search for work, is that the new economic order considers the individual to be no more than a commodity to be purchased or rejected by the powers that be. Skills and talents and physical strength mean little to machines; in the factory, Carrie operates an assembly-line mechanism that punches shoelace holes in leather. She is wholly dispensable. When she has the misfortune to fall ill, her place tending the machine is taken by another human cipher glad for the meager wage that holds body and soul together. Dreiser's unvarnished depiction of economic necessity reflects a basic truth about newly industrial America, and *Sister Carrie* is obsessive in its itemization of weekly wages and the corresponding debits that accrue for shelter, food, clothing, fuel, and—only when these other fundamentals are satisfied—entertainment.

Indeed, Dreiser was quick to perceive that amid the brick and steel and concrete of the emerging American metropolis, every avenue of diversion, including entertainment, would be commercialized to the hilt. Mass populations produced mass audiences. Their own separate individualities erased by an unfeeling industrial steamroller, these masses were turning for inspiration to celebrities, in particular to those connected with the stage, where individual personality seemed still possible and valuable. While the workers felt increasingly chained to a system not of their own devising, celebrities seemed still to be free. Dreiser's close scrutiny of this emergent American theme is one important hallmark of his modernity; his concern is never for the past but always for the present and, perhaps even more so, for what might lie in store for this land of the free, a term he was fond of using ironically. The meteoric rise to stardom of Carrie Meeber, the small-talented Wisconsin miller's daughter, her name altered to the more euphonious Carrie Madenda, is by no means accidental. Carrie is but the first in a long line of heroines of American fiction, film, and television whose stories are based upon those of the queens of manufactured glamour, a line extending from Lillian Russell to Marilyn Monroe, Madonna, and beyond.

It is becoming increasingly apparent that early rejection of Dreiser by conservative critics, a dismissal purportedly based on stylistic crudeness, was in actuality a turning away in horror, not from Dreiser the writer, but from Dreiser the messenger. What he had to tell us about the way we had organized our lives was too disquieting to be borne, and so it was denied. Time has proved the accuracy of his vision.

In Dreiser's fiction, even those occupying the tip of the industrial pyramid fight losing battles. Typically, they are hoodwinked into believing that their lives of privilege and power signify pertinence and permanence as well. The industrial system saps the freedom of their wills and turns them into pawns of "the way things are," controlling their every action no less than it controls the actions of those whom they order about in their daily lives. Dreiser, in fact, sees existence itself as ironical. In his story "Free," he depicts a power figure who realizes only toward the close of his days that he has been duped by life, set free at last—only to die.

The greatest of Dreiser's superman figures, the traction magnate Frank Cowperwood, in *The Financier* and *The Titan*, bestrides the economic world of Chicago like an invincible giant, via his streetcar monopoly gathering to himself all of the accepted prerogatives of economic triumph: lavish homes, collections of Old-Master paintings, desirable mistresses. Only in *The Stoic*, the final volume of the trilogy that tells Cowperwood's story, does the superhero discover that he has followed a will-o'-the-wisp, fully as much a puppet of the industrial system as any of his many underlings. He has been tricked by nature into building a great transportation system for the very masses he despises, and after his death the spoils of his economic victories are auctioned off, sold to the highest bidder, and dispersed. His streetcars remain; for a five-cent fare they carry Chicagoans wherever they wish to go.

That a rigid class system should have been erected in a so-called democracy—and that these classes should be separated from one another by such impassable gulfs—seemed a contradiction in terms for Dreiser, who never tired of the theme. He dwelt upon it at length in his second novel, in which the destitute Jennie Gerhardt proves irresistibly attractive to Lester Kane, son of her wealthy Cincinnati employer. Kane brings Jennie to Chicago, where the two live a secluded life as man and wife in the suburbs. Dreiser posed the central question in starkly frank terms: Might a lady's maid be permitted to marry a millionaire in America? Very probably not, was his reply. The economic gulf was too wide, the social system too inflexible. In the end, money would call the tune.

Dreiser's most successful consideration of

this new and implacable division of the classes is anatomized in *An American Tragedy*. A youthful Midwesterner, Clyde Griffiths, leaves his idealistic missionary home in Kansas City to enter the economic crucible, eventually finding his way to Chicago and then to an Eastern industrial city where he is established in a mid-management role in a factory owned by a relative. Here Clyde finds himself trapped between two worlds: as a poor relative, he lacks automatic entry into the social life of the moneyed Griffithses, but as a factory supervisor he is forbidden contact with the wage-earning workers. He is stranded between segregated classes. Clyde's dilemma comes to a climax after he breaks company rules to engage in a love affair with a working girl, impregnates her, and then is taken up by the daughter of a factory owner. Having been imbued with the conviction that money and position represent everything worth striving for—and the poor girl refusing to budge out of his life and make room for the rich girl—Clyde is led into committing the murder that wrecks his life. Awaiting the electric chair, he ponders the question of his guilt, stunned by what life has done to him. Dreiser delivers a harsh indictment of a society that, he suggests, systematically and irresponsibly makes such tragedies inevitable.

Clearly, the ideas, subjects, and dramatic situations that characterize Dreiser's novels have become staples of American fiction. Of such immensity, in fact, is Dreiser's significance to his era that it is not at all impossible that, as future literary historians delve into a reassessment of the twentieth century, the first decades, 1900–1920, may very well become known as the "Age of Dreiser and Mencken."

**SELECTED WORKS:** Dreiser's major novels include *Sister Carrie* (1900), *Jennie Gerhardt* (1911), *The Financier* (1912), *The Titan* (1914), *The "Genius"* (1915), *An American Tragedy* (1925), *The Bulwark* (1946), and *The Stoic* (1947). His short stories are gathered in *Free, and Other Stories* (1918) and *Chains* (1927). His dramatic writings are in *Plays of the Natural and the Supernatural* (1916) and *The Hand of the Potter* (1918). Dreiser's poems appear in *Moods, Cadenced and Declaimed* (1926). His autobiographical writings include *A Traveler at Forty* (1913), *A Hoosier Holiday* (1916), *A Book about Myself* (later known as *Newspaper Days*, 1922), *Dawn* (1931), *American Diaries, 1902–1926* (1982), *An Amateur Laborer* (1983), and *Dreiser's Russian Diary* (1996). Important Dreiser letters are printed in the three-volume *Letters of Theodore Dreiser* (1959), *Letters to Louise* (1959), in the two-volume *Dreiser-Mencken Letters* (1986), and in *Dearest Wilding* (1995).

Dreiser's nonfiction includes *Twelve Men* (1919), *Hey, Rub-a-Dub-Dub* (1920), *The Color of a Great City* (1923), *Dreiser Looks at Russia* (1928), *A Gallery of Women* (1929), *Tragic America* (1931), *Notes on Life* (1974), *A Selection of Uncollected Prose* (1977), *Selected Magazine Articles of Theodore Dreiser* (1985 and 1987), *Theodore Dreiser Journalism* (1988), and *Theodore Dreiser's "Heard in the Corridors" Articles and Related Writings* (1988).

**FURTHER READING:** Full-length biographies include Robert H. Elias's *Theodore Dreiser: Apostle of Nature* (1949 and 1970), W. A. Swanberg's *Dreiser* (1965), Richard Lingeman's two-volume work *Theodore Dreiser: At the Gates of the City 1871–1907* (1986), and *Theodore Dreiser: An American Journey, 1908–1945* (1990). Persons close to Dreiser have written about their experiences with him, including his widow, Helen Dreiser: *My Life with Dreiser* (1951); and his niece Vera Dreiser: *My Uncle Theodore* (1976).

Donald Pizer, Richard Dowell, and Frederic E. Rusch's *Theodore Dreiser: A Primary Bibliography and Reference Guide* (1991) is of great use in locating sources for writings by and about Dreiser. An excellent early critical study is F. O. Matthiessen's *Theodore Dreiser* (1951). Ellen Moers's *Two Dreisers* (1969) is unsurpassed as a joint study of *Sister Carrie* and *An American Tragedy*. An interesting tribute by a major fellow novelist, Robert Penn Warren, is *Homage to Theodore Dreiser* (1971). Donald Pizer's *The Novels of Theodore Dreiser* (1976) provides valuable materials concerning the circumstances surrounding the composition of Dreiser's novels, and Lawrence E. Hussman Jr.'s *Dreiser and His Fiction: A Twentieth-Century Quest* (1983) deals in a penetrating manner with Dreiser's major themes. Craig Brandon in *Murder in the Adirondacks* (1986) writes about the sources for *An American Tragedy* in a manner almost as exciting as the novel itself. A valuable and recent biographical-critical volume treating most phases of Dreiser's life and work is Philip Gerber's *Theodore Dreiser Revisited* (1992).

The Dreiser Collection at the University of Pennsylvania Library in Philadelphia is massive, including the novelist's personal library and files of correspondence with scores of his contemporaries, his notes for writing, and most of his original manuscripts and photographs, as well as copies of the many editions of his books.

PHILIP GERBER                    SUNY BROCKPORT

## BERNARD DUFFEY.
*See* appendix (1981)

## JULIA LOUISA CORY DUMONT
October 1794–January 2, 1857
(Cory also appears as "Corey" or "Carey")
BIOGRAPHY: Julia Dumont's parents, Ebenezer and Martha D. Cory, came from Rhode Island to the area around Marietta, Ohio, as two of the region's earliest settlers. Julia was born in Waterford, in Washington County. Not long before her birth, her father was found murdered, presumably by Indians. The next spring her mother packed her infant daughter into a saddlebag and survived the trip back East. Martha Cory supported herself and her daughter in Greenfield, New York, by sewing. Here Julia grew up, attended Milton Academy, where she showed literary talent, and taught school for two years before marrying John Dumont, an attorney, in August 1812.

The couple moved to Cincinnati, then in 1814 to Vevay, Indiana, where their eleven children were born, several dying in childhood. Her strong character was later written about in glowing tributes by her students EDWARD EGGLESTON and GEORGE EGGLESTON. While suffering from tuberculosis, Julia Dumont gathered together many of her stories previously published in newspapers and magazines and put together her sole book, *Life Sketches from Common Paths: A Series of American Tales* (1856). She died at Vevay in 1857.
SIGNIFICANCE: Julia Dumont was one of the better-known regional authors of her day and the first woman to attain literary prominence throughout the Ohio Valley. Unfortunately, she published only one book. However, considering the fact that she taught school continuously from 1820 to 1857 and published only in Midwestern newspapers and periodicals, she did well to collect stories into a book. The preface explains her didactic aim: to be a good moral influence particularly on young readers and to strengthen the belief in the existence and reality of good in a bad world. All the stories are intended to further these precepts.

The book is organized around a central situation, as in Chaucer's *Canterbury Tales*. An introductory episode describes a Fourth of July celebration with a group of boys playing games in a meadow near Philadelphia. A second episode describes a banquet provided for the group by one of the boys thirty-eight years later. Harley Ives, a cripple, through whom the reader had seen something of the boys at first and glimpsed their fates, now sees them again and tells a story about each. An old woman of the town, Aunt Quiet, tells some of the stories.

One story, "The Brothers," shows the brotherly love of George and William Branham. George marries and has a large family. He is occasionally forced to borrow money from his affluent bachelor brother, whom he despairs of ever being able to repay. When William brings news of the death of one of George's sons, who was learning a trade out of town, the parents are grief stricken; yet years afterward William produces the son with the explanation that he has been away at college at his wealthy uncle's expense.

"Ashton Grey" is an unrelated romantic story of a handsome, refined boatman on the Ohio River and a dreamy Annabel. Ashton rescues three children from a burning cabin and, being injured, is nursed by Annabel. The two marry over the opposition of her guardian.

Although Julia Dumont's fiction may to some extent anticipate Midwestern realism through her use of local scenes, she is best classified as a romantic and sentimentalist. She creates characters with noble demeanor, places them amid frontier crudity, and has them speak in stilted, bookish language. In her tales good always triumphs in the end.
SELECTED WORKS: *Life Sketches from Common Paths* (1856) is Julia Dumont's only book, a collection of earlier published stories. Some of her other stories were published in Midwestern newspapers, but most are now lost.
FURTHER READING: Little material about Julia Dumont is available today, but the following may be helpful: Richard Banta's *Indiana Authors and Their Books 1816–1916* (1949); Thomas Barry's "A Biographical and Biblio-

graphical Dictionary of Indiana Authors," a master's thesis, Notre Dame University (1943); Orah Briscoe's "The Hoosier School of Fiction," a master's thesis, Indiana University (1934); Meredith Nicholson's *The Hoosiers* (1900); and Benjamin Stratton Parker and Enos Boyd Heiney's *Poets and Poetry of Indiana* (1900).

ARTHUR W. SHUMAKER        DEPAUW UNIVERSITY

## PAUL LAURENCE DUNBAR

June 27, 1872–February 9, 1906

**BIOGRAPHY:** Paul Laurence Dunbar—poet, novelist, short story writer, essayist, librettist, dramatist, lecturer—was born in Dayton, Ohio. His father, Joshua Dunbar, escaped from slavery into Canada and returned to fight on the side of the Union Army. His mother, Matilda (Burton) Dunbar, also a slave, had been a widow who with her previous husband had given birth to two sons: William and Robert. She met and married Joshua Dunbar in 1871 and was employed for many years as a domestic after her freedom was granted.

Dunbar spent most of his life in Dayton, Ohio, working first as an elevator operator in the Callahan Building. It was from such a humble background that he would launch his writing career by reading a poem, at the invitation of Dr. James Newton Matthews, before the Western Association of Writers held in Dayton.

Dunbar was married briefly to the poet and short story writer Alice Ruth Moore. There were no children from the union of these two writers and there is much speculation concerning their separation and failure to reconcile. Whatever the cause, there is no substantive evidence as to what happened, and the real cause has gone into the grave with all of the Dunbar and Moore descendants.

**SIGNIFICANCE:** Paul Laurence Dunbar was and remains a central figure in the canon of African American Literature. WILLIAM DEAN HOWELLS in his 1896 *Harper's* review was correct in his assertion that Dunbar was the first African American born in the nineteenth century to exhibit exceptional literary ability. His influence is still unmeasured, for he has had a seminal influence on the use of vernacular language among the major and minor black writers of poetry and fiction. He had

a remarkable ear for detecting how language was not only used but spoken. His ability to hear the natural rhythms of daily speech as well as to imagine that of the antebellum South has influenced a variety of African American writers. With the possible exception of LANGSTON HUGHES, no other African American writer may lay claim to such an overriding influence. His influence can clearly be detected in the works of such diverse poets and novelists as Langston Hughes, GWENDOLYN BROOKS, Margaret Walker, Sterling A. Brown, Paule Marshall, Ralph Ellison, James Baldwin, RICHARD WRIGHT, Nikki Giovanni, Sonia Sanchez, Etheridge Knight, Mari Evans, and Haki Madhubuti to name only a few.

His centennial in 1972 brought about two significant conferences devoted to his work. The first was held in Dayton, Ohio, at the University of Dayton and conducted by HERBERT W. MARTIN. The second was held in Los Angeles, California, at the University of California at Irvine and conducted by Jay Martin. Those two conferences devoted themselves to the poetry, essays, and fiction of Dunbar but did not access his dramatic works. There is still work to be done in this area, for Dunbar is known to have written four full-length plays (three of which were discarded by the Library of Congress). The fourth play, *Herrick*, was recently discovered by Herbert W. Martin in the Papers of Carter G. Woodson. There are a number of interesting aspects of this play: first, it is placed in the seventeenth century; second, it has no black characters; and third, it has no dialect. In fact the whole play evokes the tone of British English. This is perhaps Dunbar's single effort to demonstrate that he could handle the English language brilliantly and that he should not be confined to the pigeonhole of dialect poet. He was anything but that. Dunbar does not escape or avoid the theme of aspiration in *Herrick*. It is a play, above all else, about social prejudices and upward mobility.

**SELECTED WORKS:** *Oak and Ivy* (1893) and *Majors and Minors* (1895) were Dunbar's first published books. It was the later book which came to William Dean Howell's attention, resulting in his *Harper's* review and the printing of Dunbar's first commercial book, *Lyrics of Lowly Life* (1896), carrying with it Howell's famous introduction.

**Paul Laurence Dunbar.**
Courtesy of the Ohio Historical Society

Dunbar collaborated with African British composer Samuel Coleridge Taylor and the African American composer Will Marion Cook on a number of musical works. With Taylor he wrote the libretti for *African Romances* (1897) and *Dream Lovers: An Operatic Romance* (1898); with Cook he wrote two musicals which played on Broadway at the turn of the century: *Clorindy, or the Cakewalk* (1898) and *In Dahomey* (1900).

In chronological order, Dunbar published the following books of short stories, novels, and poems: *Folks from Dixie* (1898), *The Uncalled* (1898), *Lyrics of the Hearthside* (1899), *Poems of Cabin and Field* (1899), *The Love of Landry* (1900), *The Strength of Gideon and Other Stories* (1900), *Candle-Lightin' Time* (1901), *The Fanatics* (1901), *The Sports of the Gods* (1902), *In Old Plantation Days* (1903), *Lyrics of Love and Laughter* (1903), *When Malindy Sings* (1903), *The Heart of Happy Hollow* (1904), *Li'l Gal* (1904), *Chris'mus Is A-comin' and Other Poems* (1905), *Howdy, Howdy, Howdy,* (1905), *Lyrics of Sunshine and Shadow* (1905), *Joggin' Erlong* (1906), *Speaking of Christmas* (1914), and *Little Brown Baby* (1938).

**FURTHER READING:** Many major and minor secondary sources have been published. There are Charles M. Austin's *Paul Laurence Dunbar's Local Roots and Much More* (1989) and Benjamin Brawley's *Paul Laurence Dunbar: A Poet of His People* (1936), while Joanne M. Braxton has supplied the scholarly community with fifty uncollected poems in her *The Collected Poetry of Paul Laurence Dunbar* (1993), as well as a biographical entry on the poet in *The Oxford Companion to African American Literature* (1997). Biographies include Virginia Cunningham's *Paul Laurence Dunbar and His Song* (1969) and Tony Gentry's *Paul Laurence Dunbar, Poet* (1989). Addison Gayle has contributed the important *Oak and Ivy: A Biography of Paul Laurence Dunbar* (1971), and two decades earlier Jean Gould wrote her biography *That Dunbar Boy: The Story of America's Famous Negro Poet* (1958). Gossie Hudson's lengthy biographical dissertation "Biography of Paul Laurence Dunbar" (1978) is still unpublished. Langston Hughes placed a biographical entry on Dunbar in his *Famous American Negroes* (1975). Pat McKissack added *Paul Laurence Dunbar A Poet to Remember* (1984) to the wealth of critical and biographical works. Herbert Martin has added a monograph: *Paul Laurence Dunbar: A Singer of Songs* (1980) as well as a video and an accompanying study guide: *Paul Laurence Dunbar: The Eyes of the Poet* (1991–94). Jay Martin and Gossie H. Hudson edited *The Paul Laurence Reader* (1975), a selection of Dunbar's most important poetry, short stories, opera libretti, essays, and letters. Jay Martin provided *A Singer in the Dawn: Reinterpretations of Paul Laurence Dunbar* (1975). Peter Revell and Pearle H. Schultz, respectively, added *Paul Laurence Dunbar* (1979) and *Paul Laurence Dunbar: Black Poet Laureate* (1974) to Lida Keck Wiggins's groundbreaking study *The Life and Works of Paul Laurence Dunbar* (1907). There is also Kathleen McGhee-Anderson's drama *Oak and Ivy*, based on the life of Dunbar, which won the 1985 Eugene O'Neill Playwright Award. It premiered in 1992 at the Crossroads Theatre in New Brunswick, New Jersey, and was produced by the Human Race Company in Dayton, Ohio, from November 17 through December 4, 1994. Dunbar's books and papers are housed in a number of places, principally at the Ohio Historical Society in Columbus, Ohio.

HERBERT WOODWARD MARTIN

UNIVERSITY OF DAYTON

## FINLEY PETER DUNNE

July 10, 1867–April 24, 1936
(Mr. Dooley)

**BIOGRAPHY:** Born in Chicago to Irish-born Peter Dunne and Ellen (Finley) Dunne, Peter Dunne adopted his mother's maiden name following her death. After graduating last in his high school class, he embarked upon a brief but spectacular journalistic career. Working at a variety of newspaper jobs, in 1893 he wrote a dialect piece for the *Sunday Post* that introduced the long series of essays by "Mr. Dooley," bartender of Archer Avenue ("Archey Road") in the Irish suburb of Bridgeport, which would later give the city its mayors Daley. The first collection of these popular essays, *Mr. Dooley in Peace and in War*, was published in 1898. The first decade of the twentieth century saw several successful Dooley anthologies. Beginning with a largely local focus, Dunne gradually widened his scope and began to comment more and more on national events. His widely read columns on the war with Spain made him a nationwide celebrity, and he departed Chicago for New York in 1900. Like George Willard, who had left Winesburg to go to "some city to get a job on some newspaper," as well as contemporaries GEORGE ADE, RING LARDNER, and many others, he had abandoned the Midwest of his youth. He would hobnob with famous writers and actors and play golf with presidents.

In 1902 he married Margaret Abbott, by whom he had four children, including screenwriter Philip Dunne. He continued to be active in editing and writing, although his permanent absence from Chicago made the creation of further Mr. Dooley pieces increasingly difficult. In spite of poor health, he enjoyed uninterrupted success and celebrity. His son Philip encouraged him to write his memoirs as he struggled with cancer in the mid-1930s. Upon his death in 1936, Dunne was honored by a heavily attended Mass in New York City's St. Patrick's Cathedral and by a memorial Mass in St. Bridget's Church on Archer Avenue.

**SIGNIFICANCE:** If Chicago was the City of the Broad Shoulders, it was the Irish like Dunne's Mr. Dooley and the other residents of Bridgeport who did much to give it those shoulders. While not a major figure of the Chicago Renaissance, Dunne was known to its principals, as he was to nearly everyone else in the city. Writing in *Chicago Renaissance*, Dale Kramer quotes FLOYD DELL as saying that Dunne lacked the "spark of reform temperament" (149). The statement does ring true: complete commitment to reform required more faith in human nature and the democratic process than either Mr. Dooley or his creator could muster. Dell did grant, however, that "Mr. Dooley is a figure which gives us in bold, clear colors the writer and his Chicago" (149).

As an Everyman commentator ("I see be th' pa-apers"), Mr. Dooley gave a dialect voice to the isolationism of the heartland, commenting satirically on the expansionist policies of "Tiddy Rosenfelt." In one of his best-known essays, "A Book Review," he concludes his deflation of the head Rough Rider's book on the Spanish-American War by observing that the title should have been "Alone in Cuba" (*Mr. Dooley's Philosophy* 2). He belittled the diplomatic capabilities of President McKinley, or "Mack," as Mr. Dooley called him, likening him to a countryman who's "been in town long enough f'r to get out iv th' way iv th' throlley ca-ar whin th' bell rings" ("On Diplomacy," *Mr. Dooley in Peace and in War* 2). Mr. Dooley treated Admiral Dewey as his "Cousin George": "Dewey or Dooley, 'tis all the same" ("On His Cousin George," *Mr. Dooley on Iverything and Ivrybody* 7).

Critical estimates of Dunne's literary skill vary: every study of American humor mentions him in considerations of two vital traditions of American humor. Walter Blair, for example, includes Dunne among the "Literary Comedians" in *Native American Humor* (103). Jennette Tandy expresses her appreciation of Mr. Dooley in *Crackerbox Philosophers in American Humor and Satire* (160–63). Scholars have even found Dooleyan influences in the works of James Joyce. Surprisingly, given the relative inaccessibility of phonetically transcribed dialect, several *Mr. Dooley* collections are still in print.

**SELECTED WORKS:** Dunne's writings include *Mr. Dooley in Peace and in War* (1898), *Mr. Dooley in the Hearts of His Countrymen* (1899), *Mr. Dooley's Philosophy* (1900), *Mr. Dooley's Opinions* (1901), *Observations by Mr. Dooley* (1902), *Dissertations by Mr. Dooley* (1906), *Mr. Dooley Says* (1910), *Mr. Dooley on Making a Will and Other Necessary Evils* (1919), and *Mr. Dooley at His Best*, edited by Elmer Ellis (1938).

**FURTHER READING:** The definitive critical biography of Dunne is Elmer Ellis's *Mr. Dooley's America: A Life of Finley Peter Dunne* (1969). Grace Eckley's Twayne book *Finley Peter Dunne* (1981) is worthwhile. Dunne's son Philip edited *Mr. Dooley Remembers: The Informal Memoirs of Finley Peter Dunne* (1963), in which essays written by the elder Dunne at the end of his life are interspersed with chapters of commentary by the son. *Mr. Dooley's Chicago,* by Barbara C. Schaaf (1977), reprints some of the Chicago essays with copious background. Charles Fanning's *Finley Peter Dunne and Mr. Dooley: The Chicago Years* (1978) chronicles that period and quotes generous excerpts from the essays, while analyzing his transition from a regional commentator to a national one (212). Focusing on the same period are James DeMuth's *Small Town Chicago: The Comic Perspective of Finley Peter Dunne, George Ade, and Ring Lardner* (1980) and Edward J. Bander's *Mr. Dooley and Mr. Dunne: The Literary Life of a Chicago Catholic* (1981). See also William Merriam Gibson's *Theodore Roosevelt among the Humorists: W. D. Howells, Mark Twain, and Mr. Dooley* (1980).

There are several articles about Dunne and Mr. Dooley, including John O. Rees's "A Reading of Mr. Dooley," in *Studies in American Humor* n.s. 7 (1989): 5–31, which argues convincingly that earlier critics misread and underestimated Dunne's artistry. Barbara C. Schaaf's "The Man Who Invented Mr. Dooley," in *Chicago Magazine* (March 1977): 116–19, 130, 217, deals with Dunne in Chicago, as does James DeMuth's "Hard Times in the Sixth Ward: Mr. Dooley on the Depression of the 1890s," in *Studies in American Humor* n.s. 3 (Summer–Fall 1984): 123–37. See also Samuel Sillen's "Dooley, Twain, and Imperialism," in *Masses and Mainstream* 1 (December 1948): 6–14; John M. Harrison's "Finley Peter Dunne and the Progressive Movement," in *Journalism Quarterly* 44 (Autumn 1967): 475–81; and John O. Rees's "An Anatomy of Mr. Dooley's Brogue," in *Studies in American Humor* 5 (Summer–Fall 1986): 145–57. J. C. Furnas addresses the relationship between Dunne and SAMUEL CLEMENS in "The True American Sage," *American Scholar* 60 (Autumn 1991): 570–74.

PAUL P. SOMERS JR.     MICHIGAN STATE UNIVERSITY

## STUART DYBEK

April 10, 1942

**BIOGRAPHY:** Poet and short story writer Stuart Dybek was born to Stanley and Adeline (Sala) Dybek in a predominantly Slavic and Hispanic working-class neighborhood on Chicago's southwest side. The product of a strict Catholic education, Dybek initially showed little interest in writing, instead developing a passion for music that would later inform much of his work as evidenced by stories such as "Chopin in Winter" and "Blight" from his collection *The Coast of Chicago* (1990).

Following graduation, Dybek attended Loyola University in Chicago, where he received a BS in 1964 and later an MA. While at school, he met Caren Bassett, and in 1966 they were married. They have two children, Anne and Nicholas.

Following graduation, he worked as a caseworker for the Cook County Department of Public Aid. From 1968 to 1970, he taught high school English on the island of St. Thomas in the Virgin Islands. In 1970 he returned to the United States to attend the Writers' Workshop at the University of Iowa. There, his interest in writing began to flourish. He graduated with an MFA in 1973 and began teaching at Western Michigan University.

Dybek has been the recipient of a number of literary awards. In 1981 he won a special citation from the ERNEST HEMINGWAY Foundation; that same year, he also received a Guggenheim Fellowship. He has won an O. Henry Prize on four separate occasions, including a first prize for the story "Hot Ice" from his collection *The Coast of Chicago.* His story "Blight," also from the collection *The Coast of Chicago,* garnered him the Nelson Algren Prize, and in 1995 he won the PEN/Bernard Malamud Prize.

**SIGNIFICANCE:** Dybek's short fiction is in many ways reminiscent of SHERWOOD ANDERSON's *Winesburg, Ohio,* both in its capacity to chart the voyage of childhood and adolescence into adulthood and in its ability to expose the ties which bind communities together.

Dybek's focus is, more often than not, the working-class neighborhood of Chicago's southwest side, a community composed largely of Hispanics and East Europeans, a neighborhood vividly brought to life with repeated references to specific street names and buildings. However, though the city is necessarily invoked, the emphasis remains the neighborhood, segregated as it is from the city at large by its unique ethnicity and low-income housing. For Dybek, the neighborhood is an essential character, every bit as important as the people who inhabit it. In pieces such as "Blight" and "Hot Ice," as well as in earlier pieces such as "The Palatski Man" and "Blood Soup" from his first collection *Childhood and Other Neighborhoods* (1980), the neighborhood participates in the story, not simply delimiting the character's role in place and time but thoroughly defining it. His characters participate in strange symbiosis with their settings, repeatedly emerging at story's end necessarily branded by that mark of insight which accompanies the transformation from child to adult.

**SELECTED WORKS:** Dybek is the author of one book of poetry, *Brass Knuckles* (1979), and two collections of short stories, *Childhood and Other Neighborhoods* (1980) and *The Coast of Chicago* (1990). His stories have appeared in numerous collections, including the 1992 *Granta Book of the American Short Story* and the *Best American Short Stories, 1996*. He has also published several as-yet-uncollected stories in various periodicals, including "Readings—Thread," in *Harper's* (September 1998): 19; "Lunch at the Loyola Arms," in the *New Yorker* (November 10, 1997): 106; "Paper Lantern," in the *New Yorker* (November 27, 1995): 82; "A Confluence of Doors," in *Plough-shares* 18.2–3 (Fall 1992): 68–72; and "I Never Told This to Anyone," in the 1992 collection *The Wedding Cake in the Middle of the Road: Twenty-Three Variations on a Theme*. He has also published a number of poems, including "Swan," in *Poetry* 171.1 (1997): 18; "Overhead Fan," in *Poetry* 169.4 (1997): 278; and "Vigil," in *Poetry* 171.4 (1998): 259. Dybek has also contributed a piece entitled "Sympathy" for the 1996 collection *Family: American Writers Remember Their Own*.

**FURTHER READING:** Thomas Gladsky considers Dybek's handling of Polish American identity in "From Ethnicity to Multiculturalism: The Fiction of Stuart Dybek," in *MELUS* 20.2 (Summer 1995): 105–18, and in "Mr. Dybek's Neighborhood: Toward a New Paradigm for Ethnic Literature," in *The Polish Diaspora: East European Monographs*, edited by James S. Pula and M. B. Biskupski (1993): 129–35. Jorge Febles reflects on America's favorite pastime in "Dying Players: Ramirez's 'El Centerfielder' and Dybek's 'Death of the Rightfielder,'" in *Confluencia: Revista Hispanica de Cultura y Literatura* 12.1 (Fall 1996): 156–67.

Dybek has given a number of personal interviews. Benjamin Seaman interviews him in "Artful Dodge Interviews: Stuart Dybek and Edward Hirsch," in *Artful Dodge* 14–15 (Fall 1988): 17–27. More recently, Mike Nickel and Adrian Smith have interviewed him in "An Interview with Stuart Dybek," in the *Chicago Review* 43.1 (Winter 1997): 87–101. For a discussion of Dybek's poetry, see Sandra Gilbert's "On Burning Ground," in *Poetry* 139 (November 1981): 35–50.

STEVE HOPKINS      UNIVERSITY OF KENTUCKY

# E-F

## CHARLES ALEXANDER EASTMAN
February 19, 1858–January 8, 1939
(Ohiyesa, Hakadah)

**BIOGRAPHY:** Born near Redwood Falls, Minnesota, of Ite Wakanhdi Ota (Many Lightnings) and Wakantankanwin (Goddess, a.k.a. Mary Nancy Eastman), he was named Ohiyesa (The Winner). Both parents claimed descent from a distinguished Sioux. Upon his mother's death, the boy was taken to Manitoba and reared in his father's family according to traditional lifeways. Later, he reluctantly returned with his father to South Dakota, where he learned English, accepted Christianity, and took the name Charles Alexander Eastman.

After attending Beloit and Knox Colleges, he graduated from Dartmouth in 1887 and three years later obtained the MD from Boston University. Finding employment as a Bureau of Indian Affairs (BIA) physician, Eastman arrived at the Pine Ridge (South Dakota) reservation in 1890 where he met Elaine Goodale, a BIA school supervisor. They married in 1891, rearing six children before separating around 1920. Eastman and Goodale were in the first party of noncombatants to visit the battlefield at Wounded Knee. Confronted by the ghastly sight, Eastman blamed BIA corruption and incompetence. For the next thirty-five years, while serving the BIA intermittently, Eastman came into frequent conflict with superiors over similar issues. He also helped to found the Boy Scouts, sought to popularize Native American legends and folklore, and worked to extend the YMCA into reservation life. In his later years, Eastman spent summers at a cabin he had built on the eastern shore of Lake Huron and winters with a son in Detroit. Following a heart attack, he died in Detroit and was buried in an unmarked grave.

**SIGNIFICANCE:** The native inhabitants of the Midwest were the focus of all Eastman's professional activities, whether with the BIA or as a political reformer and advocate of Indian rights. Moreover, his identity and personal values derived from the traditional Santee Sioux culture of the region. In eleven published books and numerous articles, Eastman's goal was, as Raymond Wilson asserts in *Ohiyesa* (1983), to enlighten whites concerning the "Indian Problem" from a Native American point of view (145).

**SELECTED WORKS:** Several of Eastman's books sought to make Native American lifeways comprehensible to his largely white readership. In this connection, one might cite the juvenile title *An Indian Boyhood* (1902), along with *Red Hunters and the Animal People* (1904) and *Old Indian Days* (1907), and the two books coauthored with Elaine Goodale Eastman: *Wigwam Evenings: Sioux Folktales Retold* (1909) and *Smoky Day's Wigwam Evenings: Indian Stories Retold* (1910). A more ambitious project was *The Soul of the Indian: An Interpretation* (1911), which aimed to show the fundamental compatibility of Native American spirituality and Protestant Christianity while excoriating the narrow-minded practices of culturally ignorant missionaries. To demonstrate that Native Americans could become acculturated without becoming so assimilated as to lose contact with their culture, Eastman published *The Indian Today: The Past and Future of the First American* (1915) and *From the Deep Woods to Civilization: Chapters in the Autobiography of an Indian* (1916), the latter work proffering the author as object lesson.

**FURTHER READING:** Before the publication of Raymond Wilson's *Ohiyesa: Charles Eastman, Santee Sioux* (1983), virtually the only secondary source was a pamphlet in the Western Writers series, *Charles Alexander Eastman (Ohiyesa)*, by Marion W. Copeland (1978). The latter provides a comprehensive discussion of Eastman's writings utilizing the trope of the "dream-vision" that Eastman himself had identified. Within the confines of the pamphlet format, Copeland's essay remains the most perceptive study of Eastman's writings to date. Also of interest are David R. Miller's unpublished University of North Dakota master's thesis on Eastman (1975) and the writings of Elaine Goodale Eastman, particularly *Pratt, The Red Man Moses* (1935) and *Sister to the Sioux: The Memoirs of Elaine Goodale Eastman, 1885–91*, edited by Kay Graber (1978).

There is no single repository of Eastman's papers, which are to be found largely among the BIA records at the National Archives in Washington and the Federal Records Centers in Kansas City and St. Louis. Other materials are at Dartmouth College, the Jones Public Library in Amherst, Massachusetts, the Minneapolis Public Library, and the YMCA Historical Library in New York.

ROGER JIANG BRESNAHAN

MICHIGAN STATE UNIVERSITY

## EDWARD EGGLESTON
December 10, 1837–September 2, 1902

**BIOGRAPHY:** Edward Eggleston's father was Joseph Cary Eggleston, a lawyer and member of the Indiana Legislature; his mother, Mary Jane (Craig), was the daughter of Indian fighter George Craig of Kentucky. His brother, GEORGE CARY EGGLESTON, was a popular novelist. Edward was born in Vevay, Indiana, and made visits to the Craig farm and elsewhere, learning much about backwoods dialect and manners.

After his father's death, his mother married a Methodist preacher, Williamson Terrell, and the family lived in New Albany and Madison, then returned to Vevay. Spending over a year in Virginia, where he visited relatives and studied at the Amelia Academy, he began, because of poor health, to educate himself by reading.

Returning to Indiana, he labored as a Bible agent until his health failed, but he regained it by outdoor work. For a few months he rode a Methodist circuit, but his health again failed, and he went to Minnesota, serving as a pastor. There, in 1858, he married Lizzie Snider.

Leaving the ministry in 1866, he moved to Evanston, Illinois, where he was an editor of Sunday School publications and published *Mr. Blake's Walking Stick: A Christmas Story for Boys and Girls* (1870). Soon he moved East and became connected with the *Independent, Hearth and Home* (1871), and *Scribner's Monthly*. His first novel, *The Hoosier School-Master*, was published in *Hearth and Home* (1871) and as a book later that year. Its success impelled the writer to issue *The End of the World* (1872), dealing with the Ohio River country, first in *Hearth and Home* and then as a book. Next came *The Mystery of Metropolisville* (1873), drawn from his experiences in Minnesota. He then yielded to a request to write *The Circuit Rider* (1874), returning to Indiana's backwoods and dramatizing the lives of circuit clergymen. That year he took his last ministerial charge, as a pastor of the Lee Congregational Church in Brooklyn. After four years of successful work, his poor health forced his resignation. The remainder of his life was devoted to study and writing.

Having collected historical materials in Europe, he gave lectures at Columbia College and elsewhere, writing several books and historical articles, some of them for young people. He lived to publish only two volumes of his ambitious history project: *The Beginners of a Nation* (1896) and *The Transit of Civilization from England to America in the Seventeenth Century* (1901). However, during these years he produced much of his best writing, such as *Roxy* (1878), *The Graysons, A Story of Illinois* (1888), and *The Hoosier School-Boy* (1883). His wife died in 1889, and in 1891 he married Frances Goode, of Madison, Indiana. He published *The Faith Doctor* (1891) and then *Duffels* (1893), a collection of short stories. Eggleston died of apoplexy at his home.

**SIGNIFICANCE:** Edward Eggleston is credited by many as beginning the realistic period in American literature with the publication of *The Hoosier School-Master* in 1871. At the very least, the Golden Age of Indiana literature began with this book. He was not the first writer to use Hoosier character and setting in fiction, but he was the first to depict them favorably. Eggleston presented life as he had seen it.

Eggleston was sympathetic to life in the American Midwest. He was a realist in his attitudes toward life and literature. He was one of the few Indiana or Midwestern writers who made a contribution in the form of dialect. His humor helped make his tales more interesting. He was a real literary pioneer who turned Indiana mud into literary gold.

Eggleston's best-known works, including *The Hoosier School-Master, The Circuit Rider, The End of the World, Roxy, The Graysons, A Story of Illinois,* and *The Hoosier School-Boy*, are all set in the Midwest.

**SELECTED WORKS:** Edward Eggleston's first and most famous book was *The Hoosier School-Master* (1871). The story is based on the experiences of his brother George while teaching at a country school near Madison, Indiana. By the use of uncouth characters, Eggleston protested against the dominance of New England in American literature. The book was translated into Dutch, German, Danish, and French.

This success prompted Eggleston to write *The End of the World* (1872), in which he uses the Ohio River country and the Millerite excitement of 1842–43 to bolster a thin plot. The book antedated MARK TWAIN in its use of a river steamboat in a Western Romance.

*The Mystery of Metropolisville* (1873), suggested by his life in Minnesota, followed shortly, though Eggleston was dissatisfied with the book. *The Circuit Rider: A Tale of the Heroic Age* (1874) came next and was set in the early Indiana backwoods, dramatizing frontier life and the hardships of circuit riders. *Roxy* (1878) dealt frankly with the problem of adultery as occurring in Vevay. *The Hoosier School-Boy* (1893) was intended to serve as a companion piece to *The Hoosier School-Master* but is largely inferior. *The Graysons, A Story of Illinois* (1888) contains a murder trial of the hero, Tom Grayson, with his attorney, ABRAHAM LINCOLN, proving a witness a liar in showing, through a calendar, that no one could have seen a murder being committed because there was no moon that night.

Readers interested in Eggleston's children's books should experience *Mr. Blake's Walking Stick: A Christmas Story for Boys and Girls* (1870) and *The Book of Queer Stories and Stories Told on a Cellar Door* (1870). Two interesting adult books are *The Faith Doctor* (1891), which is concerned with such "aerial therapeutics" as Christian Science and faith-cure, and *Duffels* (1893), a selection of short stories, a literary form in which he never distinguished himself.

**FURTHER READING:** Edward Eggleston has attracted considerable attention. An early tribute by his brother, George C. Eggleston, *The First of the Hoosiers: Reminiscences of Edward Eggleston, and of That Western Life Which He, First of All Men, Celebrated in Literature and Made Famous* (1903), deals mostly with Edward's youth. Other important early secondary sources include Crawford W. Allen's *The Contributions of Edward Eggleston to the Development of the Realistic Novel in America* (1932); Wynis Green's *Edward Eggleston: A Biographical and Critical Study* (1934); John T. Flanagan's *The Hoosier School-Master in Minnesota* (1937); William P. Randel's *Edward Eggleston's Minnesota Fiction* (1953) and *Edward Eggleston, Author of the Hoosier School-Master* (1946 and 1963); and John S. Tuckey's *Edward Eggleston as a Social Historian* (1949). More recent criticism deserving mention includes J. Richard Brown's *An Investigation of the Technique of Edward Eggleston* (1961); Thorp L. Wolford's *Edward Eggleston: Evolutionary of a Historian* (1967); Lionel Rowland's *The Idea of Progress in the Writings of Edward Eggleston* (1969); Robert R.

Craven's *Edward Eggleston's Place in American Literature* (1971); Diane D. Quantic's *Anticipations of the Revolt from the Village in Nineteenth Century Middle Western Fiction: A Study of the Small Town in the Works of Edward Eggleston, E. W. Howe, Joseph Kirkland, Hamlin Garland, William Allen White, Zona Gale, and Willa Cather* (1984); John D. Roth's *Down East and Southwestern Humor in the Western Novels of Edward Eggleston* (1974); Anne O. Morgan's *Edward Eggleston's Realistic Portrayal of Human Morality* (1977); John Garvey's *The Forgotten Realist* (1982); and Bruce E. Levy's *From Here to Modernity: Nation Building, the Writing of Place, and the Provincial Ideal in Hugh Miller and Edward Eggleston* (1993). Cornell University maintains a microfilm of Eggleston's letters and correspondences.

ARTHUR W. SHUMAKER                    DEPAUW UNIVERSITY

## GEORGE CARY EGGLESTON
November 26, 1839–April 14, 1911

**BIOGRAPHY:** George Cary Eggleston, the brother of EDWARD EGGLESTON, has usually been overshadowed by his brother but was very popular himself. His father, Joseph Cary Eggleston, was a graduate of the College of William and Mary, a lawyer and member of the Indiana legislature; his mother, Mary Jane (Craig), was the daughter of an Indian fighter and frontiersman, Captain George Craig. George was born in Vevay, Indiana. When he was seven years old, his father died. He attended primitive schools, and after a year at Indiana Asbury (now DePauw) University, he withdrew for financial reasons and taught school for a year at Ryker's Ridge. His amusing and frustrating experiences at Ryker's Ridge provided Edward material for *The Hoosier School-Master* (1871).

The next year George inherited the family plantation in Virginia and spent nine years there, attending Richmond College; he studied law and was beginning to practice when the Civil War broke out. Voting against secession, he enlisted in the Confederate Army and served with distinction in the field artillery without injury or sickness. Undaunted by the hot feeling against the South at the war's end, he was employed by a banking and steamboat company in Cairo, Illinois, where he married Marion Craggs in 1868. Later he practiced law in Mississippi, and in 1870 Eggleston went to New York with his wife and one child. Here he engaged in a journalistic career for thirty years, working as a reporter and editor of various newspapers and magazines. In 1875 he reached his highest position as literary editor of the *New York Evening Post*. In 1900 he retired from journalistic life, during which he had published fifteen books, adding twenty-eight more before he died.

**SIGNIFICANCE:** These forty-three books reveal George Eggleston as a thinker and as a person of wide interests. As such he is not easily catalogued. He was greatly interested in children's literature, particularly boys' books, for he published many adventure stories, the kind that boys would eagerly read; a few of these feature Indiana as a setting. Probably he was more interested in history, for he wrote several books concerned with specific events or periods; however, he dealt with history in a general way without spending much time doing research. The result is very readable but not necessarily complete and factual. This work was very popular, nevertheless. Then he penned many novels about Virginia, where he had spent nine glorious years, and it would be difficult to find books more favorable to a place and to a population than these. But, strangely, George Eggleston was interested enough in realism to publish at least two strongly realistic books in which he shows insight into the problems of slums and tenements. These are completely different from any of his other publications. A final group can include those books which resist classification. Some of these are set in Indiana.

We are left with the difficult question of what kind of writer Eggleston was. Since he published so few realistic works, we can hardly call him a realist; and since he penned so many romantic books, he probably should be considered a romanticist. Unfortunately, there seems to be no way of including his other books in this classification. He was very popular in his period but is less known today. His works show great humanity, a keen mind, and a warm personality. His love for his wife and the people of Virginia is evident in his romances of the South, in which his wife often figures as the heroine. In addition, he was a liberal who helped develop the warm, magnolia tradition of the antebellum South.

**SELECTED WORKS:** Examples of the children's literature that George Eggleston published are *Jack Shelby* (1906), *The Last of the*

*Flatboats* (1900), and *Long Knives* (1907), all of which have settings in Indiana. Examples of books dealing with history are *History of the Confederate War* (1910), *Evelyn Byrd* (1904), and *Southern Soldier Stories* (1898). It is not difficult to find examples of novels about Virginia, since there are so many: *Dorothy South* (1902), *The Master of Warlock* (1903), and *Two Gentlemen of Virginia* (1908) are among these. For realistic books, consider *Juggernaut* (1891) and *Blind Alleys* (1906). Samples of the books which resist classification are *The First of the Hoosiers* (1903) and *Recollections of a Varied Life* (1910).

**FURTHER READING:** A critical study devoted to George Eggleston is Louise Collinson's 1969 PhD thesis from Case Western University entitled "George Cary Eggleston: A Biographical and Critical Study." A master's thesis is Florence Abee's "Virginia Life in the Novels of George Cary Eggleston," Duke University (1938).

ARTHUR W. SHUMAKER                DePauw University

## Max(imilian) Ehrmann

September 26, 1872–September 9, 1945

**BIOGRAPHY:** Born in Terre Haute, Indiana, the son of Maximilian and Margaret Barbara (Lutz) Ehrmann, Max Ehrmann attended city schools, received the PhB degree from DePauw University in 1894, did graduate work in philosophy at Harvard University, returned home, and began to write. For a time he practiced law and served a term as deputy prosecuting attorney, but after 1912 he devoted himself entirely to writing. In 1910 he was invited to become a member of the Authors' Club of London, and in 1938 he received a doctor of literature degree from DePauw University. For nearly all his life he was a bachelor, and after being married only a few months to Bertha Pratt King, he died of a cerebral hemorrhage in Terre Haute.

**SIGNIFICANCE:** Ehrmann's first two publications appeared while he was a student at Harvard: *A Farrago* (1898), a collection of stories and sketches of student life at Harvard, and *The Mystery of Madeline Le Blanc* (1900), a well-written story of the revolution of 1830 in France. *A Fearsome Riddle* (1901) is the mystery of a peculiar connection of a faculty member of what was evidently Rose Polytechnic Institute of Terre Haute to his black servant and the strange death of the professor. *Breaking Home Ties* (1904) is a poem in blank verse based on the picture by artist Thomas Hovenden showing a son saying farewell to his family. *A Prayer and Other Selections* (1906) features his famous prayer "Desiderata," first published in 1903 when he was lonely, ill with typhoid fever, and spending three months in Columbia, South Carolina. The poem became famous when a framed copy was stolen from the Indiana Building of the St. Louis World's Fair. Its creed is work and love. In spite of the inaccurate story that the poem had been found in a church, in ten years more than a million copies were sold, and it was translated into thirty-three languages. Three volumes cover the remainder of his poetry: *Max Ehrmann's Poems* (1906), *The Poems of Max Ehrmann* (1910), and *The Poems of Max Ehrmann*, edited by Bertha K. Ehrmann (1948). Much of this material is conventional and much is in prose poetry or polyphonic prose. There are narratives, sketches, sonnets, sweetness, and melody, but also crudities, incomplete expressions, and imperfect images that mar the overall effect. Nevertheless, Ehrmann's work expresses love of humanity, strong idealism, appreciation of work, and recognition of the need for reflection and quiet in life. He is equally strong in condemning materialism and sexual immorality, defending virtue, and affirming spiritual values. Since critics tend not to find the origin of these attitudes in his days at Harvard, it appears more likely that they arose from his life in Indiana and the Midwest because they reflect Midwestern conservatism. The characters in his poems and fiction appear to be largely Midwestern. His idealism is seen in his miscellaneous works and in his dramas, such as *The Light of the Sun* (1910), *The Wife of Marobius* (1911), *Jesus: A Passion Play* (1915), and *David and Bathsheba*, published in *Drama* 28 (November 1917). Also, there are light farces, such as *The Bank Robber* and *The Plumber* (both published with other materials in 1927), and a final play, *Eternal Male and Female* (1949), on the contest between the sexes, published only in *The Wife of Marobius and Other Plays* (1911).

In addition, many of Ehrmann's pamphlets are preachments in sketch, short story, or verse against the evils of sexual immorality. His last two publications present his final works on life: *Desiderata* (1927) is a devotional creed for living, and *Worldly Wisdom* (1934), in verse based on the apocryphal book of Ec-clesiasticus, offers practical advice. The *Journal* (1952) was edited and published by his wife. His social criticism exhibits a keen sense of justice, but although his novels and plays are interesting, they have made little lasting impression. He thus did his best work in po-etry. He was a great-souled man but one whose interesting writings missed greatness.

**SELECTED WORKS:** Ehrmann's prose fiction, sketches, and mysteries include *Farrago* (1898), *The Mystery of Madeline Le Blanc* (1900), and *A Fearsome Riddle* (1901). His poetic works include *Breaking Home Ties* (1904), *A Prayer and Other Selections* (1906), *Max Ehrmann's Poems* (1906), *The Poems of Max Ehrmann* (1910), and *The Poems of Max Ehrmann*, edited by Bertha Pratt King Ehrmann (1948, 1976). His dramatic works include *The Light of the Sun* (1910), *The Wife of Marobius* (1911), and *Jesus: A Passion Play* (1915), as well as the following dramas published with other works: *David and Bathsheba* (1917), *Farces: The Bank Robber, The Plumber* (1927), and *The Eternal Male and Female* (1949).

**FURTHER READING:** The sole biography on Max Ehrmann's life is Bertha Pratt Ehr-mann's *Max Ehrmann: A Poet's Life* (1951). Criticism is largely limited to appreciative ar-ticles or reviews of one or more of his works. DePauw University Library and Archives hold copies of Ehrmann's manuscripts, type-scripts, and notes, and published copies of his poems, plays, novels, and articles, as well as his correspondence, scrapbooks, radio scripts, and reviews. The Vigo County Pub-lic Library, Indiana, has published a listing of materials and information in that library re-lating to the Max Ehrmann Centennial, held in September 1972.

ARTHUR W. SHUMAKER            DEPAUW UNIVERSITY

# LOREN COREY EISELEY
September 3, 1907–July 9, 1977

**BIOGRAPHY:** Loren Eiseley, literary natu-ralist, essayist, poet, and university professor, was born in Lincoln, Nebraska, to Clyde Ed-win and Daisy (Corey) Eiseley. He attended the Lincoln public schools, graduated from Teachers College High School in 1925, and en-tered the University of Nebraska in the fall of that same year. He attended sporadically, wrote poetry and prose, was a staff member of the *Prairie Schooner* magazine there, and met his future wife, an English major, Mabel

Langdon. Restlessness, illness, poverty, and his father's death prevented him from re-ceiving his degree until 1933. Soon after, Eise-ley began graduate work in anthropology at the University of Pennsylvania, receiving his MA in 1935 and his PhD in 1937. He married Mabel Langdon in 1938.

His academic career took the couple to the University of Kansas, then to Oberlin College, and finally to the University of Pennsylvania, where Eiseley served as chairman of the De-partment of Anthropology, as provost, and then in 1961 as the Benjamin Franklin Pro-fessor of Anthropology and the History of Sci-ence, a chair newly created for him.

His first book, *The Immense Journey*, was published in 1957, but Eiseley had been writing and publishing essays since 1942. This book, with the great success it enjoyed, changed the focus of his life and was followed by other books, including *Darwin's Century* (1958), *The Firmament of Time* (1960), *The Un-expected Universe* (1969), and his memoir *All the Strange Hours: An Excavation of a Life* (1975).

Eiseley received many honors, includ-ing election to the National Institute of Arts and Letters in 1971. He died of cancer in Philadelphia.

**SIGNIFICANCE:** In his memoir *All the Strange Hours*, Eiseley describes himself as "a creature molded of plains' dust and the seed of those who came west with the wagons" (23). He was an introspective boy and youth who liked to explore the natural world, picking up fossils and bones, looking at small creatures, and thinking. His early poems for the *Prairie Schooner* had nature as themes. Serving on the staff of that well-known regional maga-zine, Eiseley wrote reviews and edited a col-umn called "Crossroads" in which he fea-tured poems chosen from other magazines.

From 1931 to 1933, Eiseley was a member of summer expeditions for Morrill Museum collecting fossils and bones in western Ne-braska. On these expeditions Eiseley found subject matter and images for some of his fu-ture writing.

Although he spent most of his adult life in Pennsylvania, he wrote of Nebraska, "I know the taste of that dust in my youth . . . [and] No matter how far I travel it will be a fading memory upon my tongue in the hour of my death" (*All the Strange Hours* 25).

**SELECTED WORKS:** Eiseley's work includes

*The Night Country* (1971); *The Star Thrower*, a posthumous volume of both essays and poetry edited by Kenneth Heuer and with an introduction by W. H. Auden (1978); and volumes of poetry, *Notes of an Alchemist* (1972) and *All the Night Wings* (1979). *The Lost Notebooks of Loren Eiseley*, edited with a reminiscence by Kenneth Heuer and sketches by Leslie Morrill, appeared in 1987.

**FURTHER READING:** Three biographies appeared in 1983: *Loren Eiseley: The Development of a Writer*, by E. Fred Carlisle; *Loren Eiseley*, by Andrew J. Angyal; and *Loren Eiseley*, by Leslie E. Gerber and Margaret McFadden. All three are short critical works which include bibliographies, chronologies, and discussion of his work. Carlisle's book includes much material concerning Eiseley's work on the *Prairie Schooner*. Eiseley's papers are in the Loren Eiseley Conference Room at the University of Pennsylvania.

PATRICIA A. ANDERSON    DIMONDALE, MICHIGAN

# T(homas) S(tearns) Eliot

September 26, 1888–January 4, 1965

**BIOGRAPHY:** T. S. Eliot, Nobel Prize–winning poet, dominant figure in Anglo-American literary criticism, and playwright, spent only his boyhood and early adolescence in Missouri. Yet he wrote to a St. Louis newspaper in 1939 that there is something "incommunicable" in having grown up beside a big river (quoted in F. O. Matthiessen's 1935 book *The Achievement of T. S. Eliot* 155). Commenting that he had spent many years out of America, he added that Missouri and the Mississippi nevertheless "have made a deeper impression on me than any other part of the world."

Eliot's family had lived in St. Louis for two generations but spent their summers in Massachusetts and held to the ideals of their New England ancestry, including belief that religion should be expressed in public service. The poet's father, Henry Ware Eliot, was a brick manufacturer; his mother, Charlotte (Stearns) Eliot, was a poet. Thomas earned the AB at Harvard in 1909 and began graduate study in philosophy. But he abandoned his studies in 1915 and settled in England.

Eliot was already an internationally famous poet and critic when, in the 1930s, he began writing for the stage. He received the Nobel Prize in 1948, primarily for his poetry.

**SIGNIFICANCE:** Eliot gave American and European culture of his day one of its major ways of comprehending itself. Strong influences on his verse include the skeptical philosophy of F. H. Bradley and the dramatically devout poetry of Dante. Wide reading contributed to his vision of modern men and women as "hollow." Another source for this comprehension was the contrast between his experiences in Missouri and New England. In a letter of 1926 to Herbert Read, he wrote that, because of his attachment to both regions, he felt he was neither wholly a Missourian nor wholly a New Englander, the result being that he felt that he had been "never anything anywhere" (quoted by Read in "T. S. Eliot—A Memoir," in Allen Tate's 1967 essay collection *T. S. Eliot: The Man and His Work* 156).

Uncertainty about one's being and purposes is a major theme of "The Love Song of J. Alfred Prufrock," drafted in 1911 but not published until 1915, a dramatic monologue often called the first modern poem. The fog that envelops Prufrock is often taken to be that of London. Its yellow color, however, suggests that Eliot has in mind the smoke from St. Louis factories (Peter Ackroyd, in his 1984 book *T. S. Eliot* 23). In any case, the important fog is that shrouding thought and spirit. The poem's style is at one with its content, themes and imagery frequently seeming to be held together only by intimation and juxtaposition. Uncertainties such as Prufrock's have taken over the world in "The Wasteland" (1922), a 453–line poem depicting urban life as a desert. The style is even more fragmented and, though there are passages of ironic humor, the mood is close to despair.

Emphasis on the spiritual continues in "Four Quartets," poems brought together in 1943 as a meditation on time and memory. Midwestern allusions are especially prominent in the third quartet, "The Dry Salvages" (1941). This opens with the speaker's assertion that "I think the river / Is a strong brown god"; he adds that he finds it "intractable" and untrustworthy. Imagery throughout the first fourteen lines makes it clear that Eliot has in mind the Mississippi. The river flows into the ocean, the merged waters coming to represent an incomprehensible eternity in which our only hope is "spiritual illumination" (line 94).

Eliot's essays and plays confirm the views presented in his verse. The essay "Tradition and the Individual Talent" (1919), for example, argues that the job of a writer is not to express his personality but to contribute to ongoing artistic culture. The plays show continuing interest in humanity's relation to a world of spirit. In *Murder in the Cathedral* (1935), a meditation on the killing of archbishop Thomas Becket, the protagonist tries to decide whether his desire to be a martyr arises from saintliness or pride. In *The Cocktail Party* (1950), Eliot contrasts the role of the saint who undertakes a mission she knows will bring on her death and the life of a middle-class married couple. The saint's way of life is more elevated, but the couple are shown as living acceptable lives within their own sphere. Always a lover of English music halls, Eliot would be pleased to know of the success of the musical *Cats*, produced in 1981, long after his death. It is based on the light verse in Eliot's *Old Possum's Book of Practical Cats* (1939).

Some readers admire Eliot's verse techniques, and the devout may share his faith. Like MARK TWAIN, Eliot helps break the grip of moral idealism on the arts and society: both men see the ethos of the past century or more as a compound of attenuated romanticism and moral hypocrisy. Eliot's work is a presentation and profound meditation on the condition of men and women in the then new age of cities and industry, a condition he first recognizes in the St. Louis of his youth. More strongly than Twain, Eliot rejects faith in material progress. Seeking renewal, he employs aesthetic and theological traditions of Europe and Asia. His vision compels because it artfully draws on our tawdry actualities to suggest both the need for glory and the possibility of having it revealed to us.

**SELECTED WORKS:** There are no truly complete collections of Eliot's writing. *Complete Poems and Plays of T. S. Eliot: 1909–1950* (1952) is not, in fact, complete. There are also omissions from *Collected Poems 1909–1962* (1963) and from *Complete Plays* (1969).

Eliot published several collections of his essays. Among these are *The Sacred Wood* (1920), *The Use of Poetry and the Use of Criticism* (1933), and *On Poetry and Poets* (1957). The poet also published collections of social and religious criticism and commentary. Among these are *After Strange Gods* (1934), *The Idea of a Christian Society* (1939), and *Notes towards the Definition of Culture* (1948). Eliot wrote several

statements on the importance of his Midwestern years. The most easily accessible is in *American Literature and the American Language* (1953). Various writings appear in *Selected Prose of T. S. Eliot*, edited by Frank Kermode (1975).

**FURTHER READING:** Eliot asked that his executors not cooperate in the production of any biography. Limited biographical studies abound, however. Among the useful are Peter Ackroyd's *T. S. Eliot* (1984), Lyndall Gordon's *Eliot's Early Years* (1977) and *Eliot's New Life* (1988), and Tony Sharpe's *T. S. Eliot: A Literary Life* (1991).

Collections of essays about Eliot and his writings include *T. S. Eliot: The Man and His Work*, edited by Allen Tate (1966), and *The Cambridge Companion to T. S. Eliot*, edited by A. David Moody (1994). A well-known early study of Eliot's poetic career is F. O. Matthiessen's *The Achievement of T. S. Eliot* (1935). A generally approving but more analytic study is Northrop Frye's *T. S. Eliot: An Introduction* (1963).

Scholarly publications of individual poems include Helen Gardner's *The Composition of "Four Quartets"* (1978) and *The Waste Land: A Facsimile and Transcript*, edited by Valerie Eliot (1971). Several books offer interpretations of individual poems. Among the well-known ones are Elizabeth A. Drew's *T. S. Eliot: The Design of His Poetry* (1949); George Williamson's *A Reader's Guide to T. S. Eliot* (1953); and Grover Smith Jr.'s *T. S. Eliot's Poetry and Plays: A Study in Sources and Meaning* (1956). Writing for the stage is discussed in E. Martin Browne's *The Making of T. S. Eliot's Plays* (1969). A useful work for students is *T. S. Eliot: Plays, a Casebook*, edited by Arnold P. Hinchliffe (1985).

Scholars and advanced students may find helpful Donald Gallup's *T. S. Eliot: A Bibliography* (1969); Robert H. Canary's *T. S. Eliot: The Poet and His Critics* (1982); and Sebastian D. G. Knowles and Scott A. Leonard's *An Annotated Bibliography of a Decade of T. S. Eliot Criticism: 1977–1986* (1992). Correspondence appears in *The Letters of T. S. Eliot*, vol. 1 *(1898–1922)*, and vol. 2 *(1923–1927)*, edited by Valerie Eliot (1991); it is expected that this work will fill six volumes.

Eliot's manuscripts, notes, and other materials are held in numerous libraries and personal collections. The most extensive material is at the Houghton Library of Harvard University. Midwestern institutions having one or more letters or other items include the Missouri Historical Society, the St. Louis Public Library, and the libraries of Washington University, the University of Michigan, and Southern Illinois University.

BERNARD F. ENGEL    MICHIGAN STATE UNIVERSITY

## STANLEY (LAWRENCE) ELKIN
May 11, 1930–May 31, 1995

**BIOGRAPHY:** Novelist Stanley Elkin was born in New York City to Philip Elkin, a salesman who sold costume jewelry in the Midwest, and Zelda (Feldman) Elkin. In his *Stanley Elkin* (1991), critic David C. Dougherty asserts that both parents influenced Elkin in his writing (4), his father providing him with material for some of his characters, and his mother financing almost a year of travel to England and Italy so he could write his first novel, *Boswell: A Modern Comedy* (1964). In 1933 the Elkins moved to Chicago.

After graduating from Chicago's South Shore High School in 1948, Elkin entered the University of Illinois, where he published his first story, "The Dying," in *Illini Writers*. He earned a BA in English in 1952 and an MA in 1953. In 1953 he also married the artist Joan Marion Jacobson. The couple had three children, Philip Aaron (1958), Bernard Edward (1966), and Molly Ann (1967).

After serving in the U.S. Army from 1955 to 1957, Elkin pursued a PhD at the University of Illinois, which he received in 1961. He joined the English Department of Washington University in St. Louis as an instructor in 1960 and taught there until he died. The university named him Merle King Professor of Modern Letters in 1983. Elkin was the recipient of numerous awards, including a Guggenheim Fellowship for 1966–67 and the National Book Critics Circle Awards in 1983 and 1996.

In 1972 Elkin learned that he had contracted multiple sclerosis. As a result, he eventually was confined to a wheelchair. He died in 1995 of heart failure.

**SIGNIFICANCE:** Elkin has been described as an elegist, a parodist, a black humorist, a satirist, a realist, a writer of the fantastic, and a writer of Jewish American fiction. Critics generally note, however, that Elkin's novels are not particularly ethnic. In *Beyond the Waste Land* (1972), critic Raymond M. Olderman finds in Elkin's writings a touch of Whitman,

**Stanley Elkin.**
Photo © Nancy Crampton

James, Dickens, Faulkner, and Woody Allen. In *The Fiction of Stanley Elkin* (1980), Doris Bargen notes that while other writers avoided popular culture, Elkin claimed it as his territory. In *Stanley Elkin*, David C. Dougherty writes that many of Elkin's works concern characters from Midwestern cities such as Cincinnati and St. Louis, his long-time home. The novella "Van Gogh's Room at Arles" (1993) in the collection of the same name is a good example. After years of admiring Van Gogh's painting at the Art Institute in Chicago, Miller, a community college professor from Indianapolis, is permitted to stay in Van Gogh's room in that very same yellow house at Arles through the auspices of a foundation. His peculiar situation is typical of characters in Elkin's work.

**SELECTED WORKS:** Elkin's first novel, *Boswell: A Modern Comedy* (1964), announced that he was a serious writer. Other important novels include *The Dick Gibson Show* (1971), *The Franchiser* (1976), *George Mills* (1982), *Stanley Elkin's The Magic Kingdom* (1985), and *The MacGuffin* (1991). *Mrs. Ted Bliss* (1995), Elkin's final book, was chosen the best fiction book of 1995 by the National Book Critics Circle. *The Living End* (1979), considered by many critics to be his masterwork, is a collection of novellas. *Van Gogh's Room at Arles* (1993) is also a collection of novellas. *Pieces of Soap* (1992) is a collection of Elkin's essays.

**FURTHER READING:** Doris Bargen's *The Fiction of Stanley Elkin* (1980) concerns his early work. In *Reading Stanley Elkin* (1985), Peter J. Bailey maintains that Elkin is connected to Philip Roth and SAUL BELLOW but considers Elkin less of a social realist than do other critics. As a result, Bailey places him with Donald Barthleme, Robert Coover, and Thomas Pynchon. David C. Dougherty's *Stanley Elkin* (1991) provides an excellent overview of Elkin's writing career. He notes that Elkin did not accept the metafiction label attached to writers like such as Pynchon, Coover, Barth, and Nabokov, and so Dougherty attempts to view Elkin's work without labels (4). Dougherty has also published "Nemeses and MacGuffins: Paranoia as Focal Metaphor in Stanley Elkin, Joseph Heller, and Thomas Pynchon," in *The Review of Contemporary Fiction* 15.2 (Summer 1995): 70–78; the same issue of the *Contemporary Fiction* provides nine additional essays on Elkin. Other recent book-length critical studies include Lucio Benedetto's *Means of Assent: Lenny Bruce, Stanley Elkin, and the American Postmodern* (1993), Thomas Pughe's *Comic Sense: Reading Robert Coover, Stanley Elkin, Philip Roth* (1994), and Jeffrey Popovich's *Love as the Cause of Death, Death as the Cause of Love: The Fiction of Stanley Elkin* (1997). Elkin's papers are held in the Special Collections of Washington University Libraries in St. Louis.

KEVIN BEZNER      CHARLOTTE, NORTH CAROLINA

## BERNARD F. ENGEL.

*See* appendix (1991)

## PAUL (HAMILTON) ENGLE

October 12, 1908–March 22, 1991

**BIOGRAPHY:** Paul Hamilton Engle—poet, teacher, novelist, literary critic, and playwright—was born in Cedar Rapids, Iowa, the son of Thomas Allen, a livery stable owner, and Evelyn (Reinheimer) Engle, a 1932 master's degree recipient in English. Educated at Coe College in Cedar Rapids, the University of Iowa, and Columbia University, Engle attended Merton College, Oxford, as a Rhodes Scholar. There he earned a BA in 1936 and an MA in 1939.

In 1936 he married Mary Nissen, with whom he had two daughters, Mary and Sara. From 1937 through 1965 Engle was director of the Creative Writing Program at the University of Iowa. The Engles divorced in 1970. Paul married Chinese novelist Hualing Nieh in 1971, and, together with Rowena Torrevillas, they edited *The World Comes to Iowa: The Iowa International Anthology* (1987), a collection of poems, letters, essays, and stories by writers from outside the United States that celebrates the twentieth anniversary of the University of Iowa's International Writing Program, a program Engle headed from 1966 through 1977.

Engle has often been praised for his extraordinary abilities in teaching creative writing. Flannery O'Connor's University of Iowa MFA thesis, for example, has a separate page in dedication to her teacher, Engle. Once students of Engle's at Iowa and now creative writing teachers at the University of Arkansas, novelists William Harrison and Joanne Meschery often recall Engle's special teaching talents. They regard Engle's writing, especially his poetry, as equally important.

Besides his more than twenty books of poetry, including *Collected Poems* (1987) and *Selected Poems* (1990), Engle published two novels, three plays, a children's book entitled *Who's Afraid?* (1963), a book on Robert Frost, and a book on the women of the American Revolution. His writing, whether it communicates his emotional connections to American culture and geography or his intellectual attachments to language and image, usually deals with some aspect of Americana. Engle's poetry of Americana, mainly its way of absorbing direct experience into direct language, is, however, often influenced by poets from around the world, his passion for Rilke and Yeats, his students in the International Writing Program, and his influences and experiences at Oxford and abroad. He and his wife, Hualing Nieh, published their translations of the poems of Mao Tse-tung and edited a collection, *Writing from the World* (1976), of selected personal essays, poems, and short stories from world authors. Yet despite these international influences, some of Engle's poetry is greatly influenced by Walt Whitman, Robert Frost, CARL SANDBURG, and VACHEL LINDSAY.

Engle's *Worn Earth* (1932) received the Yale Series of Younger Poets Award in 1932. In 1962,

Paul Engle.
Photo © Nancy Crampton

after the private publication of his *Christmas Poems*, Engle received the Lamont Poetry Selection Award. His other awards include a Ford Fellowship in 1946 and a Rockefeller Fellowship in 1963. Engle died of a heart attack on March 22, 1991.

SIGNIFICANCE: Engle's poems and books sometimes repeat themes of nostalgia and Americana, using fixed form, rhyme, paradox, and metaphor—all with more attention to intellectual renderings than aesthetic values. But Engle's best poetry approaches that of Wallace Stevens, Rilke, or Yeats. His more lyrical and imagistic poetry appears in *A Woman Unashamed and Other Poems* (1965). Engle's poems have appeared in such publications as *Atlantic Monthly*, the *New Yorker*, and the *Kenyon Review*.

Some poems in *American Song* (1934) address Engle's Midwestern experiences. There are lyrical, imagistic, and Whitmanesque lines about an Iowa farmer and Engle's Ohio grandfather in "The Last Whiskey Cup." But perhaps foreshadowing Ferlinghetti's poems, the poems in *American Song*, such as "Coney Island," "Harlem Airshaft," and "Fire at Viareggio," evoke places outside the Midwest. The poem "America Remembers" was selected by *Poetry* magazine to represent the Chicago Century of Progress. In the more narrative volume, *Break the Heart's Anger*

(1936), "Chicago," written in Èze, France, is a narrative poem about the Illinois metropolis, its past, present, and dreams.

Engle's *Corn* (1939) contains several poems in praise of Midwestern life. "Prologue," "Corn," "The Bones of the Buffalo," "February," "March," "Farmer," and "On a Too Clear Night" address Engle's farming background and experiences in Iowa. They also capture the energy and science of Midwestern farm life in the early 1900s.

The poems in *West of Midnight* (1941) move toward shorter, more imagistic forms. See, for instance, "Against the Night," a poem that describes a couple who come to a barn to spend the night. The poem's complex action takes place over several hours, yet it is revealed in just seven quatrains of short lines. *American Child* (1945) is an interesting sonnet sequence inspired by Engle's daughters and the children of the pre-school of the University of Iowa. *Poems in Praise* (1959) contains "For the Iowa Dead," a sonnet in praise of Iowans who have died in wars. This title is repeated in the title of Engle's first produced play, *For the Iowa Dead* (1956), with music by Philip Bezanson.

*Always the Land* (1941), Engle's first of two novels, recalls some of the language associated with local color writing in its tale of the struggles and triumphs of Iowa farmer Joe Meyer. Engle's novels and poems are very seldom dark or depressing; they seek to uplift readers.

Engle's other writings with a Midwestern significance include literary criticism and nonfiction, books such as *A Prairie Christmas* (1960) and *Portrait of Iowa* (1974), with photographs by John Zielinski. Several creative nonfiction pieces by Engle appear in *This Is Iowa* (1982), edited by Clarence Andrews. Engle edited several works that concentrate on Midwestern writing: *West of the Great Water: An Iowa Anthology* (1931), with Harold Cooper; *Ozark Anthology* (1938); *Midland* (1961), an anthology of poetry and prose by Iowa students, with Henri Coulette and Donald Justice; and *Midland 2* (1970). Particularly interesting are *Reading Modern Poetry* (1968), a collection of modern poems, including such Midwesterners as Engle, EDGAR LEE MASTERS, CARL SANDBURG, and THEODORE ROETHKE, with critical explanations, and *Writing from the World* (1976), poetry and fiction and criticism in translation and in original English by members of the International Writing Program in Iowa, both of which Engle edited, the former with Warren Carrier, the latter with Hualing Nieh Engle, Burt Blume, and David Young. In addition, Engle has served as editor for a number of uncommonly valuable works in criticism. He served for six years as editor for the annual collection of O. Henry Prize Stories.

**SELECTED WORKS:** Paul Engle's most important volumes of poetry include *Worn Earth* (1932), *American Song* (1934), *Break the Heart's Anger* (1936), *Corn* (1939), *West of Midnight* (1941), *American Child* (1945), *A Word of Love* (1951), *Poems in Praise* (1959), *A Woman Unashamed, and Other Poems* (1965), *Embrace: Selected Love Poems* (1969), *Collected Poems* (1987), and *Selected Poems* (1990). His other major writings include *Always the Land* (1941), *A Prairie Christmas* (1960), *Who's Afraid?* (1963), and *Portrait of Iowa* (1974). Engle's editorial contributions include *Ozark Anthology* (1938), *Reading Modern Poetry* (1968), *Poems of Mao Tse-tung* (1972), and *Writing from the World* (1976).

**FURTHER READING:** No book-length critical studies of Paul Engle exist. Robert Ward's *MidAmerica* 16 (1989) article "The Poetry of Paul Engle: A Voice of the Midwest" provides insight into Engle's Midwestern qualities and significance (94–102). Two other widely available studies of Engle's work are Richard Weber's "Paul Engle: A Checklist," which appears in *Weber's Books at Iowa* (1965): 11–37; and Fernando Arbelaez's "La Poesia de Paul Engle," in *Boletin Cultural y Bibliografico* 11 (1969): 63–67.

WILL CLEMENS                    UNIVERSITY OF CINCINNATI

# ELIZABETH ENRIGHT (GILLHAM)
September 17, 1909–June 8, 1968

**BIOGRAPHY:** Elizabeth Enright, illustrator, fiction writer, and critic, was born in Oak Park, Illinois. She was the only child of cartoonist Walter J. and artist Maginel (Wright) Enright and niece of the architect FRANK LLOYD WRIGHT. When Elizabeth was eighteen months old, her family moved to New York City to live in the artists and writers' neighborhood around Washington Square, where she spent most of her life. Happily immersed in the arts, she grew up drawing pictures, practicing ballet, and reading children's classics, especially the fairy tales of Hans Christian Andersen and the Grimm brothers.

The best summers of her life were spent on her uncle's Wisconsin farm. Here, on their ancestral land, her grandmother Wright told her the immigrant stories of her rugged Welsh forebears and showed her the wonders of their valley's natural setting. Tales from Wisconsin's pioneer past and a deep appreciation of the natural world became integral to Enright's writing.

Trained as an artist at the Art Students' League in New York and in a Paris atelier in 1928, she began illustrating women's magazines and children's books. However, while experimenting with pictures of small jungle boys, she added a story to the illustrations and discovered she had created her first little book, *Kintu* (1935). Finding her greatest joy in writing, she gradually withdrew from the art field, having her last four books illustrated by other artists. She wrote eight major novels and two fairy tales for children as well as adult short stories published in the *New Yorker* and other magazines.

In 1930 she married Robert Marty Gillham, a television executive; they became the parents of three boys, Nicholas, Robert, and Oliver. She died at age fifty-eight in her home at Wainscot, Long Island.

**SIGNIFICANCE:** Enright, a New Yorker with deep family roots in the Midwest, places three of her children's books in the rural Wisconsin valley settled by her maternal ancestors. Her first novel, *Thimble Summer* (1938), begins as her protagonist, nine-year-old Garnet Linden, experiences one of the hottest days of a Wisconsin drought. She shakes her fist at the sky, crying out for rain to save her family's crops. After finding a silver thimble, Garnet's wishes gradually come true throughout an exciting and enchanting summer. Like many of Enright's fictional children, Garnet and her brother Jay are energetic, independent, and high-spirited. They enjoy participating in the farm activities of threshing, caring for the animals, making lime for the new barn, and winning ribbons at the county fair. When a starving, homeless orphan joins their household, they realize the richness of their secure though frugal lives in an affectionate, fun-loving family.

Enright excels in evoking the sounds, sights, and smells of a Midwestern Depression farm of the 1930s. Her characters, descendants of pioneers, retain their faith in America and democracy, as they work cooperatively with other farmers to wrest a living from the land.

Although *Thimble Summer* (1938) won the highest honors, the later Wisconsin books, *Gone-Away Lake* (1957) and its sequel, *Return to Gone-Away* (1961), are favored by critics as better-developed novels. In *Gone-Away Lake*, city-bred Portia and her naturalist cousin discover an elderly sister and brother who are living happily in an abandoned turn-of-the-century resort on the shore of a dried-up lake. The strong, loving friendships that develop between the eccentric old folks and the children, the exploration of the ghostly old mansions and the swamps and bogs, and the tales of a bygone way of life make this and its sequel fascinating, light-hearted novels. Like LAURA INGALLS WILDER and CAROL RYRIE BRINK, Enright has the gift of realism that places her in the front ranks of Midwestern writers for children.

A respected critic as well as prize-winning author, she reviewed children's books for the *New York Times*, taught creative writing at Barnard College, and directed writing workshops at universities. She was the United States' nominee for the International Hans Christian Andersen Award in 1963 for the outstanding literary quality of her complete works.

**SELECTED WORKS:** Enright's picture book, *Kintu: A Congo Adventure* (1935), has not stood the test of time. Two of Enright's three Midwestern novels are her most honored works: the self-illustrated *Thimble Summer* (1938), a Newbery Medal winner, and *Gone-Away Lake* (1957), a Newbery Honor Book. The third, *Return to Gone-Away* (1961), is the last novel she wrote, followed only by the fairy tales, *Tatsinda* (1963) and *Zeee* (1965).

*The Sea Is All Around* (1940), a powerful, poetic story, is reminiscent of Enright's summers as a lonely child on Nantucket. Her four novels about the engaging Melendy children are her most popular, beginning with *The Saturdays* (1941), her only book with a New York City setting. In the other three, *The Four-Story Mistake* (1942), *Then There Were Five* (1944), and *Spiderweb for Two: A Melendy Maze* (1951), the Melendys live deep in the country but within commuting distance of New York City.

Although seldom read today, her short stories for adults, first published in the *New Yorker, Yale Review, Harper's, Saturday Evening Post,* and other national magazines, received O. Henry Awards and were included in the annual anthologies of *Best American Short Stories* in 1950, 1952, and 1954. Of the four volumes of her collected short stories, only *The Riddle of the Fly and Other Stories* (1959) is still in print.

In her often-quoted April 1967 essay, "Realism in Children's Literature" *(Horn Book* 43: 165–70), Enright offers an analysis of her method of creating believable characters in a believable story. Her "Autobiographical Note" and "Acceptance Paper" for the Newbery Medal are reprinted in *Newbery Medal Books, 1922–1955,* edited by Bertha Mahony Miller and Elinor Whitney Field (1955).

**FURTHER READING:** Eleanor Cameron has written an informative, perceptive essay, "The Art of Elizabeth Enright," in *Horn Book* 45 (December 1969): 641–51, continuing in *Horn Book* 46 (February 1970): 26–30. In *Children's Literature Review* 4 (1980): 67–75, reviews of Enright's individual books are brought together; an "Author's Commentary" and "General Commentary" are also included. Virginia Haviland, in *Children's Literature: Views and Reviews* (1973): 78–80, 274–76, reprints two book reviews written by Enright and places her in the historical development of American realistic fiction for children.

MARY JOAN MILLER                    SPRINGFIELD, OHIO

# (KAREN) LOUISE ERDRICH
June 7, 1954

**BIOGRAPHY:** The eldest of seven children, Karen Louise Erdrich was born in Little Falls, Minnesota, and grew up in Wahpeton, North Dakota, where her parents worked for the Bureau of Indian Affairs Wahpeton Indian School. Encouraged by her parents, Ralph Louis and Rita Joanne (Gourneau), both adept storytellers themselves, Erdrich began writing as a child. As she grew up, the family made regular trips to the Turtle Mountain Chippewa reservation in north central North Dakota to visit relatives. Her grandfather, Patrick Gourneau, was tribal chair for a number of years, and Erdrich, three-eighths Chippewa, is an enrolled member of the Turtle Mountain Band of Chippewa. Later, when Erdrich created the fictional world of her novels, she was strongly influenced both by her father's German heritage and by her mother's French Chippewa culture.

A member of the first class of women accepted to Dartmouth College, Erdrich majored in English and creative writing, receiving an Academy of American Poets Prize in 1975 before she graduated in 1976. She returned briefly to North Dakota, working at a variety of jobs to support herself while she wrote, and then entered a graduate program at Johns Hopkins University as a teaching fellow in 1978. After receiving her master's degree in 1979, she served as editor of the *Circle*, the Boston Indian Council newspaper. In 1981 she married Michael Dorris, of Modoc descent, chair of Native American Studies at Dartmouth College, and her former teacher. She adopted his three adopted children, and together they would have three more children of their own.

In their writing Erdrich and Dorris have worked collaboratively, the two discussing details of characterizations and plots, with the named author of each work doing the actual writing. For the coauthored *The Crown of Columbus* (1991), the two individually wrote alternating sections as they collaborated on the work as a whole.

The family moved to Minneapolis in 1993. On April 11, 1997, Michael Dorris, from whom Erdrich had separated, committed suicide. Erdrich continues to live in Minneapolis with her children.

**SIGNIFICANCE:** Initially, Erdrich identified herself primarily as a poet and, aside from a children's writing textbook, *Imagination* (1981), her first published book was a collection of poems, *Jacklight* (1984), a reference to the spotlight used by hunters to illegally lure deer from forests. Metaphorically, the term alludes to the pernicious aspects of European-American culture which compelled many Chippewa people to leave their homeland in the Midwestern woodlands, generally to their disadvantage and sometimes to their downfall. Also featured in *Jacklight* are poem cycles centered on the Chippewa trickster Potchikoo and a German American butcher's wife, Mary Kröger. Erdrich's second collection of poems, *Baptism of Desire* (1989), expands on themes introduced in *Jacklight*.

Erdrich achieved her renown, though, mainly through her work as a writer of fiction, particularly the novel. In response to a notice for the NELSON ALGREN fiction competition, Erdrich wrote "The World's Great-

Louise Erdrich.
Photo © Nancy Crampton

est Fisherman" at her kitchen table over Christmas vacation in 1981 and won the 1982 five-thousand-dollar Nelson Algren Award. Once she had written this short story, which would form the core of the first chapter of *Love Medicine*, the entire plot of *Love Medicine* began to unfold for her along with a broad plan for a tetralogy: *Love Medicine* (1984, expanded edition 1993), *The Beet Queen* (1986), *Tracks* (1988), and *The Bingo Palace* (1994). Erdrich worked progressively back in time so that, to move chronologically through the history of multiple generations of several families from the North Dakota reservation of the Turtle Mountain Band of Chippewa and nearby German-American towns, one reads first *Tracks*, 1912–1924; then *The Beet Queen*, 1932–1972; next *Love Medicine*, 1934–1981; and finally, *The Bingo Palace*, whose action takes place from one winter to the next in the mid-1980s. Each of the novels centers around one of the four elements—earth in *Tracks*, air in *The Beet Queen*, water in *Love Medicine*, and fire in *The Bingo Palace*—motifs which serve to unify each novel, create interconnections among them, and establish symbolic links with Chippewa culture and mythology.

Erdrich has been nationally and internationally acclaimed as a writer. Readers interested in Native American history and culture are especially drawn to her work. Collectively, her novels and poetry provide a comprehensive account of the North Dakota Chippewa and Minnesota Ojibwa from the time Europeans began to arrive in the Midwest up to the present, and they illuminate a number of pertinent political and social issues.

Erdrich's novels portray many of the historical injustices suffered by the Turtle Mountain Chippewa people such as the usurpation of their land, the importation of contagious diseases and alcohol, the withholding of rations as a means of coercion, the outlawing of traditional religious practices, and the attempts to obliterate the Chippewa culture and language by sending children off to boarding school. They also portray some of the negative psychological effects, such as broken families and damaged souls, that result. It would be understandable if the tone of her novels were bitter and acerbic, but it is not. In the balance, the Chippewa people are able to survive and endure, through humor, trickster ingenuity, the healing power of love, and Chippewa spirituality.

Erdrich's descriptions of North Dakota landscapes, small-town and reservation settings, and even actual site locations, such as the Rigger Bar in Williston, the Turtle Mountain bingo hall, and Metro Drug in Fargo, are vivid and true. Her characterizations of Chippewa people include individuals who choose to retain traditional ways, those who strive to adopt the white man's ways, and those who are bicultural; and her novels might be considered "North Dakota multicultural" because they are populated as well by individuals of French, German, and Scandinavian heritage.

Erdrich is a gifted storyteller, whom critics have compared to SHERWOOD ANDERSON and William Faulkner, the latter being an acknowledged influence. Her multiple narrators and non-chronological plot sequencing are indeed reminiscent. At the same time, however, these aspects of her literary craft also have roots in traditional Native American narratives, as does the humor which pervades her work. The Lakota phrase "mitake oyasin," signifying that we are all related, seems to come literally true in Erdrich's world

as various characters are gradually revealed to be connected in surprising ways. Erdrich is able to represent the complexities of the Chippewa worldview in amazingly credible ways at those times in her novels when the mythic spiritual dimensions of the Chippewa cosmology intersect with events of this world and the two realms, for a time, coexist.

Because Erdrich's novels are much more complex than they may initially seem, some readers find them confusing. That confusion may in fact be appropriate given one of Erdrich's main themes, that life is a great mystery with important questions remaining to be resolved. The reader who persists, perhaps engaging in some background reading on Chippewa culture, will be well rewarded.

**SELECTED WORKS:** The action of Erdrich's interrelated tetralogy, *Love Medicine* (1984, expanded edition 1993), *The Beet Queen* (1986), *Tracks* (1988), and *The Bingo Palace* (1994), takes place primarily on the Turtle Mountain Chippewa reservation and in several North Dakota and Minnesota towns, as do many of the poems in *Jacklight* (1984) and *Baptism of Desire* (1989). The action of *The Crown of Columbus* (1991), a novel jointly authored with Dorris, takes place in New Hampshire and the Bahamas and thus does not particularly reflect Erdrich's Midwestern origins. *The Blue Jay's Dance: A Birth Year* (1995), a composite narrative of her reflections on motherhood, contains important biographical information. *Grandmother's Pigeon* (1996) is a children's book. In *The Tales of Burning Love* (1996), characters of Turtle Mountain Chippewa and North Dakota German origins from Erdrich's earlier novels appear again, and *The Antelope Wife* (1998), which focuses on urban Indian life in Minneapolis, extends the lives of characters and families from her first four novels, leading readers to surmise that the stories of these characters may very well continue to be revealed in future Erdrich novels.

**FURTHER READING:** Comprehensive primary information about Erdrich's life and work can be found in *Conversations with Louise Erdrich and Michael Dorris*, edited by Allan and Nancy Feyl Chavkin (1994); this volume contains twenty-three selected interviews, dating from 1985 to 1993. To better understand the Chippewa culture of Erdrich's world, readers might consult such works as Basil Johnson's *Ojibway Heritage* (1976) or GERALD

VIZENOR'S *The People Named the Chippewa* (1984). Numerous scholarly articles on various aspects of Erdrich's opus have been written. *The Chippewa Landscape of Louise Erdrich,* edited by Allan Chavkin (1999), which contains articles by scholars on a broad range of topics, is a useful resource.

JEAN T. STRANDNESS
                    NORTH DAKOTA STATE UNIVERSITY

## LOREN D. ESTLEMAN
September 15, 1952

**BIOGRAPHY:** Loren Estleman was born in Ann Arbor, Michigan, to Leauvett Charles and Louise (Milankovich) Estleman, both working-class parents, the former a truck driver and the latter a postal worker. He received his BA from Eastern Michigan University in 1974 and continued to live with his parents until his marriage to Carole Ann Ashley in 1987. Estleman and his wife now live in Whitmore Lake, a small town north of Ann Arbor.

Estleman's writing career began during college when he worked as a reporter for the *Ypsilanti Press.* Subsequently, he held reporting and editorial responsibilities with Pinckney, Ann Arbor, and Dexter, Michigan, newspapers. In 1976 Estleman's first novel appeared. It was not until 1978, when his second novel, *Sherlock Holmes vs. Dracula,* was published, that he received critical attention. A prolific writer of both novels and short fiction, Estleman is equally at home in the mystery and Western genres. He has won awards from both the Private Eye Writers of America and Western Writers of America. His books have also been nominated for American Book Award and Pulitzer Prize in Letters honors, and he has been a Michigan Arts Foundation Award laureate. In 1997 he was the recipient of the Michigan Author Award, sponsored jointly by the Michigan Center for the Book and the Michigan Library Association.

**SIGNIFICANCE:** In his Detroit novels and stories, Estleman's skillful evocation of the diverse faces of that city, from gritty warehouse and factory districts to affluent neighborhoods, reveals the author's admiration for Detroit and its inhabitants. A number of critics, as well as Estleman himself, have noted that Detroit, more than just a backdrop, is critically important to his stories.

Estleman's style, most noticeable in his series of Amos Walker books, is consciously patterned on that of Raymond Chandler's and Dashiell Hammett's 1940s mystery novels. In those, a cynical and seedy private investigator walks mean streets and deals with the dark underside of a large and sinister city similar to Detroit. Estleman's interest in *film noir,* characterized by atmospheric use of shadow, nighttime scenes, and dark rain-washed streets, has considerably influenced his writing.

The critical reception of Estleman's books has generally been positive, although some critics have complained about his Chandler-Hammett style as being too cliched and imitative.

**SELECTED WORKS:** Estleman's major mystery series deals with his Detroit private investigator, Amos Walker: *Motor City Blue* (1980), *Angel Eyes* (1981), *The Midnight Man* (1982), *The Glass Highway* (1983), *Sugartown* (1984), *Every Brilliant Eye* (1986), *Lady Yesterday* (1987), *Downriver* (1988), *General Murders* (1988), *Silent Thunder* (1989), *Sweet Women Lie* (1990), *Never Street* (1997), *The Witchfinder* (1998), *The Hours of the Virgin* (1999), and *A Smile on the Face of the Tiger* (2000). His Detroit series, initially projected as a trilogy of novels depicting dramatic eras in Detroit's history, now comprises six titles: *Whiskey River* (1990), *Motown* (1991), *King of the Corner* (1992), *Edsel* (1995), *STRESS* (1996), *Jitterbug* (1998), and *Thunder City* (1999). Estleman's interesting concept of casting a retired Detroit Mob hit man as hero resulted in a three-book Peter Macklin series: *Kill Zone* (1984), *Roses Are Dead* (1985), and *Any Man's Death* (1986). One further Detroit novel, *Peeper* (1989), features a sleazy, unscrupulous, overweight private investigator.

**FURTHER READING:** Despite his popularity and critical recognition, no full-length scholarly work has been done on Estleman's writings. There are, however, two useful shorter studies: Michael Kummel's "Der Held und Seine Stadt: Anmerkungen zur Topographie in einigen modernen Kriminalromanen," in *Die Horen: Zeitschrift für Literatur, Kunst, und Kritik* 32.4 (1987): 31–41; and Joseph Hynes's "Looking for Endings: The Fiction of Loren D. Estleman," in *Journal of Popular Culture* 29 (Winter 1995): 121–27. Besides the many reviews of his books, interviews occasionally reveal sides of Estleman's creative methodology and a few biographical details. Two of the better ones are James Kindall's "Murder, Mystery and Mean Streets," in *Detroit Magazine* (*Detroit Free Press*) (March 8, 1987): 10–24; and Keith Kroll's "The Man from Motor City," in *Armchair Detective* 24 (Winter 1991): 4–11.

ROBERT BEASECKER

GRAND VALLEY STATE UNIVERSITY

## MARIE HALL ETS
December 16, 1893–January 17, 1984

**BIOGRAPHY:** Marie Hall Ets, acclaimed author and illustrator of children's books, was born to Walter Augustus and Mathilde (Carhart) Hall in North Greenfield, Wisconsin. Her father, a medical doctor who became a minister, frequently moved his large family from one Wisconsin town to another. The happiest memories of Marie's childhood were of idyllic family summers in the North Woods, where she would disappear into the forest to observe the animals. The wonders of the Wisconsin wilderness deepened her reverence for nature and her affection for all creatures, sentiments that would find expression in many of her books.

Her unusual artistic ability was recognized when she was a first grader. In her teens, after a year at Lawrence College in Wisconsin, she studied interior design in New York, continuing later in life with graduate work in art at the Art Institute of Chicago and Columbia University. She received her PhB at the University of Chicago in 1924 while living as a volunteer social worker at the Chicago Commons Settlement House from 1919 to 1929. Stricken with a chronic disease while establishing a children's clinic in Czechoslovakia, she left social work to try her hand at writing and illustrating children's books, a profession that engaged her for forty years.

Her first husband died during World War I. In 1929 she married Dr. Harold Ets of Chicago. After his death in 1943, she moved to New York to continue her work as an author-artist. In 1974 she retired to Inverness, Florida, where she died of arteriosclerosis at age ninety-one.

**SIGNIFICANCE:** The Midwest, Ets's home for almost fifty years, provides the setting, ideas, and animal characters for many of her twenty-one picture books. Scenes from Wisconsin's old villages and countryside appear in her first book, the tender yet comic *Mr. Penny* (1935) and its two sequels, as well as in the humorous *Mr. T. W. Anthony Woo* (1951). The deep woods of Wisconsin appear as the meeting place of a small boy and his imaginary animal friends in *In the Forest* (1944), its sequel, *Another Day* (1953), and *Just Me* (1965). Her lively, rhythmic texts accompanied by exquisitely crafted illustrations, typically in black and white, create a pleasing blend of imagination and realism.

Ets's Chicago years as an inner-city social worker influence the direction of her writing in her multicultural books. Aware of the dearth of true-to-life stories from ethnic communities, she is one of the first to write realistic portrayals of African American and Mexican American children. In addition, collaborating with a Mexican librarian on *Nine Days to Christmas* (1959), she presents the holiday festivities of a native middle-class child in Mexico City, challenging the stereotype of the Mexican as a poverty-stricken villager. She won the prestigious Caldecott Medal for her glowing, brightly colored illustrations of this traditional Mexican Christmas in a thriving, modern Mexico City.

Her books have been translated into foreign languages and have received many awards over the years. In addition to the Caldecott Medal, Ets garnered Caldecott Honor designations for the illustrations in five other books set in Wisconsin. In 1975 she was the recipient of the Kerlan Award from the University of Minnesota for the body of her work.

**SELECTED WORKS:** Ets, like WANDA GÁG in *Millions of Cats* (1928), is one of the first Midwestern author-artists to create quality picture books with an immediate, lasting appeal for preschool children. Three of her Caldecott Honor Books, *In the Forest* (1944), *Play with Me* (1955), and *Just Me* (1965), are considered nursery classics along with *Another Day* (1953). Her longer stories for primary age children include *Mr. Penny* (1935), *Mr. Penny's Circus* (1961), and two other Caldecott Honor Books, *Mr. Penny's Race Horse* (1956) and *Mr. T. W. Anthony Woo* (1951). Ets's multicultural works include the story of an African American boy in Harlem, *My Dog Rinty* (1946), written with Ellen Tarry, and two books based on her experiences with a Spanish American boy in California, the lyrical *Gilberto and the Wind* (1963) and the grimly realistic *Bad Boy, Good Boy*

(1967). Two books relate to the Chicago area: Ets's pioneer sex education work, *The Story of a Baby* (1939), based on an awe-inspiring exhibit of the development of a human embryo at the 1933 Chicago World's Fair, and *Oley, The Sea Monster* (1947), the humorous story of a creature sighted in the Chicago River. Her best-known work, coauthored by Aurora Labastida, is the Caldecott Medal–winner of 1960, *Nine Days to Christmas* (1959).

**FURTHER READING:** Lee Bennett Hopkins interviewed Ets for his article in *Books Are by People* (1969): 61–63. Her "Caldecott Award Acceptance" and May Massee's "Biographical Note" are found in *Horn Book* 36 (August 1960): 209–16. A summary of her life and an analysis of her books are given in *Children's Literature Review* 33 (1994): 64–68. Ets's papers are located in the Kerlan Collection at the University of Minnesota in Minneapolis.

MARY JOAN MILLER                    SPRINGFIELD, OHIO

## DAVE (PEARSON) ETTER
March 18, 1928

**BIOGRAPHY:** Dave Etter was born in Huntington Park, California, to Harold Pearson and Judith (Goodenow) Etter. In an autobiographical essay for the Spring 1983 *Spoon River Quarterly*, Etter recalls an uneventful, middle-class childhood followed by high school years devoted to becoming "a serious student—of girls and baseball" (15–16). After two years at a junior college, Etter transferred to the University of Iowa, from which he graduated with a history major in 1953. Two years in the U.S. Army followed, then three years working at various odd jobs around the country. At age thirty, Etter returned to the Midwest, where he wrote in the *Spoon River Quarterly*, "I always felt I truly belonged" (19). Settling in Evanston, then Geneva, then Lily Lake, then Elburn, Illinois, Etter worked a succession of white- and blue-collar jobs: at Encyclopedia Britannica, Northern Illinois University Press, and the warehouse of McDougal, Littell, and Company textbook publishers. Etter retired in 1996 and moved from Elburn to Lanark, Illinois. He and his wife Margaret Ann (Cochran), married in 1959, are the parents of two children, George and Emily.

While recovering from pneumonia in an army hospital, Etter had chanced on a small, illustrated edition of Robert Frost's poetry; by the time he rejoined his unit, he had decided to become a poet. Etter began with little magazines, then published his first book, *Go Read the River*, in 1966. Etter has since published twenty-four books and chap books. His work has appeared in sixty textbooks and anthologies, including LUCIEN STRYK's *Heartland: Poets of the Midwest* (1967). Etter has won a CARL SANDBURG Award, a Midland Authors prize, and an Illinois Sesquicentennial Citation.

**SIGNIFICANCE:** Etter's acknowledged influences include Midwestern regionalists such as SHERWOOD ANDERSON, CARL SANDBURG, VACHEL LINDSAY, RICHARD BISSELL, and EDGAR LEE MASTERS; other American regionalists such as Faulkner and Frost; foreign writers including Lorca, Pasternak, and the French surrealists; and jazz musicians such as Thelonious Monk, Ornette Coleman, and John Coltrane. His poems—earthy, blue-collar, candid—are localized in the rural Midwest in and around his adoptive Illinois: "Two Beers in Argyle, Wisconsin," "In Guttenberg, Iowa," "After a Long Night in Keokuk," and "Hannibal, Missouri: Summer 1846." *Home State* (1985) is a collection of one hundred prose-poems, reverent and irreverent observations on Ulysses Grant and Adlai Stevenson, on Chicago and Beardstown and Cairo, on barns, courthouse clocks, Interstate 80, and the Hiram Walker Distillery in Peoria. Etter's ear for Midwest idiom and cadence is unmatched among contemporaries, as the poems of *Alliance, Illinois* (1983) attest: "But, hey, pay no mind to me, May" ("Stella Lynch" 46); "You know, I sorta, kinda like it" ("Howard Drumgoole" 55); "Mister, he was an awkward, gangly son of a gun / and, if it's truth you're looking for, / just a little bit on the homely side too" ("Vernon Yates" 69).

*Alliance, Illinois* is Etter's most widely known collection: 222 poems, mostly dramatic monologues, set in the fictional town of Alliance, Sunflower County, Illinois, about fifty miles southwest of Chicago. Recommending it in the Pushcart Press series of "Writer's Choice" advertisements during August 1983, Raymond Carver called *Alliance* "hands down the most impressive long work of poetry I've read in years." Beneath deceptively simple surfaces, Etter's poems conceal subtle structures of sound and imagery: they are heavily alliterative and carefully patterned. Most reward extensive formalist analysis, as do the arrangements of poems in his books. Etter's dialogue poems are encyclopedias of Midwest colloquialisms, and, as Victor Contoski observed in a Fall 1984 *New Letters* review, "No writer since Walt Whitman has used the catalogue so effectively . . . to bring the outside world into his poems" (104).

Etter's work is nostalgic, filled with jazz musicians, abandoned train depots, 1940s trademarks, and 1950s baseball players. Punk rock, cellular phones, and jet airplanes do not exist in Etter's world. "If there is such a thing as a tone which is both amused and elegiac, Etter's poems have it," Robert C. Bray observes in *Rediscoveries* (158). Many critics have noted the combination of Masters's social insights, Lindsay's lightheartedness, and Anderson's psychology. The irreverent combination of humor, idiom, rhythm, sex, and sometimes slightly grotesque character constitutes a recognizable "Dave Etter poem." Such poems have influenced writers male and female, black and white, academic and nonacademic and won for Etter an unusually diverse following among poets, academics, and the general public.

**SELECTED WORKS:** Etter is prolific, even for a poet. *Alliance, Illinois* (1983) and *Selected Poems* (1987) will carry a reader through his early and middle work, the best of which appeared in shorter earlier books such as *Go Read the River* (1966), *The Last Train to Prophetstown* (1968), *Alliance, Illinois, Cornfields* (1980), *West of Chicago* (1981), and *Home State* (1985). Etter's best work since 1987 is found in *Carnival* (1990), and *How High the Moon* (1996). The 441-page *Sunflower County* (1994) is an expanded version of *Alliance, Illinois*.

**FURTHER READING:** James T. Jones's entry in *Dictionary of Literary Biography* offers a fine overview of Etter's work, placing it in the context of earlier Illinois and Midwest poets (87–94). Less extended essays include NORBERT BLEI's hilarious "Lost in Elburn," in *Door to Door* (1985); Robert C. Bray's more serious "Down the Road from Spoon River," in *Rediscoveries: Literature and Place in Illinois* (1982); Victor Contoski's "Dave Etter: The Art of Simplicity," in *Late Harvest: Plains and Prairie Poets*, edited by Robert Killoren (1977); and David Pichaske's close reading of "Stubby Payne: Stocking Tops," in *Indiana Review* (Fall 1985): 71–81. The Spring 1983 *Spoon River Quar-*

*terly*, a special Dave Etter issue, contains Etter's self-interview and autobiographical essay "The Road to the Poem" and reprints important reviews and interviews by Norbert Blei, Robert C. Bray, Victor Contoski, Jim Elledge, and Dan Jaffe.

DAVID PICHASKE     SOUTHWEST STATE UNIVERSITY

# RONALD L. FAIR
October 27, 1932

**BIOGRAPHY:** African American novelist and poet Ronald Fair was born in Chicago, the son of Herbert and Beulah (Hunt) Fair. In his early years, Fair worked for the U.S. Naval Reserve from 1950 to 1953. He then attended the Stenotype School of Chicago from 1953 to 1955 and subsequently worked as a court reporter for the city of Chicago from 1955 to 1967. Married at age twenty in 1952 to Lucy Margaret Jones, Fair became the parent of two sons, Rodney and Glen. In 1968, divorced from Lucy, Fair married Neva June Keres, with whom he became the parent of a third child, Nile.

Working in Chicago as a court reporter provided a good job for Fair, but the success of his novels, *Many Thousand Gone* (1965) and *Hog Butcher* (1966), and his novellas, *World of Nothing: Two Novellas* (1970), prompted thoughts of supporting himself and his family from his writings. Fair also began to plan to leave Chicago, then a turbulent city filled with anguished ghettoes that blew up in flames every summer beginning with the assassination of Martin Luther King Jr. on April 4, 1968. The civil rights movement's rhetoric of racial harmony and interracial forgiveness seemed to give way to numerous militant voices in Chicago. Elijah Muhammad's Nation of Islam with its uncompromising paper, *Muhammad Speaks*, vied with the Chicago Black Panther Party's highly vocal leaders Mark Clark and Fred Hampton, who were brutally killed by the Chicago police in December 1969. For a writer, even a socially conscious writer, Chicago demanded extreme commitment. Chicago's Black Arts Movement set standards not only for the art of black writers but for their personal lives. When Fair divorced his African American wife for a European woman, he found himself under fire from militant black students at Northwestern University in Evanston, Illinois, just north of Chicago. Fair, who was to guest-lecture at the elite University on Chicago's North Shore for a semester in 1968, was forced to abandon his teaching position, a position that had probably opened up for him because black militants were pressuring institutions to open their doors to minorities. Fair, who empathized with Chicago's poor ghetto dwellers but was unwilling to commit to a rhetoric of violence, began to look toward Europe.

In December 1971, Fair had already visited the Ohio-born black detective fiction writer CHESTER HIMES at his home in Moraira, Spain. There, Himes advised him to leave Chicago. While visiting Himes, Fair and his wife stopped in Paris long enough to find the city beautiful, but perhaps because Paris was expensive, and like Chicago, a place of student uprising and unrest, Fair preferred the French countryside. In mid-January 1972, however, Fair found himself and his wife not in France but in Sweden. The Swedish Institute of Letters had offered to assist them in the relocation of his family to that country. But Fair hated Sweden's "cold, cold" climate (Fabre, *From Harlem to Paris* 291). Following the success of his third novel, *We Can't Breathe* (1972), Fair decided to go to France with his second wife, Neva, to house-sit for a French academic couple who were spending a semester in the United States. For a brief period, Fair and Neva lived in seclusion in the country home, only sixty miles from Paris, between Fontainebleau and Sens. By mid-May, Neva was expecting his third child, a baby Fair wanted to be born in amicable France, away from racially torn Chicago (Fabre, *La Rive Noire* 288). Fair sought the peace and quiet he needed to write, but the writings that ensued would continue to be about the Midwestern city he had abandoned. Like many Midwestern urban writers, from SHERWOOD ANDERSON to THEODORE DREISER, Fair had a love-hate relationship with the city. He invited his mother and his children from his first marriage to spend the summer in rural Les Bergeries, far from urban tensions while he worked on versions of a new novel, "The Migrants."

Fair determined to remain abroad, but commercial interest in "Soul Literature" was on the decline. Talks about a French publication of *We Can't Breathe* (1972) by Flammarion resulted in nothing (Fabre, *From Harlem to Paris* 292). Fair moved on to Switzerland, then later settled in Finland. Fair, like Chicago writer RICHARD WRIGHT, became an expatriate for life. Like most black expatriates, Fair left the United States for multiple personal, political, and racial reasons. In Europe, Fair fled Chicago's white racism and black militancy not to pursue a new diasporic black identity as Wright had done, but to find spiritual growth. In 1980 Fair took up sculpture and "gave his life to Jesus" (*From Harlem to Paris* 292).

Recipient of numerous awards, Fair was a major figure in Midwestern letters in the late 1960s and early 1970s. In 1970 he received the National Institute of Arts and Letters Award for his two novellas in *World of Nothing*, "World of Nothing" and "Jerome." In 1972 the American Library Association awarded Fair its Best Book Award for his autobiographical novel, *We Can't Breathe*. In 1974 the National Education Association awarded Fair a fellowship, and the following year he was the recipient of a Guggenheim Foundation Fellowship. Ronald Fair has taught literature as a visiting author at Chicago's Columbia College, at Northwestern University (Fall 1968), and at Wesleyan University (Middletown, Connecticut).

SIGNIFICANCE: Fair is often placed in the tradition of Richard Wright and GWENDOLYN BROOKS because of his focus on Chicago as a setting and his literary experimentation. Like UPTON SINCLAIR, Dreiser, JAMES T. FARRELL, and NELSON ALGREN, Fair is considered a writer who works from a naturalistic tradition, stressing impersonal forces and the lack of agency in human life when confronted by those forces. Yet Fair, like Wright, Algren, and even Brooks, often veers from naturalism to existentialist absurdism. Fair's style bears comparison to the black Chicago novelist and filmmaker MELVIN VAN PEEBLES and to the novelist and librettist Leon Forrest. Using epic narrative styles, rooted in ancient Western and African traditions, Fair laces contemporary mimetic experience with hyperbole, irony, and fantasy. True to his Midwest origins, Fair brings to his writings the savvy, style, and flavor of Chicago jazz, blues, and gospel aesthetics.

*Many Thousand Gone* (1965), Fair's first novel, aptly subtitled "an American fable," is a self-described metaphorical tale that illuminates the rural past of black history by focusing on one town where blacks remain in slavery until 1938. The allegory encompasses every variety of oppression existing in the South from the 1830s to the 1960s by presenting a Southern microcosm as the object of its biting satire. In this novel, the black female heroine, Granny Jacobs, a resident in a small imaginary county in Mississippi, arranges the escape of Jesse, her great-grandson. Jesse, the last pure black male in Jacobs County, goes on to become a writer. Jesse and Granny Jacobs communicate furtively through Preacher Harris, the only black in the county who can read and write. When Granny Jacobs learns that Jesse has published a book and that his picture will appear in Chicago's *Ebony* magazine, *Ebony* and Chicago become symbols of rescue from Southern oppression. Granny and Preacher Harris decide to write to the president and to appeal for help for the blacks of the town. Granny's appeal causes an uproar in the community and brings about a dramatic climax to the novel. With its somberly humorous depiction of rapes, lynchings, and racist murders, the novel critiques the weakness of the nation as a whole by dealing with how Southern blacks are treated. *Many Thousand Gone* brought Fair national acclaim.

For his second novel, *Hog Butcher* (1966), Fair shifts from the South to Chicago. With its corrupt power structure Chicago is exposed as a failed "Promised Land." Fair's Chicago is a smoldering urban volcano, filled with degradation and violence, particularly for black males. In *Hog Butcher*, a ten-year-old boy, Wilford Robinson, and his pal, Earl, of Chicago, witness the accidental shooting of their friend, Cornbread, an eighteen-year-old high school basketball star, by two policemen, one black and one white. The two policemen mistake the innocent teenager for a burglary suspect. The neighborhood is incensed, a small riot erupts, and the policemen are beaten. The bulk of the novel deals with the attempts of the Chicago power structure to whitewash the incident by preparing a story for the witnesses. The boys are to testify at the coroner's inquest to help shield the police and at the same time to degrade their friend, Cornbread. Some contemporary critics complained that the novel oversimplified the corruption of the white power structure. Later critics accused the novel of being out of step with its militant time. For instance, C. W. E.

Bigsby's study *The Second Black Renaissance: Essays in Black Literature* (1980) faults *Hog Butcher* from a Black Arts perspective, charging that Fair's anger belongs to the civil rights protest tradition, because the novel shrinks from its militant potential, moving "from threatened apocalyptic revolt to individual transformation" (160, 180).

The two novellas in *World of Nothing* (1970), both set in Chicago, expose religious hypocrisy. In "Jerome," a story of sin and corruption, Fair attacks the type of church that uses white middle-class values for its own hypocritical ends. Jerome, the title character, is the out-of-wedlock son of Father Jennings, who plots to have Jerome put away because Jerome unsettles and seems to accuse him. The title novella, "World of Nothing," a first-person narrative, depicts the grittier side of Chicago and relates the life of two men who are roommates sharing the bottle and the street. The narrator and his friend Top live from one moment to the next. A vivid treatment of ghetto life, this compassionate book is serious as well as comic. The friends' "nothing world" is peopled with derelicts, whores, petty thieves, outcasts, and miscasts. Laced with a deceptively light tone, the novella's narrator seems to revel in his hedonistic life, enjoying the pleasures his environment offers. One critic, Robert E. Fleming, notes, however, that juxtaposed with the sordid side of ghetto life, Fair is exposing how even tragedy can beget happiness and beauty (*College Language Association Journal* 15 [June 1972]: 485).

Fair's autobiographical fourth work, *We Can't Breathe* (1972), is a classic novel about black migration. It relates the story of a young boy who grows up in 1930s Southern poverty, then migrates to the North's urban violence. Like Richard Wright's Bigger and his friends, Fair's protagonist and his gang roam the streets, scavenging, killing rats, smashing wine bottles, and finding games in the filth. *We Can't Breathe*, however, ends with the hero, Ernie Johnson, giving up his life as the leader of a street gang to become a writer as he becomes more aware of his surroundings and their effect. *We Can't Breathe* straddles genres between autobiographical elliptical narrative and obsessive fiction. It depicts families whose lives are destroyed, wasted and blasted by justice denied. Honest, full of brilliant revelations, the novel is praised for not being one of those classic black books that tells about black loss and defeat in America. *We Can't Breathe* is seen as presenting a successful struggle against the odds.

Following his self-imposed exile to Finland, Fair has focused on poetry, publishing *Excerpts* in 1975 and *Rufus* in two editions, in 1977 and 1980. Fair's unpublished novel, "The Migrants," and his poetry, the last of his writings so far, remain rooted in African American themes of history, alienation, the blues, and Chicago's Midwestern aesthetics of "Soul," a 1960s–1970s mixture of blues, jazz, and gospel improvisation that yokes fantasy and naturalism, comedy and irony. Fair's stylistic roots reach beyond literature to include Chicago's rich musical admixture of bluesmen Howlin' Wolf and Muddy Waters, jazz musicians Phil Cohran and Earl Fatha Hines, gospel vocalists Mahalia Jackson and Albertina Walker, and "soul singers" Curtis Mayfield and Mavis Staples. Like another improvisational Chicago fiction writer, Leon Forrest, Fair's artistry and ethos arises from Chicago street language, urban oral traditions, culture, and style.

**SELECTED WORKS:** Fair's prose, poetry, and fiction include the novels *Many Thousand Gone: An American Fable* (1965) and *Hog Butcher* (1966), republished as *Cornbread, Earl and Me* (1975); the book *World of Nothing: Two Novellas* (1970), containing the title volume, *World of Nothing* and *Jerome*; a third novel, *We Can't Breathe* (1972); and two volumes of poetry, *Excerpts* (1975) and *Rufus* (1977, 1980). *Hog Butcher* was made into a feature film, retitled *Cornbread, Earl and Me*, in 1975. Fair's fiction, poetry, and commentary appear in the following periodical publications: "Excerpts from *Voices*: The Afro-Americans," *Black American Literature Forum* 13 (Summer 1979): 93–95; and "Fellow Writers Comment on Clarence Major's Work: A Review of *All-Night Visitors*," *Black American Literature Forum* 13 (Summer 1979): 73. Fair continues his theme of escape from the South in the poem "The Domestic," *Black American Literature Forum* 14 (Winter 1980): 173–74. In his short story "The Walk," *Callaloo* 3 (February–October 1980): 1–3, he sends his boy protagonist into hellish pits of ghetto violence, then rescues him with a transcendent family gathering.

**FURTHER READING:** Michel Fabre's study of black expatriates *La Rive Noire: De Harlem à la Seine* (1985), translated and published as *From Harlem to Paris* (1985), offers insight into Fair's decision to live abroad based on extensive personal correspondence between Fair and Fabre. C. W. E. Bigsby's trenchant study *The Second Black Renaissance: Essays in Black Literature* (1980) analyzes writers who chose between strident black nationalism and continued commitment to interracial harmony, placing Fair in the latter category. Robert E. Fleming stresses Fair's versatile move from myth and fantasy to the comic and the tragic in his essay "The Novels of Ronald L. Fair," in *College Language Association Journal* 15 (June 1972): 477–87. Phyllis R. Klotman traces the "black man running" metaphor, describing it as a form of aggression, not escape, in her essay "The Passive Resistant in *A Different Drummer, Day of Absence* and *Many Thousand Gone*," in *Studies in Black Literature* 3 (Autumn 1972): 7–11.

MARIA K. MOOTRY
UNIVERSITY OF ILLINOIS AT SPRINGFIELD

## JANET AYER FAIRBANK
June 7, 1878–December 28, 1951

**BIOGRAPHY:** Born in Chicago to prominent parents, Benjamin and Janet (Hopkins) Ayer, Fairbank was the older sister of Pulitzer Prize–winning writer MARGARET AYER BARNES. Janet was educated in private schools, attended the University of Chicago, and married Kellogg Fairbank in 1900, having three children with him, Janet, Kellogg, and Benjamin. Women's suffrage, national party politics, and various patriotic causes engaged much of her time and energy. She served during World War I on the Women's National Liberty Loan Committee and was a member of the Illinois Committee of the Women's Division of the Council for National Defense. During the period before World War II, she worked with the national America First Committee. Though her earlier political activity had been in the Democratic Party as a member of the executive committee of the party's national committee in 1919–20, Illinois national committeewoman from 1924 to 1928, and delegate to the party's national convention in 1931, she supported and campaigned for Republican Wendell Willkie in 1940. Her greatest philanthropic work was for the Chicago Lying-in Hospital, on whose board she served for twenty-four years.

**SIGNIFICANCE:** Fairbank's fiction, which emphasizes character depiction rather than dramatic action, is cast in the form of traditional leisurely novels, mostly set in Illinois. Women are usually the focus of her novels. Central is her trilogy consisting of *The Cortlandts of Washington Square* (1923); *The Smiths* (1925), a runner-up for a Pulitzer Prize; and *Rich Man, Poor Man* (1936). These novels study a Chicago family and effectively depict the growth of Chicago as a dynamic city while touching on such historical phenomena as progressive politics, especially the campaign for women's suffrage. Particularly insightful is the portrayal of Ann Smith in *The Smiths*. Her marriage, which she had thought would be a yoking of equals, turns out to be quite the reverse, as her husband shuts her out of much of his life. Nevertheless, she grows in strength and character, just as the young city of Chicago in which she lives grows in vitality and wealth. Fairbank's finest novel, *The Bright Land*, portrays the life of a young woman who escapes from a grim New England family life to marriage in Galena, Illinois, and follows that city through years of prosperity and then decline. For Abby-Delight Flagg, like Ann Smith a native Easterner brought to the Midwest by her marriage, Galena is wild and frightening at first but actually turns out to offer an easier life than had the bleak New England of her birth. Change is the central theme of this novel, as Fairbank skillfully describes periods of prosperity in the life of this river town which are followed by its gradual decline, with the novel ending in Abby-Delight's lonely widowhood. In both the trilogy and the Galena novel, the setting is as much a character, as finely delineated and precisely depicted, as any of the human personae. Fairbank's view of her Illinois settings is largely hopeful and optimistic but she does not blink at depicting corruption and injustice.

*Rich Man, Poor Man*, sometimes described as Fairbank's "suffrage novel," makes some use of Fairbank's experience as a worker for that cause, but the suffrage theme is relatively minor in the book as a whole and is not as favorably depicted as might have been expected. The author's insider knowledge of party politics is used notably in *The Lions' Den* (1930), the story of an idealistic young Wisconsin congressman who finds his integrity tested by the corruption he meets. Like Fairbank's female protagonists, he grows in maturity and courage.

Fairbank's fiction is largely forgotten today, but her novels remain engrossing and realistic studies of Midwestern society and history during the nineteenth and early twentieth centuries. Her presentation of the lives of middle-class Midwestern women during the period is exceptional.

**SELECTED WORKS:** Fairbank's output was, not surprisingly for such an active woman, relatively small. The novels that give the best idea of Fairbank's depiction of Chicago and Illinois are *The Cortlandts of Washington Square* (1923), *The Smiths* (1925), *The Bright Land* (1932), and *Rich Man, Poor Man* (1936). The *Lions' Den* (1930) also centers on portraying Midwestern character. *In Town and Other Conversations* (1910), her first substantial publication, is a collection of brief dramatic sketches. *The Alleged Great-Aunt* (1935) is a mystery story, written by H. K. Webster and completed by Fairbank and her sister, Margaret Ayer Barnes.

**FURTHER READING:** Little scholarly attention has been paid to Fairbank's work. Interested readers might see the *Wilson Library Bulletin* (December 1983). Two essays by Mary Jean DeMarr have appeared in *MidAmerica* 11 (1984): 34–41; and 12 (1985): 32–44.

MARY JEAN DeMARR    INDIANA STATE UNIVERSITY

# PHILIP JOSÉ FARMER
January 26, 1918
(Paul Chapin, Herald Childe, Charles Creed, Martin Eden, Rod Keen, Harry Manders, William Norfolk, Jonathan Swift Somers III, Leo Queequeg Tincrowdor, Kilgore Trout, John H. Watson, M.D.)

**BIOGRAPHY:** Philip José Farmer was born in north Terre Haute, Indiana, to George and Lucile (Jackson) Farmer. He moved at age five to Peoria, Illinois, and graduated from Peoria Central High School in 1936, two years ahead of pioneer feminist Betty Friedan. Farmer completed a freshman year at the University of Missouri, but, short of money, he returned to Illinois and got a job at Keystone Steel and Wire in Bartonville, south of Peoria. In 1941 he started evening classes at Bradley Polytechnical Institute, where in 1942 he met and married Betty Virginia Andre. Farmer spent 1942–43 in the U.S. Army Air Force, then returned to Peoria and his studies at Bradley. In 1950 he completed a bachelor's degree in English and creative writing, part of a group of GIs he described in "The Peoria-Colored Writer" as "a pre-Beatnik community" (xi).

Farmer established his reputation in 1952 with publication of "The Lovers" in *Startling Stories*. The story won Farmer his first Hugo Award and was later expanded into a novel. It changed the course of science fiction writing with its explicit depiction, in the sanitized 1950s, of raw sex between a puritanically conditioned male human and a libidinous female alien. His career seemed assured in 1953 when he won a four-thousand-dollar prize from Shasta Publishers for a novel he called *I Owe for the Flesh*. Shasta first withheld his check pending manuscript revisions, then admitted the prize money did not exist. Then Farmer's literary output slowed as he worked to feed himself and his family.

In 1957 Farmer left Peoria for Los Angeles to consolidate his career as a science fiction writer while doing technical writing for McDonnell-Douglas. He returned in 1969 to be closer to his son Philip Laird, born in 1942, and daughter Kristen, born in 1945, "convinced that a writer could live more cheaply and peacefully in Peoria (though he'd have to lose certain things)" (*Grand Adventure* 235).

Farmer became, finally, a prolific author, whose dozens of books have won three Hugo Awards and been translated into many foreign languages. The French especially value his work and place him beside Isaac Asimov, Robert A. Heinlein, and KURT VONNEGUT JR. in the first rank of science fiction writers. His books have been readily available in mass distribution paperbacks, with popular titles like *To Your Scattered Bodies Go* (1971) reaching thirty printings.

SIGNIFICANCE: Filled with sex, violence, and fictitious religion, Farmer's work appeals to Freudians, Jungians, and science fiction readers, with whom he has achieved the status of a cult writer. Postmodernist critics appreciate his penchant for writing fictional biographies that deconstruct pop icons like Tarzan, Doc Savage, and Sherlock Holmes, and for inventing fictional constructs who then invent fictional constructs of their own. Many Farmer novels, for example, contain a science fiction writer with initials P. J. or P. J. F.: Peter Jarius Frigate, who lives in twentieth-century Peoria in the Riverworld series (1971–80), or Paul Janus Finnegan in the World of Tiers series (1965–69). His work is filled with puns. It is commercial in the best sense—lively, imaginative, compelling—and in the worst sense—often slapdash, superficial, formulaic.

Farmer is, in Leslie Fiedler's words, a cultural imperialist with "a gargantuan lust to swallow down the whole cosmos, past, present, and to come, and to spew it out again" in his own novels ("Thanks for the Feast" 239). He is the creator of at least three fictional universes in three cycles of novels and stories before 1975. In the worlds of Wolff-Kickaha, Wold Newton, and Riverworld, the living mingle with the dead, historical personages with fictional characters.

Many fictional Farmer geographies vaguely resemble Peoria, and Farmer often makes explicit mention of that city and surrounding communities. *Fire and the Night* (1962) is set in Peoria of the 1940s. This mainstream novel recounts the love affair between Danny, a white steelworker in Bartonville, and a beautiful, fundamentalist Christian, African American woman named Vashti. Busiris, the city in which *Traitor to the Living* (1973) is set, is a "middle-sized, mid-Illinois city" on the Illinois River—Peoria exactly, with its river bluffs, Knollwoods subdivision, and "Traybell" University (8). Farmer created the name Busiris by combining the name of his alma mater with the Egyptian land of the dead. The Wolff-Kickaha universe derived its name from the Kickapoo Indian tribe and Kickapoo Creek outside Peoria.

Like many of his novels, *The Lovers* (1961) presents Farmer's indictment of life at Bradley, where "the semi-robots kill the human beings one way or another" ("Peoria-Colored Writer" xiii). Free-thinking, "indiscrete" linguistics professor Hal Yarrow, spied upon by a frigid and generally phobic wife and oppressive college administrators, volunteers for a dangerous mission to a distant planet to escape the entire anti-drink, anti-sex crowd. There he finds salvation in sex with an extraterrestrial. In a larger sense *The Lovers* is a critique of Puritan Peoria and the whole prairie-Puritan Middle West from the viewpoint of Farmer's college crowd of proto-Beatniks. Farmer is cited by Russel Letson in "The Worlds of Philip Jose Farmer" as calling the novel "a projection of our capacity for cutting ourselves off from the life-giving sources of joy and love to be found in sex and genuine spirituality—to turn toward rigidity and repression, the Church and puritanism" (126).

Farmer's celebration of all animal vitality is the reverse side of his indictment of the Middle West as a Land of the Dead, where, Thomas Wymer says, "fear of sexuality fosters repression, ignorance, and ultimately self-destruction" ("Trickster" 42). "It is doubtful," Farmer wrote wryly in the Peoria Bicentennial History of Peoria (1975) of the film version of A Feast Unknown, "that the movie will be shown in Peoria" (44).

**SELECTED WORKS:** Important early works include A Feast Unknown (1969), The Image of the Beast (1968), The Lovers (1961), Night of Light (1966), and Flesh (1960, expanded 1968), which borders on pornography. Farmer's most significant work is the Riverworld trilogy: To Your Scattered Bodies Go (1971), The Fabulous River Boat (1971), and The Magic Labyrinth (1980).

**FURTHER READING:** The only book-length study of Farmer to date is Mary T. Brizzi's A Reader's Guide to Philip José Farmer (1980). Contemporary Literary Criticism 19 excerpts critical articles up to 1981. Farmer's own self-appraisal may be found in an essay titled "The Peoria-Colored Writer," printed as the introduction to the short story collection The Grand Adventure (1984): vi–xiv. Significant articles include Edgar L. Chapman's "From Rebellious Rationalist to Mythmaker and Mystic: The Religious Quest of Philip José Farmer," in The Transcendent Adventure, edited by Robert Reilly (1985); Leslie Fiedler's "Thanks for the Feast," reprinted from the Los Angeles Times in The Book of Philip José Farmer (1973): 232–39; Russell Letson's "The Faces of a Thousand Heroes: Philip José Farmer," in Science Fiction Studies 4 (1977): 35–41, and his "The Worlds of Philip José Farmer," in Extrapolation 18.2 (May 1977): 124–30; Claudia Jannone's "Venus on the Half Shell as Structuralist Activity," in Extrapolation 17.11 (May 1976): 110–16; and Thomas L. Wymer's "Philip José Farmer: The Trickster as Artist," in Voices for the Future: Essays on Major Science Fiction Writers 2, edited by Thomas Clareson (1979): 34–55. A good bibliography is Thomas L Wymer's "Speculative Fiction, Bibliographies, and Philip José Farmer," in Extrapolation 18 (1976): 59–72.

DAVID R. PICHASKE    SOUTHWEST STATE UNIVERSITY

## ELIZA FARNHAM
November 17, 1815–December 15, 1864

**BIOGRAPHY:** Eliza Wood Burhans Farnham, the daughter of Cornelius and Mary (Wood) Burhans, led a varied, fascinating life that took her to both coasts as well as to the Midwest. Born at Rensselaerville, New York, she was separated from her siblings when her mother died in 1820 and lived with her grandfather and then with her atheistic aunt in Maple Springs, New York. In his Old Northwest 7 (1981–82) essay, "Eliza Farnham's Life in Prairie Land," JOHN HALLWAS writes that although Farnham was denied early schooling, she compensated by reading widely (296). Through her aunt's early influence, Eliza became a progressive thinker and developed her own atheistic tendencies. After leaving her aunt's home, Eliza obtained some formal education with her brother's help and taught school for about two years.

In 1831 her sister married and moved to a homestead near Groveland in Tazewell County, Illinois. Eliza followed in 1835 and lived in Illinois for four and a half years. Her experiences during this time are chronicled in Life in Prairie Land (1846). In July 1836 she married Thomas Jefferson Farnham, a lawyer, and lived with him in Tremont and then Peoria, Illinois. According to Hallwas, Eliza returned to Groveland in 1838 to nurse her ailing sister until she died. Eliza's own first-born child died two weeks later due to disease caused by a drought. Eliza continued to live in Peoria while Thomas, who had become a well-known Western explorer and travel writer, was on an expedition in Oregon. When the West Coast excursion ended in 1840, they moved to New York. Settling near Poughkeepsie, they never returned to Illinois.

Eliza's later life was richly diverse and active: she spoke out about women's roles in society and became matron of the female division of Sing Sing prison, where she instituted controversial reforms. In New York, she became acquainted with William Cullen Bryant and visited a literary salon frequented by Edgar Allan Poe and Margaret Fuller. When her husband died in 1848 while traveling in San Francisco, she arranged for several marriageable women to go with her to male-dominated California and then operated a farm in Santa Cruz County for several years. In March 1852 she married William Fitzpatrick, an Irishman, but was divorced from him in 1856. Upon returning East, she was a volunteer nurse at Gettysburg. There, she contracted an illness and later died of consumption at age forty-nine at Milton-on-the-Hudson, New York.

**SIGNIFICANCE:** *Life in Prairie Land,* while little known, is a significant work of early Midwestern literature. The book combines elements of autobiography, fiction, and travel writing as well as social and natural history to present both a spiritual response to the Great Plain and an astute observation of its perils. While her memorable first view of the prairie's beauty is described in romantic tradition, this approach is balanced with a realistic view of the hardships inherent in pioneer life.

The book is distinctive for its vivid portrayal of the prairie as Farnham found it in the 1830s as well as for its sensitive depiction of early Illinois culture and the interaction between prairie people and the interminable plain surrounding them. "This [latter] aspect of the book," Hallwas writes, "is its greatest claim to a position of importance in early Midwestern literature" (*Old Northwest* 309).

**SELECTED WORKS:** *Life in Prairie Land* was reissued in a 1988 Prairie State Books edition by the University of Illinois. While it is Farnham's most significant work, it was followed by several other volumes: *California In-doors and Out* (1856); *Eliza Woodson: Or, The Early Days of One of the World's Workers* (1864); and *Woman and Her Era* (1864), which established her as an early proponent of female rights.

**FURTHER READING:** John Hallwas's article "Eliza Farnham's Life in Prairie Land," in *Old Northwest* 7 (1981–82): 295–324, provides the most comprehensive treatment of Farnham's life and work, as well as her contributions to the Midwestern literary tradition. He has also written the introduction to the 1988 Prairie State Books edition. In *Writing Illinois: The Prairie, Lincoln, and Chicago* (1992), James Hurt provides valuable interpretation of the work, as does Robert C. Bray in *Rediscoveries: Literature and Place in Illinois* (1982). Feminist critic Annette Kolodny also treats the book in *The Land before Her: Fantasy and Experience of the American Frontiers, 1630–1860* (1984). See also *Notable American Women* 1 (1971): 598–600; *Dictionary of American Biography* 3 (1958): Part 2,

282; and Helen B. Woodward's essay "Biology Triumphant: Eliza Woodson Farnham," published in *The Bold Women* (1953).

Farnham's correspondence is collected at Harvard College Library, California State Library, Boston Public Library, and the New York State Library.

BARBARA BURKHARDT          UNIVERSITY OF ILLINOIS

## JAMES T(HOMAS) FARRELL
February 27, 1904–August 22, 1979

**BIOGRAPHY:** James Thomas Farrell was born in Chicago to lower-middle-class Irish American parents, James Francis and Mary (Daly) Farrell. Farrell's father was a teamster. Farrell sympathetically associated his father with the aspirations and trials of working men all over the world. On both sides of his family Farrell was connected to the cultural, social, and economic milieu associated with the lower end of Chicago's Irish American middle class. This same milieu provided the setting and thematic focus of Farrell's most significant fiction.

Because of his family's financial difficulties, Farrell was sent to live with his maternal grandparents at the age of three. His grandparents' place in the 4900 block on Indiana Avenue was also home to and supported by Farrell's Uncle Tom and Aunt Elizabeth. The economic security and creature comforts of his new home, which included central heating and plumbing, were in marked contrast to the dangerously primitive conditions of his parents' home at 45th Place and Wells. Critics and Farrell himself have attributed considerable significance to this forced relocation. On the one hand his new household's economic stability nurtured a reflective capacity that more than likely would not have been possible in his own family's more brutal circumstances. On the other hand, it inevitably denied him a normal childhood. He was, in a sense, forced to be an objective observer not only of his own family but also of himself in relation to his adopted family. From a very early age he had a sense of not exactly belonging, of being different.

In September 1911, Farrell began elementary school at Corpus Christi Parochial Grammar School located just off Grand Boulevard on 49th Street. Near the end of his fourth year, his grandmother, Uncle Tom, Aunt Ella, and he moved into the neighborhood depicted in *Studs Lonigan*. In May 1917, the Dalys moved nearby to 5816 South Park Avenue where their apartment looked out on Washington Park. Farrell lived here for many years. He completed his elementary education at St. Anselm's Parochial Grammar School, where he was known for his athletic prowess.

In 1919 Farrell enrolled in St. Cyril High School, where he chose the four-year Classical course, a clear sign of his aspirations. His was a successful high school career. He not only became a star athlete, winning seven varsity letters in baseball, football, and basketball, he also showed early literary ambitions. He was the sports editor of the St. Cyril *Oriflamme* where several of his first stories appeared, one featuring Danny O'Neill.

During his high school years and after his graduation in 1923, Farrell worked at the Amalgamated Express Company providing much needed money for both his families. His working experience, however, made him desire a different sort of future. He enrolled first in an evening pre-law course at De Paul University where he first read THEODORE DREISER. The strain of work and school proved too much so he went to work at a gas station, saved his money, and entered the University of Chicago in June 1925. His eight quarters of work there changed his life. The world of ideas, hard work, and self-discipline became his new faith, offering a way out of what more and more seemed like a hostile and spirit-draining environment. Such a liberal salvation is thematically central to both the Danny O'Neill and Bernard Carr novels. More importantly, it was at the university that he discovered his vocation. After taking James Weber Linn's composition course, he left for New York in July 1927 determined to be a writer. There he worked as a salesman while he wrote. Returning to Chicago and to the university in January, he wrote critical articles and book reviews for university publications and for Chicago and New York newspapers. In September 1929 he began work on *Studs Lonigan*.

After secretly marrying Dorothy Patricia Butler in the spring of 1931, Farrell and his new wife departed on the H.M.S. *Pennland* for France. Literarily, his year in France was successful and productive. Perhaps energized by Ezra Pound's faith in his talent, he revised *Young Lonigan*, wrote nearly all of *Gas-House McGinty*, published stories in a number of magazines, completed a number of others, and found time to read a great deal. Arriving back in America in April 1932, Farrell was nearly broke but clearly on his way as a successful writer.

After returning from Europe, Farrell settled in New York and became part of the New York literary and cultural scene. The transformation of Chicago city boy to successful New York writer is chronicled in the Bernard Carr trilogy, which dramatizes with very little disguise nearly all of Farrell's aesthetic and political struggles during these years.

The 1930s, his most influential decade, saw the publication of *Gas-House McGinty* (1933), *Studs Lonigan* (1935), and the first two Danny O'Neill novels. He wrote regularly for leftist periodicals such as *Partisan Review*, *Anvil*, and *Socialist Call*. Because of his proletarian origins and subject matter, Farrell was hailed early in his career by leftist critics such as Granville Hicks and Michael Gold. Farrell, however, soon found himself at odds with the ideological constraints of these critics. His *A Note on Literary Criticism* (1937), a thoughtful meditation on Marxist criticism and a plea for pluralism in literature and for the independence of the artist, resulted in his being vilified by the very critics who had initially established his reputation.

When Farrell died on August 22, 1979, in New York City, he had published more than fifty books, including twenty-five novels and fifteen volumes of short stories. A man of extraordinary energy, he was, at his death, approximately one third of the way through an enormous cycle of poems, plays, and fiction (*A Universe of Time*) projected to run to thirty volumes. His prodigious social and literary criticism, relentlessly poured out over five decades, touched on a remarkable range of subjects.

**SIGNIFICANCE:** At first critics tended to see Farrell strictly as a naturalist, a successor to James Joyce and Theodore Dreiser in their attention to the debilitating effects of a squalid urban environment on the city's inhabitants. But if Farrell was a naturalist, he was not one who saw his characters merely as the victims of biological or economic forces over which they had no control. He might be considered a cultural naturalist of sorts in that he was especially sensitive to the imprisoning force of his culture's parochial fictions. Farrell, however, always gave us the sense that his characters had choices to make and that they were significant choices. Heavily influenced by the Chicago school of sociology, associated with Robert Park, E. W. Burgess, and Frederick Thrasher, and, even more significantly, by John Dewey and George Herbert Mead, Farrell's fictions can be seen as studies of the self formed by the urban experience. *Studs Lonigan* dramatizes the tragic result of succumbing to a limiting and suffocating culture; the Danny O'Neill pentalogy and the Bernard Carr trilogy trace the liberation from and triumph over that same culture.

Farrell's reputation has never recovered the status originally conferred on him by the left-leaning critical establishment of the 1930s. At first these critics celebrated him as an authentic proletarian writer who depicted the corrosive effects of a decaying capitalist society on working men and women. But Farrell's own quarrels with Marxist aesthetics and the fact that his fiction did not exactly conform to Marxist formulas led to a mutual estrangement. Abandoned by those who had equated his literary merit with his subject matter, Farrell has found no competing group ready to champion him. While it seems clear now that Farrell's literary reputation rests strictly on *Studs Lonigan*, it is also true that Farrell is, in one important sense, the most significant urban writer of the first half of the century. Writers such as Dreiser and SHERWOOD ANDERSON wrote about Chicago from the outside. Their characters, drawn by the city's promises and disillusioned by the urban experience, never entirely apprehend the city from within. Even more than JOHN DOS PASSOS, with whom Farrell shared significant similarities, he was entirely in possession of and possessed by his Chicago experience. Inspired by CARL SANDBURG's *Chicago* (1916) and Sherwood Anderson's *Tar: A Midwest Childhood* (1926), Farrell became a novelist of the city. His fictions record the peculiar American longing for significance as they were expressed by the people of his thoroughly realized Chicago youth. His characters are Chicago versions of Anderson and F. SCOTT FITZGERALD's grotesques. If Gatsby's tragedy is his refusal to accept his parentage and his concomitant insistence on pursuing his dream, Studs's tragedy is the acceptance of his parentage and failure to attempt his dream.

Quite apart from whatever literary merit Farrell is finally accorded, his work has immense sociological significance. On the one hand, his Chicago novels and hundreds of short stories provide a painstakingly thorough social history, a documentation of the myriad ways life was lived and imagined in Chicago in the early decades of the century; on the other hand, his Danny O'Neill and Bernard Carr novels along with his journalism, literary criticism, and letters provide a thorough and complex study of the political and aesthetic struggles of a Midwestern urban writer in the early half of this century.

**SELECTED WORKS:** *Studs Lonigan*, comprising *Young Lonigan: A Boyhood in Chicago Streets* (1932), *The Young Manhood of Studs Lonigan* (1934), and *Judgement Day* (1935), was first published as a trilogy in 1935 and reissued in 1978 with an epilogue by Farrell. Constructed out of Farrell's personal experience, the trilogy covers a fifteen-year period opening with Studs's graduation from St. Patrick's Grammar School on June 16, 1916, and ending with his death in August 1931. The young Studs Lonigan was an actual friend of Farrell's, one of the first boys he met when Farrell moved into the 58th Street neighborhood depicted in *Studs Lonigan*. His death in 1929 shocked Farrell into understanding his estrangement from the limiting, imprisoning culture of his youth. The trilogy, starting with the young boy's optimism and concluding with his enfeebled death in the early dark days of the Depression, represents the larger experience of the nation itself.

Studs's acquiescence in and submission to his suffocating cultural environment contrasts significantly with Danny O'Neill's experience recorded in a series of five novels: *A World I Never Made* (1936); *No Star Is Lost* (1938); *Father and Son* (1940); *My Days of Anger* (1943); and *The Face of Time* (1953). While Studs's is the fate that Farrell escaped from, Danny O'Neill is clearly a thinly disguised version of Farrell's own liberation, a sort of portrait of the artist as he grows up on the south side of Chicago. Coming from the same neighborhood as Studs, Danny O'Neill wins out over the same forces that Studs gave in to. The five novels trace Danny's development over eighteen years, from his insecurities as a five-year-old in 1909 to his bold departure for New York City in 1927 to become a writer. Not as artistically successful as *Studs Lonigan*, the Danny O'Neill novels present a wider social landscape. Danny overcomes not just the narrowness of Studs's world but also the genteel pretensions of his maternal grandparents. Danny's early unhappiness, his sense of rejection and not fitting in, is transformed into the source of his determination, a measure of his superiority to the world he leaves behind.

The Bernard Carr trilogy consists of *Bernard Clare* (1946), *The Road Between* (1949), and *Yet Other Waters* (1952). A libel suit forced Farrell to change the name to Carr after the first novel. These novels, covering the years between 1927 and 1936, examine the development of the city-bred, working-class artist as he struggles to overcome his origins and the frustrations of political entrapments, materialism, and domesticity. As Danny O'Neill overcame his Chicago boyhood, Bernard Carr overcomes the New York City leftist culture of the 1930s. He is a version of Farrell, an artist dedicated to the truth and suspicious of all formal systems.

Those interested in Chicago life and Chicago fiction will want to look at *Gas-House McGinty* (1933), a novel depicting the working life of the expressmen at the Amalgamated Express Company where Farrell and his father had both worked. *Boarding House Blues* (1961) and *New Year's Eve, 1929* (1967) are both set in Chicago bohemian circles. *Ellen Rogers* (1941), Farrell's first thorough examination of a woman character, offers an interesting comparison to Dreiser's *Sister Carrie* (1900). Most of Farrell's more than two hundred short stories are located in the same Chicago settings found in *Studs Lonigan* and the Danny O'Neill novels. Of especial interest are *Calico Shoes and Other Stories* (1934) and *Guillotine Party and Other Stories* (1935). *A Note on Literary Criticism* (1937) makes the case for artistic freedom from propagandistic Marxist aesthetics.

**FURTHER READING:** EDGAR M. BRANCH is the leading Farrell scholar. His *James T. Farrell* (1971), in the Twayne Authors series, is a thorough and intelligent summary of the themes and techniques of the principal novels and short stories as well as of Farrell's journalism and literary criticism. He is especially good at providing close biographical connections to Farrell's work. In "James T. Farrell: Aspects of Telling the Whole Truth," in *American Literary Naturalism* (1956), Charles Walcutt connects Farrell to the naturalist tradition. Alfred Kazin relates Farrell to left-wing Depression naturalism in *On Native Grounds* (1942). Joseph Warren Beach's "James T. Farrell: The Plight of the Poolroom Loafer" and "James T. Farrell: The Plight of the Children," in his *American Fiction* (1941), provide an early but astute analysis of the fiction. Richard Mitchell's "*Studs Lonigan*: Research in Morality," in *Centennial Review* 6 (Spring 1962): 202–14, looks at Dewey's influence on *Studs Lonigan*. Two important works examine Farrell's special relationship to the urban setting: Blanche Gelfant's "James T. Farrell: The Ecological Novel," in *The American City Novel* (1954), and Lewis F. Fried's "James T. Farrell: The City as Society," in *Makers of the City* (1990). The most significant collection of Farrell's papers is at the University of Pennsylvania.

CLARENCE LINDSAY          UNIVERSITY OF TOLEDO

**FEIKE FEIKEMA.**
*See* Frederick Manfred

**EDNA FERBER**
August 15, 1885–April 16, 1968
**BIOGRAPHY:** Edna Ferber, short story writer, novelist, and playwright, was born in Kalamazoo, Michigan, to Hungarian-born Jacob Charles Ferber, a storekeeper, and Milwaukee-born Julia (Neumann) Ferber. Ferber lived in Chicago and in Ottumwa, Iowa, before moving with her family to Appleton, Wisconsin. She recalled her youth as marked by Chautauquas, political rallies, parades, and circuses. In Appleton, she began work as a journalist at age seventeen, continued in Milwaukee and Chicago, and began publishing short stories and a novel, *Dawn O'Hara, The Girl Who Laughed* (1911), about a newspaperwoman in Milwaukee.

Her Emma McChesney stories included *Roast Beef, Medium: The Business Adventure of Emma McChesney* (1913), *Personality Plus: Some Experiences of Emma McChesney and Her Son, Jock* (1914), and *Emma McChesney and Co.* (1915), about an independent and successful salesperson. With the success of these stories, Ferber moved to New York to work as a playwright as well. Like WILLIAM DEAN HOWELLS and HAMLIN GARLAND, Ferber moved from small town to city and then East, as her work acquired popularity; she also lived in Europe.

Ferber published eleven story collections and thirteen novels, as well as several plays written with George S. Kaufman; more than two dozen films were made of her work, though she did not write the screenplays. Ferber never married. In New York, she was regarded as the epitome of Midwestern civility: plain-spoken, understated, self-determined, and polite. She died of cancer in her New York home.

**SIGNIFICANCE:** Throughout her career, a portion of Ferber's work portrayed her Midwestern background, but not exclusively; in fact, her greatest popularity came with Hollywood films of *Showboat* (1926) and *Giant* (1952), although adaptations of her work also included such characteristic Midwestern novels as *So Big* (1924), winner of the Pulitzer Prize, and *Come and Get It* (1935). Ferber used her own experiences and familiar locales, but she researched extensively and traveled in preparing stories. Ferber was an acknowledged sentimentalist about the Midwest, particularly its frontier days. While she possessed an accurate ear for dialect, she used it only occasionally; and while she attested to the exploitation, peril, and ugliness of Wisconsin lumbering, for example, she thought the lumber barons and other industrialists were bold and daring pioneers: "rich and roistering men," she said of Barney Glasgow and his like in *Come and Get It*, "who had come up from the rough background of farm, mills, and woods . . . . They were like ignorant children with the power of gods" (46, 66). As with lumbering, Ferber found an epic setting in the Oklahoma land rush and oil boom of *Cimarron* (1930) and lumbering and gold of the Pacific Northwest in *Great Son* (1945).

However, her sentimentalism was not entirely sweet, but indignant and angry as well, and Ferber resented characterization of herself as a writer of entertaining melodrama. In *So Big*, the Illinois farm wife Selina Peake DeJong is ridiculed for her enthusiastic exclamation with the mocking, often repeated parody, "cabbages is beautiful," but that sentiment is fully justified by her injurious physical labor and indomitable will to make the farm pay. Moreover, several short

stories in *One Basket* (1947) show the limited career and social opportunities of small-town Wisconsin, particularly for young women. Ferber's Midwestern characters, especially those of the middle class, are typically resilient survivors.

**SELECTED WORKS:** *Fanny, Herself* (1917) is set in Winnebago, Wisconsin, the name for a fictionalized Appleton that Ferber also used in other work, such as *Come and Get It* (1935). *The Girls* (1921), a story of three generations of unmarried women, is set in Chicago, as are some of the stories in *Buttered Side Down* (1912). Ferber's novels often chronicle several generations, typically showing a decline of the pioneer boldness she portrayed as grandly heroic even when unethical. In *So Big* (1924), college-educated Dirk DeJong is socially embarrassed by his farm background and personally ashamed at how poorly his business wealth compares to his mother's prosperous farm. In *Come and Get It* and *Great Son* (1945), Ferber shows three generations: the ruthless and god-like frontiersmen, their offspring for whom wealth comes too easily, and ultimately those of the third generation which recognize the need to regain the pioneer temperament. According to Mike Melendy of *Great Son*, "My crowd, we've got no place to go but up. My great grand-pappy and Grandpa Vaughn Melendy and all that gang just came along in covered wagons and grabbed the stuff with their bare hands, and then they hitched machinery to it, and so now we just sit on our cans and our job is to get up every now and then and oil the machinery" (209).

Ferber wrote two volumes of autobiography: *A Peculiar Treasure* (1939) and *A Kind of Magic* (1963). There are many foreign translations of Ferber's novels.

**FURTHER READING:** Ferber has always received contemporary book, theater, and film reviews but little academic criticism. Her biography was written by a niece, Julie Goldsmith Gilbert, *Ferber: A Biography* (1978), and is not intended for literary study. Rogers Dickinson's *Edna Ferber* (1925) contains a biographical sketch and an informative bibliography for magazine pieces. The Appleton Public Library maintains a Ferber web page with a bibliography of Ferber's fiction, films, and reference works on Ferber at www.apl.org. Some manuscripts, correspondence, and personal copies of Ferber's books are held at the University of Wisconsin and the State Historical Society of Wisconsin.

THOMAS PRIBEK

UNIVERSITY OF WISCONSIN–LACROSSE

## ARTHUR DAVISON FICKE
November 10, 1883–November 30, 1945

**BIOGRAPHY:** Arthur Davison Ficke was born in Davenport, Iowa, to Charles A. and Frances (Davison) Ficke. He received his early education there, graduating from Davenport High School in 1900 and from Harvard in 1904, where he was class poet and president of Harvard's literary magazine, the *Advocate*. After attending law school at the University of Iowa and teaching briefly in the Department of English there, he married Evelyn Blunt in 1907; one son, Stanhope, resulted from this marriage.

Although Ficke dutifully began practicing law with his father in Davenport, he continued to write poetry and make frequent trips to Chicago to socialize with FLOYD DELL, EDGAR LEE MASTERS, SHERWOOD ANDERSON, THEODORE DREISER, and other writers and artists. He was most likely SUSAN GLASPELL'S inspiration for Seymour Standish, the businessman-poet who leads a double life in her 1922 comedy *Chains of Dew*.

In 1916, annoyed by the trend toward free verse, prosaic themes, and graphic language that he felt characterized the new poetry, Ficke and his Harvard friend Witter Bynner perpetrated the *Spectra* hoax, publishing a collection of verse as Anne Knish and Emanuel Morgan, respectively. The poetry in *Spectra* purported to be the radical versifying of a Spectric school of poetry but in reality was a parody of Imagism, Vorticism, and other such new styles of verse.

While Ficke was serving in France during World War I he met Gladys Brown, an ambulance driver, whom he married in 1923 after divorcing his first wife in 1922. Later that decade the Fickes purchased a country place, Hardhack, near Hillsdale, New York, where they spent almost all of their summers. After contracting tuberculosis in 1930, Ficke became a semi-invalid and took his own life at age sixty-two while suffering from throat cancer.

**SIGNIFICANCE:** A poet since adolescence, Ficke played an active role in the literary Midwest during the second decade of the twentieth century. In 1912 his sonnet "Poetry" was the first poem to appear in the inaugural issue of HARRIET MONROE's *Poetry* magazine; in 1913 the entire February issue of *Poetry* was devoted to the poems of Ficke and Bynner. In 1914 he traveled to Des Moines to speak at the Iowa Homecoming of Authors and Artists, and in 1917 his poetry was included in the Iowa Press and Authors Club's *Prairie Gold*. His work also appeared in MARGARET ANDERSON's *Little Review*, in the *Dial*, and in JOHN T. FREDERICK's *Midland*.

Yet Ficke was, perhaps, most Midwestern in his rejection of the cultural limitations he felt Midwestern life imposed; almost nothing he wrote carries any Midwestern flavor. The sonnet sequences in which he specialized were often paeans to Love, Nature, Beauty or persons he admired and suggested little, if any, sense of place. Unlike his friend, Floyd Dell, Ficke hated Davenport. To Ficke, Davenport represented the harsh accents and crude manners of his German relatives; the authoritarian presence of his father, a onetime mayor of that city; his stifling law practice; his socialite wife and her philistine friends. Practicing a classical poetics in which exalted subject matter, traditional schemes of rhyme and meter, poetic diction, and devices such as personification and apostrophe were prominent, Ficke used poetry to escape what he referred to in his journal as "that loathsome atmosphere of small-town business and domestic infelicity." Ficke also distanced himself from the Midwest through his extensive world travels, his collection of Japanese prints, and his study of Eastern religions, constructing a cosmopolitan and sophisticated persona in the many witty letters he wrote to friends such as Dell, Bynner, Masters, Dreiser, Edna St. Vincent Millay, and Robinson Jeffers.

**SELECTED WORKS:** Ficke published one work of fiction, *Mrs. Morton of Mexico* (1939); three plays, *The Breaking of Bonds* (1910), *Mr. Faust* (1913), and *The Road to the Mountain* (1930); and two books on Japanese prints, *Twelve Japanese Painters* (1913) and *Chats on Japanese Prints* (1915). He published seventeen volumes of verse: *Arthur Ficke–Tom Metcalf; Their Book* (1901), *From the Isles* (1907), *The Happy Princess* (1908), *The Earth Passion, Boundary, and Other Poems* (1908), *Sonnets of a Portrait-Painter* (1914), *Islands in the Mist: A Sonnet Sequence* (with Mary Aldis, 1914), *The Man on the*

*Hilltop, and Other Poems* (1915), *Spectra: A Book of Poetic Experiments* (1916), *An April Elegy* (1917), *Sonnets of a Portrait-Painter and Other Sonnets* (1922), *Out of Silence, and Other Poems* (1924), *Selected Poems* (1926), *Christ in China* (1927), *Mountain against Mountain* (1929), *The Hell of the Good: A Theological Epic in Six Books* (as Edouard de Verb, 1930), *The Secret and Other Poems* (1936), and *Tumultuous Shore, and Other Poems* (1942).

**FURTHER READING:** William Jay Smith's *The Spectra Hoax* (1961) is the only book-length study of Ficke. Biographical information can be found in Gladys Brown's "Arthur Davison Ficke and His Friends," in *Yale Library Gazette* (January 1949): 140–44, and in William Roba's "Twins in My Cradle: Arthur Davison Ficke, Iowa Poet," in *Books at Iowa* (November 1983): 48–56. G. Thomas Tanselle looks closely at Ficke's best-known sonnet sequence in "Ficke's *Sonnets of a Portrait Painter*: Textual Problems in a Modern Poet," in *Yale Library Gazette* (June 1961): 33–39. Kay Rout's "Arthur Davison Ficke's 'Ten Grotesques,'" in *Midwestern Miscellany* 8 (1980): 20–27, looks at Ficke's early work, and Marcia Noe examines the Ficke-Masters relationship in "Missed by Modernism: The Literary Friendship of Arthur Davison Ficke and Edgar Lee Masters," in *Western Illinois Regional Studies* (Fall 1991): 71–79. Most of Ficke's papers are at the Beinecke Library, Yale University. Others are held at the Newberry Library, Chicago; the University of Michigan library; and the University of Iowa library.

MARCIA NOE
        THE UNIVERSITY OF TENNESSEE AT CHATTANOOGA

## EUGENE FIELD
September 2 (3?), 1850–November 4, 1895
**BIOGRAPHY:** Newspaperman, humorist, poet, and short story writer, Eugene Field was born in St. Louis, Missouri, to lawyer Roswell M. and Frances (Reed) Field, both Vermont natives. When his mother died in 1856, he and his younger brother, Roswell, were sent to Amherst, Massachusetts, to be raised by a cousin, Mary Field French. Privately educated, Field entered Williams College in 1868, but when his father died in 1869, he returned to the Midwest to enter Knox College in Illinois. He stayed only one year before enrolling at the University of Missouri, where his brother was a student. Field never re-ceived a degree. After briefly considering acting as a career, he decided to travel with money left him by his father. He sailed to Europe with a college friend, the brother of Julia Sutherland Comstock, whom Field married in 1873, a marriage which produced eight children.

In that same year Field became a reporter for the *St. Louis Evening Journal*, beginning a journalistic career that took him to the *St. Joseph* (Missouri) *Gazette*, back to the *St. Louis Journal* and *Times-Journal*, on to the *Kansas City Times*, then to the *Denver Tribune* in 1881, and finally in 1885, to the morning edition of the *Chicago Daily News*.

In Chicago, Field wrote his witty and popular column "Sharps and Flats," gathered his writings into books, and became well known throughout the country. By 1889 his health began to suffer, and he took his family to live in Europe during 1889–90. Returning to Chicago and his work, Field died in his sleep in 1895 from a heart attack, only a few months after moving his family into their first purchased home in Chicago's Buena Park.

**SIGNIFICANCE:** During his lifetime and immediately following his death, Field enjoyed great popularity. His column, "Sharps and Flats," contained, in both prose and verse, satiric, sentimental, and humorous comments on Chicago's and the nation's political or cultural affairs. He was especially adept at parody and dialect; his verse often was similar to or a parody of his fellow Midwesterner JAMES WHITCOMB RILEY. Field was also a master of occasional verse, a genre which is usually short lived. His "Little Willie" verses are reminiscent of some of MARK TWAIN's risqué writings and are also examples of an earthiness often found in Midwestern speech.

Field particularly enjoyed literary hoaxes. Always playful, these hoaxes sometimes continued for weeks in his column. In one instance he wrote verses which he attributed to Judge Thomas M. Cooley of Michigan, an eminent lawyer who had been appointed by President Cleveland to the Interstate Commerce Commission. Field then wrote letters praising and criticizing the verses.

Often he wrote about people in the theater, a group happy to have their names before the reading public. Field never lost his love for the theater and delighted in reciting

**Eugene Field.**
Courtesy of the University of Kentucky Libraries

for his friends. His writings brought him in touch with the hopes and fears of his time, and his playful, boyish quality appealed to a Midwestern innocence which was fast being lost as the nineteenth century neared its end. He entertained his readers and his listeners, and they loved him for it.

Today, however, it is his verse for children which remains the best known of Field's writings. In the years following his death, this verse gained such popularity that schools were named for Field, monuments were erected in his honor, and "Eugene Field Days" were held with children reciting his verse. His children's poems, "Wynken, Blynken, and Nod (Dutch Lullaby)," "The Duel," "Jest 'Fore Christmas," "The Sugar-Plum Tree," and "Little Boy Blue," still appear in anthologies, and several have been illustrated and appear as individual picture books which have, in turn, been made into short films.

**SELECTED WORKS:** *A Little Book of Profitable Tales* (1889, 1891) contains the story "Ezra's Thanksgivin' Out West," in which Ezra writes about his lonely Thanksgiving in Kansas and how he is "powerful sick of it" (167–68). This story and those in his *Second Book of Tales* (1896) show a more serious side of Field than is found in his newspaper columns, *Sharps*

*and Flats* (1900), collected in two volumes by his friend Slason Thompson.

Field's *Hoosier Lyrics* (1905) shows his skill with Midwestern dialect, rhythm, and rhyme. This volume contains verse with such titles as "Chicago Newspaper Life," "Kansas City vs. Detroit," "To the Detroit Baseball Club," and the parody "Hoosier Lyrics Paraphrased," in which one hears the rhythms of James Whitcomb Riley, Henry Van Dyke, and other poets of the era. *A Little Book of Western Verse* (1889, 1891) includes poems ranging from the sentimental "Little Boy Blue" to the humorous "Little Mack," a verse employing Midwestern rhythmic speech and colloquial language. This and his *Second Book of Verse* (1892) show his skill with parody, humor, satire, dialect, rhyme, and rhythm. *Culture's Garland* (1887) is subtitled *Being Memorials of the Gradual Rise of Literature, Art, Music and Society in Chicago and Other Western Ganglia* and is made up of humorous sketches and verse. Two of his collections of children's verse are *Love Songs of Childhood* (1894) and *Lullaby Land: Songs of Childhood* (1896, 1898). *The Love Affairs of a Bibliomaniac* (1896) is a collection of personal essays full of quiet wit showing Field's love of books. Writing in 1945, Midwesterner JOHN T. FLANAGAN commented on Field's gift for satire and for toying with words (*University of Kansas City Review* 11.3 [Spring 1945]: 167–72). Flanagan went on to regret that only a "handful of children's poems, a few tales, several satires and imitations survive after a full half century" (172).

**FURTHER READING:** Robert Conrow's *Field Days* (1974) provides a very readable account of Field and his times and contains a long list of collections of Field's papers. Two earlier biographies were written by men who knew Field. These are Charles H. Dennis's *Eugene Field's Creative Years* (1924) and Slason Thompson's *Life of Eugene Field, the Poet of Childhood* (1927). Two other studies, both theses, are Lyle O. Morey's "Eugene Field, A Critical Study" (1953) and Alison M. Scott's "Eugene Field, Chicago's Bibliophilic Journalist" (1982). A children's biography, *Eugene Field: The Children's Poet* (1994), by Carol Greene, is the most recent book on Field.

Numerous libraries maintain Field's manuscripts, letters, and documents, but the Humanities Research Center at the University of Texas holds the largest collection. Other libraries are the Henry E. Huntington Library, Princeton University Library, the Denver Public Library, the Newberry Library, and the New York Public Library. The Eugene Field House and Toy Museum in St. Louis has a small collection of his papers.

PATRICIA A. ANDERSON     DIMONDALE, MICHIGAN

## DOROTHY (DOROTHEA FRANCES CANFIELD) FISHER

February 17, 1879–November 9, 1958
(Dorothy Canfield, Stanley Crenshawe)

**BIOGRAPHY:** Though Dorothy Canfield Fisher, novelist, short story writer, and educator, had ancestral roots in Vermont, she was born in Lawrence, Kansas, and spent her formative years in the Midwest. She was the second child of James Hulme Canfield and Flavia (Camp) Canfield. Her only sibling, James, was five years older than she.

From the University of Kansas, where her father was an economics professor, Dorothy moved with her family in 1891 to Lincoln, where Professor Fisher had been appointed Chancellor of the University of Nebraska. There, while still in high school, she met her brother's college classmate WILLA CATHER. Dorothy and Willa collaborated on a ghost story that appeared in the university literary magazine of 1894; this early acquaintance ripened into friendship that endured despite a period of alienation from 1905 to 1921. In 1895 the Fishers moved to Columbus, Ohio, where Dr. Fisher served as President of the Ohio State University until 1899. At Ohio State Dorothy earned an undergraduate degree in French; in 1904 she received her PhD in French from Columbia. Then, instead of accepting an offer to teach French at Western Reserve University in Cleveland, she took a position at the experimental Horace Mann School in New York, at the same time beginning to write professionally. Soon she was publishing short stories, some with grimly realistic Midwestern settings, in such magazines as *Munsey's* and *Harper's*. Though she did not publish fiction under her married surname until 1940, she wedded John R. Fisher, an aspiring writer himself, in 1907. In the same year her first novel, *Gunhild*, was published, the story of a displaced Norwegian American who emigrates to Norway and becomes homesick for her Kansas birthplace.

Following marriage, the Fishers moved to their permanent home, a property in Arlington, Vermont, which Dorothy had inherited. They had two children, Sally and James. In 1916 the Fisher family, children included, left their home to spend three years in France doing war work.

Fisher wrote ten novels after *Gunhild*, more than a hundred short stories, and numerous works of nonfiction. These last include books that reflect, as do several of her novels, her enthusiasm for the Montessori teaching method, an enthusiasm dating from 1911, when she visited Dr. Maria Montessori's schools in Rome. She was also a strong supporter of public education, serving for twenty-five years on the Book-of-the-Month Club's selection board. Following a stroke in 1953, she was felled by a final stroke on November 9, 1958.

**SIGNIFICANCE:** Devoted to marriage and domesticity yet an unswerving advocate of the rights and responsibilities of women as workers and citizens, a highly educated writer of popular, romantic fiction containing subtleties and complexities commonly associated with *belles lettres*, Fisher was an author full of paradoxes. A displaced New Englander at heart, even though born in the Midwest, she typically used Midwestern settings as places from which one is transplanted, if fortunate, to other, better places for personal development. In *The Squirrel Cage* (1912), set in the Ohio town of Endbury, the heroine is not among those who escape. Though she marries the town's most eligible bachelor, her marriage is doomed from the start by his relentless pursuit of success at the cost of human relationships. The protagonist of *The Bent Twig* (1915) is more fortunate. Moving from the false sophistication and materialism of La Chance, a Midwestern university town, to rural Vermont, she learns to her amazed delight that there are far more idealistic and considerate suitors in the world than the petted, wealthy brute to whom she had been briefly engaged in La Chance.

In Fisher's view, the Midwest is not a good place to grow up, as illustrated by her juvenile classic, *Understood Betsy* (1917), the story of a spoiled, neurasthenic Midwestern orphan who begins to find independence, self-confidence, and personal fulfillment only when she spends a summer on her relatives' farm in Vermont. In sum, Fisher's Midwest is associated with materialism and with the frustration of legitimate aspirations in the realm of the spirit.

**SELECTED WORKS:** Besides *Gunhild* (1907), convoluted in its development, the reader may wish to sample *The Squirrel Cage* (1912), *The Bent Twig* (1915), *Understood Betsy* (1917), or *The Deepening Stream* (1930), an autobiographical novel about a girl who grows up in college towns. Some of Fisher's stories are collected in *A Harvest of Stories from a Half Century of Writing* (1956); one of the most discussed is "Sex Education." The best known of Fisher's Montessori books are *A Montessori Mother* (1912), reissued in 1965 as *Montessori for Parents*, and *The Montessori Manual* (1913, 1965).

**FURTHER READING:** The best biography to date is Ida H. Washington's *Dorothy Canfield Fisher* (1982), which may be supplemented by Mark J. Madigan's critical introduction to *Keeping Fires Night and Day: Selected Letters of Dorothy Canfield Fisher* (1993). Important Fisher papers are in the Wilbur collection of the Bailey Howe Library at the University of Vermont. The World Catalog lists a *Dorothy Canfield Newsletter* started in Vermont in 1993.

PAUL W. MILLER                    WITTENBERG UNIVERSITY

# F(RANCIS) SCOTT (KEY) FITZGERALD

September 24, 1896–December 21, 1940

**BIOGRAPHY:** Francis Scott Key Fitzgerald was born in St. Paul, Minnesota, the son of Edward Fitzgerald, a distant relation of Francis Scott Key, and Mollie (McQuillan) Fitzgerald, the daughter of a prosperous, self-made wholesale grocer.

Fitzgerald attended the St. Paul Academy and completed his secondary schooling at the Newman School of Hackensack, New Jersey. In the fall of 1913 he entered Princeton University. In October 1917 Fitzgerald received an army commission as second lieutenant and left Princeton without taking a degree. The following summer, while stationed near Montgomery, Alabama, he met Zelda Sayre, the daughter of a prominent Southern judge. Following his discharge from the army in 1919, Fitzgerald worked for an advertising agency in New York, though he soon quit his job and returned to St. Paul. There he reworked an earlier version of *This Side of Paradise* (1920). A discursive, loosely autobiographical account

of Fitzgerald's Princeton years, the novel was accepted by Charles Scribner's Sons. A week following its publication on March 26, 1920, Fitzgerald married Zelda Sayre in New York City, the first official chapter in one of the most flamboyant and publicly scrutinized marriages in American literary history. Scott and Zelda's only child, Frances Scott (Scottie) Fitzgerald, was born in St. Paul in October 1921.

The following year marked the publication of Fitzgerald's second novel, *The Beautiful and the Damned* (1922), and a second collection of stories, *Tales of the Jazz Age* (1922), which, like other collections published during his lifetime—*Flappers and Philosophers* (1921), *All the Sad Young Men* (1926), and *Taps at Reveille* (1935)—drew selectively from Fitzgerald's evolving body of magazine fiction.

During the first decade of their marriage, Scott and Zelda spent alternating periods in the United States and Europe, including an extended stay in France and Italy (1924–26) during which Fitzgerald met and developed a legendary and much documented friendship with fellow Midwesterner ERNEST HEMINGWAY. Equally notable was Scribner's publication of *The Great Gatsby* (1925), now regarded as Fitzgerald's finest novel and one of the enduring novels in American literature, though original sales were disappointing.

Whatever their public celebrity, Scott and Zelda's marriage was frequently beset by domestic quarrels and constant struggle to meet expenses incurred by the reckless extravagance of their lifestyle. Matters were further complicated by Scott's alcoholism and Zelda's increasing mental instability, which eventually led to a series of nervous breakdowns and to her institutionalization in Asheville, North Carolina. In spite of such pressing difficulties, Fitzgerald, motivated as much by a lifelong dedication to his craft as by escalating financial responsibilities, continued to write. Considering his own discouraging personal circumstances, he managed to produce an impressive volume of work, including his fourth novel, *Tender Is the Night* (1934), a prodigious amount of magazine fiction, and a remarkable series of autobiographical essays, "The Crack-Up," "Pasting It Together," and "Handle with Care," which chronicle the period of Fitzgerald's physical and emotional "crack-up" during 1935–36.

**F. Scott Fitzgerald.**
Courtesy of Princeton University Library

Following his recovery, Fitzgerald worked as a scriptwriter in Hollywood. There he met and became romantically involved with gossip columnist Sheila Graham. Though he managed only one screen credit, *Three Comrades* (1938), Fitzgerald's Hollywood experience inspired a series of stories recounting various episodes in the checkered career of the fictive Hollywood screenwriter Pat Hobby, later collected as *The Pat Hobby Stories* (1962), and the unfinished novel *The Last Tycoon* (1941). Fitzgerald died of a heart attack in December 1940.

**SIGNIFICANCE:** In addition to the American South, East, and West, Fitzgerald's fiction draws significantly upon the Midwest and, more specifically, St. Paul, where the author spent his childhood and adolescent years. Most notable in this regard are the nine Basil Duke Lee stories, written during 1928–29. These stories evoke the social milieu, the class consciousness, and the prevailing fads, fashions, and courtship rituals of Fitzgerald's boyhood in St. Paul. The basis for a number of the stories can be traced directly to Fitzgerald's own early personal history. For example, the infamous Book of Scandal in "The Scandal Detectives" was inspired by Fitzgerald's "Thoughtbook," randomly composed by Fitzgerald during his early adolescence.

Capitalizing upon the success of the Basil Lee stories, Fitzgerald composed a second series of stories, the Josephine stories (1930–31), featuring Josephine Perry, the beautiful, independent, and capricious daughter of a prominent Chicago family and modeled after Fitzgerald's college sweetheart, Ginevra King, whom he first met in St. Paul in early January 1915. Compared to the Basil Lee stories, these five stories, which recount Josephine's various romantic conquests and disappointments in settings ranging from Chicago/Lake Forest to the East Coast, reveal a cumulative sense of "emotional bankruptcy," the title of the final story in the series, a notion that had long intrigued Fitzgerald and would reappear more elaborately in *Tender Is the Night* and the "crack-up" essays.

The Basil and Josephine stories, with their recurring focus on the youthful escapades of the rich or nearly rich, depict a Midwest far different from the provincial small-town or rural tradition of WILLA CATHER, SHERWOOD ANDERSON, SINCLAIR LEWIS, and EDGAR LEE MASTERS, or the industrial-naturalistic tradition of THEODORE DREISER, UPTON SINCLAIR, FRANK NORRIS, and JAMES FARRELL. The country club, so often a determinant of social status in Fitzgerald's fiction, serves as a pivotal thematic focus in a number of Fitzgerald's "Midwestern fictions," including the memorable "Bernice Bobs Her Hair." There, the opening country club dance proves instrumental in Bernice's eventual transformation from a dull, unpopular visiting relation from Eau Claire into a social vamp. A similar setting figures even more significantly in "Winter Dreams," in which Dexter Green's romantic, and eventually his self-made financial, fortunes are intimately related to an experience at the age of fourteen when, working as a caddy at a prestigious country club near Black Bear Lake, Minnesota, he happens to meet the wealthy and incomparably lovely Judy Jones and impulsively quits his job on the spot.

While the upper Midwest may serve as the unifying setting in "Bernice Bobs Her Hair," "Absolution," whose protagonist would later serve as a prototype for Jay Gatsby, and many of the "Basil" and "Josephine" stories, it is often placed in co-lateral or even tri-lateral relation to other regions such as the South ("The Ice Palace"); the East ("Winter Dreams," "The Freshest Boy"); and the East and West ("The Diamond as Big as the Ritz"). But Fitzgerald achieves his most sophisticated and complex management of contrasting regional settings in *The Great Gatsby*. There Fitzgerald draws a number of antithetical relations between the idealism and visionary self-aspiration of the mythic American West and the sham and vulgar materialism of the "civilized" present symbolically signified by the modern wasteland of the urban industrial East. By the end of the novel, the enervating and corrupting influence of the East becomes fully evident to the peripheral observer and narrator, Nick Carraway. Ultimately confronted by an historical, ideological, and personal impasse, Carraway thus observes that he, no less than Gatsby and other transplanted Westerners in the novel, "possessed some deficiency . . . [that rendered him] subtly unadaptable to Eastern life" (177). Fittingly, then, he decides to return to his home in Minnesota to recover, if only in his imagination, the unspoiled innocence of his Midwestern childhood.

Like Nick Carraway's status as narrator, the Midwest plays a peripheral though significant role in *The Great Gatsby* and an equally significant role in Fitzgerald's fiction as a whole, even in those novels and stories in which the Midwest serves neither as primary nor secondary setting. For if, according to Matthew J. Bruccoli, aspiration, mutability, and loss are the dominant thematic motifs in Fitzgerald's work, such motifs can ultimately be traced to Fitzgerald's boyhood in St. Paul. There, acutely conscious of his parents' often precarious financial status and his own precarious placement in the established social hierarchy, he developed a painful sense of social inferiority. That, in turn, stimulated the compensatory dreams of love, success, and achievement that dominate his life and fiction. As such, Fitzgerald's treatment of the Midwest is neither cynical, critical, nor antiprovincial. It is rather the point of departure in Fitzgerald's own self-fashioned quest for achievement and success. Thus, if not necessarily the "stuff dreams are made of," still for

Fitzgerald and so many of his protagonists, the Midwest is ultimately the place where those dreams were imaginatively formed and shaped, if only to be played out elsewhere, most often to disillusioning and disappointing effect.

**selected works:** Generally recognized as the richest and most artfully crafted of his novels, *The Great Gatsby* (1925) also remains his most popular and widely read novel. *This Side of Paradise* (1920), *The Beautiful and the Damned* (1922), *Tender Is the Night* (1934), and the unfinished *The Last Tycoon*, edited by Edmund Wilson (1941), are nonetheless significant as a chronicle of American sociocultural history through the first four decades of the twentieth century. More personally, they offer a reconstruction of key events in Fitzgerald's life as well as a record of Fitzgerald's lifelong fascination with the novelistic form.

Though Fitzgerald consistently staked his critical reputation on his novels, he produced more than 160 stories. Nearly all were published in such mass-circulation magazines as the *Saturday Evening Post*, and such stories as "Babylon Revisited" still endure as masterpieces of the genre. Collections of Fitzgerald's stories published during his lifetime include *Flappers and Philosophers* (1921), *Tales of the Jazz Age* (1922), *All the Sad Young Men* (1926), and *Taps at Reveille* (1935).

Notable collections of stories published since Fitzgerald's death include Arthur Mizener's *Afternoon of an Author* (1957), a selection of previously uncollected stories and essays; *The Basil and Josephine Stories*, edited by Jackson R. Bryer and John Kuehl (1973); *The Pat Hobby Stories* (1962); and *The Price Was High: The Last Uncollected Stories of F. Scott Fitzgerald*, edited by Matthew J. Bruccoli (1979).

Drawing on Fitzgerald's personal essays, notebooks, and correspondence, Edmund Wilson's collection *The Crack-Up* (1945) chronicles Fitzgerald's autobiographical reading of his early success, his eventual "crack-up," and the aftermath.

**further reading:** Though Fitzgerald's critical reputation had reached a nadir by the time of his death in 1940, he is currently regarded as one of the major American fiction writers of the twentieth century. Arthur Mizener's *The Far Side of Paradise* (1951, rev. 1965), the first full-length biography of Fitzgerald, was a signal event in the revival of interest in Fitzgerald. Andrew Turnbull's biography *Scott Fitzgerald* (1962) is equally noteworthy and, more recently, Matthew J. Bruccoli's *Some Sort of Epic Grandeur: The Life of F. Scott Fitzgerald* (1981), drawing extensively upon Fitzgerald's correspondence and related documentary materials and debunking various popular myths surrounding Fitzgerald, provides the most exhaustive and definitive treatment of Fitzgerald's life to date.

Major critical studies include John F. Callahan's *The Illusions of a Nation: Myth and History in the Novels of F. Scott Fitzgerald* (1972); John Kuehl's *F. Scott Fitzgerald: A Study of the Short Fiction* (1991); Richard D. Lehan's *F. Scott Fitzgerald and the Craft of Fiction* (1966); Milton R. Stern's *The Golden Moment: The Novels of F. Scott Fitzgerald* (1970); and Brian Way's *F. Scott Fitzgerald and the Art of Social Fiction* (1980).

Useful bibliographies are Matthew J. Bruccoli's primary bibliography *F. Scott Fitzgerald: A Descriptive Bibliography* (1971, sup. 1980, rev. 1987) and Jackson R. Bryer's *The Critical Reputation of F. Scott Fitzgerald: A Bibliographical Study* (1967). Significant collections of Fitzgerald's papers can be found at the Firestone Library at Princeton University and the Thomas Cooper Library at the University of South Carolina at Columbia.

MICHAEL WENTWORTH
UNIVERSITY OF NORTH CAROLINA AT WILMINGTON

## JOHN T. FLANAGAN.
*See* appendix (1977)

## ROBERT (JAMES) FLANAGAN
April 26, 1941

**BIOGRAPHY:** Son of Robert John and Minnie Jane (Treloar) Flanagan, Robert was born in Toledo, Ohio, where he was raised. Robert married Kathleen Borer on August 24, 1963. He received his BA from the University of Toledo in 1967. After positions at the Central YMCA Community College in Chicago and Slippery Rock State College in Pennsylvania, Flanagan returned to Ohio in 1969 to teach at Ohio Wesleyan in Delaware. He now directs the Creative Writing Program at Ohio Wesleyan. The Flanagans have two children: Anne, an actress and private detective in Los Angeles, and Nora, a photography editor and writer in New York City.

**SIGNIFICANCE:** In an unpublished lecture/essay entitled "Midwest Writer," Flanagan tells of his boyhood reading and his transition from exotic adventure stories to books by JAMES T. FARRELL, SHERWOOD ANDERSON, and NELSON ALGREN: "In these novels I recognized characters . . . I saw around me every day in Toledo." Such a recognition confirmed "the notion that I could focus my thinking on the local in my own writing." Thus Flanagan came personally to believe in what he calls the Midwest's value as "representative of the country in general in its cities and towns, farms and factories. Both geographically and emotionally the Midwest is that middle ground where most people live." Flanagan places many of his stories in Chicago or in the fictional town of Olentangy, Ohio, which he calls "a composite of parts of three Ohio places: Toledo, my home town, Ottawa, my wife's home town, and Delaware, our adopted home town." As a writer of prose fiction and poetry, Flanagan demonstrates what he advises: "You have to look hard at a Toledo street or an Olentangy field to see the beauty beneath its plain surface." A poetic realist, Flanagan's current work in progress is an eight-hundred-page novel about Toledo in 1954 to be called *Champions*.

**SELECTED WORKS:** Flanagan's Olentangy, Ohio, stories can be found in two collections: *Naked to Naked Goes* (1986) and *Loving Power* (1990). His novel, *Maggot* (1971) has sold more than 250,000 copies in its twelve printings. It has won praise for its honest depiction of U.S. Marine training. More important for its Midwest setting is a two-act dramatic comedy, *Jupus Redeye*, completed in 1983 and staged subsequently in Ohio and Kentucky. Of his writing of this play, Flanagan says: "Imagining my mother's life from the inside out in some way allowed me to see my own life from the center to the edge rather than the other way around" (*Contemporary Authors Autobiography Series* 17: 56). Out of numerous published poems, Flanagan himself cites the Midwest importance of *News from a Backward State* (1973) and poems collected in *Heartland II: Poets of the Midwest* (1975) and *73 Ohio Poets* (1978–79). In a letter of May 8, 1995, Flanagan offers a passage from a poem in *Heartland II*, "State Message: A Midwestern Small Town" as his credo: "(Place is the only certain / fact we can live by . . .)." In 1995 the story "Winter Term" was published in Jon Saari's edition of *Ohio Short Fiction*. In 1996 *Getting By: Stories of Working Lives*, edited by David Shevin and Larry Smith, included two chapters, as stories, from the novel in progress, *Champions*: "Champion" and "Martyrs."

**FURTHER READING:** *Contemporary Authors Autobiographies* series, volume 17, provides a warmly rich self-evaluation. Among the many reviews of Flanagan's books, a few stand out. Two reviews of *Maggot* can be found in *Book World* (November 21, 1971) and *Publishers Weekly* (October 4, 1971). An unfairly negative review of *Naked to Naked Goes* in *Southern Review* (Summer 1987) does however single out for praise as "awesomely imagined and described" a realistic depiction of a man bathing his dying mother (731). Surely such a scene so vividly imagined at once justifies and transcends regionalism.

JAMES M. HUGHES          WRIGHT STATE UNIVERSITY

## HUGH (BERNARD) FOX
February 12, 1932
(Connie Fox)

**BIOGRAPHY:** Born in Chicago to Hugh Bernard and Helen (Mangan) Fox, Hugh Fox, who also writes under the pseudonym Connie Fox, is a novelist, poet, and anthropologist whose prolific work ranges from the Midwestern immediacy of his early years and his maturity to the Latin American civilizations that have become a passionate interest. Fox was educated at Loyola University of Chicago, where he received his BA in 1954 and his MA in 1955 and at the University of Illinois, where he received a PhD in 1958. He professes neither politics nor religion. He was professor of American literature at Loyola University of Los Angeles and is currently professor of American Thought and Language at Michigan State University.

He has held numerous Fulbright appointments and research grants in Latin America and has been active in the founding and development of the Committee of Small Magazine Editors and Publishers (COSMEP). He married Lucia Alicia Ungaro in 1957; they were divorced in 1969; he married Nona Werner in 1970; they were divorced in 1988; and he married Maria Bernadette Costa on April 14, 1988. He has six children.

**SIGNIFICANCE:** Fox is one of the most prolific writers of this century, the author of sixty-two books, including six anthropological works, six works of literary criticism, twelve novels, fifty-four volumes and chapbooks of poetry, and four volumes of short fiction. He has also edited anthologies and journals and published hundreds of short works. Fox's works range widely in subject matter, technique, time, and place. However, much of his fiction, particularly the novels, is rooted firmly in the Chicago of his youth and the Michigan of his maturity. Hugh Fox's interests, knowledge, and scholarship range as widely as those of his nineteenth-century Midwestern predecessor IGNATIUS DONNELLY.

Three of his novels, which he describes as semi-autobiographical, are clear examples of his use of his Midwestern origins in his work. These are *Honeymoon* and *Mom*, published together in 1978, and his most recent novel, *The Last Summer* (1995). Each of the novels depicts a crucial point in a man's life: on his honeymoon, when he is no longer young, when he faces his death. Each, too, is a moment when he must learn to know another: his bride, his mother, his son, each of them ultimately unknowable, as is the narrator himself. Like Thomas Wolfe before him, Fox attempts to unite past and present, place and people, in an eternal now, just as in his nonfiction works he seeks an ultimate oneness in cultures remote in time, place, and circumstances.

**SELECTED WORKS:** A fine introduction to Fox's anthropological writings is *The Gods of the Cataclysm* (1976). His best poetry appears in *Apotheosis of Olde Towne* (1968), *Glyphs* (1969), and *Papa Funk* (1986). As Connie Fox, his poetry is in *Ten to the One Hundred Seventieth Power* (1986) and *Noria* (1988). His novellas, *Honeymoon* and *Mom* (1978), and his novel, *The Last Summer* (1995), are worth reading today for their insights into Midwestern life in the second half of the twentieth century.

**FURTHER READING:** Fox's works have been reviewed extensively in *Small Press Review*, *Kirkus Reviews*, and elsewhere. He is listed in *Writers Dictionary, 1998–2000* (1997): 493; *Contemporary Authors* (1992): 160; *New Revision Series 29* (1990): 148–49; and *Who's Who in U.S. Writers, Editors, and Poets*. His papers are in Special Collections, Michigan State University Libraries.

DAVID D. ANDERSON     MICHIGAN STATE UNIVERSITY

## JOHN T(OWNER) FREDERICK

February 1, 1893–January 31, 1975

**BIOGRAPHY:** Born on a farm two miles from Corning, Iowa, the only child of Oliver Roberts Frederick and May E. (Towner) Frederick, John T. Frederick worked on his father's farm from the time he could handle a hoe. He rode a pony to Corning Elementary School and later recalled that the first book he read was *Adventures of Huckleberry Finn*. He graduated from Corning High School in 1909, having been tutored in Greek and German to earn advanced credit. He entered the University of Iowa that fall, scrubbing floors and washing dishes to earn his way. He was forced to leave the university at the end of his sophomore year, and for two years he was principal, athletic coach, and sole high school teacher in Prescott, Iowa. He returned to the university in 1913 with an acute interest in American literature. He became a member of the Athelney Club of faculty and student writers, where the idea of a regional literary journal first emerged, the idea, Frederick later insisted, of his friend C. (Clark) F. (Fisher) Ansley. The journal first appeared as the *Midland* on January 6, 1915. From that point, until its demise in 1933 as a result of the Depression, the journal was his dominant interest.

He graduated in 1915, married Ester Paulus the same year, and began teaching English at the University of Iowa. In 1917 he received his MA, served as head of the English Department at the State Teachers College, Moorhead, Minnesota, for two years, returned briefly to Iowa, went to the University of Pittsburgh for a year, and then returned to Iowa as full professor. He remained there until 1930, while the *Midland* continued to grow in significance and reputation. In 1919 he bought a tract of land in Alcona County, Michigan, where he farmed with his father and two sons, John and James, and where he wrote two novels, *Druida* (1923) and *Green Bush* (1925). He also wrote textbooks and edited anthologies. In 1930, convinced that it was in the best interests of the *Midland*, he moved that journal to Chicago while he taught part-time at Northwestern University and Notre Dame, but the journal died in 1933. In 1936 he became full professor at Northwestern; he directed the WPA Writers Project in Chicago from 1937 to 1940 and, beginning in 1937, conducted a weekly book review program, *Of Men and Books*, on the CBS Radio Network for a number of years. He taught again at Notre Dame and at the University of Iowa, from which he retired on June 1, 1970. He spent most of his last years in Iowa.

**SIGNIFICANCE:** In the years during which he edited the *Midland*, John T. Frederick's name became indelibly associated with a growing national awareness of the significance of Midwestern literature. Among the writers first published in the *Midland* were JAMES T. FARRELL, PAUL ENGLE, RUTH SUCKOW, PAUL COREY, Marquis Childs, MACKINLAY KANTOR, PHIL STONG, AUGUST DERLETH, and dozens of others. Other writers previously published but little known when they first appeared in the *Midland* included William March, MARK VAN DOREN, Maxwell Anderson, LOREN EISELEY, and many others. During its lifetime the *Midland* gained a major reputation while contributing to a useful and logical definition of regionalism in American literature, making clear Frederick's lifelong conviction that regional writing is not inferior writing and asserting that it is subject to the literary standards at all times and all places.

In his introduction to his first-rate anthology, *Out of the Midwest* (1944), he expanded on that conviction, insisting that "regionalism is an incident and condition, not a purpose or motive" (xv) and that the regional writer uses "the literary substance that he knows best, the life of his own neighborhood, of his own city or state . . ." (xv).

Frederick practiced that principle in his two novels, *Druida* and *Green Bush*. Both are Midwestern farm novels in which young people must choose between farming life and joining the early-twentieth-century flight to the city. The former novel is the story of Druida, a young woman faced with the choice between two suitors, a college English professor and a young countryman. Her choice is made as the result of a mystical dream that emphasizes the wonders of the earth. She chooses the farm boy, and they go off to a new life in the newly opened Montana country.

In *Green Bush*, Frank Thompson must choose between life on the farm and his mother's wish that he become a college professor. His choice is made for the farm after a long debate with a friend.

Both novels reflect a basic dichotomy in Frederick's life at the time during which he was facing his own choice. In his case the deciding factor was the continuation of the *Midland*, and Midwestern literature is richer and more clearly defined as a result.

**SELECTED WORKS:** Frederick published four college textbooks: *A Handbook of Short Story Writing* (1924), *Good Writing* (1922), *Reading for Writing* (1935, 1941), and *Present Day Stories* (1941), an anthology, with Leo L. Ward.

**FURTHER READING:** No book has yet been published about Frederick, but one will certainly appear. Other sources are Milton M. Reigelman's *The Midland* (1975) and CLARENCE A. ANDREW's *A Literary History of Iowa* (1972). *Current Biography* (1941) and *Contemporary Authors* 111 are additional sources of information.

DAVID D. ANDERSON    MICHIGAN STATE UNIVERSITY

## ALICE FRENCH

March 19, 1850–January 9, 1934
(Octave Thanet)

**BIOGRAPHY:** Alice French was born to George Henry and Frances Wood (Morton) French in Andover, Massachusetts. When she was six, her family moved to Davenport, Iowa, where her father became a partner in a lumber mill and was elected mayor in 1861, later serving as president of the First National Bank, the Davenport and St. Paul Railroad, and the Eagle Manufacturing Company.

French was educated in the Davenport public schools and briefly studied at Vassar before enrolling in Abbott Academy in Andover, graduating in 1868. Returning to Davenport, she began to write essays and fiction, publishing her first short story in the *Davenport Gazette* in 1871.

After a trip to Europe in 1874, French returned to Davenport to resume her writing, publishing short stories as Octave Thanet, a pen name she chose to conceal her gender from editors prejudiced against female authors. Ten years later she and her longtime companion Jane Allen Crawford established a winter home in Clover Bend, Arkansas. In 1894 French and her brother traveled to Chicago to witness the Pullman strike; she made use of this material in her best-known novel, *The Man of the Hour* (1905).

During the first decade of the twentieth century, French and Crawford continued to divide their time between Davenport and Clover Bend. In 1900 she became historian of the National Society of Colonial Dames and served as president of its Iowa chapter. Her other civic activities included war relief work and frequent speaking engagements on behalf of the anti-suffrage movement.

In 1911 she received an honorary doctorate from the University of Iowa, and in 1914 she traveled to Des Moines to participate in the Homecoming of Iowa Authors and Artists. She also represented her state at meetings of the Society of Midland Authors.

Chronically obese, Alice French suffered increasingly from health problems and died at age eighty-four, almost completely blind, partially deaf, impoverished, and obscure.

**SIGNIFICANCE:** Alice French's family was Episcopalian, Republican, conservative, and rich; her fiction reflects the social attitudes and political opinions she learned at her father's knee. Writing at a time when Freudian psychology, Marxist economics, and Darwin's theory of evolution stimulated many Midwestern authors, she demonstrates in her fiction the kind of unswerving adherence to convention that would prompt the next generation of Midwesterners to revolt from the village in record numbers; she opposes women's suffrage, the free-silver movement, trade unions, socialism, and higher education for blacks. Although issues of class, race, and gender frequently inform her fiction, she is unable to conceive of these issues as complex, many-sided, and replete with ambiguity. Her labor novel, *The Man of the Hour* (1905), chronicles the maturation of a manufacturer's son who flirts with trade unionism but finally comes to understand the futility of organized labor and believe that the workers' best hope lies in the benevolence of their capitalist employers. *By Inheritance* (1910), her novel on the race question, argues that blacks are mentally inferior to whites, capable of only a limited intellectual development, and better suited to menial occupations than the professions.

Perhaps Alice French can best be appreciated for those works which realistically depict life in a postbellum Iowa river town. *Stories of a Western Town* (1893) describes both a down-to-earth Davenport thriving with new industry and an exotic Davenport, transformed for the Fourth of July into a Midwestern Venice, with its cavalcade of lighted boats on the Mis-

Alice French.
Photo courtesy of Marcia Noe

sissippi. The six stories in this volume are linked, not only by their common setting but by the appearance in each of Harry Lossing, an up-and-coming businessman and politician. Lossing's character reflects the best of his Midwestern pioneer heritage: his eye is always on the main chance, yet his decision making is informed by compassion, integrity, and respect for others. *Stories of a Western Town* can be located within the local color school of fiction writing that began with Bret Harte and includes Kate Chopin and Sarah Orne Jewett. But while the work of the latter two authors often transcends the merely local, Alice French's fiction remains firmly rooted in the upper-middle-class, Middle Western lifestyle and mind-set of her day.

**SELECTED WORKS:** Alice French's six novels are *Expiation* (1890), *The Man of the Hour* (1905), *The Lion's Share* (1907), *By Inheritance* (1910), *A Step on the Stair* (1913), and *And the Captain Answered* (1917). She also published nine short story collections: *Knitters in the Sun* (1887), *Otto the Knight and Other Trans-Mississippi Stories* (1891), *Stories of a Western Town* (1893), *The Missionary Sheriff* (1897), *A Book of True Lovers* (1897), *A Slave to Duty and Other Women* (1898), *The Heart of Toil* (1898), *The Cap-*

*tured Dream and Other Stories* (1899), and *Stories That End Well* (1911).

**FURTHER READING:** The only book-length study of Alice French is George McMichael's *Journey to Obscurity: The Life of Octave Thanet* (1965). The Newberry Library is the main repository of her manuscripts.

MARCIA NOE
THE UNIVERSITY OF TENNESSEE AT CHATTANOOGA

## ALICE (RUTH) FRIMAN
October 20, 1933

**BIOGRAPHY:** Alice Ruth Pesner was born to Joseph Pesner and Helen (Friedman) Pesner in New York City. At Brooklyn College she earned a BA in elementary education in 1954. She married Elmer Friman in 1955, followed his job to Dayton, Ohio, in 1956, and in 1960 moved to Indianapolis, Indiana. Their children are H. Richard Friman, Paul Lawrence Friman, and Lillian Elaine Wilson. She was divorced in 1975 and in 1989 married Marshall Bruce Gentry.

She worked as a professional storyteller in Dayton and Indianapolis, then in 1964 began studying English at Indiana University–Indianapolis and Butler University. After receiving her MA in English from Butler in 1971, she taught at Indiana Central, now the University of Indianapolis, and briefly at Indiana University–Purdue University–Indianapolis. In 1990 she was promoted to professor at the University of Indianapolis. She has also taught creative writing at Indiana State, Ball State, and Curtin University in Perth, Australia. She now teaches workshops.

In 1976 she began reading her poetry at the Hummingbird Cafe open reading series founded by Etheridge Knight and Mary McAnally. Her first poetry collection, *A Question of Innocence*, appeared in 1978. In 1979 she helped found the Indiana Writers' Center, now the Writers' Center of Indianapolis, which in 1993 named her Honorary Life Member. Friman's poems have been published in nine countries, in more than a hundred magazines and anthologies, including *Poetry, Ohio Review, Prairie Schooner, Field, Georgia Review, Gettysburg Review, Boulevard, New Letters, Laurel Review*, and the Midwestern anthologies *Inheriting the Land* and *The Land-Locked Heart*. She has won three prizes from the Poetry Society of America, the 1990

Midwest Poetry Prize from the Society for the Study of Midwestern Literature, a 1996–97 Individual Artist Fellowship from the Indiana Arts Commission, and the Ezra Pound Poetry Award for 1997–98 from Truman State University for her forthcoming book *Zoo*.

**SIGNIFICANCE:** Friman considers herself to be in an argument with the Midwest, for her a place of order, conservatism, and complacency. In the poem "Cardiology" in *Inverted Fire*, she describes feeling "put here without provisions / like Gulliver in a strange place" (6). She is alienated from the Midwest, but it is a productive alienation. In the Midwest Friman found motivation to write, an audience, and freedom from family. A walk through a Midwestern landscape of weeds and an occasional tree can evoke memory and start a poem. The emptied landscape serves as setting for internal emotional conflict. As Cynthia Belmont writes in a review of *Insomniac Heart* in *Cream City Review* 16.1 (1992), Friman's poetry is "centered in a complex treatment of nature's relationship with human identity, absorbed with the struggles and harmonies between body and emotional self, within nature, between nature and self" (198–99). The paradoxical combination of orderliness and stormy emotion in her poetry reflects her tentative acceptance of life in the Midwest combined with frequent travel. Friman's attention to musicality leads Sandra (Adelmund) Witt to call her, in "Reading Like a River," *Iowa Woman* 11.3 (1991), "a master of sound" (46).

**SELECTED WORKS:** Friman's troubled response to the Midwest is apparent in all her collections. *A Question of Innocence* (1978) was followed by *Song to My Sister* (1979). Friman's first full-length book was *Reporting from Corinth* (1984). *Insomniac Heart* appeared in 1990 and *Driving for Jimmy Wonderland* in 1992. *Inverted Fire*, a second full-length book, was published in 1997. Friman's essay "Inking in the Myth," *Hopewell Review* 8 (1996–97): 55–59, discusses being a poet in the conservative Midwest. She edited *Loaves and Fishes: A Book of Indiana Women Poets* (1983).

**FURTHER READING:** Scott Vannatter's University of Indianapolis MA thesis, "Definitions of Freedom: The Poetry of Alice Friman," treats the first three collections. Friman is profiled in "Alice Friman: Poems from Behind the Piano" by Barbara Koons, *Arts Insight* (May 1985): 5. A recent interview is Brooke Horvath's "A Conversation" in *Canto* 5 (1992): 57–64. Horvath also reviews *Inverted Fire* in *Indiana Review* 20.2 (1997): 171–73.

MARSHALL BRUCE GENTRY

UNIVERSITY OF INDIANAPOLIS

## HENRY BLAKE FULLER
January 9, 1857–July 29, 1929

**BIOGRAPHY:** Henry Blake Fuller, novelist and critic, was born and lived most of his life in Chicago. Because his parents, George Fuller and Mary Josephine (Sanford) Fuller, were both from New England and had deep roots there, Fuller prided himself on being a lineal descendant of New England.

Fuller grew up in Chicago amid genteel surroundings. A growing dissatisfaction with the city caused him to attend school briefly in Wisconsin, but he returned to Chicago, where in 1876 he finished high school while working at a crockery store. Balking at his father's wishes, Fuller used his earnings three years later to make the first of several trips to Europe, where he stayed for over a year. This tour and a second, shorter, trip became the basis for his first two books, the travel romances *The Chevalier of Pensieri-Vani* (1890) and *The Chatelaine of La Trinité* (1892). In the 1880s Fuller had regularly contributed satirical sketches and short stories to an old humor magazine *Life* and to the *Chicago Tribune*, but it was his first book that opened the way to near-overnight fame.

During the 1890s Fuller was welcomed into the cultured circles that formed the first generation of the Chicago Renaissance. A regular at "Little Room" gatherings in the Fine Arts Building, he soon befriended writers HARRIET MONROE and HAMLIN GARLAND. Fuller's next book, the Chicago-based novel *The Cliff-Dwellers* (1893), surprised readers who expected another idyll of Europe with its caricatures of businessmen and bankers, its vision of the city's skyscraper architecture, and its energetic satires of Chicago's booster spirit. His next novel, *With the Procession* (1895), revisited Chicago locations, this time framing an elegiac study of the dispossession of the city's settlers before the Great Fire, the generation of his father and grandfather, by the boosterism of Chicago's status-conscious upward movement. Much of the novel's action focused on the efforts of an old Chicago family, the Marshalls, to recapture its social position in a city increasingly dominated by machine politics and the nouveaux riches.

Nothing Fuller wrote after 1895 rivaled the achievement of these two Chicago novels. His opposition to the Spanish-American War, expressed in the doggerel verse of *The New Flag* (1899), opened a rift between him and the hawkish members of the Little Room. *Under the Skylights* (1901), a collection of three novellas, represented his subsequent, if equivocal, effort to bridge his differences with friends and artists from the Little Room group. To compensate for his novels' lack of commercial success, a year earlier Fuller had begun writing editorials for the *Chicago Evening Post*, and afterward he turned increasingly to writing reviews and other editorial work for supplementary income, including yeoman's service for Monroe's *Poetry*.

Because of lukewarm reviews of his novel *The Last Refuge* (1900), Fuller vowed never to write another novel, but he did write four more, including *On the Stairs* (1918), a schematic reprise of the urban milieu he had already depicted in *The Cliff-Dwellers*. *Bertram Cope's Year* (1919), a delicate and understated treatment of homosexual relations, proved explicit enough for the times to dictate private publication. Fuller lived out his final and penurious years on Chicago's south side, in boardinghouses and one-room apartments. During the 1920s, he championed young writers including LOUIS BROMFIELD, SINCLAIR LEWIS, and GLENWAY WESCOTT. He died shortly after completing two novels, *Gardens of This World* (1929) and *Not on This Screen* (1930).

**SIGNIFICANCE:** Fuller stands first in a line of Chicago writers that extends from THEODORE DREISER and on to JAMES T. FARRELL and SAUL BELLOW. If *The Cliff-Dwellers* and *With the Procession* once aligned him with WILLIAM DEAN HOWELLS, his groundbreaking representations of social class and the city's economic forces won him homage from Dreiser, who saw Fuller as the "father of American realism" (Pilkington, *Henry Blake Fuller* 109). Despite his shyness and sly satiric manner, Fuller commanded a central position in the Chicago Renaissance. Contemporary readers placed him at the head of the Chicago School of fiction

that included GEORGE ADE, Will Payne, and ROBERT HERRICK. Split as he was between Chicago and a mythic New England or Italy, his work was more complex and contradictory than his readers generally imagined. An astute observer of Chicago's cultural growth, a chronicler of its precipitous social and political changes, a sometime proponent of reform and assimilation, he nevertheless found it difficult to express the emotional life of the city's new immigrant masses or to reach with empathy beyond his own social class. He found it nearly impossible to reckon with the changing sexual mores that, by the 1920s, evoked general and bland acceptance. He was conscious of his own limitations; he was sadly aware of his unending quarrel with Chicago. A master of parody and irony, an elegant if self-conscious stylist, Fuller sought out literary strategies and forms that distanced and insulated him from the hard facts of urban and modern life. *With the Procession* remains the most accessible of his many works.

**SELECTED WORKS:** Fuller's travel romances include *The Chevalier of Pensieri-Vani* (1890), *The Chatelaine of La Trinité* (1892), and *The Last Refuge: A Sicilian Romance* (1900). His best novels and short fiction treat Chicago: *The Cliff-Dwellers* (1893), *With the Procession* (1895), *Under the Skylights* (1901), and *On the Stairs* (1918). On occasion, he tried his hand at poetry: *The New Flag: Satires* (1899) and *Lines Long and Short* (1917). Among his many editorials and essays, these are representative: "The Upward Movement in Chicago," *Atlantic Monthly* 80 (October 1897): 534–47; "Art in America," *Bookman* 10 (November 1899): 218–24; "The Melting Pot Begins to Smell," *New York Times Book Review* 21 (December 1924): 2; and "Howells or James?," edited by Darrel Abel, *Modern Fiction Studies* 3 (Summer 1957): 159–64.

**FURTHER READING:** Critical studies of Fuller and his work include Bernard Bowron Jr.'s *Henry Blake Fuller of Chicago: The Ordeal of a Genteel Realist in Ungenteel America* (1974); William Dean Howells's "Certain of the Chicago School of Fiction," in *North American Review* 176 (May 1903): 734–46; and John Pilkington Jr.'s *Henry Blake Fuller* (1970). Kenneth Scambray's *A Varied Harvest: The Life and Works of Henry Blake Fuller* (1987) stands as the most complete biography to date; in the book he gives the first serious attention to Fuller's homosexuality and how it may have affected the themes and plots of several of his works, including *The Cliff-Dwellers* and *Bertram Cope's Year*. For understanding Fuller's place in the Chicago Renaissance, see BERNARD DUFFEY's *The Chicago Renaissance in American Letters: A Critical History* (1956) and KENNY J. WILLIAMS's *In the City of Men: Another Story of Chicago* (1974). The Newberry Library in Chicago holds the largest single collection of Fuller manuscript material.

GUY SZUBERLA                    UNIVERSITY OF TOLEDO

## IOLA FULLER (GOODSPEED MCCOY)
January 25, 1906

**BIOGRAPHY:** Iola Fuller was born in Marcellus, Michigan, the daughter of Henry and Clara (Reynolds) Fuller. At the University of Michigan, where she won an Avery Hopwood Award (1939) for her novel *The Loon Feather* (1940), she received an AB (1935), an AM in English (1940), and an AM in library science (1962); she later won a Distinguished Alumnus Award (1967). She worked as a librarian, taught English at Ferris State College, and taught library science at Clarion State College. She is married to Raymond McCoy and has one son, Paul Goodspeed, from her earlier marriage.

**SIGNIFICANCE:** The narrator of Fuller's first novel, *The Loon Feather*, is Oneta, the daughter of Tecumseh. Set mainly on Mackinac Island, the book treats the relations between the Ojibways and the French trappers, fishermen, traders, and military contingent on Mackinac Island, as well as the Native Americans' unsuccessful attempts to unify themselves against the encroachment of the immigrants. *The Shining Trail* (1943) picks up the latter theme a few generations later, as BLACK HAWK tragically fails at holding his Sauk tribe together in the face of pioneers homesteading on their land on the banks of the Mississippi in what is now western Illinois. Tomah, Black Hawk's fellow chief and friend, narrates the pursuit and destruction of the entire tribe. *The Gilded Torch* (1957) relates how the explorer La Salle claimed the Louisiana Territory. The novel follows his route up the St. Lawrence River, back and forth through the Great Lakes as he was beset by various hardships, thence by river and overland to the Mississippi to discover its mouth. His relationships with traders and trappers, missionaries, and particularly with the Pottawatomie, Illinois, and Iroquois tribes along the way suggest the effects the explorers and early colonizers had upon the Northwest Territory. These three of Fuller's four novels, all of which are historical, deal with the history of the exploration and settling of the Midwest, particularly in relation to the impact on the Native American tribes.

**SELECTED WORKS:** Fuller's Midwestern novels are *The Loon Feather* (1940) and *The Shining Trail* (1943); *The Gilded Torch* (1957) takes place there as well as in Canada and south to Louisiana. The action of *All the Golden Gifts* (1966) occurs primarily in the court of Louis XIV.

**FURTHER READING:** No book-length studies and few articles have appeared on Fuller, although mention of her books appears regularly in works on Michigan writers, such as ROBERT BEASECKER's *Michigan in the Novel 1816–1996* (1998), Carol Smallwood's *Michigan Authors* (1993), and Albert G. Black's *Michigan Novels: An Annotated Bibliography* (1963).

MARY DEJONG OBUCHOWSKI

CENTRAL MICHIGAN UNIVERSITY

# G

## WANDA (HAZEL) GÁG
March 11, 1893–June 27, 1946

**BIOGRAPHY:** Artist and author/illustrator of children's books, Wanda Gág was born in New Ulm, Minnesota, to Anton and Elisabeth (Biebl) Gág, both of Central European ancestry. With her father an artist and her mother's family cabinetmakers and painters, it was not surprising that Gág's artistic talents emerged early. After her father's death in 1908, Wanda, as the oldest of seven children, helped support her German-speaking family by selling her drawings and stories to *Journal Junior*, a supplement of the *Minneapolis Journal*.

She graduated from New Ulm High School in 1912, and after teaching for one year, she studied at the St. Paul Institute of Arts and the Minneapolis School of Art. Her mother died in 1917, the same year that Gág received a scholarship to study at the Art Students' League in New York City.

As an artist Gág exhibited her etchings, woodcuts, ink drawings, and lithographs to much praise, but she received greater financial success with her illustrated children's books, beginning with *Millions of Cats* (1928), a book which has been translated into many languages. Gág followed that book with three very successful picture books and then illustrated and retold a folktale based upon a story told by her grandmother. This was *Gone Is Gone: The Story of a Man Who Wanted to Do Housework* (1935). The illustrations were remembered scenes from her New Ulm childhood.

Gág remained close to her family, especially to her youngest sister, Flavia, also a writer and illustrator of children's books. In 1943 Wanda married Earle Marshall Humphreys, a salesman who had lived with Gág in New Jersey, on a farm they called "All Creation." Gág died in a New York City hospital in 1946, having been diagnosed with lung cancer in February 1945.

**SIGNIFICANCE:** Like so many other Midwesterners, Gág felt that to succeed as an artist she needed to live in the New York City area. In her book *Wanda Gág* (1994), Karen Nelson Hoyle quotes from a letter in which Gág notes that several of her siblings moved to New York and "have been rescued from the insidious middle-class Minneapolis grip . . ." (23). Gág may have left Minnesota, but she retained a strong sense of place and a love of the countryside. Of *Gone Is Gone: The Story of a Man Who Wanted to Do Housework* (1935), Karen

Hoyle writes that the characters were based upon Gág's memories of the immigrant peoples of New Ulm (63).

Gág's Midwestern background, too, stimulated her interest in the tales of the Brothers Grimm, reading them in German to keep up with her childhood language. Her successful, illustrated *Snow White and the Seven Dwarfs* (1938) grew out of this activity, as did her *Tales from Grimm* (1936).

Most of Gág's picture books have remained in print, and although she never received a Newbery or Caldecott Medal for her books, several of her books were runners-up or Honor Books, and children and adults have found her works memorable.

Gag's autobiography, *Growing Pains: Diaries and Drawings for the Years 1908–1917* (1940), gives a remarkable account of a girl growing up in New Ulm, Minnesota, a girl who spoke no English until she entered school, a girl growing up into an artist.

**SELECTED WORKS:** Other children's books by Gág include *The Funny Thing* (1929), *Snippy and Snappy* (1931), *The ABC Bunny* (1933), *Snow White and the Seven Dwarfs* (1938), and *Nothing at All* (1941).

**FURTHER READING:** Karen Nelson Hoyle's *Wanda Gág* (1994) is a thorough, book-length critical biography of Gág. It examines her primary work and includes a selected bibliography of both primary and secondary sources, including a detailed description of the location of Gág's papers and other materials. The University of Minnesota has a large Gág collection.

An earlier and important book was written by Gág's childhood friend, Alma Scott. This is *Wanda Gág: The Story of an Artist* (1949). A more recent study concentrates on Gág as artist. This is Audur H. Winnan's *Wanda Gag: A Catalogue Raisonné of the Prints* (1993), with a foreword by David W. Kiehl. Winnan writes that Gág's work is " . . . among the most intriguing bodies of graphic art in this century" (67). This book contains many of Gág's most beautiful and interesting prints, and it also contains selected letters and diary entries from the Van Pelt Library of the University of Pennsylvania, a collection of " . . . over 100 volumes of Gág's diaries, notebooks, daybooks as well as voluminous correspondence, papers, and memorabilia" (206).

PATRICIA A. ANDERSON          DIMONDALE, MICHIGAN

## ZONA GALE
### August 26, 1874–December 27, 1938

**BIOGRAPHY:** Zona Gale, novelist, poet, short story writer, and dramatist, was born and lived most of her life in Portage, Wisconsin, the setting for nearly all of her fiction. She was the only child of Charles and Eliza (Beers) Gale, and she was encouraged by both parents to write and continue her education in a period that expected women to stay within the traditional confines of their roles as wife and mother. Gale attended the University of Wisconsin, earning a bachelor's degree in 1895 and a master's degree in literature in 1899. In 1895 she joined the editorial staff of Milwaukee's *Evening Wisconsin* and later the *Milwaukee Journal*. In 1901 she moved to New York City, becoming a reporter for the *New York Evening World* while writing stories for publication. She published her first novel, *Romance Island*, in 1906, but she became more widely known for her series of Friendship Village stories set in a thinly disguised Portage, Wisconsin. In all, she wrote thirty-four published volumes of stories, novels, plays, and essays, including one volume of poetry, *The Secret Way* (1921). She was awarded the Pulitzer Prize in 1921 for her dramatic treatment of *Miss Lulu Bett*, her 1920 novel which rivaled SINCLAIR LEWIS'S *Main Street* on the best-seller lists that year.

Gale was active in numerous progressive causes including women's suffrage, the Women's Peace Party, Robert La Follette's progressive campaign, and other social reform efforts. She was close to JANE ADDAMS and Charlotte Perkins Gilman, arranging for the publication of *The Living of Charlotte Perkins Gilman* and writing a foreword to the book in 1935. Always generous with other writers, especially those who were young and unpublished, she established scholarships at the University of Wisconsin for students who showed creative potential.

Though she traveled widely, Gale returned to Portage frequently to be with her parents. She was especially close to her mother, whose death in 1923 was traumatic for Gale and prompted a mystical strain in her work. Gale married Portage banker Will Breese in 1928, keeping her maiden name and adopting a daughter, Leslyn. She continued to write well into the next decade. She died of pneumonia in December 1938.

**SIGNIFICANCE:** In spite of the fact that Gale

has been virtually lost to modern readers, she was widely acclaimed during her lifetime, and compared to Sinclair Lewis, Ellen Glasgow, WILLA CATHER, and Eugene O'Neill. CARL VAN DOREN, in *Contemporary American Novelists* (1922), included Gale, along with SHERWOOD ANDERSON, EDGAR LEE MASTERS, and FLOYD DELL, as a writer in revolt from the sentimentalized village of traditional American fiction. While it is true that Gale's Midwestern stories convey an awareness of the foibles of small-town life, it was a misreading of her work to say she was in revolt against small-town values. Her work celebrates the sometimes primitive democratic and community-oriented values of small-town life. It was only when the community or family turned its back on an individual, as in *Birth* or *Miss Lulu Bett,* that she was critical. Two biographers, AUGUST DERLETH and Harold Simonson, place her as a Midwestern writer of the first rank, but there are few contemporary assessments of Gale's work. Historians June Sochen and Frederick Hoffman both mention Gale in their studies of 1920s literature, and Hoffman correctly notes that of all the village writers, "only Zona Gale may honestly be said to have loved the Midwestern metaphor" as representing the most admirable qualities in American small-town life (*The Twenties* 375). From the gentle satire of the Friendship Village stories to the realism of *Birth* and *Miss Lulu Bett,* Gale's work, rooted in a small Midwestern town but celebrating universal values of love and community, deserves to be rediscovered and reclaimed.

**SELECTED WORKS:** Only a few of Gale's novels have been reprinted: *Peace in Friendship Village* (1919), *Miss Lulu Bett* (1920), and *Birth* (1918); her remaining work may be found in libraries and used bookshops, primarily in the Midwest. The Friendship Village series of stories and books best exemplifies Gale's lighter touch with village life; the novels *Preface to a Life* (1926), *Faint Perfume* (1923), *Birth* (1918), and *Miss Lulu Bett* (1920) explore the darker side. Other short story collections include *Yellow Gentians and Blue* (1927) and *Old Fashioned Tales* (1933). Her political and reflective essays include *Portage Wisconsin and Other Essays* (1928) and *What Women Won in Wisconsin* (1922). Gale published one volume of poetry, *The Secret Way* (1921).

**FURTHER READING:** Two biographies of Gale exist: August Derleth's *Still Small Voice* was written and published soon after Gale's death (1940), and Harold Simonson's *Zona Gale* appeared in 1961. A summary of Gale's life and work by Nancy Breitsprecher is included in *American Women Writers: A Critical Reference Guide,* and WILLIAM MAXWELL wrote a moving tribute to Gale in *Yale Review* 76 (1987): 221–25, based on his childhood memories of her. Gale's papers may be found in the State Historical Society of Wisconsin, the Portage Library, and the Ridgely Torrence Collection in the Princeton University Library.

PAMELA NEAL WARFORD        GEORGETOWN COLLEGE

## ROBERT EDWARD GARD
July 3, 1910–December 7, 1992
(Bob Gard)

**BIOGRAPHY:** Educator, playwright, folklorist, and juvenile writer, Robert Edward Gard, better known as Bob Gard, was born in Iola, Kansas, to Samuel Arnold and Louisa Maria (Ireland) Gard. He earned a BA from the University of Kansas in 1934 and an MA from Cornell in 1938. In 1939 he married Maryo Kimball, who bore him two daughters, Maryo Gwendolyn and Eleanor Copeland.

Although Gard taught in Kansas and New York state early in his academic career, he became so rooted in Wisconsin life and lore at the University of Wisconsin, Madison, where he taught from 1945 until his retirement in 1981, that it is hard to associate him with any other state. Active in community and state organizations, he became director of the Wisconsin Idea Theatre, a statewide grassroots theater project, from 1945 on, president of the Wisconsin Arts Foundation and Council from 1957 through 1959, president of the Wisconsin Regional Writers Association from 1961 to 1964, president and editor of Wisconsin House Publications, Madison, in 1969, and cofounder of the Dale Wasserman Professional Playwright Development Laboratory at Madison in 1976. He wrote more than forty books, including regional plays and narratives (historical, legendary, and folkloristic), studies of regional theater in America, and juvenile fiction.

Following his Fulbright Professorship at the University of Helsinki in 1959–60, he was awarded the Gold Medal of Honor from the Finnish Theatre in 1961. His numerous Wisconsin honors and citations include the Governor's Award for creativity in 1967 and the Wisconsin local history award. He died in Madison at age eighty-two.

**SIGNIFICANCE:** Both as a teacher of writing and as a writer, Gard was a dedicated regionalist. The region he came to know best was the Midwest, specifically Wisconsin. In his capacity as regional writer-in-residence at the University of Wisconsin, he encouraged his many devoted students to write from their experience, and he practiced what he preached in such books as *Wisconsin Is My Doorstep: A Dramatist's Yarn Book of Wisconsin Lore* (1948); *Wisconsin Lore, Antics and Anecdotes of Wisconsin People and Places* (1962); and *Down in the Valleys: Wisconsin Back Country Lore and Humor* (1971). Seeking, like Thoreau at Walden Pond, the universal in the particulars of the region where he happened to live, Gard was by no means a narrow regionalist, as indicated by his book *Grassroots Theater: A Search for Regional Arts in America* (1955), by his chairmanship of the National Theatre Conference Appraisal Project in 1962, and by his founding of the Playwright's Workshop in Finland in the early 1960s. In addition to fostering the development of regional drama and folklore studies, Gard wrote juvenile fiction, mostly with sharply etched regional settings.

**SELECTED WORKS:** A representative selection of Gard's better-known contributions to the study of regional theater, and to drama, folklore, and juvenile fiction, includes the following: *Wisconsin Is My Doorstep* (1948); *Wisconsin Lore* (1962); *Grassroots Theater: A Search for Regional Arts in America* (1955); *Let's Get on with the Marryin'* and *Mixing up the Rent* in Alexander Drummond's *The Lake Guns of Seneca and Cayuga, and Eight Other Plays of Upstate New York* (1942); *Down in the Valleys: Wisconsin Back Country Lore and Humor* (1971); and the juvenile *A Horse Named Joe* (1956). Gard also wrote a novel in collaboration with Allen Crafton entitled *A Woman of No Importance* (1974).

**FURTHER READING:** Gard is briefly included among *Authors of Books for Young People* (1990). His obituary appeared in the December 8, 1992, *Chicago Tribune* (sec. 1:10). His papers are at the State Historical Society of Wisconsin, Madison; in the permanent collection of the University of Alberta Humanities and Social Sciences Library, Edmonton, Alberta,

Canada; and at the Steenbock Memorial Library, University of Wisconsin–Madison.

PAUL W. MILLER　　　　WITTENBERG UNIVERSITY

## (HANNIBAL) HAMLIN GARLAND
September 14, 1860–March 4, 1940

**BIOGRAPHY:** Hannibal Hamlin Garland was born on a farm near West Salem, Wisconsin, and died in Hollywood, California. His life was constant movement: westward with his restless and westering father; eastward in search of the civilization he associated with his maternal roots; back to the Middle Border to recover the source of what would be his best work; and then—like VACHEL LINDSAY, WILLA CATHER, and so many other American writers—westward again to an essentially foreign landscape and mythology which Garland never quite assimilated.

Richard Garland, Hamlin's father, left his Wisconsin farm for service in the Civil War two years after Hamlin was born. He returned at the war's end ill, disillusioned, a stranger to his son and nearly to his wife. He had barely reentered the social fabric, which included the extended family of his wife, Isabelle McClintock, when he moved in 1869, first to Minnesota, then to Mitchell County, Iowa, working a series of farms before homesteading near Osage, Iowa. Later in life, Hamlin recalled breaking prairie as a lad of nine. When in 1876 Richard became grain buyer for the Osage elevator and moved to town, Hamlin enrolled in Cedar Valley Seminary, his first real taste of culture: oratory, literature, music. But the man renting Richard's farm proved inept, and on March 27, 1877, it was back to the farm for the Garlands. Hamlin persisted in his education, graduating from Cedar Valley Seminary in 1881, the year his father moved west again to the Dakota Territory.

Hamlin did not accompany the others. He attempted to find a teaching position in several Iowa and Minnesota towns, failed, joined the family long enough to help erect a house, then headed East with his brother Franklin. This first excursion ended in disillusionment, with the brothers failing miserably in their attempt to find farm work in the Connecticut River Valley. Hamlin then returned to South Dakota to take up a claim of his own. His recollection in *A Son of the Middle Border* of a win-

Hamlin Garland.
Used by permission of Victoria Doyle-Jones

ter night on that claim is one of the great descriptions of a Midwest blizzard in American literature: temperature near forty below, the frail shanty quivering in the wind like a frightened hare, fine crystals of snow sifting down as though driven through solid boards (309–12). Determined to be done with pioneering, Garland sold his claim for two hundred dollars. He headed East once more, "absolutely alone," as he recalled in *A Son of the Middle Border*, "hungry all the time" to spend long days in the Boston library reading Darwin, Spencer, Whitman, and even the early English poets (321). Eventually Garland found employment at the Boston School of Oratory, lectured occasionally, and wrote nonfiction depictions of prairie life for *New American Magazine*. The year 1887 was pivotal for Garland: encouraged by WILLIAM DEAN HOWELLS, he returned to Iowa and South Dakota partly to visit his family and former friends, partly to gather material for his writing. He met JOSEPH KIRKLAND, whose work provided a model for his "western" fiction, and whose

stories drove him to write the realistic rural fictions which made him famous. These stories appeared first in reformist magazines including the *Arena*, then as *Main-Travelled Roads* (1891). Throughout the early 1890s, Garland spoke eloquently and angrily on subjects literary and political, observing and assisting the transformation of the Grange to the Farmer's Alliance to the Populist Party. His novel *A Spoil of Office* (1892) recounts this political development among the farmers of the upper Midwest.

In 1893 Garland moved to Chicago, drawn by the World's Columbian Exposition and intent on countering Mary Hartwell Catherwood's Romantic school of local color with his own literary "veritism," a testament to the grim realities he had known as a youth and rediscovered in 1887. Out of Garland's Chicago years came *Crumbling Idols: Twelve Essays on Art* (1894) and his best novel, *Rose of Dutcher's Coolly* (1895). The acorn, however, does not fall far from the oak: Garland soon found himself on the road again, traveling throughout the Eastern states while writing a two-volume biography of Ulysses S. Grant published by McClure in 1898. In 1898 Garland traveled overland to the Klondike and in 1899 to England. In the year 1899, he also married Zulime Taft, the sister of Chicago sculptor Lorado Taft, and published *Boy Life on the Prairie*. This book he had developed from a series of articles written at age twenty-seven for the *American Magazine* in an attempt, as he stated in his preface, to "relive the splendid days of the unbroken prairie-lands of northern Iowa."

Gradually Garland's focus shifted to the far West. A string of commercially successful but artistically mediocre novels ensued. The pattern was serial publication followed by book publication. These romances were filled with melodramatic plots, stereotypical characters, and occasional reflections of Garland's affinity with Indians and the Western working class. Garland's mother died in 1900. His father died in 1914. Each year Garland published a new book, but none of them matched either *Main-Travelled Roads* or *Rose of Dutcher's Coolly*. In 1916 Garland moved East, to New York, while refocusing his writing on the Midwest of his boyhood. *A Son of the Middle Border*, part of which had run as an article in *Collier's*, appeared in 1917. The book was not an immediate success but eventually drew audiences both public and literary. In 1918 Garland was elected to the American Academy of Arts and Letters. In 1921 he published *A Daughter of the Middle Border*, for which he received a Pulitzer Prize. A sequence of Middle Border celebrations and literary reminiscences followed, continuing through an honorary degree from the University of Wisconsin in 1926, a move to Los Angeles in 1930, and another honorary degree from Northwestern University in 1933. Garland also began exploring psychic phenomena and the occult. His final books, published in 1936 and 1939, were titled *Forty Years of Psychic Research* and *The Mystery of the Buried Crosses*.

**SIGNIFICANCE:** It is difficult indeed for any writer in America, and especially for a radical writer, to support himself and his family. Garland is to be forgiven his many commercialisms and excursions, and to be judged by those books mined from his true subject matter, namely his life on the Middle Border. Despite Robert Gish's reassessment of the Western novels, Garland's reputation as an American author is based almost exclusively on *Main-Travelled Roads*, *Rose of Dutcher's Coolly*, and *A Son of the Middle Border*.

Garland's message is most succinctly stated at the close of chapter 28 of *A Son of the Middle Border*, the summation of his 1887 visit to Wisconsin, Iowa, and Dakota: "Obscurely forming in my mind were two great literary concepts—that truth was a higher quality than beauty, and that to spread the reign of justice should everywhere be the design and intent of the artist. The merely beautiful in art seemed petty, and success at the cost of the happiness of others a monstrous egotism" (374).

Garland's main theme, then, is the truth of rural life. In his stories, rural life is harsh indeed, and those who stick it out discover, with Grant in "Up the Coulee," "that life's a failure for ninety-nine percent of us" (97). Those who send themselves, or their money, elsewhere often become easily, mysteriously successful; but women who remain become, like Agnes in "A Branch Road," too soon worn and wasted incredibly; and men, like Ed Smith in a story based upon his father's return from the Civil War, fight a daily, running, hopeless battle "against nature and against the injustice of their fellow man" (140). At worst they dwindle to garrulous caricature; at best

they rise to a magnificent but weathered type: Garland's vision is bifocal here as in so many other places.

The landscape too has its stringent beauty. "Nature was as beautiful as ever," he notes in *A Son of the Middle Border* of the 1887 visit (365). The sentiment is echoed a hundred other places in his stories and reminiscences. Garland's eloquent description of the west of southwest wind blowing on Chicago, "full of smell of unmeasured miles of growing grain in summer, or ripening corn and wheat in autumn" (*Roads* 207) is lyric, a warm balance to the blizzards of *Boy Life on the Prairie* and *A Son of the Middle Border*.

Human nature as well shows two faces in Garland's stories. For every banker, merchant, and politician who "farms the farmer" (*Son* 415), ten honest men labor heroically to support themselves and their dependants. The quintessential Garland story in this regard is "Under the Lion's Paw," in which the Haskins family, its crops devoured by grasshoppers in four successive Kansas harvests, is compensated upon its return to Iowa by a series of bountiful harvests which restore all it lost and more. Haskins is assisted by farmer Stephen Council, only to be robbed at last by landowner Jim Butler.

Hard as Garland's farmers have it, their wives have things worse. Always a mama's boy, Garland associated culture—music, poetry, literature, the East—with his mother's family and resented his father's constant uprooting of his wife, who was "not by nature an emigrant—few women are" (*Son* 43). Accordingly, Garland emphasizes the stress frontier life put on women and the heroic character of those women who bore it. "I perceived beautiful youth becoming bowed and bent," he writes of the 1887 visit (365); "I saw lovely girlhood wasting away into thin and hopeless age. Some of the women I had known had withered into querulous and complaining spinsterhood, and I heard ambitious youth cursing the bondage of the farm" (*Son* 365). In something of a shock ending for an 1891 story, Will convinces Agnes in "A Branch Road" to leave her husband, bring her child, and run away with him to the far West—a plan for renewal which, the story's conclusion makes clear, Nature approves. In another shock ending, "A Good Fellow's Wife" saves her husband from being lynched by a mob angry over the failure of his bank, starts a store of her own to sustain the family during his convalescence from a stroke, and finally, after his investments in "the copper country" pay off and he redeems himself, declines release from her little shop and return to standard married life. "Let's begin again, as equal partners," she suggests. In accepting her offer, Sanford acknowledges her status as an independent woman.

**SELECTED WORKS:** Garland's major works are *Main-Travelled Roads* (1891), *A Spoil of Office* (1892), *Prairie Songs* (1893), *Crumbling Idols: Twelve Essays on Art* (1894), *Rose of Dutcher's Coolly* (1895), *Boy Life on the Prairie* (1899), *A Son of the Middle Border* (1917), *A Daughter of the Middle Border* (1921), *The Book of the American Indian* (1923), *The Westward March of American Settlement* (1927), *Prairie Song and Western Writer* (1928), *Companions on the Trail* (1931), and *Iowa, O Iowa* (1935).

**FURTHER READING:** Donald Pizer's study *Hamlin Garland's Early Work and Career* (1960) is nicely balanced by Robert Gish's *Hamlin Garland: The Far West* (1976). Useful collections of criticism include James Nagel's *Critical Essays on Hamlin Garland* (1982) and Richard Boudreau, Charles Silet, and Robert Welch's *The Critical Reception of Hamlin Garland, 1891–1978* (1985). Garland's papers are at the University of Southern California.

DAVID PICHASKE     SOUTHWEST STATE UNIVERSITY

## WILLIAM H(OWARD) GASS
July 30, 1924

**BIOGRAPHY:** Driven by economic hardships, parents William Bernard and Claire (Sorensen) Gass moved from Fargo, North Dakota, to Warren, Ohio, just six months after William H. Gass was born. Gass's father taught engineering drawing in Warren but returned with his family to North Dakota during summers to play semi-professional baseball. William H. Gass interrupted his education at Kenyon College to join the military during World War II. Returning to Kenyon, Gass learned about the New Criticism from John Crowe Ransom and adopted some of Ransom's formalist views. He received his BA in philosophy in 1947 and began teaching philosophy at Wooster College in Ohio. During his tenure at Wooster, Gass married his first wife, Mary Patricia O'Kelley, with whom he had three children, Richard,

William H. Gass.
Photo courtesy of William H. Gass

Robert, and Susan. Meanwhile, his graduate studies at Cornell University focused on the philosophy of language and the theory of metaphorical models and culminated in a PhD in 1954.

William Gass began teaching at Purdue University in 1954. His reading of Gertrude Stein led to experimentation in recursive writing methods and to a collection of short stories published in *Accent Magazine* in 1958. Gass's first novel, *Omensetter's Luck*, was published in 1966. Soon after came the publication of *Willie Masters' Lonesome Wife* (1968), a novella, and a collection of short stories, *In the Heart of the Heart of the Country* (1968). In 1969 Gass became a professor of philosophy at Washington University in St. Louis and married Mary Alice Henderson, with whom he had twin daughters, Elizabeth and Catherine. A collection of essays, *Fiction and the Figures of Life* (1970), demonstrated Gass's aesthetic beliefs. *On Being Blue* (1976), a book-length essay, explained the relationship between words and the world. Two collections of essays, *The World within the Word* (1978) and *Habitations of the Word* (1985), featured essays previously published in other publications. His latest work of fiction, *The Tunnel* (1994), centered on the theme of the extermination of the Jews. Gass's most recent essays were collected in a volume entitled *Finding a Form: Essays* (1996). Gass has also written critical essays on Gertrude Stein and Sigmund Freud. He received a Rockefeller Foundation grant in 1966, a Guggenheim Foundation grant in 1969–70, and the National Institute of Arts and Letters Prize in literature in 1975. He was the recipient of the Society for the Study of Midwestern Literature's 1994 Mark Twain Award for distinguished contributions to Midwestern literature.

**SIGNIFICANCE:** William H. Gass is better known as critic than as fiction writer. *Fiction and the Figures of Life*, *The World within the Word*, and his philosophical inquiry *On Being Blue* analyze the ramifications of formal literary constructions that move beyond the conventions of realistic fiction. While emphasizing the importance of the author in the process of creating metaphors, Gass insists that fiction is distinct from the real world. Through the medium of art, Gass believes, the reader can effectively change his or her perception of the world. Thus, Gass invites his readers to experience the sensuous elements of language. Gass's criticism deals with the issues of modernism and postmodernism, metaphor, aesthetic construction, and the nature of style.

Gass experiments with literary styles, creating intricate and challenging fiction which demonstrates how works of art insist on their own absolute reality. He builds each story around a central metaphor and usually describes aspects of small Midwestern towns. His narrators are often transformed by discovering within themselves the same provincial elements they are revealing about their communities. Gass often focuses on the contrast between the hostile outside world and the world created by the artist. In *Omensetter's Luck*, set in a small Midwestern river town in the 1890s, Gass depicts the protagonist, Brackett Omensetter, as a kind of prelapsarian Adam whose naturalness results in isolation. *In the Heart of the Heart of the Country* is a collection of stories that explores the creative power of the imagination in spite of alienation. The novella *Willie Masters' Lonesome Wife* departs from traditional conventions of plot while focusing on the physical experience of language. Gass refrains from stereotyping the Midwest as a repressive, narrow environment. Instead, he provides original characterizations that sometimes employ several narrators and narrative styles. Although Gass's fiction has been well received by critics, it has achieved little popular success.

**SELECTED WORKS:** Critical works by William Gass include *Fiction and the Figures of Life* (1970), *On Being Blue* (1976), *The World within the Word* (1978), and *Habitations of the Word* (1985). His fiction includes *Omensetter's Luck* (1966), *Willie Masters' Lonesome Wife* (1968), and a short story collection entitled *In the Heart of the Heart of the Country*. *The Tunnel*, parts of which have been published in periodicals, was completed for publication as a book in 1994.

**FURTHER READING:** Critical appraisals of William H. Gass's work include *The Fiction of William Gass: The Consolation of Language* (1986), by Arthur M. Saltzman; *William Gass* (1990), by Watson L. Holloway; *Rethinking Character in Fiction: A Refutation of William Gass* (1983), by Vincent P. Lisella; and *The Metafictional Muse: The Works of Robert Coover, Donald Barthelme, and William H. Gass* (1982), by Larry McCaffery. Articles on Gass include Bruce Bassoff's "The Sacrificial World of William Gass: In the Heart of the Heart of the Country," in *Critique* 18 (1976): 36–58; Ned French's "Against the Grain: Theory and Practice in the Work of William H. Gass," in *Iowa Review* 7 (1976): 96–107, including a bibliography; and Richard J. Schneider's "The Fortunate Fall in William Gass's *Omensetter's Luck*," *Critique* 18 (1976): 5–20. Gass's papers are collected at the Washington University Library.

RUSSELL J. BODI        OWENS COLLEGE

## DAN GERBER
August 12, 1940

**BIOGRAPHY:** Dan Gerber, poet, novelist, story writer, and journalist, was born into the family that turned a Fremont, Michigan, canning and grocery business into Gerber Products, Inc., the world's largest producer of baby food. As son of Daniel Frank Gerber and Dorothy Marian (Scott) Gerber, he was expected to succeed his grandfather and father in the presidency of the firm. Though he worked for the company for two years and eventually accepted a position on the board of directors, he declined to pursue a full-time career in business. After completing a degree at Michigan State University, he nurtured

**Dan Gerber.**
Photo by Robert Turney. Courtesy of Dan Gerber

two other interests: writing and race car driving. His short but successful experience as a driver ended with a near fatal crash in 1966. He subsequently taught high school and college English and founded the magazine *Sumac* and the press by the same name with JIM HARRISON, whom he had known at Michigan State. Together they published some of the most notable writing of the late 1960s and early 1970s. Having raised three children in Fremont, Gerber and his wife, Virginia (Hartjen), divorced in 1992; she died in 1995. Since marrying the former Debra West in 1996, he has divided his time between Key West, Florida, and southeastern Idaho.

**SIGNIFICANCE:** The substantial portion of Gerber's writing that depicts small-town and rural locations and people places him in a Midwestern tradition harkening back to SHERWOOD ANDERSON and WILLA CATHER. Like Anderson, Gerber abandoned great expectations for success in business in order to pursue writing. He is first and foremost a poet, one who combines a transcendental vision of nature with constant awareness of life's fragility and ephemerality. In this regard his work bears a kinship not only with Whitman, Emerson, and Thoreau (each of whom he cites in his writing) but with Midwesterners THEODORE ROETHKE, ROBERT BLY, JAMES WRIGHT, and William Stafford.

Gerber's writing often dwells on the tenuousness of human relationships and the difficulty of communication, particularly between family members. Grief following or anticipating the loss of loved ones by death, divorce, or disagreement is a frequent theme, as in "The Tragedy of Action," which considers "death a robber of pleasure, / this bed a preview, / the fate of our children, / the last bath, the last meal, the last click" (*Last Bridge* 80). Characters in his fiction, most of which is set in fictional versions of Fremont, Michigan, frequently face the spectre of this mutability. The protagonist of Gerber's first novel, the comic *American Atlas* (1973) for example, responds to his father's death by leaving his family and inheritance of a large Michigan pie company to travel with a lover around the United States. The stories in *Grass Fires* (1987) are told by residents of a fictional Michigan town who cope with various forms of loneliness and inarticulation. Consolation and grace in Gerber's fiction, as in his poetry, is found in aesthetic contemplation, epiphanies in nature, memories, moments of love, art, literature, and music. In *A Voice from the River* (1990), the retired chairman of a Michigan lumber company reviews his life: his service in World War II, his stewardship of the lumber firm, his failed marriage and troubled relationships with his children, and an autumnal love affair with his daughter-in-law. Alluding to Thoreau in the book's last sentence, this character speaks for the author when he asks "Who am I . . . that this world has disappointed me?" (196). Gerber's writing answers this question by affirming life's beauty and spiritual significance.

**SELECTED WORKS:** Gerber has disavowed his first book, *The Waiting* (under the name Daniel F. Gerber Jr., 1966), as an apprentice piece. His subsequent books of poetry are *The Revenant* (1971); *Departure* (1973); *The Chinese Poems: Letters to a Distant Friend* (1978); *Snow on the Backs of Animals* (1986); *A Last Bridge Home: New and Selected Poems* (1992), which contains the best of the previous four volumes; and his last work, *The Trees, the Grass, the Leaves, the River* (1999). His works of fiction are *American Atlas* (1973), *Out of Control* (1974), *Grass Fires* (stories; 1987), and *A Voice from the River* (1990). His book of nonfiction, *Indy: The World's Fastest Carnival Ride* (1977), depicts the famous race and its accompanying hoopla. His journalism has appeared in magazines such as *Sports Illustrated, Men's Journal, Outside*, and *New York*. An essay on nature, "Walking in Tierra del Fuego," which includes descriptions of northwestern Michigan, appears in *Sacred Trusts: Essays in Stewardship and Responsibility*, edited by Michael Katakis (1993). Gerber and Harrison contributed prefatory essays to *The Sumac Reader*, a Sumac Press anthology edited by Joseph Bednarik (1996).

**FURTHER READING:** A substantial portrait, with photographs, of Gerber as "scion" of the baby food company, as well as writer, is available in Howard Muson's "The Reluctant Successor," *Family Business* (October 1990): 18–24. William Barillas's "An Interview with Dan Gerber," *Passages North* 13.1 (Summer 1992): 23–27, offers a long and meditative discussion of his life and writing; Barillas's "To Sustain the Bioregion: Michigan Poets of Place," *Mid-America* 17 (1990): 10–33, considers Gerber in the company of Theodore Roethke, Jim Harrison, and JUDITH MINTY. His work has been reviewed in such journals as *Puerto del Sol, Virginia Quarterly Review*, and *Georgia Review*. His papers are housed at Michigan State University Library, Special Collections.

WILLIAM BARILLAS

UNIVERSITY OF WISCONSIN–LA CROSSE

## PHILIP GERBER.

*See* appendix (1990)

## ALICE (ERYA) GERSTENBERG

August 2, 1885–July 28, 1972

**BIOGRAPHY:** Alice Gerstenberg, author of two novels and more than forty plays, was born in Chicago, Illinois, the only child of Julia (Wieschendorff) and Erich Gerstenberg. Alice was encouraged to pursue artistic and intellectual interests. Gerstenberg attended a private Chicago school, Kirkland, and later Bryn Mawr College, where she wrote and performed plays. Like 51 percent of her 1907 Bryn Mawr class, she remained single throughout her life.

After college, Gerstenberg spent a short period in New York where she watched David Belasco's rehearsals and then returned to Chicago. There she became very involved in the theater community. While writing her plays, Gerstenberg participated in Anna Morgan's theater, urging new playwrights to create plays and furnishing them with the opportunity to see their plays produced. Gerstenberg was a charter member of Ellen Van Volkenburg and Maurice Browne's Chicago Little Theatre. She also participated in the Society of Midland Authors and helped organize the Players' Workshop of Chicago, where she worked with BEN HECHT, MAX BODENHEIM, Kenneth Sawyer Goodman, and Elisha Cook.

Gerstenberg's first publication was *A Small World* (1908), a group of four two-act plays written at Bryn Mawr which examine the lives and choices of young college women and their fight for status, recognition, and identity. In these plays she deals with the contemporary issues of androgyny and class. She published two novels after this, *Unquenched Fire* (1912) and *The Conscience of Sarah Platt* (1915). Both were feminist and both examined Midwestern values. The first explores a young woman interested in forming a theater career in New York against her parents' wishes that she remain in the Midwest and marry an appropriately rich suitor in order to maintain their position in society. The second novel explores the effects of the genteel tradition on a middle-aged Midwestern schoolteacher who missed her opportunities in love because of her inability to express romantic feeling. Both novels deal with contemporary themes and were very popular when first published.

*Overtones* (1913) is her most frequently reprinted and performed play. HARRIET MONROE had commented on its use of "primitive selves" in *Poetry* 7.4 (1916): 196. The Washington Square Players performed the play. Edward Goodman was director, and Lily Langtry starred in the London production. *Overtones* helped push modern theater to new forms. Gerstenberg expanded and directed a three-act version at the Powers Theater in Chicago.

Another one-act play published in this group, *The Pot Boiler* or *The Dress Rehearsal*, was entered in the 1923 Little Theatre Tournament in New York and became successful. *The Pot Boiler*, a satire which uses the technique of a play within a play, role reversals, and invitations to audience participation, is a very different type of play from *Overtones*. The plot centers on the rebellion of the characters, and the audience actively responds. The play's structure anticipates the "happenings" of the 1960s as the innocent heroine repeats the novice's original question of "Shoot who?" and all the players exclaim in disgust, "Oh, shoot the author!" At this point, the audience also feels compelled to join the fun and to participate by shouting with the actor, "Shoot the author!"

Gerstenberg's first full-length play, *Alice in Wonderland*, was published in 1915, met with great success, and remained the standard until Eva Le Gallienne wrote her version in 1932. Yvonne Shafer has praised it for its quick pace, cinematic style, and early use of audience participation.

In the 1920s with Annette Washburne, Gerstenberg established the Chicago Junior League Theatre for Children and served as its director. In 1922 she founded the Playwrights Theatre of Chicago, which continued until 1945.

Gerstenberg continued to write her own plays and in 1924 published *Four Plays for Four Women*, which contains *Mah-Jongg, Their Husband, Ever Young*, and *Seaweed*, again demonstrating consciousness of region and interest in stylization, symbolism, psychology, class, and the visual effects of cheaply and effectively setting a scene with few resources and players.

Her next and final volume of plays, *Comedies All* (1930), examines the notion that even countesses can have roots and living sisters in Iowa and that individuals, young and old, fight for the right to forge their own lives. A later play, *Within the Hour* (1934), similarly examines an Iowa woman's choices. The protagonist has already sacrificed much of her youth to taking care of younger siblings after her mother's death and chooses to flee a grandfather who wants to buy her care. She finally gives herself permission to follow her heart's desire: her love and a new start in Chicago. *Time for Romance* (1940) also reflects the troubles of modern women and the choices they must make. In this play, a successful working woman needs love and finally finds time to choose it over the demands of her business.

In 1938 Gerstenberg won the Chicago Foundation of Literature Award for her work in American drama. She died of cancer in Chicago.

**SIGNIFICANCE:** Eugene O'Neill said he was influenced by the psychological dimensions of Gerstenberg's characterization. The influence of psychoanalysis was clearly apparent in Gerstenberg's *Overtones* (1913), *Alice in Wonderland* (1915), *The Buffer* (1916), and *Beyond* (1917), and it was not until O'Neill's play *Desire under the Elms* (1923) that he explored the implications of psychoanalytical theory through drama. O'Neill's interest in parapsychology also emerged in *Desire under the Elms*, but again Gerstenberg was first to examine the sixth sense in such early one-act plays as *Attuned* (1918) and *The Unseen* (1918). *Sentience* (1933), "Concordia" (unpublished, n.d.), and her religious unpublished drama, "On the Beam" (1963), also reflect her interest in the supernatural.

Gerstenberg left a strong mark on the little theater movement. She wanted theater to be available to new playwrights. She was particularly interested in giving regional playwrights the opportunity to produce their plays. Gerstenberg specialized in plays about women's issues. While her characters are usually upper-middle-class women, they reflect their times in their desire for meaning and identity outside of marriage and motherhood without sacrificing romance. Often her endings are sentimental, but she poignantly examines the trauma associated with women's pressures to marry so they can maintain social position, the economics of marriage and its effects on the entire family, and the terrible cost of forcing young women to choose.

Alice Gerstenberg believed in theater for children and in historical theater as an avenue for remembering and preserving history. She wrote many plays with regional significance, some performed on radio during the 1930s. Those interested in Gerstenberg's regional focus should look at her unpublished radio plays, "Across the River" and "Lake Front," which were sponsored by the Chicago Board of Education in 1939. These plays, as well as her unpublished play "Port of Chicago," reflect her commitment to Chicago history.

Chicago, as Gerstenberg knew, was the perfect place to begin her dramatic career, but perhaps she should have left the city. She had the opportunity to do so. In New York, she was introduced to Edward Goodman, and he asked her to help him start the Washington Square Players. When she refused, she was thinking not only of her career but of her desire to be with her family in Chicago. The city that gave her focus and power may also have served to limit it.

**SELECTED WORKS:** Gerstenberg published two novels, *Unquenched Fire* (1912) and *The Conscience of Sarah Platt* (1915). Her plays include *A Small World* (1908); an adaptation of *Alice in Wonderland* (1915); *Ten One-Act Plays* (1921); *Four Plays for Four Women* (1924); a dramatization of Lilian Bell's children's story *The Land of "Don't Want To"* (1928); the three-act version of *Overtones* (1929); *Comedies All* (1930), her final collection of one-act plays; a dramatization of Charles Kingsley's *The Water Babies* (1930); *Glee Plays the Game* (1934); and *Within the Hour* (1934).

**FURTHER READING:** Significant secondary sources include Yvonne Shafer's *American Women Playwrights 1900–1950* (1995); Mary Maddock's "Alice Gerstenberg's *Overtones*: The Demon in the Dell," in *Modern Drama* 37 (Fall 1994): 474–84; Stuart J. Hecht's "The Plays of Alice Gerstenberg: Cultural Hegemony in the American Little Theatre," in *Journal of Popular Culture* 26 (Summer 1992): 1–16; and Marilyn J. Atlas's "Alice Gerstenberg's Psychological Drama," in *Midwestern Miscellany* 10 (1982): 59–68.

The Newberry Library in Chicago has a collection of Gerstenberg's letters, some very important autobiographical fragments written in letter form, and several unpublished plays and manuscripts. The theater library at Ohio State University, the Lawrence and Lee Theatre Research Institute, houses many of her published plays. The Charvat Collection at Ohio State University has both of her novels. Gerstenberg's lengthy unpublished autobiography, "Come Back with Me," can be found at the Chicago Historical Society.

MARILYN J. ATLAS          OHIO UNIVERSITY

## SUSAN KEATING GLASPELL
July 1, 1876–July 27, 1948

**BIOGRAPHY:** Susan Glaspell was born to Elmer and Alice (Keating) Glaspell in Davenport, Iowa, and received her early education there before enrolling in Drake Univer-

**Susan Glaspell.**
Photo courtesy of the Glaspell family

sity. After graduating from Drake with a PhB in 1899, she worked as a reporter in Des Moines, covering the state house beat and writing a column, "The News Girl," before returning to Davenport to write fiction. After her short stories began appearing in such magazines as *Harper's, Youth's Companion,* and *Munsey's,* she published her first novel in 1909.

Her involvement in Davenport cultural and political activities brought her in contact with novelist GEORGE CRAM COOK, also a Davenport native, who was then married to journalist Mollie Price. The controversy surrounding Glaspell and Cook's subsequent love affair prompted their departure; they married in 1913 and settled in Greenwich Village, summering in Provincetown, Massachusetts. In 1915 they began to put on original one-act plays with a group of Provincetown artists and writers that became known as the Provincetown Players, a little theater group for which Glaspell would write and act for the next six years.

In 1922 they emigrated to Delphi, Greece, and after Cook died there in 1924, Glaspell returned to Provincetown, where she lived with novelist Norman Matson for eight years. During the latter half of the 1920s she published a biography of her late husband and an anthology of his poems, collaborated on a play with Matson, and published two novels. In 1931 she received the Pulitzer Prize for her play *Alison's House*, and her relationship with Matson ended the following year. In 1936 she moved to Chicago to direct the Midwest Play Bureau of the Federal Theatre Project, but she returned to Provincetown after a year and a half to spend the last ten years of her life writing fiction and drama. She died in Provincetown of a pulmonary embolism and viral pneumonia.

**SIGNIFICANCE:** "The Middle West must have taken strong hold of me in my early years for I've never ceased trying to figure out why it is as it is," wrote Susan Glaspell to Edmund Wilson near the end of a writing career that spanned the first half of the twentieth century. In her fiction and plays, she attempts to come to terms with the sometimes paradoxical aspects of a region that encompasses the sublimity of a great river and prairie and the tawdriness of small cities and towns, the idealism of pioneer settlers and the narrow-mindedness of their descendants, the rigid middle-class mentality of small-town Midwestern society and the independent free spirits who defy it.

Glaspell focuses all but the first of her novels on the conflict between a Midwestern community and the individuals for whom its conventions are too limiting to allow for personal development or self-expression. This theme is skillfully developed in her third novel, *Fidelity* (1915), written in the revolt from the village tradition. Images of entrapment, encirclement, and enclosure recur in this novel, which tells the story of Ruth Holland, a Freeport girl who leaves town with her married lover and returns fifteen years later to cope with the impending death of her father, as well as the effects of her return on her family, her friends, and herself.

In her last novel, *Judd Rankin's Daughter* (1945), Glaspell explores what it means to be a Midwesterner through three characters, each of whom represents a different perspective on the region. Judd Rankin is an isolationist farmer-newspaper editor. Frances Rankin Mitchell, his daughter, has married a liberal New York writer, moved to the East

Coast, and acquired a more global outlook and a resulting ambivalence about the Midwest. Cousin Adah Logan, a lifelong Iowa resident who is cultured, well traveled, and free thinking, undermines stereotypical thinking about the Midwest and represents the paradoxical aspects of the region.

Five of Susan Glaspell's plays are set in Iowa. In *Trifles* (1916) and in *Inheritors* (1921), two of the plays she wrote for the Provincetown Players, the Midwestern setting functions as a metaphor for isolation, alienation, and disengagement. The desolate Iowa farmstead on which the action of *Trifles* takes place suggests the desperate loneliness of the central character, farmwife Minnie Wright. *Inheritors* chronicles the changes in an Iowa pioneer family from 1870 to 1920, enacting the displacement of the pioneer vision by a more pragmatic outlook, as exemplified by Ira Morton, the isolationist farmer and Felix Fejevary, president of the college founded by the idealistic pioneer Silas Morton. Two other plays produced by the Provincetown Players, *Close the Book*, and *Chains of Dew*, both exploit the comic potential in the juxtaposition of Midwestern conformists and iconoclastic radicals. In *Alison's House*, Glaspell takes a more serious approach to this conflict: traditionalist family members who wish to suppress the newly discovered poems of Alison Stanhope that reveal her love affair with a married man are pitted against the proponents of free expression who fight to save them.

A chronological review of Susan Glaspell's Midwestern works reveals that her attitude toward her native region became tempered by time. Ira Morton of *Inheritors* is so stern and unyielding that he is almost a caricature of the isolationist farmer. By contrast, the spunky Judd Rankin has a sense of humor as prominent as the Iowa stubborn streak in his personality. The small-town matrons of Fidelity are self-righteous and prudish, unlike the lovely Adah Logan, who manages to be both respectable and sophisticated. There is a difference in tone as well as in character development in her later works, for by the 1930s and 1940s Glaspell had achieved enough distance from her subject to write of the Midwest with humor and insight. And even those works that are the most critical of the Midwest are suffused with an idealism that sustained Glaspell throughout her life, even as it sustained her pioneer ancestors. *Inheritors*, her harshest indictment of Midwestern isolationism, reflects this idealism in the character of Madeline Fejevary Morton, who admonishes her aunt to "be the most you can be so life will be more because you were" (154).

Like Ruth Holland, Susan Glaspell loved the Midwest, even when its people hurt her deeply; like Frances Rankin Mitchell, she questioned their self-absorption and insistence on conformity. "Now here is my own past," she wrote to Edmund Wilson about *Judd Rankin's Daughter*. "I came out of that kind of life. And as I do not agree with it, I wanted to be very fair to it; and that was not hard, for I love Judd Rankin, and I think I understand him. He's America, the old-time America. He has so much to offer us." Like Judd Rankin, Susan Glaspell has much to offer us, as Ludwig Lewisohn acknowledged when he wrote in his review of *The Verge*, "Other American dramatists may have more obvious virtues; they may reach larger audiences and enjoy a less wavering repute. Susan Glaspell has a touch of that vision without which we perish" (*Nation* 113: 708–709).

**SELECTED WORKS:** Susan Glaspell wrote more than fifty short stories. Several are set in Freeport, a Mississippi river town resembling Davenport, Iowa; a number of the stories collected in *Lifted Masks* (1912) are set in a Midwestern state capital and based on her experiences as a political reporter in Des Moines. Midwestern settings are featured in all nine of her novels: *The Glory of the Conquered* (1909); *The Visioning* (1911); *Fidelity* (1915); *Brook Evans* (1928); *Fugitive's Return* (1929); *Ambrose Holt and Family* (1931); *The Morning Is Near Us* (1940); *Norma Ashe* (1942); and *Judd Rankin's Daughter* (1945). A collection of eight plays produced by the Provincetown Players, *Plays by Susan Glaspell* (1920), includes *Suppressed Desires* and *Tickless Time* (with George Cram Cook), *Trifles, The People, Close the Book, Woman's Honor, The Outside*, and *Bernice*. Four other plays that were both produced and published are *Inheritors* (1921), *The Verge* (1922), *The Comic Artist* (with Norman Matson) (1927), and *Alison's House* (1930). *Chains of Dew*, a comedy produced by the Provincetown Players in 1922 is yet unpublished, as is *Springs Eternal*, a still unproduced comedy written in the 1940s. In 1917 Susan Glaspell adapted *Trifles* as a short story, "A Jury of Her Peers"; both works have

been frequently anthologized. In 1927 she published *The Road to the Temple*, a biography of George Cram Cook that also reveals much about her own personality and background.

**FURTHER READING:** Arthur Waterman's *Susan Glaspell* (1966), Marcia Noe's *Susan Glaspell: Voice from the Heartland* (1983), Veronica Makowsky's *Susan Glaspell's Century of American Women* (1993), and Barbara Ozielbo's *Susan Glaspell: A Critical Biography* (2000) are book-length studies of Susan Glaspell's life and works. Mary Papke's *Susan Glaspell: A Research and Production Sourcebook* (1993) includes a thorough and detailed review of Glaspell criticism as well as information on the production history of her plays. See also *Susan Glaspell: A Collection of Critical Essays*, edited by Linda Ben-Zvi (1995). The largest collection of Glaspell's papers can be found in the Berg Collection of the New York Public Library. Other libraries with significant holdings are the Houghton Library, Harvard University; the Barrett Library, University of Virginia; the Beinecke Library, Yale University; the Newberry Library; and the National Archives.

MARCIA NOE

THE UNIVERSITY OF TENNESSEE AT CHATTANOOGA

# HERBERT GOLD
March 9, 1924

**BIOGRAPHY:** The eldest of four sons born to Samuel S. and Freida (Frankel) Gold, in Cleveland, Ohio, Herbert Gold felt his early formal education was equaled by his education as a reluctant apprentice greengrocer in his father's Lakewood, Ohio, store (see *Fathers: A Novel in the Form of a Memoir*, 1967). Introduced there to the dynamics of commercial endeavor, the idiosyncrasies of customers, the passions of employees and their employer, the young Gold first met the world of adults, their longings, fears, strengths, and failures through the store. It was there too, perhaps among the turnips and stacks of canned peaches, that a keen eye for setting and character and an even keener ear for language, dialects, and word play began to develop.

Writing already in grammar school, Gold worked on the student newspaper at Lakewood High School, from which he graduated in 1942. Following service (1943–46) during World War II, Gold received both a BA (1946) and an MA (1948) from Columbia University. In 1951 a Fulbright Fellowship culminated in a *licence ès lettres* from the Sorbonne. The year 1951 also saw the publication of Gold's first novel, *Birth of a Hero*, and the first of several teaching assignments accepted by Gold through the years.

In 1948 Gold married Edith Zubrin with whom he had two children before the couple divorced in 1956. A second marriage to Melissa Dilworth in 1968 produced three children and ended in divorce in 1975.

Numerous fellowships and awards include the Ohioana Book Award (1957) for *The Man Who Was Not with It* (1956, published as *The Wild Life* in 1957), the California Literature Medal Award (1968) for *Fathers* (a best-seller), and the Commonwealth Club Award for best novel (1982) for *Family: A Novel in the Form of a Memoir* (1981). Moving like some of his characters from the Midwest to New York and California, Gold has resided in San Francisco for a number of years.

**SIGNIFICANCE:** Born and raised where coal and iron, wheat and soybeans, and a cornucopia of peoples converge on the southern shores of Lake Erie, his eye and ear honed there, Herbert Gold stands as a Midwestern author in multiple respects: as a native son, as a chronicler of life across generations in the urban Midwest, and through his characters. In their longings, disappointments, and journeys, Gold proves himself a Midwesterner as much by pen as by birth. In addition to *Fathers*, novels with Midwestern settings include *The Optimist* (1959), *Therefore Be Bold* (1960), *My Last Two Thousand Years* (1972), and *Family* (1981).

In *Fathers*, young Herbert first encounters the world of men at the Russian baths near Cleveland's Public Square or, as the novelist puts it, "the Cuyahoga Russki Svitz (Indian, Russian and Yiddish words, in that order)" (123). In that observation, as in so many strokes of Gold's pen, we at once encounter Cleveland, the Midwest, and urban America through the author's affinity for the details of language, culture, and place, hallmarks for which he is widely recognized.

**SELECTED WORKS:** The lives of Gold's often complex characters are rooted in the dialectic of human existence; loves dissolve, marriages end, life intrudes upon dreams. *He/She* (1980), *Girl of Forty* (1986), *Birth of a Hero* (1951), *Salt* (1963), and *The Optimist* (1959) present the hopes and frailties of romantic

Herbert Gold.
Photo © Nancy Crampton

love and love's ambitions. In *Therefore Be Bold* (1960), a father's anti-Semitism intrudes upon a youthful courtship. In *The Prospect before Us* (1954), regarded as Gold's most "stylized" novel, the nascent interracial romance of a marginalized couple is cut short by tragedy brought on by economic hardship. Set in a fleabag hotel, *The Prospect before Us*, like *The Man Who Was Not with It* (1956), which takes place on the carnival circuit, allows Gold to situate colorful dialogue in a colorful setting. Autobiographical explorations of kinship are to be found as two of the titles suggest, in *Fathers: A Novel in the Form of a Memoir* (1967), *Family: A Novel in the Form of a Memoir* (1981), and also, if less directly, in *My Last Two Thousand Years* (1972), in which Gold examines his life in the wider context of Jewish history.

Gold's nonfiction works include *The Age of Happy Problems* (1962), *A Walk on the West Side: California on the Brink* (1981), *Best Nightmare on Earth: A Life in Haiti* (1991), and *Bohemia: Where Art, Angst, Love and Strong Coffee Meet* (1993). Collections of short stories are published as *Fifteen by Three* (1957, with R. V. CASSILL and James B. Hall), *Love and Like* (1960), *The Magic Will: Stories and Essays of a Decade* (1971), *Stories of Misbegotten Love* (1985), and *Lovers and Cohorts: Twenty-Seven Stories* (1986). A children's book, *The Young Prince and the Magic Cone,* appeared in 1973.

**FURTHER READING:** Harry T. Moore has written on "The Fiction of Herbert Gold," in *Contemporary American Novelists* (1964). *Writers Digest* 52 (September 1972) published "An Exclusive Interview with Herbert Gold" by Robert Kiener. Two interesting essays situate Gold's work in Midwestern literature and have been published through the Society for the Study of Midwestern Literature. They are Ellen Serlen's "The American Dream: From F. Scott Fitzgerald to Herbert Gold," *MidAmerica* 4 (1977): 122–37; and DAVID D. ANDERSON's "Sherwood Anderson, Wright Morris, Herbert Gold and the Midwest–San Francisco Connection," *Society for the Study of Midwestern Literature Newsletter* 2 (Summer 1992): 23–35. *Contemporary Authors* devotes several pages to Gold (45, 1995, 150–54), and a concentration of his papers is housed in the Butler Library at Columbia University.

DAVID PERUSEK            KENT STATE UNIVERSITY

## PHILIP A. GREASLEY.

*See* appendix (1999)

## ANDREW M. GREELEY

February 5, 1928

**BIOGRAPHY:** Novelist, poet, priest, sociologist, journalist, Andrew M. Greeley was born in Oak Park, Illinois, son of Grace (McNichols) and Andrew Thomas Greeley and grandson of Irish immigrants. Ordained a priest in 1954, his first clerical appointment was at Christ the King parish in southwest Chicago. He is the author of more than a hundred books, ranging from sociology, theology, meditations, and fiction to geography. He holds a PhD in sociology from the University of Chicago, where he has held faculty and research positions. His first novel and first collection of poetry appeared in 1979, the year he accepted a professorial appointment for alternate terms at the University of Arizona. His first best-selling novel, *The Cardinal Sins,* which brought him celebrity and notoriety, appeared in 1981. Though denied tenure at the University of

Andrew Greeley.
Photo courtesy of Andrew Greeley

Chicago during the 1960s, Greeley in 1984 donated $1.5 million to the university to establish a Catholic Studies chair. Although his novels, translated into nine languages, caused him some difficulty in the archdiocese, Greeley in 1986 established a million-dollar Catholic Inner-City School Fund to provide scholarships for Chicago minorities. He was the recipient of the Society for the Study of Midwestern Literature's 1987 Mark Twain Award for distinguished contributions to Midwestern literature. Named professor of social science at the University of Chicago in 1991, he continues with his work at the University of Chicago's National Opinion Research Center and at the University of Arizona.

**SIGNIFICANCE:** As human love in Greeley's novels is the microcosm of divine love, so the microcosm for this century's human experience is the Midwestern city Chicago, particularly its Irish Catholic community, which reflects the nation's rise to affluence since

1945. Even when his characters are elsewhere, the source of the story is Chicago, its people, its sports teams, its churches; for example, his twenty-sixth novel, *Irish Gold* (1994), is set in Ireland, where Dermot Coyne, an accidental millionaire from the Chicago Stock Exchange, solves the mystery of his grandparents' permanent exile from Ireland during the troubles following 1916. The Chicago of most of his novels revolves around the often incompetent, politicized Catholic archdiocese, the pettiness of University of Chicago faculty politics, the city government that ward-healing Dick Daley built and revisionist Jane Byrne renamed, and the Chicago Board of Trade. The real life of the novels is in the largely ethnic Chicago parishes that define a Midwestern Irish Catholicism and which provide the loci for an almost Dickensian quest for salvation, where sexual, even adulterous, love can be redemptive, though degenerate sexuality, often accompanied by deadlier sins, is both morally and, at times, physically destructive, as in *Thy Brother's Wife* (1982).

Greeley's satire is at times reminiscent of Henry Fielding's, as with a "new-church" holiday liturgy in *Ascent into Hell* (1983), where "the reader wore a Santa Claus costume and the director of song a south-sea sarong, for which she lacked the figure. The bread of the Eucharist was brandied plum pudding and the wine was steaming wassail" (152).

In Greeley's theology, sinners are welcomed by a forgiving, loving God into the New Jerusalem, which is metamorphosed into his. Ron Grossman in a *Chicago Tribune* article, "Publish or Parish," reports Greeley's hyperbolic account, resulting from a hypnotherapy trance, of the Midwestern metropolis: "I saw this mystical looking city on a lake, and realized it had to be an even better Chicago . . . . That's when I grasped that heaven is like the West Side" (August 18, 1992: sec. 5.1–2).

**SELECTED WORKS:** *Death in April* (1980) deals with his grail quest theme, which in this novel is a satisfying physical as well as spiritual love. *The Cardinal Sins* (1981) launched Greeley's success and is especially interesting for its handling of international intrigue in the Vatican. *The Irish Americans: The Rise to Money and Power* (1981) is a sociological study that defines scientifically the Irish affluence that prevails in the novels; of critical interest

is a chapter on Irish American writers, many out of the Midwest. The Passover trilogy, *Thy Brother's Wife* (1982), *Ascent into Hell* (1983), and *Lord of the Dance* (1984), deals with commitment, divine mercy, and new beginnings. *Virgin and Martyr* (1985) is a novel about the traumatic times in the Church following Vatican II. It introduces Greeley's Blackie Ryan, the detective-cleric who subsequently appears in a number of Greeley's mysteries, including his own series with titles taken from the Beatitudes. *The Cardinal Virtues* (1990) explores a suburban pastor's emotional fatigue and problems of faith. *The Sense of Love* (1992) is a collection of poems divided into three sections, "Eros," "Philos," and "Agape"; a foreword by Robert McGovern places him in the tradition of Anglo-Roman priest-poets from Donne, Herbert, and Robert Herrick to the present. *Fall from Grace* (1993) examines sexual abuse of children by priests and wife-beating in Catholic marriages. *Irish Gold* (1994) is an historical novel about the assassination of Irish Republican Brotherhood leader Michael Collins, recreated in the present through an investigation by rich Irish-Chicagoan Dermot Coyne and a marriageable teenage girl from the west of Ireland, Nuala Anne McGrail.

**FURTHER READING:** Greeley is often the subject of newspaper and magazine feature stories. Book-length studies include John Kotre's *The Best of Times, the Worst of Times: Andrew Greeley and American Catholicism 1950–1975* (1978); Ingrid H. Shafer's *Eros and the Womanliness of God: Andrew Greeley's Romances of Renewal* (1986); a Festschrift including the work of David Riesman, Hans Kung, Jacob Neusner, Mary Durkin, and Martin E. Marty in honor of Andrew Greeley on his sixtieth birthday; *The Incarnate Imagination: Essays in Theology, the Arts and Social Sciences*, edited by Ingrid H. Shafer (1988); *Andrew Greeley's World: An Anthology of Critical Essays 1986–1988*, also edited by Ingrid H. Shafer (1989); and Elizabeth Harrison's *Andrew M. Greeley, An Annotated Bibliography* (1994).

ROBERT MCGOVERN                    ASHLAND UNIVERSITY

# (ROBERT) BOB (BERNARD) GREENE (JR.)
March 10, 1947

**BIOGRAPHY:** Bob Greene was born in Columbus, Ohio, the son of Robert Bernard

Greene and Phyllis Ann (Harmon) Greene. After graduating from Northwestern University in 1969, he began work as a reporter for the *Chicago Sun-Times*. Within two years he had moved to the *Chicago Tribune*, where he continues to work as a columnist specializing in human interest and slice-of-life stories. His success at the *Tribune* led to a regular column entitled "American Beat" for *Esquire* magazine and a job as a contributor to ABC TV's *Nightline*. Greene married Susan Bonnet Koebel in 1971.

**SIGNIFICANCE:** Greene's career has been one of early and steady success, anchored by, but not limited to, his regular contributions to the *Chicago Tribune*. While the majority of his books are compilations of previously published newspaper columns, he has also published several autobiographical, diary-based works, longer meditations on subjects that began in his column, and portraits of his interaction with musical and sports celebrities.

Response to Greene's work has been mixed, with his admirers complimenting his perception and willingness to focus on and tell stories others might find mundane. More critical reviews have accused Greene of focusing too heavily on himself and his own responses to a story, a charge leveled more frequently in discussions of his recent pair of books describing his friendship with Chicago Bulls basketball star Michael Jordan.

Throughout his career Greene has shown a willingness to take a strong and vocal stand on controversial issues. Examples include an early column condemning hunting and his book *Homecoming* (1989), which chronicled letters Greene received from Vietnam veterans answering his question, "Were you ever spat upon?" More recently Greene has focused publicity on the Illinois Supreme Court's refusal to grant a best interest hearing to the child known as "Baby Richard," who was ordered to be removed from his adoptive parents' home and returned to his biological father. Although some readers and peers questioned the propriety of a newspaper columnist taking the role of advocate, others credit Greene for drawing attention to a perceived miscarriage of justice.

Greene's column in the *Chicago Tribune*, like the body of his work, retains a strong Midwestern flavor by mixing stories about average Americans with stories of celebrities

and politicians and by emphasizing positive, human interest stories that might not be deemed worthy of note in a large metropolitan newspaper.

**SELECTED WORKS:** Compilations of Greene's newspaper material can be found in *Johnny Deadline, Reporter: The Best of Bob Greene* (1976), *American Beat* (1983), *Cheeseburgers: The Best of Bob Greene* (1985), and *He Was a Midwestern Boy on His Own* (1991). He used his own journals as the impetus for *Running: A Nixon-McGovern Campaign Journal* (1973), *Good Morning, Merry Sunshine: A Father's Journal of His Child's First Year* (1984), and *Be True to Your School: A Diary of 1964* (1987). The latter works border on oral history, an interest that is confirmed in the previously mentioned *Homecoming: When the Soldiers Returned from Vietnam* (1989) and the question book *To Our Children's Children: Preserving Family Histories for Generations to Come* (1993). By far Greene's most popular books have been his celebrity profiles that often focus as much on Greene as they do on the celebrity subject. Greene's acquaintance with the rock group Alice Cooper is documented in *Billion Dollar Baby* (1974), while his friendship with Michael Jordan has led to *Hang Time: Days and Dreams with Michael Jordan* (1992) and *Rebound: The Odyssey of Michael Jordan* (1995).

**FURTHER READING:** Studies on Bob Greene include Richard Shereikis's "Farewell to the Regional Columnist: The Meaning of Bob Greene's Success," in *MidAmerica* 8 (1986): 125–33, and Steve Jones's coverage of Greene in *A Sourcebook of American Literary Journalism: Representative Writers in an Emerging Genre*, edited by Thomas Bernard Connery (1992).

KENNETH R. MOREFIELD    TOCCOA FALLS COLLEGE

## (PEARL) ZANE GREY

January 31, 1872–October 23, 1939

**BIOGRAPHY:** The son of Lewis M. and Alice Josephine (Zane), Zane Gray changed the spelling of his last name because he thought an "e" was more distinguished than an "a." Born in Zanesville, Ohio, he went from Zanesville High School to the University of Pennsylvania. After graduation in 1896, Grey established a dental practice in New York City. In 1905 he married Lina Elise and they would have three children. *Betty Zane* (1903) began the three-volume Ohio River trilogy, which also includes *The Spirit of the Border* (1906) and *The Last Trail* (1909). Grey's great and continuing popularity depends on later books about the Far West, especially *Riders of the Purple Sage* (1912) and *Desert Gold* (1913). In 1918 Grey moved to California and continued a life of world travel designed to research his eighty-five books of which seventy-five are still in print in 1995. More than forty million book sales are estimated thus far. Zane Grey died in Altadena, California, in 1939.

**SIGNIFICANCE:** Zane Grey's successful career as a writer of Westerns began with his own Midwestern family history. In the *New York Times* of May 17, 1998, Deanne Stillman notes how she as a child would "escape the gray skies and frozen shores of northern Ohio by huddling under . . . covers with a flashlight and reading Zane Grey" ("Leaving the Freeway, Paying the Price"). The irony is that the escapist West began only a few miles south near Wheeling, West Virginia. Zane Grey's mother, Alice Josephine Zane, was the daughter of Colonel Ebenezer Zane, the founder of Wheeling who established Zane's Trace across Ohio in 1797. *Betty Zane* (1903) is the story of the author's great-great-aunt who is credited with saving Fort Henry (presently the site of Wheeling) during the Western border wars of the American Revolution. *The Spirit of the Border* (1906) fictionalizes the actual history of Gnadenhutten and the massacre of the Moravian Indians there near the present Ohio city of Coshocton. A great-great-uncle, Jonathan Zane, and his partner, Lewis Wetzel, are honorable men caught in the middle between the savage white settlers and the Indian defenders of that land which itself became known as the Middle Ground between the Bloody Ground of Kentucky and the British territories in Canada. *The Last Trail* (1909) focuses on the villainy of the victors, personified by Simon Girty. Zane Grey's familial Ohio "Middle Ground" (see Richard White's 1991 book, *The Middle Ground*) is the genesis of further Western and still continuing American territorial imperatives.

**SELECTED WORKS:** Primary is the Ohio trilogy mentioned above: *Betty Zane* (1903); *The Spirit of the Border* (1906), and *The Last Trail* (1909).

**FURTHER READING:** Most important is Stephen J. May's *Zane Grey: Romancing the West* (1997). The 1989 revised edition of Carlton Jackson's *Zane Grey*, in the Twayne U.S. Authors series, is useful. Jackson cites a Zane

Grey description of a desert night in *The Last of the Plainsmen* (1908) that may reveal Zane Grey's version of our famed Midwestern restlessness: "How infinite all this is! How impossible to understand!" (251). Also important for further study are G. M. Farley's *Zane Grey: A Documented Portrait* (1986) and Charles McKnight's *Our Western Border* (1876), a major print source for the Ohio River trilogy. Zane Grey papers can be found at the Ohio Historical Society Center in Columbus, in the possession of Zane Grey's son, Dr. Loren Grey, and at the National Road–Zane Grey Museum in Zanesville, Ohio.

JAMES M. HUGHES          WRIGHT STATE UNIVERSITY

# PAUL GRUCHOW
May 23, 1947

**BIOGRAPHY:** Born on a farm near Montevideo, Minnesota, to Marie (Halvorson) and Howard Gruchow, Paul Gruchow received his elementary education in a one-room country school. While still in high school he worked for the *Montevideo American News*. At the University of Minnesota from 1965 to 1969, he majored in humanities and edited the *Minnesota Daily* from 1968 to 1969. On September 7, 1968, he married Nancy Harding. The couple have two children, Laura and Aaron.

Because his seriously ill father had neither money nor insurance, Gruchow left school in 1969 several courses short of a degree. He worked as a legislative assistant to Representative Donald Fraser, first in St. Paul and then in Washington, D.C. He returned to Minnesota as news and public affairs director of Minnesota Public Radio from 1972 to 1973, later moving to an editorial position with *Minneapolis–St. Paul Magazine*. In 1976 Gruchow became managing editor and part owner of the *Worthington* (Minnesota) *Daily Globe*, recognized during the decade of his tenure as one of the area's outstanding small-town newspapers.

In 1986 Gruchow sold his interest in the *Globe* and, retaining ownership of a farm outside Worthington, moved to Northfield, Minnesota, to pursue work as a full-time writer and operate a bookstore, Author's Ink. From 1988 to 1992 he served on the Minnesota Humanities Commission, including two terms as chair. Gruchow has served on the boards of many organizations related to nature, conservancy, and food production. He has intermittently taught at Worthington Community College, St. Olaf College, and Concordia College in Moorhead. He is presently engaged in walking, over the course of several seasons, the Continental Divide.

**SIGNIFICANCE:** "What I hope to accomplish in my writing is a very simple thing," Gruchow told Laurie Hertzel in *Minnesota Monthly* (July 1994); "I want to encourage people to pay attention." Gruchow is a thoughtful reader, a sharp observer, a gifted storyteller, and an eloquent stylist who writes with a journalist's economy and clarity. His essays and articles have appeared in *Sierra, Audubon, Nature Conservancy*, the *Utne Reader*, the *New York Times*, and thirty anthologies. Five have been cited as "Notable Essays" in *The Best American Essays* volumes.

Gruchow writes in the tradition of Thoreau, ALDO LEOPOLD, Dillard, and other naturalist-philosophers. *Journal of a Prairie Year* (1985) is a collection of meditations on the Minnesota prairie around Chippewa County and Worthington, set loosely into a sequence of seasons. Much of it recalls what Gruchow in *Grass Roots* (1995) termed "that brief time when I was a country boy and lived in the outdoors essentially as one might occupy a living room" (203). *The Necessity of Empty Places* (1988) is a more structured series of essays in the Gretyl Ehrlich–John McPhee–Wallace Stegner tradition. Using data, anecdote, and rumination, Gruchow argues the value of wilderness in American experience and imagination. In the text of *Travels in Canoe Country* (1990), a celebration of Minnesota's Boundary Waters structured on the canonical hours, a latent mysticism rises finally to the surface of Gruchow's writing. *Grass Roots* collects previously published essays, including "Bones," which appeared in 1988 in *Minnesota Monthly* and then in *The Best American Essays 1989*. The book won a 1996 Minnesota Book Award and a Critics Choice Award from the *San Francisco Review of Books*.

**SELECTED WORKS:** *Journal of a Prairie Year* (1985), *The Necessity of Empty Places* (1988), and *Grass Roots* (1995) are all significant nonfiction works. Gruchow provided text for *Minnesota: Images of Home*, a book of Jim Brandenburg's photographs, privately printed in an edition of two thousand by the Blandin Foundation in 1990, and for another coffee-table book of photos, *Travels in Canoe Country* (1990). In January 1995, Gruchow began his "Cannon River Letter," a self-published bimonthly booklet of essays, poems, journal entries, and recommendations in "What I've Been Reading." *Boundary Waters: The Grace of the Wild* was published in 1997.

**FURTHER READING:** The only serious consideration of Gruchow's work to date is Ronald Barron's *A Guide to Minnesota Authors* (1993). In 1996 cinematographer Jon Hanson produced a short tape on Gruchow for the Minnesota Writers Project.

DAVID PICHASKE          SOUTHWEST STATE UNIVERSITY

# EDGAR A(LBERT) GUEST
August 20, 1881–August 5, 1959

**BIOGRAPHY:** Edgar A. Guest, born in Birmingham, England, to Edwin and Julia (Wayne) Guest, came to the United States in 1891 and was naturalized in 1902. In 1895 he began his lifelong career with the *Detroit Free Press*, rising from copyboy through police writer and exchange editor to verse columnist. His weekly "Chaff" became the daily "Breakfast Table Chat," which eventually was syndicated in more than three hundred newspapers. He published more than twenty volumes of those verses, beginning with *Home Rhymes* in 1909. He married Nellie Crossman in 1906, and they had two children, Janet Guest Sobell and Edgar "Bud" Guest Jr. He died of a cerebral hemorrhage in Detroit.

**SIGNIFICANCE:** Guest took up such homely subjects as his titles suggest: "The Apple Tree," "Care-Free Youth," "When Pa Comes Home," and "Little Fishermen," along with meditations such as "Kindness," "Patriotism," and "My Soul and I." God, country, family, and home dominated his topics. The title verse of his *A Heap o' Livin'* (1916) remains his best-known and best-loved poem. In the tradition of JAMES WHITCOMB RILEY and EUGENE FIELD, he used the Midwestern idiom, as in these lines from *The Path to Home* (1919), "Bud Discusses Cleanliness," the voice being that of Guest's son Bud: "First thing in the morning, last I hear at night, / Get it when I come from school: 'My, you look a sight! / Go upstairs this minute, an' roll your sleeves up high, / An' give your hands a scrubbing, an' wipe 'em till they're dry!'" (72). The location of the homes and farms of his subjects is undoubtedly also

Midwestern but universal enough to appeal to much of small-town America.

Critics of poetry had little time for Guest's versification and sentimentality, but he achieved immense popularity during his lifetime, *A Heap o' Livin'* selling more than a million copies. Modestly, he wished to be in the ranks of Robert Louis Stevenson and Robert Burns, though writing on less elevated subjects. In "Bread and Jam," a poem in *A Path to Home*, he indicated that he would be content to write even on humble topics if he could be another Whittier (90–91). Guest's "James Whitcomb Riley" (*A Heap o' Livin'* 54–56) eulogizes that poet, whom he also greatly admired.

**SELECTED WORKS:** A few of Guest's many volumes include *Home* Rhymes (1909), *A Heap o' Livin'* (1916), *Just Folks* (1917), *The Path to Home* (1919), *Life's Highway* (1924), and *Living the Years* (1949).

**FURTHER READING:** Guest's work receives only minor mention, if any, in literary criticism. Information on him appears in such reference works as Carol Smallwood's *Michigan Authors* (1993) and in Royce Howes's *Edgar Guest: A Biography* (1953). The *Detroit Free Press* (August 6, 1959) carried several appreciative articles and an obituary (1, 2, 3, 4, 6, 8, 40) attesting to the affection in which he was held.

MARY DeJONG OBUCHOWSKI
CENTRAL MICHIGAN UNIVERSITY

## JUDITH (ANN) GUEST
March 29, 1936

**BIOGRAPHY:** Born in Detroit to Harry Reginald and Marion Aline (Nesbit) Guest, Judith Guest graduated from the University of Michigan in 1958, taught school in Detroit suburbs, and worked for newspapers in the Chicago area. Her first novel, *Ordinary People* (1976), was an immediate success both as a book and as a screenplay. Her other novels include *Second Heaven* (1982), *Errands* (1997), and, with Rebecca Hill, *Killing Time in St. Cloud* (1988). She has also written screenplays and contributed to periodicals. She divides her time between Edina, Minnesota, and Harrisville, Michigan.

**SIGNIFICANCE:** Guest set all of her books in the Midwest. *Ordinary People* takes place, nominally, in Lake Forest, Illinois. The lifestyle and activities of Conrad Jarrett and his family reflect those of such a Midwestern upper-middle-class community. In *Second Heaven*, the decisions of the adult characters to live in Detroit shape their lives and evolve from their personalities. One of the reasons Mike Atwood's wife has divorced him is that he would not leave Detroit, because "the truth was, he loved this city; it was his hometown, and if it had a reputation, if they called it Motown or Murder City, he couldn't care less" (33). Cat Holtzman also elects to move into the city from Bloomfield Hills after her divorce. The third protagonist is Gale Murray, another teenager, abused by his parents. Gale brings the two adults together as they try to help him through the downtown courts and detention center into a potentially better environment with them. In *Killing Time in St. Cloud*, a psychological thriller, the wintry Minnesota landscape provides complications which enhance the tension in this fast-paced mystery. The incidents that frame *Errands*—the death of Keith Browning and the interlude in which his wife, Annie, finally comes to terms with her grief—take place in Harrisville, on Michigan's Lake Huron coast. The core events, in which their children work through their problems, occur in a Detroit suburb where, although the children are safe enough from adult hazards at night, they create their own potential disasters. Their daughter struggles with school and eventually succeeds, a son resists the temptations of juvenile delinquency, and another son recovers from a fishing accident.

**SELECTED WORKS:** All four novels center upon troubled adolescents and their relationships with the people around them. In *Ordinary People* (1976), Conrad Jarrett struggles with his brother's death, his own mental illness, and his parents' problems. The issue in *Second Heaven* (1982) is child abuse; in *Killing Time in St. Cloud* (1988), it is the effects of psychosis which, undetected in childhood, lead to devastating consequences in adulthood. Grief, anger, and healing, the ways in which the death of Keith Browner affects his wife, Annie, and three children, shape *Errands* (1997).

**FURTHER READING:** No full-length work has yet appeared on Judith Guest.

MARY DeJONG OBUCHOWSKI
CENTRAL MICHIGAN UNIVERSITY

# H

## FRANCIS HACKETT
### January 21, 1883–April 24, 1962

**BIOGRAPHY:** Francis Hackett, the son of John and Bridget (Doheny) Hackett, was born in Kilkenny, Ireland. He received a traditional Roman Catholic education which ended with his attendance at Clongowes Wood College from 1897 to 1900. When he was eighteen years old, disillusioned by the refusal of the Irish to mobilize against the British and questioning the power of the Roman Catholic Church, he emigrated to the United States.

After several jobs in New York City, he moved to Chicago. He worked at odd jobs although his real interest was journalism. He eventually became a reporter for William Randolph Hearst's *Chicago American*. During this period, he lived at Hull House, which was a refuge for immigrants in the city. As a Fabian socialist and as an intellectual, Hackett, who believed that rebellion was a means by which men and women could alter the world and their destinies, found the atmosphere of Hull House stimulating.

When he was fired from the *Chicago American*, Hackett soon found employment as a literary critic at the distinguished *Evening Post*. Its popular literary section was expanded into a supplement known as the *Friday Literary Re-view*, which initially appeared on March 9, 1909, and consisted of eight tabloid pages. Hackett was its first editor, and FLOYD DELL was his assistant. He left the *Friday Literary Review* in 1911 and returned to New York, where he directed his energies to the writing of history, biography, and fiction; however, he was part of the group that launched the *New Republic* in 1914 as a progressive weekly. As its literary editor until he resigned in 1922, he was able to address an intellectual elite as he had done in Chicago.

Hackett eventually returned to Ireland but shortly thereafter moved to Denmark, his wife's home. During World War II, Hackett and his wife, Signe Toksvig, fled to the United States but later returned. He died in Virum, Denmark, of heart failure.

**SIGNIFICANCE:** The literary page of Chicago's *Evening Post* attempted to elevate the taste of the city's elite. Hackett addressed some issues popular in British journals. He brought an unmistakable cosmopolitan air to a newspaper which emphasized financial news and which was read avidly by businessmen as well as by their families. Not satisfied with pandering to the city's mercantile class, he wanted to educate without alienating the newspaper's public or its advertisers.

At a time when much literary criticism had a tendency to be genteel and respectful of the status quo, Hackett was iconoclastic. His political ideas, however, did not jeopardize his commitment to literary standards, and there was a certain earnestness about his work that helped to make it so influential at the time. He was idealistic and refused to be pressured by owners or editors. He reviewed the work of a diverse group, including that of George Bernard Shaw, Henrik Ibsen, H. G. Wells, John Galsworthy, Anatole France, G. K. Chesterton, Friedrich Nietzsche, H. L. Mencken, Jack London, and Maxim Gorky. He also examined Chicago's realistic writers, who were gaining national recognition. He was especially supportive of ROBERT HERRICK, Arthur Eddy, and other novelists who attacked the materialism of the city and who deplored apparent social stratifications. Moreover, Hackett had little tolerance for those who sentimentalized life.

*The Friday Literary Review* became increasingly influential. Its reviews were instrumental in supporting both book reading and book buying in Chicago and elsewhere. Despite his role as a major participant in the Chicago Renaissance, Hackett was never a part of the city's bohemian culture. Furthermore, he was a peripheral member of the Little Room, which gave him access to the business and cultural elite in Chicago. Writing of Hackett's Chicago years, Dale Kramer observed in his *Chicago Renaissance: The Literary Life in the Midwest 1900–1930* (1966): "In London he would have had access to bourgeois publications with audiences ready for his wit and erudition. Here . . . he was a kind of missionary to the heathen" (105).

In time, Hackett's influence was widespread, and he became a conduit for the creation of literary reputations. When SHERWOOD ANDERSON sent his Winesburg stories to Hackett for a reading, Hackett suggested that Ben Heubsch, whose publishing company was issuing the work of some of the nation's avant-garde writers, consider Anderson's tales. Calling the stories *Winesburg, Ohio*, Heubsch published the work in 1919.

Many literary historians date the Chicago Renaissance from the *Evening Post*'s launching of the *Friday Literary Review* with Francis Hackett as its editor. Certainly Hackett made a significant contribution in making the Midwest a center for outstanding critical work.

**SELECTED WORKS:** Hackett was a prolific writer whose work included biographies and several histories of Ireland. Among his novels is *Queen Anne Boleyn* (1939), based upon historical sources. His autobiography, *I Chose Denmark* (1940), reveals much about his own intellectual life and development and explains why he elected to return to Europe. In 1941 he issued *What "Mein Kampf" Means to America* as a warning to the United States.

**FURTHER READING:** The Chicago literary scene and Francis Hackett's role in it are described in some detail in Floyd Dell's *Homecoming: An Autobiography* (1933). References to Hackett also appear in most works relating to the early period of the Chicago Renaissance. Letters, manuscripts, and documents relating to Hackett are held in several research libraries in the United States. Perhaps the largest concentration of materials can be found at the University of Minnesota; however, material specifically relating to the period from 1909 to 1920 is in the Alice Corbin Henderson Collection at the University of Texas at Austin.

KENNY J. WILLIAMS                    DUKE UNIVERSITY

## E(MANUEL) HALDEMAN-JULIUS
July 30, 1889–July 31, 1951

**BIOGRAPHY:** Editor, publisher, writer, and founder of the world-famous Little Blue Books, Emanuel Haldeman-Julius was born in Philadelphia of working-class, immigrant parents, David and Elizabeth (Zolajefsky) Julius, and became a socialist while a teenager. In 1915 he moved to Girard, Kansas, and joined the staff of the *Appeal to Reason* (1990), the socialist newspaper with the largest circulation in the world at that time. In 1916 he married (Anna) Marcet Haldeman, the daughter of a local banker. The couple joined their names and were both known thereafter as Haldeman-Julius. In 1919 he purchased the *Appeal to Reason* and its printing plant with a down payment borrowed from his wife. He began to publish the Little Blue Books, which sold for as little as five cents apiece. Sales expanded, and over the next thirty years hundreds of millions of copies were sold. Titles included reprints of classic stories, Haldeman-Julius's own writings, and "how to do it" books. He had a strong interest in free thought and published Thomas Paine and ROBERT INGERSOLL, and modern writers such as CLARENCE DARROW and Bertrand Russell. Ex-priest Joseph McCabe, whom he billed as "the world's greatest scholar," was one of his most prolific authors, and VANCE RANDOLPH, the noted folklorist, also wrote Little Blue Books. Haldeman-Julius published the complete plays of Shakespeare, Oscar Wilde, and the Greek tragedians.

In 1921 he and Marcet collaborated on a novel, *Dust*; they also wrote short stories and another novel, *Violence*; but the Little Blue Books—2,203 titles in various series—were their most popular sellers. Marcet died in 1941; a year later Haldeman-Julius married his secretary, Susan Haney. He ran afoul of the Federal Bureau of Investigation in the late 1940s after attacking the bureau in a Little Blue Book that described it as "a Gestapo in knee pants." By the end of the decade, America was entering the Cold War and the McCarthy Era, and the Little Blue Book business lagged. J. Edgar Hoover called in the Internal Revenue Service and investigations began. Depressed by the investigations into his affairs, Haldeman-Julius was found dead in his swimming pool in 1951. His death may have been due to a heart attack, or he may have committed suicide. The exact cause of his death is not known. His son, Henry Haldeman-Julius, continued to sell Little Blue Books from the stock in the building that had housed the *Appeal to Reason* and the book company. This structure and the remaining Little Blue Books and other publications were destroyed by fire on July 4, 1978.
**SIGNIFICANCE:** The *Appeal to Reason* put Girard, Kansas, on the map of the American Socialist Party before and during World War I, and Emanuel and Marcet Haldeman-Julius continued that tradition with the Little Blue Books. Socialism and free thought, historically strong in the Midwest, had a center in Girard. With his publications, Haldeman-Julius reached millions of Americans, including Kenneth Rexroth, who related in *An Autobiographical Novel* how he traveled the roads of the West one summer selling Little Blue Books and discussing them with the people he met along his way.
**SELECTED WORKS:** With Marcet as coauthor, Haldeman-Julius published the novels *Dust* (1921) and *Violence* (1929). *The First Hun-*

*dred Million* (1928) and *My First and Second Twenty-Five Years* (1949) relate his experiences as publisher of the Little Blue Books. "The Village Atheist," in *Freethought on the American Frontier*, edited by Fred Whitehead and Verle Muhrer (1992), is representative of Haldeman-Julius's philosophy.
**FURTHER READING:** *"Yours for the Revolution": The Appeal to Reason*, edited by John Graham, discusses the historical background of the Little Blue Books. An excellent source for the publishing history of the various Little Blue Book series is Richard Colles Johnson and G. Thomas Tanselle's "The Haldeman-Julius 'Little Blue Books' as a Bibliographical Problem," in *Papers of the Bibliographic Society of America* 64 (1970): 29–78. Sue Haldeman-Julius's "An Intimate Look at Haldeman-Julius," in *Little Balkans Review* 2.2 (Winter 1981–82): 1–19; and Mark Scott's "The Little Blue Books in the War on Bigotry and Bunk," in *Kansas History* 1 (1978): 155–76, are useful sources. The Haldeman-Julius Collection of the Leonard H. Axe Library at Pittsburg State University in Pittsburg, Kansas, has the most complete holdings of Little Blue Books and other publications of Haldeman-Julius. Many of his private papers and business correspondence are also in this collection. The Lilly Library at Indiana University also has an extensive collection of Little Blue Books and approximately one-third of Haldeman-Julius's private papers.

TOM L. PAGE                    WICHITA STATE UNIVERSITY

## DONALD (ANDREW) HALL (JR.)
September 20, 1928

**BIOGRAPHY:** Born in New Haven, Connecticut, the son of Donald Andrew, a businessman, and Lucy (Wells) Hall, Donald Hall received a BA from Harvard in 1951 and a bachelor of literature degree from Oxford University in 1953. He taught in the Department of English at the University of Michigan from 1957 to 1975 and has done extensive editorial and consulting work as poetry editor for *Paris Review* and elsewhere. He has contributed to periodicals and written books of poetry, fiction, nonfiction, criticism, drama, children's books, and textbooks for literature and writing and has edited anthologies. His honors include Guggenheim Fellowships and many poetry awards. He was married to Kirby (Thompson) from 1952 to 1969, with whom he had two children, Andrew and Philippa. In 1972 he married Jane Kenyon, who died in 1995. In 1975 he bought Eagle Pond Farm in Danbury, New Hampshire, which had belonged to his grandparents, and he still resides there.

**SIGNIFICANCE:** The variety and range of Hall's work defies formulation; in fact, his poetry, like his fiction, maintains a balance between the classic and the contemporary in form as it does in language, tone, and theme, moving from the irreverent wit to the darkness of mortality. His interviews with poets such as Frost and T. S. ELIOT, most recently published as *Their Ancient Glittering Eyes* (1992), textbooks, including *Writing Well* (1973), and anthologies have secure places in classrooms. He has written several children's books, including *Ox-Cart Man*, illustrated by Jane Cooney (1979), which received the 1980 Caldecott Medal.

Hall's roots remain firmly in New England, and a recurrent theme in his poems and stories has to do with the cycle of generations and the links to his New Hampshire ancestors. However, references to his Michigan days emerge in his books and capture the scents and sounds of a Midwestern college town. The title poem of *Kicking the Leaves* (1978) begins on a football Saturday in Ann Arbor. Satiric images of faculty gatherings at the University of Michigan, memories of family occasions during those years, and fragmentary accounts of travel in the Midwest appear in both his prose and his poetry.

**SELECTED WORKS:** Material from Hall's early book *String Too Short to Be Saved: Childhood Reminiscences* (1961; expanded 3rd ed., 1979) became the drama *The Bone Ring* (1987). He ventured into the world of art and biography with *Henry Moore: The Life and Work of a Great Sculptor* (1966). Among his books of poetry are *Exiles and Marriages* (1955), *The Alligator Bride: Poems New and Selected* (1969), *The Town of Hill* (1975), *Kicking the Leaves* (1978), and *The Happy Man* (1986). *The Museum of Clear Ideas* (1993) illustrates one of Hall's great loves, baseball. His books on poets and poetry include *Marianne Moore: The Cage and the Animal* (1970) and *Goatfoot Milktongue Twinbird: Interviews, Essays, and Notes on Poetry, 1970–1976* (1978) and its sequel *The Weather for Poetry: Essays, Reviews, and Notes on Poetry, 1977–1981* (1982), and *Their Ancient Glittering Eyes* (1992).

Donald Hall.
Photo © Nancy Crampton

His children's books include *Andrew and the Lion Farmer*, illustrated by Jane Miller (1959) and by Ann Reason (1961); *Ox-Cart Man*, illustrated by Jane Cooney (1979); *The Farm Summer 1942* and *I Am the Dog, I Am the Cat*, both illustrated by Barry Moser (both 1994); and *Lucy's Summer* and *Lucy's Christmas* (1994).

**FURTHER READING:** *The Day I Was Older: On the Poetry of Donald Hall*, edited by Liam Rector (1989), brings together essays on Hall by a variety of poets and critics.

MARY DEJONG OBUCHOWSKI
CENTRAL MICHIGAN UNIVERSITY

## JAMES HALL
July 29, 1793–July 5, 1868
(Orlando)

**BIOGRAPHY:** James Hall was born in Philadelphia to John and Sarah (Ewing) Hall. After a bad experience at a Philadelphia academy, he was educated at home by his mother. At age nineteen he enlisted in the military, serving for five years. He left the army in 1818, shortly after having been admitted to the bar and after having been court-martialed and later pardoned by President Monroe. After a brief stint writing for the *Pittsburgh Gazette*, he set off for the West in 1820, traveling down the Ohio River on a keelboat, a journey which would acquaint him with the material with which he would make his mark as an American writer.

At the end of Hall's journey lay Shawneetown, Illinois, where Hall would begin to build his career as a man of law and letters. In Shawneetown he served as prosecuting attorney and circuit judge and edited a newspaper, the *Illinois Gazette*. In 1823 he married Mary Harrison Posey; four children resulted from this union. In 1827 the Halls moved to Vandalia, Illinois, at that time the state capital. There Hall served as state treasurer, published a newspaper, the *Illinois Intelligencer*, and founded the *Illinois Monthly Magazine*, the first literary magazine west of the Ohio. Hall was also one of the founders of the Antiquarian and Historical Society of Illinois.

The year 1832 marked the lowest point in Hall's life. His wife died, he lost his job as state treasurer, and he was forced to sell his press and give up his newspaper to pay his debts. Hall responded to these crises by moving to Cincinnati to rebuild his life. There he published his *Illinois Monthly Magazine* as the *Western Monthly Magazine*, built its subscription list to three thousand, and found a new career opportunity in banking and finance. From 1836 until his retirement in 1865 Hall was associated with the Commercial Bank of Cincinnati, serving as cashier, as president, and as a member of the board of directors. In 1839 he married Mary Louise Anderson Alexander and fathered four more children. He died at his country home near Cincinnati.

**SIGNIFICANCE:** As one of the Ohio Valley's earliest men of letters, James Hall played a pivotal role in the construction of that region for Eastern audiences, representing it as a place of breathtaking beauty, unbelievable fertility, and relentless violence. Although his fictional works contain many characteristics of romantic literature, they also foreshadow the work of prairie realists such as DAVID ROSS LOCKE and JOSEPH KIRKLAND in their descriptions of the manners and customs of Ohio Valley pioneers. Readers who want to know how log cabins were furnished, what settlers ate at community feasts, what happened at camp meetings, and how coon

James Hall.
Photo courtesy of David D. Anderson

hunts were conducted can find the details in Hall's works.

Hall's travel narrative, *Letters from the West* (1828), is an account of his keelboat journey down the Ohio, mixing personal adventures and observations with frontier folklore. Later books include both folkloric elements and realistic accounts of frontier life; they also introduce several regional character types to the American reading public. *The Western Souvenir*, a gift book he put out in 1828, includes his story "The Bachelor's Elysium," first published in 1823, featuring a rough-edged backwoodsman who suggests James Fenimore Cooper's Natty Bumppo. *The Western Souvenir* also contains a story by Morgan Neville in which Mike Fink and his keelboat make their first appearance in American literature. Another story in that volume, Hall's "The Indian Hater," introduces the title character, an antecedent of Robert Montgomery Bird's Nathan Slaughter in *Nick of the Woods* (1837), and serves as a source for Herman Melville's 1857 novel *The Confidence-Man*.

Hall's only novel, *The Harpe's Head* (1833), builds on the legends that grew up around outlaws Micajah and Wiley Harpe to create yet another backwoods character type: the bloodthirsty lowlife who lives on the fringes of the frontier, raping, robbing, and murdering for sport. This novel also features a prototype of Huckleberry Finn in the orphan Hark Short, who prefers the freedom of the forest to the more confining life of the prairie community.

**SELECTED WORKS:** Among Hall's books on frontier life are one miscellany, *The Western Souvenir* (1828); one travel narrative, *Letters from the West* (1828); one novel, *The Harpe's Head* (1833); and four books of tales: *Legends of the West* (1832), *The Soldier's Bride and Other Tales* (1833), *Tales of the Border* (1835), and *The Wilderness and the Warpath* (1846).

**FURTHER READING:** There are three book-length studies of Hall: JOHN FLANAGAN'S *James Hall, Literary Pioneer of the Ohio Valley* (1941), Randolph Randall's *James Hall: Spokesman for the New West* (1964), and Mary Burtschi's *James Hall of Lincoln's Frontier World* (1977). Most of Hall's papers can be found at the Cincinnati Historical Society.

MARCIA NOE

THE UNIVERSITY OF TENNESSEE AT CHATTANOOGA

## JAMES NORMAN HALL

April 22, 1887–July 6, 1951

**BIOGRAPHY:** Born in Colfax, Iowa, to Arthur Wright and Ellen (Young) Hall, James Norman Hall began writing in his youth, earning the appellation of woodshed poet by scribbling verse on his family woodshed. He graduated from Grinnell College in 1910 and moved to Boston, where he was a social worker for four years. He then toyed with the idea of becoming a sheepherder in Montana before choosing to enlist in the British infantry. Hall reenlisted as an aviator with the Escadrille Lafayette. In 1925 he married sixteen-year-old Sarah Winchester, the part-Polynesian daughter of a Liverpool sea captain.

Except for the publication of a few poems, Hall's writing career began with *Kitchener's Mob* (1916), a narrative of his experiences in the trenches of France. Another war narrative, *High Adventure* (1918), followed before he coauthored *Lafayette Flying Corps* (1920) with Charles Bernard Nordhoff. After their initial collaboration, Hall and Nordhoff set off for Polynesia intent on writing a series of articles and a book. Both would spend the majority of their lives in Polynesia, publishing essay collections and juvenile fiction until beginning their most successful collaboration, the

Bounty trilogy. *Mutiny on the Bounty* (1932) quickly became a best-seller and a popular movie. The successive novels in the trilogy, *Men against the Sea* (1934) and *Pitcairn's Island* (1936), were likewise popular. Hall died of coronary failure at his home in Arue, Tahiti, in 1951.

**SIGNIFICANCE:** Although best-remembered for the Bounty trilogy, Hall is a keen social critic who celebrates a Midwestern past even while living in the South Seas. The distinction between his boyhood Iowa home and Polynesia blurs in many of his works. *On the Stream of Travel* (1925) laments the loss of Iowa as it extols Polynesia. Hall's identification of Polynesia with the Midwest may seem paradoxical. However, in *Tale of a Shipwreck* (1934), for example, Hall praises Polynesia for a pace of life he associates with his boyhood home, now being destroyed by an army of Babbitts. In his 1978 *James Norman Hall*, Robert Roulston elaborates, "Hall in a sense never left rural Iowa because he . . . regained many of its most cherished qualities in the South Seas" (119).

The humor and irony of Hall's attachment to Iowa is reflected in *Oh Millersville!* (1940). This poem was published as the work of Fern Gravel, a little girl who lived in turn-of-the-century Iowa. In this literary hoax, Hall acknowledges the narrowness of small-town life even as he mourns its passing. Hall also emphasizes Midwestern themes in *Mid-Pacific* (1928), *Under a Thatched Roof* (1942), and his autobiography, *My Island Home* (1952). In the concluding chapter of the autobiography, Hall writes, "Iowa, for all the years I have been away from it, has always been, and still is, home for me" (328–29).

Hall's popularity dropped sharply after his death. He is known chiefly for the historical novels coauthored with Nordhoff. However, his essay collections and autobiography provide a stirring indictment of progress echoed in the works of his contemporaries.

**SELECTED WORKS:** Hall's nonfiction works include *Kitchener's Mob: Adventures of an American in Kitchener's Army* (1916), *High Adventure: A Narrative of Air Fighting in France* (1918), *On the Stream of Travel* (1926), *Mid-Pacific* (1928), *Flying with Chaucer* (1930), *Mother Goose Land* (1930), *The Tale of a Shipwreck* (1934), *Doctor Dogbody's Leg* (1940), *Under a Thatched Roof* (1942), *Lost Island* (1944), *The Far Lands* (1950), and *The*

*Forgotten One, and Other True Tales of the South Seas* (1952). Hall's autobiography, *My Island Home* (1952), was published posthumously. Hall's first volume of poetry is *The Friends* (1939). Other poetry includes *Oh Millersville!* (1940), *A Word for His Sponsor, a Narrative Poem* (1949) and *Her Daddy's Best Ice Cream* (1952). Novels written with Charles Nordhoff include *Lafayette Flying Corps* (1920), *Faery Lands of the South Seas* (1921), *Falcons of France: A Tale of Youth and the Air* (1929), *Mutiny on the Bounty* (1932), *Men against the Sea* (1934), *Pitcairn's Island* (1934), *The Hurricane* (1936), *The Dark River* (1938), *No More Gas* (1940), *Botany Bay* (1941), *Men without Country* (1942), and *High Barbaree* (1945).

**FURTHER READING:** Robert Roulston's *James Norman Hall* (1978) provides a good analysis of major works as well as substantial biographical information. Robert Leland Johnson's *The American Heritage of James Norman Hall, the Woodshed Poet of Iowa and Co-Author of Mutiny on the Bounty* (1969) offers a perspective on Hall's family roots and social context but assumes a certain familiarity with Hall's works. Other works include Paul Briand's *In Search of Paradise: The Nordhoff-Hall Story* (1966). Hall's papers are located in the Burlington Library of Grinnell College.

JOHN L. SUTTON                    NEW YORK UNIVERSITY

## JOHN T. HALLWAS.
*See* appendix (1994)

## JANE HAMILTON
July 13, 1957

**BIOGRAPHY:** Born in Oak Park, Illinois, to Allen and Ruth (Hubert) Hamilton, novelist Jane Hamilton comes by the craft of fiction naturally, for her mother and grandmother were writers. "I wanted to write fiction pretty much all along," she says. "I thought that was what you were supposed to do if you were a girl child." Hamilton has lived in the Midwest all of her life; small towns in Illinois and Wisconsin figure prominently as settings for her fiction. Growing up in Oak Park, she recalls, was not really a small-town experience but "a great place, green and beautiful and sheltered, yet it offered access to the huge world of the city, so that I could be in one place and yet experience a completely different place."

After graduating from Carleton College in Northfield, Minnesota, in 1979, Hamilton wanted to enroll in a graduate program in creative writing, "but no one would have me." She headed east instead to follow up on the possibility of a New York City publishing job, stopping in Rochester, Wisconsin, to visit a friend whose cousin owned an apple orchard there. She found that she liked the people, the farm life, and, most of all, the cousin, Robert Willard, whom she married three years later. Also in 1982 she published her first short story and began a lengthy term of service as president of the Rochester Library Board.

As an emerging novelist, Hamilton found Midwestern farm life especially conducive to fiction writing. "It was good to be in a place that was off the beaten path in terms of writing. I was not as self-conscious as I would have been had I lived in New York City." Throughout the 1980s and 1990s, Hamilton combined fiction writing with marriage and motherhood, giving birth to a son and a daughter. Her first novel, *The Book of Ruth* (1988), won the Pen/Hemingway Award, the Banta Award, and the Great Lakes Colleges New Writers Award. The recipient of a grant from the National Endowment for the Arts in 1993, Hamilton published her second novel, *A Map of the World*, the following year. Her third novel, *The Short History of a Prince*, was published in 1998.

**SIGNIFICANCE:** When asked what Midwestern authors have most influenced her work, Hamilton cites WILLA CATHER and JANE SMILEY, writers who, like Hamilton, focus on the cultural changes the Midwest has experienced over time and on nonconformists who are treated insensitively and sometimes even demonized by their more conventional neighbors. Like Cather's Claude Wheeler, SINCLAIR LEWIS's Carol Kennicott, and SHERWOOD ANDERSON's Wing Biddlebaum, Jane Hamilton's central characters are Midwestern misfits; Hamilton's intelligent, perceptive, and articulate reflections on what, how, and why they suffer give her fiction unusual depth and resonance.

Ruth Grey, the first-person narrator of Hamilton's *The Book of Ruth*, grows up in a little country town in northern Illinois, hungry for praise and attention, in a fatherless home headed by an abusive and neglectful mother. Relegated to remedial classes and ostracized by her schoolmates, Ruth achieves a sense of self-worth for the first time when she falls in love with Ruby Dahl, a drug and alcohol abuser who is allergic to work and prone to violence. Their subsequent marriage ends in disaster; when a family fight escalates, Ruby beats up Ruth and bludgeons his mother-in-law to death with a poker, events which force Ruth to critically reexamine her life in order to reconstruct it.

The fate of the misfits in Hamilton's second novel, *A Map of the World*, comments more directly on the changing character of the Midwest. In a brilliantly ironic inversion that emphasizes the death of the agrarian dream, it is dairy farmers Alice and Howard Goodwin who are the persecuted misfits in a rural Wisconsin community that is rapidly becoming suburban in economy, values, and lifestyle. Their dream of sustaining a livelihood by farming is destroyed by two crises: a neighbor's child drowns in their farm pond and a student at the school where Alice works as a nurse accuses her of molesting him. Although Alice is acquitted and the Goodwin family survives these ordeals intact, they lose their farm, an event that comes to symbolize not only the many losses that occur in this novel—losses of innocence, trust, friendship, community, and values—but also the loss of a rural identity and economy that in an earlier day had been the Midwest's strongest cultural characteristic.

*The Short History of a Prince* is Hamilton's most complex and nuanced treatment of the Midwestern misfit. In this novel she moves the reader back and forth in time between 1972 and 1996, rendering the coming of age of Walter McCloud as he comes to terms with his sexual orientation as a gay man and his lack of talent for the ballet that he loves so passionately. As Walter grows to manhood and trades his dream of a professional future in ballet for a job teaching English and directing school plays in a small Wisconsin town, he experiences betrayal, neglect, humiliation, and rejection before achieving self-acceptance and reconciliation with his family.

**SELECTED WORKS:** Hamilton has published three novels: *The Book of Ruth* (1988), *A Map of the World* (1994), and *The Short History of a Prince* (1998). She has also published four short stories: "My Own Earth," *Harper's* 265 (November 1982): 39–49; "Aunt Marji's Happy Ending," *Harper's* 267 (December 1983): 56–60; "When I Began to Understand Quantum Mechanics,"

*Harper's* 279 (August 1989): 41–49; and "Rehearsing the Firebird," *Harper's* 280 (June 1990): 62–69.

**FURTHER READING:** No critical studies of Hamilton's works have yet been published. Articles in the popular press include Viva Hardigg's "Mapping America's Heart," *U.S. News and World Report* 116 (June 13, 1994): 82; and Patrick McCormick's "Thrice-Told Tales," *U.S. Catholic* 62 (May 1997): 46–49. See also interviews in *Writer's Digest* 7 (October 1990): 28–29 and *Publishers Weekly* 245 (February 2, 1998): 68–69.

MARCIA NOE

THE UNIVERSITY OF TENNESSEE AT CHATTANOOGA

## VIRGINIA (ESTHER) HAMILTON
March 12, 1936

**BIOGRAPHY:** Virginia Hamilton, celebrated children's book author and folklorist, was born on an Ohio farm near Yellow Springs. Youngest of the five children of Kenneth James and Etta Belle (Perry) Hamilton, she became deeply attached to her Perry extended family and to their land settled by her fugitive slave grandfather, Levi Perry. Perry, his part-Cherokee wife, and their many descendants wrested a living from the fertile Ohio soil but found their joy and recreation in family storytelling. Captivated by tales from the past, gossip, jokes, superstitions, and tall tales related at family gatherings, as well as biblical narratives heard in the churches, Hamilton began to think in terms of stories at an early age. From her talented, well-read father she learned to value their African American heritage, a topic she would explore in her research and writing; his heroes, W. E. B. DuBois and Paul Robeson, would become the subjects of her first two biographies; her father's advice, to be not only the best but to be original, would encourage her to break with the genteel literary tradition and dare to create innovative books that are uniquely her own.

After three years at Antioch College followed by two years at Ohio State University, she left the Midwest for New York City. While devoting herself to writing, she took courses at the New School for Social Research and worked part-time. In 1960 she married New York teacher, poet, and anthologist Arnold Adoff. They became the parents of a biracial daughter and son. In 1967 Hamilton was

**Virginia Hamilton.**
Photo by Jimmy Byrge. Courtesy of Virginia Hamilton

launched as a professional writer when Macmillan published her first children's book, *Zeely*, an Ohio girl's coming-of-age story that was named an American Library Association Notable Book. It was followed by a mystery set in Yellow Springs, *The House of Dies Drear* (1968), an award winner that received favorable reviews. In 1969 Hamilton and her family moved from New York to Ohio, where they built their permanent home on two acres of the original Perry farm, land rich in childhood and family memories,

Publishing at least one book a year since 1967, Hamilton has received many awards for her unique achievements in children's literature and in folklore. Her honors include the International Hans Christian Andersen Medal, the National Book Award, two Coretta Scott King Awards, the Newbery Medal, the Regina Medal, two Ohioana Book Awards, the LAURA INGALLS WILDER Award, and a grant from the John D. and Catherine T. MacArthur Foundation. She was awarded the Society for the Study of Midwestern Literature's 1999 Mark Twain Award for distinguished contributions to Midwestern literature. Hamilton continues to create multicultural books that receive the highest praise for literary excellence.

**SIGNIFICANCE:** Hamilton leaves little doubt of the importance of her home place to her work. Speaking to educators in Fairborn, Ohio, on February 24, 1995, she declared, "Everything I write comes out of Ohio."

Placing most of her fiction in rural or small-town Ohio, she breaks new ground by portraying African Americans like her ancestors and herself as the settlers and long-time residents of Ohio land. Coining the term "parallel culture" for such distinctive nonwhite, ethnic, or multiracial communities, she is one of the first Midwestern writers to create children's novels, biographies, and story collections from within her own African American culture. Dismissing the terms "minority" and "majority," she portrays parallel cultures as diverse but as fully equal to American cultures of European descent.

As an African American storyteller writing in the oral tradition, Hamilton weaves stories within stories, creating a narrative from a variety of characters, time frames, plots, and subplots. Quoting directly from the conversations and inner thoughts of her African American characters, she approximates their speech in a reasonably colloquial dialect, distinguishing between city and "Ohio country" vernacular. Their stories are rich in proverbs, riddles, songs, folk spirits, ghostly apparitions, and legendary heroes from the African American tradition, elements of a folklore new to Midwestern literature. The themes focus on the importance of a strong family, a knowledge of ancestors and ethnic heritage, preservation of the land, and freedom for all people. Like her fellow-Ohioan TONI MORRISON, she draws upon the riches of the African American experience, contemporary and historical, to create powerful stories of universal significance.

Hamilton's strong Ohio settings lend credibility to both her fantasies and her realistic stories. Many of her characters live on Perry-like farms or in towns with thinly veiled street names of Yellow Springs, colleges like Antioch, and the limestone ledges and caves of a nearby glen. The influence of the Ohio locale, along with an environmental warning, is further confirmed by the extremes of climate described so convincingly in the drought conditions of *Drylongso* (1992) and the early spring floods in *Plain City* (1993).

**SELECTED WORKS:** *W. E. B. DuBois* (1972) and *Paul Robeson: The Life and Times of a Free Black Man* (1974) are her earliest biographies honoring African American leaders. Her "Ohio" novels for children include *Zeely* (1967), the two mysteries, *The House of Dies Drear* (1968) and *The Mystery of Drear House* (1987), the Newbery Medal–winner *M. C. Higgins the Great* (1974), *Cousins* (1990), *Plain City* (1993), and *Second Cousins* (1998). Books that feature characters with unusual psychic power are represented in the time-space trilogy, *Justice and Her Brothers* (1978), *Dustland* (1980), and *The Gathering* (1981), as well as in *Sweet Whispers, Brother Rush* (1982) and *Drylongso* (1992). In *The Magical Adventures of Pretty Pearl* (1983), Hamilton brings together her love of fantasy, myth-making, and African American history and folklore to create a complex and powerful novel for readers of all ages. The joys of a strong supportive family are showcased in the humorous *Willie Bea and the Time the Martians Landed* (1983) and in the holiday festivities of 1890 in *The Bells of Christmas* (1989), a picture book. Two realistic novels for young adults are *A Little Love* (1984), a girl's search for her father, and *A White Romance* (1987), a suspenseful story of biracial friendships. In the 1980s Hamilton created a new genre called "liberation literature," defined by Rudine Sims Bishop in the August 1995 *Horn Book* as "literature about . . . individuals who, against great odds, pursued their freedom" (444). Beginning with the folktale collection *The People Could Fly* (1985) and continuing with the slave biographies *Anthony Burns: The Defeat and Triumph of a Fugitive Slave* (1988) and *Many Thousand Gone: African Americans from Slavery to Freedom* (1993), she makes available to readers of all ages the liberating stories that belong to America's folklore and history. Enlarging her scope to include other parallel cultures, she published *In the Beginning: Creation Stories from around the World* (1988) and *The Dark Way: Stories from the Spirit World* (1990). More story collections, all beautifully and aptly illustrated, include *Her Stories: African American Folktales, Fairy Tales, and True Tales* (1995), *When Birds Could Talk and Bats Could Sing* (1996), and *A Ring of Tricksters: Animal Tales from America, the West Indies and Africa* (1997). *Jaguarundi* (1995), a spectacular picture book, continues the African American freedom theme along with an environmental message in an animal migration story. Virginia Hamilton invites her readers to enjoy her "virtual home" at www.VirginiaHamilton.com.

**FURTHER READING:** In *Virginia Hamilton: Ohio Explorer in the World of Imagination* (1979), a monograph published by the State Library of Ohio, Marilyn Apseloff gives a perceptive analysis of the significance of Ohio in Hamilton's writings. *Virginia Hamilton* (1994), by Nina Mikkelson, is a thorough, scholarly, book-length study of the writer as a storyteller and cultural teacher; a chronology, photos, biography, and bibliography are helpful inclusions. Kent State University Library and Central State University Library, both in Ohio, serve as repositories for Hamilton's papers.

MARY JOAN MILLER SPRINGFIELD, OHIO

## PATRICIA HAMPL
March 12, 1946

**BIOGRAPHY:** Patricia Hampl, a St. Paul native, grew up an avid reader. Her parents, Stanley, a florist, and Mary (Marum) Hampl, a librarian at Macalester College, nurtured her literary bent. After an undergraduate education at the University of Minnesota, where she received encouragement as a fledgling writer from GARRISON KEILLOR, who edited the school's literary magazine, Hampl entered the University of Iowa Writers' Workshop, earning an MFA in 1970. She returned to Minnesota to pursue a career as a writer, publishing essays, poetry, fiction, and memoirs. She was founding editor of what is now the *Minnesota Monthly*, the magazine of Minnesota Public Radio. After winning writing grants from the National Endowment of the Arts and other agencies for her poetry, she joined the English faculty at the University of Minnesota, where she continues to teach creative writing.

Hampl has published several volumes of poetry, and her work has appeared in leading magazines such as *American Poetry Review, New Yorker, Paris Review,* and others. In 1981 she received a Houghton Mifflin literary fellowship to support the writing of *A Romantic Education* (1981), a ruminative memoir about her St. Paul upbringing and Czech family history; a later reminiscence, *Virgin Time* (1992), addresses her Catholic girlhood and explores the life of the spirit. *Spillville* (1987) is an imaginative recreation of a summer spent in the Midwest by composer Antonin Dvorak. In 1990 Hampl received a prestigious MacArthur Fellowship; she was awarded a Fulbright Fellowship to Prague, Czech Republic, in 1995. She lives in the St. Paul of her formative years.

**SIGNIFICANCE:** Patricia Hampl's evocations of St. Paul and of the northern Midwest are among the most palpable literary treatments of the region. Her work reflects the characteristic mix of nostalgia and discontent that has fueled so many heartland writers. *A Romantic Education* in particular captures that emotional paradox, with its wry celebration of Minnesota's icy winters and its humorous rendition of "the provincial anguish" of Midwestern identity (50). The Hampl family home was in a middle-class neighborhood adjacent to the famous Summit Avenue where F. SCOTT FITZGERALD and James J. Hill had resided. As a child, Hampl walked to school along the avenue, awed by its roster of august names and by the towering presence of the St. Paul Cathedral at the crest of the hill. These influences remained with her, compelling much of her later writing, including *A Romantic Education* and *Virgin Time.*

In a recent addition to her cluster of memoirs, "In the Mountain Ranges and Rain Forests of St. Paul," Hampl articulates the ways in which the "ordinariness" of life in that Midwestern city propelled her to imagine the rich extremes of the world's landscapes and climates, which in turn have come to be enfolded into her vision of St. Paul's own venues. As a whole, Hampl's writing gives us the contemporary Midwestern sensibility as freshly and acutely as the work of any writer.

**SELECTED WORKS:** Hampl's poetry has been collected in two volumes, *Woman Before an Aquarium* (1978) and *Resort and Other Poems* (1983), and her edited collection of sacred poetry, *Burning Bright: An Anthology* (1995). Her three book-length memoirs are *A Romantic Education* (1981) and *Virgin Time* (1992), and *I Could Tell You Stories: Sojourns in the Land of Memory* (1999). "In the Mountains and Rain Forests of St. Paul" appeared in *Imagining Home: Writing from the Midwest,* edited by Mark Vinz and Thom Tammaro (1995).

**FURTHER READING:** There is no significant critical literature on Hampl at present. In addition to reviews of her various books, there are entries in *Contemporary Authors* 104 (1982): 193–94; and *Contemporary Authors, New Revision Series* 21 (1987): 168. A useful piece is Hampl's article "Meridel Le Sueur, Voice of the Prairie," in *Ms.* 4.2 (August 1975): 62–66, 95–96. Additional information is included in "Views from the Hill," in *Growing Up in the Midwest,* edited by CLARENCE ANDREWS (1981).

LIAHNA BABENER CENTRAL WASHINGTON UNIVERSITY

# LORRAINE HANSBERRY

May 19, 1930–January 12, 1965

**BIOGRAPHY:** Lorraine Hansberry was the youngest of four children of Carl A. Hansberry and Nanny (Perry) Hansberry. Hansberry's mother, a social and political activist to whom *A Raisin in the Sun* (1959) is dedicated, was born in Columbia, Tennessee; the influence of her mother's Southern roots as well as her activism pervades Hansberry's writings. Her father, a successful Chicago real estate agent, challenged restrictive real estate covenants by buying a home in a neighborhood "restricted" to whites. The family withstood a brick-throwing white mob and won legal vindication before the Supreme Court in *Hansberry v. Lee* (1940), which outlawed restrictive covenants. The Hansberry home was a meeting place for African American thinkers and activists. *A Raisin in the Sun,* with its portraits of aspiring intellectuals as well as working-class people, each responding to segregation and racism in an individual way, reflects the variety of people she met and the contradictions of life in a Midwestern ghetto, the south side of Chicago.

After attending the University of Wisconsin, Hansberry moved to New York in 1950, where she was a reporter for Paul Robeson's newspaper, *Freedom.* She married Robert Nemiroff in 1953; although the couple was divorced in 1964, they remained friends and coworkers, Nemiroff continuing his collaboration even after her death as her literary executor.

*A Raisin in the Sun*, completed in 1957, opened at the Ethel Barrymore Theatre on Broadway on March 11, 1959, where it ran for 538 performances. It won the New York Drama Critics Circle Award as Best Play of the Year over Tennessee Williams's *Sweet Bird of Youth* and Eugene O'Neill's *A Touch of the Poet*. *The Sign in Sidney Brustein's Window* ran on Broadway for 101 performances, closing in 1965 on the night of Hansberry's death from cancer. *To Be Young, Gifted, and Black* opened in New York in 1969, and *Les Blancs* in 1970; both plays were adapted by Robert Nemiroff after Hansberry's death.

**SIGNIFICANCE:** Although *A Raisin in the Sun* is generally considered one of the classics of American drama, the play's presentation of African American life has aroused controversy from its opening. In *The Crisis of the Negro Intellectual* (1967), Harold Cruse condemned the play as a "glorified soap opera" (278) whose characters "mouth middle-class ideology" (280). On the other hand, C. W. E. Bigsby in *Confrontation and Commitment* (1967) argued that the play's emphasis on the "parochial injustices of racial intolerance" (172) kept Hansberry from reaching the universality of great drama. Hansberry's own view of her accomplishment in *A Raisin in the Sun* has won wide acceptance: the play indeed focuses on the specific dilemmas facing African Americans in the Chicago of the 1950s, but the probing of the dilemmas facing the Younger family has a universal resonance.

Just as Eugene O'Neill's *Long Day's Journey into Night* achieves general significance probing conflicts whose particular tensions reflect the culture of New England Irish Catholicism, so Hansberry's dramatization of the Younger family's conflicts is not limited but deepened through the concreteness of its presentation of African American life in Chicago. Hansberry's play vividly recreates the south side of the 1950s, where African Americans of all classes and pursuits were packed together: young urban intellectuals like Beneatha and Asagai, working-class people like Walter, Mama, and Ruth, and upper-class families like the Murchisons. Hansberry's realism insures that the play's conclusion, in which the Youngers move to a white neighborhood, is anything but a fairy-tale

happy ending. Hansberry herself urged those who see the move as guaranteeing that the Youngers would live "happily ever after" to "come live in one of the communities where the Youngers are going" (*A Raisin in the Sun and The Sign in Sidney Brustein's Window* xiv).

The twenty-fifth anniversary edition of *A Raisin in the Sun and The Sign in Sidney Brustein's Window* (1987) includes an essay by Amiri Baraka in which he admits that those, like himself, who had once criticized *A Raisin in the Sun* as ideologically dated had "missed the essence of the work." Baraka adds that "what is most telling about our ignorance is that Hansberry's play still remains overwhelmingly popular and evocative of black and white reality" (19). In an essay included in the same edition, John Braine asserts, against the consensus of the Broadway critics, that *The Sign in Sidney Brustein's Window* "is a great play" (159).

The other plays, essays, and poems Hansberry completed in her short life include much compelling material, as the success of *To Be Young, Gifted, and Black*, a collection of Hansberry's writings edited by Robert Nemiroff, demonstrates. *A Raisin in the Sun* is, however, unquestionably both Hansberry's masterpiece and the work most clearly identified with her Midwestern origins.

**SELECTED WORKS:** The text of *A Raisin in the Sun* was published in 1959, and the script of *The Sign in Sidney Brustein's Window* appeared in 1965. *Les Blancs: The Collected Last Plays of Lorraine Hansberry*, a posthumous volume edited by Robert Nemiroff (1972), includes *Les Blancs, What Use Are Flowers?* and *The Drinking Gourd. The Movement: Documentary of a Struggle for Equality* (1964) is a book of photographs of the civil rights struggle chosen by the Student Nonviolent Coordinating Committee with text by Hansberry. *Toussaint*, a play Hansberry left unfinished, is included in *9 Plays by Black Women*, edited by Margaret Wilkerson (1968). *To Be Young, Gifted, and Black: Lorraine Hansberry in Her Own Words*, edited by Robert Nemiroff (1969), includes excerpts from a wide range of Hansberry's works. An "expanded 25th anniversary edition" of *A Raisin in the Sun*, edited by Robert Nemiroff (1987), includes the text of *The Sign in Sidney Brustein's Window* and essays by Amiri Baraka, Frank Rich, John Braine, and Robert Nemiroff. Lorraine Hansberry's papers will be deposited at the Schomburg Center for Research and Black Culture in New York City.

**FURTHER READING:** Anne Cheney's *Lorraine Hansberry* (1984) is both a biography and a critical study. Steven R. Carter's *Hansberry's Drama: Commitment amid Complexity* (1991) focuses on Hansberry as a playwright. Margaret Wilkerson's "Lorraine Vivian Hansberry" appears both in *Black Women in America*, edited by Darlene Clark Hine (1993), and in *Notable Women in the American Theatre*, edited by Robinson, Roberts, and Barranger (1989). For a work emphasizing Hansberry as a thinker rather than a literary figure, see Ben Keppel's *The Work of Democracy: Ralph Bunche, Kenneth B. Clark, Lorraine Hansberry, and the Cultural Politics of Race* (1995).

SANDRA SEATON    CENTRAL MICHIGAN UNIVERSITY

## HARRY HANSEN

December 26, 1884–January 2, 1977

**BIOGRAPHY:** Born in Davenport, Iowa, to German immigrant parents Christine (Jochims) and Hans Hansen, Harry Hansen attended public schools in that city before embarking on a writing career that would span eight decades and include work as a reporter, historian, translator, columnist, editor, novelist, and book reviewer. After working as a beat reporter for newspapers in Davenport, he enrolled in the University of Chicago, graduating in 1909. Then, after a short stint in public relations for the university, he hired on with the *Chicago Daily News* in 1911 to write book reviews and later became literary editor of that publication. He served as a foreign correspondent for the *Daily News* during World War I, surviving capture by the Germans to cover the Versailles Peace Conference. He married Ruth McLernon in 1914; the couple had two daughters, Ruth and Marian.

In 1926 the Hansens moved to Westchester County in New York after he became literary editor of the *New York World*, writing a literary column, hosting a weekly radio program, and reviewing more than four hundred books a year for the next twenty years. From 1933 to 1940 he edited the annual volume of the O. Henry Memorial Award short stories, and from 1948 to 1965 he edited the *World Almanac*. In 1965 he began to edit the American Guide series of state histories. He suffered a stroke on December 22, 1976, and died in St. Clare's Hospital in New York several days later.

**SIGNIFICANCE:** Hansen's job as a book reviewer in Chicago during the second decade of this century put him in contact with the major figures of the Chicago Renaissance, many of whom he regularly drank and dined with at Schlogl's Restaurant. His reminiscences of this period were published in *Midwest Portraits* (1923), which offers profiles of CARL SANDBURG, FLOYD DELL, EDGAR LEE MASTERS, SHERWOOD ANDERSON, ROBERT HERRICK, HARRIET MONROE, Lew Sarett, Wallace Smith, and BEN HECHT. Hansen published his memoirs of growing up in the Midwest in his essay "A Davenport Boyhood," which appeared in the April 1956 issue of *The Palimpsest*, and in his only novel, *Your Life Lies Before You* (1935). Told from the point of view of cub reporter David Kinsman, the novel paints a vivid picture of riverfront life in turn-of-the-century Davenport; the novel, as well as the essay, records the rich cultural legacy of Davenport's German forty-eighters: singing societies, shooting contests, beer gardens, torchlight parades, gymnastic displays, band concerts, oratory contests, masked balls, and Shakespearean productions at the Turner Hall.

**SELECTED WORKS:** Hansen's account of the Versailles Peace Conference can be found in *The Adventures of the Fourteen Points* (1919). *Midwest Portraits* (1923) and *Carl Sandburg: The Man and His Poetry* (1925) are of interest to scholars of the Chicago Renaissance. *Your Life Lies Before You* (1935) and "A Davenport Boyhood" (1956) are valuable documents of Davenport social history. Hansen also published *The Chicago* in the Rivers of America series (1942) and *The Story of Illinois* (1956), as well as a one-volume history, *The Civil War* (1961).

**FURTHER READING:** See William Roba's 1979 thesis "A Literary Pilgrim: Harry Hansen and Popular American Book Reviewing" (University of Iowa 1979) and also his "Harry Hansen's Literary Career," in *Books at Iowa* 35 (November 1981): 19–33.

MARCIA NOE

THE UNIVERSITY OF TENNESSEE AT CHATTANOOGA

## CURTIS (ARTHUR) HARNACK

June 27, 1927

**BIOGRAPHY:** Curtis Harnack was born in Le Mars, Iowa. After his father, Henry, died when Harnack was six months old, he lived on a farm near Remsen in Plymouth County, Iowa, with his mother, Caroline (Lang), three siblings, and an aunt and uncle and their three children. Educated in Iowa schools, he read widely and began writing stories while in grade school. Many of his rural growing-up experiences are recounted in *We Have All Gone Away* (1973) and *The Attic* (1993), both demonstrating his deep Iowa roots. After serving in the U.S. Navy from 1945 to 1946, he earned a BA from Grinnell College in 1949 and an MA from Columbia in 1950. Once in graduate school at Columbia, he considered himself separated enough from his own roots to return to familiar Midwestern authors: WILLA CATHER, RUTH SUCKOW, HAMLIN GARLAND, SHERWOOD ANDERSON, ERNEST HEMINGWAY, F. SCOTT FITZGERALD, and others, whom he has continued to read throughout his career.

Following brief positions with the United Nations Secretariat and as an admissions counselor, Harnack taught English at Grinnell, the Writers Workshop at the University of Iowa, the University of Tabriz in Iran as a Fulbright Professor in 1958–59, and Sarah Lawrence College. From 1971 to 1987, he served as executive director of Yaddo, an artists' colony in Saratoga Springs, New York. Married to writer Hortense Calisher, he lives in New York City and at his country home in Eagle Bridge, New York.

**SIGNIFICANCE:** In *The Attic*, Harnack writes, "I found that I could write best about Iowa if I remained physically distant from it . . . I always regarded myself as an Iowan who happened to live elsewhere, who returned home as often as he could" (vi). Having gained the requisite distance, Harnack has set almost all of his work in Iowa even though he resists being labeled an Iowa author as too limiting. His three novels in which some of the same characters reappear, *The Work of an Ancient Hand* (1960), *Love and Be Silent* (1962), and *Limits of the Land* (1979), are all set in or near the fictional northwest Iowa town of Kaleburg. Even his socio-historical work, *Gentlemen on the Prairie* (1960) records adventures of a group of British who settle in Iowa. In both fiction and autobiography, he tells stories typical of small rural towns and farms where family, hard work, religion, community, and the land are primary values and where people struggle with economic crises, weather, neighbors, families, and themselves. Staples of the Midwestern scene, including small-town centennial celebrations, wedding parties, and Fourth of July festivities, as well as religious antipathies, political disagreements, and harvest unpredictabilities, are all recurrent in Harnack's work.

**SELECTED WORKS:** Harnack's autobiographical works, *We Have All Gone Away* (1973), and *The Attic: A Memoir* (1993), focusing on his childhood in Iowa, are particularly rich in Midwestern details. Though partially autobiographical, *Persian Lions, Persian Lambs: An American's Odyssey in Iran* (1965) does not explore the Midwestern scene. His three novels, *The Work of an Ancient Hand* (1960), *Love and Be Silent* (1962), and *Limits of the Land* (1979), offer valuable insights into small-town Iowa life, as do some of the stories in *Under My Wings Everything Prospers* (1977). *Gentlemen on the Prairie* (1985) views Iowa from still another perspective, that of British settlers. During the 1950s, Harnack contributed several articles on Iowa history to the *Iowan*; among these are "An Amazing English Colony of Northwest Iowa" in the *Iowan* 2 (April–May 1954): 10–13, 42–44, and "The Iowa Underground Railroad" in the *Iowan* 4 (June–July 1956): 20–23, 44, 47.

**FURTHER READING:** Harnack's work is mentioned in Midwestern literary surveys, including CLARENCE ANDREWS's *A Literary History of Iowa* (1972). An informative interview is Judith Gildner's "Iowans in the Arts: Curtis Harnack," in *Annals of Iowa* 43 (Summer 1975): 39–48. Rockwell Gray offers an extended review of *We Have All Gone Away* in "Three Midwestern Writers," in *Great Lakes Review* 3 (Summer 1976): 74–93. Many of Harnack's papers are in Special Collections at the University of Iowa. His will stipulates that all of his literary papers will eventually go there.

SARA McALPIN BVM                              CLARKE COLLEGE

## JIM (JAMES THOMAS) HARRISON
December 11, 1937

**BIOGRAPHY:** Jim Harrison was born in Grayling, Michigan, and grew up near Reed City and Haslett. His parents, Winfield Sprague Harrison, an agriculturalist, and Norma Olivia (Wahlgren) Harrison, encouraged their son's interest in nature and love for literature. A brief bohemian period in New York and Boston initiated him into the writer's life. He married Linda King in 1960; they have two daughters. He earned degrees in English at

Michigan State University (BA 1960, MA 1966), where he met writers THOMAS MC-GUANE and DAN GERBER, who became his close friends. A year teaching at the State University of New York at Stony Brook convinced him that he was unsuited to academic life. He has since resided in Lake Leelanau, Michigan, where he first supported his family as a laborer and increasingly as a freelance journalist. He made his first mark on the literary world with his books of poetry; on McGuane's suggestion, he wrote *Wolf* (1971), thus beginning a more widely recognized career as a novelist. In addition to his fiction, poetry, and essays, Harrison has cowritten several motion pictures, including *Cold Feet* (1989), *Revenge* (1990), and *Wolf* (1994), the last of which is unrelated to his novella with the same title. His work has achieved both wide popularity and critical respect. In 1990 he received the Society for the Study of Midwestern Literature's Mark Twain Award for distinguished contributions to Midwestern literature.

**SIGNIFICANCE:** Most of Harrison's writing is set in the Midwest, particularly in his native Michigan. His first books of poetry established the rural focus and autobiographical basis of his work. The poem "Sketch for a Job Application Blank" from *Plain Song* (1965), for example, considers his northern Michigan childhood and Swedish and German Mennonite ancestry. While the free-verse technique of this and other poems derives from the experimentalism of Pound, Yeats, and ELIOT, Harrison found the Modernist example insufficient. As he wrote in his master's thesis, published in *Just before Dark: Collected Nonfiction* (1991), "My family background was essentially Populist and it was impossible for me to become comfortably absorbed in . . . [the Modernists'] concerns" (199). He discovered a more congenial spiritual influence in foreign poets, notably Rilke, Rimbaud, and Neruda. Harrison's poetry responds to Neruda's call for an "impure poetry," described by the Chilean Nobel laureate as "impure as a suit or body . . . stained by food and shame, a poetry with wrinkles, observations, dreams, waking, prophesies, declarations of love and hatred, beasts, blows, idylls, manifestos, denials, doubts, affirmations, taxes" (*Passions and Impressions*, ed. Matilde Neruda and Miguel Otero Silva, trans. Margaret Sayers Peden, 1993; 128). Harrison's internationalism parallels that of

many other American poets of the 1960s, including his fellow Midwesterners ROBERT BLY and JAMES WRIGHT, who share his pastoralism. His Michigan origin and spiritual apprehension of nature have also occasioned many comparisons to THEODORE ROETHKE, whose Michigan poems and late "North American Sequence" prefigure some of Harrison's best poetry, including the long poem "The Theory and Practice of Rivers."

Harrison's fiction, like his poetry, is a major contribution to the Midwestern pastoral tradition which includes HAMLIN GARLAND, WILLA CATHER, and ERNEST HEMINGWAY. Comparisons to Hemingway are invited by his northern Michigan settings and love for fishing and hunting. Some of his fictions, particularly *Wolf* (1971), *Sundog* (1984), and the novellas "Brown Dog" (1990) and "The Seven-Ounce Man" (1994), are pastorals in the Cooper/Hemingway tradition, featuring male characters escaping from civilization into wilderness, sex, and occasionally violence. On that basis Harrison's writing was stigmatized for a time as "macho," a charge leveled particularly against the trilogy of novellas *Legends of the Fall* (1978). But as more careful readers such as William H. Roberson have shown, most of Harrison's male characters "do not represent the epitome of manliness and virtue. They are not leaders; they are lost." Those few characters who might be described as macho "reach no fulfillment or strength" because Harrison portrays machismo as "ultimately sentimental and thus self-destructive" (236).

Harrison's pastoral fiction actually tends less to romances of male flight than to a Virgilian concern with troubled love, aging and death, desire for wider knowledge, and intense awareness of local landscape and history. *Farmer* (1976), about a Michigan schoolteacher and farmer torn between his love for one woman and sexual attraction to another, is closer in spirit to Cather's *O Pioneers!* than to Hemingway's "Big Two-Hearted River." *Dalva* (1988) ended the stereotyping of Harrison's fiction with its use of a woman narrator, praised as authentic by noted women writers including LOUISE ERDRICH. In *Dalva*, a Nebraska woman searches for the son she gave up at birth while she allows an historian, her sometime lover, to uncover her family history of Plains Indians and pioneers. Like much of Harrison's poetry and nonfiction, *Dalva* confronts America's "soul history" of environmental abuse and "the blood of over two hundred Native American civilizations we destroyed" (*Just before Dark* 300). The theme continues in *The Road Home* (1998), a sequel to *Dalva* narrated by Dalva and by four members of her family. The central motif in that most recent novel, as in all of Harrison's work, is the healing of historical wounds, personal and public, by visionary and naturalistic means. "I continue to dream myself back to what I lost," Harrison declares, "and continue to lose and regain, to an earth where I am a fellow creature and to a landscape I can call home. When I return I can offer my family, my writing, my friends, a portion of the gift I've been given . . ." (*Just before Dark* 317).

**SELECTED WORKS:** Harrison's books of poetry are *Plain Song* (1965), *Locations* (1968), *Outlyer and Ghazals* (1971), *Letters to Yesenin* (1973), *Returning to Earth* (1977), *Selected and New Poems* (1982), *The Theory and Practice of Rivers* (1985), *The Theory and Practice of Rivers and New Poems* (1989), *After Ikkyu and Other Poems* (1996), and *The Shape of the Journey: New and Collected Poems* (1998). His works of fiction are *Wolf* (1971), *A Good Day to Die* (1973), *Farmer* (1976), *Legends of the Fall* (three novellas: "Revenge," "The Man Who Gave Up His Name," and "Legends of the Fall"; 1978), *Warlock* (1981), *Sundog* (1984), *Dalva* (1988), *The Woman Lit by Fireflies* (three novellas: "Brown Dog," "Sunset Limited," and "The Woman Lit by Fireflies"; 1990), *Julip* (three novellas: "Julip," "The Seven-Ounce Man," and "The Beige Dolorosa"; 1994), *The Road Home* (1998), *The Beast God Forgot to Invent* (novellas: title story, "Westward Ho," "I Forgot to Go to Spain"; 2000), and *The Boy Who Ran to the Woods* (2000). His essays appear in *Just before Dark: Collected Nonfiction* (1991). Uncollected essays may be found in periodicals including *Sports Illustrated* and *Esquire*, for which he wrote a column, "The Raw and the Cooked," from 1991 to 1993. His books in translation are especially popular in France, Germany, and Italy.

**FURTHER READING:** A detailed profile of Harrison may be found in *Current Biography Yearbook* (1992). He often receives celebrity treatment in the popular press in the United States and abroad, as in Robert Cross's "Siren song: Will success lure poet/novelist Jim Harrison out of his Midwestern lair?" in *Chicago Tribune Magazine* (August 30, 1992): 10: 14–18, 24; and François Granon's "Jim Harrison: Cigarettes, whisky et p'tites pépées" in *Télérama Paris* (July 28, 1993): 12–17. Terry W. Phipps portrays him in photographs as well as text in "Image Matters to Jim Harrison," in *Book: The Magazine for the Reading Life* (October–November 1998): 42–49. The essential interview is Jim Fergus's "The Art of Fiction CIV: Jim Harrison," *Paris Review* 107 (1988): 52–97; also see Hank Nuwer's "The Man Whose Soul Is Not for Sale," in *Rendezvous: Idaho State University Journal of Arts and Letters* 21.1 (Fall 1985): 26–42. His books regularly receive notice in periodicals including the *New York Times Book Review*, the *Nation*, and *Time*. A selection of major reviews may be found in *Contemporary Literary Criticism* 66. A useful, though dated, index of primary and secondary materials is Tom Colonnese's "Jim Harrison: A Checklist," in *Bulletin of Bibliography* 39.3 (September 1982): 132–35.

Literary scholars have begun to examine Harrison's work in depth; notable early studies are John Rohrkemper's "'Natty Bumppo Wants Tobacco': Jim Harrison's Wilderness," in *Great Lakes Review* 8.2–9.1 (Fall 1982–Spring 1983): 20–28; Thomas Maher Gilligan's "Myth and Reality in Jim Harrison's *Warlock*," in *Critique* 25.3 (Spring 1984): 147–53; William H. Roberson's "'Macho Mistake': The Misrepresentation of Jim Harrison's Fiction," in *Critique* 29.4 (Summer 1988): 233–44; Aleksandra Gruzinska's "E. M. Cioran and *The Man Who Gave Up His Name* by Jim Harrison," in *Journal of the American-Romanian Academy of Arts and Sciences* 12 (1989): 83–93; William Barillas's "To Sustain the Bioregion: Michigan Poets of Place," in *MidAmerica* 17 (1990): 10–33; Robert Johnson's "Brown Dog's Insight: The Fiction of Jim Harrison," in *Notes on Contemporary Fiction* 27.1 (1997): 2–4; and James I. McClintock's "*Dalva*: Jim Harrison's 'Twin Sister,'" in *Journal of Men's Studies* 6.3 (Spring 1998): 319–30. The first book on Harrison is from France: Brice Matthieussent's biographical and critical "dictionary" *Jim Harrison, de A à W* (1995); the first book in English is Edward C. Reilly's *Jim Harrison* (1996). While most of Harrison's papers and manuscripts remain inaccessible, Special Collections at the Michigan State University Library holds an extensive collection of books, letters, and related materials.

WILLIAM BARILLAS

UNIVERSITY OF WISCONSIN–LA CROSSE

**DIANA C. HASKELL.**
*See* appendix (1988)

**LINDA HASSELSTROM**
July 14, 1943
BIOGRAPHY: Poet and essayist Linda Hasselstrom was born in Houston, Texas, to John
and Florence (Baker) Hasselstrom. She came
to South Dakota at age four, moved at age
nine to a ranch when her mother remarried,
and spent her youth riding and writing. After graduation from high school, she enrolled
at the University of South Dakota, where she
worked on the night staff of the *Sioux City
Journal.* Hasselstrom received her BA in 1965
and an MA from the University of Missouri–
Columbia in 1969(?). She married Daniel Lusk
in 1966. She taught at Columbia College in
Missouri from 1966 to 1969 and at the University of Missouri–Columbia from 1969 to
1971. In 1971 Hasselstrom and her husband returned to South Dakota, founding the arts
magazine *Sunday Clothes* and Lame Johnny
Press, while helping her parents on the ranch
in Hermosa, South Dakota. In 1983 Hasselstrom published, through Lame Johnny
Press, *Horizons: The South Dakota Writers' Anthology.* In 1984 Holcomb Press published her
first poetry book, *Caught by One Wing.* In 1987
she published the three books which
launched her literary career: a second volume
of poems, *Roadkill,* a collection of ranching essays, *Going Over East,* and a year-long sequence of journal entries mined from the diaries she had kept since age nine, *Windbreak.*

Hasselstrom was divorced in 1972 and married George R. Snell in 1979; much of *Land Circle* (1991) recounts her grief over George's
death in 1988 of Hodgkin's disease. By 1994,
when after a long court battle she received title to the South Dakota ranch she had inherited, Hasselstrom had moved to Cheyenne,
Wyoming, to devote most of her attention to
writing, teaching, and speaking.

Hasselstrom received a National Endowment for the Arts Fellowship in 1984 and a
South Dakota Arts Council Fellowship in 1989.
She was awarded a Governor's Award in Arts
in 1989 and the Elkhorn Poetry Prize in 1991.
She was South Dakota Author of the Year in
1989, and in 1990 she became the first woman
to receive a Western American Writer Award.
SIGNIFICANCE: One of those rare writers
who is also a worker, Hasselstrom com-
mands the same respect accorded MERIDEL
LE SUEUR and TOM McGRATH, and for the
same qualities: stoic acceptance of the interwoven inevitabilities of life and death,
combined with the lyric faith of a poet. Hasselstrom indulges neither herself nor others:
"The poems are in the scars," she writes in
"Hands," "and in what I recall of all this,
when my hands are too battered to do it any
more" (*Bones* 50). Hasselstrom exhibits a certain disdain for writers and readers with
more grants than scars, and her feminism
owes more to self-reliance than theory. "Labor should be both physical and mental in
order to keep all circuits healthy," she says
in *Land Circle* (65).

Beyond the routine of ranch life, Hasselstrom's favorite subject is the Great Plains' special need for building and sustaining community, whether fighting prairie fires, birthing
and slaughtering cattle, or supporting the
county fair. The first section of *Land Circle* is
subtitled "Where Neighbor Is a Verb." A militant environmentalist, Hasselstrom also understands that the ranching, farming, and mining jobs that support rural people inevitably
have an impact upon the environment, and
that compromise is the foundation of community. A worker's writer, Hasselstrom is direct, honest, and intimately familiar with
the landscapes and mythologies in which she
trades. Her best work exhibits a sparse minimalism which reflects her prairie landscape,
and a delicate balance between style and content which we have come to recognize as
characteristically Midwestern.

SELECTED WORKS: The journal *Windbreak:
A Woman Rancher on the Northern Plains* (1987)
remains Hasselstrom's defining work to date,
although *Land Circle* (1991) presents a more
mature vision in essays and poems. Early
essays on ranching are collected in *Going
Over East: Reflections of a Woman Rancher* (1987).
*Dakota Bones* (1993) reprints the complete contents of *Caught by One Wing* (1984) and *Roadkill* (1987), adding fifteen later poems. *The Book
Book: A Publishing Handbook* (1979), published
by Hasselstrom on her Lame Johnny imprint,
reflects Hasselstrom's commitment to the
small press movement. *Roadside History of
South Dakota* (1994) is a traveler's guide to the
state's history and geography, its towns and
people. In 1997, with coeditors Gaydell Collier
and Nancy Curtis, Hasselstrom published the

anthology *Leaning into the Wind: Women Write from the Heart of the West.*

**FURTHER READING:** Criticism is limited to articles, some in popular media: "Journal of a Woman Rancher," in *Life* (July 1989); Paul Higbee's "At Home on the Range," in *South Dakota Magazine* (September–October 1992); John Murray's interview in the *Bloomsbury Review* (July–August 1992); and Geraldine Stanford's "The Dichotomy Pulse: The Beating Heart of Hasselstrom Country," in *South Dakota Review* 30 (Autumn 1992): 130–55.

DAVID PICHASKE        SOUTHWEST STATE UNIVERSITY

## JON HASSLER

March 30, 1933

**BIOGRAPHY:** Jon Francis Hassler was born in Minneapolis, Minnesota, to Leo Blaise and Ellen (Callihan) Hassler. He grew up in the small towns of Staples and Plainview, Minnesota, then received a BA from St. John's University in 1955 and an MA from the University of North Dakota in 1960. He taught at a series of high schools, then at Bemidji State University, Brainerd Community College, and since 1980 at St. John's University, all in Minnesota. Hassler lives in Sauk Rapids, Minnesota.

Although he thought of himself as a writer at age six, Hassler did not begin to publish professionally until age thirty-seven, first short stories, later novels. He drew on the people and scenes he had come to know in the small towns and villages of rural Minnesota. He told Ronald Barron in *A Guide to Minnesota Authors*, "my experience is related to my fiction the way grass is related to milk. I'm the cow" (77). Since publishing his first novel at forty-three, Hassler has emerged as one of the upper Midwest's most solid writers of novels in the traditional mode.

*Staggerford* (1977) was chosen Novel of the Year by Friends of American Writers; Hassler received a Guggenheim Fellowship to complete *The Love Hunter* (1981); *Grand Opening* (1987) won a Society of Midland Authors Award. He was the recipient of the Society for the Study of Midwestern Literature's 1997 Mark Twain Award for distinguished contributions to Midwestern literature.

**SIGNIFICANCE:** The focus of most Hassler novels is ordinary people caught in extraordinary circumstances: Irish priests, retired teachers, small-town shopkeepers at the cross-roads of their lives. Frequently his work involves the chasms separating and the bridges joining generations. Age is a recurrent subject, as is the closing down of small-town society. Hassler is sometimes overly optimistic, and some characters border on stereotype, but he writes out of his own experience, and with the grace of John Cheever, his major model.

*Staggerford* (1977) chronicles one week in the life of English teacher Miles Pruitt, adding colorful sketches of small-town life and people. *Simon's Night* (1979) records a week in the life of Simon Shea, retired professor from a small Minnesota college, as he enters and subsequently exits the Norman (Rest) Home, populated with eccentrics of various races and genders. In *The Love Hunter* (1981), Hassler "toughened his tone, complicated his plot, and dared more difficult themes," wrote Barton Sutter in the *Minneapolis Tribune* of June 28, 1981 (14G). Hassler recounts the plan of Chris MacKensie to murder his best friend, Larry Quinn, who is dying of multiple sclerosis, on a duck hunting trip to Canada. MacKensie is also in love with Quinn's wife. The darker side of small-town life is again depicted in *Grand Opening* (1987), the story of the Foster family, which moves from Minneapolis to Plum, Minnesota, seeking the simple life as operators of a grocery store. Small-town life is neither as simple nor as sunny as the Fosters expect, and their relationship suffers from the tensions of their experience.

In *North of Hope* (1990) Hassler recounts the crisis of faith experienced by Father Frank Healy at a rural parish on the Basswood Indian reservation. Instead of rural peace, Healy finds the girl he loved in high school, now married, and northern Minnesota drugs, death, and despair. Similarly in *Dear James* (1993), Agatha McGee, forcibly retired from Staggerford's failing St. Isidore Elementary School, finds her friends less supportive than she had expected. She escapes the small-town Midwest for Italy, only to encounter an unorthodox affection and new troubles, with Father James O'Hannon, whom Agatha had met previously in Ireland in *The Green Journey* (1985).

A writer of solid prose and an old-fashioned storyteller, Hassler creates Dickensian characters and is capable of extended scenes similar to those in a nineteenth-century social novel. A smoother stylist than either SIN-

CLAIR LEWIS or SHERWOOD ANDERSON, Hassler lacks the former's gift for satire and the latter's insights into complex human psychology. While not entirely glossing over the sores of Midwest life, Hassler's novels reflect a faith that elicits from reviewers words like "inspiring," "marvelous," and "uplifting." The *New York Times* book review excerpted on the cover of *Dear James* may best characterize Hassler's work: "A gentle examination of the fragile but enduring strengths of small town life through characters so exquisitely rendered that even a first time visitor to Staggerford will come to love them as old friends."

**SELECTED WORKS:** Hassler is best known for his social novels set entirely or in part in the towns and villages of out-state Minnesota: *Staggerford* (1977), *Simon's Night* (1979), *The Love Hunter* (1981), *Grand Opening* (1987), *North of Hope* (1990), *Dear James* (1993). *Rookery Blues* appeared in 1995. *Four Miles to Pinecone* (1977) and *Jemmy* (1980) are juvenile novels. NBC-TV aired a television movie version of *A Green Journey* in 1990. Hassler's long novels are available in mass-distribution paperbacks from Ballantine Books.

**FURTHER READING:** A 1988 television interview with Jon Hassler, number 10 in the Northern Lights and Insights series, is available from Hennepin County (Minnesota) Library. In 1990 the Dinkytown Antiquarian Bookstore published Larry Dingman's interview with Hassler as a chapbook. Ronald Barron's *A Guide to Minnesota Writers* (1993) provides a useful overview of the man and his work. John Hynes's "Midwestern Loneliness: The Novels of Jon Hassler," in *Commonweal* (November 3, 1995): 8–12, stresses Hassler's Catholic faith, as does Anthony Low's "Jon Hassler: Catholic Realist," in *Essays on Values in Literature* 47 (1994): 59–71. A similar approach characterizes chapters on Hassler in two omnibus books: W. Dale Brown's *Of Fiction and Faith: Twelve American Writers Talk about Their Vision and Work* (1997) and Kevin and Marilyn Ryan's *Why I Am Still Catholic* (1998). Hassler's papers are at the St. Cloud State University Library.

DAVID PICHASKE    SOUTHWEST STATE UNIVERSITY

# HARLAN (HENTHORNE) HATCHER

September 9, 1898–February 25, 1998

**BIOGRAPHY:** Born in Ironton, Ohio, to Robert Elison and Linda (Leslie) Hatcher, Harlan Hatcher had a diverse career as literary scholar and teacher, academic administrator, novelist, literary critic, and cultural historian, all of which was rooted in his native Midwest. He received the AB in 1922, the AM in 1923, and the PhD in 1927, all from Ohio State University, and did further graduate work at the University of Chicago. Although he lectured widely in the United States and abroad, his academic career was entirely at two institutions, Ohio State University, where he served as assistant professor and professor of English, dean of the College of Arts and Sciences, and vice president between 1928 and 1951, and the University of Michigan, where he served as president from 1951 to 1967, when he became president emeritus. He served in the U.S. Army in World War I and the navy in World War II.

Hatcher married Anne Gregory Vance on April 3, 1942, and had two children, Robert and Anne. He published his first book, *The Versification of Robert Browning*, in 1928, and a standard study, *Creating the Modern American Novel* (1935, 1965), as well as a standard anthology, *Modern Drama* (1944), but his three novels and nearly a dozen other works are rooted in his native Ohio, the Midwest, and the Great Lakes.

Hatcher served as director of the Federal Writers' Project in Ohio from 1937 to 1938 and edited *The Ohio Guide*, produced by the Federal Writers' Project and published in 1940. He also served on numerous governmental and private boards, commissions, and study groups. He was awarded the MidAmerica Award from the Society for the Study of Midwestern Literature in 1980. In his last years he worked to increase the holdings of the University of Michigan Library, and the Graduate Library is named in his honor. He died of heart disease at the age of ninety-nine.

**SIGNIFICANCE:** Hatcher's three novels, *Tunnel Hill* (1931), *Patterns of Wolfpen* (1934), and *Central Standard Time* (1937) are all set in the Ohio Valley and based primarily on his youthful and family experiences, especially in Ironton. Two, *Tunnel Hill* and *Patterns of Wolfpen*, explore the development of the rural Ohio River Valley, and *Central Standard Time* is based on the transition of a Midwestern town as it became industrialized. The three, defining the transition of the region

**Harlan Hatcher.**
Photo courtesy of the Bentley Historical Library,
University of Michigan

from wilderness to industrialization, foreshadow the substance of his later historical studies.

Equally evident in his novels is his growing interest in the Ohio past, an interest that was intensified by his experience with the Federal Writers' Project in developing *The Ohio Guide* and other publications, and this interest directed much of his later creative and scholarly work, producing first of all his major historical and cultural study, *The Buckeye Country: A Pageant of Ohio* in 1940. This was followed by *The Great Lakes* (1944) and *Lake Erie* (1945), both of which are pioneering historical-cultural studies on the Great Lakes and which led to his later *A Pictorial History of the Great Lakes* (1963). More than any other historical writer, Hatcher made the Great Lakes the subject of serious historical research. His *The Western Reserve: The Story of New Connecticut in Ohio* (1949) is equally important in examining the impact of New England's culture on the emerging Old Northwest and Midwest.

**SELECTED WORKS:** His novels *Tunnel Hill* (1931), *Patterns of Wolfpen* (1934), and *Central*

*Standard Time* (1937) reflect his Ohio and Midwestern present. Much of his nonfiction, including *The Buckeye Country* (1940), his editorship of *The Ohio Guide* (1940), *The Great Lakes* (1944), *Lake Erie* (1945), and *A Pictorial History of the Great Lakes* (1963), are preoccupied with the past. *The Persistent Quest for Values: What Are We Seeking?* (1966) is a philosophical exercise that reflects his own perceptions of contemporary life.

**FURTHER READING:** No books and few articles have appeared on Hatcher's work, but he is listed in *Who's Who in America, Contemporary Authors, Michigan Authors,* and *Ohio Authors and Their Books.* A fine appraisal of his novels can be found in Roger J. Bresnahan's "Harlan Hatcher's Midwestern Novels," in *MidAmerica* 11 (1984): 69–80. Most of his papers can be found in the library of the University of Michigan.

DAVID D. ANDERSON    MICHIGAN STATE UNIVERSITY

## HARLAN (HENTHORNE) HATCHER.

*See also* appendix (1980)

## WALTER (EDWIN) HAVIGHURST

November 28, 1901–February 3, 1994

**BIOGRAPHY:** A novelist, critic, and literary and social historian of the Midwest, Walter Edwin Havighurst was born in Appleton, Wisconsin, the son of Freeman Alfred and Winifred (Weter) Havighurst. He grew up in the Fox River Valley where, he liked to recall in conversation, "French explorers passed on their way to the Mississippi." Although he based his earliest writings on his brief career as a merchant seaman, he later insisted many times that the place of his origins, "midland America," was his true, inexhaustible source and stimulation. He received the BA from the University of Denver in 1924, and after attending King's College, London, 1925–26, he received the MA from Columbia University in 1928. He became an assistant professor at Miami University, in Oxford, Ohio, in 1928, where he spent his academic career, retiring as research professor emeritus in 1969.

He married Marion Boyd, a writer who became his collaborator on several books. She died in 1974. Havighurst made his home in Oxford, Ohio, until his last years, when he moved to Richmond, Indiana. He died in Richmond of heart disease.

Walter Havighurst.
Photo courtesy of David D. Anderson

Havighurst's work, particularly his cultural and social histories, has received much critical acclaim and a number of awards, including the Ohioana Library Association medal (1946, 1950); Friends of American Writers Award (1947); Society of Midland Authors Prize (1971); and the MidAmerica Award of the Society for the Study of Midwestern Literature (1979) for distinguished contributions to the study of Midwestern literature.

**SIGNIFICANCE:** Havighurst has described the best of his own work as focusing on "the region between the Ohio River and the Great Lakes," the area that provided the setting and the historical context of his best novel, *The Quiet Shore* (1937). The novel traces three generations of an Ohio family living on the south shore of Lake Erie between the end of the Civil War, when the area was settled, and the onset of the Depression of the 1930s. In the novel the area moves from a wilderness to a stable society, and the life of the family from a primitive rural existence to financial security and urban relationships, with the inevitable conflicts that complicate family life as the result of those changes.

Havighurst's historical works are equally rooted in the transition of the state, reflecting his desire to understand what the state had been and what it still tried to become. Significant historical works are *Wilderness for Sale* (1956), *Land of the Long Horizons* (1960), *The Heartland* (1962, 1974), and *Ohio: A Bicentennial History* (1976), all of which explore the history that had inspired *The Quiet Shore* and his other novels.

**SELECTED WORKS:** Havighurst's works include *Pier 17* (1935), *The Quiet Shore* (1937), *The Winds of Spring* (1940), *High Prairie*, with Marion Havighurst (1944), *Land of Promise* (1946), *Signature of Time* (1949), *Song of the Pines*, with Marion Havighurst (1949), *The Heartland* (1962, rev. 1974), and *River to the West* (1970).

**FURTHER READING:** No book and few critical articles about Havighurst have appeared, but he received attention in biographical sources, including *Who's Who in America* and *Who's Who in the Midwest*, and is listed in *Contemporary Authors New Revised Series* 29 (1990): 189–90, William Coyle's *Ohio Authors and Their Books, 1796–1950* (1962): 283–85, and in the Michigan Association for Media in Education's *Michigan Authors*, 2nd edition (1980): 166–67, and other works. His papers are in the Miami (Ohio) University Library.

DAVID D. ANDERSON    MICHIGAN STATE UNIVERSITY

## WALTER (EDWIN) HAVIGHURST.
*See also* appendix (1979)

## JOHN HAY
October 8, 1838–July 1, 1905

**BIOGRAPHY:** Statesman, biographer, and poet, John Hay was born in Salem, Indiana, and grew up in Spunky Point, later renamed Warsaw, Illinois. The fourth of six children of New Englander parents Dr. Charles Hay and Helen (Leonard) Hay, John Hay received his education from schools in Pittsfield and Springfield, Illinois, and from Brown University, where he graduated in 1858 as the class poet. Soon after he returned to Springfield and studied law in his uncle's office, where he became acquainted with ABRAHAM LINCOLN. After campaigning for Lincoln in the 1860 presidential election, Hay was appointed White House secretary. During this time he published some of his poetry and began writing short fiction. After the Civil War, Hay enjoyed several government stints in Europe and drew upon such experiences for his book *Castilian Days* (1871).

In 1870 Hay returned to the United States and began writing editorials for the *New York Tribune*. Around this time he also published "Little Breeches" (1870) and "Jim Bludso, of the Prairie Belle," two poems which garnered Hay much popular and critical acclaim for his use of Midwestern subjects and regional dialect. In 1871 he published these ballads and a variety of other poems in the collection *Pike County Ballads and Other Pieces* (1871). In 1874 Hay married Clara Louise Stone, daughter of Cleveland magnate Amasa Stone, and settled in Cleveland to assist in his father-in-law's financial affairs. They had four children.

As labor disputes erupted throughout the country in the 1870s and 1880s, Hay again turned his attention to politics and became a staunch advocate of capitalism and a critic of labor unions. He gave vent to these sentiments in *The Bread-winners*, a novel published anonymously in serial form in 1883–84 and in book form in 1884. The novel caused a minor stir in the literary circles that year for its polemic against labor and its advocacy of class division, but it probably caused just as much controversy because readers were curious to know who the author was. Hay was not identified with certainty as the novel's author until after his death. For the remainder of the 1880s, Hay worked with John G. Nicolay on what would become their ten-volume opus on Lincoln. After serving in other government posts abroad, Hay was appointed Secretary of State under McKinley in 1898 and served in that post until his death. He died in Newbury, New Hampshire, after a long illness. **SIGNIFICANCE:** Hay has had a double-edged influence on Midwestern literature. His most famous poems, from *Pike County Ballads*, bask in rural Illinois dialect and surroundings and provide rather optimistic portraits of a preindustrial, egalitarian Middle America. In *The Bread-winners*, however, Hay embraces the East-coast and European training of the novel's hero, Arthur Farnham, while criticizing Midwesterners for their provinciality. Accordingly, throughout the novel Hay mocks any pretensions of social advancement, privileges inherited through wealth and station, and dismisses out of hand the grievances of labor unions. Noted in its time as one of the first

American novels to treat organized labor, the novel was a popular and critical success, helped in part by a generally glowing review by Hay's friend WILLIAM DEAN HOWELLS. Hay's reputation as a writer today best rests on his and Nicolay's multivolume biography of Lincoln. **SELECTED WORKS:** Hay's *Poems* (1890) contains "Jim Bludso," "Little Breeches," and other Pike County ballads. Early in his career he published two short stories set in the Midwest, "The Foster-Brothers" in *Harper's New Monthly Magazine* 39 (September 1869): 535–44, and "The Blood Seedling" in *Lippincott's Magazine* 7 (March 1871): 281–93. *The Bread-winners* was published in book form in 1884, and his and Nicolay's *Abraham Lincoln: A History* appeared in 1890. **FURTHER READING:** William Roscoe Thayer's *The Life and Letters of John Hay* (1915) and Tyler Dennett's *John Hay: From Poetry to Politics* (1933) are informative, laudatory biographies, while Kenton J. Clymer's *John Hay: The Gentleman as Diplomat* (1975) is a more critical biography. Howard I. Kushner and Anne Hummel Sherrill's *John Milton Hay: The Union of Poetry and Politics* (1977) provides a good overview of the poetry. Charles Vandersee's "The Great Literary Mystery of the Gilded Age," in *American Literary Realism 1870–1910* 7 (1974): 245–72, is a detailed account of the reception and controversies of *The Bread-winners*, and Robert Dunne's "Dueling Ideologies of America in *The Bread-winners* and *The Money-Makers*," in *American Literary Realism 1870–1910* 28 (1996): 30–37, examines the political and cultural criticism behind Hay's novel and one of several novels that rebutted it. Most of Hay's papers are located at Brown University and the Library of Congress.
ROBERT DUNNE
                              CENTRAL CONNECTICUT STATE UNIVERSITY

# ROBERT HAYDEN
August 4, 1913–February 25, 1980
**BIOGRAPHY:** Robert Hayden was born as Asa Bundy Sheffey on August 4, 1913, in Detroit, Michigan. His name was changed to Robert Hayden by foster parents William and Sue Ellen (Westerfield) Hayden of Detroit. He received his BA from Detroit City College, now Wayne State University, in 1936. Hayden's research on the history of blacks in America for the Federal Writers' Project in Detroit (1936–40) gave him the passion and knowl-

edge which shine forth in his later writings. In June 1940 he married Erma Morris.

Following the completion of his MA at the University of Michigan (1944), Hayden entered into an academic career. For twenty-three years he was a member of the English Department at Fisk University (1946–69) and for the next eleven years, until his death, at the University of Michigan. His greatest formal honor was being appointed, in 1976, as the consultant in poetry to the Library of Congress; this position has subsequently been renamed as poet laureate of the United States.

**SIGNIFICANCE:** Robert Hayden wrote finely crafted and deeply meaningful poems. His writings present the powerful theme of a black man's search for identity in the streets and fields of white America. This quest for personal identity takes Hayden to the filth and blindness on board the slave ship where "Deep in the festering hold thy father lies, / the corpse of mercy rots with him, / rats eat love's rotten gelid eyes . . ." ("Middle Passage," *Angle of Ascent* 122). It also encompasses the contemporary scene of his "Witch Doctor," the jive black man religious leader who "dances, dances, ensorcelled and aloof. / The fervid juba of God as love, healer, / conjiver. And of himself as God" (*Angle of Ascent* 109).

Robert Hayden's perspective is that of a Detroit-born man. He seeks identity and meaning in brotherhood, a brotherhood found in shared historical themes and stories and in the personal touch of human lives. His search is that of an educated Midwestern black man. Hayden's poetry is a world of quiet narrative and observation, a truly aesthetic world. Where there is excitement and passion, it is distanced excitement and passion belonging generically to the story and its characters. Hayden sees himself in others, digging into the ruins of his racial heritage and into the world of people surrounding him. He gives us a kaleidoscope which uses faces, rather than bits of broken glass, for the basic stuff of design. The result is a quiet though ever-changing vision of persons, a tumbling wheel of snapshots, always searching, always personal.

As a Midwestern poet Hayden took his search for identity to Caribbean islands as well as to the circus sideshow of Aunt Jemima ("Aunt Jemima of the Ocean Waves"). Hayden also explored his identity within the heritage of famous ancestors like Harriet Tubman in "Runogate, Runogate" and Frederick Douglass in his poem "Frederick Douglass."

Robert Hayden's poems always seek two identities: that of his own person and identity as a poet. He wants to be known as an artist, not a black artist. In *Kaleidoscope, Poems by American Negro Poets* (1967), he says that a Negro writer is often seen as a "spokesman for his race . . . a species of race-relations man, the leader of a cause, the voice of protest" (introduction). In the powerful concluding stanzas of "Words in the Mourning Time," Hayden states his case as man and poet: "We must not be frightened nor cajoled / into accepting evil as deliverance from evil. / We must go on struggling to be human, / though monsters of abstraction / police and threaten us. / Reclaim now, now renew the vision of / a human world where godliness / is possible and man / is neither gook nigger honey wop nor kike / but man / permitted to be man" (*Words in the Mourning Time* 49).

**SELECTED WORKS:** Robert Hayden edited and wrote the introduction to *Kaleidoscope: Poems by American Negro Poets* (1967). He also edited and wrote the preface of *The New Negro* (1968). These works provide an important first-person account of Hayden's feelings about "black poetry." Other important prose pieces are found in *Collected Prose*, edited by Frederick Glaysher (1984).

Hayden's poetry is available to us in *Selected Poems* (1966), *Words in the Mourning Time* (1970), and *The Night-Blooming Cereus* (1972). *Angle of Ascent: New and Selected Poems* (1975) is a valuable book which contains many of his previously published poems. Finally, an excellent collection is available in *Robert Hayden: Collected Poems*, edited by Frederick Glaysher (1985).

**FURTHER READING:** At least two books have been written about Robert Hayden. They include George Ronald's *From the Auroral Darkness: The Life and Poetry of Robert Hayden* (1984) and *Robert Hayden* (1984). References to and studies on Hayden abound in a wide variety of books, particularly books on African American writers. Among these are Addison Gayle's *The Black Aesthetic* (1971), Donald B. Gibson's *Modern Black Poets: A Collection of Critical Essays* (1973), Roger Whitlow's *Black American Literature* (1973), and John O'Brian's *Interviews with Black Writers* (1973). Other studies of Hayden's work include more than thirty articles in at least twenty-five periodicals.

CHARLES CAMPBELL          SPRING ARBOR COLLEGE

## JAMES HEARST
August 8, 1900–July 23, 1983

**BIOGRAPHY:** James Hearst was born outside Cedar Falls, Iowa, on the farm that his grandfather had settled in 1859. James was raised on the Hearst Farm, attended a one-room country school, pitched semi-pro baseball, helped farm the family farm until 1941, wrote thirteen books of poetry and three of prose, had more than six hundred poems published in journals during his lifetime, and was a professor at the University of Northern Iowa for thirty-four years. All this he did despite diving into the Cedar River and breaking his neck at the age of nineteen and spending the rest of his life in a wheelchair. Hearst published his first poem in 1924, but a book of poetry did not appear until 1937. His thirteenth book of poems was published by the Iowa State Press in 1979.

**SIGNIFICANCE:** PAUL ENGLE once said that Hearst was the best farm poet in America. Many other writers and critics have echoed that judgement over the years. Hearst said that it took him twenty years to find his voice. That is perhaps an overstatement, for by the 1930s he was writing poems characterized by a Midwestern vernacular. Like Frost, Hearst was writing a poetry that Emerson and Whitman had championed more than a century earlier. In his best poems Hearst sounds like a sensitive man talking to you about the joys and heartaches of farming the land in a language that a Midwestern farmer would really use. Yet, like so many good poets, his poetry also achieves universal human significance.

**SELECTED WORKS:** Hearst's works include *Country Men* (1937), *Man and His Field* (1951), *Limited View* (1962), *A Single Focus* (1967), *Snakes in the Strawberries* (1979), *Seleccion de Poemas de James Hearst* bilingual edition (1992), and a collection of poems published posthumously entitled *A Country Man* (1993).

**FURTHER READING:** RUTH SUCKOW's foreword to *Country Men* (1937) provides valuable insight into Hearst's poetry, as does Theodore Hadden's "James Hearst: The Poetry of an Iowa Farmer," in *Late Harvest: Plains and Prairie Poets* (1977). See also Robert Ward's *James Hearst: A Bibliography of His Work* (1980); "Farm-ing the Land and Writing Poetry," in *Poet and Critic* (1983); "Farming as Ritual in the Poetry of James Hearst," in *Nebraska Humanist* (1985); and "James Hearst: A Poet of Iowa and the World," in *Expressions* 11 (1988).

ROBERT J. WARD     UNIVERSITY OF NORTHERN IOWA

## WILLIAM LEAST HEAT-MOON
August 27, 1939
(William Lewis Trogdon)

**BIOGRAPHY:** A native Missourian born in Kansas City, the son of Ralph G. and Maurine (Davis) Trogdon, William Trogdon earned a BA (1961), MA (1962), and PhD (1973) in literature and a BA (1978) in photojournalism from the University of Missouri–Columbia and taught at Stephens College until he was laid off in 1978. Separated from his wife Lezlie and jobless, Trogdon took off in his van named "Ghost Dancing" on a fourteen-thousand-mile journey, experiencing the lower forty-eight states via backroads, collecting oral histories of authentic American places and peoples. His record of that journey, *Blue Highways*, was published while he worked on a loading dock. After three years of rejections, Trogdon adopted the name "Heat-Moon," drawing upon the name his family used, particularly in Boy Scouts, to honor their part-Osage heritage. Being the youngest in the family, William was "Least Heat-Moon." After he revised *Blue Highways* to include discussion of this heritage, he replaced "Trogdon" with "Least Heat-Moon" on the title page; the manuscript was accepted and published in 1982. The book was a best-seller, garnering Least Heat-Moon writing assignments in magazines such as the *Atlantic* and the *New Yorker* and allowing him to work on his second book, *PrairyErth (a deep map)* (1991). Currently, Least Heat-Moon teaches journalism at the University of Missouri–Columbia. Following the divorce of his first wife, Lezlie, in 1978, Trogdon married Linda Keown.

**SIGNIFICANCE:** Least Heat-Moon avoided much discussion of himself as a Midwesterner in *Blue Highways*, opting for an outsider persona, a traveler to places that represented an authentic America unfamiliar to him. However, his second book, *PrairyErth (a deep map)*, is a deep evocation of a specifically Midwestern place, Chase County, Kansas. In this book, Least Heat-Moon is not only an historical chronicler and a thoughtful philosopher on the meaning of place but also a writer with a keen sensibility to what the Midwestern prairie is all about.

To know Chase County, Kansas, as comprehensively as possible, to "draw" the titular "deep map," the author spent a number of months tramping the county, observing its natural landscape, reading local history, and talking with local people, the reports of which make up much of the contents of the book. To guide his travels, he followed the township grid mapping, but Least Heat-Moon soon discovered how inappropriate such arbitrary lines were to an understanding of place. The natural features of this prairie led him to connect with its deepest geography, including the prehistoric mountains that undergird the flat grasslands. The current inhabitants of the county, predominantly of European background, are not in tune with the geological heritage of their land, he discovers, nor with the deep human history that the memory of the land contains.

Ultimately, after all the hundreds of conversations and miles of foot travel, Least Heat-Moon taps into the Native American understanding of the place as the truest. Taking a psychic journey into the "dreamtime" of the Kansa, Least Heat-Moon attunes himself to the memory of the original landscape before European alteration, where the truest knowledge of Kansas occurs, the most authentic symbiotic relationship between people and land. The lesson of the book is that only through native memory can a full "deep map" be drawn.

**SELECTED WORKS:** Least Heat-Moon's three books, and his major works, are *Blue Highways: A Journey into America* (1982), *Prairy-Erth (a deep map)* (1991), and *River Horse: The Logbook of a Boat across America* (1999). His short writings include further travel writing: "Journeys into Kansas," in *Temperamental Journeys: Essays on the Modern Literature of Travel*, edited by Michael Kowalewski (1992); and "Up among the Roadside Gods," an essay on Japan, in *Time* (August 1, 1983): 80–81. Other topics include Native American politics, which he covers in "The Native Son," in *Esquire* (December 1984): 502–507; and microbreweries, with "A Glass of Handmade," in *Atlantic* (November 1987): 75–79+.

**FURTHER READING:** Very little academic scholarship exists on Least Heat-Moon besides a couple of articles: Hank Nuwer's "William Least Heat-Moon: The Road to Serendipity," in *Rendezvous: Journal of Arts and Letters* 21 (Fall 1985): 79–91; and some discussion in David L. Newquist's "The Violation of Hospitality and the Demoralization of the Frontier," in *Midwestern Miscellany* 21 (1993): 19–28. An interview by Daniel Bourne appears in *Artful Dodge* 20–21 (1991): 92–120. Articles in popular magazines include an interview in *People* (April 18, 1983): 72–74; and Alvin P. Sanoff's "Whispers from the Kansas Tallgrass," in *U.S. News and World Report* (November 11, 1991): 58–59.

Thomas K. Dean                    University of Iowa

## Ben Hecht
February 28, 1894–April 18, 1964

**BIOGRAPHY:** Ben Hecht, journalist, novelist, playwright, and screenwriter, began writing as a police reporter and feature writer for the *Chicago Daily News* and in all his work in various genres remained true to his beginnings at the time of the Chicago Renaissance. He was born to Joseph and Sarah (Swernofsky) Hecht on the Lower East Side of New York but moved to Racine, Wisconsin, with his family while still in grade school. In the summer of 1910, Hecht enrolled in the University of Wisconsin, but after only a few days in college he moved to Chicago and began his long development as a newspaperman and writer. In 1915 he married Marie Armstrong and was acquiring a remarkable circle of friends that included Sherwood Anderson, Carl Sandburg, Margaret Anderson of the *Little Review*, and Vincent Starrett, one of the most bookish of the Chicago journalists. Hecht's journalism rapidly became more literary and innovative so that by 1921, according to the Albert Halper anthology, *This Is Chicago*, he had created a "new kind of Chicago journalism" in his feature columns and reviews (314).

Hecht's timeliness and hard-driving reportorial style also won him immense early fame as a novelist with *Erik Dorn* (1921) and as a playwright with *The Front Page* (1928) in collaboration with Charles MacArthur. In 1924 his marriage broke up and he moved to New York City. Then from 1926 onward, he alternated between New York and Hollywood where he wrote many screenplays. Always sensitive about the image of the Jew in middle America, Hecht became an eloquent

Zionist once fears of the Holocaust began to be confirmed in the 1930s. He had been a foreign correspondent right after World War I in Berlin, where he had picked up ideas on Dadaism and modernist writing to fuel the Chicago Renaissance. But by the end of his career he wrote in order, as he said, "to damn the Germans" as much as he could in his books (*A Child of the Century* 268). Hecht died of a heart attack in the midst of new and energetic writing projects in New York City with his second wife and fellow screenwriter Rose Caylor, whom he had married in 1924.

**SIGNIFICANCE:** It is delightful to read Hecht's later autobiographical books *A Child of the Century* (1954) and *Gaily, Gaily* (1963), although William MacAdams in his recent biography admits that Hecht would tend "to fictionalize his life" in these books (262). But even though some facts may not be reliable in this later reporting, Hecht did not concoct any half truths when he wrote about Chicago, about Jazz Age decadence, or about the glitter of stage and film. He also wrote honestly about race. In fact, the truth about Jewishness and its relation to the Chicago Midwest in Hecht's work may be his finest contribution to our thought and literature in this century. Even as early as *Erik Dorn*, which was hailed as a precursor of a new American novel when it appeared, the concreteness of sexual experience and of racial origins was central to Hecht's writing. In that book he wrote about Chicago reporters having "a common almost racial sophistication stamped their expression," (15) and then a few pages farther on in the book, "Yesterday a bacchanal of flesh, to-day a bacchanal of words" (21–22).

Hecht was very sensitive to setting and to the appearance of the human body, so perhaps the Chicago Midwest of the 1920s was his perfect background. Later in one of his books attacking the Germans, *A Guide for the Bedevilled* (1944), with its fierce and energetic Zionist rhetoric, his memories of murderers in the Cook County Jail link his Chicago beginnings to his fine writing on Nazism. Hecht learned to write vividly about the sensuousness of the body, and he had a strong commitment to his own racial origins. These ancient sources of strength in writing, combined with a lively wit, drive his prose. In much of his writing there is the suggestive link of liberation politics, sexual freedoms, and the

teeming world he had first come to know as a young police reporter in Chicago and that he and MacArthur may have captured with most verve in *The Front Page*. But most critics agree that he never fully realized the potential promised by his early Chicago work or by his commitment to liberation causes.

**SELECTED WORKS:** Hecht's best novels are *Erik Dorn* (1921), *Count Bruga* (1926), and *A Jew in Love* (1931). *The Front Page* (1928) is the best of his plays. In addition to the autobiographical works mentioned above, his biography *Charlie: The Improbable Life and Times of Charles MacArthur* (1957) is interesting. He has a substantial list of screenplays to his credit and important short sketches and stories, of the latter two categories most notably *1001 Afternoons in Chicago* (1922) and *The Collected Stories* (1945).

**FURTHER READING:** *The Five Lives of Ben Hecht* (1977) by Doug Fetherling; *Ben Hecht, Hollywood Screenwriter* (1985) by Jeffrey Brown Martin; and *Ben Hecht: The Man behind the Legend* (1990) by William MacAdams, are all useful studies of his work. The anthology edited by Albert Halper, *This Is Chicago* (1952), places some of Hecht's short sketches nicely into the context of Chicago writing in his time.

DONALD M. HASSLER      KENT STATE UNIVERSITY

## HEHAKE SAPA.

*See* Black Elk

## ERNEST (MILLER) HEMINGWAY
July 21, 1899–July 2, 1961

**BIOGRAPHY:** Ernest Hemingway, short story writer, novelist, war correspondent, and sportsman was the second child of Dr. Clarence Edmonds Hemingway and Grace (Hall) Hemingway of Oak Park, Illinois, now a Chicago suburb. Ernest had four sisters, Marcelline, Ursula, Madelaine (Sunny), and Carol, and a brother, Leicester. From his mother he acquired his love of the arts, including music, painting, and literature. From his father he learned fishing and hunting on the family's summer vacations at Walloon Lake near Little Traverse Bay and Petoskey in northern Michigan. The Hemingways of the village of Oak Park were staunch members of the First Congregational Church, from whose guilt-ridden Protestant heritage Ernest struggled unsuccessfully to escape. Hemingway attended Oak Park High School, where he was active in a variety of extracurricular activities that included drama, sports, and school publications, including columns and stories written in imitation of RING LARDNER.

Following graduation in 1917, the young writer went to work as a reporter for the *Kansas City Star*. In 1918 having volunteered as an ambulance driver for the American Red Cross, he was severely wounded by enemy mortar fire at Fossalta di Piave, Italy. In 1919 he returned home to recuperate, first in Oak Park, later in Michigan. That summer he took a restorative fishing trip to the Big and Little Fox Rivers near Seney on the Upper Peninsula, a trip that in 1924 inspired him to write "Big Two-Hearted River." Having tried his hand at story writing in Petoskey late in 1919, Hemingway soon moved to Toronto, where he got a job writing human interest stories for the *Star Weekly*.

Early in 1921, Hemingway met SHERWOOD ANDERSON, his first, perhaps also his most important, literary mentor. That fall, following his marriage to Hadley Richardson of St. Louis at the little Methodist church in Horton Bay near Walloon Lake, Ernest and his bride took Anderson's advice to travel to Paris rather than Italy, Hadley's preference. In December, after Hemingway was hired as the *Toronto Daily Star*'s first European correspondent, he and Hadley sailed for France, Anderson having graciously written them letters of introduction to Gertrude Stein, Ezra Pound, and James Joyce. They arrived in time to celebrate Christmas in Paris, their home base in Europe until 1928, though they actually spent less than three years in that city.

Clearly, Paris was the place where Hemingway had his first success and recognition as a writer. Learning what he could about style from Stein, Pound, and Joyce as well as Anderson, he moved from 1922 to 1924 in the direction of artistic compression to a kind of literary minimalism. In *Hemingway: A Biography* (1985), Jeffrey Meyers quotes him as saying, "I always try to write on the principle of the iceberg. There is seven-eighths of it underwater for every part that shows" (139). Among the products of this discipline, rigorously pursued in the Paris period, were such masterpieces of fiction as *In Our Time* (1925), *The Sun Also Rises* (1926), and *A Farewell to Arms* (1929). In this period he also wrote *The Torrents of Spring* (1926), a vicious parody, set in Petoskey, Michigan, of Anderson's *Dark Laughter*.

**Ernest Hemingway.**
Photo © Helen Pierce Breaker.
Courtesy of the John F. Kennedy Library

Anderson was the first of a whole cavalcade of Hemingway's mentors and friends to be repudiated and mocked by "Papa," as his chums and protégés called him. In January 1926, in a letter written on a skiing trip with his wealthy Irish Catholic friend Pauline Pfeiffer, he claimed to be a Catholic. The following January he was divorced by Hadley; in May he married Pauline in a fashionable Catholic church in Paris, his marriage to Hadley, followed by the birth of their son John (Bumby) in 1923, having been interpreted by the Church as a non-event.

In 1928 Hemingway and his pregnant new wife moved from France to Key West, Florida, which became the base for his peregrinations until 1939. Also in 1928, his father committed suicide, an event that haunted the author's life as it obsessed his writing. Early in the Key West period, Pauline bore Hemingway a son, Patrick, followed by another, Gregory, in 1931, but the marriage gradually deteriorated until by the end of 1938, it existed in name only. Besides taking up deep-sea fishing in the Key West years, Hemingway wrote a book about bullfighting, *Death in the Afternoon* (1932). Then, following his first big-game hunting safari, he wrote *Green Hills of Africa* (1935). Two of his best short stories, "The

Short Happy Life of Francis Macomber" and "The Snows of Kilimanjaro," also came out of that African experience. In 1937–38 he covered the Spanish Civil War for the North American Newspaper Alliance, an assignment which prepared him to write his most controversial novel, *For Whom the Bell Tolls* (1940). Toward the end of his residence in Key West, Hemingway became increasingly disillusioned with Pauline as well as with the Catholicism he had adopted shortly before their marriage. To ease his discontent with this second marriage, he took refuge in ever-more-open infidelities.

In 1939, Hemingway established himself in a new locale, Cuba, where he lived for about twenty years in the Finca Vigia (Lookout Farm) twelve miles southeast of Havana. In 1940, soon after his divorce from Pauline, he married Martha Gellhorn, an ambitious, sophisticated journalist, novelist, and war correspondent who soon became as much Hemingway's rival as his loving helpmate. In 1945 he divorced her, and in 1946 he replaced her with his fourth and final wife, Mary Welsh, also a writer, who outlived him. Having involved himself in World War II by submarine hunting in the Caribbean, serving as a war correspondent in Europe, and participating in the Normandy invasion and liberation of Paris, he became for a time more of an American military icon than a serious writer as his creativity languished or declined. But following the disaster of *Across the River and into the Trees* (1950), he recouped his reputation by writing *The Old Man and the Sea* (1952), and in 1954, after revisiting Africa and surviving two plane crashes, he was awarded the Nobel Prize for literature. He spent his last years struggling unsuccessfully to overcome physical and mental illness exacerbated by alcohol and by a lifetime of accidents and injuries, many of them serious. Hemingway also tried to complete *A Moveable Feast* (1964), *Islands in the Stream* (1970), and *The Garden of Eden* (1986), works that were ultimately published after his death. In 1958, just before Castro came to power, Hemingway and his wife left Cuba for Ketchum, Idaho, where they lived until his suicide in 1961 by a shotgun blast to the head. His suicide by this means inevitably recalled his father's suicide in 1928 with a revolver.

**SIGNIFICANCE:** Although the centrality of violence and war and the severely tested hero in Hemingway's fiction has not been effectively challenged, recent discussion has shifted to the inner struggle of Hemingway the man, as revealed especially by the later fiction. Turning attention from Hemingway the consummate storyteller and spare stylist to Hemingway the man, this approach has been encouraged by the renewed respectability of biographical, including psychological and psychoanalytic, criticism since the 1960s, by the opening to the public of the Hemingway Collection at the John F. Kennedy Library in the 1980s, and by feminist, specifically androgynous, criticism. This last variant of biographical criticism has seized upon androgyny, the blend of a person's female and male attributes, as a key to understanding Hemingway's character and creativity as well as his treatment of women. Interest in the life has also been whetted by Scribner's posthumous publication of Hemingway's unfinished manuscripts.

Not surprisingly, if indeed "the child is father of the man," both the internal and external conflicts engaging Hemingway are foreshadowed in his early Midwestern years, divided between his androgynous upbringing in Oak Park and his partial escape from that world during summers in Michigan. Modeled on such ideals as those afforded by Frances Hodgson Burnett's *Little Lord Fauntleroy* and the muscular Christianity of Dinah Craik's *Lord Halifax, Gentleman*, Ernest's Oak Park upbringing, approved of by his father, involved a dominant mother's genteel blending of feminine and masculine versions of manhood and womanhood in her sons as well as her daughters. In pursuit of this suburban ideal of the day, Mrs. Hemingway dressed little Ernest and his older sister Marcelline as twins, either in frilly dresses or natty sailor suits. In contrast, Ernest's summers in Michigan came to represent a dominantly masculine escape from Oak Park, sometimes with his father but often without, into an unspoiled wilderness that afforded such pleasures as hunting, fishing, hiking, and consorting with Ojibway Indians. With hunting came violence, and as he got older, adolescent sexual initiation, as recollected in such autobiographical stories as "Ten Indians" (1927) and "Fathers and Sons" (1933).

According to Mark Spilka, Hemingway did not find that childhood androgyny fulfilled its early promise of happiness; on the contrary, he soon perceived it to be a wounding condition that he must resist by plunging into "manly" sports like boxing, dedicating himself to writing as an athletic discipline and choosing violence, blood sports, physical conflict, and war as the subject matter of his fiction. His lifelong reputation for being a "tough guy" possessing traditionally masculine interests and skills would suggest that his pursuit of twenty-four-carat masculinity was successful. Furthermore, most of his published writings from *In Our Time* (1925) to *The Old Man and the Sea* (1952) would seem in their autobiographical dimensions as well as their choice of subject matter to guarantee the almost stereotypical masculinity of the author behind the image. Thus in "Big Two-Hearted River" (1925), arguably the best of the early autobiographical stories reflecting Hemingway's youthful self-image as Nick Adams, we already meet the Hemingway hero, wounded not by androgyny but by the war that is never mentioned in so many words. He is seeking the quiet healing promised by a trout stream in northern Michigan. Later, in his novels, Hemingway recreated this hero in the characters of Jake Barnes, Frederic Henry, and Robert Jordan, and in such heroes as Wilson in "The Short Happy Life of Francis Macomber" and Santiago in *The Old Man and the Sea*, characters who provide examples of "grace under pressure," of courageous and honorable behavior in the course of being savaged by the world and by life. Though the later examples of Hemingway heroes are tested far from Nick's beloved woods in northern Michigan, Hemingway passionately seeks equivalents of Michigan's wilderness to mirror and explore his characters' souls in Spain, Africa, and off-shore Cuba.

Though earlier commentators had found more than aggressive heterosexuality in Hemingway's psychosexual makeup, some even finding or claiming to find evidence of covert or overt homosexuality, it was not until 1986, with publication of a drastically cut, unfinished manuscript of *The Garden of Eden*, that critics began a systematic search for early manifestations of androgyny in Hemingway's life and works. They also sought evidence that the succession of wives and mistresses in his life, like the destructive wife and nurturing mistress of David Bourne in *The Garden*,

were projections of Hemingway's secret muse, sometimes destroying, sometimes fueling the creativity that gave meaning to his life. In effect, David Bourne, Hemingway's patently autobiographical protagonist in *The Garden of Eden*, is a new Adam. He has replaced the old Nick Adams, whose cherished code of correct masculine behavior had little applicability to his successor's female role playing, sexual experimentation, and loss of creativity accompanied by guilt as David faced the loss of his Garden of Eden. In pursuit of the new "androgynous" Hemingway, with all its implications for his life and art, critics have also doubled back on his writing career to find evidence of ambivalent attitudes toward homosexuality, lesbianism, and bisexuality as early as "A Simple Enquiry" (1927) and "The Sea Change" (1931).

Finally, interest in Hemingway's life and work has been kept alive since his suicide in 1961 by personal revelations in several other posthumous publications authorized by Scribner's from 1964 to the present, and with more still likely to be forthcoming. This process, which has been aptly called "the emptying of the vault," not only involved publication of *A Moveable Feast* (1964), *Islands in the Stream* (1970), and *The Garden of Eden* (1986), but also *The Nick Adams Stories* (1972) with eight new Nick Adams stories, and *The Complete Short Stories of Ernest Hemingway* (1987) with a few more questionable additions, signifying that the vault must be almost empty. Even so, Hemingway's long African journal, of which only a quarter had been published, has recently appeared under the title *True at First Light* (1999), edited by his son Patrick.

As revealing as these posthumous writings have been, none was ready for publication at the time of Hemingway's death. Consequently, in order to convince readers that they were getting authentic Hemingway, his posthumous editors have felt obliged to understate the amount of editorial tinkering and cutting required to prepare these manuscripts for press. While the vault was being emptied, the problems of editing became more and more formidable, as reviewers of *The Garden* learned to their amazement when they compared its published text to manuscript versions. Though Scribner's had claimed that the printed text was in every significant respect all the author's, they neglected to mention that Tom Jenks, its editor, had cut the manuscript from two hundred thousand to seventy thousand words, in the process eliminating a subplot and three characters providing an essential counterpoint to the main plot. Thus it is little wonder that while some scholars have welcomed every scrap of posthumous publication to date for its biographical significance, others have seen the trade publication of these unfinished, inferior products as violating the author's intentions and possibly diminishing rather than enhancing his reputation as a writer.

**SELECTED WORKS:** Among Hemingway's short story collections, the first published in the United States, *In Our Time* (1925), stands out. From this collection, "Indian Camp," "The Doctor and the Doctor's Wife," and "Big Two-Hearted River," set in Michigan, are rich in regional and autobiographical significance. Later short stories of note include "The Short Happy Life of Francis Macomber" and "The Snows of Kilimanjaro," reprinted in *The Complete Short Stories of Ernest Hemingway* (1987). Among the novels, *The Sun Also Rises* (1926) and *A Farewell to Arms* (1929) call attention to the 1920s as a time of amazing creativity for Hemingway. Later landmarks of his achievement as a novelist include *For Whom the Bell Tolls* (1940) and his popular short novel, *The Old Man and the Sea* (1952). *A Moveable Feast* (1964), though vicious in its portrayal of Hemingway's Paris contemporaries, is a brilliant re-creation of his life there in the 1920s. Finally, *The Garden of Eden* (1986), far from completion at Hemingway's death, nevertheless provides insights into his previously private life. Hemingway's verses and some of his letters may be found in his *Complete Poems* (1983) and *Selected Letters, 1917–1961* (1981).

**FURTHER READING:** Among older biographies of Hemingway, the following deserve special mention: Carlos Baker's *Ernest Hemingway: A Life Story* (1969, 1980), Jeffrey Meyers's *Hemingway: A Biography* (1985), and Kenneth Lynn's *Hemingway* (1987). Important critical approaches to the life and works have been provided by Philip Young's *Ernest Hemingway: A Reconsideration* (1966), Mark Spilka's *Hemingway's Quarrel with Androgyny* (1990), Robert E. Fleming's *The Face in the Mirror* (1994), and *The Cambridge Companion to Hemingway*, edited by Scott Donaldson (1996). Paul Smith's *A Reader's Guide to the Short Sto-*

*ries of Ernest Hemingway* (1989) is useful for reference. In 1999 *Hemingway: The Final Years*, the last volume of Michael S. Reynolds's exhaustive five-volume biography, was published. The most useful videotape on Hemingway's early years is GENE DENT's *Up in Michigan* (1983). This twenty-nine-minute video is available at Bowling Green State University, Bowling Green, Ohio, and in other film collections. A somewhat dated but still useful reference is Constance Cappel Montgomery's *Hemingway in Michigan* (1966). Its account of Hemingway's early years needs to be supplemented by Michael S. Reynolds's *The Young Hemingway* (1986). The best collection of Hemingway papers is at the John F. Kennedy Library, Boston, with additional materials at the Scribner Archives in Princeton University Library.

PAUL W. MILLER                    WITTENBERG UNIVERSITY

# CAROLINE LEE (WHITING) HENTZ
June 1, 1800–February 11, 1856

**BIOGRAPHY:** Born in Lancaster, Massachusetts, to John and Orpah Whiting, Caroline Lee Hentz spent her youth writing poems and stories to amuse family and friends. When she was seventeen, she began teaching at Lancaster Common School. In 1824 she married Nicholas Marcellus Hentz. He taught French in Northampton and later at the University of North Carolina, where they moved in 1826. In 1832 Caroline and her husband founded a popular female seminary in Cincinnati. While in Cincinnati, Hentz frequented a small literary circle known as the Semi-Colons, which was headed by Dr. DANIEL DRAKE. Another member of this circle was Harriet Beecher Stowe. The two met in this circle and debated on public issues, influenced, no doubt, by the fervent abolitionist climate of Cincinnati. Caroline followed her husband to a number of teaching posts in both the Midwest and South and assisted in his teaching. When Nicholas became seriously ill in 1849, Caroline Lee Hentz turned her talent for writing into a profession to support her husband and three children. One daughter, Julia Louisa Keyes, became a published poet. Hentz died, shortly after her husband, in Marianna, Florida, from pneumonia.

Hentz's fist published works were plays; *DeLara* (performed in 1831 but not published until 1843) was followed quickly by *Werden-*

berg (1832) and *Lamorah* (1832). Hentz's first novel, *Lovell's Folly* (1833), received little notice; she returned to serious writing with the publication of *Aunt Patty's Scrap Bag* (1846). Hentz wrote a prodigious amount of fiction in the last ten years of her life, many of which have been characterized as domestic novels or plantation romances.

**SIGNIFICANCE:** Hentz is primarily remembered for the proslavery novel *The Planter's Northern Bride* (1854) because it directly rebuts Harriet Beecher Stowe's *Uncle Tom's Cabin* (1852). In this and her other novels, Hentz's Southern characters travel to the Midwest or New England in order to contrast the conditions of slave labor in the South with "wage slavery" in the North. Hentz demonstrates that conditions for the poor are far worse in Northern urban centers than they are for slaves in the South. Hentz's depiction of the Midwest relies on the myth of the Vanishing Indian. In "A Soldier's Bride," from the collection *Lost Daughter* (1857) set in Ohio, Hentz presents the loyal Indian, Sakamaw. After he is killed, Hentz proclaims that with Indians eliminated from the "frontiers of the West . . . [t]he wilderness began to blossom 'like the rose'" (119). Kathryn Lee Seidel's 1985 study, *The Southern Belle in the American Novel*, contends that Hentz was "one of the three most popular American authors as late as 1892" (11). Her most successful novel, *Linda* (1850), went through thirteen editions in two years. In *A Literary History of Alabama: The Nineteenth Century* (1979), Benjamin Buford Williams downplays Hentz's literary merit but adds, "One cannot argue with the financial success she enjoyed with her domestic fiction, but her works must remain a curiosity of mid-nineteenth century tastes" (175).

**SELECTED WORKS:** Hentz's plays include *DeLara, or, the Moorish Bride* (1831); *Werdenberg, or the Forest League* (1832); and *Lamorah, or the Western Wild* (1832). Her novels include *Lovell's Folly* (1833); *Linda, or, the Young Pilot of the Belle Creole* (1850); *Rena, or the Snow Bird* (1851); *Marcus Warland, or the Long Moss Spring* (1852); *Eoline, or the Magnolia Vale, or The Heiress of Glenmore* (1852); *Helen and Arthur, or Miss Thusa's Spinning Wheel* (1853); *The Planter's Northern Bride* (2 vols., 1854); *Robert Graham: A Sequel to Linda* (1855); and *Ernest Lindwood* (1856). Short story collections include *Aunt Patty's Scrap Bag* (1846), *The Victim of Excitement* (1853), *Wild*

*Jack; or, the Stolen Child, and Other Stories* (1853), *Courtship and Marriage, or, the Joys and Sorrows of American Life* (1856), *The Banished Son; and Other Stories of the Heart* (1856), *The Lost Daughter; and Other Stories of the Heart* (1857), and *Love after Marriage; and Other Stories of the Heart* (1857).

**FURTHER READING:** Only a few sources treat Hentz in much detail. Benjamin Buford Williams's *A Literary History of Alabama: The Nineteenth Century* (1979) contains an informative section entitled "Caroline Lee Hentz: Alabama's First Best-Selling Author." Mary Ann Wimsat's "Caroline Hentz's Balancing Act," in *The Female Tradition in Southern Literature*, edited by Carol S. Manning (1993): 161–75, offers an interesting analysis of Hentz as professional author. Other sources include a chapter entitled "E.D.E.N. Southworth and Caroline Lee Hentz," in Nina Baym's *Woman's Fiction: A Guide to Novels by and about Women in America, 1820–1870* (1978); Rhoda Coleman Ellison's *Early Alabama Publications: A Study of Literary Interests* (1943); Miriam J. Shillingsburg's "The Ascent of Woman, Southern Style: Hentz, King, Chopin," in *Southern Literature in Transition*, edited by Philip Castille and William Osborne (1983); and Kathryn Lee Seidel's *The Southern Belle in the American Novel* (1985). E. D. Mansfield also offers a valuable personal reminiscence of the literary circle Hentz frequented in Cincinnati in *Mansfield's Personal Memories, Social, Political and Literary, 1803–1843* (1879: 261–76). Caroline's son, Charles Hentz, has written an unpublished autobiography. This autobiography, as well as Caroline's unpublished diary, is located in the North Carolina Collection of the Library of the University of North Carolina at Chapel Hill.

JOHN L. SUTTON            NEW YORK UNIVERSITY

## JOSEPHINE (FREY) HERBST
March 5, 1892–January 28, 1969

**BIOGRAPHY:** Born in Sioux City, Iowa, to William Benton Herbst, a farm equipment salesman, and May (Frey) Herbst, both of whom were born in the East and were of German Swiss ancestry, Josephine Herbst became an important radical novelist and journalist. Known as Josie, she attended high school in Sioux City, graduating in 1910. Then she attended four different colleges: Morningside College in Sioux City; the University of Iowa, where she determined to be a writer;

the University of Washington in Seattle; and finally the University of California, from which she received her BA in 1918. She had begun reading the *Masses* in college and became interested in radical causes while at Berkeley, an interest that dominated her professional life in the 1930s.

By 1920 Josie had moved to New York where she held a number of jobs, including one as an editorial reader for H. L. Mencken. After an affair with Maxwell Anderson that ended in a pregnancy and an abortion, she went to Europe to write, first in Berlin and then in Paris, where she met JOHN HERRMANN of Lansing, Michigan. He was a young writer who, like Herbst, was in rebellion against the Midwestern mores of his parents. They lived together in France and the United States for two years before succumbing to parental pressure and marrying in 1926. They lived in an old stone house in Edwinna, Pennsylvania, until their separation in 1934. They divorced in 1940, but Josie remained in the house in Edwinna. She apparently remained in love with Herrmann, visiting his grave in Lansing after his death in 1959 and shortly before her own death ten years later.

Herbst published her first novel, *Nothing Is Sacred*, in 1928 and her second, *Money for Love*, in 1929. In 1933 she published the first volume of a trilogy, *Pity Is Not Enough*, followed by *The Executioner Waits* (1934) and *Rope of Gold* (1939). In 1930 she and John Herrmann attended the International Congress of Revolutionary Writers in Kharkov, USSR, and Josie moved farther left in her sympathies while Herrmann became a Communist Party member. His association with the Ware Group in Washington, a branch of the Communist underground, with Alger Hiss, Whittaker Chambers, and others, came between them, contributing to their separation.

Herbst's growing prominence as a writer and her stay in Spain during the Spanish Revolution led to suspicions that she, too, was a Communist Party member, although there is no evidence that she became one. In 1942 she was fired from a job with the Office of Facts and Figures of the Donovan Committee, a forerunner of the Office of Strategic Services, the OSS. She published a novel, *Somewhere the Tempest Fell*, in 1947, and she was refused a passport in 1951 and in 1954. She was interviewed by the FBI during the Hiss case in 1949

and warned Herrmann, who had fled to Mexico and remained there until his death in 1959.

In her last two decades, Herbst became modestly prominent as a writer. She became friendly with such young writers as John Cheever and SAUL BELLOW, and she became a member of such literary establishments as Yaddo. She died of cancer in 1969 and returned in death to the Sioux City, Iowa, of her birth.

**SIGNIFICANCE:** Josephine Herbst, like John Herrmann, remained in quiet rebellion against the Midwestern middle-class values of her family all her life, and most of her work reflected that rebellion in its strong autobiographical dimensions. Her first published novel, *Nothing Is Sacred* (1928), is set in Sioux City, centering on the illness and death of her mother in 1925; so personal and detailed was the novel, not only in her descriptions of her mother's illness but in its portrayal of her embezzling brother-in-law, that the family found it offensive. Her second novel, *Money for Love* (1929), the story of a young Midwestern woman in the East, is based on her successful attempt to sell Maxwell Anderson's letters back to him to start her new life with John Herrmann. Both novels began the course that her future novels were to take: the dispassionate reporting of intimate details; the clear definition of the middle-class Midwestern value system against which she was in revolt; the complexity of the social and family systems her people were caught up in; and her growing sense of moral decay in American life.

Her trilogy, *Pity Is Not Enough* (1933), *The Executioner Waits* (1934), and *Rope of Gold* (1939), is the intensely autobiographical story of the growth of social consciousness of a young woman, Victoria. In the first book, she learns about the future of capitalism, and in the second book she marries Jonathan Chance, who bears a strong resemblance to John Herrmann. In the third novel they become committed radicals dedicated to change. In the background of the three novels, Herbst graphically portrays the social and economic history of the Midwest from post–Civil War capitalistic abuses through the emergence of post–World War I radicalism, the outbreak of the Depression of the 1930s, and the search for change, even as growing international threats became apparent.

The trilogy, Herbst's best work, provides

a history of a turbulent era and the people who sought to make it orderly and humane. It transcends the proletarian ideology with which it is associated to become a complex portrayal of the elements that shaped the lives of its people and directed the course of the times and the place in which it is set.

**SELECTED WORKS:** The trilogy, *Pity Is Not Enough* (1933), *The Executioner Waits* (1934), and *Rope of Gold* (1939), deserves reprinting as a unit. Also valuable are the three parts of her memoirs that have been published in journals: "The Starched Blue Sky of Spain," in *Noble Savage* 1 (September 1960): 76–117; "A Year of Disgrace," in *Noble Savage* 3 (March 1961): 128–60; and "*Yesterday's Road,*" in *New American Review* 3 (April 1968): 84–104. These were collected, together with the previously unpublished "The Magicians and Their Apprentices," in *The Starched Blue Sky of Spain and Other Memoirs* (1991). Her novella "Hunter of Doves," in *Botteghe Oscure* (Spring 1954), is a moving, fictional portrayal of her friend Nathanael West. Her novels, *Nothing Is Sacred* (1928), *Money for Love* (1929), and *Somewhere the Tempest Fell* (1947), the latter set in Chicago, reflect the conflict between traditional Midwestern values and Eastern sophistication that characterized much of her relationship with her past and her family.

**FURTHER READING:** Elinor Langer's *Josephine Herbst: The Story She Could Never Tell* (1984), the only biography of Herbst, is a thorough and sympathetic study. Herbst also is prominent in literary and biographical studies of leading writers of the 1920s and 1930s, including ERNEST HEMINGWAY, and more recently John Cheever and Saul Bellow. Her papers are in the Beinecke Library of Yale University, where a bibliography of her published work, compiled by Martha Pickering with Herbst's cooperation, is available.

DAVID D. ANDERSON    MICHIGAN STATE UNIVERSITY

## ROBERT HERRICK
April 26, 1868–December 23, 1938

**BIOGRAPHY:** Robert Herrick was born in Cambridge, Massachusetts, the next to the youngest of five children. His father, William Augustus, could trace his ancestors back to the early days of Salem and was distantly related to Nathaniel Hawthorne. Harriet Peabody (Emery) Herrick, Robert's mother, came from people of the laboring class who had achieved a respected social status over the years. Kenneth Lynn observes that Herrick wrote almost nothing about his childhood but that his novels are "peculiarly personal documents" whose protagonists have much in common with Robert Herrick himself (*The Dream of Success*, 210). Blake Nevius has noted that Herrick's early life was dominated by his mother's social ambitions, which were a major source of conflict within the family. In fact, Herrick's own family represented a microcosm of American society. In *The Development of a Novelist*, Nevius asserted that "the ruling passion that drove Harriet Herrick and destroyed the family harmony was one that on a broader scale was transforming American life" (16).

Robert Herrick was educated at Harvard, completing a master's degree there. From 1890 to 1893 he taught English composition and literature at Massachusetts Institute of Technology. In 1893 he was approached by William Raney Harper, who persuaded him to accept a teaching position at the University of Chicago. Although Herrick disliked Chicago from the very beginning and would no doubt have agreed with Jack London's footnote in *The Iron Heel* (1907) calling Hell "a pocket edition of Chicago" (309), he remained there almost his entire career. In 1894 Herrick married his first cousin, who was living in Chicago. Her name was Harriet Peabody Emery, ironically the same name as his mother and grandmother. The couple had no children, and the marriage became an unhappy one. Herrick wanted a divorce, but his wife was uncooperative because of advice she had received from a lawyer. The divorce was granted in 1916, but the experience provided Herrick with two important subjects for his fiction: marriage and lawyers.

Herrick published approximately twenty novels, most of which were focused on the changing values of American society. Herrick was on leave from the University of Chicago and living in Europe prior to America's entering World War I. He wrote essays for the Chicago papers advocating that America enter the war quickly. When America finally entered the war, he came back disillusioned, fearing that his country would imitate the worst features of fascism. Herrick's last novel was a little-known utopian novel called *Sometime* (1933). Clearly, in all of his previous works, Herrick demonstrated that powerful materialistic values were destroying America. In the first half of *Sometime*, Herrick established what he believed was necessary for a healthy society, but by the end of the novel that society was in danger of falling prey to the same materialistic values that were threatening America.

In the mid-1920s, the Macmillan Publishing Company was eager to publish an academic novel. When Herrick's name was mentioned as a possible author, the editors were afraid that Herrick would take advantage of the situation to pay back his enemies. Herrick assured the editors that such would not be the case; however, even though *Chimes* (1926) is set in a fictional college called Eureka College, the novel is a thinly disguised portrayal of the University of Chicago, and the faculty and administration are rather easy to identify.

Herrick's reputation was at its peak around 1910, but from then on it declined, and he is regarded as a minor figure in American literature today. During the last three years of his life, he served as secretary to the governor of the Virgin Islands, where he died of a heart attack in 1938.

**SIGNIFICANCE:** Although Herrick was born in the East and spent his early life there, he lived most of his adult life in Chicago. Several of his novels are set in Chicago, the most noteworthy being *Memoirs of an American Citizen* (1905), which portrays the corruption of the meat-packing industry. Herrick was one of a group of writers who set their novels in Chicago, apparently in the belief that if they could understand Chicago, they could understand what was going on in the rest of America. WILLIAM DEAN HOWELLS thought highly enough of Herrick's work to call Herrick a successor to Henry James ("The Novels of Robert Herrick," *North American Review* 189 [1909]: 812–20).

Unfortunately, Herrick made a decision around that time that his message was far more important than the skill of writing, and his later works failed to achieve the bright promise that Howells had predicted. Scholars agree that Herrick's works after 1910 are sprawling, formless, and disorganized; in fact, he even lifted materials from his early published works. At one time in his career, Herrick was praised by Lewis Mumford for his "unflinching honesty" (*The Golden Day* 210) in

facing the serious problems of American life. Although he saw much to praise in Herrick's work, Granville Hicks believed that Herrick's failure was his narrow opposition to industrialism, causing him to reject industrialism outright instead of working to humanize it. As Hicks wrote in "Robert Herrick, Liberal," "The great novels, when they come, will humanize industry; Herrick, in his heart, rejects it" (*New Republic* 67 [June 17, 1931]: 130). For Hicks, then, Herrick's liberalism was not a fruitful solution to the problems of industrialism in America.

Although Herrick is not a major figure today, he is significant for addressing many of the problems of his day that are still with us: the role of government in American life, pollution, the evils of industrialism, the exploitation of natural resources, the problems of marriage, and the question of women's rights. To read Herrick's novels is to gain insight into what America has become in the latter part of the twentieth century.

**SELECTED WORKS:** The best of Herrick's novels and the one that has been issued in paperback and that is thus available for classroom use is *The Memoirs of an American Citizen* (1905), an exposé of the meat-packing industry at the top level. With UPTON SINCLAIR'S *The Jungle* (1906), also set in Chicago, and *Memoirs*, readers can gain much insight into the corruption of this industry and the human misery that resulted from it. *The Common Lot* (1904) is about a young architect in Chicago who compromises his integrity for financial gain. *Together* (1908) is a fictional study of five marriages, only one of which proves successful. *Together* is perhaps Herrick's most controversial novel because of its criticism of the institution of marriage in the early twentieth century. The women receive the greater share of the blame for the failure of the marriages, since Herrick portrays them as self-seeking social climbers who drive their husbands to push for more money which, in turn, will bring them social advantages. *Together* is essentially Herrick's commentary on the women's rights movement. His position is clear that in seeking freedom, women were abandoning their function of child bearing and their role as man's comrade in the struggle that is life. *The Healer* (1911) is about a physician who has the gift of healing but who betrays that gift and loses it entirely when he

puts money and social prestige ahead of healing. *The Healer* is typical of many of Herrick's
novels which involve professional men
tempted by money and social standing to
compromise their ideals and sell out their integrity and their talent. *Chimes* (1926) is more
interesting as an exposé of the University of
Chicago than as a literary work.

**FURTHER READING:** Most of the scholarly
work devoted to Herrick was done prior to
1970. The best source for information about
him, since no full-length biography has
been written, is Blake Nevius, whose dissertation, "The Novels of Robert Herrick, a Critical Study" (1947); his essay "The Idealistic
Novels of Robert Herrick," in *American Literature* 21 (March 1949): 56–63; and his book
*Robert Herrick: The Development of a Novelist*
(1962) represent a thorough and balanced
scholarly treatment of the man and his work.
In addition to the scholarly works mentioned
earlier, one could consult the following for
valuable insights into Herrick's fiction: Har-
ald Nielsen's "Robert Herrick," in *Poet Lore* 19
(September 1908): 337–63; Edwin Bjorkman's
*Voices of Tomorrow: Critical Studies of the Spirit in
Literature* (1913); Newton Arvin's "Homage to
Robert Herrick," in *New Republic* 82 (March 6,
1935): 93–95; Heinrich Ludeke's "Robert Herrick, Novelist of American Democracy," in *English Studies* 18 (April 1936): 49–57; and Russell
Blankenship's literary history *American Literature* (1949). Herrick's papers are located in
three libraries: the University of Chicago, the
Newberry Library in Chicago, and the Princeton Library.

LOREN LOGSDON                    EUREKA COLLEGE

## JOHN HERRMANN
November 9, 1900–April 9, 1959

**BIOGRAPHY:** John Herrmann, novelist,
short story writer, and literary expatriate,
was born into a prosperous Lansing, Michigan, family of merchant tailors. His father,
Henry Herrmann, was of German ancestry;
his mother, Florence (Ludwig) Herrmann,
was of Pennsylvania Dutch and New England origins. He was educated in the Lansing
public schools and the University of Michigan and later at George Washington University and in Munich, Germany. His vacations
were spent in northern Michigan, and later
he worked as a traveling seed salesman; both
experiences became the basis for his later

fiction. He also worked as a newspaperman
in Lansing and Washington, D.C.

In the early 1920s, he went to Paris to become a writer. There he met ERNEST HEM-
INGWAY, Gertrude Stein, and others and
worked on the staff of *Transition*, in which he
published his first fiction. In 1924 he met
JOSEPHINE HERBST, and they lived together
without marrying until 1926, when, in response to family pressures, they married.
They separated in 1934 and were divorced in
1940, when Herrmann was married to Ruth
Tate, with whom he had a son, John. In 1930
he and Herbst attended the International
Congress of Revolutionary Writers in
Kharkov, USSR, and Herrmann returned a
dedicated Communist Party member. In the
early 1930s he was part of the Ware Group of
the Communist underground with Whittaker
Chambers, Alger Hiss, and others in Washington, D.C. He served in the U.S. Coast
Guard in World War II, and when the Hiss
case began to break in 1948, he went to Mexico, where he remained until his death in
Guadalajara on April 9, 1959.

**SIGNIFICANCE:** Herrmann drew heavily on
his experience in Michigan and the Midwest
for three novels, a prize-winning novella,
and twelve or more short stories. His first
novel, *What Happens?* (1926), was published by
Robert McAlmon in Paris; based on his Lansing youth, it was banned from import into the
United States as "obscene," an order that was
appealed by prominent writers and critics
but was upheld. His second novel, *Summer
Is Ended* (1932), is set in Lansing and Detroit;
and his third, *The Salesman* (1939), is the story
of a troubled traveling salesman. It bears
more than a passing resemblance to Arthur
Miller's *Death of a Salesman*. His novella, "The
Big Short Trip," shared the Scribner's Prize of
1932 with Thomas Wolfe's "A Portrait of Bas-
com Hawke." Herrmann's work has been
favorably compared to that of SHERWOOD
ANDERSON, Ernest Hemingway, and other
Midwestern writers. Like theirs, Herrmann's
work was firmly rooted in the Midwestern
experiences of his youth, and although he left
the Midwest in fact, he remained a Midwestern writer. However, he wrote little after 1940, and his promise was never realized.

**SELECTED WORKS:** Herrmann's three novels, *What Happens?* (1926), *Summer Is Ended*
(1932), and *The Salesman* (1939), are somewhat

dated. His best work is in his novella, "The Big Short Trip" (*Scribner's*, August 1932) and in his short fiction, most notably "The Gale of August Twentieth" (*Scribner's*, October 1931), "The Man Who Had Two Stars" (*Scribner's*, August 1931), and "Two Days from the South" (*Scribner's*, May 1936).

**FURTHER READING:** No book about Herrmann has been written, but he is mentioned in many histories, biographies, and autobiographies of the 1920s and 1930s. His relationship with Josephine Herbst is treated extensively in Elinor Langer's *Josephine Herbst* (1984). Short pieces include DAVID D. ANDERSON's "John Herrmann, Midwestern Modern, Part I," in *Midwestern Miscellany* 17 (1990): 26–33; and "John Herrmann, Midwestern Modern, Part II: The Alger Hiss Case and the Midwestern Literary Connection," in *Midwestern Miscellany* 19 (1991): 42–52. Also valuable is William McCann's "Lansing's Forgotten Novelist of the Lost Generation," in *Society for the Study of Midwestern Literature Newsletter* 11 (Summer 1981): 43–46.

DAVID D. ANDERSON    MICHIGAN STATE UNIVERSITY

# JIM HEYNEN

July 14, 1940

**BIOGRAPHY:** Poet turned fiction writer Jim Heynen was born in Sioux County, Iowa, to Hilbert and Alice (Klein) Heynen. He grew up on a farm and in the Dutch Reformed Church. He left the countryside for Calvin College (BA, 1960), then graduate studies at the University of Iowa (MA, 1965, plus sixty hours of doctoral studies) and the University of Oregon (MFA, 1972). Heynen worked a sequence of jobs, some teaching or related to writing and some not, in Michigan, Idaho, Oregon, and Minnesota. He married three times: to DeLaine Blick in 1960, to Carol Jane Bangs in 1973, and to Sally Williams in 1990. He now lives in St. Paul, Minnesota, while teaching at St. Olaf College. He is the father of two children, Emily Jane (1975) and William Geoffrey (1978).

Heynen's publishing career followed the paradigm of many contemporary writers. He began publishing small chapbooks of poems with literary presses, then moved to literary fictions from better-known small presses, culminating in a major collection from a prestigious house, followed by some nonfiction and a juvenile novel. His stories appear regularly in the *Georgia Review*. *One Hundred Over 100* (1990), a commercial venture somewhat outside Heynen's normal range, contains Heynen's interviews with one hundred people over the age of one hundred. Heynen received two fellowships from the National Endowment for the Arts (poetry in 1974, fiction in 1985) and in 1977 was a U.S.–U.K. Bicentennial Fellow to Norwich, England. *You Know What Is Right* won a Northwest Booksellers Association Award in 1986, and *One Hundred Over 100* was a finalist for an American Book Associations Award in 1990.

**SIGNIFICANCE:** Heynen has written, "I am interested in developing a distinctively rural American esthetic, one which I would not call a sentimental ruralism, but rather a clear and even harsh acceptance of the earth and animal presence in our historical and contemporary lives" (*Contemporary Authors* 77–80: 237). In his work, most of it firmly rooted in the countryside of Iowa, Minnesota, and South Dakota, he has only partially succeeded: the minister's wife who sweetens parishioners' coffee with a few drops of breast milk (*The Man Who Kept Cigars in His Cap* 17) and the mound of coins which "glow like a collection plate" in a gas station urinal (*You Know What Is Right* 74) are but the more bizarre examples of surrealistic presences in his stories. Still, Heynen's Dutch Reformed background keeps intruding, and we understand that in a crisis his farm boys "know what is right" and will do it. Heynen can, however, be whimsical about the church and critical of the rural community, with which he carries on a lover's quarrel.

Heynen's best work to date is his short fiction: one- and two-page stories of farm life, some nearly legends or fables, often pitting the gang of young country boys against the older men or town folks. The boys confront life's vicissitudes and wonders with that matter-of-fact directness often associated with rural life, a practicality which constitutes the basis of Heynen's rural aesthetic. His novel *Being Youngest* (1997) is told in the first person by Henry and Gretchen, the youngest children in two neighboring farm families. Heynen recounts the real and imagined indignities they suffer in a world of Brownie cameras and Schwinn bicycles, the revenges they exact, and their battle against a sinister old couple who, among other eccentricities, share a set of false teeth.

SELECTED WORKS: Heynen's poems are contained in several small chapbooks, including *Sioux Songs* (1976) and *Notes from Custer* (1976) and in the hardback collection *A Suitable Church* (1981). His short fictions appeared first in two smaller volumes, *The Man Who Kept Cigars in His Cap* (1979) and *You Know What Is Right* (1985), then in the 224-page *The One-Room Schoolhouse* (1993), which went to five printings in paperback. His juvenile novel, *Being Youngest*, published in 1997, also appeared in paperback. *One Hundred Over 100* (1990) has proved a very successful venture as well.

FURTHER READING: *Contemporary Authors* 77–80 contains a brief review of Heynen's life and work (237).

DAVID PICHASKE      SOUTHWEST STATE UNIVERSITY

## CHESTER HIMES
July 29, 1909–November 12, 1984

BIOGRAPHY: An African American writer three generations removed from slavery, Chester Bomar Himes was born in Jefferson City, Missouri, to Joseph Sandy Himes and Estelle (Bomar) Himes. He moved with his family to Cleveland, Ohio, in 1914 where he graduated from Glenville High School in 1926. He enrolled at Ohio State University in 1926, having scored fourth highest on the standardized entrance examination. However, he withdrew from the university at the end of his third semester and returned to Cleveland, where he became increasingly immersed in criminal activity. This involvement eventually led to a conviction of armed robbery in 1928 resulting in a sentence of twenty to twenty-five years in the Ohio State Penitentiary.

He began writing in prison, and his first story, "To What Red Hell," an account of the 1930 fire at the penitentiary in which hundreds of inmates were killed, was published in *Esquire* in 1934. While in prison, Himes published stories in several other magazines. He was paroled in 1936, returned to Cleveland, and continued writing while working at various other jobs to support himself and his wife, Jean Lucinda Johnson, whom he married in 1937. His marriage to Johnson lasted fourteen years. He married Leslie Packard in 1965.

He moved to California in 1940 and later to New York, publishing three novels, *If He Hollers Let Him Go* (1945), *Lonely Crusade* (1947), and *Cast the First Stone* (1952), before leaving the United States for Paris in 1953. He remained abroad for the rest of his life. It was in Paris that he began writing the detective fiction which earned him critical success in France and popular appeal internationally. He died from Parkinson's disease in Moraira, Spain, where he had spent the last fifteen years of his life.

SIGNIFICANCE: Himes is best known as a writer of detective fiction as well as novels which address race relations in the United States. With the exception of *The Third Generation* (1954), much of which, because of its autobiographical nature, is set in St. Louis and Cleveland, none of his books are set in the Midwest or are concerned with specifically Midwestern themes. However, Himes should not be considered a Midwestern writer merely by birth. It is generally acknowledged that much of his fiction is autobiographical. Himes had significant life experiences as a child and young adult living in the Midwest. These experiences formed his worldview and convey Midwestern influences to his writing.

SELECTED WORKS: Novels such as *If He Hollers Let Him Go* (1945) and *The Primitive* (1955) are exemplary of Himes's "protest" fiction. In these works he closely examines and criticizes race relations in America. Although Himes was reluctant to write popular detective fiction, he was quite successful at it, and his novels written between 1957 and 1969 show an evolution from the basic formula of that genre to a unique adaptation which manages to reflect on American race relations.

FURTHER READING: Himes wrote two autobiographies: *The Quality of Hurt: The Autobiography of Chester Himes* (1971) and *My Life of Absurdity: The Autobiography of Chester Himes* (1976). Both offer a frank look at his life and the unique experiences that shaped and influenced his writing. *Conversations with Chester Himes*, edited by Michel Fabre and Robert E. Skinner (1995), is a compilation of interviews with the writer. Critical interpretation can be found in James Sallis's "In America's Black Heartland: The Achievement of Chester Himes," in *Western Humanities Review* 37.3 (Autumn 1983): 191–206; as well as in *Native Sons: A Critical Study of Twentieth-Century Negro American Authors*, by Edward Margolies (1968). Also by Edward Margolies with Michel Fabre is *The Several Lives of Chester*

*Himes* (1997), which places Himes's work within the context of his life experiences. Many of Himes's papers are held at the Beinecke Rare Book and Manuscript Library, Yale University.

MARY B. DUNNE                    BOSTON UNIVERSITY

## HOLLING C(LANCY) HOLLING
August 2, 1900–September 7, 1973
(Holling Allison Clancy)

**BIOGRAPHY:** Holling Allison Clancy was born in Henriette, Michigan, in a rural area of Jackson County. Holling legally changed his surname to his grandfather's in 1925. His father, Bennet A. Clancy, and mother were both educators who provided Holling with a wealth of reading, information, and encouragement. His grandfather was an early Michigan pioneer who fostered a love for the natural world and Native American traditions. Holling spent much of his childhood drawing, writing, and doing research. At ten, he was writing and illustrating his own stories because he had decided there was a great need for good children's books.

Holling graduated from high school in Leslie, Michigan, in 1917, worked in a factory, on an ore boat, and as a taxidermist at the Chicago Field Museum. He graduated from the Art Institute in Chicago in 1923, taught on a University World Cruise and worked for an advertising firm. In 1925 he married Lucile Webster, an artist. She would collaborate with Holling on many of his children's books. Holling died in Leslie, Michigan, and is buried close to his birthplace. An image of the canoe "Paddle-to-the-Sea" is engraved on his tombstone.

**SIGNIFICANCE:** Holling created award-winning children's books that were beautifully illustrated and meticulously researched. Holling emphasized the importance of conserving the environment, protecting wildlife, and respecting the views and heritage of Native Americans. Holling also had a deep respect for the abilities and interests of his young readers. His books follow a predictable format of a central story unified around a single imaginative character or figure. His stories are detailed with historical, cultural, geographical, and scientific facts. Printed pages of text alternate with full-color illustrations, while margin notes and drawings add further details.

*Paddle-to-the-Sea* (1941) describes the progress of a small wooden man in a canoe carved by a Native American boy as it moves through the Great Lakes and along the St. Lawrence Seaway. The text and illustrations portray the landscapes, wildlife, industries, and inhabitants of the area around the lakes. In *The Tree in the Trail* (1942), Holling shows Native American life on the Great Plains as it occurs around a cottonwood sapling in what became Kansas. Buffalo hunts, the advent of the horse, and the development of the Santa Fe Trail surround the tree, which sprouted before explorers came to North America. *Minn of the Mississippi* (1951) begins with the geology of northern Minnesota and the biology of the development of reptile eggs. It traces the adventures of a contemporary snapping turtle down the Mississippi. All of Holling's books offer a wealth of information to the young people who read them, and these three in particular provide an abundance of lively detail about areas of the Midwest.

**SELECTED WORKS:** Holling wrote more than thirteen works, of which the best known include *The Book of Indians* (1935); *Paddle-to-the-Sea* (1941), runner-up for the 1942 Caldecott Medal for illustrations in a children's book; *Tree in the Trail* (1942); *Seabird* (1943), runner-up for the Newbery Medal in 1949; *Minn of the Mississippi* (1951), runner-up for the Newbery Award in 1952; and *Pagoo* (1957).

**FURTHER READING:** Although no book-length work has appeared on Holling, two helpful articles are M. Clyde Armstrong's "Holling Clancy Holling," *Horn Book* 31 (April 1955): 135–43, and Terry Borton's "The Teaching of *Paddle-to-the-Sea*," *Learning* 8 (January 1977): 26–31. Holling's manuscripts are at the University of Oregon Library in Eugene.

JEAN LAMING           MIDLAND PUBLIC SCHOOLS

## WILLIAM JON (BILL) HOLM
August 25, 1943

**BIOGRAPHY:** William Jon Holm of Minnesota, not to be confused with Oscar William Holm of Washington state, is the child of first-generation Icelandic-Americans Bill Holm, Sr., and Jonina (Sigurborg) Josephson. He grew up rural, Midwestern, Lutheran, and fiercely independent in an old, crooked, white farmhouse north of Minneota, Minnesota. Praised as a youth for his precocious bookishness, Holm first encountered what he calls "America" in Minneota High School: football and cheerleaders and the business of getting ahead. Deciding that all he really wanted was the sight of Minneota receding in the rearview mirror of his car, Holm enrolled at Gustavus Adolphus College (BA, 1965) and then at the University of Kansas on his way to becoming "a famous author, a distinguished and respected professor at an old university, surrounded by beautiful women, witty talk, fine whiskey, Mozart" ("The Music of Failure" 56). Holm left Kansas having completed his course work but not a dissertation. He taught at Hampton Institute, Virginia, at Lakewood Community College, Minnesota, and at the University of Iceland on a Fulbright (1978) before returning to the family home in Minneota and a position at the recently founded Southwest State University, where in Whitmanesque defiance of state regulations, he maintains the school's only office in which smoking is permitted. Although Holm failed in his quest for a professorship at an old and respected university, he was awarded the Fulbright to Iceland, a visiting professorship in Xian, in the People's Republic of China in 1986, two Bush Arts Fellowships in poetry (1982 and 1996), and a National Endowment for the Arts Fellowship in prose in 1987. As a famous writer he makes frequent visits to the Pacific Northwest and has lectured in Madagascar, Iceland, Alaska, Canada, and the Lower 48.

SIGNIFICANCE: Strongly influenced by ROBERT BLY and CAROL BLY, whose friendship dates to his college years, Holm has his quarrels with the Midwestern village. Like Robert, he can be grand; like Carol, he can be quarrelsome. Like Thoreau, whom he often quotes, Holm can see the world in the south forty; like Emerson, Holm can read a mute gospel in a ruined barn. Beneath his flamboyant personality, gruff preaching, and harsh criticism, however, Holm harbors enormous affection for Minneota, "his not much of a sacred place," for "stuff nobody wants to look at" and "subjects nobody wants to read about" (Landscape 7). The title essay of his Music of Failure is, in fact, a celebration of failed lives in a failed town in a failed section of what Holm reads as a failed country, leading, finally, to the conclusion that "Whatever failure is, Minneota [America] is not it . . . . The heart can be filled anywhere on earth" (87). That theme is the

burden of other essays in this volume including "The Grand Tour" of southwest Minnesota sites and scenes, and of the book Boxelder Bug Variations (1985), a collection of poems, keyboard variations, and short prose meditations which is, according to Ronald Barron in A Guide to Minnesota Authors, "Holm's testimonial to the importance of persistence and the dangers of an overemphasis on the importance of self" (82). The beauty of Midwestern decay and loss echoes through his texts for Bob Firth's photographs in the coffee table book Landscape of Ghosts (1993): essays on old windows, ruined barns, trashed outhouses, old fieldstones, junked cars, peeling billboards, broken windmills, and neglected graveyards. His 1996 collection of personal essays is titled, significantly, The Heart Can Be Filled Anywhere on Earth. Holm's prairie populism is best seen in "A Circle of Pitchforks," a poem on the Farmer's Holiday movement of the 1930s first published in the Nation, reprinted in The Dead Get by with Everything (1990): "Come to an old cafe / in Ghent, or Fertile, or Halloway . . . . / These are the men wrecking the ship of state" (30).

From his experiences in Xian, Holm wrote Coming Home Crazy (1990), winner of the Minnesota Book Award in the area of biography. The true importance of this, his most celebrated work, may be that it sharpened his perception of Minneota: as he said, "the only way to see a place clearly is to move a few thousand miles away now and then" (Landscape 144).

SELECTED WORKS: In addition to two small poetry chapbooks, two small Christmas essays, and a long poem titled Playing Hayden for the Angel of Death (1997), Bill Holm has published two significant books of poetry: The Dead Get by with Everything (1990) and Boxelder Bug Variations: A Meditation on an Idea in Language and Music (1985), which ran successfully as a dinner theater musical in Minneapolis. Holm is best known for his prose works, especially Coming Home Crazy: An Alphabet of China Essays (1990), The Heart Can Be Filled Anywhere on Earth (1996), Landscape of Ghosts (with Bob Firth, 1993), and his first and in many respects still his best book, The Music of Failure (1985), reprinted in a cloth edition by Saybrook Press in 1987 as Prairie Days.

FURTHER READING: Criticism of Holm's work is limited to magazine articles and reviews. Most useful are William Sounder's

"Mr. Big," in *Minnesota Monthly* (February 1989): 24–32, and "Holm at Last," in *St. Paul Pioneer Press Dispatch* (February 16, 1990): 1D. Ronald Barron's *A Guide to Minnesota Authors* (1993: 82–83) contains a good overview of Holm and his work. Several television interviews exist, including a Minnesota Public Television program titled "Not Quite American" (1990) and a Steve Benson interview in the Northern Lights series produced by the Hennepin County (Minnesota) Library in 1994. The most useful perspective on Holm's art may be his own essay "Is Minnesota in America Yet?" in Tammaro and Vinz's *Imagining Home* (1995).

DAVID PICHASKE     SOUTHWEST STATE UNIVERSITY

## EMERSON HOUGH
June 28, 1857–April 30, 1923

**BIOGRAPHY:** Emerson Hough was born in Newton, Iowa, to Joseph Bond and Elizabeth Hough. His parents had recently moved from Virginia, arriving in Iowa in 1852, six years before its statehood. After graduating from the State University of Iowa in 1880, Hough worked briefly as a surveyor in central Iowa. Dissatisfied, he became an attorney and soon after moved to New Mexico. He moved back to Iowa a year and a half later and gave up law.

After short stints with the *Des Moines Times* in 1884 and in Ohio with the *Sandusky Register,* Hough moved to Chicago, where he took charge of *Forest and Stream*'s "Chicago and the West" column. Known as a writer of Western novels and histories, Hough began by writing Kansas county histories featuring the contributor's prominent pioneer ancestors. Hough is quoted in Delbert Wylder's *Emerson Hough* (1981) as calling this writing "boom literature," narratives of the rapid immigration to and development of communities on the Kansas Plains (24). He married Charlotte Amelia Cheesebro in 1897.

Hough died in Chicago of heart and respiratory complications in 1923.

**SIGNIFICANCE:** In many of his works, Hough recognizes the role of Midwesterners in shaping Western culture and history. *The Passing of the Frontier* (1918) and *The Covered Wagon* (1922) feature heroines from the Midwest. *The Covered Wagon* is also Hough's most famous novel; W. H. D. Koerner illustrated this novel with a painting of the heroine, Mollie, entitled "The Madonna of the Prairies." It

became a powerful image for the westward migration of settlers from the Midwest to Oregon. In *The Passing of the Frontier,* Hough argues, "The chief figure of the American West . . . [is] the gaunt and sad-faced woman sitting on the front seat of the wagon . . . . There was the seed of America's wealth" (93). The fact that the cultural caretakers in these westward journeys are Midwestern daughters reflects the importance Hough accorded the Midwest.

While Hough's novels have been described as Westerns, many of them are set on the Plains. Hough treated the Midwest as a middle ground from which to shape an identity between Easterner and Westerner. This is reflected in the title of his first novel, *The Girl at the Halfway House* (1900), set in Kansas. More often, however, Hough relied on characters from the Midwest to transform the West. The values of a New Mexico community in *Heart's Desire* (1905) are shaped by a Kansas family; the social compact is formed "In the home of the girl from Kansas" (25). In *The Story of the Cowboy* (1897), Hough parodies himself as both the Western lawyer and, at the same time, the transplanted Midwesterner; the shingle outside the lawyer's office reads, "John Jones, Attorney-at-Law, Real Estate and Insurance. Collections promptly attended to at all hours of the day and night. Good Ohio cider for sale at 5 cents a glass" (239). Midwesterners figure prominently in Hough's West.

Hough's works enjoyed praise from Theodore Roosevelt and HAMLIN GARLAND, as well as wide popularity during his lifetime.

**SELECTED WORKS:** Hough's novels and historical works include *The Story of the Cowboy* (1897), *The Girl at the Halfway House* (1900), *The Way to the West and the Lives of Three Early Americans: Boone, Crockett, Carson* (1903), *Heart's Desire* (1905), *The Story of the Outlaw* (1907), *The Way of a Man* (1907), *54–40 or Fight* (1909), *The Purchase Price* (1910), *John Rawn* (1912), *The Magnificent Adventure* (1916), *The Man Next Door* (1917), *The Broken Gate* (1917), *The Way Out* (1918), *The Passing of the Frontier; a Chronicle of the Old West* (1918), *The Sagebrusher* (1919), *The Covered Wagon* (1922), and *North of 36* (1923).

**FURTHER READING:** Delbert Wylder's *Emerson Hough* (1981) offers the only critical book-length treatment of Hough. It provides biographical information as well as an analysis of Hough's Western and historical novels. Lee Alexander Stone's *Emerson Hough: His Place in American Letters* (1925) offers little in the way of analysis. Significant articles on Hough include Dorys Crow Grover's "W. H. D. Koerner and Emerson Hough: A Western Collaboration," in *Montana: The Magazine of Western History* 29 (April 1979): 2–15; Carole Johnson's "Emerson Hough's American West," in *Books at Iowa* (November 1974): 26–42; John Miller's "Emerson Hough: Merry Christmas Sued You Today," in *Indiana University Bookman* 8 (March 1967): 23–35; Delbert Wylder's "Emerson Hough and the Popular Novel," in *Southwestern American Literature* 2 (Fall 1972): 83–89; and Wylder's "Emerson Hough's Heart's Desire," in *Western American Literature* 1 (Spring 1966): 44–54. Hough's papers are located in the Emerson Hough Collection in the Iowa State Department of History and Archives.

JOHN L. SUTTON          NEW YORK UNIVERSITY

## EDGAR WATSON HOWE
May 3, 1853–October 3, 1937

**BIOGRAPHY:** The most cynical and iconoclastic of the prairie realists, Edgar Watson Howe was born in Wabash County, Indiana, to Henry Howe, a farmer and Methodist preacher, and Elizabeth (Irwin) Howe. When Howe was a toddler, the family moved to Harrison County, Missouri. When he was in his early teens, his father ran off with his sister-in-law, and Howe began to support himself through newspaper work. Thus, Howe came to the writing profession in much the same way as did Benjamin Franklin, MARK TWAIN, WILLIAM DEAN HOWELLS, and other American authors; he first learned the printing trade, later became a reporter, and then began to think of writing fiction.

Howe traveled throughout the Midwest and West as a young printer and reporter, working on a number of different newspapers, before marrying Clara Frank in 1873 and settling in Atchison, Kansas. The couple had five children; they were divorced in 1901. In 1877 Howe founded the *Atchison Globe*, which he edited and published for more than thirty years. He also published a magazine, *E. W. Howe's Monthly*, for more than two decades as well as twenty-three books. He died in Atchison after suffering two strokes.

**SIGNIFICANCE:** For more than fifty years the Sage of Potato Hill reigned in Atchison as the Midwest's answer to H. L. Mencken. Only slightly less well known than his Emporia counterpart and friend WILLIAM ALLEN WHITE, Howe was famous for his sardonic, tell-it-like-it-is comments, which he called paragraphs, on organized religion, big government, feminism, prohibition, organized labor, and other perceived blights on his cultural landscape. "The first time a man kisses a woman other than his wife, he feels as sneaking as a farmer when sending his first order to Montgomery-Ward and Co. But the husband and farmer soon become hardened, and patronize not only Montgomery-Ward, but Sears-Roebuck, and others" is Howe's take on marital fidelity in *Country Town Sayings* (273). In the same book he observes, "If you have sense enough to realize why flies gather around a restaurant, you should be able to appreciate why men run for office" (116). Such observations were first published in his newspaper column, "Globe Sights," or in his *Monthly* and later in such books as *Country Town Sayings* (1911), *Ventures in Common Sense* (1919), and *The Indignations of E. W. Howe* (1933).

Howe's best-known book is his first novel, *The Story of a Country Town* (1883). This novel, which favorably impressed Twain and Howells, was one of the first books to expose the downside of the Jeffersonian dream and spark the revolt-from-the-village tradition that includes HAMLIN GARLAND, SHERWOOD ANDERSON, THEODORE DREISER, and EDGAR LEE MASTERS.

Howe's novel represents the rural villages of Fairview and Twin Mounds, Missouri, as sites of secret sin and open misery. Its double plot centers on two relatives of the first-person narrator, Ned Westlock: his father, a preacher who runs off with a congregant, and his uncle, a miller whose jealousy of his wife's former lover results in murder, suicide, and insanity. Drawing on autobiographical material for the first of these stories, Howe emphasizes the joylessness of life in the Midwestern small town and presents much of the suffering that dominates the novel as a function of the narrow minds and limited experience of his rural Midwestern characters, as well as of the spirit-deadening religion that prevailed on the prairie.

**SELECTED WORKS:** Howe published six novels: *The Story of a Country Town* (1883), *The*

*Mystery of the Locks* (1885), *A Moonlight Boy* (1886), *A Man Story* (1889), *An Ante-Mortem Statement* (1891), and *The Confession of John Whitlock* (1891). He also published four collections of short stories: *Dying Like a Gentleman and Other Stories* (1926), *The Covered Wagon and the West with Other Stories* (1928), *Her Fifth Marriage and Other Stories* (1928), and *When a Woman Enjoys Herself and Other Tales of a Small Town* (1928). S. J. Sackett considers the first of Howe's three travel books, *Daily Notes of a Trip around the World* (1907), to be among the best in the genre. Also of note are *The Anthology of Another Town* (1920), a collection of paragraphs, sketches, and stories written in response to Edgar Lee Masters's *Spoon River Anthology*, and an autobiography, *Plain People* (1929), both of which were serialized in the *Saturday Evening Post*.

**FURTHER READING:** See Calder M. Pickett's biography, *Ed Howe: Country Town Philosopher* (1968), as well as two critical studies: S. J. Sackett's *E. W. Howe* (1972) and Martin Bucco's *E. W. Howe* (1977). Howe's letters are held by the University of Kansas, Indiana University, and the University of Southern California.

MARCIA NOE
THE UNIVERSITY OF TENNESSEE AT CHATTANOOGA

# HENRY HOWE

October 11, 1816–October 14, 1893

**BIOGRAPHY:** Henry Howe was a pioneer local, state, and regional historian and collector and compiler of the recollections and experiences of nineteenth-century Americans as well as of their folklore and legends, the material that would a century later be considered oral history. He was born in New Haven, Connecticut, in 1816, the youngest of seven children of Hezekiah and Sarah (Townsend) Howe. His father was a bibliophile, bookseller, and publisher who published Noah Webster's *American Dictionary of the English Language* in 1828.

At Yale Henry Howe came under the influence of John W. Barber, an historian, artist, and engraver who shared with Howe his determination to contribute to the construction of a uniquely American identity, history, and myth. Howe was strongly influenced by Barber's *The Historical Collections of Connecticut* (1836) and *The Historical Collections of Massachusetts* (1839). Howe joined his mentor in preparing *The Historical Collections of New York* (1841)

and *The Historical Collections of New Jersey* (1844). In *The Historical Collections of Virginia* (1845) he first worked alone.

The compilation of each of the works followed the same pattern: an extensive journey through the appropriate area for up to a year, usually on horseback. During the journey to virtually every county in each state, the compiler sought out early settlers and older citizens for interviews during which recollections were recorded, as were first-, second-, and third-hand reminiscences. Old records and memoirs were culled, as were biographical sketches and historical, archaeological, geographical, geological, and other studies. Solicited and unsolicited contributions were gathered and drawings of living and historical figures as well as man-made and natural phenomena were made by the compiler. The result was organized alphabetically county by county, followed by extensive indices and appendices.

His apprenticeship served in the East, in 1846 Howe felt himself ready for what was to be his major work, *The Historical Collections of Ohio* (1847), which he completed and published the next year. He returned briefly to New Haven, where he married Frances A. Tuttle in September 1847, and returned immediately to Cincinnati, his home for the next thirty years.

In Cincinnati he became a publisher, bookseller, and compiler of more historical collections—of *The Great West* (various printings, last in 1861), of *Celebrated Travellors* (various printings, last in 1863), of *Our Whole Country* (1861), all co-compiled and edited with Barber and numerous others. In 1878 he returned to New Haven to live until 1885, when he moved to Columbus, Ohio, to complete his dream project, an updated version of *The Historical Collections of Ohio* that would demonstrate the progress made in the state in forty years. With the work completed, his personal fortune was exhausted, and he was stricken by paralysis. The work was published by state subsidy in two volumes as the *Ohio Centennial Edition* in 1890–91, one volume of which had appeared as early as 1888. Howe died in Columbus in 1893.

**SIGNIFICANCE:** Howe's various historical collections are not history as it would be written today. His major work, *The Historical Collections of Ohio*, in its two incarnations, has many shortcomings: it may be considered naive, biased, narrowly ethnocentric, unreliable, unattributed, even judgmental. But with all its shortcomings, it is a remarkable work by a remarkable observer of the transition of the state from Old Northwest to Midwest, from frontier to civilized and orderly society. It remains the most comprehensive and informative source available for the elements of that transition and the attitudes, sentiments, and convictions that made it possible.

**SELECTED WORKS:** Henry Howe's complete title of his most important work gives insight into his accomplishments. It is entitled *Historical Collections of Ohio; Containing a Collection of the Most Interesting Facts, Traditions, Biographical Sketches, Anecdotes, etc., relating to its General and Local History: With Descriptions of its Counties, Principal Towns and Villages*, illustrated by 177 engravings (1847). The title of the version published more than forty years later is even more inclusive: *Historical Collections of Ohio in Two Volumes. An Encyclopedia of the State: History both General and Local, Geography with Descriptions of its Counties, Cities, and Villages, its Agricultural, Manufacturing, Mining, and Business Development, Sketches of Eminent and Interesting Characters, etc., with Notes of a Tour over it in 1886. Illustrated by about 700 engravings. Contrasting Ohio of 1846 with 1886–1890. From drawings by the author in 1846 and photographs taken solely for it in 1886, 1887, 1888, 1889, and 1890, of Cities and Chief Towns, Public Buildings, Historical Localities, Monuments, Curiosities, Portraits, Maps, Etc. The Ohio Centennial Edition (1890–91)*. Most of Howe's other works pale in comparison, and, more than any of the other works, these two versions of his masterwork are of his own authorship.

**FURTHER READING:** No book about Howe has yet been written. Articles include Joseph P. Smith's "Henry Howe, the Historian," in the *Ohio Archaeological and Historical Quarterly* 4 (1895): 211–27; and DAVID D. ANDERSON'S "Henry Howe and Ohio's Transition from Old West to Midwest," in the *Society for the Study of Midwestern Literature Newsletter* 22 (Spring 1992): 15–23. Howe's papers are in the Ohio Historical Society, Columbus.

DAVID D. ANDERSON    MICHIGAN STATE UNIVERSITY

# WILLIAM DEAN HOWELLS
March 1, 1837–May 11, 1920

**BIOGRAPHY:** Of Welsh, Pennsylvania Dutch, and Irish stock, William Dean Howells was born in Martins Ferry, Ohio, the second of eight children of William Cooper Howells, a country editor who converted from his father's revivalistic Methodism to a milder Swedenborgianism, and Mary (Dean) Howells, whose family included several Ohio rivermen.

The family lived in Hamilton, Ohio, from 1840 until 1848, where William Cooper Howells had bought the *Intelligencer* and William Dean Howells began learning the printing trade at an early age. The fortunes of small-town newspapers and their editors were largely determined by their conformity with local political views, and the elder Howells held strong political views at odds with those of the region. These views and the strength with which he expressed them repeatedly doomed his efforts and resulted in regular family moves. Late 1850 saw the beginning of his brief experiment in creating a utopian socialist community and operating a grist and sawmill near Xenia, Ohio, at Eureka Mills, which William Dean Howells recounted autobiographically in *My Year in a Log Cabin* (1887) and fictionally in *New Leaf Mills* (1913).

The family then moved to Columbus, Ohio, where William Cooper Howells reported the proceedings of the Ohio legislature for the *Ohio State Journal* and young William Dean Howells worked as a compositor for that newspaper and began to incline toward literature. In 1852 the family left the pro-slavery Miami Valley in southern Ohio for the Western Reserve. There Howells's father, as a part owner, edited and published the *Ashtabula Sentinel* and moved it to the county seat—Jefferson. Their Republican politics now an asset, not a detriment, the Howells family soon enjoyed exclusive ownership of this successful newspaper, and William Cooper Howells became a highly regarded and politically well-connected member of the community.

Young William Dean Howells was enriched by reading works of current romantic and classic writers, such as Scott, Pope, Dryden, Poe, Irving, Cervantes, and Goldsmith. When his father took a job for part of each year publishing proceedings of the Ohio state legislature, Howells went to Columbus. Having already taught himself Spanish, he studied German privately and worked for the *Ohio State Journal* starting in late 1858. After Howells's highly successful campaign biography of

William Dean Howells.
Courtesy of the Ohio Historical Society

ABRAHAM LINCOLN in 1860, his journalistic, literary, and political status was high, and as a Lincoln supporter and an ascendant literary figure, he was rewarded with a consular appointment in Venice in 1861. In Europe he married Elinor Gertrude Mead in late 1862; the couple would have two daughters and one son.

Howells returned to the United States in the summer of 1865, worked briefly in Ohio, and then joined the editorial staff of the *Atlantic Monthly* in 1866, becoming editor-in-chief in 1871 and remaining there until 1881. This influential connection was very helpful as Howells began a long career as magazine editor and novelist, primarily in Boston and New York. In 1885 Howells began his association with *Harper's Magazine*; this relationship continued in various forms through 1920.

Howells was the first president of the American Academy of Arts and Letters, received honorary degrees from many prestigious universities in America and Britain, and was recognized by the National Institute of Arts and Letters. While wintering in Savannah during the last year of his life, Howells caught a bad cold which lingered even af-

ter he returned to New York City in April 1920. He died quietly at his home there the following month.

**SIGNIFICANCE:** Howells wrote about nearly every issue and aspect of American life. The gentle ethics of his father's Swedenborgian faith and the fervor of abolitionism helped shape his views. Increasingly, his major works, including *A Modern Instance* (1882), *The Rise of Silas Lapham* (1885), and *A Hazard of New Fortunes* (1889), dealt seriously with a complex of interrelated issues which were highly ethical in nature and intertwined social justice, the importance of individual relationship to societal values and norms, and the interplay between regional and class experiences, values, and cultures. Although an accepted Boston Brahmin and a cosmopolitan New Yorker in his later years, Howells was ready to join calls for individual cultivation with reverence for ethical standards that he tended to associate more with the underclass and cultural provinces than with prestigious American cultural centers.

Before William Dean Howells left the Midwest for Venice in 1861, he had written for a number of newspapers and magazines in Ohio and had published a collection of poems, *Poems of Two Friends* (1860), with his friend J. J. Piatt. Throughout his life, Howells was an extremely prolific writer, producing many volumes of essays and short stories as well as a large number of plays. Howells was perhaps most important as a leading advocate for emerging writers and American literary realism, which he supported with several critical works, most notably *Criticism and Fiction* (1891), as well as statements embedded in his novels.

Howells drew upon Midwestern materials for a romantic camp-meeting poem, wrote up historical research concerning the 1782 massacre of a band of Moravian Christian Indians, and reviewed histories which concerned the West and historical fiction, from Whitelaw Reid's *Ohio in the War* (1868) to historical works by William Prescott, Francis Parkman, and Theodore Roosevelt. The figure of the Indiana newspaperman Colville traveling in Italy in *Indian Summer* (1886) reflects both Midwestern and European experiences of Howells and is drawn from one of the Midwestern careers Howells might have pursued had he stayed in Columbus.

Reviewing fiction and Midwestern poetry and writing introductions to the books of others, he promoted many Midwestern writers, including PAUL LAURENCE DUNBAR, EDWARD EGGLESTON, EDGAR WATSON HOWE, MARK TWAIN, JAMES WHITCOMB RILEY, EUGENE FIELD, and HAMLIN GARLAND.

The Midwestern influence increased from 1887 to 1917, during which time Howells published five autobiographical books and three novels set partly or wholly in Ohio. The first, *My Year in a Log Cabin* (1893), revised from a magazine piece for the *Youth's Companion* (1887), recounts the year at Eureka Mills. *A Boy's Town* (1890), in the boy's story tradition started by Thomas Bailey Aldrich in New England and furthered by *Tom Sawyer* and *Huckleberry Finn*, subordinates Howells's own life to the general biographies of boys in Hamilton, Ohio, in the 1840s. Incidents in their lives are treated timelessly, yet the book resists romantic notions of childhood innocence by asserting themes of terror, confusion, cruelty, greed, and pain.

In 1893 Howells wrote of his father's occupation in "A Country Printer" and published his father's memoir in 1895. In a school reader, *Stories of Ohio* (1897), he relied heavily on standard state histories but characterized Ohio's earliest history as often stranger than that of Greece or Rome. He found the state's more recent times scarred by industrialization, particularly along the Ohio River. Natural gas fields discovered at Findlay, Ohio, provided a source for the circumstances of the Jacob Dryfoos family of "Moffit, Indiana" in *A Hazard of New Fortunes* (1889) and prompted Howells to advise his school readers that the "romance" of industrial giants had yet to be written.

Nostalgic for the Ohio life of his adolescent years, Howells projected a series of stories about the village of Jefferson, telling Brander Mathews in a letter of September 6, 1898, that its American characteristics were "unsurpassed and . . . hardly discovered" (manuscript at Columbia University). He pursued the village ideal more fully in *The Kentons* (1902), its location drawn from several north central Ohio county seats and its characters named for a frontier Indian fighter and drawn from Civil War veterans and families. A shortcoming of *The Kentons*, arguably serving to contrast Midwestern values with those of the East and of Europe, is its lapse into an old Howells convention, the novel of European travel, a genre highly popular with Eastern audiences of the period. Of relatively similar success is *New Leaf Mills* (1913), begun in 1867, which fictionalizes the failure of his father's utopian experiment.

A richer evocation of the Midwest appears in *The Leatherwood God* (1916). The basis for this novel was an historical narrative Howells had reviewed in 1871. The narrative describes an evangelist who came to eastern Ohio in 1828 claiming to be God. The supporting characters in *The Leatherwood God* included a skeptical old squire and some family members suggested by his source, as well as a gullible and slovenly couple and a frontier law student. All were drawn from figures Howells had seen on a trip near Steubenville, Ohio, in 1870. The author's knowledge of frontier desertions and inadvertent bigamy suggested a situation through which Howells could explore the mystery of this would-be God, Joseph C. Dylks, as well as of the charisma and sexual attractiveness of Dylks, the last of Howells's three Midwestern villains. On the other hand, law student James Redfield, suggested by the historical source work but also shaped after Simon Kenton and other frontiersmen, embodies the continuing appeal of secular democracy to Howells.

The settings in *The Leatherwood God* often suggest southwestern Ohio's Miami Valley, wooded and hilly but not so rugged as the historical Leatherwood Valley in southeastern Guernsey County. Howells restores the dialect of hill folk, often formalized by the historical account. The novel has been held to be among his better works, and was called by Warren French, in his June 1977 *Old Northwest* 3.2 review of the Indiana University Press edition, "the archetypal epic of the Midwestern sensibility" for its evocation of the unrestrained hopes and claims of frontier religion (200). Dylks is arguably a descendant of Melville's "Confidence-Man," and recent scholarship considers *The Leatherwood God* the best example of the American historical novel.

SELECTED WORKS: Howells's most important novels are *A Modern Instance* (1882), *The Rise of Silas Lapham* (1885), and *A Hazard of New Fortunes* (1889). Works significantly involving the Midwest include *The Kentons* (1902), *New Leaf Mills* (1913), and *The Leatherwood God* (1916).

His *A Boy's Town* (1890) describes Columbus life during his childhood, and *My Year in a Log Cabin* (1893), a revision of the 1887 *Youth's Companion* piece, recounts the family's year attempting to set up a utopian socialist community at Eureka Mills, Ohio. *Years of My Youth* (1916) incorporates earlier reminiscences and relates Howells's Ohio life to young adulthood in Columbus.

**FURTHER READING:** Major studies on Howells include Edwin H. Cady's *William Dean Howells: Dean of American Letters, 1837–1920* (1956, 1959) and his "Howells on the River," in *American Literary Realism 1870–1910* 25.3 (Spring 1993): 27–41; William Baker's "The Little Miami River Heritage of William Dean Howells," in *Antioch Review* 34 (1976): 405–16; William E. Lenz's "*The Leatherwood God*: William Dean Howells' Confidence Man," in *Old Northwest* 8.2 (Summer 1982): 119–30; and Eugene H. Pattison's "The Landscape and Sense of the Past in William Dean Howells's *The Kentons*," in *MidAmerica* 20 (1993): 48–58. Other studies focusing on Howells as a Midwesterner include David D. Anderson's "From Memory to Meaning: The Boys' Stories of William Dean Howells, Clarence Darrow, and Sherwood Anderson," in *MidAmerica* 10 (1983): 69–84; William D. Baker's "Ohio's Reaction of William Dean Howells," in *MidAmerica* 11 (1984): 117–48; and Eugene Pattison's "The Great Lakes Childhood: The Experience of William Dean Howells and Annie Dillard," in *Old Northwest* 4 (Winter 1988–89): 311–29.

EUGENE H. PATTISON                    ALMA COLLEGE

## BETTE HOWLAND
January 28, 1937

**BIOGRAPHY:** Bette Howland was born in Chicago and grew up on the west side, around Roosevelt and Crawford, a neighborhood of working-class Jews. Her parents were Sam Sotonoff, a factory worker, and Jessie (Berger) Sotonoff. She entered the University of Chicago after two years of high school and graduated in 1955. The university, still under the influence of Robert Hutchins, attracted precocious students to its program of independent learning. She married Howard Howland, with whom she had two children, Frank and Jacob, and from whom she was divorced in 1962. She worked at a number of part-time jobs, including editorial assistant and librarian, and enrolled as a graduate student at the

university in order to work with SAUL BELLOW but left without finishing her PhD. She returned to the university in 1993 for a one-semester appointment as professor of literature and remained for four years. In between, she had lived in New England, the Northwest, and New Mexico. She currently resides in southwestern Michigan.

Her writing career began in the 1950s when her early short stories were accepted in little magazines including the *Quarterly Review of Literature*, *Epoch*, and the *Noble Savage*. It continued with the publication of her autobiographical novel *W-3* in 1974. Since that time she has continued to contribute short stories, critical essays, and reviews to magazines and newspapers. She has been the recipient of fellowships and grants from the Rockefeller Foundation, the Marsden Foundation, the Guggenheim Foundation, and the MacArthur Foundation. Her most recently completed work is a short novel, *Calm Sea and Prosperous Voyage* (forthcoming).

**SIGNIFICANCE:** Howland's three volumes, *W-3* (1974), *Blue in Chicago* (1978), and *Things to Come and Go* (1983), focus in powerful ways on the themes of the city, Chicago, which she has inhabited with mixed feelings and continues to recreate in her fiction. With a keen eye, a compassionate heart, and a strong voice she dissects the troubles of her own life as they intersect with family, community, and city. The strong bonds that keep the family together in repetitive and often destructive patterns and the conflicts that emerge between the generations of the family are in the forefront of many of her stories.

Old neighborhoods in Chicago, including the west side, uptown, and the University of Chicago's Hyde Park area, are revisited. In virtually every story the center is a Jewish woman, at various stages of her life, who observes and agonizes over family relationships, feuds, and personal discontents. As she ages and they as well, the theme of death begins to take hold and a partial acknowledgment of the ties of love and connection give strong emotional richness to her stories. As her character Sally Horner says in "The Life You Gave Me," "There is nothing here I would ever choose—and nothing I can bear to part with" (*Things to Come and Go* 157).

The terrors of old age extend her concerns about the self and the family. She turns her camera eye on the misery and helplessness of old age in the city; she laments the isolation of the elderly, cut off and under attack in the decaying neighborhoods of Chicago, gathering at the public library for warmth and safety. These conditions propel the young narrator and her children to seek refuge in the country, to discover a safe place that continues to be elusive in her makeshift life.

The aging and decrepit city as paradigm of the conflicts and brutalities of human existence recurs in many stories which she locates in Chicago neighborhoods where racial tensions, high crime rates, and the perception of danger define the everyday lives of the inhabitants, often young women. The cry that resounds through her work is the dream of escape and of reconciliation. The narrator of "To the Country" speaks for the "passive population under siege" in the city, as she yearns to know, "Where is that undiscovered territory? Where the air is clear and consciences are clean" (*Blue in Chicago* 66).

Bette Howland's work is a strong and complex voice of the generation born of the Depression and of immigrant parents in the Midwest who search for meaning and belonging in the America they have inherited. Though her canon is relatively small, she has been widely reviewed and acknowledged as a perceptive observer and powerful commentator of Midwestern urban life.

**SELECTED WORKS:** Howland's major works include *W-3* (1974), *Blue in Chicago* (1978), and *Things to Come and Go* (1983). A work-in progress, *Calm Sea and Prosperous Voyage*, is a novella narrated by the Chicago woman familiar from her previous works and living now in a Midwestern university town. Her early short stories appeared beginning in 1958 in various journals and literary reviews and include "Julia," in the *Quarterly Review of Literature* 4 (1958): 274–81; "Sam Katz," in *Epoch* 2 (1958): 105–16; and "Aronesti," in *Noble Savage* 5 (1962): 102–15. Since that time she has continued to publish book reviews and critical essays in journals and newspapers.

**FURTHER READING:** Babette Inglehart's essay "Bette Howland," in *Jewish American Women Writers: A Bio-Bibliographical and Critical Sourcebook*, edited by Ann R. Shapiro (1994), contains a complete list of newspaper and magazine reviews of Howland's works as well as a critical survey of this material.

BABETTE F. INGLEHART   CHICAGO STATE UNIVERSITY

## (FRANK McKINNEY) "KIN" HUBBARD
September 1, 1868–December 26, 1930

**BIOGRAPHY:** Frank McKinney Hubbard was born in Bellefontaine, Ohio. The son of Thomas Hubbard, the publisher of the *Bellefontaine Examiner*, and Jane (Miller) Hubbard, Kin Hubbard attended local schools, learned printing in his father's print shop, and spent five years in the city post office after his father became postmaster. He also toured the South as a silhouette artist and excelled in amateur theatricals. In 1891 he was hired by the *Indianapolis News* as the first newspaper artist of Indianapolis. After three years he organized minstrel shows in Bellefontaine and worked on various newspapers. In 1901 he was re-hired by the *Indianapolis News*, where he remained for his lifetime. In 1905 Kin married Josephine Jackson, with whom he had two children.

On November 16, 1904, his sketch of a rural person appeared in the *News* along with a quip of only two sentences; the editor asked Hubbard to begin a series. The first of these appeared on December 31 and featured a ludicrous character named Abe Martin, who wore baggy pants, a ragged coat, a shapeless hat, shoes, and chin whiskers, and was placed in a rural background. Each sketch was accompanied with a sentence or two of observation on manners or contemporary life. Soon the feature was syndicated and eventually appeared in three hundred newspapers. A collection of the drawings with their accompanying sentences was published in 1906, as *Abe Martin of Brown County, Indiana*. Further Abe Martin books appeared yearly. In each Saturday edition of the *News* a dialect essay, "Short Furrows," appeared. It was also popular.

Kin Hubbard died of a heart attack at his home in Indianapolis. His death was lamented by American editorial writers and cartoonists as a national tragedy. The Brown County State Park was established in his memory, with the Abe Martin Lodge surrounded by guest cabins named for some of Kin's characters.

**SIGNIFICANCE:** Kin Hubbard's many compilations of cartoons and quips as well as collections of essays were usually issued for Christmas sale, often in almanac form. The Abe Martin Publishing Company was a name under which he distributed many of his books. The complete listing of his publications is very long.

Kin was a close observer of his time, and he expressed his feelings by criticizing life humorously through drawing, dialect, and allusion. Under a crude drawing he would place an aphorism or two providing a humorous commentary on society or reflecting Hubbard's perceptions on life. Hubbard's imaginative combination of strong dialect and colorful characters could be counted on to give new vitality to clichés. For example, in Hubbard's hands "All that glitters is not gold" becomes "Th' fust thing t' turn green in th' spring is Christmas jewelry" (Tandy 169).

His rustic characters were often composites but were recognized as being true to human nature, both in town and country. His sentences unfolded with impact in reporting situations, as with "'If she comes in t' night I'll try t' catch her in th' mornin' an' tell her,' said Mrs. Tipton Budd when somebuddy left a message for her daughter" (Tandy 169). Such compressed stories, keeping the climax for the very last, are Hubbard's primary contribution to American humor. He was also noted for coining short sayings like "Of all th' home remedies a good wife is th' best" (Blair 258) and "What this country needs is a good five-cent cigar" (Kelley 121). His humor is Midwestern or Hoosier. He was popular with JAMES WHITCOMB RILEY, GEORGE ADE, and Will Rogers.

**SELECTED WORKS:** The Abe Martin books, from *Abe Martin of Brown County, Indiana* (1906) through *Abe Martin's Wisecracks* (1930), appeared yearly and contain compilations of Hubbard's cartoons and sayings. Seven of them, plus *Short Furrows* (1912), were published by trade publishers and the rest privately, under the imprint of the Abe Martin Publishing Company. *Short Furrows* consists of dialect essays which originally appeared in the Saturday editions of the *Indianapolis News*.

**FURTHER READING:** Writing about Kin Hubbard has tended to be appreciative. Books include Blanche Stillson and Dorothy Russo's *Abe Martin—Kin Hubbard: A Checklist* (1939); Fred Kelley's *The Life and Times of Kin Hubbard,*

*Creator of Abe Martin* (1952), and *The Best of Kin Hubbard*, edited by David Hawes (1964). Discussions of Hubbard appear in Thomas Masson's *Our American Humorists* (1922), Jennette Reid Tandy's *Crackerbox Philosophers in American Humor and Satire* (1925) and Walter Blair's *Horse Sense in American Humor* (1942). At Hubbard's death there were obituaries in newspapers across the nation, as, for example, in the *New York Times*, December 27, 1930.

ARTHUR W. SHUMAKER            DEPAUW UNIVERSITY

## LANGSTON HUGHES
February 2, 1902–May 22, 1967

**BIOGRAPHY:** While Langston Hughes's prominent career as a poet, playwright, fiction writer, and essayist took him to places all over the world, his early life was spent in the Midwest. He was born in Joplin, Missouri, where he lived for a year or two before his mother, Carrie (Langston) Hughes took him to Lawrence, Kansas, where her family had lived for decades. Here, Langston grew up in near poverty with his aged maternal grandmother as his primary caretaker. His father, James Nathaniel, discouraged by racism and segregation, had left for Mexico; his mother traveled frequently in search of work.

In Kansas, Hughes first heard the blues, jazz, and orchestral music that would later play a major role in his poetry. In these early years, he also discovered reading, which helped him to cope with the hardships he endured as a child. In *The Big Sea* (1940), the first of two autobiographical volumes, he wrote of "the wonderful world of books—where if people suffered, they suffered in beautiful language, not in monosyllables, as we did in Kansas" (*The Life of Langston Hughes* xiii).

Following his grandmother's death in 1915, Hughes moved with his remarried mother to Lincoln, Illinois, where they stayed for one year. Here, he wrote his first poem. When the family moved to Cleveland, Ohio, he attended Central High School where he excelled as an athlete and writer: he published stories and poems in the monthly school magazine and was elected Class Poet as well as editor of the *Annual*. By the time he graduated from Central, he had committed himself to a writing career—one distinctly focused on African American life.

At age eighteen, Hughes wrote his most frequently anthologized poem, "The Negro

Speaks of Rivers," while crossing the Mississippi by train on his way to see his father in Mexico. After a year there, Hughes entered New York City's Columbia University in 1921 but remained for only one year. He then undertook a series of odd jobs including the position of messman on ships headed for Africa and Europe. In 1924 he jumped ship at Rotterdam and traveled to Paris, where he washed dishes in an American-run jazz nightclub. Back in the United States, Hughes's poems began to appear in W. E. B. DuBois's *Crisis* magazine. He found work as a busboy at the Wardman Park Hotel in Washington, D.C., where he met Illinois poet VACHEL LINDSAY, who encouraged and promoted his work publicly. After receiving first prize in a poetry contest in May 1925, he published, with the help of CARL VAN VECHTEN, his first book of collected verse, *The Weary Blues*, in 1926.

That same year he entered Lincoln University in Pennsylvania, one of the nation's most prestigious black colleges at the time, and earned his bachelor's degree in 1929. His biographer, Arnold Rampersad in *The Life of Langston Hughes*, considered these years important in building Hughes's relationship with Charlotte Mason, an elderly widow who became his patron for a time. Mason influenced Hughes greatly, provided generous funding for his work, and lavished him with praise and advice about his literary career. In 1930 she broke with Hughes abruptly for reasons that remain unclear. His devastation by the sudden loss of friendship and philanthropic support, along with the onset of the Depression, initiated his interest in leftist politics and proletarian revolution.

During the 1930s Hughes became an active public figure: he traveled extensively in the segregated American South, sailed to the Soviet Union in June 1932, and later in the decade served as a newspaper correspondent during the Spanish Civil War.

In 1953 Hughes was called before Senator Joseph McCarthy's subcommittee on subversive activities and testified about his involvement with communism in the 1930s. After 1960, however, he traveled to Africa and Europe numerous times on cultural grants from the State Department. Hughes died of heart failure in New York City.

**SIGNIFICANCE:** Langston Hughes became the most prominent figure of the Harlem Renaissance of the 1920s; his contributions to American literature continue from this period to the Black Arts movement of the late 1960s, making him one of the most significant black American writers of the twentieth century. His blues and jazz-based poetry poignantly portray African American experience; this inventive work, along with racial protest poems and short fiction, made him popular in his own time.

While Hughes would later encounter jazz and blues in Harlem, Paris, and New Orleans, he first heard the blues in Kansas with his grandmother when he was around six years old. Steven Tracy, in *Langston Hughes and the Blues*, asserts that the traditional folk-blues lyrics sung in this part of the country early in the century became the basis for some of his most important work (104); in *The Big Sea*, Hughes reveals that his poem "The Weary Blues" "included the first blues verse [he had] ever heard way back in Lawrence, Kansas, when [he] was a kid" (105–106). Kansas blues and jazz would continue to influence him as both he and the music idiom evolved. Hughes absorbed early blues, often performed a cappella or with makeshift instruments, as well as more sophisticated ragtime, jazz, and orchestral arrangements. In 1918 Hughes happened upon the blues again in Chicago: "All up and down State Street there were blues, indoors and out," he writes in "I Remember the Blues." "At the Grand and the old Monogram theaters where Ma Rainey sang, in the night clubs, in the dance halls, on phonographs" (Tracy 108).

Inspired by this rich musical climate, Hughes produced his own blues-based poems. His approach to incorporating folk material into his poetry often parallels the technique of city jazz musicians. As Tracy suggests, Hughes strove to represent and preserve authentic African American folk culture; at the same time, he hoped to legitimize folk material by interpreting it to the black middle class.

Chicago was important to Hughes in other ways. Here, in 1941 he founded the Skyloft Players, who performed his musical *The Sun Do More*, and he wrote a weekly column for the *Chicago Defender*, an African American newspaper, which published the first of five short stories featuring Jesse B. Semple, Hughes's "simple" Harlem folk philosopher. In *The Big Sea*, the writer also recognizes the influence of

Chicago Renaissance writers CARL SANDBURG and Vachel Lindsay.

Lindsay had direct contact with Hughes, who had left three poems—"The Weary Blues," "Jazzonia," and "Negro Dancers"—at Lindsay's table in the Wardman Park restaurant. While Lindsay gave Hughes moral support, Lindsay's Midwestern, chant-like poetry, dramatic performances, and troubadour lifestyle may also have inspired Hughes early in his career.

Sandburg, too, was influential as a balladeer who used coarse colloquialism; and by writing biographies, an autobiography, children's books, and articles, as well as poetry, Sandburg broadened his modes of literary expression—an example Hughes would follow (Tracy 142–43).

Hughes's most thoroughly Midwestern work is his sole novel, *Not without Laughter* (1930), an autobiographical fiction about a black boy who grows up in Kansas and later moves to Chicago to work as an elevator-boy at a Loop hotel. Written during the writer's years with Mrs. Mason, it secured his reputation and sales and enabled him to support himself. The work's lucid, natural, and unfurnished prose captures common African American experience and dialect and addresses issues of racial inequality without defense or resentment. While the novel is not as well known today as Hughes's poetry, it received high praise from black and white critics alike. Rampersad suggests that *Not without Laughter* is "perhaps the most appealing and completely realized novel in black fiction to that date" (*Life of Langston Hughes* 190).

**SELECTED WORKS:** Works by Hughes include *The Weary Blues* (1926); *Fine Clothes to the Jew* (1927); *Not without Laughter* (1930); *The Dream Keeper and Other Poems* (1932); *The Ways of White Folks* (1934); *The Big Sea: An Autobiography* (1940); *Shakespeare in Harlem* (1942); *One-Way Ticket* (1949); and *I Wonder As I Wander: An Autobiographical Journey* (1956).

**FURTHER READING:** Arnold Rampersad's two-volume biography, *The Life of Langston Hughes* (1986 and 1988), provides a comprehensive portrait of Hughes as a man and writer. His introduction to Hughes's *I Wonder As I Wander* (1993) is also helpful. Other important sources include Richard Barksdale's *Langston Hughes: The Poet and His Critics* (1977);

F. Berry's *Langston Hughes: Before and Beyond Harlem* (1983); R. B. Miller's *The Art and Imagination of Langston Hughes* (1989); Jemie Onwuchekwa's *Langston Hughes: An Introduction to the Poetry* (1976); and Steven Tracy's *Langston Hughes and the Blues* (1988).

The largest repository of Hughes's letters and papers is the James Weldon Johnson Memorial Collection at Yale University. Additional papers are available in the Schomburg Collection at the New York Public Library, Lincoln University Library in Pennsylvania, and Fisk University Library.

BARBARA BURKHARDT　　　　UNIVERSITY OF ILLINOIS

## IRENE HUNT
May 18, 1902

**BIOGRAPHY:** Irene Hunt, educator and distinguished author of seven children's books and a young adult novel, was born to Franklin Pierce and Sarah Ann (Land) Hunt in Pontiac, Illinois. Although 1907 is usually accepted as the year of her birth, family members, including her half-brother Loren Poe, insist that May 18, 1902, is the correct date. She was six weeks old when her parents moved to the southern Illinois village of Newton in Jasper County. After her father's death when she was seven, she spent five years with her grandparents on the family homestead. Her love of the land and her experience with country people and their folkways give her farm fiction a depth of understanding and authenticity. Her grandfather's stories of his backwoods childhood, especially the gripping accounts of his Illinois border family during the Civil War, prompted her many years later to write her highly acclaimed historical novel, *Across Five Aprils* (1964).

Hunt received her AB from the University of Illinois in 1939 and her MA from the University of Minnesota in 1946. She took graduate courses in psychology at the University of Colorado. As a teacher and consultant in the Chicago area schools for more than thirty years, she discovered that her grandfather's stories were entertaining, effective teaching tools. Responding to her students' needs and her long-standing desire to write, Hunt began her second career as a children's novelist in 1964 when her first book was published and received five awards. She retired from teaching in 1969, moved to Florida, and continued writing fiction for her enthusiastic readers in this country and abroad. In 1992, in poor health, she moved back to Illinois to be close to her family.

**SIGNIFICANCE:** Hunt's first three books are thoroughly Midwestern in their rural settings, their direct, unpretentious style, and their portrayal of strong, believable characters who speak the colorful "country" vernacular. In the first novel, *Across Five Aprils*, Hunt presents a powerfully realistic story of the tragic impact of the Civil War on her grandfather's large, close-knit farm family. Torn apart by divided loyalties, family members fight on both sides. The news of lost battles, the disappearance and death of sons, and finally the assassination of Lincoln rob war of all its romance and glory. Her second book, the deeply moving *Up a Road Slowly* (1966), won the prestigious Newbery Medal. A first-person narrative, it chronicles the growing-up years of a girl much like Hunt who suffered the trauma of a parent's death and a subsequent move to her relatives' Midwestern farm. The problems of children, teenagers, and adults are presented realistically with no easy solutions. In *Trail of Apple Blossoms* (1968), the story of Johnny Appleseed gives young children a glimpse of the eccentric folk hero who enriched the lives of the Midwestern settlers with his gifts of healing and friendship along with his apple seeds.

An admirer of CARL SANDBURG, Hunt shares his faith in the common people, celebrating their courage, perseverance, and achievements. Her memories of the grim realities of life in Jasper County and Chicago provide her with a deep compassion for both rural and urban Americans. Always an advocate for children, she portrays the suffering of those who are battered, exploited, mentally retarded, and homeless with poignant, often painful honesty.

**SELECTED WORKS:** Hunt's three Midwestern books, *Across Five Aprils* (1964), *Up a Road Slowly* (1966), and *Trail of Apple Blossoms* (1968), are considered the best examples of her work. A fourth book, *No Promises in the Wind* (1970), begins in Chicago during the Depression but moves southward as the two desperate young protagonists flee from their abusive father to seek a different life on the road. In her books set in the South, *The Lottery Rose* (1976) and *William* (1977), as well as Colorado-based *The*

*Everlasting Hills* (1985), Hunt portrays children who survive the direst of circumstances through human compassion and understanding. Her highly praised young adult novel, *Claws of a Young Century* (1980), is both a love story and an authentic account of the long struggle for women's suffrage in the early 1900s. *Preludes* (1992), a booklet published by the Newton Public Library in Newton, Illinois, is a collection of four of Hunt's earliest stories, which were originally published in *Good Housekeeping* between 1936 and 1941. Hunt gives a rhapsodic tribute to the power of books in her Newbery Award Acceptance, titled "Books and the Learning Process," printed in *Horn Book* 43 (August 1967): 424–29.

**FURTHER READING:** Hunt's nephew, Wendell Bruce Beem, portrays her as a genial, engaging, multitalented friend in "Aunt Irene," *Horn Book* 43 (August 1967): 429–33. An informative account of her life and work is given in *Dictionary of Literary Biography* 52: 202–208. A shorter treatment appears in Sheryl Lee Saunders's "Irene Hunt," in *Children's Books and Their Creators*, edited by Anita Silvey (1995): 331. Hunt's manuscripts are located in the Kerlan Collection at the University of Minnesota in Minneapolis.

MARY JOAN MILLER                    SPRINGFIELD, OHIO

# FANNIE HURST
October 18, 1885–February 23, 1968

**BIOGRAPHY:** Fannie Hurst's German Jewish American-born parents, Samuel and Rose (Koppel) Hurst, traveled from St. Louis to Rose's parents' farm in Hamilton, Ohio, near Cincinnati, for their daughter's birth. Soon after, they returned to St. Louis where Hurst was reared, attending public schools and graduating from Washington University in 1909. In that year she began to publish short stories in WILLIAM MARION REEDY'S *St. Louis Mirror*. Moving to New York to pursue her literary career, after dozens of rejections, Fannie Hurst exploded onto the New York literary scene in 1912 with several stories each in *Cavalier* and the *Saturday Evening Post*, and the following year in *Metropolitan Magazine* and *Cosmopolitan*.

She rapidly became one of the most highly paid short story writers in the world and a well-known and influential celebrity in the United States, lending her name and her labor to many social causes and civic organizations. Her secret marriage to musician Jacques Danielson, discovered five years after the fact, led to the expression "a Fannie Hurst marriage" to refer to one dedicated to keeping the dew on the rose of romance and maintaining independent identities. She was closely associated with the New Deal through her close friendship with Eleanor Roosevelt and with the women of the Heterodoxy Club in New York. Twenty-nine films were made from her fiction, and she hosted radio and television programs, including the popular program *Pleased to Meet You*. Despite her international fame, Hurst never lost touch with or interest in her family and friends in Hamilton, Ohio, and St. Louis, Missouri. Fannie Hurst died of cancer in her apartment in Manhattan.

**SIGNIFICANCE:** Many of Hurst's stories deal with the lives of urban working women, realistically portraying the abominable working conditions—including sexual harassment, inadequate health benefits, unhealthy working conditions, and age discrimination—and the courage, intelligence, and moral strength of working women. Her first-generation American protagonists struggle with the conflicts between the lure of assimilation and the pull of old-world values.

Known for her philanthropy and activism for social justice as well as for earning more money as a writer than any woman to that time, she has also been credited with being one of the creators of the field of public relations, having learned early and well that personal celebrity enhances book sales as much as good writing. She was also the first white person to recognize and encourage Zora Neale Hurston's literary work. The two women developed a relationship that has been interestingly problematized by contemporary cultural critics.

Her Midwestern fiction is set either in St. Louis and its environs, in which case the characters are identifiably ethnic; or in Ohio, where the characters are undifferentiated white people.

St. Louis figures prominently in Fannie Hurst's writing. The St. Louis in which she grew up and was educated is a city of boardinghouses, bankruptcy, intellectual education, social embarrassment, fierce ambition, and literary apprenticeship. It is also the set-

ting for most of her mother/daughter stories, of which she wrote many.

In several of her novels, especially in *Hallelujah* (1944), based in part on the life of William Marion Reedy—and in many stories, including "The Good Provider" (1914), "Hochenheimer of Cincinnati" (1915), "Oats for the Woman" (1917), "The Wrong Pew" (1917), "The Brinkerhoff Brothers" (1922), and "The Hossie-Frossie" (1928)—St. Louis is a world of tightly knit, self-centered, two- and three-generation stable families threatened by a variety of crises arising from rebellion from within their ranks or from external economic crises.

Whether Hurst's families live in the boardinghouses and apartment buildings along the streets just north of Delmar, in the mansions along the broad, tree-lined Lindell and Forest Park Boulevards east of the park, or in the large, square, over-furnished, dimly lit houses in the German south St. Louis, her St. Louisans are similar: socially conservative; unattracted to cultural, social, political, or financial risks; and family and home oriented.

The stories from the world of women working in retail stores, the fashion industry, the arts community, and the sexual trades appear to be set in New York City but are often drawn from the world she knew in St. Louis. In a 1925 interview with Catharine Cranmer in the April 1925 issue of the *Missouri Historical Review* 19.3, Hurst confided " . . . I have used St. Louis almost as freely as I have New York; and sometimes when New York was the apparent setting, the characters and locale really belonged to St. Louis" (392).

Among Hurst's clearly identifiable Ohio stories are "Back Pay" (1919), "Even as You and I" (1919), "Nightshade" (1918), "Song of Life" (1926), "Wrath" (1927), and her 1928 novel *A President Is Born*. The Ohio settings are either rural or small town, the natural world described in lush, loving terms reflecting the world she knew during the summers of her youth spent on her Koppel grandparents' farm.

**SELECTED WORKS:** Sixty-three of Hurst's more than two hundred short stories were collected in nine volumes, including *Just Around the Corner: Romance En Casserole* (1914), *Every Soul Hath Its Song* (1916), *Gaslight Sonata* (1918), *Humoresque: A Laugh on Life with a Tear*

*Behind It* (1919), and *Song of Life* (1927). Hurst's eighteen novels include the semi-autobiographical *Star-Dust: The Story of an American Girl* (1921); her own favorite, *Lummox* (1923); the thrice-filmed *Back Street* (1931); and the twice-filmed *Imitation of Life* (1933). Her autobiography is *Anatomy of Me: A Wonderer in Search of Herself* (1958).

**FURTHER READING:** *The Fannie Hurst Newsletter*, a publication of the Fannie Hurst Society, founded in 1991, was published by the English Department of Gettysburg College through 1996. Forthcoming from the University of Illinois Press are *Fannie Hurst: The Woman and the Work* and *Selected Stories of Fannie Hurst*, both edited and with introductions by Susan Koppelman. Brooke Kroeger's biography, *Fannie: The Talent for Success of Writer Fannie Hurst*, appeared in 1999. Other valuable sources include Cynthia Brandimarte's 1980 University of Texas dissertation "Fannie Hurst and Her Fiction: Prescriptions for America's Working Women" and Abe C. Ravitz's *Imitations of Life: Fannie Hurst's Gaslight Sonatas* (1997).

The bulk of Hurst's papers are in the Humanities Research Center at the University of Texas at Austin. Smaller but very important collections of her correspondences, manuscripts, books, and recordings are held at Washington University, Brandeis University, and the Library of Congress.

SUSAN KOPPELMAN                     TUCSON, ARIZONA

# I-L

## WILLIAM (MOTTER) INGE
May 3, 1913–June 10, 1973

**BIOGRAPHY:** William Motter Inge, who observed in his essay "A Level Land" that much of the "color and culture" of America's major metropolitan centers can be attributed to fugitive and "gifted misfits from the plains," was himself born in Independence, Kansas, the youngest child of Maude Sara (Gibson) Inge and Luther Clayton Inge (157). Inge was educated at the University of Kansas, where he studied drama and acting, and later at George Peabody College in Nashville, Tennessee, where, lacking the self-assurance to pursue a professional acting career, he received a master's degree in English. Inge subsequently taught English and drama at Stephens College from 1938 to 1943 and Washington University of St. Louis from 1946 to 1949 and also served as a drama critic for the *St. Louis Star-Times* from 1943 to 1946.

Inge's reputation as one of the leading American dramatists of midcentury is largely based on his Midwestern dramas of the 1950s, all of which played on Broadway and were subsequently adapted to film: *Come Back Little Sheba* (1950), *Picnic* (1953), *Bus Stop* (1955), and *Dark at the Top of the Stairs* (1958), a revision of Inge's *Farther Off from Heaven*, previously produced, through the encouragement and assistance of Tennessee Williams, in Dallas in 1947. Inge was honored by the *New York Times* following the Broadway premiere of *Come Back Little Sheba* as "the most promising new playwright of 1950," a promise fulfilled three years later when Inge received the Pulitzer Prize, the New York Drama Critics' Circle Award, and the Donaldson Award for *Picnic* ("The Most Promising Playwright," July 23, 1950: II, 1).

However, with the failure of his fifth Broadway play, *A Loss of Roses* (1960), Inge left New York for Los Angeles where he wrote the Academy Award–winning screenplay for *Splendor in the Grass* (1961). This, Inge's final artistic triumph, was followed by the two dramas *Natural Affection* (1963) and *Where's Daddy?* (1966), both of which were produced in New York to disastrous commercial and critical reception. In addition to his full-length dramas, Inge wrote numerous one-act plays, most of which date from the 1950s and the early 1960s, and the two novels *Good Luck, Miss Wykoff* (1970) and *My Son Is a Splendid Driver* (1971). Tormented throughout his adult life by alcoholism and his homosexuality and ultimately plagued by self-doubt and a sense of personal failure, Inge took his own life on June 10, 1973.

**SIGNIFICANCE:** One of the most popular dramatists of the 1950s, more significantly, Inge was the first major American playwright, according to R. Baird Shuman in *William Inge* (1965), "to examine the Midwest with insight and to write seriously of it—to have concern for the sociological uniqueness of the area and for the psychological manifestations of this uniqueness as it is revealed in the reactions of its people" (17–18). *Picnic*, arguably Inge's most popular play, poignantly reveals a sympathetic understanding of small-town Mid-America that typifies Inge's work as a whole. Hal Carter, a handsome drifter looking for work and more importantly a permanent sense of place, arrives in a small Kansas town on Labor Day. Unfortunately, through a series of unforeseen circumstances, Hal is ultimately forced to leave town. With the galvanizing, if unintended, influence of a Dionysian intruder, he—for better or worse—decisively alters the lives of the play's five female characters, including Madge, the town beauty, who likewise leaves to join Hal in Tulsa. While Hal values, as Inge does, the sense of community, ritual, and tradition inherent in small-town life, he discovers that the small town can be unsupportive of independent thought and action and equally inimical to sexual openness.

The small-town provincialism in *Picnic* recurs throughout Inge's work; but in other major works, the psychological and emotional conflicts of individual characters are resolved not through an open revolt and departure from the village but through compromise and a discovery of mutual need, as in the case of Doc and Lola Delaney in *Come Back Little Sheba* and Rubin and Cora Flood in *Dark at the Top of the Stairs*. Inge's characters also come to terms with the loneliness and failed achievement of their lives through a related sense of stoic resignation and self-acceptance typified by Deanie at the end of *Splendor in the Grass*, when, quoting from Wordsworth's "Intimations Ode," she determines to "grieve not," but "rather find strength in what remains behind." Thus, far from an unqualified rejection of small-town Mid-America, Inge downplays the small-town setting as a primary and exclusive psychological determinant but focuses rather upon his characters' capacity for personal growth and maturation within such a setting.

Inge also draws upon the Midwest in various of his one-act plays and in his two novels published shortly before his death: *Good Luck, Miss Wyckoff*, which deals with the loneliness, frustration, and eventual liberation of a small-town spinster schoolteacher, and *My Son Is a Splendid Driver*, a thinly disguised account of Inge's childhood and adolescence in Independence, Kansas. Though ultimately unable to adapt to changes in theatrical taste following the 1950s, through his sensitive and sympathetic treatment of the inhabitants of the rural and small-town Midwest, Inge may be justifiably regarded as the first notable dramatist of, and not merely from, the American Midwest.

**SELECTED WORKS:** Inge's best-known dramas are his Midwestern plays of the 1950s—*Come Back Little Sheba* (1950), *Picnic* (1953), *Bus Stop* (1955), and *Dark at the Top of the Stairs* (1958)—all of which have been published as *Four Plays by William Inge* (1979), together with an informative foreword by the author. Inge's other full-length plays include *A Loss of Roses* (1960) and *Natural Affection* (1963), both of which are set in the Midwest, and *Where's Daddy?* (1966). More varied in setting and often more graphic in content, a number of Inge's one-act plays have been published in *Summer Brave and Eleven Short Plays* (1962). Inge's "A Level Land," reprinted in *What Kansas Means to Me*, edited by Thomas Fox Averill (1990), provides a revealing, elegiac estimate of Kansas and the Great Plains. Toward the end of his life, Inge turned from drama to fiction, producing two novels: *Good Luck, Miss Wyckoff* (1970) and *My Son Is a Splendid Driver* (1971). A number of Inge's works, including a final novel, "The Boy from the Circus," completed shortly before his death, remain unpublished.

**FURTHER READING:** Arthur F. McClure's *William Inge: A Bibliography* (1982) provides a comprehensive checklist of biographical and critical studies through 1980. More recently, Maarten Reilingh's bibliographical article "William Inge," in *American Playwrights since 1945: A Guide to Scholarship, Criticism, and Performance*, edited by Philip C. Kolin (1989), presents an annotated survey of secondary sources, including general studies and analyses of individual plays, as well as a production history of Inge's work, an assessment of Inge's reputation, and future research opportunities. R. Baird Shuman's *William Inge* (1965) offers a thoughtful analysis of Inge's life and work through 1965, though Shuman's study should be supplemented by Ralph Voss's *A Life of William Inge: The Strains of Triumph* (1989), which draws extensively upon primary materials in the William Inge Collection at Independence Community College in its examination of Inge's troubled personal history. Interviews with Inge are included in *Counterpoint*, edited by Roy Newquist (1964), and *The Playwrights Speak: Interviews with 11 Playwrights*, edited by Walter Wager (1967). A special issue of *Kansas Quarterly* devoted to Inge (Fall 1986) contains a number of illuminating biographical and critical studies. The major collection of Inge's papers is located at Independence Community College, Independence, Kansas, the site as well of the annual William Inge Festival and Conference. Other collections are held at the Spencer Research Library at the University of Kansas and the Humanities Research Center at the University of Texas.

MICHAEL WENTWORTH

UNIVERSITY OF NORTH CAROLINA AT WILMINGTON

## ROBERT GREEN INGERSOLL

August 11, 1833–July 21, 1899

**BIOGRAPHY:** Robert Ingersoll was born in Dresden, New York, to John Ingersoll, a Congregational minister of Puritan descent, and Mary (Livingston) Ingersoll. The family moved to Ohio, Kentucky, Indiana, Michigan, Wisconsin, and finally to Illinois in 1843.

Largely self-educated, Ingersoll briefly taught school, then began practicing law with his brother in 1854, and later entered local politics in Peoria. Ingersoll was a colonel in the Union Army and later appointed Attorney General of Illinois, his only political office. He married Eva Parker in 1862, while on active military duty.

As knowledge of Darwinian theory spread in America, Ingersoll became a spokesman for scientific humanism and acquired notoriety as "the great agnostic," as he was often advertised before speeches. He promoted freethinking and rational criticism of the Christian religion throughout a three-decade career of lecturing, newspaper and magazine articles, and pamphlets.

An active campaigner for Republican candidates, he never held public office after becoming famous and was disappointed at failing to gain a cabinet or diplomatic assignment.

Robert Green Ingersoll.
Courtesy of the University of Kentucky Libraries

In 1878 Ingersoll moved to Washington, D.C., then in 1885 to New York, where he continued lecturing, writing, and practicing law. Ingersoll and his wife had two daughters. In 1896 he suffered a mild stroke while lecturing in Janesville, Wisconsin, finished the address, and continued speaking for several days, but his health steadily declined for several years. Shortly after a diagnosis of angina, Ingersoll died at his summer home in Dobbs Ferry, New York.

**SIGNIFICANCE:** As in the cases of WILLIAM JENNINGS BRYAN and Robert La Follette, Ingersoll's literary career was based on oratory on the Lyceum circuit and political stump. His publications developed from provocative lectures and essays such as "Superstition," "The Great Infidels," "Myth and Miracle," and "Some Mistakes of Moses," all of which he read many times. Like MARK TWAIN, he equated religious superstition to intellectual slavery and political complacency. Ingersoll campaigned for civil rights, women's suffrage, and prison reform and against imperialism.

Ingersoll was the epitome of a particular rural Midwestern character, the virtuous freethinker, a common type in small communities where an educated man might be granted some leeway from conventional morality so long as he was recognizably moral and civic-minded. Publicly and privately, Ingersoll was charming, rational, dependable, skeptical, and free from charges of personal impropriety. A literary version of the freethinker contemporary to Ingersoll is Matthew Braile in WILLIAM DEAN HOWELLS's *The Leatherwood God;* earlier Mark Twain had portrayed the freethinker as David Wilson and Judge Driscoll in *Pudd'nhead Wilson,* set before the Civil War.

Like his political and religious opposite, William Jennings Bryan, Ingersoll earned a reputation for intellectual sincerity and personal rectitude, which served him well as political speaker and lawyer addressing juries despite his reputation as an infidel. In his use of wit and homely imagery, in his sympathy for farmers and labor, and in his apparent sincerity and spontaneity, Ingersoll resembled the skilled orator Bryan.

Ingersoll wrote no memoirs and used personal references in his speeches only rarely for rhetorical effect; however, he did lecture somewhat romantically on farming in Illinois, admiring the rich soil of the middle states, the country life, and the virtue of hard labor. Among contemporary writers he admired, Ingersoll named Howells, Walt Whitman, JAMES WHITCOMB RILEY, and EUGENE FIELD.

**SELECTED WORKS:** Speeches, lectures, and articles are collected in *The Works of Robert G. Ingersoll* (1900); in addition, complete works are available on-line at www.infidels.org and www.codesh.org. *The Letters of Robert G. Ingersoll* was collected and edited by a granddaughter (1951). His lectures, published as pamphlets, are widely available in libraries.

**FURTHER READING:** Biography and interpretation of Ingersoll's place in nineteenth-century culture include DAVID D. ANDERSON's *Robert Ingersoll* (1972), Orvin Larson's *American Infidel* (1962), and Frank Smith's *Robert Ingersoll: A Life* (1990). Mark Plummer's *Robert G. Ingersoll: Peoria's Pagan Politician* (1984) exclusively concerns Ingersoll's career in Illinois. For bibliography, see Gordon Stein's *Robert G. Ingersoll: A Checklist* (1969). Ingersoll's papers are held at the Library of Congress, the Illinois State Historical Library, and the Peoria Public Library.

THOMAS PRIBEK

UNIVERSITY OF WISCONSIN–LACROSSE

## JOHN JAKES

March 31, 1932

(Alan Payne, Rachel Anne Payne, Jay Scotland)

**BIOGRAPHY:** Variously called the "godfather of the historical novel," "the people's author," and "America's history teacher," John Jakes was born in Chicago, the son of John Adrian and Bertha (Retz) Jakes. As an only child of parents who were in their forties when he was born, he shared, as a boy, many of their "adult" recreations, especially reading and visits to the movies and legitimate theater. These early activities continue to influence his writing.

Jakes graduated from the creative writing program at DePauw University in 1953. At the end of his sophomore year, on June 15, 1951, he married Rachel Anne Payne, who had been his zoology lab instructor. He completed the MA in American literature from Ohio State University in 1954 but left the PhD program to meet the demands of a growing family. His first job, from 1954 to 1960, was with Abbott Laboratories, where he rose from copywriter to product promotion manager. For the next eleven years he worked at advertising agencies in Rochester, New York, and Dayton, Ohio.

Jakes is the recipient of honorary degrees from Wright State University in 1976, DePauw University in 1977, Winthrop College and the University of South Carolina in 1993, and Ohio State University in 1996. Since 1989 he has been a research fellow in the Department of History at the University of South Carolina. In 1995 alone he received the Ohio State University College of Humanities Alumni Award, the citizen and celebrity award for library advocacy from the White House Conference on Libraries and Information Systems Task Force, and the Western Heritage Award at the National Cowboy Hall of Fame for the best Western short story of 1994. From December 1993 through January 1994 he was the subject of an exhibition at the University of South Carolina Thomas Cooper Library entitled "John Jakes: The People's Author." In October 1997 he received the Ohio State Alumni Association Professional Achievement Award.

**SIGNIFICANCE:** Jakes's early inspiration, the swashbuckling adventure films of the 1930s and 1940s, clearly influenced his mature style; Jakes often moves cinematically from scene to scene, adding descriptive detail and historical data to his narrative and creating vicarious verisimilitude for his readers. The Saturday matinees he viewed with his parents contributed another influence, for, as Jakes recalls, after seeing a film such as *Charge of the Light Brigade* or *Dodge City,* he rushed to the Chicago Public Library to find out more about Custer or Balaklava. This was the foundation for his library habit; he now spends as much time researching his historical fiction as writing it. Jakes once dreamed of being an actor and was part of a comedy team during his high school years. But when he sold his first short story about a diabolical toaster which took over its owner's body to the *Magazine of Fantasy and Science Fiction*, his career took a turn. Since that first twenty-five-dollar check, his acting has been only avocational. But theater, he argues, has practical benefits for the novelist; it provides an ear for dialogue.

During his advertising years Jakes wrote scores of books, many under pseudonyms, and experimented with a variety of genres: science fiction, mystery and suspense, fantasy, a detective series, Western short stories, historical novels, and children's fiction and nonfiction. He wrote at night, allocating whatever he earned for his four children's college educations.

His professional breakthrough came when he was approached by Lyle Kenyon Engel, creator of a frankly commercial idea, a series of historical novels timed to coincide with the American Bicentennial. The result was the Kent Family Chronicles, an enormously successful series of eight novels carrying the Kent family from the American Revolution to the end of the nineteenth century. No book in the series sold fewer than 3.5 million copies. Ironically, Jakes had earlier wanted to write about American themes, but his publishers told him that stories about "guys in three cornered hats don't make it." By the 1970s, in part because of the national disillusionment of the Vietnam-Johnson-Nixon-Watergate years, the country was, Jakes believes, ready for fiction affirming American values.

In the Kent Family Chronicles (1974–80), Jakes established a method which he continued in all his subsequent novels, the North and South series (1982–87), *California Gold* (1989), and *Homeland* (1993). He intertwines the lives of his created characters with those of actual historical figures and thus allows his families, the Kents, the Mains and the Hazards, the Chances, and the Crowns, with their dreams and aspirations, their crises and failures, their principles and their flaws, to serve as metaphors for the nation. Throughout, although Jakes refuses to gloss over America's wrongs, such as slavery, the stealing of Indian lands, and socioeconomic inequities, he affirms his strong belief in America's goals, strengths, and ideals.

Although Jakes's characters participate in events occurring in the Midwest, such as the Battle of Fallen Timbers and the great Chicago fire, the scope of his best-known novels is national, rather than regional; some of his lesser-known works are set in fantasy worlds or in outer space. Similarly, although one of his best-loved heroines, Amanda Kent of *The Seekers* (1975) and *The Furies* (1976), takes refuge for a night with a family named Lincoln, Jakes's portrayal of ABRAHAM LINCOLN is not as a Midwestern boy but as the beleaguered and haunted president of a riven nation. While Jakes's upbringing and education were Midwestern, his major works, except for *California Gold*, chronicle America's history rather than that of any particular region. This is, however, not a rejection of region so much as a reflection of a theme present in many of the Kent Family Chronicles and in *Homeland,* that one source of strength for the United States is its fusion of many nations, regions, and philosophies.

**SELECTED WORKS:** Jakes's best-known works are three continuing family sagas: the Kent Family Chronicles, the North and South series, and the Crown family saga, and the self-contained *California Gold*. The Kent Family Chronicles included eight novels: *The Bastard* (1974), *The Rebels* (1975), *The Seekers* (1975), *The Furies* (1976), *The Titans* (1976), *The Warriors* (1977), *The Lawless* (1978), and *The Americans* (1980); the North and South series included three: *North and South* (1982), *Love and War* (1984), and *Heaven and Hell* (1987); and the Crown series began with *Homeland* (1993) and continues with *American Dreams* (1998) and a projected two or three additional novels. Although many of Jakes's early books are difficult to find today, *Susanna of the Alamo: A True Story* (1986) is an example of his continuing interest in writing children's nonfiction.

**FURTHER READING:** Robert Hawkins's *The*

*Kent Family Chronicles Encyclopedia* (1979) is a helpful guide to those eight novels. The first full-length study of John Jakes is Mary Ellen Jones's *John Jakes: A Critical Companion* (1996). The major collection of Jakes's papers is at the John Jakes Archive, Thomas Cooper Library, at the University of South Carolina, Columbia, which houses manuscripts, correspondence, and promotional materials. The DePauw University Library, Greencastle, Indiana, holds final typescripts of the eight Kent Family Chronicles novels. The Archive of Contemporary History, University of Wyoming, Laramie, has a miscellaneous collection, including some pre-Kent novels.

MARY ELLEN JONES          WITTENBERG UNIVERSITY

## ORRICK JOHNS
June 2, 1887–July 8, 1946

**BIOGRAPHY:** Born in St. Louis, Missouri, to George S. and Minnehaha (McDearmon) Johns, Orrick Johns had a varied career in which he worked in advertising, helped to edit *New Masses*, served as a Communist Party operative, and, during 1935–36, directed the Federal Writers' Project in New York City. He wrote poetry, unsuccessful plays, a novel, and finally a moving memoir of himself and his father, who was editor of the *St. Louis Post-Dispatch* and a friend of Woodrow Wilson.

One of six sons, Johns lost a leg at seven when he was hit by a trolley car. After a long recovery he continued to attend the St. Louis Public Schools. Later he attended the University of Missouri and Washington University but graduated from neither. In 1910 WILLIAM MARION REEDY, editor of the *Mirror* and mentor to such young writers as ZOE AKINS and SARA TEASDALE, asked Johns to serve as drama critic. While reviewing books, drama, music, and art, Johns worked on a novel and wrote poetry.

Restless, as he was throughout his life, Johns moved to New York City in 1911. Here he wrote the poem "Second City," which won the *Lyric Year* first prize in 1912. Here, too, he met and married Peggy Baird, who later became the wife of Malcolm Cowley. Johns continued to write poetry, placing some of his poems in the early issues of *Poetry: A Magazine of Verse*. He returned to Missouri and a job in advertising for three years; then it was back to New York and more advertising until he

sailed for Europe in 1926. His marriage had long been broken.

Johns spent three years in Europe, primarily in Italy, and while he was there, someone told him that parts of California resembled Capri. He decided to visit that state, especially since he had been corresponding with a former friend from St. Louis, Caroline Blackman, who now lived with her family in Carmel. Johns took a job there as editor of the *Carmelite*, a weekly newspaper, and he and Caroline were married. A daughter, Charis, was born in 1930, but Caroline suffered from depression, entered a hospital, and Charis was taken to be raised by her grandmother. With this, Johns began a new life as a labor organizer and Communist Party member.

The Depression years found Johns active in organizing in California, St. Louis, and finally, in New York City again. He wrote for the Communist *Daily Worker* and became one of the editors of *New Masses*. He helped to organize the American Writers' Congress in 1935. He joined the WPA Federal Writers' Project and became director of the New York City Project, from which he resigned in 1937. After the death of his wife, he married Doria Berton. He died in Danbury, Connecticut, a suicide by poison, in 1946.

**SIGNIFICANCE:** Johns's memoir, *Time of Our Lives: The Story of My Father and Myself* (1937), provides an interesting and important picture of intellectual life in the Midwest and other areas from the 1850s through the New Deal. Johns's early work with *Reedy's Mirror* in St. Louis and his friendships there with other young aspiring Midwestern writers, such as Zoe Akins and Sara Teasdale, were important to his development as a lyric poet. Like them, also, he felt that he needed to go East to find success. He found some success early, placing poems in *Poetry* in Chicago and *Others* in the East; but Johns largely wrote rhyming poetry at a time when such verse was losing favor, and he wrote that he felt that the "vein was running thin" (*Time of Our Lives* 233), that he would not in the future take his "role as a poet very seriously" (*Time of Our Lives* 234). He also wrote, however, that he had been " . . . in search of a simple expression belonging to my origin" and that he " . . . wanted to write so that the people of my region could grasp and remember what I said" (*Time of Our Lives* 233).

SELECTED WORKS: Johns published three books of poetry: *Asphalt* (1919), *Black Branches* (1920), and *Wild Plum* (1926). He published a novel, *Blindfold*, in 1923. He also wrote an unpublished, unproduced play entitled "The Price of Vegetables," which dealt with farmers in Missouri. A play, *A Charming Conscience*, was produced in California and on the road beginning in 1923. *Time of Our Lives* (1937) remains his most durable work.

FURTHER READING: There has been no biography or book-length critical study on Johns. A brief biography can be found in *Twentieth Century Authors* (1942), and mention is made of Johns in books on this period. Some of these are Douglas Wixson's *Worker-Writer in America* (1994), Allen Churchill's *The Improper Bohemians* (1959), and Malcolm Cowley's *The Dream of the Golden Mountains* (1980). The Missouri Historical Society, St. Louis, has some Orrick Johns materials in various specialized collections.

PATRICIA A. ANDERSON          DIMONDALE, MICHIGAN

## JAMES JONES
November 6, 1921–May 9, 1977

BIOGRAPHY: James Jones was born to Ramon and Ada (Blessing) Jones, in Robinson, Illinois. After high school he joined the U.S. Air Force and was stationed at Schofield Barracks, Hawaii, where he transferred to Infantry and witnessed the Japanese bombing of Pearl Harbor. He was wounded in the battle of Guadalcanal and was awarded the Bronze Star and Purple Heart. Jones's war experience provided the background for his best three novels, *From Here to Eternity* (1951), *The Pistol* (1958), and *The Thin Red Line* (1962). After he was discharged he moved in with Harry E. and Lowney Handy of his hometown of Robinson, Illinois. The Handys wanted to help him in his ambition to become a writer.

After seven years and one rejected manuscript, *From Here to Eternity* won the National Book Award in 1951. Jones sold the film rights for $82,500 to Columbia Pictures and used the money to help the Handys establish a writers' colony in Marshall, Illinois. In 1957 Jones married Gloria Patricia Mosolino. In 1958 he and his wife moved to Paris, where they lived until 1974 when he returned to teach at Florida International University in Miami. In

James Jones.
Photo © Nancy Crampton

1976 Jones moved to Southampton, Long Island, where he died in 1977.

SIGNIFICANCE: Although considered one of his weaker works, Jones's second novel, *Some Came Running* (1958), most clearly draws on his Midwestern background. Critics panned the novel for its enormous length (nearly nine hundred pages), Jones's indifference to standard syntax, and his excessive philosophizing. But many of the experiences of Dave Hirsch, the protagonist, who returns a war hero to his hometown of Parkham, Illinois, to write a war novel, parallel those of Jones himself upon his return from Guadalcanal and his experiences with Lowney Handy while writing *From Here to Eternity*.

SELECTED WORKS: Jones's first novel, *From Here to Eternity* (1951) stands as his greatest achievement. His other major works include *Some Came Running* (1958), *The Pistol* (1958), *The Thin Red Line* (1962), *Go to the Widow-Maker* (1967), *The Ice-Cream Headache and Other Stories* (1968), *The Merry Month of May* (1971), *A Touch of Danger* (1973), *Viet Journal* (1974), and *WWII* (1975). *Whistle* (1978) was completed by Willie Morris from Jones's notes and tapes and published posthumously. Jones's letters have been collected in *To Reach Eternity: The Letters of James Jones* (1989), which includes a foreword by William Styron. *The James Jones Reader*, edited by James R. Giles and J. Michael Lennon (1991), contains outstanding selections from his war writings.

**FURTHER READING:** Jones is discussed in nearly every major study of post–World War II American novelists. An excellent introduction to Jones is James R. Giles's Twayne series *James Jones* (1981). Two full-length biographies have appeared: George Garrett's *James Jones* (1984) and Frank MacShane's *Into Eternity: The Life of James Jones American Writer* (1985). Yale University library has a significant collection of Jones's manuscripts, and the most extensive collection of Jones's papers is the James Jones Archives of the Humanities Research Center of the University of Texas at Austin.

KEITH FYNAARDT            NORTHWESTERN COLLEGE

## NETTIE (PEARL) JONES
January 1, 1941

**BIOGRAPHY:** Nettie Jones was born in rural Arlington, Georgia, the first of two children of Benjamin and Delonia (Mears) Jones. Taken to Detroit as a child, she attended public schools there. She received the bachelor of science degree from Wayne State University in 1962 and the Master of Education from Marygrove College, Detroit, in 1971. She subsequently moved to New York, enrolling in the New School for Social Research from 1971 through 1972 and the Fashion Institute of Technology from 1973 to 1976. At that point she returned to Michigan to live in Leelanau County, in Detroit, and in the Upper Peninsula, where in 1989 she was writer in residence at Michigan Technological University. She was married to Frank Stafford in 1958 and divorced in 1961, and to Frank W. Harris in 1963 and divorced in 1975. She has one child, Lynne Cheryl Stafford Harris. She left Michigan to attend the University of Chicago Divinity School from 1990 to 1992 and later returned to the East Coast. Her two novels, *Fish Tales* (1983) and *Mischief Makers* (1989), take place in Leelanau County and in Detroit, as well as in New York, and the mix of Leelanau Native Americans and Detroit African Americans is

vital to the writing. She has been a Yaddo Fellow and the recipient of a National Endowment for the Arts award, as well as of grants from the Michigan Council for the Arts.

**SIGNIFICANCE:**

"Am I [a Negro]?"

"Partly Negro, partly white, partly Indian."

"Good . . . I like being parts of all those people. Makes me part of everyone—American."

Like Lily in these lines from *Mischief Makers* (70), the characters in Nettie Jones's two novels are often racially indeterminate. They may also seem to be sexually ambiguous. Lewis Jones in *Fish Tales* is a woman. Kitty is a man. They think of themselves as they believe themselves to be rather than as they are seen by others. This distinction between individuality and racial or sexual stereotyping results in conflicts that permeate the books.

If, for example, being free of genetic racial determination seems American to Lily, the experience of life in America is consistently that of racial or sexual identification or both. The word "fish" in the title *Fish Tales* is described in the novel as a male homosexual term of opprobrium for women; thus, the title identifies one set of persons as labeled by another. Persons are treated as black, Indian, or white, as homosexual or as straight, and the lesson of such treatment is hatred and violence. Lily, who thinks of herself as American in part because of her racial intermixture, is killed by blacks who take her for white during a Detroit race riot.

A separate account in *Mischief Makers* tells of the Fort Pillow massacre, in which black Union troops and their white officers are disarmed and murdered by Confederate whites.

These novels are marked by eroticism as well as by racism and anger. They are distinguished from other recent fiction because Nettie Jones's racially mixed and sexually anxious characters, if burned by hatred, seek and return love as best they are able. The significance of these books lies in that opposition of hatred and race with love and singularity.

Finally, the refusal of externally imposed identity is also evident in the relationships of character and place. Setting is fully realized in Jones. Her Detroit is as vivid as that of Joyce

Carol Oates, and those parts of *Mischief Makers* set in the Traverse City area bring ERNEST HEMINGWAY's Nick Adams stories to mind: both *Mischief Makers* and the Nick Adams stories take place in part at about the same time; some story elements are similar, including childbirth and youthful initiation; and the names of places and persons, Peshawbestown in Jones and Billy Tabeshaw in Hemingway, Suttons Bay in Jones and Hortons Bay in Hemingway, but the racially mixed characters in Jones's novels are neither of nor confined by place. They migrate freely. There may be in this quality something of Jones's own experience of the black migration from the South to Detroit, Chicago, and New York, but there is also a sense of the Midwestern migrant interchanging city and country.

**SELECTED WORKS:** Jones's principal works are the novels *Fish Tales* (1983) and *Mischief Makers* (1989). Her nonfiction appears in an essay on the Clarence Thomas hearings as participatory public spectacle, "Anita and the Battle of the Bush," *African-American Women Speak Out on Anita Hill-Clarence Thomas*, edited by Geneva Smitherman (1996).

**FURTHER READING:** A good account of personal and autobiographical elements associated with the novels, especially as they relate to memories of Georgia and adolescence in Detroit, is Nettie Jones's original entry, *Contemporary Authors* 20 (1994). Sharon P. Holland compares the treatment of African American and Native American identities in Leslie Marmon Silko's *Almanac of the Dead* and Jones's *Mischief Makers* in "If You Have a History, You Will Respect Me," in *Callaloo* 17.1 (1994): 334–50. Mary Kellie Munsil completed a BA thesis, "A Reading of Signs," dealing with *Fish Tales* at Scripps College in 1986.

WILLIAM POWERS

MICHIGAN TECHNOLOGICAL UNIVERSITY

# MacKinlay Kantor

February 4, 1904–October 11, 1977

**BIOGRAPHY:** Novelist and short story writer, MacKinlay Kantor was born Benjamin McKinlay Kantor in Webster City, Iowa, to John Martin and Effie Rachel (McKinlay) Kantor. While still young, Kantor dropped his first name and added the "a" to MacKinlay to maintain the original Scottish spelling of his mother's maiden name. Kantor's parents divorced soon after his birth, and his mother, a newspaper editor, raised him. After his high school graduation, Kantor worked with his mother as a reporter for the *Webster City Daily News* from 1921 to 1925, but he eventually shifted his focus to fiction writing. In 1925 Kantor moved to Chicago where he joined the Graeme Players theatre company. There he met Florence Irene Layne, whom he married on July 2, 1926. They later had two children, a daughter, Layne Kantor Shroder, and a son, Thomas (Tim) MacKinlay Kantor.

Kantor continued to work as a journalist while writing his early novels. He served as a *Cedar Rapids Republican* reporter until 1927 and then as a columnist for the *Des Moines Tribune* from 1930 to 1931. Later, Kantor continued his longer novelistic projects while supporting his family by writing hundreds of short stories for publication in popular magazines and by serving as a scenario writer for several major film companies. During World War II, Kantor went to England to serve as a war correspondent with the Royal Air Force and the U.S. Air Force in Europe. While there, however, he volunteered for combat duty and flew as an aerial gunner. Upon his return to the United States, Kantor served in the New York City Police Department from 1948 through 1950.

Though Kantor's writing spans many genres from biography to autobiography, from children's literature to poetry, he is most known for his historical novels and for his sentimental depiction of American life. Kantor's short story "Silent Grow the Guns" won the O. Henry Award in 1935. Kantor's most acclaimed novel, *Andersonville* (1955), set in the infamous Confederate prison camp, won the 1956 Pulitzer Prize. Kantor died at home of a heart attack in Sarasota, Florida.

**SIGNIFICANCE:** Whether writing of the American Civil War, fox hunting in Missouri, or the memories of a retiring high school janitor, MacKinlay Kantor invests his stories with everyday characters and scenes of the Midwest he knew so well. For Kantor, small-town, ordinary citizens become a wealth of inspiration. Far from superheroes, Kantor's main characters are simple, Midwestern people living out simple Midwestern ideals of devotion and respect for one another and for the land. Kantor's *The Voice of Bugle Ann* (1935) details the devotion between Bugle Ann, a Missouri hound dog, and her owner, Spring Davis. Davis's love is such that he shoots a man he suspects of killing her. In *Valedictory* (1939), a retiring janitor remembers fondly the many students he has helped in his long career. Similarly, in *God and My Country* (1954), Kantor recounts the memories of a Boy Scout troop leader's forty years of service. Even *Andersonville*, Kantor's depiction of the South during the Civil War, centers not around battles and bloodshed, but around the enduring humanity of one character, Ira Claffey, a rural farmer, and his refusal to hate even those the war called his enemy. Kantor's detailing of small-town heroes and their codes of honor were not always entirely fictitious, however. In *But Look, the Morn* (1947), Kantor writes autobiographically of his small-town childhood in Webster City, Iowa.

**SELECTED WORKS:** Set in Chicago, Kantor's first published novel, *Diversey* (1928), describes the gang violence so prominent there in the 1920s. Also set in Chicago, *El Goes South* (1930) relays the experiences of a widowed man and his family. *Andersonville* (1955) remains Kantor's most acclaimed historical novel while the Civil War tale "Silent Grow the Guns" (1935) is perhaps his most noted short story. Other Civil War stories include *Long Remember* (1934), based on the battle of Gettysburg, and *Arouse and Beware* (1936), which tells of two Union soldiers' struggle to escape a Confederate prison. Kantor depicts small-town Missouri life in *Missouri Bittersweet* (1969), *The Voice of Bugle Ann* (1935), and *The Daughter of Bugle Ann* (1953). Like the autobiographical *But Look, the Morn* (1947), *Midnight Lace* (1948) is also set in Iowa and tells the story of a young woman's move from Chicago to a more rural new beginning. *Valedictory* (1939) and *God and My Country* (1954) exemplify Kantor's use of common heroes as main characters. Kantor depicts his brief employment as a New York City policeman in *Signal Thirty-Two* (1950). His experiences as a B-17 gunner and war correspondent inspired his two World War II novels, *Happy Land* (1943) and *Glory for Me* (1945). The latter novel was later adapted into the film *The Best Years of Our Lives*, which won numerous Academy Awards including Best Picture of 1946. Kantor's short stories appear in collections such as *Author's Choice, 40 Stories . . .* (1944); *Silent Grow the Guns, and Other Tales of the American Civil War*

(1958); and *The Gun-Toter, and Other Stories of the Missouri Hills* (1963).

**FURTHER READING:** Tim Kantor's biography, *My Father's Voice: MacKinlay Kantor Long Remembered* (1988), offers accounts from the author's life. Kantor's short stories are collected in numerous anthologies, including the *O. Henry Memorial Award Prize Stories of 1935* (1935), *The Pocket Book of Adventure Stories* (1945), *A Cavalcade of Collier's* (1959), and *The Pulps: Fifty Years of American Pop Culture* (1970). Kantor discusses writing *Andersonville* in his essay "The Writing of Andersonville," in *Books at Iowa* 43 (1985): 24–29. For other critical studies of *Andersonville*, see Joel Mackey Jones's 1963 Miami University master's thesis entitled "Pegasus and Clio: A Study of the Historical Novel, Focusing upon MacKinlay Kantor's *Andersonville*." For emphasis on Kantor's detective stories, see John Apostolou's "MacKinlay Kantor and the Police Novel," in *Armchair Detective* 30.2 (1997): 202. Kantor's papers and manuscripts are housed at the Library of Congress and the University of Iowa Library.

ROBIN L. KIDD          UNIVERSITY OF KENTUCKY

## GARY EDWARD KEILLOR
August 7, 1942
(Garrison Keillor)

**BIOGRAPHY:** Gary Keillor was born in Anoka, Minnesota, to working-class parents, John Philip and Grace Ruth (Denham) Keillor. In 1947 the family moved to nearby Brooklyn Park, where Keillor lived until leaving home for the University of Minnesota. After graduating with a BA in English in 1966, Keillor went on to some graduate work in English at Minnesota, freelance writing, and more work at KUOM, the University radio station, and some other public radio stations in Minnesota. Since 1970, his humorous sketches and fiction have appeared in leading magazines, including the *New Yorker, Harper's Magazine, Atlantic Monthly*, and *Time*. In July 1974, a few months after Keillor was sent to Nashville by the *New Yorker* to write about the Grand Ole Opry, live Saturday-night broadcasts of *A Prairie Home Companion*, his famous radio variety show, began. His dual career as writer and radio performer has continued more or less steadily since that time, though with several deliberate breaks from radio work. Minnesota Public Radio began nationwide broadcasts of *A Prairie Home Companion* in 1980. Soon thereafter, the news from Lake Wobegon, "my hometown," Keillor's ten- to thirty-minute monologues, became the regular centerpiece of the show. In 1985 the bestseller *Lake Wobegon Days*, a loosely novelistic rendering of Lake Wobegon material, appeared, as did Keillor's picture on the cover of *Time* magazine. The "final" performance of *A Prairie Home Companion* aired on June 13, 1987. After several months in Denmark and two years as a staff writer for the *New Yorker*, in 1989 Keillor began a similar program, *The American Radio Company of the Air*, usually broadcast from New York City. In 1993 the name *A Prairie Home Companion* returned, and many broadcasts have emanated again from St. Paul. Also, several more books have been published through the years.

Keillor has received many awards and honors for his work. In 1980 *A Prairie Home Companion* won the prestigious George Foster Peabody Award. The *Lake Wobegon Days* set of cassettes received a Grammy for best spoken-word recording of 1987. In 1994 Keillor was inducted into the Radio Hall of Fame in Chicago.

Keillor married Mary Guntzel in 1965. They had a son, Jason, and were divorced in 1976. In 1985 Keillor married Ulla Skaerved, formerly his classmate and the exchange student from Denmark at Anoka High School. They were later divorced. Keillor married Jenny Lind Nilsson, and in December 1997 their daughter Maya Grace was born.

**SIGNIFICANCE:** The diverse writings of Garrison Keillor are probably unequaled in recent decades in gaining wide popularity for Midwestern themes and subjects, even though they are perhaps secondary in that regard to his famous monologues, the "news from Lake Wobegon," and, in general, his Saturday-night *A Prairie Home Companion*. Not since Grant Wood's painting *American Gothic* has there been anything comparable to the name Lake Wobegon for evoking Iowa and Minnesota, respectively, the Midwest, and even quintessential America, for so many people and in such an entertaining yet meaningful way.

As a revival of local-color literature, Keillor's writings and storytelling portray in vivid detail the speech, dress, mannerisms, values, and attitudes of the Norwegian Lutherans and German Catholics, the middle-class towns-

**Garrison Keillor.**
Photo © Nancy Crampton

people and families on the farms surrounding little Lake Wobegon. As in earlier local-color writing, Keillor sometimes uses eccentrics, such as his Norwegian bachelor farmers, to embody and exaggerate local traits. And by close observation of the surface details of life, from interior decoration and yard art to styles of gardening and cooking, he conveys the sense of actually being there in his Minnesota homeland.

Many of Keillor's themes can be traced to Midwestern roots, to the "village myth" and its opposite, the "revolt from the village." The latter is the phrase used by critic CARL VAN DOREN in the October 12, 1921, issue of the *Nation* to characterize the new, realistic portrayal of small-town life found in works of that era, usually with Midwestern settings and even Midwestern place names for titles, such as EDGAR LEE MASTERS's *Spoon River Anthology* (1915), SHERWOOD ANDERSON's *Winesburg, Ohio* (1919), and SINCLAIR LEWIS's *Main Street* (1920). These books were in revolt against the then predominant, sentimental and idealized rendition of small-town life, usually situated again in the Midwest, provided by authors such as ZONA GALE and BOOTH TARKINGTON. According to this myth, as explained by Van Doren's follower, critic Anthony Hilfer in his 1969 book *The Revolt from the Village, 1915–1930*, the village, with its "togetherness" or sense of community, its innocence, and its simplicity, had been portrayed as the ideal antithesis to the city, with its alienation, its vice, and its complexity (3–34). Keillor's work sometimes alternates between and sometimes reconciles the two perspectives in a deft ambiguity. Reverence and nostalgia and rather gentle humor are predominant in the radio work, while witty satire is more pronounced in the writings, allowing overall the same range of response as *American Gothic*. The qualities revealed in Lake Wobegon, Minnesota, and the Midwest include a sense of community along with conformity and repression, innocence along with smugness and moral naivete, and, most elaborately developed of all, wholesome simplicity along with blandness, cautiousness, stagnation, and torpor.

Most of Keillor's work seems rooted in an ongoing analysis of his relationship to his past and his Midwestern home. Stories of entrapment and escape alternate and are mixed with stories, in an equally imaginative variety, of attempts to go back home again or, at least, to reconnect and be reconciled, almost corresponding to the way live broadcasts of *A Prairie Home Companion* have alternated in recent years between New York City and St. Paul. And for millions of readers and listeners, Keillor has provided entertainment and revelation of their own identities.

**SELECTED WORKS:** *Happy to Be Here* (1982) is an early collection of sketches and stories, most of them from the *New Yorker*. *Lake Wobegon Days* (1985) is Keillor's most popular book. *Leaving Home* (1987) brings together reworked versions of thirty-six Lake Wobegon monologues. Two later collections of stories, poems, and other short pieces, some versions of which Keillor has used on the radio, are *We Are Still Married* (1989) and *The Book of Guys* (1993). *WLT: A Radio Romance* (1991) has been called Keillor's first true novel. *The Sandy Bottom Orchestra* (1996), coauthored with Keillor's violinist wife Jenny Lind Nilsson, is a coming-of-age novel, intended especially for younger readers, of a fourteen-year-old vio-

linist named Rachel in a small Wisconsin town. *Wobegon Boy* (1997) chronicles the adventures of a middle-aged Lake Wobegon native in upstate New York, as director of a campus radio station, and back in his hometown during the 1980s and 1990s.

**FURTHER READING:** Judith Lee's *Garrison Keillor: A Voice of America* (1991) offers a thoughtful analysis of Keillor's radio work and writings. Peter Scholl's Twayne book, *Garrison Keillor* (1993), is a solid, well-researched biographical and critical study. Michael Fedo's *The Man from Lake Wobegon* (1987) is, as Peter Scholl says, "long on interviews and short on analysis" (244).

WAYNE H. MEYER          BALL STATE UNIVERSITY

# WILLIAM X(AVIER) KIENZLE
September 11, 1928

**BIOGRAPHY:** William X. Kienzle was born in Detroit, Michigan, the son of Alphonzo and Mary Louise (Boyle) Kienzle. He attended Sacred Heart Seminary High School and College, where he received a BA in 1950 and was ordained a Roman Catholic priest in 1954. He also attended the University of Detroit in 1968. As a Detroit diocesan priest, Kienzle served in five different parishes.

Kienzle's literary attachment to Detroit stems from his having grown up, gone to school, and entered the priesthood there. In 1974, he left the priesthood, not to get married but because of marriage laws and other constraining rules. The September 15, 1983, *Detroit Free Press* quotes him as saying, "I left because there are 2,414 laws and I can't think of one I like" (5B). Kienzle's editorship of *The Michigan Catholic* from 1962 to 1974 put him in contact with a copy editor for the *Free Press*, Javan Andrews, who later became his wife. She is now also his foremost editor and plot critic. From 1974 until 1977, they lived in Minneapolis, Minnesota, where Kienzle became an editor and review and feature writer for *MPLS*, a city magazine. In 1977, Kienzle accepted a teaching position at the Center for Contemplative Study at Western Michigan University and moved to Dallas, Texas, when the center moved, remaining there until 1979. Kienzle chose to write mystery novels because his experience as a priest and journalist left him with an array of anecdotal material that he could retell in this popular genre.

Kienzle was awarded the Society for the

**William X. Kienzle.**
Photo courtesy of William X. Kienzle

Study of Midwestern Literature's 2000 Mark Twain Award for distinguished contributions to Midwestern literature. He lives in Rochester, Michigan, a Detroit suburb.

**SIGNIFICANCE:** In his first novel, *The Rosary Murders* (1979), Kienzle created the character of Father Robert Koesler, the diocesan priest who became the protagonist of all his detective novels. Koesler, with his expertise in ecclesiastical matters, helps Detroit police detectives solve cases involving canon law and other complexities of the Catholic Church. *The Rosary Murders* was made into a 1987 film starring Donald Sutherland and Charles Durning, with screenplay by ELMORE LEONARD.

Aside from theological mysteries interspersed with humorous anecdotes, Bill Kienzle's work incorporates thoughtful interpretation of the office of the priesthood as well as a critique of the complex, authoritarian religious hierarchy. He notes that Detroit, as well as being the city most familiar to him, is an ideal venue for his novels. In his March 28, 1998, letter to Russell Bodi, Kienzle states, "Detroit has been in the forefront of all the blessings as well as the woes of the post-conciliar era . . . . Detroit was the birthplace of the international 'Call To Action.' Nowhere is there a more open confrontation between Catholic progressives and traditionalists. In conclusion, Detroit has become a natural setting for Catholic murder mysteries." Kienzle represents protagonists who must mediate between authoritarian Rome and democratic America. His particularly satirical view of the Catholic Church's marriage laws exemplifies his love for and his keen understanding of the Catholic Church and all its flaws. William X. Kienzle incorporates an academic's grasp of heady religious subject matter, a scholar's hand for research, and a stylist's ear for a well-turned phrase.

**SELECTED WORKS:** A William X. Kienzle novel has appeared annually since 1979. In *The Rosary Murders,* his first novel, Robert Koesler must solve a serial killing spree aligned with theological phenomena. In *Deadline for a Critic* (1987), an unpopular performing-arts critic is murdered, and Father Koesler discovers the spiritual motivation. In *Body Count* (1992), Kienzle explores the concept of the seal of confession. In *Call No Man Father* (1995), Kienzle tackles papal infallibility, demonstrating how the concept varies in interpretation. One of Kienzle's best critical illuminations of the Church's stand on controversial issues is in *The Greatest Evil* (1998), where a couple struggles with pre–Vatican II marriage laws, and a bishop excommunicates his sister, a doctor, for performing abortions. Father Koesler advises the doctor that the church's teaching on abortion is no more infallible than he or she is. Other Kienzle novels include *Death Wears a Red Hat* (1980), *Mind over Murder* (1981), *Assault with Intent* (1982), *Shadow of Death* (1983), *Kill and Tell* (1984), *Sudden Death* (1985), *Deathbed* (1986), *Marked for Murder* (1988), *Eminence* (1989), *Masquerade* (1990), *Chameleon* (1991), *Dead Wrong* (1993), *Bishop as Pawn* (1994), *Requiem for Moses* (1996), *The Man Who Loved God* (1997), and *No Greater Love* (1999).

**FURTHER READING:** Russell J. Bodi's Spring 1999 *Midwestern Miscellany* article "Priestly Sleuths: Mystery in Midwestern Urban Settings" (27: 32–40) uses the writings of William Kienzle and Andrew Greeley to exemplify the dilemma facing contemporary urban Catholic clergy in reconciling the church's dogmatism with democratic America. Bodi's "William X. Kienzle and the Seal of Confession," forthcoming in *Clues: A Journal of Detection*, examines how the seal of confession creates tension in fiction, particularly in William X. Kienzle's novels. Kienzle's first eight manuscripts have been lost in transportation during processing. The rest are housed at the University of Detroit Library.

RUSSELL J. BODI                    OWENS COLLEGE

## W(ILLIAM) P(ATRICK) KINSELLA
May 25, 1935

**BIOGRAPHY:** A Canadian whose passion for America's national pastime has inspired much of his best fiction, William Patrick Kinsella was born, raised, and educated in Edmonton, Alberta, the only child of John and Olive (Elliot) Kinsella. He has described himself as born with a compulsion to write. He has been writing fiction for most of his life although he did not publish his first book until he was forty-two. After his marriage in 1957 to Myrna Stalls, he worked at a variety of white-collar jobs to support his wife and three children while writing short stories in his spare time. The couple divorced in 1963.

In 1965 Kinsella married Mildred Clay; five years later, he matriculated at the University of Victoria, where he earned a BA in 1974. The Kinsellas then moved to Iowa City, Iowa, where he enrolled in the Writers' Workshop at the University of Iowa and taught there for two years, publishing his first short story collection, *Dance Me Outside*, in 1977. The following year the University of Iowa awarded Kinsella an MFA; also that year, Kinsella divorced his wife, married Ann Knight, and joined the Department of English at the University of Calgary, where he would teach for the next several years.

In 1982 Kinsella's first novel, *Shoeless Joe*, won the Houghton-Mifflin Literary Fellowship, enabling him to resign his university position the following year and devote himself full time to writing fiction. The success of the 1989 film *Field of Dreams*, based on this novel, enhanced Kinsella's growing literary reputation. He lives in Blaine, Washington.

**SIGNIFICANCE:** Kinsella's main subjects are baseball and Indians. Many of his early stories feature a young Cree narrator, Silas Ermineskin, who has been called a Canadian Huck Finn by some critics. Kinsella's baseball

fiction blends humor, fantasy, and realism, often depicting characters who find themselves committed to an idealistic quest. His best-known novel, *Shoeless Joe* (1982), tells the story of an eccentric Iowa farmer and an unpublished author who is visited by the spirits of the Chicago White Sox team of 1919, including Shoeless Joe Jackson, when he builds a baseball diamond in his cornfield.

In Kinsella's fiction, the state of Iowa is both a place for heroes and family reconciliation and a place where spirits of displaced Native Americans and generations of disappointed settlers and farmers coexist, brooding. The romantic Ray Kinsella of *Shoeless Joe* is not encouraged by his neighbors, and the obsessive baseball historian Gideon Clarke of *The Iowa Baseball Confederacy* (1986) is quite mad. In *Shoeless Joe*, as in other Kinsella stories, his characters, in the American Midwest and on the Cree reservations of Canada, are often motivated by a sense of need and loss, failed or fated aspiration, or broken relationships. His portrayal of Iowa, for example, is less promising than it appears in the popular film. In *Shoeless Joe*, Joe Jackson and Ray Kinsella meet with the following exchange: "'God, what an outfield,' he says. 'What a left field.' He looks up at me and I look down at him. 'This must be heaven,' he says. 'No. It's Iowa,' I reply automatically'" (16). While *Field of Dreams* changes the dialogue slightly to suggest that Iowa could be heaven, Kinsella's novel, with its strong negative portrayal of agribusiness and the farm community establishment, leaves the proposition dubious. *The Thrill of the Grass* (1984) provides an often sad account of minor league towns in Iowa and Canada but contains a fantastic triumph of fans who secretly replace an artificial turf with real grass.

**SELECTED WORKS:** Kinsella's short story collections include *Dance Me Outside* (1977), *Scars* (1980), *Shoeless Joe Jackson Comes to Iowa* (1980), *The Moccasin Telegraph and Other Tales* (1983), *The Thrill of the Grass* (1984), *The Alligator Report* (1985), *The Fencepost Chronicles* (1986), *Red Wolf, Red Wolf* (1987), *The Further Adventures of Slugger McBatt* (1988), *The Dixon Cornbelt League* (1993), and *Brother Frank's Gospel Hour* (1994). His novels include *Shoeless Joe* (1982), *The Iowa Baseball Confederacy* (1986), *Box Socials* (1992), and *The Winter Helen Dropped By* (1995).

**FURTHER READING:** Don Murray's *The Fic-*

tion of *W. P. Kinsella: Tall Tales in Various Voices* (1987) is the only book-length study of Kinsella's work. Recent articles include Neil Randall's "*Shoeless Joe*: Fantasy and the Humor of Fellow-Feeling," in *Modern Fiction Studies* 33 (Spring 1987): 173–82; Bryan Garman's "Myth Building and Cultural Politics in W. P. Kinsella's *Shoeless Joe*," in *Canadian Review of American Studies* 24 (Winter 1994): 41–62; and Clarence Jenkins's "Kinsella's *Shoeless Joe*," in *Explicator* 53 (Spring 1995): 179–80. Interviews include R. C. Fedderson's "Interview with W. P. Kinsella," in *Short Story* 1 (Fall 1993): 81–88. Ann Knight has published *W. P. Kinsella: A Partially-Annotated Bibliographical Checklist, 1953–83* (1983). Some of Kinsella's manuscripts can be found at the National Library of Canada in Ottawa.

THOMAS PRIBEK
UNIVERSITY OF WISCONSIN–LACROSSE

## RUSSELL (AMOS) KIRK
October 19, 1918–April 29, 1994

**BIOGRAPHY:** Russell Kirk was born in Plymouth, Michigan, the first child of Russell Andrew and Marjorie Rachel (Pierce) Kirk. He earned a BA in history from Michigan State College, now Michigan State University, in 1940 and an MA in history from Duke University in 1941. Kirk joined the army in 1942 and served through 1946. After World War II, Kirk came to Michigan State as an assistant professor teaching the history of civilization. In 1948 he departed for St. Andrews University in Scotland, receiving his doctor of letters degree in 1952. His doctoral dissertation was published as *The Conservative Mind* (1953).

Kirk's first book, *Randolph of Roanoke: A Study in Conservative Thought*, was published in 1951, but it was his second book, *The Conservative Mind*, which made his reputation as a leading conservative thinker. Kirk's conservatism is a matter of temper and sensibility more than doctrine. The book reflects this orientation with chapters on such literary figures as Walter Scott, Samuel Coleridge, James Fenimore Cooper, James Russell Lowell, Henry Adams, Paul Elmer More, and Irving Babbitt, as well as George Santayana and T. S. ELIOT. In 1953 Kirk resigned from Michigan State and moved to Mecosta, Michigan, where he spent the rest of his life. In 1955 he began writing a column, "From the Academy," for the then-new conservative journal *National Review*. Kirk himself founded and edited two journals, *Modern Age* (1957) and the *University Bookman* (1960). In 1961 Kirk wrote *Old House of Fear*, a Gothic novel that sold more copies than anything else he ever wrote.

Kirk became a Roman Catholic in 1964 and in the same year married Annette Courtemanche. They had four daughters. Kirk received at least eleven honorary doctorates, and in 1989 he was awarded the Presidential Citizen's Medal for Distinguished Service to the United States. His last major publication was an autobiographical work, *The Sword of Imagination: Memoirs of a Half-Century of Literary Conflict* (1995). In that book Kirk describes himself not as a political figure but as a "a man of letters" (1) who has "drawn the sword of imagination" in battle against "the follies of the time" (476). Russell Kirk died at his home, Piety Hill, on Friday, April 29, 1994.

**SIGNIFICANCE:** As a political figure, Russell Kirk was best-known as the leading voice of what came to be known as "paleoconservatism," in contrast not only to liberalism but also to "neoconservatism." He has often been credited or blamed for providing the intellectual starting point for the revival of political conservatism in recent decades. Kirk's lasting significance, however, is cultural rather than political. His most important book, *The Conservative Mind*, avoids narrow partisanship. Taking Edmund Burke as the founder of modern conservatism, Kirk praises Burke's emphasis on "the moral imagination, which sets men apart from beasts" (59). Utilitarianism is excoriated for ignoring "the immense variety of human motives" (100) dramatized in the novels of Bentham's contemporary, Walter Scott. Kirk condemns modern intellectuals not so much for their leftist opinions as for their neglect of "the imagination, the powers of insight and wonder, and the whole realm of being that is beyond private rational perception" (416). In essays collected in works such as *Beyond the Dreams of Avarice* (1956), *Confessions of a Bohemian Tory* (1963), and *The Intemperate Professor* (1965), Kirk united literary flair with powerful social and cultural criticism of contemporary life.

Kirk's third-person memoir, *The Sword of Imagination*, seems likely to achieve a high rank among American intellectual autobiographies. In that work Kirk describes himself as "a Michigan backwoodsman" (184) who delights in his "Mecostan existence unpolluted by carbon monoxide and other progressive poisons" (164). Kirk's romantic "Gothic mind" (68) may seem at odds with his Midwestern roots. Kirk himself, however, finds Midwestern reality just as strange and romantic as, for example, the South of Flannery O'Connor. Comparing O'Connor's "Southern Gothic" fiction to his own, Kirk comments that he "well understood her fantastic and her depraved characters, their twisted faith and all, because precisely such people lived about him in Mecosta County; they emerged repeatedly in his own stories" (183).

Russell Kirk, like his fellow Midwesterners Paul Elmer More and Irving Babbitt, affirms a temper and spirit apparently at odds with the dominant trends in American society. Kirk's best work, however, like the best of More and Babbitt, may well survive.

**SELECTED WORKS:** New editions of Kirk's most important book, *The Conservative Mind*, have appeared regularly since its first publication in 1953; later editions are subtitled *From Burke to Eliot* rather than the original *From Burke to Santayana*. Kirk's most sustained work of literary criticism is *Eliot and His Age: T. S. Eliot's Moral Imagination in the Twentieth Century* (1971). *The Roots of American Order* (1974) traces the Western cultural heritage to its origins. *The Politics of Prudence* (1993) includes essays and speeches on political issues. Some of Kirk's best writing occurs in his essay collections on literary and cultural topics, such as *Beyond the Dreams of Avarice* (1956), *Confessions of a Bohemian Tory* (1963), *The Intemperate Professor, and Other Cultural Splenetics* (1965), *Enemies of the Permanent Things* (1969), and *Decadence and Renewal in the Higher Learning* (1978). Kirk published three novels: *Old House of Fear* (1961), *A Creature of the Twilight* (1966), and *Lord of the Hollow Dark* (1979), as well as three short story collections: *The Surly Sullen Bell* (1962), *The Princess of All Lands* (1979), and *Watchers at the Strait Gate* (1984). Kirk's autobiography, *The Sword of Imagination: Memoirs of a Half-Century of Literary Conflict*, was published in 1995.

**FURTHER READING:** *The Unbought Grace of Life: Essays in Honor of Russell Kirk*, edited by James E. Person Jr. (1994), is a Festschrift including essays by Forrest McDonald, Robert Nisbet, and Peter Stanlis, among others. The fall 1994 issue of *Intercollegiate Review* is dedicated to "Russell Kirk: Man of Letters," with essays assessing his achievement by figures such as George Panichas, Roger Scruton, and Gerhart Niemeyer.

JAMES SEATON                MICHIGAN STATE UNIVERSITY

## CAROLINE KIRKLAND
January 11, 1801–April 6, 1864

**BIOGRAPHY:** Although the Midwestern frontier inspired her first three books, it is probable that Caroline Kirkland would have become an author even had she never accompanied her husband to the Michigan wilderness. Her mother, Eliza (Alexander) Stansbury, raised eleven children yet found time to read novels and write poems, sketches, and stories; her paternal grandfather, Joseph Stansbury, was a Tory satirist who published his verses in the *Royal Gazette*.

Kirkland's father, Samuel Stansbury, enrolled his eldest child in a Quaker school run by his sister, Lydia Mott, where she learned French, Latin, Greek, and German. In 1819, while teaching school in upstate New York, she met William Kirkland, then teaching at Hamilton College; they married in 1828 and opened their own school in nearby Geneva, where four children were born to them.

In 1835 the Kirklands accepted positions at the Detroit Female Seminary and began buying land in Michigan near Ann Arbor, where they founded the town of Pinckney. They moved there in the fall of 1837; shortly thereafter, Kirkland began to write stories and sketches based on the pioneering experiences that would inspire her first three books.

Personal and financial considerations prompted the Kirklands to return to the East, and in 1843 they opened a school in New York City. After William died in 1846, Caroline spent her seventeen-year widowhood writing, editing, traveling, teaching, presiding over a literary salon, and working for the Union cause during the Civil War. She died in New York City of a stroke after supervising a fund-raiser for the U.S. Sanitary Commission.

**SIGNIFICANCE:** Caroline Kirkland is one of the first American authors to write from the perspective of the Western settler. Writing against the romantic tradition then in vogue in American literature, she anticipates in her three Midwestern books the prairie realism of EDGAR WATSON HOWE, DAVID ROSS LOCKE,

EDWARD EGGLESTON, and her own son, Illinois novelist JOSEPH KIRKLAND.

*A New Home—Who'll Follow?* (1839) is considered the most unified and best written of her three frontier works. Like her contemporary Margaret Fuller, who writes about her experiences in the same region in *Summer on the Lakes* (1843), Kirkland emphasizes the natural garden-cultural desert dichotomy as characteristic of the frontier Midwest. Her realistic portrayal of frontier democracy in a thinly disguised Pinckney emphasizes the beauties of the natural scene as well as the infelicities of pioneer life: prostrating agues, unpalatable food, unscrupulous land sharks, and, in particular, the crude manners of her pipe-smoking, snuff-taking, meddlesome, gossipy neighbors.

Her descriptions of the latter so antagonized the Pinckney community that Kirkland's second book, *Forest Life* (1842), focuses on the Michigan frontier region in general rather than on a particular village. These essays, sketches, and stories are energized and informed by the tension between city and country, Yankee and British, East and West, aristocracy and democracy. Kirkland chronicles such frontier happenings as a political parade through the forest, a donation party at a clergyman's home, a mill-raising, and a shivaree. Her satirical pen skewers her Michigan neighbors, emphasizing their propensity to fell every tree, their lust for pork, and their compulsion to ape New York fashions and manners. *Western Clearings* (1845), her third frontier book, is a compilation of plotless sketches and lively, opinionated essays spiced with frontier dialect and unflinchingly exact descriptions of the people of Michigan Territory.

**SELECTED WORKS:** In addition to the three books on frontier Michigan, Kirkland published three miscellanies: *The Evening Book* (1852), *A Book for the Home Circle* (1853), and *Autumn Hours and Fireside Reading* (1854). She also edited two volumes of verse, *Garden Walks with the Poets* (1852) and *The School-Girl's Garland* (1864), and published a book of travel sketches, *Holidays Abroad; or Europe from the West* (1849). She published two books for young people, *Spenser and the Faery Queen* (1854) and *Personal Memoirs of George Washington* (1857), as well as a plea for the rehabilitation of female convicts, *The Helping Hand* (1853).

**FURTHER READING:** The only book-length study of Kirkland is William S. Osborne's *Caroline M. Kirkland* (1972). Annette Kolodny devotes a chapter to Kirkland in *The Land Before Her* (1984). *Legacy* 8.2 (1991): 133–40 includes a profile of Kirkland by Stacy Spencer; *Legacy* 12.1 (1995): 17–37 contains Dawn Keetley's "Unsettling the Frontier: Gender and Racial Identity in Caroline Kirkland's *A New Home—Who'll Follow?* and *Forest Life*." Kelli A. Larson looks at Kirkland's work from a feminist perspective in "Kirkland's Myth of the American Eve: Re-Visioning the Frontier Experience," in *Midwestern Miscellany* 20 (1992): 9–14.

Kirkland's papers are widely scattered. The largest collections of her letters can be found at the New York Public Library, the Massachusetts Historical Society, and the Cornell University Library. Some manuscripts are held by the Cincinnati Historical Society and the Newberry Library.

MARCIA NOE
THE UNIVERSITY OF TENNESSEE AT CHATTANOOGA

## JOSEPH KIRKLAND
January 7, 1830–April 28, 1893

**BIOGRAPHY:** Joseph Kirkland was born in Geneva, New York, to William and CAROLINE (STANSBURY) KIRKLAND. One of the earliest novelists and historians of the Midwest, he was introduced to his future subject matter in 1835 when, as a toddler, he moved with his family to Michigan Territory, where his mother, Caroline, wrote three books describing Michigan frontier culture.

Although the family moved back to New York in 1843, and Kirkland subsequently held a number of jobs, including sailor, auditor for the Illinois Central Railroad, and coal mine supervisor, the early influence of his educator/writer parents was strong. After resigning his Union Army commission, Kirkland moved to Tilton, Illinois, and married Theodosia Wilkinson in 1863. The following year he founded a Midwestern literary periodical called the *Prairie Chicken*.

In 1868 Kirkland moved his family to Chicago and subsequently began a successful legal practice there. He also played an important role in the first phase of the Chicago Renaissance: founding the Chicago Literary Club, serving as literary editor of the *Chicago Tribune*, and writing three novels, three works on the history of Chicago, and nu-

**Joseph Kirkland.**
Courtesy of the University of Kentucky Libraries

merous articles, stories, essays, and reviews. He also served as a literary mentor to the fledgling novelist HAMLIN GARLAND, who modeled his own stories of Midwestern misery on Kirkland's fiction. Kirkland died of a heart attack at his home in Chicago.

**SIGNIFICANCE:** Joseph Kirkland was one of the prairie realists who exposed in their novels the limitations of the Jeffersonian dream of the West. Like EDWARD EGGLESTON, EDGAR WATSON HOWE, Hamlin Garland, and DAVID ROSS LOCKE, he provided an unvarnished account of nineteenth-century rural life in the Midwest and laid the groundwork for the revolt from the village movement of early-twentieth-century Midwestern literature.

Kirkland's three novels are set in Illinois. *Zury: The Meanest Man in Spring County* (1887) is one of the earliest fictional portraits of the Midwestern farmer: frugal, forehanded, practical, and hardworking. Moreover, this novel, as well as its sequel, *The McVeys: An Episode* (1888), is valuable for the detailed record it provides of Midwestern frontier life and language. Hamlin Garland called *Zury* "the best picture of pioneer Illinois life yet written" and praised Kirkland's realistic rendering of regional dialect (*Roadside Meetings* 106). Kirk-

land's fictionalized account of his experiences in the Union Army, *The Captain of Company K* (1891), is set in Chicago and in Cairo at the Union training camp; in its realistic depiction of battle conditions it anticipates *The Red Badge of Courage.*

**SELECTED WORKS:** Kirkland published six books: the three Illinois novels discussed above as well as *The Story of Chicago* (1892) and *The Chicago Massacre of 1812* (1893). With John Moses he edited *The History of Chicago, Illinois* (1895).

**FURTHER READING:** The only book-length study of Kirkland's work is Clyde E. Henson's *Joseph Kirkland* (1962). Ronald Grosh's three-part article on early American literary realism, published in volumes 15, 16, and 17 of *Mid-America*, discusses Kirkland's work as part of the tradition of the prairie realists. Kirkland's papers can be found in the Newberry Library, Chicago.

MARCIA NOE
THE UNIVERSITY OF TENNESSEE AT CHATTANOOGA

## WILLIAM KLOEFKORN
August 12, 1932

**BIOGRAPHY:** "I'm drawn quite often to the small town and the farm because that's where most of my early epiphanies occurred," Kloefkorn told J. V. Brummels in 1983 (*On Common Ground* 31). Born in Attica, Kansas, to Katie Marie (Yock) and Ralph Kloefkorn, Bill Kloefkorn spent his childhood in Wichita during World War II. After graduating from Emporia State College in 1954, Kloefkorn entered the Marine Corps, where as a lieutenant he commanded an anti-tank assault platoon. He then taught high school for several years, returned to Emporia State for the MA, and joined the English Department at Wichita State University. In 1962 he moved to Nebraska Wesleyan University, where he taught English until his retirement in 1998.

Despite his teaching position, Kloefkorn is a down-to-earth person whose hobbies include kite building, whittling walking sticks, and hog calling. He won the Nebraska state hog-calling championship in 1978. In 1982 Kloefkorn was named Nebraska State Poet. He and his wife, Eloise, whom he married in 1953, are the parents of four children and the grandparents of nine.

**SIGNIFICANCE:** "I started writing poetry when I finally realized that my small-town years, the experiences I had accumulated over those years, might be worth writing about," Kloefkorn told J. V. Brummels (*On Common Ground* 30). Realism, humor, and sensitivity to the smallest nuances of Midwestern life characterize Kloefkorn's work, although over the course of twenty published books he has grown more comfortable with his own voice and less reliant on a persona. *Alvin Turner as Farmer* (1977) recounts the history of a Kansas dirt farmer modeled largely on the poet's grandfather. *Platte Valley Homestead* (1981) chronicles the battles of nineteenth-century German immigrants Jacob and Anna with a hostile environment. In other collections Kloefkorn adopts the personae of an adolescent male, or an aging, comfortably married middle-class man. In later books such as *Collecting for the Wichita Beacon* and *A Life Like Mine,* Kloefkorn drops the personae and explores a personal past recounted in the poet's own voice. In *Dragging Sand Creek for Minnows* (1992) the poet adopts, in various poems, the voices of a child, adolescent, parent, spouse, and even grandparent. Despite the personal roots of his poetry, Kloefkorn's world is at the same time his own, ours, our collective parents' and grandparents'. His work is accessible without being simplistic.

Kloefkorn's primary subject is life in Great Plains villages and farmyards. "These are where very basic things happen: birth, death, sun rising, sun going down," Kloefkorn says (*On Common Ground* 31). The poet is engaged, however, in a pioneer's quarrel with his social and geographical environment. His work conveys a sense of belonging to, and being renewed by, nature, as well as a sense of alienation and hardship. In *Alvin Turner,* adversity is symbolized by rock, which Turner must learn to plow around, not through. In *Platte Valley Homestead,* adversity is water, which Jacob must learn can purify as well as drown. Kloefkorn's quotidian is not without spiritual, usually biblical, significance and yields readily to archetypal interpretation. "I grew up singing hymns loaded with rock and water metaphors," says Kloefkorn (*On Common Ground* 32). Marriage is a repeated motif in his poetry, most fully explored in *Honeymoon* (1982). For Kloefkorn, as for his acknowledged models Geoffrey Chaucer and Wendell Berry, a healthy marriage is a metaphor for a sound

relationship with the environment and for all intimate social relationships.

**SELECTED WORKS:** *Alvin Turner as Farmer* (1977) remains one of Kloefkorn's most important works; other collections include *Uncertain the Final Run to Winter* (1974), *loony* (1975), *ludi jr* (1976), *Stocker* (1978), *Leaving Town* (1979), *Not Such a Bad Place to Be* (1980), *Platte Valley Homestead* (1981), *Houses and Beyond* (1982), *Honeymoon for Doris (1933–2032)* (1982), *A Life Like Mine* (1984), *Collecting for the Wichita Beacon* (1984), *Drinking the Tin Cup Dry* (1989), *Where the Visible Sun Is* (1989), *Dragging Sand Creek for Minnows* (1992), *Going Out, Coming Back* (1993), *Burning the Hymnal* (1994), and (with David Lee) *Covenants* (1996). No volume of collected or selected poems has been published.

**FURTHER READING:** Useful essays on Kloefkorn's work include DAVE ETTER's "Master Poem Maker on the Great Plains" and Mark Sanders's "Rocks, Water, and Fire: Kloefkorn's Use of Symbol," in *On Common Ground: The Poetry of William Kloefkorn, Ted Kooser, Greg Kuzma, and Don Welch,* edited by J. V. Brummels and Mark Sanders (1983). Sanders's essay is followed by an interview; other published interviews include David Cicotello's "Stay against Chaos," in *Midwest Quarterly* (Spring 1983): 274–82, and Kenneth Robbins's "A Conversation with William Kloefkorn," in *South Dakota Review* (Fall 1994): 89–100. *Burning the Hymnal* contains a bibliography of published poems through early 1993. Jane Pierce wrote a master's thesis entitled "William Kloefkorn: His Works and His Women" at South Dakota State University (1985).

DAVID PICHASKE        SOUTHWEST STATE UNIVERSITY

## JOHN (IGNATIUS) KNOEPFLE
February 4, 1923

**BIOGRAPHY:** John Knoepfle, poet, prose writer, folklorist, translator, and professor of literature and creative writing, was born in Cincinnati, Ohio, to a Swiss father, Rudolph Knoepfle, and an Irish Catholic mother, Catherine (Brickley) Knoepfle. Rudolph traveled the Midwest selling and arranging film programs for theaters. John, the youngest of four brothers, was educated at St. Xavier High School and the University of Cincinnati, receiving a PhB in 1947, an MA in 1949, and a PhD in 1967 at St. Louis University. Between 1956 and 1991 he taught at several schools in the Midwest including Ohio State University, Southern Illinois University Residence Center at East St. Louis, St. Louis University High School, and Maryville College of the Sacred Heart in St. Louis. At St. Louis University he was director of creative writing, and at Sangamon State University, professor of literature. He was affiliated with Mark Twain Institute, Washington University College, and the State University of New York at Buffalo. He worked as a producer-director for WCET educational television in 1954–55, and between 1954 and 1960 he made fifty one-hour audio tape recordings of rivermen of the inland rivers, "The Knoepfle Collection." Between 1965 and 1970 he was a consultant to Project Upward Bound, a federal poverty program enabling high-risk high school students to study at universities. A second group of Midwestern materials, "The Peoria-Miami Language Collection" comprising Jesuit, Native American, and Anglo-American sources collected by Knoepfle, is in his possession. He and his wife, Margaret (Sower) Knoepfle, have traveled widely to research the history of Illinois cities and towns. They have been married since 1956 and have four children; a fifth is deceased. John and Margaret reside in Auburn, Illinois.

**SIGNIFICANCE:** Knoepfle has admitted the influence of Melville, Frost, and William Carlos Williams on his writing. His interest in the language of the Midwest was stimulated significantly by his experiences in taping the rivermen, by his teaching people who lived and spoke in East St. Louis, and by his particular sensitivity to the vernacular, which he developed researching the historical records of Midwestern settlers, Native Americans, and the Jesuits. From these sources, in a language spare, intense, and often meditational, he has built his most effective poetic statements of Midwestern life. Like EDGAR LEE MASTERS, VACHEL LINDSAY, and CARL SANDBURG before him, Knoepfle includes himself with the people, though his scope is broader than that of Masters and his sense of the riverlife keener. His spiritual and literary identifications with the river are evident in "church of rose of lima, cincinnati" and "june night on the river" in *Rivers into Islands* (1965). In his masterwork, *poems from the sangamon* (1985), direct speech of his Midwestern persona integrates with locale in "marquette in winter camp, chicago river,

John Knoepfle.
Courtesy of John Knoepfle

1675," "lunchroom, new berlin," and "kickapoo dance." Figures as diverse as Chief BLACK HAWK, Richard Nixon, and a member of a posse that captured Big Harpe, an Ohio River outlaw, appear in *selected poems* (1985).

Knoepfle makes use not only of actual characters from Midwestern and national records but also of place, poignantly rendered. As a major Midwestern poet and writer about the life of the Midwest, he names anew major cities—Springfield, Chicago, St. Louis, Cincinnati—as well as counties and towns of Illinois—McLean, Sangamon, Menard, Edwardsville, Normal, and Buckles Grove. Throughout his poetry Knoepfle brings together historic past and present successes and failures to cause Americans to rediscover who we are. In "decatur" in *sangamon* he assays past and present struggles of laborers inland. In "confluence" the Sangamon, Illinois, and Mississippi Rivers are great connectors of his Midwestern vision. In his poems pertaining to ABRAHAM LINCOLN in *poems from the sangamon* and *the chinkapin oak* (1995), Knoepfle's commonality merges with Lincoln's and those of people of Illinois and the nation, revealing the depth and extent of historical consciousness informing much of his writing. His numerous awards from the people of Illinois and the 1986

Mark Twain Award for distinguished contributions to Midwestern literature from the Society for the Study of Midwestern Literature attest to his significance.

SELECTED WORKS: Knoepfle's full expression of his poetic art and best treatment of Midwestern culture appears in *poems from the sangamon* (1985). His *selected poems* (1985) brings together many of his best poems before 1985. *Rivers into Islands* (1965) and *the intricate land* (1970) show Knoepfle's deep attachment to the rivers, land, and people of the Midwest. *Begging an Amnesty* (1994) broadens scope from the Midwest to the American West. Knoepfle's most recent poetry appears in *the chinkapin oak* (1995), which deals with a year in the life of Springfield, Illinois. Important smaller publications are *Voyages to the Inland Sea* (1971), with Lisel Mueller and DAVE ETTER, and the meditational *Poems for the Hours* (1979). *T'ang Dynasty Poems* and *Song Dynasty Poems* (both 1985) contain seventy-three and fifty-three Chinese poems respectively, translated by Knoepfle and his colleague Wang Shouyi. A significant group of Midwestern folktales is *Dim Tales* (1989). A Haikai No Renga form, *Illinois Fields in Summer*, with Harris Hatcher and Deborah Newbolt, appeared in *Sangamon Poets 13* (1993). In a series of "Green Snake Interviews" appearing in *Kansas Quarterly* (Winter–Spring 1990): 88–103, readers will find "memories of kansas," "taping the rivermen," and "the prairie poets" forthcoming.

FURTHER READING: The chief study of Knoepfle's poetry is the doctoral dissertation by John Frederick Garmon, "Aspects of Place in the Poetry of John Knoepfle" (Ball State University, 1979). Its bibliography is complemented by background material in "John Knoepfle Memoir," with Margery Towery, and "The John Knoepfle Collection" at the University of Illinois at Springfield. Relevant articles that deal wholly or in part with Midwestern concerns include James F. Scott's "The Metropolitan Sensibility: Notes on Four Poets of St. Louis," in *Cross Currents* 15 (1965): 487–91; Raymond Benoit's "The Reflective Art of John Knoepfle," in *Minnesota Review* 8.3 (1968): 254–57; Ralph Mills Jr.'s "Some Notes on John Knoepfle's Poetry," in *Northeast* 3.6 (Winter 1978–79): 31–45; Helen Mandeville's "New Poems by John Knoepfle," in *Late Harvest: Plains and Prairie Poets*, edited by Robert Killoren (1977); Norman Hinton's "The Poetry of John

Knoepfle," in *Western Illinois Regional Studies* 8.2 (1985): 34–52; Theodore Haddin's "John Knoepfle's Historical Consciousness and the Renaming of America," in *Chariton Review* 12.2 (1986): 87–93; Todd Moore's "The Language of Prairies: The Poetry of John Knoepfle," in *Spoon River Poetry Review* 20.2 (1995): 157–61. Also strategic for Knoepfle's Midwestern image are Dan Jaffe's review article in *Great Lakes Review* 10.1 (1976): 94–98; Michael Kincaid's "Indian Pictures on a Rock," in *Illinois Writer's Review* (Spring–Fall): 2–6; Anne C. Bromley's review article in *Prairie Schooner* (Winter 1989): 22–27; Patricia Rice's "A Poet Finds Fertile Ground in the Farm Belt," in *St. Louis Post-Dispatch* (May 20, 1986): 3D; and Dan Guillory's "Poet of the Prairie," in *Illinois Times* 2.14 (1985): 28–29. James McGowan celebrates Knoepfle's Midwestern folklore and language in discussing *Dim Tales* in *Illinois Writer's Review* 9.2 (1990): 5–9. A film documentary, *Inland Voyages: The Poetry of John Knoepfle*, directed and produced by James F. Scott (1995), is available at St. Louis University.

The Knoepfle Collection of audio cassettes and transcripts of rivermen is in the Division of Inland Rivers, Public Library of Cincinnati and Hamilton County, Ohio, as well as in the archives of the University of Illinois at Springfield. The Peoria-Miami Language Collection of Jesuit, Central Algonquian, French, and Anglo-American sources will be placed in the Illinois State Museum Annex.

THEODORE HADDIN
THE UNIVERSITY OF ALABAMA AT BIRMINGHAM

# HERBERT KRAUSE
May 25, 1905–September 22, 1976

BIOGRAPHY: Born on a small farm in Otter Tail County, Minnesota, to Arthur and Bertha (Peters) Krause, Herbert Krause resolved at age ten to become a writer, a decision that would one day crystallize into the desire to do for German American farm people what OLE RÖLVAAG had done for their Norwegian American counterparts. In 1931 Krause took the first steps toward achieving this goal when he matriculated at St. Olaf College, where Rölvaag was on the faculty; however the author of *Giants in the Earth* died before Krause could meet him. But even without Rölvaag's mentoring, Krause was able to begin his first novel at St. Olaf. He also wrote a one-act tragedy, "Bondsmen to the Hills," which was produced in Cape Girardeau, Missouri, in 1936, winning first prize in the Midwestern Folk Drama Tournament.

In 1933 Krause was graduated *magna cum laude* from St. Olaf with a BA and began graduate work the following year at the University of Iowa, where he earned an MA in 1935. In 1939 he began a thirty-six-year academic career at Augustana College in Sioux Falls, South Dakota, serving as head of the Department of English from 1939 until 1945 and as writer in residence from 1945 until 1976.

During the 1960s Krause was awarded a Fulbright Fellowship to South Africa and a three-year Rockefeller Professorship in the Philippines; he then returned to South Dakota to concentrate on Western Studies. In 1970 he became founding director of the Center for Western Studies at Augustana, serving in that post until his death. He also served on the executive council of the Western Literature Association from 1971 until 1974. Krause died in Sioux Falls of congestive heart failure.

**SIGNIFICANCE:** Krause's novels are in the tradition of prairie realists such as HAMLIN GARLAND; his literary landscape extends from St. Paul to the Pockerbrush hills of western Minnesota. His farm novels *Wind without Rain* (1939) and *The Thresher* (1946) emphasize how inhospitable a homogenous Midwestern farm community can be to individuals who are in any way different from the norm. These novels are episodic, structured on the cycle of the seasons and the rhythms of nature, here portrayed as occasionally beautiful but most often cruel, violent, and exacting, and functioning, together with the bank and the church, as a despotic Trinity against which the farmers must struggle for autonomy and survival. Winner of the Friends of American Writers Award for the best Midwestern novel of 1939, *Wind without Rain* chronicles the coming of age of first-person narrator Jepthah Vildvogel and his three brothers under the harsh tutelage of their rock-ribbed German Lutheran father.

*The Thresher* is similarly structured, focusing on the orphan Johnny Schwartz's struggle through childhood, adolescence, and young adulthood to win acceptance from the German American farm community into which he was adopted. Krause's historical novel, *The Oxcart Trail* (1954), is set in Minnesota Territory during the 1850s. While relating fugitive Shawnie Dark's adventures there, Krause renders in meticulously accurate detail not only the gritty realities of pioneer life in St. Paul but the conflicts between abolitionist and copperhead, trapper and farmer, Indian hater and missionary, Chippewa and Sioux, and, most importantly, white settler and Indian that defined life on the Minnesota frontier.

**SELECTED WORKS:** Krause was the author of three novels, *Wind without Rain* (1939), *The Thresher* (1946), and *The Oxcart Trail* (1954); two unpublished plays, including *Bondsmen to the Hills* (1936); and a number of essays, articles, and reviews. He also published a book of verse, *Neighbor Boy* (1939), edited a short story collection, *Fiction 151–1* (1968), and, with Gary D. Olson, edited *Prelude to Glory* (1974), a newspaper account of Custer's 1874 expedition to the Black Hills.

**FURTHER READING:** Good sources on Krause include Arthur Huseboe's monograph *Herbert Krause* in the Boise State University Western Writers series (1985); Judith Janssen's essay "Black Frost in Summer: Central Themes in the Novels of Herbert Krause," in *South Dakota Review* 5 (Spring 1967): 55–65; and Kristoffer Paulson's "Ole Rölvaag, Herbert Krause, and the Frontier Thesis of Frederick Jackson Turner," in *Where the West Begins*, edited by Arthur Huseboe and William Geyer (1978). Good discussions of Krause's fiction are also found in Roy Meyer's *The Middle Western Farm Novel in the Twentieth Century* (1965) and the Western Literature Association's *A Literary History of the American West* (1987). Krause's papers are held by the Center for Western Studies at Augustana College in Sioux Falls, South Dakota.

MARCIA NOE
THE UNIVERSITY OF TENNESSEE AT CHATTANOOGA

## CAROLINE VIRGINIA KROUT
October 13, 1852–October 9, 1931
(Caroline Brown)

**BIOGRAPHY:** Caroline Krout was born in Crawfordsville, Indiana, and attended first a local subscription school, then a public school. Her father, Robert Kennedy Krout, was eccentric; and her sister, Mary Hannah Krout, became one of the leading feminists of the United States. When Caroline was sixteen, her mother died, leaving Caroline to take care of the house and four younger children. When, three years later, a younger sister took over these tasks, Caroline taught for five years in Crawfordsville until her health failed. When she was ill, she contributed feature articles and short stories to Chicago newspapers. After partly recovering, she was an assistant court reporter in town and then served on the staff of the Newberry Library in Chicago. When her health again failed, she returned to Crawfordsville, wrote stories for periodicals, then turned to novel writing, adopting her mother's maiden name, Caroline Brown, as a pseudonym. Her shyness and the fact that she discovered belatedly that her nearly completed second novel, *On the We-a Trail* (1903), was on the same subject as *Alice of Old Vincennes* (1900), a novel being published by MAURICE THOMPSON, a fellow townsman, discouraged her creativity. In fact, she was so aware of her own literary faults and so sensitive to criticism that she finally gave up writing and lived her last twenty years with her sisters in the family home, where she died.

**SIGNIFICANCE:** Caroline Krout was very Midwestern in the way she used Indiana history. Her first novel, *Knights in Fustian: A War Time Story of Indiana* (1900), is in mythical Middle County of southern Indiana. Frank Neal, son of a prosperous farmer, returns on furlough from the Union Army to recover from his experience as a prisoner of war at Andersonville. He and the heroine, Lucy Whittaker, suffer from troubles with the subversive Knights of the Golden Circle. Frank and a federal detective foil a plot to seize control of the state, and the Knights are dispersed by troops dispatched by Governor Oliver P. Morton. Then Lucy and Frank become engaged. Governor Theodore Roosevelt of New York wrote to the author, complimenting her on the presentation of the Indiana Copperheads and life in the Indiana farming communities. Although the author gives weak characterization and the account is better as history than as a novel, the book sold well.

Krout's second novel, *On the We-a Trail, A Story of the Great Wilderness* (1903), tells how a pioneer girl, Ferriby Benhem, is the only survivor of an Indian attack on her family's cabin, for she had been at a spring getting water. Dazed, she wanders in the forest until she is rescued and taken to Vincennes, where a French family cares for her. The taking of the fort from the British by George Rogers Clark's men is woven into the tale; however, the book abounds in adventure and description but suffers from an air of unreality in some of the action and description, caused partly by lack of detail and sufficient analysis of character. *Bold Robin and His Forest Rangers* (1905) consists of six stories for young people inspired by Mrs. Lew Wallace and perhaps by the interest in archery in Crawfordsville. *Dionis of the White Veil* (1911) is a well-written romance recounting the attempt of a group of priests and nuns to found the first Jesuit mission at the mouth of White River. The Chevalier Fauchet falls in love with a novice who is to take the veil in a week and wrests her away just in time.

Caroline Krout, therefore, is an author who is interested in history as a strong background for her work. Perhaps she depended on romantic adventure stories as the action of her works. She has many faults, yet many portions of her novels move well. Her descriptions of nature are well done, and she succeeds in digging materials from native soil.

**SELECTED WORKS:** Since there are only four books to consider, perhaps all could be examined, in the following order: *On the We-a Trail* (1903), *Knights in Fustian* (1900), and *Dionis of the White Veil* (1911). If there is interest in juvenile literature, the last book, *Bold Robin and His Forest Rangers* (1905), could then be read.

**FURTHER READING:** There is no book of biography or criticism on Caroline Virginia Krout, but there are some articles available, including reviews of her books. Books containing general treatments of her are William Burke and Will Howe's *American Authors and Books, 1640 to the Present Day* (1962); and Dorothy Russo and Thelma Sullivan's *Bibliographic Studies of Seven Authors of Crawfordsville, Indiana* (1952). Also, there is a very interesting article in Ronald E. Banta's *Indiana Authors and Their Books, 1816–1916* (1949), as well as a general treatment in Arthur Shumaker's *A History of Indiana Literature* (1962).

ARTHUR W. SHUMAKER          DEPAUW UNIVERSITY

# DON KURTZ

August 1, 1951

**BIOGRAPHY:** Donald Lester Kurtz, son of Frances and Lester T. Kurtz, was born in Urbana, Illinois, and grew up in the farming regions of rural Illinois and Indiana. Kurtz's father was a professor of agronomy at the

University of Illinois for more than forty years. Kurtz earned a BS in psychology from the University of Illinois in 1972 and an MA in bilingual education from New Mexico State University in 1979. He married Elizabeth Gutierrez in 1986. Kurtz won a National Endowment for the Arts Fellowship for fiction in 1992 and a fellowship from the Bread Loaf Writer's Conference in 1995. He presently teaches Spanish and is the coordinator of foreign studies at New Mexico State University in Las Cruces, New Mexico.

**SIGNIFICANCE:** If one of the fundamental characteristics of rural Midwestern writing is a recognition of the tension in human life caused by societal and economic change, then Don Kurtz's novel *South of the Big Four* (1995) stands as an excellent example of this theme in contemporary Midwestern writing. Although this is Kurtz's only novel to date, successful writer Robert Boswell, author of *Mystery Ride* and *Crooked Hearts*, has called *South of the Big Four*, "a work of lasting literary merit" (jacket note).

The title refers to the rule of ag-loan bankers in the northern Indiana county where good farm land meets swampy gumbo: "Don't make farm loans south of the Big Four Railroad." *South of the Big Four* is successful in its evocation of life on the Midwestern farm because Kurtz is so unsparingly honest in his description of contemporary northern Indiana farm culture. The story begins with Art Conason's return to his boyhood home on the farm that he had left to work on Great Lakes iron freighters. As Art attempts to find his way back into relationships with his family, his hometown, and the land, Kurtz is able to explore a whole range of typical emotional and psychological responses associated with homecoming: nostalgia for youth on the family farm, hatred of the same, ambivalence, and confusion. After two unsatisfactory affairs and another failed try at farming, the answers Art finds are not simple ones. He is able to more fully understand the forces that destroyed his father's farm because, like him, Art has gotten caught up in the failing farm operation of Gerry Maars, for whom he works as a hired hand, once again, south of the Big Four. In the end, Kurtz's novel does not lament the passing of the family farm model, nor does it expose the destructive power of the same; rather, it suggests that Art, like other survivors of cultural change, must recognize and accept the state of things as they have become.

**SELECTED WORKS:** *South of the Big Four* is Kurtz's only novel to date. Other publications include the following short stories and novel segments: "Three" in *Puerto del Sol* 32:1 (Spring 1997); "Home" in the *Iowa Review* 21:1 (Winter 1991); "Roger's Dad" in the *Iowa Review* 18:3 (Fall 1988); "The Right to Bear Arms" in the *O. Henry Festival Stories 1987*. He has also published an "Interview with Ricardo Aguilar Melantzón" in *Puerto del Sol* 29:1 (Spring 1994) and coauthored *Trails of the Guadalupes: A Hiker's Guide to the Guadalupe Mountains National Park* (1978) with William D. Goran.

**FURTHER READING:** Reviews of *South of the Big Four* in major newspapers and magazines include a full-page essay review by Sandra Scofield in the *Boston Globe* (February 7, 1995) and by Michael S. Manley in *Sycamore Review* 8:1 (Winter–Spring 1996): 136–39. Other reviews include *New Yorker* (July 31, 1995): 79; *American Book Review* (June–July 1996): 21; *Chicago Tribune* (August 4, 1995): sec. 2.3; and *Washington Post Book World* (November 19, 1995). No articles or book-length studies of Kurtz's work have yet appeared.

KEITH FYNAARDT                    NORTHWESTERN COLLEGE

# MARGO LaGATTUTA
September 14, 1942

**BIOGRAPHY:** Born in Detroit, Michigan, to Edwin Olaf Grahn, a designer, and Elizabeth (True) Grahn, a painter, Margo LaGattuta is a well-known, active, and popular Michigan poet. She grew up in Detroit and Bloomfield Hills and graduated from Seaholm High School in 1960. She continued her education at Western Michigan University (1960–62) and Pratt Institute (1962–64). She completed her BA in English at Oakland University in 1980 and received the MFA in writing from Vermont College in 1984.

The mother of three sons, Mark, Erik, and Adam, from her marriage to Stephen LaGattuta (November 14, 1964–June 1988), she is an adjunct writing instructor at Oakland Community College as well as Midwest editor for Plain View Press in Austin, Texas. LaGattuta also teaches local and national workshops under the business name "Inventing the Invisible." She appears regularly on Michigan radio and television and writes a weekly column, "Notes on Creativity," for *Phenomenews*, a Detroit newspaper. She has received the Midwest Poetry Award of the Society for the Study of Midwestern Literature (1991) and was a 1997 nominee for a Pushcart Press Prize. **SIGNIFICANCE:** In a recent letter, she writes that "I have written poetry all my life and have been published in literary magazines and journals since the late 70s." She has published five collections of poetry: *Diversion Road* (1983); *Noedgelines* (1986), a collaboration of art and poetry with artist Chris Reising; *The Dream Givers* (1990); *Embracing the Fall* (1994); and *Wind Eyes* (1977), an anthology with seven other women writers. She has edited anthologies, including *Variations on the Ordinary* (1995), *Almost Touching* (1996), and *Up from the Soles of Our Feet* (1977).

Margo LaGattuta's poems "reflect a Midwest rural-suburban landscape," she writes, and that landscape, she says, is as often inner as it is external, as surreal as it is real. The Midwest Poetry Festival Prize Poem "Embracing the Fall" moves from the physical act of falling as the result of a slippery sidewalk or floor to the psychological and spiritual act of recovered equilibrium; "Looking for Elvis in Kalamazoo" moves from foolishness to fantasy; "Alone in America," "Remortgaging My House," and "On My Birthday, Bats" are reflections of the search for equilibrium in a contemporary Midwestern landscape that joins the outer reality with the inner. **SELECTED WORKS:** LaGattuta's volumes of poetry include *Diversion Road* (1983), *Noedgelines* (1986), *The Dream Givers* (1990), *Embracing the Fall* (1994), and *Wind Eyes* (1977). Her contributions to anthologies and literary magazines are extensive, including work in the 1984 *Anthology of Magazine Verse*, *State Street Press Anthology* (1989), and *Passages North Anthology* (1990), an anthology of Michigan verse, as well as in *Woman Poet*, *Green River Review*, *Passages North*, and others, but each of her collections is a good representation of the depth and breadth of her work. **FURTHER READING:** LaGattuta is listed in *Contemporary Authors* 115 (1985): 283 and in *Contemporary Authors New Revision Series* 38 (1993): 221–22. She has also been the subject of numerous news items in the *Detroit Free Press*, *Detroit News*, *Michigan Daily*, and many other papers, largely in Michigan.

DAVID D. ANDERSON    MICHIGAN STATE UNIVERSITY

## ROSE WILDER LANE
December 5, 1886–October 30, 1968

**BIOGRAPHY:** Born at De Smet, South Dakota, to Almanzo James and LAURA ELIZABETH (INGALLS) WILDER, Rose Lane early in life knew about the hardships of the frontier. Her parents were sturdy, American pioneers, who broke the way for the white race westward across the continent. From her Midwestern mother she obtained a life-long love of the Midwest, beauty, and books. In 1894 she moved, with her parents, from De Smet to Mansfield, Missouri, where she lived until 1903 when she went to Crowley, Louisiana. There she stayed with an aunt and went to high school. The Louisiana experience was the beginning of her worldwide adventures. After graduation, she worked as a telegrapher at Western Union in Kansas City, Missouri. From there she went to San Francisco where she became one of the first real estate women in America. Also as a reporter, she went to work for the *San Francisco Bulletin*. On March 24, 1909, she married Gillette Lane. In 1918 she divorced him; there were no children. After the divorce she accepted an American Red Cross job as a publicist, living in Europe and the Near East for the next three years.

After returning to America, she became a self-supporting freelance writer. She wrote for *Saturday Evening Post*, *Ladies' Home Journal*, *Redbook*, *Travel*, *Good Housekeeping*, *Country Gentleman*, *McCall's*, *Woman's Day*, *Sunset*, and *Esquire*. Sometimes she lived at Mansfield with her parents; at other times she lived on the East Coast or in Europe. Her Mansfield days ended in 1938 when she bought a farm in Danbury, Connecticut, where she resided to the end of her life.

In 1926 while living at Rocky Ridge Farm, Mansfield, with her parents, she encouraged her mother to write her childhood memories of the Midwestern prairie. Those memories became the famous Little House books. Rose also used her Midwest experience by writing *Let the Hurricane Roar* (1933). It is the story of her grandmother's survival on the Midwestern prairie. Rose continued to write and report throughout her life, serving as the oldest woman war correspondent in the Vietnam War. It was also in 1968 during the war that she died quietly at her Danbury farm. **SIGNIFICANCE:** Writer, telegrapher, reporter, real estate agent, publicist, activist, European traveler, Rose Wilder Lane opened up new careers for women. However, much of her fame is intertwined with that of her famous mother, Laura Ingalls Wilder, and her Little House books. She encouraged her mother to write them, and she edited and marketed them for her. Her expertise made them possible. Her own book, *Let the Hurricane Roar* (1933), written about the Midwestern frontier is a classic. The book was later republished as *Young Pioneers*. Although it was supposedly an adult novel, its length and style make it a classic junior novel. It captures the homesteading spirit through the narration of a young frontier girl. Her short stories collected from the various slick magazines for which she wrote are published in a 1935 volume, entitled *Old Home Town Stories*. Having grown up in the small town of Mansfield, Rose knew all about the narrow and crippling effects of small-town life. Ernestine, an adolescent girl, observant, bookish, and typical of Rose herself, narrates the stories. She also wrote the biographies of Henry Ford (1917) and Herbert Hoover (1920). A versatile writer, she wrote novels, biographies, short stories, and nonfiction articles.

**SELECTED WORKS:** Her major works include *Diverging Roads* (1919), *The Peaks of Shala: Being a Record of Certain Wanderings among the Hill-Tribes of Albania* (1922), *He Was a Man* (1925), *Cindy: A Romance of the Ozarks* (1928), *Let the Hurricane Roar* (1933), *Old Home Town Stories* (1935), and *Free Land* (1938).

**FURTHER READING:** William Holtz's *The Ghost in the Little House: A Life of Rose Wilder Lane* (1993) provides a major biography.

LELAND MAY

NORTHWEST MISSOURI STATE UNIVERSITY

## JOSEPH LANGLAND
February 16, 1917

**BIOGRAPHY:** Born of Charles M. and Clara Elizabeth (Hille) Langland and raised on a farm on the Iowa side of the state line between Minnesota and Iowa, south of Spring Grove, Joseph Langland went to Santa Ana College in California in the midst of the Great Depression from 1935 to 1936. In 1938 he continued his education at the University of Iowa, where he earned a BA in 1940 and an MA in 1941. At twenty-five he began service in the U.S. Army as an infantry soldier and officer in the allied campaigns in France and Germany during World War II. Captain Langland served in the Allied military government of Bavaria from 1945 to March 1946 and was among the troops that opened up the concentration camps in the spring of 1945. After the war Langland resumed graduate studies and teaching at the University of Iowa. He was professor of English at the University of Wyoming at Laramie from 1948 through 1959, and from 1959 until his retirement in 1979 he was professor of English at the University of Massachusetts at Amherst. Langland married the artist Judith Gail Wood in 1943. They have three children.

**SIGNIFICANCE:** Joseph Langland's roots in a rural Iowa farming community with a strong Norwegian American ethnic awareness and his celebration of landscape and nature in many of his poems define him as a Midwestern poet, just as EDGAR LEE MASTERS is defined by his Spoon River locality or CARL SANDBURG in those parts of his poetry where he celebrates Midwestern landscape and life. Many of Langland's poems have grown out of recollections from childhood and adolescence on the home farm and have innocence and initiation as main themes, particularly the poems in the "Sacrifices" section of *The Wheel of Summer*. They reflect a young man's experience of the facts of life, like birth, death and suffering as remembered and evoked by a mature and sophisticated intellect. Other poems are more in the great tradition of English poetry and reflect the poet's wide range of intellectual and cultural pursuits and cosmopolitan experiences. Their meanings, however, typically grow out of a keen sense of place, of sympathetic observation of everyday things and events. Langland has an acute ear for the speech rhythms of the rural Midwest, and music often informs his poems, a quality he often brings out in his own public readings—and occasional singing—of them. The oral character of his poems is often counterbalanced by use of sophisticated stanza forms and unexpected imagery.

**SELECTED WORKS:** Langland's published books of poetry are *The Green Town* (1956) and *The Wheel of Summer* (1963), which were among the nominees for the National Book Award; the latter won the Melville Cane Award. A sequence from *The Wheel of Summer* was published separately under the title *The*

*Sacrifice Poems* in 1975. *Any Body's Song* (1980) was one of the five books selected for the National Poetry series. Recent collections are *A Dream of Love* (1986), *Twelve Poems with Preludes and Postludes* (1988), and *Selected Poems* (1991). Most of his poems were originally published in various magazines and journals, particularly in the *New Yorker* and the *Massachusetts Review*, and also in *Poetry,* the *Nation,* the *Atlantic,* the *Partisan Review,* the *Hudson Review,* and many others. He has coedited an anthology of poetry, *Poets' Choice* (1962), and translated (with Tamas Aczel and Lazlo Tikos) and edited a volume titled *Poetry from the Russian Underground* (1973).

**FURTHER READING:** Langland is the subject of entries in *Contemporary Poets* (1991), *Directory of American Poets and Fiction Writers, Who's Who in America* (1996), *Writers' Directory,* and *Who's Who in Writers, Editors and Poets.*

ARNE NESET          STAVANGER COLLEGE (NORWAY)

## RING(GOLD WILMER) LARDNER
March 6, 1885–September 25, 1933

**BIOGRAPHY:** Ring Lardner was born and grew up in Niles, Michigan, a small town north of South Bend, Indiana. His father, Henry Lardner, was a well-to-do businessman; his mother, Lena (Phillips) Lardner was a preacher's daughter and a devout Episcopalian, a singer, and an amateur poet.

Ring, the youngest of their six children, experienced a happy childhood: comfortable and secure, if somewhat isolated. He was educated at home by his mother until he was twelve, and then by a tutor. During these years, he seldom left the family's Bond Street mansion and its spacious, wooded grounds. At Niles High School, he played football and sang in a quartet. Because the family's fortunes began to decline in 1902, his father sent him and his brother Rex to Chicago's Armour Institute (later, the Illinois Institute of Technology), hoping to make the two young men into engineers. Neither lasted the year. Ring returned to Niles to work at odd jobs; he also wrote and performed in amateur musicals. In the fall of 1905, when an editor from the *South Bend Times* sought to employ the absent Rex, Lardner puffed his nonexistent credentials as a reporter and landed the job for himself. He became the *Times* sports writer, and, if his mock autobiography "Who's Who—and Why" is credited, he doubled up as a "society reporter,

court-house man," and drama critic (*Some Champions* 2).

Within two years, he was writing for the faltering *Chicago Inter-Ocean.* By 1908 he was reporting on the world champion Cubs for the *Chicago Tribune.* His ambitions and rapid advancement were fueled by a long-term romance with Ellis Abbott of Goshen, Indiana, whom he married in June 1911. Lardner began writing the daily column "In the Wake of the News" for the *Tribune* in 1913. He filled the space with doggerel verse, family gossip, parodies, children's stories, short stories, and occasionally direct commentary on sports. For the *Saturday Evening Post* in 1914, he created Jack Keefe, a semi-literate baseball player and a type-character known in the 1920s as a wise boob. The first series of these stories was collected in *You Know Me, Al* (1916); other, later Keefe stories or "Busher Letters" were compiled in *Treat 'Em Rough* (1918) and *The Real Dope* (1919).

Ring and Ellis had four sons: John Abbott, James Phillip, Ringgold Wilmer Jr., and David. To accommodate their growing family, the Lardners bought a home in Riverside, a far western suburb of Chicago. The experience spurred the writing of *Own Your Own Home* (1919). These sequenced stories, first published in *Redbook* in 1915, tracked the crude and vainglorious strivings of Fred and Grace Gross, a Chicago policeman and his wife, both bent on establishing their social status in the suburbs. *Gullible's Travels, Etc.* (1917), a collection of five interrelated short stories, followed the thwarted social ambitions of the Gullibles, Joe Gullible and his "Missus." So successful was Lardner's magazine writing that in 1919 he resigned from the *Tribune* and began writing a widely syndicated column called "Weekly Letter."

In the same year he and his family moved to the East Coast, eventually buying a home in Great Neck, Long Island. The trip was commemorated in two richly comic, fictional works: *The Young Immigrunts* (1920) and *The Big Town* (1921). Lardner soon came to know Robert Benchley, Dorothy Parker, Alexander Woollcott, and other Algonquin wits, though he never became one of the Round Table regulars. More important to him was the friendship of F. SCOTT FITZGERALD, a fellow Midwesterner and a Great Neck neighbor in 1922–23. Fitzgerald pressed Maxwell Perkins, his editor at Scribners, to publish *How to Write Short Stories (With Samples)* (1924), a collection of previously published work that established Lardner's importance as a writer.

The mid to late 1920s are generally regarded as his best years as a short story writer; "Haircut," his widely anthologized tale of vicious pranks and small-town Michigan, dates from this period, as do the equally dark satires "Love Nest" and a "A Day with Conrad Green." Despite growing alcoholism and recurring pulmonary problems in the late 1920s, Lardner continued to produce a steady flow of stories, magazine articles, and theatrical writings. His efforts at theatrical writing yielded one hit in collaboration with George S. Kaufman: *June Moon* (1929), a play based on his short story about a hack Chicago songwriter, "Some Like Them Cold." As the Depression began to trim his income, Lardner resumed his column writing for the Bell Syndicate and took on radio criticism for the *New Yorker*. For the *Saturday Evening Post* Lardner wrote a new group of "Busher Letters" collected in *Lose with a Smile* (1933) and a series of autobiographical pieces including "Some Champions." According to Jonathan Yardley, during the last months of his life he was at work on a serious play that was to be an "interlocking study of alcoholism and family relationships" (374). Lardner died of a heart attack at his home in East Hampton, New York.

**SIGNIFICANCE:** Lardner's literary reputation, his fame, and his fees for magazine stories all peaked in the mid-1920s. H. L. Mencken, the powerful tastemaker of the 1920s, praised his stories and, in his preface to the *American Language* (1921), lauded his "authentic American" language. Edmund Wilson, to disabuse readers of the notion that Lardner was a mere humorist or a hack baseball writer, declared him a "serious writer," saying that he possessed a "talent for social satire and observation" equal to that of his fellow Midwesterners, SHERWOOD ANDERSON and SINCLAIR LEWIS (*Shores of Light* 94–95). That Lardner had an ear for Midwestern slang and reproduced its subtlest idioms and that he understood the American character and catalogued its principal character types have been evident to readers as different as Virginia Woolf, Clifton Fadiman, and JOHN BERRYMAN. His small-town salesmen, meter readers, and clerks; his big-city prizefighters, police detectives, and

baseball players; and his nurses, secretaries, and suburban homeowners may be grotesque or, as Wilson put it, "queer cases," but they bear an unmistakable stamp of reality.

Lardner owed much to the example of two Chicago columnists, GEORGE ADE and FINLEY PETER DUNNE. In their turn, the generation of ERNEST HEMINGWAY, F. Scott Fitzgerald, and JAMES T. FARRELL drew on Lardner's hard-bitten satire and his finely tuned sense of Midwestern speech. Lardner's sometimes sentimental or Victorian view of women and his reticence and general inhibitions about sex have dated some of his stories. And yet his place as a major American humorist and as one of our most important short story writers remains secure.

**SELECTED WORKS:** Lardner, guided by the heavy hand of F. Scott Fitzgerald, produced *How to Write Short Stories* (1924), a well-sifted collection, including such standards as "Champion" and "Some Like Them Cold." *Round Up* (1929) was a much fuller compilation and in many ways became the definitive and seminal selection of his work. Maxwell Geismar's *The Ring Lardner Reader* (1963) and Babette Rosmond and Henry Morgan's *Shut Up, He Explained* (1962) are handy miscellanies, sources for his "nonsense plays," critical essays, mock-autobiographies, parodies, and nonstandard short fiction. *Some Champions*, edited by Matthew J. Bruccoli and Richard Layman (1976), gathered previously uncollected sketches, columns, and short stories. Of Lardner's interrelated tales, *You Know Me, Al* (1916) and *Gullible's Travels, Etc.* (1917) are generally regarded as his best; until recently they were available in reprints from the University of Chicago Press. Though also of interest and still humorous, *Own Your Own Home* (1919) and *The Big Town* (1921), two other interrelated tales, have attracted little critical attention and less current favor.

**FURTHER READING:** Jonathan Yardley's *Ring: A Biography of Ring Lardner* (1977) stands as the most complete biography to date; it also offers perceptive readings of the fiction. Edmund Wilson's 1924 essay "Mr. Lardner's American Characters" (reprinted in *The Shores of Light*, 1952) and Virginia Woolf's 1925 essay "American Fiction" (reprinted in *The Moment and Other Essays*, 1952) charted the major directions for much subsequent Lardner criticism. Clifton Fadiman's "Ring Lardner and the

Triangle of Hate," in *Nation* 136 (March 22, 1933): 315–17, and John Berryman's "The Case of Ring Lardner," in *Commentary* 25 (November 1956): 416–23, are also significant resources. Norris Yates's chapter in *The American Humorist* (1964), "The Isolated Man of Ring Lardner," expanded on Woolf's notion that his characters were "isolates" and refined Wilson's view of Lardner's character types as representations of the "mass man" (165–93). Leverett T. Smith Jr.'s article "The Diameter of Frank Chance's Diamond: Ring Lardner and Professional Sports," in *Journal of Popular Culture* 6 (Summer 1972): 133–56, supplies a useful study of Lardner's understanding of baseball and other games that he covered. The bulk of Ring Lardner's papers are at the Newberry Library in Chicago.

GUY SZUBERLA                    UNIVERSITY OF TOLEDO

# NELLA LARSEN
April 13, 1891–ca. March 30, 1964

**BIOGRAPHY:** Much of Nella Larsen's personal history has been shrouded for years in vague and contradictory details, a great deal of the confusion produced by Larsen herself. But extensive work by scholars has helped to tie many loose strands in Larsen's life. Larsen was born Nellie Walker in 1891 in Chicago, the only child of Mary Hanson Walker, a white Danish woman, and Peter Walker, a black man from the present-day Virgin Islands. Larsen stated that her father died when she was two years old and that her mother later married Peter Larson, a white Danish man with whom she had a second daughter. During Larsen's childhood, she and her family lived in several ethnically diverse areas; however, when they moved to more affluent white neighborhoods, Larsen, the only member of her immediate family who was identified as "colored," began to question her racial identity.

Larsen, whose family adopted the current spelling of the last name in 1907, attended Chicago public schools until 1907, when she was enrolled in Fisk University. Larsen remained at Fisk for one year, an experience which fomented in her a sense of loneliness and ambivalence regarding her racial identity.

From 1912 to 1915, Larsen studied nursing in New York City and then became head nurse at the Tuskegee Institute. She returned to New York in 1916, where she continued to work as a nurse. In 1919 Larsen married Dr. Elmer Samuel Imes, a distinguished black physicist. They divorced in 1933.

The creative force of the Harlem Renaissance signaled for Larsen the inauguration of new careers, first as a librarian for the New York City Public Library, and then as a writer, both of which gave Larsen access to the Harlem literati. Larsen's brief tenure as a writer began with the publication of short pieces and flourished with the 1928 publication of her first novel, *Quicksand*. Another critical success, *Passing*, was published in 1929. Her promise as a writer was further recognized when she was awarded the Harmon Award's Bronze Medal that same year. Larsen's prominence as a writer became short lived when, in 1930, she was accused of plagiarizing a work by Sheila Kaye-Smith for her short story "Sanctuary." Although Larsen denied the charges, she was never able to fully recover from the blow to her career and her confidence as a writer.

In 1930 Larsen went to Europe on a Guggenheim Fellowship, where she worked on a third novel that was never published. Despite a promising and powerful start, Larsen was never able to recoup her position as a writer. During the 1930s Larsen broke her ties with the literary scene, and by 1944 she resumed her career as a nurse, seemingly abandoning her writing altogether. Alone and unrecognized for her literary contributions, Larsen died of heart disease at some point before March 30, 1964, when her body was found in her Manhattan apartment.

**SIGNIFICANCE:** Larsen's prominence as a writer of the Harlem Renaissance and her position as one of the few successful black women novelists of the period have been increasingly recognized by scholars. While it is in New York that Larsen emerges as a writer, Chicago still plays a role in her works, particularly in *Quicksand* and *Passing*. In the semi-autobiographical *Quicksand*, Larsen examines the conflicts of identity, isolation, and displacement, themes established early on in the Chicago setting, as the protagonist, Helga Crane, is rejected by the white members of her family and by a city that makes it a struggle for her to find any "acceptable" job. In *Passing*, early scenes in a Chicago cafe underscore the conflicts of social identity and "passing," which are explored throughout the novel. Although Larsen's novels are set in numerous locales, Chicago appears as one of the places where Larsen's characters try to establish and accommodate racial, class, and public identity in a segregated city.

**SELECTED WORKS:** Larsen published several short stories, including some under the names Nella Larsen Imes and Allen Semi—Nella Imes in reverse—but it is in *Quicksand* (1928) and *Passing* (1929) that she provides a brief but focused study of class and race in the Midwest, specifically in segregated Chicago. Both novels are available in *Quicksand and Passing*, edited by Deborah E. McDowell (1986), and in *An Intimation of Things Past: The Collected Fiction of Nella Larsen*, edited by Charles R. Larson (1992). The latter work also includes her early short stories, as well as "Sanctuary," the subject of Larsen's plagiarism controversy.

**FURTHER READING:** Thadious M. Davis's *Nella Larsen: Novelist of the Harlem Renaissance* (1994) is a detailed biography which ties together many of the loose biographical strings while offering a good critical overview of Larsen's fiction, including *Quicksand* and *Passing*. Cheryl Wall discusses the issue of identity in "Passing for What? Aspects of Identity in Nella Larsen's Novels," in *Black American Literature Forum* 20 (Spring–Summer 1986): 97–111. Hiroko Sato analyzes Larsen in the larger perspective of the Harlem Renaissance in "Under the Harlem Shadow: A Study of Jessie Fauset and Nella Larsen," in *The Harlem Renaissance Remembered*, edited by Arna Bontemps (1972). David Levering Lewis's *When Harlem Was in Vogue* (1979) provides a detailed overview of the Harlem Renaissance, including Larsen's participation in the movement. Most of Larsen's correspondence is in Yale University's Beinecke Library and in the New York Public Library.

ARLENE RODRÍGUEZ
SPRINGFIELD TECHNICAL COMMUNITY COLLEGE

## CLARA E(LIZABETH) LAUGHLIN
August 3, 1873–March 3, 1941

**BIOGRAPHY:** Clara Elizabeth Laughlin, author and travel writer, made Chicago her home for most of her itinerant life. Born in New York City, she moved with her family to Milwaukee in 1876. Three years later, her father's broken fortunes repaired, the family moved to a comfortable house on Chicago's near north side. Her father, Samuel Wilson Laughlin, was born near Belfast, Ireland; he was a businessman who, in various enterprises, won and lost several modest fortunes. Laughlin remembered him in her autobiography, *Traveling through Life* (1934), as an "ardent Briton" who never became an American citizen (22). Her mother, Elizabeth Abbott Laughlin, grew up in New York City and instilled in her daughter an insatiable love of travel. At age six or seven, she traveled with her mother to Europe, the first of many such trips she was to make. Laughlin graduated from Chicago's North Division High School in 1890. She expected to complete her education in Switzerland, but her father's death early in 1891 foreclosed that possibility. Instead, at the age of seventeen, she began her career as a professional writer for the *Interior*, a Presbyterian literary and religious weekly published in Chicago.

Laughlin soon worked her way up from routine book reviewing to the responsible editorial post she held for close to twenty years. Her autobiography shows her to have been shrewd and knowledgeable about the economics of magazine publication. From her magazine's narrow base, she built a network of contacts among leading editors and publishers of the new "cheap magazines," soon counting Edward Bok and S. S. McClure as close friends. For *Harper's Weekly, Harper's Bazaar*, and *Scribner's*, she wrote editorial and opinion pieces for twenty dollars each. For *McClure's* and *Good Housekeeping*, she produced a steady stream of short stories, advice columns, and popular biographies. Her friendship with JAMES WHITCOMB RILEY led her to the compilation of an anthology of his poetry and prose and a book of warm reminiscences.

Younger than most of the artists, architects, and writers who made up Chicago's Little Room group, she nevertheless became a regular at the Friday afternoon teas during the 1890s and after. Seeing the need for a counterpart to HAMLIN GARLAND's all-male Cliff-Dwellers Club, in 1915 she organized Chicago's Cordon, a club of women artists, sculptors, and writers.

Though she wrote numerous stories of love and marriage, she never married, saying in her autobiography that "a woman no longer feels called upon to defend her unmarried state" (91).

During World War I, she wrote a daily column for the *Chicago American*. In 1921 she published a long-running serial story in the *Chicago Daily Tribune* under the heading "Men Are Like That." Beginning with *So You're Going to Paris* in 1924, Laughlin wrote two dozen or more travel guides. The series spelled an end to her serious writing. So successful were these books that she established a profitable travel agency with offices in Chicago, Paris, and Los Angeles. For a brief time she broadcast travelogues on WMAQ, a Chicago radio station.

**SIGNIFICANCE:** When Laughlin died, the *New York Times* obituary saluted her as an authority on travel but gave only passing attention to her achievements as a novelist and short story writer. Sidney Bremer, in *Urban Intersections* (1994), has stressed the importance of Laughlin's contributions to Chicago's "residential novel," women's novels such as *"Just Folks"* (1910) that value community, ethnically mixed neighborhoods, and "social work interactions between classes" (93). Set on Chicago's near west side, in the neighborhood of Hull House, *"Just Folks"* tells the story of Beth Tully, a probation officer, who chooses to live among the immigrants and poor. Laura Hapke's critical study *Tales of the Working Girl* (1992) notes Laughlin's novel *The Work-a-Day Girl* (1913) and the type-figures it defines. One chapter of Laughlin's novel *Felicity: The Making of a Comedienne* (1907) and her *Penny Philanthropist* (1912) rely upon a Chicago setting and infusions of urban realism. At her best, as in *"Just Folks,"* Laughlin's writings eschew sentimental formulas and see the city steadily and whole.

**SELECTED WORKS:** No biography on Laughlin has appeared, though her own autobiography, *Traveling through Life* (1934), and her introspective essay *The Evolution of a Girl's Ideal* (1902) provide a reasonably full record of her life. Of her many novels, those set in Chicago—*"Just Folks"* (1910) and *The Penny Philanthropist* (1912)—hold the most interest. A chapter in *Felicity: The Making of a Comedienne* (1907) and *The Work-a-Day Girl* (1913) also use the urban Chicago locale. Laughlin, who knew James Whitcomb Riley through the So-

ciety of Midland Authors, placed particular value on *The Golden Year* (1898), her compilation of his poetry and prose. Their friendship also led to her *Reminiscences of James Whitcomb Riley* (1916). Her most popular works are the two dozen or more travel guides in the series she began with *So You're Going to Paris* (1924).

**FURTHER READING:** Brief biographical and bibliographical articles on Laughlin appear in *Current Biography* 2 (1941): 495, and in *American Authors and Books: 1640–1940* (1943): 413. Laughlin's interest in the role of working women and their social status is recognized in Laura Hapke's *Tales of the Working Girl* (1992) and Sidney Bremer's *Urban Intersections* (1994). The spring 1995 issue of the *Illinois Historical Journal* includes Judith Raferty's "Chicago Settlement Women in Fact and Fiction," which considers Laughlin and the "New Woman" (37–58).

GUY SZUBERLA                    UNIVERSITY OF TOLEDO

# LOIS (LENORE) LENSKI
October 14, 1893–September 11, 1974

**BIOGRAPHY:** Lois Lenski, author and illustrator of more than a hundred children's books, was born into a Lutheran pastor's family in Springfield, Ohio. Six years later the family moved to the small farming village of Anna, Ohio, where the scholarly Reverend R. C. H. Lenski and his wife, Marietta (Young) Lenski, ministered to the close-knit German American community for twelve years. In their lively and stimulating parsonage home the five Lenski children learned to value family loyalty, to cherish books and learning, and to welcome all kinds of people into their lives.

Lenski majored in education at Ohio State University, graduating in 1915 with a BS. Determined to become an artist instead of a teacher, she attended classes at the Art Students' League in New York for four years. The following year she studied in London, where she began illustrating children's books.

Returning to New York in 1921, she married her former teacher, muralist Arthur Covey, a widower and father of two children. Lenski continued to illustrate children's books by other authors, fifty-seven in all, and began her own career as a writer with two books about her Ohio childhood published in 1927 and 1928. In 1929, after son Stephen was born, the Covey family moved into a 140–

year-old farmhouse that provided the stimulus and setting for the first of Lenski's seven meticulously researched historical novels.

In 1941, when Lenski's failing health prompted the family to spend their winters in the South, she discovered unique groups of people living in isolated, little-known areas of America. The children in these communities became the subjects of her celebrated regional books.

In 1951 Lenski and her husband moved into their retirement home in Tarpon Springs, Florida. Covey died there in 1960, Lenski in 1974 at the age of eighty.

**SIGNIFICANCE:** Although Lenski left Ohio at age twenty-two, she carried with her the Midwestern values of her childhood. Like her parents she devoted her life to her work, writing true stories of America's common people.

Lenski saw herself as a pioneer, setting out in a new direction of realism and egalitarianism in fiction for children. In *Adventure in Understanding* (1968), she wrote: "I would like to see in children's books a stronger accent on a true and balanced realism, which recognizes the worth and dignity of every human being" (83).

Lenski reached her full maturity as a realistic writer in her regional books. While making extended visits to the remote places where culturally diverse Americans had settled, she heard the dramatic stories of their lives. Like the Midwestern pioneers, they too had struggled against tremendous odds in an unfamiliar, often hostile environment to realize their dreams. Writing from her notebooks and sketches, Lenski was able to make the characters and plots come alive. She broke unwritten taboos by using serious themes, violent episodes, villainous characters, and colorful, ungrammatical colloquial language in books for children. A contemporary critic, May Hill Arbuthnot, commented in *Children and Books* (1957) that the realism in Lenski's regionals was grimmer than anything since *Tom Sawyer*. She praised Lenski for giving children glimpses of underprivileged families whose lives seem sordid but are glorified by "love that binds them together through thick and thin" (423).

For more than fifty years Lenski's books were popular not only with children but also with librarians, teachers, and parents. She received honorary doctorates from Wartburg College, in Iowa, the University of North Carolina at Greensboro, Capital University, in Ohio, and Southwestern College, in Kansas. She is remembered today as an innovator who dared give her readers vivid portrayals of people from humble origins, of diverse races, faiths, lifestyles, and cultures who made vital contributions to a dynamic America.

**SELECTED WORKS:** In her article "My Ohio Beginnings," *Ohioana Quarterly* (Spring 1970): 25–30, she reveals the strong influence of her Ohio years. Her first and only Ohio books, *Skipping Village* (1927) and *A Little Girl of 1900* (1928), are important because they reveal the direction of her later work, the daily experience of ordinary American families. Lenski's many picture books, created to amuse her young son, are best represented by the famous "Mr. Small" series, including *The Little Family* (1932) and *The Little Auto* (1934). Her first historical work, *Phebe Fairchild: Her Book* (1936), was a Newbery Honor Book. The second, *A-Going to the Westward* (1937), chronicles the journey of a family traveling to the Ohio country in a covered wagon in 1811. Her first regional work, *Bayou Suzette* (1943), won the Ohioana Award; the second, *Strawberry Girl* (1945), was awarded the coveted Newbery Medal. She declared her *Prairie School* (1951), an exciting account of a year of blizzards in the Dakotas, to be the "truest" of all her books. Her autobiography, *Journey into Childhood* (1972), gives an excellent account of her childhood and her life as an author and artist. *Adventure in Understanding: Talks to Parents, Teachers and Librarians* (1968) is a collection of her speeches made between 1944 and 1966. In 1987 Giles Laroche illustrated a Lenski poem in the colorful picture book *Sing a Song of People*, a celebration of city life.

**FURTHER READING:** *The Dictionary of Literary Biography* 22: 241–52, and *Something about the Author* 26: 134–42, treat Lenski's life and work. She donated her papers to at least eighteen libraries in the United States. The Edward H. Butler Library of the State University College at Buffalo, New York, holds book manuscripts and sketches, as well as first editions of all her books. The Lenski materials in the library of the University of Oklahoma are part of a larger collection showing the history of illustrated children's books. Other libraries with sizable holdings are Florida State University in Tallahassee, William Jewell College in Liberty, Missouri, the University of Minnesota in Minneapolis, and Capital University in Columbus, Ohio. The Clark County Public Library in her hometown of Springfield, Ohio, also has a substantial collection of Lenski materials, including more than a hundred autographed copies of her books, foreign language editions, original drawings, manuscripts, scrapbooks, and family photographs.

MARY JOAN MILLER                    SPRINGFIELD, OHIO

## ELMORE LEONARD JR.
October 11, 1925

BIOGRAPHY: Elmore Leonard, copywriter and writer of Westerns, hard-boiled crime stories, and film scripts, was born in New Orleans, Louisiana, to Elmore Leonard Sr. and Flora (Rive) Leonard. Because the elder Leonard was a scout for new General Motors dealerships, the family moved several times before settling in Detroit in 1934. A Roman Catholic, Leonard Jr. attended parochial school, graduating from the Jesuit-run University of Detroit High School in 1943. He was then drafted for military service in the U.S. Navy, serving as a Seabee in the Pacific theater. On July 30, 1949, he married Beverly Cline, with whom he had five children. Having majored in English and philosophy at the University of Detroit, he received his PhB there in 1950. His first job was at the Campbell-Ewald Advertising Agency in Detroit, where he remained as a copywriter until 1961. His writing career has extended from 1951, when he had his first Western story published, to the present. Divorced from Beverly Cline in 1977, he married Joan Shepard on September 15, 1979; she died on January 13, 1993. On August 19, 1993, he married Christine Kent, with whom he lives in Bloomfield Village near Detroit. There he continues to write screenplays as well as novels.

SIGNIFICANCE: Leonard's writing may be roughly divided into three periods. The first period was 1951 to 1969, when he wrote Western stories and novels and freelance industrial and educational films. The second, of special interest in the context of Midwestern literature, was 1969 to 1981, when he wrote crime stories mostly with Michigan, especially Detroit, settings. The third was 1981 to the mid-1990s, when he wrote crime stories set mainly in Florida, where his mother owned a motel and where he vacationed. This third period,

Elmore Leonard Jr.
Photo © Nancy Crampton

on up to the present, has been the time of his greatest success, when he has been receiving lucrative writing and screen contracts and such honors as the Edgar Allan Poe Award from the Mystery Writers of America (1984).

Leonard's talent, hard work, persistence, and keen business sense enabled him to capitalize on the popularity of the Western in American popular culture of the 1950s. In the Western's period of declining popularity in the 1960s, Leonard was perceptive and nimble enough to switch to writing crime novels, then replacing Westerns in popularity. In the process he adapted some of the conventions of the period Western to those of the urban crime novel, which he aptly called the "eastern western" (Geherin 66). He saw that urban "civilization" in cities like Detroit was fully as corrupt and lawless as anything in the Wild West, and that the individual seeking even a modicum of justice in the contemporary world faced a greater challenge than the hero of *High Noon*.

For our purposes, *City Primeval: High Noon in Detroit* (1980) may be sufficiently representative of the broad outlines of Leonard's 1969–81 crime novels, with their predominantly Midwestern settings. In the manner of *Gunfight at the O.K. Corral*, the action in *City Primeval* leads inevitably to a shoot-out between the good detective Raymond Cruz and the Oklahoma Wildman, Clement Mansell. By his own count Mansell has stolen 266 cars and committed nine murders, including the recent killing of a Detroit judge. But because the police can't prove Mansell guilty of the crimes they know he committed, the law can't touch him in the lawless city of Detroit. The only way to justice in this eastern western is the way of the personal vendetta, to which Cruz finally resorts, shooting Mansell to death as the criminal reaches inside his jacket for what turns out to be only a bottle opener. The book ends as Cruz pares his nails with the sharp edge of Mansell's bottle opener, recalling for the reader Gregory Peck's similar action in *The Gunfighter*, alluded to earlier in the novel.

**SELECTED WORKS:** Notable for their Michigan settings as well as for their increasingly complex characterization and structure, Leonard's urban crime novels composed in the second period, from 1969 to 1981, include *The Big Bounce* (1969), *Fifty-Two Pickup* (1974), *Swag* (1976), *Unknown Man No. 89* (1977), *The Switch* (1978), *City Primeval: High Noon in Detroit* (1980), and *Split Images* (1981), a transitional work so far as setting is concerned, beginning in Palm Beach, Florida, then moving to Detroit. What is clear in his Michigan crime novels is his rejection of the myth of Midwestern wholesomeness and rectitude. Yet his all but totally cynical portrayal of human nature is mitigated by vestiges of goodness and mercy revealed in the worst of mankind. Far from being challenged, this dark view of human nature is confirmed in both his early Westerns and his more recent crime novels, set in Florida and elsewhere. Clearly Leonard in his gritty Michigan novels has rejected the American myth of Progress along with the notion that the Midwest, at least as represented by Detroit's mean streets, is a place of innocence and homely virtue.

Those wishing to sample Leonard's early Western fiction might try *Hombre* (1961), listed by the Western Writers of America as one of the twenty-five best Western novels of all time (1977). Those wishing to read his more recent fiction might look into *Riding the Rap* (1995) or *Out of Sight* (1996).

**FURTHER READING:** To date only one book on Leonard has appeared, an interesting biography by David Geherin based on his interviews with Leonard as well as extensive research. Entitled *Elmore Leonard*, it was published in 1989.

PAUL W. MILLER                    WITTENBERG UNIVERSITY

## ALDO LEOPOLD
January 11, 1887–April 21, 1948

**BIOGRAPHY:** Aldo Leopold was born to Carl and Clara (Starker) Leopold in Burlington, Iowa. The son of a well-to-do desk manufacturing family, Leopold spent his childhood absorbing the Mississippi Valley landscape, keeping careful records of its flora and fauna, and paving the way for his career as a naturalist. As a teenager, Leopold attended the Lawrenceville School in New Jersey, pegged by other students as the somewhat peculiar naturalist from the Midwest. His marriage to Estella Bergere on October 9, 1912, produced three sons and two daughters. Leopold was one of the earliest graduates of Yale University's forestry program, earning a bachelor's degree in 1908 and a master's in 1909. He began his career as a forester in 1909, spending fifteen years in Arizona and New Mexico. Because of an illness, he took a desk job at the Forest Products Laboratory in Madison, Wisconsin, in 1924, though he went back to the field surveying game a few years later. He was professor of wildlife management, virtually inventing the profession, at the University of Wisconsin–Madison from 1933 until his death of a heart attack while fighting a grass fire in 1948. Leopold gained national prominence as a presidential and United Nations adviser on conservation and wildlife management, and he was a cofounder of the Wilderness Society in the 1940s. The fame of *A Sand County Almanac* (1949) was posthumous, and the book earned the Burroughs Medal of the John Burroughs Memorial Association for the distinguished book in the field of nature writing in 1977.

**SIGNIFICANCE:** Aldo Leopold's work in the fields of modern forestry, ecology, and environmental writing is foundational, and it is important to realize how fundamental his Midwestern experience was to that national influence. He grew up in a transitional time,

**Aldo Leopold.**
Photo by Robert McCabe. Courtesy of the University
of Wisconsin–Madison Archives

in the sense that he was a child during the years that FREDERICK JACKSON TURNER'S "frontier thesis" of 1893 influenced thinking about the fate of Americans' relationship with the land. As a child in Iowa growing up on the Mississippi, Leopold had formative impressions of nature and human uses of it in a region midway between the swiftly industrializing East and the closing frontier of the West. After life and work experience in all three regions, seeing the spectrum of development across the country, Leopold returned to the middle ground of the Midwest and developed his "land ethic" on his family's worn-out sand farm in central Wisconsin. Although Wisconsin's environmental degradation at that point was nowhere near the levels of much of the East, Leopold still experienced firsthand the exploitation of regional natural resources through his family's desk company and the degradation of farmland literally in his own backyard, sensitizing him to the need for an ethic of environmental care.

In his idea of a "land ethic," Leopold defines humanity's relationship with the land as an extension of ethical systems, which are limitations placed on individual action for the sake of cooperative interdependence, developed over centuries. The first and second levels of ethical systems developed philosophies about the relationships between individuals and then between individuals and societies. In a move that Leopold calls ecological, the next step in the evolutionary process is to develop a sense of relationship between humans and the land, including the animals and plants indigenous to it. Like other ethical systems, the "land ethic" assumes that members of the system form a community. The biological community of interdependent beings would today be called an "ecosystem," and Leopold claims that the members of that community have rights above and beyond humanity's designs on them. Economic self-interest in relation to the land is too short-sighted, according to Leopold, because it does not hold the health of a biotic community, its ability to sustain self-renewal, as a paramount value. The land ethic asserts the immorality of any human action harmful to the biotic community's beauty or its ability to renew itself. Humanity has an obligation to sustain the natural community of which it is a part.

Since Leopold developed these ideas in large part through experiencing his own Midwestern place, his work presents interesting ideas for considering one's own regional place, as well as helping readers to understand the natural relationships informing the Midwestern landscape. *A Sand County Almanac* presents not only numerous specific details about the native flora and fauna that inhabit and characterize the Midwest but also invites readers to consider their own relationships to the natural community about them.

**SELECTED WORKS:** Leopold's major work is *A Sand County Almanac*, published posthumously in 1949. It was originally published with *Sketches Here and There,* and it has been reprinted numerous times; some reprinted versions include essays from *Round River: From the Journal of Aldo Leopold,* itself originally published in 1953. Other essay collections are *Aldo Leopold's Wilderness: Selected Early Writings by the Author of A Sand County Almanac,* edited by David E. Brown and Neil B. Carmony (1990); *The River of the Mother of God and Other Essays,* edited by Susan L. Flader and J. Baird Callicott (1991); *Aldo Leopold's Southwest,* edited by David E. Brown and Neil B. Carmony (1995); and *For the Health of the Land* (1999), a major new collection of previously uncollected essays, many previously unpublished.

**FURTHER READING:** The standard biography of Leopold is Curt Meine's *Aldo Leopold: His Life and Work* (1988). A book-length study of Leopold's intellectual development is Susan L. Flader's *Thinking Like a Mountain: Aldo Leopold and the Evolution of an Ecological Atti-*

tude toward Deer, Wolves, and Forests (1974). A book of essays celebrating the Leopold Centennial is *Aldo Leopold: The Man and His Legacy*, edited by Thomas Tanner (1987). Recent analyses of Leopold's work can be found in *For Love of the World: Essays on Nature Writers*, by Sherman Paul (1992); *Nature's Kindred Spirits: Aldo Leopold, Joseph Wood Krutch, Edward Abbey, Annie Dillard, and Gary Snyder*, by James I. McClintock (1994); and *Companion to "A Sand County Almanac": Interpretive and Critical Essays*, edited by J. Baird Callicott (1987). A recent essay specifically on Leopold's Midwestern landscapes is William Barillas's "Aldo Leopold and Midwestern Pastoralism," in *American Studies* 37.2 (Fall 1996): 61–81. Leopold's papers are deposited in the University of Wisconsin Archives in Madison, the State Historical Society of Wisconsin Archives in Madison, the United States Forest Products Laboratory Library in Madison, and the Leopold Library of the Department of Forestry and Resource Management at the University of California–Berkeley.

THOMAS K. DEAN                    UNIVERSITY OF IOWA

## MERIDEL LE SUEUR

February 22, 1900–November 14, 1996

**BIOGRAPHY:** Meridel Le Sueur, poet, journalist, novelist, historian, short story writer, socialist, and feminist, was born in Murray, Iowa. Her stepfather, Arthur Le Sueur, was a lawyer heavily involved in socialism; her mother, Marian Wharton, was a politically active socialist and feminist. Spending most of her childhood and adolescence in Texas and Oklahoma, Meridel Le Sueur settled in St. Paul, Minnesota, where her parents introduced her to such Midwestern reform movements as the populists and the Industrial Workers of the World. Having quit school at a young age, she traveled to New York and California, where she worked in the silent film industry, waited tables, and did factory work. These experiences provided her with material for her political journalism and early short stories about common folk.

Le Sueur found the 1920s a period of political repression. However, the 1930s would be for her a political crucible. With the onset of the Great Depression, she returned to the Midwest, where she chronicled the effects of the economic collapse on farmers and the urban poor, and where she believed in the pos-

sibility of social change. During this time she also reported on labor strikes, soil erosion, and unemployment. Her reportage, pieces that combined factual reporting with the narrative techniques of fiction, captured the plight of people in the Depression, especially their experiences in relief agencies and on breadlines.

Because of her socialist leanings, Le Sueur was politically harassed during the Cold War period of the 1940s and 1950s. Her publishing, though, found a new audience in the politically active 1960s. Consequently, many of her repressed works were reprinted in the 1970s and 1980s, attracting a new generation of politically minded Americans.

An important female figure in the literary history of her time, Le Sueur died in Hudson, Wisconsin, on November 14, 1996.

**SIGNIFICANCE:** Le Sueur's reputation as an important figure in the literary history of the Midwest rests on her use of Midwestern people and culture in many of her short stories and in much of her reportage of the 1930s. Drawing heavily on her experiences in Minnesota, Kansas, Illinois, and Wisconsin, she forged a career as both a journalist and a fiction writer who understood the Midwest as a significant site of analysis in American literary history. Her speech to the American Writers Congress of 1935, "Proletarian Literature and the Middle West," outlined her Midwest aesthetic, one issued from the Midwestern working class. Her involvement in relief agencies, labor strikes, and breadlines in St. Paul provided the background for one of her most stirring pieces of reportage, "Women on the Breadlines" (1932), and for her novel *The Girl* (1936). In these essays and stories, she wrote of the working-class Midwesterner victimized by class hegemony. The publication of *Salute to Spring* (1940), a collection of her Midwestern journalism and stories, and *North Star Country* (1945) marked high points in her career. The latter book, a history of the Midwest based on oral folktales, attests to her abiding interest in American Midwestern traditions.

**SELECTED WORKS:** Le Sueur's works most fully typifying her Midwest aesthetic are *The Girl* (1936), *Salute to Spring* (1940), and *North Star Country* (1945). Depression-era writings, "Women on the Breadlines" (1932), "Cows and Horses Are Hungry" (1934), "I Was Marching" (1934), and "They Follow Us Girls" (1935), are noteworthy for their political commentary and for their use of Midwestern people and settings. Her often-anthologized "Annunciation" (1935), using rich and concise prose, describes the transformation of a woman during pregnancy.

**FURTHER READING:** Elaine Hedges's *Ripening: Selected Works, 1927–1980* (1982) and Neala Schleuning's *America: Song We Sang without Knowing* (1983) remain the best treatments of Le Sueur's canon and aesthetics to date. Articles worthy of note include Blanche Gelfant's "'Everybody Steals': Language as Theft in Meridel Le Sueur's *The Girl*," in *Tradition and the Talents of Women*, edited by Florence Howe (1991), and Roberta Maierhofer's "Meridel Le Sueur: A Female Voice of the Thirties," in *Women in Search of Literary Space* (1992). Constance Coiner's *Better Red: The Writing and Resistance of Tillie Olsen and Meridel Le Sueur* (1995) is the most recent analysis of Le Sueur's works and those of her colleague TILLIE OLSEN.

JAMES M. BOEHNLEIN          UNIVERSITY OF DAYTON

## (Harry) Sinclair Lewis
February 7, 1885–January 10, 1951
(Tom Graham)

**BIOGRAPHY:** Sinclair Lewis, America's first winner of the Nobel Prize for literature, was admirably suited to become America's critic, especially of the Midwestern small town and its bourgeois values. He was born and spent his youth in his birthplace, Sauk Centre, Minnesota, a windswept, bleak prairie town whose economic base was wheat. He was the youngest of three boys born to Edward J. and Emma F. (Kermott) Lewis, a couple who had met while teaching school in Elysian, Minnesota. After the marriage, Edward went on to study medicine and became a doctor. When Harry—as his family called him—was six, in June 1891, his mother died of tuberculosis. Twelve days later his father married Isabel Warner, the daughter of the household where the elder Lewis had boarded when he was a medical student. In *Sinclair Lewis, An American Life*, Mark Schorer notes that the adult Lewis called her "more mother than step-mother, psychically my own mother" (18).

From his earliest days, Sinclair Lewis could never meet the expectations of his father, the town doctor, nor fit into the life of his village. Tall and gangly, with a head too large for his thin body and, from his early teens on, a face covered with acne, his homely appearance was exaggerated by his tendency to act the buffoon. By the time he went to college, he was eager to escape the confines of Sauk Centre. As preparation for college, he spent a year at Oberlin Academy, and in July 1902 he was admitted to Yale University. He entered Yale with great expectations and a number of romantic illusions about college life. He worked as a freshman on the *Yale Courant*, and his first published story, "The Coward Minstrel," appeared on June 18, 1904, during his second year there. However, despite this early success with the college newspaper, the next six years saw a long, slow disaffection with college life. In October 1906 Lewis left Yale to "bum" around the country. During his hiatus from college he shipped out on a cattle boat, the *Georgian*, and worked as a cattle feeder on the passage to England and back, doing very dirty, even dangerous, work. During this period he continued to write both poetry and short fiction, and his first commercially published short story appeared in the *Pacific Monthly* in 1905. In 1906 Lewis spent a month at UPTON SINCLAIR's communal settlement, Helicon Hall, in Englewood, New Jersey. Eventually he returned to Yale and took his AB degree in June 1908.

He spent the years after college moving from one newspaper job to another, holding none of them for more than a few months. Lewis began his journalistic career in the editorial offices of the Waterloo, Iowa, *Daily Courier*, but he soon returned to New York. It wasn't until he became an editor for the Frederick A. Stokes Company in 1910 that he stayed in one place for more than a year. All the while he continued his freelance writing, publishing short stories and two long serialized stories which appeared in the *Nautilus*. His first book, *Hike and the Aeroplane*, a children's story, was commissioned by Stokes and published under the pseudonym Tom Graham in August 1912.

The acceptance of a short story, "Nature, Inc.," by the *Saturday Evening Post* in 1915 marked a turning point in Sinclair Lewis's life. He had already published two novels, *Our Mr. Wrenn* in 1914 and *The Trail of the Hawk* in 1915. Beginning with "Nature, Inc.," Lewis wrote sixteen short stories in a period of eighteen months. In the next four years he wrote forty-four stories, all of which were accepted for publication by well-known periodicals of the day. Between 1915 and 1920, more than fifty Lewis short stories appeared in magazines including the *Metropolitan, Smart Set,* and *Red Book,* and his name became a byword at the *Saturday Evening Post.* These stories brought him national recognition as a writer and allowed him to explore the concerns and ideas that would dominate all of his later fiction.

In February 1914, the same month that *Our Mr. Wrenn* was published, Lewis announced his engagement to Grace Hegger, a pretty, vain, and spirited woman whose poise and chic had captured his admiration. He went to work for George H. Doran Co., writing promotional material for their best-selling list of British authors. In 1915 he and Grace Hegger were married. The marriage produced one child, Wells Lewis, born July 25, 1917.

The long apprenticeship of Sinclair Lewis came to its full flower in the decade of the 1920s with the publication of five major novels: *Main Street* (1920), *Babbitt* (1922), *Arrowsmith* (1925), *Elmer Gantry* (1927), and *Dodsworth* (1929). *Main Street* was published by Harcourt, Brace, and it met with almost instantaneous success and was acclaimed by the critics. It was voted a Pulitzer Prize in 1921, but the trustees of Columbia University overruled the jury's decision and awarded the prize to Edith Wharton's *Age of Innocence* instead. *Babbitt* followed in 1922 and garnered even more critical notice. Lewis, who was noted for meticulous research, collaborated with PAUL DE KRUIF, also a critic of the medical establishment, on *Arrowsmith,* and the Pulitzer Prize was awarded to Lewis for *Arrowsmith* in 1926. However, he refused to accept it, mostly out of pique at what had happened with the earlier award. In the midst of all of this success, Lewis separated from Grace Hegger Lewis in 1925, and they were divorced in April 1928. In the meantime he met Dorothy Thompson in July 1927 in Rome. She was then chief of Central European Service in Berlin, serving as a correspondent to the *Philadelphia Public Ledger* and the *New York Evening Post.* Thompson was a brilliant journalist who had the respect of all her male colleagues, and Lewis pursued her ardently and relentlessly until she agreed to marry him in May 1928. They had one son, Michael Lewis, who was born on June 20, 1930.

The awarding of the 1930 Nobel Prize marked the beginning of Lewis's decline, both as a writer and as a man. *It Can't Happen Here* (1936) owes much of its success to the times in which it was written and to the Federal Theatre WPA play production, which opened simultaneously in fifteen cities across the nation. Only *Cass Timberlane* (1945) emerges as a work of quality comparable to the novels in the decade of the 1920s.

Sinclair Lewis's personal life was marked by disintegrating relationships, such as his break with Alfred Harcourt, which also terminated his publishing relationship with Harcourt, Brace, and the dissolution of his marriage to Dorothy Thompson. His drinking and restless wandering made him an abusive, exhausting, and irritating companion. He left Thompson in April 1937, saying that "her work had ruined their marriage" (Schorer 628–29). They were divorced in January 1942. His only respite from a harried existence seemed a brief fling with the theater and his romance with the seventeen-year-old ingenue, Marcella Powers. He met Rosemary Marcella Powers in August 1938, while acting in Eugene O'Neill's *Ah, Wilderness!* at the Provincetown Playhouse. She remained a somewhat intermittent companion until her marriage in 1947, and they continued friends until his death. Wells Lewis, his son with Grace Hegger Lewis, was killed by a sniper's bullet during World War II, in October 1944.

Sinclair Lewis died in Rome of "paralysis of the heart," according to the death certificate, on January 10, 1951. He was to be buried there until his older brother, Claude, intervened, had him cremated, and had his ashes returned to a grave in Sauk Centre. His biographer, Mark Schorer, closes his account with: "All of the ancient history of the West lay around him. And in the ruin on the bed lay another West, Sauk Centre, Minnesota. He had never left home . . ." (814).

**SIGNIFICANCE:** Sinclair Lewis is remembered today as the writer who made Americans stop and take a hard look at themselves. His "Pentateuch," *Main Street, Babbitt, Arrowsmith, Elmer Gantry,* and *Dodsworth,* the major work for which he received the Nobel Prize for literature in 1930, attacked America's most venerated institutions. Out of Lewis's own alienation from Sauk Centre, Minnesota, there grew a satiric eye that could examine and dissect American life in all its varied manifestations. The small town as the seedbed of American democracy, where independent, resourceful citizens helped and supported one another in times of triumph and tragedy, was shown to be a suffocating, maiming environment. The village as a kind of extended family and the source of America's moral strength and self-reliance was revealed as a collection of petty, fearful individuals, intent on securing their lives with arbitrary conventions and on pursuing with single-mindedness the trappings of social status. Carol Kennicott's walk down Main Street became America's first critical look at one of its most cherished myths.

*Main Street* is an anatomy of provincialism. In it Lewis examines subject by subject what makes up life in America's Gopher Prairies: the small-town streets, the gossip, the parties, the efforts at cultural reform, even summer vacations at the lake. *Main Street* is the symbol of dullness, conventionality, and sterility. The theme of *Main Street* is the uniformity and negativity spread by the "village virus" (Schorer 102).

The 1920s were imbued with a sense of destiny. The great middle class was realizing the fruits of the Industrial Revolution, and postwar prosperity was filtering down to the individual businessman. The villages were growing up into mid-size towns with subdivisions and tract houses. Cars and fancy plumbing were within the reach of all but the lower classes, and feeding American acquisitiveness had become a business in itself. Gopher Prairie had become Zenith.

With the publication of *Babbitt*, Lewis forced America to acknowledge its materialism, and with that its shallowness, and to recognize how its devotion to industrial progress had skewed its values. "Babbittry" became an instant label for all the distorted principles the age had produced. Lewis's portrayal is a superficially authentic but actually distorted account of life in an industrial and commercial society dominated by the profit motive and standardization.

No American institutions escaped Sinclair Lewis's penetrating examination, not science nor religion. In *Arrowsmith*, for which he declined the Pulitzer Prize, Lewis attacked the medical establishment, from the general practitioner to the public health official to the lofty towers of pure research. In *Elmer Gantry*

he forced America to examine religious fundamentalism and the chicanery of the revivalist. And, though it differs in both tone and technique from the other novels, in *Dodsworth* he examined the institution of marriage—the relationship of American men to their women—and he did so by juxtaposing America to the older civilizations of Europe. If the 1920s represent the young nation's "coming of age," then Sinclair Lewis played a powerful role in its maturation.

Time and retrospection show clearly that Lewis reached the pinnacle of his powers as an author in the 1920s. Although he enjoyed an immense popularity as a novelist through the 1930s and 1940s, he never again attained the artistic level that he achieved in the major novels of the 1920s. His caricatures in the late novels were often too broad and the satire degenerated into burlesque. Yet Lewis retained his instinct for recognizing where America was going astray. His warning about fascism, *It Can't Happen Here* (1935), was taken to heart; *Kingsblood Royal* (1947) is credited with being among the first attacks on America's racism. Throughout his life Sinclair Lewis's books continued to sell more than one hundred thousand copies and to be picked by the Book-of-the-Month Club and the Literary Guild for their membership.

Only two novels stand out in Lewis's later years as having the same power and artistic merit as his earlier novels: *It Can't Happen Here* and *Cass Timberlane*. *It Can't Happen Here* is a satiric analysis of the major threats to the free spirit in America: big business, mass taste and values, the forces of conformity, and political demaguery. The relationship of *It Can't Happen Here* to the great novels of the 1920s is strong. The rise of the "Corpos" is merely an extension of Babbitt's Good Citizens League. *Cass Timberlane* is possibly the best book of this later period. It is both the anatomy of a Midwestern town, Grand Republic, and the chronicle of a marriage. Cass typifies the highest order of native man both in descent and profession, and Lewis's treatment of both him and his city is kinder than his treatment of Babbitt or Zenith.

William Couch Jr. points out in "The Emergence, Rise and Decline of the Reputation of Sinclair Lewis," a dissertation completed at the University of Chicago in 1954, that Lewis's point of view is romantic but his fictional presentation is essentially naturalistic. This places Lewis in an interesting relation to the literary controversy between romance and realism. Lewis's values were formed in an earlier period than those of the young writers during and just after World War I. Both his characters and his vision of America represent an older version of the American Dream. Lewis had internalized the values of his Midwestern background: the idealism of the nineteenth century, the sense that the average man can act nobly and unselfishly and in ways that are beneficial to his community. He retained all his life the values of the pioneering spirit, still strong in his prairie town when he was a boy. This was the positive element in his largely negative presentation of American life. His books call for a return to the heroic virtues of the pioneers so that the fulfillment of the American Dream can be realized. He is a romantic who located his romantic dreams in the region he satirized, the American Midwest.

The Nobel Prize Committee recognized in Sinclair Lewis a man who had embraced the archetypal American myths. His "art" lay in his ironic perspective, his ability to depict through satire how far the Babbitts had strayed from their philosophical and moral roots.

Lewis's contribution to American literature is in many ways remarkable. He has recorded the reign of grotesque vulgarity in this country in a way that a man with different talents working in a different genre could not have done. It is no mean feat to have created a man and a town that, in themselves, comprise the characteristics of a type so completely that thereafter this kind of man and this kind of town are known by their names. Because of Lewis the words "Babbitt" and "Main Street" have been added to the American vocabulary as precise and definite things.
**SELECTED WORKS:** Sinclair Lewis's major works are *Main Street, The Story of Carol Kennicott* (1920), *Babbitt* (1922), *Arrowsmith* (1925), *Elmer Gantry* (1927), and *Dodsworth* (1929). *It Can't Happen Here* (1935) and *Kingsblood Royal* (1947) are of special interest because of Lewis's prescience about America's problems (fascism and racism). Of his works written before 1920, *Our Mr. Wrenn* (1914) is worth reading. The best of the later novels is *Cass Timberlane, A Novel of Husbands and Wives* (1945). The best

collection of Lewis's short fiction is *I'm a Stranger Here Myself and Other Stories*, edited by Mark Schorer (1962).
**FURTHER READING:** The major biography is Mark Schorer's *Sinclair Lewis, An American Life* (1961). Grace Hegger Lewis wrote an account of her marriage to Lewis, *With Love from Gracie: Sinclair Lewis, 1912–1925* (1955), and Vincent Sheean describes the years Lewis spent with Dorothy Thompson in *Dorothy and Red* (1963). Richard Lingeman is the author of a new biography to be published by Random House. A quarterly newsletter is published by the Sinclair Lewis Society located in the Department of English at Illinois State University. The newsletter contains articles, critical essays and reviews, and a continuing checklist of Lewis materials.

The most complete checklist of Sinclair Lewis's work is Stephen R. Pastore's *Sinclair Lewis: A Descriptive Bibliography* (1997). Sheldon Norman Grebstein's *Sinclair Lewis* (1962) and D. Dooley's *The Art of Sinclair Lewis* (1967) are extended critical works. An excellent collection of shorter critical analyses is Mark Schorer's *Sinclair Lewis: A Collection of Critical Essays* (1962). Harrison Smith has edited *From Main Street to Stockholm: Letters of Sinclair Lewis, 1919–1930* (1951). In 1995 the Minnesota Historical Society acquired Lewis's correspondence with George Horace Lorrimer, longtime editor of the *Saturday Evening Post*. These letters cover the years 1915 to 1936. Lewis's letters to Marcella Powers, covering the last twelve years of his life, are held at St. Cloud State University, Minnesota. The major collection of Sinclair Lewis material is at Yale University.
CLARA LEE R. MOODIE
CENTRAL MICHIGAN UNIVERSITY

## ABRAHAM LINCOLN
February 12, 1809–April 15, 1865
**BIOGRAPHY:** Abraham Lincoln, sixteenth president of the United States, was born to Thomas and Nancy (Hanks) Lincoln, in a log cabin on the Nolin River in Hardin County, Kentucky. Both parents were of Virginia origins; their story, multiplied many times, was that of the Westward movement. Both parents were humble people, of doubtful literacy, who replicated the pioneer experience, their lives dominated by the harsh reality of the West, the drive to move on, and the fundamental revivalist religion and Democratic political faith

that gave intellectual and emotional stability to their lives. Both doctrines were to be influential in Abraham Lincoln's formative years in Kentucky and later in Indiana.

At the Nolin River farm Lincoln learned to walk and talk; when he was two, the family moved to a larger farm, but no better physical circumstances, on Knob Creek. There Lincoln attended an A.B.C. subscription school, a primary school supported by parents' fees, for a few weeks in the fall of 1815 and again in 1816. The family moved across the Ohio River in the winter of 1816, and in the winter of 1820 he attended Andrew Crawford's school in Spencer County, Indiana, for a few weeks; in 1822 he attended "blab" school, a bookless school emphasizing memorization and recitation, for about four months. In 1824 he completed his formal education, a total of about two years, with about six months at Azel Dorsey's school.

In Indiana his mother died in 1818; in 1819 his father married Sarah Bush Johnson, a Kentucky widow who was to give Abraham much encouragement and support. Lincoln worked as a farmhand and later as a ferryman on the Ohio. In 1828 he traveled to New Orleans as a crew member on a flatboat, returning by land, and the next year he clerked in a store. In 1830 the family moved on to the prairies of Macon County, Illinois, where Lincoln became the "railsplitter" to fence the new acreage. In 1831, legally an adult, he made another flatboat trip to New Orleans, but on his return he left the farm forever, moving instead to the thriving frontier village of New Salem, Illinois.

When asked in 1860 to describe those early years, Lincoln quoted Thomas Gray; they were, he said, "the short and simple annals of the poor" (CARL SANDBURG, *The Prairie Years* 2, 1926, 356). His cousin Dennis Hanks later described the experience more graphically: "We weren't much better off'n the Indians, 'ceptin' we took an interest in politics and religion" (Rufus Rockwell Wilson, *Lincoln among His Friends*, 1942, 22). But both descriptions neglected to come to terms with whatever it was that happened to Lincoln during those years that gave him a determination to rise in the open society of rural Illinois, a drive that was to create the most durable myth of the West and of the nation, that of the individual's opportunity to rise as far as one's tal-

Abraham Lincoln.
Courtesy of the Chicago Historical Society

ent, energy, and ambition would take him. In Lincoln's case, that rise was literally from the log cabin of his birth, youth, and young manhood to the White House of his maturity.

In New Salem, Lincoln cast his first vote; he became an unsuccessful candidate for the Illinois State Legislature; he served as a militia captain in the BLACK HAWK War; he became known as a storyteller; he read voraciously; and he became a storekeeper and later postmaster. In 1834 Lincoln became a surveyor, gained election to the Illinois Legislature as a Whig, thus rejecting his father's Democratic faith, and became something of a Deist, thus rejecting his parents' religious faith. Admitted to the bar in 1836, he moved to Springfield in 1837 as New Salem began its decline. He practiced law and served in the legislature until 1842. Then he married Mary Todd on November 4, 1842, and practiced law on the central Illinois legal circuit until 1847. In 1846 he had been elected to Congress, where he served one term, 1847–48; when he was not reelected, he returned to the practice of law in Illinois until 1860.

The decade of the 1850s was crucial for the nation and for Lincoln as the slavery crisis intensified. Reluctantly, as the Whigs foundered on the slavery issue, he became a Republican; he became known statewide, and by 1858, nationally, as a simple but eloquent prairie lawyer as the result of his unsuccessful campaign for the Senate against Stephen Douglas that year. Early in 1860 he was invited to speak at the Cooper Union in New York and then in New England. On May 18, 1860, a dark-horse candidate, he became the Republican nominee for the presidency, and on November 6, he was elected, receiving a minority of popular votes in a three-way race but an impressive electoral majority.

From his inauguration on March 4, 1861, through his renomination and reelection in 1864, to his death in 1865, Lincoln's life, his thinking, and his writing were synonymous with the prosecution of the Civil War, the outbreak of which had greeted his election and inauguration, a fact which produced some of his most eloquent speeches and profound writings. Although strongly anti-slavery from his youth, perhaps one of the reasons he had rejected his father's Democratic politics, his major concern as president was the restoration of the Union. His second concern was a profound compassion for the cost of the war in human terms. Both concerns were the result of his formative years in Indiana and Illinois, the years that saw the Old Northwest become the Midwest by midcentury. The area was strongly nationalistic and convinced of the innate worth of the individual human being. It was convinced, too, of the ultimate divine justice with which human affairs were arbitrated. All these influences are reflected in his writings, each of which became more profound, more compassionate, and more convinced of divine justice as the war progressed. He died of an assassin's bullet on April 15, 1865, as the war was coming to an end.

**SIGNIFICANCE:** Of all Lincoln's writings, the four great utterances of the war years— the Emancipation Proclamation of September 22, 1862, to become effective on January 1, 1863; the Gettysburg Address of November 19, 1863; the letter to Mrs. Lydia Bixby of November 21, 1864; and the Second Inaugural Address of March 4, 1865—illustrate most clearly Lincoln's command of language, the depth of his compassion, and the strength of his convictions, and all of them are firmly rooted in the experiences and influences of his youth and young manhood.

The Emancipation Proclamation is a document that is completely legal and rational, with all its language devoted to one purpose: that of his constitutional right and power, as commander in chief, to declare the slaves in those states in rebellion to be free as an aid to prosecution of the war. At the same time, however, the document declares that it is "an act of justice" as well as of constitutional legality (Lincoln, *Works* 6, 30).

The Gettysburg Address, the letter to Mrs. Bixby, and the Second Inaugural Address are documents that have their roots in the war, but each transcends war and human suffering to find a meaning more profound, more compassionate, and more universal than the bloodshed and suffering that engendered them. The Gettysburg Address defines the meaning of the battle and its cost in human suffering, but it also defines the tragedy and ultimate triumph of human life. The letter to Mrs. Bixby, who had lost five sons in the war, glimpses, out of pure compassion, the graves dug in grief and out of which a solemn pride emerges. The Second Inaugural Address, the greatest of all Lincoln's utterances, compounds righteousness, humility, forgiveness, retribution, and absolution in an eloquent definition of the Civil War, the American experience, and the ultimate universal reality. In it Lincoln returns, for a deeply felt moment, to the profound confidence in divine justice that marked the religious experience of his youth.

Without these four documents Lincoln's literary reputation would be that of an eloquent American president, perhaps ranking with Theodore Roosevelt or Woodrow Wilson. With them, it is as lofty as it is secure. In each of these documents, he transcended the reality of the moment to interpret the universal experience in words that are simple, deeply felt, and profound, and in so doing each document gives its own testimony of Lincoln's greatness as man and as writer.

**SELECTED WORKS:** Lincoln's complete writings from early copybook verse to his last public address on April 11, 1865, are included in *The Collected Works of Abraham Lincoln*, with supplements, edited by Roy P. Basler with Marian Delores and Lloyd A. Dunlap (1953). Other collections are *Created Equal? The Com-*

*plete Lincoln-Douglas Debates of 1858,* edited by Paul M. Angle (1958); and *The Literary Works of Abraham Lincoln,* edited by DAVID D. AN-DERSON (1970).

**FURTHER READING:** The best one-volume life of Lincoln remains *Abraham Lincoln,* by Benjamin P. Thomas (1952). Other, more extensive or more specialized works are *Abraham Lincoln: The Prairie Years,* in two volumes (1926), and *Abraham Lincoln: The War Years,* in four volumes (1936), both by Carl Sandburg. *Abraham Lincoln* (1970), by David D. Anderson, is a study of Lincoln as a literary artist.

Lincoln's papers are widely dispersed, and many libraries have small collections, but the largest and most important collections are in the Library of Congress, the Illinois State Historical Library, the Henry E. Huntington Library, the National Archives, and the Brown University Library.

DAVID D. ANDERSON    MICHIGAN STATE UNIVERSITY

## (NICHOLAS) VACHEL LINDSAY
November 10, 1879–December 5, 1931

**BIOGRAPHY:** Vachel Lindsay, poet, essayist, visual artist, and film theorist, was born in Springfield, Illinois. His parents were Vachel Thomas Lindsay and Esther Catherine (Frazee) Lindsay. The Lindsays had three living children, Olive, Vachel, and Joy, while three children died in infancy. Lindsay's father hoped that young Vachel would follow in his footsteps and attend medical school, but after three years at Hiram College, Vachel quit his medical studies and went on to study art at the Chicago Art Institute (1901–1903) and the New York School of Art (1903–1905). While studying art, Lindsay worked at various menial jobs. His teachers were not impressed with Lindsay's drawing, but he sold several poems to the magazine *Critic,* and he handmade a book of poems, *Where Is Aladdin's Lamp,* in 1904.

Estranged from his parents and destitute, in 1906 Lindsay decided to set out on a walking trip to share his poems and art with the people he met along the way, in what he described as a campaign for beauty, democracy, and civilization. He walked from Florida to Grassy Springs, Kentucky, where he stayed with his aunt, Eudora Lindsay South. He returned to his home in Springfield in 1908, where he undertook a series of lectures at the YMCA. He published several pamphlets, and

in 1910 he published a volume of poems, *The Village Magazine,* which was well received. In 1912 Lindsay undertook a walking trip to the West. This time he carried with him a small volume of poems entitled *Rhymes to Be Traded for Bread,* which he intended to trade for his keep along the way. This trip is chronicled in his book of prose, *Adventures while Preaching the Gospel of Beauty* (1914). By then, Lindsay had developed the oratorical lecture and reading style that made him a popular figure on the lecture circuit and on college campuses. With the publication of *General William Booth Enters into Heaven and Other Poems* in 1913, and *The Congo and Other Poems,* with an introduction by HARRIET MONROE in 1914, Lindsay's reputation as a literary artist was assured. Monroe was an admirer of Lindsay's and had invited him to send her poems for *Poetry,* the magazine she edited. He received prizes from the magazine in 1913 and again in 1915. It was at one of Harriet Monroe's dinner parties in Chicago that Lindsay met William Butler Yeats in March 1914.

Lindsay was a prolific poet and essayist and a very energetic lecturer. The new art of the film caught his interest, and in 1915 he published *The Art of the Moving Picture. The Chinese Nightingale and Other Poems* was published in 1917, and *Collected Poems* in 1923. By the 1920s, however, his reputation waned. The death of his mother in 1922 was a serious loss for Lindsay. He suffered a physical breakdown in 1923 and was forced to cancel a tour. Lindsay married Elizabeth Conner in 1925, and the couple had two children: Susan Doniphan and Nicholas Cave Lindsay. He had problems supporting his family in the late 1920s and suffered from serious bouts of depression. His death in 1931 was officially attributed to a coronary thrombosis, but according to several biographers, including EDGAR LEE MASTERS and Mark Harris, he committed suicide by drinking a bottle of lye.

**SIGNIFICANCE:** Vachel Lindsay was famous in his day for his revival of poetry as a spoken art. He increased interest in poetry and folklore as an oral art in the Midwest through the use of dramatic delivery and popular themes. Lindsay drew on the work of Walt Whitman and MARK TWAIN, and from the self-improvement and community service outlook of his parents, especially his mother's, to develop a vision of Springfield, the Midwest, and America as another Garden of Eden. His *Adventures while Preaching the Gospel of Beauty* (1914) and *The Golden Book of Springfield* (1920) attest to this vision. In his talks, lectures, and energetic readings throughout the country, Lindsay spread his "gospel of beauty" and the populist values he had learned while growing up in Springfield and had formulated while on his walking tours. For Lindsay, the people and towns of the Midwest held within them higher values of civilization that needed only to be developed and popularized.

In *The Golden Book of Springfield*, a work of prose, Lindsay envisioned a Springfield of the future: a city greatly transformed architecturally, but a city whose people were yet in need of improvement. Should the reforms he envisioned materialize, both the people and the town would flower. Although his reputation suffered in his lifetime, it is secure today even though some critics feel that he took an uncritical standpoint toward American history in general and "manifest destiny" in particular. While chiefly remembered as a poet, Lindsay also was a man of ideas, as much of his work testifies. His vision for society had its roots in the abolitionist and populist traditions of the Midwest, and it is in this light that his work has been reevaluated.

**SELECTED WORKS:** There are several collections of Lindsay's poetry. The latest, *The Poetry of Vachel Lindsay*, 3 vols., and *The Prose of Vachel Lindsay*, were published by Spoon River Poetry Press, Granite Falls, Minnesota, edited by Dennis Camp (1984–88). *Adventures, Rhyme and Design: Early Writings* (1968) is a useful work. *The Art of the Moving Picture* (1915) was reprinted in 1970 with an introduction by Stanley Kauffmann.

**FURTHER READING:** Lindsay has had several distinguished biographers; see Mark Harris, *City of Discontent* (1952); Anna Massa, *Vachel Lindsay: Fieldworker for the American Dream* (1970); and Edgar Lee Masters, *Vachel Lindsay: A Poet in America* (1935). Marc Chenetier edited *Letters of Vachel Lindsay* (1979). The University of Virginia has the most extensive holdings of Lindsay materials, and the Lindsay House in Springfield, Illinois, has materials of scholarly interest.

TOM L. PAGE                           WICHITA, KANSAS

## MALCOLM LITTLE.
*See* Malcolm X

## DAVID ROSS LOCKE
September 20, 1833–February 15, 1888
(Petroleum V. Nasby)

**BIOGRAPHY:** Born in Vestal, New York, to laborer and self-proclaimed temperance man Nathaniel Reed Locke and Hester (Ross) Locke, David Ross Locke began as a printer's apprentice at age twelve. Moving to Ohio in 1853, he edited newspapers in Plymouth and Bucyrus. In 1855 he married Martha H. Bodine, by whom he had three sons. In 1861 he relocated to Findlay and bought the *Hancock Jeffersonian*. While livening up the paper's contents to increase circulation, he refined a vernacular narrator from his earlier columns into Petroleum V. (Vesuvius) Nasby, an ignorant, racist, sexist Copperhead preacher from Confedrit X Roads who was to make his creator famous. In 1865 he became editor of the Toledo *Blade*, which he would make known throughout the region and even the nation.

After the Civil War, Locke led a busy and influential life as a popular lecturer, reformer, New York newspaper editor, and businessman. He reprinted pseudo-Oriental stories which had appeared in his short-lived *Locke's National Monthly* as *The Morals of Abou Ben Adhem* (1875). *Nasby in Exile* (1882) collects a series of travel essays in Locke's own persona with his own democratic sympathies. No copy survives of his plays, *Inflation* (1876) or *Widow Bedott*, which was successfully performed in 1879. Lecture audiences demanded to hear his poem, *Hannah Jane*, separately published in 1882. On February 15, 1888, he died in Toledo of tuberculosis.

**SIGNIFICANCE:** Barely twenty when he emigrated to Ohio, Locke already possessed the commitment to the temperance movement and the principles of the burgeoning Republican Party which would make him at home in his adopted region. The Nasby essays, of which ABRAHAM LINCOLN was very fond, were influential in maintaining Union morale. In his discussion of the literary comedians in *Native American Humor*, Walter Blair lists among Nasby's admirers General Ulysses S. Grant and James Russell Lowell (109–10). Locke was a friend and soul mate of the radical Republican cartoonist Thomas Nast, who illustrated some of Locke's books. A satirist rather than an entertainer, Locke through the Nasby Letters struck brutal and powerful blows against the

Confederacy and its Democratic sympathizers, verbal equivalents of Nast's uncompromising cartoons which, likewise, never hesitated to wave the bloody shirt. These essays recall the passions aroused in the Midwest by a Civil War now nearly forgotten. His two novels, *A Paper City* (1879) and *The Demagogue*, published posthumously in 1891, are representative but not exceptional examples of Midwestern realism.

**SELECTED WORKS:** Collections of Nasby letters include *The Nasby Papers* (1864); *Divers Views, Opinions, and Prophecies of Yours Trooly, Petroleum V. Nasby* (1866); *Androo Johnson, His Life* (1866); *Swingin' 'Round the Cirkle* (1867); *Ekkoes from Kentucky* (1868); *The Impendin Crisis uv the Democracy* (1868); *The Struggles (Social, Financial and Political) of Petroleum V. Nasby* (1872); *Inflation at the Cross Roads* (1875); *The President's Policy* (1877); *The Democratic John Bunyan* (1880); *The Nasby Letters* (1893); and *The Struggles of Petroleum V. Nasby*, edited by Joseph Jones (1963). *Nasby in Exile; or, Six Months of Travel* (1882) does not use the Nasby persona. *The Morals of Abou Ben Adhem* (1875) is a collection of pseudo-Oriental tales, while *A Paper City* (1879) and *The Demagogue* (1891) are novels. *Hannah Jane* (1882) is a poem. Several of these titles are still in print: *Nasby in Exile*, a reproduction of the 1882 edition (Irvington, N.Y.: n.d.); *A Paper City*, a reprint of the 1879 edition (1986); *Morals of Abou Ben Adhem*, a reprint of the 1875 edition (Irvington, N.Y.: n.d.); *Swingin' Round the Cirkle*, a reprint of the 1867 edition (1986); and *The Demagogue: A Political Novel*, a reprint of the 1891 edition (1986).

**FURTHER READING:** The definitive biography of Locke is John M. Harrison's *The Man Who Made Nasby: David Ross Locke* (1969). Cyril Clemens's earlier work, *Petroleum Vesuvius Nasby* (1936), utilizes some questionable sources. James C. Austin's Twayne book, *Petroleum V. Nasby (David Ross Locke)* (1965), is useful. Some shorter studies are helpful: James C. Austin's "The World of Petroleum V. Nasby: Blacks, Women, and Political Corruption," *MidAmerica* 3 (1976): 101–22; Ronald Grosh's "Civil War Politics in the Novels of David Ross Locke," *MidAmerica* 13 (1986): 19–30; and DAVID D. ANDERSON, "The Odyssey of Petroleum Vesuvius Nasby," *Ohio History* 74 (1965): 232–46.

PAUL P. SOMERS JR.    MICHIGAN STATE UNIVERSITY

**LARRY LOCKRIDGE.**
*See* appendix (1998)

**ROSS (FRANKLIN) LOCKRIDGE JR.**
April 25, 1914–March 6, 1948

**BIOGRAPHY:** Ross Lockridge Jr., novelist, was born in Bloomington, Indiana, son of Ross Lockridge, an historian, and Elsie (Shockley) Lockridge, a psychologist. After moving to Indianapolis and then Fort Wayne, Indiana, his family returned in 1924 to Bloomington, where Lockridge continued his formal schooling, excelling in all subjects. He frequently accompanied his father on his excursions throughout Indiana, during which Ross Senior, well known as "Mr. Indiana," evoked local heroes in public oratorical performances that he termed "historic site recitals."

Entering Indiana University in 1931, Ross Lockridge Jr. spent his junior year abroad at the Sorbonne, taking highest honors among foreign students. Returning to Indiana University, where he was known as "A plus Lockridge," he graduated with the highest academic average ever accumulated there. In 1937 he married his high school sweetheart, Vernice Baker, while teaching as a graduate student in the Department of English and writing a four-hundred-page epic poem, "The Dream of the Flesh of Iron" (unpublished).

Accepting a scholarship to Harvard in 1940, he announced that he would write a doctoral dissertation on Walt Whitman. Actually, he began writing, in 1941, a novel based in part on his mother Elsie Shockley's side of the family. In 1946, now the father of four children, he carried the twenty-pound manuscript of *Raintree County* to Houghton Mifflin's offices in a battered suitcase. Accepted within five weeks, the novel, prior to publication, was excerpted in *Life* magazine, won an enormous prize given by MGM along with a movie contract, and was the Main Selection of the Book-of-the-Month Club. Lockridge revised the novel in a lake cottage in Manistee, Michigan, and visited Hollywood with his wife late in 1947. He and his family then moved back to Bloomington.

Published on January 5, 1948, *Raintree County* received mostly lavish reviews. But Lockridge was already deeply depressed for a multitude of reasons that eluded the public eye. Two months following publication, and one day before his novel was announced the number one national best-seller, he took his own life by carbon monoxide poisoning. His obituary was carried on the front page of the *New York Times*.

**SIGNIFICANCE:** In *Raintree County*, Ross Lockridge unabashedly aspired to write the Great American Novel, not a regional novel, but he anchored his 1,060–page narrative in nineteenth-century Midwestern history, folklore, and landscape. The novel incorporates many rites, customs, and linguistic practices of Hoosier culture in a carnivalesque atmosphere and has been called, by Joel Jones and Charles Trueheart, at least the "Great American Studies Novel."

Set in a mythical Indiana county based partly on Henry County, Indiana, the novel tells the life story of John Wickliff Shawnessy in a series of flashbacks occasioned by the events of a single day, July 4, 1892. It thus owes much to Joyce—as well as to such Midwestern writers as SHERWOOD ANDERSON, MARK TWAIN, JOHN DOS PASSOS, THEODORE DREISER, HAMLIN GARLAND, ERNEST HEMINGWAY, RING LARDNER, SINCLAIR LEWIS, ABRAHAM LINCOLN, EDGAR LEE MASTERS, and BOOTH TARKINGTON. But Lockridge attempted an encyclopedic fiction that would be more accessible than *Ulysses*, as William York Tindall noted early on, to the common reader. Its form is cinematic, indebted to *Intolerance* and *Citizen Kane*; its plot is based on Hawthorne's story, "The Great Stone Face"; and its themes reflect Lockridge's absorption in myth, environment, sexuality, and the need for reaffirmation of American idealism in the midst of cultural decline.

**SELECTED WORKS:** *Raintree County* (1948) is Ross Lockridge's only novel. At his death he left a large archive of unpublished material, some of which is now in the Lilly Library of Indiana University and the Houghton Library of Harvard University. Most materials remain, as of this writing, in the possession of his family.

**FURTHER READING:** Book-length studies include Larry Lockridge's full-scale critical biography, *Shade of the Raintree: The Life and Death of Ross Lockridge, Jr.* (1994), and John Leggett's *Ross and Tom: Two American Tragedies* (1974), which narrates Lockridge's life as well as that of Thomas Heggen, author of *Mister Roberts*. A notable doctoral dissertation is

**Ross Lockridge Jr., 1946.**
Photo by Francis (Jeff) Wylie.
Courtesy of Larry Lockridge

Delia Clark Temes's "The American Epic Tradition and *Raintree County*" (University of Syracuse, 1973).

Early journalistic reviews and review essays include James Baldwin's negative "The American Myth," in *New Leader* (April 10, 1948): 10, 14; Howard Mumford Jones's "Indiana Reflection of U.S. 1844–92," in *Saturday Review* 31 (January 3, 1948): 9–10, which observed that the novel had ended a long slump in American fiction; Nanette Kutner's "Ross Lockridge, Jr.: Escape from Main Street," in *Saturday Review* 31 (June 12, 1948): 6–7, 31, which includes a portrait of Lockridge's final days; Charles Lee's "Encompassing the American Spirit," from the *New York Times Book Review* (January 4, 1948): 5, 21, the review Lockridge himself liked best; and William York Tindall's "Many-leveled Fiction: Virginia Woolf to Ross Lockridge," in *College English* 10 (November 1948): 65–71.

Journalistic reviews and review essays on the occasion of the novel's republication in 1994, simultaneous with publication of *Shade of the Raintree*, include Richard Bausch's "Success and the American Novelist," in the *Los Angeles Times Book Review* (May 15, 1994): 2;

Bruce Cook's "*Raintree* Revisited," in the *Chicago Tribune Books* (May 29, 1994): 3; Scott Donaldson's "Nowhere to Go but Down," in the *Washington Post Book World* (April 10, 1994): 11; Christopher Lehmann-Haupt's "Novelist's Work and Death," in the *New York Times* (May 2, 1994): C13; Tim Page's "In Search of *Raintree County*," in *Newsday* (November 17, 1994): 1, 4–5, 7 (pt. 2); and Charles Trueheart's "The Great American Studies Novel," in *Atlantic Monthly* (September 1994): 105–11. Of the score of major 1994 reviews, only Trueheart's is, on balance, negative; several critics reconfirm Lockridge's early high estimate of his own novel, which remains, however, in problematic relationship to the American canon.

Notable critical essays include Daniel Aaron's "On Ross Lockridge's *Raintree County*," in *Classics of Civil War Fiction*, edited by David Madden and Peggy Bach (1991): 204–14; Joseph Blotner's "*Raintree County* Revisited," in *Western Humanities Review* 10 (Winter 1956): 57–64, and his introduction to *Raintree County* (1984): xiii-xvii; Fred Erisman's "*Raintree County* and the Power of Place," in *Markham Review* 8 (Winter 1979): 36–40, which makes a case for the novel as ecological fiction; Park Dixon Goist's "Habits of the Heart in *Raintree County*," in *MidAmerica* 13 (1986): 94–106; Donald Greiner's deeply considered "Ross Lockridge and the Tragedy of *Raintree County*," in *Critique: Studies in Modern Fiction* 20 (1978): 51–63; Joel Jones's "The Presence of the Past in the Heartland: *Raintree County* Revisited," in *MidAmerica* 4 (1977): 112–21; Leonard Lutwak's "*Raintree County* and the Epicising Poet in American Fiction," in *Ball State University Forum* 13 (Winter 1972): 14–28, which contains a close structural analysis; Darshan Singh Maini's "An Ode to America: A Reconsideration of *Raintree County*," in *Essays in American Studies*, edited by Isaac Sequeira (1992): 142–49; and Gerald Nemanic's "Ross Lockridge, *Raintree County*, and the Epic of Irony," in *MidAmerica* 2 (1975): 35–46. DAVID D. ANDERSON has edited a collection of critical essays, *Myth, Memory, and the American Earth: The Durability of Raintree County* (1998).

LARRY LOCKRIDGE                    NEW YORK UNIVERSITY

## EDMUND G(EORGE) LOVE
February 12, 1912–August 30, 1990

**BIOGRAPHY:** Edmund G. Love was born in Flushing, Michigan, son of Earl Dalzell Love and Muda (Perry) Love. Love's family moved from Flushing to Flint, Michigan, approximately ten miles, when he was about ten years old. The rest of his youth, apart from a year in military school, was spent in Flint during that city's heyday as a growing automobile manufacturing center. He received his AB degree in 1935 and his MA in 1940 from the University of Michigan.

From 1935 until he entered the army, Love taught English at Flint Northern High School. Although he was a decorated combat soldier in the Pacific theater, Love's main assignment was as military historian, a work he continued for three years after his discharge in 1946. Love became a freelance writer, producing his major works between 1957 and 1973. During his last years he wrote a series of principally historical and autobiographical articles for the *Flint Journal*.

His first marriage, which ended in divorce, produced a son and daughter. In 1959 he married Anna Virginia Wurts, who died shortly after Love's death. He died at a Flint hospital, mainly from the infirmities of age, after a brief illness.

**SIGNIFICANCE:** Love's most successful book, *Subways Are for Sleeping* (1957), has nothing directly to do with the Midwest but is perhaps the first book to portray the almost universal problem of urban homelessness. It was adapted into a successful Broadway play. Love wrote three highly autobiographical novels set in Michigan. *The Situation in Flushing* (1965), which became a best-seller, depicts life in a Midwestern village in the years immediately before World War I. It portrays village life partially from the viewpoint of a child and also captures the nostalgia that anyone who experienced that halcyon era must have felt. *A Small Bequest* (1973) narrates the effort of two teen-age boys to investigate a bequest in the form of lake property in northern Michigan. The third of the three Michigan books, and the most historically significant, *Hanging On* (1972), details Love's experiences from approximately the age of seventeen, in 1929, to 1940, when he was twenty-eight. At the beginning of the story, Love's father, who owned a lumberyard, was a prosperous member of the upper-middle economic class. What follows is the struggle of this middle-class family to "hang on," somehow keeping the family together during the ten-year economic crisis now known as the Great Depression.

Most of Love's books are largely autobiographical. His strength was straightforward narrative with engaging vividness and power. *The Situation in Flushing* is a near classic with universal appeal. Most events in the story are probably unique to a small Midwestern village, from a youngster who knows by sound the number of each railroad engine coming into town to a massive homecoming/reunion honoring the community's sole black family. *A Small Bequest* depicts a common phenomenon in any resort area, the natives' tendency to take advantage of summer visitors. The depression of the 1930s affected the entire nation, indeed, most of the world, but nowhere more severely than in the American Midwest, where both agriculture and industry entered a life-and-death struggle. Love describes a youth's effort to understand the tide of economic events, to get an education, to hold his job as a teacher—in short, despite all difficulties, to hang on.

Edmund Love's writing is in the tradition of nineteenth-century Midwestern storytelling: pictorial, detailed, diverting, memorable—a carryover from the era before high-circulation magazines, motion pictures, and the modern media usurped people's leisure hours. If patient good humor, fortitude, and keen observation are typical Midwestern traits, then Love's writings are indeed representative.

**SELECTED WORKS:** Love's writing skills were disciplined by the writing of three official military histories of operations in the Pacific theater. His work as military historian resulted in *The 27th Infantry Division in World War II* (1949), *The Hourglass: A History of the 7th Infantry Division in World War II* (1950), *Seizure of the Gilberts and Marshalls* (with Philip A. Crowl, 1955). Later he wrote vivid accounts, both amusing and bemusing, of his military service in *War Is a Private Affair* (1959) and *Arsenic and Red Tape* (1960). Then came *Subways Are for Sleeping* and *An End to Bugling* (1963). After *The Situation in Flushing*, Love wrote his only historical novel, *A Shipment of Tarts* (1967), set mainly on the Ohio River, about an actual event that occurred during the Civil War. Ex-President Eisenhower reportedly purchased fifty copies of the book to give as Christmas presents to friends. It is a funny story, timeless so long as there are military organizations, prostitution, and civilians. In addition to *The Situation in Flushing, Hanging On; Or How to Get through a Depression and Enjoy Life* (to give the book's complete title), and *A Small Bequest*, Love's last book, *Set Up* (1980), a detective mystery also set in Michigan, involves a robbery in Flint, although the setting is incidental.

**FURTHER READING:** For Love's obituary, see the *Flint Journal,* August 31, 1990; also the *Society for the Study of Midwestern Literature Newsletter* 20.3 (Fall 1990). Love's papers are located in the Bentley Historical Library at the University of Michigan.

THEODORE R. KENNEDY

MICHIGAN STATE UNIVERSITY

## ROBERT MORSS LOVETT
December 25, 1870–February 8, 1956

**BIOGRAPHY:** Robert Morss Lovett, a professor of English at the University of Chicago from 1893 to 1936, was born in Boston, the son of Augustus Sidney, a businessman and veteran of the Civil War. Lovett grew out of the pious Congregationalism of his mother, Elizabeth (Russell), and attended Harvard, from which he graduated in 1892. In 1893 he joined the faculty of the year-old University of Chicago, boldly conceived by President William Rainey Harper and lavishly endowed by John D. Rockefeller, situated on the Midway of the Columbian Exposition. Lovett caught his first sight of the university's gothic buildings when, as he puts it in his autobiography, "the city was emerging from its triumph of the . . . Exposition into the financial panic of 1893" (53). The contrast between the "artificial glory" of the fair and the "squalor" and strife of the "real city" planted the seed of Lovett's enduring political activism (54).

In 1895 Lovett married Ida Mott-Smith, who had been a student at the Harvard Annex (later Radcliffe). During World War I, he became a vocal advocate of a just peace, an unpopular position in the Chicago of a superpatriotic era. He was the father of two daughters. His only son, Robert, was killed in action at Belleau Wood in 1918. From 1921 to 1937, Lovett lived in Hull House, where his wife served as an aide to JANE ADDAMS. In 1939 he was appointed government secretary of the Virgin Islands by Harold L. Ickes, secretary of the interior, one of his former students. Lovett served five years in this post. Under attack in Congress for his alleged radicalism, Lovett was denied his salary by the House of Representatives, an action that was eventually overturned in the Supreme Court. In 1946 he retired to Lake Zurich, Illinois. He died in a Chicago hospital at the age of eighty-five.

**SIGNIFICANCE:** In company with his faculty colleagues ROBERT HERRICK and WILLIAM VAUGHN MOODY, Lovett brought the Harvard of President Charles William Eliot, George Lyman Kittredge, and George Santayana to the heart of the thriving Midwest at the end of the nineteenth century. For the next fifty years he sent forth from Chicago his urbane, iconoclastic, and forceful views as teacher, scholar, and public advocate. Lovett was one of the catalytic agents of the Chicago Renaissance. He was closely associated with SHERWOOD ANDERSON as well as novelist Herrick and poet and playwright Moody. He formed a club at which students might hear the comments of HARRIET MONROE, the editor of *Poetry,* and readings from CARL SANDBURG, EDGAR LEE MASTERS, and Robert Frost, among others. Lovett encouraged JAMES T. FARRELL to turn his short story about Studs Lonigan into a novel and tried to find a publisher for Meyer Levin's first book. He collaborated with Moody on *A History of English Literature* (1902), which was reprinted in innumerable editions, and edited a number of literary texts and anthologies. In the 1920s and 1930s, Lovett took up in words and action such causes as the Sacco-Vanzetti case; the Flint, Michigan, sitdown strikes; and the Spanish Civil War. His writings appeared in journals of opinion, and while on a series of leaves from the university, he served in New York as editor of the *Dial* in 1919 and as associate editor of the *New Republic* from 1921 to 1929.

**SELECTED WORKS:** Lovett's autobiography, *All Our Years* (1948), and the briskly informative *A History of English Literature,* written with Moody, are most important. He wrote a study entitled *Edith Wharton* (1925) and earlier in his career, with limited success, published two novels, *Richard Gresham* (1904) and *A Winged Victory* (1907), and a play, *Cowards* (in *Drama,* August 1917). Among many articles which remain uncollected, his essay "The Future of the Middle West," in the *New Republic* (November 8, 1939): 54–56, stands out as a call for a revival of the Middle West's earlier vitality.

Lovett believed that to reestablish its "distinctive" nature the region had to resist the incursion of financial absenteeism, political corruption, labor strife, and "standardizing and uniforming tendencies" in literature and art.

**FURTHER READING:** *All Our Years* is essential to an understanding of Lovett's personal character, his achievements, and the literary and cultural milieu of Chicago during the first half of the twentieth century. The autobiography may be supplemented by Jefferson B. Fletcher's "Salute to Bob Lovett," in *New Republic* (September 27, 1943): 420–23; by the obituary in the *New York Times* (February 9, 1956): 31; and by the entries in *Current Biography* (1943): 461–65, and the *Dictionary of American Biography* 6 (1956–60): 391–92. Lovett's papers are in the library of the University of Chicago.

NEALE REINITZ          THE COLORADO COLLEGE

## DELLA THOMPSON LUTES

ca. 1871–July 13, 1942

**BIOGRAPHY:** Della Thompson grew up on a farm in Summit Township in Jackson County, Michigan, the only child of Elijah Bonnet Thompson, of New York state, and Almira Frances (Bogardus) Thompson, of Detroit. Completing high school in Jackson at sixteen, she became accredited to teach in country schools. Those years were the source of her retrospective writing. She taught in Jackson County and then in Detroit for a few years. In 1893 she married Louis Irving Lutes and had two sons, the older being killed in a shooting accident when he was seven.

She said that her first writing for money appeared in the *Detroit Free Press.* In October 1905, the *Delineator* began her six-part story, "Deestrick No. 5." Her first book, *Just Away: A Story of Hope* (1906), was prompted by the death of her son, Ralph, and dedicated "To the mothers who sorrowed with me in my sorrow" (7). Impressed by this work, the publishers invited her in 1907 to Cooperstown, New York, to join the editorial staff of their journals *American Motherhood, Table Talk,* and *Today's Housewife.* In 1924 she became housekeeping editor of *Modern Priscilla* and manager of the Priscilla Proving Plant, in Newton, Massachusetts.

Her writing was directed by her editorial responsibilities until the Priscilla organization disbanded after the 1929 stock market crash, her articles, pamphlets and books being mainly concerned with home-making topics. Still, her stylistic qualities of common sense and often pungent wit grew during these years.

The appearance of her essay "Simple Epicure" in the *Atlantic* of March 1935 began her success with a larger public. This essay and others which quickly followed provoked an unusually broad reaction from the magazine's readers, a great many of whom were men. These essays were collected and published in 1936 as *The Country Kitchen;* the book established her as a best-selling, sought-after writer and speaker. During her last years, her surviving son, Robert, became her leg man, researching her last books. She died on July 13, 1942, at Cooperstown, New York. Her ashes were returned, as she wished, to Michigan for interment at Horton.

**SIGNIFICANCE:** Della Lutes's writing is significant for its rendering of the end-of-the-century cultural period, as her readers recognized when her articles and books appeared during the 1930s and 1940s. Appealing to natives of rural Michigan and the Midwest, her books brought letters of praise from every part of the nation and from other countries, including Russia. Detailing the landscapes through the changing seasons, her stories also brought alive local politics, schooling, architecture and interior decoration, moral standards, social attitudes, and, in a unique way, the food as "prepared by late nineteenth century southern Michigan farm wives" ("A Word. . . ." 31). Her readers commended her writing particularly for its affectionate, realistic, and accurate recording of rural family life as it was lived in America at the end of the nineteenth century.

Her contribution to Michigan is commemorated by an elementary school named after her in Oakland County and by the use of excerpts from *The Country Kitchen* in the nineteenth-century floor opened in the State Museum of Michigan in 1994.

**SELECTED WORKS:** *The Country Kitchen* (1936) was followed by five additional books offering "vignettes," as she described them, of rural life: *Home Grown* (1937), *Millbrook* (1938), *Gabriel's Search* (1940), *Country Schoolma'am* (1941), and *Cousin William* (1942).

**FURTHER READING:** Biographical and critical information is to be found in three works by Lawrence R. Dawson: "'A Word for What Was Eaten': An Introduction to Della T. Lutes and Her Fiction," in *Midwestern Miscellany* 9 (1981): 31–42; "Della Thompson Lutes: A Preliminary Bibliography," in *Bulletin of Bibliography* 39 (December 1982): 184–90; and the introduction to the reprint of *The Country Kitchen* (1992): ix-xxii. The principal repository of her papers is the archive of the Clarke Historical Library, Central Michigan University, Mt. Pleasant, Michigan.

LAWRENCE R. DAWSON

CENTRAL MICHIGAN UNIVERSITY

# M-N

## CHARLES (GORDON) MACARTHUR

November 5, 1895–April 21, 1956

**BIOGRAPHY:** Charles MacArthur was born in Scranton, Pennsylvania, the fifth child of William and Georgiana (Welstead) MacArthur. His father, a farmer turned evangelist, sent fourteen-year-old Charles to Nyack, New York, to the Wilson Memorial Academy for ministerial and missionary training. After three years, the rigorous academic regime proved too constraining to his exuberant nature. Charles went to Chicago to work for the *City Press,* a daily newspaper. His notable reporting abilities led him to write for the *Chicago Herald-Examiner* and later the *Chicago Tribune,* becoming Chicago's first hundred-dollar-a-week reporter.

His military experience covered three wars. In 1916 MacArthur joined the Illinois Militia to pursue Pancho Villa in Mexico. In World War I, he served in the Rainbow Division, seeing action in the Meuse-Argonne and at Château-Thierry. This venture led to his humorous book, *A Bug's Eye View of the War* (1919), later entitled *War Bugs* (1929). In World War II, unable to join soldiers on the front lines, MacArthur became a lieutenant

colonel and assistant to the chief of the Chemical Warfare Service.

After World War I, MacArthur returned to his work as a reporter for the *Herald-Examiner* and later served on the editorial staff of the *Chicago Tribune.* During these years he met and married Carol Frink, whom he divorced in 1926 after a lengthy separation. MacArthur sold short stories to *Smart Set,* prompting editor H. L. Mencken to praise his exuberance and virtuosity. He relocated to New York in 1922 to write for Hearst publications, soon meeting Robert Benchley, who introduced him to the Algonquin Round Table, an influential group who met at the Algonquin Hotel and produced sophisticated, intellectual humor. He promptly became a member in good standing among this noted group of wits.

In 1928 MacArthur collaborated with fellow Chicagoan BEN HECHT on *The Front Page,* a Broadway play based on their experiences in the pressroom of Chicago's criminal court building. The play was a critical and financial hit, often revived on stage, and made into film three times. Once his career as playwright was established, he married actress Helen Hayes. Success led him to Hollywood, where he wrote scenarios and screenplays, such as *The Sin of Madelon Claudet* (1931), which won an Academy Award for his wife. Collaboration on this film won MacArthur and Noel Coward an Oscar for best story. His collaborators included Ben Hecht, Edward Sheldon, Sidney Howard, and Nunnally Johnson. The MacArthurs had one daughter, Mary, and an adopted son, James, who became a film and television actor. Charles MacArthur died on April 21, 1956, of intense internal hemorrhage.

**SIGNIFICANCE:** Like RING LARDNER, CARL SANDBURG, and Ben Hecht, Charles MacArthur drew on his Chicago experiences to create fictional work. MacArthur's playwriting reflects the turbulent, high-spirited, sometimes melodramatic style often associated with sensationalist newspapermen. As he often draws from everyday life to create some of his roguish characters, he presents lively action and sometimes coarse dialogue. His characterizations represent real people who have become recognized as universal types. His most famous play, *The Front Page*, mimics the hard-hitting dialogue and the violence that tough, cynical Chicago newsmen wrote about. The comedy is set on the evening before a convicted murderer's execution. "Rope," a short story, is about the life of a professional hangman and demonstrates MacArthur's tendency to use gallows humor. His writing also includes scenarios for motion pictures including *Barbary Coast* (1935), *Wuthering Heights* (1939), and *Gunga Din* (1939).

**SELECTED WORKS:** *War Bugs* (1929) is a collection of personal narratives based on his field artillery experience in World War I. *The Stage Works of Charles MacArthur*, edited by Arthur Dorlag and John Irvine (1974), a limited edition, contains eight MacArthur plays. *Lulu Belle* (1926), a collaboration with the bedridden Edward Sheldon, is a melodrama about a black courtesan who marries a French viscount. *Salvation* (1928), a collaboration with Sidney Howard, is about a woman evangelist. The play suffers from nearly unrelieved seriousness. *The Front Page* (1928) is the first of five combined efforts with fellow Chicagoan, Ben Hecht. The successful comedy is a departure from traditional American stagework, since its lively action becomes central to the play. MacArthur and Hecht combined wits in *Twentieth Century* (1932), a cynical lampoon of the theater world set on

a train from Chicago to New York. Collaborating with Hecht, and starring MacArthur's wife, Helen Hayes, *Ladies and Gentlemen* (1939) portrays a jury room love triangle which includes the defendant. MacArthur helped direct this play which was not a critical success. *Johnny on a Spot* (1942), a political farce rejected by critics and audiences, stands as MacArthur's only solo play script. *Swan Song* (1946), another Hecht collaboration, is a ponderous melodrama about a psychotic musician. It was critically unsuccessful in spite of witty dialogue that includes several attacks on critics. *Stag at Bay* (1954), actually begun with Nunnally Johnson in 1939 but not performed until 1974, is based on an anecdote about John Barrymore.

Screenplays include *The Sin of Madelon Claudet* (1931), with Noel Coward, and *Rasputin and the Empress* (1933). Screenplay collaborations with Ben Hecht include *Crime without Passion* (1934), *Barbary Coast* (1935), *The Scoundrel* (1935), *Once in a Blue Moon* (1935), *Wuthering Heights* (1939), and *Gunga Din* (1939). The screenplay for *The Senator Was Indiscreet* (1948) completes the list.

**FURTHER READING:** Ben Hecht's *Charlie: The Improbable Life and Times of Charles MacArthur* (1957) contains colorful reminiscences of life in Chicago, New York, and Hollywood. *Front Page Marriage* (1982), by Jhan Robbins, is a biography of MacArthur and his wife. With the help of Mary Kennedy, Helen Hayes's *Star on Her Forehead* (1949) provides memories of MacArthur. *A Gift of Joy* (1965), by Helen Hayes and Lewis Funke, *On Reflection* (1969), with Doty Sanford, and *Twice Over Lightly* (1972), with Anita Loos, are also recollections of Hayes's life with MacArthur. Other sources include Bennett Cerf's *Bumper Crop* (1956), Richard Corliss's *Talking Pictures: Screenwriters in the American Cinema* (1974), and Robert Drennan's *The Algonquin Wits* (1968). MacArthur's manuscripts are in the Harvard University Library. His papers are at the Wisconsin Center for Theatre Research at the University of Wisconsin–Madison.

RUSSELL J. BODI           OWENS COLLEGE

# WILLIAM (BRIGGS) MACHARG

September 18, 1872–February 21, 1951

**BIOGRAPHY:** William MacHarg was born in Dover Plains, New York, the son of Frances Eunice (Briggs) and William Storrs MacHarg.

He attended the University of Michigan and worked for the *Chicago Tribune*. For most of his career, however, he wrote novels and stories, many of which appeared in magazines. His best-known work resulted from a collaboration with his brother-in-law, EDWIN BALMER, who married MacHarg's sister, Katharine.

**SIGNIFICANCE:** A collection of short mystery stories, *The Achievements of Luther Trant* (1910), was the most popular of MacHarg and Balmer's joint products at the time. The Chicago psychologist of the title uses the methods of his field to solve crimes. In one story, "The Man Higher Up," an early form of the lie detector appears. Nevertheless, the most lasting of their books is *The Indian Drum* (1917), an adventure involving rivalries among the shipping empires of Chicago, incorporating lore of the Great Lakes. Chicago, Lake Michigan, and Little Traverse Bay are the major locales for its action, and a supposed Indian legend dominates the plot. Betrayal, corruption, romance, the wreck of a car ferry, and a chase on an icy shoreline provide suspense. The authors probably drew on the great storms of 1885, 1905, and 1913 for details of the shipwrecks. The book has sustained such interest that, once the copyright expired, it was reissued in almost identical form but with a new title and author.

**SELECTED WORKS:** MacHarg's collaboration with Balmer resulted in *The Achievements of Luther Trant* (1910), *The Indian Drum* (1917), and *The Blind Man's Eyes* (1916), another mystery. Alone, MacHarg wrote *Peewee* (1921), a novel about the adventures of a child from a Chicago orphanage; and a book of short detective stories, *The Affairs of O'Malley* (1940), which also appeared under the title of *Smart Guy* (1951). Many of his short stories which appeared in magazines remain uncollected.

**FURTHER READING:** Short biographical and bibliographical entries appear on MacHarg in such reference works as Chris Steinbrunner and Otto Penzler's *Encyclopedia of Mystery and Detection* (1976) and ROBERT BEASECKER'S *Michigan in the Novel, 1816–1996* (1998). Information on MacHarg appears in the Edwin Balmer entry in *Twentieth Century Crime and Mystery Writers*, edited by John M. Reilly (1980). CLARENCE ANDREWS discusses *The Indian Drum* in *Michigan in Literature* (1992).

MARY DEJONG OBUCHOWSKI

CENTRAL MICHIGAN UNIVERSITY

## MACK-KE-TE-BE-NESSY.
*See* Andrew Blackbird

## ARCHIBALD MACLEISH
May 7, 1892–April 20, 1982

**BIOGRAPHY:** Born in Glencoe, Illinois, of socially conscious patrician parents, Archibald MacLeish succeeded in half a dozen careers while pursuing two frequently competing goals: to write great poetry and advance great causes. His father, Andrew, a dry-goods merchant emigrated from Scotland, had risen from poverty to found the Chicago department store Carson, Pirie, Scott and Co., and was a founding board member and first vice-president of the University of Chicago. His mother, Martha (Hillard) MacLeish, whose family traced its roots to Elder Brewster of the Mayflower, had taught at Vassar College and became the first woman president of Rockford College in Illinois. "Archie" recreated his Midwestern childhood at "Craigie Lea," the family home on Lake Michigan, in the outstanding mature poems "Ancestral" and "Eleven."

At Yale, congenial, competitive MacLeish played football and edited the *Yale Lit*; immediately after graduation in 1915 he entered Harvard Law School. In 1916 he married singer Ada Hitchcock, and his first book of poems was published in December 1917, shortly after he enlisted in the U.S. Army during World War I. As a second lieutenant commanding field artillery in France, he put his battery into position during the Second Battle of the Marne and was transferred stateside to be an artillery instructor just before a German attack killed half the unit. He also lost an aviator brother, grieving for him in poems "Kenneth" and "Memorial Rain." MacLeish finished law school after the war, briefly taught international law at Harvard, and practiced law for three years.

In 1923 he abruptly gave up law and moved his young family to Paris, where—among American expatriates—he published five collections that include some of his best poems. He also became a lifelong friend of ERNEST HEMINGWAY. Returning to the United States in 1928, MacLeish wrote *Conquistador* (1932), a long Pulitzer Prize–winning poem on the Spanish conquest of Mexico. During the Depression, he wrote full time for the business magazine *Fortune*, while exposing the faults of capitalism in a drama, *Panic*

Archibald MacLeish.

Photo © Nancy Crampton

(1935), and in poetry with *America Was Promises* (1939).

The Roosevelt administration appointed MacLeish to several posts: librarian of Congress (1939–44), assistant director of the Office of War Information (1942), assistant secretary of state (1944–45), and chairman of the American Delegation to the Founding Conference of UNESCO (1945). No other well-known American writer has risen so high in public service as MacLeish did, nor suffered so much antagonism for his good fortune from literary people, many of whom resented his close connection with the New Deal. After more than a decade of censure from both ends of the political spectrum, MacLeish was targeted by the McCarthy investigations, and he successfully counterattacked by publishing articles and initiating public petitions.

By 1948 MacLeish had given up government responsibilities to begin a second "renaissance" in his own writing. The MacLeishes owned a farm near Conway, Massachusetts, the town where his Brewster grandparents had spent their last days. Used mainly as a summer home during the two decades MacLeish worked in New York and Washington, the newly winterized Uphill Farm became the MacLeishes' permanent home for the rest of Archibald's life. New work appeared in *Collected Poems* (1952), which won a Pulitzer Prize. His widely acclaimed play *J.B.* (1958), retelling the biblical story of Job, won a third Pulitzer and enjoyed a successful Broadway run.

MacLeish taught from 1949 to 1972 as writer-in-residence at Harvard and wrote critical essays published in *Poetry and Experience* (1960). Habitually guarded in personal matters, he revealed new aspects of himself in later poems published in *The Wild Old Wicked Man* (1968). Some of his most candid autobiographical essays in *Riders on the Earth* (1978) focused on his years in Paris and Illinois. His health declined rapidly in the early 1980s, and he died at Massachusetts General Hospital in Boston, on April 20, 1982, of pneumonia contracted after an operation.

**SIGNIFICANCE:** Sixty years ago, scholar-critic Cleanth Brooks included MacLeish with Frost and Auden in a triumvirate of poets whose work in the modern tradition was likely to endure. Yet today MacLeish is conspicuous among those who have been decanonized. His accidental good fortune in birth, education, and association with the powerful have worked against him, inspiring the censure of envious writers and critics, particularly during and since World War II. Yet MacLeish's contributions to American and Midwestern letters have permanent significance.

First, some of his poems have been—to take Robert Frost's words—hard to get rid of: "You, Andrew Marvell," "Ars Poetica," "The End of the World," and "What Any Lover Learns." Besides these, "Immortal Autumn" and "Landscape as a Nude" are masterful regional poems conveying a distinctly Midwestern experience. Like Ernest Hemingway, MacLeish lived most of his cosmopolitan life outside the Midwest yet cherished a youthful awareness of his birthplace. Crows, oaks, cornfields, and the Lake Michigan shoreline remained an active part of his lifelong mental imagery.

Second, MacLeish had a knack for turning up in the right place at the right time. He matured as a writer in Paris at an important time for American letters. Touring the United States during the 1930s for his *Fortune* articles, he wrote such poems as "America Was Promises" and "The States Talking" in pursuit of Whitman's and CARL SANDBURG's democratic ideal of being a representative poet portraying ordinary people's sufferings and aspirations. These free-verse panoramas, which include Midwestern scenes and idiom, had an impact on contemporaries but survived no better than most other twentieth-century poets' attempts at being representative. Other partially successful enterprises—his verse dramas of the 1920s and 1930s and some of the first radio plays broadcast in America—are nevertheless cultural landmarks. As librarian of congress, he played a strong administrative role in turning a disorganized, venerable Washington institution into a research library. He was also the primary agent in getting Ezra Pound released from St. Elizabeth's Hospital in 1958. As writer in residence at Harvard for twenty-three years, MacLeish pioneered on-campus creative writing programs.

Finally, MacLeish kept developing as a writer, even into old age. His writing style has been compared to an Aeolian harp, changing melody with each change of wind. His ear for the music of language served well in successive experiments with Imagism, the high modernism of T. S. ELIOT and Ezra Pound, the populist free verse of VACHEL LINDSAY and Kenneth Fearing, and the surrealism of the post–World War II era. His need for approbation made him cautious until about the 1950s, when he began caring less about what others thought of his work and more of writing to his own standards. The play *J.B.* incorporates his best poetic resources in thoroughly idiomatic prose on themes important to him. The late poems published in *The Wild Old Wicked Man* (1968), along with earlier ones published after his death, reveal a personal voice which his principal biographer, Scott Donaldson, believes has been underrated.

**SELECTED WORKS:** The most important of MacLeish's sixteen poetry collections are: *Streets in the Moon* (1926), *New Found Land* (1930), *Conquistador* (1932), *Poems, 1924–1933* (1933), *America Was Promises* (1939), *Collected Poems: 1917–1952* (1952), *Songs for Eve* (1954), *Collected Poems* (1962), *The Wild Old Wicked Man and Other Poems* (1968), *The Human Season: Selected Poems, 1926–72* (1972), and *Collected Poems, 1917–1984* (1985). A representative selection from twenty-eight books of prose is: *The Irresponsibles* (1940), *A Time to Speak* (1941), *A Time to Act* (1943), *Poetry and Opinion: The Pisan Cantos of Ezra Pound* (1950), *Poetry and Journalism* (1958), *Poetry and Experience* (1960), and *Riders on the Earth: Essays and Recollections* (1978). The standard source for correspondence is *Letters of Archibald MacLeish,* edited by R. H. Winnick (1983), who also taped many interviews. Bernard A. Drabeck and Helen E. Ellis published their interviews in *Archibald MacLeish: Reflections* (1986). The most important of MacLeish's seventeen dramatic publications are: *J.B.: A Play in Verse* (1958) and the stage version of this play (1959) substantially altered by director Elia Kazan; *Scratch* (1971), based on a short story by Stephen Vincent Benet; and *Six Plays* (1980).

**FURTHER READING:** Signi Lenea Falk's *Archibald MacLeish* (1965) is the first literary biography and Scott Donaldson's *Archibald MacLeish: An American Life* (1992) is the most comprehensive and important to date. More useful and objective than most works of its kind, the autobiography *Martha Hillard MacLeish* (1949) describes Archibald's early traits, his childhood reading, and his mother's program of early education. Helen E. Ellis, Bernard Drabeck, and Margaret E. Howland have compiled *Archibald MacLeish: A Selectively Annotated Bibliography* (1995). Extended critical appraisals include Cleanth Brooks's *Modern Poetry and the Tradition* (1939), Denis Donoghue's *The Third Voice* (1959), Allen Tate's *Essays of Four Decades* (1970), Grover Smith's *Archibald MacLeish* (1971), and Donald Hall's *The Weather for Poetry* (1982). Special MacLeish collections of manuscripts and other materials can be found at the New York Public Library Berg Collection, the Library of Congress, and Yale and Harvard University libraries.

EDWARD MORIN                    WAYNE STATE UNIVERSITY

## SISTER MARY MADELEVA
May 24, 1887–July 25, 1964

**BIOGRAPHY:** Sister Mary Madeleva, whose secular name was Mary Evaline Wolff, was born in Cumberland, Wisconsin, the daughter of August Wolff, a harness maker, and his wife, Lucy (Arntz) Wolff. She attended local schools then spent a year at the University of Wisconsin and obtained her BA degree in 1909 from St. Mary's College, Notre Dame. Other degrees received were an MA from the University of Notre Dame in 1918, the PhD from the University of California at Berkeley in 1925, the doctor of literature degree in 1938 from Manhattan College in New York City, and the LLD from Indiana University in 1958. She attended Oxford University in 1933–34 and taught at several academies and colleges. Her travels took her to Europe and the Holy Land, and she lectured extensively in the United States, in Canada, and at Oxford University. She held various administrative positions in educational institutions, and as a member of the Sisters of the Congregation of the Holy Cross she was president of St. Mary's College, Notre Dame, from 1934 to 1961.

**SIGNIFICANCE:** As a Catholic nun, Sister Madeleva has called attention to the Midwest through her publications. Not only is her work religious in nature, but it also mirrors her background. Few nuns have written noteworthy literature, and her contributions are significant. Her verse reveals her as a person of sensitive spirit and great depth who searches always for better communication with God. The poetry is simple, fastidious, beautifully turned, and usually cast in conventional form, though she does have some free verse. Her best form is the sonnet. In general, Sister Mary Madeleva used her poetry as a vehicle in her quest to enhance her communication with God.

**SELECTED WORKS:** Her first volume, *Knights Errant and Other Poems* (1923), shows Sister Mary Madeleva's deeply spiritual nature. The subject matter is primarily religious, as in "A Young Girl Writes to Her Father," and the reader discovers that the father is God. A later volume, *A Question of Lovers and Other Poems* (1935), again presents love, mostly spiritual, as a major theme and examines her travel experiences; this book includes some of her exquisite sonnets. *Selected Poems* (1939) is her first long publication. *A Song of Bedlam Inn and Other Poems* (1941) contains lyrics. *The Last Four Things: Collected Poems* (1959) is the most complete and probably the best edition of her work.

In addition to her poetry she published *Chaucer's Nuns and Other Essays* (1925); *Pearl, A Study of Spiritual Dryness* (1925); *A Lost Language and Other Essays on Chaucer* (1951); and her autobiography, *My First Seventy Years* (1959).

Less important works, such as *Penelope and Other Poems* (1927), demonstrate that she was still a novice in writing, yet she had a sure touch in her sonnets. *The Happy Christmas Wind and Other Poems* (1936) is a collection of religious verse; *Christmas Eve and Other Poems*

(1938) is a similar small volume. *Gates and Other Poems* (1938) reflects her travels in the Holy Land and elsewhere. *Selected Poems* (1939) includes much material issued previously along with new lyrics and sonnets. *Four Girls and Other Poems* (1941) commemorates the Marianites in 1841. *American Twelfth Night and Other Poems* (1955) is dedicated to Saint Mary's College and contains only religious verse.

**FURTHER READING:** *Sister Mary Madeleva* (1961) is written by Barbara Jencks. Gail Mandell's *Madeleva: One Woman's Life* (1994) is helpful, as is Maria Werner's *Sister Mary Madeleva Wolff, CSC: A Pictorial Biography* (1993). The most recent source is Gail Mandell's *Madeleva: A Biography* (1997).

ARTHUR W. SHUMAKER                    DEPAUW UNIVERSITY

# CHARLES MAJOR
July 25, 1856–February 13, 1913

**BIOGRAPHY:** Charles Major was born in Indianapolis. His English father, Stephen Major, born in Ireland, came to the United States, becoming a judge of Indiana's Fifth Judicial Circuit; his mother was Phoebe (Gaskill) Major. When Charles was thirteen, the family moved to Shelbyville, Indiana, where he spent the rest of his life. In high school he was attracted to English literature and history, and he was graduated with the school's first graduating class in 1872, giving a brilliant class oration. After graduating from the University of Michigan in 1875, he read law in his father's office and became more interested in history. He was married to Alice Shaw and elected city clerk in 1885, and he served a term in the Indiana legislature in 1887. From 1902 until his death, he was a trustee of Purdue University. Though he spent most of his time in law, he also devoted himself to the study of history, particularly of the English and French Renaissance. He died of a liver disease.

Major conceived his first novel, *When Knighthood Was in Flower* (1898), two years before it was published. He found the plot and characters readily, coming from English history. When Mary Tudor, sister of Henry VIII of England, married Louis XII, king of France, she was in love with Charles Brandon; following her husband's death, she wrote to Brandon that to marry her he should come to Paris before Henry could prevent their marriage. From these scraps of history, Major composed his novel. After a rejection from *Harper's*, in 1897 a salesman for the Bowen-Merrill Publishing Company of Indianapolis came to his office. Major asked him to take the manuscript back to his company. Fortunately, Bowen-Merrill approved it, and the book was an immediate, overwhelming success. The eager public soon discovered the identity of the author, who had used a pseudonym; the book received quick and enthusiastic reviews and became a best-seller. The famous Shakespearean actress Julia Marlowe quickly asked for dramatic rights, and soon Major allowed Paul Hester to dramatize the novel; with Miss Marlowe assuming the part of Mary Tudor, it became a popular stage play. When it played at English's Theater in Indianapolis, a special train was run from Shelbyville to Indianapolis, and Major was called to the stage to make a speech.

After this experience, Major tended to do less legal work. He published many other books. *Dorothy Vernon of Haddon Hall* (1902), next in popularity to *Knighthood*, utilizing the period of conflict between Queen Elizabeth I and Mary Queen of Scots, was also a best-seller successfully dramatized by Paul Hester. Less popular romances followed: *Yolanda, Maid of Burgundy* (1905), set in sixteenth-century France; *A Gentle Knight of Old Brandenburg* (1909), an account of the boyhood of Frederick the Great; *The Little King: A Story of the Childhood of Louis XIV, King of France* (1910); and *The Touchstone of Fortune: Being the Memoir of Baron Clyde, Who Lived, Thrived, and Fell in the Doleful Reign of the So-Called Merry Monarch, Charles II* (1912). However, Major also wrote about Indiana, as in *The Bears of Blue River* (1901), his best-known book about the state; *Uncle Tom Andy Bill* (1908), and *A Forest Hearth: A Romance of Indiana in the Thirties* (1903), which was practically a failure because the author attempted to transplant all the machinery of European romance to early Indiana. His mediocre last book was *Rosalie* (1925), revised and published by his wife and a friend, Test Dalton. Yet, in spite of the repetition of his favorite plot of European romance, he had become a famous writer.

**SIGNIFICANCE:** There are two possible reasons why Major wrote novels set in Indiana. Either as an imaginative writer he found his state background to be drab and provincial, and to distance himself from it he penned his European romances; or, even though he loved the romances, he found himself much attracted to Indiana and its people and to the Midwest, since his environment had given him the values which he placed in the novels and in all his works. Although Charles Major wrote about Indiana, his greatest significance as a writer was his success as an historical novelist. From bits of history he constructed plots that present passionate lovers whose marital union is prevented by some outside force, which finally is overcome. Also, usually he does not sufficiently develop his characters, and most remain stock types. Despite Major's tremendous knowledge of political history, he sometimes errs on social history. Nevertheless, what is now a hackneyed plot, a stock character, or a melodramatic device was much newer in Major's day, and readers tended to ignore these faults. The books on Indiana did not employ this usual stylized form and simply tell a story. Major's romantic works were widely imitated, and seeing that the public liked spirited romances, he gave them what they wanted. He was a minor Sir Walter Scott.

**SELECTED WORKS:** Few reviews of Charles Major's books can be found today, yet his books were very popular. *When Knighthood Was in Flower* (1898) was the nation's best-seller for fifteen months with a total of 200,000 copies sold in two years. The researcher should start with this book, should follow with *Dorothy Vernon of Haddon Hall* (1902), and then with *The Bears of Blue River* (1901). Major's other books are of less importance.

**FURTHER READING:** Howard Baetzhold's article "Charles Major: Hoosier Romancer," in *Indiana Magazine of History* (March 1955): 31–42, is a general review of Major. Edmund Wells's *The Literary and Cultural Implications of Charles Major's Use of Religious Materials in His Novels* (1951) should be interesting, as is Hortense Montgomery's *Biography of Charles Major* (1930). Two additional biographies are Kenneth Fallis's *When Charles Major Was in Flower: A Biography of the Shelbyville Author* (1898) and William Turner's *The Charles Major Family* (1975). *Who's Who in America* for 1912–13 contains a summary, as do obituaries, such as the unsigned article "Novelist Dead at His Indiana Home," in the *Indianapolis News* (February 13, 1931): 1, as well as "Mr. Nicholson's Tribute" on page 18. Some editions of *Knighthood* contain an article, "The Author and the

Book," by MAURICE THOMPSON. Various anthologies include Major. William Hepburn's pamphlet "The Charles Major Manuscripts in the Purdue Libraries" (1946), reprinted from *Indiana Quarterly for Bookmen* 2.3 (July 1946): 71–81, presents the large holdings of Major materials in the Purdue Libraries, including the manuscripts of his ten novels in holograph and typescript and corrected galley and page proofs as well as all material available by and about him until 1925. Major's private library is included here. This is the best collection of Major materials.

ARTHUR W. SHUMAKER          DEPAUW UNIVERSITY

## MA-KA-TAI-ME-SHE-KIA-KIAK.
*See* Black Hawk

## MALCOLM X
May 19, 1925–February 21, 1965
(Malcolm Little, El-Hajj Malik El-Shabazz)
**BIOGRAPHY:** Malcolm X was born Malcolm Little in Omaha, Nebraska, to the Reverend Earl and Louise (Norton) Little. His father was a Baptist minister and an organizer for Marcus Garvey's Universal Negro Improvement Association. The family suffered grievously from racism while living in the Midwest. Ku Klux Klan harassment forced them to leave Omaha in 1929, and they moved to Milwaukee, Wisconsin, then to Lansing, Michigan, where their house was burned down by the Black Legion, a KKK-like hate group. Two years later, after relocating to East Lansing, the Reverend Little died in a streetcar accident. Malcolm later expressed a suspicion that his father had been murdered by racist whites. The state welfare system dispersed the impoverished family to foster homes and institutions, and Malcolm's mother was eventually placed in the state mental hospital at Kalamazoo.

After experiencing more racism in the Michigan public schools, Malcolm dropped out of the eighth grade and moved to Boston to live with a half sister. He became involved in criminal activities in Boston and New York and acquired the nickname "Detroit Red" for his Michigan origins. While imprisoned from 1946 to 1952 in Massachusetts on burglary charges, he read widely and became a follower of the Nation of Islam, the sect led by Elijah Muhammad and known popularly as the Black Muslims. After converting, Mal-

colm dropped the name Little and replaced it with the letter X, symbolizing the absence of his African name. Late in life he took the name El-Hajj Malik El-Shabazz. Soon after leaving prison, he became a leading Nation of Islam minister, organizing temples in Detroit and other cities. Malcolm became the group's leading orator and drew much media attention for his refutation of the nonviolent methods of other civil rights leaders.

In 1958 Malcolm X married Betty Shabazz, with whom he had six children. By 1964 he had become disillusioned with Elijah Muhammad. He denounced many Nation of Islam tenets and became an orthodox Muslim. He traveled in Africa and the Middle East and focused on issues of colonialism and economic exploitation. The following year he was assassinated while giving a speech in New York City. Three Nation of Islam members were convicted of his murder.

**SIGNIFICANCE:** Although Malcolm X left the Midwest to become a national and international leader, his *Autobiography* (1965) powerfully describes his origins and his work in the region. Angry about his family's bitter experience of racism in the Midwest, Malcolm X nevertheless celebrates the spirit and dignity of Midwestern African Americans who endured in the face of discrimination.

In his *Autobiography*, Malcolm X examines the Depression-era African American communities in Lansing and East Lansing, Michigan, where an extremely impoverished lower class coexisted uneasily with an "integrationist-seeking" middle class (5). He relates his experiences in the Detroit ghetto and tells of his efforts to redeem "our brainwashed black brothers and sisters" from the scourges of self-destructive crime and chemical addiction (195). He also describes with pride his work for Nation of Islam temples in Detroit and Chicago in the 1950s and 1960s and their efforts to improve the spiritual, social, and economic situation of African Americans.

**SELECTED WORKS:** *The Autobiography of Malcolm X* (1965), written with the assistance of Alex Haley, was published in the months following Malcolm's death and is an enduring classic of the genre. Malcolm's speeches appear in a number of different collections, including *Malcolm X Speaks* (1965) and *By Any Means Necessary*, edited by George Breitman (2nd ed., 1992); *Two Speeches by Malcolm X*

(1965); *Malcolm X on Afro-American History* (3rd ed., 1990); *The End of White World Supremacy*, edited by Benjamin Goodman (1970); *Malcolm X: The Last Speeches*, edited by Bruce Perry (1989); and *Malcolm X: Speeches at Harvard*, edited by Archie Epps (rev. ed. 1991).

**FURTHER READING:** Biographical studies of Malcolm X include George Breitman's *The Last Year of Malcolm X* (1967), John Henrik Clarke's *Malcolm X: The Man and His Times* (1969), Peter Goldman's *The Death and Life of Malcolm X* (rev. ed. 1979), Bruce Perry's *Malcolm: The Life of a Man Who Changed Black America* (1991), Rodnell P. Collins's *Seventh Child: A Family Memoir of Malcolm X* (1998), and Louis A. DeCaro's *On the Side of My People: A Religious Life of Malcolm X* (1996). See also James Baldwin's drama based on the *Autobiography*, *One Day When I Was Lost* (1972); Carson Clayborne's *Malcolm X: The FBI File* (1991); Michael Friedly's *Malcolm X: The Assassination* (1992); the film by Spike Lee, *Malcolm X* (1992); and Michael Eric Dyson's *Making Malcolm* (1995).

WILLIAM OSTREM                    PRINCETON, NEW JERSEY

## DAVID MAMET
November 30, 1947

**BIOGRAPHY:** Born in Chicago, David Mamet and his younger sister Lynn were raised first in the city's predominantly Jewish south side and, after Mamet turned thirteen, in Olympia Fields, a suburb Mamet dubbed "New South Hell." Mamet is very much an urban writer, and "the city," usually Chicago, figures in a dehumanizing and even brutal way in his writing, generating rhythm and energy. After a private secondary school experience in Olympia Fields, Mamet earned a degree in literature and theater from Goddard College, Vermont, in 1969. He thought all along that school was tedious and sought to create an alternate world, a need also spawned as a way of detaching himself from the domestic abuses he chronicles in his memoir *The Cabin* (1992).

David Savran, in his book *In Their Own Words: Contemporary American Playwrights* (1988), pegs Mamet as "the American theater's foremost warrior-philologist" (132). Mamet credits his teacher-mother, his labor lawyer–father, their divorce when he was ten, and years of piano lessons with developing his ear for both the combative and the musical power of language. Mamet worked as a busboy at Chicago's improvisational theater, Second City, before teaching and studying acting in New York. Then he returned to Chicago to work as a cabdriver, short-order cook, and high-pressure salesman for an unscrupulous real estate firm. During a teaching stint at Goddard College, he founded the St. Nicholas Company to stage his early works, but it was back in Chicago that he wrote a string of major plays, including *American Buffalo* (1977), *Sexual Perversity in Chicago* (1978), *A Life in the Theatre* (1978), and *Glengarry Glen Ross* (1984), for which he won the Pulitzer Prize.

After his divorce from actress Lindsay Crouse, with whom he had one daughter, Willa, Mamet married Rebecca Pidgeon, a British musician, and began to divide his time between Massachusetts and Vermont.

**SIGNIFICANCE:** Mamet has made it clear that the rhythms of the modern urban environment, his deconstruction of the American Dream, and the darkly prophetic nature in his work were fostered by such Midwestern writers as FRANK NORRIS, THEODORE DREISER, WILLA CATHER (his daughter is named Willa), SINCLAIR LEWIS, and UPTON SINCLAIR. His particular stamp is gritty urban dialogue in a dog-eat-dog world, with characters often speaking right past each other in broken, cryptic, elided speech.

A freighter cruising the Great Lakes is the setting for *Lakeboat* (1981), one of Mamet's earliest plays, which focuses on eight crew members completing seemingly purposeless tasks as they reveal lives consumed with sex, gambling, drinking, and fighting. Little men with dead-end lives who contemplate thievery in a junk shop inhabit *American Buffalo*, a play highly naturalistic in style and tone. The heavy use of street slang and compulsive obscenities in both these and later plays is the song of the alienated and dispossessed of the inner city, where expletives voice anguish over the loss of warmth and humanity.

Chicago as setting and also as landscape of the mind figures largely in Mamet's most important work. An article in the *New York Times Magazine* by Samuel G. Freedman, "The Gritty Eloquence of David Mamet" (April 21, 1985): 32 ff., testifies to the directness and "loathing of pretense" that Mamet's "street denizens" inherited from

SAUL BELLOW's Augie March and JAMES T.
FARRELL's Studs Lonigan (32). Freedman
also highlights Mamet's "fondness for blue-
collar America" (40) and the ways in which
Mamet's life experiences—salesman in a
shady real estate firm, playing poker in a
junk shop with ex-convicts—inform the action in plays such as Glengarry Glen Ross and
American Buffalo. Mamet's screenplay to The
Untouchables (1985) is an especially strong example of how the Chicago setting infuses his
work. Stark naturalism—including a pes-
simistic sense of the possibilities of human
relationships—is a vital underpinning of his
art, and vigilant, even ruthless, revision is
his self-imposed method. That Mamet admires his money-grubbing petty hustlers,
who perversely betray each other as they
operate on the edge of the law, is shown
in the vital, urgent language he has them
speak, a language which in its brutal objectivity and biting irony keeps others and even
self at a cold distance.

Because the presence of the City of the Big
Shoulders cannot be underestimated in his
work, it is fitting that the Off-Loop theater
district of Chicago was for many years the
testing-ground of Mamet's drama, paving the
way for his successes in New York and securing his national reputation. Mamet has
also succeeded in crossing genres, having
produced a fragmented and elusive novel,
several collections of essays, children's books,
and numerous screenplays. His novella
Passover (1995) gives a haunting and threatening meaning to a holiday observance.

**SELECTED WORKS:** Mamet's best-known
and most frequently produced plays are *American Buffalo* (1977), *Sexual Perversity in Chicago*
and *The Duck Variations* (1978), *A Life in the
Theater* (1978), *Lakeboat* (1981), *Glengarry Glen
Ross* (1984), *Speed-the-Plow* (1988), and *Oleanna*
(1992). Later productions are *The Cryptogram*
(1994) and *Ricky Jay and His 52 Assistants* (1994).
*A Whore's Profession: Notes and Essays* (1994) collects four previously published books: *Writing
in Restaurants* (1986), *Some Freaks* (1989), *On Directing Film* (1991), and *The Cabin* (1992). His
novel, *The Village* (1994), garnered mixed reviews. Among his screenplays are *Homicide,
House of Games, The Verdict* (an Oscar nominee
for Best Adaptation), *Things Change, Hoffa,
Malcolm X, We're No Angels, Glengarry Glen
Ross, Vanya on 42nd Street,* and *The Edge.*

**FURTHER READING:** Mamet and his career
are both relatively young, and no full-scale
biography has yet been published. C. W. E.
Bigsby's *David Mamet* (1985) is the first book-
length study of Mamet's art. Dennis Carroll's
*David Mamet* (1987) examines Mamet's career
in terms of his themes: business, sex, learning, and communication. Gay Brewer's book
*David Mamet and Film: Illusion/Disillusion in a
Wounded Land* (1993) explores Mamet's combined role as director and screenwriter in
two films. Anne Dean's *David Mamet: Language
as Dramatic Action* (1990) and Leslie Kane's
accessible, scholarly, and compelling *David
Mamet: A Casebook* (1992) examine the plays in
terms of technique and method; both offer
useful bibliographies.

JILL B. GIDMARK          UNIVERSITY OF MINNESOTA

## FREDERICK MANFRED

January 6, 1912–September 7, 1994
(Feike Feikema)

**BIOGRAPHY:** Frederick Manfred was born
Feike Feikema, the eldest of six sons of Feike
Feikema and Aaltje (Alice) (von Engen) Feikema, on a farm near Doon, Iowa. Both of
Manfred's parents had a strong sense of their
Frisian ancestry, and they raised him in the
strict religious tradition of the Dutch Calvin-
ists. Despite his upbringing, during his years
at Calvin College in Grand Rapids, Michigan,
Manfred began to question his traditional
beliefs and finally rebelled against them.
His early novels of the World's Wanderer
trilogy—*The Primitive* (1949), *The Brother* (1950),
and *The Giant* (1951)—describe these experiences through an autobiographical protagonist. Yet Manfred considered his years at
Calvin intellectually challenging, and he was
pleased to be asked to return to the campus
many times to speak about his writing.

After college Manfred traveled to both
coasts working at odd jobs, and at one point
he gained the real-life experience of a hobo
that he would chronicle in his first novel *The
Golden Bowl* (1944). However, by 1940 Manfred's poor eating habits forced him to enter
the Glen Lake Tuberculosis Sanatorium, in
Oak Terrace, Minnesota. After his recovery
two years later, he was again able to use this
experience in his second novel *Boy Almighty*
(1945).

Manfred's early career was highlighted by
the critical success of *The Golden Bowl* and his

third novel, *This Is the Year* (1947), both of which received positive reviews from major novelists, including SINCLAIR LEWIS, and nominations for national prizes. Critics strongly disliked the autobiographical ruminations of the World's Wanderer trilogy, however, and Manfred lost a critical acclaim that he would not recover, even with his later success in the Buckskin Man Tales. In 1949 he was appointed writer in residence at Macalester College in St. Paul, where he worked for a year. In 1952 he changed his name to Frederick Manfred because he thought the strong ethnic sound of his name was damaging his popular appeal. His first novel under his new name, *Lord Grizzly* (1954), was highly acclaimed and his most successful.

In 1960 he moved to Luverne, Minnesota, where he lived in a house he planned and helped construct on a bluff overlooking the Big Rock River near the Blue Mounds. Here he continued a disciplined writing life with an astounding output for three more decades until his death from cancer in 1994. He won the Mark Twain Award of the Society for the Study of Midwestern Literature in 1981.

Frederick Manfred.
Photo courtesy of Archives, Calvin College

**SIGNIFICANCE:** In all, Manfred published some thirty-two works of fiction, poetry, and nonfiction, and nearly every work is intrinsically bound to the Midwest. Manfred made his life's work the evocation of the spirit of a specific locale of the Midwest: "Siouxland," an area including portions of Iowa, South Dakota, Nebraska, and Minnesota, or the watershed of the Big Sioux River. Manfred spent his literary life populating this region, and he often said that he did not choose to write about Siouxland, but that it chose him to have its stories told. His historical novels of the Buckskin Man Tales tell the stories of Siouxland from the time of the Sioux Indians until the twentieth century, where his farm novels begin. They include the remarkable stories of No Name, a young Sioux Indian in search of a vision that will bring him an identity, and of mountain man Hugh Glass's ordeal after being attacked by a grizzly bear. His farm novels, *The Golden Bowl, This Is the Year*, and *Green Earth*, are also significant accounts of the settling of the Midwest and of the farming practices of the twentieth century. They are remarkable for their frank treatment of the physical details of farm life and their use of the vernacular of farmers. In these novels, unlike his more autobiographical ruminations, Manfred was able to effectively combine his experience growing up on the farm and his knowledge of Frisian mythology with his sensitivity to the spirit, the place of Siouxland. Manfred often shows how these competing mythologies—one of the European settler and one of the rocks and prairies and the landscape itself—would come in conflict with each other. The farm practice that had developed from European notions of land use and tillage is clearly displayed in a character such as Pier Frixen, the protagonist of *This Is the Year*, and Pier fails to produce a healthy life, family, or culture because he does not listen to the land. Manfred was a giant of the Midwest in both his physical stature and his immense canon. The latter stands as a testament to his aspiration of evoking the spirit of Siouxland.

**SELECTED WORKS:** Manfred's series of historical novels—the Buckskin Man Tales, *Lord Grizzly* (1954), *Riders of Judgement* (1957), *Conquering Horse* (1959), *Scarlet Plume* (1964), and *King of Spades* (1966)—are generally considered his major achievement. His other major novels include *The Golden Bowl* (1944), *This Is the Year* (1947), *Morning Red* (1956), *Green Earth*

(1977), and *Of Lizards and Angels* (1992). Manfred's work also includes books of poetry, short stories, and nonfiction. An important interview has been published as *Conversations with Frederick Manfred* (1974), moderated by John R. Milton. *Prime Fathers* (1985) collects a series of essays in tribute to other Midwestern writers Manfred admired. His early letters have been collected in *The Selected Letters of Frederick Manfred 1932–1954*, edited by Arthur R. Huseboe and Nancy Owen Nelson (1989).

**FURTHER READING:** Joseph M. Flora's *Frederick Manfred* (1974) of the Western Writers series provides a useful introduction, and Robert C. Wright's *Frederick Manfred* (1979), in the Twayne U.S. Authors series, is the only full-length study to date although several theses and dissertations that treat Manfred's work exclusively have appeared. *Frederick Manfred: A Bibliography and Publishing History* (1981) was compiled by Rodney J. Mulder and John H. Timmerman. Manfred's papers are collected at the University of Minnesota Library, Minneapolis.

KEITH FYNAARDT			NORTHWESTERN COLLEGE

## DON(ALD ROBERT PERRY) MARQUIS

July 29, 1878–December 29, 1937

**BIOGRAPHY:** Don Marquis, journalist, poet, playwright, short story writer, and novelist, may be best known as the columnist who created "Archy and Mehitabel." He is inevitably identified with New York, but he was born and raised in Walnut, Illinois, in Bureau County, some fifty miles east of Moline and the Mississippi River. Marquis remembered Walnut in his unpublished "Egobiography" as "a little town with muddy streets"; he went to its Baptist Sunday School and clerked for the stores on Main Street, according to Edward Anthony in his 1962 *O Rare Don Marquis* (21, 27). His parents were James Stewart Marquis, who eked out a living in Walnut as a country doctor, and Virginia (Whitmore) Marquis. He graduated from Walnut High School in 1894 and attended, for the three months his money lasted, nearby Knoxville College Academy in Galesburg, then held odd jobs as a clerk at the village drug store, teacher, chicken-plucker, railroad section hand, and printer and writer for Bureau County's weekly newspaper.

He moved in 1900 to Washington, D.C., to work for the Census Bureau and then as a reporter for the *Washington Times*. From 1902 to 1907 he wrote columns and editorials for Atlanta papers. In 1907 he joined Joel Chandler Harris as a contributing editor for his newly formed *Uncle Remus's Magazine*. Harris encouraged him to write and publish short fiction. Marquis married the young short story writer Reina Melcher in 1909. They had two children, Robert and Barbara. Harris's death in 1908 spurred Marquis to leave Atlanta for New York, where in 1912, after several years as a freelance writer, he began writing "The Sun Dial," a column in the *New York Evening Sun*. He had published his first novel, *Danny's Own Story*, in 1912, in an homage to MARK TWAIN's *Huckleberry Finn* and a recasting of Walnut's sturdy townsfolk and grotesques. Though writing a column afforded him a steady and fairly comfortable income, Lynn Lee in *Don Marquis* (1981) reports Marquis as complaining that he had "buried a part of himself every day in his column" (24). Still, Marquis wrote or compiled from columns more than thirty books, including four novels and six plays. *The Old Soak* (1921), written first as a series of columns attacking Prohibition, became a popular and critically acclaimed Broadway play.

Reina died suddenly in 1923; three years later Marquis married the actress Marjorie Potts Vonnegut. Marquis's final years were painfully hard; he suffered temporary blindness in 1932, and a stroke in 1936 confined him to a wheelchair and seriously afflicted his speech. Marjorie died in 1936. A year later, heavily in debt and paralyzed, Marquis died in Forest Hills, New York. Until the end he remained hard at work on his last novel, *Sons of the Puritans* (1939).

**SIGNIFICANCE:** Edward Anthony reports that Marquis feared, with good reason, that he might be remembered only for that "Goddam Cockroach" (410). His serious efforts, like the short-lived plays *The Dark Hours* (1924) and *Out of the Sea* (1927), may have stated his theological speculations and metaphysical doubts eloquently, but daily readers of his column paid far more attention to the wisdom and wisecracking of Archy, the vers libre writing roach. They also made the collections of his columns like *Archy and Mehitabel* (1927) bestsellers. Archy and his companion Mehitabel, the flapper and alley-cat, have secured an honored place for Marquis in the anthologies and histories of American humor. Norris Yates, in his chapter on Marquis in *The American Humorist* (1964), concluded that as Archy, as "The Old Soak," as Mehitabel, or as other characters, he could be "skeptic . . . dreamer, philosopher, and vagabond" (216). Marquis, in short, spoke best through his comic masks. Walter Blair and Hamlin Hill, contrasting him with other period columnists in *America's Humor* (1978), praised his unique power to comment "almost daily on the stupidities and asininities of his time" (406). Of late, critics including Lynn Lee have called attention to Marquis's sharp frontal attacks on racism in the short story "Carter," first published as "The Mulatto," and in *Danny's Own Story*, both reenactments of the mob violence and lynching that he witnessed during the Atlanta race riot of 1906 (Lee, *Don Marquis* 103). "Carter" was collected in *Carter, and Other People* (1921).

Defining Marquis's relation to the Midwest and Midwestern literature seems more problematic because he left Walnut in his twenties and never returned. As a young man, he had read and admired GEORGE ADE and EUGENE FIELD, Chicago newspaper columnists who early set a pattern for his own column writing. Like them he found the small-town ethos in the city, locating counterparts for the Walnut villagers and their prejudices in urban settings. Yates, like others, concluded that "in Marquis' fiction all the small towns are essentially the Walnut, Illinois of his boyhood" (214). His first novel, *Danny's Own Story*, invoked small-town "Illinoise" and recalled, in loving and comic detail, a village of "only three hundred soles" (8–9). Stressing his affinities to Mark Twain, his friend and fellow columnist Christopher Morley argues in *The Best of Don Marquis* (1946) that Marquis carried the Midwest and "rustic Middle West dialect" with him to New York and into his writing (xii).

**SELECTED WORKS:** Marquis's best-known books remain *Archy and Mehitabel* (1927), *Archy's Life of Mehitabel* (1933), and *Archy Does His Part* (1935), collected in *The Lives and Times of Archy and Mehitabel* (1940). Other humorous and satiric works include *Hermione and Her Little Group of Serious Thinkers* (1916); the two Clem Hawley books, *The Old Soak, and Hail and Farewell* (1921) and *The Old Soak's History of the World* (1924); and plays, *The Old Soak: A Comedy in Three Acts* (1926) and *Everything's Jake*

(1930). He also wrote novels, such as *Danny's Own Story* (1912), and short stories, such as *Carter, and Other People* (1921). *The Dark Hours, Five Scenes from History* (1924), and *Out of the Sea* (1927) represent his serious drama. In *Sons of the Puritans* (1939) he returned to the Midwest for its setting.

**FURTHER READING:** Edward Anthony's somewhat sprawling *O Rare Don Marquis* (1962) remains the only comprehensive biography. It includes, in long uninterrupted quotations, sections from Marquis's informative and unpublished third-person "Egobiography." Lynn Lee's *Don Marquis* (1981) distills Anthony and offers summaries and criticism of Marquis's principal writings. *The Best of Don Marquis*, edited and introduced by Christopher Morley (1946), provides an accessible and generous anthology of Marquis, ranging from his Archy and Mehitabel poems through the theological and utopian speculations of *The Almost Perfect State* (1927). Norris Yates's chapter in *The American Humorist* (1964), "The Many Masks of Don Marquis" (195–210), and Walter Blair and Hamlin Hill's brief commentaries in their 1978 *America's Humor* (405–409, 411, 439, 462) are instructive on his relation to traditional "crackerbox humor" and to other 1920s columnists. *Selected Letters of Don Marquis*, edited by William McCollum Jr. (1982), samples his correspondence and supplies useful identifications and annotations of forgotten friends. Marquis's papers are located in several libraries, including the Butler Library, Columbia University; the New York Public Library; the Henry E. Huntington Library, San Marino, California; the Walter Hampden Memorial Library of the Players Club, New York City; the Houghton Library, Harvard University; and the Library of Congress. The largest number have been collected at the Linderman Library, Lehigh University.

GUY SZUBERLA                    UNIVERSITY OF TOLEDO

# HERBERT WOODWARD MARTIN
October 4, 1933

**BIOGRAPHY:** Herbert Woodward Martin—poet, teacher-scholar, singer-actor, and opera librettist—was born in Birmingham, Alabama. His father, David Nathaniel Martin, a foundry worker, and his mother, Willie Mae (Woodward) Martin, a domestic who was trained as a beautician, introduced him to literature and music at an early age. Herbert

Martin read widely, including the works of PAUL LAURENCE DUNBAR and tales of terror. Martin's striking resemblance to Dunbar and his amazing vocal range and performing skills may have drawn him to a literary life even from the earliest years. His family moved to Toledo, Ohio, when he was twelve. In 1960 he began to write poetry as an undergraduate at the University of Toledo, from which he graduated with a BA in 1964. He published his first book at the end of the decade while living in Grand Rapids, Michigan. Martin holds several advanced degrees including master's degrees from SUNY Buffalo in 1967 and the Breadloaf School at Middlebury College in 1972, and the doctorate from Carnegie Mellon University in 1979. He has published and performed widely throughout the world. His most noteworthy positions include a Fulbright Professorship in Hungary, a visiting distinguished professorship at Central Michigan University, and appointments as poet in residence and professor of English at the University of Dayton for twenty-five years. He is married to poet-teacher Elizabeth Altman Martin; they have two daughters and two grandchildren.

**SIGNIFICANCE:** Martin's poems capture the vitality of human voices from classical antiquity to today. His characters speak with the intensity of love and grief among American slaves and cowboys, city dwellers and rural folk, revolutionaries and domestics; his poems convey the silence of prayers, the shouting of revolutionaries, the contrapuntal dialogue of embattled lovers. Classical music, painting, and sculpture figure prominently in his poems—as do family rituals, traditions, dreams, and rhythmic silence. He writes often of memory and celebration, human need, commitment, and an effort to reach out to others. His poems are meant to be heard, performed the way he does best, in person in his readings or on videotape. His most recent works capture voices he remembers from his earliest days in Alabama and Ohio and while traveling the world; he introduces us to passengers aboard slave ships, Vietnam soldiers, and victims of AIDS and cancer. Martin's life and writings focus on the Midwestern city of Dayton, Ohio—home also of his inspiration Paul Laurence Dunbar. Martin is the poet laureate of Dayton and poet in residence at the Dunbar House in Dayton.

Herbert Woodward Martin.
Photo by Larry Burgess. Courtesy
of University of Dayton Public Relations

In performance, Martin has interpreted Shakespeare, modern drama, and the Broadway musical. He is in great demand for readings of his own work and for his one-man show on Dunbar. Martin has also collaborated with Adolphus Hailstork on an opera, *Paul Laurence Dunbar: Common Ground* (1995). His scholarship on American literature is considerable; his monograph on Dunbar contributed greatly to an understanding of the poems in dialect and standard English. A steady increase in the outpouring of poetry, performance, and scholarship suggests that the full measure of Martin's achievement cannot yet be fully determined.

**SELECTED WORKS:** Martin's poems have appeared in more than seventy literary magazines and journals as well as in a dozen anthologies. His volumes of poetry include *New York: The Nine Million* (1969), *The Shit-Storm Poems* (1972), *The Persistence of the Flesh* (1976), and *The Forms of Silence* (1980). He has published ten articles on African American literature; a monograph, *Paul Laurence Dunbar: A Singer of Songs* (1979); two videos: *Paul Laurence Dunbar* (1984) and *PLD: The Eyes of the Poet* (1992); and the libretto for the opera *Paul Laurence Dunbar: Common Ground* (1995). In 1972 he organized the Dunbar Centennial at the University of Dayton, a gathering of more than twenty-five poets and scholars. Works in progress include several volumes of poems: *The Last Days of William Short, Final W.*, *The Log of the Vigilante*, *The Bones of the Bargain*, *The Edge of Being*, and *Early Songs, Midnight Music*; the libretto for the opera *It Pays to Advertize* (1995);

a new show, *Langston and Company*; and an edition of lost Dunbar plays and stories, *The Dramatic and Other Uncollected Works of Paul Laurence Dunbar* (forthcoming).

**FURTHER READING:** No book about Martin has been written, but his poems have been included and discussed in a dozen literary anthologies with national or regional focus. Ronald Primeau's "Slave Narrative Turning Midwestern: Deadwood Dick Rides into Difficulty," in *MidAmerica* 1 (1974): 16–35, discusses the Midwestern qualities of Martin's Deadwood Dick poems. In the last ten years numerous articles have brought Martin critical acclaim and notoriety for his own poems, his scholarship on Dunbar, and his performances. Selected articles include "Dunbar's Poetry Lives through UD Prof," in the *Dayton Daily* (February 6, 1987); "The Poet and His Song," in *Dimensions* (University of Dayton [Summer 1990]: 1); "Star Professors," in *Ohio Magazine* (April 1992): 30–33; "Poet Herbert Woodward Martin as Paul Laurence Dunbar," in *Humanities* (July–August 1994): 32–33; "A Poet Gives Life to His Fascination," in *Chronicle of Higher Education* (November 3, 1993): A5; and "Doctor Martin and Mister Dunbar," in *Ohio Magazine* (February 1995): 23–27. Martin's collected papers are housed in the Herbert Woodward Martin Collection at the University of Toledo.

RONALD PRIMEAU    CENTRAL MICHIGAN UNIVERSITY

## MICHAEL MARTONE
August 22, 1955

**BIOGRAPHY:** As an essayist, editor, poet, and writer of short fiction, Michael Martone has focused exclusively on the Midwest and, more specifically, his home state of Indiana. Martone was born in Fort Wayne, Indiana, to Anthony and Patricia (Payne) Martone. Martone's father was a telephone company switchman and his mother an English teacher in the public schools. From 1973 to 1976, Martone attended Butler University; in 1977, however, he transferred to Indiana University, where he received his BA in English at the end of the year. After a year working at a hotel in Fort Wayne, Martone enrolled in the writing program at Johns Hopkins University and was awarded an MA in fiction writing in 1979. From 1980 to 1988, Martone taught English at Iowa State University and also served as the editor of *Poet and Critic*. Martone married

Theresa Pappas, a poet, in 1984, and together, while at Iowa State, they published a series of chapbooks under the imprint of Story County Books. Since leaving Iowa State University, Martone has written on agricultural issues for the *North American Review* and served as Briggs-Copeland Lecturer on Fiction at Harvard University. Currently, Martone is professor of English at the University of Alabama.

**SIGNIFICANCE:** Although it is quite early in Martone's career, it is clear that his fiction and nonfiction, as well as his skills as an editor, have had a considerable impact on both contemporary Midwestern writing and the study of Midwestern regionalism. Martone has often commented that his writing inevitably ends up being about place, and, as the subtitle of a collection he has edited, *A Sense of Place: Essays in Search of the Midwest* (1988), suggests, Martone's literary preoccupation invites the reader to search for the mythic Midwest that exists somewhere in the wide open places between small towns in Indiana and Iowa. An unusual characteristic of Martone's fiction involves his use of real historical figures within fictional narratives; he layers fact and fiction in such a way that the myth transcends both the real and the fictional, leaving only the human. His first collection of stories, *Alive and Dead in Indiana* (1984), makes use of such famous persons as Alfred Kinsey, Ezra Pound, and James Dean, while his second collection of fiction, *Fort Wayne Is Seventh on Hitler's List* (1990), composed of original stories as well as work from the first collection, extends Martone's notion of what may be left behind when historical figures are reduced to a series of dates and accomplishments. It is Martone's practice to work around the actual history one finds in textbooks, concentrating on the possibilities just beyond the purview of the reader. In his editorial introduction to *Townships* (1992), Martone contends that the Midwest "began as a highly abstract work of the imagination and lingers so today" (5), and in his own work, there is attempt after attempt to bring what is Midwestern into clearer focus, to add specificity to a region that seems to defy any single definition, a region that Martone approaches with wonder and reverence and art.

**SELECTED WORKS:** Martone began his career as a poet and has published two volumes,

*At a Loss* (1977) and *Return to Powers* (1985). His fiction, which has received more attention and greater praise from critics, includes *Alive and Dead in Indiana* (1984), *Safety Patrol* (1988), *Fort Wayne Is Seventh on Hitler's List* (1990), and *Seeing Eye* (1995). Martone's work as an editor of *A Sense of Place: Essays in Search of the Midwest* (1988) and *Townships* (1992) displays his fascination with the imaginative task of defining the Midwest.

**FURTHER READING:** To date, Martone's work has not been the subject of scholarly attention; this may be attributed to his resistance to the long form. His work, however, has received high praise in book reviews from such noted critics as Peter S. Prescott, and he has received numerous awards and grants, including the Pushcart Prize on three separate occasions, the Margaret Jones Fiction Award, mention in both the *Best American Short Stories of 1981* and the *Best American Essays of 1986*, and a Creative Writing Fellowship Grant for Fiction from the National Endowment for the Arts.

TODD F. DAVIS          GOSHEN COLLEGE

## EDGAR LEE MASTERS
August 23, 1868–March 5, 1950
(Dexter Wallace, Webster Ford)

**BIOGRAPHY:** Edgar Lee Masters was born in Garnett, Kansas, to Hardin Wallace Masters, a lawyer, and Emma Jerusha (Dexter) Masters but raised in the central Illinois towns of Petersburg and Lewistown, two Corn Belt county seats which figure prominently in his many writings. After graduation from Lewistown High School in 1886, Masters worked in his father's law office and on the *Lewistown News* before attending the preparatory school of nearby Knox College during the 1889–90 school year.

Masters passed the Illinois bar in 1891 and briefly practiced law with his father before moving to Chicago in 1892. There he continued his work as an attorney and married Helen Jenkins in 1898. In 1903 Masters began a lucrative law practice with the famous criminal lawyer CLARENCE DARROW but eventually quarreled with Darrow over the division of a legal fee and established his own practice in 1911.

Dissatisfied with both the law and his marriage, Masters turned frequently to reading and part-time writing. Between 1896 and

Edgar Lee Masters.
Photo courtesy of Hilary Masters

1912, he published five pamphlets on literary and political subjects and a dozen other small volumes—poems, plays, and a book of essays—and in 1914 began serial publication in *Reedy's Mirror* of the verses that became *Spoon River Anthology*. Published in book form in 1915, *Spoon River* became an overnight best-seller and brought Masters international popular and critical attention.

In 1919 Masters encountered a wealthy young widow named Lillian Wilson and abandoned his wife and three children, Hardin, Marcia, and Madeline, to pursue her. He slowly abandoned his law practice as well, and in 1920 published the first of several novels in order to help support himself. He was divorced in 1923, but his plans to marry Lillian Wilson failed to work out, and he moved to New York City.

In 1926 he married a twenty-seven-year-old actress from Kansas City, Ellen Coyne. They decided that their New York apartment was too small for a family, and Ellen Masters returned to her Kansas City parents to await the birth of their son Hilary in 1928. This separation and Ellen's 1929 graduate studies in English created stress between Masters and his wife, and the couple began to drift apart. The strains grew greater in the 1930s when Masters moved to New York's Hotel Chelsea and began a romantic liaison with his typist, Alice Davis.

Masters wrote at a prodigious rate during his New York years, sometimes publishing two or three books a year. Unfortunately, he never duplicated the success of *Spoon River Anthology* and spent several of his later years in near poverty. In 1943 he was hospitalized with pneumonia and malnutrition and never fully regained his strength. His wife, Ellen, by then a teacher, cared for him through his death in 1950.

SIGNIFICANCE: Masters was one of the most prolific Midwestern authors, publishing fifty-three books during his long lifetime, including twenty-nine volumes of verse, seven novels, seven plays, five biographies, a book of essays, and his autobiography as well as two histories, and one edited volume of Emerson's works. He was also the author of at least eight pamphlets and a large number of newspaper and magazine pieces in addition to book prefaces and miscellaneous prose and poetry in Festschrifts. A posthumous collection of poems added a fifty-fourth volume to this remarkable output.

Many books by Masters deal with a three-county area in west-central Illinois where the Sangamon and Spoon Rivers wend their way through the prairie on their way to the Illinois River. All of the books important to his literary reputation come from this general area, including the one that made him world famous, *Spoon River Anthology*.

*Spoon River Anthology* sprang from and celebrated life in the Midwest as an authentic experience and could only have been written by a Midwesterner. *Spoon River* tore the mantle of innocence from the American village by portraying realistically the lives and deaths of people in the village of Spoon River—a fictive community based on Masters's hometowns of Petersburg and Lewistown. Depicted in 243 free verse "epitaphs," Spoon River's inhabitants gossiped freely about themselves and their neighbors—and in so doing completely destroyed the stereotype of the American village as a place where meaningful lives were lived out in harmony and purpose.

Most of the Spoon River poems were less than a printed page, but in these few lines Masters caught the essence of the speaker's existence, as well as his or her relation to others, with unprecedented frankness and recognition of life's many ironies. Midwestern settings and subjects show up repeatedly in many other books by Masters, including all seven of his novels, but for one reason or another none of his later books ever came close to rivaling *Spoon River*. For one thing, the timing of *Spoon River Anthology* had been fortunate. Masters was never fully at home with the nation's drift toward industrialization, urbanization, and sophistication, and after World War I and the Roaring Twenties, he grew increasingly out of step with the times.

A second problem in his later writings was that Masters often failed to objectify his material as he had done so well through the use of dramatic monologues in *Spoon River*. Instead, he cluttered his work with highly subjective and inartistic outbursts. Poor reviews and poor sales characterized many of these post–*Spoon River* works, and because Masters lacked the ability to criticize his own work, he tended to blame others rather than himself for what became one of the longest literary declines in American letters.

SELECTED WORKS: In the forty books that Masters published after *Spoon River*, he returned repeatedly to the Midwest and to central Illinois for his characters, themes, and settings. His 1920 epic of America, *Domesday Book*, a work which Masters referred to as his "finest achievement" in Kimball Flaccus's New York University dissertation, "Edgar Lee Masters: A Biographical and Critical Study" (1952): 217, is situated in large part in central Illinois, as is his first and best novel, *Mitch Miller* (1920), which relies heavily on Petersburg. His hometowns of Petersburg and Lewistown also helped provide Masters with a second volume of epitaphs, *The New Spoon River* (1924), a less successful treatment of the same geographical area as *Spoon River Anthology*. His most controversial biography, *Lincoln: The Man* (1931), takes place partially in Petersburg and in nearby New Salem and Springfield. Springfield is also the principal town for Masters's most successful biography—of his writer-friend VACHEL LINDSAY in *Vachel Lindsay: A Poet in America* (1935). Much of Masters's autobiography, *Across Spoon River* (1936), also occurs in Illinois. His last significant work, *The Sangamon* (1942), was a combination family history and a history of the river that flows through his home of Petersburg.

**FURTHER READING:** Useful critical commentary on Masters and his many books appears in John H. and Margaret Wrenn's *Edgar Lee Masters* (1983); Ronald Primeau's *Beyond Spoon River: The Legacy of Edgar Lee Masters* (1981); and JOHN T. FLANAGAN's *Edgar Lee Masters: The Spoon River Poet and His Critics* (1974). An indispensable guide to the Spoon River poems is *Spoon River Anthology: An Annotated Edition*, edited by JOHN E. HALLWAS (1992). There is no full-length biography of Masters, but partial views appear in Hilary Masters's *Last Stands: Notes from Memory* (1982); Hardin Masters's *Edgar Lee Masters: A Biographical Sketchbook about a Famous American Author* (1978); and Herbert K. Russell's "Edgar Lee Masters," in *Dictionary of Literary Biography* 54: 293–312. The bulk of Masters's manuscripts, papers, and letters are at the University of Texas at Austin, with supplementary materials at Harvard, Yale, Princeton, Dartmouth, Georgetown University, the University of Chicago, and the Newberry Library, Chicago.

HERBERT K. RUSSELL        JOHN A. LOGAN COLLEGE

## JACK MATTHEWS
July 22, 1925

**BIOGRAPHY:** Jack Matthews was born in his family's house at 164 Glencoe Road, in Clintonville, a suburb north of Columbus, Ohio. His parents, John and Lou (Grover) Matthews, were born and reared in rural Gallia County in southern Ohio. While Jack was in high school, his father, an attorney with a passion for baseball, turned gentleman farmer—a return to his rural ties—and moved the family to a 121–acre farm in Delaware County, northeast of Columbus. There, in the wild pasture land and woods surrounding Alum Creek, the young author stored many images for later stories and poems.

Matthews served from 1943 to 1945 with the Coast Guard Cutter *Maclaine*, an antisubmarine patrol ship, and was stationed at Point Higgins outside Ketchikan, Alaska. After World War II, he attended Ohio State University, concentrating in creative writing, at the time a rare and unpopular major, and completed a graduate curriculum emphasizing Greek, philosophy, and literature. In 1947 he married Barbara Reese and settled near Columbus.

Jack and Barbara have three children, Cynthia, Barbara Ellen, and John. During the 1950s and 1960s Matthews helped support his family and his writing by loading produce on the dock at the Big Bear supermarket off Olentangy River Road in Columbus, inspiring his novel *The Tale of Asa Bean* (1971). He also worked as an encyclopedia and Fuller Brush salesman, private investigator, piano salesman, and postal worker at the Spring Street Station in Columbus.

Matthews's first story, "The Lieutenant," appeared in an Irish periodical, *Envoy*, in June 1951. Soon after, his stories began appearing in *Accent*, *Chicago Review*, *Southwest Review*, and *Sewanee Review* with writers such as J. F. POWERS, Wallace Stevens, Iris Murdoch, T. S. ELIOT, Donald Hall, and Isaac Rosenfeld. Following publication of his first volume of stories, *Bitter Knowledge* (1964), the author joined the full-time faculty of Ohio University and moved to Athens. Since then, he has published six novels, six story collections, a collection of poems, two plays, and several volumes of essays. He continues to serve on the faculty of Ohio University as distinguished professor of English.

**SIGNIFICANCE:** While reviewers such as Doris Grumbach praise Matthews's stories for their "straightforward language" developing "ominous overtones" (*New York Times*, August 18, 1985: 9), two of Matthews's early novels in particular, *Hanger Stout, Awake!* (1967) and *The Charisma Campaigns* (1972), explore the comic possibilities of an edenic Midwestern innocence. Clyde Stout, for instance, a high school dropout who worships a Chevy and a hard-hearted girl, is swindled by a gambler who uses Clyde's talent for hanging by his hands for long intervals to win bets. *The Charisma Campaigns*, nominated for the National Book Award by Walker Percy, concerns one Rex McCoy, a successful used-car dealer in a small Ohio town whose hypnotic power over buyers is nearly his undoing.

Matthews's later novels, for instance *Pictures of the Journey Back* (1973) and *Sassafras* (1983), give compelling historical and cultural depth to the Midwest. The author draws, for example, on burial practices of Plains Indians to inform *Sassafras*, material the author gathered because of his rigorous passion for book collecting, expressed in volumes of essays, such as *Booking in the Heartland* (1986).

**SELECTED WORKS:** Matthews's major works include novels, *Hanger Stout, Awake!* (1967), *The Tale of Asa Bean* (1971), *The Charisma Campaigns* (1972), *Pictures of the Journey Back* (1973), *Sassafras* (1983); and story collections, *Bitter Knowledge* (1964), *Tales of the Ohio Land* (1980), *Dubious Persuasions* (1981), *Crazy Women* (1985), *Ghostly Populations* (1986), *Dirty Tricks* (1990), and *Storyhood as We Know It and Other Stories* (1993). His nonfiction and essays concerning the author's passion for collecting old and rare books in the Midwest are also notable and include *Collecting Rare Books for Pleasure and Profit* (1977), *Booking in the Heartland* (1986), *Memoirs of a Bookman* (1989), and *Booking Pleasures* (1996).

**FURTHER READING:** Although no book has been written on Jack Matthews's work, his fiction has received wide critical notice, such as D. J. Gordon's review of *Hanger Stout, Awake!* in the *Yale Review* 57 (1967): 114; Martin Levin's review of *The Charisma Campaigns* in the *New York Times Book Review* (March 19, 1972): 41; Tom O'Brien's review of *Dubious Persuasions* in the *New York Times* (February 17, 1982): 12; and Doris Grumbach's review of *Crazy Women* in the *New York Times* (August 18, 1985): 9.

WENDELL MAYO  BOWLING GREEN STATE UNIVERSITY

## WILLIAM MAXWELL
August 16, 1908–July 31, 2000

**BIOGRAPHY:** William Maxwell—novelist, short story writer, essayist, and fiction editor—was born in Lincoln, a town of twelve thousand people in central Illinois. His father—a successful fire insurance salesman—traveled extensively throughout the state, and young Maxwell was exceptionally close to his mother. When she died during the 1918 influenza epidemic, Maxwell was only ten; five years later he moved to Chicago with his newly remarried father and family. In "A Note about the Author" in *The Chateau* (1961), Maxwell has said that the loss of his mother "made a novelist" of him, and much of his fiction recaptures emotions surrounding this early tragedy.

In 1930 he graduated from the University of Illinois at Urbana–Champaign with a scholarship to Harvard. After receiving his master's degree at Cambridge in 1931, he returned to Urbana, where he taught literature and pursued a PhD until 1933, when he decided to turn his attention exclusively to writing. His first novel, *Bright Center of Heaven*, appeared in 1934. Two years later—with his second novel accepted for publication at Harper's—he began his forty-year career at the *New Yorker*, first as a member of the art department and later as a fiction editor, helping to shape the work of such writers as John Updike, Eudora Welty, J. D. Salinger, John Cheever, and Vladimir Nabokov.

Since his retirement from editing in 1976, the magazine has continued to publish his stories and essays. As an artist Maxwell flourished in later life, producing some of his most powerful work in his seventies and eighties. In 1995 he received the Society for the Study of Midwestern Literature's Mark Twain Award for outstanding contributions to Midwestern literature, the Penn Malamud Award for short fiction, and the National Critics Circle Award for distinguished achievement in publishing. Maxwell died at his home in New York, preceded in death by Emily, his wife of fifty years.

**SIGNIFICANCE:** William Maxwell's Midwestern youth has provided the foundation for a nationally prominent literary career that has spanned six decades. Although he has lived in New York since the mid-1930s, he has continued to capture the place he calls his "imagination's home" with a spare style that reflects the unadorned, subtle beauty of the prairiescape (Burkhardt, *Tamaqua* [Fall 1992]: 9). Even at the *New Yorker*, he most often published pieces that recall the Illinois town he knew in the 1910s and 1920s. The family and community, the simple, everyday details that make up what he called in personal correspondence "the Natural History of home," weave through four novels—including the American Book Award–winning *So Long, See You Tomorrow*—and numerous short stories. Yet while his work emanates from the Midwestern landscape, language, and culture that shaped his childhood, the intellectual and psychological life of his adulthood in New York and abroad also inform his work and contribute universal relevance and a distanced, intelligent voice to his canon.

*They Came Like Swallows*, Maxwell's first novel to tell the story of his mother's death, first brought him a national audience in 1937. It was followed in 1945 by *The Folded Leaf*, an intensely personal, psychological drama in-

**William Maxwell.**
Photo © Nancy Crampton

volving a pair of young male students at a large Midwestern university in the 1920s. Set in Draperville, a fictional town modeled on Lincoln, *Time Will Darken It* appeared in 1947 as the author's first mature work to center on adulthood rather than childhood.

In the 1970s Maxwell published *Over by the River* (1977), a collection of stories set in Illinois, New York, and France, as well as *Ancestors* (1971), a nonfiction family history. *So Long, See You Tomorrow*, perhaps his finest novel, appeared in 1980. In this late work, Maxwell brings fresh perspective to his Midwestern youth, taking full advantage of the more detached view afforded by passing decades, diverse life experiences, and geographic distance. The strengths of his earlier work are heightened: the deceptive simplicity and intelligent, straightforward style; the powerful understatement; and the ability to lay bare tragedy and truth without sentimentality. Here Maxwell tightens the thread that holds his fiction taut: the delicate, even precarious, balance between life's exhilaration and haunting sadness, between events and interpretation.

*So Long* can be considered a significant work of postmodern sensibility, yet it exudes a distinctly Midwestern mood and quality. As in all Maxwell's Lincoln fiction, his fidelity to the common cadences of early-century, Illinois idiom is painstaking, and his eye for cultural detail is meticulous. The silent Midwestern landscape itself becomes part of the narrative tone and framework. Like an unresolved chord, it creates an underlying, unrelenting tension that courses beneath Maxwell's restrained yet graceful prose.

**SELECTED WORKS:** Maxwell's fiction includes *Bright Center of Heaven* (1934); *They Came Like Swallows* (1937); *The Folded Leaf* (1945); *Time Will Darken It* (1948); *The Chateau* (1961); *Ancestors* (1971); *Over by the River and Other Stories* (1977); *So Long, See You Tomorrow* (1980); *Billie Dyer and Other Stories* (1992); and *All the Days and Nights: The Collected Short Stories* (1995). Maxwell has also published a collection of essays entitled *The Outermost Dream: Essays and Reviews* (1989).

**FURTHER READING:** Articles and interviews include Bruce Bawer's "States of Grace: The Novels of William Maxwell," in *New Criterion* (May 1989): 26–38; James Hurt's "William Maxwell: The Illinoisan and the New Yorker," in *Selected Paper in Illinois History* (1981); and Richard Shereikis's "William Maxwell's Lincoln, Illinois," in *MidAmerica* 19 (1987): 101–12. George Plimpton's interview with Maxwell for the *Paris Review* is available in *Writers at Work: The Paris Review Interviews* (1986). "Imagining the Middle West: An Interview with William Maxwell" (9–25) and Barbara Burkhardt's "Behind the Writer's Window: Visiting with William Maxwell" appear in the Fall 1992 issue of *Tamaqua* (71–87). Ben Yagoda's *About Town: The New Yorker and the World It Made* (2000) includes Maxwell, with particular emphasis on his career as an editor. His obituary was published in the *New York Times* (August 1, 2000): A24.

BARBARA A. BURKHARDT    UNIVERSITY OF ILLINOIS

## ROBERT (MENZIES) McALMON
March 9, 1895–February 2, 1956

**BIOGRAPHY:** Robert McAlmon, writer and publisher, was born in Clifton, Kansas, the youngest of ten children born to John Alexander McAlmon, a Presbyterian minister, and Bess (Urquhart) McAlmon. Soon after Robert was born, his impoverished family moved to a succession of small towns in South Dakota, which he described in *Being Geniuses Together, 1920–1930* (1968) as a "wild and dreary plains state" (158). Later the family moved to Minneapolis, where McAlmon attended East High School (1910–12) and in the fall of 1913 studied at the University of Minnesota. In 1917 he moved with his family to Los Angeles, where he intermittently attended the University of Southern California until 1920. After a brief stint in the Army Air Corps, he became serious enough about writing to submit poems to HARRIET MONROE, who in March 1919 published six of them in *Poetry*. In 1920, after dropping out of college, he headed for Chicago, which he soon left for Greenwich Village. There, with the support of his friend William Carlos Williams, he began publishing the works of such writers as Marianne Moore, Ezra Pound, and Wallace Stevens in the short-lived little magazine *Contact*.

In 1921 McAlmon achieved a kind of celebrity by marrying Winifred Bryher, a young English writer who had come to the United States with Imagist poet H.D. (Hilda Doolittle). Because Bryher, whose legal name was Annie Winifred Ellerman, turned out to be the daughter of an immensely wealthy shipping magnate, the marriage was written up in a Los Angeles Sunday supplement and in the *New York Times*. Bryher's father, Sir John Ellerman, generously subsidized McAlmon, first in London, where he met T. S. ELIOT, and later in Paris, where he met Joyce, Pound, and Sylvia Beach, among other expatriates. Besides writing poems and short stories, he was enabled by his new affluence to publish his own work and that of several avant-garde literary figures in Contact Editions. Important literary innovators published by McAlmon included Ezra Pound, Gertrude Stein, and ERNEST HEMINGWAY, whose first little book, *Three Stories and Ten Poems* (1923), made both its author and publisher famous. McAlmon was divorced from Bryher in 1927. In 1929 he brought out his last Contact books. By this time he was drinking heavily and becoming less creative and productive. When the expatriate movement collapsed in the late 1920s, he remained in Europe. His greatest achievement of the next decade was completion by 1934 of *Being Geniuses Together*, an insightful memoir of the expatriate movement not published until 1938. In 1940 McAlmon managed to escape to the United States from occupied France via Lisbon. He spent his remaining unhealthy, unhappy years first in Texas, then Mexico, and finally California, where he died of pneumonia in Desert Hot Springs.

SIGNIFICANCE: Although today McAlmon is probably better known for his discriminating publication of important American expatriate writers than for his own writing, his continuing ties with the Midwestern plains of his youth are most evident in his autobiographical short stories, even those composed during the latter days of his expatriation. Thus, though capable of writing brilliantly about homosexual and heterosexual decadence in Berlin, about rich and indolent American vacationers on the Riviera, and about the expatriate movement in Paris, his "spiritual environment" remains the Midwest of the plains from *A Hasty Bunch* (1922), his first collection of stories, to *Indefinite Huntress and Other Stories* (1932), his last. The typical protagonist of his stories is a magnetically charming boy or youth in rebellious if not reckless pursuit of experience forbidden to self-respecting members of his narrowly conformist, small-town Midwestern family— experience of low life on the road or in strange cities, of early sexual initiation, of racial barriers crossed, or the exploration of death in his wonderfully evocative story "The Jack Rabbit Drive" (1929). Talented beyond many of his literary rivals in presenting the unvarnished realities of everyday life, McAlmon ultimately falls short of their achievement because of his impatience with detail and his unwillingness to take the pains necessary to produce great art.

SELECTED WORKS: Anyone seeking to capture the flavor and style of McAlmon's writing should look into his Berlin stories in *Distinguished Air* (1925), recently republished under the title *Miss Knight and Others* (1992); his *Being Geniuses Together* (1938), republished in 1968 and again in 1984 under the title *Being Geniuses Together, 1920–1930*, with alternate chapters and an afterword by Kay Boyle. Another important source is his *McAlmon and the Lost Generation: A Self-Portrait*, edited by Robert E. Knoll (1962). This volume contains his memorable story "The Jack Rabbit Drive" (11–20) along with a selection of McAlmon's other writings. Anyone interested in exploring the specifically Midwestern dimensions of McAlmon's art might read some of his small-town stories in *A Hasty Bunch* (1922) or the grim portraits of Midwestern life in *Village: as it happened through a fifteen year period* (1924), ostensibly set in Wentworth, North Dakota, but actually Madison, South Dakota. According to writer Gore Vidal in his foreword to McAlmon's *Miss Knight and Others*, the high school football hero Eugene Collins in *Village*, with whom the autobiographical protagonist Peter Reynalds is in love, was closely modeled on Vidal's father, Eugene Vidal. Evidently he and other members of the Vidal family resident in Madison when McAlmon lived there are faithfully encapsulated in *Village* like flies in amber (xi-xii).

**FURTHER READING:** Besides reading McAlmon's *Being Geniuses Together, 1920–1930* (1968), those interested in his biography and critical reputation should consult Sanford J. Smoller's somewhat romantic and speculative *Adrift among Geniuses: Robert McAlmon, Writer and Publisher of the Twenties* (1975). On the question of McAlmon's date of birth and attendance at the University of Minnesota, see James K. P. Mortensen's "Robert McAlmon's Birth Date," in *American Notes* and *Queries* 22.3–4 (1983): 47. Correcting other authorities, Mortensen has found public records which establish that McAlmon was born on March 9, 1895 (not 1896), and that he attended the University of Minnesota in the fall term, 1913 (not 1916). The largest collection of McAlmon's papers is at Southern Illinois University, Carbondale, with supplementary materials at the Beinecke Library, Yale University.

PAUL W. MILLER                    WITTENBERG UNIVERSITY

## (JOHN) ROBERT MCCLOSKEY

September 15, 1914

**BIOGRAPHY:** Celebrated author and illustrator of children's books, Robert McCloskey was born and raised in Hamilton, Ohio, the town that informed his boys' stories. His parents, Howard and Mable (Wismeyer) McCloskey, encouraged him in his boyhood fascination with musical instruments, mechanical inventions, and art, which became his vocation. As a teenager, deeply involved in community and school activities, McCloskey taught harmonica and soap carving at the YMCA and contributed his art work to the publications of Hamilton High School. After graduating in 1932, he accepted a scholarship at the Vesper George School of Art in Boston, where he studied for three winters, followed by two years at the National Academy of Design in New York.

In 1935 he began his long and cordial association with May Massee, the arbiter of taste in children's books at Viking Press. Three years later, when he showed her his text and drawings of a small-town Ohio boy, she accepted them for his first book, *Lentil*, published in 1940. On November 23 of the same year, he married Margaret (Peggy) Durand, who is featured in his books along with their daughters Sarah (Sal) and Jane. In 1945, after three years in the U.S. Army, McCloskey moved his family to their summer cottage on one of the Scott Islands in Maine, the setting of three of his best-loved picture books. During the next thirty years, he came into prominence as one of the most admired author-illustrators of juvenile books. He received honorary doctorates from Miami University in Oxford, Ohio, in 1964 and Mount Holyoke College in 1967. Pursuing interests outside the children's book field since 1970, he reported he was working on an autobiography in 1995.

**SIGNIFICANCE:** McCloskey's works are firmly rooted in three places he loves: the Mid-American small town of his childhood, urban Boston, and the Maine islands in Penobscot Bay. His three Midwestern books, hailed as authentic Americana in the patriotic fervor of the 1940s, place him in the tradition of MARK TWAIN as a humorous realist and a teller of boys' stories and tall tales. From the familiar war monument and public buildings of his boyhood Hamilton he creates the perfect setting for his works: the archetypal small town named Alto, Ohio, in the picture book *Lentil* (1940), and Centerburg in the stories of *Homer Price* (1943) and *Centerburg Tales* (1951). In *Lentil*, the tone of comic exaggeration is enhanced by the bold, cartoon-like drawings of the parade of townspeople who are saved from public disgrace by Lentil's harmonica playing. In *Homer Price*, the hilarious episodes become even more preposterous, though rooted in everyday reality. In *Centerburg Tales*, Grandpa Hercules' exuberant accounts of his youthful exploits are clearly in the American tall-tale genre. Only the children of the town, however, appreciate his wildly imaginative stories that cannot be "scientifically proved in the laboratory" (77).

The first reviewers of *Homer Price* welcomed the ingenious and imperturbable Homer into the literary lineage of the typical American boy, Tom Sawyer. Homer, like Tom, is a dauntless adventurer, thereby becoming a well-known participant in the life of his town. Centerburg is a public-spirited, egalitarian community of lively citizens with several comic eccentrics among them. Except for the college-educated robber and the judge, everyone uses the Midwestern vernacular, rich in slang and humorous folk sayings. Led by Uncle Ulysses, the local apostle of the machine age, the town celebrates its one hundred and fiftieth anniversary by adding a suburb of a hundred and one identical prefabricated houses. McCloskey's satiric tone suggests his increasing concern over America's desecration of the natural landscape in the name of progress.

McCloskey, important today as the creator of undisputed classics for children, is the only author-artist to win two Caldecott Medals and three Caldecott Honors for his distinguished illustrations. His literary style is also widely praised: the folksy humor and authentic language of the Midwestern stories and his sensitive narratives of family life in a Maine island setting. In *Time of Wonder* (1957), considered by many his greatest achievement, he evokes the eternal mystery and power of the changing seasons in prose as rhythmic, precise, and suggestive as poetry. **SELECTED WORKS:** Between 1940 and 1970 McCloskey published a total of six picture books and two story collections. He also illustrated ten children's books by other writers. His most successful collaborations include a collection of American tall tales, *Yankee Doodle's Cousins* (1941), by Anne Malcolmson; the Caldecott Honor Book *Journey Cake, Ho!* (1953), by Ruth Sawyer; and four books of the Henry Reed series, beginning with *Henry Reed, Inc.* (1958), by Keith Robertson.

Of his three Midwestern books, *Lentil* (1940), *Homer Price* (1943), and *Centerburg Tales* (1951), *Homer Price* received the Young Readers' Choice Award. Set in Boston, his first Caldecott Medal winner, *Make Way for Ducklings* (1941), was celebrated as a small miracle

of perfection on its fiftieth birthday in 1991. His Maine picture books draw on the everyday experiences of the McCloskey family as they live safe and secure in their island home. *Blueberries for Sal* (1948) and *One Morning in Maine* (1952) are both Caldecott Honor books; *Time of Wonder* (1957), with full-color illustrations, won McCloskey his second Caldecott Medal. In his last book, *Burt Dow, Deep-Water Man: A Tale of the Sea in the Classic Tradition* (1963), McCloskey returns to the fantasy and broad humor of the tall-tale genre. In his second Caldecott Medal acceptance speech, published in the *Horn Book* of July 1958, he expresses his outrage at the aesthetic deterioration of America by machine-inspired designs (245–51).

**FURTHER READING:** *Robert McCloskey* (1990), by Gary D. Schmidt, is a comprehensive and meticulously researched biographical and critical work. Schmidt provides a chronology, pictures, and an excellent selected bibliography of primary and secondary works. He places McCloskey's work in the larger context of children's literature and emphasizes his affirming vision of the warmth and security of family life and "the permanence and significance and beauty of the world" (149). An earlier critic, May Hill Arbuthnot in *Children and Books* (1957), although recognizing the theme of reassurance in the picture books, notes the "astringent humor" in the Homer Price tales, including the "caustically amusing" satire in the stories of the uncontrollable doughnut machine and the invasion of mass-produced housing into a natural area (410–11).

In 1965 a motion picture, *Robert McCloskey*, was directed by Morton Schindel of Weston Woods Studios. Weston Woods produced other films of McCloskey's books including *Make Way for Ducklings* (1955), *Lentil* (1956), *Time of Wonder* (1961), *Blueberries for Sal* (1967), and *Burt Dow: Deep-Water Man* (1983).

McCloskey donated the majority of his papers to the May Massee Memorial Collection in the WILLIAM ALLEN WHITE Library of Emporia State University, Emporia, Kansas. He gave hundreds of sketches made for *Make Way for Ducklings* to the Boston Public Library. The Lane Public Library in Hamilton, Ohio, holds the original illustrations McCloskey created for *Yankee Doodle's Cousins* (1941), by Anne Malcolmson as well as a collection of memorabilia, pamphlets, and local newspaper clippings. A map of present-day Hamilton highlighting six local landmarks that appear in the illustrations of *Lentil* is available to the public.

MARY JOAN MILLER                    SPRINGFIELD, OHIO

## GEORGE BARR McCUTCHEON
July 26, 1866–October 23, 1928

**BIOGRAPHY:** George Barr McCutcheon was the son of John Barr McCutcheon, a political office holder in Tippecanoe County, Indiana, a veteran of the Civil War, and a farmer. His mother was Clara (Glick) McCutcheon. His brothers were famous; Ben Frederick McCutcheon became the commercial editor of the *Chicago Tribune*, and John Tinney McCutcheon was a cartoonist.

George Barr McCutcheon was born in Tippecanoe County. He went to a country school and the Lafayette schools. He attended Purdue University from 1883 to 1885, where he reported Purdue news to the *Lafayette Journal* and later became a reporter on the *Journal*. From 1893 to 1901 he served as city editor for the *Lafayette Daily Courier*. Following several rejections, his second novel, *Graustark: The Story of a Love behind a Throne* (1901), was sold for five hundred dollars and began his production of successful romantic novels and other books. With that, he resigned his editorship, moved to Chicago, and settled down to publishing at least one book a year.

In 1904 McCutcheon and Mrs. Marie Van Antwerp Fay were married, and the couple lived in New York City. He maintained a close friendship with GEORGE ADE and BOOTH TARKINGTON but lived mostly in his writings. Publishing forty-eight works, he sold more than five million copies. Dying suddenly at a luncheon, he was buried in Lafayette.

**SIGNIFICANCE:** McCutcheon began a tradition with his romances, particularly the Graustark series of books, which owed something to the romantic interest engendered by *Prince Otto* (1885), by Robert Louis Stevenson, and *The Prisoner of Zenda* (1894), by Anthony Hope. *Graustark* told the story of how a young, red-blooded American male fell in love with a dazzlingly beautiful princess traveling incognito in America. Following her home to a tiny mythical Balkan kingdom, he discovered the beauty, mystery, and hidebound traditions of her country, where, using American ingenuity, he was able to subdue her enemies and win the lady as his bride. Through this book

and through the later books of the series, *Beverly of Graustark* (1904), *Truxton King* (1909), *The Prince of Graustark* (1914), *Land of the Setting Sun* (1924), and *The Inn of the Hawk and Raven* (1927), the author gave the impression that the European male was small, villainous, and inferior to Americans.

Nevertheless, McCutcheon, though writing most of his books in this romantic style, did pen some other types, such as *Brewster's Millions* (1903), a comic fantasy, in which Montgomery Brewster suddenly inherits a million dollars from his grandfather then receives word that a forgotten uncle has left him seven million dollars provided that on his coming twenty-sixth birthday he is absolutely penniless. Of course, he qualifies. *Mr. Bingle* (1915) shows McCutcheon's love for Charles Dickens; *The Day of the Dog* (1904) tells the story of how a lawyer, who reveals the rascality of an attractive widow's brother-in-law, is forced to flee an infuriated bulldog but solves the problems and wins the lady. Though McCutcheon claimed that he preferred realism to romanticism, his only book that attains it is *Mary Midthorne* (1911). Siblings Eric and Mary Midthorne are first tyrannized by their aunt and uncle but finally attain happiness. McCutcheon has gone down in history as a strong romantic and an authority on the Balkans.

**SELECTED WORKS:** McCutcheon's most famous works are the Graustark series, beginning with *Graustark* (1901), *Beverly of Graustark* (1904), *Truxton King* (1909), *The Prince of Graustark* (1914), *Land of the Setting Sun* (1924), and *The Inn of the Hawk and Raven* (1927), which should be read first of all the Graustark books. In all his novels McCutcheon gave the impression that the European male was small, villainous, and inferior to Americans; that Russia, Austria, and Germany were sources of mischief; but that France and England were peacemakers. There were other kinds of books that he issued, however, such as *Brewster's Millions* (1903), a comic fantasy; *Mr. Bingle* (1915), inspired by Charles Dickens; *Mary Midthorne* (1911), a book set in Indiana that is surprisingly realistic; *Viola Gwyn* (1922), set in Lafayette, Indiana; and *The Day of the Dog* (1904), which features an Indiana town. McCutcheon also wrote several unpublished plays.

**FURTHER READING:** Discussions of McCutcheon's work include James Hart's *The*

*Popular Book* (1950); Grant Knight's "The Pastry Period in Literature, the Graustark Novel Was Well-Intentioned to a Fault," in *Saturday Review of Literature* 27 (December 16, 1944): 5–7, 22–23; A. B. Maurice's "History of Their Books," in *Bookman* 68 (January 1929): 528–29; and A. L. Lazarus and Victor Jones's *Beyond Graustark: George Barr McCutcheon, Playwright Discovered* (1981). This last book may be the most helpful of all, for it provides a complete, detailed account of McCutcheon's life and books including his many unpublished plays. McCutcheon's papers can be found in the Purdue University Library.

ARTHUR W. SHUMAKER          DEPAUW UNIVERSITY

# THOMAS (MATTHEW) MCGRATH
November 20, 1916–September 20, 1990

**BIOGRAPHY:** Poet Thomas McGrath was born near Sheldon, North Dakota, to James and Catherine (Shea) McGrath. He grew up on a family farm in the Red River Valley during the agricultural depression of the 1920s. After high school, McGrath studied intermittently at Moorhead State University, then took a BA from the University of North Dakota (1939) and an MA from Louisiana State University (1940), where he studied with Cleanth Brooks and met Alan Swallow, editor-publisher of the Swallow Press. McGrath taught briefly at Colby College and in 1942 married the first of his three wives, Marian Points. He served in the U.S. Army Air Corps from 1942 to 1946 and spent 1947–48 at Oxford as a Rhodes Scholar. In 1952 he married for the second time to Alice Greenfield. McGrath's refusal in 1953 to testify before the House Committee on Un-American Activities did not result in a jail sentence, but it did cost him his job at Los Angeles State University. During the 1950s, McGrath alternated periods of working blue-collar jobs, traveling, and writing film scripts, juvenile novels, criticism, and poetry. In 1960 he returned to teaching, this time at C. W. Post College in Hunter, New York. There he met and married (1960) his third wife, Eugenia Johnson, and founded the journal *Crazy Horse*. The couple had one son, Thomas Samuel Koan, nicknamed "Tomasito," who appears in many of his poems. In 1962 McGrath returned to the Midwest to teach at North Dakota State University; in 1969 he crossed the state line to Moorhead State University in Minnesota.

McGrath spoke in *Epoch* 22 (1973) of writers returning from the big cities "to Nebraska or Arizona or wherever," because "they find the unknown lands in which they were born democratic for the reasons I have tried to sketch out" (211). In 1981 McGrath retired from Moorhead to Minneapolis, to a neighborhood close to his old leftist friend MERIDEL LE SUEUR.

Although his work was highly regarded by poets—especially DONALD HALL, ROBERT BLY, and Kenneth Rexroth—McGrath never established himself with academics or major commercial houses. The reason, Fred Whitehead suggests in the Fall 1982 *North Dakota Quarterly*, was his "life-long opposition from and to this [literary] establishment, on artistic and political grounds" (6). During his lifetime McGrath received the acclaim of two Bush Fellowships (1976, 1981), a Guggenheim Fellowship (1967), and three National Endowment for the Arts Fellowships (1974, 1982, 1987). His *Selected Poems* (1971) won a Lenore Marshall/*Nation* Prize, a Minnesota Book Award, and nomination for a National Book Critics Circle Award in poetry. Despite this acclaim, the life-long Marxist is not well represented today in major American textbook-anthologies.

**SIGNIFICANCE:** MICHAEL ANANIA, many years Alan Swallow's poetry editor, recalls riding in a Chicago cab with Swallow, discussing the design of *Letter to an Imaginary Friend, Part I*. Anania argued for a large-format book to accommodate, unbroken, McGrath's unusually long lines; Swallow opposed the idea because of added costs. The cab driver, although he'd caught no names, did understand the subject of their discussion. "Poetry, eh?" he interrupted, leaning back over the seat; "As far as I'm concerned there's only one poet in this country worth a damn, and that's Tom McGrath."

McGrath published more than a dozen collections of poetry, seven with Swallow, beginning with *To Walk a Crooked Mile* (1947). A technically sophisticated and highly skilled poet, he grounded much of his work, especially the early portions of his *Letter to an Imaginary Friend*, in narrative and in the agrarian populist tradition associated with northwestern Minnesota and the Dakotas. Sheldon, North Dakota, was still prairie populist territory in the early years of this century, and

McGrath's account of coming of age amid the workers' strikes and labor battles among the Red River Valley farmworkers (*Letter*, part 1) is as compelling as anything in Steinbeck. The local scene, however, is but a metaphor for America: as McGrath put it, "North Dakota / is everywhere" (*Letter* 103).

Letter also incorporates elements of Christianity and of classical and Native American mythology, emphasizing the dehumanizing effects of industrialized capitalism, the corruption of American ideals in the twentieth century, and the continuing class struggle in this country and abroad. "In this most readable of epics," wrote J. P. White in the *New York Times Book Review* (March 10, 1991), "history and eternity roll up their shirt sleeves and go to work in the grease of dreams" (24). Placing *Letter* in the context of Whitman's "Song of Myself," Olson's *The Maximus Poems,* and Williams's *Paterson,* Diane Wakoski observed that McGrath's poem is "an attempt to see America, American history, and mythology, as well as economics and politics, through a semi-autobiographical screen . . ." (*Revolutionary Poet* 59). Part I, she believes, contains "some of the most vivid and beautiful writing that has ever been done about the American midwest" (60).

**SELECTED WORKS:** *Letter to an Imaginary Friend, Parts I–IV*—published separately in 1962, 1970, 1985, and collectively in 1997—constitutes one long poem, McGrath's magnum opus. *Letter* should be supplemented by *The Movie at the End of the World* (1972), which, McGrath claimed in the preface, "gathers together most of the short poems I want to save" (vi) and by *Selected Poems: 1938–88* (1991).
**FURTHER READING:** Ronald Barron's *A Guide to Minnesota Writers* (1993) provides a good overview of McGrath's life and work. The most useful of his many interviews are those with Mark Vinz in *Voyage to the Inland Sea* 3 (1973): 33–48; James Bertolino for *Epoch* 22 (1973): 207–19; and Reginald Gibbons and Terence Des Pres for *TriQuarterly* 70 (Fall 1987): 38–102. *TriQuarterly* 70 also contains Terrence Des Press's excellent analysis "Thomas McGrath" (158–92). The Fall 1982 *North Dakota Quarterly* is a Festschrift edited by Fred Whitehead celebrating McGrath's life and work. See also James Vinson's *Contemporary Poets* (1980) and Terrence Des Pres and Reginald Gibbons's *Thomas McGrath: Life and the Poem*

(1987). *The Revolutionary Poet in the United States* (1988) contains fourteen essays by FREDERICK C. STERN, STUDS TERKEL, Diane Wakoski, HAYDEN CARRUTH, Gene Frumkin, and others and an annotated bibliography by Carla Kaplan. The major collection of McGrath's papers is in the library at North Dakota State University.
DAVID PICHASKE          SOUTHWEST STATE UNIVERSITY

# THOMAS (FRANCIS) McGUANE (III)
December 11, 1939
**BIOGRAPHY:** Thomas McGuane, novelist, essayist, scriptwriter, and short story author, was born into an Irish Catholic family in Wyandotte, Michigan. Thomas Francis McGuane Jr., his father, was a financially successful automobile parts manufacturer, while the former Alice Torphy, his mother, had been an English major in college. After originally attending public school, McGuane was sent to Cranbrook, a private boarding school, in Bloomfield Hills, Michigan. His interest in nature became evident early in his life through summer vacations in northern Michigan. This interest included fishing and hunting, which often play significant roles in his writings. Following an unsuccessful beginning at the University of Michigan, McGuane attended Olivet College, a small liberal arts school also in Michigan, for one year. Then he went to Harvard summer school, taking a class in writing fiction. In 1962 he received his BA from Michigan State University. There he also met fellow author JIM HARRISON, who became a close friend. McGuane then earned an MFA from Yale in 1965, lived in Spain and Italy for a time, and was awarded a Wallace Stegner Fellowship at Stanford.

McGuane became notorious as a celebrity figure for a few years; this period included his brief second marriage to actress Margot Kidder. Having visited and fallen in love with Montana as a teenager, McGuane used earnings from his first published book, *The Sporting Club* (1969), to buy the first in a series of ranches. He spends some time in Florida but lives primarily in Montana mountain country. Beside writing and ranching there, he raises cutting horses with his third wife, Laurie Buffett.
**SIGNIFICANCE:** McGuane's Midwestern roots and sensibilities inform all of his writ-

ing, most noticeably his first two novels; *The Sporting Club* is set in Michigan, as is much of *The Bushwhacked Piano* (1971). Both works satirize middle-American lifestyles and values, focusing on what their author sees as a declining culture. This thematic emphasis continues in McGuane's work following these two books, though as his writing career has progressed, he has moved away from explicit satire.

Only two short stories in *To Skin a Cat* (1986), "A Skirmish" and "Sportsmen," are set in the northern Midwest. Most of his other work is set primarily in Florida or Montana. Still untapped critical approaches to these other writings include what they might reveal about being an expatriate Midwesterner, about the author's residual Midwestern sensibilities as exemplified by characters in the texts, and about how these sensibilities influence his portrayals of other regions and their people.

McGuane is a serious writer and an interesting sociocultural critic, particularly of the modern West and its ties to America as a whole. His actual and fictional moves to the Rocky Mountain West follow not only the historical drift of America itself but also the pattern of a large number of authors with Midwestern roots and writings. Given the details of McGuane's life and the nature of his writings, a number of reviewers and critics have remarked on his strong, likely self-fostered, parallels to another writer whose beginnings were Midwestern, ERNEST HEMINGWAY.

**SELECTED WORKS:** McGuane is best known for his novels, *The Sporting Club* (1969), *The Bushwhacked Piano* (1971), *Ninety-Two in the Shade* (1973), *Panama* (1978), *Nobody's Angel* (1982), *Something to Be Desired* (1984), *Keep the Change* (1989), and *Nothing but Blue Skies* (1992). He has also published a book of nonfiction, *An Outside Chance: Classic and New Essays on Sport* (1990), and a collection of short stories, *To Skin a Cat* (1986). Other short stories have appeared in periodicals. He has written or co-written scripts for five films: *Ninety-Two in the Shade* (1975), *Rancho Deluxe* (1975), *The Missouri Breaks* (1976), *Tom Horn* (1980, with Bud Shrake), and *Cold Feet* (1989, with Jim Harrison).

**FURTHER READING:** The sole book-length work on McGuane is *Thomas McGuane* (1991), by Dexter Westrum; it includes material on all of McGuane's published works except *Nothing but Blue Skies*. Also of interest are Jerome Klinkowitz's *The New American Novel of Manners: The Fiction of Richard Yates, Dan Wakefield, and Thomas McGuane* (1986) and Gregory L. Morris's "How Ambivalence Won the West: Thomas McGuane and the Fiction of the New West," in *Critique: Studies in Contemporary Fiction* 32.3 (Spring 1991): 180–89.

DAVID N. CREMEAN   BLACK HILLS STATE UNIVERSITY

## WILLIAM (HOLMES) MCGUFFEY

September 23, 1800–May 4, 1873

**BIOGRAPHY:** Born in a log cabin in Washington County, Pennsylvania, to Alexander, a farmer, and Anna (Holmes) McGuffey, William Holmes McGuffey attended Old Stone Academy and Washington College, graduating with honors in 1826. McGuffey's career as a Midwestern educator was illustrious, including appointments as professor of ancient languages at Miami University, Oxford, Ohio (1926), and head of Miami University's Department of Mental Philosophy and Philology (1832). He was also named president of Cincinnati College in 1836 and of Ohio University, Athens, Ohio, in 1839. In his later years, McGuffey was a member of the faculty at the University of Virginia.

In 1833 he was ordained a Presbyterian minister. He married Harriet Spinning in 1827. They had five children, two daughters and three sons. The year after Harriet's death in 1850, he married Laura Howard. One daughter marked the second marriage.

During his lengthy career McGuffey started Master McGuffey's Subscription School in September 1814, experimented with educational methods, and helped establish the common school in Ohio. He wrote his first reader in 1833 by compiling his daily lessons. The contents included original works, classic and contemporary selections from other books, and adaptations. As a writer of textbooks for children, he was concerned about the age, pursuits, and aptitude of his young pupils. While his six readers, primers, and spellers were more informative than entertaining, they helped to open the publishing industry to the marketability and profitability of books written specifically for children. The successful McGuffey texts provided the nation's schools with uniform lessons. More than one hundred and twenty million copies of the reader were sold, but McGuffey's efforts were not always rewarded. He was accused of copyright violations and did not receive the royalties from the sale of his works that writers expect today. His original contract gave him a royalty of 10 percent of sales until the royalties reached one thousand dollars (Westerhoff 57). He died of congestion of the brain in Charlottesville, Virginia.

SIGNIFICANCE: McGuffey's works are built on the foundation of his classic education in Greek, Latin, Hebrew, ancient studies, and philosophy; however, he uses his pioneer spirit to explore new territory in educational theory. His readers contain selections that would appeal to students and parents living in the Midwest. The stories, poems, and essays include history, ethics, religion, biology, geography, and manners. In addition to building reading skills, McGuffey's readers promote character building, strong multigenerational family ties, and patriotism. They reflect a moral philosophy that encourages strong discipline—the tools required of a culture of pioneers who were creating and expanding a new nation. Characters in his selections, like Midwestern homesteaders, seize opportunity, display personal responsibility, and serve their community.

Although McGuffey's series of elementary readers spanned six levels, he compiled only the first four books: *McGuffey's First and Second Eclectic Readers* (1836) and *McGuffey's Third and Fourth Eclectic Readers* (1837). The series was revised in 1857 and 1879. The 1879 editions found in bookstores and libraries today do not reflect the Midwestern influence that McGuffey gave to the first editions. These readers are more cosmopolitan in tone and serve the needs of an emerging multicultural population that developed as a result of the industrial revolution and the policy of open immigration. Their focus is on cooperation, compromise, and assimilation rather than personal character and achievement.

SELECTED WORKS: McGuffey began his writing career with *The First Eclectic Reader* (1836). He completed nine volumes of readers for students in the first grade through high school. Some of the readers were compiled with his brother, Alexander Hamilton McGuffey.

FURTHER READING: Dolores Sullivan's *William Holmes McGuffey: Schoolmaster to the Nation* (1994) provides a careful biography. Additional sources include Harvey John Westerhoff III's *McGuffey and His Readers* (1978), Alice McGuffey Ruggle's *The Story of the McGuffeys* (1950), and Harvey Minnich's *William Holmes McGuffey and His Readers* (1936). McGuffey's papers are held in the DeGrummond Collection at the University of Mississippi Library and in the Walter Havighurst Collection, Miami University, Oxford, Ohio.

SUSAN BOURRIE     EASTERN MICHIGAN UNIVERSITY

## SAMUEL MERWIN
### October 6, 1874–October 17, 1936

BIOGRAPHY: Samuel Merwin was born in Evanston, Illinois, to Orlando H. and Ellen (Bannister) Merwin, and was the nephew of women's rights advocate Frances E. Willard. He attended schools in Evanston, including Northwestern University, where he seems to have taken literary courses from 1896 to 1897 but did not graduate. While a student, he wrote several musical comedies which were produced locally and gave him his lifelong interest in theater and drama. He married his college sweetheart, Edna Fleshiem, in 1901, and the couple had two sons and adopted a third.

Merwin's interest in writing began during his high school years when he submitted satires to boys' magazines, but the fortuitous collaboration with his boyhood friend and college associate, Henry Kitchell Webster, in writing two successive novels brought both of them early popularity before they embarked upon separate careers.

After moving to New York, he worked as an editor for *Success Magazine* from 1905 until its demise in 1911. The Merwins ultimately settled in Concord, Massachusetts, where he continued to produce a steady flow of novels through the 1920s. Earlier trips to Paris and China provided backgrounds and themes for some of his books, but by the 1930s Merwin concentrated his energies on drama and overseeing his own playhouse in Concord. His death from an apparent heart attack occurred while dining in New York at Player's, his favorite club.

SIGNIFICANCE: Merwin's literary success, whether initially with his friend Webster or later on his own, was consistent. He was equally proficient in writing popular novels that dealt with small-town social life in the Midwest as he was in those that encompassed politics and big business in Chicago. Unlike some of his contemporaries, who used similar plots and settings, Merwin gave strong and independent roles to his female characters. His own literary theory was that to produce any work worth reading an author must get inspiration from violent reactions, not from the ordinariness of everyday life.

Criticism of his novels as they were published was generally positive and stressed the ability of Merwin to create believable characters. More than one reviewer compared him favorably to Balzac. His books remain readable and entertaining today, especially the regional novels which contain valuable renderings of the Midwestern scene.

**SELECTED WORKS:** Merwin's first two novels, written in collaboration with Henry Kitchell Webster, look at two Illinois businesses: *The Short Line War* (1899) deals with railroad construction and rivalries, and *Calumet "K"* (1901) follows the troubled construction of a grain elevator. In *His Little World* (1903), *The Whip Hand* (1903), and *The Merry Anne* (1904), Merwin uses the lumber industry as a background, with substantial scenes set in Chicago, Michigan, and on the Great Lakes. *The Citadel* (1912) traces the political career of an Illinois congressman, and small-town life in Illinois is the subject of *Temperamental Henry* (1917), *Henry Is Twenty* (1918), and *Goldie Green* (1922).

**FURTHER READING:** Although Merwin was popular in his day, very little has been written on either his life or his works, aside from contemporary reviews, and no scholarly assessment has appeared to date. Besides the entry for Merwin in *Twentieth Century Authors* (1942), which supplies the general outline of his life and career (950), there exists the promotional tract *A Chat about Samuel Merwin* (1921), by Robert C. Holliday and issued by Bobbs-Merrill, Merwin's publisher at the time. It contains a sketchy account of his life and excerpts from reviews of a select number of his novels. His obituary in the *New York Times* offers additional biographical and literary information (October 18, 1936): sec. II: 8.

There are significant collections of Merwin's papers at the New York Public Library and Harvard University; Merwin-related material can also be found among the Concord Players collection at the Concord (Massachusetts) Free Public Library and in the Bobbs-

Merrill Company papers at the Lilly Library, Indiana University.

ROBERT BEASECKER

GRAND VALLEY STATE UNIVERSITY

## OSCAR MICHEAUX
January 2, 1884–March 25, 1951

**BIOGRAPHY:** Novelist and filmmaker Oscar Micheaux was the fifth of thirteen children born to Calvin Swann Micheaux and Bell Willingham, "near the Ohio River, about forty miles above Cairo" according to *The Conquest: The Story of a Negro Pioneer* (1913), Micheaux's autobiographical novel (10). He spent his childhood and early adolescent years in Metropolis, Massac County, Illinois, where his father was a farmer. Metropolis was his hometown, but he disapproved of farming, the church, and most of the other rural African Americans because Micheaux felt they lacked an appropriate vision to improve the lives of the majority of African Americans. When Micheaux left his family farm in Illinois to make his own way in the world at the age of seventeen, his philosophy of work and life had already begun to develop from his experiences in the Midwest. His early careers as Pullman porter in Chicago and farmer and entrepreneur in South Dakota also helped create a philosophy that influenced both his novels and films.

Recognized mostly for his thirty films that span the years 1919 through 1948, he began as a novelist in 1913 with the publication and marketing of his first book, *The Conquest*. Micheaux traveled from door to door to sell his book to local farmers in South Dakota. He later founded his own book company, the Western Book Supply. Micheaux died of a heart attack in 1951 at the age of sixty-seven in Charlotte, North Carolina. He was buried in his adopted hometown of Great Bend, Kansas. Because of his contributions to the film industry, the Oakland Museum's Cultural and Ethnic Guild in Oakland, California, has honored him through the creation of an annual Filmmaker's Hall of Fame award, the Oscar Micheaux Award. He also received a star on the Hollywood Walk of Fame in 1986.

**SIGNIFICANCE:** Oscar Micheaux's novels describe the life of African Americans in the Midwest at the turn of the century. He refers to Devereaux, Micheaux's fictional autobiographical character, and his family's move to

Metropolis as designed "not so much to get off the farm, or to be near more colored people . . . as to give the children better educational facilities. The local colored school was held in an old building made of plain boards standing straight up and down with batten on the cracks" (*The Conquest* 12). His experience in Chicago as a Pullman porter and his rural experience in the Midwest were the sources of his fictional, detective, and autobiographical novels. Devereaux's courtship of Orlean, his wife, took place in Chicago. He describes Chicago as "the Mecca for southern Negroes" (*The Conquest* 220). Micheaux's account of Devereaux's courtship of Orlean and his description of the famous *Chicago Tribune* and Chicago's social life were probably a result of his early experience as a Pullman porter. His philosophy, which complemented Booker T. Washington's, embraced the American work ethic and cultural assimilation as solutions for uplifting the black race.

Micheaux's novels concentrated on Midwestern America and the frontier life in South Dakota. These provided a regional backdrop to the negative conditions that African Americans experienced in the free cities in the Midwest during slavery, while also painting an unfavorable picture of African American characters who hindered their own success by what Micheaux's fictional representative describes as "[their] failure to grasp the many opportunities that presented themselves" (*The Conquest* 17).

Although in *The Conquest* we meet the Nicholson brothers, members of the South Dakota gentry who used their political power to help develop the railroad in some of the smaller cities, Micheaux's concentration on the life of the black middle class remained consistent throughout all of his novels. Micheaux ignored racial injustices and the daily problems of African American life. Unlike other black writers, the focus of Micheaux's novels was on the character flaws of African Americans.

In retrospect, Micheaux's success in overcoming many of the obstacles that prevented African Americans from owning land or businesses in the unsettled frontier during this period in American history seems commendable. Joseph A. Young in *Black Novelist as White Racist: The Myth of Black Inferiority in the Novels of Oscar Micheaux* (1989), however, considered Micheaux a failure at age twenty-

nine because of his inability to create the epic novel, the departure of his wife, and the loss of his land in South Dakota (32). Young also attributed Micheaux's failure as a writer to his resolution to depict African Americans in his novels as either good or bad according to popular American myths of black inferiority.

**SELECTED WORKS:** Micheaux's first novel, *The Conquest: The Story of a Negro Pioneer* (1913), written under the name Devereaux, was autobiographical. Micheaux's second book was a detective novel called *The Forged Note: A Romance of the Darker Race* (1915). Some critics feel that Micheaux continued his autobiography in *The Homesteader* (1917). Because of his film career, Micheaux did not write his next novel, *The Wind from Nowhere*, until 1941. In the 1940s Micheaux wrote three other novels, *The Case of Wingate* (1944), *The Story of Dorothy Stanfield, Based on a Great Insurance Swindle, and a Woman!* (1946), and *The Masquerade: An Historical Novel* (1947).

**FURTHER READING:** The only critical study of Micheaux's novels is Joseph A. Young's *Black Novelist as White Racist*. George W. May's *History of Massac County, Illinois* contains a biographical chapter about Micheaux. Many of Micheaux's novels are featured in the rare book collection at the Cannady Center at the University of Toledo.

For an analysis of Micheaux's films, see Donald Bogle's *Toms, Coons, Mulattoes, Mammies, and Bucks: An Interpretive History of Blacks in American Films* (1973), Thomas Cripps's *Slow Fade to Black: The Negro in American Film, 1900–1942* (1977), and Henry T. Sampson's *Blacks in Black and White: A Source Book on Black Films* (1977). Other writers to consult are Charles J. Fontenot Jr., Arlene Elder, Daniel J. Leab, Howard A. Phelps, and Hugo Gloster.

IMELDA HUNT          OWENS COMMUNITY COLLEGE

## PAUL W. MILLER.

*See* appendix (1997)

## JUDITH MINTY

August 5, 1937

**BIOGRAPHY:** Judith Minty, poet, was born and raised in Detroit, Michigan, the daughter of Karl Makinen, an electrical engineer of Finnish descent, and Margaret (Hunt) Makinen, of mixed Mohawk, English, and Irish ancestry. Although her ethnically diverse family assimilated into the dominant white soci-

**Judith Minty.**
Photo by Robert Turney. Courtesy of Judith Minty

ety of Detroit, she discovered her Finnish and Native American heritage as an adolescent. Her father introduced her to the North Woods country of Michigan's Upper Peninsula where he had grown up, the son of an immigrant blacksmith. She was educated in the Detroit Public Schools and later earned degrees from Ithaca College and Western Michigan University. In 1954 she married businessman Edgar Minty, with whom she raised three children. After winning the United States Award of the International Poetry Forum for her first book, *Lake Songs and Other Fears* (1974), Minty taught at various colleges and universities, her longest-held position being that of professor and director of creative writing at Humboldt State University from 1982 through 1993. Throughout her years teaching, she maintained a home in New Era, Michigan, where she currently resides.

**SIGNIFICANCE:** Minty's poetry emerges from a strong Michigan and Great Lakes sense of place. From the region's waters, valleys, and woods she has derived a personal mythology that has itself become part of the Midwestern cultural landscape. Lake Michigan has long stood in her writing for the simultaneously beneficent and destructive power of

nature, a power Minty alternately characterizes as masculine or maternal. She approaches nature with ritual circumspection, as in "Lake Michigan": "I strip off my clothes, / fall into the waves. I will / go deep, let it lick my skin, / feel its pulse as we sink again together" (*Lake Songs* 7). Much of her poetry has this tone of homecoming, of a return to elemental forces shaping her life and the lives of her parents, children, and friends. Acknowledged influences on Minty's poetry of psychic autobiography include JIM HARRISON, Etheridge Knight, ROBERT BLY, JAMES WRIGHT, and Diane Wakoski, all of whom have strong Midwestern connections. Yet Minty speaks in her own distinctive first-person voice, as close to incantation as to free verse, to Native American lore and the Finnish Kalevala as to Walt Whitman. She is a poet of spirit and body, person and place.

**SELECTED WORKS:** Minty's books are *Lake Songs and Other Fears* (1974), *Yellow Dog Journal* (1979, revised edition 1992), *Letters to My Daughters* (1980), *In the Presence of Mothers* (1981), *Counting the Losses* (1986), *Dancing the Fault* (1991), and *The Mad Painter Poems* (1996). *Killing the Bear*, a limited edition book of prose, appeared in 1999. A useful explanation of her writing process, focusing on the genesis of her poem "The End of Summer," appears in *Fifty Contemporary Poets: The Creative Process*, edited by David McKay (1977).

**FURTHER READING:** Editor Elaine Dallman's *Woman Poet: The Midwest* (1987): 92–101 offers three resources: Shirley Clay Scott's "Dancing the Fault: The Poetry of Judith Minty"; Karen Carlton's "Interview with Judith Minty"; and Helen Collier's "Judith Minty: Biographical Notes." For close readings, see Marilyn Zorn's "Mother Lore: A Sequence for Daughters," in *Great Lakes Review* 6.1 (1979): 37–39; Natalie Harris's "New Life in American Poetry: The Child as Mother of the Poet," in *Centennial Review* 31.3 (Summer 1987): 240–54; and William Barillas's "To Sustain the Bioregion: Michigan Poets of Place," in *Mid-America* 17 (1990): 10–33. Additional interviews include Karla Hammond's "An Inteview with Judith Minty," in *Hawaii Review* 12 (Fall 1981): 103–12; and Foley Schuler's "Talking to the Earth: An Interview with Judith Minty," in *Sky* 2.1 (Spring 1994): 34–41.

WILLIAM BARILLAS

UNIVERSITY OF WISCONSIN–LA CROSSE

## HOWARD MOHR
March 20, 1939

**BIOGRAPHY:** Howard Mohr was born to Ralph and Rosie Mohr in Des Moines, Iowa. He took his BA at Abilene Christian University in 1961 and his MA at the University of Arkansas in 1964. He left the University of Iowa without completing his PhD in English to teach American literature, popular culture, and writing workshops at Southwest State University in Minnesota from 1970 to 1981. Joining other area writers in a grant-funded project titled Poetry Outloud, Mohr brought culture to southwestern Minnesota schools, nursing homes, and parks. The colorful tour is graphically described in Bill Holm's essay "On Tour in Western Minnesota" in *Music of Failure* (1985). The group's appearance on "*A Prairie Home Companion*" in 1976 resulted in Mohr's career as a writer for the show and a record-setting nine-year leave from the university. It also resulted in his first book, *How to Tell a Tornado* (1982), a collection of poems both comic and serious, and satirical pieces in prose. Mohr's long-running "Companion" spots for Minnesota Language Systems, described on book and cassette as "the simple cassette-tape and study guide for visitors from out of state, so they don't stick out like a sore thumb," became the heart of his book *How to Talk Minnesotan* (1987). This best-seller was followed in 1989 by *A Minnesota Book of Days (And a Few Nights)*, a 365–day calendar of Gopher State oddities and eccentrics, and a running satirical commentary on enthusiasms from vegetarianism to the Men's Movement. Today Mohr lives with his wife, Jody, and daughter Susan on the southwestern Minnesota prairie, where all 360 degrees of the horizon can be clearly seen and studied, and where a rusty '46 Dodge pickup stares at them through the kitchen window from its permanent parking spot at the edge of the grove. The Mohrs have a compost heap, eight outdoor cats, a thirty-year-old horse, and just about the right number of possums, skunks, and groundhogs. Visitors from the big city always ask, "What do you do out here for fun?" Howard says, "This is it. You're doing it now."

**SIGNIFICANCE:** Mohr created more than two hundred scripts and ad spots for "*A Prairie Home Companion*," including "Raw Bits," "Bigger Hammer Hardware," "Penta-gon Overstocks," "Slo-Decay Snack Cakes," "One-Minute Romances," and "The College of Lo-Technology." His humorous essays appeared in the *St. Paul* magazine throughout the 1980s. His best work is short satires of Minnesota foibles like "Being Positive," "Waving, Its Ins and Outs," and "This Is the Best Way [to give directions]." Mohr's combination of the American tall tale with a characteristically Midwestern deadpan understatement makes him a devastatingly funny speaker and writer, sensitive to the nuances of Minnesota idioms, vocabulary, and communication habits. His sense of the absurd pushes the Minnesota quotidian nearly to surrealism, as when fictional associate professor M. Toby Johnson ends his preface to *How to Talk Minnesotan* with, "I couldn't say enough good about [this book] if I tried." But always a reader is left with the thought, "Yes, that's exactly the way it goes around here."

**SELECTED WORKS:** *How to Tell a Tornado* (1982) may be Mohr's best book, but read also *How to Talk Minnesotan* (1987) and *A Minnesota Book of Days (And a Few Nights)* (1989). A musical called *How to Talk Minnesotan: The Musical* opened on January 25, 1997, at the Plymouth (Minnesota) Playhouse for an extended run. Also in circulation are a Minnesota Public Radio audiotape based on the book, a Twin Cities Public Television video also from the book, and a compact disc cast album from the musical.

**FURTHER READING:** No significant discussion of Mohr's work exists at this writing. In 1983 Katherine Allen of Minnesota Public Television produced a half-hour video record of the Poetry Outloud project titled *A Nest of Singing Birds*.

DAVID PICHASKE            SOUTHWEST STATE UNIVERSITY

## HARRIET MONROE
December 23, 1860–September 26, 1936

**BIOGRAPHY:** Harriet Monroe—Chicago poet, dramatist, and the editor of *Poetry: A Magazine of Verse*, which she founded and edited until her death—was the second of four children born in Chicago, Illinois, to Henry Stanton Monroe, a lawyer and intellectual, and Martha (Mitchell) Monroe, a less-educated woman. Her parents educated her in the classical and European style popular in the 1870s.

Monroe attended Moseley Public Grammar School and at twelve studied at the Dearborn Seminary. She read the art histories, classics, and poetry she found in her father's library and in 1877 enrolled at the Visitation Convent in Georgetown, where she continued to be encouraged to read and write poetry. In 1879, then nineteen years old, she left Washington, D.C., and returned to Chicago. There she served as a freelance cultural correspondent for the *Chicago Tribune,* and later, spending a year in New York City, she became the *Tribune's* art, drama, and music critic. She also lectured and taught.

In 1889 her first poem, "With a Copy of Shelley," appeared in *Century,* an important nineteenth-century magazine. She also published a few poems in other significant journals such as the *Atlantic* and the *Fortnightly Review.* That summer she wrote "Valeria," a verse play which she printed privately in 1891 with a selection of her poems. She wrote a dedication poem for Chicago's new auditorium and when Chicago was chosen as the site for the Columbian Exposition, she created a long poem, "The Columbian Ode," celebrating her admiration of the city. In 1896 she completed a biography of her brother-in-law, architectural pioneer John Wellborn Root, honoring his theories and lamenting his early death. She also published *The Passing Show: Five Modern Plays in Verse* in 1903 and a long poem, *The Dance of the Seasons.*

The absence of venues welcoming poetic innovation frustrated and discouraged Monroe. Therefore she decided, with the help and advice of HOBART CHATFIELD-TAYLOR, publisher of *America,* to begin a magazine independent of the marketplace. She solicited poems from a select group and allowed Ezra Pound to be her foreign correspondent. With Alice Corbin Henderson as her assistant editor, and Edith Wyatt, HENRY BLAKE FULLER, and Hobart Chatfield-Taylor on an advisory board, she published the highest-quality poetry she could find, judging each piece on its own merit.

When not editing, Monroe worked on her own poetry and nonfiction. *You and I* was published in 1914; *The Difference and Other Poems* was published in 1924; *Poets and Their Art* in 1926, and then revised and republished in 1932; *Chosen Poems* in 1935; and her autobiography, *A Poet's Life: Seventy Years in a Changing World,* in 1938. She also edited with Alice Corbin Henderson an important poetry anthology, *The New Poetry,* in 1917; it was revised and enlarged in 1923 and again in 1932. By the end of the 1920s, the poetic innovations Monroe had fought to make mainstream had become so, but during the next decade, out of rhythm with American poetry, she rejected the experimental forms and political content of W. H. Auden and Stephen Spender's poems. In 1936 Monroe was America's representative at the International Association of Poets, Playwrights, Editors, Essayists, and Novelists Conference (PEN) in Buenos Aires. On her way home, in Peru, she suffered a cerebral hemorrhage, died, and was buried in Arequipa.

**SIGNIFICANCE:** *Poetry: A Magazine of Verse* provided early and continuing recognition for a rising generation of poets who were experimenting with form, sound, concreteness, and modern subject matter. These poets included Midwesterners such as CARL SANDBURG, EDGAR LEE MASTERS, and VACHEL LINDSAY, who won the magazine's annual award. The journal also served as a forum for poetic theory and helped put the Midwest, particularly Chicago, on the map as a literary center. Monroe appreciated Pound's talents and connections, but she would not let him turn her journal into one that omitted regional poets. Her concept of the best in modern poetry included representation of the Midwest. Monroe felt deep affection toward her city and helped create the atmosphere necessary for great poetry to be written and new waves of talent to appear. Her verse plays, including *Valeria* and *The Passing Show,* mix the ancient and the modern and explore issues of geography and identity. Such poetry as "The Hotel," "Chicago 1933," and "Lake Michigan" examine the culture and geography of the modern Midwest. Her writings study human-made constructions, female mythic images, and earthly transcendence without losing sight of her time and place.

While loyal to Chicago, Monroe never fetishized locale; she simply examined it and chose to be loyal to her own. She critiqued the turn-of-the-century's romance with growth or evaluated the beauty of the Great Lakes as she searched for a usable past and a way to capture her sense of the Midwest. A Chicagoan and a revolutionary, Harriet Monroe was loyal to art; an Emersonian, she was loyal to her own gender, time, and place.

Chicago was her home and her artistic center. With her journal, she helped to foster the poetry renaissance of the 1910s, and with her poetry and plays she contributed to it.

**SELECTED WORKS:** Harriet Monroe's responses to regionalism are reflected in "The Columbian Ode" (1893); *You and I* (1914); *The Difference and Other Poems* (1924); *Poets and Their Art* (1926, 1932); *The New Poetry: Seventy Years in a Changing World*, edited with Alice Corbin Henderson and introduced by Monroe (1917, 1923, 1932); and *A Poet's Life: Seventy Years in a Changing World* (1938), where she discusses her relationship to Chicago, the Midwest, and regionalism. Her editorials are also very helpful in understanding her relationship to art.

**FURTHER READING:** Countless literary historians and scholars have analyzed *Poetry*'s influence on modern poetry and Monroe's role as editor. Most famous are Daniel J. Cahill's *Harriet Monroe* (1973) and Ellen Williams's *Harriet Monroe and the Poetry Renaissance: The First Ten Years of Poetry, 1912–1922* (1977).

Other explorations of her work include Stanley K. Coffman's *Imagism: A Chapter for the History of Modern Poetry* (1951); *After the Genteel Tradition: American Writers 1910–1930*, edited by Malcolm Cowley (1964); BERNARD DUFFEY's *The Chicago Renaissance in American Letters: A Critical History* (1956); John Gould Fletcher's *Life Is My Song* (1937); Horace Gregory's "The Unheard of Adventure—Harriet Monroe and Poetry," in *American Scholar* 6 (Spring 1937): 195–200; Gregory and Marya Zaturenska's *A History of American Poetry: 1900–1940* (1942); Harry Hansen's *Midwest Portraits: A Book of Memories and Friendships* (1923); Dale Kramer's *Chicago Renaissance* (1966); and Charles Allen and Carolyn F. Ulrich's *The Little Magazine: A History and Bibliography* (1946).

Edgar Lee Masters's "The Poetry Revival in the United States," in *American Mercury* 26 (July 1932): 272–80, and Morton Dauwen Zabel's *Literary Opinion in America* (1951) provide two important Midwestern points of view.

More recent perspectives include Marilyn J. Atlas's "Harriet Monroe, Margaret Anderson, and the Spirit of the Chicago Renaissance," in *Midwestern Miscellany* 9 (1981): 43–53; William Drake's *The First Wave* (1987); *1915: The Cultural Moment*, edited by Adele Heller and Lois Rudnick (1991); *The Old Guard and the Avant-Garde: Modernism in Chicago, 1910–1940*, edited by Sue Ann Prince (1990); Jayne E. Marek's *Women Editing Modernism: "Little" Magazines and Literary History* (1995); and Marilyn J. Atlas's "Harriet Monroe at the Crossroads: A Study of Harriet Monroe's 'The Turbine,'" in *MidAmerica* 22 (1995): 69–82.

The most significant collection of Monroe's papers can be found at the University of Chicago's Joseph Regenstein Library.

MARILYN J. ATLAS                    OHIO UNIVERSITY

# WILLIAM VAUGHN MOODY
July 8, 1869–October 17, 1910

**BIOGRAPHY:** Born in Spencer, Indiana, to Francis Burdette Moody, a retired captain of a Mississippi River steamer, and Henrietta Emily (Stoy) Moody, of pioneer stock, William Vaughn Moody grew up in New Albany, Indiana, where he started writing poetry at age fifteen. In high school he edited two school papers, and after graduation he studied art for a year in Louisville and also taught in a country school for a year. Preparing for admission to Harvard by studying at Riverview Academy, New York, he supported himself by teaching.

In 1889 he enrolled in Harvard and completed the four-year course in three years, while earning his way and helping a sister financially. Moody served as an editor of the *Harvard Monthly*, associating with fellow students ROBERT HERRICK and George Santayana. Having finished graduation requirements, he spent his senior year in Europe, tutoring a wealthy boy, returning to read his class day poem at graduation in 1893. He spent the next two years at the Harvard Graduate School, earning his way by doing editorial work for Bulfinch's *Mythology* and by acting as teaching assistant in the English departments of Radcliffe College and Harvard. In 1895 he joined the faculty at the University of Chicago. After several leaves of absence, he finally left the university in 1902 and rededicated himself to poetry.

Though always strong physically, in 1905 the dramatist had a growth removed from his leg. Then in 1908 he suffered a bad case of typhoid fever and convalesced on an island near the Maine coast, where he was nursed by Harriet Converse Brainerd, whom he later married. He became very sick while visiting in London, returned to this country, and died with a brain disease in 1910.

**William Vaughn Moody.**
Courtesy of the University of Kentucky Libraries

**SIGNIFICANCE:** Moody's writings merit analysis. All Moody's drama revolves around one problem, the eternal question of sin. Moody distinguishes between absolute evil and the sense of sin as evil, and he attacks this sense of sin. His central idea is the inseparable unity of God and human beings. *The Fire Bringer* (1904) shows how Prometheus stole fire from heaven for humankind to use but concentrates on human reaction to the unsuccessful attempt to destroy human dependence on the Almighty. In *The Masque of Judgement* (1900), the theme is re-invoked, showing that God would destroy Himself in destroying humans. *The Faith Healer* (1909) deals with the problem of love and sex and dedication to a calling. *The Great Divide* (1906) is important in contrasting the cultures of America's long-settled, cultivated East and its emerging "West."

As the center of a group of poets, Moody demonstrated the unity of thought and craft and pleasure in the physical world. He excelled in his use of condensed, thought-laden language, and he destroyed any verse that he considered imperfect. He mingled lyricism and spiritual philosophy, but he never claimed to know the goal of creation. Moody was a teacher, editor, scholar, poet, and dramatist; but the critics seem to have largely ignored the first three except for occasional mention of his scholarly editions.

**SELECTED WORKS:** Moody's first imaginative book was *The Masque of Judgement, A Masque-Drama in Five Acts, and a Prelude* (1900); it was followed by *The Fire Bringer* (1904). Both were part of a projected dramatic verse trilogy on a Promethean theme. *The Great Divide, A Play* (1909) was produced in Chicago in 1906 as "The Sabine Woman" and, after revision, in New York. This first prose play made him famous. His second drama in prose, *The Faith Healer, A Play in Four Acts* (1909), inspired by newspaper accounts of a faith healer, was not as successful as *The Great Divide*, yet it confirmed Moody as a leading American dramatist. He finished only one act of the *Death of Eve* (1912) projected as the final play of the dramatic trilogy. *Gloucester Moors, and Other Poems* (1910); *Poems and Plays*, in two volumes (1912); *Some Letters of William Vaughn Moody* (1913); *Selected Poems of William Vaughn Moody* (1931); and *Letters to Harriet* (1935) completed his major publications.

**FURTHER READING:** Several books focus particularly on William Vaughn Moody's drama. The best of these are Charles Davis's *The Poetic Drama of Moody* (1900); T. H. Dickinson's *Playwrights of the New American Theatre* (1925); Martin Halpern's *William Vaughn Moody* (1964); and A. H. Quinn's *A History of American Drama from the Civil War to the Present Day* (1927). High-quality works dealing more broadly with Moody's life and works include Maurice Browne's *Estranging Dawn: The Life and Works of William Vaughn Moody* (1973); Henry Dodds's *William Vaughn Moody: A Study* (1973); Henry David's *William Vaughn Moody* (1934); E. Lewis's *William Vaughn Moody* (1914); Bliss Perry's "Memoir of William Vaughn Moody," in *Proceedings of the American Academy of Arts and Letters* 5 and 6 (1913); Robert Lovett's *Selected Poems of William Vaughn Moody* (1931); and Daniel Mason's *Some Letters of William Vaughn Moody* (1913).

ARTHUR W. SHUMAKER      DEPAUW UNIVERSITY

## JULIA A. (DAVIS) MOORE
December 1, 1847–June 5, 1920
**BIOGRAPHY:** Julia A. Davis, born in Plainfield Township, Michigan, near Grand Rapids in Kent County, lived there until her family

moved to a farm near Algoma (which is no longer on the map) and then to Edgerton, north of Rockford. She married Fred Moore when she was eighteen, and they later settled near Manton, in Wexford County. She was called "The Sweet Singer of Michigan," after the best-known title of her book of verse. Moore composed verses on topics such as local places, country life, and the deaths of children. She also wrote occasional patriotic verse. In 1876 a Grand Rapids publisher brought out *The Sentimental Song Book* and reissued it as *The Sweet Singer of Michigan* in 1878. The poems appeared with variations in several other editions, including several by a publisher named Ryder, of Cleveland. The 1878 *A Few Choice Words to the Public, with New and Original Poems* consists mainly of ironically flattering reviews, along with poems.

The success of the poems depended largely on their unintentional humor, by way of awkward versification and outrageous pathos. Their forms often reflected those of ballads and current popular songs, and she intended some of the poems to be sung. She accepted invitations to read in public in Grand Rapids, not aware that the audiences came to ridicule her. When Moore's husband realized that her sponsors were using her as a laughingstock, he forbade her to write any more. After his death, she published some short fiction, including a romantic novel about the American Revolution, *Sun and Shadow* (1915). She died at her home near Manton.

**SIGNIFICANCE:** The title of Moore's *The Sweet Singer of Michigan* brought some notoriety to her state. She memorialized the Grand Rapids area in a number of her verses, notably one about the Cricket Club, and particularly praised the Civil War dead from the area. Saccharine descriptions of her childhood on a Michigan farm and sincere, if awkwardly worded, tributes to her parents are typical subjects of her poems. Disasters including a smallpox epidemic and the Great Fire, both in Chicago, also supplied material for her pen. But it was her versified obituaries, especially those of children, that her critics satirized most gleefully. The best-known parody of Moore, by MARK TWAIN, appeared in the character of Emmeline Grangerford in *Huckleberry Finn*. BILL NYE gave over a whole chapter of *Bill Nye and Boomerang* (1881) to treat her with humor and high disfavor.

In "The Author's Early Life," Moore asserted, "It was my heart's delight / To compose on a sentimental subject / If it came in my mind just right" (*Sentimental Song Book* 49). Responding to her critics, she wrote in "Address to the Public," "Literary is a work very difficult to do" (*A Few Choice Words* 6). The following stanza from "Little Andrew" provides a typical example of such work; this child drowned, Moore wrote, when "his life was two years old," and "His parents never more can see him / In this world of grief and pain, / And Oh! they will not forget him / While on earth they do remain" (*Sentimental Song Book* 12).

Moore's verse has both appalled and delighted her readers, often for the same reasons. Her descriptions of Michigan and her funereal attitudes leave her nickname firmly, if ironically, established.

**SELECTED WORKS:** Moore's literary output was limited but appeared greater because many of the same poems appeared in many editions, which bore various titles, with different, sometimes inaccurate, dates. *The Sentimental Song Book* (1876) and *The Sweet Singer of Michigan* (1878) were the earliest, and an 1877 volume of *The Sentimental Song Book* was a particularly handsome edition with marbleized binding in a slipcase. *A Few Choice Words to the Public, with New and Original Poems* also appeared in 1878. Her novel, *Sunshine and Shadow*, appeared first serially in the *Cedar Springs Clipper* in 1880 and as a book in 1915.

**FURTHER READING:** A. H. Greenly's article "*The Sweet Singer of Michigan*, Bibliographically Considered," in *Papers of the Bibliographic Society of America* 39 (1945): 91–118, and Walter Blair's Introduction to his edition of *The Sweet Singer of Michigan: Poems by Mrs. Julia A. Moore* (1928) provide sound material on Moore. *Mortal Refrains, The Complete Collected Poetry, Prose, and Songs of Julia A. Moore, The Sweet Singer of Michigan*, edited by Thomas J. Riedlinger (1998), gives access to Moore's publications. The Michigan State University library houses the largest collection of materials on her.

MARY DEJONG OBUCHOWSKI

CENTRAL MICHIGAN UNIVERSITY

# WRIGHT MORRIS

January 6, 1910–April 25, 1998

**BIOGRAPHY:** Wright Morris was born in Central City, Nebraska, his mother, Grace (Osborn) Morris, dying within a week of his birth. In Wright's childhood, his father, Will, often left him with families in small towns, then in Omaha, before moving to Chicago for Morris's high school years. His education at Pomona College in California ended with an extended stay in Europe. In 1934 he married Mary E. Finfrock and embarked upon a dual career as writer and photographer. The first of twenty novels, *My Uncle Dudley*, appeared in 1942. Morris's travels, especially his cross-country photography trip in the early 1940s and sojourns in Mexico and Europe, provided much material for his fiction. He was the recipient of the Society for the Study of Midwestern Literature's 1982 Mark Twain Award for distinguished contributions to Midwestern literature and of three Guggenheim Fellowships, including one to take the Nebraska home place photographs in 1947, and exhibited widely, including a retrospective at the San Francisco Museum of Modern Art (1992). Morris taught at San Francisco State University from 1962 to 1975. After his divorce from his first wife in 1961, he was married to Josephine Kantor. Morris died in Mill Valley, California, on April 25, 1998.

Wright Morris.
Photo by Barbara Hall. Courtesy of Josephine Morris

**SIGNIFICANCE:** Morris's works centering on Midwestern identity remain compelling. Part of his aesthetic motive was to salvage things on the brink of disappearing by showing intimate details of American cultural objects; thus his early experiments combining writing and photography were crucial, especially for his emphasis on texture, spatial conceptualizations of time, and visual perception as a metaphor for imagination. Critics sometimes focus on Morris's pessimism, but his efforts to analyze American consciousness and to explore imaginative alternatives were acute and made with humor and ironic empathy.

Morris's dominant early theme is found in *The Man Who Was There* (1945), *The Home Place* (1948), and *The World in the Attic* (1949), where his protagonists search for identity through recovery of meanings imbedded in childhood artifacts and experiences. *The Home Place*, a photo-text novel, brings Clyde Muncy and his family back from New York to the rural Nebraska structures and objects pictured beside the prose, thus paralleling Morris's own need to respond to the "problem of being. Of knowing you are there" (76). In *The Works of Love* (1951), the protagonist Will Brady

is based on Morris's father; Brady's absurd faith in the American Dream which seduces and betrays him is underscored by Morris's dedication of the work to LOREN EISELEY and SHERWOOD ANDERSON. A later counterpart, the memoir *Will's Boy* (1981), poignantly recalls Morris's own childhood and adolescence while insisting that memory is recoverable only through imaginative reconstruction.

In the 1950s Morris turned to the possibilities of imaginative transformation to combat the conformities and distractions enervating American culture. *The Field of Vision* (1956), which won a National Book Award, is a critique of the stifled Midwest. It is set in a Mexican bullfight arena, where the McKees meet their old friend Boyd and an assortment of other odd characters. At thematic center are the blandishments of consumption and conflicting notions of the good life. In the sequel, *Ceremony in Lone Tree* (1960), some of the same characters and others come together in Nebraska for Scanlon's ninetieth birthday; with real-life murderer Charles Starkweather lurking in the wings, the novel satirizes misuse of the Western myth.

*Plains Song for Female Voices* (1980), for which Morris won the American Book Award, sketches the Midwest's twentieth-century emotional development primarily through three generations of women in the Atkins family. The conflict between nostalgia and small-town nausea, first noted in *The World in the Attic*, remains, but now more emphasis is placed on womanly oppositions to the failure of the promises that initially mobilized many American pioneers.

**SELECTED WORKS:** Morris produced nearly forty books, beginning with *My Uncle Dudley* in 1942. His novels dealing most explicitly with Midwestern themes are *The Man Who Was There* (1945); the photo-text *The Home Place* (1948); *The World in the Attic* (1949); *The Works of Love* (1951); *The Field of Vision* (1956) and its sequel, *Ceremony in Lone Tree* (1960); and *Plains Song for Female Voices* (1980). Other novels include *Man and Boy* (1951) and *The Deep Sleep* (1953), on the American family as matriarchy; *The Huge Season* (1954), juxtaposing the McCarthyite 1950s and the Jazz Age; *Love among the Cannibals* (1957), *What a Way to Go* (1962), *Cause for Wonder* (1963), *In Orbit* (1967), and *The Fork River Space Project* (1977), exploring various imaginative evolutionary transformations; *One Day* (1965), on the cultural meanings of John F. Kennedy's assassination; *Fire Sermon* (1971) and *A Life* (1973), on memory and the rituals of old age; and *War Games* (1972), first written in the 1950s and containing early versions of several Morris themes. There are three memoirs: *Will's Boy* (1981); *Solo: An American Dreamer in Europe: 1933–1934* (1983); and *A Cloak of Light: Writing My Life* (1985). *The Territory Ahead* (1958), Morris's most important critical book, considers canonical American writers and their historic struggle with the burdens of the mythic past. Also provocative is *Earthly Delights, Unearthly Adornments: American Writers as Image-Makers* (1978). Of interest are Morris's editing of *The Mississippi River Reader* (1962) and his introduction to the University of Chicago Press edition of Sherwood Anderson's *Windy McPherson's Son* (1965). Among his photo-texts are *The Inhabitants* (1946), *God's Country and My People* (1968), and *Love Affair: A Venetian Journal* (1972). The exhibition catalog *Origin of a Species* (1992) includes appreciative essays. Morris collected his essays on photography in *Time Pieces: Photographs, Writing, and Memory* (1989), and his short stories in *Collected Stories 1948–1986* (1986). Granville Hicks collected primarily Midwestern work in *Wright Morris: A Reader* (1970).

**FURTHER READING:** There are several books on Morris's work, although most are dated. The first critical book, David Madden's *Wright Morris* (1964), is still helpful. Two books from the University of Nebraska Press remain essential: G. B. Crump's *The Novels of Wright Morris: A Critical Interpretation* (1978) and Robert Knoll's *Conversations with Wright Morris: Critical Views and Responses* (1977), the latter with an excellent bibliography by Robert I. Boyce. Leon Howard's University of Minnesota pamphlet *Wright Morris* (1968) and Roy K. Bird's *Wright Morris: Memory and Imagination* (1985) are useful. Most current, from the perspective of the end of Morris's writing career, is Joseph J. Wydeven's *Wright Morris Revisited* (1998). Diane Quantic's "The Unifying Thread: Connecting Place and Language in Great Plains Literature," in *American Studies* 32 (Spring 1991): 67–83, and Reginald Dyck's "Revisiting and Revising the West: Willa Cather's *My Antonia* and Wright Morris' *Plains Song*," in *Modern Fiction Studies* 36 (Spring 1990): 25–37, consider Morris specifically in Western-Midwestern terms. Three studies on the aesthetic relationship between Morris's fiction and his photographs are Peter Halter's "Distance and Desire: Wright Morris' *The Home Place* as 'Photo-Text,'" in *Etudes Textuelles* 4 (October–December 1990): 65–89; Colin Westerbeck's "American Graphic: The Photography and Fiction of Wright Morris," in *Multiple Views,* edited by Daniel P. Younger (1991): 271–302; and Joseph Wydeven's "Focus and Frame in Wright Morris's *The Works of Love*," in *Western American Literature* 32 (Summer 1988): 99–112. Olga Carlisle and Jodie Ireland conducted the interview "Wright Morris: The Art of Fiction CXXV," in *Paris Review* 33 (Fall 1991): 52–94. The Bancroft Library at Berkeley has a voluminous collection of Morris's manuscripts.

JOSEPH J. WYDEVEN          BELLEVUE UNIVERSITY

## TONI MORRISON (CHLOE ANTHONY WOFFORD)

February 18, 1931

**BIOGRAPHY:** Toni Morrison, winner of the 1993 Nobel Prize for literature, is another of America's Midwestern writers whose pen name has almost completely obscured that of her birth, Chloe Anthony Wofford. She was born in Lorain, Ohio, a small town near the shores of Lake Erie, to George and Ramah

(Willis) Wofford. Morrison's maternal grand-parents, Ardelia and John Solomon Willis, were Alabama sharecroppers. John Solomon had mined coal in Kentucky before moving to Lorain, where Ramah, Morrison's mother, was born. Morrison's father worked as a ship-yard welder, steel-mill welder, car washer, and construction worker.

The second of four children, Chloe grew up in a stable, supportive environment. The Woffords loved music and storytelling and moved comfortably from the natural to the supernatural. Her mother cleaned houses, but she also sang in the church choir and was involved with her community. Morrison's Midwestern family values included endur-ance, spirituality, and a love of language.

Morrison received her BA from Howard University in 1953. During her undergraduate years she became known as Toni rather than Chloe. She majored in English, minored in the Classics, and dreamt of being a teacher. In 1955 she was awarded an MA from Cornell University, where she wrote her thesis on the theme of suicide in Virginia Woolf and William Faulkner. From 1955 to 1957 she was an English instructor at Texas Southern Uni-versity in Houston. Next, she taught at Howard University from 1957 until 1964. In the late 1950s at Howard, she met and influenced Amiri Baraka, Andrew Young, and Claude Brown. She taught Stokely Carmichael. She left Howard because she failed to get tenure, not having the requisite PhD. But it was there that she began to define herself as a writer of fiction.

Toni married Harold Morrison, a Jamaican architect, in 1958; the couple had two sons, Harold Ford and Slade Kevin. By 1964, when she divorced, she was already writing fiction. After her divorce and a year-and-one-half stay with her family in Lorain, she found a job with Random House in Syracuse. Soon she left Syracuse to become a senior editor with Random House in New York City. There she helped Toni Cade Bambara, Gayle Jones, and Angela Davis publish their work.

In 1970 Morrison published her first novel, *The Bluest Eye*, and accepted a professorship at the State University of New York at Purchase for the 1971–72 academic year. In 1973 she pub-lished her second novel, *Sula*, which was ex-cerpted in *Redbook*, nominated for the Na-tional Book Award, and chosen as an alternate

**Toni Morrison.**
Photo © Nancy Crampton

Book-of-the-Month Club selection, launching Morrison into the national arena and garner-ing her regional accolades, including the 1975 Ohioana Book Award.

In 1976–77 Morrison was a visiting lecturer at Yale University. In 1980 President Carter ap-pointed her to the National Council on the Arts. In the following year, she published *Tar Baby*, which spent four months on the best-seller list. Morrison appeared on *Newsweek*'s cover. She was also elected to the American Academy and Institute of Arts and Letters. From 1984 through 1989 she was the Schweitzer Professor of the Humanities at State Uni-versity of New York at Albany. *Beloved*, her Pulitzer Prize–winning novel, was published in 1987. In 1988, along with the Pulitzer, she won the Robert F. Kennedy Award, the Melcher Award, the Before Columbus Foun-dation Award, and the Elizabeth Cady Stan-ton Award.

Presently, she is the Robert F. Goheen Pro-fessor of the Humanities at Princeton, a po-sition she has held since 1989. In that year, she won the Modern Language Association of America's Commonwealth Award in litera-ture. The next year she was awarded the Chi-anti Ruffino Antico Fattore International Literary Prize. In 1992 she published *Jazz* and *Playing in the Dark: Whiteness and the Literary Imagination*, a book of literary criticism. That year Morrison also edited *Race-ing Justice, En-Gendering Power: Essays on Anita Hill, Clarence Thomas, and the Construction of Social Reality*. She received the Society for the Study of Midwestern Literature's 1997 Mark Twain Award for distinguished contributions to Midwestern literature. Her seventh novel, *Paradise*, was published in 1998.

**SIGNIFICANCE:** All of Toni Morrison's fiction is in some way about geography and her experiences in the small Midwestern town of her childhood, Lorain, Ohio. During a 1997 lecture at Michigan State University when asked about *Paradise,* Morrison responded to questions about the church in this community by stating that, of course, her prototype came from the church in Lorain, Ohio, her church, her church steps, her mother's voice as she sang in the choir.

Morrison writes from what she knows, and before she knew the South or the East, she knew Ohio and the Midwest. When she accepted the Nobel Prize in 1993, Morrison acknowledged how much regionalism had forged her identity. She said she could claim representation in so many areas: "I'm a Midwesterner and everyone in Ohio is so excited." She went on to name other regions, other groups with whom she identified and who claimed her, and humorously added: "I know it seems like I'm spreading like algae when I put it this way, but I'd like to think of the prize being distributed to these regions and nations and races."

Morrison moved beyond her Midwestern residence and direct focus on the Midwest, but her images and sense of people were first formed in Lorain. Her first, second, third, fifth, and seventh novels are centered in this region. In *Black Women Writers at Work*, edited by Claude Tate (1983), Morrison demonstrates the depth of her relationship to this region, saying "I am from the Midwest so I have a special affection for it. My beginnings are always there. . . . No matter what I write, I begin there. . . . It's the matrix for me. . . . Ohio also offers an escape from stereotyped black settings. It is neither plantation nor ghetto" (117–31).

In *Song of Solomon* (1978) Morrison first leaves the Midwest. In this novel she best portrays the duplicity of the Midwest's physical landscape. The narrator suggests that truly landlocked people know they are, but people who live in the Great Lakes region are confused because their border is not a coast. The narrator suggests that they seem to be able to live a long time believing they are at the frontier "where final exit and total escape are the only journeys left" (163). When they find out this is not so, "the longing to leave becomes acute, and a break from the area, therefore, is necessarily dream-bitten, but necessary nonetheless" (163). Not only the Great Lakes region but geography generally is duplicitous for African Americans who are expected to own little or nothing and to go nowhere. Pilate, the spiritual matriarch of the novel, reminds her nephew, Milkman, that in the 1910s, passenger trains were not even available to them.

Morrison's first novel, *The Bluest Eye*, is set in Lorain. Pecola Breedlove, a young black girl, becomes mentally ill because she feels that having blue eyes, or being Caucasian like Shirley Temple and Dick and Jane, will save her from loneliness. Claudia, the narrator, looks back at her sister's preadolescent self, remembering their long vanished comfort with themselves: "We felt comfortable in our own skins, enjoyed the news that our senses released to us, admired our dirt, cultivated our scars, and could not comprehend this unworthiness" (45). Few adults in Lorain feel worthy. Yet Miss Marie, a prostitute, a woman with no status in Lorain, manages to feel pride. Her laugh portrays an inner landscape richer than Lorain's where in 1941, the year Pecola goes mad, even the marigolds would not grow. Here is the way the narrator describes Marie's laugh to the reader: "From deep inside her laughter came the sound of many rivers, freely, deeply, muddily, heading for the room of an open sea" (45). Because Marie has no status in the white or black culture, she is free to return to a deeper place, and for her place is fertile, beautiful, and dynamic.

As Claudia narrates the "how" of her childhood, she creates many aspects of Lorain for the reader: an ice cream shop, a candy store, a coal company, an orange sky, a fear of the "outdoors," of being without community. Like Miss Marie, Claudia knows her town's values are cracked. Claudia knows that what she wants from Christmas is not commercialized, that what she wants is to "feel" something on Christmas day (21).

*The Bluest Eye* ends in the realization that the land as we know and create it can function as a distortion for which we are individually and culturally responsible. Claudia narrates an ending to the novel, condemning the soil, the town, and herself for not being able to help Pecola: "This soil is bad for certain kinds of flowers. Certain seeds it will not nurture, certain fruit it will not bear and when the land kills of its own volition, we acquiesce and say the victim had no right to live. We are wrong, of course, but it doesn't matter. It's too late. At least on the edge of my town, among the garbage and the sunflowers of my town, it's much, much, much too late" (160). The Midwest has failed Pecola, and Claudia ends the novel depressed by the loss.

In Morrison's second novel, *Sula*, the earth is no more nurturing than in *The Bluest Eye*. Here Morrison creates a Midwestern city, Medallion, which she places in Ohio. African Americans live in the Bottom, where the land is so hilly that planting is backbreaking and the soil insists on sliding down and wasting seeds. But unlike Medallion, the Bottom is not hot and dirty with progress. The narrator notes: " . . . those heavy trees that sheltered the shade up in the Bottom were wonderful to see" (6).

*Sula* begins in 1920, a year when World War I is still taking its toll. Shadrack, a wounded soldier, returns half mad with the horror of seeing a man die grotesquely, and Plum returns a junky. The world outside the Bottom is perverse; the world within is as powerfully and beautifully grotesque as *Winesburg, Ohio*'s misshapen apples.

Sula leaves town to attend college but finds no comfortable place in the world and returns. Sula has no center, no speck around which to grow (103), and comes back to a community also without a center. The novel reflects Morrison's continuing experiments with being landlocked physically, mentally, and spiritually.

Filled with destruction, *Sula* appropriately ends with the breaking of landscape, with the grotesque images of people marching on Suicide Day to destroy a tunnel that should have led to jobs for African Americans but did not. With Shadrack as their leader, the people kill, as best they can, the Midwestern tunnel they

were forbidden to build. But they go too deep and too far. The earth shifts and some individuals drown; others are killed by falling matter and still others become entrapped. The enclosed space, the false promises, and the useless deaths all serve as proper closure for a Midwestern novel with no healthy outlets.

Morrison's first two novels are about Midwestern places: one Lorain, the other imaginary, perhaps a suburb of Cleveland. *Song of Solomon* is set in another unnamed Midwestern locale, this time probably Detroit. Pilate, the central female character, loves geography. In her twenty years of wandering, she takes her geography book wherever she goes and keeps it, along with a rock from each place she has lived, and what she thinks are the bones of the man her brother murdered. When she settles, it is in the Midwestern town where her brother lives.

Guitar, Milkman's brilliant, if misguided, friend, realizes the importance of place. On the run from Pilate's daughter, Hagar, Milkman stops at Guitar's home and requests something to drink. Guitar offers him loose tea and a lecture which reveals Morrison's view of the importance of geography: "Bet you thought tea grew in little bags . . . . Like Louisiana cotton. Except the black men picking it wear diapers and turbans. All over India that's all you see. Bushes with little bitsy white tea bags blossoming. Right?" Milkman asks for tea without geography and Guitar adds, "No geography? Okay, no geography. How about some history in your tea? or some sociopolitical—No. That's still geography. Goddamn Milk, I do believe my whole life's geography" (114).

Morrison's novels demonstrate interest in literary traditions, but she adds uniquely to these traditions, integrating music and magic with realism; integrating African myth, orality, and slave narratives with psychological, domestic, and protest traditions. Morrison is always sensitive to dialect, intonation, shifting and layered perspective. And she is always very conscious of place, of region. Milkman, in search of what he thinks is his father's gold and then in search of his father's relatives, travels to Boston, Massachusetts; Danville, Pennsylvania; and Shalimar, Virginia, where he learns about the texture of place, people, pleasure, and his own internal landscape.

Geography and ownership have their limits in this novel. Appropriating the land, trying to own and control it, will not do. One must be an ethical custodian. No one place can absolutely harbor African Americans. There is no permanent land, and loyalty to place can be as destructive as Circe's relationship to her employer's home: she is willing to spend the last years of her life making sure her employer's home is destroyed. Yet loyalty to place can be as healing as Solomon's flight home: he leaves twenty-one children and flies out of slavery back to Africa because he belongs there, and because he can. In *Song of Solomon* happiness comes from repeating the songs that make up one's history. Pilate, the spiritual center of the novel, tries to explain that the only home one can have in this world is oneself (138). Morrison's very geographic novel, *Song of Solomon,* ends with flight.

*Tar Baby* is no less geographical. Morrison sets this novel in the Caribbean. American cities such as Baltimore, Philadelphia, New York, and Eloe are used to explore the novel's conflicting viewpoints and the characters' conflicting natures. The Midwest is almost purposefully left out, but Morrison continues to examine rural versus urban values.

Physical reality of place remains important, even when not absolutely as important as the inner landscape. In *Beloved,* Morrison continues her geography lessons. Here, Ohio serves as a representative place between North and South where African Americans live in communities and struggle for personal freedom and earthly future. Once again, Morrison has returned to Ohio to examine the necessity and methodology of living on this earth.

In *Beloved,* Morrison enters the Ohio of the 1850s to examine the ravages of slavery. She examines place in layers, forcing readers to reevaluate their sense of the real and viable; she casts down boundaries to prove their fragility in a world where roots and structure change with one's perspective. The dynamic pattern here is the myth of return, of inheriting the kingdom, of finally owning a place to make one's life. Place is defined in complex terms. As Sethe tries to explain to her daughter, Denver, time is a concept in which she does not believe, and place, therefore, can continue to exist as long as memory exists. While this negative space where the past lives is omnipresent and demanding, in *Beloved* it is a lesser place and one the liv-

ing characters must reckon with but reject. The past demands body and voice, but ultimately the dead must give way so the living may continue.

The home in Ohio where Sethe lives, 124 Bluestone, once belonged to Baby Suggs, Sethe's mother-in-law, whose tie is not only to the house but to the world outside, a forested world in which she preached. This place was in nature, a "green blessed place . . . misty with plant steam and the decay of berries" (89). This emerald forest is also part of Morrison's Midwest. The world at the end of Sethe's porch, although dangerous, does not swallow Denver up; it allows her adulthood and control.

Sethe's home is, by the end of the novel, the haven it once was when slaves like Paul D longed to "get North. Free North. Magical North. Welcoming, benevolent North" (112). It is differently magical, a place where two fragmented adults learn to live in the present and make a future. First Denver, then Paul D, and hopefully, finally Sethe have gotten to a place where they can love anything they choose, where they no longer need permission for desire, a place where each can truly be free, in 124 Bluestone, at the Godwins', in Cincinnati, in the Midwest.

*Jazz* is another seemingly non-Midwestern story, but the Midwest is symbolically present. The setting is the city of Jazz, New York, the "City," as Morrison's narrator calls it. The time is 1926, and "spirit" seems to live here in the present and to be an integral part of the musical, rhythmic, and alive city. Virginia is where the novel's main characters, Violet and Joe, meet, but they live in the City, a melting pot for all that is American. It is to this America that the escapees from Springfield, Ohio, Springfield, Indiana, and Greensburg, Indiana, come (33). So, while the story literally takes place in the East, figuratively we are surrounded by Midwesterners. Some are victims of the East St. Louis race riots, and some are searching for better economic opportunities. These characters, these Midwesterners, bring their region with them.

*Paradise*, set in Ruby, Oklahoma, is Morrison's latest novel. Ruby is a second-generation black town. Its ancestor, Haven, was founded during Reconstruction by black men who fled from segregationist politics and the resurgence of the Ku Klux Klan. They came to Oklahoma to escape the prejudice of the Deep South. Afraid of corruption, the patriarchs of the town try to avoid the changing values of their progeny, so they attempt to reestablish themselves in Ruby. Place, as always with Morrison, does not simply offer safe haven. One brings one's corruption and paranoia along. The self-righteous people of the community have troubles, search for scapegoats, and end committing atrocities, because they are disturbed and misguided. They attack women living seventeen miles from their town, women in a "convent," because they are afraid of their own natures.

In *Paradise*, Morrison again explores the relationship between place and troubled people. Wherever Morrison's characters take us, landscape and the exploration of place are there, as is the Midwest, for Toni Morrison is rooted in Lorain and it is with her Midwestern town that she must make her personal peace.

**SELECTED WORKS:** Morrison's novels include *The Bluest Eye* (1970), *Sula* (1973), *The Song of Solomon* (1978), *Tar Baby* (1981), *Beloved* (1987), *Jazz* (1992), and *Paradise* (1998). Trudier Harris's article "The Worlds That Toni Morrison Made," which appears in *Georgia Review* 49.1 (Spring 1995): 314–30, includes Toni Morrison's Nobel Prize acceptance speech. Toni Morrison has been widely interviewed. *Conversations with Toni Morrison*, edited by Dane Taylor-Guthrie (1994), is valuable because of its variety. Morrison reveals her Midwestern focus in *Black Women at Work*, edited by Claudia Tate (1983); and in Robert Stepto's interview with her, "'Intimate Things in Place': A Conversation with Toni Morrison," which first appeared in *Massachusetts Review* 18 (Autumn 1977): 473–89. Another early and excellent interview is one she gave JANE BAKERMAN, "The Seams Can't Show: An Interview with Toni Morrison," in *Black American Literature Forum* 12 (Summer 1978): 56–60.

**FURTHER READING:** Many articles and many critical books have been written on Toni Morrison's work. *Toni Morrison: Critical Perspectives Past and Present*, edited by Henry Louis Gates Jr. and K. A. Appiah (1993), contains reviews, essays, and interviews and a very thorough bibliography up to 1992.

More than five hundred articles, chapters, and books on Toni Morrison's work are listed on the on-line MLA bibliography (1980–98), and new books and articles are continually

being published. In 1996 the Society for the Study of Midwestern Literature published a special Toni Morrison issue of *Midwestern Miscellany*, number 24; it contains several articles that consider Morrison's relationship to the Midwest. Patrick Bryce Bjork's *The Novels of Toni Morrison: The Search for Place within the Community* (1994) is valuable, as is Jocelyn Chadwick-Joshua's chapter, "Metonymy and Synecdoche: The Rhetoric of the City in Toni Morrison's *Jazz*," in Yoshinobu Hakutani and Robert Butler's *The City in African-American Literature* (1995): 169–80. Charles Scruggs's "The Invisible City in Toni Morrison's *Beloved*," in *Arizona Quarterly* 48.3 (1992): 95–132; Darlene E. Erickson's "Toni Morrison: The Black Search for Place in America," in *Dolphin* 20 (Spring 1991): 45–54; Katherine Leake's article "Morrison's *Beloved*," in *Explicator* 53.2 (1995): 120–23; Patricia McKee's "Spacing and Placing Experience in Toni Morrison's *Sula*," in *Modern Fiction Studies* 42.1 (Spring 1996): 1–30; and Melvin Dixon's *Ride Out the Wilderness, Geography and Identity in Afro-American Literature* (1987) all consider place in Morrison's writings.

Toni Morrison's manuscripts are located at Princeton University's Special Collections Department, but they are not currently open to the public.

MARILYN J. ATLAS                    OHIO UNIVERSITY

## WILLARD F. MOTLEY
July 14, 1909–March 4, 1965
(Bud Billiken)

**BIOGRAPHY:** Though during his lifetime the dust jackets of Willard Motley's novels routinely listed his date of birth as 1912, he was in fact born in Chicago on July 14, 1909. According to Craig Abbott, Motley was raised "as if his mother [Florence or Flossie Motley] were his sister and as if his grandparents—Archibald John Motley and Mary Frederica Huff—were his parents" (*Dictionary of American Biography*: Supplement 7: 557). The family included his uncle, the painter Archibald John Motley Jr. (1891–1981), whom biographers, following Willard's lead, sometimes treated as his older brother. Archibald John Motley, the man he always called his father, was a Pullman porter who brought his family from New Orleans to Chicago's southwest side around 1900.

Motley once recalled that his grandfather bought their home in Englewood (350 W. 60th) with the "nickel-and-dime-and quarter tips" he had saved over the years. There, the Motleys were the only black family in a neighborhood dominated by Irish and German immigrants. When Chicago suffered through several murderous days of race riots in 1919, as much later described in Willard Motley's "Let No Man Write His Epitaph of Hate for Chicago," the family's neighbors warned a menacing white mob away from the home of the "colored family down the street" (*Chicago Sun-Times,* August 11, 1963, sec. 2, 1–4). During the following nights his grandfather and a white neighbor, each with a rifle, guarded the Motley home.

His family was Roman Catholic, of Creole extraction, and fairly comfortable lower-middle-class. While no record of Motley's having attended parochial schools exists, he was baptized when he was two weeks old. He graduated from Englewood High School in 1929, but, apart from a brief and quixotic effort to join the University of Wisconsin football team in 1933, he spent no time in college.

Between December 9, 1922, and July 3, 1924, Motley wrote a children's column, "Bud Says," for the *Chicago Defender.* "Sister and Brother," his first published short story, had appeared in the *Defender* starting on September 23, 1922. As "Bud Billiken," he answered readers' letters, sent birthday greetings, commented on Chicago, and published several of his own short stories. To this precocious beginning act came no immediate sequel. Motley published little, and almost nothing noteworthy, until the 1940s. At Englewood High School and throughout the 1930s, he wrote short stories, but, though he submitted many to popular magazines and to Chicago and New York newspapers, he placed none. During the Depression years, Motley was unemployed or worked odd jobs; in 1936 and again in 1938, he and a friend took trips by "jalopy" to the West Coast. On his first hobo trip, he wound up in a Cheyenne jail for a month. Motley kept careful and detailed notes of the trips and unsuccessfully attempted to shape "Adventures" or "Adventures and Misadventures"—his alternate working titles for these travel narratives—into a book.

In 1939 Motley moved into a slum apartment at 1410 Union, near Chicago's Maxwell Street Market and not far from Hull House. At the Hull House Settlement he met two other writers, William P. Schenk and proletarian novelist Alexander Saxton. Together the three founded the literary monthly *Hull House Magazine*; "Pavement Portraits," prose poems that Motley contributed in 1939–40, marked an important turning point toward the writing of *Knock on Any Door* (1947).

From 1940 to 1942 he was employed by the WPA Writers' Project, documenting in reports and photographs the housing conditions in Chicago's "Little Italy." This work brought him into renewed contact with JACK CONROY and NELSON ALGREN. He met still other WPA writers including Horace Cayton, St. Clair Drake, RICHARD WRIGHT, and Frank Yerby.

From 1941 to its publication in 1947, he worked steadily on *Knock on Any Door*, initially titled "Leave without Illusions." Motley revised and edited thousands of pages from his notes and diaries; he had investigated the city's court and prison systems, its pool halls, taverns, and Madison Avenue's Skid Row. These experiences were hammered into the story of Nick Romano—the tragic life and death of a former altar boy and Italian immigrant's son who killed a brutal cop, was convicted, and died in the electric chair.

The immediate critical acclaim and massive sales of the novel made Motley a celebrity overnight. Two long, documentary novels on Chicago followed: *We Fished All Night* (1951) and *Let No Man Write My Epitaph* (1958). His 1951 novel, a densely plotted exposé of Chicago political corruption, centers on the story of Chet Kosinski—an amateur actor, World War II veteran, and politician who, to erase his ethnic past and further his career, reinvents himself as Don Lockwood. *Let No Man Write My Epitaph*, focusing on narcotics addiction, continued the narrative of *Knock on Any Door* through the interlocked stories of Nellie, Nick Romano's lover, their illegitimate son Nick Jr., and his younger brother Louie Romano. In 1951 Motley traveled widely in Mexico and in 1952, taking up permanent residence there, bought a home outside Mexico City. His last novel, the posthumously published *Let Noon Be Fair* (1966), reflected his sympathetic understanding of Cuernavaca, the Mexican city where he last lived. Motley never married but adopted a Mexican boy, Sergio Lopez, as his son. He died in Mexico City from the effects of intestinal gangrene poisoning.

**SIGNIFICANCE:** With the publication of *Knock on Any Door*, Motley was hailed as THEODORE DREISER's successor and a leading figure in a Chicago school said to include Nelson Algren, JAMES T. FARRELL, Meyer Levin, and Richard Wright. Horace Cayton, writing in the *New Republic* of May 12, 1947, contended that his novel had shown "greater artistry" and "more sensitivity" than Dreiser's *American Tragedy*. But reviewers, including his friend Nelson Algren, decided his subsequent novels did not fulfill the promise of his first book, and they increasingly placed him—and his novels of thick social documentation—at the dead end of the naturalistic novel's tradition. Further, Motley's criticism of CHESTER HIMES and James Baldwin, and then the charge that he had written "raceless" novels, led to his eclipse in many histories of African American literature. *Knock on Any Door* endures as a passionate testimony to Chicago's violent racial and ethnic divisions, even as it restates Motley's belief, through subtle irony and pounding rhetoric, in "the brotherhood of man" (419).

**SELECTED WORKS:** *Knock on Any Door* (1947) and "The Almost White Boy," a short story first published in *Soon, One Morning: New Writing by American Negroes* (1963), stand as vital social protests and compelling stories of Chicago's multiethnic diversity and racial divisions. *The Diaries of Willard Motley*, edited by Jerome Klinkowitz (1979), culls the many volumes Motley filled between 1926 and 1943. *The Diaries* indexes Motley's growth as a writer and traces the origins of *Knock on Any Door*. Motley's "Let No Man Write His Epitaph of Hate for Chicago," in the *Chicago Sun-Times* (August 11, 1963): sec. 2, 1–4, records valuable biographical information and helps define his position on civil rights in relation to James Baldwin, MALCOLM X, and others. *Knock on Any Door* proved popular enough to be made into a 1949 film starring Humphrey Bogart. In 1960 *Let No Man Write My Epitaph* was made into a film starring James Darren and Shelley Winters.

**FURTHER READING:** Robert E. Fleming's *Willard Motley* (1978) remains the most complete critical and biographical study. For a more recent treatment of Motley's fiction, see John Conder's "Selves of the City, Selves of the South," in *The City in African-American Literature*, edited by Yoshinobu Hakutani and Robert Butler (1995): 110–22. Most of Motley's papers are deposited at Northern Illinois University and the University of Wisconsin. Craig S. Abbot and Kay Van Mol's "The Willard Motley Papers at Northern Illinois University," in *Resources for American Literary Study* (1978): 3–26, offers a guide to that collection.
GUY SZUBERLA                          UNIVERSITY OF TOLEDO

# JOHN MUIR
April 21, 1838–December 24, 1914

**BIOGRAPHY:** Born in Dunbar, Scotland, to pious, working-class parents, Daniel and Ann (Gilrye) Muir, John Muir immigrated to Fountain Lake, Wisconsin, with his family in 1849. Raised under the stern guidance of his Calvinist father, Muir spent his childhood in relentless toil on the family's farm. By his teens, however, Muir showed considerable mechanical genius, and in 1860, at the age of twenty-two, he left home to exhibit several mechanical inventions at the Wisconsin State Fair. Enrolling at the University of Wisconsin, Muir busied himself with the study of science as well as literature, especially the works of Transcendentalist writers Emerson and Thoreau. After completing his studies at the university, Muir worked as a factory mechanic in Indianapolis, Indiana, until an industrial accident left him temporarily blinded in March 1867.

Following recovery of his eyesight, Muir turned his back on his career as a mechanic and inventor and dedicated his life to the study of nature. In September 1867 he embarked on a thousand-mile walk to the Gulf of Mexico, a trip which would take him through Indiana, Kentucky, Tennessee, Georgia, and Florida and which, more importantly, would lead him toward a view of nature in which humans played only one small role among millions of other species. The following year, Muir made his first trip to California, where he would reside for the remainder of his life. The wilderness of the Sierras provided him with the inspiration and raw material for a new career as a writer, and by the early 1870s, Muir's articles on the mountains of the West were being published regularly in the nation's press.

In 1880 he married Louise Strentzel and began an ill-fated attempt at farming. Even during this time as a fruit grower, however, much of Muir's attention was on the wilderness. In 1889 he began a public campaign to protect the Yosemite region as a national park. Three years later, he helped to organize the Sierra Club and became the era's leading proponent of conservation causes. Following a lengthy and ultimately unsuccessful battle to save Yosemite's Hetch Hetchy Valley from destruction by a reservoir dam, Muir died in Los Angeles on December 24, 1914.

**SIGNIFICANCE:** Although Muir has traditionally been viewed as a Western writer, his is a career firmly grounded in the Midwest. As Muir states in *The Story of My Boyhood and Youth* (1913), the love and respect for the natural world which would become so evident in famous works such as *The Mountains of California* (1894) began with boyhood excursions into what he termed in *The Story of My Boyhood and Youth* "the glorious Wisconsin wilderness" (52). Here, young Muir first intuited the Romantic notion of the divine in nature which would later lead him to devote his life and his talents as a writer to protecting the natural world.

Perhaps more importantly, Muir's years in the Midwest allowed him to witness firsthand the environmental degradation which civilization, agriculture, and industry brought with it, such as the wholesale destruction of the passenger pigeon by Wisconsin farmers, a spectacle which he describes in *The Story of My Boyhood and Youth*. Two decades of early life in the Midwest instilled in John Muir both a love for wild nature and a desire to protect it at all costs, setting the stage for a career that would make him one of America's preeminent nature writers and wilderness advocates.

**SELECTED WORKS:** Readers interested in Muir's Midwestern youth will find his memoir *The Story of My Boyhood and Youth* (1913) rewarding. A more nature-centered view of parts of the Midwest appears in *A Thousand-Mile Walk to the Gulf* (1916). Muir's best Western wilderness writings are contained in *My First Summer in the Sierras* (1911) and *The Mountains of California* (1894).

**FURTHER READING:** William Cronon discusses the environmental legacy of Muir's Midwestern childhood, along with those of FREDERICK JACKSON TURNER and ALDO LEOPOLD, in his article "Landscape and Home: Environmental Traditions in Wisconsin," in *Wisconsin Magazine of History* 74.2 (Winter 1990–91). Two other excellent, more general,

sources on Muir are Stephen Fox's *John Muir and His Legacy: The American Conservation Movement* (1981) and Roderick Nash's chapter on Muir in his work *Wilderness and the American Mind* (1967). Many of Muir's papers are housed at the Holt-Atherton Pacific Center for Western Studies at the University of the Pacific.

ROD PHILLIPS          MICHIGAN STATE UNIVERSITY

## BHARATI MUKHERJEE
July 27, 1940

**BIOGRAPHY:** Born in Calcutta to Sudhir Lal and Bina (Banerjee) Mukherjee, a Brahmin family, Bharati Mukherjee grew up in India, England, and Switzerland. She received degrees from the Universities of Calcutta, Baroda, and Iowa, the last where she met novelist Clark Blaise, whom she married in 1963. They have two sons, Bart Anand and Bernard Sudhir. After working in a number of colleges and universities in Canada and the United States, Mukherjee currently teaches at the University of California at Berkeley. She has received numerous awards and honors, including a Guggenheim Foundation Award (1978) and a National Book Critics Circle Award for fiction (1988).

**SIGNIFICANCE:** Although her life has been cosmopolitan, Mukherjee's Midwestern experience in Iowa has been significant, and some of her most important writing focuses on the immigrant experience in Iowa. Emerging from a patriarchal Indian society, Mukherjee's women attempt to develop individual identity in the ostensibly freer atmosphere of the United States. Often what they experience, however, is rootlessness, exploitation, even violence, contrasted with the traditional idea of Midwestern rootedness and stability. Iowa offers an especially dramatic setting for these themes. From the short story collection *The Middleman and Other Stories* (1988), Jasmine, a housekeeper from Trinidad, in "Jasmine" and Maya Sanyal in "The Tenant," a university professor and an itinerant tenant, search for connection through shallow sexual relationships. Maya Sanyal's best hope for a stable relationship seems to be with a fellow Indian she meets briefly at the Chicago airport, where people come and go but do not stay.

One of Mukherjee's most important novels, and her most significant Midwestern

Bharati Mukherjee.
Photo © Nancy Crampton

work, is *Jasmine* (1989). The title character, who comes to America to honor her assassinated husband's greatest wish, goes through a number of identity transformations, illustrating the rootlessness of the Indian immigrant. In Iowa, she is "Jane," wife of the town banker. Her identity remains fluid, however, as she leaves both Iowa, land of deep-rooted crops, and her paraplegic husband, tragically confined to his wheelchair, to return to her relationship with Taylor, a Columbia professor. In the process, she becomes "Jasmine" again.

This novel contributes significantly to Midwestern literature by broadening the stereotypical portrayal of the supposedly monocultural Midwest to include Indian, Vietnamese, and Hmong immigrants, as well as the other, more long-standing cultures of Iowa, such as that of the Mennonites. Perhaps even more important, Mukherjee dramatizes the depths of drama and violence of supposedly "flat" Midwestern experience, suggesting comparisons between the murders and suicides of the farm crisis of the late 1980s and political violence in India and the Vietnam War. In many ways, though, the novel also reaffirms traditional "American" themes in Jasmine's restlessness on the Midwestern "frontier," and at the end she "lights out for the territory" of Cal-

ifornia with her former lover. The novel also suggests that the Midwest is merely a stopping place on the way to somewhere else. The novel, and much of Mukherjee's work, presents a combination of traditional Midwestern portraiture and radical revisioning.

**SELECTED WORKS:** Mukherjee's most significant works set in the Midwest include the novel *Jasmine* (1989) and the short stories "The Tenant" and "Jasmine," both in the collection *The Middleman and Other Stories* (1988). "Jasmine" and *Jasmine* are not about the same characters, though the thematic ideas are somewhat similar. Mukherjee's other fictional works include *The Tiger's Daughter* (1971), *Wife* (1975), *Darkness* (1985), *The Holder of the World* (1993), and *Leave It to Me* (1997). Mukherjee has also written nonfiction, including *Kautilya's Concept of Diplomacy: A New Interpretation* (1976) and, with her husband Clark Blaise, *Days and Nights in Calcutta* (1986) and *The Sorrow and the Terror: The Haunting Legacy of the Air India Tragedy* (1987).

**FURTHER READING:** Two book-length works on Mukherjee include a collection of essays edited by Emmanuel S. Nelson, *Bharati Mukherjee: Critical Perspectives* (1993), which includes a number of pieces dealing with *Jasmine* and some significant discussion of the stories "The Tenant" and "Jasmine"; and *Bharati Mukherjee* (1995), by Fakrul Alam, in the Twayne U.S. Authors series. Significant articles in journals include Arvindra Sant-Wade and Karen-Marguerite Radell's "Refashioning the Self: Immigrant Women in Bharati Mukherjee's New World," in *Studies in Short Fiction* 29.1 (Winter 1992): 11–17, and Kristin Carter-Sanborn's "'We Murder Who We Were': *Jasmine* and the Violence of Identity," in *American Literature* 66.3 (September 1994): 573–93.

THOMAS K. DEAN                    UNIVERSITY OF IOWA

## PETROLEUM V. NASBY.
*See* David Ross Locke

## JOHN G(NEISENAU) NEIHARDT
January 8, 1881–November 4, 1973

**BIOGRAPHY:** Born on a farm near Sharpsburg, Illinois, southeast of Springfield, John G. Neihardt published works in a large number of literary genres during his long life. His largely unsuccessful father, Nicholas Neihardt, later deserted the family in Kansas

John G. Neihardt.
Courtesy of the Nebraska State Historical Society

City, Missouri. But he did name his son after John Greenleaf Whittier, giving the boy the poet's first two names, though Neihardt later changed his middle name. His mother, the former Alice Culler, took her children to live with her parents in the Great Plains, and Neihardt grew up primarily in Kansas and Nebraska. In 1892, while sick with a fever, he had a mystical experience that led to his poetic interests. After graduating with a BS from Nebraska Normal College in 1897, Neihardt embarked on a trail of jobs ranging from farming and clerking for a man who traded with Indians to editing and teaching.

Mona Martinsen, a Midwestern-Western sculptor studying under Rodin in Paris, read some of Neihardt's early poetry while in France; after a courtship by mail, the two married when she returned to the states in 1908. Together they had four children; she died in 1958. His early experiences living with Omaha and Sioux Indians and later ones working for the Bureau of Indian Affairs whetted and added to his knowledge of Native Americans of the Plains, one of the primary subjects of his writings.

His career as a published author began in 1900 and continued until his death. During his lifetime Neihardt received many honors and held many prestigious appointments including poet laureate of Nebraska (1921), professor of poetry at the University of Nebraska, Lincoln, poet in residence at the University of Missouri–Columbia, chancellor of the Academy of American Poets from 1959 to 1967, and Fellow of the International Institute of Arts and Letters.

**SIGNIFICANCE:** As is the case for so many Midwestern writers—as well as other writers primarily associated with a region—Neihardt has received relatively scant attention as an ambitious and at times highly successful writer. Currently, most critical attention focuses on *Black Elk Speaks*, yet a number of his other works are as deserving of attention. His writings deal with the white settlers and Native Americans of the Midwestern or Western Plains and tend to fuse devices of classical literature with those of folklore and history. The Unitarian Neihardt's highly eclectic religious view of life emphasizes the need for his characters to overcome adversity and thereby create order. As Vine Deloria Jr. states in the introduction to *A Sender of Words*, "Two major themes ran through Neihardt's work: the exploration of the High Plains and western mountains and a profound universal mysticism that found unique expression in the various religions of mankind" (2).

Perhaps ultimately most important, Neihardt's literary efforts made him the first relatively successful artist to attempt a frontier epic. As such, he can perhaps duly be entitled "the progenitor of Western poetry." This distinction makes Neihardt's writing simultaneously Midwestern literature since much of it takes place in and evinces the society of the region at once Midwestern and Western, revealing vital interconnections between both.

As a body of work, like that of most creators of a distinctive literary line or subject, Neihardt's writing generally bends noticeably toward the romantic and sentimental. Yet the best of his writing produces a powerful response in the reader.

**SELECTED WORKS:** Neihardt is most famous for *Black Elk Speaks* (1932), his personally molded account of talks with the famous Sioux Indian using BLACK ELK's son as an interpreter. However, Neihardt published in diverse genres during his long life. The other main work for which he is best known, *A Cycle of the West* (1949), consists of a five-part epic poem primarily concerned with mountain men and Native Americans. It brings together the separately published *The Song of Hugh Glass* (1915), *The Song of Three Friends* (1919), *The Song of the Indian Wars* (1925), *The Song of the Messiah* (1935), and *The Song of Jed Smith* (1941). He also wrote in the following genres: novels, the best of which is *When the Tree Flowered* (1951), his last important work; short stories about the frontier, in collections *The Lonesome Trail* (1907) and *Indian Tales and Others* (1926); lyrical poems, gathered in his *Collected Poems* (1926); nonfiction, such as *The River and I* (1910); literary criticism, particularly his artistic credo, *Poetic Values: Their Reality and Our Need of Them* (1925); a biography of Jedediah Smith, *The Splendid Wayfaring* (1920); and verse plays, including a pair published together as *Two Mothers* (1920). Neihardt also wrote a two-volume autobiography focusing on his younger days, *All Is but a Beginning* (1972), and the posthumously published *Patterns and Coincidences* (1978).

**FURTHER READING:** *A Sender of Words: Essays in Memory of John G. Neihardt*, edited by Vine Deloria Jr. (1984), consists of fourteen essays on Neihardt and includes essays by such renowned fellow authors as Vine Deloria Jr., Dee Brown, Frank Waters, N. Scott Momaday, and FREDERICK MANFRED. Lucile F. Aly, who has written a number of shorter pieces on Neihardt, also penned *John G. Neihardt: A Critical Biography* (1977). Blair Whitney's Twayne volume, *John G. Neihardt* (1976), offers another book-length treatment of the author. Solid shorter pieces concerned with the author include the following essays: David L. Newquist's "The Violation of Hospitality and the Demoralization of the Frontier," in *Midwestern Miscellany* 21 (1993): 19–28; G. Thomas Couser's "Black Elk Speaks with Forked Tongue," in *Studies in Autobiography* (1988); Aly's "John G. Neihardt," in *A Literary History of the American West* (1987), "Poetry and History in Neihardt's Cycle of the West," in *Western American Literature* 16.1 (1981): 3–18, and "John G. Neihardt and the American Epic," in *Western American Literature* 13 (1979): 309–25; and Paul A. Olson's "The Epic and Great Plains Literature: Rolvaag, Cather, and Neihardt," in

*Prairie Schooner* 55.1–2 (1981): 263–85. The author's papers are available at the University of Missouri's Neihardt Memorial Collection.

DAVID N. CREMEAN    BLACK HILLS STATE UNIVERSITY

## MEREDITH NICHOLSON
December 9, 1866–December 22, 1947

**BIOGRAPHY:** Meredith Nicholson was born in Crawfordsville, Indiana, the son of Edward Willis Nicholson, a respected farmer and a member of LEW WALLACE's company of Montgomery Guards who served throughout the Civil War. Meredith's mother, Emily, was the daughter of an early settler and editor. When Meredith was about five, the family moved to Indianapolis, where he lived most of his life, while maintaining close ties with Crawfordsville. He left high school during his first year, taking a series of small jobs and starting to study law.

When JAMES WHITCOMB RILEY sought him out to congratulate him on getting a poem published in the *Cincinnati Enquirer*, the two became fast friends, and Nicholson, thus inspired, contributed to Indianapolis newspapers, particularly the *Indianapolis News*, where he worked from 1884 through 1897. His first book, *Short Flights* (1891), was a collection of mediocre poems, which prompted Wabash College to award him an AM degree.

In 1896 he married Eugenie Kountze of Omaha, Nebraska, who bore him three children. After he passed an unsuccessful year as a stockbroker, the couple spent three years in Denver, Colorado, where he served as the unhappy treasurer and auditor of a coal-mining company. Suffering from homesickness, he wrote his study of Indiana, *The Hoosiers* (1900), and soon Wabash College awarded him the doctor of literature degree. The couple returned to Indianapolis, where his wife provided the means by which he could attempt to make a career of writing. Unfortunately, his new book, *Poems* (1906), was like his first and was known only for a poem on James Whitcomb Riley. Thus, he turned to prose. His first novel, *The Main Chance* (1903), was a best-seller. His greatest success, *The House of a Thousand Candles* (1905), sold more than two hundred and fifty thousand copies in the United States. Then Nicholson issued collections of his essays previously published in periodicals and also four novels that did not add to his stature.

He was elected to Phi Beta Kappa and the National Institute of Arts and Letters. He received honorary degrees from Indiana and Butler Universities and Wabash College. His wife died in 1931, and his marriage to Dorothy Wolfe Lannon in 1933 ended in divorce ten years later. Nicholson served as American envoy to Paraguay, Venezuela, and Nicaragua. The cordial, genial, optimistic Nicholson was a famous figure everywhere he went. He died in Indianapolis.

**SIGNIFICANCE:** Meredith Nicholson achieved little fame as a poet, for his verse was not particularly original in thought or expression. It is fortunate that he turned to prose as his medium. His best writing is to be found in his novels, such as *The Main Chance* and *The House of a Thousand Candles*, which brought him more notice, perhaps, than anything else he published. His attempt to write realistic fiction could not be much of a success, since he always provided a happy ending. His few dramas are interesting, such as *Honor Bright* (1923), first produced at the Murat Theater in Indianapolis. His essays are serious and sincere, and in them one finds the real Nicholson.

**SELECTED WORKS:** Nicholson's first novel, *The Main Chance* (1903), was an indictment of big business in Omaha, Nebraska. The next, *Zelda Dameron* (1904), was set in Indianapolis. *The House of a Thousand Candles* (1905), a romantic thriller, was translated into five languages, was dramatized, and inspired two motion pictures. *A Hoosier Chronicle* (1912) dealt with the campus and early history of Wabash College. Then he turned to issuing collections of essays defending the American village as a bulwark of democracy. These volumes are *The Hoosiers* (1900), a good early study of the state; *The Valley of Democracy* (1918); *The Man in the Street, Papers on American Topics* (1921), and *Old Familiar Faces* (1929). Here the real Nicholson stresses three ideas: the desirability of decentralization of government, the necessity of separating municipal government from partisan politics, and the importance of all people's participation in a democracy. He reiterated these themes in his speeches. His last books were of several types, such as *Honor Bright* (1923), a three-act comedy written with Kenyon Nicholson (no relative), and three pseudo-realistic novels. His last work was *The Cavalier of Tennessee* (1928), an historical novel about Andrew Jackson.

**FURTHER READING:** Criticism of Nicholson is limited. Nevertheless, the following materials may be useful: Charles Baldwin's *The Men Who Make Our Novels* (1924); Richard Banta's *Indiana Authors and Their Books* (1949); James Hart's *The Popular Book* (1950); Grant Knight's *The Strenuous Age in American Literature* (1954); Meredith Nicholson's own *American Man of Letters* (n.d.); Meredith Nicholson's "Confessions of a Best Seller," in *The Provincial American and Other Papers* (1912): 219 ff.; Fred Pattee's *The New American Literature, 1890–1930* (1930); Dorothy Russo and Thelma Sullivan's *Bibliographical Studies of Seven Authors of Crawfordsville, Indiana* (1952); Jean Sanders's unpublished DePauw University thesis, "Meredith Nicholson, Hoosier Cavalier" (1952); and Russell Smith's "The Play Boy of the Wabash," in *Bookman* 52 (October 1920): 133–36. The Indiana State Library has a good collection of Nicholson's books and papers. Many of his books there contain his handwritten notes.

ARTHUR W. SHUMAKER        DEPAUW UNIVERSITY

# LORINE NIEDECKER

May 12, 1903–December 31, 1970

**BIOGRAPHY:** Lorine Niedecker was born in Fort Atkinson, Wisconsin, near her parents' home on Blackhawk Island, which is actually a small promontory jutting into Lake Koshkonong close to where the Rock River flows into the lake. She spent the great majority of her days in this watery place. Her father, Henry E. Niedecker, was a commercial fisherman and the proprietor of a combination bait shop and tavern on the island. Her mother, Theresa (Kunz) Niedecker, was a housewife. In 1922 Niedecker began studies at Beloit College but left after two years when her mother's already poor health declined further and Lorine felt needed at home. Her marriage in 1928 to Frank Hartwig, a road contractor, ended in separation two years later. From 1938 to 1942 Niedecker worked in Madison in the Federal Writers' Project. From the 1920s through the early 1960s, she held various jobs in Fort Atkinson, as public library assistant, stenographer, proofreader, and kitchen and cleaning assistant at the hospital, among others. Her 1963 marriage to Al Millen, a housepainter from Milwaukee, lasted until her death in 1970.

Niedecker became interested in new currents in modern poetry early on. She exchanged many letters with other objectivist poets over the years, in particular with Louis Zukovsky. Yet in near-isolation she determinedly developed her craft. The first slender collections of Niedecker's poems were published by small presses in Illinois and Scotland when she was forty-three and fifty-eight years old. A few others followed during the last few years of her life. In 1985, fifteen years after her death, her complete collected writings were published. Only recently has her work received the critical recognition it deserves.

**SIGNIFICANCE:** The work of Lorine Niedecker manifests her integrity. In her plain and simple living and in her spare and highly compressed poetry, she pares things down to their minimal, most meaningful essentials. In her everyday life she could afford no extra money or time for the nonessential, much less the superfluous. Her poems reflect a similar approach. Nor did she have to travel far to find her essential subject matter. Her work shows a deeply rooted, lifelong attachment to place, to her particular Midwestern home on Blackhawk Island.

A few poems delve into regional history, dealing with early settlers and Native Americans, such as the Sauk chief BLACK HAWK himself and his uprising in the 1830s against the advance of white civilization. A few poems deal with Niedecker's own place in her contemporary human community or, better, with her literal and figurative location on the outskirts of Fort Atkinson. They portray the poet's discomfort with or downright distrust of the town and the civilized. Also, from a feminist perspective, Niedecker explores some of the subtle strictures as well as hard burdens placed upon women. But it is the natural world around Blackhawk Island that provides the primary subject matter and the basic source of sustenance for this poet.

The poems abound in natural sights and sounds, images of plants and animals (especially birds), lake and river, marsh and shore. There are reflections upon the experience of her fisherman father and his family on the island. This poetry is not pastoral, however, portraying a lovely life in the country. Recurrent spring flooding and other hardships imposed by nature are prominent. But natural imagery provides the means of expression of who and what she was, including her most significant and hard-won identity as a poet.

According to the title poem of the 1961 collection *My Friend Tree* (1), even a tree turns out to be too solid, too material, and an obstruction to a more basic vital force: "My friend tree / I sawed you down / but I must attend / an older friend / the sun." Hard choices and sacrifice were required to achieve the distinctive poetic voice and deeply felt enlightenment that reward her careful readers.

**SELECTED WORKS:** Two recent collections are *From This Condensery: The Complete Writing of Lorine Niedecker*, edited by Robert J. Bertholf (1985), and *The Granite Pail: The Selected Poems of Lorine Niedecker*, edited by Cid Corman (1985). A later small collection is *Harpsichord and Salt Fish*, edited by Jenny Penberthy (1991).

**FURTHER READING:** The summer 1975 issue, number 16, of the little magazine *Truck* is devoted to Niedecker. Two recent books document Niedecker's correspondence with fellow poets: *"Between Your House and Mine": The Letters of Lorine Niedecker to Cid Corman, 1960 to 1970* (1986) and *Niedecker and the Correspondence with Zukovsky, 1931–1970* (1993). The latter includes a lengthy biographical and critical introduction by the editor, Jenny Penberthy, as well as an extensive bibliography, including a list of the various library collections holding Niedecker's papers. Chief among these are the Humanities Research Center, University of Texas at Austin, which holds some Niedecker manuscript poems and her letters to and from Zukofsky, and the Berg Collection, New York Public Library, which holds her letters to Corman.

WAYNE H. MEYER                    BALL STATE UNIVERSITY

# HUGH NISSENSON
March 10, 1933

**BIOGRAPHY:** Hugh Nissenson was born in New York City to Charles Arthur and Harriette (Dolch) Nissenson. He received his BA from Swarthmore College in 1955. A full-time freelance writer, Nissenson was the Wallace Stegner Literary Fellow at Stanford University in 1961–62. He currently resides in New York City.

**SIGNIFICANCE:** In 1985 Nissenson published *The Tree of Life*, which received the 1986 Ohioana Book Award for fiction. This novel seemed to represent a new departure for Nissenson, who had previously emphasized Israel and the Jewish immigrant experience in New York. In a February 11, 1997, telephone interview, Nissenson explained the naturalness of this change. Always interested in MARK TWAIN, he was specifically inspired by reading Robert Price's 1954 biography *Johnny Appleseed: Man and Myth*. Suddenly the importance of American history to Jewish immigrants found a focus on a frontier hero and frontier conditions reminiscent of those Nissenson had encountered in Israel. John Chapman's Swedenborgian religiosity echoed frontier Maine's Jonathan Fisher's Congregationalism.

Based on three years of research, Nissenson creates an ex-minister, Thomas Keene, who has emigrated from New England to the Ohio of 1811 and 1812. There, Keene and his now "curdled faith" confront Delaware Indian raids, sexuality with a freed slave from Kentucky, and the "religious mania" of Johnny Appleseed. These confrontations are expressed in a diary with poetic and artistic elements. Nissenson used A. A. Graham's *History of Richland County, Ohio* (1880) extensively.

*The Tree of Life* is intended to form the second volume of a planned trilogy, *American Visions*. The first volume is the novel *My Own Ground* (1976), about the Jewish experience in New York. The forthcoming third volume, *The Song of the Earth*, will be a work of science fiction set in twenty-first-century Nebraska. The trilogy will, in Nissenson's terms, fulfill his "passionate interest in the American Protestant tradition" from its Jewish analogues to its once traditional and futuristic stylistic innovations.

**SELECTED WORKS:** Three volumes of short stories show Nissenson's range as well as his focus. *A Pile of Stones* (1965) and *In the Reign of Peace* (1972) lead to the 1988 *The Elephant and My Jewish Problem: Selected Stories and Journals*. The inclusion of the word "Journals" here reflects the other abiding interest of Nissenson's career: the diary as narrative. Thus *Notes from the Frontier*, a 1968 account of Nissenson's experiences on the Israel–Syria border, anticipates both the subject matter and format of 1985's *The Tree of Life*.

**FURTHER READING:** Among many book reviews, special attention might be given to the 1985 reviews of *The Tree of Life* in the *New York Times* (October 14), the *Chicago Tribune Book World* (October 27), the *New York Times*

*Book Review* (October 27), and *Village Voice* (October 22). A doctoral dissertation on Nissenson is under way in Italy, testifying to European interest in a writer who, in a letter of May 30, 1995, asserts: "*The Tree of Life* is my contribution to American literature about the Midwest—and the birth of our civilization."

JAMES M. HUGHES          WRIGHT STATE UNIVERSITY

## JEANNETTE COVERT NOLAN
March 31, 1897–October 12, 1974
(Caroline Tucker)

**BIOGRAPHY:** Jeannette Nolan, writer of adult and juvenile fiction and nonfiction, much of which is Midwestern in subject matter, was the granddaughter of Jacob Covert, who owned and edited a newspaper in Washington, Indiana, and also edited a paper in Evansville. Her father, Charles Grant Nolan, was city editor of the *Evansville Tribune* and became mayor of Evansville. Her mother was Grace Louise (Tucker) Covert. At the age of nine Jeannette received from *St. Nicholas* magazine a silver badge to reward her for publishing her first poem. In high school at Evansville she was editor of the school paper and also editor of the yearbook.

When she graduated, the family could not afford to send her to college, so she obtained instead a position on the *Evansville Courier*, where she wrote the advice to the lovelorn column. A year later she transferred to the *Journal-News*. After three years of newspaper work she married Val Nolan, a young attorney in town. The couple had three children, two boys and a girl. Because one of the children developed mastoid trouble, Jeannette Nolan took the children to Florida for several winters. There, her interest in fiction increased, and she sold her first story to *St. Nicholas*. In 1933 the family moved to Indianapolis, where Val Nolan served as a U.S. district attorney until his death in 1940. Jeannette Nolan then decided to concentrate on writing. The family moved to Bloomington but in 1945 returned to Indianapolis, where she occasionally taught classes in juvenile writing at a branch of Indiana University. For two years she wrote a column, "Lines with a Hoosier Accent," for the *Indianapolis Star*.

Many honors came to this writer. Her work was included in school readers and anthologies and was made into radio presentations. At least ten of her books were published in England; seven were Junior Literary Guild selections. Her *George Rogers Clark, Soldier and Hero* (1954) received the Indiana University award for the best juvenile book written that year by an Indiana author, and in 1961 she again received this award for *Spy for the Confederacy: Rose O'Neal Greenhow* (1961). In 1959 she was recognized by Theta Sigma Pi as an outstanding woman author. She died in Indianapolis having produced one of the longest lists of publications of any Indiana author.

SIGNIFICANCE: Jeannette Nolan writes about Indiana and the Midwest in a large number of her books whether or not she places her story in a recognizable location. She uses settings and characters that she knows, changing many of them somewhat to fit the book. For example, her novel *Second Best* (1933) is set in an Indiana town, *Gather Ye Rosebuds* (1946) uses Evansville, Indiana, and *This Same Flower* (1948) can be placed in the state. Also, as she solves her plots, her attitudes reflect the Midwestern emphasis on common sense. This is equally true of her biographies. There she uses real facts alone or adds some fiction: *James Whitcomb Riley* (1964), *Eugene Field* (1940), *George Rogers Clark* (1954), *O. Henry* (1943), *Clara Barton* (1941), *Stephen A. Douglas* (1964), *Florence Nightingale* (1949), *Ulysses S. Grant* (1952), *Joan of Arc* (1953), and *Dolley Madison* (1958). Nolan writes clean, well-constructed prose and appeals to common sense, and her works can be considered as belonging to various classes. The juveniles can be divided into fiction, biography, and a combination of the two, while the adult publications are expository books and novels.

SELECTED WORKS: Examples of her works in juvenile fiction are *Treason at the Point* (1944) and *The Victory Drum* (1953). Her juvenile biographies include *O. Henry* (1943); *The Story of Clara Barton of the Red Cross* (1941); *James Whitcomb Riley, Hoosier Poet* (1941); and *The Story of William Sydney Porter* (1943). Her list of juvenile fictional biography is very long; examples are *Red Hugh of Ireland* (1938), *The Gay Poet: The Story of Eugene Field* (1940), *Abraham Lincoln* (1953), and *Dolley Madison* (1958). Her juveniles are well constructed and very interesting to readers of any age. Examples of her adult expository books are *Hoosier City: The Story of Indianapolis* (1943), *The Shot Heard Round the World* (1963), *Indiana: States of the Nation* (1969), and *Getting to Know the Ohio River* (1973).

Her ten adult novels begin with *Second Best* (1933), a dramatic story of a girl in a small Indiana town who wishes to go on the New York City stage but whose domineering father says no, so she stays home and marries her second choice. Her last adult novel is *This Same Flower* (1948) which shows how a young lady in answering an advertisement for a private secretary finds herself in the midst of the suffragette movement.

FURTHER READING: Criticism of Nolan's work lies almost entirely in articles written for newspapers and magazines, usually not long after she published a book. Although these articles usually contain some biographical material, they also discuss the book and often remark about her writing in general. See, for example, articles in the Indianapolis newspapers.

ARTHUR W. SHUMAKER          DePauw University

## (Benjamin) Frank(lin) Norris
### March 5, 1870–October 25, 1902

BIOGRAPHY: Frank Norris was born in Chicago, Illinois, to Gertrude (Dogget) Norris and Benjamin Franklin Norris. In 1884 the family moved to Oakland, California, and the following year to San Francisco, where he attended Belmont Academy but subsequently transferred to the San Francisco Art Association to study painting. In 1887 he enrolled in the Kensington School of Art in Chicago; later that same year, his family accompanied him to Paris, where he studied art at the Julian Academy.

Norris matriculated at Berkeley in 1890, failing the mathematics portion of the entrance exam but proving his dedication to professional writing by submitting to the admissions board *Yvernelle*, a verse romance published privately in 1892. While at Berkeley, Norris contributed to the *Occident*, a student paper, the *San Francisco Argonaut*, the *Overland Monthly*, and the *San Francisco Wave*. He also developed a deep interest in the novels of Zola and met Joseph Le Conte, a professor who helped to shape his views on naturalism.

In 1894 Norris's parents divorced, and he left Berkeley without a degree. That same year, he entered Harvard, where he began drafts of *Vandover and the Brute* (1914) and

*McTeague* (1899). He continued to publish in West Coast periodicals.

Norris was hired in 1896 by the *San Francisco Chronicle* to cover the conflict between the Boers and the English in South Africa and wrote a number of travel essays before African fever forced his return to San Francisco. Once he regained his strength, he was hired by the *San Francisco Wave*.

In 1897 Norris completed *McTeague*, inspired by the 1893 murder of charwoman Sarah Collins by her husband in a San Francisco kindergarten. Also that year, Norris is thought to have suffered a nervous breakdown from overwork.

In 1898 he was hired by *McClure's Magazine* to cover the Spanish-American War. In Cuba he met fellow correspondents Stephen Crane and Richard Harding Davis but quickly contracted malaria and was forced to return to San Francisco. Also that year, Doubleday and McClure published his novel *Moran of the Lady Letty* and the following year *McTeague*. In 1899 Norris first conceived of "The Epic of the Wheat Trilogy," a projected series of three novels. The first was to deal with the growth of wheat in the American West, the second with its distribution via the Chicago commodities exchange, and the third with its eventual consumption in Europe.

In 1900 Norris married Jeanette Black, became a manuscript reader for Doubleday, Page and Company, and wrote the first novel of the trilogy, *The Octopus*, which was published the next year. Throughout 1902 Norris began to research and write the second book of the trilogy, *The Pit*, all the while producing short stories and essays. Jeanette, the Norrises' only child, was born that year. The family then moved to San Francisco, where Norris began to plan the third novel of the trilogy, *The Wolf*. Norris died in San Francisco of peritonitis that developed after surgery for appendicitis.

**SIGNIFICANCE:** In order to understand Frank Norris's vision of the Midwest, it is crucial to understand his brand of naturalism. For Norris, naturalism was not ultra-realism as some suggest. Instead, Norris was averse to overly factual accounts masquerading as literature and spoke in favor of a new synthesis of realism and romanticism. Norris even commented that realism was a more formidable obstacle for naturalism to circumvent than romanticism. *The Pit*, Norris's Chicago novel, evidences the fusion of these two modes.

From the beginning of the novel, the workaday world of the Chicago business district is linked with the more pristine realm of music and drama of the shimmering opera house, where Laura Dearborn, new to the city from the New England countryside, sits annoyed, unable to lose herself in the production because of stockbrokers discussing the news of the day. Laura fails to realize the seriousness of the narrative she cannot help but overhear. So excited to witness the celestial artistry of her new city that outshines the cultural resources of her Boston home, she does not recognize that the *real* life of the city inheres in the stockbrokers' conversation, which is closer to her than the stars on the stage. Ironically, Laura will learn the power of the market the hard way when her future husband, Curtis Jadwin, is sucked down into the pit of financial ruin.

In Norris's view Chicago is the epicenter of the Midwest, the region that nourished the world, especially Europe. The point of convergence of that most essential crop, wheat, Chicago's markets vibrate with the pulse of nature. Hence it is no surprise that the central action in the novel involves Curtis Jadwin's speculative ventures in this commodity. All of his hereditary gifts are brought to bear in the highest drama, which transpires on the floor of the commodities exchange. Cleverly manipulating the market with the skill of a born virtuoso and for a time "cornering wheat," Jadwin raises himself to the status of hero through his temporary conquest, but Norris is no pure romantic. Jadwin is tumbled from his lofty perch, wiped out in a matter of seconds by the crashing force of an oceanic wheat crop that drives prices down. Though he is the wealthiest and most respected man in the Midwest, he is reduced to nothing—instantaneously, remorselessly, and indifferently.

Jadwin's ruin attests to the potency of Midwestern production. No barrier can withstand the eastward flow of wheat to the hungry. Gretry, Jadwin's broker, sees the folly in "fighting against the earth itself" and urges Jadwin to sell (347). By this time, however, the market has taken its toll, and Jadwin is unable to think rationally. Tremendous success has convinced him of his invulnerability, and though he knows the wheat yield will be up as a result of his efforts to raise its selling price, he asserts himself against all reason.

CLARENCE ANDREWS calls *The Pit* the best fictional study of the Chicago Board of Trade (*Chicago in Story* 98). But as FLOYD DELL points out, the real attraction of this best-selling novel of 1903 was Norris's capacity for seeing and his reporting instinct, which amounted to genius. Dell proclaimed that in *The Pit*, "[b]etter than in any book written by a real Chicagoan, he gives . . . a sense of Chicago's streets and buildings and business" (*Chicago in Story* 98). Dell is implying that Norris's not being a resident of the great city was to his literary advantage. Even though he was born there, Frank Norris left before the mythos surrounding Chicago had a chance to dissipate so that he never became desensitized to the city's illusory grandeur. Norris was just enough of a romantic to accept Chicago in all of its glory, to elevate rather than debunk, as real Chicagoans were apt to do.

**SELECTED WORKS:** Norris published seven novels: *Moran of the Lady Letty* (1898), *McTeague* (1899), *Blix* (1899), *A Man's Woman* (1900), *The Octopus* (1901), *The Pit* (1903), and *Vandover and the Brute* (1914). Eight collections of his short stories and essays appeared after his death: *A Deal in Wheat and Other Stories of the New and Old West* (1903), *The Responsibilities of the Novelist and Other Literary Essays* (1903), *The Joyous Miracle* (1906), *The Third Circle* (1909), *The Surrender of Santiago* (1917), *Frank Norris of "The Wave"* (1931), *The Literary Criticism of Frank Norris* (1964), and *A Novelist in the Making* (1970). Norris also published a single book of poems: *Yvernelle: A Legend of Feudal France* (1892). His letters are available in *Frank Norris: Collected Letters*, edited by Jesse S. Crisler (1986).

**FURTHER READING:** Three short biographies are André Poncet's *Frank Norris* (1977), Franklin Walker's *Frank Norris* (1932), and Charles G. Norris's *Frank Norris* (1914). The only full-length biography available is Warren French's *Frank Norris* (1962). Joseph McElrath's *Frank Norris: A Descriptive Bibliography* (1992) is an important primary bibliography. Four significant books of criticism are Jennifer Boyd's *Frank Norris: Spatial Form and Narrative Time* (1993), which deals with how Norris renders time and space in his narratives; Barbara Hockman's *The Art of Frank*

*Norris, Storyteller* (1988), which disagrees with typically naturalistic interpretations and focuses on the self's vulnerability; William B. Dillingham's *Frank Norris: Instinct and Art* (1969), which discusses the way personality and masculinity contribute to Norris's style; and Donald Pizer's *The Novels of Frank Norris* (1966), which looks at Norris's writings in light of Joseph Le Conte's teachings. The largest collection of Norris's papers is at the Bancroft Library of the University of California, Berkeley.

SCOTT DENT
THE UNIVERSITY OF TENNESSEE AT CHATTANOOGA

# KATHLEEN NORRIS
July 27, 1947

**BIOGRAPHY:** Kathleen Norris, the daughter of John Heyward Norris and Lois Ferne (Totten) Norris, was born in Washington, D.C. As a child and young adult, she lived in Virginia, Illinois, Vermont, and New York but spent many of her summers at her grandparents' house in South Dakota. She received a BA from Bennington College in 1969 and worked in New York City until 1974, when she and her husband, poet David J. Dwyer, returned to live on the family farm.

Since moving to South Dakota, Norris has been president and manager of Leaves of Grass, Inc. (1974–); assistant librarian of Lemmon, South Dakota, Library (1976–); and poet in residence for the North Dakota Arts Council (1979–). Her increasing focus on spirituality and its links to place led her in 1986 to become an oblate of the Benedictine Assumption Abbey. Similarly, she has spent two nine-month terms in residence at the Institute for Ecumenical and Cultural Research at St. John's Abbey and University in Collegeville, Minnesota.

She has received grants from the Guggenheim and Bush Foundations; *Dakota* (1993) received several awards, including the Society of Midland Authors Annual Award.

**SIGNIFICANCE:** The High Plains of the western Dakotas are at the heart of Kathleen Norris's writings, particularly her three volumes of essays: *Dakota* (1993), *The Cloister Walk* (1996), and *Amazing Grace* (1998). In these works, place is an immediate physical presence, yet at the same time, as her subtitle to *Dakota* asserts, "a spiritual geography." Norris parallels living in the solitude, harshness, and stark beauty of the northern Midwest to the discipline of reflective monastic life. The challenges such a place makes lead to an intensification of daily experience and the development of a deeply meditative space and process. Looking at historical and current demographics, definitions of the frontier and marginality, as well as her family history as shaped by this place, Norris celebrates the value of living here, working to create a moral ethos and a sustaining community. Her physical descriptions are concrete and local.

Like other poets and mystics, she links the sacred to the ordinary. In *Dakota*, for example, brief almost imagistic "Weather Reports" are interspersed with longer essays, linking immediate sensations and experiences to larger philosophic issues. Similarly, *The Cloister Walk* is shaped around the liturgical year, during which time Norris examines writing and monasticism as parallel vocations. In its consideration of celibacy, commitment, martyrs, religious saints, and metaphor as a mode of knowing, it also raises questions of gender within the material and spiritual worlds. However, Norris remains a mystic and poet, not a theologian.

Norris's poetry mirrors the concerns of her essays. In her last two books, *The Middle of the World* (1981) and *Little Girls in Church* (1995), the majority of poems are situated in the Midwest. Frequently female personae reveal themselves in stark but poignant descriptions and ruminations on their place, both on the land and in their families. In *Little Girls in Church*, her strongest collection of poems, Norris has her speakers interact and react to mythic, historic, and literary representations of women. In acknowledging the sacred in the humble and homely lives of these women, her spiritual quest takes on a feminist shading. Whether in poetry or prose, Norris celebrates the power of place to both shape and mirror the spiritual journey and growth of the individual.

**SELECTED WORKS:** Norris has published three nonfiction books: *Dakota: A Spiritual Geography* (1993), *The Cloister Walk* (1996), and *Amazing Grace* (1998). She has also published three books of poetry: *Falling Off* (1971), *The Middle of the World* (1981), and *Little Girls in Church* (1995). Many of her poems have appeared first in chapbook editions, including *From South Dakota* (1978), *The Year of Common Things* (1988), *How I Came to Drink My Grand-Mother's Piano* (1989), *All Souls* (1993), and *The Astronomy of Love* (1994). She is also the editor of a collection of essays which continues to focus on place: *Leaving New York: Writers Look Back* (1995).

**FURTHER READING:** Critical commentary is still mainly in the form of reviews. Among those that treat place as a particular element in her writing are Elizabeth Bartelme's discussion of *Dakota*, "Praying in Place," in *Commonweal* 120 (May 7, 1993): 23–24, and Robert Coles's evaluation of *The Cloister Walk*, "A School for Love," in the *New York Times Book Review* (May 5, 1996): 12. Although there has been as yet no lengthy scholarly treatment of her work, an entry on Norris appears in *Contemporary Authors* 120.

MELODY M. ZAJDEL   MONTANA STATE UNIVERSITY

## STERLING NORTH

November 4, 1906–December 22, 1974

**BIOGRAPHY:** Sterling North, editor, critic, poet, biographer, and novelist for both children and adults, was well prepared for a literary career by his richly rewarding Midwestern childhood. Born near the town of Edgerton in the fertile farm country of southern Wisconsin, he was the fourth and last child of college-educated parents David Willard and Elizabeth (Nelson) North. His father, a farm-owner devoted to nature and Native American lore, encouraged his son to study the natural world and to tame wild animals, including the raccoon that inspired North's masterpiece, *Rascal: A Memoir of a Better Era* (1963). His multitalented mother, who died when he was seven, instilled in him her passion for poetry, biology, and history. Like his sister Jessica, a poet, he began writing verse at an early age, publishing his first poem in *St. Nicholas* magazine when he was eight.

While working his way through the University of Chicago, from 1924 to 1929, he edited the literary magazine, wrote lyrics for musicals, and published poems and short stories in national journals. He married his high school sweetheart, Gladys Dolores Buchanan, in his junior year. They had two children, David Sterling and Arielle, for whose pleasure North began writing juvenile books.

After receiving his AB in 1929, he began

his long newspaper career working as a cub reporter for the *Chicago Daily News*, rising to the position of literary editor in three years. He left the Midwest in 1943 to serve as literary editor of the *New York Post* and later of the *World Telegram and Sun*. In 1957 he became founder and editor of North Star Books, a series of American historical books for children, published by Houghton Mifflin. He lived with his family on a twenty-seven-acre farm outside of Morristown, New Jersey, where he died of a stroke at age sixty-eight.

SIGNIFICANCE: Although North lived in the East his last thirty-one years, he maintained his Midwestern identity in his way of life and in his writings. His commitment to country living, the natural environment, and democratic ideals continued in New Jersey, where he lived and worked on his farm, enjoying the daily visits of deer, raccoons, foxes, and birds. Both his children's books and his adult novels continued to be set in the rural Midwest and to portray characters who love the land, lakes, streams, and abundant wildlife. Two of his finest biographies for children celebrate the lives of ABRAHAM LINCOLN and MARK TWAIN, famous Americans who experienced Midwestern boyhoods and values.

North's reputation today rests principally on two of his children's books that are deeply rooted in the fields, forests, and marshes of southern Wisconsin: *Rascal: A Memoir of a Better Era* and *The Wolfling: A Documentary Novel of the Eighteen-Seventies* (1969). Both works, aptly illustrated by John Schoenherr, tell the true, poignant coming-of-age stories of a boy who raises a newborn animal from the wild to become his cherished, close companion. The books also present a realistic yet nostalgic portrait of an era in Midwestern history: a place, a people, and their values. In the autobiographical *Rascal* North recreates the events of 1918 and 1919, his twelfth year, when he adds a raccoon kit to his already large family of pets. The kit soon becomes his best friend, eating, sleeping, biking, and fishing with him, and camping with him and his father in the magnificent Wisconsin North Woods. The boy's ultimate decision to release his raccoon in the wild marks an important and difficult step on his path toward maturity.

In *The Wolfling* North narrates in fictional form the dramatic events of 1873, the thirteenth year of his father, David Willard North, a farm boy who daringly invades the den of a timber wolf to claim one of her whelps. His devotion to the young wolf-dog leads to confrontations with his stern, Bible-quoting father and certain members of their conservative farming community. He finds vital support and inspiration, however, from their brilliant neighbor, the great Swedish American naturalist Thure Kumlien, who shares with the boy his immense knowledge of the natural world and his passion to preserve the unspoiled rivers and forests of the Midwest. North excels in his depiction of his immigrant ancestors: their suspicion of higher education, their belief in the common man and the work ethic, their loyalty to family, community, and their adopted land.

North was a writer of prodigious energy with a wide range of literary activities and talents. Throughout his life he reached a large audience as a syndicated columnist, literary critic in prominent newspapers, popular lecturer, author of poems, articles, and short stories that appeared in the *Dial*, *Atlantic Monthly*, *Harper's*, *Nation*, *Reader's Digest*, and other periodicals. He edited some thirty books and wrote thirty more that were published between the years 1929 and 1969. Several won national awards including the 1964 Lewis Carroll Shelf Award, the 1964 Newbery Honor, and the 1965 Aurianne Award. His best-sellers were translated into more than fifty languages.

SELECTED WORKS: North's best-known works, written for children but enjoyed by readers of all ages, are the two winners of the Dutton Animal Book Awards, *Rascal: A Memoir of a Better Era* (1963) and *The Wolfling: A Documentary Novel of the Eighteen-Seventies* (1969). Another story of a Midwestern farm boy and his pet, *So Dear to My Heart* (1947), was a bestseller along with *Rascal* and was made into a popular film in 1948, as was *Rascal* in 1969. Convinced that American children needed not only books that would entertain but also those that would give a deeper, richer sense of our nation's history, he wrote six biographies of outstanding Americans including *Abe Lincoln: Log Cabin to White House* (1956), *Thoreau of Walden Pond* (1959), and *Mark Twain and the River* (1961). Among his adult novels,

North's favorites were *Plowing on Sunday* (1934), *Night Outlasts the Whippoorwill* (1936), and *Seven against the Years* (1939). His power as a nature writer is revealed in his book of essays, *Hurry, Spring!* (1966).

**FURTHER READING:** Informative accounts of North's life and writings are found in many literary reference works including *American Novelists of Today* (1951): 326; *Third Book of Junior Authors* (1972): 210–11; *Something about the Author* 45 (1986): 155–62; and the third edition of *Twentieth-Century Children's Writers* (1989): 725–26. The majority of North's papers are held in the Manuscript Collection of the Boston University Library.

MARY JOAN MILLER                    SPRINGFIELD, OHIO

## (EDGAR WILSON) "BILL" NYE
August 25, 1850–February 22, 1896

**BIOGRAPHY:** Bill Nye, as he signed his humorous newspaper columns, was born in Shirley, Maine, the oldest of three sons, to Franklin and Elizabeth (Loring) Nye. In 1854 the family moved to the St. Croix Valley in Wisconsin, where Nye's meager public school education was supplemented by tutoring in law. He taught public school and wrote for local newspapers. Nye became editor of a paper in Laramie, Wyoming, in 1876. There he became justice of the peace and postmaster, and in 1881 he began his own paper, the *Boomerang*, which acquired a national circulation because of his humorous columns. In 1884 he returned to the St. Croix, a more congenial climate to his poor health, and began lecturing as well as writing newspaper columns. Nye moved to New York to become a full-time lecturer, then to Asheville, North Carolina, for his health. He lectured frequently with JAMES WHITCOMB RILEY, who also suffered from ill health. Nye died from complications of meningitis, a disease that had afflicted him throughout his adult life, at a time when his popularity as a comic writer and performer was nearly as great as MARK TWAIN'S. His one novel had been lost in manuscript and two plays were unsuccessful. Nye and his wife, Clara Frances (Smith), had five boys and two girls.

**SIGNIFICANCE:** The pen name Bill Nye is taken from a character in "The Heathen Chinee," by Mark Twain and Bret Harte. Like Twain, a friend and admirer, Nye was a master of poker-faced exaggeration and self-

**Bill Nye.**
Courtesy of Thomas Pribek

satire, writing newspaper burlesques at a time when small-town papers in the Midwest often had a staff humorist.

The lecture stage was even better suited to portraying a persona whose humor is based partly on not overtly recognizing his own humor. The character, if successful, seemed naturally funny, not calculated. This literary version of Western and Midwestern humor, developed by newspaper writers and lecturers such as Nye, was understated in tone, colloquial in language and subject, and subversive of proper values and manners. On stage, the seemingly dim-witted, uncultured Nye used singers or the sentimental poet Riley as foils, whose contrast made the apparently unpracticed and unorganized speaker seem even more amusing. Nye used his rural Midwestern roots for a persona who was skeptical and irreverent, gullible, homely and decent, lowbrow, awkward, and often the butt of his own jokes.

Newspaper humorists and comic lecturers like Nye reflected a cultural maturity in the

Midwestern character. On the one hand, they poked fun at pretension, snobbery, and anything suggesting Eastern arrogance, while on the other hand they laughed at Midwestern vulgarity to suggest that folks there were tough enough and self-secure enough to take a joke. A typical lecture had little continuity and sometimes avoided the announced topic. The speaker's apparent oratorical incompetence served as a unifying comic device. Nye was renowned for presenting pure nonsense free of crudity.

**SELECTED WORKS:** Collections of newspaper pieces and lectures are *Bill Nye and Boomerang* (1881), *Forty Liars and Other Lies* (1882), *Baled Hay* (1884), *Remarks, by Bill Nye* (1887), *Bill Nye's Chestnuts, Old and New* (1888), *Bill Nye's Thinks* (1888), *Bill Nye's Redbook* (1891), *Bill Nye's Sparks* (1891), and *Bill Nye's History of the United States* (1894). *A Guest at the Ludlow* (1896) and *Bill Nye's History of England* (1896), published shortly after his death, suggest his great popularity at the time. Several books with James Whitcomb Riley contain material published elsewhere.

**FURTHER READING:** David B. Kesterson's *Bill Nye* (1981) is a critical biography. Nye's style as writer and performer is described in Thomas Pribek's "Bill Nye as Comic Lecturer," in *Old Northwest* 13 (1987): 131–41. An autobiography, *Bill Nye: His Own Life Story* (1926), compiled by Frank Wilson Nye, consists of sketches from Nye's lectures and columns. Letters and other papers by Nye are held at the University of Wyoming Library.

THOMAS PRIBEK

UNIVERSITY OF WISCONSIN–LACROSSE

# RUSSEL B. NYE.
*See* appendix (1978)

# O-R

## JOYCE CAROL OATES
June 16, 1938
(Rosamond Smith)

**BIOGRAPHY:** Novelist, short story writer, critic, poet, editor, and dramatist, Joyce Carol Oates was born in Millersport, New York, to working-class parents. Her father, Frederic J. Oates, was a tool-and-die designer, her mother, Carolina (Bush) Oates, a homemaker. Oates's family lived on her grandparents' farm in Erie County, New York. This background may partially account for her sensitivity to the struggles of working-class characters portrayed in some of her fiction, but Oates describes her own relatively quiet life as "a study in conventionality" (Johnson, *Understanding* 23).

As a child she enjoyed reading and soon began writing her own stories. She first submitted a novel for publication when she was fifteen, but the publishing company found the book too depressing for a young adult market. Oates earned a scholarship to Syracuse University, was the valedictorian of her class, and graduated Phi Beta Kappa in 1960.

Although Oates has called upstate New York "Midwestern," her direct connection to the Midwest begins with her graduate school experience. In 1961 she earned a master's degree in English from the University of Wisconsin. There she met Raymond J. Smith Jr., whom she married on January 23, 1961. After a year in Texas, the couple relocated to Detroit in 1962, a choice that had a profound effect on Oates's fiction. She wrote that Detroit "made me the person I am, consequently the writer I am—for better or worse" ("Visions of Detroit" 308).

Oates taught at the University of Detroit, as an instructor from 1962 to 1965, then as an assistant professor until 1967. A move across the Detroit River brought her to the University of Windsor in Ontario, where she and her husband both taught until 1978. During this period, Oates published an average of two books per year, including her highly acclaimed novels of psychological and social realism set in Detroit. In 1978 Oates was appointed writer in residence at Princeton University. She became a professor there in 1981 and currently serves as Roger S. Berlind Distinguished Professor.

Between 1963 and 1996, Oates won twenty-five first-place O. Henry Short Story Awards, including two special awards for continuing achievement. During the same time period, she also placed stories in sixteen of the annual Best American Short Stories anthologies, and she served as the editor of the 1979 volume.

Among her many other awards are these: a National Book Award for *them* in 1970, grants from the National Endowment for the Arts in 1966 and 1968, the Bobst Award for Lifetime Achievement in fiction in 1990, the Bram Stoker Award for Lifetime Achievement in 1994, a 1996 Bram Stoker Award for Superior Achievement in a novel, *Zombie*, and in 1996 a PEN/Malamud Award for Lifetime Achievement in the short story.

**SIGNIFICANCE:** Oates is the most prolific of major contemporary American writers. By 1995, thirty years into her career, she had authored more than seventy-five books and edited several more. She is noted for her exploration of the dark side of the human psyche and her ability to render a sense of the terror underlying ordinary living. Early critical response placed Oates in the company of American Southern writers, especially William Faulkner, Eudora Welty, and Flannery O'-Connor, because of the apparently sudden eruptions of violence in the fictional, rural Eden County settings of her short stories.

Oates's fiction reflects a Midwestern focus beginning with the stories in *The Wheel of Love* (1970) and *Marriages and Infidelities* (1972) and with her National Book Award–winning novel *them* (1969). Her work of this period shows a shift in emphasis, away from characters isolated by their rural surroundings to characters isolated by social and psychological forces within crowded urban or affluent suburban areas. Settings include unspecified Ohio cities and the Madison, Wisconsin, of her graduate student experience. Such settings provide a backdrop for characters ill at ease with some aspect of their lives. Some academics and professionals, for example, concentrate on their careers while repressing personal emotions. Others are adolescents or housewives neglected by career-obsessed husbands and fathers and consequently unfulfilled both emotionally and professionally.

Setting becomes a more central concern in her works about Detroit, especially the Detroit immediately before and after the 1967 riots. Oates wrote in an essay in the 1986 *Michigan Quarterly Review* that Detroit is "the quintessential American city" (308). This label, however, is no accolade. In *them*, as in three of her most frequently anthologized short stories, life in Detroit is a struggle. Jules Wendall in *them*, for example, struggles for a sense of per-

Joyce Carol Oates.
Photo © Nancy Crampton

sonal dignity and identity because the social order Detroit represents is in its death throes. At the conclusion of *them*, Loretta Wendall, Jules' mother, finds that Detroit is "a carnival that had gotten stuck." A few characters manage to find a pocket of fragile and perhaps self-deluding safety in a Catholic university, as do Sister Irene in "In the Region of Ice" and Father Hoffman, Ilena's nemesis, in "The Dead." Others retreat to the suburbs of Grosse Pointe or Bloomfield Hills, most notably the narrator in "How I Contemplated the Detroit House of Correction and Began My Life Over." Greg Johnson, Oates's authorized biographer, argues that these stories are notable for their "riveting psychological intensity and an authoritative, all-inclusive vision of what American experience is really like for people who suffer various kinds of emotional turmoil and who, like the title characters in *them*, become emblematic of America as a whole" (*Understanding* 16).

Oates's later work includes a series of novels that explore the possibilities and limitations of various sub-genres, especially the gothic. With *Childwold* (1976) Oates returns to her rural Eden County, New York. Most of the fiction since the late 1970s has New York or

New England settings. One of the exceptions is *Zombie* (1995). This novel was first inspired by a spate of serial killings that occurred some twenty years earlier in Michigan. Oates disclosed in an interview at San Francisco's City Arts and Lecture series that she "wanted to write a novel about the terror and the despair of living in the community where this was going on and being so helpless" (http://www .salon1999.com/06/departments/litchat.html). Oates, however, discarded her early drafts, judging them unsuccessful, and returned to work on this project again only much later.

**SELECTED WORKS:** Among more than twenty short story collections, *The Wheel of Love* (1970) and *Marriages and Infidelities* (1972) have the greatest concentration of stories with Midwestern settings. Among the novels, *them* (1969), with its Detroit setting, is part of a trilogy that aims at a comprehensive view of American social landscapes. The other books in the trilogy are *A Garden of Earthly Delights* (1967), with a rural focus, and *Expensive People* (1967), set in suburbia. *Do with Me What You Will* (1973) returns to urban Detroit. Oates's essay "Visions of Detroit" is in the *Michigan Quarterly Review* 25 (1986): 308–11.

**FURTHER READING:** Greg Johnson offers a thorough reading of Oates's work during her Midwestern years in his *Understanding Joyce Carol Oates* (1987). He concentrates on the short fiction in *Joyce Carol Oates: A Study of the Short Fiction* (1994). Written after Johnson studied the Oates's manuscript collection at Syracuse University, he brings to this analysis an awareness about Oates missing from much earlier Oates criticism: she revises extensively. Johnson has also written about Oates's later novels in *A Reader's Guide to the Recent Novels of Joyce Carol Oates* (1996).

Eileen Teper Bender's study of Oates's novels, *Joyce Carol Oates: Artist in Residence* (1987), includes an insightful analysis of how Detroit figures in *them*. James R. Giles also writes about *them* in "Suffering, Transcendence, and Artistic 'Form': Joyce Carol Oates's *them*," in *Arizona Quarterly* 32 (1976): 213–26.

Margaret Rozga's essay "Threatening Places, Hiding Places: The Midwest in Selected Stories by Joyce Carol Oates" appeared in *Midwestern Miscellany* 18 (1990): 34–44. Rozga also writes about "The Lady with the Pet Dog" and "The Dead" in "Joyce Carol Oates: Reimagining the Masters, or A Woman's Place Is in Her Own Fiction," in *American Women Short Story Writers: A Collection of Critical Essays*, edited by Julie Brown (1995).

Articles on other Detroit stories include Sue Simpson Park's "A Study of Counterpoint: Joyce Carol Oates's 'How I Contemplated the World from the Detroit House of Correction and Began My Life Over Again,'" in *Modern Fiction Studies* 22 (1976): 213–24, and an analysis of "In the Region of Ice," William Liston's article entitled "Her Brother's Keeper," in *Southern Humanities Review* 11 (1977): 195–203.

Biographical information about Oates can be found in *Current Biography Yearbook* (1994) and in *Contemporary Authors* (1995). Updated information is available on the Joyce Carol Oates home page: http://storm.usfca .edu/%7Esoutherr/toc.html.

Oates's papers and manuscripts are located at Syracuse University.

MARGARET ROZGA

UNIVERSITY OF WISCONSIN–WAUKESHA

# (WILLIAM) TIM(OTHY) O'BRIEN
October 1, 1946

**BIOGRAPHY:** Tim O'Brien was born in Austin, Minnesota, to William Timothy and Ava Eleanor (Schultz) O'Brien, both naval veterans of World War II. When O'Brien was nine, the family moved cross-state to Worthington, which figures prominently in his writing. From Worthington, O'Brien went to Macalester College, where he developed a reputation as a social and educational reformer and was elected student-body president. A month after graduating *summa cum laude* in 1968, O'Brien received his draft notice. He spent that summer pounding the typewriter in his Worthington home, caught between conflicting claims of conscience and community. Finally O'Brien enlisted. He joined the 198th Infantry Brigade in Vietnam in February 1969 and left Vietnam in March 1970, with a Purple Heart, the rank of sergeant, an honorable discharge, and his material and a mission as a writer.

Although enrolled in a Harvard graduate program in government, O'Brien spent the summers of 1971 and 1972 interning with the *Washington Post,* for which he worked full time in 1973–74. After separate publication in several newspapers and magazines, including *Playboy*, his Vietnam memoirs became his first book, *If I Die in a Combat Zone,* which was published in 1973, the year he married Ann Elizabeth Weller. A second novel, *Northern Lights,* was published two years later to mixed reviews. In 1976 O'Brien left Harvard without a degree to pursue his writing career, settling in the Boston area. Chapters from what would become *Going after Cacciato* (1978) won O. Henry Awards in 1976 and 1978; the book itself received a long and admiring review from John Updike in the *New Yorker* and won the 1978 National Book Award over John Irving's *The World according to Garp. The Nuclear Age* (1985), O'Brien's tale of a draft-dodger-turned-terrorist, met with mixed reviews, but *The Things They Carried* (1990) won the National Magazine Award in fiction for its title section, published first in *Esquire,* then made the *New York Times Book Review*'s "Editor's Choice: Best Books of 1990." A collection of twenty-two interlocked stories, it is probably O'Brien's most compelling work to date. *In the Lake of the Woods* (1994), a mystery set in northern Minnesota, went to three printings in hardback before appearing in paperback.

Among his many literary awards, O'Brien has received fellowships from the Guggenheim Foundation and the National Endowment for the Arts.

**SIGNIFICANCE:** O'Brien's work is bipolar. His primary material is undeniably the Vietnam War and its short- and long-term impact on those who fought it. However, two of his novels are set in Minnesota and another in Montana. Even Vietnam—the outer edge of reality—is measured against a physical and moral landscape back home, a center, a geography familiar to residents of the Middle Border. "His book could stand very honorably as an unsensational and sensitive introduction to American 'provincial' life," notes Rosellen Brown in her February 7, 1976, *New Republic* review of *Northern Lights* (27).

O'Brien's work also exhibits stylistic and thematic dualities: his formal experiments, surrealism, and insistence on the impossibility of knowing suggest postmodernism and magical realism, but his work owes more to ERNEST HEMINGWAY than to Joseph Heller. O'Brien's repeated insistence on ideas in fiction—what Daniel Zins in "Imaging the Read: The Fiction of Tim O'Brien" calls "the exploration of substantive, important human

values" (2)—is an assertion of Midwest realism in an age still under the influence of postmodernist stylistics.

*Northern Lights,* a coming-of-age novel set in Sawmill Landing, Minnesota, describes the rivalry between Paul Milton Perry and his Vietnam veteran older brother Harvey; Paul's difficulties with his wife, Faith, and his attraction to the young, free-spirited, and thoroughly intimidating Addi; and Paul's passage to Hemingwayesque manhood during the brothers' ski excursion through the uncharted Arrowhead region. This long, climactic scene is one of Minnesota's finest blizzard survival stories. Sawmill Landing has a fictional history nearly as good as that of GARRISON KEILLOR's Lake Wobegon, and O'Brien includes a number of Iowa jokes popular among Minnesotans.

Minnesota's Boundary Waters and the town of Worthington play prominent roles in *If I Die in a Combat Zone* and *The Things They Carried.* The section "On the Rainy River," with O'Brien in the Boundary Waters contemplating desertion to Canada, is, however, a fiction. The narrator's childhood memories in *Going after Cacciato* are of western Wisconsin. O'Brien set *The Nuclear Age* in Fort Derry, Montana, but returns to Minnesota for his structurally innovative mystery *In the Lake of the Woods,* a sensitive examination of the disastrous effects of My Lai on the career, marriage, and life of fictional magician-lawyer-lieutenant governor John Wade.

O'Brien's Midwest functions as a system of values. It can be bedrock baseball practical, dead-end normal, nice bordering on prissy, nearly mad with patriotic and evangelical fervor. Yet it is also patient, compassionate, enduring, and, in its own way, sane. Small-town Midwest values offer something against which O'Brien can rebel: the Lutheran minister-father planning his nuclear fallout shelter in *Northern Lights,* the uncomprehending hometown patriotism of *Northern Lights* and *The Things They Carried,* the smothering neighborliness of *In the Lake of the Woods.* However, they also offer ballast which keeps O'Brien the novelist from spinning off into inconsequential mysteries of pure text.

**SELECTED WORKS:** No collection of O'Brien's stories has been published; Ian McMeechan lists uncollected stories to 1990 in "Tim O'Brien," *Contemporary Novelists* (5th ed., 1991),

705–706. O'Brien's major works are *If I Die in a Combat Zone, Box Me Up and Ship Me Home* (1973; revised ed. 1979), *Northern Lights* (1975, presently out of print), *Going after Cacciato* (1978), *The Nuclear Age* (1985), *The Things They Carried* (1990), and *In the Lake of the Woods* (1994).

**FURTHER READING:** Steven Kaplan's *Understanding Tim O'Brien* (1995) offers the only book-length study to date and a bibliography. Ronald Baron's *A Guide to Minnesota Authors* (revised ed., 1993) and *Current Biography Yearbook* 56 (1995): 441–45 contain shorter overviews of O'Brien's career. Article-length critiques include Maria S. Bonn's "Can Stories Save Us?" in *Critique* (Fall 1994): 2–14, and Daniel Zins's "Imaging the Read: The Fiction of Tim O'Brien," in *Hollins Critic* (June 1986): 1–12. Collected reviews and criticisms may be found in *Contemporary Literary Criticism* 7, 19, and 40.

DAVID PICHASKE          SOUTHWEST STATE UNIVERSITY

## MARY OLIVER
September 10, 1935

**BIOGRAPHY:** Born in Cleveland, Ohio, to Edward William and Helen M. (Vlasak) Oliver, Mary Oliver attended Ohio State University and Vassar College. She has taught as a visiting professor at Case Western Reserve University, the University of Cincinnati, Bucknell University, and Sweet Briar College. She now teaches at Bennington College.

Oliver held fellowships from the National Endowment for the Arts (1972–73) and the Guggenheim (1980–81). She won the Pulitzer Prize in 1984 for *American Primitive* and the National Book Award for poetry in 1992 for *New and Selected Poems*.

**SIGNIFICANCE:** Oliver writes mainly about her encounters with nature and the resulting insights into the interconnections among all elements of the natural world.

Several of the early poems are set in Ohio. The title poem of her second volume, *The River Styx, Ohio* (1972), presents a bleak encounter with multiple levels of mortality. The speaker drives through Ohio in October with her aging mother and grandmother, sees bankrupt farms, and looks "for freedom, but the measure's set" (*New and Selected Poems* 240).

Other poems examine facts of American history for insight into what so set the measure against freedom. "Tecumseh" in *American Primitive* (1983) is one of these. The speaker compares "wounds of the past" to "litter that snags among the yellow branches" (77). As she imagines the Indian leader Tecumseh's struggle for freedom, however, she finds a glimmer of hope in the fact that "his body could not be found" (78). This opens the possibility of Tecumseh's being found again, still "so angry" (78).

Poems in subsequent volumes value learning from both history and nature and move toward seeing a more fluid boundary between one's self and the natural world. The conclusion, for example, to "White Flowers" in *New and Selected Poems* celebrates being near "that porous line / where my own body was done with / and the roots and the stems and the flowers / began" (59).

**SELECTED WORKS:** Oliver's first volume of poems, *No Voyage, and Other Poems*, was published by Dent in 1963 and reissued in an expanded edition by Houghton in 1965. Her books with the strongest Midwestern flavor are *The River Styx, Ohio, and Other Poems* (1972), *The Night Traveler* (1978), *Sleeping in the Forest* (1979), and *American Primitive* (1983). *New and Selected Poems* (1992) includes poems from all of her earlier volumes.

**FURTHER READING:** No book-length studies of Oliver's poetry have yet been published. Douglas Burton-Christie argues, in his article "Nature, Spirit, and Imagination in the Poetry of Mary Oliver" (*Cross Currents* 46 [Spring 1996]: 77–88), that Oliver sees and appreciates natural things in their particularity as well as for their symbolic significance."

In her extended article "Into the Body of Another: Mary Oliver and the Poetics of Becoming Other," Vicki Graham compares the relationship to nature depicted in Oliver's work to that found in Native American poets. Both express a desire for unity with the natural world, but Oliver pulls back from the melding of her individual psyche with natural forms. This well-reasoned argument is found in *Papers on Language and Literature* 30.4 (Fall 1994): 352–73.

Janet McNew sees Oliver as representing a more feminist conception of nature rather than viewing the natural world as "Other." Her views are presented in "Mary Oliver and the Tradition of Romantic Nature Poetry," in *Contemporary Literature* 30 (1989): 59–77.

In his review of *American Primitive*, Bruce Bennett sees Oliver's work as comparable to

James Wright's in its "emotional intensity, directness and clarity, as well as the way they evoke Ohio, explore American themes and incorporate the visionary" ("Three Poets," in *New York Times Book Review,* July 17, 1983, 101).

MARGARET ROZGA

UNIVERSITY OF WISCONSIN–WAUKESHA

## TILLIE (LERNER) OLSEN
January 14, 1912 or 1913

**BIOGRAPHY:** Tillie Olsen was born in Nebraska in 1912 or 1913; she says "she comes from a family that didn't have birth certificates" (Orr 25). Her parents, Samuel and Ida (Beber) Lerner, were Russian Jews who emigrated after the 1905 revolution to New York and then to Nebraska. She grew up in a radical Jewish community in Omaha, to which her family of active socialists moved before she began elementary school. Her education, frequently interrupted by illness and the necessity to work for family support, ended after eleventh grade. In an ongoing struggle for economic security, Olsen worked as a waitress, packing house worker, cook, warehouse checker, hotel room cleaner, and journalist. She joined the Young Communist League in 1931; assisted with labor organizing, for which she was jailed; and participated in numerous activities supporting justice for the working class. She moved to California in 1933 and in 1944 married Jack Olsen, with whom she had established a relationship in the 1930s; he died in 1989. Olsen began writing in young adulthood, notably journals, a novel, and political pieces; however, the need to support her family of four daughters prevented her from giving significant time to writing until the 1950s and 1960s.

Immediately before and since the 1962 book publication of four previously published short stories, grants from the Guggenheim and Ford Foundations, National Endowment for the Arts, the MacDowell Colony, and others enabled her to dedicate more time to writing. In the past three decades, Olsen has been writer in residence at Amherst and Massachusetts Institute of Technology, visiting lecturer at Stanford and the University of California, San Diego, International Visiting Scholar for several Norwegian universities, and visiting professor at various other universities. She has also received a number of impressive awards and honors including

Tillie Olsen.
Photo © Nancy Crampton

honorary degrees and a citation for distinguished contribution to American literature from the American Academy and National Institute of Arts and Letters.

**SIGNIFICANCE:** Despite her relatively small total output including journalistic works and fiction, Olsen has achieved a remarkably distinguished position as spokeswoman, model, and mentor for women writers. She has both uncovered the works of women ignored, lost, and devalued in the past and championed the writing of women struggling to emerge in the present. Social class and gender are ultimately more significant in her writing than region, though her Midwestern roots are evident in several works, especially *Yonnondio* (1974), which she began writing at age nineteen but was not able to continue until forty years later. In this novel the Holbrook family fights an endless war against brutal poverty, stretching from the coal mines of Wyoming to the tenant farms of South Dakota and into Midwestern urban packing houses.

The stories collected in *Tell Me a Riddle* (1962) include many autobiographical experiences, though Olsen resists explicit linking of fiction to her life. Most important to her as a feminist working-class writer is revealing in uniquely powerful prose the drudgery, futility, pain, energy, endurance, and ultimate survival in lives of those trapped on the margins. Striving constantly to erase the silences imposed upon the oppressed and inarticulate, especially on women, Olsen offers vivid portraits, including those of Anna Holbrook, who is crushed repeatedly by poverty and abuse; the mother-narrator in "I Stand Here Ironing," haunted by regrets in raising her daughter; the Russian immigrant grandmother in "Tell Me a Riddle," who yearns to live at the end according to her *own* rhythm. Olsen has been especially acclaimed for honoring people on the edges of society, believing in their potential, giving them voice, and writing their truths. The words of Margaret Atwood convey the conviction of many readers: for Olsen "'respect' is too pale a word: 'reverence' is more like it" (Pearlman and Werlock ix).

**SELECTED WORKS:** *Tell Me a Riddle* (1962), a collection of four stories, is Olsen's highly praised first publication. "Requa," in *Iowa Review* (Summer 1970), is the first part of a novella, not yet completed. Her "Biographical Interpretation" accompanies the re-publication of *Life in the Iron Mills* by Rebecca Harding Davis (1972), a work which Olsen rescued from obscurity. Among Olsen's works, the novel *Yonnondio: From the Thirties* (1974) focuses most explicitly on the Midwestern scene. *Silences* (1978), a widely read and acclaimed collection of essays and lectures, explores the multiple struggles of women writers. *Mother to Daughter, Daughter to Mother* (1984) is a daybook and reader "selected and shaped" by Olsen. Her "Mothers and Daughters" (with daughter, Julie Olsen Edwards) appears in *Mothers and Daughters: That Special Quality, An Exploration in Photographs*, coedited with Edwards and Estelle Jussim (1987).

**FURTHER READING:** Valuable book-length studies include Abigail Martin's *Tillie Olsen* (1984), Elaine Neil Orr's *Tillie Olsen and a Feminist Spiritual Vision* (1987), Mickey Pearlman and Abby H. P. Werlock's *Tillie Olsen* (1991), Mara Faulkner's *Protest and Possibility in the Writing of Tillie Olsen* (1993), and *The Critical Response to Tillie Olsen*, edited by Kay Hoyle Nelson and Nancy Huse (1994). The latter is an especially helpful overview with an excellent, extensive bibliography. A study by Constance Coiner, *Better Red: The Writing and Resistance of*

*Tillie Olsen and Meridel Le Sueur* (1995), links two women writers who have dedicated their careers to giving voices to the silenced poor. The principal repository of Olsen's papers is the Stanford University Library. Selected papers, especially those related to *Yonnondio*, are in the Berg Collection of the New York Public Library. The Harry Ransom Humanities Research Center at the University of Texas, Austin, holds a typed manuscript of *Yonnondio*.

SARA MCALPIN BVM        CLARKE COLLEGE

## SIGURD F(ERDINAND) OLSON
### April 4, 1899–January 13, 1982

**BIOGRAPHY:** Born in Chicago to Lawrence J. and Ida May (Cedarholm) Olson, Sigurd Olson remained a Midwesterner throughout his life. In 1921 he married Elizabeth Dorothy Uhrenholdt, with whom he had two children, Sigurd Thorn and Robert Keith. Olson attended Northland College in Wisconsin from 1916 to 1918. He received a bachelor's degree from the University of Wisconsin in 1920 and an MS from the University of Illinois in 1931. He taught biology at Ely Junior College in Minnesota from 1922 to 1935, also serving as department head and then as dean from 1936 to 1945. During World War II, Olson served in the U.S. Army Information and Education Division. During his subsequent career as a freelance writer, lecturer, and environmentalist, Olson was a consultant to the U.S. Department of the Interior and numerous organizations and publishers. Olson is most noted for his efforts on the Quetico-Superior Council to preserve the Minnesota-Ontario North Woods as wilderness, culminating in the Wilderness Act of 1964. He was also president of the National Parks Association from 1954 to 1960.

Olson's writings and activities brought him much honor, including awards from the American Library Association, the Boy Scouts of America, the Isaak Walton League, and the Sierra Club, and honorary degrees from Northland College, Carleton College, Macalaster College, and Hamline University. He died after suffering a heart attack while snowshoeing near his home in Ely.

**SIGNIFICANCE:** Sigurd Olson is the most significant literary voice defining the Superior National Forest region of Minnesota ecologically, aesthetically, and spiritually. From his first major book, *The Singing Wilderness* (1956), Olson advocated a felt union with wilderness, positing that, with mindful attunement to the wilderness, one can almost literally hear it "singing" and effect a communion with the earth, providing peace and contentment. Olson's message is ethical as well as spiritual, for this attunement will give humanity pause as it attempts to manipulate an environment that should not, and ultimately cannot, be controlled.

Olson's message is no mere ecological abstraction, however. He grounds his ideas, literally, in the woods, lakes, and muskeg of a very specific place: the Minnesota North Woods. During his life, he traveled, by foot and canoe, thousands of miles of the Superior region. His intimate knowledge of the region and its expression in writing go beyond reportage of natural detail. Olson peels back layers of memory as he reveals understanding of self, place, history, and myth.

A typical essay describes a natural scene and then moves on to more metaphysical connections with the landscape, as when canoe paddler, paddle, and water are tightly merged in what Olson calls "the Way of the Canoe." Olson often connects the described experience with a personal memory, especially in an attempt to recapture a childlike wonder. He expresses an affiliation with the eighteenth-century voyageurs, the ancient Ojibwe residents, or the deepest mythological connection of all, Olson's ancient Finnish ancestors. Ultimately, the most transcendent connection with the earth is with the prehuman; listening to a frog chorus, for example, connects one with a music from the past more pure than anything possible in the modern day. Olson often comes full circle in his essays, returning to a transcendent ideal, moving beyond the ancient frog chorus to a world of spirit and peace that approaches God. Perhaps more than anyone else, Sigurd Olson is able to take his readers through layers of memory and experience, grounded in a wholly Midwestern place, that provide a literary journey from the decidedly local to the unquestionably transcendent.

**SELECTED WORKS:** Olson's major books include *The Singing Wilderness* (1956), *Listening Point* (1958), *The Lonely Land* (1961), *Runes of the North* (1963), the autobiography *Open Horizons* (1969), *Sigurd F. Olson's Wilderness Days* (1972),

and *Of Time and Place* (1982). Some of Olson's earlier writings were collected by Voyageur Press of Stillwater, Minnesota, in two volumes of *The Collected Works of Sigurd F. Olson*, edited by Mike Link: *The Early Writings: 1921–1934* (1988) and *The College Years: 1935–1944* (1990).

**FURTHER READING:** The major source on Sigurd Olson is David Backes's biography *A Wilderness Within: The Life of Sigurd F. Olson* (1997). Olson is discussed at some length in environmental histories including R. Newell Searle's *Saving Quetico-Superior: A Land Set Apart* (1977) and John C. Miles's *Guardians of the Parks: A History of the National Parks and Conservation Association* (1995). One of the few articles on Olson is Sanford E. Marovitz's "The Romantic Echoes of Sigurd F. Olson: Conservationist with a Fly Rod," *Old Northwest* 16.2 (Summer 1993): 107–19. Sigurd Olson's papers are archived at the Minnesota Historical Society in St. Paul.

THOMAS K. DEAN                    UNIVERSITY OF IOWA

## DONALD S. PADY.
*See* appendix (1984)

## SARA PARETSKY
June 8, 1947

**BIOGRAPHY:** Detective story writer Sara Paretsky was born in Iowa to David and Mary (Edwards) Paretsky and raised in Lawrence, Kansas. She took her undergraduate degree from the University of Kansas in political science in 1967 and in 1977 earned both an MBA and a doctorate in history from the University of Chicago. Paretsky settled in that city, married Courtenay Wright, with whom she has had three children, and entered the corporate domain, where she held several managerial positions in large businesses.

During these years, from 1977 to 1986, Paretsky worked independently on a second career as a novelist. An avid reader of detective fiction, she gravitated to the mystery genre. In 1982 she published *Indemnity Only*, the first in a highly successful series of novels featuring private investigator V. I. Warshawski. By 1986 she had retired from business to devote herself exclusively to writing, and she has now authored eight full-length Warshawski mysteries and numerous short stories featuring the character. She continues to live and write in Chicago. Paretsky is the cofounder of Sisters in Crime, a national association dedicated to advancing opportunities for women mystery writers. She has been widely honored for her fiction and in 1988 was given the Silver Dagger Award by the Crime Writers Association. She received the Society for the Study of Midwestern Literature's 1996 Mark Twain Award for outstanding contributions to Midwestern literature.

**SIGNIFICANCE:** Sara Paretsky is among the most important and influential crime writers practicing today. Her novels are at the vanguard of feminist revisions of the hard-boiled mystery tradition. Paretsky's interest in creating a feminist detective was prodded by her experiences in the patriarchal world of corporate business, where she witnessed egregious gender inequities. Influenced by her reading of writers such as Raymond Chandler and Dashiell Hammett, she set out to challenge those authors' misogynist portrayals of women as conniving temptresses. Paretsky created the tough-talking, streetwise V. I. as a female revision of the prototypical hard-boiled sleuth, but her character was endowed from the beginning with a nuanced personal history and a complex nature that transcends her formulaic roots. As a feminist, Warshawski's professional mission is ultimately to assist, vindicate, or redeem society's victims, usually women. Paretsky deftly interweaves V. I.'s familial life and female friendships into the narrative, making a convoluted matrix of human relationships in which reside both the mystery at hand and its solution.

Paretsky's corporate background has also inspired her plots, many of which focus on institutional wrongdoing. *Indemnity Only* (1982) addresses corruption in the insurance business; *Deadlock* (1984) probes financial misdeeds among shipping magnates; *Killing Orders* (1986) discovers criminal linkages between the Catholic Church, organized crime, and high finance. Subsequent novels uncover villainy in established spheres such as medicine (*Bitter Medicine*, 1987); industry (*Blood Shot*, 1988); politics and law enforcement (*Burn Marks*, 1990); and urban social services (*Guardian Angel*, 1992; and *Tunnel Vision*, 1994). Underlying the exposure of criminality in traditional institutions is Paretsky's articulation of the kind of humane ethic often seen as endemic to heartland values, along

Sara Paretsky.
Courtesy of Sara Paretsky

with a feminist celebration of a communal rather than a hierarchical social order.

The Chicago setting of Paretsky's fiction has impressed that city sharply in the literary imagination of her readership. From V. I.'s apartment near Wrigley Field to her motorized treks along the lakeshore, through the Loop, and around the serpentine network of freeways, the detective's daily odysseys through the city endow the novels with a piquant sense of place that rivals the regional sensibilities of the best American authors.

**SELECTED WORKS:** Paretsky's eight V. I. Warshawski novels include *Indemnity Only* (1982); *Deadlock* (1984); *Killing Orders* (1986); *Bitter Medicine* (1987); *Blood Shot* (1988; published as *Toxic Shock* in England); *Burn Marks* (1990); *Guardian Angel* (1992); and *Tunnel Vision* (1994). She has also published a number of uncollected short stories, an anthology of Warshawski tales, *Windy City Blues* (1995), and several edited collections of mystery stories by various hands, including *Beastly Tales* (1989), *A Woman's Eye* (1990), and *Women on the Case* (1997). A 1998 novel, *Ghost Country*, departs from the street-wise world of V. I. to the domain of magic and miracles and introduces a pair of moneyed sisters who prove unlikely but capable sleuths.

**FURTHER READING:** Paretsky's fiction is frequently discussed in critical studies of feminist detection and mentioned regularly in the popular press. While there is no booklength study of Paretsky, substantive treatments of the author and her work include JANE S. BAKERMAN's "Living 'Openly and with Dignity': Sara Paretsky's New-Boiled Feminist Fiction," in *MidAmerica* 12 (1985): 120–35; Maureen Reddy's *Sisters in Crime: Feminism and the Crime Novel* (1988); Kathleen Klein's *The Woman Detective: Gender and Genre* (1988); Linda S. Wells's "Popular Literature and Postmodernism: Sara Paretsky's Hard-Boiled Feminist," in *Proteus* 6.1 (Spring 1989): 51–56; Patricia E. Johnson's "Sex and Betrayal in the Detective Fiction of Sue Grafton and Sara Paretsky," in *Journal of Popular Culture* 27.4 (Spring 1994): 97–106; and Rebecca A. Pope's "'Friends Is a Weak Word for It': Female Friendship and the Spectre of Lesbianism in Sara Paretsky," in *Feminism and Women's Detective Fiction*, edited by Glenwood Irons (1995).

LIAHNA BABENER

CENTRAL WASHINGTON UNIVERSITY

## GORDON (ALEXANDER BUCHANAN) PARKS

November 30, 1912

**BIOGRAPHY:** Gordon Alexander Buchanan Parks, photographer, writer, film director, and poet, was born in Fort Scott, Kansas. His parents, Andrew Jackson Parks and Sarah (Ross) Parks, were poor African Americans who struggled to raise a large family. Early in life he was aware of the racist attitudes that divided the small town and that sometimes were directed against him, his family, and his friends. After his mother's death, he moved to Minneapolis to live with a sister and continue his high school education. As a student, he enjoyed music and liked to draw and to write, and he resolved to become an artist, although he knew he would have to fight against discrimination to win artistic recognition.

While working as a sleeping-car porter on the Northern Pacific run to Seattle, he bought a camera and studied photography. After some success with his camera work in Min-

neapolis, he moved with his family to Chicago in 1940, where he was offered space in an art center in which to work as a photographer. The following year he won a Julius Rosenwald Fellowship to work as a staff photographer for the Farm Security Administration in Washington, D.C. Mentored by Roy Stryker, director of the FSA, Parks went on to photograph a segregated group of African American pilots—the 332nd Fighter Group. After the war, Stryker worked for Standard Oil, and he brought Parks, barred by Jim Crow from the major magazines, along with him. In 1947 Parks published his first book, *Flash Photography*, and in 1949 he was given the now famous assignment by *Life* magazine (a first for an African American) to photograph gang members in Harlem. His photography led to a full-time job with *Life* that would last for twenty years and take him to all parts of the world.

In 1963 Parks published *The Learning Tree*, an autobiographical novel about growing up as an African American in Kansas; *A Choice of Weapons*, the first part of his three-volume autobiography, was published in 1966. *The Learning Tree* was made into a movie directed by Parks in 1968, and he made several other films for Hollywood, including *Leadbelly* in 1975. He married Sally Alvis in 1933, whom he divorced in 1961. They had three children, Gordon Jr., Toni, and David. He was subsequently married to Elizabeth Cambell in 1962 (divorced in 1973) and Genevieve Young (divorced in 1977). His daughter, Leslie, is the child of his marriage to Elizabeth Cambell.

He has composed concertos and sonatas performed in the United States and Europe and has received many honors. In 1991 he was awarded the President's Medal by Wichita State University, Wichita, Kansas.

**SIGNIFICANCE:** *The Learning Tree* is drawn from Parks's early life in Fort Scott, Kansas, and is an American classic of its time and place. Its depiction of an African American family's life in a small Midwestern town bordering an ex-slave state is the story of the family's struggle to maintain dignity and self-respect as human beings and citizens. The boy, Newt, fights to become a man in the racist culture of the town. Parks's autobiography, *A Choice of Weapons*, recounts his struggle as a young man to reject the social definition of "black" and to succeed as an artist in the white societies of Minneapolis and Chicago. His later autobiographical works, *To Smile in Autumn* (1979) and *Voices in the Mirror* (1990), lack the force of his earlier work and are somewhat repetitive. *The Learning Tree* is regarded as his masterpiece and as a key narrative of the African American experience of growing up in the Midwest.

**SELECTED WORKS:** Parks's first published book is *Flash Photography* (1947). *The Learning Tree* (1963), a novel, is a classic of African American literature. *A Choice of Weapons* (1966), *To Smile in Autumn* (1979), and *Voices in the Mirror* (1990) constitute an autobiographical trilogy. *In Love* (1971) and *Moments without Proper Names* (1975) are volumes of poems, and *Shannon* (1981) is Parks's second novel.

**FURTHER READING:** Parks has given many interviews and is the subject of a number of magazine stories; for example, see C. Gerald Fraser's "Gordon Parks: An Artist Reminisces" in the December 3, 1975, *New York Times* (36). His works have been reviewed in the *New York Times Book Review* and other magazines. Terry Harnan writes about Parks's work with film in *Gordon Parks: Black Photographer and Film Maker* (1972).

TOM PAGE                    WICHITA STATE UNIVERSITY

## GARY PAULSEN

May 17, 1939
(Paul Garrison)

**BIOGRAPHY:** Gary Paulsen, a versatile, prolific author best known for his young adult novels, was born in Minneapolis, Minnesota, to Oscar and Eunice (Moen) Paulsen, both of Scandinavian descent. While his father served as a U.S. Army officer abroad during World War II and his mother worked in a munitions plant, Paulsen was cared for by his Norwegian American grandmother and his aunts, nurturing women who appear later in his fiction. The deeply traumatic events in his life beginning about age seven and continuing through adolescence are laid bare in his candid autobiography for adults, *Eastern Sun, Winter Moon* (1993). Living with his alcoholic parents first in the Philippines and later stateside, he received little schooling, was barely able to graduate from high school in Thief River Falls, Minnesota, and failed his courses at Bemidji State University, 1957–58. A person of prodigious energy and physical endurance, Paulsen began supporting himself at age fifteen, left home at seventeen, and throughout his life gained valuable firsthand experience of a variety of jobs: farmer, trapper, hunter, carpenter, army sergeant, aerospace engineer, editor, teacher, sculptor, sled dog breeder and trainer, as well as author.

Paulsen's apprenticeship as a writer began abruptly in 1965 when he moved to Hollywood to work on a men's magazine. He published his first book in 1966. Despite early failure in marriage and years of alcohol addiction, he wrote 140 fiction and nonfiction books, two plays, and hundreds of magazine articles in the next thirty-one years. He drew largely from the great variety of his own life experiences in his writing.

In 1971 he married the gifted artist Ruth Ellen Wright, illustrator of many of his books. With their son James they settled in northern Minnesota in 1979 where Paulsen became devoted to raising and running sled dogs, the subject of many of his books. Twice during the 1980s he raced his dogs across Alaska in the 1,180 mile Iditarod. In 1991, after he was diagnosed with heart disease, the family moved to a ranch in New Mexico, where Paulsen has continued to write at breakneck speed.

**SIGNIFICANCE:** Although Paulsen's fictional landscape extends far beyond the boundaries of the Midwest, much of his most powerful writing is drawn from his many years of experience with the places and people in his home state of Minnesota. His exact knowledge of the minute details of life in a small town, on a family farm, or in the vast wilderness and woods of the north country empowers him to create strong realistic settings for his Midwestern fiction. His characters, especially ordinary farm folk living on their ancestral land, come to life as rugged, resourceful individuals who find joy and contentment in their lives in spite of grueling work and hardships. Like Paulsen himself they are skilled hunters and trappers who live close to the earth, attuned to the rhythm of the seasons and the deep relationship between man and nature.

Paulsen's teenage protagonists often reflect his own painful adolescence in northern Minnesota. Escaping from troubled homes, usually in cities, they retreat to the healing environment of a family farm or the untamed wilderness where the forces of nature may threaten their very survival before transforming them into more mature human beings with direction in their lives. Their stories often emerge as fast-paced action novels like thirteen-year-old Brian's in the best-seller *Hatchet* (1987) or as the less suspenseful but equally powerful rite-of-passage experience of the youth in *The Foxman* (1977).

Paulsen's literary achievements have been widely recognized since 1985 when *Dogsong*, his first Newbery Honor Book, was published. His books have sold more than eight million copies and his best-sellers are translated into fifteen languages. More than a dozen of his titles have been placed on the annual lists of the American Library Association's Best Books for Children and Best Books for Young Adults. In 1997 he received the Margaret A. Edwards Award for his lifetime contribution to books for teenagers.

**SELECTED WORKS:** In the children's book *The Cookcamp* (1991), Paulsen re-creates a summer spent with his grandmother and a crew of road builders in the north woods of Minnesota when he was five. His memories of his adolescent visits with farm relatives have yielded the hilarious *Harris and Me: A Summer Remembered* (1993); the strong anti-war novel *The Foxman* (1977); and the meditative *The Winter Room* (1989), a Newbery Honor Book that affirms the bonding power of family storytelling. Paulsen's deep admiration for the Midwestern family farm as a way of life is expressed in two adult books: *Farm: A History and Celebration of the American Farmer* (1977) and the strongly autobiographical *Clabbered Dirt, Sweet Grass* (1992), which is illustrated by the luminous paintings of Ruth Wright Paulsen. *Eastern Sun, Winter Moon: An Autobiographical Odyssey* (1993) and *Father Water, Mother Woods: Essays on Hunting and Fishing in the North Woods* (1994) are important to read for an understanding of Paulsen's traumatic childhood and adolescence. His experiences running and racing sled dogs in Minnesota and Alaska in the 1980s are celebrated in the stunning picture book for children, *Dogteam* (1993), in *Woodsong* (1990) for young adults, and in his memoir, *Puppies, Dogs, and Blue Northers* (1996), all illustrated by Ruth Wright Paulsen. *Winterdance* (1994), written for adults, is a comprehensive nonfiction treatment of Paulsen's 1983 trans-Alaskan Iditarod race. *Dogsong* (1985) also had its origin in the Idi-

tarod when he met a young Inuit boy who became the protagonist in this suspenseful coming-of-age novel. His most popular survival story, *Hatchet* (1987), has two powerful sequels, *The River* (1991) and *Brian's Winter* (1996). One of Paulsen's most gripping historical novels, *Nightjohn* (1993), has its source in the account of an escaped slave who risked his life to return to the Southern plantation to teach his people to read. The story of one of his students, *Sarny: A Life Remembered* (1997), is a worthy sequel. In the powerfully realistic Civil War novella *Soldier's Heart* (1998), Paulsen reveals the horror and futility of war. Paulsen's own passion for reading and his concerns about the declining literacy rate of children have inspired him to create two entertaining, easy-to-read paperback series, the *Culpepper Adventures* and the *Gary Paulsen World of Adventure*.

**FURTHER READING:** *Presenting Gary Paulsen* (1996), by Gary M. Salvner, is a perceptive, comprehensive book-length biographical and critical study in Twayne's Young Adult Authors series. A preface, chronology, selected bibliography, photos, list of awards, and index are useful features. Informative accounts of Paulsen's life and works are found in many literary reference works including *The 100 Most Popular Young Adult Authors: Biographical Sketches and Bibliographies*, by Bernard A. Drew (1996), and *Children's Literature Review* 19 (1997). In *School Library Journal* (June 1997): 24–29, David Gale interviews Paulsen in "The Maximum Expression of Being Human," a title that reflects Paulsen's definition of learning through the reading of books (27).

MARY JOAN MILLER                    SPRINGFIELD, OHIO

# DONALD CULROSS PEATTIE
June 21, 1898–July 22, 1967

**BIOGRAPHY:** Donald Culross Peattie, botanist, nature writer, novelist, and historian, was born in Chicago into a literary family. His father, Robert Burns Peattie, was editor of the *Chicago Tribune's* literary page, and his mother, Elia (Wilkinson) Peattie, was a well-known *Tribune* book reviewer as well as a novelist. Young Peattie worked as a reporter and attended the University of Chicago (1916–18), then worked for a publisher in New York and finished his education at Harvard, where he graduated *cum laude* in 1922. Interested in natural science and literature, he worked as a botanist for the Department of Agriculture but left in 1926 to do freelance writing. He married novelist Louise Redfield in 1923, and they had four children.

Peattie wrote a nature column for the *Washington Star* from 1924 to 1935, and his first book, *Cargoes and Harvests*, focused on economic botany, appeared in 1926. Two years later he took his family to southern France, where they lived at Vence and Menton for five years while he struggled to launch his career as a fiction writer. He wrote a few unimportant novels there and a popular history of Vence, published in 1930, which appeared in a revised, American edition as *Immortal Village* (1945). After returning to America, the Peatties moved to the Chicago area, settling at Kennicott's Grove, a Glenview nature preserve where Louise had been raised. She set one of her novels there, and Peattie produced a classic of American nature writing, *An Almanac for Moderns* (1935), based on his observations there. It was widely acclaimed and gave him a national reputation. He wrote several other nature-related books at the Grove, including *Green Laurels: The Lives and Achievements of the Great Naturalists* (1935), *A Book of Hours* (1937), and *A Prairie Grove* (1938). He also wrote a nature column for the *Chicago Daily News* as well as historical books for children.

In the late 1930s the Peatties moved to Santa Barbara, California, where he wrote a column called "The Nature of Things" for *Bird Lore* and produced such well-received books as *Flowering Earth* (1939), a volume of popular science; *The Road of a Naturalist* (1941), his spiritual autobiography; and *American Heartwood* (1949), a volume of historical sketches. He also wrote two field guides to North American trees and other books. His articles for *Reader's Digest*, *Saturday Evening Post*, and other magazines made him familiar to a broad readership.

**SIGNIFICANCE:** Most of Peattie's books are of little literary interest, but *A Book of Hours* is a readable series of essays on the human spiritual condition, and *A Prairie Grove* is an inventive combination of fiction, regional history, and reflective nature writing. The latter explores and imagines the natural and human past of a stretch of wild landscape near Chicago. However, *An Almanac for Moderns* is clearly Peattie's greatest work. It consists of 365 short, often poetic essays that reflect the observations, biological knowledge, and philosophical outlook of a twentieth-century man who knows that he lives in a universe without purposeful design and without special regard for humankind. Nevertheless, during the cycle of the year, from one spring to the advent of another, he achieves a sense of harmony with the natural world and acceptance of his condition.

**SELECTED WORKS:** *Cargoes and Harvests* (1926), *An Almanac for Moderns* (1935), *Green Laurels* (1935), *A Book of Hours* (1937), *A Prairie Grove* (1938), *Flowering Earth* (1939), *The Road of a Naturalist* (1941), and his well-written guides to North American trees (1950; 1953) are his best works.

**FURTHER READING:** William H. O. Scott's "Donald Culross and Louise Redfield Peattie: A Bibliography," in *Bulletin of Bibliography* 46 (March 1989): 10–30, is the only work of scholarship on the author. Peattie's papers are at the University of California, Santa Barbara Library.

JOHN E. HALLWAS    WESTERN ILLINOIS UNIVERSITY

## ELIA W. PEATTIE

January 15, 1862–July 12, 1935
(Sade Iverson)

**BIOGRAPHY:** Elia W. Peattie—journalist, novelist, and book critic—was born in Kalamazoo, Michigan, the daughter of Amanda (Cahill) and Frederick Wilkinson. Her family moved from Kalamazoo to Chicago shortly after the Chicago fire of 1871. Peattie's unpublished memoir, "The Star Wagon," makes clear that her childhood was an unhappy one. Sidney Bremer's introduction to Peattie's 1914 novel *The Precipice* (reprinted 1989) depicts her father as overbearing and ambitious, failing in ill-conceived business ventures, and dooming the family to genteel poverty and her mother to "bitter work" and "heavy domestic burdens" (xviii). Elia was forced to quit school before completing the seventh grade.

She married Chicago journalist Robert Burns Peattie in 1883; at about the same time she became a reporter for the *Chicago Tribune*, the first woman to report for that paper and, by some accounts, Chicago's second female reporter. For the *Tribune* she wrote society notes and interviewed visiting literary celebrities. After the Peatties moved to Omaha, where her husband was managing editor of the *Omaha World Herald*, she wrote editorials for that paper and founded and edited its women's pages from 1889 until the mid-1890s. Her populist editorials inspired WILLIAM JENNINGS BRYAN to call her "the first Bryan man" (Bremer xiii-xiv).

By 1898 the Peatties had returned to Chicago, where she first freelanced for the reform-minded *Chicago Daily News*. However, she soon returned to the *Tribune*, writing more than one hundred short stories for that publication in 1899. Between 1901 and 1917, first as a reviewer and then as review editor for the *Tribune*, she exercised considerable power. On Sunday afternoons the family's home on South Shore Drive became a literary salon; an invitation implied acceptance into the inner circle of the Chicago Renaissance. A member of the Little Room salon, an active participant in women's clubs and other groups dedicated to cultural uplift, Peattie promoted the arts, civic betterment, and feminist causes in Chicago. Her writings on JANE ADDAMS and the settlement house movement did much to define that cause for a popular audience.

Peattie was a prolific writer throughout her career, contributing numerous short stories and articles to the *Atlantic Monthly* and other periodicals, even as she turned out her daily quota of column inches for newspapers. In the midst of novel writing, lecturing, reviewing, and heavy-duty journalistic production, she raised four children: Edward, Barbara, Roderick, and DONALD CULROSS PEATTIE, the naturalist and writer. In 1917, when her husband became a correspondent for the *New York Times*, the Peatties moved to New York; in 1920 they retired to Tryon, North Carolina, where he died in 1930. Elia W. Peattie died at age seventy-four at her son Roderick's summer home in Wallingford, Vermont.

**SIGNIFICANCE:** BERNARD DUFFEY and Dale Kramer emphasize Peattie's importance as an opinion maker; in *The Chicago Renaissance in American Letters* (1954), Duffey stresses the conservative tendencies in Peattie's writings and the genteel influence of her criticism and review policies (57, 257). Kramer, in *Chicago Renaissance* (1966), relates how Peattie fought a rearguard action against the encroachments of realism and the early moderns from the *Tribune's* literary pages (253–54). Writing under

the pseudonym of Sade Iverson, she once passed off her poem "The Milliner" as a genuine example of avant-garde literature. MARGARET ANDERSON, taken in by the hoax, published Peattie's free-verse tale in the first volume of the *Little Review*.

In more recent assessments, Peattie emerges as a serious and socially conscious writer. Her genteel and reformist impulses animate statements like her essay on Chicago and its upward movement, "The Artistic Side of Chicago," published in the December 1899 issue of the *Atlantic Monthly* (828–34). But her social consciousness and reformer's will, almost inevitably, are hedged round by commercial considerations. Often because her family needed the money, she wrote sentimental magazine fiction, formulaic poetry, girls' books, and a popular history, *The Story of America* (1899).

Still, in stories like "Jim Lancy's Waterloo" from her collection *A Mountain Woman* (1896), she conveys the hard facts of farm and frontier life in the Midwest in terms and with a force that rival HAMLIN GARLAND's *Main Travelled Roads*. Her tales of grinding poverty, unremitting toil, and unyielding loneliness tell the stories of people in Iowa and Nebraska who have, in the words of one character, "well, kind of lost our grip" (*A Mountain Woman* 50). *The Precipice* (1914), her most important novel, is largely set in turn-of-the-century Chicago and shows, in Sidney Bremer's words, a "multiplicity of responses to women's changing roles" (xxii). Just before and after World War I, Peattie wrote, for women's clubs and other private performances, several one-act plays, including those collected in *The Wander Weed and Seven Other Little Theater Plays* (1923).

**SELECTED WORKS:** Peattie is the author of two novels, *The Judge* (1890) and *The Precipice* (1914). In 1896 she published a collection of short stories, *A Mountain Woman*, that focuses on the cultural conflict between city life and frontier society and undermines the cult of domesticity. Other interesting works are *The Wander Weed and Seven Other Little Theater Plays* (1923) and "Times and Manners" (1918), a one-act pageant that traces the changing status of women from classical to modern times.

**FURTHER READING:** Peattie's contribution to the Chicago Renaissance is discussed briefly in Bernard Duffey's *The Chicago Renaissance in American Letters* (1954) and in Dale Kramer's *Chicago Renaissance* (1966). See also BURTON RASCOE's *Before I Forget* (1937) for an assessment by one of her contemporaries. Sidney Bremer's introduction to *The Precipice* (1914; reprinted 1989) supplies the fullest commentary on the novel and the most useful biographical sketch of Peattie to date. Bremer draws on Peattie's unpublished memoir "The Star Wagon," a private manuscript held by Mark R. Peattie. Bremer also discusses *The Precipice* in relation to Chicago fiction in *Urban Intersections* (1992). Guy Szuberla in "Peattie's *The Precipice* and the Settlement House Novel," in *MidAmerica* 20 (1993): 59–75, comments on the relation of her novel to Jane Addams and the settlement house movement.

GUY SZUBERLA                    UNIVERSITY OF TOLEDO

## GEORGE W(ILBUR) PECK
September 28, 1840–April 16, 1916

**BIOGRAPHY:** George W. Peck was born in Henderson, New York, the oldest of three children of David B. and Alzina P. Peck. The family moved to Cold Spring, Wisconsin, when he was three, and Peck lived most of his life in that state. He attended public school until he was fifteen and was then apprenticed in the printing trade. He married Francena Rowley in 1860, and the couple had two sons.

He was part-owner of a newspaper when he enlisted in the Wisconsin Volunteer Cavalry as a private, later rising to the rank of lieutenant. He owned newspapers and held several political offices in Ripon, Madison, and LaCrosse and achieved a national readership when he moved *Peck's Sun*, a weekly of political satire and humorous columns, from LaCrosse to Milwaukee. He was mayor of Milwaukee and twice governor of Wisconsin, from 1890 to 1895. Peck promised to repeal an English-only school law, to reapportion voting districts, and to eliminate monetary profits allowed to cabinet secretaries, all of which he accomplished.

A popular entertainer with populist appeal, Peck foreshadowed the career of Illinois-native Ronald Reagan, even joking that a "boy" of his temperament would become president. He last ran for office in 1904, losing the governorship to Robert LaFollette. In retirement, Peck was still a popular raconteur at several fashionable Milwaukee hotels. Af-

ter an illness of six months, Peck died and was buried in Milwaukee.

**SIGNIFICANCE:** Peck was one of many columnists and publishers of small newspapers to acquire popularity and prominence as a writer of humorous sketches and populist editorials. His first book, *Adventures of One Terence McGant* (1871), is partly satire of the Grant administration by a witty Irish rough who foreshadows FINLEY PETER DUNNE's Mr. Dooley. In addition, like many others, he lectured with a self-satirical comic persona that owed much to ARTEMUS WARD and MARK TWAIN. As a performer, his most popular stage material consisted of anecdotes from *How Private Geo. W. Peck Put Down the Rebellion* (1887). He characterized himself as a good-hearted, innocent country boy who helped preserve the Union by avoiding battle and playing pranks instead, many rebounding on himself. His language is slang and his values as much prejudice as principle.

Through sketches in *Peck's Sun* and more than a dozen book collections, he created and developed the prankish career of Hennery, "Peck's Bad Boy," a troublemaker to all employers, reputable people, adults and authority figures, and most especially his father. A familiar figure in American humor, Hennery, like Huck Finn, clashes with the excesses and pretensions of the civilized world. A group calling themselves "Peck's Bad Boys" promoted his candidacy for governor in 1890.

Peck defined the Bad Boy in a dedication to the "Typical American Boy" in Peck's *Uncle Ike and the Red-Headed Boy* (1899): he takes hard knocks in work and play, refuses to cry when hurt, experiences life by "mixing up with the world," and becomes equally adept at fighting, doctoring, loving, laughing, and praying. Usually his pranks hit deserving targets, including himself, but sometimes they hurt innocent bystanders as well. Peck's version of Western and Midwestern humor is a coarser sort than that of BILL NYE and ROBERT BURDETTE. Popular humorists often scoffed at the sentimentality and optimism of Horatio Alger; however, Peck's satire would today be called politically incorrect. In addition to satirizing stereotypes of family, church, and commerce, he ridiculed immigrants, blacks and other ethnic groups, country folk, and others, some of whom were his political supporters. His persona was referred to as a boy,

George W. Peck.
Courtesy of Thomas Pribek

but it characterized a manhood defined by ability both to drink strong liquor and to take a joke without flinching. Peck's Bad Boy character continued after the author's death in stories, plays, and even Hollywood films by other writers.

**SELECTED WORKS:** The Bad Boy sketches were frequently reprinted in book collections under various titles but contained some of the same material, including *Peck's Bad Boy and His Pa* (1883), *The Grocery Man and Peck's Bad Boy* (1883), *Peck's Bad Boy Abroad* (1904), *Peck's Bad Boy with the Circus* (1906), *Peck's Bad Boy with the Cowboys* (1907), and *Peck's Bad Boy in an Airship* (1908). Other collections are *Peck's Fun* (1879), *Peck's Sunshine* (1882), *Mirth for the Millions* (1883), *Peck's Boss Book* (1884), *Peck's Compendium of Fun* (1886), *Sunbeams* (1900), and *Peck's Red-Headed Boy* (1901). Peck's own sketch of his career appears in his gazetteer *Wisconsin* (1906).

**FURTHER READING:** A brief introduction and selection appear in Richard Boudreau's *The Literary Heritage of Wisconsin, I* (1986), JACK

CONROY's *Midland Humor* (1947), and B. A. Botkin's *A Treasury of American Folklore* (1944). The State Historical Society of Wisconsin holds copies of Peck's newspapers, manuscripts, and official documents. The Milwaukee Public Library has holdings as well.

THOMAS PRIBEK

UNIVERSITY OF WISCONSIN–LACROSSE

## MARK PERLBERG

February 19, 1929

**BIOGRAPHY:** Mark Perlberg was born in Palisade, New Jersey, to parents Rene (Levinson) and Emmanuel Perlberg. He attended Hobart College, where, on graduation, he won their 1950 poetry prize. He attended Columbia University from 1950 to 1952, where he received the Department of English's coveted Van Rensselaer Award for "the best example of English lyric verse." MARK VAN DOREN, in correspondence with the publisher, quoted on the dust jacket of Perlberg's first book, has said, "No poet of our time is more generous in his affections."

An important influence on his verse, Chinese and Japanese visual art and poetry, derives from his U.S. Army service in Korea and Japan from 1952 to 1954. In 1953 he married Anna Nessy Backer, whom he had met at Columbia. They have two daughters, Katherine, born in 1957, and Julie, born in 1960.

Perlberg has held a number of positions as a writer and editor. He moved to Chicago in 1956, serving as a *Time* magazine correspondent there until 1961. He has also been a senior editor for the *World Book Yearbook* (1961–66), principal editor at *Encyclopedia Britannica* (1967–72), and a freelance editor and writer in Chicago. He is the author of two well-received books of poetry as well as of many magazine publications. His poetry has received several literary awards, including the Illinois Arts Council Literary Award (1977 and 1979). Publication of his third book is projected for 2000.

Perlberg is also a founding member and was long-time president of the Poetry Center of Chicago, associated with the Art Institute of Chicago. The center was cofounded in 1974 by Perlberg and Chicago poets Lisel Mueller, Paul Carroll, Paul Hoover, and MAXINE CHERNOFF to bring major American and international poets to the Midwest.

**SIGNIFICANCE:** The strength of Perlberg's

beautifully wrought early poems is their exploration of the ways mood or memory can be written in the colors or light of exactly defined spaces or times. One of his favorite devices is the space of light marked by tree or line or shadow: "In the square of sunlight / On the polished floor / The three-blossomed amaryllis / Throws its shadow as in an act of will" (*Burning Field* 25). Sharp lines across sunlight portion out luminous spaces: "The snow, like fragments of burned-out stars, / Lies within the blue parentheses of two tree shadows. / Morning light rises and fills space" (*Burning Field* 34). The effect is often like calligraphy floating above a crisp Japanese landscape.

Sometimes the stark lineations are frames, or doorways, that invite the reader to travel across thresholds, as in "For a Dead Lady" (*Burning Field* 1–3), for whom death comes as a warm cottage whose door is bathed in light. But Perlberg's poetry is not static or only evocative, like an Asian painting; it is also full of stories and journeys into memory, childhood, parenthood, age. In one of his finest lyrics, "The Garden" (*Feel* 1–2), a grown woman comforts her dying mother by returning the gift of fairy tale, painting at her bedside a story of death as a garden that shows how writing, narrative, is itself a journey that can close a circle and surprise us with meanings.

The thresholds in poems like "The Edge of the Forest" may also exclude: "Like the witch in a fairy tale, / she opened the kitchen door / and shoved her small son and daughter / out on the back stoop" (*Toystore* ms.). Perlberg's literary children often rage against adults who abandon them—or seem to refuse to share what they know before they leave. His recent work, *The Impossible Toystore: Poems* (2000), confronts the anger and perplexity of a young boy struggling to explain the mystery of parental figures who recede across boundaries, leaping away over hedgerows, sinking down into easy chairs, hiding in their letters, escaping on their deathbeds. But with the wisdom and occasional humor of maturity, he sees that what parents conceal is often only the deeper mystery of their simple human frailties. His most thoughtful poems challenge the great painters, writers, leaders of the past—from Martin Luther King Jr. and Dietrich Bonhoeffer to Brueghel

and Klee—to yield some of their inscrutability to the almost runic power of poetry. As in so much of the best American poetry, Perlberg's verse explores the beauty of vivid particulars, which respond to his questionings not in abstractions but only as they are occasions for surprising story or purity of language.

**SELECTED WORKS:** Mark Perlberg has published three volumes of poetry, *The Burning Field* (1970), *The Feel of the Sun* (1981), and *The Impossible Toystore: Poems* (2000). His poems have appeared in *Chicago Review*, the *New Yorker*, the *Hudson Review*, *Poetry*, and *Prairie Schooner*, as well as in numerous anthologies, including *Sunflower Splendor: Three Thousand Years of Chinese Poetry*, which featured some of his translations from the Chinese.

**FURTHER READING:** In an analysis of Mark Perlberg's first volume, reviewer James Finn Cotter remarks in the *Hudson Review* 35 (1982) on the tense oppositions in Perlberg's work between "the fragility of human consciousness and the mastery of human speech" (471–72). And poet WILLIAM STAFFORD is quoted on the dust jacket of *The Feel of the Sun* saying that Perlberg's work displays "a devotion to precious things in a world lighted by values." Chicago poet Lisel Mueller has praised his "astonishing purity of language" in her review in the *Chicago Daily News* (April 4, 1971): Arts 2. Other reviews include Bill Ott's review of Chicago poets John Frederick Nims, Mary Kinzie, and Perlberg in the *Chicago Tribune* (August 29, 1982): Book World 2.

MARK KIPPERMAN    NORTHERN ILLINOIS UNIVERSITY

# HARRY MARK PETRAKIS
June 5, 1923

**BIOGRAPHY:** Although Harry Mark Petrakis was born in St. Louis, he spent his early years in Chicago's Greektown, where much of his fiction is set. His parents were Mark and Stella (Christoulakis) Petrakis, the former a Greek Orthodox priest. Aspiring to a writing career since childhood, Petrakis attended the University of Illinois and then worked at a number of jobs, as a steelworker, laborer, speechwriter, lunchroom owner, tailor's assistant, and real estate salesperson among others, all the while serving a ten-year literary apprenticeship. Petrakis published his first short story in 1957; since that time he has published eight novels, four collections of short stories, two works of autobiography, and a collection of essays. He has been nominated twice for the National Book Award and has won an Atlantic First Award and a Benjamin Franklin Citation as well as awards from the Friends of American Writers, the Society of Midland Authors, the Friends of Literature, and the Friends of the Chicago Public Library. He was the recipient of the Society for the Study of Midwestern Literature's 1988 Mark Twain Award for distinguished contributions to Midwestern literature.

Petrakis has taught American literature at Columbia College in Chicago and fiction writing workshops for Rochester University, Indiana University, Ball State University, Illinois Wesleyan University, and the University of Wisconsin–Rhinelander. He has served as writer in residence for the Chicago Public Library and the Chicago Board of Education. Since 1945 he has been married to Diana Preparos; they have three sons. The Petrakises reside in Chesterton, Indiana.

**SIGNIFICANCE:** Petrakis's main subject is the Greek immigrant experience in the United States; most of his stories and novels are set amid the coffeehouses, restaurants, and grocery stores of Chicago's Greektown, the area bounded by Harrison, Halsted, Polk, and Blue Island that is sometimes called the Delta.

Petrakis's fiction is characterized by the tension between the rich cultural resources of his ancestral Greece and the sterile materialism of the Chicago in which Greek immigrants struggle to achieve the American Dream. More often than not, Petrakis characterizes the Greektown in which his fiction is set as ugly, bleak, deteriorating, and depressing; contrasted with this alienating environment are the soul-restoring blue skies, fragrant mountains, and sparkling seas of Greece. Thus, the Chicago cityscape functions as an objective correlative for the arduous and mind-numbing life that Greek immigrants must lead as they seek to prosper in America. Kostas and Katerina Volakis, whose story is told in *The Odyssey of Kostas Volakis* (1963), eventually achieve a comfortable, middle-class lifestyle in Chicago; however, their first home is a sunless room on the fourth floor of a tenement. Told of Lake Michigan's beauty at sunset, Kostas sets out to see it but loses his way in the labyrinth of the Loop's

**Harry Mark Petrakis.**
Courtesy of Harry Mark Petrakis

tall, ugly buildings. Similarly, Leonidas Matsoukas, protagonist of *A Dream of Kings* (1966) schemes desperately to raise the funds he needs to take his severely disabled son Stavros to Greece, where, he believes, Stavros's only hope for a cure lies in the healing sun of his homeland. *In the Land of Morning* (1973) features veteran Alex Rifakis, returning from Vietnam to Chicago's Greek American community, who sees only decay, misery, and hopelessness in his old neighborhood and abandons Chicago for a new life in Arizona at the end of the novel.

**SELECTED WORKS:** Almost all of the short stories published in *Pericles on 31st Street* (1965) and *The Waves of Night, and Other Stories* (1969) take place in Chicago's Greek community; these stories were later published in *A Petrakis Reader* (1978) and, along with a few more recent efforts, in *Collected Stories* (1987). Seven of Petrakis's eight novels are also set there, in whole or in part: *Lion at My Heart* (1959), *The Odyssey of Kostas Volakis* (1963), *A Dream of Kings* (1966), *In the Land of Morning* (1973), *Nick the Greek* (1979), *Days of Vengeance* (1983), and *Ghost of the Sun* (1990). Petrakis's finest novel, *The Hour of the Bell* (1976), is set in Greece and deals with the 1821 Greek war of independence. Petrakis also published two autobiographical works, *Stelmark* (1970) and *Reflections: A Writer's Work—A Writer's Life* (1983), as well as a nonfiction collection, *Tales of the Heart: Dreams and Memories of a Lifetime* (1999).

**FURTHER READING:** There are no book-length studies of Petrakis's fiction. Interviews with Petrakis appear in the *Chicago Review* 28.3 (1977): 97–119 and in *MELUS* 17.3 (Fall 1991–Spring 1992): 95–107. Petrakis's use of Greek myths and themes is examined in Katherine Zepantis's "Gender, Myth, and Memory: Ethnic Continuity in Greek-American Narrative," in *MELUS* 20:3 (Fall 1995): 47–65; and Alexander Karanikas's "Harry Mark Petrakis: A Study in Greek Ethnicity" appears in *MELUS* 5:1 (1978): 14–30. See also Athena G. Dallas-Damis's "The Greek Heritage and Its Impact on the Greek American Writer," in *The Greek American Community in Transition,* edited by Harry J. Psomiades and Alice Scourby (1982): 217–29. An article that focuses on the Chicago setting of Petrakis's fiction is Helen Geracimos Chapin's "'Chicagopolis': The Double World of Harry Mark Petrakis," in *Old Northwest* 2 (1976): 401–13.

MARCIA NOE
THE UNIVERSITY OF TENNESSEE AT CHATTANOOGA

## DAVID GRAHAM PHILLIPS
### October 31, 1867–January 24, 1911

**BIOGRAPHY:** David Graham Phillips was born in Madison, Indiana, one of five children of David Graham Phillips Sr. and Margaret (Lee) Phillips. A lifelong bachelor, Phillips remained extremely close to his older sister Carolyn Phillips Frevert all his life. Phillips attended Asbury (later DePauw) University in Greencastle, Indiana, where he met Albert J. Beveridge, who was to become a lifelong friend. Leaving Asbury, Phillips graduated from Princeton in 1887.

Phillips returned to the Midwest as a reporter in Cincinnati. In 1890 he left the *Cincinnati Commercial Gazette* to join Charles A. Dana's *New York Sun.* His success at the *Sun* led to an offer in 1893 to become the London correspondent for the *New York World* of Joseph Pulitzer. Phillips wrote for the *World* for nine years, becoming one of the most famous reporters of the time.

After 1902 Phillips devoted most of his en-

David Graham Phillips.
Courtesy of the University of Kentucky Libraries

ergies to writing fiction, but his most famous reportage, "The Treason of the Senate," appeared in 1906 in a series of articles in *Cosmopolitan,* then published by William Randolph Hearst. The series vehemently indicted the most powerful senators as traitors to the nation for serving wealthy corporations rather than the people.

Phillips's heavy-handed assault provoked President Theodore Roosevelt to condemn as "muckrakers" those who assumed that wealth in and of itself was a sign of criminality. The prestige of the muckrakers never recovered from Roosevelt's critique, all the more telling because of Roosevelt's own willingness to denounce "malefactors of great wealth" (*Presidential Addresses and State Papers* 6: 1359). Phillips himself returned to fiction, continuing to publish novel after novel. He was murdered in 1911 by Fitzhugh Goldsborough, who wrongly believed that Phillips had been attacking the Goldsborough family in his fiction. *Susan Lenox,* generally regarded as Phillips's best novel, was published posthumously in 1917.

**SIGNIFICANCE:** Phillips's muckraking journalism, including "The Treason of the Senate" and *The Reign of Gilt* (1905), has historical interest but little intrinsic importance. Although H. L. Mencken once asserted that Phillips was the leading American novelist of the time on the basis of *The Hungry Heart* (1909) and *The Husband's Story* (1910), neither these two novels, nor the posthumous *Susan Lenox* (1917), nor any other of Phillips's many novels seem likely candidates for revival. Mencken appreciated Phillips's journalistic realism but ignored his sentimental love stories and his lack of interest or ability in the craft of fiction.

In both his journalism and his fiction Phillips remained loyal to the Midwestern small-town values he had absorbed in Madison, Indiana. Phillips's *The Second Generation* (1907) suggests that the biggest mistake wealthy Midwesterners can make is to send their children East in search of culture. Judge Torrey speaks for the author when he exclaims "That *damned* East! We send it most of our money and our best young men; and what do we get from it in return? Why, sneers and snob-ideas" (155). Phillips was unable, however, to work out a way of reconciling his feeling that great wealth and power were sources of corruption with his Social Darwinist belief that the acquisition of wealth and power was the inevitable result of natural superiority. *The Second Generation* illustrates Phillips's dilemma; the novel both celebrates the determination of the first generation of Midwestern entrepreneurs and suggests that their newfound wealth virtually ensures that the "second generation" will forsake the Midwestern work ethic in favor of Eastern snobbery.

**SELECTED WORKS:** Phillips's two most important writings as a muckraker are *The Reign of Gilt* (1905) and "The Treason of the Senate" (1906). Phillips's first novel, *The Great God Success* (1901), written under an assumed name, was followed by *Golden Fleece* (1903), *The Cost* (1904), and *The Plum Tree* (1905). All three, like *The Deluge* (1905), expose the corruption of business and politics. Phillips's later fiction deals with the personal costs of commercial civilization and focuses on the new, uncertain status of women. *The Second Generation* (1907), *The Hungry Heart* (1909), *The Husband's Story* (1910), and *Susan Lenox* (1917) all share this emphasis.

**FURTHER READING:** Two biographies discussing both Phillips's journalism and his fiction are *David Graham Phillips* (1966), by Abe Ravitz, and *Voice of the Democracy* (1978), subtitled *A Critical Biography of David Graham Phillips: Journalist, Novelist, Progressive*, by Louis Filler. The David Graham Phillips Papers are held at the Princeton University Library.

JAMES SEATON            MICHIGAN STATE UNIVERSITY

## MARGE PIERCY
March 31, 1936

**BIOGRAPHY:** Marge Piercy was born and raised in a working-class neighborhood in Detroit, Michigan, a city that she says formed her and made her a novelist. Her father, Robert Douglas Piercy, was a heavy-machinery repairman and Piercy, along with her mother, Bert Bedoyna (Bunnin) Piercy, traveled summers throughout Michigan and Ohio to jobs with him. To her mother, Piercy attributes her love of plants and nature, an observant eye, a quick imagination, and a strong communal, feminist viewpoint. Detroit gave Piercy her first lessons in class consciousness. In her essay "Inviting the Muse," in *Parti-Colored Blocks for a Quilt* (1982), she summed up her early life as "skimpy, hard, surrounded by violence outdoors and containing familial violence within, a typical patriarchal working-class family in inner-city Detroit" (6).

Piercy dates her beginnings as a writer to fifteen, when her family moved to a house in which she had a room of her own. After high school she won a scholarship to the University of Michigan, where she felt out of place but excelled academically. At Michigan, she garnered academic honors and received the Avery and Jule Hopwood Award for both poetry and fiction in 1956 and again for poetry in 1957. She received her AB in 1957, married, and moved to Chicago. She earned her MA from Northwestern University in 1958, then dropped out of school to support her husband. While in Chicago, Piercy held a number of jobs, including secretarial work and teaching at the Gary Extension of Indiana University. During this period (1958–63), Piercy divorced her first husband and became active in local and national political movements. Her concerns regarding urban renewal, civil rights, the anti-war movement, and local political processes are reflected in her first published books, *Going Down Fast* (1969) and *Dance the Eagle to Sleep* (1970). Piercy has said that during this period right after college she needed to reestablish her roots, which she identified as Midwestern and populist. In part, she had to unlearn some of the class and aesthetic strictures she had acquired in academe and return to the voice and perspective of her younger self.

Since 1963 Piercy has made her living as a social and political organizer, novelist, poet, and reviewer. She worked for Students for a Democratic Society (1965–69) and the North American Congress on Latin America (1966–67), moving from Detroit to New York City. By 1969 Piercy's primary political work shifted to the women's movement, a shift strongly reflected in the publication of her third novel, *Small Changes* (1973), and all subsequent works. She has served on the editorial boards of feminist journals, such as *Aphra* (1975–77), *Sojourner* (1976–present), and *Tikkun* (1988–present).

Piercy has lived not only in Detroit and Chicago but also in New York City, San Francisco, and Paris. With her third husband, Ira Wood, whom she married in 1982, she lives in Wellfleet, Massachusetts, the landscape of which she often contrasts with the Midwest. **SIGNIFICANCE:** Midwestern identification is central to Piercy's development as a writer, particularly as a novelist. Her portrayal of urban life takes much from her personal experiences in Detroit and Chicago. Her awareness of class and gender restrictions, her opposition to dehumanized or over-industrialized life, her first explorations of power within the family, society, and political structures—all have their root in the Midwest of her first thirty-four years.

Piercy's novels portray the Midwest of rust-belt cities and working-class neighborhoods against which her protagonists rebel and from which they leave, determined to find better, more liberating space. Many of her protagonists directly echo or parallel Piercy's experiences of family life, work, college, and political awakening. For example, Piercy calls her first published novel, *Going Down Fast*, her "love-hate musing on Chicago" (*Parti-Colored Blocks for a Quilt* 214). Certainly her knowledge of Chicago history and politics underlies this study of urban renewal, in which incidents repeatedly highlight the discrepancy between those with power and those without. Detailed descriptions of both the decaying neighborhood and

its inhabitants, who seem to be in dead-end jobs and relationships, bring alive the socioeconomic as well as emotional plight of Midwestern inner cities. She evokes this world well in many of her novels, including *The High Cost of Living* (1978), *Braided Lives* (1982), and *Gone to Soldiers* (1987).

Midwestern cities in Piercy's novels are centers of physical and metaphorical corruption and decay. This is apparent even in her science fiction work, such as *He, She and It* (1991). In this novel, the Yakamura-Stichen dome, in the middle of Nebraska, is a corporate enclave in the middle of a North American, very Midwestern wasteland. Even more unsettling is the literal battleground of the "Glop," the toxic and violent megalopolis which stretches between enclaves and is the living space for the expendable poor. Filled with gang wars, constant assaults on the individual, drugs, homelessness, and hunger, the "Glop" is Piercy's dystopic extension of contemporary urban life. Piercy's strongest indictment against the Midwest is that it has been so corrupted and polluted, become so rigid in class and gender roles, that it lacks the power to be regenerated from within. Her characters must leave if they are to develop fully or launch an assault against these values.

Although the Midwest is oppressive, it is also a source of strength for many of Piercy's characters. It is within the families and cities of their childhood that they learn to stand up for beliefs, to fight for rights, to count on community to pull them through tough times, to be activists, and to nurture the small plots of nature available to them. Piercy's working-class heroines grow out of experiences of hardship and loss common in the urban Midwest. They emerge from these roots frequently wounded but always resilient and claiming power over their lives. Her protagonists are survivors and scrappers who overcome the dinginess of their surroundings and the disapproval of their families. Both the obstacles and the people who surmount them are products of the Midwest Piercy knows well and presents vividly.

**SELECTED WORKS:** Although Piercy has written fourteen novels, the ones with the strongest Midwestern base include *Going Down Fast* (1969), *Dance the Eagle to Sleep* (1970), *Small Changes* (1973), *The High Cost of Living* (1978), *Vida* (1979), *Braided Lives* (1982), *Gone to*

*Soldiers* (1987), and *He, She and It* (1991). Her other novels explore her common themes but do so primarily outside a Midwestern setting. These novels are *Woman on the Edge of Time* (1976), *Fly Away Home* (1984), *Summer People* (1989), *The Longings of Women* (1994), *City of Darkness, City of Light* (1996), and *Storm Tide* (1998), which she coauthored with Ira Wood. Her book of essays, *Parti-Colored Blocks for a Quilt* (1982), provides valuable biographical and critical information about Piercy along with the significance of the Midwest in her personal and artistic development.

Additionally, Piercy has published thirteen volumes of poetry. *Circles on the Water: Selected Poems* (1982) gives a good overview of her works from 1968 to 1982. Some of the imagery is urban and Midwestern, but that element is not as strong in her poetry as in her novels. In *Breaking Camp* (1968) Piercy chronicles her move from Chicago to New York City, but her imagery is not so sharply Midwestern, remaining on a less localized plane.

Piercy shows her editorial skills and her work as a feminist literary critic in her anthology *Early Ripening: American Women's Poetry Now* (1988). With her third husband, Ira Wood, she coauthored a play, *The Last White Class* (1978).

**FURTHER READING:** The most useful biographical source remains Piercy's own *Parti-Colored Blocks for a Quilt* (1982). Two critical books on Piercy begin to assess her career and achievements: *The Repair of the World: The Novels of Marge Piercy* by Kerstin W. Shands (1994) and *Ways of Knowing: Critical Essays on Marge Piercy*, edited by Sue Walker and Eugenie Hamner (1984). Other studies of Piercy are spread through mixed author texts and are available as individual articles and reviews. Piercy's manuscript collection and archives are housed in the Harlan Hatcher Graduate Library at the University of Michigan.

MELODY M. ZAJDEL    MONTANA STATE UNIVERSITY

## STANLEY (ROSS) PLUMLY
May 23, 1939

**BIOGRAPHY:** Born in Barnesville, Belmont County, Ohio, the son of Herman and Esther (Wellbaum) Plumly, Stanley received his BA from Ohio's Wilmington College in 1962. He has an MA and work toward a PhD at Ohio University in Athens, where he taught from 1970 to 1973. Since 1974 Plumly has taught at the University of Iowa and the University of Michigan. Currently Plumly is professor of English at the University of Maryland, where he founded the MFA program and served as director of Creative Writing. He has been poetry editor of the *Ohio Review* and *Iowa Review* as well as contributing editor of *The Pushcart Prize Anthology*. As of 1997, Plumly has received more than thirty-five awards and honors. These range from the 1972 Delmore Schwartz Memorial Award (Best First Book of Poems) through many Pushcart Prizes, two NEA grants, a Guggenheim, a National Book Critics Circle Award nomination and a 1991 Robert Frost Fellowship.

**SIGNIFICANCE:** Stanley Plumly is a respected and widely published poet. Two poems from *Giraffe* (1973) suggest the ways Ohio and the Midwest continue to affect Plumly's writing. In "Buckeye" Plumly simply asserts: " My father came to Ohio / the year the war ended" (11). That simple biographical fact is placed in an ambiguous context in that poem's last line: "Ohio being north of the way things were" (11). Another poem, "At the Hub's Farm, May," seems to affirm both Midwestern roots and displacement: "I wanted country weather. / My Quaker uncle still works / these Ohio hills at the ass end / of a plow horse" (10). Of course, by 1973, Plumly was himself in the process of leaving "these Ohio hills." In a 1995 interview with David Biespiel in the *American Poetry Review*, Plumly recollects the complexity of his Ohio genesis as he responds to a question about James Wright: "He and I were born in the same county, very different parts of the county, different worlds, really. It could have been a much wider geographic gap than county-wide . . . . the terrain of that river-country county . . . the Belmont County countryside . . . at the edge of two worlds, pastoral and industrial . . . . I grew up in a Quaker part of the county; it's up country, very pastoral . . . . I'm much more of a country poet than James Wright really is" (49). Plumly's 1995 claim that he remains in part "a country poet" testifies to the lasting power of that Ohio region that also produced Zane Grey and James Wright. Skeptical readers may wish to read a very urban poem, "Fifth and 94th," which was published first in the *New Yorker* and then reprinted in Howard Moss's 1980 *New York: Poems,* and see if they can discover an Ohio Quaker sensitivity!

**SELECTED WORKS:** Plumly's published volumes of poetry are *In the Outer Dark* (1970), *Giraffe* (1973), *How the Plains Indians Got Horses* (1975), *Out-of-the-Body Travel* (1977), *Summer Celestial* (1983), *Boy on the Step* (1989), *The Marriage in the Trees* (1997), and *Now that My Father Lies Down Beside Me: New and Selected Poems, 1970–2000* (2000). Projected is a prose work to be called *Posthumous Keats: A Meditation on Mortality*.

**FURTHER READING:** The best sources for more information about Plumly may be his interviews. The aforementioned interview with David Biespiel (and Rose Solari) can be found in the *American Poetry Review* 24.3 (May–June 1995): 43–50. Others of note are the earlier interview in the Fall 1983 *Crazyhorse* and the "conversation" with Lisa Meyer in *Boston Review* (Summer 1996). Ohio University at Athens is the repository for Stanley Plumly's papers.

JAMES M. HUGHES          WRIGHT STATE UNIVERSITY

## SIMON POKAGON

Spring, 1830–January 28, 1899

**BIOGRAPHY:** The Native American author of the autobiographical novel *Queen of the Woods* (1899) was born in southwestern Michigan. His father was Leopold Pokagon, a leader of Michigan Potawatomi Indians, who was influential in negotiating amendments to the 1833 Treaty of Chicago that finally enabled the "Pokagon Band" to remain in their Michigan homeland. Like his father, Simon successfully worked to avoid removal from Michigan to Kansas and Oklahoma. Simon's mother, Elizabeth, came from another family of Indian leaders.

Speaking only the native language until he was twelve, Simon went on to study three years at Notre Dame, a year at Oberlin, and two years at Twinsburg, Ohio. After school he settled in southwestern Michigan, in the back country near Black River, some distance north of his birthplace. Here he met Lonidaw Sinagaw, whose English name was Angela. They married and had four children. Settling in the back country provided the story of *Queen of the Woods* (1899), which the book's preface calls a "real romance." Sincere profession of the Catholic faith functioned along with settlement to establish responsible family life and ward off the threat of eviction from the land they loved. Simon administered tribal affairs, wrote magazine articles, and made speeches,

including a presentation at the Columbian Exposition or Chicago World's Fair of 1893. From its base in Michigan's Cass County, his band of Native Americans continued organizing and achieved federal tribal recognition as the Pokagon Band of Potawatomi Indians in 1994.

Some years after his first wife died on December 1, 1871, Simon Pokagon married again; his second wife's name was Victoria. Pneumonia caused Simon Pokagon's death in 1899.

**SIGNIFICANCE:** Simon Pokagon wrote, in David H. Dickason's phrase, "to maintain and defend his own native values . . ." (136). In his article "Chief Simon Pokagon: 'The Indian Longfellow'" in the *Indiana Magazine of History* (June 1961), Dickason admires in *Queen of the Woods* "the novelty of its contents and depth of its feeling" (128). Further, noting "some deficiencies in verbal mechanics" in Pokagon's personal correspondence, Dickason believes that "Pokagon doubtless had considerable editorial assistance" (128) in producing his published works. Yet Dickason terms such criticism "picayune" in comparison to his appreciation of *Queen of the Woods* as "a unique document from a genuine Indian source" (128).

*Queen of the Woods* is a sourcebook for the value of nature in a specifically Midwestern mode. In a wilderness of dense green forest and blue water everywhere, Lonidaw (Loda) displays wonderful rapport with animals: for instance, she can call to herself a flock of passenger pigeons; and a white deer jealously remains near her. Loda achieves eminence by perfecting widely held traits among natives. Her character and the respect it engenders offer a glimpse into a world where being a part of life's network is more important than amassing possessions.

However, paradise does not stay perfect. The story concludes with loved ones lost to drink and with a passionate plea for sobriety. Having seen Indian leaders such as Topenabee debilitated by drunkenness, Pokagon places his story in the broadly based nineteenth-century movement advocating temperance.

*Queen of the Woods* presents the world of the *anishinabay*, people of the Algonquian languages. The language is also named Ojibway (Chippewa) after the largest tribal group who speak it. *Queen of the Woods* is significant in that it gives a taste of this language by incorporating several native words on each page of the story. The book also contains a brief grammar and vocabulary. An owl is "*ko-ko-ko*," and passenger pigeons are "*o-me-me-og*." Their names sound like their calls in a language whose expressions are imagery of sight and sound, minimizing abstractions. Down to its very word-forms, *Queen of the Woods* creates a lively experience of being at home in the natural world, a characteristically Native American set of attitudes and skills that Simon Pokagon worked effectively to preserve in the Midwest.

**SELECTED WORKS:** *O-gi-ma-kwe Mit-i-gwa-ki* (*Queen of the Woods*) was published by Hardscrabble Books of Berrien Springs, Michigan, in 1972, reprinting the 1899 edition first published at Hartford, Michigan. This reprint lacks only the original appendix that tells the story of Pokagon's unsuccessful efforts to hold a congress of Indian nations at the 1893 Columbian Exposition.

Pokagon wrote nature studies such as "Wild Pigeons of North America," in *Chautauquan* 22 (November 1895): 202–206, and "An Indian's Observations on the Mating of Geese," in *Arena* 16 (July 1896): 245–48. Yet Pokagon's journal articles emphasize issues of Indian culture. Declaring the futility of warfare in "The Future of the Red Man," in *Forum* 23 (July 1897): 698–708, Pokagon goes on to note how superficial writing about Indian treachery and cruelty increases racial hatred. He carries this theme into "Indian Native Skill," in *Chautauquan* 26 (February 1898); here those who dig up Indian graves read "in the battle-axe and spear of stone and in the arrow-head and knife of flint" the savage character of Indians (540–52). Nevertheless, in "An Indian on the Problems of His Race," in *Review of Reviews* 12 (December 1895): 694–95, Pokagon writes that schooling will enable Indian people to handle the inevitable changes of advancing civilization. His other magazine articles include "Indian Superstitions and Legends," in *Forum* 25 (July 1896): 618–29; "The Massacre of Fort Dearborn at Chicago," in *Harper's New Monthly Magazine* 98 (March 1899): 649–56; "Our Indian Women," in *Chautauquan* 22 (March 1896): 732–34; "The Pottawatomies in the War of 1812," in *Arena* 26 (July 1901): 48–55; "Simon Pokagon on Naming the Indians," in *Review of Reviews* 15 (September 1897): 320–21.

In addition, the original publisher of *Queen of the Woods*, Charles C. Engle of Hartford,

Michigan, also published five booklets on Indian themes written by Pokagon, four of which have survived. Three are in the Ayer Collection of Chicago's Newberry Library: *The Red Man's Greeting* (1893), also in the files of the Chicago Historical Society; *Pottawatamie Book of Genesis—Legends of the Creation of Man* (1901), also reprinted in Charles S. Winslow's *Indians of the Chicago Region* (1946); and *Lord's Prayer in Algonquin Language* (not dated). A fourth booklet, *Algonquin Legends of South Haven* (not dated), is found in the files of the Chicago Historical Society.

**FURTHER READING:** James Clifton's *The Pokagons, 1633–1983: Catholic Potawatomi Indians of the St. Joseph River Valley* (1984) emphasizes political and legal activism surrounding Indian treaties and the threatening environment of the Indian Removal Act of 1830. Clifton, Cornell, and McClurken's *People of the Three Fires: The Ottawa, Potawatomi, and Ojibway of Michigan* (1986) provides an overview, including cultural dynamics. Reprinted in a limited edition in 1976, Cecilia Buechner's *The Pokagons* (1931) gives a religious interpretation of the Pokagons' movements. Roy H. Pearce's *The Savages of America: A Study of the Indian and the Idea of Civilization* (reprinted as *Savagism and Civilization: A Study of the Indian and the American Mind*, 1965) shows what a task it was for an American Indian to portray for the majority of readers a truly Native American version of humanity. Helen Hornbeck Tanner's *Atlas of Great Lakes Indian History* (1987) graphically portrays history with a large collection of maps. Two native writers were Pokagon's contemporaries. ANDREW J. BLACKBIRD, also a Michigan Indian, wrote his *History of the Ottawa and Chippewa Indians of Michigan* (1887, limited reprints in 1967 and 1977). WILLIAM W. WARREN's *History of the Ojibway Nation* (1885, reprinted as *History of the Ojibway People* in 1984) chronicled Indian warfare in northern and central Wisconsin, adding important observations of culture in the only existing volume of a planned four-volume series.

JEFFREY A. JUSTIN          MUSKEGON, MICHIGAN

## PATRICIA POLACCO
July 11, 1944

**BIOGRAPHY:** Award-winning writer and illustrator of children's books, Patricia Polacco was born in Lansing, Michigan, to William F. Barber, a television station employee, and

Mary Ellen (Gaw) Barber, a teacher. Patricia and her brother, Richard, spent their early years in Union City, Michigan, a farm community south of Battle Creek, where their mother's Russian immigrant parents lived. After their parents' divorce, Patricia lived with her mother in Florida and later in Oakland, California. Summers were spent with her father in Williamston, a rural community east of Lansing, Michigan.

Despite struggles with dyslexia, Polacco earned the BFA and MFA from Monash University in Melbourne, Australia, and the PhD from the Royal Melbourne Institute of Technology. In 1979 she married Enzo Mario Polacco. She has two children, Traci Denise and Steven John.

Although a freelance writer and illustrator for years, Polacco did not create her first children's book until 1987. Since then she has written prolifically. Her honors include *Rechenka's Eggs* (1988), the International Reading Association Best Picture Book; *The Keeping Quilt* (1988), the Sydney Taylor Award; *Just Plain Fancy* (1990), the *School Library Journal* Best Book of the Year; *Some Birthday!* (1991), IRA/CBC Children's Choice and the Parents' Choice Award; *Chicken Sunday* (1992), the Educators for Social Responsibility Award, Golden Kite Award for Illustration, Society of Children's Book Writers and Illustrators Award; *Mrs. Katz and Tush* (1992), Honor Picture Book of the JANE ADDAMS Children's Book Award; *My Rotten Redheaded Older Brother* (1994), the American Library Association's Notable Children's Book, *School Library Journal* Best Book, American Pick of the List Book; *Pink and Say* (1994), the American Library Association Notable Book, *Publishers Weekly* Best Book, CBC Notable Children's Book in the Field of Social Studies, and Irma S. and James H. Black Award for Excellence in Children's Literature.

After decades outside the Midwest, Polacco has returned to Union City. She lives at Meteor Ridge Farm, its name based on the meteor that landed on the family's farm and became the subject of her first children's book, *Meteor* (1987).

**SIGNIFICANCE:** Polacco writes and illustrates children's picture books that use simple stories and common people to entertain while teaching life lessons based on her family traditions and stories and her rural Midwestern childhood. These books reflect strong appreciation of family. The rich, colorful drawings depict characters with charming faces full of expression and personality. The stories and illustrations portray a positive, often humorous, view of humanity through children's eyes.

Like *Meteor*, many of her books depict love and appreciation for Polacco's mother's family and Union City. *The Keeping Quilt* (1988) illustrates identification with the family's Russian heritage in portraying a quilt passing from generation to generation. In *Thunder Cake* (1990), a Russian grandmother's love and wisdom help overcome fear of thunder; Uncle Vova, in *Uncle Vova's Tree* (1989), demonstrates the value of tradition. *The Bee Tree* (1993) presents a grandfather passing on the joy of reading. *My Rotten Redheaded Older Brother* draws on nostalgic memories of sibling rivalries with Polacco's teasing-yet-loving brother at her grandmother's.

Several books, including *Babushka's Doll* (1990), *Babushka's Mother Goose* (1995), *Babushka Baba Yaga* (1993), and *Rechenka's Eggs* (1988), trace their origins to Russian tales. The accompanying drawings of contented, well-lined faces of the aged as well as the young make Polacco's books unique and easily recognizable.

Polacco's identification with her father's acculturated-Irish family is also clear in several delightful books depicting summers in small-town Williamston. These stories, like her other works, present simple experiences of rural children in unpretentious Midwestern families. *My Ol' Man* (1995) provides an enduring picture of her father's happy-go-lucky lifestyle and grace under pressure following loss of his job. *Some Birthday!* (1991) recalls a childhood birthday with a fun-loving father who thrilled his daughter with a dark-night outing. His gift of riding lessons in Lansing, in *Mrs. Mack* (1998), gives readers a look at the lessons a girl learns from horses and humans one summer in Michigan.

Polacco's writings repeatedly portray diverse multicultural values, traditions, and lifestyles. *Pink and Say* (1994) retells Polacco's father's tale of an ancestor saved by a black Civil War soldier. *Chicken Sunday* (1992) is a story about Polacco's childhood love for her "adopted" black gramma. *Boat Ride with Lillian Two Blossom* (1988) is her father's recollection of a childhood adventure with a local Native American woman; *Just Plain Fancy* (1990) is an Amish story; and *Tikvah Means Hope* (1994) relates a Jewish tale. All these, like Polacco's Russian books, encourage children to broaden their life perspectives.

**SELECTED WORKS:** Children's books written and illustrated by Polacco include *Meteor* (1987), *Boat Ride with Lillian Two Blossom* (1988), *The Keeping Quilt* (1988), *Rechenka's Eggs* (1988), *Uncle Vova's Tree* (1989), *Babushka's Doll* (1990), *Just Plain Fancy* (1990), *Thunder Cake* (1990), *Appelemando's Dreams* (1991), *Some Birthday!* (1991), *Chicken Sunday* (1992), *Mrs. Katz and Tush* (1992), *Picnic at Mudsock Meadow* (1992), *Babushka Baba Yaga* (1993), *The Bee Tree* (1993), *My Rotten Redheaded Older Brother* (1994), *Pink and Say* (1994), *Tikvah Means Hope* (1994), *Babushka's Mother Goose* (1995), *My Ol' Man* (1995), *Aunt Chip and the Great Triple Creek Dam Affair* (1996), *I Can Hear the Sun* (1996), *The Trees of the Dancing Goats* (1996), *In Enzo's Splendid Gardens* (1997), *Mrs. Mack* (1998), *Thank You, Mr. Falker* (1998), *Luba and the Wren* (1999), *Welcome Comfort* (1999), *The Butterfly* (2000), and *The Calhoun Club* (2000). She illustrated *Casey at the Bat* (1988), by Thayer Ernest Lawrence. Polacco's *Firetalking* (1994) offers biographical information. "The Sydney Taylor Book Award Speeches," in *Judaica Librarianship* 5.1 (1989–90): 50–53, carries Polacco's award acceptance speech.

**FURTHER READING:** Studies of Polacco's writings include Kay E. Vandergrift's "Peacocks, Dreams, Quilts, and Honey: Patricia Polacco, A Woman's Voice of Remembrance," in *Ways of Knowing: Literature and the Intellectual Life of Children*, edited by Kay E. Vandergrift (1996): 259–88; *Something about the Author* 74 (1993): 193–200; and *Children's Books and Their Creators* (1995): 531–32.

MARSHA O. GREASLEY

WOODFORD COUNTY (KENTUCKY) SCHOOLS

## GENE STRATTON PORTER
August 17, 1863–December 6, 1924

**BIOGRAPHY:** Geneva Grace Stratton's love for nature began with her birthplace, a farm near LaGro in Wabash County, Indiana. Her father, Mark Stratton, a farmer and lay minister, encouraged her to study and nurture wildlife, particularly birds. Her mother, Mary (Shallenberger) Stratton, taught her how to grow flowers. Having changed her

name to Gene, she married pharmacist and banker Charles Dorwin Porter in 1887 and bore a daughter, Jeannette, in 1888, in Geneva, Indiana.

A pioneering photographer, wearing trousers and high boots and enduring sunburn, insect attacks, and the effects of poisonous plants, among other hazards, she explored the marshes, meadows, and woods with her massive equipment. On glass plates, she preserved images of wildlife native to the region. Under the name Gene Stratton-Porter, she first published articles on birds and camera usage, then short fiction, and eventually a total of more than twenty books. Outraged by the changes the lumbering, oil, and farming interests had made to the landscape, she moved her family north to a lake near Rome City, Indiana, where she had planned and built a house she called "Wildflower Woods" and "Limberlost North." Later, in California, Porter began a new venture, making films of her novels. She died in an automobile accident in Los Angeles.

**SIGNIFICANCE:** Porter set many of her most significant works on Indiana farms and in uncultivated landscapes. Her characters, endowed with qualities derived from their pioneer parents and grandparents, embody the ethics of hard work, hospitality, and community, as well as their opposites, in a range of personalities. Themes of preserving and appreciating the environment and of caring for one's neighbor, derived from and supported by a deep religious belief, underlie the lively plots of her novels and the themes of her nonfiction.

Porter's first book, *The Song of the Cardinal* (1901), protests the casual killing of songbirds while presenting an engaging portrait of a year in the life of a cardinal. Finding that she could capture a large audience and that she had a flair for storytelling, she decided to try via fiction to induce her readers to appreciate nature. The money her novels brought financed the more expensive illustrated nature volumes. Porter said that she intended to use "a slight romance as a sugar coating, in my effort to entice the household afield" ("My Life and My Books," *Ladies' Home Journal* 38 [September 1916]: 13). For example, in *Freckles*, a one-armed city orphan conquers his fear of the outdoors as he patrols the Limberlost as guard for a lumber company; El-nora Comstock, the *Girl of the Limberlost*, pays her own school expenses by collecting moths and crafting objects from the Indiana woods; David Langston, *The Harvester*, collects herbs from the same territory to bring a sick and distraught young woman to glowing health. The protagonist of *Laddie* converts a British aristocrat to love of the rich farmland in the Wabash Valley. Romance comes to all of them. Clearly, the formula worked; the sales figures of her novels at times matched those of Dickens's fiction.

Porter's editorials for *McCall's* (which she wrote to revive its sagging reputation) reinforce darker subthemes dealing with divorce, illegitimacy, alcoholism, responsibility for children's upbringing, the rights of women to inheritance, and political corruption, all of which evolved from the community values inspired by her background. The articles advocated a healthy lifestyle, conveniences to ease the lives of rural women, a single standard, cooperation within the home, and political responsibility, all subtly conveyed in the fiction and developed in greater depth in her magazine columns. Her store of articles lasted three years beyond her death.

Indiana's Limberlost figures prominently as setting in Porter's earliest and best-known fiction, *Freckles*, *A Girl of the Limberlost*, and *The Harvester*, and in one of her later novels, *The White Flag* (1923). Most of her nature books, including *Moths of the Limberlost* (1912) and *Music of the Wild* (1910), also revolve around the Indiana landscape and its wild inhabitants, portraying the beauty of the outdoors and urging conservation. *Laddie: A True-Blue Story* (1913) fictionalizes her parents' experiences homesteading in LaGro and her own girlhood on their farm, recording the lifestyle of a rural child of late-nineteenth-century Indiana.

Porter's homes at Geneva and Rome City, the latter a preserve for wildflowers and other native plants, remain open as museums.

**SELECTED WORKS:** Porter's best-known Indiana fiction includes *Freckles* (1904), *A Girl of the Limberlost* (1909), *The Harvester* (1911), and *Laddie: A True Blue Story* (1913). *At the Foot of the Rainbow* (1907), *Michael O'Halloran* (1915), and *A Daughter of the Land* (1918) also have Midwestern settings. *The Keeper of the Bees* (1925), set in California, and *The White Flag* (1923) are among her later books. *Moths of the Limberlost* (1912), *Music of the Wild* (1910), and *Homing with the Birds* (1919) typify her books combining photography and nature lore and describe Indiana locations and situations. She wrote both short and book-length poems, notably *The Fire Bird* (1922).

**FURTHER READING:** Jeannette Porter Meehan's biography of her mother, *The Lady of the Limberlost: The Life and Letters of Gene Stratton-Porter* (1928), is the primary resource for readers of this author. A more recent biography, *Gene Stratton-Porter: Novelist and Naturalist*, by Judith Reick Long, appeared in 1990. Bertrand F. Richards's Twayne book, *Gene Stratton Porter* (1980), and David G. MacLean's *Gene Stratton-Porter: A Bibliography and Collector's Guide* (1976) are also valuable. Sydney Landon Plum's introductions to the selections in *Coming through the Swamp: The Nature Writings of Gene Stratton Porter* (1996) provide useful insights.

MARY DEJONG OBUCHOWSKI

CENTRAL MICHIGAN UNIVERSITY

# DAWN POWELL

November 28, 1896(?)–November 14, 1965

**BIOGRAPHY:** Dawn Powell, novelist, dramatist, and short story writer, was born in Mount Gilead in northern Ohio. Powell cited 1897 as her birth year, but increasing evidence indicates that she was born in 1896. Roy Powell, a traveling salesman, often left Dawn, her two sisters, and her mother, Hattie Sherman Powell, awaiting infrequent support. When Dawn was six, her mother died and the girls lived with various relatives in Ohio until Dawn was eleven, when her father remarried. Powell later said: "My stepmother, one day, burned up all the stories I was writing, a form of discipline I could not endure. With thirty cents earned by picking strawberries, I ran away, ending up in the home of a kindly aunt at Shelby, Ohio" (Josephson 33). Powell was awarded a scholarship to Lake Erie College; after graduating in 1918, she went to New York. In 1920 she married Joseph Roebuck Gousha, an advertising executive and former music critic. Their son, Joseph, was born a year later. Complications during birth left "Jojo" mentally disabled and he spent much of his life in institutions, giving Powell impetus to work to pay for his care. The marriage survived until Gousha's death in 1962 despite perpetual financial woes and Powell's close friendship with Coburn Gilman, a wise-cracking magazine editor. Although Powell attracted a loyal following, she never achieved enough success to eliminate financial concerns. In addition to fifteen novels, Powell wrote short stories, magazine articles, book reviews, and Hollywood scripts. In the 1930s, the young, avant-garde Group Theater produced two of her plays, *Jig Saw* and *Big Night*, both of which had short runs. Powell played as hard as she worked, holding forth at the Hotel Lafayette near Washington Square, much as Dorothy Parker held sway at the Algonquin. Powell's cafe circle included JOHN DOS PASSOS, Edmund Wilson, and Malcolm Cowley; other friends and admirers included ERNEST HEMINGWAY, E. E. Cummings, and Van Wyck Brooks. Powell described her work as "neither literary nor intellectual" (Josephson 18) and acknowledged that she alienated middle-class readers with her satire; "You both confuse and anger people if you satirize the middle class," she told Robert Van Gelder. "It is considered jolly and good-humored to point out the oddities of the poor or of the rich . . . . I go outside the rules with my stuff, because I can't help believing that the middle class is funny, too" (133). Of her form of humor, she wrote: "I believe true wit should break a wise man's heart. It should strike at the exact point of weakness and it should scar. It should rest on a pillar of truth and not on a gelatine base, and the truth is not so shameful that it cannot be recorded" (*New York Times*, November 16, 1965). In 1963 Powell received the Margaret Peabody Waite Award for lifetime achievement. Powell died of cancer at St. Luke's Hospital in New York City.

**SIGNIFICANCE:** Powell called herself a "permanent visitor" in New York. Although she never returned to the Midwest to live, she could not shake the Ohio dust, and her novels frequently mirror her duality as Midwesterner and New Yorker. "Coming as I do from many generations of small town American people," Powell wrote, "I am basically interested in the problems of the provincial at home and in the world, in business, love, and art. I would like to portray these Americans as vividly as Balzac did his French provincials at home and in Paris" (*American Novelists of Today* 1951). Powell's New York novels usually feature a Midwesterner seeking fame, fortune, or freedom in the city.

**SELECTED WORKS:** Powell disavowed her first novel, *Whither* (1927), and followed it with five Ohio novels: *She Walks in Beauty* (1928), *The Bride's House* (1929), *Dance Night* (1930, 1994), *The Tenth Moon* (1932), and *The Story of a Country Boy* (1934). A decade later, she rounded out her Ohio novels with *My Home Is Far Away* (1944, 1995). Her New York novels are *Turn, Magic Wheel* (1936, 1994), *The Happy Island* (1938), *Angels on Toast* (1940, 1990; revised as a paperback titled *A Man's Affair* in 1956), *A Time to Be Born* (1942, 1991), *The Locusts Have No King* (1948, 1990), *The Wicked Pavilion* (1954, 1990), *A Cage for Lovers* (1957), and *The Golden Spur* (1962, 1990). Her short stories are collected in *Sunday, Monday and Always* (1952). *Jig Saw* (1933, 1934) is her only published play.

**FURTHER READING:** Key sources include Tim Page's *Dawn Powell: A Biography* (1998) and *The Diaries of Dawn Powell 1931–1965* (1995). Powell is mentioned in several of Edmund Wilson's journals (*The Thirties, The Forties, The Fifties, The Sixties*). Two key essays are Gore Vidal's "Dawn Powell: The American Writer," in *At Home* (1990), and Matthew Josephson's "Dawn Powell: A Woman of Esprit," in *Southern Review* 9.1 (January 1973): 18–52. Also of note is Robert Van Gelder's short interview "Some Difficulties Confronting the Satirist," in *Writers and Writing* (1946): 132–34. Marcelle Smith Rice provides a critical study of Powell's work in the Twayne *Dawn Powell* (2000). Powell's papers are at Columbia University.

MARCELLE SMITH RICE
NORTH CAROLINA STATE UNIVERSITY

## J(AMES) F(ARL) POWERS
July 8, 1917–June 12, 1999

**BIOGRAPHY:** Novelist and short story writer J. F. Powers was born in Jacksonville, Illinois, the son of James and Zella (Routzong) Powers. When he was eight, the family moved to Rockford and later to Quincy, Illinois, and then to Evansville, Indiana. Powers attended Quincy College Academy, graduating in 1935, and then followed his family, who had moved to Chicago.

Since Powers could not afford to attend college full time, he took night school classes at the Chicago Avenue branch of Northwestern University while working at a variety of jobs that included selling books at Marshall Field, selling insurance, and chauffeuring a businessman through the South. After Bergen Evans, Powers's composition professor, encouraged him to write fiction, he began submitting stories to *Accent* and published his first short story in that quarterly in 1943. *Accent* also published "Lions, Harts, Leaping Does," which was selected for the *O. Henry Prize Stories of 1944* and for *Best American Short Stories of 1944*.

In 1940 Powers registered as a conscientious objector, but when he was called up for service in 1943, he was denied conscientious objector status and sent to the Sandstone federal prison in Minnesota. After serving thirteen months there, he was paroled to work as a hospital orderly in St. Paul. Shortly thereafter, he met Betty Wahl, a fledgling novelist from St. Cloud, and married her in 1946; subsequently the couple had five children.

In 1947 Powers began teaching writing courses at St. John's University in Collegeville, Minnesota, and published his first book, *Prince of Darkness and Other Stories*. "The Valiant Woman," perhaps his best-known story from this collection, won the O. Henry Award that year. The following year Powers received a National Institute of Arts and Letters grant and a Guggenheim fellowship; he would later hold Rockefeller–University of Iowa Writers' Workshop and Rockefeller–*Kenyon Review* fellowships.

Although Powers was reluctant to take teaching jobs because they left him little time to write, he taught at Marquette University from 1949 to 1951; at the University of Michigan from 1956 to 1957; and at Smith College from 1965 to 1966. The year 1956 saw the publication of a second short story collection, *The Presence of Grace*, and in 1963 his first novel, *Morte D'Urban* (1962), won the National Book Award.

In an effort to live more cheaply, safely, and simply, the Powers family made four trips to Ireland, residing there for a cumulative total of fourteen years. "Tinkers," the last story in Powers's third short story collection, *Look How the Fish Live* (1975), reflects this experience, as does Betty's novel *Rafferty* (1969).

After the family returned from Ireland in 1975, Powers accepted the position of Regents' Professor of English at St. John's University; thirteen years later he lost his beloved wife of forty-two years to cancer. Powers retired in 1993. He died of natural causes at his home in Collegeville, Minnesota, on June 12, 1999. **SIGNIFICANCE:** The central figures in Powers's fiction are usually Catholic priests. Father Urban Roche, the star performer of the

struggling Order of St. Clement, is the protagonist of Powers's first novel, *Morte D'Urban*. Father Urban's preaching has won influential friends for the Clementines among Chicago businessmen, notably Billy Cosgrove. However, Father Urban is transferred to rural Minnesota in what he regards as a jealous move by his superior, Father Boniface. There he joins Father Wilfrid and Brother Harold in their efforts to convert a recently acquired county poorhouse into a retreat house for priests and their parishioners. Months later Father Urban, with help from Billy Cosgrove, purchases an adjoining farm and constructs a golf course to attract a better class of men to the refurbished retreat house. Here he discovers that wealthy patrons can be cruel and mean-spirited. Knocked out after a bishop's stray golf ball strikes him in the head, he experiences a spiritual rebirth, which his fellow Clementines recognize by electing him Provincial of the Order of St. Clement.

Powers's second novel, *Wheat That Springeth Green*, was not published until 1988, twenty-six years after *Morte D'Urban*. This novel focuses on Joe Hackett, the pampered son of a well-to-do coal dealer in an Illinois town. Although he is much influenced by a very worldly, non-Catholic uncle, he decides to become a priest instead of a businessman. He wants, he says, to get a lot of fun out of life while he performs good works so he will be assured of a high place in heaven. When he enters the seminary, Joe puts his secular adolescence behind him and determines to become a saintly priest. For a time he wears a hair shirt in his pursuit of holiness and is labeled "Holy Joe," and "a spiritual athlete" (42, 46) by his more worldly fellow seminarians. Joe's increasing abhorrence of the materialism threatening the Church peaks at his ordination during a confrontation with the money-grubbing pastor of his home parish, Father "Dollar" Bill Stock. But when Joe is sent out as an assistant to the most contemplative priest in the diocese, he learns the realities of a priest's life. Father Van Slaag spends so much time on his knees that they have developed horny gray calluses. While their priest prays, his parishioners are left to their own devices. To fill this void, Joe begins to work with the people of the parish and finds that he can ably do the job of a parish priest. When he gets his own parish, Joe draws a hippie assistant pastor who wears sandals and jeans and initiates guitar masses; Joe's resulting discomfort reflects the conflict between traditional Catholicism and post–Vatican II reformism.

Through his priest characters Powers examines the conflict between spiritual and temporal values in the present-day Mammon-dominated world. He decries the way society works by replicating its petty power struggles and paralyzing bureaucracies in the Midwestern parishes his priests serve, writing ironically, satirically, and often humorously about the greed and boosterism they encounter daily. HAYDEN CARRUTH, reviewing *Morte D'Urban* in the *New Republic* (September 24, 1988): 147, lauds Powers for having "revived the satire of the Great Age . . . within a modern context of style and attitude" (24–25).

Powers is not a skeptic, however. He continues to believe in the power of his church to save the world from "dreck." Powers sets his fiction within convincingly recognizable small towns and small-town parishes in Minnesota. Though his shopping malls and discount houses are not exclusively Midwestern phenomena, they are certainly Midwestern in the way that they highlight the materialism and conformism that are so closely associated with Middle America. Writing about one of Powers's best stories, "Lions, Harts, Leaping Does," Julian Moynahan, in the *New York Review of Books* 35 (December 8, 1988), praises Powers's "severely restricted imagery—Minnesota imagery—of snow falling on bare frozen fields as night comes, of an ancient high-shouldered canary escaping its cage and out through a window deliberately opened into the icy dark" (52). Because Powers has always had a keen ear for the speech of ordinary people and the ability to write convincing dialogue, the language his people speak is Midwestern language and remarkably true.

**SELECTED WORKS:** Powers has published three short story collections: *Prince of Darkness and Other Stories* (1947), *The Presence of Grace* (1956), and *Look How the Fish Live* (1975). His two novels are *Morte D'Urban* (1962) and *Wheat That Springeth Green* (1988). In 1991 the Minnesota Center for Book Arts reprinted a 1943 short story, "The Old Bird, A Love Story." The publication, with woodcuts by Barbara Har-

man, was published in a limited edition of forty copies and a standard edition of two hundred and sixty copies.

**FURTHER READING:** Excellent sources on Powers are John V. Hagopian's critical biography *J. F. Powers* (1968) and a collection of essays edited by Fallon Evans, also called *J. F. Powers* (1968). A helpful bibliography is Jeffrey Meyers's "J. F. Powers: Uncollected Stories, Essays and Interviews, 1943–1979," published in the *Bulletin of Bibliography* 44 (March 1987): 38–39. Ross Labrie's *The Catholic Imagination in American Literature* (1988) contains a brief chapter on Powers's fiction. Interviews with Powers include John DuBois's "Gruff Novelist Charms Critics," *St. Cloud Times* (October 2, 1988): 1c-8c; Bob Lundegaard's "A Long Time between Books," *Minneapolis Star Tribune* (October 9, 1988): 1–6ex; Colman McCarthy's "A Minnesota Writer Does More with Less," *Minneapolis Star Tribune* (June 8, 1988): 13a; Michael Powers's "An Interview with J. F. Powers," *Lower Stumpf Lake Review* 16 (Spring 1979): 53–59; John Rosengren's "Awesome Powers," *Minneapolis–St. Paul Magazine* (January 1989): 81–83; Anthony Schmitz's "The Alphabet God Uses: A Conversation with J. F. Powers," *Minnesota Monthly* 22 (December 1988): 35–39; Robert T. Smith's "Novelist Offers Look at Society through Men of Cloth," *Minneapolis Star Tribune* (January 16, 1992): 5b; and Dave Wood's "J. F. Powers's Book Surprises," *Minneapolis Star Tribune* (January 16, 1992): 1e-3e. A large and varied collection of Powers's papers is held by the University of Illinois Archive in Urbana, Illinois.

CLARENCE A. GLASRUD

MINNESOTA STATE UNIVERSITY

MARCIA NOE

THE UNIVERSITY OF TENNESSEE AT CHATTANOOGA

# JAMES (OTIS) PURDY

July 17, 1914

**BIOGRAPHY:** Although James Purdy, short story writer, playwright, novelist and poet, has usually given his birth date as 1923, in fact he was born in 1914 to William B. Purdy and Vera (Otis) Purdy in Hicksville, Ohio. James was the second of three sons born to the Purdys, the oldest of whom, Richard (1909–67), became a briefly successful actor. The youngest brother, Robert, was born in Findlay in 1921, where the family moved following William's failure in Hicksville as a banker and financier. After Purdy's mother divorced his father in 1930, William worked as a real estate agent in Bowling Green, his hometown, where James went to college.

After graduating from Bowling Green State College in 1935, James Purdy studied at the University of Chicago, earning his AM in 1937. While there, he met Chicago artist Gertrude Abercrombie, novelist Wendell Wilcox, and Chicago industrialist and author Osborn Andreas, who in the 1950s became Purdy's patron. Subsequently he served in the U.S. Army, studied Spanish at the University of Chicago during the 1944–45 academic year, and studied at the University of Pueblo, Mexico, in the summer of 1945. In 1945–46 he taught English at the Ruston Academy in Havana, Cuba, followed by nine and one-half years of teaching Spanish at Lawrence College in Appleton, Wisconsin. Then, with the encouragement of Osborn and Miriam Andreas, and with support from the Andreas Foundation, he returned to Chicago to pursue writing.

In 1957 he moved to New York City, eventually settling in Brooklyn Heights, his present home. There he reportedly lives a reclusive life, writing in a small apartment, nourished by the memories and ghosts of his early life in the Midwest, which he never visits. The rare interviews he grants are devoted to fulminating against the New York literary establishment and the media and to evading direct questions about his early life in Ohio and the possible autobiographical significance of his fiction.

**SIGNIFICANCE:** Although Purdy has written plays and poetry as well as fiction, the bulk of his writing consists of short stories and novels. From his first critical notices in the early 1960s to the present, he has successively been labeled a postmodernist, a Gothic writer, and more recently, a gay writer, but none of these labels quite does justice to the variety and distinctive texture of his work. What is fair to say, however, is that the Midwestern, realistic elements in his early fiction and his later, obsessive, fictional reworking of early experiences in Hicksville, Findlay, and Bowling Green, Ohio, have been scarcely noted.

Beginning with *The House of the Solitary Maggot* (1974), the realistic elements in Purdy's fiction, though not abandoned, become so overlaid with fantasy, horror, and personal mythmaking as to be much diminished in significance. In the process, Purdy's critical reputation, at a high point in the early 1970s, has gradually declined.

**SELECTED WORKS:** One of Purdy's best works of fiction is his first collection of short stories, *Don't Call Me by My Right Name and Other Stories* (1956), reissued in 1957 as *Color of Darkness*. Most of these early stories are set in small towns recalling the realistic fiction of SHERWOOD ANDERSON's *Winesburg, Ohio*, but with a cutting edge of cynicism and suffering not found in Anderson.

Three works with Chicago settings also deserve attention here: *Malcolm* (1954); the nightmarish, surrealistic novella *63: Dream Palace* (1957); and the long, terrifying *Eustace Chisholm and the Works* (1967), a story of two ill-fated love triangles culminating in indescribably brutal sadomasochism. This last may well be Purdy's most powerful novel. Like most of his novels, each of the Chicago works has a youth in it who has lost his father by death, divorce, or long, unexplained absence. And despite the dream-like quality of these works, their realism is apparent in the fact that Chicago streets and landmarks and such characters as the painter Gertrude Abercrombie, also alluded to in *Gertrude of Stony Island Avenue* (1997), the writer Wilcox, and the patron Andreas and his wife, Miriam, are clearly identifiable in them, though distorted for dramatic effect.

Finally, two realistic novels, even richer in autobiographical significance, should be mentioned: *The Nephew* (1960), set in Rainbow Center, a thinly disguised Bowling Green, Ohio; and *Jeremy's Version* (1970), set in Boutflour (Findlay) with flashbacks to Hittisleigh (Hicksville), Purdy's birthplace. Though both these novels dwell on painful aspects of disintegrating family life in a small town, they also have moments of optimism and mellow, nostalgic humor at odds with Purdy's characteristic pessimism and acerbic, baleful wit.

**FURTHER READING:** The first book on Purdy's fiction was Bettina Schwarzschild's *The Not-Right House* (1968), followed by Henry Chupack's *James Purdy* (1975) and Stephen Adams's *James Purdy* (1976). Of these three, Adams's book provides the most thorough appreciation and analysis of Purdy's art to date. While neither Schwarzschild nor Adams tackles Purdy's biography, Chupack includes biographical information, some of it incorrect. To establish the biographical context of the Chicago novels, Paul Miller has written "James Purdy's Fiction as Shaped by the American Midwest: The Chicago Novels," in *American Literature in Belgium* (1988): 149–61. An interesting recent commentary on Purdy is provided by James Morrison's "James Purdy (1927–)," in *Contemporary Gay American Novelists* (1993): 328–39. Some of Purdy's manuscripts are at the Beinecke Library (Yale) and the University of Texas.

PAUL W. MILLER          WITTENBERG UNIVERSITY

## (ERNEST) "ERNIE" (TAYLOR) PYLE

August 3, 1900–April 18, 1945

**BIOGRAPHY:** Ernie Pyle was born in a farmhouse near the small town of Dana, Indiana. His parents, William Clyde and Maria (Taylor) Pyle, were sharecroppers for the Sam Elder family, a fairly affluent family who lived in the area. After graduating from Bono High School in the spring of 1918, he entered the U.S. Naval Reserves hoping eventually to get into the action of World War I. The Armistice, however, was signed before he completed his training. Pyle enrolled in Indiana University in the fall of 1919 and decided to study journalism. He eventually became the city editor for the *Indiana Daily Student*. Six months before he was scheduled to graduate, Pyle got his first job as a reporter for the *LaPorte Herald*. Approximately four months later, the *Washington Daily News*, one of the Scripps Howard newspapers, offered him a $2.50–a-week raise to come work for them. On July 7, 1925, Pyle married Geraldine (Jerry) Siebolds, a civil service worker originally from Afton, Minnesota.

From 1928 to 1932, Pyle wrote the first daily column ever devoted entirely to the new industry of aviation. He eventually became the managing editor of the *Daily News*, a job that he especially hated because he was constantly behind a desk and was unable to do the traveling and reporting that he loved so much. In 1935 the Scripps Howard executives allowed him to become a "roving reporter." He could go where he wished and write what he wished as long as he turned in six columns a week. The following five years took Pyle and his wife all over the United States, Central America, and South America. It was during this time that he became known as the "Hoosier Vagabond" and perfected his abilities at using plain, everyday language to tell the human interest stories of ordinary people.

Pyle had his first experiences as a war correspondent in November 1940 when he went to London to cover the Battle of Britain. When the United States officially entered World War II after the attack on Pearl Harbor, he tried to join the army but was too old. He then became an official civilian war correspondent for the Scripps Howard news service. Beginning in November 1942, Pyle covered the action in North Africa. He then went to Sicily and Normandy beach one day after D-Day, and he eventually accompanied the Allies during the liberation of Paris. He was awarded the Pulitzer Prize in May 1944. After a few months of rest back in the United States, Pyle began his coverage of the war in the Pacific in January 1945. He was there for only four months when he was killed by Japanese machine-gun sniper fire on the tiny island of Ie Shima, approximately three miles west of Okinawa.

**SIGNIFICANCE:** Pyle's background and upbringing as a Hoosier farm boy perfectly laid the groundwork for his eventual style of writing which was to make him so popular. As a child, he and his family epitomized the normal, everyday people he eventually sought to glorify. He had little use for the rich and famous, possibly due in part to the extreme insecurity he felt in childhood as a country boy around the town kids in Dana. Neither his family nor his education in a small, local, country school fostered an environment for learning the flowery language and the grand words which were the norm in newspapers in the early part of this century. Pyle, of course, took these experiences and attitudes with him to Indiana University.

Many editors of the *Indiana Daily Student* considered Pyle's writing too simplistic, but public opinion and readership statistics would prove otherwise. His human-interest columns eventually captured the attention and heart of an entire nation. Whether he was reporting on the experimental flight of a new airplane, chronicling the story of the last living slave, or reporting the carnage he saw at Normandy, Ernie Pyle always put himself in the shoes of those people about whom he was reporting. He demanded no special favors or treatment and became extremely uncomfortable the few times it was offered. Because of Pyle's unpretentious style, readers, regardless of class, color, economic, or social distinctions, felt they were living his experiences vicariously through him. He was their eyes and ears to places, events, and people otherwise beyond the scope of their own experiences.

Although Pyle's trips back home to Dana grew very infrequent, he never forgot his family or his roots. The humor, triumphs, and tragedies of his family life were fair game in his columns, ranging from his aunt's recipe for preserving fried chicken to his mother's death while he was in England. Readers throughout the country thought of his family as their own, and soon the tiny town of Dana and the entire Pyle family were receiving national attention. In turn, Indiana has worked tirelessly to preserve the memory of one of its favorite sons. Perhaps the most fitting tribute to Pyle is found at his alma mater. A journalism scholarship is named for him at Indiana University, and the Indiana University School of Journalism is located in Ernie Pyle Hall. This and many other tributes in Indiana and throughout the country will ensure that the spirit of an extremely gifted journalist is preserved for years to come.

**SELECTED WORKS:** Pyle's major writings include *Ernie Pyle in England* (1941), *Here Is Your War* (1943), *Brave Men* (1944), *Last Chapter* (1946), and *Home Country* (1947). More recently, David Nichols has edited *Ernie's War: The Best of Ernie Pyle's World War II Dispatches* (1986) and *Ernie's America: The Best of Ernie Pyle's Travel Dispatches* (1989).

**FURTHER READING:** Book-length works considering Ernie Pyle include Lee Graham Miller's *The Story of Ernie Pyle* (1950), Barbara O'Connor's *The Soldiers' Voice: The Story of Ernie Pyle* (1996), and James Tobin's *Ernie Pyle's War: America's Eyewitness to World War II* (1997). In addition, Pyle's original columns and his private correspondence are available for study at the Ernie Pyle State Historic Site in Dana, Indiana.

KRISTA ANN GREENBERG

UNIVERSITY OF INDIANAPOLIS

# (JOHN) HERBERT QUICK

October 23, 1861–May 10, 1925

**BIOGRAPHY:** Herbert Quick was born on a farm in Grundy County near Steamboat Rock, Iowa, the son of Martin and Margaret (Coleman) Quick who married, each for a second time, on a pioneer journey westward from New York. In his autobiography, *One Man's Life* (1925), Quick describes himself as a "true son of the prairie" (39) whose ancestors "were, with one or two exceptions, Dutch" (7); a bit of Irish ancestry came from his mother's side. As an infant, Quick suffered infantile paralysis, which excluded him from certain youthful activities and gave him "a rather odd walk" (51) for life. Neither disease nor limited schooling prevented him from reading voraciously, thereby adding a large literary reservoir to his personal experience.

During his varied career he was author, editor, teacher, school principal, lawyer, mayor (of Sioux City, Iowa, from 1898 to 1900), lecturer, businessman, Red Cross executive, and organizer of the Federal Farm Loan Bureau. A voluminous writer of editorials and articles, as well as books, Quick spent much of his life in Iowa but moved permanently in 1912 to a country estate in Berkeley Springs, West Virginia, where he lived with his wife, Ella D. Corey, whom he married in 1890, his daughter Margaret, and son Edward. He died of heart failure in Columbia, Missouri, after a university lecture there.

**SIGNIFICANCE:** Quick devoted most of his early literary career to journalistic writing; as editor of a national farm paper, *Farm and Fireside*, from 1909 to 1916, he consistently championed movements and actions benefiting farmers. Though Quick did not become a serious imaginative writer until he was forty years old, he produced several volumes, the most important and successful of which are three novels—*Vandemark's Folly* (1922), *The Hawkeye* (1923), and *The Invisible Woman* (1924)—which constitute the Iowa trilogy and provide a social history of the challenging pre–Civil War trek from central New York to Monterey County, Iowa, through the clearing and settling of the prairies, to the establishment of small rural towns in the late nineteenth century.

Fremont McConkey, the would-be literary artist and strongly autobiographical hero of *The Hawkeye*, speaks Quick's own conviction: "I know that if the artist born in Iowa could only be allowed such a life of the soul as would impel him to respect his Iowa materials, and to ponder them long enough and deeply enough, every element of great art would be found here" (476–77). Although the artist Quick is sometimes overwhelmed by the social historian, he succeeds in giving his native state a past not previously acknowledged. Focusing on Iowa while also embracing a larger Midwestern scene, Quick offers vividly authentic accounts of converting virgin prairies into crop-producing fields, the ceaseless struggles of farming, the political and economic intricacies of small-town living, concern for preserving natural resources, and the ongoing need for social reform. With a vision somewhat brighter and more melodramatic than that of HAMLIN GARLAND, SHERWOOD ANDERSON, and RUTH SUCKOW, he writes consistently with a passionate affirmation of ordinary rural people.

**SELECTED WORKS:** Quick tells his life story to approximately 1890 in *One Man's Life: An Autobiography* (1925). His major fictional works form the Iowa or Hawkeye trilogy: *Vandemark's Folly* (1922), *The Hawkeye* (1923), and *The Invisible Woman* (1924). Novels and semi-fictional works which focus on reform issues are *Aladdin and Co.: A Romance of Yankee Magic* (1904), *The Broken Lance* (1907), *The Brown Mouse* (1915), and *The Fairview Idea: A Story of the New Rural Life (1919)*. Additional novels are *Double Trouble or, Every Hero His Own Villain* (1906) and *Virginia of the Air Lines* (1909). Nonfictional works include *American Inland Waterways* (1909), *On Board the Good Ship Earth: A Survey of World Problems* (1913), *The New Farm Wife* (1919), and *The Real Trouble with Farmers* (1924). Connected short stories appear in *Yellowstone Nights* (1911) and a dramatic piece is *There Came Two Women* (1924). Quick's last book, *Mississippi Steamboatin': A History of Steamboating on the Mississippi and Its Tributaries* (1926), was written with his son, Edward.

**FURTHER READING:** Doctoral dissertations include Carl Lee Keen's "The Fictional Writings of Herbert Quick" (1967); Frederick Garver Morain's "Herbert Quick: Iowa Agrarian" (1970); Richard Whitt Ferguson's "Herbert Quick and the Search for a New American Frontier: A Biography" (1978); and Charlene M. Hawks's "Herbert Quick: Iowan" (1981). A chapter on Quick appears in Clarence Andrews's *A Literary History of Iowa* (1972): 66–77.

The bulk of Quick's papers were deposited by his daughter Margaret Quick Ball in 1973 in the Iowa State Department of History and Archives in Des Moines. Selected papers are also in the Lilly Library at Indiana University in Bloomington, Special Collections at the University of Iowa Library in Iowa City, and public libraries in Grundy Center, Mason City, and Sioux City, Iowa.

SARA MCALPIN BVM               CLARKE COLLEGE

## DUDLEY FELKER RANDALL
January 14, 1914–August 5, 2000

**BIOGRAPHY:** Dudley Felker Randall, librarian, poet in residence, visiting lecturer, poet, editor, publisher, and poet laureate of Detroit, was born in Washington, D.C. His father, Arthur George Clyde Randall, was a Congregational minister; his mother, Ada Viola (Bradley), was a teacher. Randall spent most of his life in Detroit, Michigan, working first as a foundry worker for the Ford Motor Company and then as a postal carrier and clerk. He served in the U.S. Army in the South Pacific during World War II. At the conclusion of the war he resumed his position at the post office while enrolling in Wayne State University, where he received his BA in 1949. He studied library science at the University of Michigan and was awarded an MA in 1951. He worked as librarian, associate librarian, assistant branch librarian, and branch librarian at Lincoln University, Morgan State College, and Wayne County Federated Library System, where he was the head of the reference-interlibrary loan department from 1963 through 1969. At the University of Detroit he served as both reference librarian and poet in residence.

Randall's Detroit years were his most productive and influential. During these years he published six books of poetry: *Poem Counterpoem* (1966) with Margaret Danner; *Cities Burning* (1968); *Love You* (1970); *More to Remember: Poems of Four Decades* (1971); *After the Killing* (1973); and *A Litany of Friends: New and Selected Poems* (1981). He also contributed to a variety of anthologies and texts, and more importantly, edited *The Black Poets* (1971); *Homage to Hoyt Fuller* (1984), and *For Malcolm: Poems on the Life and Death of Malcolm X* (1967).

During the 1960s, 1970s, and 1980s, Randall steadily garnered honors. He was the winner of the Tompkins Prize in 1962 and 1966 from Wayne State University. In 1978 he was awarded an honorary Doctor of Letters from the University of Detroit and named that city's poet laureate by Mayor Coleman Young in 1981. He has received an Arts Award in literature, a Creative Artist Award in literature, and a National Endowment for the Arts Fellowship as well as a Senior Fellowship in 1981. In 1989 the Society for the Study of Midwestern Literature gave him its Mark Twain Award.

Randall lived in Detroit with his second wife, Vivian Spencer, until his death of congestive heart failure in Southfield, Michigan. His marriage to Ruby Hands ended in divorce. He had one daughter, Phyllis Sharon.

**SIGNIFICANCE:** Randall was the most influential publisher of new voices in black American poetry beginning in 1965 and ending in the mid-1980s. His achievement in terms of Midwestern literature can be seen in his ability to discover and publish a vast array of black authors during this period. His agenda simply was to give voice to those writers who had no other outlet. No other individual may lay claim to such an overriding influence. During that period the Broadside Press, which Randall founded in 1963, was the first to publish Sonia Sanchez, Etheridge Knight, Nikki Giovanni, Haki R. Madhubuti, James A. Emanuel, Sarah Webster Fabio, Lance Jeffers, Audre Lorde, Doughtry Long, James Thompson, Keorapetse Kgositsile, and Houston A. Baker Jr. Randall also published works by such established writers as GWENDOLYN BROOKS, Margaret Walker, and ROBERT HAYDEN. In an April 11, 1982, *Detroit Magazine* article entitled "The Courtly Librarian Who Became the Ben Franklin of Black Poetry," Suzanne Dolezal writes that Randall "became dedicated to giving the emerging black poetry the forum it needed" (6). Dolezal continues, expressing the importance of Randall's distinguished career. She writes, "Beyond Randall's contributions as a poet, his role as editor and publisher . . . [has proved] invaluable to the Afro-American community" (6) and to the larger canon of American literature.

**SELECTED WORKS:** Randall's major poetic works include *Poem Counterpoem* (1966), *Cities Burning* (1968), *More to Remember: Poems of Four Decades* (1971), *After the Killing* (1973), *A Litany of Friends* (1983), and *Homage to Hoyt Fuller* (1984). As an editor, as a contributor,

and as a collaborator with other anthologists, his total output can rightly include the following: *For Malcolm: Poems on the Life and Death of Malcolm X* (1969), *Black Poetry: A Supplement to Anthologies Which Exclude Black Poets* (1969), *The Black Poets* (1971), *The Black Aesthetic* (1971), *A Capsule Course in Black Poetry Writing* (1975), *Broadside Memories: Poets I Have Known* (1975), and *Golden Song: The Fiftieth Anniversary Anthology of the Poetry Society of Michigan* (1985). His poetry has been widely anthologized and published in many periodicals.

**FURTHER READING:** R. Baxter Miller's *"Endowing the World and Time": The Life and Work of Dudley Randall* (1986) is so far the only full-length study which examines the poet's poetry and his relationship to other African American poets from 1940 to 1960. There is also D. H. Melhem's *Dudley Randall: A Humanist View* (1983), which examines the poet's poetry and his poetic technique as well as his treatment of African Americans. Four significant interviews have been granted: A. X. Nicholas's "A Conversation with Dudley Randall" (1971), Hoyt Fuller's "Interview with Gwendolyn Brooks" (1973), *Black World's* "Black Publisher, Black Writer: An Answer" (1975), and Charles H. Rowell's "In Conversation with Dudley Randall" (1976), each of which examines his observations and changing opinions on the state of American and African American poetry. The books published while he was publisher-editor of Broadside Press as well as the important papers associated with those years are housed in the Rare Books Room in the William S. Carlson Library on the campus of the University of Toledo.

Two August 10, 2000, *Detroit Free Press* articles mark Randall's death. The first, "Dudley Randall: Poet, publisher, inspired others," is an obituary and appreciation of Detroit's poet laureate. This article, by Ben Schmitt and Cassandra Spratling, details Randall's life and the emergence of his Broadside Press in response to the 1963 bombing of a Birmingham, Alabama, church. The authors cite the importance of Randall and his press in encouraging and publishing African American writers. The second article, "Poet laureate Dudley Randall dies at 86," is unsigned. It excerpts Randall's poem "Detroit Renaissance," reflecting his commitment to Detroit and to using literature to transform pain and loss into beauty, hope, and inspiration.

HERBERT WOODWARD MARTIN

UNIVERSITY OF DAYTON

## VANCE RANDOLPH

February 23, 1892–November 1, 1980

**BIOGRAPHY:** Born in Pittsburg, Kansas, of professional parents, John and Theresa (Gould) Randolph, Vance Randolph spent his first twenty years in Pittsburg, a Midwestern border city full of political shenanigans and Western frontier attitudes. He attended public schools in the city where his father was a lawyer and his mother a schoolteacher and librarian. In 1910 he enrolled for undergraduate work at Pittsburg's State Manual Training Normal School, now Pittsburg State University. He graduated in 1914 with most of his course work centered in the natural sciences. For graduate work in the fall of 1914, he entered Clark University, Worcester, Massachusetts, where his courses centered in psychology with an emphasis upon psychoanalysis. He graduated with an MA in 1914.

In 1923 Randolph was offered an assistant instructor position in psychology at the University of Kansas for a salary of $800. He accepted the offer but worked only during the academic year of 1924. He gave up the position in order to continue his writing career, which he had already begun in southern Missouri. Randolph had actually come to the Ozarks in the early 1920s, arriving in the small town of Pineville, Missouri. Here Randolph began his research into the traditional life ways of the Ozark Midwestern mountain people.

Randolph's ability to observe and listen helped him develop the skills needed to become a Midwestern folklorist of central and southern Missouri and northern Arkansas. Because all of his tales came from the preceding locations, he was classified as an Ozark folklorist. Robert Cochran, a professor of English at the University of Arkansas, says in his biography *Vance Randolph: An Ozark Life* (1985) that there are two groups of people to whom Randolph appeals, "the first, a diverse band, is comprised of celebrators of the Ozark region, people who for reasons of residence, family connection, patriotic ardor, huckster greed or some mix thereof have made it their business to publicize the virtues of the area.

The second group of fans is more homogeneous, composed of scholars, folklorists, cultural geographers, Americanists, students of regional dialect and anthropologists" (12). The latter have studied him for his methodological innovations and for the tenacity with which he pursued his work.

**SIGNIFICANCE:** Randolph's methods of recording folklore were more casual than those of most other folklorists. Most of his collected tales were first set down in longhand and typed a few hours later while the details were still fresh in his mind. His transcripts were not literary adaptations; he did not add embellishments, characters, or incidents or try to improve the original narrator's style. He simply set down each item as accurately as he could, giving his writings the feel of the Ozark dialect. His folklore tales distinctively characterize the hill people of the Midwestern state of Missouri.

In the early part of his career, the 1930s and 1940s, his first works were ignored or severely criticized as not being academic. By the mid-1950s he was recognized as an excellent folklorist; by the 1970s he was a regional Midwestern Ozark patriarch who was praised nationally.

**SELECTED WORKS:** Randolph's major folklore works include *A Reporter in the Ozarks* (1931), *Ozark Mountain Folks* (1932), *From an Ozark Holler: A Collection of Stories* (1933), *Ozarks Outdoors: Hunting and Fishing* (1934), *Ozark Anthology* (1940), *Wild Stories from the Ozarks* (1943), *Tall Tales from the Ozarks* (1944), *Ozark Folksongs* (1946), *We Always Lie to Strangers* (1951), *Who Blowed up the Church House* (1952), *The Devil's Pretty Daughter* (1955), *The Talking Turtle* (1957), *Sticks in the Knapsack* (1958), *Ozark Folklore: A Bibliography* (1972), and *Pissing in the Snow* (1976).

**FURTHER READING:** Robert Cochran's *Vance Randolph: An Ozark Life* (1985) provides a major biography. Robert Cochran and Mike Luster's *For Love and for Money: Vance Randolph, an Annotated Bibliography* (1979) provides major criticism.

LELAND MAY

NORTHWEST MISSOURI STATE UNIVERSITY

## (ARTHUR) BURTON RASCOE

October 22, 1892–March 19, 1957

**BIOGRAPHY:** Arthur Burton Rascoe was

born in Fulton, Kentucky, the son of Matthew Lafayette and Elizabeth (Burton) Rascoe. After attending the Carr Institute School, he went to high school in Shawnee, Oklahoma. The discovery of oil on the family farm gave him a sense of independence. His interest in journalism led him to work for the *Shawnee Herald*. He moved to Chicago in order to attend the University of Chicago, where he became a campus correspondent and proved to be an aggressive reporter.

During the course of his life Burton Rascoe was a columnist, a critic, an editor, and a freelance writer. His job at the *Chicago Tribune* began while he was still a student at the University of Chicago. Believing that activities of the academic world were too often ignored by the general press, he profiled many of the works of professors to popularize them through news reports. Because of his own impressive performance, he was hired as a full-time reporter in 1913 after two years at the university. He had a varied career at the *Tribune*. Not only did he become the assistant editor for the Sunday paper, he was also both the drama and literary critic. Moreover, he translated French, German, and Latin works as demanded by the editorial department.

As a result of some disparaging remarks that he made about Mary Baker Eddy and the Christian Science Church, Rascoe was fired from the *Tribune* and left the city in December 1920. At first he returned to his home in Oklahoma and then moved to New York City, as had many others associated with the Chicago Renaissance. Once again, he worked for several journals. He was an associate editor of *McCall's Magazine* from 1921 to 1922 and became the literary editor of the *New York Tribune* from 1922 to 1924. A few years later (1927–28), he was selected to edit the *Bookman*, a significant journal of literary criticism which had been established in 1895 and existed until 1932. He brought a degree of flamboyance to what had been a staid journal.

From the 1920s, he held various editorial positions, often simultaneously, and wrote syndicated columns. Probably his most noteworthy commentary, "Daybook of a New Yorker," was syndicated and appeared in more than four newspapers. He died in New York City.

**SIGNIFICANCE:** Both FRANCIS HACKETT and Burton Rascoe took literature seriously and wanted their readers to do so as well. At a time when literary criticism was often genteel and moralistic, Rascoe's courageous work in Chicago and later in New York often flaunted traditions. Like Hackett at the *Evening Post*, Rascoe did much to free literary criticism from a type of censorship that came not only from the city's ecclesiastical establishment but also from the influential club women whose husbands were powerful businessmen. Rascoe made the issue one of general public interest when, in 1913, he publicized attempts by the Chicago Women's Club to ban those authors whose works were thought to be obscene or too explicit in their descriptions. As might be expected, Rascoe aptly noted in his autobiography, *Before I Forget* (1937), that any attempt to censor a work would merely lead to its increased popularity (193).

As the editor of the Saturday book page, he was extremely witty and introduced what was known as the "high brow" page. In her autobiography, *Many Lives—One Love* (1972), Fanny Butcher defines the high brow page as "the entire front page of a Sunday feature section . . . printed in wider columns than the rest of the paper, and it contained manna for those striving to read about ideas" (114). *Tribune* readers were introduced to the varied work of Joseph Conrad, George Bernard Shaw, H. G. Wells, and Vicente Blasco-Ibáñez, as well as having the opportunity to read articles by H. L. Mencken, Edith Wharton, Harold MacGrath, and George Jean Nathan. He was an early advocate of some writers who have since become part of the canon of modern American literature. For example, he campaigned for the recognition of James Branch Cabell, SHERWOOD ANDERSON, and THEODORE DREISER, although the three writers were often considered to be either purveyors of immorality or pornography. He was a vocal and influential supporter of the judgment of HARRIET MONROE, whose *Poetry: A Magazine of Verse* was issuing the work of a diverse group of modern poets which included T. S. ELIOT, Conrad Aiken, MAXWELL BODENHEIM, Rabindranath Tagore, Ezra Pound, and Alfred Kreymborg.

In order to keep books "newsworthy," Rascoe deliberately created literary confrontations that occasioned responses, letters to the editor, and general interest in the argument that he had fostered. As a result, Chicago became the center of a particular type of literary criticism that was read almost as avidly as the news. In fact, in many instances, it was THE news.

Rascoe was highly supportive of Chicago writers and of the period that has become known as the Chicago Renaissance, an era that began approximately with the publication of HENRY BLAKE FULLER'S *The Cliff-Dwellers* in 1893 and ended with the great exodus of a number of writers from the city in the 1920s. Without abandoning what he perceived to be literary standards, Rascoe argued the case for the work of Midwestern writers. He championed the work of CARL SANDBURG, EDGAR LEE MASTERS, and VACHEL LINDSAY. His concern for regional writers went beyond the pages of the *Tribune* and his life in Chicago. In the February 1924 issue of the *Bookman*, Rascoe's column, "Literary Spotlight," focuses on Henry Blake Fuller, who is viewed as a stylist *par excellence*, even though Rascoe did not share Fuller's dim view of the city.

In retrospect, the later Chicago book critic Vincent Starrett records in his *Born in a Bookshop: Chapters from the Chicago Renascence* (1965) that some thought of Rascoe as "the liveliest book critic in Chicago." In fact, with the exception of H. L. Mencken, he was "the most influential book critic in the country" (134).

**SELECTED WORKS:** Rascoe was the author of numerous books of criticism and reminiscences. Among the most significant are *Theodore Dreiser* (1925), *Titans of Literature* (1932), *Prometheans* (1933), *The Smart Set Anthology* (1934), and *The Joys of Reading* (1937). *Belle Starr* (1941) is billed as "a biography of a Southwest Bandit Queen." Both *Before I Forget* (1937) and *We Were Interrupted* (1947) are autobiographies.

**FURTHER READING:** While most references to Burton Rascoe deal with his years in New York, his Chicago years have not been totally overlooked. His days in the Midwest are treated especially by Emmett Dedmon in *Fabulous Chicago* (1953), Vincent Starrett, *Born in a Bookshop: Chapters from the Chicago Renascence* (1965), Fanny Butcher, *Many Lives—One Love* (1972), and by Lloyd Wendt in *Chicago Tribune: The Rise of a Great American Newspaper* (1979). Other participants in the Chicago Renaissance frequently mention him. Libraries and research centers throughout the country hold numerous Rascoe letters and materials. Perhaps the largest collections are at the University of Oklahoma, the University of Pennsylvania, the University of Texas, and the University of Virginia.

KENNY J. WILLIAMS                    DUKE UNIVERSITY

## OPIE PERCIVAL (POPE) READ
December 22, 1852–November 2, 1939
(Crawfish)

**BIOGRAPHY:** Opie Read—journalist, humorist, novelist, and lecturer—was born in Nashville, Tennessee, the youngest of eleven children. His father, Guilford Read, manufactured carriages there until competition forced him to move his work to Gallatin, some fifty miles away. His mother, Elizabeth (Wallace) Read, so family legend had it, was descended from English nobility. In Gallatin, the young Opie heard Brer Fox and Brer Rabbit stories, grudgingly attended Sunday School, and dutifully studied his McGuffey reader. Under the pseudonym of "Crawfish," he published his first sketches in the nearby Franklin, Kentucky, *Patriot*. For two years he worked his way through Gallatin's Neophogen College as a typesetter for the school magazine. His hard-won education prepared him for his wander years as printer, editor, and publisher in Tennessee, Ohio, Kentucky, and Arkansas.

In 1881 Read married Ada Benham, and the following year, backed by her brother, Arkansas businessman P. D. Benham, he launched the weekly *Arkansas Traveler*. This periodical, filled with his humorous sketches and dialect stories, rankled sensibilities throughout the Midwest. In his autobiography *I Remember* (1930), Read recounts how its popularity had overwhelmed a small Little Rock post office by 1887, and how, listening to the advice of traveling men, Read and Benham moved with their magazine to Chicago that year (288).

Read would reside in Chicago with his wife and eight children for the next fifty years, playing a central role in the first phase of the Chicago Renaissance. Steering clear of the Little Room and other genteel literary groups, he gravitated to the bohemian Whitechapel Club and to the Press Club, where he drank and swapped stories with GEORGE ADE, EUGENE FIELD, FINLEY PETER DUNNE, and other Chicago journalists.

Influenced by his new environment, Read steadily shifted the *Traveler*'s focus toward Chicago and the Midwest. Though the magazine prospered, he grew tired of the weekly grind as jokesmith and yarnspinner, and increasingly he used serial installments from his novels to meet demand for copy. When Benham married and moved to St. Louis in 1892, Read gave up his post as editor; for the next twenty years he made his living writing novels and traveling the lecture circuit. In 1914 Read gave up novel writing to concentrate on golf, speech making, and the Chautauqua circuit. His wife died in Chicago in 1928; he died ten years later, from a concussion incurred in a fall at the south side Chicago home of Mrs. Ben King, widow of the Michigan poet, an old friend whose poetry he had helped publish in 1898.

**SIGNIFICANCE:** Opie Read's initial fame, and perhaps his enduring significance, rests upon his humorous tales of Arkansas squatters, stories that packed folk wisdom into earthy epigrams and sly punch lines. His railroad fiction, page-turning novels produced to be consumed and tossed aside on transcontinental journeys, soon fell out of favor and out of print. *A Kentucky Colonel* (1890) and *The Jucklins* (1896), million-plus best-sellers, now attract little interest, though some scholars judge *My Young Master* (1896) to be a powerful anti-slavery novel. His Chicago novels focus on old, settled families rather than the city's new immigrants and their sons and daughters. *The Colossus* (1893), a story of a department store magnate and his long-lost son, cranks up a plot of doubled and masked identities, high-society life, and the rough-hewn democracy of the Chicago Press Club. Chicago, as a character in *Judge Elbridge* (1899) says, exists in "the nervous atmosphere of adventure and bold trickery. The spirit of this town hates the stagnant; we wipe our muddy feet on tradition. To us the pig squeal of the present is sweeter than the flute of the past" (18). Read defined Chicago and the Midwest defiantly and often humorously against the aristocratic prejudices and illusions of the Old South and over and above what he likes to call a "puritanic" New England.

**SELECTED WORKS:** Of the thirty-five to forty novels Opie Read published, four—*The Colossus* (1893), *Judge Elbridge* (1899), *The Mystery of Margaret* (1906), and *The New Mr.*

*Howerson* (1914)—make concentrated use of Chicago settings. Read divides the action of *A Tennessee Judge* (1893) between Chicago and Gallatin while *A Yankee from the West* (1898) focuses on the Midwest and rural Illinois. *The American Cavalier* (1904), his only collection of essays, includes one on "The Chicago Man," calling the city "a great melodrama" (63). His autobiography *I Remember* (1930) details his years as a journalist and humorist.

**FURTHER READING:** Maurice Elfer's biography, *Opie Read* (1940), provides an account by one of Read's contemporaries; Robert L. Morris's appreciation, *Opie Read: American Humorist* (1965), remains the best single source for biographical information and comment on Read. Vincent Starrett's "Opie Read and the Great American Novel," in *Buried Caesars* (1923), pays generous tribute to his talents as a novelist and measures his lost popularity.

GUY SZUBERLA    UNIVERSITY OF TOLEDO

## WILLIAM MARION REEDY

December 11, 1862–July 28, 1920

**BIOGRAPHY:** Born in St. Louis, Missouri, of Irish immigrant parents Patrick Reedy and Ann (Marion) Reedy, William Marion Reedy became an influential publisher and earned a national and international reputation in literature. Reedy attended public schools, then Christian Brothers College, a Catholic preparatory school. At age fourteen he was admitted to St. Louis University where he studied both the arts and business, graduating in 1880 with a master of accounts degree.

Reedy worked as a reporter for the *Missouri Republican*, then for the *St. Louis Globe-Democrat*. He tried unsuccessfully to enter ward politics and freelanced as a writer, contributing to *Brann's Iconoclast* of Waco, Texas. Reedy reported for the *Star-Sayings*, later the *St. Louis Star*, and served as its editor for a time. In 1891 he helped found the magazine that became *Reedy's Mirror*. Begun as a journal of society, the *Mirror* under Reedy's editorship gradually changed from a gossip sheet to a sophisticated literary magazine; it lasted from February 1891 to September 1920.

Reedy's public social life was criticized and his standing suffered in some social circles. His first marriage to Agnes "Addie" Baldwin, a prostitute, in November 1893 ended in divorce in February 1896. His second marriage in March 1897 to Eulalie "Lalite" Bauduy, daughter of a socially prominent family, ended with her death in November 1901. In 1909 Reedy married Margaret Helen Chambers, a former madam, with whom he lived a happy and stable life.

Reedy died from a heart attack in San Francisco on July 28, 1920, during a trip to attend the Democratic National Convention. The *Mirror* closed shortly after his death.

**SIGNIFICANCE:** William Marion Reedy's work, centered in St. Louis, Missouri, led the national and international transformation in taste that paved the way for contemporary evaluation in prose fiction and the evolutionary changes in poetry that marked the emergence of modern poetics. In the process, he focused attention on Midwestern writers and literature. More than chronicling political events and literary developments at the turn of the century, the *Mirror*, in its transformation from society paper to critical magazine, brought literature and philosophy into the public realm, making it more accessible to the average person. In publishing and promoting writers, many of them Midwestern, Reedy encouraged a cultural atmosphere that fostered the growth of poetry and fiction. In advocating modern poetry, maintaining professional relationships with influential poets Ezra Pound, Amy Lowell, and HARRIET MONROE, Reedy participated in the literary trend that revived poetry in the early twentieth century.

The *Mirror* became a forum for political issues and literature and gained an international following. Reedy introduced several writers and poets to the public: ZOË AKINS, FANNIE HURST, ORRICK JOHNS, SARA TEASDALE, and EDGAR LEE MASTERS. He promoted realism and naturalism in the fiction of THEODORE DREISER, Kate Chopin, ALICE FRENCH, and AMBROSE BIERCE. Poets whose careers Reedy assisted include VACHEL LINDSAY, John Hall Wheelock, Yone Noguchi, and Babette Deutsch. Reedy also published such European and British writers as Joseph Conrad, Cunninghame Graham, and John Galsworthy. Reedy was accepted in literary circles for his critical expertise, as evidenced by his selection in 1919, along with Bliss Perry of Harvard and Jessie B. Rittenhouse of the Poetry Society of America, as a judge for the first Columbia Poetry Prize, which later became the Pulitzer Prize for poetry.

**SELECTED WORKS:** The *Mirror* contains most of Reedy's best writing, and twenty-seven volumes of the periodical are held at the St. Louis Public Library. Incomplete indexes of the magazine are held at the St. Louis Public Library, the Mercantile Library of St. Louis, and the University of Pennsylvania. Reedy produced one novel, *The Imitator* (1901), and collections of essays including *The Law of Love: Being Fantasies of Science and Sentiment . . .* (1905) and *A Golden Book and the Literature of Childhood* (1910). From 1899 to 1902 Reedy issued three *Mirror Pamphlet* series, which offered essays reprinted from the magazine and addresses from his speaking engagements. Typical of the pamphlets are *The Story of the Strike* (1900), on the street railway workers' strike, and *A Nest of Singing Birds* (1901), on local poets. Other publications include *Friendship's Garland, or the Escape Valve of an Enthusiast* (1899), *The Myth of the Free Press: An Address Delivered before the Missouri Press Association at Excelsior Springs, Mo., May 28, 1908* (1908), and *'Frisco the Fallen* (1916), a pamphlet reprinted as *The City That Has Fallen* (1933). Reedy contributed introductions for several books: Walter Pater's *Marius the Epicurean* (1900), Ernest McGaffey's *Sonnets to a Wife* (1901), William Hazlitt's *Liber Amoris* (1908), Robert Burns's *The Jolly Beggars, A Cantata* (1914), and Witter Bynner's *The Beloved Stranger* (1919).

**FURTHER READING:** Ethyl M. King's *Reflections of Reedy: A Biography of William Marion Reedy of Reedy's Mirror* (1961) reviews the contents of the *Mirror*. Max Putzel's *The Man in the Mirror: William Marion Reedy and His Magazine* (1963) provides an excellent bibliography that includes manuscript and letter collections. The St. Louis Public Library holds the Reedy Collection.

NANCY E. MCKINNEY
    SOUTHERN ILLINOIS UNIVERSITY AT CARBONDALE

## CONRAD (MICHAEL) RICHTER
October 13, 1890–October 30, 1968

**BIOGRAPHY:** Conrad Richter, journalist, novelist, short story writer, and essayist, was born and died in Pine Grove, Pennsylvania, a rural area between Harrisburg and Allentown. From a family of clergy, his father, John Absalom Richter, served as a Lutheran minister, pastoring in a number of small coal mining towns. The author's mother, the former

Charlotte Esther Henry, served as a minister's wife and homemaker. Richter graduated from high school at fifteen, marking the end of his formal education, but he pursued a program of self-education, reading widely.

Early on, Richter engaged in numerous occupations, ranging from farmworker and door-to-door salesman to bank teller and clerk. When only nineteen, he began newspaper work, which took him to several Pennsylvania newspapers: the *Johnstown Journal and Leader*; the *Patton Courier*, which he edited; and the *Pittsburgh Dispatch*. This newspaper work strongly influenced his writing style and supplied him with a deep pool of personalities and sensibilities. For two years he worked as a private secretary in Cleveland, Ohio, where in 1913 he began publishing short stories, a genre of writing he engaged in throughout his life. In Reading and Harrisburg, Pennsylvania, Richter participated in publishing ventures, including his own *Junior Magazine* for about a year.

Richter married Harvena Achenbach in 1915; a daughter, Harvena, was born in 1917. In 1928 the family moved West, to Albuquerque, New Mexico. There, writing finally became Richter's full-time career. With the success of *The Sea of Grass* (1937), he became an established author. The Richters remained in Albuquerque until 1950, when they moved back to Pine Grove, where the author continued writing until his death.

**SIGNIFICANCE:** In his lifetime, Richter not only won the prestigious 1960 National Book Award for *The Waters of Kronos*, considered by many critics his best book, but also the 1951 Pulitzer Prize for *The Town*, though it is commonly held that the Pulitzer was awarded for the entire Ohio trilogy. The trilogy was set in the Midwest and peopled by Midwestern characters. In the quarter-century since his death, his writings have received intermittent critical attention. His penchant for privacy and lack of self-promotion have undoubtedly contributed to this situation.

Richter's Midwestern interests are planted most noticeably in his fiction set in the region, yet they also function just beneath the surface of his Southwestern fiction, particularly in his romanticizing of the West. In fact, his writing as a whole tends to be strongly romantic and nostalgic. Early in life he developed and published on his self-made, idiosyncratic personal philosophy, which attempts to reconcile science and metaphysics and informs his fictional work. In addition to allowing for romanticism and emphasizing a nostalgic view of people in the past as superior to those of the present, it is distinctly American and Midwestern in emphasizing hard work, the character-enhancing nature of difficult times, the individual, and harmonious communities. Consequently, although Richter's writings reveal his extensive historical research, avoid overt moralizing, and are in many ways realistic, even the best of his fiction frequently seems excessively romantic.

Nonetheless, the author has produced a considerable fictional legacy. Critical attention has focused primarily on his regionalism as a Midwestern and Southwestern writer as well as on autobiographical, historical, and thematic elements. But much remains to be more thoroughly explored in Richter's fictional worlds, particularly his frequent use of "outsiders" as narrators and the elements that make his Midwestern writings distinctively Midwestern.

**SELECTED WORKS:** Richter set most of his noteworthy works in the states of Ohio and Pennsylvania. The former works reflect Midwestern characters, dialects, occupations, and attitudes toward the land and a changing Midwest both in history and in Richter's own times. His historical Ohio trilogy, collected into one volume as *The Awakening Land* in 1966 and made into a television film in 1979, consists of *The Trees* (1940), *The Fields* (1946), and *The Town* (1950). These works focus on the expanding Midwestern frontier during the 1800s. His more contemporary Pennsylvania trilogy, incomplete because he was working on the third volume when he died, consists of two books: *The Waters of Kronos* (1960) and *A Simple Honorable Man* (1962). Still widely read, particularly as adolescent fiction, *The Light in the Forest* (1953) is also set in the Midwest; its focus is on the tensions experienced by a young white boy kidnapped and adopted by Delaware Indians in frontier times.

In addition, two of his Southwestern novels bear reading: *The Sea of Grass* (1937) and *The Lady* (1957). Finally, his published work includes several other novels, some short story collections as well as scattered uncollected stories, and nonfiction elucidating his personal philosophy: *Human Vibrations* (1925) and *Principles in Bio-Physics* (1927), along with a philosophical novel, *The Mountain on the Desert* (1955).

**FURTHER READING:** One of the most interesting and informative books published about Richter is his daughter Harvena's *Writing to Survive: The Private Notebooks of Conrad Richter* (1988), which in addition to selected materials from those notebooks offers supporting text by Harvena herself. Much of the book provides information relevant to Richter's Midwestern biographical and literary concerns. Other books of value include the following: Edwin W. Gaston's *Conrad Richter* (1989); Marvin J. Lahood's *Conrad Richter's America* (1975); and Clifford D. Edwards's *Conrad Richter's Ohio Trilogy: Its Ideas, Themes, and Relationship to Literary Tradition* (1970).

Two articles focusing on Midwestern concerns, both by Marvin J. Lahood, are "Conrad Richter and Willa Cather: Some Similarities," in *Xavier University Studies* 9.1 (1970): 33–46; and "*The Light in the Forest:* History as Fiction," in *English Journal* 55 (1966): 298–304. Seven of Richter's manuscripts are located at various libraries: one at the University of California, Research Library Special Collections; two at Princeton University; three at the Fred Lewis Pattee Library, Pennsylvania State University; and one at Alderman Library, University of Virginia.

DAVID N. CREMEAN   BLACK HILLS STATE UNIVERSITY

## WALTER B. RIDEOUT.

*See* appendix (1983)

## JAMES WHITCOMB RILEY
October 7, 1849–July 22, 1916

**BIOGRAPHY:** James Whitcomb Riley was born in Greenfield, Indiana, the third child of Reuben A. and Elizabeth (Marine) Riley. During the Civil War, Reuben served as a captain of cavalry and later as a political speaker, while Elizabeth was a sympathetic and kindly mother. James Whitcomb Riley attended the Greenfield schools, where a teacher gave up hope of teaching him mathematics and interested him in literature.

After leaving school at sixteen, he read law in his father's office, then became a sign painter and an advance agent for a wagon show, for which he painted advertisements. He graduated to writing lyrics for the songs

James Whitcomb Riley.
Courtesy of the University of Kentucky Libraries

of the show and developed his acting ability. His first poem was published in the fall of 1870, in the *Greenfield Commercial*, and in 1872 he had several published by the *Indianapolis Saturday Mirror*. In 1873 he served briefly as editor of the Greenfield paper and saw several of his poems published by various newspapers; then as a reporter on the *Anderson Democrat*, he broke into the literary world rather ingloriously.

To prove his theory that to be successful and popular a poem needs only to be known as the work of a genius, he wrote "Leonainie" in the manner of Edgar Allan Poe and sent it signed with Poe's initials to the *Kokomo Dispatch*, saying that he had found it on the flyleaf of an old dictionary. When it was published, many critics accepted it as a true poem of Poe, holding to their opinions even after Riley admitted the hoax.

The *Anderson Democrat* fired him, but he was promptly hired by the *Indianapolis Journal*. Riley remained there from 1877 to 1885, writing routine assignments and also verse, which he organized into a series credited to "Benjamin F. Johnson, of Boone," that included his famous poem, "When the Frost

Is on the Punkin'." His first book was a short paper-backed collection of the *Journal* series, entitled *The Old Swimmin' Hole, and 'Leven More Poems*, by Benjamin F. Johnson, of Boone (1883), which was financed by Riley and the business manager of the *Journal*. The thousand copies were quickly sold, and a second edition was published by Merrill, Meigs and Company; this company and its successor, the Bobbs-Merrill Company, became Riley's regular publishers.

Leaving the *Journal*, Riley became a loved and famous writer and finally an institution. He published many volumes of his verse and also some prose, and several editions of his collected works appeared. He increased his popularity, not only with residents of Indiana but all over the country, by giving readings, sometimes with others, such as BILL NYE, MARK TWAIN, and EUGENE FIELD. He wrote much in dialect and was sometimes controversial, yet most readers accepted his work. When he died in Indianapolis on July 22, 1916, some thirty-five thousand people passed his bier under the dome of the Indiana state capitol.

**SIGNIFICANCE:** The general public has tended to accept Riley as a poet whose works represent wholesomeness, a sure feeling for character, common sense, and humor intertwined with pathos. At his lectures this immaculately dressed, dapper little man held his audiences in the palm of his hand when he recited his poetry, making them laugh or weep. Many critics have called him the most gifted American poet in his giving of readings, and for years he was a guest in the White House. His subject matter is often childlike adults or mischievous children with begrimed faces, topics of universal appeal. Riley had a good ear for dialect, particularly that of his less-educated contemporaries. Readers have enjoyed his poetry with its usual romantic portrayal of a life that never was. Critics condemn Riley for sentimentalism, and some argue that the dialect he uses is not true to the region where his speakers live. They criticize him for always looking backward, for never recognizing the problems of his era, and for portraying only simple characters. Although some critics have dismissed him as sub-literary, insincere, and an artificial entertainer, his defenders reply that a writer who has been so popular with millions of people in differ-

ent walks of life must contribute something of value, that his faults, if any, can be ignored. Thus, his popularity remains, not only with Midwesterners but nationally. Analyses and tributes to Riley have been written by HAMLIN GARLAND, William Lyon Phelps, Bliss Carmen, and many others.

**SELECTED WORKS:** It is difficult to suggest any particular books of Riley's for further reading, since tastes differ. His most popular poems are "Little Orphant Annie," "The Old Swimmin' Hole," "The Old Man and Jim," "When the Frost Is on the Punkin'," "Knee Deep in June," "The Raggedy Man," "The Object Lesson," and "Out to Old Aunt Mary's." There have been numerous publications since *The Old Swimmin' Hole, and 'Leven More Poems* (1883). Several books caught the public fancy, perhaps for a particular reason, such as *Juvenile Poems of James Whitcomb Riley*, chosen by William Lyon Phelps (1938). Complete editions of Riley are *Complete Works*, by Edmund H. Eitel, in six volumes (1913); and *Complete Works, Including Poems and Prose Sketches*, in ten volumes (1916). Some of Riley's publications contain a single poem and are deluxe with a great deal of art work.

**FURTHER READING:** Though a number of critics of Riley's day and afterward did not bother with Riley, those who did wrote a good deal of criticism. Some of the best sources are as follows: Bliss Carman's *James Whitcomb Riley, An Essay* (1925–26); Richard Crowder's *Those Innocent Years; the Legacy and Inheritance of a Hero of the Victorian Era* (1957); Marcus Dickey's *The Youth of James Whitcomb Riley* (1919) and *The Maturity of James Whitcomb Riley* (1922); Hamlin Garland's *Commemorative Tribute to James Whitcomb Riley, Read in the 1920 Lecture Series of the American Academy of Arts and Letters* (1922); the Indiana State Teachers Association's *In Honor of James Whitcomb Riley* (1906); Clara Laughlin's *Reminiscences of James Whitcomb Riley* (1916); Edwin Markham's *Concerning James Whitcomb Riley* (1949); Daniel Marsh's *The Faith of the People's Poet, James Whitcomb Riley* (1920); EDGAR LEE MASTERS'S "James Whitcomb Riley, a Sketch of His Life and An Appraisal of His Work," in *Century Magazine* (October 1927): 714; and "James Whitcomb Riley" in *Century Magazine* (October 1927): 704–15; Minnie Mitchell's *James Whitcomb Riley As I Knew Him, Real Incidents in the Early Life of America's Beloved Poet* (1949);

Jeannette Nolan's *Poet of the People; an Evaluation of James Whitcomb Riley* (1951); Louise Richards's "James Whitcomb Riley on a Country Newspaper," in *Bookman* (September 1904): 18–24; Peter Revell's *James Whitcomb Riley*, Twayne U.S. Authors series 159 (1970); and Anthony Russo and Dorothy Russ's *A Bibliography of James Whitcomb Riley* (1944). His papers can be found in many libraries.

ARTHUR W. SHUMAKER                    DEPAUW UNIVERSITY

## LES ROBERTS
July 18, 1937

**BIOGRAPHY:** Novelist Les Roberts was born to Lester Nathaniel Roubert, a dentist, and Eleanor (Bauch) Roubert in Chicago, Illinois, and changed his name to Roberts in 1968. He attended the University of Illinois at Champaign–Urbana and Roosevelt University from 1954 to 1956, served in the U.S. Army from 1960 to 1962, and married Gail Medland in 1957; the two divorced in 1980. Roberts has two children, Valerie Lynne and Darren Jon, and a granddaughter, Shea Holland Thompson.

Roberts has held positions as a television writer and producer, including assignments with *The Jackie Gleason Show*, *The Andy Griffith Show*, *The Man from UNCLE*, *The Lucy Show*, *When Things Were Rotten*, and *The Hollywood Squares*. He has held adjunct teaching appointments with Case Western Reserve University, Glendale Community College, and Notre Dame College of Ohio.

A Chicago native living in Los Angeles, Roberts had already written two of his six California detective novels featuring Saxon when he visited Ohio and fell in love with Cleveland and the surrounding area. He relocated permanently in 1990.

Roberts received the 1986 Best First Private Eye Novel Award from the Private Eye Writers of America for *An Infinite Number of Monkeys*, and the 1992 Cleveland Arts Prize for Literature.

**SIGNIFICANCE:** In 1988 St. Martin's Press published *Pepper Pike*, which introduced Cleveland private detective Milan Jacovich, a Slovenian American Vietnam veteran, former Kent State football star, ex-cop, ex-husband of a Serbian-descended strong-willed woman, and father of two boys. Jacovich longs for more than every-other-Sunday fatherhood, hangs out in the east side Slovenian Croatian neighborhood of his birth, eats Klobasa sandwiches, stays in touch with friends of thirty years standing, crosses philosophical swords with devilish mob big-wigs, and undercuts with ironic self-mockery every macho value readers have come to expect hard-boiled detectives to champion. Each of his thus-far failed romances provides the reader with a guided tour of another aspect of Cleveland society, culture, and cuisine.

Les Roberts makes Cleveland a character all its own in the Milan Jacovich novels. He explores its inner-city neighborhoods, hardworking immigrant families, and beautiful, lushly forested suburbs with an honest but loving eye. He guides readers through the history of local industry and politics, troubled racial and ethnic relations, local restaurants, cultural institutions, and architecture, weaving the details into his plots so that it is clear that, as he stated in a 1994 conversation with Susan Koppelman, "the stories couldn't take place in quite the same way anywhere else."

**SELECTED WORKS:** The Cleveland novels include *Pepper Pike* (1988), *Full Cleveland* (1989), *Deep Shaker* (1991), *The Cleveland Connection* (1993), *The Lake Effect* (1994), *The Duke of Cleveland* (1995), *Collision Bend* (1996), *The Cleveland Local* (1997), *A Shoot in Cleveland* (1998), and *The Best Kept Secret* (1999). A Cleveland novella entitled *A Carol for Cleveland* was published in 1991.

**FURTHER READING:** Roberts's papers are in the Popular Culture Library at Bowling Green State University.

SUSAN KOPPELMAN                       TUCSON, ARIZONA

## DON ROBERTSON
March 21, 1929–March 21, 1999

**BIOGRAPHY:** Don Robertson was born in Cleveland, Ohio, the son of Carl Trowbridge Robertson and Josephine (Wuebben) Robertson. Carl Robertson worked as an associate editor for the *Cleveland Plain Dealer*. Don Robertson served from 1946 to 1948 in the U.S. Army, after which he attended Harvard University for one year. He then worked as a reporter for the *Cleveland Plain Dealer* until 1955; then he was promoted and worked as a copy editor for two years. During his years at the *Plain Dealer*, Robertson attended Western Reserve University (1953–57). After graduation, he became a reporter for the *Cleveland News*, where he worked for two years. From 1959 to 1960, Robertson became the executive assistant to the Attorney General of Ohio. In 1963 Robertson returned to the *Cleveland Plain Dealer*, where he worked until 1966. He was a columnist for the *Cleveland Press* from 1968 until 1982. During this time he also hosted a television talk-show and reviewed movies and plays. In 1963 he married Shari Kah, whom he later divorced. His second marriage in 1987 was to Sherri Ann Heideloff. He died of lung cancer on his seventieth birthday.

Don Robertson won the Mark Twain Award from the Society for the Study of Midwestern Literature in 1991. He won the Putnam Award in 1964 for *A Flag Full of Stars* and the Cleveland Arts Prize in 1966.

**SIGNIFICANCE:** Robertson received most critical attention for his fictional account of the boyhood and coming of age of Morris Bird III. Called the Cleveland trilogy, these novels include *The Greatest Thing since Sliced Bread* (1965), *The Sum and Total of Now* (1966), and *The Greatest Thing That Almost Happened* (1970). They are all set in Cleveland, Ohio, during the years 1944 and 1953, and each features a major event in the city's history: the refinery explosion, the Indians winning the pennant, and the Korean War. This trilogy, his most significant fictional accomplishment, is an intimate depiction of Robertson's familiar Cleveland landscape. It is likely to assume an important place in American boyhood fiction. In *Midwestern Miscellany* 20 (1992), David D. Anderson, referring to the trilogy, says, "Robertson's contributions to the sub-genre of the boys' story take it as far as it can go as romance becomes an unknown reality, as Morris Bird III moves from the promise of fulfillment almost happening into an unacceptable, yet inevitable end" (56). Reviewers of the trilogy praise Robertson for his development of minor characters and compare his work to that of MARK TWAIN, BOOTH TARKINGTON, J. D. Salinger, and others. Robertson often uses multiple points of view to tell the story of Morris Bird's life and death. The coming of age trilogy portrays young Morris's encounters with themes of heroism, loss, greed, and death. Robertson mixes humor and pathos, sometimes creating heavy-handed sentimentality. While his minor characters have been praised for their genuineness, other characters have been called stereotypical and ineffective.

Robertson's other notable work, *Paradise Falls* (1968), encompasses thirty-five years in

Don Robertson.
Courtesy of Sherri Robertson

the life of a small Ohio town from the end of the Civil War to the beginning of the twentieth century. Praised for its story line, it was also cited for its vulgarity and violence. Other subsequent works have also been repudiated for their sordid and violent tendencies. Robertson's most recent novel is *Prisoners of Twilight* (1989).

**SELECTED WORKS:** Robertson's first three novels, *The Three Days* (1959), *By Antietam Creek* (1960), and *The River and the Wilderness* (1962), deal primarily with Civil War themes. *A Flag Full of Stars* (1964) centers on the 1948 election of Harry Truman. The Cleveland trilogy includes *The Greatest Thing since Sliced Bread* (1965), *The Sum and Total of Now* (1966), and *The Greatest Thing That Almost Happened* (1970). *Paradise Falls* (1968) is a lengthy novel about the emergence of America as an industrial power. Other works include *Praise the Human Season* (1974), *Miss Margaret Ridpath and the Dismantling of the Universe* (1977), *Make a Wish* (1978), and *Mystical Union* (1978), portions of which appeared in the play *Mystical Union*, first performed in 1977 in Chagrin Falls, Ohio. *The Greatest Thing That Almost Happened* was adapted as a movie for television.

**FURTHER READING:** Critiques of Don Robertson's work appear in *Best Sellers*, July 1,

1965; December 1, 1970; and May 1978. David Anderson's article "Don Robertson's Cleveland Trilogy" appears in *Midwestern Miscellany* 20 (1992): 50–56.

RUSSELL J. BODI                          OWENS COLLEGE

## LUIS J. RODRÍGUEZ

July 9, 1954

**BIOGRAPHY:** Luis J. Rodríguez, poet, nonfiction author, and journalist, was born in El Paso, Texas. His parents, Alfonso and Maria Estela (Jimenez) Rodríguez, immigrated to the United States from Mexico. In 1956 his family moved to the Watts community of Los Angeles. By the age of fifteen he was writing in earnest, working skilled trade jobs and then in journalism. Assignments took him to Mexico, to Central America, and to the Midwest. After moving to Chicago in 1985, he published poems, stories, and memoirs in both major daily newspapers and national literary journals such as the *Nation, TriQuarterly*, and the *Americas Review*. He has been married three times: to Camilla Martínez in 1974 (divorced 1979), to Paulette Theresa Donalson in 1982 (divorced 1984), and to Maria Trinidad Cardenas in 1988. He has a son and a daughter by Martínez and a son by Cardenas. Traveling around the Midwest and beyond, he gives poetry readings, teaches, and speaks to teenagers about his former street gang experience, all the while editing his own Tia Chucha Press, one of the Midwest's leading venues for poets of color. He is frequently interviewed on National Public Radio and on television talk shows including *Good Morning America*.

**SIGNIFICANCE:** Chicano writing is often associated with the Southwestern United States, bordering Mexico. Many Mexicans, however, immigrated farther north, to the Midwest. Rodríguez's poems and stories inform this regional neglect. Influenced by authors as diverse as Jimmy Santiago Baca and CARL SANDBURG, Rodríguez has exposed not only racism and violence but the scholarly marginalization that has obscured other significant Midwestern Latino writers, such as SANDRA CISNEROS and Ana Castillo. In "Walk Late Chicago," one of the defining poems in his first collection, *Poems across the Pavement* (1989), Rodríguez narrates his readers through streets walked by the homeless of Chicago, through the "empty zero of a late night walk / in this

cold town," something never faced by the homeless of the Southwest (34). In his gang memoir, *Always Running* (1993), the pervasiveness of the L.A. gang problem is only fully explored when Rodríguez realizes that his son Ramiro, in whom burns "a small but intense fire," has joined a Chicago street gang (251).

**SELECTED WORKS:** Rodríguez's books of poetry are *Poems across the Pavement* (1989), *The Concrete River* (1991), and *Trochemoche* (1998). His memoir of gang life is *Always Running: La Vida Loca, Gang Days in L.A.* (1993). His children's book is *América Is Her Name* (1998), illustrated by Carlos Vásquez.

**FURTHER READING:** Rodríguez's writing is frequently reviewed in the *New York Times*, the *Los Angeles Times*, the *Village Voice*, and the *Chicago Reader*. Vicente Perez reviews *Always Running* in *Americas Review* 22.1–2 (Spring–Summer 1994): 277–79; Sesshu Foster reviews *Poems across the Pavement* and *The Concrete River* in the same issue (279–82). An analysis of *Always Running* may be found in editor Frank N. Magill's *Masterpieces of Latino Literature* (1994). Two profiles of Rodríguez are Scott Collins's article "Up from the Streets," in the *Chicago Tribune* (October 17, 1993): 5, 1; and Mark Cromer's "From La Vida Loca to La Dolce Vita," in the *Los Angeles Times* (July 25, 1996): E1. Rodríguez speaks to the importance of education in combating gang violence in an interview with Anita Merina, "Meet Luis Rodríguez—Peacemaker," in *NEA Today* 14.6 (February 1996): 7. A video portrait, titled *Luis J. Rodríguez* and released by the Lannon Foundation in 1993, features an interview and a poetry reading.

MARCUS CAFAGÑA

SOUTHWEST MISSOURI STATE UNIVERSITY

## THEODORE ROETHKE

May 25, 1908–August 1, 1963

**BIOGRAPHY:** Born in Saginaw, Michigan, into a family which had emigrated from Germany and established a large and highly respected florist business, Theodore Roethke helped his father and played in the greenhouses as a child. His parents were Otto and Helen (Huebner) Roethke. He graduated from the University of Michigan in 1929 and attended Harvard before returning to Michigan, from which he received an MA in 1936. Roethke taught at Lafayette College in Pennsylvania and at Michigan State University, where in 1935 he had the first of several mental breakdowns. He also taught at Penn State, at Bennington, and finally at the University of Washington, where he spent most of his teaching career. He was a pioneer in the teaching of creative writing in colleges. With the friendship and encouragement of both young and established poets, he began publishing poems in the early 1930s, leading to his first book, *Open House*, in 1941. Many awards and much critical acclaim followed, including Guggenheims, a Fulbright, the Eunice Tietjens Memorial Prize, a Pulitzer Prize for *The Waking*, the Bollingen Prize, and National Book Awards for *Words for the Wind* and *The Far Field*. In 1953 he married Beatrice O'Connell, a former student at Bennington. He died of a heart attack in a friend's swimming pool near Seattle.

**SIGNIFICANCE:** The plant nurseries where Roethke worked and played as a boy and the nearby fields and river contributed images and settings for many of his poems. Although he did not believe that Saginaw society provided a stimulus for himself as artist or materials for his writing, its landscape did; the wildlife of eastern Michigan and the domestic plant life of his father's business permeate the whole of his body of poetry.

Roethke's poetry is broad in range and depth, covering themes from love in various forms to humor, compassion, self-disgust, spiritual search, and redemption. As Jay Parini convincingly argues in *Theodore Roethke: An American Romantic* (1979), the poet's primary philosophical orientation was to the romanticism of Emerson, Thoreau, and Whitman. From these American sources, Roethke drew his sense of the "poet as prophet . . . a priest of the imagination" who seeks in nature an expanded definition of selfhood (Parini 31). Imagery of nature and landscape pervades Roethke's work regardless of theme or poetic form, from his tightly crafted poems in the manner of Yeats and Auden to his modern free verse and late experiments with Whitman's long line. His experience with landscape covers both coasts and some of Europe, but the figures that dominate—the birds, rocks, running water, roads, fields, trees, even the air—have their sources in Roethke's Midwest.

The motif of a journey that is at once geographical and psychological is announced in *Open House*. Although the poems in this first

Theodore Roethke.
Courtesy of Special Collections Division,
University of Washington Libraries

volume tend to the metaphysical, a few anticipate the emphasis on place of Roethke's later work. Notable among these are "The Premonition," "The Light Comes Brighter," "Mid-Country Blow," "Highway: Michigan," and "Night Journey," the last of which, an impression of a cross-country train trip, suggests the central role that nature and landscape would play in the poet's developing vision.

Roethke focuses more directly on his early life in his second book, *The Lost Son and Other Poems* (1948). The cluster known as the greenhouse poems takes both name and nominal subject from his experiences there. "Frau Bauman, Frau Schmidt, and Frau Schwartze," for example, describes German immigrant women in their old-world clothes, laboring in the glass houses. "Root Cellar," "Big Wind," and "Child on Top of a Greenhouse" also touch on various aspects of the life of a florist's child.

The greenhouse poems define his empathy with the plant world as well as reveal his skill at horticultural processes. His affinity with living things, from the microscopic and primordial to animals and ecosystems, may have been inherent but was surely nurtured by his daily contact with soil, water, and plants. In "Cuttings (*later*)," he says, "I can hear, underground, that sucking and sobbing. / In my veins, in my bones I feel it—" (*Collected Poems* 37). And in "Moss Gathering," he equates stripping moss from the riverbank with stripping flesh from the earth. While these poems portray nature literally, their images imply more than the simply descriptive. Plants, sky, road, and field suggest universal themes such as death wishes, Oedipal conflict, and yearning for transcendental experience. These correspondences become more explicit in "The Lost Son," the book's long title poem, which depicts an emotional and spiritual crisis played out near the Tittabawassee River, beginning in the cemetery where Roethke's father was buried and where the poet's ashes would later be interred. Many critics have stressed the centrality of "The Lost Son," not only to Roethke's career but to American poetry in the twentieth century. The impact of this poem depends as much on its environmental and autobiographical specificity as on its technical innovation and use of mythological symbols and Freudian psychology.

Midwestern agrarian ideals are curiously modified in the greenhouse setting: Roethke portrays his father as a stern but nurturing yeoman farmer, whose crop of flowers feeds the human spirit rather than body. The greenhouse reverses the metaphor for American pastoralism announced in the title of Leo Marx's famous book, *The Machine in the Garden: Technology and the Pastoral Ideal in America* (1964). A "garden in the machine," Roethke's greenhouse reconciles technology and agriculture, utility and aesthetic values. As Roethke told his British audience in a 1953 radio address included in *The Poet and His Craft: Selected Prose of Theodore Roethke* (1966), the greenhouses were to him both "heaven and hell, a kind of tropics created in the savage climate of Michigan, where austere German-Americans turned their love of order and their terrifying efficiency into something truly beautiful" (8). His mixed feelings for his father and for the greenhouses are reconciled in such late poems as "Otto" and "The Rose," both from *The Far Field* (1964). These characterize the greenhouse keeper as a model for the poet, his cultivation of flowers paralleling the son's writing as a spiritual pursuit and labor of love. In "The Rose," for example, Roethke remembers how the "roses, / White

and red, in the wide six-hundred-foot greenhouses / . . . seemed to flow toward me, to beckon me, only a child, out of myself" (*Collected Poems* 203).

Roethke's late residence in Washington state is so evident in his last poems that a valid claim can be made for him as an incipient Pacific Northwest poet. It would be more accurate, however, to say that he was stretching his poetic range and contextualizing his place of origin within a broader continental vision. The poems in *The Far Field* repeatedly shift from Washington, Rocky Mountain, and Great Plains scenes back to the Saginaw Valley of Michigan. Engaged in "Meditation at Oyster River," his thoughts return to "the first trembling of a Michigan brook in April" and "the Tittebawasee [*sic*], in the time between winter and spring" (*Collected Poems* 191). "The Far Field" and "The Rose" similarly find him back in the greenhouses and surrounding country. In "All Morning" he describes birds feeding behind his house in Seattle, but as the poem goes on, the birds merge with those of all times and places, and he says, "It is neither spring nor summer: it is Always!" (*Collected Poems* 235). In the book's final poem, "Once More, the Round," he employs the concept of the dance, which appears throughout his work, to unify the themes of love, nature, and vision, as well as the unity of all things. The images, like the themes, run full circle.

**SELECTED WORKS:** Roethke's major books of poetry are *Open House* (1941); *The Lost Son and Other Poems* (1948); *Praise to the End!* (1951); *The Waking, Poems: 1933–1953* (1953); *Words for the Wind* (1958); *I Am! Says the Lamb* (1961), children's poems; and *The Far Field* (1964). Two collections are *The Collected Poems of Theodore Roethke* (1968) and *Theodore Roethke: Selected Poems*, edited by Beatrice Roethke (1969). Resources include *On the Poet and His Craft: Selected Prose of Theodore Roethke* (1966) and *Selected Letters of Theodore Roethke* (1968), both edited by Ralph J. Mills Jr., and *Straw for the Fire: From the Notebooks of Theodore Roethke, 1943–63*, edited by David Wagoner (1972).

**FURTHER READING:** The definitive biography of Roethke remains Allan Seager's *The Glass House: The Life of Theodore Roethke* (1968). Gary Lane has done *A Concordance to the Poems of Theodore Roethke* (1972). Three bibliographies are *Theodore Roethke: A Manuscript Checklist* (1971) and *Theodore Roethke: A Bibliography*

(1973), both by James R. McLeod; and Keith R. Moul's *Theodore Roethke's Career: An Annotated Bibliography* (1977). Introductions include *Theodore Roethke* (1963), by Ralph T. Mills Jr.; Karl Malkof's *Theodore Roethke, An Introduction to the Poetry* (1966); and George Wolff's Twayne book, *Theodore Roethke* (1981). *"The Edge Is What I Have": Theodore Roethke and After* (1977), by Harry Williams, speaks to a "Roethkean mode" that shaped the writing of subsequent Midwestern poets Robert Bly and James Wright; and Jay Parini's *Theodore Roethke: An American Romantic* (1979) is also useful. Books which shed light on Roethke's use of his Michigan background include *Theodore Roethke: The Garden Master* (1975), by Rosemary Sullivan; *Theodore Roethke: Poetry of the Earth . . . Poet of the Spirit* (1981), by Lynn Ross-Bryant; *Theodore Roethke's Far Fields: The Evolution of His Poetry* (1989), by Peter Balakian; and *Theodore Roethke and the Writing Process* (1991), by Don Bogen. The proceedings of a symposium on Roethke held in Saginaw in 1967 featuring Allan Seager, Stanley Kunitz, and John Ciardi, "An Evening with Ted Roethke," appear in the *Michigan Quarterly Review* 6.4 (Fall 1967): 225–45, and, with additions, in *Profile of Theodore Roethke*, edited by William Hayden (1971). John Rohrkemper, in "'When the Mind Remembers All': Dream and Memory in Theodore Roethke's 'North American Sequence,'" *Journal of the Midwest Modern Language Association* 21.1 (Spring 1988): 28–37; and William Barillas, in "To Sustain the Bioregion: Michigan Poets of Place," *MidAmerica* 17 (1990): 10–33, also consider Midwestern roots of Roethke's poetry.

An additional resource is David Myers's film *In a Dark Time* (1964), re-released in 1966 as *Theodore Roethke*. Filmed in Seattle, it shows Roethke reading his poetry and responding to his students. Roethke's papers are in the Suzallo Library at the University of Washington.

WILLIAM BARILLAS

UNIVERSITY OF WISCONSIN–LA CROSSE

MARY DEJONG OBUCHOWSKI

CENTRAL MICHIGAN UNIVERSITY

## OLE EDVART RØLVAAG
April 22, 1876–November 5, 1931
(Paul Morck)

**BIOGRAPHY:** Ole Edvart Pedersen was born at Rølvaag, Donna Island, in northern Norway, to Ellerine Pedersdotter and Peder Benjamin Jakobsen, fisherman. He was the third of seven children. In childhood he absorbed regional myths and folklore. He had little schooling as a youth in Norway, but his family home was literate and lively, and a public library supplied reading materials. For six years as a young man he made annual fishing expeditions to banks off the Lofoten Islands, where on one occasion a fierce storm at sea almost cost him his life.

His ambition to write formed early and was a factor in his leaving his beloved homeland at age twenty for the New World. For two years he worked on farms in rural South Dakota, then entered Augustana Academy at Canton, South Dakota. There he changed his name from the patronymic Pedersen to Rølvaag. He graduated from the academy in 1901 and enrolled at St. Olaf College in Northfield, Minnesota, receiving a BA in 1905. At these institutions established by Norwegian Lutherans, he nurtured his goal of keeping alive, through teaching and writing, his Norwegian cultural heritage. A year of post-graduate study at the University of Oslo qualified him for a post as teacher of Norwegian at St. Olaf, and there he remained, eventually as chairman of the Department of Norwegian, until his retirement from teaching in the year of his death.

In 1908 Rølvaag married Jennie Berdahl of Garretson, South Dakota, daughter of pioneers, with whom he had three sons and one daughter: Olaf Arnljot died of illness at the age of six; Karl Fridtjof became governor of Minnesota; Paul Gunnar died by drowning at the age of five; and daughter Ella Valborg has been a source of valuable help to Rølvaag scholars. Rølvaag had already written ten novels in Norwegian about his countrymen in America when in 1923 news that Norwegian writer Johan Bojer was planning a novel on immigrant themes spurred him to begin his masterpiece, *Giants in the Earth*. Published in Norway in two volumes in 1924 and 1925, it was translated into English and published in the United States in a single volume in 1927. *Giants* won instant acclaim in both countries. *Peder Victorious* followed in 1929 and *Their Father's God* in 1931, completing Rølvaag's prairie trilogy. Recurring periods of heart ailment gave Rølvaag premonitions of an early death, which came in 1931 at the age of fifty-five.

SIGNIFICANCE: At once a Norwegian and an American Midwestern writer, Rølvaag is the preeminent interpreter in Norwegian and American fiction of European immigrant settlers on the Midwestern prairie frontier. He wrote in his native Norwegian and sought collaboration in preparing English translations. Critics of Rølvaag's work comment on the ways he combines realism with myth as he explores the physical, psychological, and moral effects of frontier and post-frontier life. Rølvaag dramatizes the tension between a Norwegian focus on inherited cultural traditions and an American focus on the promise of future prosperity and happiness. His reputation rests primarily on *Giants in the Earth* (1927; Norwegian: *I de Dage*, 1924–25), which his collaborator on the translation, Lincoln Colcord, describes as "European in its art and atmosphere" and "distinctly American in everything it deals with" (Introduction xi).

Rølvaag borrowed both the English and the Norwegian titles of his major novel from Gen. 6:4, "There were giants in the earth in those days." The "giants" may be taken to be the hostile natural forces encountered by the pioneers, or they may be the heroic pioneers themselves. Set in South Dakota in the 1870s, the novel embodies features of myth, epic, and tragedy. It is enriched by direct and indirect reference to both Norwegian folklore and American Edenic myths. It shares epic qualities with writings of his Midwestern contemporaries, writers WILLA CATHER and JOHN G. NEIHARDT. In episodes of planting, harvesting, fur-trading, capturing wild fowl, and general enterprise, Per Hansa becomes the hero of an epic quest, who can, like the Ash Lad of Norwegian story, achieve more than ordinary men. Per Hansa is the epic hero as well in the American application of the biblical myth of the Promised Land, the founding of a new social order in a new world, while through Per's wife Beret, Rølvaag dramatizes the toll exacted of the settlers. The epic turns to tragedy when Per Hansa, at Beret's urging, skis off to his death in a blizzard in a heroic endeavor to bring a minister for a sick friend.

The novel also adheres to conventions of Midwestern realistic fiction. The conflicts are both psychological and cultural. Per Hansa lives and dies facing west; Beret yearns east-

O. E. Rølvaag.
Photo courtesy of St. Olaf College Archives

ward toward the culture and religion of Norway. Some readers attribute Per Hansa's death to Beret's religious fanaticism, others to Per Hansa's failure to realize his own limits. Younger readers tend to identify with the heroic Per Hansa; many older readers tend to feel greater appreciation for the tragic Beret.

The two novels that complete Rølvaag's prairie trilogy focus on the next stages of settlement and on the children of the original settlers. Nevertheless, *Peder Victorious* (1929; Norwegian: *Peder Seier*, 1928) and *Their Father's God* (1931; Norwegian: *Den Signede Dag*, 1931) also continue Beret's story. By the end of *Peder Victorious*, Beret, though filled with forebodings, acquiesces in the marriage of her Americanized son Peder to Susie, the daughter of Irish Catholic immigrants. In *Their Father's God*, Beret's struggles to maintain Norwegian language, culture, and religion contribute to the difficulties of Peder and Susie. The conflict of cultures, as well as the contrasting personalities of the young couple, leads eventually to the failure of the marriage. Although didactic at times and lacking the epic and mythic dimensions of *Giants in the Earth*, *Peder Victorious* and *Their Father's God* have interest as Midwestern novels of social and psychological realism.

**SELECTED WORKS:** In addition to the trilogy, some of Rølvaag's earlier works are available in English translations. *The Third Life of Per Smevik* (1971; Norwegian: *Amerika Breve*, 1912) is told in letters, mostly between a young immigrant and his father in Norway. In *Pure Gold* (1930; Norwegian: *To Tullinger*, 1920), Lars and Lizzie Houglum, a young Norwegian couple lacking in cultural and personal identity, are destroyed by their materialistic greed. Romantic in its first section on Nils Vaag's childhood in Norway, *The Boat of Longing* (1933; Norwegian: *Laengselens Baat*, 1921) portrays the hero searching for artistic and cultural identity amid naturalistic scenes in Minneapolis and rural Minnesota. In a climactic episode, Nil's roommate reads him a poem about the Ash Lad, leading eventually to Nils's recognizing the course he must follow in pursuing his goal. Rølvaag has said, "I have put more of myself into that book than into any other" (Haugen 62).

**FURTHER READING:** The standard biography is Theodore Jorgenson and Nora O. Solum's *Ole Edvart Rølvaag: A Biography* (1939). An excellent brief introduction to Rølvaag's works in English is Ann Moseley's *Ole Edvart Rølvaag* (1987). Einar Haugen's *Ole Edwart Rølvaag* (1983) is more comprehensive, covering untranslated published and unpublished work as well as works available in English. Paul Reigstad's *Rølvaag, His Life and Art* (1972) is the earliest full-scale critical appreciation. As the title indicates, Harold P. Simonson's *Prairies Within: The Tragic Trilogy of Ole Rølvaag* (1987) examines the prairie trilogy. The essays in *Ole Rølvaag, Artist and Cultural Leader*, edited by Gerald Thorson (1975), appraise aspects of the work and career. The major collection of manuscripts and papers is in the St. Olaf College Library.

ROBERT NARVESON

UNIVERSITY OF NEBRASKA, LINCOLN

# E(DWARD) MERRILL ROOT

January 1, 1895–October 27, 1973

**BIOGRAPHY:** E(dward) Merrill Root was born in Baltimore, Maryland, to Edward Talmadge and Georginna (Merrill) Root. He graduated from Amherst College in 1917, spent the next year at the University of Missouri, donated his services to the Friends' Reconstruction Unit in France, and in 1919–20 attended Andover Theological Seminary. In 1920 Root was appointed assistant professor of English at Earlham College, became professor in 1930, and remained a member of that faculty until he retired from active teaching in 1960. In addition to teaching, he held positions as one of the editors of *The Poetry Folio* and *The Measure* and received many prizes for his poetry. He studied with Robert Frost and Alexander Meiklejohn, lectured at a number of colleges, and took part in radio and television programs. His wife was the former Dorothy McNab. E. Merrill Root died in Portland, Maine.

**SIGNIFICANCE:** Root was a prolific writer known primarily as an excellent poet although he also wrote biography, analytical and polemical works, and collections of essays. His approach to poetry remained largely consistent throughout his lifetime with successive volumes reflecting heightened mastery. Some of his best work appears in sonnet form.

His first book, *Lost Eden and Other Poems* (1927), is a collection of mostly short pieces which provide evidence of a sensitive spirit seeking spiritual values and beauty. The verse is rhymed in various patterns, and he uses the sonnet effectively. There is a strong appreciation of nature, fancy, protest, sympathy for the underdog, and anti-war feeling. *Bow of Burning Gold* (1929) shows improvement in quality. Root expresses his rebellion against the present when he looks for a new country complete with a new Columbus who will rediscover America. In this book he shows, also, his fascination with the historic and his sympathy with victims of the machine world. His touch is surer here and his diction is very well chosen. *Dawn Is Forever* (1938) shows his imagination and love of the outdoors together with his love of poetry, though some of his poems lack clarity. *Before the Swallow Dares* (1947) attracted even better criticism and reviews than his first three volumes of poetry. The subjects cover philosophy, nature, love, humor, and history. Examples are "God's Fool (Columbus Dying)" and "The Iron

Door," recalling the Civil War fight between the Monitor and Merrimac, beautiful poems to those he loves, and also sonnets of exquisite beauty. In *The Seeds of Time* (1950) there is the same wild wonder at life, love, nature, and the universe; this volume also includes a sonnet sequence written to his wife. *The Light Wind Over* (1950) contains many of the same thoughts found in his other books and presents a sonnet sequence on love. *Ulysses to Penelope* (1951) is composed of a beautiful sonnet sequence. The work is very idealistic; the poet imagines himself to be Ulysses voyaging forever toward the lost Penelope, the star toward which he steers, representing his greatest dream. In *Out of Our Winter* (1956) and *Shoulder the Sky* (1961) one finds more of Root's previously expressed ideas and verse forms. In the former he includes poems against commissars, while the latter contains "Major Testament," listing his gifts to others at his death. *Of Perilous Sea* (1964) has Root's long poem on the loss of the Titanic; *Like White Birds Flying* (1969) presents many good poems including "Woman and Man," a sequence of fourteen sonnets on married love. *Children of the Morning* (1974) carries many references to religious beliefs and appreciates the "hard hate" of those who defend the status quo.

**SELECTED WORKS:** Root's volumes of poetry include *Lost Eden and Other Poems* (1927), *Bow of Burning Gold* (1929), *Dawn Is Forever* (1938), *Before the Swallow Dares* (1947), *The Seeds of Time* (1950), *The Light Wind Over* (1950), *Ulysses to Penelope* (1951), *Out of Our Winter* (1956), *Shoulder the Sky* (1961), *Of Perilous Sea* (1964), *Like White Birds Flying* (1969), and *Children of the Morning* (1974). Of these, *Before the Swallow Dares* is generally considered his best collection of verse.

Root's non-poetic writings include *Frank Harris* (1947), a biography of appreciation; *Collectivism on the Campus: The Battle for the Mind in American Colleges* (1955); *Brain-washing in the High Schools: An Examination of Eleven American History Textbooks* (1958); and *America's Steadfast Dream* (1971), a collection of essays. *The Way of All Spirit* (1940) is a philosophical work which presents his "I am" as existing in eternity. Along with *America's Steadfast Dream*, it is considered his best prose work.

**FURTHER READING:** Root's books were extensively reviewed at the time of their first publication, but there is virtually no recent criticism. Randolph Gilbert's *Four Living Poets* (1944, reprinted 1970) contains an essay in appreciation of Root.

ARTHUR W. SHUMAKER                    DEPAUW UNIVERSITY

## (MICHAEL) MIKE ROYKO
September 19, 1932–April 29, 1997
(Slats Grobnick)

**BIOGRAPHY:** Born in Chicago of Michael Royko Jr., a Ukrainian immigrant, and Helen (Zak) Royko, Mike Royko attended Wright Junior College, the University of Illinois, and Northwestern University without receiving a degree. Royko had two children with his first wife, Carol Joyce Duckman, whom he married in 1954 and who died in 1979. He married his second wife, Judith Arndt, in 1985, and they had two children.

During his Korean War tour of duty in the U.S. Air Force, he volunteered to edit the base newspaper, lying about experience with the *Chicago Daily News* to bolster his credentials. He became a newspaper satirist when he eventually did get a job as a columnist with the *Daily News* in 1959, moving to the *Chicago Sun-Times* in 1978 when the *Daily News* closed. Leaving the *Sun-Times* in protest when it was purchased by Rupert Murdoch, Royko wrote his column for the *Chicago Tribune* from 1984 until early 1997. He won the Heywood Broun Award in 1968, the Pulitzer Prize for commentary in 1972, the University of Missouri School of Journalism Award in 1979, the H. L. Mencken Award in 1981, the Ernie Pyle Award in 1982, and the lifetime achievement award from the National Press Club in 1990. Royko was named to the Chicago Press Club's Hall of Fame in 1980, and he was four times named the best columnist in America by the *Washington Journalism Review*. Royko died of heart failure following surgery for an aneurysm.

**SIGNIFICANCE:** Mike Royko's columns centered on the experience and common sense of ordinary working people in Chicago. His ability to mimic in print the "back of the yards" Irish dialect of Mayor Richard M. Daley contributed to his ability to use humor as a vehicle for strong social commentary in the tradition of MARK TWAIN and others. Royko's white ethnic characters, such as his Slats

Grobnick, mimic Chicago's Eastern European demographics, thus harkening back to an earlier Chicago newspaperman, FINLEY PETER DUNNE, whose Mr. Dooley and an Irish immigrant cohort served similar satiric purposes. Like Dunne, Royko could and did comment on national issues, but much of his satire has an intensely local, Chicago quality. Fundamentally, Slats reflects a distrust of elites and the government that is emblematic of the Midwestern heartland.

**SELECTED WORKS:** Royko has published several collections taken from his columns over the years: *Up against It* (1967), *I May Be Wrong, but I Doubt It* (1968), *Slats Grobnick and Some Other Friends* (1973), *Sez Who? Sez Me* (1982), *Like I Was Sayin'* (1984), and *Dr. Kookie, You're Right* (1989). He also published *Boss:*

*Richard J. Daley of Chicago* (1971), a caustic portrait of Chicago's colorful mayor and his powerful, often corrupt, political machine.

**FURTHER READING:** Numerous profiles of Royko and brief reviews of his books have appeared in the popular press. Sustained studies have yet to be written. Three informative essays are Roger J. Bresnahan's "Mr. Dooley and Slats Grobnick: Chicago Commentators on the World around Them," in *Midwestern Miscellany* 14 (1986): 34–46; Paul P. Somers Jr.'s "Mike Royko: Midwestern Satirist," in *Mid-America* 10 (1983): 177–86; and Richard Shereikis's "Farewell to the Regional Columnist: The Meaning of Bob Greene's Success," in *MidAmerica* 13 (1986): 122–35.

ROGER JIANG BRESNAHAN

MICHIGAN STATE UNIVERSITY

# S

## CARL (AUGUST) SANDBURG
January 6, 1878–July 22, 1967

**BIOGRAPHY:** Born in Galesburg, Illinois, of working-class Swedish immigrant parents, August and Clara (Anderson) Sandburg, Carl Sandburg began working at age thirteen following elementary school graduation, taking on a wide range of early jobs. These jobs and several youthful forays across the country by rail and on foot as a hobo broadened Sandburg's experience and helped forge his populist worldview. Enlistment in Company C of the Sixth Illinois Volunteers in 1898 and service in Puerto Rico during the Spanish-American War provided further experiences and allowed Sandburg to attend Lombard College in Galesburg, Illinois, on scholarship for one year. His prior military service also led to a brief unsuccessful appointment at the U.S. Military Academy at West Point, following which Sandburg returned to Lombard, where he studied until 1902. The Lombard experience was important for Sandburg. There he met and studied under Philip Green Wright, his mentor and publisher for four volumes of apprentice writings.

Sandburg's experiences as a hobo traveler and his increasing dedication to social causes and class justice led him to become an organizer for the Social Democratic Party in Milwaukee, Wisconsin, from 1907 to 1912. There, he met his future wife, Lillian Steichen, whom he called Paula. They married on June 15, 1908; together they had three daughters, Margaret, Janet, and Helga.

Sandburg wrote for several Milwaukee newspapers while continuing his work for the Social Democratic Party. In 1910 he was named secretary to Emil Seidel, Milwaukee's socialist mayor, a position Sandburg held through 1912. From there he continued his journalistic connection with Milwaukee newspapers, periodicals, and magazines before leaving for Chicago in 1912, the year *Poetry: A Magazine of Verse* began publication. In Chicago, Sandburg wrote for *Day Book, System*, and other Chicago newspapers, including the *Chicago Daily News* and the Newspaper Enterprise Association, for which he served as foreign correspondent in Stockholm, Sweden, in 1918. Sandburg joined the staff of the *Chicago Daily News* in 1917 and remained through 1932, serving progressively as labor and social issues reporter covering the Chicago race riots of 1919, editorial writer, motion picture editor, and columnist.

Winning *Poetry*'s 1914 Levinson Prize for poems that formed the nucleus of his first vol-

**Carl Sandburg.**
Courtesy of Special Collections,
Western Illinois University

ume of mature poetry, *Chicago Poems* (1916), brought Sandburg his first significant poetic recognition. This prize also solidified his connection to other emerging poetic voices, including Chicago Renaissance writers and others rejecting nineteenth-century poetic styles and forms. *Chicago Poems* received strong notice, positively as a leading exemplar of the new poetry and negatively as completely unpoetic. Additional volumes of poetry followed every few years. Growing fame and royalties increasingly provided a financial base independent of journalism. After 1932 Sandburg supported himself almost exclusively with royalties from independent writing and income from readings and musical performances. He proved versatile and productive, with strong credentials in many areas beyond poetry and journalism. He wrote biography, collected and wrote folk music, experimented in American idiom, and completed a novel and an autobiography.

Sandburg's early rural Midwestern life and his experiences as hobo, socialist organizer, urban journalist, and war correspondent provided literary and historical subjects

and themes. These experiences also stimulated his lifelong fascination with American vernacular and folk song. Throughout his life, Sandburg remained staunchly dedicated to working-class values and suspicious of the elite. Despite his socialist sympathies, he separated himself from those opposing the American war effort. Sandburg remained always a staunch patriot, lifting Americans' spirits during the Depression and fostering support for America's war effort in World War II.

His many awards included *Poetry's* 1914 Levinson Prize, the Poetry Society of America Prize in 1919 and 1921, the Pulitzer Prize for Poetry in 1950, the Gold Medal for History from the American Academy of Arts and Letters in 1950, and the Gold Medal for Poetry from the Poetry Society of America in 1953. He was the Phi Beta Kappa poet at Harvard in 1928 and received honorary degrees from many American and international colleges and universities including Northwestern, Harvard, Yale, New York University, Syracuse, and Dartmouth.

Sandburg lived almost exclusively in the Midwest until the early 1940s, when he and his family moved to a country estate and working farm, Connemara, in Flat Rock, North Carolina. He died there on July 22, 1967, following multiple heart attacks in his final weeks. He is buried at Remembrance Rock, the Carl Sandburg birthplace, in Galesburg, Illinois.

**SIGNIFICANCE:** Carl Sandburg has made major contributions to Midwestern and American life and culture. His landmark multivolume biography of ABRAHAM LINCOLN (1927, 1939) remains one of the premier pieces of Lincoln biography and American historical writing. Sandburg's *American Songbag* (1926) and *New American Songbag* (1927) marked him as a student of American idiom and folk music just as several volumes of stories for children made his place in children's literature. Sandburg's versatility also extended to a novel, *Remembrance Rock* (1948), and an autobiography, *Always the Young Strangers* (1953).

Throughout Sandburg's career, his canvas centers almost exclusively on the Midwest and the laboring people of its small towns and cities. Their indomitable courage, spirit, and zest for life despite challenge and injustice typify for him America's greatness. Sandburg's intense, continuing focus on Midwestern life and people raises public awareness of abusive early-twentieth-century industrial and agrarian working conditions. His advocacy of common people and his attacks on exploitative management earn widespread public respect and appreciation.

Like the Utopian Socialists, Emerson, Thoreau, and Whitman, Sandburg believes unquestioningly in the potential of "common" people, and like Whitman, he maintains great faith in democratic possibilities. His writings reflect his excitement at life's possibilities and the appropriateness of democratic aspiration. Sandburg's fierce intellectual and social independence grows from this same root. He believes that if human beings partake of godliness, they should look deep into themselves, not others, for solutions to human problems. Throughout, Sandburg's writings express passionate excitement and intensity of a crusade based on infinite faith in the common people of the Midwest, the nation, and the world.

Sandburg also follows Whitman's intellectual and literary lead in radical poetic innovation. Carrying forward his experiences in Mid-America's small towns, as a socialist organizer, an American soldier at war, and an urban journalist reporting on war and social issues, he focuses attention on working-class people, a poetic subject and audience largely ignored by earlier genteel American romantic writing. He follows Whitman's lead in celebrating common people, the democratic "grass" from which great nations rise and prosper.

Sandburg adopts Whitman's aggressively realistic focus, forcing readers accustomed to genteel euphemism in poetry to confront harsh realities and real language. In "Song of Myself" from *Leaves of Grass*, Whitman had consciously rejected nineteenth-century norms for radical poetic subjects and language, declaring, "What is commonest, cheapest, nearest, easiest, is Me" (14.259), and aggressively used realistic language that outraged genteel sensibilities, "sound[ing his] . . . barbaric yawp over the roofs of the world" (52.1333). Sandburg too asserts the gritty realities of early-twentieth-century urban and rural life in his poetry. He consciously baits the literary establishment by starting *Chicago Poems*, his first mature collection of poetry, with

extreme non-genteel language and reference: "Hog butcher for the World" (*Collected Poems* 3). Sandburg's poetry luxuriates in Mid-American regional dialect and working-class slang.

His poetic principles are equally liberating. He rejects syllabic verse, rhyme, and poetic diction, the hallmarks of nineteenth-century genteel romantic verse, to foster a new Whitmanic poetics based in the oral speech patterns, vocabulary, and experience of American working people. Sandburg follows Whitman finally in his devotion to democracy and Abraham Lincoln, the ultimate symbol of democratic greatness rising out of Midwestern frontier obscurity.

Sandburg carries Whitman's worldview and poetics into a new era, one of rampant technology, robber barons, class warfare, hideous urban-industrial working conditions, and organized conspiracies of corporations, government, political parties, and courts to keep laboring masses from reaping their just rewards and living lives of dignity. Therefore, he moves beyond Whitman's uncritical celebration of American life to emphatic, direct confrontation of social conditions and abuses and active advocacy for society's victims.

Sandburg's poetic style is not, however, exclusively Whitmanic. Occasionally, his poetry presents a vastly different voice deriving from the then-emerging Imagist movement. Poems such as "Fog" and "Nocturne in a Deserted Brickyard" reject the wordy didacticism of much neoclassical and romantic verse as well as the syntax and ordering techniques characteristic of Whitmanic oral poetry. Instead, they approach wordlessness in presenting experiential moments of beauty or mood. Here, long poetic lines, slang, and class-struggle references are absent. In their place come pictures created using very precise language, the smallest number of words possible, and metaphoric comparison.

Sandburg is somewhat atypical as a Midwestern writer in his strong emotional and experiential ties with teeming industrial cities as well as with rural towns and landscapes. In both environments, he finds beauty, serenity, and joy as well as pain, betrayal, and harsh reality. He loves the working people of the Midwest's small towns as well as their urban counterparts. He advocates for both, respecting their dignity and individuality, immigrant origins, and working-class status.

Sandburg's rural and urban portraits portray common people of strength, dignity, and worth. His city poems emphasize and celebrate multiethnic Mid-American life.

Sandburg's contributions to Midwestern and American literature and society are many. He has advanced realistic poetry and literature and has fostered the emergence of modern poetry from stagnant nineteenth-century forms. He is among the American poets responsible for advancing early understanding and appreciation of free verse. His poetry celebrates Mid-America's common people, their dialects, vocabulary, and speech patterns. It captures images of great beauty and poignancy in everyday experience and expresses its vision with language striking in its elegance, simplicity, and experiential force. He advocates for working-class Midwesterners and Americans and makes their lives, dreams, challenges, and greatness his themes. Sandburg's democratic vision, his crusade for working people, and his strong patriotism have advanced social justice and inspirited Americans through depression and world wars. He has sustained Americans with his high romantic vision of humanity. Even though common people, as portrayed in Sandburg's verse, are often caught in an immoral society or an incoherent universe of naturalistic forces of superhuman scale, his poetry retains an unshakable vision of human greatness, integrity, and fruitful possibility. It asserts the transcendent family of man.

Critical reaction to Sandburg's poetry has been mixed. In the early years his poetry produces great shock through its direct, highly realistic language and portrayal of life as well as through nontraditional Whitmanic and imagistic poetics. As such, this poetry is attacked by literary traditionalists wishing to retain nineteenth-century genteel romantic norms and by advocates of avant-garde, elite, intellectual Eliot-like poetry. On the positive side, his work is regularly praised for the strength and impact of its images, language, portrayal of realistic situations, innovative poetic structures, and speech rhythms.

As time passes, Sandburg's language, characters, situations, and poetic structuring methods lose some of their early shock value. Other poets and prose writers increasingly adopt realistic language and situations and write more about people previously ignored by genteel literature. Critical response becomes more lukewarm, or even worse, less frequent, suggesting that Sandburg's poetic approaches are no longer seen as being in the forefront of the twentieth-century poetic revolution. Despite growing criticism, he continues to experiment. He breaks new ground in applying jazz rhythms to poetry, testing the limits and structuring of the Whitmanic oral poetic line, and working to elevate working-class American slang and dialect speech to the poetic expression of democratic humanity.

Although critics increasingly dismiss Carl Sandburg as a minor figure, his poetry strikes a responsive chord with Americans generally. His poetry celebrates and inspirits people often overlooked in life and literature. His Lincoln biography provides an unmatched scholarly and empathic presentation of Illinois' martyr to the Union and America's model of democratic and patriotic greatness. Sandburg's absorption in the uniqueness and fecundity of American slang and language patterns has fostered new awareness of the richness of our language and new pride in our diversity.

Carl Sandburg's major awards and honors are legion. His most significant recognition, however, is the high regard that generations of Americans have maintained for him and his writings. In speaking with love, respect, and admiration of Midwestern laboring people, he has expressed American democratic greatness and asserted human dignity and universality.

**SELECTED WORKS:** Sandburg's poetic works include *Chicago Poems* (1916); *Cornhuskers* (1918); *Smoke and Steel* (1920); *Slabs of the Sunburnt West* (1922); *Selected Poems of Carl Sandburg* (1926); *Good Morning, America* (1928); *The People, Yes* (1936); *Poems of the Midwest*, an aggregation of *Chicago Poems* and *Cornhuskers*; *Complete Poems* (1950); *The Sandburg Range* (1957); *Harvest Poems* (1960); and *Honey and Salt* (1963).

Sandburg's journalistic and historical writings are many and span decades. Most important perhaps of his journalistic writings are the stories reprinted as *The Chicago Race Riots, July 1919* (1919). Sandburg stands among the most important Lincoln biographers with his *Abraham Lincoln: The Prairie Years* (1927), *Abraham Lincoln: The War Years* (1939), *A Lincoln and Whitman Miscellany* (1938), and *A Lincoln Preface* (1953).

His *Rootabaga Stories* (1922) and *Rootabaga Pigeons* (1923) reflect Sandburg as a children's writer. His *American Songbag* (1926) and *New American Songbag* (1927) record Sandburg's interest in American folk songs and language patterns. *Remembrance Rock*, commissioned in 1943 and published in 1948, is Sandburg's only novel.

*Always the Young Strangers* (1953) provides an autobiographical account of his early years. Sandburg's early letters to his mentor, Philip Green Wright, are collected in *Carl Sandburg, Philip Green Wright, and the Asgard Press* (1975). *The Poet and the Dream Girl: The Love Letters of Lilian Steichen & Carl Sandburg*, edited by Margaret Sandburg (1999), provides another perspective. A much broader collection appears as *The Letters of Carl Sandburg* (1968).

**FURTHER READING:** Biographical, bibliographical, and critical studies on Sandburg are abundant, although critical interest has waned in recent years. Penelope Niven's *Sandburg: A Biography* (1991) is the standard biography. Milton Meltzer's *Carl Sandburg: A Biography* (1999) and Philip Yannella's *The Other Carl Sandburg* (1996) provide the newest studies of the poet. Harry Golden's *Carl Sandburg* (1961) and North Callahan's *Carl Sandburg: Lincoln of Our Literature* (1970) are also valuable book-length biographies although they are somewhat idealizing in their treatment. Several extended biographical works, reminiscences, and commentaries on Sandburg have been written by members of his family, including Paula and Margaret Sandburg and Edward Steichen. Dale Selwak's *Carl Sandburg: A Reference Guide* (1988) offers a recent bibliography. Richard Crowder (1964), Mark Van Doren (1969), and Gay Wilson Allen (1972) have each written extended critical studies entitled *Carl Sandburg*. Van Doren's volume is also useful in its bibliography of Sandburg materials at the Library of Congress. The Carl Sandburg Collection at the University of Illinois (Urbana-Champaign) is the primary Sandburg repository. Page one of the *New York Times* for Sunday, July 23, 1967, provides an extended obituary as well as related stories detailing Sandburg's poetic approaches, literary significance, and impact on America (1, 62). Sandburg's home, Connemara, in Flat Rock, North Carolina, contains a large number of books and manuscripts written by Sandburg as well as his still uncatalogued personal library.

PHILIP A. GREASLEY          UNIVERSITY OF KENTUCKY

## SCOTT RUSSELL SANDERS
October 26, 1945

**BIOGRAPHY:** Scott Russell Sanders was born in Memphis, Tennessee, in 1945, to Greeley Ray and Eva (Soloman) Sanders and spent his early childhood in Tennessee farming communities. In 1951 Sanders's family moved from Tennessee to rural Portage County, Ohio, where he lived until enrolling at Brown University in 1963. Sanders's Ohio years were spent living near the Ravenna Arsenal, a weapons production plant where his father worked; these childhood experiences of rural and military life became frequent subjects of his later essays and fiction. After graduating from Brown in 1967, Sanders married and began studying for a PhD at Cambridge University. While there, he published his first short stories. After receiving his doctorate in 1971, Sanders joined the English Department at Indiana University, where he still teaches. He has published novels, collections of essays and short stories, and literary criticism.

**SIGNIFICANCE:** Sanders's writing consistently calls for people to take responsibility for the places in which they live; he strongly opposes all wars and nuclear weapons. His experience growing up in small, close-knit farming communities gave him a sense of commitment to local life, while his years at the weapons arsenal during the height of the Cold War showed him the fragility of human existence. These themes dominate his work, which frequently focuses on Ohio and Indiana, where he has spent most of his life.

Sanders's earliest writing was fiction. His short stories about rural life began appearing in literary magazines in the early 1970s and were collected in *Fetching the Dead* (1984). His wide reading in Ohio history resulted in *Bad Man Ballad* (1986), a novel based on an 1813 murder in the Ohio region where he grew up, and *Wilderness Plots* (1983), a collection of tales from settlement of the Ohio Valley. He has also published science fiction, both stories and novels.

Despite his prolific writing of fiction, Sanders is best known as an essayist. In his essays, he provides a strong sense of Midwest regional life, blending autobiography, docu-

**Scott Russell Sanders.**
Photo by Eva Sanders Allen.
Courtesy of Scott Russell Sanders

mentary, and meditations on the need for human commitment to a particular place. *In Limestone Country* (1991) is a book about the limestone industry in his current home, southern Indiana. *The Paradise of Bombs* (1987) is a collection of essays that explores his childhood at the Ohio weapons arsenal and his rural background. *Secrets of the Universe* (1991) focuses on family life and place, while *Staying Put* (1993) is more polemic, arguing for human rootedness and centeredness. *Writing from the Center* (1995) explores the writing life from a Midwestern perspective; and *Hunting for Hope* (1998) explores the challenges of maintaining hope in today's world. His essays on Midwestern and rural life have made Sanders a leading practitioner of the emerging genre of creative nonfiction, and most critical attention focuses on his essays. *The Paradise of Bombs* won the Associated Writing Programs Award for Creative Nonfiction in 1987, and *Staying Put* won the 1994 Ohioana Book Award for Nonfiction.

**SELECTED WORKS:** Sanders's collections of short stories include *Wilderness Plots: Tales*

*about the Settlement of the Ohio Land* (1983) and *Fetching the Dead* (1984); his historical novel is *Bad Man Ballad* (1986). His science fiction novels are *Terrarium* (1985), *The Engineer of Beasts* (1988), and *The Invisible Company* (1989). His nonfiction books include *Stone Country* (1985), later revised as *In Limestone Country* (1991); *The Paradise of Bombs* (1987); *Secrets of the Universe* (1991); *Staying Put: Making a Home in a Restless World* (1993); *Writing from the Center* (1995); and *Hunting for Hope* (1998). Sanders has also written books for children, including *Aurora Means Dawn* (1989), *Warm as Wool* (1992), and *Here Comes the Mystery Man* (1994).

**FURTHER READING:** William Nichols undertakes an overview of Sanders's entire oeuvre in *American Nature Writers*, edited by John Elder (1996). Patrick Parrinder examines Sanders's fiction in "Swan Songs," in *Poetry Nation Review* 14.3 (December 1987): 53–54. Kevin Walzer discusses Sanders's nonfiction in "Staying Put: The Invisible Landscape of Scott Russell Sanders's Nonfiction," in the *Journal of Kentucky Studies* 11 (September 1994): 117–25. Kent Ryden discusses Sanders's essays in the context of regional writing in *Mapping the Invisible Landscape: Writing, Folklore and the Sense of Place* (1993). Sanders has not designated a repository for his papers.

KEVIN WALZER                    CINCINNATI, OHIO

## MARI(E SUSETTE) SANDOZ

May 11, 1896–March 10, 1966
(Mary S. Macumber)

**BIOGRAPHY:** Born in Sheridan County, Nebraska, at the time a frontier area, Sandoz grew up in primitive conditions. Her father, Jules Ami Sandoz, the subject of *Old Jules* (1935), was an eccentric and sometimes cruel frontiersman of Swiss origins and a lasting influence, both negative and positive. Her mother, Mary Elizabeth (Fehr) Sandoz, had less impact. In this dysfunctional family, Mari bore heavy responsibilities from early childhood onward. Though Swiss German was the language in her home, Mari became an avid reader of English materials and taught herself about the world by reading anything she could find. She learned about her region by listening to stories of Indians and settlers told by old-timers.

Having achieved an eighth-grade education, she became a country schoolteacher in 1913 and married Wray Macumber in 1914. Divorced in 1919, she moved to Lincoln, Nebraska, where she took a secretarial course and enthusiastically entered the cultural life of this university community. By 1923 she considered herself a writer, and the rest of her life is essentially her literary biography. Though she moved to New York City in 1943, she retained close ties to Nebraska, always her literary and historical subject. She died of cancer in New York City and was buried, at her request, on the family homestead in the Nebraska sand hills.

**SIGNIFICANCE:** Sandoz was a novelist, biographer, historian, and writer of children's books, all of these deeply rooted in her western Nebraska, which she depicted in all its harshness and beauty. As a biographer she perceptively examined such dissimilar subjects as her own father, whom she both admired and feared, and Crazy Horse, the Oglala chief. The latter work, *Crazy Horse, the Strange Man of the Oglalas: A Biography* (1942), was influenced by stories she had heard in childhood. Sandoz made significant contributions to the study of the economic and social history of her region in *The Buffalo Hunters: The Story of the Hide Men* (1954), *The Cattlemen: From the Rio Grande across the Far Marias* (1958), and *The Beaver Men: Spearheads of Empire* (1964). The locale she portrays is on the border between Midwest and West, and her work is significant for readers and scholars interested in both regions.

Her fiction is almost entirely rooted in actual historical fact. *Slogum House* (1937), a striking portrait of a powerful and ruthless woman, gives an unvarnished picture of frontier brutality. *The Tom-Walker* (1947), *Miss Morissa: Doctor of the Gold Trail* (1955), and *Son of the Gamblin' Man: The Youth of an Artist* (1960) all examine aspects of this bleak land: war veterans striving to make lives despite corruption surrounding them, struggles of a woman doctor on the frontier, and the attempt, finally successful, of a sensitive boy to escape an acquisitive and unintentionally destructive father. *Son of the Gamblin' Man*, among her lesser-known works, is particularly interesting as a gloss on an interesting and stereotypical event in Nebraska history and as the thinly fictionalized biography of Robert Henri, who despite uncongenial origins became a leading painter and teacher of artists. In this novel Sandoz explores a num-

Mari Sandoz.
Courtesy of the Nebraska State Historical Society

ber of recurring themes and concerns, including the violence of the frontier, conflicts between groups, the change from wilderness to a settled society, and frontier hostility to the artistic temperament.

Sandoz portrays the landscape and history of western Nebraska, principally the sand hills, with unmatched honesty and clarity. The University of Nebraska has kept much of her work available.

**SELECTED WORKS:** *Capital City* (1939) is a satiric novel intended as a companion to *Slogum House* (1937). *Cheyenne Autumn* (1953), *Love Song to the Plains* (1961), *The Story Catcher* (1963), and *Sandhills Sundays, and Other Recollections* (1966) in varied ways reveal the author's continuing fascination with Nebraska.

**FURTHER READING:** Several helpful critical studies exist. A fine literary biography and the principal secondary source for information on Sandoz is *Mari Sandoz: Story Catcher of the Plains* (1982), by Helen Winter Stauffer. Laura R. Villiger's *Mari Sandoz: A Study in Post-Colonial Discourse* (1994) examines Sandoz's work in light of recent literary theory. Both the University of Nebraska and the Nebraska State Historical Society hold significant collections of her manuscripts, letters, and other papers.

MARY JEAN DEMARR    INDIANA STATE UNIVERSITY

## HELEN HOOVEN SANTMYER
November 25, 1895–February 21, 1986

**BIOGRAPHY:** Helen Hooven Santmyer, novelist and memoirist, was born in Cincinnati, Ohio, the eldest of three children of Joseph and Bertha (Hooven) Santmyer. When the author was five, her family moved to her great-grandparents' home in Xenia, a short distance from Dayton and Springfield. Helen grew up in that small conservative town, a bastion of Republican and Presbyterian respectability. Though the family did not consider themselves more than adequately well off, her father's work as a pharmaceutical salesman enabled them to live comfortably and to send Santmyer, an admirer of Louisa May Alcott, to Wellesley to study. After taking her bachelor of arts there in 1918, she stayed on for a year to work for a suffragist group, then moved to New York in 1919 to take a job at *Scribner's Magazine* for two years.

Summoned back to Ohio by her father, Santmyer taught in the local high school for a year, then returned to Massachusetts to teach for two years at Wellesley. After this, according to an agreement they had made, her father sent her to England for three years of study at Oxford. With her bachelor of letters in hand, Santmyer returned to Ohio. In the early 1930s she moved to California with her parents, but they returned to Ohio once more when her father retired.

In 1936 Santmyer was hired as dean of women at Cedarville College, a few miles from Xenia. During a seventeen-year tenure there she became head of the English Department. When in 1953 the Presbyterian school was sold to the Baptist Church, Santmyer left to become a reference librarian for the Dayton/Montgomery County Public Library, a post she held until her retirement in 1959.

For many years she shared a house in Xenia with her friend and mentor Mildred Sandoe until Santmyer's health failed and both women moved to a nursing home in that town. It was here that she finished her best-known novel, . . . *And Ladies of the Club* (1982). Santmyer died in Xenia from complications of chronic emphysema.

**SIGNIFICANCE:** Helen Santmyer wrote her novels and the memoir *Ohio Town* to preserve the essence of small-town Mid-America, which she thought of as the daily life of ordinary people who tried to uphold a standard of honesty and scrupulous behavior in the chaotic times following the Civil War, the times of despair during the Great Depression, and in times of progress and favorable growth. Her values were largely modeled on the beliefs of the Presbyterian Church and the politics of the Republican Party, though she was more progressive and liberal than many people in her community. Though she denied having written . . . *And Ladies of the Club* as a refutation of SINCLAIR LEWIS's *Main Street,* she did express distaste for the latter novel, for she recalled her own childhood as happy, and felt that Lewis had pictured small-town life as too stifling. Her first two novels, *Herbs and Apples* (1925) and *The Fierce Dispute* (1929), were only mildly praised. During her stay in California she wrote descriptive essays about Xenia, the first of which appeared in the *Antioch Review*, that were published as the book *Ohio Town* by Ohio State University Press in 1962. That book received the Florence Roberts Head Award from the Ohioana Library Association in 1964, a fact which pleased Santmyer greatly.

The two-decades-long creation of . . . *And Ladies of the Club* came next, and its republication by Putnam's in 1984 made an "overnight" sensation. Santmyer herself believed that most of the excitement was the result of her age—eighty-eight—when the book made the best-seller list. Though seldom critically lauded, the book was appreciated for its detailed examination of the political, religious, racial, educational, and social mores of citizens of "Waynesboro," her pseudonym for Xenia. The characters exhibit many of the author's own prejudices and predispositions, but they are well-drawn and ultimately interesting in their own right. For example, characters take both sides of the issue of education for women, and some represent the blue-collar (Democratic) side of labor issues, while the depiction of treatment of servants and minorities is characteristic of the times. Black characters usually speak in dialect (which is skillfully done) even though the author was undoubtedly aware of an educated class of blacks at nearby Wilberforce University. The period's treatment of the Irish, generally assumed to be Catholic, is also pivotal to the story. In similar ways she included such topics as the opinion of small-town Midwesterners by a "sophisticated" California lawyer, the labyrinth of Ohio politics, the problems of small businesses in depression times, and the survival strategies of rural and small-town Ohio in wars and natural disasters.

The panoramic novel . . . *And Ladies of the Club*, its now-republished predecessors, and its posthumous successor have been enjoyed by a wide cross-section of people interested in the minutiae of turn-of-the-century life in the Midwest. On the strength of that work and the preservation of history that it represents, Santmyer was awarded honorary doctorates by both Ohio State University and Wright State University.

**SELECTED WORKS:** Santmyer's novels are *Herbs and Apples* (1925), *The Fierce Dispute* (1929), . . . *And Ladies of the Club* (1982), and *Farewell Summer* (1988, posthumous). Her memoir of the city of Xenia is *Ohio Town* (1962).

**FURTHER READING:** Joyce Crosby Quay's brief *Early Promise, Late Reward: A Biography of Helen Hooven Santmyer* (1995) is the only book-length study to date. Articles of criticism have appeared in recent years in various journals: *Ohio Town* was reviewed in 1963 by Eldon C. Hill in *Indiana Magazine of History* and in 1964 by James Iverne Dowie in *History News*; in 1984, after the publication of . . . *And Ladies of the Club*, there were dozens of reviews. While Gene Lyons, writing for *Newsweek*, and Michael Malone, for the *Nation*, generally did not care for it, there were primarily favorable reviews by VANCE BOURJAILY in the *New York Times Book Review*, Francis X. Marnell in *National Review*, and Cynthia Grenier in the *American Spectator*. A considerable collection of Santmyer's other writing, some previously published in *Scribner's*, *Antioch Review*, and *Midland*, is kept in the rare books collection at Ohio State University. It includes poetry, stories, and articles on such subjects as Ann Morrow Lindbergh, Defoe, Chaucer, Shakespeare, Pirandello, and journalism in southwest Ohio. Folders of her correspondence with publishers, a household inventory, some pictures, and collected fan mail from . . . *And*

*Ladies of the Club* are among the still-uncatalogued material.

AMY JO ZOOK        URBANA UNIVERSITY

## BIENVENIDO N(UQUI) SANTOS
March 22, 1911–January 7, 1996
(Tomas F. Mendoza, Ursulo S. Dabu, C. Kabiling Santos, Eugenio Lingad, Ben Santos)

**BIOGRAPHY:** Born in Manila of Tomas and Vicenta (Nuqui) de los Santos, Santos earned his BSE in English in 1932 at the University of the Philippines. A year later he married his college sweetheart, Beatriz Nidea, and both began public school teaching; they had two daughters and a son. Awarded a government scholarship, he obtained an MA in English at the University of Illinois in 1942, followed by a summer writing fiction under Whit Burnett. Throughout World War II, he served the Philippine Commonwealth government-in-exile as clerk, speechwriter, editor of *Philippines* magazine, and public speaker—an assignment that led to the memorable story, "Scent of Apples." Following the war, he studied poetry with I. A. Richards before going home.

Returning in 1958 as a Rockefeller grantee at Paul Engle's writers' workshop at the University of Iowa, Santos thereafter split his time between the Philippines and the United States. From 1973 until 1982, Santos was Distinguished Writer in Residence at Wichita State University, with additional stints at Iowa State and Ohio State. He died of undisclosed causes at Daraga in the Province of Albay, Philippines, in the house with a view of Mount Mayon volcano that he and Beatriz had built but hardly lived in.

**SIGNIFICANCE:** Santos is known for depicting alienated Filipinos in America, especially in the Midwest. In an interview published in *Conversations with Filipino Writers* (1990), Santos indicated that he thought Midwesterners represented what was best about America and thus formed the perfect foil for his exploration of the exile's predicament.

**SELECTED WORKS:** Those works set in the Midwest are the novel *The Man Who (Thought He) Looked Like Robert Taylor* (1983), set in Chicago; and *Scent of Apples: A Collection of Stories* (1979), which won the Before Columbus Foundation's American Book Award. Santos's story "Immigration Blues," which won the University of Missouri New Letters Prize in 1977, received honorable mention in *Best American Short Stories, 1978*. Among the stories frequently anthologized are "Scent of Apples," set in Kalamazoo, and "The Contender" and "The Day the Dancers Came," both set in Chicago. Santos is the author, as well, of four additional novels: *The Volcano* (1965), *Villa Magdalena* (1965), *The Praying Man* (1982), and *What the Hell for You Left Your Heart in San Francisco* (1987); two additional short story collections, *Brother, My Brother* (1960) and *Dwell in the Wilderness* (1985); two volumes of poetry, *The Wounded Stag* (1956) and *Distances: In Time* (1983); and a memoir, *Memory's Fictions* (1993). His collected papers are at Wichita State University.

**FURTHER READING:** There is no book-length study of Santos, although Leonor Aureus-Briscoe has been working on a biography since 1982. Published interviews with Santos include Lynn M. Grow's "The Harrowed and Hallowed Ground: An Interview with Bienvenido N. Santos," in *Wichita State University Bulletin* 53:4 (1977): 3–22; and those included in Edilberto N. Alegre and Doreen G. Fernandez's *The Writer and His Milieu: An Oral History of the First Generation of Writers in English* (1984), 217–58; and Roger J. Bresnahan's *Conversations with Filipino Writers* (1990), 88–114.

ROGER JIANG BRESNAHAN

MICHIGAN STATE UNIVERSITY

# HENRY ROWE SCHOOLCRAFT
## March 28, 1793–December 10, 1864

**BIOGRAPHY:** Henry Rowe Schoolcraft, explorer, travel writer, and ground-breaking ethnologist, was born just west of Albany, New York, to an ambitious middle-class family that had fought as Anglo-Americans against what they viewed as the "savage, barbarian" Indians on the revolutionary frontier (Mosser 9). His father, Lawrence Schoolcraft, traced ancestry back to the Dutch period; his mother, Margaret (Rowe) Schoolcraft, could claim descent from a James Calcraft, a British officer sent to fight in Canada prior to 1712. By the end of his life, Schoolcraft had grown beyond this European heritage to become the foremost commentator on Native Americans as complex sets of peoples.

Schoolcraft took courses at both Union College and Middlebury College but could not afford degree education and had to work in his father's glass-making industry as a young man. He was essentially self-trained in the science of the day as a mineralogist and geologist, and as early as 1808 he was organizing literary groups and trying to write. These dual early interests foreshadowed his later accomplishments as scientist and writer.

In 1818 he set off for southern Missouri and produced his first book from his travel and mineralogical observations, *A View of the Lead Mines of Missouri* (1819). The book quickly established his reputation as a natural scientist and travel writer and earned him a position on exploring expeditions led by Lewis Cass, governor of the Michigan territory. Schoolcraft produced three more travel narratives in the next decade and a half based on expeditions to the Lake Superior region led by Cass and, finally, by himself. On the 1832 trip that he led, the great scientific achievement was the discovery of the true source of the Mississippi River.

But his writing was most important to him, and gradually Schoolcraft trained himself to be an accurate and sensitive observer of Native American Indian culture. In 1823 he married Jane Johnston, the granddaughter of a Chippewa chief, and hence was given the opportunity through his wife's family to develop his innovative methods of recording oral history and ethnography. Later he applied these methods to the Iroquois tribes of his native New York state as well as to the Lake Superior tribes. By the end of his career he had compiled a massive and important study of the complex American Indian culture. Cass had early appointed him Indian agent for the Lake Superior tribes and later superintendent of Indian Affairs for all of Michigan. Jane Johnston Schoolcraft died in 1842. A few years later, Henry married a Southerner, Mary E. Howard, and he helped her at the end of his life in research and publication of works, under her name, that sought to defend Southern slave culture. Schoolcraft died in Washington, D.C., with a solid reputation as a writer and scientist.

**SIGNIFICANCE:** Schoolcraft was years ahead of his time in developing methods for "salvage ethnography" and oral history (Mosser 231). His ability to change as a writer and his ambition account for this achievement. At first his books reflected neither sympathy for nor knowledge of Native Americans beyond the frontier bias of his father and brothers.

Following the trilogy of his travel books, from the original Cass expedition to his 1832 Lake Itasca expedition, and concurrent with his political work as Indian Administrator for Cass, however, a change occurred. His later volumes were chiefly ethnographic works and sympathetic popularizations of Native American Indian cultures and religions.

All his life Schoolcraft wanted to write as well as be a scientific observer, and he was able to adapt and change. *Algic Researches, Comprising Inquiries Respecting the Mental Characteristics of the North American Indian: First Series: Indian Tales and Legends*, in two volumes (1839), is an ethnographic collection growing from the Algic Society of Detroit that Schoolcraft founded in 1832 and is probably his best book. Schoolcraft coined the term *Algic* by combining "Algonquin" and "Atlantic" to suggest that the Lake Superior Chippewa tribes had roots going back to the Atlantic coast tribes. The ethnographic truth of lineage among these various tribes as hypothesized by Schoolcraft has been generally accepted by modern researchers despite continuing discussion over language derivations. Thus, the usual misconception that Longfellow, who used Schoolcraft's Algic book for his poem *Hiawatha* (1855), transplanted his characters incorrectly from the Atlantic coast to Lake Superior is farther from ethnographic "truth" than necessary. D. P. Mosser's 1991 dissertation, "Henry Rowe Schoolcraft: Eyewitness to a Changing Frontier," makes it clear that Schoolcraft's ideas are being taken seriously now. At the very least he was an immensely prolific and influential writer on the Midwest, its land, and its indigenous peoples.

**SELECTED WORKS:** Schoolcraft's first travel book on Missouri as well as the trilogy of travel books from the Cass expeditions were well received in the nineteenth century and are now being reprinted beautifully by Michigan State University Press. *Algic Researches . . .* (1839) was the first of several ethnographic as well as popular works that culminated in *Historical and Statistical Information Respecting the History, Condition, and Prospects of the Indian Tribes of the United States*, 6 parts (1851–57).
**FURTHER READING:** Richard C. Bremer's *Indian Agent and Wilderness Scholar: The Life of Henry Rowe Schoolcraft* (1987) and a new doctoral dissertation by D. P. Mosser, "Henry Rowe Schoolcraft: Eyewitness to a Changing

Frontier" (1991), are the most valuable secondary sources. The best collection of Schoolcraft papers and of material by him, in the Papers of the United States Office of Indian Affairs, 1797–1920, is housed in the Manuscripts Division of the Library of Congress. The Minnesota Historical Society and the Huntington Library in San Marino, California, also have important Schoolcraft materials.

DONALD M. HASSLER          KENT STATE UNIVERSITY

## AMY JO SCHOONOVER (ZOOK)
April 25, 1937

**BIOGRAPHY:** Born in Glen Ellyn, Illinois, to John Dale Schoonover and Alice (Fletcher) Schoonover, both musicians, Amy Jo Schoonover spent much of her youth from age three in Texas, where she attended school in Abilene, graduating from high school there in 1955. She attended Hardin-Simmons University in Abilene from 1955 to 1958. After moving to Ohio, she received the BA in English from Wittenberg University in 1969. She received the MA in 1982 and the PhD in 1993, both in English from West Virginia University.

The mother of three children from her first marriage to Boyd McCarty of Urbana, Ohio, which ended in divorce in 1972, she married Samuel J. Zook Jr. of West Liberty, Ohio, later that year; they reside in Mechanicsburg, Ohio. In a personal letter to David D. Anderson she writes, "I began writing at ten, and published my first poems in my early teens . . . when I moved to Ohio I was a full-time parent and part-time student and teacher . . . . [I] Began serious writing again in 1971." She has taught at a variety of schools.
**SIGNIFICANCE:** Schoonover has published five volumes of poetry in addition to literally hundreds of poems in a wide variety of journals. Her work is firmly rooted in the time and place of her adult experience. Her best work, collected in *New and Used Poems* (1988), for which she was named Ohio Poet of the Year for 1988 by the Ohio Poetry Day Association, is rich with the imagery of place, largely that of rural and small-town Ohio. At the same time each of her poems is a manifestation of the poet's urge to know what lies beyond the sharply etched appearance. In "Ohio Cabin" she recreates an imaginary but realistic past; in "Decoration Day Parade" she recreates the reality of the past; in others, she is vividly personal, both in her imagery and

in the details of her poetry, as in "Monday Blues," the lament of a rural Ohio housewife-poet.

**SELECTED WORKS:** Schoonover's volumes of verse include *Echoes of England* (1975), *A Sonnet Sampler* (1979), *A New Page* (1979, revised and enlarged 1984), and *Threnody* (1994). She contributed to and edited a revised edition of *The Study and Writing of Poetry* (1983, 1996), a collection of essays by and about women poets.

**FURTHER READING:** Schoonover is listed in *The Directory of American Poets and Fiction Writers, 1997–1998* (1997): 251, and in *Who's Who in Writers, Editors, and Poets, 1992–1993* (1992): 547. Her works, particularly *New and Used Poems*, have been widely reviewed.

DAVID D. ANDERSON    MICHIGAN STATE UNIVERSITY

## CARL SCHURZ
March 2, 1829–May 14, 1906

**BIOGRAPHY:** Born in the village of Liblar, in the Rhineland, to Christian Schurz, a schoolteacher, and Marianne (Jussen) Schurz, a journalist and public speaker, Carl Schurz was educated at the University of Bonn. There he became a student revolutionary and was forced to flee without finishing a degree. He married Margaretha Meyer in 1852, just before immigrating to the United States. After living in Philadelphia and acquiring facility with English, Schurz and his wife bought a farm in the Milwaukee area in 1855. Schurz quickly acquired prominence as the Republican Party's anti-slavery speaker to German immigrants in Wisconsin and nearby states. A major general in the Union army, he later served in the Senate and the administrations of ABRAHAM LINCOLN and Rutherford B. Hayes.

Schurz was correspondent or editor for papers in New York, Detroit, and St. Louis; he was also editorial writer for *Harper's Weekly* and a lecturer throughout his political and journalistic career. From 1869 Schurz lived principally in Washington and New York, where he died of pneumonia. Schurz and his wife had three daughters and two sons.

**SIGNIFICANCE:** Schurz's Midwestern residence influenced his entire career. After arriving in the United States, he had visited relatives in Illinois, Wisconsin, and Missouri, but he was appalled by slavery and found Milwaukee congenial and stimulating because of the immigrant enthusiasm and apparently classless society that he envisioned in America. As political speaker and lyceum lecturer, his principal themes paralleled those of the Populists and later the Progressives: civil service, monetary reform, anti-imperialism, Negro suffrage, and civil rights. In the Senate, Schurz was an outspoken critic of corruption in the Grant administration. As President Hayes's secretary of the interior, Schurz argued for a more generous Indian policy. Often breaking with the Republicans, Schurz ultimately endorsed the candidacy of WILLIAM JENNINGS BRYAN.

As a lecturer, Schurz's popularity was similar to Bryan's: he could project sincere altruism, enthusiasm for his principles, optimism, and amiability. In *Reminiscences* (1908), his stories of traveling the rural Midwestern lecture circuit by horse, carriage, and steamer are as historically informative and amusing as similar anecdotes by MARK TWAIN and BILL NYE. Schurz called his "rough adventures [in the Midwest] the most interesting and cheering of my early American experiences. I saw what I might call the middle-class culture in process of formation." Schurz observed that Eastern stereotypes of Midwestern small towns belied their "intellectual and moral energy" (*Reminiscences* II, 158–59).

**SELECTED WORKS:** Schurz's political writings include *The Speeches of Carl Schurz* (1865), *The Life of Henry Clay* (1887), "Abraham Lincoln: An Essay," in *The Writings of Abraham Lincoln* (1905), and *Speeches, Correspondences, and Political Papers* (1913). *The Reminiscences of Carl Schurz*, in two volumes (1908), unfinished at his death, consists of personal anecdotes and reflections covering his years to 1869. In addition, Schurz's early Midwestern years are described in *Intimate Letters of Carl Schurz, 1841–1869* (1928). A prolific letter writer, Schurz usually recorded his lectures and political work on the road.

**FURTHER READING:** Biographies with emphasis on early life, Midwestern residence, and Civil War years are Chester Easum's *The Americanization of Carl Schurz* (1929), Joseph Schafer's *Carl Schurz: Militant Liberal* (1930), and Claude Fuess's *Carl Schurz, Reformer* (1932). A complete biography is Hans Trefousse's *Carl Schurz* (1982). Schurz's papers are held at the Library of Congress and the State Historical Society of Wisconsin.

THOMAS PRIBEK

UNIVERSITY OF WISCONSIN–LACROSSE

## BARBARA J(UNE NORRIS) SCOT
February 16, 1942

**BIOGRAPHY:** Barbara J. Scot was born in Scotch Grove, Iowa, the daughter of Robert and Kathleen (Hughes) Norris. Abandoned by her father when she was very young, Scot was raised by her mother, a schoolteacher whose struggle to support two children was increased by the huge debt Robert left for the family.

Scot received a BA in English from Coe College in Cedar Rapids, Iowa, in 1963, and she earned an MA from the University of Iowa in 1965. She taught high school for twenty-six years, most of them in Oregon, where she has lived since 1972. She took an MA in history from Portland State University in 1975. In 1990 Scot went to Nepal to teach for a year, and she records this experience in her first book, *The Violet Shyness of Their Eyes: Notes from Nepal* (1993). In the spring of 1993, Scot decided to revisit Scotch Grove in an attempt to gain a new understanding about the life of her mother, who died of a heart attack in 1963. The return to Iowa led Scot to write her second book, the autobiographical *Prairie Reunion* (1995), which was a *New York Times* Notable Book. Scot married Jim Trusky in 1979 and has two sons, Taig and Lon Murphy, from an earlier marriage.

**SIGNIFICANCE:** Although *The Violet Shyness of Their Eyes* contains several references to her Iowa childhood, Barbara Scot's significance as a Midwestern writer comes primarily from *Prairie Reunion*. In this book Scot returns to her native Scotch Grove, Iowa, and begins searching for answers to questions concerning the failed relationship of a mother she adored and a father she never knew. By investigating the history of her family, the community, and the land itself, Scot locates the values which shape not only her parents' lives but also her own life and the lives of others growing up in communities like Scotch Grove: reverence for the land, respect for family and the community, and adherence to the teachings of the church fathers. Scot herself has mixed feelings about the effect of such values on individuals living in the Midwest. For example, strict Protestant morality and a patriarchal family structure often make life difficult for community members, women in particular; but these ideals were part of a system of beliefs that could be passed from one generation to the next to provide order and tradition in an otherwise changing world. Scot learns that her mother lived her life according to these values so that she could someday teach them to her children.

The land itself plays a key role in the story, but Scot does not share her ancestors' preoccupation with owning and maintaining land. In fact, *Prairie Reunion* explores both archaeological and cultural history of the Scotch Grove area to show that the land itself has outlasted all groups of people who temporarily lived on it.

**SELECTED WORKS:** *The Violet Shyness of Their Eyes: Notes from Nepal* (1993) and *Prairie Reunion* (1995) are the two books Scot has written.

**FURTHER READING:** No book-length study or articles have appeared on Scot. Informative book reviews of *Prairie Reunion* are found in the September 17, 1995, *New York Times Book Review*: 11, and the September 1, 1995, *Washington Post*: 3F.

MATTHEW J. DARLING          MARQUETTE UNIVERSITY

## RUTH SEID
July 1, 1913–April 4, 1995
(Jo Sinclair)

**BIOGRAPHY:** Born in Brooklyn of working-class Eastern European Jewish immigrant parents, Nathan and Ida (Kravetsky) Seid, Ruth Seid began working at the age of seventeen. In 1936 she started on the Foreign Language Newspaper Digest of the Works Progress Administration in Cleveland, the classic beginning for so many writers of her era. She had already taken her pseudonym, a name to honor UPTON SINCLAIR and SINCLAIR LEWIS while it camouflaged her gender and ethnicity. Later, while employed by the WPA, she met her first beloved, Helen (Adler) Buchman, a married mother of two children, started writing for the Red Cross chapter in Cleveland, and moved into the Buchman household as a family member. During the years from 1942 to 1970, she lived with them in Cleveland Heights, Shaker Heights, and Novelty, Ohio, and worked as a freelance writer and gardener to help feed the family. Helen died prematurely in 1963, leaving Sinclair alone to cope with her alcoholism, depression, and suicidal impulses.

During her more than twenty years with Helen, Sinclair published four novels and wrote hundreds of essays, short stories, and plays, one of which was actually produced. After Helen's death, she rewrote *Approach to the Meaning* five times but never published a novel again. However, she did complete her memoir in 1972.

In 1973 she moved in with Joan (Mandell) Soffer, in Jenkintown, Pennsylvania. On April 4, 1995, Sinclair died after a decade of various debilitating ailments. She had been working for twenty years on a novel about being a homosexual in straight America.

**SIGNIFICANCE:** Jo Sinclair is explicitly a Midwestern writer. Her work is set either in a fictionalized Cleveland or other Midwestern cities like Detroit or in the Ohio countryside that she both adored and hated for its fecundity and harshness. Helen had taught her to love gardening; homegrown vegetables and flowers play a central role in Sinclair's texts. Her early stories and collages about the WPA explore the ambivalence of a working-class woman needing public assistance. *Wasteland* (1946), *Sing at My Wake* (1951), and *Anna Teller* (1960) explicitly treat the WPA, which broadened her horizons from the Cleveland ghetto of her childhood to the world at large; she had had no idea how many ethnic groups there were in Cleveland—"'[m]elting pot' in library books turned into real people, who became friends as she learned their ways" (*Seasons* 3). Her third novel, *The Changelings* (1955), continues her preoccupation with class issues as it accurately describes Jewish, or white, flight from the inner city as African Americans claim the neighborhoods.

Her novels and stories are also important Jewish texts because they depict the transition of unwanted *shtetl* immigrants to middle-class Americans, who either struggle with or simply live out their otherness in the predominantly gentile Midwest. Sinclair's roots were urban and her texts show appreciation for the amenities of Cleveland, not least in the autobiography where she talks about the rye bread, kosher hot dogs, bagels, and lox: "those city things we like and can't buy out here in 'goy' territory" (96). *Wasteland* is a psychological novel, written during the peak of that genre, which explores internalized anti-Semitism when anti-Jewish feelings were at their highest after World War II.

Finally, Sinclair is important as a lesbian writer. *Wasteland* is the first fully developed, positive portrayal of a lesbian in twentieth-century American literature. The coming-out stories of the last two decades of the century need the historical contexts of Sinclair's texts. By fictionalizing her own sensitivities and experiences, Jo Sinclair challenges American identity from the Depression through the Cold War as Americans shifted from a prescribed monoculturalism to an acceptance, if not celebration, of diversity.

Jo Sinclair was Cleveland's most celebrated author, an honor not yet surpassed. She won the ten-thousand-dollar Harper Prize in 1946 for *Wasteland*, which catapulted her into fame. The Ohioana Library Association gave her an honorable mention for *Wasteland* and the best fiction award for *The Changelings* and *Anna Teller*. In 1970 Boston University bought her manuscripts to form the cornerstone of its new Special Collections, which was unique in the country by focusing solely on American culture. A "ghetto punk" had become a national literary icon during the 1940s and 1950s, and her legacy would survive, ironically, at a university library while she herself was a "graduate" of the Cleveland Public Library.

**SELECTED WORKS:** Sinclair's major novels include *Wasteland* (1946), *Sing at My Wake* (1951), *The Changelings* (1955), and *Anna Teller* (1960). From the late 1930s to the early 1960s, Sinclair published more than fifty stories and essays in a wide variety of publications which included *New Masses*, *Junior Red Cross Journal*, *Esquire*, *Chicago Jewish Forum*, *Today's Woman*, *Collier's*, *Reader's Digest*, and *Skyline*, a quarterly of Cleveland College. In 1950 *The Long Moment*, a play Sinclair had written for Karamu House about a black musician contemplating passing for white, had an eight-week run at the experimental Brooks Theatre of the Cleveland Play House. In 1993 the Feminist Press published *The Seasons: Death and Transfiguration* to kick off their new series of memoirs. This book is deeply rooted in Ohio's landscape and Ohio's culture.

**FURTHER READING:** An early article is "John Brown (né Jake Braunowitz) of the [sic] *Wasteland* of Jo Sinclair (née Ruth Seid)," by Ellen Serlen Uffen, printed in *Midwestern Miscellany* 16 (1988): 41–51. The republications of *Wasteland* (1987), *The Changelings* (1983), and

*Anna Teller* (1992) all contain useful commentaries on the novels. Recent short discussions include Jan Clausen's "Testament of Friendship," in a review of *The Seasons* in the *Women's Review of Books* (December 1992): 7–8; Elisabeth Sandberg's "Jo Sinclair: A Gardener of Souls," in *Studies in American Jewish Literature* 12 (1993): 72–78; Gay Wilentz's article "(Re)Constructing Identity: 'Angled' Presentation in Sinclair/Seid's *Wasteland*," anthologized in Barbara Frey Waxman's *Multicultural Literatures through Feminist/Poststructuralist Lenses* (1993): 84–103; Wilentz's entry on Sinclair in *Jewish-American Women Writers: A Bio-Bibliographical Critical Sourcebook* (1994): 397–406; and Elisabeth Sandberg's entry in *Contemporary Jewish American Novelists* (1996): 375–84. In 1995 Barbara Chiarello wrote a master's thesis at the University of Texas at Arlington entitled "The Space between Revealing and Concealing: '*Wasteland*' by Jo Sinclair," and in 1996 Amy Robin Jones wrote a dissertation at the University of Colorado called "'There Is No Place': Geographical Imagination and Revision in Novels by Ann Petry and Jo Sinclair." The only dissertation devoted strictly to Jo Sinclair is "Jo Sinclair: Toward a Critical Biography" (1985), by Elisabeth Sandberg; it is based on the manuscripts at Mugar Memorial Library at Boston University.

ELISABETH SANDBERG          WOODBURY UNIVERSITY

# (ARNOLD) ERIC SEVAREID
November 26, 1912–July 9, 1992

**BIOGRAPHY:** Arnold Eric Sevareid was born in Velva, North Dakota, the younger son of Alfred and Clare (Hougen) Sevareid. The Sevareid family moved to Minneapolis, Minnesota, when Eric was a teenager, after his father's bank failed. Upon graduation from high school, Sevareid convinced the *Minneapolis Star* to underwrite a two-thousand-mile canoe trip from Minneapolis to Hudson Bay, during which he corresponded with the paper. Later, he worked for the *Minneapolis Journal* while studying at the University of Minnesota. Sevareid wrote for the Paris edition of the *New York Herald Tribune* while studying in that city and began signing his stories "Eric." In 1939 he was recruited by Edward R. Murrow as a radio reporter for CBS News and covered many of the major events of World War II. Sevareid continued with

CBS as the Washington bureau chief. Later, on television, he was best known for elegantly written, formally delivered commentaries on the *CBS Evening News*.

Sevareid took strong positions in favor of civil rights and negotiating an end to the Vietnam War. His ability to project fairness and sound judgment helped to make editorial commentary a regular feature of network news. He was also the moderator and narrator of many regular and special programs, author of a syndicated column, and winner of numerous awards for journalism. Sevareid was compelled to retire from broadcasting upon reaching CBS's mandatory age limit, but he continued writing. He considered himself more a writer than a broadcaster.

He married three times and had three children. Sevareid died of stomach cancer in Washington, D.C.

**SIGNIFICANCE:** His first book, *Canoeing with the Cree* (1935), the adventures of his trip from Minneapolis to Hudson Bay, retraces and relives early Midwestern history of fur traders and Indians. *Not So Wild a Dream* (1946), memoirs published after World War II, contains reflections upon his Midwestern upbringing. His career was lived in major cities of Europe and America, because for a boy of his generation with worldly ambition, "we knew that the last of the frontiers had disappeared . . . . It was the East that was golden" (11), as it was for contemporaries GLENWAY WESCOTT and F. SCOTT FITZGERALD.

Sevareid avoided the Norwegian speech of his parents and grandparents. However, like Fitzgerald's Nick Carraway, Sevareid maintained a self-consciously Midwestern, nonjudgmental attitude, while his appearance and manner of fair-mindedness, as well as his Midwestern accent, helped form the ideal for a broadcast journalist in the early days of television. Until recently, broadcasters learned or preserved the measured, undramatic cadence and reduced vowel sounds of Midwestern speech, for a journalistic equivalent of the poker-faced, unsmiling earnestness in Midwestern and Western humor. Murrow called Sevareid "the gloomy Dane" for his deep voice and solemn delivery (*The Murrow Boys* 253).

In the introduction to *This Is Eric Sevareid* (1964), he described himself as liberal on domestic affairs and conservative on foreign affairs, which may serve as one definition of

Midwestern temperament, embodied earlier by WILLIAM JENNINGS BRYAN. In various commentaries, Sevareid acknowledged that he possessed a Midwestern and Scandinavian restraint that suggested stuffiness but that masked a sentimental optimism about ordinary people and democracy. In *Not So Wild a Dream*, Sevareid took SINCLAIR LEWIS's position, in *It Can't Happen Here*, that Midwestern small-town life's social democracy, rooted in economic privation, provided a buffer against fascism.

**SELECTED WORKS:** *Canoeing with the Cree* (1935) and *Not So Wild a Dream* (1946) are autobiography about Sevareid's youth and early career. Several collections of columns and essays include *In One Ear* (1952) and *Small Sounds in the Night* (1956). Another collection, *This Is Eric Sevareid* (1964), contains commentary on growing up in Minnesota and North Dakota. "The American Dream," an essay in *The Midwest*, edited by Ronald Szymanski (1979), reaffirms Sevareid's optimism for traditional values and his Midwestern upbringing.

**FURTHER READING:** Sevareid is prominently featured in Stanley Cloud and Lynne Olson's *The Murrow Boys* (1996). A biography by Raymond Schroth, *The American Journey of Eric Sevareid* (1995), covers Sevareid's character and career with emphasis on the model of journalistic integrity Sevareid embodied. There are chapters on Sevareid in Ron Barron's *Guide to Minnesota Writers* (1987), and Genevieve Rose Breen and Carmen Nelson Richards's *Minnesota Writes* (1945). Sevareid's papers in the Library of Congress contain his professional documents, including manuscripts, transcripts, and letters, but little from his personal life. The Minnesota Historical Society maintains a file of newspaper clippings on Sevareid's life and career.

THOMAS PRIBEK

UNIVERSITY OF WISCONSIN–LACROSSE

# KARL SHAPIRO
November 10, 1913–May 14, 2000

**BIOGRAPHY:** Karl Shapiro was born to Sarah (Omansky) and Joseph Shapiro in Baltimore, Maryland, and attended Baltimore city schools. While at the University of Virginia, Shapiro felt alienated, ostracized because of his Jewish identity, not only by the white Christian population but by German Jews as well. One of Shapiro's most fre-

quently anthologized poems, "University" (1942), reflects this sense of alienation, which resulted in Shapiro's changing the spelling of his first name from "Carl" to "Karl" in 1920 in a deliberate attempt to Germanize himself.

In 1935 Shapiro published his first book, *Poems*, which won him the scholarship that made possible his enrollment at the Johns Hopkins University, where he studied from 1937 to 1939. He would later joke that the prize-winning collection was inspired by the unlikely combination of Shakespearean sonnets and the poetry of William Carlos Williams. Shapiro even sent Williams a copy of *Poems*, to which the older poet responded kindly, although without praising the quality of Shapiro's verse.

Even though Shapiro attended three high schools and two universities, he never earned a degree. The institution from which he came closest to graduating was the Enoch Pratt Library in Baltimore, where he was studying to be a librarian when he was drafted in 1941. Stationed in the miserably hot South Pacific from 1941 to 1945, Shapiro produced what many critics believe are some of the best war poems ever written by an American; the resulting volume, *V-Letter and Other Poems* (1944), won the Pulitzer Prize in 1945.

Also that year Shapiro married Evalyn Katz, with whom he would produce three children. In 1946 Shapiro was released from military service, and that same year he was appointed consultant in poetry at the Library of Congress. The most famous decision he made while he was consultant was voting against Ezra Pound, who in 1948 was up for the Bollingen Prize for *Pisan Cantos*. Shapiro found it difficult to separate the poet Pound from the criminal, anti-Semitic Pound; years later Shapiro speculated that Pound's rhetoric was the same as that which had led to the Holocaust.

Shapiro spent the late 1940s, 1950s, and 1960s carving out a niche for himself in academia and the poetry establishment. He taught writing courses at the Johns Hopkins University from 1947 to 1956 and edited *Poetry: A Magazine of Verse* from 1950 to 1956. He then moved on to the University of Nebraska, where, as professor of English, he edited *Prairie Schooner* from 1956 until 1966. That year he joined the faculty at the Chicago Circle Campus of the University of Illinois, and in 1968 he left Chicago to become a professor of English at the University of California–Davis.

In 1967 Shapiro divorced Evalyn Katz and married Teri Kovach, the inspiration for a book of poems, *White-Haired Lover* (1966); the marriage ended in 1982. In 1985 Shapiro married Sophie Wilkins and retired from the University of California–Davis; Karl and Sophie resided in Davis, California, until his death.

Shapiro has received numerous awards, including two Guggenheim Fellowships, a grant from the American Academy of Arts in 1944, a Pulitzer Prize in 1945, an honorary membership in Phi Beta Kappa at Harvard in 1949, and a Bollingen Prize in 1969.

**SIGNIFICANCE:** Karl Shapiro once asserted, "I detest New England, admire the Midwest, and love Northern California" (Reid 37). When pressed, he admitted that, if anything, he felt Southern. Thus tracing Shapiro's Midwesternness is a difficult task. He spent ten years at the University of Nebraska and two in Chicago with the University of Illinois, but his work reveals no real connection to the heartland region. Instead, when considering Shapiro, other issues come to the forefront, particularly the ways in which his Jewish identity and his sense of his relationship to poets of previous generations inform his poetics.

A case in point is Shapiro's decision to send a copy of his first published work, *Poems*, to William Carlos Williams, which was probably an allusion to the way that Williams submitted his own first published work, also titled *Poems*, to Ezra Pound. Shapiro's acknowledgment of Williams sheared a path back toward a reclamation of Walt Whitman and uninhibited speech, and in many ways, this defiant stand was not without a price. Throughout his career, Shapiro has been threatened by marginality.

It is true that Shapiro espoused Whitman and Williams as the fathers of American verse, downplayed the contributions of Ezra Pound and T. S. ELIOT, and, in his critical theory, preferred experimental to classical form. But Shapiro, too, was guilty of the classicism of which he accused others. In "Pact in Wartime," Selden Rodman writes that "Shapiro's style is on the classical side. The images are often violent but are always contained in a strict pattern" (834). For example, two of Shapiro's most frequently anthologized poems, "Auto Wreck" and "The Leg," are fresh in their utilization of stark imagery to render real and present experience but employ fairly traditional rhyme schemes and meter. In fact, many critics consider Shapiro more of a classical poet than an innovator like Whitman or Williams.

Paradoxically, the Shapiro whom many viewed as somewhat conservative issued critical pronouncements calling for more originality in poetry. Yet further evidence of Shapiro's poetic conventionality is found in the negative comments he leveled at Beat poets. Shapiro criticized writers such as Allen Ginsberg for taking too many liberties, even though he had promoted the irreverent style himself. As Shapiro grew older, his insistence that the poet break with tradition waned.

Perhaps the single most formative quality of Shapiro's work was his Jewish identity. Shapiro was not particularly religious; rather, he saw his Jewishness as a metaphor for all forms of subordination. He spoke of how even his sense of himself as a Southerner had been shaped by his Jewishness: the South is also "the other" in a biased hegemonic relationship, and, like Jews, Southerners are also outsiders.

Though often anthologized, Shapiro could probably have been more commercially successful had his work been more mainstream. Volumes such as *Adult Bookstore* (1976) affirm the strength of his dissent from academic thinking, even while interviews reveal his bitterness about being increasingly supplanted in prestigious anthologies such as the *Oxford Book of American Verse*.

**SELECTED WORKS:** Shapiro published numerous books of poetry: *Poems* (1935), *Person, Place, and Thing* (1942), *The Place of Love* (1942), *V-Letter and Other Poems* (1944), *Trial of a Poet and Other Poems* (1947), *Poems 1940–1953* (1953), *The House* (1957), *Poems of a Jew* (1958), *The Bourgeois Poet* (1964), *Selected Poems* (1968), *White-Haired Lover* (1968), *Adult Book Store* (1976), *Collected Poems: 1948–1978* (1978), *Love and War, Art and God* (1984), *Adam and Eve* (1986), *New and Selected Poems: 1940–1986* (1987), and *The Old Horsefly* (1992). He wrote only one novel, *Edsel* (1971), and published two plays: *The Tenor* (1956) and *The Soldier's Tale* (1968). Shapiro produced a great deal of nonfiction: *Essay on Rime* (1945), *English Prosody and Modern Poetry* (1947), *A Bibliography of Modern*

*Poetry* (1948), *Beyond Criticism* (1953), *In Defense of Ignorance* (1960), *Start with the Sun: Studies in Cosmic Poetry* (1960), *Prose Keys to Modern Poetry* (1962), *A Prosody Handbook* (1965), *To Abolish Children and Other Essays* (1968), and *The Poetry Wreck: Selected Essays 1950–1970* (1975). His autobiographical works include *The Younger Son, Poet: An Autobiography in Three Parts* (1988) and *Reports of My Death* (1990).

**FURTHER READING:** Two helpful bibliographies are William White's *Karl Shapiro: A Bibliography* (1960) and Lee Bartlett's *Karl Shapiro: A Descriptive Bibliography 1933–1977* (1979). Joseph Reino's *Karl Shapiro* (1981) and *Seriously Meeting Karl Shapiro*, edited by Sue B. Walker (1993), are book-length studies. Some important essays on Shapiro are Sam Bradley's "Shapiro Strikes at the Establishment," *University of Kansas City Review* 29 (1963): 275–79; Richard Slotkin's "The Contextual Symbol: Karl Shapiro's Image of 'The Jew,'" *American Quarterly* 18 (1966): 220–26; Alfred S. Reid's "The Southern Exposure of Karl Shapiro," *Southern Humanities Review* 6 (1972): 35–44; Selden Rodman's "Poet in Wartime," *New Republic* 107 (December 21, 1942): 834; Richard Jackson's "Signing the Syllables: The Poetry of Karl Shapiro," *South Carolina Review* 13 (Fall 1981): 109–20; and Kathy Rugoff's "T. S. Eliot's Cultural Elitism: An Indictment by Charles Olson and Karl Shapiro," *Connecticut Review* 14 (Fall 1992): 61–68. The Wayne State University Library, the Lilly Library of Indiana University, and the Library of Congress hold many of Shapiro's papers.

SCOTT DENT

THE UNIVERSITY OF TENNESSEE AT CHATTANOOGA

## SAM SHEPARD

November 5, 1943

**BIOGRAPHY:** Sam Shepard, considered by many to be one of the preeminent American playwrights of his generation, was born Samuel Shepard Rogers VII in Fort Sheridan, Illinois, to parents Samuel Shepard Rogers and Elaine (Schook) Rogers. His father was a career army officer, and the family lived on army bases in Illinois, South Dakota, Utah, Florida, and Guam. Upon his father's retirement, the family moved to southern California, where Shepard spent most of his childhood and adolescence. At age nineteen he joined an acting troupe and made his way to New York City, where he embarked on a ca-

Sam Shepard.
Photo © Nancy Crampton

reer as a playwright. In 1964 he changed his name to Sam Shepard. In the hospitable atmosphere of Greenwich Village of the 1960s, he had his avant-garde, one-act plays produced at off-off-Broadway theaters. His plays, which number more than forty, have won many awards, including a Pulitzer Prize and eleven Obie Awards for best off-Broadway play of the season. In 1994 he was inducted into the Theater Hall of Fame.

Shepard has also had a successful career as a screen actor and has starred in or directed several films shot on location in the Midwest. In *Country* (1984) he played an Iowa farmer facing loss of his land during the farm debt crisis of the 1980s. In the Michael Apted film, *Thunderheart* (1992), he starred as a corrupt FBI agent investigating the 1975 killing of federal agents at the Pine Ridge Sioux Indian reservation in South Dakota. *Far North* (1988), a film written and directed by Shepard, is set in the northern Minnesota woods and the city of Duluth.

**SIGNIFICANCE:** In his introduction to Shepard's *Seven Plays* (1981), Richard Gilman writes that Shepard's work deals with "the death (or betrayal) of the American dream [and] the decay of our national myths" (xi). In his exploration of those myths, Shepard saturates his plays with the icons of American culture: cowboys, Indians, gangsters, rock stars, and movie stars. Shepard particularly punctures the myth of the West as a place of limitless opportunity and resources. As Austin in *True West* (1980) comments, "There's no such thing as the West anymore. It's a dead issue. It's all dried up" (*Seven Plays* 35).

Although the Southwest and Far West figure much more prominently in Shepard's work than the Midwest, the latter region has still played a role as a setting in his work. In this respect the mythology of the Middle West is no different for Shepard than that of the Far West; it too has come to bear little resemblance to its postwar reality. In the 1978 Pulitzer Prize–winning play *Buried Child*, which has the most recognizably Midwestern setting of any of his plays, the agricultural bounty of an Illinois farm serves as an ironic backdrop to the story of a family's spiritual poverty. *Buried Child* is one of a string of five "family" plays—beginning with *Curse of the Starving Class* (1974) and also including *True West* (1980), *Fool for Love* (1983), and *A Lie of the Mind* (1985)—that mark a change in Shepard's style away from avant-garde experimentation and toward greater realism. Shepard's 1996 story collection, *Cruising Paradise*, sets a number of its tales in the Midwest, particularly South Dakota.

**SELECTED WORKS:** Shepard's plays include Obie Award winners *Chicago* (1965), *La Turista* (1968), *The Tooth of Crime* (1972), *Curse of the Starving Class* (1974), *Buried Child* (1978; also Pulitzer Prize), and *Fool for Love* (1983; screenplay and actor, 1985). Shepard was awarded the New York Drama Critics' Circle Award for best new play for *A Lie of the Mind* (1985). His other plays include *Cowboys* (1964), *4-H Club* (1965), *Operation Sidewinder* (1970), *Geography of a Horse Dreamer* (1974), *True West* (1980), *States of Shock* (1991), *Simpatico* (1994), and *Eyes for Consuela* (1998). Collections of his plays include *The Unseen Hand and Other Plays* (1971), *Angel City and Other Plays* (1976), *Seven Plays* (1981), *Fool for Love and Other Plays* (1984), and *Plays* (3 vols., 1996).

Shepard has also written two collections of stories and poems, *Hawk Moon* (1973) and *Motel Chronicles* (1982); a journal, *Rolling Thunder Logbook* (1977); and a collection of "tales," *Cruising Paradise* (1996). His film work includes credits as director and screenwriter for *Far North* (1988) and as co-screenwriter for *Zabriskie Point* (1970) and *Paris, Texas* (1984; Golden Palm, Cannes Film Festival). As an actor he has starred in many films, including *Days of Heaven* (1978), *Frances* (1982), *The Right Stuff* (1983; Academy Award nomination, best supporting actor), *Country* (1984), *Steel Magnolias* (1989), and *Thunderheart* (1992).

**FURTHER READING:** Shepard has already been the subject of many book-length studies. These include *American Dreams: The Imagination of Sam Shepard*, edited by Bonnie Marranca (1981); *Inner Landscapes: The Theater of Sam Shepard* (1984), by Ron Mottram; *Sam Shepard* (1985), by Don Shewey; *Sam Shepard* (Western Writers series, 1985), by Vivian M. Patraka and Mark Siegel; *Sam Shepard: The Life and Work of an American Dreamer* (1986), by Ellen Oumano; *Sam Shepard* (1992), by Martin Tucker; *Sam Shepard* (1992), by David J. DeRose; *Rereading Shepard: Contemporary Critical Essays on the Plays of Sam Shepard*, edited by Leonard Wilcox (1993); *Sam Shepard and the American Theatre* (1997), by Leslie A. Wade; and *The Theatre of Sam Shepard* (1998), by Stephen J. Bottoms. See also Gerald Weales, *The Jumping-Off Place: American Drama in the 1960's* (1969).

WILLIAM OSTREM                    PRINCETON, NEW JERSEY

## JEAN SHEPHERD

July 26, 1929–October 16, 1999

**BIOGRAPHY:** The son of Jean P. and Anne (Heinrichs) Shepherd, Jean Shepherd was born in Chicago and was raised in nearby Hammond, Indiana, the setting for much of his short fiction. During his adolescent years, Shepherd worked part time as a sports journalist for a Hammond radio station and was also featured in numerous juvenile roles on network radio in Chicago, including the part of Billy Fairchild in the long-running popular serial *Jack Armstrong, All-American Boy*.

Following World War II, during which he served in the Signal Corps, Shepherd studied acting at the Goodman Theatre in Chicago and psychology and engineering at Indiana University. He left school in 1949 to pursue a career in radio, serving as a staff member of WLW in Cincinnati from 1951 to

1953. There he also hosted *Rear Bumper*, a late-night comedy show on WLW TV. Shepherd then moved to Philadelphia, where he worked at radio station KYW from 1954 to 1957. He made the move to New York in 1957, where his *Night People* on radio station WOR established Shepherd's reputation as a consummate performer-raconteur.

Through the late 1950s and 1960s Shepherd appeared in four one-man shows at Carnegie Hall as well as in numerous off-Broadway productions. Shepherd's reputation as a popular humorist was further enhanced by the frequent appearance of his stories and essays in the *Village Voice*, *Playboy*, and *Car and Driver*; four collections of new and previously published material; and a number of television series, including *Shepherd's Pie* and *Jean Shepherd's America*. A number of Shepherd's stories, including "Wanda Hickey's Night of Golden Memories," "The Star-Crossed Romance of Josephine Cosnowski," and "Ollie Hopnoodle's Haven of Bliss," have also been adapted as feature-length television dramas, and since its theatrical release in 1983, Shepherd's immensely popular *A Christmas Story* has become a seasonal classic. *It Runs in the Family*, later retitled *My Summer Story*, was released as a sequel to *A Christmas Story* in 1994.

**SIGNIFICANCE:** Though the greater part of Shepherd's adult life was spent on the East Coast, his childhood and adolescence in the urban-industrial Midwest of Chicago and Hammond, Indiana, provided the occasion and imaginative impetus for much of his short fiction. Shepherd also frequently exploited the sociocultural and geographical contrasts between the East and Midwest to notable comic effect. Typically, the narrator, presumably Shepherd himself, who managed a successful professional career back East and an accompanying sense of worldly and cultural sophistication, escaped the frustration, complexity, and frenetic pace of his lifestyle by returning to the imagined innocence and simplicity of his childhood or adolescent years in the Midwest. During the course of such recollective narratives, the topical focus of which ranged from county fairs and family vacations to the senior prom and assorted romantic disasters, the young Shepherd, with the undiscouraged resiliency and unsoiled optimism of a Harold Lloyd or Buster Keaton, somehow survived the amusing disappointments and vicissitudes of "kidhood."

Shepherd's short fiction, like his essays, further revealed the author's obsessive fascination with the effluvia of American popular culture, including, but by no means limited to, Flash Gordon zap guns, Melvin Purvis G-Man escape-proof handcuffs, and Little Orphan Annie decoder rings. With the possible exception of Woody Allen, Shepherd was unrivaled among American humorists in his nostalgic reconstruction of the popular rituals, icons, music, media heroes, and send-away contests that typified working-class family life in the 1930s and 1940s.

Stylistically, Shepherd's humor was characterized by a colloquial, idiomatic vigor, an outrageous hyperbole reminiscent of MARK TWAIN and RING LARDNER, a rhapsodic fondness for American kitsch, a keen sense of irony, and an attention to the absurd incongruities both of his own personal history and the modern scene. However, Shepherd's capacity for comic self-parody was perhaps the most distinctive and engaging aspect of his work, for more often than not the butt of Shepherd's humor is the author himself, though the reader is willingly implicated as well. As such, Shepherd, whatever his intimate affiliation with the Midwest, is ultimately a man for all regions.

**SELECTED WORKS:** Shepherd's status as a major American humorist is based largely on four collections of stories and essays. The first of these, *In God We Trust, All Others Pay Cash* (1966), is a series of youthful and loosely autobiographical reminiscences occasioned by the narrator's return from New York to his hometown of Hammond, Indiana, and his reunion, over the course of an afternoon, with a childhood friend who now owns the neighborhood bar. The second is *Wanda Hickey's Night of Golden Memories and Other Disasters* (1971), another series of juvenile and adolescent misadventures. *The Ferrari in the Bedroom* (1972) is a compilation of humorous essays and satiric sketches on such wide-ranging and improbable topics as drive-in confessionals, the Johnson Smith mail-order catalog, television fishermen, and New York cabbies. *A Fistful of Fig Newtons* (1981) is another collection of "autobiographical fictions" that draws upon Shepherd's army, college, and childhood experiences.

FURTHER READING: L. Moody Simms Jr.'s entry on Shepherd in the *Encyclopedia of American Humorists*, edited by Steven H. Gale (1988), provides a brief but informative overview of Shepherd's life and writings. Though critical scholarship on Shepherd is surprisingly limited, the following studies assess selected works and Shepherd's qualities as an American humorist and cultural commentator: Peter Scholl's "Jean Shepherd: The Survivor of Hammond," in the *Great Lakes Review* 5.1 (1979): 7–18; James F. Smith's "Humor, Cultural History and Jean Shepherd," in the *Journal of Popular Culture* 16.1 (1982): 1–12, and "Wanda Hickey's Night of Golden Memories and Other Disasters" in the *Proceedings of the Fifth National Convention of the Popular Culture Association*, compiled by Michael T. Marsden (1975): 203–32; and Joseph F. Trimmer's "Memoryscape: Jean Shepherd's Midwest," in *Old Northwest* 2 (1976): 357–69.

MICHAEL WENTWORTH
UNIVERSITY OF NORTH CAROLINA AT WILMINGTON

**Alix Kates Shulman.**
Photo © Nancy Crampton

## ALIX KATES SHULMAN
August 17, 1932

**BIOGRAPHY:** Born in Cleveland, Ohio, Alix Kates Shulman was the daughter of Samuel S. and Dorothy (Davis) Kates. She had an older brother, Robert Davis Kates, who died of cancer in 1989, and she has a younger sister, Linda Trichter Metcalf. She earned an associate of arts degree from Bradford Junior College in 1951 and a bachelor of arts degree in 1953 from Western Reserve University, now Case Western Reserve University. At the age of twenty, she fled Ohio and a suffocating, short-term suburban marriage to chart a more free-spirited course of political activism and feminist conscious-raising in New York's Greenwich Village. She remarried and joined her second husband Jerry Shulman on his Fulbright year in Europe in 1956–57. Though his business effectively detached Jerry from family life and though they eventually divorced, the couple had two children together, Stevie, who became a scientist, and Amy. While raising her children in Manhattan, Shulman had a number of freelance jobs, including teaching writing and literature at New York University, and she published her first novel at the age of forty. By the time she was sixty, she was a grandmother and had published three children's books in addition to two books on Emma Goldman, four novels, and a book of memoirs.

If one hallmark of Midwestern behavior is to leave the Midwest, then Shulman displays this tendency, abandoning her Ohio origins for the more cosmopolitan New York City and subsequently finding solace and wholeness on a remote island off the Maine coast. Over her own personal objections, early in their marriage her husband had decided to purchase the "nubble," a primitive cabin without electricity or water on rugged Long Island in Maine. Ironically, it was there, during many solitary months over a number of years, that Shulman gained the appreciation of nature and the perspectives on life that form the basis of her most successful work, her memoir, *Drinking the Rain* (1995). Writing retreats have included MacDowell Colony and the Millay Colony, and she has held teaching posts at Yale, the University of Southern Maine, the University of Colorado, and the University of Hawaii, where she held the Citizen's Chair in 1991–92.

**SIGNIFICANCE:** The value of Shulman's fiction for Midwestern readers is that her heroines, as their author had done, leave the Midwest as they attain adulthood, the geographical rite of passage mirroring physical and emotional maturity. The plot of *On the Stroll* (1981), Shulman's third novel, is typical: sixteen-year-old, small-town Robin runs away to New York and tries to lose herself in the fevered backstreets of Times Square. As if it were a fulfillment of a dream or at least an accomplishment, Shulman maintains that, in leaving Cleveland and her family of origin, she was also "placing my childhood values on hold" (*Drinking the Rain* 95). Embracing new values in New York, including the women's movement, bohemia, her writing life, political protest, seemed to estrange her from her old values until she eventually reconciled the two.

Shulman is Midwestern in her reluctance to uproot things she has come to rely on, which explains the fact that she endured her second marriage for so long before agreeing to a divorce. If the presentation of her own character and others in *Drinking the Rain* is not always likable, there is energy in their aggression and passion. If they are vulnerable and victimized, they also reveal an inner strength and survival mentality characteristic of the Midwest.

**SELECTED WORKS:** Shulman's book-length works fall into three categories. Least significant are her books for children: *Bosley on the Number Line* (1970), *Awake or Asleep* (1971), and *Finders Keepers* (1972). Her political nonfiction includes *To the Barricades: The Anarchist Life of Emma Goldman* (1971) and *An Emma Goldman Reader: Selected Writings and Speeches of Emma Goldman* (1972). Her novels, perhaps the most widely read of her publications, include *Memoirs of an Ex-Prom Queen* (1972), *In Every Woman's Life . . .* (1987), *Burning Questions* (1978), and *On the Stroll* (1981). Her memoir, *Drinking the Rain* (1995), is not only a beautifully evocative piece of nature writing and a meaningful reflection on male and female relationships but also the best source of information about the author's life.

**FURTHER READING:** It would seem that, while Shulman has taken feminism seriously, perhaps feminist writers have not returned the compliment. There is little important critical work that has been written about her, nothing of book—or even of chapter—length. In *Images of Women in Fiction: Feminist Perspectives* (edited by Susan Koppelman Cornillon, 1972), Ellen Morgan's essay "Humanbecom-

ing: Form and Focus in the Neo-Feminist Novel" (183–206) devotes seven pages to exploring the patriarchal mechanisms that oppress Sasha Davis, the heroine of *Memoirs of an Ex-Prom Queen*. Josephine Hendin's *Vulnerable People: A View of American Fiction since 1945* (1978) devotes a scant three paragraphs to that character (176–77).

Book reviews in the *New York Times*, the *Los Angeles Times*, the *Boston Globe*, the *San Francisco Chronicle*, and the *Chicago Tribune* have tended to give more favorable note to *Drinking the Rain* than to Shulman's earlier works. Alden Whitman, in writing for the *Nation* (April 15, 1978): 440–42, in the most extensive assessment of her early work, discusses how Shulman fictionalizes human learning in both *Burning Questions* and *Memoirs of an Ex-Prom Queen*. Two reviews in the *Hudson Review* (William H. Pritchard, 31: 3 [Autumn 1978]: 520–21; and Patricia Meyer Spacks, 25: 3 [Autumn 1972]: 498–99) are particularly unforgiving of Shulman's "superficial perception" and "annoying prose." But *Drinking the Rain*, the more mature, more thoughtful, less strident later memoir, has much broader appeal. Doris Grumbach credits it with "sustained grace" (*Boston Globe*, May 7, 1995, 50: 3, 20), and Rebecca Radner calls it a "voyage of discovery in a stimulating, bracing story" (*San Francisco Chronicle*, April 16, 1995, 3: 1, 8).

JILL B. GIDMARK          UNIVERSITY OF MINNESOTA

## ARTHUR W. SHUMAKER.
*See* appendix (1985)

## CLIFFORD D. SIMAK
August 3, 1904–April 25, 1988

**BIOGRAPHY:** Born on a farm near Millville, Wisconsin, to John Lewis and Margaret (Wiseman) Simak, science fiction writer and journalist Simak was educated at the University of Wisconsin, married Agnes Kuchenberg in 1929, and fathered two children. He worked for small-town newspapers in Iowa, Minnesota, Missouri, and North Dakota before being employed at the *Minneapolis Star and Tribune* in 1939, where he rose over the years to become news editor and then writer of a science column. In the late 1970s he gave up journalism in order to concentrate on writing science fiction. He has won a number of awards for outstanding work in the genre and was inducted into the Science

Fiction Hall of Fame in 1973. Simak died in Minneapolis.

**SIGNIFICANCE:** The impact of the Midwest in Simak's science fiction is notable. The Millville of his birth and boyhood appears frequently, sometimes under its own name and sometimes in transparent disguise. Critics have argued that even the communities he creates on imagined worlds are thinly masked versions of Millville. His stress on nature, on the loveliness of the Midwestern landscape, and on the importance of living in harmony with nature make him unusual within the genre. Simak is less dependent on either science and technology or space adventure than many of his colleagues within the field; his gentle philosophy and emphasis on the best within humanity, developed from his Midwestern roots, have made him something of an oddity as a science fiction writer, but an oddity with a persistent appeal to a wide public.

**SELECTED WORKS:** Among Simak's more popular works and illustrating the variety of his fiction are *The Creator* (1946), *Cosmic Engineers* (1950), *Time and Again* (1951), *City* (1952), *Ring around the Sun* (1953), *Time Is the Simplest Thing* (1961), *All the Traps of Earth* (1962), *Way Station* (1963), *Worlds without End* (1964), *All Flesh Is Grass* (1965), *The Goblin Reservation* (1968), *Destiny Doll* (1971), *A Choice of Gods* (1972), *Cemetery World* (1973), *Shakespeare's Planet* (1976), *Mastodonia* (1978), and *The Visitors* (1980).

**FURTHER READING:** Several critical examinations of Simak's work are useful. Among these are William Lomax's "The 'Invisible Alien' in the Science Fiction of Clifford Simak," in *Extrapolation* 30.2 (1989): 133–45; Paul Walker's "Clifford Simak: An Interview," in *Luna Monthly* 57 (1975): 1–6; Mary Jean DeMarr's "Clifford Simak's Use of the Midwest in Science Fiction," in *MidAmerica* 22 (1995): 108–21; and entries in several specialized biographical reference works: Thomas D. Clareson's "Clifford D. Simak: The Inhabited Universe," in *Voices for the Future: Essays on Major Science Fiction Writers* (1976): 64–87; and Bud Foote's "Clifford D. Simak's Way Station: The Hero as Archetypal Science Fiction Writer, the Science Fiction Writer as Seeker for Immortality," in *Immortal Engines: Life Extension and Immortality in Science Fiction and Fantasy*, edited by George Slusser and others (1996): 193–200.

MARY JEAN DEMARR    INDIANA STATE UNIVERSITY

## JO SINCLAIR.
*See* Ruth Seid

## UPTON (BEALL) SINCLAIR (JR.)
September 20, 1878–November 25, 1968
(Clarke Fitch, Frederick Garrison, Arthur Stirling)

**BIOGRAPHY:** Upton Sinclair, novelist and politician, was born in Baltimore, Maryland, the only son of Upton and Priscilla (Harden) Sinclair. When he was eight, his family moved to New York City, where Sinclair later enrolled in public schools after being homeschooled by his mother until he was ten. Sinclair enrolled in the City College of New York in 1892, where he completed his AB in 1897. While an undergraduate, he began publishing jokes and pulp fiction stories in adventure magazines and dime novels to help support his family. He enrolled in graduate courses at Columbia University from 1897 through 1901 but left without completing a graduate degree.

Before leaving Columbia, Sinclair had married his first wife, Meta Fuller, in October 1900. Meta and Sinclair shared the author's only child, David, before divorcing in 1913. The divorce was followed by Sinclair's marriage to Mary Craig Kimbrough, which lasted from April 1913 until her death in April 1961. In October 1961, Sinclair married Mary Elizabeth Willis, with whom he lived until her death in December 1967.

The socialist allegiances so evident in many of Sinclair's novels inspired him to establish a Utopian experiment in Englewood, New Jersey, which he called Helicon Hall, and later, to run, though unsuccessfully, as a Socialist Party candidate for several New Jersey and California political offices throughout the 1920s and 1930s. Perhaps the most memorable campaign, though, came in 1934 as Sinclair shifted party allegiances to run as the Democratic candidate for governor of California. According to political scholar Greg Mitchell, Sinclair's 1934 EPIC (End Poverty in California) campaign marked the beginning of the modern media-centered political race.

After a lifetime of publishing and political activism, Sinclair died in a New Jersey nursing home at the age of ninety.

**SIGNIFICANCE:** After leaving Columbia in 1901, Sinclair devoted his full attention to writing. His publication of *The Jungle* in 1906 garnered national attention due to its shocking depiction of the Chicago meat-packing industry as well as for the health inspections and Pure Food and Drug Act which it helped to precipitate. In the novel, Sinclair details the hardships of a Lithuanian immigrant, Jurgis Rudkis, and his family, who come to Chicago expecting opportunities for a better life. Through Jurgis's experiences, Sinclair very graphically reflects the common Midwestern theme of working-class mistrust for the rich, powerful, well-connected elite. Jurgis represents a type of turn-of-the-century Midwestern "everyman" who believes, at first, that his strong work ethic will lead to eventual rewards for his family. However, his efforts result only in hardship and, eventually, an understanding of the oppressive and corrupt power of Packingtown's political and business leaders. Jurgis works amidst diseased beef, dangerous machines, and absent safety standards; his wife, Ona, is the victim of her boss's unwanted sexual advances; the family is forced to live in a deteriorating tenement house which had been painted to appear new; and Jurgis's young son drowns in the street. Ultimately, Jurgis turns to socialism as the only means by which poor workers can fight the oppressive conditions of Packingtown and express their distrust and contempt for the political system and the leaders of the Chicago beef machine.

**SELECTED WORKS:** Sinclair remains most widely known for *The Jungle* (1906). Still, it was his later work, *Dragon's Teeth* (1942), the third volume in his eleven-volume Lanny Budd series, which was awarded the Pulitzer Prize in 1943. The series centers on Budd and provides a sketch of major American and European political and historical events from 1915 to 1950. In particular, *Dragon's Teeth* describes Hitler's rise to power in Germany. Similar in proletarian theme to *The Jungle* are *King Coal* (1917), which depicts a strike of California coal workers; *The Brass Check* (1920), centering on the ill effects of capitalism on journalism; and *Oil!* (1927), which exposes the oppressive practices of Californian oil monopolies. As a political figure, Sinclair offers further insight into his socialist ideology in *We People of America, and How We Ended Poverty: A True Story of the Future* (1935). He details the reasons for his 1934 campaign failure in *I, Candidate for Governor, and How I Got Licked* (1935). Sinclair's works are collected in *An Upton Sinclair Anthology*, edited by George Schreiber (1934).

**FURTHER READING:** Upton Sinclair's *Autobiography* (1962) as well as William A. Bloodworth Jr.'s *Upton Sinclair* (1977), Jon A. Yoder's *Upton Sinclair* (1975), FLOYD DELL's *Upton Sinclair: A Study in Social Protest* (1927), and Leon Harris's *Upton Sinclair: American Rebel* (1975) offer comprehensive details of the author's life. For emphasis on Sinclair's role as a socialist writer, see Rabindra Nath Mookerjee's *Art for Social Justice: The Major Novels of Upton Sinclair* (1988). For more specific focus on *The Jungle*, particularly on its historical accuracy, see Walter James Miller's *Upton Sinclair's The Jungle: A Critical Commentary* (1983), Louise Carroll Wade's "The Problem with Classroom Use of Upton Sinclair's *The Jungle*," in *American Studies* 32.2 (Fall 1991): 79–102, and James Harvey Young's "The Pig That Fell into the Privy: Upton Sinclair's 'The Jungle' and the Meat Inspection Amendments of 1906," in the *Bulletin of the History of Medicine* 59.4 (Winter 1985): 467–80. For discussion of Sinclair's EPIC campaign, see Greg Mitchell's "Media Politics, Keeping Sinclair from Governor," in *American Heritage* 39.6 (September–October 1988): 34–41, and his "Upton Sinclair's EPIC Campaign," in *Nation* 239 (August 4–11, 1984): 75–78. Dorys Crow Grover offers a discussion of Sinclair's continuing popularity in her essay "Upton Sinclair, Never Forgotten," in *MidAmerica* 22 (1995): 41–49, while Ivan Scott considers the declining popular and critical attention currently being paid to Sinclair in *Upton Sinclair, the Forgotten Socialist* (1997). Sinclair's manuscripts and other papers are housed in the Lilly Library at Indiana University.

ROBIN L. KIDD                    UNIVERSITY OF KENTUCKY

# CHARLES ALLEN SMART
November 30, 1904–March 11, 1967

**BIOGRAPHY:** Born in Cleveland, Ohio, to George and Lucy (Allen) Smart, Charles Allen Smart was educated in the Cleveland Public Schools and at Harvard University, where he received his BA *cum laude* in 1926. He worked as an editorial assistant at Doubleday, Page and Company and Doubleday, Doran from 1927 through 1930 and taught English at Choate School from 1932 through 1934.

He published his first novel, *New England Holiday* (1931), with modest success and his second, *The Brass Cannon* (1933), to lesser response. In 1934 Smart and his sister inherited two farms in Ross County, Ohio, and with the Depression continuing unabated, he returned there to farm and write. He married Margaret Warren Hussey on January 1, 1935. In 1938 Smart published *R.F.D.*, a collection of essays which was a major success. He farmed until 1942 and published *Rosscommon* (1940), a novel, and *Wild Geese and How to Chase Them* (1941), a collection of essays.

Smart entered the U.S. Navy in 1942, participating in the Normandy invasion. After the war he was writer in residence at Ohio University from 1946 through 1954 and published *Sassafras Hill* (1947), a novel, and *The Green Adventure* (1954), a play. In the 1950s he began to spend winters in Mexico and he wrote several books on that country. He lived near Chillicothe, Ohio, until his death in 1967.

**SIGNIFICANCE:** Charles Allen Smart was one of many aspiring young writers who sought literary success in the East, and, as his first two novels suggest, he had begun to think of himself as an Easterner. But chance, in his return to Ohio, provided him with a literary place and a subject matter. *R.F.D.* records his discovery of Ohio farm life and his identity as an Ohio dirt farmer. With the aid of a hired man, he planted and tilled the soil, cared for his sheep, learned about and practiced conservation, and came to know and respect his neighbors.

Perhaps the time and the circumstances aided his success, but the book was a bestseller and a Book-of-the-Month Club selection; it was published in England by Oxford University Press as *The Adventures of an American Farmer* (1938). The well-written creation of a time and place now gone, it bears rereading.

Although he attempted to recreate his success with *Wild Geese and How to Chase Them* (1941) and to use his new subject matter in fiction, his success was minor, but, like Thoreau, he had clearly found a literary place and a subject matter as well as a literary identity.

Smart's Mexican works are less interesting than *R.F.D.*, although *At Home in Mexico* (1957) attempts to emulate it. *Viva Juarez!*, a biography, won the Ohioana Library Award for 1964. *The Long Watch* (1968) is an interesting memoir.

**SELECTED WORKS:** Among Smart's writings are *New England Holiday* (1931), *Brass Cannon* (1933), *R.F.D.* (1938), *Rosscommon* (1940), *Wild Geese and How to Chase Them* (1941), *Sassafras Hill* (1947), *The Green Adventure, a Play* (1954), *At Home in Mexico* (1957), *Viva Juarez!* (1963), and *The Long Watch* (1968).

**FURTHER READING:** Smart is listed in *Contemporary Authors, Permanent Series* and in *Who Was Who in America*. An interesting summary essay by William B. Thomas appears in the *Society for the Study of Midwestern Literature Newsletter* 3 (Fall 1973): 1–2. Smart's obituary is carried in the *New York Times*, March 14, 1967, and a retrospective essay appears in *Best Sellers*, June 1, 1968. His papers are in the Ohio University Library.

DAVID D. ANDERSON　　MICHIGAN STATE UNIVERSITY

# JANE (GRAVES) SMILEY
September 26, 1949

**BIOGRAPHY:** Jane Smiley was born in Los Angeles, California, the daughter of James La Verne Smiley and Frances Nuelle (Graves) Smiley, and grew up in St. Louis, Missouri. She is the author of novels which explore the complexities of interpersonal relationships in settings as diverse as a fourteenth-century Nordic settlement and Manhattan in the 1980s. Smiley earned a BA in English at Vassar College in 1971. While at Vassar she married John Whiston. After graduating from Vassar she enrolled at the University of Iowa, where she earned an MA in 1975 and a PhD in 1978. She was also awarded an MFA degree in 1976 from the University of Iowa's Writers' Workshop. Also during this time, in 1975, she divorced Whiston and later married William Silag in 1978. They have two daughters, Phoebe and Lucy. She became an assistant professor at Iowa State University in 1981 and continues to teach there. She married Stephen M. Mortensen in 1987 and has one son by that marriage, Axel James Mortensen.

Smiley wrote a novel for her senior thesis at Vassar and has continued to write since then. She has been critically noted for her thorough research which produces accurate details that serve as a backdrop for her stories. This is particularly evident in her first published novel, *Barn Blind* (1980), and her story of a fourteenth-century colony of Norse settlers in *Greenlanders* (1988). Most of her work centers on the bonds, seemingly solid but secretly fragile, between family members: husband and wife, parent and child, sister

Jane Smiley.
Photo © Nancy Crampton

and brother. Works such as *At Paradise Gate* (1981), her collection of short stories *The Age of Grief* (1987), and her two novellas, *Ordinary Love* and *Good Will* (1989), share themes of testing the bonds of family relationships.

Smiley won the Pulitzer Prize for her novel *A Thousand Acres* (1991). She has described this and the novel which followed, *Moo* (1995), as her tragic and comic novels about American agriculture. Indeed, both have been likened to Shakespearean prose in subject and style. *A Thousand Acres* takes place on an Iowa farm and tells the story of family rivalry and coming to terms with past wrongs. *Moo*, which takes place at a Midwestern university, is a satire that explores and exposes the quirks and intrigues of the academic world. Smiley published *The All-True Travels and Adventures of Lidie Newton* in 1998; this novel presents slavery and abolition in mid-1800s Kansas Territory.

**SIGNIFICANCE:** Smiley's connection with the Midwest is personal, professional, and creative. She was raised in Missouri, was educated mainly at Midwestern schools, and lived until recently in the Midwest. With the exception of *Duplicate Keys* (1984) and *Greenlanders*, Smiley has set her writings in the Midwest. While Smiley imbues her fiction with universal themes such as the dynamics of family relationships and personal conflict, she places them in the Midwestern milieu of prairies and farmland.

**SELECTED WORKS:** Smiley has been simultaneously criticized for letting detail get in the way of her stories and praised for their fascinating accuracy. *Barn Blind* (1980), *Greenlanders* (1988), and *The All-True Travels and Adventures of Lidie Newton* (1998) are particularly good examples of Smiley's attention to and use of detail. *Horse Heaven* (2000) is Smiley's newest work. *A Thousand Acres* is probably the most critically praised of her volumes.

**FURTHER READING:** Because Smiley is still a productive writer, most critical study of her work is found in recent literary and academic journals. For more about her writing to date, read Tim Keppel's "Goneril's Version: *A Thousand Acres* and *King Lear*," in *South Dakota Review* 33.2 (1995): 105–17; and JANE BAKERMAN's "'The Gleaming Obsidian Shard': Jane Smiley's *A Thousand Acres*," in *MidAmerica* 19 (1992): 127–37. See also Bakerman's "Renovating the House of Fiction: Structural Diversity in Jane Smiley's *Duplicate Keys*," in *MidAmerica* 15 (1988): 111–20. An interview with Smiley is included in *Listen to Their Voices*, by Mickey Pearlman (1993).

MARY B. DUNNE                    BOSTON UNIVERSITY

# WILLIAM STAFFORD
January 17, 1914–August 28, 1993

**BIOGRAPHY:** One of America's most prolific poets, William Stafford was born in Hutchinson, Kansas, to Earl and Ruby Nina (Mayher) Stafford. The Staffords lived in several small plains towns where William attended public schools. In 1937 he graduated from the University of Kansas with a BA; he earned an MA from Kansas in 1946 and a PhD from the University of Iowa in 1954.

In the years preceding World War II, Stafford held several jobs on farms and in oil refineries. When the war came, he worked for the Church of the Brethren and other organizations promoting peace. Because Stafford was a conscientious objector, he also labored in civilian public service camps until the war ended. He would later recount his experiences during the war years in *Down in My Heart* (1947), one of his five works of non-fiction.

Stafford married Dorothy Hope Frantz in 1944; they had two sons and two daughters. In 1948 he became a professor at Lewis and Clark College in Portland, Oregon. Except for two years when he taught at other colleges, he remained at Lewis and Clark until he retired as professor emeritus of English in 1980.

Stafford was the recipient of many honors and awards, including the National Book Award for *Traveling through the Dark* (1962), a National Endowment for the Arts grant (1966), and a Guggenheim Fellowship (1966). He was named poet laureate of Oregon from 1975 through 1990, consultant in poetry at the Library of Congress (1970–71), and U.S. Information Agency lecturer.

Stafford died in 1993 of myocardial arrhythmia in Lake Oswego, Oregon.

**SIGNIFICANCE:** William Stafford appreciated his Midwestern roots. The most notable evidence for this may be his tendency to compare unfavorably the materialism of the modern world with the simple family life he knew in Kansas. The voice in Stafford's poems is usually familiar and colloquial, engendering a sense of quiet reflection upon a purer, less frantic time and place. Life in Kansas was not perfect but it was adequate, and he suggested that he would not wish to come from anywhere else (Krauth 96).

Stafford's poetry bears the unmistakable imprint of the Midwest. Traditional Midwestern landscapes and themes predominate, as Stafford often looked to his family and native Kansas home as a setting for his poems. Although usually not explicitly identified, geographical location can be intuited from descriptions of nature. For example, one of Stafford's most famous poems, "Midwest," utilizes several distinctly Midwestern images, such as "the ultimate wind," and "the whole land's wave" (*Stories That Could Be True* 29). A recurring poetic interest in Native Americans and a feeling of repulsion at the destruction of the environment are also observable in Stafford's work. In the poem "One Home," the speaker opens with the statement, "Mine was a Midwest home—you can keep your world" and ends by saying "Wherever we looked the land would hold us up" (*Stories That Could Be True* 29–30).

Stafford's aesthetic is deeply indebted to his ruminations on the heartland. He remarks in an early poem, "Vocation," "Your job is trying to find out what the world is trying to be" (*Stories That Could Be True* 107). He frequently refers to attempting to get at the pattern behind everyday places and events. The process by which Stafford came into knowledge of the Midwestern world involved patience, a crude form of meditation, and considerable trial and error. Marc Hudson comments on Stafford's technique, saying that "[t]he trick is noninterference: the writer does not judge or discriminate, but passively records the results of the process" (99). Stafford compared it to fishing, a pastime he enjoyed, asserting that in order to succeed you have to be willing to fail and cannot always be thinking about what you are doing. The result of Stafford's "letting the poem write itself" approach has been that critics praise his best poems but berate him for the profusion of bad ones. It has been suggested that he will never fully ascend from the ranks of minor poets because there is so much mediocre material to sift through to find the real jewels.

It was not until 1960, when Stafford was in his mid-forties, that he published his first book, *West of Your City*. Getting such a late start could account for the unremarkable constancy critics perceive in Stafford's poetry. It is virtually impossible to distinguish later poems from earlier ones because of a conspicuous absence of overall development, a characteristic some have pointed to as further evidence of Stafford's minor status.

**SELECTED WORKS:** Stafford published many books of poetry. Some of the better-known ones are *West of Your City* (1960), *Traveling through the Dark* (1962), *The Rescued Year* (1966), *Allegiances* (1970), *Someday, Maybe* (1973), *Stories That Could Be True* (1977), *A Glass Face in the Rain* (1982), *Listening Deep* (1984), *Wyoming* (1985), and *An Oregon Message* (1987). Stafford also wrote several books of nonfiction. The most famous of these, *Down in My Heart* (1947), details Stafford's experience as a conscientious objector during World War II. In a more recent autobiographical work, *Writing the Australian Crawl* (1978), Stafford discusses his views of the poet's vocation.

**FURTHER READING:** Some important books are David Carpenter's *William Stafford* (1986), Judith Kitchen's *Understanding William Stafford* (1989), Lars Nordstrom's *Theodore Roethke,*

*William Stafford, and Gary Snyder: The Ecological Metaphor as Transformed Regionalism* (1989), Denise Low's *The Kansas Poems of William Stafford* (1995), and Tom Andrews's *On William Stafford* (1995).

Several helpful essays and articles are Robert Creeley's "'Think what got away. . . ,'" *Poetry* 102 (April 1963): 42–48; James Dickey's "William Stafford," in *Babel to Byzantium* (1968): 139–40; Richard Hugo's "Problems with Landscapes in Early Stafford Poems," *Kansas Quarterly* 2 (Spring 1970): 26–47; William Heyen's "William Stafford's Allegiances," *Modern Poetry Studies* 1 (1970): 307–18; Sister Bernetta Quinn's "Symbolic Landscapes," *Poetry* 118 (August 1971): 288–90; Leland Krauth's "'A Visioned End': Edgar Lee Masters and William Stafford," *MidAmerica* 11 (1984): 91–107; Thomas E. Benediktsson's "Montana Eclogue: The Pastoral Art of William Stafford," in *World, Self, Poem: Essays on Contemporary Poetry from the "Jubilation of Poets,"* edited by Leonard M. Trawick (1990): 196–202; David Axelrod's "Poetry of the American West," *Western American Literature* 31 (November 1996): 255–63; and Marc Hudson's "The Prodigal Poet," *Sewanee Review* 106 (Winter 1998): 97–102.

Four interviews are Sam Bradley's "Reciprocity vs. Suicide: Interview with William Stafford," *Trace* 46 (1962): 223–36; Nancy Bunge's "People Are Equal: An Interview with William Stafford," *American Poetry Review* 10 (1981): 8–11; Jeff Gundy's "If Struck I Should Give Off a Clear Note: A Conversation with William Stafford," in *Paint Brush* 17 (Spring 1990): 39–51; and David Elliott's "'At Home in the Dark': An Interview with William Stafford," *Michigan Quarterly Review* 30 (Spring 1991): 277–89.

Major collections of Stafford's papers are located at Indiana University's Lilly Library, Washington University Library in Saint Louis, and the University of Nevada Library in Reno.

SCOTT DENT

THE UNIVERSITY OF TENNESSEE AT CHATTANOOGA

## LUTHER STANDING BEAR
December 1868(?)–February 20, 1939

**BIOGRAPHY:** Luther Standing Bear, a Teton Lakota (Sioux) writer, leader, and activist, was born to Mato Najin (Standing Bear) of the Brule One Horse Band, his father, and

Wastewin (Pretty Face) of the Swift Bear Band on the Rosebud reservation in South Dakota. Named Ota K'te (Plenty Kill), he was raised as a traditional warrior-hunter, and in 1879 he killed his first and only buffalo before electing to join the first class of the Carlisle Indian School in Pennsylvania. Half of the Plains Native Americans perished in that Euro-American environment while he was there. At the school, he chose the name Luther from a list provided and was given his father's name as a surname.

Upon leaving the school, Luther Standing Bear worked at Wanamaker's department store before returning to the Dakota Territory to be an assistant teacher on the Rosebud reservation. In 1887 he moved west to the neighboring Pine Ridge reservation, where he joined the Oglala Band of Tetons and took a land allotment. He married a Lakota half-blood, Mary DeCory, and in 1902 joined Buffalo Bill Cody's Wild West Show, with which he was involved in a train wreck near Chicago in April 1903. Although he was made a chief in 1905, he sold his allotment and bought a house in Sioux City, Iowa, where he worked as a clerk in a wholesale firm. After a brief job on a ranch in Oklahoma, he moved to California in 1911 and appeared in films for producer Thomas Ince. He later opened his own business in Venice, California, and became involved in lecturing and organizing Native American rights groups. In 1925 he sold his business and began his first book, after the publication of which he returned to Pine Ridge in 1931. There he devoted his remaining years to writing and working in behalf of Native American people. He became a key figure in movements to reform government Indian policy during the Hoover and Roosevelt administrations.

**SIGNIFICANCE:** Luther Standing Bear is part of a small group of transitional Native American writers who were born and raised in the preliterate traditions of their cultures but became multilingual and literary and wrote accounts of their history and people in English. Standing Bear's works are important primary intellectual documents. They delineate the vital relationships that people indigenous to the Dakotas had with the land and the landscape, which informs traditional oral and written literature as the setting, the subject, and often the structure of the story cycles. They provide texts of first-hand authority. When compared with accounts by other Native Americans, they establish a concordance against which accounts by translators and collaborators may be critically assessed for reliability and integrity in the portrayals of culture and history.

Standing Bear's works are written ostensibly as correctives to the errors and distortions of Euro-American accounts and are, consequently, organized by anthropological categories such as religion, kinship, and material culture, as contained in Euro-American accounts. However, Standing Bear's writing is cast in the forms of the extended episodic narratives which characterize Native American oral histories and stories. In these forms relationships between humankind and nature are emphasized over the categories into which people and natural objects might be grouped so that landscape, region, and the relationships people have experienced with the land are the essential context of the stories. To the Teton Lakota, the landscape is the matrix of spiritual history.

Standing Bear's Tetons moved from the central Midwest, where they were primarily agriculturalists, to the western part of the Midwest, where they adopted the horse and bison culture. Their thought and literature, however, retained the agricultural perspective in their cosmology, as reflected in the stewardship they practiced with the bison herds and all of nature on the plains, and which traditional Tetons reflect currently in their spiritual and aesthetic concepts.

Luther Standing Bear's writing gives an account of how the values and concepts of the Teton people were derived from the geography of the Midwest and how those values and concepts have been threatened and undermined by Euro-American domination. The Lakota regarded the land as the direct gift from their creator, who provided them with its regional features. In the practice of agriculture and hunting they viewed what was provided to them as a sacrament. Luther Standing Bear's work is among the first delineations of Lakota beliefs and values which his people believed to be implicit in the Midwestern landscape. His writing also depicts the threat posed by Euro-American subjuga-tion. To Luther Standing Bear and the Tetons, the Midwest is the particular, unique gift given them, and it defines their particular relationship to their creator and the universe.

**SELECTED WORKS:** *My People, the Sioux,* edited by University of Michigan ethnologist E. A. Brininsteel (1928), was designed as a corrective to the then very influential Euro-American accounts of history and ethnology of the American Indians, particularly the Lakota. *My Indian Boyhood* (1931) is a recasting of the same materials for children, but it also provides a valuable explanation of the Lakota concept of developmental psychology in children and contrasts it with Euro-American concepts. *The Land of the Spotted Eagle* (1933), written after Standing Bear's return to Pine Ridge with the assistance of Melvin Gilmore, a Los Angeles friend, and a niece, Warcazi-win, is a more intellectually aggressive and aesthetically oriented book; it confronts the destruction by white culture and recalls the culture which was destroyed. *Stories of the Sioux* are Luther Standing Bear's renderings of traditional oral tales he recalled being told by tribal storytellers, his grandmother prominently among them.

**FURTHER READING:** No book-length studies have been completed on Luther Standing Bear's life or work. One essay devoted to his work is Frederick Hale's "Acceptance and Rejection of Assimilation in the Works of Luther Standing Bear," appearing in *Studies in American Indian Literatures* (Winter 1993): 25–41. Most commentaries mentioning Standing Bear are critical studies of Native American autobiographies. Brief but contributory studies include H. David Brumble III's *American Indian Autobiography* (1988) and *An Annotated Bibliography of American Indian and Eskimo Autobiographies* (1981); Gerald Vizenor's "The Ruins of Representation: Shadow Survivance and the Literature of Dominance," in the *American Indian Quarterly* (Winter 1993): 7–24; Janette K. Murray's "An Overview of Literature by Dakota/Lakota Authors," in Arthur Huseboe's *An Illustrated History of the Arts in South Dakota* (1989); and A. LaVonne Brown Ruoff's "Old Traditions and New Forms," in *Studies in American Indian Literature: Critical Essays and Course Designs*, edited by Paula Gunn Allen (1983).

DAVID L. NEWQUIST     NORTHERN STATE UNIVERSITY

**FREDERICK C. STERN.**
*See* appendix (1992)

**NANCY Y(OUNG) STONE**
December 15, 1925
**BIOGRAPHY:** Nancy Stone, children's novelist, was born in Crawfordsville, Indiana, the
daughter of William Foster, a journalist, and
Mary Emma (Engle) Young, and graduated
from Antioch College in 1948. Between 1944
and 1955, she worked in journalism, publishing, and secretarial fields. In 1947 she married
William Royal Stone, and they had two children. After receiving an MA from Western
Michigan University in 1970, she taught English there until 1988. She lives in Florida.
**SIGNIFICANCE:** All three of Stone's books
portray aspects of Michigan's natural resources, the development of its industries,
and the people who, in the 1870s, watched or
helped to make the changes that dominated
that period. *Whistle Up the Bay* (1966) depicts
the hardships of three orphan boys, the sons
of immigrants to Antrim County, Michigan.
Their struggles to live by farming and working in a logging operation reflect the evolution of the land from forest to fields, which
will not support ordinary crops, to orchards.
Betty Beebe, the illustrator of both this book
and of *The Wooden River* (1973), knew the actual family and its experiences with tragedy
and the generosity of neighbors. Rose Mac-
Laren, the ten-year-old narrator of *The Wooden
River*, spends a winter at a lumber camp near
Bay City. She observes and questions, learning and thus teaching young readers about
the cookhouse and the jobs of the inkslingers
(camp bookkeepers and managers of stores)
and shanty boys, showing their rough life,
and, as Stone notes in her introduction to the
book, "they were also dogged, hard-working,
adventurous and often self-sacrificing. Without them, the growing edge of the frontier
might have stalled and died" (4). *Dune Shadow*
(1980) treats a less positive aspect of logging,
its damage to the Lake Michigan dunes. Lumbering removed the trees whose roots kept
the sand from shifting. Through the eyes of
Selena Rawlings, who is thirteen, the book
shows the destruction of a village that the industry had originated, as the dunes knock
houses from their foundations and crush
other buildings in sand. The residents flee,
helping each other to find new lives, but the
book ends on a warning note on protecting
the fragile environment. All of the novels
tell compelling stories, rich in the details of
housekeeping, clothing, occupations, and geography of the time and region.
**SELECTED WORKS:** Stone's books, *Whistle
Up the Bay* (1966), *The Wooden River* (1973), and
*Dune Shadow* (1980), describe aspects of the
development of Michigan as a state in the
nineteenth century.
**FURTHER READING:** No book-length work
has appeared on Stone. For a discussion of the
books as they portray Michigan, see Carol
Smallwood's *Michigan Authors* (1993), Robert
Beasecker's *Michigan in the Novel, 1816–
1996* (1998), and Mary DeJong Obuchowski's
"Nancy Y. Stone, Michigan Author," in the
*Michigan Historical Review* 21 (Spring 1995):
136–42.
MARY DEJONG OBUCHOWSKI

CENTRAL MICHIGAN UNIVERSITY

**PHIL(IP) (DUFFIELD) STONG**
January 27, 1899–April 26, 1957
**BIOGRAPHY:** Born at the great bend of the
Des Moines River on a farm that had been in
his family since the early days of Iowa state-
hood, Phil Stong, the son of Benjamin J. and
Evesta (Duffield) Stong, wrote well in several
genres about his origins, his state, and the
importance of being a regional writer. His an-
cestors on both sides of the family had been
Iowa settlers. His great-grandfather, James
Duffield, was claimed by Stong to have made
the first wagon track west of the Des Moines
River in Iowa.

Stong graduated from Drake University in
1919, went to New York City, and took classes
at Columbia for a year, then returned to the
upper Midwest and taught high school in the
Duluth iron country. Some of his fiction is
salted with experiences among the Finns and
Swedes on the iron range. He writes vividly
in his early autobiography, *If School Keeps*
(1940), about his conscious decision "not to
teach but to do" (197). Though he was back
in Des Moines offering journalism classes at
Drake, he chose in 1923 to work exclusively
as a writer and editor. In 1925 he married Virginia Maude Swain.

Stong had already begun to submit his
work to JOHN T. FREDERICK's journal *The Midland* and continued to mine his Iowa memories for material until the great success of *State*

*Fair* (1932) enabled him to quit his newspaper work. He later made a major editorial contribution by gathering the first serious collection of fantasy and science fiction, *The Other Worlds* (1941). His newspaper work had taken him from the *Des Moines Register* to the Associated Press and the *New York World*. He won the *New York Herald Tribune* prize for juvenile fiction in 1939. *State Fair* was made three times into a film, the most recent a 1962 musical version by Oscar Hammerstein II. Stong published more than a dozen other novels, including juveniles, an important historical novel, *Buckskin Breeches* (1937), based on his family's pioneer move to Iowa, and personalized history books on Iowa and on California. By the time of his relatively early death from heart failure in New York, he was an influential member of the literary establishment but continually drew material from the small-town environment of places similar to Keosauqua, Iowa, where he had been born.

**SIGNIFICANCE:** The great year for Stong as a writer and editor had the unfortunate coincidence of coming right at the start of World War II, but his several books of 1940 define vividly his solid vision of Iowa history and values; even the introduction to his fantasy anthology, written at this time, nicely relates the genre back to Keosauqua fantasies. It is from his autobiography, however, and his history of Iowa at its centennial, *Hawkeyes* (1940), as well as from his 1937 historical novel *Buckskin Breeches*, that the reader may sense most clearly what Stong accomplishes. He expresses a strong vision of the Midwestern values of stoic acceptance and yet adventuresome movement. Even though he claims in his history that Iowa writers use mainly corn and hogs to create their effects, Stong has managed to weave literary pastoral ambivalence, by which the country is idealized from a city point of view, and a stoicism into his strongest novels, beginning with *State Fair*.

But the effect of Stong's pastoralism is perhaps strongest in *Stranger's Return* (1933), where in the end the torn lover and Iowa farmer, Guy, must leave his farm and become a "stranger" himself in the city and a teacher rather than a doer. In other words, Stong has clearly thought through the distinction between the stolidness of the great hog Blue Boy in *State Fair* and the adventuresomeness, even sexual adventuresomeness, of the

newspaperman, Pat Gilbert, who would write about him.

Near the end of his life, Stong published a sequel to his fabulous success, in which the newspaperman comes back; but his real strength of theme and image were back in the pastoral ambivalence that were expressed in his fiction of the early Depression years. Stong's fiction is never dustbowl realism, but its semi-pessimistic stoicism and good humor do find a perfect setting in these hard times.

**SELECTED WORKS:** Stong is best known for his quintessential Midwestern work, *State Fair* (1932). *Stranger's Return* (1933), *Buckskin Breeches* (1937), and *Hawkeyes* (1940) are also central in defining Stong's vision of Iowa and the Midwest. The important sequel to *State Fair* is *Return in August* (1953). Stong also published a science fiction collection, *The Other Worlds* (1941), and an award-winning juvenile work, *The Hired Man's Elephant* (1939). Other important novels include *Week End* (1935); *Ivanhoe Keeler* (1939), an historical novel; *Iron Mountain* (1942); and *Blizzard* (1955). Two other historical works by Stong are *Marta of Muscovy* (1945) and his final work, a personalized account of the California gold rush, *Gold in Them Hills* (1957). Stong's autobiography is entitled *If School Keeps* (1940).

**FURTHER READING:** The best source for Stong's development as a writer is his own autobiographical work cited above. For his theory of fiction see his "Foreword" to *The Other Worlds* (1941), pages 1–16. See also the *Saturday Review of Literature* 18 (July 30, 1938): 1 ff. Stong's papers and archives are in the Special Collections of the Cowles Library at Drake University.

DONALD M. HASSLER          KENT STATE UNIVERSITY

## GENE STRATTON-PORTER.
*See* Gene Stratton Porter

## LUCIEN STRYK
April 7, 1924

**BIOGRAPHY:** Lucien Stryk, poet and translator, was born in Kolo, Poland, to Emil and Celia (Meinstein) Stryk. In 1928 the family immigrated to the United States and settled in Chicago, where, as Stryk recounts in his long poem "A Sheaf for Chicago," he lived a childhood amidst the rubble of the Midwestern metropolis: "We gathered fenders, axles, blasted hoods / To build Cockaigne and

Never-never Land" (23). From 1943 to 1945 Stryk served with the U.S. Army artillery in the South Pacific.

Upon his return from the war, Stryk entered Indiana University, graduating with a BA in English in 1948. He pursued his studies in literature and philosophy at the Sorbonne under the auspices of the University of Maryland's foreign studies program, and in 1950 he received a master's degree in foreign study. Stryk furthered his education at Queen Mary College, University of London, and in 1951 while in England he married Helen Esterman, continuing to reside in London until 1954. Stryk returned to the United States with his family in 1955 and enrolled at the University of Iowa, where he received an MFA in 1956.

From 1956 to 1958, Stryk held a visiting lectureship at Niigata University in Japan, a post that stimulated his deep interest in Asian literature and Zen philosophy. In 1958 he began teaching at Northern Illinois University as a professor of English and Asian literatures; he retired from full-time teaching in this capacity in 1991, with an agreement to teach an occasional course in poetry writing. Throughout his distinguished career, Stryk has received numerous awards and grants, including a National Endowment for the Arts Poetry Fellowship, a Rockefeller Foundation Fellowship, a Ford Foundation Fellowship, a Fulbright grant and lectureship, and a National Institute of Arts and Letters Award. Stryk continues to live and write in DeKalb, Illinois.

**SIGNIFICANCE:** Stryk has garnered many accolades and grants for his translations of Japanese poetry, including his work on the haiku of Basho and Issa, the Zen poetry of Shinkichi Takahashi, and, perhaps most notably, *The Penguin Book of Zen Poetry* (1977) for which he received the Islands and Continents Translation Award. His own poetry, however, remains firmly situated in the Midwest.

Stryk's devotion to place grows naturally out of his dedication to Zen principles, and, as he suggests in the introduction to his second edited collection of Midwestern Poetry, *Heartland II: Poets of the Midwest* (1975), if one is to find peace as a poet or philosopher or human, then one must, as the Zen master Ch'ingyuan explains, see "mountains as mountains, waters as waters" (xxxviii). For Stryk then, there can be no richer place on earth than the Midwest for the creation of poetry: the vast sprawl of cities connected by rail and commerce, the dark, furrowed fields undulating with growth to the farthest horizon, and towns rising up out of nowhere, their quiet streets offering passage into what is most human and telling about our condition.

As an editor of two landmark collections of Midwestern poetry—*Heartland* (1967) and *Heartland II* (1975)—and as the author of such poems as "Farmer," "Scarecrow," "Return to DeKalb," and "Fishing with My Daughter in Miller's Meadow," Stryk searches the Midwestern landscape not for spectacle but for daily life. It is in daily living that Stryk moves, capturing in minimalist lines in "Fishing with My Daughter in Miller's Meadow" the wonder of a father holding his daughter's hand, walking through a meadow filled with fresh manure and grazing horses, or in "Farmer" magnifying the farmer's eyes that are "bound tight as wheat, packed / hard as dirt" (*Collected Poems* 2). Stryk, in an essay entitled "Making Poems" which is collected in *Encounter with Zen*, explains that the writing of poetry demands one to engage in "pure seeing," and from such seeing, Stryk creates a poetry of simple Midwestern images that illustrate clearly the beauty, diversity, and breadth of life in the heartland.

**SELECTED WORKS:** Stryk's *Collected Poems: 1953–1983* (1984) proffers a fine retrospective of his career as author, translator, or editor of more than thirty-one books of poetry, while suggesting the scope of his achievement. Although the works included in *Collected Poems* are not set exclusively in the Midwest, the vision of life found in this collection is shaped by Stryk's life there. As he explains in the introduction to *Heartland II*, "As one who has worked for a number of years, in Asia and the United States on the translation and interpretation of Zen poetry, I am sometimes asked why in the face of such 'exotic' pursuits I have an interest in the poetry of my region—or, worse, why my own poetry is set for the most part in small-town Illinois. To one involved in the study of a philosophy like Zen, the answer to such questions is not difficult: one writes of one's place because it is in every sense as wonderful as any other, whatever its topography and weathers, and because one cannot hope to discover oneself elsewhere" (xxii). Since the publication of *Collected Poems*, Stryk has published several books of poetry including *Bells of Lombardy* (1986), *Of Pen and Ink and Paper Scraps* (1989), and *And Still Birds Sing: New and Collected Poems* (1998), all of which continue to focus on the relationship between Zen philosophy and Stryk's Midwestern heritage. In addition to his own poetry, he has also recently translated three new collections of haiku and Zen poetry and edited a volume of poems selected for their impact on his own poetic vision, *The Gift of Great Poetry* (1992).

**FURTHER READING:** A collection of Stryk's worksheets has been established at the University of Buffalo, while a manuscript collection is presently housed at Boston University. *Zen, Poetry, the Art of Lucien Stryk,* edited by Susan Porterfield (1993), stands as the most significant critical work to date. There have been, however, several fine articles featuring Stryk's work, among them Daniel L. Guillory's *MidAmerica* essay "The Oriental Connection: Zen and Representations of the Midwest in the Collected Poems of Lucien Stryk," 13 (1986): 107–15; and Jay S. Paul's *Chicago Review* essay "Renewal of Intimacy: Lucien Stryk's Metaphor of Comprehension," 32.2 (1980): 30–40. For the most complete bibliography to date, consult Craig S. Abbott's "Lucien Stryk: A Bibliography," found in *Analytical and Enumerative Bibliography* 5.3 and 5.4 (1991): 160–265.

TODD F. DAVIS                     GOSHEN COLLEGE

# RUTH SUCKOW

August 6, 1892–January 23, 1960

**BIOGRAPHY:** Ruth Suckow was born in Hawarden, Iowa, the daughter of William John and Anna (Kluckhohn) Suckow. Her father was a Congregational minister of German extraction who served pastorates in such Iowa towns as Hawarden, LeMars, Algona, Fort Dodge, Manchester, and Davenport. Her education came from Iowa public schools, Grinnell College, the Curry School of Expression in Boston, and the University of Denver (BA 1917, MA 1918).

Having learned bee-keeping while in Denver, she established her "Orchard Apiary" in Earlville and began her career as a writer in 1918 with the publication of several poems. H. L. Mencken was impressed by her early fiction and encouraged her literary efforts. For some months in 1921 and 1922, she was associated with JOHN T. FREDERICK and *The Midland.* In 1921 she began publishing short fiction in such leading magazines of the day as *Smart Set, Century, American Mercury,* and *Harper's*; many of these stories were later included in book-length collections. By 1924 she turned to longer fiction, the form for which she is best known.

She married Ferner Nuhn, another Iowa writer, on March 11, 1929; they had no children. The couple moved about for a number of years, living variously in New Mexico, Iowa, Virginia, and Arizona, as well as at Yaddo and the MacDowell Colony, but they finally established a home in Claremont, California, in 1952, where Suckow died eight years later.

**SIGNIFICANCE:** Suckow's small-town Iowa background was crucial for her fiction. Like her contemporary, SINCLAIR LEWIS, she provided an unvarnished view of her Midwest, though her writings are less satiric than his. Both short stories and novels portray families, and particularly the women of those families, struggling with various forms of impoverishment—financial, spiritual, aesthetic, and emotional—always against the backdrop of an unnourishing Midwest. The Iowa lives depicted in her writings are narrow. The culture is materialistic, and the aspirations of her characters are restricted. Her old-fashioned German farmers and their families are simple people whose daily lives are toil-laden and often unrewarding. Her modern young women search both for work that will fulfill them and for love; they fail to combine these goals successfully and end in loneliness and frustration. For many characters, one single episode or moment—a wedding in *The Folks* (1934) is a particularly dramatic example—becomes a touchstone against which all the rest of life is measured and found wanting. The style used in examining these characters and their simple and very ordinary experiences is appropriately flat and unadorned, describing emotionally bleak lives in direct prose.

Suckow's first novel, *Country People* (1924), depicts German farmers whose economic rise does not bring happiness. Four novels presenting middle- or working-class small-town families follow; female characters are the center of all of these, and their quests for happiness end in disillusionment or loneliness, though not necessarily in despair or even great unhappiness. These are not truly examined lives. *The Odyssey of a Nice Girl* (1925), *The Bonney Family* (1928), and *Cora* (1929) form a closely related grouping with many parallels, almost as if Suckow were placing these mainly middle-class Iowa families in a variety of situations so as to examine them and their provincial small-town lives fully. In each of these, young women grow to maturity searching for identity and for some beauty or meaning in their lives. These young women face conflict between career and conventional marriage. Suckow sees no easy solution—perhaps no solution at all—to this conflict, and her young women, although apparently successful, are generally left with unfulfilled yearnings. The shallow culture and the lack of true courage it inculcates in its women seem to be responsible.

Related to the above mentioned three novels is *The Kramer Girls* (1930), which depicts a family of three sisters—one of the elder two illustrating conventional domesticity and femininity, the other a strong and masculine woman. The younger, whom they rear and in whom they invest all their dreams, is sheltered by her elders. Like all of Suckow's young women, she must choose between family and career; like all of them, her choices are restricted by the lack of opportunities her world—and she—envisage. Suckow's Iowa is accurately rendered, with such special Iowa phenomena as high school girls' basketball and chiropractic medical education among the details portrayed. In her Midwest, the American dream has constricted to a narrow round of conventionality, boredom, lack of beauty, and pettiness.

Her most ambitious and finest novel, *The Folks*, brought to their highest level the skills Suckow had been practicing in her earlier fiction. This long and complex work follows the lives of members of a small-town family, particularly its children, showing how each fails to live up to his or her promise and revealing as well how mystified the parents are by the desires and actions of their offspring. While the children try to break away from their stultifying Iowa background, the parents have little notion of anything beyond their gray lives and never understand the vague yearnings of their offspring.

Suckow's final two novels are not up to the level of her earlier fiction, but they also present interesting studies of small-town Iowa life. *New Hope* (1942) and *The John Wood Case* (1959) dramatize paradoxes: the contrast between innocence and experience is present in each. These novels are thematically based rather than character-driven, as her earlier fiction had been, but they rely no less strongly on sharp delineation of the Iowa scene and culture. Both, however, reveal the descent of the old American dream into bathos in Suckow's Iowa.

Realistically and ambivalently drawn Iowa backgrounds are crucial for all of Suckow's work. Her sense of detail is impeccable, and her scenes are effectively rendered. Her characters tend to be shallow, not very well able to articulate their deepest yearnings. The Iowa of her fiction is intellectually and spiritually narrow, and her characters seek for a fulfillment that, to their bewilderment, always eludes them. A deep sense of place, however, gives this fiction a conviction and interest that belie the decline in its creator's reputation. Once well known, widely read, and highly respected, Suckow is today largely forgotten.

**SELECTED WORKS:** Suckow's apprentice novel was *Country People* (1924). *The Odyssey of a Nice Girl* (1925), *The Bonney Family* (1928), *Cora* (1929), *The Kramer Girls* (1930), and *The Folks* (1934) are works of her period of mastery. Her late novels, *New Hope* (1942) and *The John Wood Case* (1959), show a diminution of her powers but portray Iowa scenes and characters well. *A Memoir* (1952) sketches her youth and Iowa background effectively. Collections of shorter pieces, particularly short stories but sometimes also including novels and memoirs, are *Children and Older People* (1931), *Carry-Over* (1936), and *Some Others and Myself* (1952).

**FURTHER READING:** Book-length studies of Suckow's work are Leedice McAnelly's *Ruth Suckow* (1969) and Margaret Stewart Omrécanin's *Ruth Suckow: A Critical Study of Her Fiction* (1972). In addition, there are Abigail Ann Hamblen's short monograph, *Ruth Suckow* (1978), a chapter devoted to her in CLARENCE ANDREWS's *A Literary History of Iowa* (1972), and a series of essays in *MidAmerica* (1986, 1988, 1989, 1991, and 1992), by Mary Jean DeMarr, each examining one of Suckow's novels or several short stories. Suckow's papers are widely scattered, but major holdings are at the University of Iowa, which has twelve manuscripts, 145 letters, and miscellaneous materials.

MARY JEAN DEMARR     INDIANA STATE UNIVERSITY

## LOUIS (HENRI) SULLIVAN
### September 3, 1856–April 14, 1924

**BIOGRAPHY:** Louis Sullivan, the son of Patrick and Andrienne Françoise (List) Sullivan, was born in Boston. He early exhibited an interest in bridges and buildings. After two years of study at the Massachusetts Institute of Technology, he moved to Philadelphia when he was seventeen years old to work in the office of Frank Furness, one of that city's major architects. Shortly thereafter, in 1873, Sullivan moved to Chicago at a time when the city was rebuilding after the devastation of the fire of 1871. Once again, he found work in the office of an architect. This time he was associated with William Le Baron Jenney, one of the pioneers of the Chicago School.

From the post-fire era to the magnificence of the World's Columbian Exposition through the period of the Chicago Renaissance, Sullivan understood the city better than some of the natives and realized that those attempting to pattern Chicago after the imagined genteel qualities of the East were missing the essential nature of the city. In his *Autobiography of an Idea* (1924), Sullivan recalled his early impressions of the city. Writing in the third person, he said: "Louis thought it all magnificent and wild: A crude extravaganza: An intoxicating rawness: A sense of big things to be done. For 'Big' was the word. 'Biggest' was preferred, and the 'biggest in the world' was the braggart phrase on every tongue . . ." (200).

In search of further formal architectural training, Sullivan attended the Ecole des Beaux Arts during 1874–75. While he enjoyed his time in Paris, he rebelled against the neoclassical tradition in architecture which the school espoused. He himself was strongly influenced by the work of Henry Hobson Richardson (1838–86), who used a Romanesque pattern that came to be called Richardsonian.

In 1881 he joined with Dankmar Adler, the German engineer, to form the firm of Adler and Sullivan, where FRANK LLOYD WRIGHT worked from 1887 to 1893. During this period, Sullivan became an occasional member of Chicago's Little Room, a loose organization with no formal structure but which generally met on Friday afternoons following the symphony. It began as a social gathering which included businessmen and their wives, literary artists and their critics, builders, painters, and sculptors. He was also caught up in the excitement engendered by the World's Columbian Exposition of 1893, which marked a significant event in Chicago's history. Sullivan's Transportation Building remains one of the outstanding structures of the fair; however, unlike many participants and visitors, Sullivan was not impressed by the exposition. Because of its imitative nature, he saw it as the end of the innovative period of American architecture and declared in his *Autobiography of an Idea*: "The damage wrought . . . will last for half a century from its date if not longer . . ." (325).

The Adler-Sullivan partnership was dissolved in 1895 but not before producing some of the outstanding buildings of the Chicago School. By 1899 he had created the Schlesinger and Mayer Department Store, an important building designed for retailing. Now known as Carson Pirie Scott and Co., this building is merely a reflection of a period which includes the notable structures of the Chicago School produced in the 1880s and 1890s. By 1900 Sullivan's greatest period as a designer had come to an end, yet he continued to produce primarily small bank buildings in the Midwest.

His professional successes were not accompanied by personal ones. His marriage to Margaret Hattaborough in 1899 was burdened with problems. They separated in 1917 and later divorced. His last years were filled with illness, regrets, and disillusionment. He did not realize that commercial architecture in the United States had been guided by his designs and his writings. He died in Chicago of heart failure and is buried in the city's famous Graceland Cemetery.

**SIGNIFICANCE:** Although he was not a Midwesterner by birth, Sullivan lived and worked in Chicago long enough to be securely identified with the Midwest in general and with Chicago in particular, where he executed significant architectural innovations that led to the Chicago School of Architecture. As was true for many entrepreneurial businessmen and innovative architects, Sullivan benefited from the fire of 1871. Chicago provided a laboratory for him to execute many of his ideas on design and ornamentation.

Sullivan made cogent and revealing comments about American buildings that ultimately could be taken as perceptive observations on American civilization. He believed in a functional approach to architecture, but he also believed that utilitarianism meant neither a lack of beauty nor an absence of ornament. His use of ornamentation was rooted in his love for nature, about which he wrote in almost Whitmanesque terms. He was extremely fond of Whitman's work, and some observers might think of him as a poet in stone.

He was a prolific writer and wrote many explanations of his approach to construction as well as to design. He insisted upon looking forward rather than on imitating old styles. His mandate "form follows function" appeared in "The Tall Office Building Artistically Considered," in *Lippincott's Magazine* (March 1896), and was revolutionary in its democratic approach to architecture. Moreover, in an effort to humanize buildings, Sullivan was convinced that any structure ought to mirror the lives of people who had to use the building and should reflect the structure's purpose. Consequently, in many lectures, articles, and several books, he articulated the aesthetic possibilities of the nation's technological culture at a time when others were imitating earlier historic periods in their designs.

**SELECTED WORKS:** Aside from individual lectures, many of which appeared in the leading journals of the day and are in the Burnham Library of the Art Institute of Chicago, Sullivan's major works are *The Autobiography of an Idea* (1924) and *Kindergarten Chats and Other Writings* (1934), which initially appeared in serial form and whose sections were later edited and issued as a book.

**FURTHER READING:** Both Albert Bush-Brown's *Louis Sullivan* (1960) and Willard Connely's *Louis Sullivan As He Lived* (1960) give excellent biographical surveys of Sullivan. Hugh Morrison's *Louis Sullivan: Prophet of Modern Architecture* (1935) and Hugh D. Duncan's *Culture and Democracy: The Struggle for Form and Architecture in Chicago and the Middle West during the Life and Times of Louis Sullivan* (1965) emphasize Sullivan's role as an architectural leader. Both Sherman Paul's *Louis Sullivan: An Architect in American Thought* (1962) and KENNY J. WILLIAMS's *In the City of Men: Another Story of Chicago* (1974) examine Sullivan's role as a writer as well as the influence of Chicago on him. In *Genius and the Mobocracy* (1949), Frank Lloyd Wright presents a student's commendation to his teacher. Sullivan's papers are located in the Burnham Library of the Art Institute of Chicago and in the Avery Architectural Library of Columbia University. Additional miscellaneous items may be found in the archives of the American Institute of Architects in Washington, D.C.

KENNY J. WILLIAMS          DUKE UNIVERSITY

## MARY SWANDER
November 5, 1950

**BIOGRAPHY:** Mary Swander was born in Carroll, Iowa, in Carroll County, the same county where her Irish great-grandparents had homesteaded and shared their cabin with Native Americans. Her father, John Chester Swander, sold electrical substations, and her mother, Rita (Lynch) Swander, was an elementary schoolteacher. Swander's primary role model was her grandmother, who ran two farms and walked the beans with a corn knife until she was eighty. From her, Swander learned about anatomy and metaphor, survival, death, and daily miracles. Her primary literary influence was Flannery O'-Connor. Both grew up Catholic, graduated from the Iowa Writers' Workshop, and acquired chronic illnesses in their early adult lives; both knew the power of the rural grotesque to probe to the center of things. The strange, spiritual visions of these two writers, centered profoundly in the concrete, were partly born of common pasts.

While trying to support her writing, Swander became a desk clerk at a motel in Iowa, worked in a Pediatric Intensive Care Unit, taught at Lake Forest College in Illinois, had a practice in hypnotherapy and therapeutic massage that took her on tour with the Winnipeg Ballet, and assisted a veterinarian. Presently, she teaches at Iowa State University in Ames, Iowa. She has worked in the Poets-in-the-Schools program in Iowa and has been a visiting writer at Interlochen, Hiram College, Stephens College, the University of New Mexico, and the University of Alabama.

At age thirty-three, she suffered an overdose of allergy vaccine that led to an environmental illness that persists to this day. During her vacations and holidays she lives in a converted schoolhouse in Kalona, Iowa, among the Amish. Here she grows a com-

Mary Swander.
Photo by Jon Van Allen. Courtesy of Mary Swander

pletely organic garden, raises sheep and a one-eyed pygmy goat, and whittles life to its most simple lines. Swander's preoccupation with rural life in Iowa, as well as the central issue of recovery, has frequently brought abundance to her own life and direction to her art.

Her work has earned her the RUTH SUCKOW Award, the Johnson Brigham Award, the *Nation*-Discovery Award, the CARL SANDBURG Award, two Ingram Merrill Foundation grants, grants from the Iowa Arts Council, the Literary Arts Award from the Chicago Public Library, a National Endowment for the Arts Creative Writing Fellowship, and the Quill and Travel Award from the Garden Writers Association of America for best magazine writing. In the fall of 1994 Swander received a prestigious Whiting Award for "exceptional talent and promise."

**SIGNIFICANCE:** Swander welcomes Iowa into her work with rare persistence, loyalty, joy, and outrageous humor. She finds the Iowa countryside an inexhaustible resource. From her very first published essay in 1974, "A Monarch Roosting Tree in Iowa," to her 1995 book, *Out of This World: A Woman's Life among the Amish* (retitled *Out of This World: A Journey of Healing* in the 1996 paperback), Iowa has remained Swander's center, the

source of her material and her vision. Even in *Succession* (1979), an early volume of poetry that explores her Irish roots, stories and images of the Lynches in fifteenth-century Ireland mesh with the lives and cells of descendants who live on back country roads in Iowa. *Driving the Body Back* (1986), a book of poetry that won acclaim from poets David Wojahn, STANLEY PLUMLY, and David St. John, is a holy journey into the most extravagant and poignant corners of the Midwest, a journey filled with feed and seed stores, twisters, chickens, cafés, roadside grottoes, butcher shops, funeral homes, and extravagant personalities. The metaphysical and concrete join once more in a work of nonfiction written with Jane Staw, *Parsnips in the Snow: Talks with Midwestern Gardeners* (1990), a book which was named one of the best of 1990 by *Publishers Weekly*. Iowa themes are dramatically evoked in *Dear Iowa*, a play written in collaboration with Christopher Frank and first produced in Iowa in 1991. In her most recent volume of poetry, *Heaven-and-Earth House* (1994), as well as in *Out of This World*, Swander continues to explore the mysteries of place within the more particular surroundings of the Amish countryside.

Swander's collection *Land of the Fragile Giants: Landscapes, Environments, and Peoples of the Loess Hills*, edited with Cornelia F. Mutel (1994), quite literally relates to Midwestern soil. *Bloom and Blossom: The Reader's Guide to Gardening* (1997), a collection of poetry, fiction, and essays by America's literary gardeners, continues to reveal the profound connections of people to the earth. Her most recent collection, *The Healing Circle: Authors Writing of Recovery*, edited with Patricia Foster (1998), records fourteen stories of illness and healing including Swander's own tribute to her neighbors in rural Iowa who helped her recover from viral myelitis. Currently she is working on a novel set at the time of the Midwestern floods of 1993, as well as other books.

Talking in a 1984 interview for *Iowa Woman* about her return to Iowa after short stays elsewhere, Swander says, "When I came back to Iowa I think I finally realized that my subject matter was here right now" (28). The Midwestern landscape, open and secure, and the rural people she has known and lived among center Swander's work again and again. A prolific and agile writer, Swander finds an inexhaustible source of wealth in the small corners of her native state. It is significant that in her essay "West of Eden" she describes the geography of Iowa as imitating "the layout of the nation with the Atlantic and Pacific Oceans" (*Townships* 169). Ironically, to Swander, looking hard at Iowa is the best way of seeing America whole, a way, finally, of understanding the world itself more clearly.

**SELECTED WORKS:** Swander's collections of poetry include *Needlepoint* (1977), *Succession* (1979), *Driving the Body Back* (1986), *Lost Lake* (1986), and *Heaven-and-Earth House* (1994). Her dramatic adaptation of *Driving the Body Back* was produced by the Riverside Theatre of Iowa City in 1988. Another play, *Dear Iowa*, was written with Christopher Frank and first produced in Iowa in 1991. In 1982 she published a collection of stories, *Partners*, about her experiences working for a veterinarian. Her nonfiction features *Parsnips in the Snow: Talks with Midwestern Gardeners* (with Jane Staw, 1990) and *Out of This World* (1995), as well as essays in prominent collections about place, such as *A Place of Sense: Essays in Search of the Midwest* (1988), *Townships* (1992), *Iowa: A Celebration of Land, People, and Purpose* (1995), *Family Reunion* (1995), and *Imagining Home* (1995). Swander has also edited several collections, including *The Land of the Fragile Giants: Landscapes, Environments, and Peoples of the Loess Hills* (1994), an illustrated work about the Loess Hills in western Iowa, edited with Cornelia F. Mutel (1994); *Bloom and Blossom: The Reader's Guide to Gardening* (1997); and *The Healing Circle: Authors Writing of Recovery*, edited with Patrica Foster (1998). She crosses easily and naturally from one genre to another, seeing no clear lines between prose and poetry, and has published essays, poems, articles, and short stories in magazines such as *Nation*, the *New Yorker*, the *New Republic*, *Poetry*, and the *New York Times Sunday Magazine*.

**FURTHER READING:** No book about Swander has yet been written, but she is mentioned in several key references, including *Contemporary Authors, New Revision Series* 48: 431–33. Significant short pieces about Swander's work include Joyce Dyer's "Portrait of an Iowa Poet," in *Iowa Woman* 5.2 (1984): 28–33 (reprinted in *A Retrospective Anthology of Our First Fifteen Years: Iowa Woman* 15.3 [1995]: 22–26); Joyce Dyer's review of *Driving the Body Back*, in *Poet and Critic* 18.1 (1986): 54–60; Eliz-

abeth Spires's "Crossing the Divide: Mary Swander's *Driving the Body Back*," in *Antioch Review* 45.1 (1987): 84–89; and James Grove and Steven Horowitz's "Interview: Mary Swander," in *Iowa Woman* 13.4 (1993): 13–20.

JOYCE DYER                     HIRAM COLLEGE

## GLENDON (FRED) SWARTHOUT
April 8, 1918–September 23, 1992

**BIOGRAPHY:** Glendon Swarthout was born near Pinckney, Michigan, the only child of Fred Harrington and Lila (Chubb) Swarthout, both descendants of early Michigan settlers. As a bank cashier his father worked in several Michigan towns, but Glendon grew up in Lowell, Michigan. During his high school and college years he played in one of the many small dance orchestras of that era. He attended the University of Michigan, receiving his BA degree in 1939. Swarthout worked for a time in business and advertising, and in 1940 he married Kathryn Vaughn. After working two years in the Willow Run airplane factory, he entered the U.S. Army Infantry. Among his duties was investigating reports and writing citations for military medals. From 1946 through 1948, he was a teaching fellow at the University of Michigan. He received his MA degree there in 1946 and in 1948 won the Hopwood fiction award. During most of the next three years he was an instructor at the University of Maryland and also lived for a few months in Mexico. He also for a time worked in business and advertising. In 1951 Swarthout joined the Michigan State University Department of Communication Skills and earned his PhD degree in English from Michigan State University in 1955. In 1959 Swarthout left the Midwest to serve as a lecturer in the Department of English at Arizona State University, a role he continued until 1963. He returned to teaching part time from 1982 until 1986. Each of his experiences became the basis for a later novel.

Four of Swarthout's novels and one of his short stories were made into motion pictures. The first, in which he also acted as script consultant, was *They Came to Cordura* (1958). The second and most successful of the screen adaptations of his work was *Where the Boys Are* (1960). *Bless the Beasts and Children* (1970) directed attention to the Department of the Interior's inhumane method of thinning the buffalo herds. *The Shootist* (1975) became

John Wayne's last motion picture. One of Swarthout's short stories, "Seventh Cavalry," was retitled as the motion picture "A Horse for Mr. Custer." Additionally, Swarthout collaborated with his wife, Kathryn, in the writing of six children's books.

The Western Writers Association conferred the Spur Award on Swarthout for *The Shootist* in 1975 and the same award in 1988 for *The Homesman*. The latter novel also won a Wrangler Award from the Western Historical Society. Earlier, in 1972, he was recognized as a gold medalist by the National Society of Arts and Letters. The association conferred on him the first Owen Wister Lifetime Achievement Award in 1991, when Swarthout made his last public appearance. In 1992, suffering from emphysema he died at his home in Scottsdale, Arizona. He was survived by his widow and his son Miles.

**SIGNIFICANCE:** Anyone born during the first quarter of the twentieth century was inevitably marked by the great economic depression of the 1930s; then World War II profoundly and permanently changed society. Both of these influences color Swarthout's novels, particularly those set in the Midwest. *Welcome to Thebes* (1962) and *Loveland* (1968) show how the problems of adults affect their children, especially adolescents trying to adapt to an adult world. Swarthout's first novel, *Willow Run* (1943), takes the reader inside the pulsing, powerful environment of a wartime weapons factory. Although *They Came to Cordura* (1958) is set in Mexico at the time of the 1916 border dispute, its analysis of the roots of courage clearly grew out of Swarthout's wartime experiences. Teaching freshman honors English classes gave Swarthout insight into the postwar mentality of college students, and *Where the Boys Are* (1960) presaged the explosion that was to erupt in American colleges a decade later. *The Melodeon* (1977) is a farewell tribute to his Michigan antecedents and reflects his awareness of their tradition of understanding and concern for others. It was reissued in paperback under the title *A Christmas Gift* (1992).

With the conspicuous exception of *The Melodeon*, all Swarthout's novels are infused with a sardonic spirit, in response to human cruelty and viciousness. Yet the tone of his work is fundamentally dispassionate and characterized by a clear, uncluttered, pictor-

ial style. He was a great admirer of ERNEST HEMINGWAY and Somerset Maugham, whose influence is clear in his writing.

**SELECTED WORKS:** *Willow Run* (1943), like many first novels, was not successful in penetrating the implications of events described. *They Came to Cordura* (1958) brought Swarthout national attention for the impact of the story and the power of his writing. *Where the Boys Are* (1960) and the motion picture based on it focused attention on the lemming-like spring vacation trip college students were making to Fort Lauderdale, Florida. *Welcome to Thebes* (1962) caused Swarthout some difficulty, probably because it was drawn from an unhappy interval in his youth. *Cadillac Cowboys* (1964) is a somewhat satirical narrative of efforts to preserve the so-called romantic era of the old West. *The Eagle and the Iron Cross* (1966) focuses on German prisoners of war held in the American Southwest. Outrage over the government's callous and inhumane disposal of buffalo inspired *Bless the Beasts and Children* (1970), prompting a change in the practices. In *The Tin Lizzie Troop* (1972) Swarthout returned to the 1916 "border skirmish" with Mexico, describing the shift of Eastern soldiers from horses to Model T Fords. *Luck and Pluck* (1973) derived in part from Swarthout's brief venture into the world of advertising. John Wayne seemed appropriate for the lead role in the motion picture adaptation of *The Shootist* (1975), where a gunman had, like Wayne, to face death from cancer. *The Melodeon* (1977) may well join other perennial Christmas stories as a somewhat nostalgic salute to the courage, consideration, and hardships of an earlier generation. *Skeletons* (1979) is a mystery set in the Midwest, though the setting is incidental to the story. *The Old Colts* (1985), a colorful story about Bat Masterson and Wyatt Earp, was inspired by a holographic manuscript purportedly written by Masterson. Swarthout's last major work, *The Homesman* (1988), depicts the consequences of the hardships of those who first moved out to settle in the West. *Pinch Me: I Must Be Dreaming* (1994) was published posthumously.

**FURTHER READING:** A critical account of Swarthout's work may be found in *Contemporary Literary Criticism* 35 (1985): 398. The Swarthout papers are at Arizona State University.

THEODORE R. KENNEDY

MICHIGAN STATE UNIVERSITY

# T-Z

## (NEWTON) BOOTH TARKINGTON

July 29, 1869–May 19, 1946

**BIOGRAPHY:** Booth Tarkington was born in Indianapolis into the prosperous Midwestern middle class. His father, Judge John Stevenson Tarkington, practiced law in Indianapolis and had been a captain of an infantry company during the Civil War. His mother, Elizabeth Booth Tarkington, had attended St. Mary-of-the-Woods College in Terre Haute and possessed intelligence and ambition. In the family home in Indianapolis, Booth educated himself by reading in his father's library. He spent two years each at Phillips Exeter Academy, Purdue, and Princeton, participating in dramatics, glee club, and journalism.

He then spent five years attempting to find himself as a writer or illustrator, but almost all his submissions to publishers brought rejection slips. Even *Monsieur Beaucaire* (1900) and *The Gentleman from Indiana* (1899) shared this fate. However, unknown to Booth, his sister, Hauté, took the manuscript of *Monsieur Beaucaire* to New York and tried to interest a publisher, S. S. McClure, in it. McClure was not much interested, but he did want to see the novel about Indiana that she had mentioned, so she telegraphed Booth to send it to him.

Two weeks later a letter arrived from HAMLIN GARLAND, a reader for McClure, saying, "You are a novelist" (Woodress 74). These words and the offer to publish changed Tarkington's life. Invited to New York to cut the manuscript for publication as a serial for *McClure's Magazine*, Tarkington found himself transported in a dream world of opened doors, friendly editors and publishers, and famous authors who greeted him as an equal.

Tarkington's novel *The Gentleman from Indiana* was romantic and sentimental, telling how a promising college graduate buys a broken-down county newspaper and revitalizes it, is nearly killed by mobsters, but finds himself a state hero and the nominee of his party to Congress. His next novel, *The Two Vanrevels* (1902), based on his mother's memory of her education at St. Mary-of-the-Woods, was a best-seller.

On June 18, 1902, Tarkington married Laurel Louisa Fletcher and put his name on the ballot for the Indiana House of Representatives; he conducted no campaign but was elected. This experience provided the background for *In the Arena: Stories of Political Life* (1905), in which he dramatized the inner, often dirty workings of a legislature. He and his wife spent 1903 and 1904 in Europe, then settled briefly in New York.

Next Tarkington published *The Beautiful Lady* (1905), concerning an impoverished Italian nobleman, and *The Conquest of Canaan* (1905), the story of an Indiana attorney. *His Own People* (1907) told the story of a smug, naive, Midwestern young man who, exhilarated by Roman society, was fleeced at poker and returned home where he belonged. Another novel was *The Guest of Quesnay* (1908), about a dissolute, rich, young American who lost his memory in an automobile accident.

A play that he and Harry Leon Wilson had been writing, *The Guardian* (1907), was produced and published as *The Man from Home* (1908). It featured an Indiana booster and was an instant success. From 1907 through 1910 Tarkington worked on drama with Harry Wilson, with decreasing success. A novelette reflecting these experiences was *Harlequin and Columbine* (1925).

Tarkington's travels made him frequently absent from home, and in 1911 his wife was awarded a divorce. Tarkington suffered in public esteem but reorganized his life and went back to work as a writer with even greater success. On November 6, 1912, he and Susanah Robinson, of Dayton, were quietly married and came to live in Indianapolis, where she managed the household, cushioned Booth from the distractions of ordinary living, and helped him give up alcohol.

*The Flirt* (1913) was written in a new manner: letting his characters do what they wished. His heroine, Cora Madison, was beautiful but selfish, the first of his Becky Sharp characters. But the Penrod stories were Tarkington's real find. Beginning with "Penrod and the Pageant," they succeeded because Tarkington believed boys should be presented as they are, not as adults would like them to be. Tarkington also attacked the problems of industrialism. *The Turmoil* (1915) sharply criticized materialism and big business. Three other novels were similar: *The Magnificent Ambersons* (1918), *Alice Adams* (1921), and *The Midlander* (1924). In these four novels, Tarkington made his most significant contribution to American literature as a social historian. He constructed chronicles of Hoosier families and their relationship with big business. Both *Al-*

**Booth Tarkington.**
Courtesy of Princeton University Library

*ice Adams* and *The Magnificent Ambersons* won the Pulitzer Prize.

In his second period of playwriting he turned out farces and comedies of manners, with varying success. In all he showed optimism and ability to entertain. Academic honors came from DePauw, Princeton, Columbia, and Purdue. Some collections of short stories were published.

Yet Tarkington continued to produce novels. *The Plutocrat* (1927) presented an American millionaire manufacturer, Earl Tinker, a noisy yet likable braggart who lied to his wife, got drunk, and pursued women. *Young Mrs. Greeley* (1929) was about living in an apartment house; *Mirthful Haven* (1930), probably his most bitter book, examined the antagonism between the natives of Kennebunkport, Maine, and the summer residents. The novelist then returned to his all-consuming love, Indiana, in *The Heritage of Hatcher Ide* (1941). *The Fighting Littles* (1941) set forth much of Tarkington's anti–New Deal convictions; *Kate Fennigate* (1943) told how a woman made her husband a business success. His last novel, *The Show Piece* (1947), dealt with egoism.

Booth Tarkington died at his second beautiful Indianapolis home on May 19, 1946.

**SIGNIFICANCE:** One is struck by Tarkington's great ability and versatility. He combined many kinds of materials into popular and artistic successes. Although he wrote to entertain, he always tried to say something worthwhile. As a humanitarian he interested himself in people and in character, and the older Tarkington particularly disparaged overemphasis on plot. His characters are recognizable, for he fastened upon the enduring in human nature. Tarkington recorded the life of Hoosiers and residents of Indianapolis as well as the composite life of America.

His literary attitude is difficult to discern. Even though he began as a romanticist and continued this approach in some later writing, the bulk of his production was somewhat realistic in dissecting life as influenced by economic and social forces. His romanticism and realism were seldom extreme, the exceptions being *Monsieur Beaucaire* (1900) and *In the Arena: Stories of Political Life* (1905). He was never attracted to naturalism. Although his plays were often built on a social problem, they were usually light comedies or entertaining farces. None was a serious study of a great problem. Tarkington was the most prolific Hoosier dramatist and one of the most popular playwrights in the first third of the twentieth century. His stories were set in many Midwestern locales, and he used Indiana settings more than any other Hoosier author except perhaps JAMES WHITCOMB RILEY. Often he portrayed the American traveler abroad in unflattering colors, as in *His Own People* (1907), *The Plutocrat* (1927), *Claire Ambler* (1928), and *The Man from Home* (play 1908, novel 1915). Tarkington maintained a quiet optimism, believing that underneath the many changes in society the best in humanity is still strong and cannot be crushed.

For some, Tarkington will always be associated with books of childhood and youth, and although he shared the leadership of Indiana literature with GEORGE ADE and MEREDITH NICHOLSON, for many he will remain the best of all the Indiana authors.

**SELECTED WORKS:** Booth Tarkington wrote voluminously. Most notable are *The Gentleman from Indiana* (1899), *Monsieur Beaucaire* (1900), *The Two Vanrevels* (1902), *In the Arena: Stories of Political Life* (1905), *Guest of Quesnay* (1908), *The Man from Home* (1908), *Penrod* (1914), *The Magnificent Ambersons* (1918), and *Alice Adams* (1921). Other novels include *Claire Ambler* (1928), *Mirthful Haven* (1930), *Penrod: His Complete Story* (1931), and *The Heritage of Hatcher Ide* (1941).

**FURTHER READING:** Book-length studies of Tarkington include Dorothy Russo and Thelma Sullivan's *A Bibliography of Booth Tarkington, 1869–1946* (1949); Keith Fennimore's *Booth Tarkington* (1974); Asa Dickinson's *Booth Tarkington: A Sketch* (1928); Robert Holliday's *Booth Tarkington* (1918); *The Gentleman from Indianapolis: A Treasury of Booth Tarkington*, edited by John Beecroft (1957); Susanah Mayberry's *My Amiable Uncle: Recollections about Booth Tarkington* (1983); James Woodress's *Booth Tarkington, Gentleman from Indiana* (1955); and Adam Sorkin's *Booth Tarkington and Sinclair Lewis: Two Realists as Social Historians* (1973). The Indiana State Library has many Tarkington letters, but the main collection of Tarkington manuscripts is located at the Princeton University Library.

ARTHUR W. SHUMAKER          DEPAUW UNIVERSITY

## SARA TEASDALE
August 8, 1884–January 29, 1933

**BIOGRAPHY:** Sara Teasdale, lyric poet, was born in St. Louis, Missouri, into a prosperous, middle-class family. Her father, a businessman, John Warren Teasdale, and her mother, Mary Elizabeth (Willard) Teasdale, were already in their forties and had three teen-aged children. Sara, always considered frail, was raised in a pampered, protective atmosphere and tutored at home until she was nine. Then, she attended private schools, graduating from Hosmer Hall in 1903. The family's summers were spent in Charlevoix, Michigan. Travel and new locales seemed to improve Teasdale's health, and in 1905 her mother took her on a five-month trip to Europe and the Middle East. Her health problems were probably emotionally based. Throughout her life she continued to suffer from bouts of depression and ill health and to periodically seek relief in travel or in visits to a sanitarium in Cromwell, Connecticut, where she first spent time in 1908. She also sought relief in writing.

It was with a group of young women school friends that Teasdale first published poems and sketches. The group, calling themselves the Potters, produced a monthly magazine called *The Potter's Wheel*. WILLIAM MARION REEDY, the St. Louis publisher of the weekly newspaper the *Mirror*, asked to reprint her sketch titled "The Crystal Cup" and later printed her poems and gave her encouragement. In 1907 she had her first collection, *Sonnets to Duse and other Poems*, privately printed.

Through her writing, Teasdale made new St. Louis friends, ZOË AKINS and ORRICK JOHNS, both developing writers; and through correspondence she began a long-distance relationship with poet John Myers O'Hara, who had moved from Chicago to New York. Also through letters she met Marion Cummings Stanley, a philosophy instructor at the University of Arizona, with whom Teasdale spent the winter of 1908, a woman who helped her in her determination to be a poet.

In 1911 Teasdale published her second book, *Helen of Troy and Other Poems*. She was also invited to join the Poetry Society of America, and on her visit to New York, she met Jessie B. Rittenhouse and John Hall Wheelock, poets who would remain life-long friends. She also had a disappointing first meeting with John Myers O'Hara.

Teasdale traveled to Chicago in 1913 and there met HARRIET MONROE of *Poetry* magazine and one of her assistants, EUNICE TIETJENS, who introduced her to some of the writers active in the Chicago Renaissance. Later that year, the poet VACHEL LINDSAY wrote to Teasdale, having learned of her from Monroe. The two met in 1914 and remained friends until his death by suicide in 1931.

Teasdale's relationships with men formed the theme of many of her lyrics. She had fallen in love in 1912 with an Englishman, Stafford Hatfield, and she was greatly attracted to John Hall Wheelock, but in 1914 she married a St. Louis businessman, Ernest Filsinger; the marriage was less than successful.

In 1915 she published her highly successful *Rivers to the Sea*, and in 1916 she and her husband moved to New York City. In 1917 she published an anthology, *The Answering Voice: One Hundred Love Lyrics by Women*, and her own *Love Songs*, which won the Columbia Poetry Prize in 1918.

Her health continued to be a problem, and Teasdale sought relief in travel, making trips to England and France, often with women friends. In 1926 a university student, Margaret Conklin, entered her life, again through correspondence, and provided needed support. Perhaps trying for a new beginning, Teasdale divorced Ernest Filsinger in 1929. She traveled to England in 1931 and 1932, researching a book on Christina Rossetti, but her ill health and depression continued, and in 1933 she died from an overdose of sleeping pills. Her ashes were buried in Bellefontaine Cemetery in St. Louis.

**SIGNIFICANCE:** Little in Teasdale's work is identifiably Midwestern, although some of her lyrics about the sea may stem from summers spent near Lake Michigan. Her poetry, popular with critics and general readers during the World War I years and the 1920s and 1930s, started to lose critical favor in the 1940s as poetic styles changed. Today her poetry is largely ignored, although interest in her life has resulted in biographical studies. Many feminist critics have ignored her poetry, although some general readers still seek out and collect her work, possibly because, as Carol B. Schoen writes in her critical biography *Sara Teasdale* (1986), it appeals to "all those who instinctively value the 'magic of melody'" (176).

**SELECTED WORKS:** Seven volumes of Teasdale's lyrics appeared during her lifetime: *Sonnets to Duse and Other Poems* (1907), *Helen of Troy and Other Poems* (1911), *Rivers to the Sea* (1915), *Love Songs* (1917), *Flame and Shadow* (1920), *Dark of the Moon* (1926), and *Stars To-Night* (1930). An eighth, *Strange Victory* (1933), was completed before her death. *Flame and Shadow* and *Dark of the Moon* are interesting for the use of different techniques. She also published two anthologies, *The Answering Voice: One Hundred Love Lyrics by Women* (1917; revised 1928) and *Rainbow Gold: Poems Old and New Selected for Girls and Boys* (1922). *The Collected Poems of Sara Teasdale* appeared in 1937 and was reissued with an introduction by Marya Zaturenska in 1966. William Drake edited and introduced *Mirror of the Heart: Poems of Sara Teasdale* (1984).

**FURTHER READING:** Three biographies have appeared, each building upon the earlier. They are *Sara Teasdale, A Biography*, by Margaret Haley Carpenter (1960); *Sara Teasdale: Woman and Poet*, by William Drake (1979); and *Sara Teasdale*, by Carol B. Schoen (1986). Jean Gould includes a chapter on Teasdale in her *American Women Poets* (1980), and William Drake provides insights about Teasdale, her relationships, and her poetry in *The First Wave* (1987). Collections of her papers are held at the Beinecke Library at Yale University and at the Wellesley College Library. The Missouri Historical Society has a collection of letters and memoirs from St. Louis friends.

PATRICIA A. ANDERSON        DIMONDALE, MICHIGAN

## (LOUIS) STUDS TERKEL
May 16, 1912

**BIOGRAPHY:** Louis Terkel was born in New York City, the youngest son of Samuel and Anna (Finkel) Terkel, a Jewish family whose origins can be traced to the Russian-Polish border. Early family life was difficult because of his father's illness and early death and his mother's emotional volatility. When Terkel was about eight, the family moved to Chicago and managed small hotels. Terkel's self-selected nickname, Studs, reflects his admiration for James T. Farrell's *Studs Lonigan*. Terkel earned his PhB (1932) and JD (1934) from the University of Chicago but never practiced law. He married Ida Goldberg on July 2, 1939. The couple have one son, Paul.

Studs Terkel gained public attention through the stage, which gave way to roles in radio soap opera, as jazz disk jockey, radio and television host, actor, and interviewer. His first television series, *Studs' Place*, begun in 1950, was canceled, and he was blacklisted in 1953 for refusal to disavow petitions he had signed or to disclose names to the House Un-American Activities Committee. Terkel's association with Chicago's fine arts radio station, WFMT, began in 1953 and continued through his final radio program on January 1, 1998. He is now engaged in a two-year process of preparing the Studs Terkel Archive, a massive collection of interviews to be held by the Chicago Historical Society.

Terkel has received many awards, including nomination for the 1975 National Book Award for *Working* and the 1985 Pulitzer Prize in nonfiction for *The Good War*. In May 1997 he was inducted into the American Academy of Arts and Letters. He received a medal for Distinguished Contribution to American Letters from the National Book Foundation in November 1997.

**SIGNIFICANCE:** Studs Terkel's significance lies in his representation of the Chicago lo-

**Studs Terkel.**
Photo © Nancy Crampton

cale, his celebration of Mid-American lives, and his classically Midwestern inclination toward the thoughts and words of "common" people. His primary artistic venues have been his WFMT Chicago radio broadcasts and his nine volumes of oral history.

Terkel is an oral historian although he disavows the term. In Ronald J. Grele's 1985 collection *Envelopes of Sound: The Art of Oral History*, he defines the oral historian as one whose works "begin to affect the consciousness of teller and hearer, and of the community itself" and form "a context . . . for the dialogue . . . . [a] dialectic between the telling of the story and the inquisitive and critical mind" (vii). In extended interviews with Tony Parker, published as *Studs Terkel: A Life in Words* (1996), Terkel refers to his works as "memory books" (139) because they impressionistically capture individuals' memories, which may be accurate or inaccurate but are nonetheless "true" in embodying their passions and pains (86). Each of these memories is highly particular, intense, and experiential.

Terkel is an informed, engaged, passionate Midwestern social critic who seeks opportunity and social justice for all. He laments society's focus on material possessions, the increasing isolation and segmentation of America's populations, and the great and growing divide between the "haves" and "have nots." He regrets the loss of a caring, concerned society and the resulting loss of dignity by those at the bottom. He advocates renewed social cohesiveness and celebrates the human spirit, as did his predecessors in oral form, Walt Whitman and CARL SANDBURG.

Terkel is vibrant, enthusiastic, spontaneous. He loves words and ideas and talks unabashedly to himself and anyone who will listen. He speaks for Everyman and feels irony in his personal acclaim for depicting lives of forgotten, unheralded Americans.

As interviewer, Terkel mixes highly conscious techniques and unconscious rapport with a readiness to listen respectfully to individuals expressing widely divergent views and ideologies. Terkel's questions are as soft, broad, and inviting as possible. He avoids "yes" and "no" questions and listens intently, ready with a sympathetic follow-up to encourage free extended talk. Almost inevitably, his subject's eloquent expression of deepest beliefs and passions follows.

Terkel's artistry actively transforms diffuse oral interviews into eloquent literary expression. Selection and compression are key. Raw single interview transcripts typically cover sixty pages but when edited comprise only four to five pages. He seeks moments of feeling tone and passion, moments when subjects fully express themselves intensely, passionately, and poetically.

Terkel stitches individual interviews together with a guiding prologue calling attention to cogent thinkers and recurring themes. He further sets the tone of each interview with spare yet telling thumbnail sketches of the speaker, setting, or situation. References to history, literature, drama, or music provide further dramatic intensity or contrast.

Terkel focuses on situations and experiences common to all of an age, class, or time. Yet while *abstract* issues—war, depression, work, aspirations—are regularly considered, Terkel's subjects always present them in highly specific experiential contexts that make them "real," emotive, and meaningful to readers.

Ultimately, Terkel writes his "memory books" like an impressionist painter paints, juxtaposing luminous moments, similar or opposing colors, patches of emotional light or darkness. He creates what at first seem amorphous, meaningless blotches yet which take on meaning, form, and order in combination with those surrounding them. In the process, plain speech of common Mid-Americans is metamorphosed into intense, graphic moments of emotional truth; life becomes art; prose rises to poetry.

**SELECTED WORKS:** Studs Terkel's oral histories include *Division Street: America* (1967); *Hard Times: An Oral History of the Great Depression* (1970); his National Book Award–nominated *Working: People Talk about What They Do All Day and How They Feel about What They Do* (1974); *American Dreams: Lost and Found* (1980); his Pulitzer Prize–winning *"The Good War": An Oral History of World War Two* (1984); *The Great Divide: Second Thoughts on the American Dream* (1988); *Race: How Blacks and Whites Think and Feel about the American Obsession* (1992); *Coming of Age: The Story of Our Century by Those Who've Lived It* (1995); and *My American Century* (1997). His *Talking to Myself: A Memoir of My Times* (1977) is not an autobiography in the normal sense of the word. While this volume does capture several seminal moments in Terkel's life, it is not chronologically arranged, and it provides considerably more coverage to others than to himself. *Chicago* (1986), a joint effort by Terkel and several photographers, captures the moods and the feel of the city while providing historical and biographical segments. Studs Terkel participates in two extended discussions on oral history in Ronald J. Grele's *Envelopes of Sound: The Art of Oral History* (1985). He appears as interview subject in multiple chapters of Tony Parker's *Studs Terkel: A Life in Words* (1996). Hundreds of audio and video tapes exist, capturing the discussions of Studs Terkel and his subjects.

**FURTHER READING:** Tony Parker's *Studs Terkel: A Life in Words* (1996) provides an abundance of interviews and articles about Terkel along with multiple interviews with him. Ronald J. Grele's compilation of essays and discussions, *Envelopes of Sound: The Art of Oral History* (1985), provides extended expert opinion and discussion on the nature and qualities of oral history. The Studs Terkel Archive, a collection of more than seven thousand hours of interviews now being organized, will be placed with the Chicago Historical Society upon completion in the year 2000.

PHILIP A. GREASLEY          UNIVERSITY OF KENTUCKY

## OCTAVE THANET.
*See* Alice French

## F(RANKLIN) RICHARD THOMAS
August 1, 1940

**BIOGRAPHY:** F. Richard Thomas was born in Evansville, Indiana, the son of Franklin Albert and Lydia (Klausmeier) Thomas, and educated in Indiana public schools. He went to Purdue University with the purpose of becoming a chemical engineer, but in his freshman year he learned that he was destined to become a writer. After wandering Europe for six months between his sophomore and junior years, he returned to marry Sharon Myers in 1962 and to take his AB in English in 1963, followed by an MA in 1964 and a PhD from Indiana University in 1970.

While pursuing a successful academic career, including his current position as professor of American thought and language at Michigan State University, and spending several years in Denmark as a Fulbright Lecturer, Thomas has published extensively as a scholar, a poet, an anthologist, and most recently, a novelist. His scholarship includes *Literary Admirers of Alfred Stieglitz* (1983), a study of the photographer as an influence upon his literary contemporaries, and an edited volume, *Americans in Denmark* (1990), consisting of essays by expatriate artists and writers. As an anthologist and contributor, he coedited *The Day After Yesterday* (1971), a collection of Midwestern poems, with Charles B. Tinkham. He also coedited *Stoney Lonesome* (1971), a collection of Indiana poems, with Roger Pfingston and Richard Pflum, and *The Land Locked Heart* (1980), poems from Indiana, with Michael Wilkerson. He has edited *Centering: a magazine of poetry* since 1973 and is editor-publisher of Years Press. His several hundred poems in anthologies and journals as well as his more than eight volumes of poetry mark him clearly as an Indiana poet and poet of the greater Midwest.

**SIGNIFICANCE:** Thomas describes himself as a domestic poet, the meaning of which becomes clear in each of his collections. He is a poet of people and place and of the close, often ambiguous and mysterious relationship between them. His people are family and friends; his poems are of his father dying in the midst of a vivid dream; of his children on a windswept northern beach; of himself at midlife. His place is that in which life is not merely lived but experienced: the southern Indiana of his youth, the increasingly abstract Michigan of his maturity, the far places that become one in his travels.

In spite of their apparent diversity of focus, Thomas's poems emerge as a remarkably unified vision of the poet's world, as in *Frog Praises Night* (1980), which he presents with commentary on the individual poems addressed to people in his life as well as the extended section "My Self." Presented in the manner of a poetry reading, the collection leads the reader into the individual poems and the oneness of the poet's perception and sensibility. In *Miracles* (1995) the poet leads his reader from memory to imagination and sheer fantasy in the countries of his mind. Thomas is an authentic Midwestern poet who demonstrates most clearly in his work the richness of the Midwestern poetic sensibility.

**SELECTED WORKS:** Thomas's poetry collections include *Frog Praises Night* (1980), *Alive with You This Day* (1980), *Heart Climbing Stairs* (1986), *Corolla, Stamen, and Style* (1986), *The Whole Mustery of the Bregn* (1988), and *Miracles* (1995). His novel *Prism: The Journal of John Fish* (1992) reflects Thomas's interest in the ambiguous wonder of human life.

**FURTHER READING:** Thomas is listed in *Contemporary Authors, New Revision Series* 29 (1990): 418–19, and in *Who's Who in the Midwest, Who's Who in U.S. Writers, Editors, and Poets,* and other sourcebooks. See Marilyn J. Atlas's "Clear Water from a Porcelain Spigot: A Review Essay of *Alive with You this Day,*" in *Society for the Study of Midwestern Literature Newsletter* 10.1 (1980): 44–49, for a valuable reading of Thomas's poetry.

DAVID D. ANDERSON     MICHIGAN STATE UNIVERSITY

## EARL THOMPSON
ca. 1931–November 9, 1978

**BIOGRAPHY:** Earl Thompson, novelist and journalist, was born to unemployed parents in his maternal grandparents' farmhouse on the outskirts of Wichita, Kansas. Little is known of Thompson's early years, although he spent the major portion of his childhood with his grandparents. He attended public schools in Wichita and at the age of fourteen, in early 1945, lied about his age and joined the U.S. Navy. While in the navy he served aboard ship in Shanghai and there observed the social and political upheaval of the Chinese Revolution. He returned to Wichita, but, bored by a succession of petty jobs, he enlisted in the U.S. Army. While in the army Thompson continued his education, read widely, and served in the Korean War.

Thompson attended the School of Journalism at the University of Missouri on the GI Bill. After several newspaper jobs, he moved to New York City and opened a commercial print shop in Brooklyn. There he wrote his first novel, *A Garden of Sand* (1970). Thompson published two other novels, *Tattoo* (1974) and *Caldo Largo* (1976), before his death of a heart attack at the age of forty-seven in Sausalito, California. *A Garden of Sand*, *Tattoo*, and *The Devil to Pay* (1981) constitute his autobiographical Jack Andersen trilogy. Thompson's actual birth date and the names of his close relatives are not known. Thompson was married twice and had three children.

**SIGNIFICANCE:** Rejected by many publishers, *A Garden of Sand* was mainly autobiographical and written in the style of the American naturalists. Because of its mother-son incest theme, it created a sensation when it was finally published. It was nominated for a National Book Award. In the Jack Andersen trilogy, Thompson depicts his childhood and early years, and the working and underclass people he knew in the industrial city of Wichita, Kansas, during the 1930s and 1940s. The realistic sensibility evident in his writing has its roots not only in his early life in Wichita, but in his experience in the army and navy of the 1940s and 1950s. Thompson came of age in the armed forces during World War II and the Korean War, and much of *Tattoo* and *The Devil to Pay* is devoted to this experience. The protagonist of *Caldo Largo*, Thompson's single non-autobiographical novel, is a Korean War veteran motivated by his military experience to live as an outsider.

Thompson's trilogy is important as a literary record of the transition from the culture of the Old West to a Midwestern culture in Kansas, with its relative loss of personal freedom. Notable for its force is the characterization in the trilogy of Jack's grandfather, John MacDeramid. An old frontier settler, rancher, lawman, and farmer with populist convictions, MacDeramid is estranged from the life of the new Midwestern factory city: "The Air Capital," as described by boosters of its aircraft industry. In MacDeramid's lifetime, Kansas changed from a Western, frontier state to a Midwestern place of conformist farmers and urban factory workers, and he rails against the changes in society since his youth. Young Jack's life is a manifestation of this social change. Thompson's novels remain in print and have became internationally known.

**SELECTED WORKS:** Thompson published three novels in his lifetime. *A Garden of Sand* (1970) was his first published fiction, followed by *Tattoo* (1974) and *Caldo Largo* (1976). *The Devil to Pay* was published posthumously in 1981.

**FURTHER READING:** Little has been written about Thompson. Two short pieces are "Backstage with Esquire," appearing in *Esquire* (September 1970), and Tom Page's "The Case of Earl Thompson," in *People's Culture*, n.s. 22 (1994).

TOM L. PAGE            WICHITA STATE UNIVERSITY

## (JAMES) MAURICE THOMPSON
September 9, 1844–February 15, 1901

**BIOGRAPHY:** James Maurice Thompson was born to Diantha (Jaeger) Thompson and Matthew Grigg Thompson in Fairfield, Indiana. His father was pastor of the Primitive Baptist Church. Maurice's brother, Will Henry Thompson, who later wrote two famous poems about the Civil War, was soon born. By 1854 their father inherited a plantation with slaves in Georgia; he left the ministry and had his sons tutored. When the Civil War began, the two boys enlisted in the Confederate Army. Maurice returned, recovering from a wound, found the family destitute, and soon went to Calhoun, Georgia, where he studied engineering, read law, and was admitted to the bar. After Maurice had made some scientific surveys, the two boys walked north, arriving in Crawfordsville, Indiana, where they were received well and were given jobs as engineers on a railroad being constructed. Here Maurice married Alice Lee and settled in town, and the two brothers opened a law office in 1871. For a time Maurice was a partner of his former enemy, General Lew Wallace, and in 1879 he was elected to the Indiana legislature. In 1884 he gave up law for literature but served two terms as Indiana State Geologist. His family wintered in the South. In 1900 Wabash College awarded Maurice a doctor of letters degree, and when he died of pneumonia in 1901, in Crawfordsville, the local G.A.R. post attended his funeral, and local schools observed a day in his honor.

**SIGNIFICANCE:** Thompson published many books: geology, nature sketches, juveniles, literature, and art. He is remembered primarily as a poet and a writer of romances. The first of his imaginative works, *Hoosier Mosaics* (1875), made him famous. It was a collection of gracefully written dialect sketches and stories faithfully depicting Indiana people and places. Thompson wrote two collections of verse, *Songs of Fair Weather* (1883) and *Poems* (1892). These consisted largely of nature poetry of unequal merit but interwoven with delicacy, awe, and wonder. His romantic novels are of the same type and are sentimental, colorful stories of the South. Thompson's short stories depicting his boyhood in a slave state are collected in *Stories of the Cherokee Hills* (1898). The interest of the book lies mostly in externals, but its strong movement and suspense carry the reader. Because of his popularity and his significant literary output, including *Alice of Old Vincennes* (1900), he now found himself one of the leaders of Midwestern literature.

Retiring by nature and declining lectureships, Maurice Thompson was a thorough romanticist, and as a nonresident literary editor of the *Independent* he spoke for morality in literature and against realism. His verse is mostly mediocre; in his novels he was a Southern romanticist working in the North, who helped in the rebirth of romance.

**SELECTED WORKS:** Thompson's best works, *Alice of Old Vincennes* (1900) and *Hoosier Mosaics* (1875), are his most Midwestern and most lasting literary efforts. *A Banker of Bankersville* (1886) and *Rosalynde's Lovers* (1901) are also set in Indiana. *Stories of the Cherokee Hills* (1898) offers short stories dealing with life in the South. *Songs of Fair Weather* (1883) and *Poems* (1892) are Thompson's forays into poetry. Interestingly, he earned great nonliterary fame through his publication of two volumes on archery: *The Witchery of Archery: A Complete Manual of Archery* (1878) and *How to Train in Archery: Being a Complete Study of the York Round* (1879). Thompson wrote the second volume on archery with his brother Will.

**FURTHER READING:** Many books contain sections on Maurice Thompson; one of the first was Meredith Nicholson's *The Hoosiers* (1900). Then came obituaries in the press, such as the *Indianapolis Sentinel* (February 16, 1901) and the *Indianapolis News* (February 15 and February 16, 1901). Charles F. Smith included him in *Reminiscences and Sketches* (1908), and Dorothy R. Russo and Thelma L. Sullivan covered him in detail in their *Bibliographical Studies of Seven Authors of Crawfordsville, Indiana* (1952). Louis D. Rubin did something of the same in *A Bibliographical Guide to the Study of Southern Literature* (1969). George A. Schumaker offered *Maurice Thompson, Archer and Author* (1968), and Otis B. Wheeler published *The Literary Career of Maurice Thompson* (1965). Also, Mary Gaither issued a new edition of *Alice of Old Vincennes* in 1985. In addition, a number of letters of Thompson can be found in the Indiana State Library manuscript collection.

ARTHUR W. SHUMAKER          DEPAUW UNIVERSITY

## EMMA SHORE THORNTON
July 10, 1908–March 24, 1998

**BIOGRAPHY:** Emma Shore was born to Henry W. and Bertha (Lott) Shore on a farm in Ransom Township near Rushmore in southwestern Minnesota. When she was ten, her family moved to Worthington, Minnesota, where most of her public schooling took place. After graduating from Morningside College in Sioux City, Iowa, in 1930, she taught English and history for three years in Parker, South Dakota. She also worked with historical documents for the WPA and was executive secretary of the YWCA in Newton, Iowa.

In 1936 she married George Thornton, a doctoral student in psychology at the University of Nebraska. They spent 1939 through 1944 at Purdue University. During this period, while participating in a university writing group, she started to write. Poetry was her primary medium though she also wrote prose, some of the latter in collaboration. While at Purdue, the Thorntons adopted their first child, James. The family then spent two years in Ann Arbor, Michigan, while George obtained a law degree from the University of Michigan. During this sojourn, Emma taught at a country school. In 1946 the Thorntons moved to East Lansing, Michigan.

The Thorntons' second child, Becky, was adopted in 1948.

From 1961 until her retirement in 1976 she taught in the Department of American Thought and Language at Michigan State University. She retired as an assistant professor emerita of that institution. Emma Thornton died of ALS, also known as Lou Gehrig's disease, at her home in East Lansing.

**SIGNIFICANCE:** Thornton's poems resonate exquisitely with Midwestern place and person. In a review article of her poetry in the *Worthington* (Minnesota) *Globe* (March 30, 1982), PAUL GRUCHOW called her poems "sophisticated, zestful, affectionate, curious about everything, possessed of a sense of humor, thoughtful, modest . . . ." The reviewer continued: "[Her poems are] artful, but in a completely unpretentious way. They are simple, direct, unsentimental, unflinchingly plainspoken." In other words, they typify the Midwestern persona. Her nonfiction works focus essentially on Midwestern grassroots people who might otherwise have remained in obscurity.

**SELECTED WORKS:** Thornton's works include *Heirs and Assigns Forever: The Life of Robert Shore, Minnesota Pioneer* (1950); *Ideas Have Consequences: 125 Years of the Liberal Tradition in the Lansing Area* (1973); *Poems: A Collection of Poems by Emma Shore Thornton* (1975); *The Stone in My Pocket: New and Collected Poems* (1981); *A Populist Assault: Sarah E. Van De Vort Emery on American Democracy, 1862–1895,* with Pauline Gordon Adams (1982); *Loleta Dawson Fyan and the Evergreen Tree: The Story of Library Extension in Michigan* (forthcoming); and *This Spiral of Life: Poems* (1994). All of Thornton's articles deal with Midwestern themes and people. Several were coauthored with Pauline Adams.

**FURTHER READING:** Very little extended criticism exists of Emma Shore Thornton's writing. Her papers are held by George Thornton.

PAULINE GORDON ADAMS

MICHIGAN STATE UNIVERSITY

## JAMES THURBER

December 8, 1894–November 4, 1961

**BIOGRAPHY:** James Thurber, one of the great American humorists, was born in Columbus, Ohio, the city with which his name has most frequently been associated in

**James Thurber, 1958.**
Photo by Douglas Glass. Courtesy of Rosemary Thurber

spite of his long Eastern residence and employment at the *New Yorker*. His parents, Charles L. and Mary (Fisher) Thurber, were of pioneer Ohio ancestry, although his father was born in Indiana. His father was interested in the stage and the law and was a professional Republican political activist for most of his life. His mother was of the wealthy, prominent Fisher family of Columbus. James was the second of three sons. When James was seven, the family moved briefly to Falls Church, Virginia, after Charles took a minor post in the McKinley administration. There, James was blinded in his left eye by an arrow shot by his brother, Robert. Eye problems were to plague him for the rest of his life, leading ultimately to his blindness.

The family returned to Columbus in 1903, where James attended the public schools and in 1913 entered Ohio State University. There he began writing for the *Ohio State Lantern*, the campus paper, and the *Sun-Dial*, the student monthly. He became friends with Elliott Nugent at Ohio State and became the *Sun-Dial's* editor early in 1918, but he left the university in June 1918 without a degree, unwilling to meet his science, drill, and gym requirements. Rejected by his draft board and by enlistment officers, he became a code clerk for the State Department, first in Washington and then at the American embassy in Paris. He returned to Columbus in 1920 and became first a clerk in a state office and then a reporter for the *Columbus Dispatch*. He also began writing and directing musical comedies for the Scarlet Mask Club of Ohio State University. He worked on five between 1921 and 1925.

On May 20, 1922, he married Althea Adams in a fashionable wedding that surprised his friends. She gave birth to a daughter, Rosemary, on October 7, 1931. She and James were divorced in 1935. Thurber continued writing for the *Dispatch* until 1924, including a critical literary column "Credos and Curios." When the column was canceled in 1924, he resigned to become a freelance writer, served as Columbus correspondent for the *Christian Science Monitor*, and wrote political features. In May 1925 he went to France to write a projected novel, but it would not come, and in April 1926 he returned to New York, where he became a reporter for the *Evening Post*. The next year he met E. B. White and Harold Ross and went to work for the *New Yorker*, a move that was to shape and direct his career.

In 1929 Thurber published his first book, *Is Sex Necessary?* in collaboration with E. B. White, and in 1931 he published his first cartoons in the *New Yorker* as well as his second book, *The Owl in the Attic and Other Perplexities*, a collection of pieces that had previously appeared in the *New Yorker*. That pattern, together with his growing interest in cartoon illustrations, marked the course of his career through the next decade. In 1933 he published *My Life and Hard Times*, and on June 25, 1935, he married Helen Muriel Wismer. Thurber published his most famous work, "The Secret Life of Walter Mitty," in the *New Yorker* in the March 18, 1939, issue. At the end of the decade he had a series of gallery showings of his drawings. His increasing eye trouble led to eye operations for cataracts and trachoma, and ultimately to a nervous breakdown as he feared that he could no longer work.

During the 1940s Thurber's writing, drawing, and publication rate continued apace, although his eyesight continued to deteriorate. In 1945 he published *The Thurber Carnival*,

and in the early 1950s, as Senator Joseph McCarthy and McCarthyism began to cast their long shadows over the arts, publishing, and educational worlds, he became outspokenly opposed to both, particularly on the Ohio State University campus.

Although by 1947 Thurber could no longer see well enough to draw and his production rate began to drop off, he published some of his best writing and drawings, including *The Thirteen Clocks* (1950), *Thurber's Dogs* (1955), and his memoir, *The Years with Ross* (1959). His particular combination of words and line drawings in his inimitably wry style began to attract increasing attention and garner rising numbers of honors. On October 4, 1961, in New York, he was stricken with a blood clot on the brain, and, although surgery was successful, he died of pneumonia on November 4, 1961. He is buried in Green Lawn Cemetery in Columbus.

SIGNIFICANCE: Although Thurber disliked comparisons between his work and that of others, especially MARK TWAIN, the relationship is clear. Thurber's best work is darkly humorous, and his people are largely antiheroic misfits, the best example of whom is Walter Mitty. Thurber's characters are the type who people the banks of Twain's Mississippi and later the streets and shops of SHERWOOD ANDERSON's *Winesburg, Ohio*, and other Midwestern towns and cities. Thurber's people are drawn from life, particularly from members of the Thurber family in Columbus in the early years of the twentieth century.

Two posthumous collections of Thurber's works, *Credos and Curios* (1962) and *Thurber and Company* (1966), have been published as well as a number of biographies and critical biographies, and many of his other works have been reissued. Collectively, these provide testimony to the durability of his work and the universality of its appeal. In both prose and drawings, Thurber created a unique world of his own, rooted in the Midwestern reality of Columbus in his youth. Transcending that reality is his perennial little man, with the little dog that may be his only friend. He speaks to and for his age, with clear insight into the chaos of the larger world that threatens him. Thurber's work is a microcosm of the human condition; the chaos that threatens has always existed and will continue, even as his people, the Walter Mittys of every age, continue to muddle through, buoyed by the few momentary triumphs that enable them to go on.

**SELECTED WORKS:** No complete collected edition of Thurber's works has yet appeared, although *The Works of James Thurber* was published in 1985 in one volume. It includes ninety-two stories. His best works include *The Owl in the Attic and Other Perplexities* (1931); *My Life and Hard Times* (1933); *The Male Animal*, a play, with Elliott Nugent (1940); *The Thurber Carnival* (1945); *The Thirteen Clocks* (1950); and *The Years with Ross* (1959). Other important titles are *Fables for Our Time* (1940), *Thurber Country* (1953), and *Further Fables for Our Time* (1956). He published a total of twenty-seven books, including two posthumously.

**FURTHER READING:** Thurber has been the subject of a number of biographies and essays, and he plays a prominent part in most studies of American humor. Among the best biographical and critical works are Robert E. Morsberger's *James Thurber* (1964); Richard C. Tobias's *The Art of James Thurber* (1969); Burton Bernstein's *Thurber: A Biography* (1975); and Charles S. Holmes's *The Clocks of Columbus* (1972). Also useful are Sara Eleanora Toombs's *James Thurber: A Research Guide* (1986, 1988), a doctoral dissertation, and Robert Emmet Long's *James Thurber* (1988). The James Thurber Collection is in the Ohio State University Library in Columbus.

DAVID D. ANDERSON    MICHIGAN STATE UNIVERSITY

## EUNICE (HAMMOND) TIETJENS
July 29, 1884–September 6, 1944
(Eloise Briton)

**BIOGRAPHY:** Eunice Hammond, a Midwestern poet, playwright, and journalist, a promoter of the "new" poetry movement and longtime affiliate of HARRIET MONROE and *Poetry*, was born in Chicago to Idea Louise (Strong) Hammond, a talented painter and lifelong world traveler, and William Andrew Hammond, a prominent banker. Eunice was the eldest of four children. She attended schools in north suburban Evanston until she was thirteen when her father drowned and her mother took the children to Europe.

She lived in Paris, Geneva, and Dresden and became fluent in several Romance languages. Eunice enrolled in courses at the College de France and the Sorbonne and graduated from the Froebel Kindergarten Institute of Dresden.

Still in Europe at nineteen, she married Paul Tietjens, an American composer, creator of the score for L. FRANK BAUM's *The Wizard of Oz*. Together, they returned to the United States, briefly living in Michigan and New York. She gave birth to two daughters, Idea and Janet. The eldest, Idea, died at four. Their marriage disintegrated and the year after their daughter's death, they separated. In 1914 she and her two-year-old returned to Evanston.

For a short period she conducted a French Kindergarten in Evanston but quickly became involved in creative writing, particularly in poetry. Friends with Margery Currey and FLOYD DELL, she became a significant member of the Chicago Renaissance. EDGAR LEE MASTERS, a lifelong friend, gave her a copy of the Bhagavad Gita, reinforcing her belief that spirituality and beauty were of utmost importance. During that period she also met Harriet Monroe, began working on the *Poetry* staff, and formed friendships with CARL SANDBURG, ARTHUR DAVISON FICKE, and SARA TEASDALE. Several of her poems appeared in *Poetry*.

In 1916 she traveled with her mother, first to the West Coast and then to China. The idea was attempting to keep Eunice from publishing overtly sexual poetry which prompted her, for a short while, to publish under the name Eloise Briton. Tietjens's poetry blossomed during this period, and *Profiles from China*, her best book of poetry, appeared in 1917. These poems were written in free verse. Another book of poetry, poems written earlier, *Body and Raiment*, appeared in 1919. By then, Eunice Tietjens had stopped publishing under her pseudonym.

Later in 1916, she returned to her editorial duties at *Poetry*. She wrote various features for the *Chicago Daily News*. After World War I began, she requested to be sent to Europe as a war correspondent. By October 1917, she was in Paris and did not return to the Midwest until 1919. It was during this time that she put *Body and Raiment* together. She and her daughter spent the following summer in a shack at the Indiana dunes, which serves as the setting for *Jake* (1921), her only adult novel.

Cloyd Head, playwright, became her husband and lifelong collaborator in 1920. They had two children, a son, Marshall, and a daughter who died at birth. Together they lived in the Chicago area. During this period at the University of Chicago's Poetry Club, she met many younger Midwestern poets, among them George Dillon, Elizabeth Madox Roberts, Janet Lewis, Elder Olsen, and GLENWAY WESCOTT, and she supported their work. In 1922 she and Cloyd Head stayed at the MacDowell Colony in Petersboro, New Hampshire, and she became closely associated with Mary and Padraic Colum, Edwin Arlington Robinson, and Elinor Wylie.

In 1923 Tietjens was back in Paris, where she met Ezra Pound and Ford Madox Ford. Later, she and her husband went south to the Riviera and then Tunisia. In 1925 they returned to America and settled in Rockland County, New York. Norman Bel Geddes produced the play *Arabesque*, which she and Head wrote, but the play closed in less than a month. In 1926 they were once again in North Africa after which Tietjens put together her anthology, *Poetry of the Orient* (1928). They returned to Chicago in 1927 because Head was offered the position of business manager for the Goodman Memorial Theatre at the Art Institute of Chicago. Tietjens wrote some children's literature and compiled a new collection of her own poetry, *Leaves in Windy Weather* (1929). Shortly after, they left Chicago again to live in the South Seas, returning to find Chicago much affected by the Great Depression. They then moved to Florida, where between 1933 and 1935 Tietjens taught at the University of Miami. After a long, painful struggle with cancer, she returned to Chicago, where she died in 1944. At her request, her ashes were strewn in the Indiana dunes.

**SIGNIFICANCE:** While Tietjens's novel, *Jake,* is an interesting exploration of passionate love, filial obligations, jealousy, and control and is partially set in the Indiana dunes, her significance is as a poet who helped establish free verse, legitimize new subjects, and increase the international flavor and geographical focus of the 1910s poetry renaissance. Tietjens wrote and published articles on polyphonic verse and primitive chanting, contemporary issues of her day. Her poems, such as "The Bacchante to Her Babe," "The Drug Clerk," and "The Steam Shovel," were published in newspapers and journals and were anthologized by editors, such as William S. Braithwaite and Harriet Monroe. Tietjens's writing was translated into French and German. She was the first of the *Poetry* staff, other than Ezra Pound, then living in England, to leave America. As her engagement ring helped pay for the publication of MARGARET ANDERSON'S *Little Review*, so her love of poetry, the Midwest, and the world helped an era find its wings.

Many of her most successful poems capture the vividness of people and places. In her introductory poem to *Body and Raiment*, "A Plaint of Complexity," the poem's persona complains about having too many selves to know the one, about being a child of too many cities. This persona acknowledges a Chicago self, modern, technological, feminist, androgynous, fragmented, and lonely.

In *Profiles from Home: Sketches in Free Verse of People and Things Seen in the United States* (1925), Tietjens explores her America. Tietjens's introductory poem is situated in California, and she divides the poem into three sections, "From Plains and Valleys," "From the Wilds," and "From the Cities." In this volume, she tries to capture ethnicity, as in "The Jew," and she is very aware that different spaces demand different tones. "The Moon on Caravans" is set in a camping area in Iowa which connects Montana to Chicago and Indiana to Denver. "In a Shoe Shop" takes place in Wisconsin, and "In the Wheat Country" explores Kansas from a plush seat on a train. She finds beauty in a farm wife from Indiana in "The Visit," examining the language of place and the vitality that is everywhere if one is able to see it. Tietjens moves between classes, personalities, and locales. In poems such as "My Grandmother," a narrator sees her grandmother's face in her own and analyzes how New England and Illinois come together and form her. Whether examining people in the dunes or in the North Country, whether exploring urban society life, a Chicago skyscraper, the countryside, baseball, the theater, or a New York politician, Tietjens is at home with multicultural America and its diverse landscape. Simultaneously Midwestern, American, and international, Eunice Tietjens explores identity and geography in all of her art.

**SELECTED WORKS:** Tietjens's major work includes four books of verse: *Profiles from China* (1917), *Body and Raiment* (1919), *Profiles* *from Home* (1925), and *Leaves in Windy Weather* (1929). Her novel, *Jake* (1921), is another major work, as is her anthology of Eastern poetry, *Poetry of the Orient* (1928). Her autobiography, *The World at My Shoulder* (1938), is an invaluable resource on her life as well as the history of the Chicago Renaissance. Her play, *Arabesque*, written with Cloyd Head, also deserves attention. Tietjens's children's literature received much praise from her contemporaries. In 1932 *Boy of the South Seas* (1931) won the prestigious Newbery Honor Book Award. Among her children's texts one should look at *Boy of the Desert* (1928); *The Romance of Antar* (1929); *The Jaw-Breaker's Alphabet* (1930), written with her daughter Janet; and *The Gingerbread Boy* (1932).

**FURTHER READING:** A fine unpublished dissertation by Willie Nell Stallings Love, University of Maryland (1960), examines both Tietjens's life and work. The Newberry Library in Chicago has a collection of her letters and manuscripts. Harvard University Library, the Library of Congress, the University of Chicago Library, and Yale also have manuscripts and letters.

MARILYN J. ATLAS                    OHIO UNIVERSITY

## SUSAN ALLEN TOTH
June 24, 1940

**BIOGRAPHY:** Susan Allen Toth was born and raised in the Midwestern college town of Ames, Iowa, the home of Iowa State University where her parents, Edward Douglas Allen, an economics professor, and her mother, Hazel Allen, an English professor, were both employed. Toth later attended Smith College, Northampton, Massachusetts, majoring in English and graduating *magna cum laude* in 1961. She subsequently received an MA in English at the University of California–Berkeley in 1963 and a PhD in English at the University of Minnesota in 1969. Since 1969 she has been a member of the English faculty at Macalester College in St. Paul, Minnesota, where she teaches American literature, modern and historical fiction, women's literature, and creative writing.

**SIGNIFICANCE:** *Blooming: A Small-Town Girlhood* (1981) is a classic account of a small-town girlhood in the American Midwest of the 1950s. It represents Toth's fullest treatment of the Midwest, as she perceptively, and often humorously, recounts her childhood and ado-

Susan Allen Toth.
Photo © Nancy Crampton

lescence in Ames, Iowa. From the vantage point of distance and maturity, Toth recognizes the provincialism, the lack of diversity, and the potentially enervating routine of small-town life in the Midwest; but unlike SINCLAIR LEWIS and EDGAR LEE MASTERS, Toth also discovers that such disadvantages are far outweighed by the constructive influence of familiar places, friends, and social rituals, all of which contribute to a sense of security, permanence, and identity. The sequel, *Ivy Days: Making My Way Out East* (1984), is primarily an account of Toth's undergraduate days at Smith College. The Midwest figures indirectly, though significantly, in the work as Toth poignantly recalls her homesickness and voices a persistent sense of social and geographical dislocation. Still, whatever her perceived sense of inadequacy, the values of community, friendship, personal integrity, and self-responsibility nurtured back home in the Midwest combine with her own intelligence and unflagging self-motivation to enable her social and academic success at Smith.

Currently residing in Minnesota, just one state north of her native Iowa, Toth's personal journey has come full circle. In the many stories and essays written since *Ivy Days*, Toth has dealt less frequently and directly with the Midwest. Still, in such essays as "How to Prepare for Your High-School Reunion," Toth returns to the small-town Midwest of her childhood. She herself often writes about the landscape, folkways, and simple pleasures of her adopted state. Toth credits E. B. White and Sarah Orne Jewett as the greatest influences on her own prose.

**SELECTED WORKS:** Toth's best-known works are *Blooming: A Small-Town Girlhood* (1981) and *Ivy Days: Making My Way Out East* (1984). Her collection *How to Prepare for Your High-School Reunion and Other Midlife Musings* (1988) includes new and previously published essays on subjects ranging from picking raspberries and attending movies to garage sales, learning to ski, and Minnesota weather. *My Love Affair with England: A Traveler's Memoir* (1992), *England As You Like It: An Independent Traveler's Companion* (1995), and *England for All Seasons* (1997) recount Toth's travels in England over a thirty-year period.

**FURTHER READING:** Regrettably, Toth has received little critical attention, though Patricia L. Sharda's essay "Susan Allen Toth," in the *Dictionary of Literary Biography Yearbook* (1986): 335–42, does provide a perceptive analysis of *Blooming* and *Ivy Days*, together with an interview with Toth.

MICHAEL WENTWORTH
UNIVERSITY OF NORTH CAROLINA AT WILMINGTON

# ROBERT TRAVER.
*See* John Donaldson Voelker

# WILLIAM LEWIS TROGDON.
*See* William Least Heat-Moon

# SOJOURNER TRUTH
ca. 1797–November 26, 1883
**BIOGRAPHY:** An integral figure in the cause of abolition and women's rights, Sojourner Truth was born a slave, named Isabella, in Hurley, New York, one of twelve or thirteen children of her parents, James and Elizabeth. Sold several times to New York Dutch owners before she was a teenager, raped by one of her masters, she gave birth to five children from a slave marriage to a man named Thomas. In her later years, however, she would say that she gave birth to thirteen children during her lifetime. In 1827 she fled with one of her children after her master reneged on a promise to free her one year before an emancipation statute went into effect in New York. Soon after, she settled in New York City as a domestic, taking the name of her employer, Van Wagenen.

In 1843, after an intense involvement with evangelical sects, Truth again changed her name to reflect what she saw as God's mission for her. To support herself as an itinerant preacher, in 1850 she dictated her autobiography, because she was illiterate throughout her life, and sold copies as she traveled first through Connecticut and Massachusetts and then throughout the Midwest. In 1863 she gained nationwide attention when Harriet Beecher Stowe published an article in the *Atlantic Monthly* titled "Sojourner Truth, The Libyan Sibyl," which recounted a meeting the two had had ten years earlier. The next year Sojourner Truth met ABRAHAM LINCOLN, and after the Civil War she led a campaign to have African Americans settle in the Midwest.

From the 1850s until her death, Truth resided in various locales in the Midwest, settling permanently in Battle Creek, Michigan. At the same time she fought racist social practices and legal policies against African Americans, suffering beatings on several occasions as a result. She also spoke out ardently on behalf of women's rights. At a women's rights convention in Akron, Ohio, in 1851, she gave her most famous speech, which was inaccurately transcribed in Southern dialect by Frances Dana George, and in 1858, during an Indiana speech, she bared her breast to prove that she was a woman. After a long illness, she died in Battle Creek.

**SIGNIFICANCE:** Sojourner Truth was reported to be a dynamic speaker whose actions and words helped to vitalize both the women's rights movement and the nineteenth-century civil rights movement in the North, particularly in the Midwest. Despite the inaccuracies in transcriptions of her speeches and the gaps in her *Narrative* resulting from her transcriber Olive Gilbert's attempts to censor some details "from motives of delicacy" (Washington xxx), a reader of her works may still sense the power of her oratory in cutting through social conventions and making commonsense pleas, such as her famous line from the Akron speech, "Ar'n't I a woman?" (Washington 117). Her literary influence on the Midwest may be slight, but her social influence is significant, for she helped extend to the Midwest two of the leading civil rights causes of the nineteenth and twentieth centuries.

**SELECTED WORKS:** Olive Gilbert's *Narrative of Sojourner Truth* (1850) is the major work associated with Sojourner Truth; Frances W. Titus added an appendix in the 1884 edition which included speeches by and about Truth. Margaret Washington has edited a critical edition of Truth's *Narrative* and speeches (1993). Several of her speeches are frequently anthologized in American literature and women's literature anthologies.

**FURTHER READING:** Harriet Beecher Stowe's influential article on Truth is "Sojourner Truth, The Libyan Sibyl," in the *Atlantic Monthly* (April 1863): 473–81. Reliable biographies of Sojourner Truth include *Sojourner Truth: A Life, a Symbol* (1996), by Nell Irvin Painter; *Sojourner Truth: Slave, Prophet, Legend* (1993), by Carleton Mabee with Susan Mabee Newhouse; and *Glorying in Tribulation: The Lifework of Sojourner Truth* (1994), by Erlene Stetson and Linda David. For a larger perspective of Truth and other abolitionists involved in the women's movement, see Jean Fagan Yellin's *Women and Sisters: The Antislavery Feminists in American Culture* (1989). Primary materials on Truth are to be found in several locations, principally in the Detroit Public Library, the Bentley Historical Library at the University of Michigan, and the Library of Congress.

ROBERT DUNNE

CENTRAL CONNECTICUT STATE UNIVERSITY

## JIM TULLY

June 3, 1888–June 22, 1947

**BIOGRAPHY:** Jim Tully, novelist and journalist, was born in a log cabin near St. Marys, Auglaize County, Ohio, to an Irish American laboring family which had come to Ohio to dig canals in the mid-nineteenth century. His father, James, was a laborer; his mother Bridget (Lawler) Tully, died before he was six, and he received his only formal education between six and eleven in a Catholic orphanage in Cincinnati. Between eleven and twelve he was a bound-boy on an Auglaize County

farm. At twelve he ran away and was in turn a hobo, a laborer, a link heater in a chain factory, a circus roustabout, and a prize fighter. Always a voracious reader, when he was knocked unconscious for twenty-four hours at age twenty-one, he decided to write.

While working as a tree surgeon, a chain inspector, and finally a reporter in Akron, Ohio, Tully wrote his first novel, *Emmett Lawler* (1922), which was one hundred thousand words long in one paragraph. Discovered by Rupert Hughes, who taught him paragraphing, and by H. L. Mencken and Charlie Chaplin, he was simultaneously a novelist, journalist, scriptwriter, ghost writer, and press agent, a regular contributor to many journals, and by 1942, the author of thirty volumes of fiction, autobiography, biography, screenplays, and some nine hundred stories, sketches, and articles in journals as diverse as *Esquire, Photoplay*, and the *American Mercury*. Married twice, he died of heart disease at his home in Holmby Hills overlooking Toluca Lake. He is buried in Forest Lawn Cemetery, in Glendale, California, among stars and tycoons.

**SIGNIFICANCE:** Tully's best fiction is rooted firmly in his Ohio boyhood and his years on the road. Strongly autobiographical, his writings celebrate the people he knew and admired in his youth, people whose origins were as humble as his own. His works, long out of print in the United States, were considered American classics in the Soviet Union. Particularly important is his recreation of the experiences and people whom a later generation would describe as proletarian. Those novels set in St. Marys, Ohio, in the last years of the nineteenth century demonstrate the fate of the unskilled workers—his father was a ditchdigger and his grandfather was a canaldigger—who are left behind as western Ohio becomes a stable society in the years before the onset of industrialism.

**SELECTED WORKS:** His novels, all autobiographical, include *Emmett Lawler* (1922), *Beggars of Life* (1924), *Jarnegan* (1925), *Black Boy* (1926), *Circus Parade* (1927), *Shanty Irish* (1928), *Shadows of Men* (1929), *Blood on the Moon* (1931), *Ladies in the Parlor* (1934), and *Biddy Brogan's Boy* (1942).

**FURTHER READING:** No books and few essays on Tully and his works have appeared, although much of his short fiction appeared in the *American Mercury* and most of his longer works were widely reviewed. Recent studies are David D. Anderson's "A Portrait of Jim Tully: An Ohio Hobo and Hollywood," in the *Society for the Study of Midwestern Literature Newsletter* 12 (Spring 1982), and Anderson's "An Ohio Boyhood in Jim Tully's Fiction," in the *Society for the Study of Midwestern Literature Newsletter* 24 (Fall 1994). His papers are largely in the library of the University of Southern California. Princeton University Library and the University of Virginia Library also have substantial collections. Supplementary material is held at the St. Marys, Ohio, Public Library.

David D. Anderson   Michigan State University

## FREDERICK JACKSON TURNER
November 14, 1861–March 14, 1932
**BIOGRAPHY:** Frederick Jackson Turner was born in Portage on the Wisconsin frontier to Andrew Jackson and Mary Olivia (Hanford) Turner. He enrolled in the University of Wisconsin in 1878 and received a doctorate in history from the Johns Hopkins University in 1890. He then returned to the University of Wisconsin, eventually becoming head of the Department of History. In Madison, Turner married Caroline Mae Sherwood in 1889, and the couple had three children, Dorothy, Jackson, and Mae. As his fame as an historian grew, Turner repeatedly turned down positions at other universities until he moved to Harvard University in 1910, the year he served as president of the American Historical Association. He left Harvard in 1924, returning to Madison for three years, until age and ill health persuaded him to become a research associate at the Huntington Library in California, where he remained until his death in 1932. Turner was posthumously awarded the Pulitzer Prize in 1933 for *The Significance of Sections in American History*.

**SIGNIFICANCE:** Frederick Jackson Turner has been widely considered one of the United States' foremost historians. His writings on the frontier and geographic sections in American history broke new ground in historical studies and have generated continuing vigorous debate.

Turner's favorite section was his native Midwest, and his writings show an undisguisable, sometimes partisan, love for that re-

gion. He was one of the first historians to consider the Midwest a vital area of study for American history, yet he insisted that the region formed only a part of the American experience. While Turner wrote mainly about the Midwest and the frontier, he was continually interested in the whole of American history, and he studied the Midwest as only a single, if somewhat overlooked, ingredient of that story.

Turner is best known for his frontier thesis, which he first stated in 1893 at the World's Columbian Exposition in Chicago and spent much of his career expanding and defending. In the Midwestern frontier, Turner saw many elements he considered vital to American character: abundant free land, struggle against a "savage," purifying environment, frequent migrations, and a vigorous, individualistic democracy fostered by a lack of "civilized" control. Turner discounted the influences of the East and Europe and saw Westerners' isolation from these areas as protecting their egalitarian values. To disenchanted Easterners and Europeans, the frontier was a safety valve that offered new opportunity while stripping these settlers of their Old World airs. While he emphasized the "common man," Turner too often glazed over the subjugation of Indians, and he also saw the influx of new immigrants in the late nineteenth and early twentieth centuries as threatening *his* Midwest. In this light, many see Turner's Midwest as less democratic than he had suggested.

Turner never intended his work to explain fully the Midwest or the frontier. Critics point out that his romantic language and unsupported statements accomplish that intention for him. Yet Turner wanted only to stimulate interest in Western history and provide a base from which others could continue his work. He found the writing of history very frustrating, and he preferred instructing students on the value of Western history so that they might build upon his foundation.

**SELECTED WORKS:** While Turner promised eager publishers myriad books, he produced a relatively small body of published works. These books are essentially collections of Turner's earlier essays in slightly modified form. *The Frontier in American History* (1920) is considered his most important book, containing his famous 1893 frontier thesis and other articles about the Midwest and the frontier. *The Significance of Sections in American History* (1932) is his other noteworthy work. Turner labored on *The United States: 1830–1850: The Nation and Its Sections* at the time of his death, and it was published posthumously in 1935.

**FURTHER READING:** Ray Allen Billington's *Frederick Jackson Turner: Historian, Scholar, Teacher* (1973) is the major biography, using Turner's abundant academic and personal papers. Richard Hofstadter's *The Progressive Historians: Turner, Beard, Parrington* (1968) is also notable. Writings on Turner's frontier thesis are voluminous. Billington's *The American Frontier: Attack and Defense* (1958) provides an early overview. Vernon E. Mattson and William E. Marion's annotated *Frederick Jackson Turner: A Reference Guide* (1985) is a chronological guide to all of Turner's writings and the literature about him and his works up to 1982. The one-hundredth anniversary of Turner's frontier thesis in 1993 brought reappraisals of Western history and of Turner's views about the West. John Mack Faragher's "The Frontier Trail: Rethinking Turner and Reimagining the American West," *American Historical Review* (February 1993), is a good starting point. "New" Western historians largely reject Turner's thesis, instead seeing much organized settlement of the West and stressing the importance of the West's many ethnic groups. Patricia Nelson Limerick's *The Legacy of Conquest: The Unbroken Past of the American West* (1987) and Richard White's *"It's Your Misfortune and None of My Own": A New History of the American West* (1991) are the most notable examples. Finally, see Stephen Aron's "Lessons in Conquest: Towards a Greater Western History," *Pacific Historical Review* (May 1994), which advocates a combination of the views of Turner and the new Western historians. Turner willed the Henry E. Huntington Library, San Marino, California, all of his letters, documents, and books. Much smaller holdings can be found at the Houghton Library, Harvard University, the State Historical Society of Wisconsin, and the Archives of the University of Wisconsin.

STEVEN N. ALLEN            UNIVERSITY OF KENTUCKY

# MARK TWAIN.
*See* Samuel Langhorne Clemens

# JONATHAN LOUIS VALIN
November 23, 1948

**BIOGRAPHY:** The son of Sigmund and Marcella (Fink) Valin, Jonathan was born and raised in Cincinnati. He attended the University of Chicago (MA, 1974) and Washington University in St. Louis (doctoral study from 1976 to 1979). On January 3, 1971, Jonathan married Katherine Brockhaus. The Valins live in Cincinnati. *Extenuating Circumstances* (1989) won the Shamus Award for best novel.

**SIGNIFICANCE:** Jonathan Valin's Harry Stoner series of detective novels may form the best fictional portrait of Cincinnati, Ohio's Queen City. It is ironic that a city which, as John Clubbe notes in *Cincinnati Observed* (1992), prides itself on its traditional propriety is best understood through the crime fiction not only of Valin, but of Jim DeBrosse, A. M. Pyle, and Sharon Gwyn Short. Valin and his protagonist, Harry Stoner, know their city and record with geographic accuracy what Alvin Harlow in *The Serene Cincinnatians* (1950) called its "apparently inconsistent tangle of past, present and future" (16). In an interview with *Cincinnati Magazine* (1986), Valin distinguishes between the importance of "a sense of place" in detective fiction and the Cincinnati in his head ("The Mystery Men" [March 1986]: 79). The Cincinnati in Valin's head is slanted toward those who have been victimized by the rich and powerful. A passage describing Mt. Adams in *Day of Wrath* (1982) illustrates Valin's slant: "Every evening a blonde haze hung above the hill—the distillation of all the bar lights and restaurant lights and house lights on the hill's ritzy peak. Half-way down the slope, the money stopped and the lights began to go out" (95). Valin persists in paying attention to the often violent conflict between those at the top and those at the bottom.

**SELECTED WORKS:** The titles of Valin's novels often have double meanings that reflect both the social and prophetic dimensions of his work. *Final Notice* (1980) refers both to a neighborhood library's overdue book notice and the missed warning signals of a serial killer. In 1982 *Day of Wrath* used a teenage runaway to chart the apocalyptic implications of Cincinnati's rigid class structure. *Fire Lake* (1987) uses the title of a Bob Seger rock song's reference to the Book of Revelation to explore the aftereffects of the 1960s counterculture. *Missing* (1995) refers not only to a missing person but to the element that may be missing in what Edmund White in *States of Desire* (1980) calls his "hometown's" obsession with respectability: "the most one might ask for is compassion for those never or no longer respectable" (173).

**FURTHER READING:** In addition to book reviews and the *Cincinnati Magazine* article mentioned above, the following are useful: "Scene of the Crime . . . Novel," *Ohio Magazine* 18.10 (March 1996): 28–33; an interview with David A. Bowman in *Armchair Detective* 20.3 (Summer 1987): 228–38; and Janet Wiehe's "Jonathan Valin: Stellar Mystery Writer," in *Ohioana Quarterly* 26.1 (Spring 1983): 4. There is no information at this time concerning the repository of Valin's papers.

JAMES M. HUGHES          WRIGHT STATE UNIVERSITY

## CARL VAN DOREN
September 10, 1885–July 18, 1950

**BIOGRAPHY:** A popular and respected literary historian who helped bring critical attention to American fiction during the first half of this century, a time when American letters were commonly regarded as a minor offshoot of the British tradition, Carl Van Doren was born in Hope, Illinois, the eldest of five sons of Charles Lucius and Dora Anne (Butz). He spent his early years in the village of Hope and then on a farm nearby, after which the family moved to Urbana, where Van Doren attended high school and later graduated from the University of Illinois in 1907. He earned his doctorate from Columbia University in 1911 and was immediately hired as a professor there. He soon left his full-time teaching duties and became literary editor at the *Nation* and *Century Magazine* in the 1920s. By 1930 he had already authored biographical treatments of Thomas Love Peacock (1911) and Jonathan Swift (1930); two book-length collections of essays that were written for journals and newspapers, *The Roving Critic* (1923) and *Many Minds* (1924); a short-story collection; and a novel. But his lasting contributions to American literature, particularly to writings from the Midwest, came from such critical works as *The American Novel* (1921), *Contemporary American Novelists 1900–1920* (1922), and *The Cambridge History of American Literature* (1917) which he co-edited.

During the 1930s and 1940s Van Doren edited literature anthologies, wrote a glowing biography of SINCLAIR LEWIS (1933), authored the autobiographical *Three Worlds* (1936), and wrote several historical treatments of the American Revolution and the early Republic, his most famous being *Benjamin Franklin* (1938), which won a Pulitzer Prize. He died in Torrington, Connecticut, from a heart attack.

**SIGNIFICANCE:** Van Doren championed the merits of American literature at a time when few critics or scholars had given it much serious attention. In doing so, he brought notice to such Midwestern writers as LEWIS, ANDERSON, DREISER, LINDSAY, JOSEPH KIRKLAND, ROBERT HERRICK, ZONA GALE, and GEORGE ADE. Regarding himself as more a literary historian than a critic, Van Doren steered clear of partisan quarrels arising from the different interpretive theories then in vogue, such as New Criticism and psychoanalysis. Instead, he opted for a humbler, if vague, measure of evaluation, what he called "the fourth dimension in criticism"; next to questions about whether a literary work was good, beautiful, or true was a fourth one, "Is it alive?" (*Roving Critic* 16). Perhaps because he did not engage in academic criticism, his reputation is difficult to measure today, but he did have a great influence on generations of American writers during his lifetime.

**SELECTED WORKS:** Van Doren's *The American Novel* (1921) and *Contemporary American Novelists 1900–1920* (1922) provide what were then fresh insights into several Midwestern writers. His *Sinclair Lewis* (1933), effusive in its praise of its subject, drew criticism for claiming that Lewis was more a realist than a satirist. On Van Doren's methods of criticism and his wide range of thoughts on American letters, see his collections of essays *The Roving Critic* (1923) and *Many Minds* (1924). His only attempts at fiction are the character-driven short stories in *Other Provinces* (1925) and the novel *The Ninth Wave* (1926). The first part of Van Doren's autobiography, *Three Worlds* (1936), is an intimate glimpse of his boyhood life in Illinois. Excerpts from several of his works can be found in the Viking Portable Library's *Carl Van Doren: Selected by Himself* (1945).

**FURTHER READING:** Little critical work has been done on Van Doren since his death. A substantial entry on him in *Twentieth-Century*

*Literary Criticism* provides excerpts of Van Doren's critical reception during his lifetime. Of particular interest is Charles I. Glicksberg's "Carl Van Doren: Scholar and Skeptic," in *Sewanee Review* 46.2 (1938): 223–34. It provides a solid assessment of his career up to 1938. Some of Van Doren's papers can be found in the University of Illinois–Urbana archives.

ROBERT DUNNE

CENTRAL CONNECTICUT STATE UNIVERSITY

## MARK VAN DOREN
June 13, 1894–December 10, 1972

**BIOGRAPHY:** Pulitzer Prize–winning poet, playwright, critic, and short story writer, Mark Van Doren was the fourth of five sons of Charles Lucius Van Doren, a physician, and Dora Anne (Butz) Van Doren. He was born in Hope, Illinois, and spent much time on the family farm near there. Van Doren attended elementary and high school in Urbana, Illinois, where the family moved in 1900, and he went on to the University of Illinois. There he received his BA in 1914 and his MA in 1915, with a thesis on Thoreau, which was published as *Henry David Thoreau: A Critical Study* in 1916. His first published poem appeared in *Smart Set* in 1915.

He followed his older brother Carl to Columbia University in 1915 to pursue a PhD, but in September 1917 he entered the U.S. Army, to serve until December 1918. He did not serve overseas, and he returned to Columbia early in 1920. He received his doctorate in 1920 with a dissertation on John Dryden, which was published that year as *The Poetry of John Dryden*. Van Doren joined the Columbia English Department that fall as an instructor. As a temporary literary editor of the *Nation* that summer, he met Dorothy Graffe, a future novelist, whom he married on September 1, 1922. He remained at Columbia until his retirement in 1952, becoming a full professor in 1942. From 1924 to 1928 he was again literary editor of the *Nation*, and from 1935 to 1938 he was the journal's movie critic.

During his career at Columbia, Van Doren became a legendary teacher, and he was a prolific writer of criticism, poetry, essays, and short fiction. His *Collected Poems, 1922–1938* (1939) won the Pulitzer Prize in 1940; it was updated as *Collected and New Poems, 1924–1963* in the latter year. His stories were collected in *Collected Stories* in three volumes in 1962,

and the *Essays of Mark Van Doren, 1924–1972* appeared in 1980.

**SIGNIFICANCE:** Mark Van Doren spent his academic career and his scholarly and creative life as an impeccable member of the Eastern intellectual and critical establishment. He returned to the Midwest only rarely for lectures and family funerals, but his Midwestern origins are evident in his fiction and poetry from his first published work to his last. In both fiction and verse, Van Doren's clear, integrated reflections of the rural Illinois sights, sounds, and experiences of his youth were augmented by his later discovery of rural northwest Connecticut. In both verse and fiction he avoided the fragmentation of modernism at the same time that he reflected a clear relationship between the poet and the natural world. His long narrative poems, *Jonathan Gentry* (1931) and *The Mayfield Deer* (1941), are attempts to recreate the essence of the American rural experience as it came into being in the movement to America, to the Midwest, and into the modern age. The three parts of *Jonathan Gentry*—"Ohio River 1800," "Civil War," and "Foreclosure"—are in effect an American epic; that poem and *The Mayfield Deer*, the story of John Richman, a hunter born out of his time, are attempts to create epic poetic themes out of his own experience. Neither, however, was critically successful.

His lyric celebrations of nature, the rural experience, and intimations of the supernatural beyond them have been his most consistently successful works. His best short fiction reflects his ongoing concerns with the relationship between individual human lives and the natural world, the world of time and place, of which they are a part.

**SELECTED WORKS:** Van Doren's best verse appears in *Collected and New Poems, 1924–1963* (1963) and in *Good Morning: Last Poems* (1973). *Collected Stories* (1962) contains his best prose fiction, and *The Essays of Mark Van Doren, 1924–1972* (1980) contains much of his best criticism. His *Liberal Education* (1943) and *The Noble Voice: A Study of Ten Great Poems* (1946), republished as *Mark Van Doren on Great Poems of Western Literature* (1962), give insight into the mind and techniques of Van Doren as a teacher. Also available is *The Autobiography of Mark Van Doren* (1958).

**FURTHER READING:** No books have yet appeared on Van Doren's life and works, but he is the subject of numerous interesting essays, including John Peale Bishop's "The Poetry of Mark Van Doren," in his *Collected Essays* (1948), and numerous references in biographies and autobiographies, including Thomas Merton's *The Seven Story Mountain* (1948) and Mortimer Adler's *Philosopher at Large: An Intellectual Autobiography* (1977). Van Doren's works have been extensively reviewed, and introductions to his collections are often perceptive. His papers are in the Butler Library, Columbia University.

DAVID D. ANDERSON    MICHIGAN STATE UNIVERSITY

## MONA VAN DUYN
May 9, 1921

**BIOGRAPHY:** Born in Waterloo, Iowa, to businessman Earl George and Lora (Kramer) Van Duyn, Mona Van Duyn earned a BA from Iowa State Teachers College, now the University of Northern Iowa, in 1942 and an MA from the University of Iowa in 1943. She married Jarvis A. Thurston, an English professor, on August 31, 1943, and with his help published her first book of poems, *Valentines to the Wide World*, in 1959. She taught from 1943 to 1945 at the University of Iowa, from 1946 to 1950 at the University of Louisville, and from 1950 to 1967 at Washington University. With her husband, she founded and edited *Perspective: A Quarterly of Literature* from 1947 to 1967.

**Mona Van Duyn.**
Photo courtesy of Mona Van Duyn

Mona Van Duyn has received numerous awards, including the 1991 Pulitzer Prize for poetry, the HARRIET MONROE Memorial Prize from *Poetry* magazine (1968), the Bollingen Prize (1970), and a National Book Award (1971). In 1972 Van Duyn received a Guggenheim Fellowship. She is a chancellor of the Academy of American Poets and a member of the American Academy of Arts and Letters. In 1992 she was honored by being named to serve as national poet laureate. She received the Society for the Study of Midwestern Literature's 1993 Mark Twain Award for distinguished contributions to Midwestern literature. Van Duyn currently resides in St. Louis.

**SIGNIFICANCE:** Although the label offends her, Van Duyn is considered a domestic poet. It is an appropriate label, however, because her poems have a homey, sentimental feel. Unlike the writings of Robert Creeley, Colette Inez, and Emily Dickinson, who could also be labeled domestic poets, Van Duyn's work lacks an overriding philosophy or a spirited self-examination. She writes about anything that amuses her. Her poems concern her everyday life. She writes of her godson's christening, her puppy, a trip to the zoo with her husband, and a "First Trip through the Automatic Carwash." Except for an occasional detail of place, little of the Midwest is present in her poetry. *Firefall* (1993) offers somewhat of a departure. These short poems sometimes surprise, both in form and content. As a formalist, she is most often listed with writers such as Anthony Hecht, John Hollander, and Richard Wilbur.

**SELECTED WORKS:** Van Duyn's early poetry includes *Valentines to the Wide World* (1959), *A Time of Bees* (1964), *To See, To Take* (1970), and *Bedtime Stories* (1972). These poems have been collected in *Merciful Disguises: Poems Published and Unpublished* (1973, reprinted 1982) and more recently in *If It Be Not I: Collected Poems 1959–1982* (1993), including poems from her 1982 collection *Letters from a Father and Other Poems*. Her latest work includes *Near Changes* (1990) and *Firefall* (1993). She has also published two works of literary criticism, *An Essay on Modern Poetry and Poems* (1943) and *Matters of Poetry* (1993).

**FURTHER READING:** Valuable insight into Van Duyn's work can be found in *Discovery and Reminiscence: Essays on the Poetry of Mona Van Duyn*, edited by Michael Burns (1998). Also helpful are Marianne Abel's interview with Van Duyn, "Conversations with Pulitzer Prize Winners Jane Shorer and Mona Van Duyn," in *Iowa Woman* 11.3 (Autumn 1991): 18–23, and Stacy Tuthill's *Laurels: Eight Women Poets* (1998), with its treatment of Van Duyn and seven other women who served as consultants in poetry or poets laureate to the Library of Congress. Additional sources include William Logan's "Late Callings," in *Parnassus: Poetry in Review* 18–19.1–2 (1993): 317–27, and Constance Hunting's "Methods of Transport," in *Parnassus: Poetry in Review* 16.2 (1991): 377. Information on Van Duyn's appointment as poet laureate can be found in *Newsmakers* 2 (1993): 129.

KEVIN BEZNER        CHARLOTTE, NORTH CAROLINA

## MELVIN VAN PEEBLES
August 21, 1932

**BIOGRAPHY:** Born in Chicago, Illinois, Melvin Peebles grew up in Phoenix, Illinois. He attended Thornton High School in south suburban Chicago and Virginia State College in Institute, West Virginia, and earned a bachelor's degree in literature from Ohio Wesleyan University in Delaware, Ohio, in 1953. His special interests were singing and composing. While still an undergraduate, Peebles made two short films, *Sunlight* (1951) and *Three Pickup Men for Herrick* (1951). Upon graduating, Peebles enlisted in the U.S. Air Force, but after three and a half years as a flight navigator, he could not find employment with commercial airlines. To make a living, he worked for the Chicago post office, then moved to San Francisco, where he worked as a cable-car gripman, published his first book, and made three film shorts. In 1957 he published *The Big Heart*, a portrait of cable cars illustrated with photographs by Ruth Bernard.

Unable to get Hollywood interested in his films, in 1959 Peebles expatriated to Holland to study astronomy in graduate school. In the Netherlands, Peebles added the "Van" to his name, studied with the Dutch National Theatre, and toured as an actor in Brendan Behan's play *The Hostage*. Van Peebles left Holland for Paris when he learned that the French film directors' union would give a union card to any writer who wished to make a film on his own. Van Peebles used the French system of supporting film *auteurs* to realize his frustrated ambitions to become a published writer. In Paris, Van Peebles wrote and published five works in French. His autobiographical first novel, *Un ours pour le F.B.I.* (1964), was translated and published as *A Bear for the FBI* (1968). Van Peebles's autobiography, *Un Américain en enfer* (1965), was translated and published as *The American: A Folk Fable* (1965). Next, Van Peebles published *Le Chinois du XIVe* (1966), a collection of short stories. The following year, he published two works jointly: *La Fête à Harlem* and *La Permission* (1967). For two hundred thousand dollars, Van Peebles made his first feature-length movie, *The Story of a Three Day Pass* (1967), based on *La Permission*. *The Story of a Three Day Pass* won the Critics' Choice Award for first place as the French entry in the San Francisco Film Festival in 1967. Ironically, the United States had no minority filmmakers in Hollywood at that time.

Following Van Peebles's *succès d'estime*, Hollywood's Columbia Pictures selected him to direct the satire *Watermelon Man* (1970), a comedy about a white bigot who awakes one morning to find himself turned black. With his Columbia Pictures salary and a fifty-thousand-dollar loan from Bill Cosby, Van Peebles produced his film *Sweet Sweetback's Baadasssss Song* (1971) for five hundred thousand dollars. *Sweetback* grossed over ten million dollars. Following *Sweetback*'s success, Van Peebles mounted a Broadway production of *La Fête à Harlem* under the title *Don't Play Us Cheap* (1972). A year later, the novel was translated and published as *Harlem Party* (1973). A few months later, Van Peebles made a film based on the novel, returning to his Broadway title, *Don't Play Us Cheap* (1973).

In the 1970s Van Peebles used music from *Sweetback* to make the music recording *Ain't Supposed to Die a Natural Death*. He also produced two records with Atlanta, *What the **** You Mean I Can't Sing* and *Don't Play Us Cheap (Yeah!)*. In 1976, for General Electric Theater, he composed the song "Just an Old Sweet Song."

Van Peebles also directed and wrote three plays: *The Hostage* (Dutch National Theatre Tour) (1964); the musical play *Ain't Supposed to Die a Natural Death* (1971); and *Don't Play Us*

*Cheap* (1972). First produced as a Broadway musical, the film *Don't Play Us Cheap* (1973) was directed, written, and composed by Van Peebles, with Esther Rolle among the actors. In 1973 Van Peebles went on a nationwide tour with his last stage work of the 1970s, a one-man show *Out There by Your Lonesome* (1973). Throughout the 1970s, Van Peebles maintained a high profile, developing an engaging controversial public folk-hero persona by appearing regularly on television programs, including *AM, NY* (1970s); *Free Time* (1971); *Black Journal* (1971, 1975, 1976); *One to One Telethon* (1974); *The Bachelor of the Year, World Wide Special* (1974); and Chicago's *Kup's Show* (1975).

In the mid-1970s, Van Peebles wrote television scripts about black middle-class family life for NBC, including *Just an Old Sweet Song* (1976) and the highly regarded *Sophisticated Gents* (1981). His bold achievements were not ignored. In the 1970s, he received the Belgium Film Festival First Prize and the NAACP Award for best film director. In 1976 he was inducted into the Black Filmmakers' Hall of Fame.

By the 1980s, Van Peebles resumed working with his son Mario, who had appeared in *Sweetback*. Van Peebles wrote, produced, and starred with Mario in the play *The Waltz of the Stork* (1982) with Bob Carten and C. J. Critt. Then, setting aside his cultural interests, Van Peebles became an options trader on the floor of the American Stock Exchange in 1983. Drawing on this experience, he published two books, *Bold Money: A New Way to Play the Options Market* (1986) and *Bold Money: How to Get Rich in the Options Market* (1987).

In the late 1980s and into the 1990s Van Peebles continued collaborative work with Mario. He directed the comedy film *Identity Crisis* (1989), written by and starring Mario. He appeared in Mario's all-black Western film *Posse* (1993). In 1995 Van Peebles published the novel *Panther* (1995) about the Black Panthers, the basis for Mario's film *Panther* (1995). Two years later, Melvin Van Peebles acted in *Riot* (1997), a movie about the 1992 Los Angeles uprising.

By the 1990s, Van Peebles's work received renewed attention with the second wave of black filmmaking. The Museum of Modern Art honored Van Peebles with a retrospective showing of his film repertoire.

**SIGNIFICANCE:** *Sweetback* (1971) was the first film to feature a black American urban vaga-bond as a hero. With *Sweetback,* Van Peebles set a precedent for independent artists and the mass cinema by his provocative cinematic technique and his bold self-promotion. He fused gospel choric voices and a jazz score with an episodic plot. Although set in Los Angeles, *Sweetback*'s innovation lies in its melding of Chicago "soul" gospel and blues culture with counterculture politics to forge a unique expressive art. A political diatribe and an existential tale of an anti-hero, *Sweetback* was written and produced in response to one of the most overt uses of police force during the turbulent 1960s. On December 4, 1969, Black Panther Party leaders Mark Clark and Fred Hampton were killed in a raid by police in Chicago, Illinois. The same ambiance of bloody violence, impending victimhood, and overwhelming odds informs the life of Van Peebles's hero, Sweetback, from his sordid childhood origins to his fugitive status at film's end. Van Peebles's populist sentiments link him to other Midwestern social critics, from CARL SANDBURG and SHERWOOD ANDERSON to Haki Madhubuti. Ironically, *Sweetback* ushered in a wave of imitative, lucrative urban "blaxploitation" films whose glorification of pimps, crime, and deviant urban life-styles seemed devoid of any aesthetics or political commentary. In the mid-1970s, some of Van Peebles's work was cited for its lack of emphasis on race. *Hot Tickets* (1996) quotes critic Clive Barnes on Van Peebles's Broadway musical, *Don't Play Us Cheap* (1973). Barnes described the work as "fun all the way . . . that rare thing—a black play that does not feel the need to mention a white all evening."

**SELECTED WORKS:** Van Peebles's prolific output draws heavily on his own Midwestern and expatriate experiences. Because he was first published only in French, Van Peebles often shifts languages and genres. He reworks his autobiography into fiction, fiction into drama, drama into screenplays, and plays into films. His first book was an autobiography, *Un ours pour le F.B.I.* (1964), translated as *A Bear for the F.B.I* (1968). An autobiographical novel, *Un Américain en enfer* (1965), was translated as *The American: A Folk Fable* (1965). Van Peebles's comic yet piquant collection of short stories about Paris street workers and bistro workers, *Le Chinois du XIVe* (1966), remains untranslated into English. Van Peebles's novel *La Fête à Harlem* (1967) was translated into English as the novel *A Harlem Party* (1973), then adapted to the Broadway musical play *Don't Play Us Cheap* (1972) and the film *Don't Play Us Cheap* (1973). *La Permission* (1967) translated into English became the prize-winning film *Story of a Three Day Pass* (1967), an expatriate story of interracial romance dramatizing a black soldier's decision to take his white girlfriend on a weekend holiday despite his superior officer's disapproval. *Sweet Sweetback's Baadasssss Song* (1971) was a *tour de force*, written, produced, directed, filmed, edited, scored, and starring Van Peebles. The following year, Van Peebles published *The Making of Sweet Sweetback's Baadasssss Song* (1972), reprinted in a collector's edition by NEO Press in 1995. *Ain't Supposed to Die a Natural Death* (1973) was a Van Peebles Broadway musical controversial in its discussions of sexuality and life in the black ghetto. Van Peebles wrote for the films *Greased Lightning* (1977), *Vrooom Vrooom Vrooom* (1995), *Panther* (1995), and *Riot* (1997).

**FURTHER READING:** Information about Melvin Van Peebles's writing, filmmaking, directing, producing, composing, and editing can be found on the Internet Movie Database LTD. Discussion of *Sweetback* and other Van Peebles work is found in Edward Mapp's *Black Image* (1993); Edward Guerrero's *Framing Blackness* (1993); John Gray's *Blacks in Film and Television* (1994); Nelson George's *Blackface* (1994); Donald Bogle's *Toms, Coons, Mulattoes, Mammies, and Bucks* (1973) and *Blacks in American Films and Television: An Encyclopedia* (1988); Jack Salzman, David Lionel Smith, and Cornel West's *Encyclopedia of African-American Culture and History* (1995); Manthia Diawara's anthology of critical essays *Black American Cinema* (1993); Mark A. Reid's study of independent black films *Redefining Black Films* (1993); and in on-line newsletters, including *Scoop (The National Alliance of Postal and Federal Employees)*.

MARIA MOOTRY

UNIVERSITY OF ILLINOIS AT SPRINGFIELD

## CARL VAN VECHTEN
June 17, 1880–December 21, 1964

**BIOGRAPHY:** Born in Cedar Rapids, Iowa, the late, third child of Charles and Ada Amanda (Fitch) Van Vechten, Carl Van Vechten developed from an early age the interests and outlooks that would shape his multifarious career as New York novelist, art and music critic, essayist, photographer, and unparalleled champion of new and neglected writers and artists. Although the cultural constraints of the town held him only through high school, Carl benefited from the influence of his literary-minded parents, who devoted a great deal of time to their youngest child, whose two siblings, Emma and Ralph, were sixteen and eighteen at the time of his birth. His mother was responsible for the state's appropriation of funds to construct the Cedar Rapids Free Public Library, where Carl first read such writers as Henry James and George Bernard Shaw. The theatricals and light operas at Greene's Opera House in Cedar Rapids inspired him to write and act in his own plays presented in the Van Vechten parlor or barn. In his biography, *Carl Van Vechten and the Irreverent Decades*, Bruce Kellner writes that young Carl compensated for a lack of local musical offerings by playing the piano works of Schubert, Beethoven, and Bizet on the family grand (15).

In 1899 Carl entered the University of Chicago and voraciously absorbed the city's cultural atmosphere. He visited art galleries, attended concerts of the Chicago Symphony orchestra, and heard ragtime. Studying under the novelist ROBERT HERRICK, Carl began to write enthusiastically and in his senior year composed music. Following graduation, he began his journalistic career writing for the *Chicago American*. Two years later, when one of his columns offended the wife of the paper's business manager, Carl left his position and traveled to New York in early 1906 (Kellner 22).

Late that year Van Vechten was hired by the *New York Times* as assistant music critic. Following his 1907 marriage to Cedar Rapids friend Anna Elizabeth Snyder he became the *Times* correspondent in Paris from 1908 to 1910, when he became acquainted with Gertrude Stein. In 1912 he divorced Anna and in 1914 married Fania Marinoff, with whom he had a lasting union. A New Yorker for the rest of his life, Van Vechten became a fixture of Manhattan's literary and music scenes for more than fifty years.

His first book of essays, *Music after the Great War*, appeared in 1915 followed by five other essay collections championing the work of progressive European composers of the teens and twenties, as well as blues and jazz.

Between 1922 and 1930 he produced seven novels, all but one set in New York, Paris, or Hollywood during the 1920s. *The Tattooed Countess* (1924), his only novel set in the Midwest, recounts the return from Paris of a middle-aged American countess to her Iowa hometown. Set in 1920s Harlem, Van Vechten's *Nigger Heaven* (1926) inspired diverse reactions from both the African American and white communities and became a best-seller.

After publishing his seven novels, Carl started a new career as a portrait photographer and from 1932 to 1964 compiled an extensive photographic record of the artists and writers of the mid-twentieth century. Continuing to work as both photographer and critic in his later years, he also established a number of important library collections, including the James Weldon Johnson Memorial Collection of Negro Arts and Letters, one of the premier cultural archives in the nation. Van Vechten died in his sleep in New York two months after his fiftieth wedding anniversary.

**SIGNIFICANCE:** Carl Van Vechten's exit from the "City with the Big Shoulders" in 1906 preceded both Carl Sandburg's arrival and HARRIET MONROE's founding of *Poetry* magazine by six years. He just missed the surge of literary activity that came to be known as the Chicago Renaissance, including the publication of VACHEL LINDSAY's and EDGAR LEE MASTERS's best-known works between 1913 and 1915.

Van Vechten's one truly Midwestern work, *The Tattooed Countess*—like *Main Street* and *Winesburg, Ohio* before it—depicts the provincialism of small-town Mid-America. Yet unlike other 1920s chroniclers of the Midwest, Van Vechten treats the region's life and society with a lightness and humor that contrasts the foreboding intensity of SINCLAIR LEWIS and SHERWOOD ANDERSON. "Like the worthy but sometimes depressing authors of *Winesburg, Ohio, Main Street*, and *O Pioneers!*" wrote Lewis in the *Saturday Review of Literature*, "[Van Vechten] has entered upon the middle west—and he has made it at once real and amusing."

Despite this successful contribution to the Midwestern novel tradition, and unlike the writers that followed him in Chicago, Van Vechten did not become identified with this regional work. His vast, eclectic contributions to both the arts and letters eclipse *The Tattooed Countess*; likewise, his early journalism covering Chicago's turn-of-the century social world constitutes but a footnote in his long and varied career.

A close look at his work, however, reveals that the fundamental sensibilities, interests, and passions that fueled his primary career achievements emanate from his early heartland experience. Like other writers from the region, he was influenced both by the restrictions and the opportunities of the small, Midwestern town. During his Iowa youth, he obtained scores for the newest, most challenging musical works and played them long before they were performed professionally in the Cedar Rapids area (Kellner 15). This penchant for discovering and sharing new artistry became a dominant force in his life and led to some of his most significant contributions to twentieth-century arts and letters. After a 1913 visit to Gertrude Stein in Paris, for example, he championed her work in America where she was then an obscure, unread writer. And, recognizing the achievement of *Moby Dick*, he awakened new interest in Herman Melville's later works.

As a Midwestern youth, he was exposed to an interesting artistic mix. Although limited, the offerings at the local opera house provided both classic and popular productions on one stage—from Romeo and Juliet to the musicals of Eddie Foy. His early exposure to this juxtaposition may have served as the basis for his highly eclectic critical approach: in his seven books of criticism, he praises the artistic merits of the blues and jazz alongside those of classical symphonies, operas, and ballets. Bessie Smith's blues receive the same serious, aesthetic evaluation as Sergei Rachmaninoff's symphonies and Strauss's waltzes.

His intense, lifelong interest in African Americans and their arts also finds its beginnings in the Midwest. In Cedar Rapids, he heard Sissieretta Jones sing in her traveling musical production. Following his parents' lead, he addressed African Americans respectfully as Mr. and Mrs., a rarity in turn-of-the-century Mid-American homes. And, as Edward Lueders notes, for four years as a student in Chicago Van Vechten accompanied his black housekeeper to the Baptist church and played piano for the services. These early, positive experiences with African Americans in the Midwest inspired his work as a legendary promoter of African American artists. A major influence on the Harlem Renaissance of the 1920s, he was responsible for the appearance of poetry by LANGSTON HUGHES and Countee Cullen in *Vanity Fair* and for the publication of Hughes's first collection, *The Weary Blues,* by Alfred Knopf.

Although not typically considered a Midwestern writer, Van Vechten captured small-town and urban Midwestern life at the turn of the twentieth century with a light, amused style that is his own. More importantly, his Midwest experience imprinted him with outlooks and passions that helped him to shape the national cultural life of his time.

**SELECTED WORKS:** Published within one decade, Van Vechten's often semi-autobiographical, jazz-age novels include *Peter Whiffle: His Life and Works* (1922), *The Blind Bow-Boy* (1923), *The Tattooed Countess* (1924), *Firecrackers: A Realistic Novel* (1925), *Nigger Heaven* (1926), and *Parties: Scenes from Contemporary New York Life* (1930). His nine volumes of musical and literary criticism include *Music after the Great War and Other Studies* (1915), *The Music of Spain* (1918), *Red: Papers on Musical Subjects* (1925), and *Excavations: A Book of Advocacies* (1926), as well as the posthumously published *"Keep Inchin' Along": Selected Writings of Carl Van Vechten about Black Arts and Letters,* edited by Bruce Kellner (1979). Van Vechten also penned an autobiography, *Sacred and Profane Memories* (1932). Several volumes of his photographic work were published posthumously, including *Portraits: The Photography of Carl Van Vechten* (1975), *The Dance Photography of Carl Van Vechten* (1981), and *Generations in Black and White: Photographs by Carl Van Vechten* (1993).

**FURTHER READING:** Bruce Kellner's *A Bibliography of the Work of Carl Van Vechten* (1980) provides a compilation of Van Vechten's books, pamphlets, and voluminous contributions to periodicals and newspapers, as well as a full listing of his photographic portrait work with eighteen sample photographs. Kellner also wrote a biography, *Carl Van Vechten and the Irreverent Decades* (1968), in which he devotes chapters to his subject's years in both Cedar Rapids and Chicago, and edited *Letters of Carl Van Vechten* (1987). Klaus W. Jonas published the earlier *Carl Van Vechten: A Bibliography* (1955). Other book-length studies include Hisao Kishimoto's *Carl Van Vechten: The Man and His Role in the Harlem Renaissance* (1983) and Edward Lueders *Carl Van Vechten* (1965). Book articles devoted to Van Vechten's work include Corrine E. Blackmer's "Selling Taboo Subjects: The Literary Commerce of Gertrude Stein and Carl Van Vechten," in *Marketing Modernisms: Self-Promotion, Canonization, Rereading* (1996), and Donald Pizer's "The Novels of Carl Van Vechten and the Spirit of the Age," in *Toward a New American Literary History: Essays in Honor of Arlin Turner* (1980).

The New York Public Library holds Van Vechten's manuscripts and correspondence pertaining to his books. The American Literature Collection of the Beinecke Library at Yale University houses most of his correspondence and materials on his literary acquaintances, his major gift of the James Weldon Johnson Collection of Negro Arts and Letters, and his Anna Marble Pollack Memorial Library of Books about Cats. The Fisk University Library has additional Van Vechten materials on Negro culture, his Florine Stettheimer Memorial Library of Books about the Fine Arts, and his George Gershwin Memorial Collection of Music and Musical Literature.

The Museum of the City of New York has approximately three hundred Van Vechten photographs of theatrical personalities, while the Museum of Modern Art has nearly the same number of Van Vechten photographs of dancers and choreographers. The University of New Mexico Jonson Gallery houses the Jerome Bowers Peterson Memorial Collection of Photographs of Negro Notables by Van Vechten.

BARBARA A. BURKHARDT       UNIVERSITY OF ILLINOIS

## THORSTEIN (BUNDE) VEBLEN
July 30, 1857–August 3, 1929

**BIOGRAPHY:** Economist and social critic, Thorstein Veblen was born on a farm in Wisconsin of parents of Norwegian immigrant background, Thomas Anderson Veblen and Kari (Bunde) Veblen. He graduated from Carleton College in Minnesota in three years and studied philosophy at Johns Hopkins and Yale, where he took his PhD in 1884. Unable to find a teaching job, he returned to his father's farm and spent the next seven years reading and talking with the local farmers.

His father encouraged him to return to university life, as he was no help on the farm, and he entered Cornell in 1891 as a graduate student. When James Laurence Laughlin moved to the new University of Chicago in 1892, he took Veblen with him as a fellow in economics. In 1896, when he was thirty-nine, he was promoted to instructor. He published *The Theory of the Leisure Class: An Economic Study of Institutions*, his best-known work, in 1899. He was promoted to assistant professor in 1900.

As a university professor, Veblen was not a success. He married Ellen Rolfe in 1888 but was asked to leave the University of Chicago after an adulterous affair. He took a position as an associate professor at Stanford in 1906, and again he was forced to leave for the same reason. By 1911 he was a lecturer at the University of Missouri. Ellen divorced him, and he married Anne Bradley Bevans, a former student, in 1914. Anne died in 1920. Veblen gave up teaching in 1926 after a stint at the New School for Social Research in New York and moved to a cabin by the sea in California, where he died in 1929.

SIGNIFICANCE: Veblen shared the outlook of Midwestern farmers in his antipathy toward the big interests, trusts, and banks of the Eastern establishment of his day, and he translated this attitude into a trenchant analysis of the economic and social systems. In *The Theory of the Leisure Class*, Veblen argued that while the industrial system required efficiency and a division of labor, the masters of industry were concerned with pecuniary emulation and conspicuous consumption (1918 ed., 22–34, 68–101, passim). Applying Social Darwinism to his analysis, Veblen asserted that the wealthy were survivors of a barbarian past. In 1904 he published *The Theory of Business Enterprise* in which he analyzed the industrial process and the organization of business and finance.

In *The Higher Learning in America* (1918), Veblen made the case that educational priorities in American universities were set by the corporate interests on which they were financially dependent. Veblen's work was popular among socialists and the literary world, and he was regarded as a brilliant social critic. He influenced the development of the Midwestern institutionalist school of economics and the social thought represented by Midwestern literary realists. With the publication of *An Inquiry into the Nature of Peace and the Terms of Its Perpetuation* (1917), Veblen found an international audience as well. In this work, he argued that peace was possible only if rights of ownership were limited.

SELECTED WORKS: *The Theory of the Leisure Class* (1899) and *The Theory of Business Enterprise* (1904) are Veblen's most important works and are still read. Also interesting are *The Higher Learning in America* (1918), *The Instinct of Workmanship and the State of the Industrial Arts* (1914), *Imperial Germany and the Industrial Revolution* (1915), and *The Place of Science in Modern Civilization and Other Essays* (1919). Veblen continued to publish in the 1920s, but in his work of that period he tended to restate his earlier views.

FURTHER READING: The classic work on Veblen is *Thorstein Veblen and His America*, by Joseph Dorfman (1934). Much has been written about him and his ideas; some of the leading works are David Riesman's *Thorstein Veblen: A Critical Interpretation* (1953); *Thorstein Veblen: A Critical Reappraisal*, edited by Douglas F. Dowd (1958); and David Seckler's *Thorstein Veblen and the Institutionalists* (1975). Useful as an introduction to his writings is *The Portable Veblen*, edited by Max Lerner (1948). Rick Tilman's *The Intellectual Legacy of Thorstein Veblen: Unresolved Issues* (1996) draws on Carleton College's Thorstein Veblen Collection and the Joseph Dorfman Papers in the Butler Library at Columbia University.

TOM L. PAGE                              WICHITA, KANSAS

# WILLIAM HENRY VENABLE
April 29, 1836–July 6, 1920

BIOGRAPHY: Descended from Quakers who became Universalists, William Henry Venable was born to William and Hannah (Baird) Venable in Waynesville, Ohio, and raised on the family's farm near Ridgeville, about thirty-eight miles north of Cincinnati. Before taking up farming, his father taught school, and at seventeen the son followed that profession, teaching at Sugar Grove and then training with a teachers' institute at Miami University and in the National Normal School in Lebanon, Ohio, from which he graduated in 1860. Venable married Mary Vater in 1860.

Venable held several overlapping teaching and administrative positions with Ohio schools. He taught at the Lebanon Normal

School, then became principal at the Jennings Academy in Vernon, Indiana. He then taught for many years at the Chickering Institute in Cincinnati, ultimately becoming its principal and proprietor. When the school failed at some personal cost to him, he taught at Hughes High School and from 1895 at Walnut Hills High School, both in Cincinnati.

Venable received the AM from DePauw in 1864. He organized the Cincinnati Society of Political Education and served as its first president in 1880, was first president of the Teachers' Club of Cincinnati in 1891, and president of the Western Association of Writers in 1895. Ohio University honored him with the LLD in 1886 and the University of Cincinnati with the LittD in 1917. He left teaching in 1900 but continued to write. He died in Cincinnati on July 6, 1920.

**SIGNIFICANCE:** Whig politics, abolitionism, Mexican war protests, wide reading, and love of rural nature shaped Venable's lifelong outlooks. He saw the arrival of the first railroad in the Miami Valley and gained wider horizons on his father's commercial trips by wagon to Cincinnati. Imitating plays he saw there, young "Tip," who was named after William Henry Harrison, practiced oratory in the local woods and was moved by the Hungarian quest for independence led by Kossuth.

Venable's contributions to Midwestern literature stem from forty years in education, thirty-eight of them in Cincinnati. He helped form the city's school system, publishing a collection of papers on education and two textbooks in history, *A School History of the United States* (1872) and *Tales of Ohio History for Home and School* (1896). In 1898 he edited standard editions of the poems of Burns, Byron, and Wordsworth. He wrote of visits to writers' homes in accounts for the Walnut Hills High School literary magazine, and his works on Ohio Valley literary history are invaluable guides to Ohio writers. His books of poetry earned him the epithet "The Teacher-Poet." "The Teacher's Dream," a vision of influences on future leaders, and "Is Yonder the Place?" an account of returning to a childhood home after several years, are good examples of his homely rural verse; its style influenced his friend and protégé JAMES WHITCOMB RILEY. His correspondence with literary men and women of his day was extensive.

He tried an historical novel with *A Dream of Empire; or, the House of Blennerhassett* (1901) based on accounts of an Irish exile who settled near Marietta and lost his estate in Aaron Burr's conspiracy of 1805–1806. The novel delineates stereotypical regional characters in settings which are often symbolic or didactic, becoming most real when they are localized near Cincinnati. A more vital fiction, the boys' life novel, *Tom Tad* (1902), combined experiences from his childhood with those of his sons. The latter novel included many of the "Tom Tad" stories and lectures given at school and educational meetings for some years. It delineates Cincinnati social classes and dramatizes a boy's struggles with bullies, tyrannical teachers, river floods, and losses through death. Cincinnati and river settings and routes into the city are carefully detailed in both novels. *A Buckeye Boyhood* (1911) collected and expanded his previous accounts of idyllic childhood and adventures near Ridgeville.

**SELECTED WORKS:** Venable's poems include an undated broadside, "The Founders of Ohio," *June on the Miami, and Other Poems* (1872, reprinted in 1877 and 1912), *Melodies of the Heart, Songs of Freedom, and Other Poems* (1884), *The Teacher's Dream and Other Songs of School Days* (1889), *The Last Flight* (1894), *Saga of the Oak, and Other Poems* (1904), and *Cincinnati, a Civic Ode* (1907). The literary histories include *Early Periodical Literature of the Ohio Valley* (1888), *Footprints of the Pioneers in the Ohio Valley* (1888), *Beginnings of Literary Culture in the Ohio Valley* (1891), and *Ohio Literary Men and Women* (1904). In addition to the two history texts he published a reminiscence, *Down South before the War* (1889), and a commemorative work, *Ohio Centennial Anniversary Celebration* (1903). His fiction includes *A Dream of Empire or, the House of Blennerhassett* (1901) and *Tom Tad* (1902) as well as a few children's stories. In *A Buckeye Boyhood* (1911), he recollected his early life in the Miami Valley.

**FURTHER READING:** References to William Henry Venable appear in Henrietta Brady Brown's *The Ancestors and Descendants of William Henry Venable* (1904); in Henry Howe's *Historical Collections of Ohio, II* (1891), 732; and in the proceedings of the *Ohio Centennial Anniversary Celebration at Chillicothe, May 20–21, 1903*, edited by E. O. Randall. A large collection of Venable's papers is at the Ohio Historical Society in Columbus.

EUGENE H. PATTISON                              ALMA COLLEGE

## GERALD VIZENOR
October 22, 1934

**BIOGRAPHY:** When Gerald Vizenor was only two, his half-white father, Clement Vizenor, a painter and paperhanger, was murdered in a Minneapolis alley. Gerald spent the next six years rotating among his Anishinabe grandmother, his mother, LaVerne (Peterson), and various foster families. When he was eight his mother married Elmer Petesch, whom she later deserted, although Vizenor remained with Petesch until his stepfather died in a fall down an elevator shaft. Vizenor joined the National Guard, serving on active duty in Japan from 1952 to 1955. Upon returning to Minnesota, he worked for the American Indian Employment and Guidance Center in Minneapolis and as a *Minneapolis Tribune* reporter. After earning a degree from the Native American Studies Department of the University of Minnesota, Vizenor taught at the University of California at Berkeley, and the University of California at Santa Cruz, spending 1983 in China as an exchange teacher to Tianjin University.

Vizenor's second novel, *Griever* (1987), won the Fiction Collective Prize and the American Book Award of the Before Columbus Foundation. His original screenplay *Harold of Orange* was named "best film" at the San Francisco American Indian Film Festival. In 1989 he received a California Arts Council Literature Award.

**SIGNIFICANCE:** Alan Velie called Vizenor "the Isaac Bashevis Singer of the Chippewas" (*Four* 126), and indeed he is one of the most productive, innovative, and accomplished of Native American writers. His *Wordarrows* (1978) is a Singer-like collection of snapshots of life on Minneapolis's Franklin Avenue, the city's "urban reservation." The mixed blood Indian—Vizenor's term is "crossblood"—becomes in Vizenor's early work a cultural hero rather than the traditional outcast. Also prominent in Vizenor's work and thought is the figure of Wenebojo, the trickster—sometimes two tricksters, benign and dangerous, sometimes a single figure combining all Wenebojo's aspects, sometimes a combined Chippewa-Chinese trickster. The trickster figures in Vizenor's childhood recollections, *Interior Landscapes* (1990), as an antidote to life-destroying, overly serious "terminal beliefs." In *Griever: An American Monkey King in China*, the trickster is a gadfly to pompous American teachers. In *The Heirs of Columbus* (1991), he is a comic reinvention of America. *The Trickster of Liberty* (1988) is a history of the White Earth reservation in northern Minnesota. "In all his works," Alan Velie writes, "Vizenor deals with the delicate subjects of race relations, color, and ethnic identity. But he does not deal with them delicately. He slashes away at prejudices and 'terminal beliefs' with merciless satire, exposing and ridiculing whites, full bloods, and mixed-bloods. His friends are no safer than his enemies . . ." (*Writers* 699).

Although Vizenor's fiction exhibits deconstructionist and postmodern qualities, and although Vizenor is himself an academic, he once told the *Minneapolis Star-Tribune*'s Mary Ann Grossman, "I want to turn around the *New Yorker* approach to the short story or the writing school traditional approach to writing; their work is dull, dry, and worn out. You won't find that traditional numbness in Native American literature" (3D).

**SELECTED WORKS:** One of Vizenor's best and most accessible works is *Interior Landscapes: Autobiographical Myths and Metaphors* (1990), which incorporates material from his essay in *Growing Up in Minnesota* (1976). Also interesting are *Wordarrows: Indians and Whites in the New Fur Trade* (1978), *Earthdivers: Tribal Narratives on Mixed Descent* (1981), and *The Trickster of Liberty: Tribal Heirs to a Wild Baronage* (1988). More challenging because of their postmodern structure are *Darkness in Saint Louis Bearheart* (1978) and *Griever: An American Monkey King in China* (1987). *The Heirs of Columbus* (1991) retreats to a kind of Native American, Edward Abbey–style gonzo-Nativism.

**FURTHER READING:** Brief discussions of Gerald Vizenor may be found in Ronald Barron's *A Guide to Minnesota Writers* (1993) and Alan Velie's "Gerald Vizenor," in *Twentieth-Century Western Writers*, edited by Geoff Sadler (1991: 697–99). Mary Ann Grossman's "Talking Leaves Voices New Popularity of Indian Literature" (*St. Paul Pioneer Press*, September 22, 1991: 1D, 3D) is brief but illuminating. Louis Owens's *Other Destinies: Understanding the American Indian Novel* (1992) and Alan Velie's *Four American Indian Literary Masters* (1982) provide more detailed interpretations of a complex and difficult writer.

DAVID PICHASKE          SOUTHWEST STATE UNIVERSITY

## JOHN DONALDSON VOELKER
June 29, 1903–March 19, 1991
(Robert Traver)

**BIOGRAPHY:** John Donaldson Voelker was born to George Oliver and Annie (Traver) Voelker in Ishpeming, near Marquette in Michigan's remote Upper Peninsula, more than four-hundred miles from Lansing, the state's capital. Voelker's father was a tavern owner who loved the UP's natural beauty and sublimity. His mother was a music teacher; her maiden name contributed to Voelker's eventual pen name, Robert Traver. Voelker's UP upbringing taught him love of nature, admiration for individualism, respect for Native Americans and ethnic minorities, distrust of government, and distaste for corporate exploitation.

After spending 1922–24 at Northern Michigan Normal School, Voelker completed the bachelor of laws degree at the University of Michigan in 1928 and returned to the UP to practice law. In 1930 he married Grace Taylor. The couple had three children: Elizabeth, Julie, and Grace. Voelker served as Marquette County Prosecutor from 1934 to 1953 and was named to the Michigan Supreme Court, serving from 1957 through 1960. He resigned at age fifty-seven to return to literature and semiretirement in the UP. Voelker's greatest literary success came with *Anatomy of a Murder* (1957), a national best-seller and the source of Otto Preminger's 1959 movie. He was awarded the Society for the Study of Midwestern Literature's 1983 Mark Twain Award for distinguished contributions to Midwestern literature. John Donaldson Voelker died of a heart attack in his beloved UP on March 19, 1991.

**SIGNIFICANCE:** Eleven books, including novels, collections of essays and stories, musings on trout fishing and life, and a weekly *Detroit News* newspaper column mark Voelker's literary production. As a Michigan Supreme Court justice, Voelker authored many legal opinions.

Voelker's legal opinions and his literary works are characteristically Midwestern in their attitudes toward people, society, life, and literature. They express love for unspoiled nature and rural life. They respect individualism and common people, are skeptical about government, and resent the hegemony of cultural, economic, and political centers. They repeatedly attack corporate exploitation of

John Donaldson Voelker.
Photo by Frederick M. Baker Jr.
Courtesy of Frederick M. Baker Jr.

land and people. Voelker's books express suspicion of technology, particularly in the hands of those valuing profit over human life. The UP and, more broadly, Michigan, provide inspiration, settings, situations, and themes.

Voelker's stories and essays insistently mingle law, nature, and society. They reveal anarchic, destructive impulses in individuals and society, present law as an imperfect yet important tool for minimizing damage, and repeatedly stress the tragic human loss inherent in imprisonment, the death-centeredness of government and society, and the restorative power of nature. In *Trout Madness* (1960) Voelker asserts, "I love the environs where trout are found, which are invariably beautiful, and hate the environs where crowds of people are found, which are invariably ugly" (34).

Using protagonists and narrators closely approximating their author, Voelker's writings confront central social issues through novels, stories, and essays with realistic detail, imaginatively compelling plots, sardonic humor, a teaching orientation, and typically positive outcomes in the popular literary tradition. His most successful novel, *Anatomy of a Murder*, fits this pattern neatly.

**SELECTED WORKS:** Voelker's novels include *Danny and the Boys* (1951), *Anatomy of a Murder* (1957), *Hornstein's Boy* (1962), *Laughing Whitefish* (1965), and *People versus Kirk* (1981). *Troubleshooter: The Story of a Northwoods Prosecutor* (1943), *Small Town D.A.* (1954), and *The Jealous Mistress* (1968) present essays, reminiscences, semi-fictionalized stories, and opinions based on Voelker's experiences as a Michigan prosecuting attorney and judge. *Trout Madness* (1960), *Anatomy of a Fisherman* (1968), and *Trout Magic* (1974) showcase the author's love of nature for itself and as a respite from personal and social pressures.

**FURTHER READING:** No biography on Voelker exists; criticism is limited to scattered articles. Most helpful is John C. Hepler's essay "Penman for the People: Justice Voelker," published in *MidAmerica 6* (1979): 127–40. Information on John Donaldson Voelker as justice of the Supreme Court of Michigan is available through the State of Michigan Library at 525 W. Ottawa in Lansing, Michigan. Copies of his legal opinions can be found in any law library maintaining the *Michigan Reports*. Biographical information on Justice Voelker is available in the annual editions of the *Michigan Manual*.

PHILIP A. GREASLEY      UNIVERSITY OF KENTUCKY

**Kurt Vonnegut.**
Photo © Nancy Crampton

## KURT VONNEGUT

November 11, 1922

**BIOGRAPHY:** Kurt Vonnegut Jr., who after the publication of *Slapstick* in 1976 dropped the "Jr." from his name, was born in Indianapolis, Indiana, to Kurt Sr. and Edith (Lieber) Vonnegut. The Vonnegut family, who owned Vonnegut Hardware in Indianapolis, claimed a position of prominence in this Midwestern city both financially and socially in the late nineteenth and early twentieth century. Vonnegut's father and grandfather were influential architects in the burgeoning city of Indianapolis, designing many business and government buildings before the Great Depression as well as the Vonnegut family residences. World War I seriously altered the financial prosperity enjoyed by the Vonneguts and the depression effectively ended Vonnegut's father's employment as an architect.

After graduating from Shortridge High School in Indianapolis, Vonnegut attended Cornell University and served as editor for the daily paper, the *Sun*. In 1943 Vonnegut enlisted in the U.S. Army, never to return to Cornell and his undergraduate studies in chemistry and biology. In 1944 Vonnegut was captured by German troops at the Battle of the Bulge and interned as a prisoner of war in Dresden, Germany, an event that is the basis for his most important work, *Slaughterhouse-Five* (1969).

Vonnegut survived the bombing of Dresden and returned to the United States, marrying Jane Marie Cox in 1945. The following year he returned to the Midwest as a resident for the last time, enrolling as a graduate student in anthropology at the University of Chicago; he also worked as a police reporter for the Chicago City News Bureau. In 1979 Vonnegut and Jane Marie divorced; in that same year he married photographer Jill Krementz. The two marriages produced three biological and four adopted children. Vonnegut has since lived in Schenectady, New York, in several villages on Cape Cod, and in New York City. He presently resides in Manhattan where he completed the novel *Timequake* (1997), which he claims is his last.

**SIGNIFICANCE:** Vonnegut, whose work for years was available only in paperback having been marketed as science fiction, has been heralded since the early 1970s as one of the most important postmodern innovators in contemporary American fiction. While formally his work is considered postmodern because of its use of achronological narrative structure and its lack of concern with traditional generic boundaries, thematically Vonnegut remains closely aligned with his Midwestern heritage.

Vonnegut consistently uses his own family history, his experiences growing up in Indianapolis, and the Midwestern values propagated in his youth to create plots that for all of their postmodern complexity remain concerned with notions of family, religion, and the improvement of the human condition. Perhaps Malachai Constant in *The Sirens of Titan* (1959) states best what is arguably Vonnegut's most essential and compelling theme: "It took us that long to realize that a purpose of human life, no matter who is controlling it, is to love whoever is around to be loved" (313).

All thirteen of Vonnegut's novels contain at least one character who in some way has a connection to the Midwest. *Breakfast of Champions* (1973) and *Deadeye Dick* (1982) are set in Midland City, Ohio, which is also the hometown of James Wait in *Galápagos* (1985) and where Eugene Debs Hartke, Jr., moves with his family when his father takes a position with Robo-Magic Corporation in *Hocus Pocus* (1990). *God Bless You, Mr. Rosewater* (1965) is set exclusively in Indiana, moving back and forth between Rosewater County, Indiana, and Indianapolis, and in *The Sirens of Titan* (1959) when Malachai Constant, after traveling throughout the universe, is given the choice to be left anywhere in the world, he explains that Indianapolis is the place for him.

Vonnegut's fictional world weaves itself into real Midwestern towns and events to create a montage of characters, plots, and places that recur in many of his works. Although Vonnegut has not lived in the Midwest for many years, he consistently pays homage to his roots. In his nonfiction collected in *Wampeters, Foma and Granfalloons* (1974), *Palm Sunday* (1981), and *Fates Worse Than Death* (1991), he points to the importance of his Indianapolis heritage; while recounting his family history and his youth in the

Midwest, he proudly asserts that his own themes, considered radical by some, are merely the idealistic product of his junior civics lessons at Shortridge High School. Like the writer he most admires, MARK TWAIN, Vonnegut, although far from the geographical locale of the Midwest, continues to mine the spirit of the place.

**SELECTED WORKS:** While all of Vonnegut's work remains in print, *Mother Night* (1961), *Cat's Cradle* (1963), *God Bless You, Mr. Rosewater* (1965), *Slaughterhouse-Five* (1969), *Deadeye Dick* (1982), *Galápagos* (1985), and *Bluebeard* (1987) have garnered the most critical attention. Other novels by Vonnegut include *Player Piano* (1952), *The Sirens of Titan* (1959), *Breakfast of Champions* (1973), *Slapstick* (1976), *Jailbird* (1979), *Hocus Pocus* (1990), and *Timequake* (1997).

As previously noted, Vonnegut's nonfiction, including *Wampeters, Foma and Granfalloons* (1974), *Palm Sunday* (1981), and *Fates Worse Than Death* (1991), is of particular interest to scholars exploring his Midwestern background. Especially valuable is the second chapter of *Palm Sunday* (1981), succinctly entitled "Roots."

**FURTHER READING:** While no biography exists of Vonnegut's life, many scholarly works and edited collections do exist. Among the best critical collections are *The Vonnegut Statement*, edited by Jerome Klinkowitz and John Somer (1973); *Vonnegut in America*, edited by Jerome Klinkowitz and Donald L. Lawler (1977); *Critical Essays on Kurt Vonnegut*, edited by Robert Merrill (1990); *The Critical Response to Kurt Vonnegut*, edited by Leonard Mustazza (1994); and Klinkowitz's *Vonnegut in Fact: The Public Spokesmanship of Personal Fiction* (1998). Lawrence Broer's *Sanity Plea: Schizophrenia in the Novels of Kurt Vonnegut* (1994) and Mustazza's *Forever Pursuing Genesis: The Myth of Eden in the Novels of Kurt Vonnegut* (1990) are exemplary thematic studies of Vonnegut's work to date. For the best introductions to Vonnegut's oeuvre, consult Jerome Klinkowitz's *Kurt Vonnegut* (1982), James Lundquist's *Kurt Vonnegut* (1977), and William Rodney Allen's *Understanding Kurt Vonnegut* (1991).

TODD F. DAVIS                                    GOSHEN COLLEGE

# DAN WAKEFIELD
May 21, 1932

**BIOGRAPHY:** Dan Wakefield, novelist, journalist, and television playwright, was born to

Benjamin H. and Brucie (Ridge) Wakefield in Indianapolis, Indiana, where he attended Shortridge High School. After spending a year at Indiana University, Wakefield left Indianapolis to study at Columbia University in New York City, graduating in 1955. He chronicles his tenure in New York City's Greenwich Village in his recent work of creative nonfiction, *New York in the Fifties* (1992). From 1956 to 1959, Wakefield was a staff writer for the *Nation*, and since 1959 he has made his living as a freelance writer with occasional stints as a visiting lecturer at such schools as the University of Massachusetts, the University of Illinois, and the University of Iowa.

Since leaving New York City to make his residence in Boston, Wakefield has returned to the Midwest only for short visits, but he maintains a relationship with other writers from the region, including fellow Shortridge High alumnus KURT VONNEGUT. Like Vonnegut, although he has lived his adult life in the East, Wakefield exhibits qualities from his Midwestern heritage in his fiction and nonfiction alike. Besides winning the DeVoto Fellowship to the Bread Loaf Writers Conference, the Neiman Fellowship at Harvard University, and a Rockefeller Foundation grant for imaginative writing, Wakefield received a nomination for the National Book Award in 1970 for *Going All the Way*. Wakefield has been the distinguished visiting writer at Florida International University since 1995. His most recent work of nonfiction, *Creating from the Spirit: A Path to Creative Power in Art and Life*, was published in 1997 to critical praise.

**SIGNIFICANCE:** First as a journalist for the *Nation* and later as a respected writer of nonfiction works dealing with topics as diverse as Spanish Harlem and television soap operas, Wakefield at all times writes out of personal experience, investing his prose with his own voice, his own subjectivity. His nonfiction rests firmly in the school of New Journalism made popular by writers such as Tom Wolfe and Hunter S. Thompson, and, as such, his own Midwestern history pushes his prose in directions that encompass life in Indiana during the 1940s and 1950s. Books such as *Between the Lines* (1966) and *Returning: A Spiritual Journey* (1988) are firmly situated in Wakefield's youth, and, as he tells it, his youth was spent dreaming of the writing life while he worked for the school newspaper at Short-

**Dan Wakefield.**
Photo © Nancy Crampton

ridge High School and later for the *Indianapolis Star*. Wakefield's novels, as Jerome Klinkowitz suggests in *The New American Novel of Manners* (1986), are all about finding a way home, a notion that is attributed to Wakefield's Midwestern understanding of place and community.

Wakefield's most important novel, *Going All the Way* (1970), is set in Indianapolis and follows the absurd mishaps of two young veterans of the Korean War as they attempt to negotiate the repressive atmosphere of Midwestern life in the 1950s. The novel's main character, Sonny Burns, searches incessantly for the perfect come-on line in order to break through the conventions of the day in hopes that he will be introduced to the forbidden world of sex. Wakefield, however, turns Sonny's search on its head in a series of tragically funny misadventures that culminate with a car accident, leaving Sonny in traction. *Going All the Way* ends with what Sonny believes is his beginning, a move away from Indianapolis to New York. Having said that, it is clear that Sonny's Midwestern past, like Wakefield's own past, cannot be left behind so simply; a train ride to the East may create geographical distance, but the Midwest Sonny wishes to move beyond has less to do with the lay of the land and more to do with the boundaries of his own spirit.

**SELECTED WORKS:** Wakefield's best nonfiction is found in *Between the Lines: A Reporter's Personal Journey through Public Events* (1966) and *Returning: A Spiritual Journey* (1988). Also of note is a piece written by Wakefield for *The Vonnegut Statement* (1973) entitled "In Vonnegut's Karass"; the essay is a personal memoir describing Wakefield's dreams of the writer's life and the hopeful possibilities Vonnegut's career held out to the fledgling author. Of Wakefield's five novels, *Going All the Way* (1970), *Starting Over* (1973), and *Home Free* (1977) have received the highest critical praise.

**FURTHER READING:** Wakefield's work has not been the subject of much scholarly discussion. The most significant writing thus far includes Kurt Vonnegut's short essay "Oversexed in Indianapolis," collected in *Wampeters, Foma and Granfalloons* (1974): 117–19, and Jerome Klinkowitz's long chapter, "Dan Wakefield: Finding the Way Home," in *The New American Novel of Manners* (1986): 60–111, as well as his experimental essay, "At Home with Dan Wakefield," included in *Literary Subversions: New American Fiction and the Practice of Criticism* (1985): 149–63.

TODD F. DAVIS                          GOSHEN COLLEGE

## LEW(IS) WALLACE
April 10, 1827–February 15, 1905

**BIOGRAPHY:** Lew Wallace, novelist and poet, led a romantic and impetuous life as a soldier, lawyer, diplomat, and author. His father, "Colonel" David Wallace, attended and taught mathematics at West Point, studied law, served in the legislature, and became lieutenant governor and finally governor of Indiana in 1837. Born in Brookville and living there and in Indianapolis, Lew disliked formal education, was often truant from school, and learned from reading and rambling in the woods. After playing a part in Robert Dale Owen's *Pocahontas*, he started thinking and acting dramatically. He and another boy ran off from home, attempting to join the Texans as they battled the Mexicans, but they were interrupted and returned home. His first position was doing copy work in the county clerk's office and reporting deliberations of the Indiana House of Representatives. He studied law but failed the bar examination because his time was spent organizing a company for the Mexican War. He was, however, elected second lieutenant. After seeing no

action, he returned, passed his bar exam, moved to Corydon, and then organized in Crawfordsville a military company, the Montgomery Guards, known as the Zouaves, because of their Algerian French uniform. In 1852 he married Susan Arnold Elston of Crawfordsville, a writer who became an excellent wife. When the Civil War commenced, the Indiana governor, Oliver P. Morton, appointed Wallace adjutant general of the state, and in a few days he had assembled 130 companies and was made colonel to command the Eleventh Regiment. He became a major general but still did not have a strong role in the war. During the last of it he engaged in military and diplomatic activities, trying to bring Texas into the union, sending munitions to the Mexicans, and assuming a commission of major general in the Mexican Army. After returning home, he was defeated for election to Congress but served as governor of New Mexico territory and as minister to Turkey. He died in Crawfordsville of what was diagnosed as atrophy of the stomach.

**SIGNIFICANCE:** Like the books of many nineteenth-century Midwestern writers, Wallace's works are highly romantic, featuring exotic settings, sensational actions, and heroic characters, such as in his poetry: *Commodus, An Historical Play* (1876) and *The Wooing of Malkatoon* (1898). Wallace's novels include *The Fair God; or The Last of the 'Tzins* (1873); *Ben-Hur, a Tale of the Christ* (1880); and *The Prince of India or Why Constantinople Fell* (1893). *The Fair God* tells a story of love and ambition mixed with the history of Mexico in a glittering parade of splendid scenes, costumes, and heroic actions, which contrast the decaying pagan civilization and the supposedly Christian civilization of the invading Spanish forces. Critical reception was mostly favorable. *The Prince of India* was not very interesting to readers despite its consistent recourse to vigorous, marvelous, and exotic elements. But in *Ben-Hur,* Wallace reached his zenith. After listening to Colonel Robert Ingersoll's agnosticism, Wallace, though never a church member, turned his book into a defense of Christianity. It had everything— Jesus, a Jew as hero, a Roman as villain—and the author mixed it all with local color, miracles, daring and villainous actions, history, pageantry, biblical narratives, vengeance, and excitement. *Ben-Hur* was his greatest success.

Wallace was a very gifted amateur. Through *Ben-Hur* and *The Fair God* he led millions to appreciate literature and art, and he was Midwestern in his life and also in his choice of the exotic and heroic.

**SELECTED WORKS:** Lew Wallace's significant works include *The Fair God* (1873), *Ben-Hur* (1880), and *The Prince of India* (1893). His major poetic efforts are *Commodus, An Historical Play* (1876) and *The Wooing of Malkatoon* (1898). Wallace's autobiography is *Lew Wallace, an Autobiography* (1906).

**FURTHER READING:** Two biographies exist on Lew Wallace: Irving McKee's *Ben-Hur Wallace* (1947) and Robert E. and Katharine M. Morsberger's *Wallace: Militant Romantic* (1980). These can be supplemented with Dorothy R. Russo and Thelma L. Sullivan's *Bibliographical Studies of Seven Authors of Crawfordsville, Indiana* (1952), and the article in R. E. Banta's *Indiana Authors and Their Books, 1816–1916* (1949). The Indiana State Library has many of Wallace's letters; several other libraries also hold Wallace letters.

ARTHUR W. SHUMAKER      DEPAUW UNIVERSITY

## ROBERT JAMES WALLER

August 1, 1939

**BIOGRAPHY:** Robert James Waller, the only son of Robert and Ruth Waller, grew up in rural Rockford, Iowa. When he was not helping his father, a chicken wholesaler, Waller was developing his musical and athletic talents. In 1957 he entered the University of Iowa on a basketball scholarship. A year later, disillusioned with college athletics, Waller transferred to the University of Northern Iowa to pursue a degree in mathematics and economics. After receiving his PhD in business management from Indiana University in 1968, Waller joined the management faculty of the University of Northern Iowa. In 1979 he, became dean of the university's business school.

Waller's literary career started locally in 1983 when he began contributing essays to the *Des Moines Register*. In 1985 job stress prompted him to step down as business dean and return to teaching. Discouraged by his students' lack of interest, Waller took an unpaid leave of absence in 1991. In a two-week period, inspired by a trip to Madison County, Waller wrote his first novel, *The Bridges of Madison County*. Within nine months of its first printing, the novel

topped the best-seller list and remained there for the better part of two years. Three subsequent novels and much popular attention have followed.

**SIGNIFICANCE:** While other publishers rejected the first novel of this little-known Iowa professor, Warner Books agreed to publish *The Bridges of Madison County* because of the appeal of its Midwestern values. Whether this novel does in fact reflect Midwestern values has been hotly debated. An August 9, 1993, *U.S. News and World Report* article by John Leo questions the novel's plot: Francesca Johnson, a forty-five-year-old farmer's wife, embraces her sense of responsibility and duty to family only after having a four-day extramarital affair with a fifty-two-year-old photographer, Robert Kincaid (N6). Other recurrent criticisms leveled by the literary establishment have focused on the excessive prose and formulaic characters and plots marking *Bridges* as well as Waller's subsequent novels, *Slow Waltz in Cedar Bend* (1993), *Border Music* (1995), and *Puerto Vallarta Squeeze* (1995).

Despite critical labeling of Waller as a sentimental middle-aged hippie who has marketed his way to stardom, Waller is unapologetic. He sees his novels and essays as assertions of literary and philosophical positions much needed in our time.

While criticisms are plentiful with regard to Waller's fiction, his three essay collections are well respected and comprise his most lasting and unquestioned contributions to Midwestern life and literature. These essays range from personal anecdotes on his life, disquisitions on the importance of family, and expressions of fervent belief in the life-sustaining power of romance to eloquent appeals for the preservation of nature and Iowa lifestyles. Midwestern values and beliefs are strongly asserted in these short autobiographical essays. Waller emphasizes the need to return to basic feelings and loyalties like love and family—and to romance.

Waller's essays, like his fiction, assert the importance of personal and literary romanticism. As such, his writings reflect the romantic resurgence evident in later twentieth-century literature. He rejects limits imposed by realistic literature's forms, techniques, and values, saying in his essay "Romance" in *Just beyond the Firelight* (1988) that "romance got lost along the way, drowned in the roar of our times, beat out by overly analytic teachers, drummed out by those who scoff at romantics as foolish and weak" (56). Waller sees human beings as more than their genetics and environment and believes that even within the limits imposed by day-to-day existence, people can achieve lives of transcendent meaning and value. He says, "romance is practical. It fuels your life and propels your work with a sense of vision, hope and caring" (57).

**SELECTED WORKS:** Waller began his literary career writing essays for the *Des Moines Register*. His most successful pieces written between 1983 and 1989 have been collected in three volumes of essays. The first two collections, published by Iowa State University Press, are *Just beyond the Firelight* (1988) and *One Good Road Is Enough* (1990). Warner Books published the third collection, *Old Songs in a New Cafe*, in 1994.

Undoubtedly, his most commercially successful work remains his first novel, *The Bridges of Madison County* (1992). The movie version, starring Meryl Streep and Clint Eastwood, became a top summer movie hit of 1995.

Waller's second novel, *Slow Waltz in Cedar Bend* (1993), enjoyed almost equal success to *Bridges*, but *Border Music* (1995) and *Puerto Vallarta Squeeze* (1995) attracted little favorable attention and considerable criticism for their sensationalism and formulaic writing, elements testing even the most faithful of Waller's fans.

**FURTHER READING:** Critical commentary on Waller's fiction includes Jennifer A. Chavez's 1995 University of New Mexico master's thesis, "A Rhetorical Criticism of *The Bridges of Madison County*: Narrative Rationality and the Evolution of Consciousness," as well as Bonnie Brennon's "Bridging the Backlash: A Cultural Material Reading of *The Bridges of Madison County*," in *Studies in Popular Culture* 19.1 (October 1996): 59–78. *Current Biography Yearbook* (1994): 604–607 provides an extensive biographical statement.

TRACEY HOLMES            UNIVERSITY OF KENTUCKY

## ARTEMUS WARD.
*See* Charles Farrar Browne

## THEODORE "TED" WARD
September 15, 1902–May 8, 1983

**BIOGRAPHY:** The author of twenty-two plays, Theodore Ward was born in Thibodeaux, Louisiana, the eighth of eleven children of Everett and Mary Louise (Pierre) Ward. In 1940 he married Mary Sangigian; the couple had two children. Ward studied creative writing at the University of Utah and at the University of Wisconsin under a ZONA GALE scholarship. In 1945 he won a scholarship for a Theater Guild playwriting seminar, during which Ward revised his original draft of *Our Lan'* (1941). *Big White Fog*, Ward's first play, was produced by the Federal Theatre Project in Chicago in 1938. *Our Lan'*, Ward's best-known play, opened on Broadway at the Royale Theatre in 1947. Ward, who was one of the organizers of the Harlem Negro Playwrights Company (1940) with LANGSTON HUGHES, Paul Robeson, and RICHARD WRIGHT, founded the South Side Center for the Performing Arts in Chicago in 1967. From 1938 until his death, Ward served as a mentor for several generations of African American playwrights, actors, and directors in Chicago and New York. Ward won the Theatre Guild Award in 1947 for *Our Lan'*. He was awarded a Guggenheim Fellowship for 1947–48. Theodore Ward died of heart failure in Chicago in 1983.

**SIGNIFICANCE:** Theodore Ward's best-known plays are *Our Lan'*, set in the Georgia Sea Islands after the Civil War, and *Big White Fog*, which forcefully depicts the dilemmas facing the Masons, an African American family who left the South for a better life in Chicago, a city which turns out to be immersed in what young Les Mason calls "a big white fog" (*Big White Fog*, in *Black Theatre USA* 297). Ella Mason protests to her husband, Victor, a Garveyite, that his "fine talk about freedom and giving the children a chance to be somebody" in the Midwest has turned out to be "a stack of lies" (*Big White Fog*, in *Black Theatre USA* 291). His mother-in-law considers Victor a "black crank" because of his faith in Garvey and especially because the reality of Chicago has proven very different from what Victor had promised with "his fool talk 'bout we goin' find freedom up here in the North" (*Big White Fog*, in *Black Theatre USA* 287–88). Victor's brother-in-law, Dan, asserts that blacks at least have the opportunity to make money in Chicago but loses his own money with the onset of the depression. As the play ends, only the possibility of a socialist revolution seems to offer hope.

**SELECTED WORKS:** *Big White Fog* appears in *Black Theatre USA*, edited by James V. Hatch and Ted Shine (1996). The full text of *Our Lan'* appears in Kenneth Rowe's *A Theater in Your Head* (1960), which also includes Rowe's commentaries on individual passages and scenes. Unpublished plays that received productions include *Sick and Tiahd* (alternate title: *Sick and Tired*, 1937), *Even the Dead Arise* (1938), *Skin Deep* (1939), *Deliver the Goods* (1942), *John Brown* (alternate title: *Of Human Grandeur*, 1950), *Throwback* (1951), *Whole Hog or Nothing* (1952), *The Daubers* (1953), and *Candle in the Wind* (1967).

**FURTHER READING:** Owen E. Brady's "Theodore Ward's *Our Lan'*: From the Slavery of Melodrama to the Freedom of Tragedy" appears in *Callaloo* 7.2 (Spring–Summer 1984): 40–56. Ward's treatment of African American women in *Big White Fog* is discussed by Anthony Barthelmy in "Mother, Sister, Wife: A Dramatic Perspective," *Southern Review* 221.3 (Summer 1985): 770–89. The Schomburg Center for Research in Black Culture at the New York Public Library holds a collection of Ward's papers. Manuscripts of Theodore Ward's plays are stored in the Hatch-Billops Collection in New York.

SANDRA SEATON    CENTRAL MICHIGAN UNIVERSITY

## WILLIAM W(HIPPLE) WARREN
May 27, 1825–June 1, 1853

**BIOGRAPHY:** Born one-quarter Native American in 1825, the son of a successful trader among the Ojibway (also called Chippewa) of northern Wisconsin, William W. Warren completed in 1852 a single book eventually published as *History of the Ojibways, Based upon Traditions and Oral Statements* (1885). The author's preface states that he had planned additional volumes presenting Ojibway "customs, beliefs, and rites," their "mythological traditions," and important biographies. Warren, however, died at twenty-eight after completing the first of the series. Fortunately, his *History* incorporates something of his other projects.

From childhood Warren was a fluent speaker of Indian language and "deemed it a duty to save their traditions from oblivion" (25). After schooling at his grandfather's in Clarkson, New York, Warren attended the Oneida Institute near Utica for two years until 1841. Returning to the Lake Superior country, he married Matilda Aitkin, a trader's

daughter, became official interpreter for treaty negotiations, and was eventually elected to the Minnesota House of Representatives.

**SIGNIFICANCE:** Appreciating the indigenous culture on its own terms, Warren still saw himself as a Christian. Like many contemporaneous writers of American and European history, he presents Indian history as a chronological account of political alignments and battles. History thus becomes the affairs of men at war. The Ojibway battled the Iroquois and the Foxes and then engaged the "Dakotas" (Warren never uses "Sioux") in more protracted guerrilla war for the rich hunting grounds of the upper Mississippi.

The Ojibway struggled for possession of the upper Midwest after their migration up the Saint Lawrence from the Atlantic Ocean. The defensible shores of Madeline Island and the nearby Chequamegon Peninsula, now Wisconsin, became the center of the Ojibway world. It was a world of conflict, and Warren says that not only tribes, but clans also fought with each other. Presenting these tragedies, Warren does not idealize his subject.

One-third of Warren's book discusses Ojibway origins, the clan system, an Ojibway religion ("Midewiwin"), and other customs such as the vision quest. Warren's comments about membership in clans, which in the Ojibway world are patrilineal groups denominated by various animals, emphasize the connection between people and nature. Such comments are important because indigenous people identified themselves more by clan than by the tribes through which nonnatives knew them. Today, Indians viewing themselves as members of the crane clan or the marten clan can thereby facilitate participation in silent but living nature, one reason Indian culture is valued. Warren also grouped Indian people by related languages. By this criterion, the Algonquin or "Algic" group, including the Ojibway, constitutes the largest extended family of related Indian cultures in North America, extending across the upper Midwest.

Regarding Midewiwin, Warren declares that "Missionaries, travelers and sojourners amongst the Ojibways" have found it to be "foolish and unmeaning ceremonies" (66). However, Midewiwin is a mystery religion of progressive initiations, containing rules of life for this world, rites of empowerment and healing, and the path to continued life in the spirit world. Warren describes how fratricidal conflict caused abuses of this religious institution. Nevertheless, noting similarities to contemporaneous spiritualism, Warren says, "There is much yet to be learned from the wild and apparently simple son of the forest . . . derived from their religious beliefs" (67).

**SELECTED WORKS:** Warren wrote a series of weekly articles for the *Minnesota Democrat* from February 11 to April 1, 1851; these were reprinted in the *Minnesota Archaeologist* 12: 45–91, 95–107 and 13: 5–21 (April and October 1946 and April 1947). Here Warren writes that in gathering information he confirmed its validity by seeking additional informants from different villages, thereby anticipating sound modern methodology. Reprinted in 1984 as *History of the Ojibway People,* Warren's book was originally published in 1885 as volume 5 of the Collections of the Minnesota Historical Society.

**FURTHER READING:** W. Roger Buffalo-head's thoughtful introduction in the 1984 reprint of Warren's *History* furnished several points for this present article on Warren, recommending Robert F. Berkhofer's *The White Man's Indian* (1978) for a discussion of non-Indian perceptions during the nineteenth century. Reprinted in 1965 as *Savagism and Civilization: A Study of the Indian and the American Mind,* Roy H. Pearce's *The Savages of America* (1953) covers non-Indian perceptions from the beginning of European settlement; in the face of censure for being primitive, described by Pearce, Warren's claim that Ojibway religion has something to teach becomes a defense of Indian humanity. An appreciative voice is that of Frances Densmore; her two-volume *Chippewa Music* (1910, 1913) and *Chippewa Customs* (1929) benefited from the assistance of Warren's sister, Mary Warren English.

A number of non-Indian writers have written on the Midewiwin. Helen Hornbeck Tanner published *The Ojibwas: A Critical Bibliography* (1976). A lengthy bibliography is found in Christopher Vecsey, *Traditional Ojibwa Religion and Its Historical Changes* (1983). However, one Ojibway author describes Midewiwin as a living practice; in *The Mishomis Book: The Voice of the Ojibway* (1979), available from Indian Country Communications in Hayward, Wisconsin, Edward Benton-Banai presents the Midewiwin as a network of positive re-lationships, natural and spiritual, nurturing the continuance of life.

JEFF JUSTIN                                    MUSKEGON, MICHIGAN

## THEODORE WEESNER
July 31, 1935

**BIOGRAPHY:** Theodore Weesner, novelist and short story writer, grew up in Flint, Michigan. His father, William Weesner, previously a railroad brakeman in Kansas, worked for Chevrolet Motor Company; his mother, Margaret (McInnes), was formerly a barmaid. His parents, both alcoholics, divorced when the future writer was two years old, each assuming custody of two children. Weesner was raised by his father and step-mother. A troubled adolescent, he was arrested several times, twice remanded to juvenile detention, and sentenced to three years' probation for car theft. His father committed suicide in 1951. After being suspended from high school, the seventeen-year-old Weesner enlisted in the army and was stationed in West Germany. Responding positively to the discipline and educational opportunity offered by the military, he went on to earn degrees at Michigan State University (BA, 1959) and the University of Iowa (MFA, 1964), where his classmates included Raymond Carver and Joy Williams. He married Sharon Long in 1963; she bore two sons and a daughter before her death in 1988. Weesner's best-selling first novel, *The Car Thief* (1972), won the Great Lakes Colleges Award and led to Guggenheim and National Endowment for the Arts grants. He has taught at the University of New Hampshire, Carnegie Mellon University, and Emerson College.

**SIGNIFICANCE:** Weesner's writing dwells on the damaged among us, especially adolescents being shaped by adverse social environments. Noting his treatment of social class in America, critics have compared him favorably to an earlier Midwesterner, THEODORE DREISER. Weesner has drawn extensively from his youth in the automobile industry city of Flint; he described *The Car Thief,* for example, to Nicholas Basbanes of *Publishers Weekly* as "pretty much a straight-line autobiographical novel" (46). But the book endures not only as a naturalistic document of life in the 1950s, but as a sparely written, quietly moving picture of a troubled sixteen-year-old who "borrows" cars to escape, if temporarily, the painful reality of his drab and lonely life. As Roger Sale writes in *On Not Being Good Enough: Writings of a Working Critic* (1979), "Weesner knows when to blurt out, when to back off, and the cumulative effect of his apparently simple sentences is sometimes staggering" (19).

In Alex Housman, the protagonist of *The Car Thief*, Weesner created a prototype for other characters with autobiographical underpinnings. *The Car Thief* ends with Alex in the army, having left high school and his past as a petty criminal for a new life. Though the protagonist of *A German Affair* (1976) does not share Alex's name, his story logically follows: a working-class Midwestern youth seeks initiation into adulthood while serving as a soldier in postwar Germany. Weesner's other Flint novel, *Winning the City* (1990), reads in part as a prequel to *The Car Thief*; its central character, Dale Wheeler, also lives with his alcoholic autoworker father in Flint. Dale believes that success in basketball will turn his life around, and his father's as well. But what follows is a painful lesson in social inequity, class warfare in miniature: a factory supervisor in his father's auto plant effectively buys the team and Dale loses his rightful position to the man's sons. The team he joins to compete against his own classmates is made up of boys like himself, sons of transplanted Southerners in the industrial Midwest—the same people portrayed in novels by HARRIETTE ARNOW and JACK CONROY.

Weesner's Midwestern context is also evident in the stories of *Children's Hearts* (1992), two of which had been incorporated into *The Car Thief*. Four stories feature Glenn Whalen, another quasi-autobiographical character. In "Driver's Ed," Weesner completes the imaginative re-creation of his early life much as does ERNEST HEMINGWAY in the story "Fathers and Sons." Like Hemingway's alter ego Nick Adams, Glenn remembers his father, privately as well as aloud to his young son, who is accompanying him on a driving trip. But whereas Hemingway implies the suicide of Nick's father and has Nick's son express the desire to visit his grandfather's grave, Weesner places his characters in the graveyard, searching for the marker while discussing the man's self-destruction.

Weesner's connection to the Midwest thus continues, though like Glenn Whalen and many characters in his recent fiction, he has made New Hampshire his home. *The True Detective* (1987), a realistic crime novel in the tradition of Dreiser's *An American Tragedy*, was researched and originally set in Detroit, where the actual case occurred. The characterization in *Novemberfest* (1994) of a middle-aged New Hampshire college professor echoes Weesner's earlier protagonists: Glen Cady grew up in Flint, Michigan, had an alcoholic father, and served in Germany during the 1950s. Differences, of course, abound between Glen, the earlier characters, and their author. Yet like other important Midwestern writers, Weesner has transformed his own experience into art by seeking the universally human in the particular, personal, and local.

**SELECTED WORKS:** Weesner's first stories appeared in *The Saturday Evening Post*, *New Yorker*, *Esquire*, and other periodicals between 1965 and 1970, leading to the publication of his first novel, *The Car Thief* (1972), followed by *A German Affair* (1976), *The True Detective* (1987), *Winning the City* (1990), *Novemberfest* (1994), and *Harbor Lights* (2000). *Children's Hearts*, a collection of short stories, appeared in 1992.

**FURTHER READING:** In *On Not Being Good Enough: Writings of a Working Critic* (1979), Roger Sale discusses Weesner among talented contemporary novelists, major and lesser known. For an interview-based portrait of the author, see Nicholas Basbanes's "Theodore Weesner: 'I Became an Over-Achiever,'" in *Publishers Weekly* (December 12, 1994): 46–47. His books regularly earn notice in periodicals such as the *New York Times Book Review*, *USA Today*, and the *Chicago Tribune*.

WILLIAM BARILLAS

UNIVERSITY OF WISCONSIN–LA CROSSE

# GLENWAY WESCOTT

April 11, 1901–February 22, 1987

**BIOGRAPHY:** Glenway Wescott—poet, short story writer, novelist, critic, and popular spokesman for arts—was born the first of six children on a small farm in Kewaskum, Wisconsin, to Josephine (Gordon) and Bruce Peters Wescott. Disliking farmwork, he left home in 1913 to live with relatives, then attended the University of Chicago for two years, where he began writing stories of rural Wisconsin, stayed briefly with poet YVOR WINTERS, and met VACHEL LINDSAY, CARL SANDBURG, and EDGAR LEE MASTERS.

In 1920 Wescott returned home to Wisconsin for a visit, then began a series of moves to New York and then to sites in Europe. Wescott consciously made the grand tour and associated with the American expatriate community while writing poetry, as well as works of fiction that made use of his Wisconsin roots. During this time he met ERNEST HEMINGWAY, who modeled the character of Robert Prentiss in *The Sun Also Rises* on Wescott.

Wescott returned to the United States in 1934, settling three years later on a brother's farm in New Jersey while maintaining an apartment in New York. He moved to another farm when the property was flooded for a reservoir. In the four decades from the end of World War II until his death, he published no fiction, concentrating on reviews, critical essays, and editorial work. As president of the National Institute of Arts and Letters, he conducted a lecture tour and was himself a frequent college lecturer. In the 1950s, Wescott told an interviewer for Wisconsin Public Radio, "I think I'm a talker. That's a very special destiny."

Wescott survived a stroke at his home in New Jersey but died eighteen months later in New York.

**SIGNIFICANCE:** The fact that he was a rural Midwestern native was central to Wescott's fiction, he claimed, even though he chose to live elsewhere most of his life. *Good-bye, Wisconsin* (1928), a collection of short stories, contains an opening sketch that defines a pose of the ex-Midwesterner: "There is no Middle West. It is a certain climate, a certain landscape; and beyond that, a state of mind of people born where they do not like to live" (39). However, in his interview with Wisconsin Public Radio in Madison, Wescott said he never intended that pretentious narrator's pose to be taken as seriously as it was. He insisted that permanent relocation was "no drama." Rather, "I followed my vocation and my opportunities as a young man," building upon his interests in art that had begun in Kewaskum.

In the 1920s, Wescott made summer visits to the family farm and created a fictional expatriate persona, Alwyn Tower, first appearing in *The Grandmothers* (1927). The Midwest as frontier was history to Wescott. In his day, however, the region offered neither challenge for survival nor culture for imagination. While he called his frequent trips abroad his greatest education, he told his interviewer in Madison that "subject matter is the heart of any aesthetic." Wescott's style for Midwestern stories is self-consciously poetic with lavish description, brooding and reflective, and with lesser emphasis on plot and dialogue. His typical narrator is respectful but alienated by temperament and experience from earlier generations: he has visited a Midwestern home but experienced it principally in imagination.

Wescott was an autobiographical writer, determined to create fiction from his Midwestern roots and adult experiences. *The Apple of the Eye* (1924) is set in the eastern Wisconsin of Wescott's birth. The story recounts a family history of failed, even fatal, romances, owing to repressive material ambitions and religion. Dan Strane, disappointed by his family and disliking farmwork, resolves that only a university education can help his young man's restlessness and questionings about his own life.

In *The Grandmothers*, Alwyn Tower, in Europe but haunted by long-dead family, realizes he must learn his ancestors' stories in order to form and understand his own character. He imaginatively reconstructs a family history from memory, personal possessions, and stories from his grandmothers. Alwyn realizes he has created an account of pioneer life in the Midwest, where despite the gradual softening of life, most farms and businesses failed and most families lived unhappily, resigned and brooding though not in outright conflict. Tower realizes that his life, separated from the older frontier setting, will take a different direction. In *The Pilgrim Hawk* (1940), set in France, the narrator is a matured Alwyn Tower, still reflecting in part upon his family.

*The Babe's Bed* (1930), a small, private publication, was Wescott's last book set in Wisconsin; it too was narrated by an expatriate. *Apartment in Athens* (1945), set during World

War II, was his only best-seller and his last published work of fiction.

**SELECTED WORKS:** Wescott's novels include *The Apple of the Eye* (1924), *The Grandmothers* (1927), *The Babe's Bed* (1930), *The Pilgrim Hawk* (1940), and *Apartment in Athens* (1945). He has a collection of short stories entitled *Good-bye, Wisconsin* (1928). Wescott published two books of verse: *The Bitterns* (1920) and *Natives of Rock: XX Poems* (1925). He also published *A Calendar of Saints for Unbelievers* (1932) and *Twelve Fables by Aesop* (1954). *Images of Truth: Remembrances and Criticism* (1962) is a memoir of literary acquaintances. Wescott published one volume of his journals, *The Best of All Possible Worlds* (1975), and arranged for posthumous publication of another, *Continual Lessons: The Journals of Glenway Wescott 1937–1955* (1990).

**FURTHER READING:** William Rueckert's *Glenway Wescott* (1965) is a critical biography tracing Wescott's development from fiction writer and poet to public spokesman for literature and art. Ira Johnson's *Glenway Wescott: The Paradox of Voice* (1971) is a detailed critical study of each book of fiction. Frank Gado's *First Person: Conversations on Writers and Writing* (1973) contains an interview with Wescott. *Continual Lessons*, edited by Robert Phelps and Jerry Rosco, contains a completed chronology of Wescott's life and provides an index of his literary acquaintances, some of whom wrote about Wescott. Rosco has also written "Glenway Wescott: The Poetic Career of a Novelist," in the *Chicago Review* 37 (1990): 113–30. Kegan Doyle's "The Moral of Glenway Wescott: The Closet and the Second Act," appearing in the *Canadian Review of American Studies* 28 (1998): 43–61, attributes Wescott's departure from rural Wisconsin to a desire for a society more tolerant of homosexuality.

Wescott's manuscripts, letters, and other materials are held by the State Historical Society of Wisconsin; libraries of the University of Wisconsin and the University of Maryland; and the New York Public Library.

Thomas Pribek

University of Wisconsin–LaCrosse

## (Mary) Jessamyn West

July 18, 1902–February 23, 1984

**BIOGRAPHY:** Jessamyn West was born near North Vernon, Indiana, of Eldo Ray and Grace Anna (Milhous) West, Quakers. Reportedly, she was named after her grandfather, Jesse G. Milhous. Her mother's side was of predominantly Irish descent. In *Double Discovery* (1980), she described her father's people as western Celts whom "the invaders of England had been unable either to kill or to drive across the sea to Ireland" (6). Her father also had Indian blood from a maternal grandmother. His half-Indian mother was a stern and formidable woman, Miss West said in *Hide and Seek* (1973), who "could throw a 100–pound sack of wheat across her shoulder and walk off with it as easily as another woman could shoulder a baby" (71). This image of oneself as related to stubborn people who survived in spite of opposition may have helped the author through the most serious illness of her life, tuberculosis.

West spent her earliest years doing farmwork. When she was seven years old, her family moved to southern California, eventually settling in Yorba Linda. The local scenes in Indiana and southern California, experiences of schooling at Whittier College (AB 1923) and Fullerton Junior College, and her Quaker orientation were to provide the basis for her writing. In college she met her future husband, Harry Maxwell (Max) McPherson, whom she married in 1923. They adopted a child, Ann Cash.

Jessamyn West was a secretary and schoolteacher during the early years of her marriage. In 1929 she went to Oxford University for the summer session; before classes began, she visited Ireland and Scotland and later went to Paris; her horizons newly widened, she attended graduate school at the University of California at Berkeley, preparing for a doctorate in English. But her academic career was cut short by her discovery that she was the victim of bilateral tuberculosis. Arising one morning, she abruptly hemorrhaged, and thus began several years of "horizontal life," as she called it, during which she made a slow recovery against the odds.

But the disease carried one blessing in disguise: it began her writing career. The first story West ever published was "99.6," an account of the experience of a bedridden consumptive. It appeared in *Broun's Nutmeg* of June 10, 1939. But another seed had been planted. Depressed, West says she could neither live in the "past" of her marriage, her travels, and her studies, which were "impossible or forbidden now," nor in the present from which she was "locked away," nor in the uncertain future, so her mother "gave [her] her own life, as a young woman, as Grace Milhous, a Quaker girl on a farm in southern Indiana at the turn of the century" (*Woman* 46–47). Thus, said West, tuberculosis "forced me, through deprivation, to the one act which I had been for so long simultaneously avoiding and loving—the writing of a story" (*To See the Dream* 258).

In 1940 the McPhersons moved to Napa, California, their home for the rest of their lives. It was six years before her first short story collection, *The Friendly Persuasion*, appeared in 1945. With that, Jessamyn West was firmly set in her choice of a career. Several more short story collections, novels, screenplays, and an operetta followed. She also found time to teach at writers' conferences at Bread Loaf, Indiana University, Notre Dame, University of Colorado, University of Utah, University of Washington, and Stanford.

West died of a stroke in Napa, California.

**SIGNIFICANCE:** Jessamyn West's first short story collection, *The Friendly Persuasion* (1945), was a very successful, idyllic collection of Quaker stories that drew heavily on family history and stories told by her mother. The central figure in this "love poem to Indiana," Jess Birdwell was modeled both on Henry David Thoreau and on her great-grandfather, Joshua Vickers Milhous, including his Quaker minister-wife and his purchase of a forbidden organ (Shivers 55). Except for a few germs of information like these and the use of the names of actual family members, the stories in *The Friendly Persuasion* are the fruit of West's imagination.

Her first novel, *The Witch Diggers* (1951), set in 1899 Indiana, is a grim tale of disappointment and tragedy. The title comes from two cultists living in the County Home who believe the Devil long ago buried Truth somewhere in the earth and that it is the duty of those who know this truth to dig until they find it so that mankind may be happy again. Similarly, characters like the central female figure, Cate Conboy, look everywhere for happiness and end up losing their chance for it because of that very preoccupation. The novel was competent and praised in reviews, but never popular. It did not contain any characters with which people could identify.

Unfortunately, Jessamyn West had become stereotyped by her first collection and the film based upon it as "the sweet singer of Quakerdom, the good gray novelist" (*To See the Dream* 57). Anything untypical was not read by her fans. Throughout her career this stereotype followed her. Although she wrote ever more realistic stories and novels, she maintained the image of a sheltered housewife of Quaker origins. She might, as late as *Leafy Rivers* in 1967, create worldly Midwestern Quakers who are not especially pacifist, who have no characteristic manner of language or dress, and who avoid all silent meetings, but they were still present as the central figures in her tales of nineteenth-century Indiana. Over time, West began to fall into the formula writing that Hollywood had encouraged of her as a screenwriter. She began to produce a series of formulaic stories in which problems are all solved in the time allotted for the action, there is adequate raw sex and some violence, and the villains pay in the end while virtue is affirmed.

*Cress Delahanty* (1953) was one of West's more popular story collections. It was chosen as a Book-of-the-Month Club selection. The collection is organized by the seasons, like Thoreau's *Walden*. Some of the autobiographical details in *Cress* underline a similarity in experiences and perhaps personality between author and character.

Her third collection, *Love, Death and the Ladies' Drill Team* (1955), is set in modern California. In these bleak tales characters manifest their distance from wholesomeness by a disregard or even hatred for human beings and nature. Consistent with her admiration for Thoreau, West often used characters' attitudes toward nature as markers for their humanity.

A story collection bringing the Birdwell family up to date and filling in the gaps left by *The Friendly Persuasion*, *Except for Me and Thee* (1969), sold quite well, probably because it maintained the tone and plot of the former collection. West's growing awareness of racial issues during the 1960s was reflected in her inclusion of African American slavery in "Neighbors," the longest episode in the book. Perhaps also recalling the Hollywood producer's complaint that Jess Birdwell had never been tested in his faith, West created a moral conflict for his wife. The crisis for the Quaker Eliza Birdwell comes when she has to admit that a Higher Law takes precedence over the Fugitive Slave Law, which protects slavery. She accepts responsibility for saving a slave couple from recapture, forsaking her usual conservative respect for constitutional authority. West explores the reality that part of the Underground Railroad passed through Quaker territory and might have occasioned painful choices by its citizens.

West's second novel, *South of the Angels* (1960), uses the Yorba Linda of her girlhood as a setting. The book is marked by the cycle of nature, the agriculturally based Tract where the earliest settlers stayed, conflicts over water, a few Quaker families, a lot of fornication and infidelity, and neatly balanced births and deaths. Asa Brice, a major character, is clearly modeled after Thoreau.

The novel *A Matter of Time*, serialized in *Redbook* in 1966, West feared was so controversial that it would never be published. The central character, Tassie (Tasmania), talks with her sister Blix as Blix lies dying of cancer and finally makes the decision to commit suicide rather than to endure the pain. West allows Blix a painless and uneventful death in a lovely green silk dress, but she still depicts the ex-Quaker Murphy family as inadequate spiritually, partly because of their removal from the Midwest to the West. Reviewers found moral ambiguity at the novel's core. The obvious conflict between "physician-assisted suicide" and conservative religion is muted by the author's apparent endorsement of Blix's decision.

In 1975 Jessamyn West published what is probably her most powerful novel, *The Massacre at Fall Creek*. This fictionalized treatment of a true event on the Indiana frontier of 1824 portrays the intermingled racism and sense of Manifest Destiny that led otherwise reputable family men to take part in the murder of unarmed men, women, and children in an attack disguised as a social visit. West not only condemns their actions but also their executions. On the other hand, since the Indians expect a blood sacrifice, West makes it clear that it is the men's duty to die to prevent an attack on the settlement. While she presented capital punishment as unavoidable, she made it clear in a later interview that she saw it as useless, never solving anything. The issues

raised in *The Massacre at Fall Creek* take the reader beyond character and plot and into the greater society while still reflecting the Midwestern Quaker base of the author's moral position.

West brings another moral question squarely onto Midwestern soil. The nineteenth-century land issues raised again beginning in 1968 with the formation of the American Indian Movement and the 1973 resistance of Native Americans at Wounded Knee, South Dakota, the site of the final massacre of the Indian wars in 1890, are relevant in this novel. These issues are played out in the Indiana of an earlier time. Whereas "preachers spoke of the West as if it was the Promised Land," it was not possible to take the land without killing or cheating its original inhabitants (*Massacre* 292). Old John Wood, contemplating the gallows, expresses his complicity in immoral dealings from the first time he bought Indian land back in New York state up to his involvement in the massacre at Fall Creek. The sense of entitlement that he and others felt remains prevalent at the time of the trials and executions of these, the first white men to die in the United States for killing Indians. The resistance of whites to the hangings is strong. They feel "Indian-killing [is] on a par with ridding the country of wolves and copperheads"; hence, as a general principle, "No white man shall die for an Indian" (288). The novel raised questions arising from the clash of cultures throughout the history of westward expansion, as the author intended (314).

West's most enduring creations are the Quaker figures in *The Friendly Persuasion* and *Except for Me and Thee*. She was at her best in covering ground that reflected old family stories and fond recollections of the Indiana of her earliest childhood. Her other stories, though extremely traditional in technique, are skillfully written; they were not compelling, however, to audiences who looked for faster pacing and greater irony of characterization during the postwar era and especially up through the 1960s. West will be remembered as a minor writer who used two different yet familiar locales for sources of color: southern California and back home in Indiana.

**SELECTED WORKS:** West's works with a Midwestern setting include *The Friendly Per-*

*suasion* (1945); *The Witch Diggers* (1951); *The Quaker Reader* (1962), which she edited; *Leafy Rivers* (1967); *Except for Me and Thee* (1969); *Crimson Ramblers of the World; Farewell* (1970); and *The Massacre at Fall Creek* (1975). Among her personal writings are *To See the Dream* (1957), *Hide and Seek* (1973), *The Woman Said Yes* (1976), and *Double Discovery* (1980). In 1970 West made a short videotape entitled *Jessamyn West: My Hand, My Pen* in which she discussed her feelings about writing. A PBS interview with Robert Cromie on *Bookbeat* (May 26, 1975) is available on audiotape.

**FURTHER READING:** Alfred S. Shivers's *Jessamyn West* (1972, 1992, CD-ROM version, 1995) and Ann D. Farmer's *Jessamyn West* (1982) are the only full-length critical studies. Farmer has also coedited with Philip O'Brien *Jessamyn West: A Descriptive and Annotated Bibliography* (1998). All of West's work has been reviewed, as has the film *Friendly Persuasion*. Among the most interesting critical articles are DAVID ANDERSON's "The Way It Was: Jessamyn West's *The Witchdiggers*," in the *Society for the Study of Midwestern Literature Newsletter* 13.2 (Summer 1983): 38–46; JANE S. BAKERMAN's "Surrogate Mothers: The Manipulation of Daughters in Works by Jessamyn West," in *Midwestern Miscellany* 10 (1982): 49–58; JOHN T. FLANAGAN's "The Fiction of Jessamyn West," in the *Indiana Magazine of History* 67 (1971): 299–316, and his "Folklore in Five Midwestern Novelists," appearing in the *Great Lakes Review* 1.2 (1975): 43–57; Kathleen Rout's "Death in Indiana: *The Massacre at Fall Creek* by Jessamyn West," in *Indiana Social Studies Quarterly* 38.1 (Spring 1985): 19–25, and her article "The Social Morality of *The Massacre at Fall Creek*," in the *Society for the Study of Midwestern Literature Newsletter* 13.3 (1983): 1–11.

KATHLEEN K. ROUT        MICHIGAN STATE UNIVERSITY

# RAY LEWIS WHITE.
*See* appendix (1987)

# WILLIAM ALLEN WHITE
February 10, 1868–January 29, 1944
(Will A. White, W. A. White, The Sage of Emporia, The Emporian)

**BIOGRAPHY:** Born in Emporia, Kansas, of Allen and Mary Ann (Hatton) White, William Allen White grew up an only child in Emporia and in El Dorado, sixty miles south. His father, who died when the boy was fourteen, was a storekeeper and part-time country doctor who for a time operated a hotel, served as mayor of El Dorado, and dabbled in real estate. His mother, who died in her nineties, always lived with her son or close by.

Upon graduating from high school, White attended the College of Emporia and the University of Kansas, though he did not earn a degree. From the time he was seventeen, he made his living as a journalist, working successively on the *Lawrence Journal*, the *El Dorado Republican*, and the *Kansas City Journal* and later the *Star*, before buying the *Emporia Gazette*, a daily paper of which he was editor and publisher from 1895 until 1944. While working in Kansas City he met Sallie Lindsay, a schoolteacher. They married in 1893 and had two children, William Lindsay and Mary.

White knew every U.S. president from William McKinley to Franklin Roosevelt and counted among his friends and professional colleagues many of the eminent men and women of his time, including writers and journalists Ida Tarbell, RAY STANNARD BAKER, EDNA FERBER, Lincoln Steffens, Mark Sullivan, BRAND WHITLOCK, Walter Lippmann, Drew Pearson, CARL SANDBURG, Josephus Daniels, and S. S. McClure, in addition to such political friends as Henry Wallace, Alf Landon, Harold Ickes, Robert M. La Follette, senior and junior, and especially Theodore Roosevelt.

Less than two weeks short of his seventy-sixth birthday, he died in Emporia of a heart attack, apparently induced by advanced prostate cancer for which he had undergone surgery at the Mayo Clinic. His widow and his son edited *The Autobiography of William Allen White*, which was published posthumously in 1946 and awarded the Pulitzer Prize.

**SIGNIFICANCE:** The *Emporia* (Kansas) *Gazette* was the rostrum from which William Allen White's opinions spread far and wide for most of the first half of the twentieth century. Despite his 1896 editorial, "What's the Matter with Kansas?" that brought White to national attention for its attack on William Jennings Bryan's populism, White became a staunch supporter of Progressivism. Fundamental to his mature outlook was the value he placed on middle-class gentility, by which he meant small-town America—particularly as found in the Midwest. The Midwestern town represented for him the necessary balance between the forces of industrial capital and the working class.

White's finest hour came in his vigorous assault, beginning with *Gazette* editorials in 1921, on the Ku Klux Klan—a crusade that led him to run for governor of Kansas in 1924 so that his anti-Klan message would reach a broader state and national audience. As expected, White did not win the election, but he was widely credited with deflating Klan intentions in Kansas. In *A Man from Kansas* (1945), David Hinshaw credits White with being "the first American newspaper editor of much consequence to attack" the Klan (239).

When his teenage daughter died after running into a low-hanging branch while riding her horse, he composed "Mary White," a tribute that has become his most widely reprinted writing. Another famous editorial, which White ran on the front page of the *Gazette* in 1922, won a Pulitzer Prize. That editorial, "To an Anxious Friend," argued for broad freedom of expression, particularly in times of social unrest.

SELECTED WORKS: William Allen White's fiction attempts to show the virtues of small-town American life—a thrust that was also present in much of his editorial writing. His two novels, *A Certain Rich Man* (1909) and *In the Heart of a Fool* (1918), are loosely plotted romantic melodramas. The theme of *A Certain Rich Man* was summed up by Vernon Lewis Parrington as "fear of the economic city that draws the village into its web" (*Main Currents of American Thought* III: 374). *In the Heart of a Fool* juxtaposes a slick, materialistic corporation lawyer with an idealistic artisan. White also published five collections of short fiction, most notably *The Real Issue: A Book of Kansas Stories* (1896) and *The Court of Boyville* (1899), both depicting Midwestern village life.

White wrote several political books, including works on Woodrow Wilson, Alf Landon, and two on Calvin Coolidge, plus several volumes of political and social commentary reprinted from his editorials and magazine writings. His opinions and editorials are collected in two volumes: *The Editor and His People: Editorials by William Allen White, Selected from the Emporia Gazette*, edited by Helen Ogden Mahin (1924); and *Forty Years on Main Street*, compiled by Russell Fitzgibbon (1937). His letters, edited by his friend Walter Johnson, were published posthumously as *Selected Letters of William Allen White, 1888–1943* (1947).

FURTHER READING: The definitive study of William Allen White is that of E. Jay Jernigan, *William Allen White* (1983), in the Twayne series. A more recent sketch, *William Allen White* (1993), by Diane Dufva Quantic, in the Boise State University Western Writers series, is notable for its cogent critiques of White's fiction, despite the brevity afforded by the format. The comprehensive and most thoroughly documented biography, however, is *William Allen White's America* (1947), by Walter Johnson, which quotes extensively from primary sources and contains a very useful index. An abridged version of *The Autobiography of William Allen White* (1990) has been edited by Sally Foreman Griffith, who is the author of a study of his journalism: *Home Town News: William Allen White and the Emporia Gazette* (1989). A study focusing particularly on White's behind-the-scenes political career is John DeWitt McKee's *William Allen White: Maverick on Main Street* (1975).

A listing of White's books, articles, editorials, and poems, compiled by Walter Johnson and Alberta Pantle, was published as "A Bibliography of the Published Works of William Allen White," in the *Kansas Historical Quarterly* 13 (1947). "GLR Bibliography: William Allen White," compiled by Donald S. Pady and published in the *Great Lakes Review* 5 (1978), is especially notable for a checklist of secondary sources listing such ephemera as reviews of White's books, works by others in which White is mentioned, his obituaries, and tributes by numerous friends and admirers. The two-volume *A Bibliography of William Allen White* (1969), compiled by Gary Mason et al., is a finding list for the William Allen White collection at Emporia State University. Nelson R. Burr has compiled a similar finding list, *William Allen White: A Register and Index of His Papers in the Library of Congress* (1978). White's papers are at Emporia State University and the Library of Congress.

ROGER JIANG BRESNAHAN

MICHIGAN STATE UNIVERSITY

## (JOSEPH) BRAND WHITLOCK
March 4, 1869–May 24, 1934

BIOGRAPHY: Brand Whitlock, journalist, lawyer, novelist, diplomat, was born in Urbana, Ohio, the son of the Rev. Elias Whitlock and Mollie Lavinia (Brand) Whitlock. Young Whitlock grew up in his father's successive Methodist ministerial homes in such Ohio towns as Delaware, Findlay, and Kenton, spending summers with his beloved maternal grandfather in Urbana. Whitlock graduated from high school in Toledo, Ohio. Inspired by his grandfather, Joseph Carter Brand, a fiery abolitionist and three-term mayor of Urbana, Whitlock rejected the more traditional values of his family by not going to college and by becoming a Democrat in a family of staunch Ohio Republicans.

As a youth of eighteen, he began working as a journalist for the Toledo *Blade*. His life thereafter as a reformer may be conveniently divided into two periods, from 1890 to 1897, and from 1897 to 1914, following which he gradually became disillusioned with reform and with American democracy (1914–34).

In the first period, working as a reporter in Chicago and Springfield for the *Chicago Herald* (1891–93), becoming a lawyer (1894), and starting to write short stories, he came under the influence of controversial reform Governor John P. Altgeld, the labor lawyer CLARENCE DARROW, and such fellow members of the bohemian Whitechapel Club as budding satirists GEORGE ADE and FINLEY PETER DUNNE. In this period Whitlock came to sympathize with the poor and downtrodden, exploited by machine politics, rampant capitalism, and a criminal justice system that favored the upper class. Also in this period (1892) he married Susan Brainerd of Springfield, who died four months afterward. Three years later he married her sister Ella, who outlived him. They had no children.

In the second period of reform, from 1897 to 1914, Whitlock moved to Toledo, Ohio, to practice law and become a supporter of reform Mayor Samuel "Golden Rule" Jones, from whom, following Jones's sudden death in 1904, he soon took over the reins of office for four terms. Equally important, he published four novels and two collections of short stories, beginning with *The Thirteenth District* (1902), a novel exposing machine politics and political corruption in Illinois and Washington. In this second period, the underpinnings of Whitlock's reform gradually shifted from Jeffersonian idealism to devout though cerebral Christianity based on his reading of Tolstoy and the words of Jesus.

Following his appointment as minister and later ambassador to Belgium (1914–21), the life of Whitlock underwent a sea change. Glorying in the freedom of his new position, which promised to be a sinecure, he plunged into a new novel, to be called *J. Hardin and Son*, which was interrupted one third of the way through by the war and by his exhausting years of work in Belgian relief. In this period he was lionized by the Belgians and thoroughly Europeanized. He shifted his faith and allegiance to the aristocracy, gradually losing his belief in reform, in democracy, and in America. Retiring in 1921 to spend summers in Belgium and winters in France, he completed *J. Hardin and Son* in 1923. This novel was followed by some half dozen others of indifferent quality, including the expatriate novels *Uprooted* (1926) and *Transplanted* (1927), and his last and unfinished work, *The Buckeyes*, a fictionalized account of his grandfather's early life in Urbana that was posthumously published in 1977. Whitlock also wrote a substantial biography of Lafayette, published in 1929. He died following cancer surgery in the British colony of Cannes in southern France.

SIGNIFICANCE: Though Whitlock is remembered for his contributions to reform, both in such topical protest novels as *The Turn of the Balance* (1907) and as mayor of Toledo fighting the monopolistic Toledo Railways and Light Company, his enduring contribution to Midwestern letters is his realistic portrayal in fiction of Macochee, Ohio, a thinly disguised Urbana. Macochee first appears as the setting of *The Happy Average* (1904), then in seven short stories in *The Gold Brick* (1910) and *The Fall Guy* (1912), again in *J. Hardin and Son*, and finally in *The Buckeyes*.

In *J. Hardin and Son*, Whitlock's best novel, Macochee is the home of a skilled carriage maker who becomes a victim of the national trusts and mass production that prepared the way for the automotive age. This novel also traces the corollary disaster of Hardin's son Paul, corrupted by the easy money of the new age of oil and financial speculation in northern Ohio. Influenced by the reticent realism of William Dean Howells but going beyond it to explore such indelicate topics as lynching and adultery in the town, this novel might have received the attention it deserved had its composition and publication not been delayed by the war and its aftermath. By 1923, however, the realism of *J. Hardin and Son,* though still impressive on its own terms, had paled by comparison with such bolder modernist works as SHERWOOD ANDERSON's *Winesburg, Ohio* (1919) and SINCLAIR LEWIS's *Main Street* (1920).

In retrospect, one can see that Whitlock was an American at war with himself, simultaneously loving and loathing the underclass, whose cause he championed, and the egalitarian democracy whose great potentialities he tested as mayor of Toledo. Though he retained to his death a nostalgic attachment to the beautiful rural landscapes of Ohio, his rejection of American society, including the spirit of the Midwest, was by 1921 all but complete. As he wrote in his *Journal* (1936) of December 23, 1921, "As for America, I have no desire to live there. The things I like, admire, esteem, are not respected there. A graceful life is thus impossible; there refinement, culture, literature, art, are almost unknown . . . . Now the spirit of vulgarity prevails . . . above all, dominating all, that provincial, nonconformist, puritanical Middle-West spirit" (720–21).

**SELECTED WORKS:** For a sampling of Whitlock's early fiction, combining elements of romance, realism, and protest, see *The Thirteenth District* (1902), *The Happy Average* (1904), or *The Turn of the Balance* (1907). Among the Macochee fictions, *J. Hardin and Son* (1923) stands out, with *The Buckeyes* (1977) providing insights into Macochee-Urbana's politics and abolitionism from 1836 to 1845. Among Whitlock's nonfiction writings, *Forty Years of It* (1914), *Belgium: A Personal Narrative* (1919), and *The Letters and Journal of Brand Whitlock* (1936) have both biographical and historical interest. **FURTHER READING:** Three good book-length accounts of Whitlock's life and achievements have been written: David D. Anderson's *Brand Whitlock* (1968), Robert M. Crunden's *A Hero in Spite of Himself* (1969), and Jack Tager's *The Intellectual as Urban Reformer* (1968). Also, Paul W. Miller has written introductions to editions of *J. Hardin and Son* (1982) and *The Buckeyes* (1977). The largest collection of Whitlock manuscripts is in the Library of Congress, with supplementary materials owned by the Champaign County Historical Society in Urbana, Ohio. In 1992 Bowling Green State University produced a twenty-nine-minute video

by Gene Dent entitled *The Reluctant Hero: Brand Whitlock.*

PAUL W. MILLER    WITTENBERG UNIVERSITY

# ELLA WHEELER WILCOX
November 5, 1850–October 30, 1919
(Eloine)

**BIOGRAPHY:** Ella Wheeler was born in rural Johnstown Center, Wisconsin, twelve miles outside Madison, and, as she later recalled, a five-mile ride bareback to the nearest post office and mailbox. Her parents were New Englanders who had trekked cross-country from Vermont to improve the family fortunes. Her father, Marcus Hartwell, a dancing instructor, businessman, and speculator, tried but generally failed to secure for his wife and four children a comfortable middle-class life. Sarah (Pratt) Wheeler succeeded in exciting her precocious daughter's interest in sentimental novelists such as "Ouida" and E. D. E. N. Southworth and in the standard household poets: Byron, Moore, Scott, and Shakespeare. Ella Wheeler's erratic formal education ended in 1867 after one homesick and unhappy term at the University of Wisconsin in Madison.

From age thirteen on, she bombarded newspapers and magazines, mostly in the East, with her poems and essays. Under the nom de plume of Eloine, she published her first essay in the *New York Mercury.* For her earliest publications she won prizes—magazines, books, pictures, and bric-a-brac that filled her parents' small prairie home. When still in her teens, she earned her first check in payment for poetry from *Frank Leslie's Magazine.* She soon became famous in "the West," which for her was a world bounded by Milwaukee and Chicago. For a brief time, she was said to have headed the "Milwaukee School of Poetry," a group that included her friend Hattie Tyng Griswold and a half-dozen other minor figures. The poet JAMES WHITCOMB RILEY, reading her poetry and following her career from Indiana, saw her as his Elizabeth Barrett and, having met her in Milwaukee in 1880, proposed marriage. After a long silence, she refused him.

*Poems of Passion* (1883) made her nationally known. Jansen and McClurg had published her first collection of poetry, *Drops of Water,* in 1872 but, believing this second book immoral,

Ella Wheeler Wilcox.
Courtesy of the University of Kentucky Libraries

turned it down. Another Chicago publishing house, Belford, Clarke, published it; the book, marked by its earnestness rather than streaks of eroticism, commanded enormous sales. In 1884 she met and married Robert Wilcox, a manufacturer of sterling silver works of art. They married in Milwaukee and then moved to his home in Connecticut. They divided their year's residence between New York City and Short Beach, Connecticut; their homes became salons for local society and young poets including ZONA GALE and Ridgely Torrence. In 1887 Ella Wheeler gave birth to her only child, a son who lived but a few hours. After her husband's death in 1916, her previous interest in spiritualism and theosophy intensified, and she claimed to have had astral communications with Robert. She died, it is generally believed, from exhaustion, having spent herself entertaining and preaching sexual restraint to the American troops in France during World War I.

SIGNIFICANCE: Wilcox wrote and published some forty books, but her reputation and popularity declined precipitously in the age of Frost, Pound, and ELIOT. Four lines from "Solitude" (first published in *Poems of Passion* and reprinted in many collections) ensure a continuing half-life for her verse in anthologies and books of quotations: "Laugh and the whole world laughs with you; / Weep and you weep alone. / For the sad old earth must borrow its mirth. / It has trouble enough of its own." That the platitudes and verses in *Poems of Passion* stirred editorial writers such as Charles Dana to condemn the book angrily, that five hundred citizens of Milwaukee staged a testimonial dinner answering such attacks, can hardly be believed or understood today. Except for their occasional references to Midwestern place names and rural landscapes, the verses of Wilcox are notably lacking in Midwestern significance. Instead, in such collections as *Poems of Passion, Poems of Pleasure* (1888) and *Poems of Power* (1901), she became the high priestess of sentimental verse with erotic overtones that aspired to universal, rather than merely regional or temporal, significance. For some sense of her youthful response to the barren intellectual and social life of rural Wisconsin in the 1860s and 1870s and to the Milwaukee literary groups fueling her powerful literary ambitions, one must turn to the opening chapters of her autobiography, *The World and I* (1918). For Wilcox, as her marriage to a wealthy Easterner and her subsequent residence in Connecticut and New York may suggest, the Midwest constituted only a very limited source of poetic inspiration.

SELECTED WORKS: Ella Wheeler Wilcox was a highly prolific author. Editions of *The Collected Poems of Ella Wheeler Wilcox* were published in 1917 and 1924. Wilcox's autobiography, *The World and I*, appeared in 1918. This autobiography reprints her most quoted and representative poems complete or in generous excerpts—"Solitude," "The Voluptuary," "Illusion," and "The Queen's Last Ride" among them. As such it is a useful introduction to both Wilcox and her poetry.

FURTHER READING: Jenny Ballou's *Period Piece: Ella Wheeler Wilcox and Her Times* (1940) itself has become dated but remains the most complete biography of Wilcox. More recent studies of Wilcox and her work include Malcolm Pittock's "In Defense of Ella Wheeler

Wilcox," appearing in the British *Durham University Journal* 34 (1973): 86–89; and Laura C. Wendroff's 1992 University of Michigan dissertation, "Race, Ethnicity, and the Voice of the 'Poetess' in the Lives and Works of Four Late-Nineteenth-Century Women Poets, Frances E. W. Harper, Emma Lazarus, Louise Guiney, and Ella Wheeler Wilcox." The State Historical Society of Wisconsin collections holds a large number of Wilcox letters.

GUY SZUBERLA                    UNIVERSITY OF TOLEDO

## LAURA INGALLS WILDER

February 7, 1867–February 10, 1957

**BIOGRAPHY:** Born at Lake Pepin, Wisconsin, to Charles Phillip and Caroline Lake (Quiner) Ingalls, Laura Ingalls Wilder came to know the hardships of Midwestern frontier living at an early age. At the age of three her family moved westward through Kansas, Minnesota, and the Dakota Territory, homesteading as they traveled. Finally, the family settled in De Smet, South Dakota, where in 1882 at the age of fifteen she began teaching and at the same time became engaged to Almanzo James Wilder, whom she married three years later on August 25, 1885. Life for the couple was one continuous disaster: their crops were destroyed by the elements, fire burned their house, and the drought years of 1892–94 caused the young couple and their only child, Rose, born on December 5, 1886, to move southward to Missouri. In the summer of 1894, they arrived at Mansfield, Missouri, and purchased a small farm where Laura and Almanzo spent the rest of their long lives.

In 1915 Laura expressed to her daughter, ROSE WILDER LANE, who was a reporter for the *San Francisco Bulletin*, that she had a desire to write. Her wish came true that year when she had an article published in the *Missouri Ruralist*. The article led to an editorship on the home page which lasted for twelve years. As early as 1926 Rose encouraged her to write her prairie childhood memories. In 1930 Laura gave her first manuscript, *The Little House in the Woods*, to Rose, who edited it and by 1932 had found a publisher for it. Seven more Little House books were to follow to complete the series. Before her death, she became a literary phenomenon, lionized in the American literary imagination. Libraries have been named for her in Detroit,

Pomona, California, and Mansfield, Missouri. In 1954 the American Library Association established the Laura Ingalls Wilder Award for authors or illustrators of children's books and presented its first medal to Laura herself. At her Mansfield farm, she lived her life peacefully and unpretentiously, enjoying the accolades which came to her. In 1949 Almanzo, at age ninety-two, died; in 1957, at age ninety, she also died at their farm home in Mansfield, Missouri.

**SIGNIFICANCE:** Wilder's early South Dakota experiences, as a child of homesteaders, provided her with the material for her realistic, classic Little House books. Always the tales are the autobiographical happenings of Laura's life in the Dakota Territory. The books have a mythic quality, showing the human struggle repeating itself in a Midwestern setting. Laura, herself, is an archetype. As soon as she overcomes one frontier problem, she encounters another. She is always progressing toward the world of maturity, but never quite enters it. The Little House books are legendary, read by young people throughout the world.

**SELECTED WORKS:** Wilder's major works include *Little House in the Big Woods* (1932), *Farmer Boy* (1933), *Little House on the Prairie* (1935), *On the Banks of the Plum Creek* (1937), *By the Shores of Silver Lake* (1939), *The Long Winter* (1940), *Little Town on the Prairie* (1941), *These Happy Golden Years* (1943), *On the Way Home: The Diary of a Trip from South Dakota to Mansfield, Missouri in 1894*, edited by Rose Wilder Lane (1962), *The First Four Years*, edited by Roger L. MacBride (1971), and *West from Home: Letters of Laura Ingalls Wilder*, edited by Roger L. MacBride (1974).

**FURTHER READING:** Donald Zochert's *The Life of Laura Ingalls Wilder* (1976) provides a major biography. Critical studies include Sheila Black's *Laura Ingalls Wilder: American Authoress* (1987); *The Plum Creek Story of Laura Ingalls Wilder*, by William T. Anderson (1987); *The Horn Book's Laura Ingalls Wilder*, edited by Anderson (1987); and *Laura Ingalls Wilder*, by Janet Spaeth (1987). Manuscript collections exist at the Laura Ingalls Wilder Home and Museum, Mansfield, Missouri; the Pomona Public Library, California; and the Detroit Public Library.

LELAND MAY

NORTHWEST MISSOURI STATE UNIVERSITY

## THORNTON WILDER
April 17, 1897–December 7, 1975

**BIOGRAPHY:** Thornton Wilder was one of five children born in Madison, Wisconsin, to Amos P. Wilder, a devout Congregationalist whose sense of duty and Puritan conscience sprang from the austere discipline of New England Calvinism, and to Isabella (Niven) Wilder, the daughter of Reverend Thornton M. Niven, Presbyterian minister in Dobbs Ferry, New York. Wilder's father was editor of the *Wisconsin State Journal*.

From an early age Thornton was exposed to progressive political ideals and Christian values. He experienced an intellectually stimulating and happy childhood, which included schooling in China, where his father was posted as consul general. In Shanghai he attended a German school, beginning a lifelong fascination with German culture and language. After further schooling in Ojai, California, and Oberlin College, Wilder took his BA degree at Yale University in 1920. There he wrote and published his first full-length play, *The Trumpet Shall Sound* (1920).

Following a brief tour of duty with the Coast Artillery in 1918–19, Wilder embarked on what became a lifetime of lengthy visits to Europe, the first to Rome, where he studied at the American Academy, with subsequent trips to Germany to attend theater productions by Max Reinhardt, Bertolt Brecht, and others. Greek and Roman history were also Wilder's passion; he set his first novels, *The Cabala* (1926) and *The Woman of Andros* (1930), in classical times. His fascination for exotic settings led him to set *The Bridge of San Luis Rey* (1927) in Peru, a novel that won him wide readership, the Pulitzer Prize, and handsome royalties. His cosmopolitanism and humanity gained him friends and admirers among general readers and literary peers, such as ERNEST HEMINGWAY, Gertrude Stein, Alexander Woollcott, and Max Reinhardt. Wilder served in the U.S. Army Air Intelligence during World War II. Immensely popular in America, his plays won acclaim in postwar Germany, where he was awarded the Frankfurter Friedenspreis in 1957. Wilder lectured at the University of Chicago between 1930 and 1936, and at Harvard University in 1950–51. An enthusiastic, seasoned traveler, he was admired and welcomed as an unofficial American ambassador of cultivated intelligence, good-natured love of life, and cosmopolitan humanism, in the manner of his beloved Goethe.

**SIGNIFICANCE:** Sections of Wilder's plays and novels are situated in the Midwest. Yet he was not a novelist of place or region so much as he was of ideas and innovative approaches to his material. Wilder returned again and again to convictions and ideals grounded in the enduring values associated with Midwestern small-town life and character. His later work fits ordinary events and everyday lives into *theatrum mundi*, a world theater of macrocosmic significance. The poignant, bittersweet commentaries on common people's lives, for which his best plays, *Our Town* (1938), *The Skin of Our Teeth* (1942), and his Depression-era novel *Heaven's My Destination* (1935) are known, elide all evidence of his infatuation with foreign locales and long-ago times. His literary versatility in giving dramaturgical treatment, based upon European models, to commonplace American subjects, revealed itself first in *The Long Christmas Dinner and Other Plays* (1931).

Edmund Wilson's urging, and a hostile review of his novel *The Woman of Andros* (1930), by Mike Gold, a formidable voice of the left in the 1930s, prompted Wilder to pursue his exploration of American themes and settings. *Heaven's My Destination* is a SINCLAIR LEWIS-like look at a Midwestern type, the Bible-toting businessman-optimist. While Lewis's George Babbitt is no more or less than a creature of place and time, Wilder's George Brush is a funny-sad commentary on ruling obsessions that exclude human commitments in any place and any time. At the conclusion of the novel we know that Brush, despite all that he has encountered, will continue to place principle before people.

Not the fact of birth in Wisconsin, then, but Wilder's humane vision of ordinary people marks a Midwestern sensibility which has gone to school at the finest institutions of learning and culture in the American East and Europe. Its distinction lies in the common person's enduring faith in neighborliness, goodness, and egalitarianism as irreducible constituents of existence. The poignant attachment to the commonplace, the simple direct language, and sturdy faith in those whose lives are seldom recorded make for powerful, affective, enduring drama in his best plays. These qualities were stitched into a speech on democratic culture, delivered in German Frankfurt in 1957, faulting elitism represented by the Anglophilic poet T. S. ELIOT. Wilder loved European literature, assimilating Brecht's open dramaturgy and Lope de Vega's theatricalism into his work, yet, as he had written much earlier at Oberlin, he was "too much of an American and a middlewesterner to ever really go for the Continental Method in earnest" (Harrison 44).

**SELECTED WORKS:** *The Long Christmas Dinner and Other Plays* (1931) signaled Wilder's attention to American themes and settings. The play *Our Town* (1938), for which Aaron Copland later wrote a musical score, brought him worldwide recognition. It remains one of the most frequently performed plays in American high schools. *The Skin of Our Teeth* (1942) won a Pulitzer Prize, and *The Matchmaker* (1955) became the hit Broadway musical *Hello, Dolly!* Wilder's best-known novels include *The Bridge of San Luis Rey* (1927), *Heaven's My Destination* (1935), *The Eighth Day* (1967), and the semi-autobiographical *Theophilus North* (1973).

**FURTHER READING:** Gilbert A. Harrison's *The Enthusiast: A Life of Thornton Wilder* (1983) is a primary biographical resource. Critical studies include David Castronova's *Thornton Wilder* (1986), Linda Simon's *Thornton Wilder: His World* (1979), Rex Burbank's *Thornton Wilder* (1978), and *Critical Essays on Thornton Wilder*, edited by Martin Blank (1996). A new collection of essays on Wilder is *Thornton Wilder: New Essays*, edited by Martin Blank, Dalma Hunyadi Brunauer, and David Garrett Izzo (1998). On his German reception, see Horst Oppel's *Thornton Wilder in Deutschland* (1977). In addition, Amos Niven Wilder's *Thornton Wilder and His Public* (1980), Donald Gallup's *Journals of Thornton Wilder, 1939–1961* (1985), and *Conversations with Thornton Wilder* (1992) are valuable. Of special usefulness is Claudette Walsh's *Thornton Wilder: A Reference Guide, 1926–1990* (1993).

DOUGLAS WIXSON

UNIVERSITY OF MISSOURI AT ROLLA

# NANCY WILLARD
June 26, 1936

**BIOGRAPHY:** Nancy Willard was born and raised in Ann Arbor, Michigan, the daughter of Hobart Hurd, a professor of chemistry, and Marge (Sheppard) Willard. She received her

Nancy Willard.
Photo by Eric Lindbloom. Courtesy of Nancy Willard

AB and PhD degrees from the University of Michigan and an MA from Stanford University. Willard has taught creative writing at Vassar College since 1965 and at the Bread Loaf Writers' Conference. She married Eric Lindbloom in 1964, and they have one son. A prolific writer, she is perhaps best known for her many children's books, on which she has collaborated with a variety of illustrators, and for which she, and they, have won numerous awards, including both the Newbery Medal and Caldecott Honor Awards in 1982 for *A Visit to William Blake's Inn: Poems for Innocent and Experienced Travelers*, illustrated by Alice and Martin Provenson (1981).

Early in her career, Willard published literary criticism, which emerges again in her later essays on creative writing. Her poetry has won honors, notably the Avery Hopwood Award at the University of Michigan and the Devins Memorial Award for *Skin of Grace* (1967). *Water Walker* (1989) was nominated by the National Book Critics Circle. She has written extensively in prose, both fiction and nonfiction. Willard has illustrated the books of other writers but not her own until the 1994 *Alphabet of Angels*, for which she arranged and took the photographs, and *The Magic Cornfield* (1997).

**SIGNIFICANCE:** In writing for both children and adults, Willard blends genres of prose and poetry, fiction and nonfiction. At the same time, she merges memory, dream, realistic detail, and the fantastic, the mythical, and the mystical.

Willard's childhood in Michigan, with summers spent at the family cottage near Oxford, provides the lazy summer atmosphere characteristic of the area, as well as anecdotes, landscapes, flora, and fauna for such works as her children's fantasy series called *The Anatole Trilogy* (1974, 1979, and 1982). Baseball, railroads, and Native American legends provide Midwestern topics and details for her fiction and nonfiction. Several of her early short stories, such as those gathered in *The Childhood of the Magician* (1973), and both of her novels for adults, *Things Invisible to See* (1984) and *Sister Water* (1993), take place primarily in Ann Arbor. They capture the essence of that college town, with landmarks, especially the Huron River, readily identifiable. Dimensions of place enhance her writing; for instance, in *The Mountains of Quilt* (1987) the names of the magicians—Elyria, Detroit, Cleveland, and Sandusky—come from Ohio and Michigan stations on the Lakeshore Limited railroad line which runs from New York to Chicago. In such ways, she transforms familiar places and everyday objects and events into the magical and reveals spiritual dimensions hidden in the material world.

Several of her Bread Loaf lectures, gathered in *Telling Time: Angels, Ancestors, and Stories* (1993), bring together childhood scenes, family relationships, reading, dreams, tales about ancestors, and the ways in which language and the mind form them into "once upon a time" (244). These essays and another collection of fiction and nonfiction, *Angel in the Parlor* (1983), are also invested with a sense of family and of place. They include reminiscences of summer days on an Ann Arbor porch swing, family reunions in Iowa, an uncle's general store in Wisconsin, ghost stories at camp in southern Michigan, and the sense of an angel's presence at Sunday dinner with relatives. There, she transforms the particulars of quirky and imperfect people into universal qualities, and locations in the Midwest become regions of the heart.

**SELECTED WORKS:** Willard's poetry includes *Skin of Grace* (1967), *Household Tales of Moon and Water* (1982), and *Water Walker* (1989). *The Childhood of the Magician* (1973) consists of

short stories, and *Things Invisible to See* (1984) and *Sister Water* (1993) are novels.

Of well over twenty books for children, many lavishly illustrated, a few are *The Well-Mannered Balloon*, illustrated by Haig and Regina Shekerjian (1976); *Simple Pictures Are Best*, illustrated by Tomie dePaola (1977); *The Voyage of the Ludgate Hill*, illustrated by Alice and Martin Provenson (1987); and *Pish Posh, Said Hieronymus Bosch*, illustrated by Leo and Diane Dillon (1991). Willard illustrated *Alphabet of Angels* (1994) and *The Magic Cornfield* (1997) herself; the latter features postcards from places with such names as Sleepy Eye, MN; Morning Sun, IA; and Peculiar, MO. *The Anatole Trilogy* includes *Sailing to Cythera and Other Anatole Stories* (1974), *The Island of the Grass King: The Further Adventures of Anatole* (1979), and *Uncle Terrible: More Adventures of Anatole* (1982), all illustrated by David McPhail. For *Beauty and the Beast* (1992), she and the illustrator, Barry Moser, traveled to Michigan to see her great-grandmother's house in Union City. Willard adapted another fairy tale, *East of the Sun and West of the Moon*, also illustrated by Barry Moser (1989), into a drama. She wrote *The Highest Hit* (1978) for young people.

*Cracked Corn and Snow Ice Cream: A Family Almanac* (1997), illustrated by Jane Dyer, takes the form of a farmers' almanac intended for children. It also contains interviews of Dyer and Willard family members from Iowa.

*A Nancy Willard Reader: Selected Poetry and Prose*, with photographs by Eric Lindbloom (1991), gathers a sampling of her poetry, essays, and short fiction. *Angel in the Parlor: Five Stories and Eight Essays* (1983) and *Telling Time: Angels, Ancestors, and Stories* (1993) are collections of her prose.

**FURTHER READING:** Although no book-length study of Willard's work has appeared as yet, some of the articles which explore dimensions of her writing include Francine Danis's "Nancy Willard's Domestic Psalms," in *Modern Poetry Studies* 9 (Spring 1978): 126–34; Barbara Lucas's "Nancy Willard," in *Horn Book* 58 (August 1982): 374–79; and Nancy Crim's "When Things Invisible Become Visible: A Writer and Her Readers," in *English Journal* 79 (December 1990): 16–19. Willard's 1982 Newbery acceptance speech appears in *Horn Book* 58 (August 1982): 369–73. Reference works which focus on her as a Michigan author include ROBERT BEASECKER's *Michigan* in the Novel, 1816–1996 (1998) and Carol Small-wood's *Michigan Authors* (1993). Collections of Willard's papers can be found in the University of Michigan Library and the Kerlan Collection at the University of Minnesota.

MARY DEJONG OBUCHOWSKI

CENTRAL MICHIGAN UNIVERSITY

## KENNY JACKSON WILLIAMS.

*See* appendix (1986)

## MEREDITH (ROBERT) WILLSON

May 18, 1902–June 15, 1984

**BIOGRAPHY:** Born in Mason City, Iowa, son of John David Willson, a lawyer, and Rosalie (Reiniger) Wilson, Meredith Willson played flute and piccolo in local bands. Graduating from Mason City High School in 1919, he attended Damrosch Institute (now Julliard School of Music) from 1919 to 1922. He married Elizabeth Wilson in 1920; they divorced in 1948. He married Ralina Zarova in 1948; she died in 1966. In 1968 he married Rosemary Sullivan, who survived him.

Willson joined John Philip Sousa's band in 1922, toured with it for three years, and continued performing with it in New York until 1924. He played flute with the New York Philharmonic Symphony Orchestra and New York Chamber Music Society from 1924 to 1929, when he moved to the West Coast to lead orchestras on network radio stations.

Willson was music director of NBC's *Maxwell House Coffee Time*, 1937–42; a major in the U.S. Army and head of the music division of Armed Forces Radio Service, 1942–45; master of ceremonies of *The Meredith Willson Show* in 1949; and music director and personality for network radio on *The Big Show*, 1950–52, and *Music Room*, 1953. He also wrote many popular songs, two symphonies, scores for Chaplin's *The Great Dictator* (1940) and the film version of Lillian Hellman's *The Little Foxes* (1941), and a novel—*Who Did What to Fedalia?* (1952).

A genial raconteur, Willson told anecdotes about his Midwestern boyhood on radio and television, and in three autobiographies: *And There I Stood with My Piccolo* (1948), *Eggs I Have Laid* (1955), and *"But He Doesn't Know the Territory"* (1959). According to David Ewen in *The Story of America's Musical Theatre* (219), the well-known Broadway writer-composer Frank Loesser was so amused by

Willson's yarns that he suggested Willson use this material for a musical comedy. Willson wrote the book, lyrics, and music of *The Music Man*, with help on the story from Franklin Lacey, and the show opened on Broadway on December 19, 1957.

*The Music Man* took audiences by storm, running until 1961 for 1,375 performances—Broadway's fifth-longest-running play. In competition with Bernstein and Sondheim's *West Side Story*, *The Music Man* won all of the awards in its opening season: Drama Critics' Circle Awards for best musical, best music, and best lyrics; five Tony Awards; and best musical awards from *Variety* and *Sign* magazines. In 1962 a successful movie and Willson's novel based on the story were released.

Willson wrote the songs for another Broadway success, *The Unsinkable Molly Brown* (1960), and the book, lyrics, and music for his third Broadway musical, *Here's Love* (1963), based on the 1947 film *Miracle on 34th Street*. The last musical for which Willson wrote book, lyrics, and music was the unsuccessful *1491*, produced in Los Angeles in 1969. An autobiography in progress with a working title *More Eggs—As Laid by Meredith Willson* remained unpublished when he died of heart failure at St. John's Hospital in Santa Monica.

**SIGNIFICANCE:** Meredith Willson's versatility in musical performance, composition, and mass media production have distracted critical attention from his substantial achievements as a writer. His literary reputation rests upon his masterpiece, *The Music Man*, and the neglected autobiographies. These works also show him to be quintessentially Midwestern—a keen observer of small-town folkways with a superb ear for regional dialects and a genius for shaping character and story in the casual tradition of MARK TWAIN.

*The Music Man* stands as a landmark apart from the many explorations of Americana that flooded Broadway after the success of *Oklahoma!* in 1943. Willson's unoperatic style piqued the interest of theatergoers with an opening chorus of businessmen chattering without melody or rhyme to the rhythm of a moving train, a thumping march ("76 Trombones") as musical centerpiece accompanied by brass band, a title character talking through major songs played by an actor (Robert Preston) whose lengthy stage and movie credits included no previous musicals, and an unabashed barbershop quartet singing in close harmony without intended satire. The quartet intermittently comments on the action in the manner of a Greek chorus.

A witty, nostalgic panorama of a Midwestern small town in 1912, *The Music Man* features Harold Hill, a swindler who convinces townspeople of River City, Iowa, to lift the moral tone of their community by sponsoring a boys' uniformed band. Hill intends to abscond with their money as soon as band instruments are shipped and paid for but falls in love with town librarian Marian Paroo; hilarious consequences follow, capped by a romantic ending.

The play excels in theatricality, characterization, and authentic regionalism. In this labor of love, Willson drew upon his memories of Mason City and early experiences with music that led him to pursue it as a career. Jolly, deal-making Mayor Shinn and gossipy matrons of the town are life-like antagonists of Harold Hill, the city slicker from Gary. Fast, light, bigger than life, the play has well-integrated dramatic scenes as exemplified by the serious personal discussions between the leads Hill and Marian and the turning point of the play when Hill admits lying to young Winthrop Paroo and must decide whether to continue a life of lying. With superb stagecraft and musicality, the play says something significant about the human condition.

Willson's autobiographies are charming, humorous sketches and short essays about personal and professional relationships. Poles apart from the self-absorbed virtuoso performance of his contemporary Oscar Levant, Willson radiates good nature and an empathy with ordinary people that are reminiscent of Washington Irving and Oliver Goldsmith. *And There I Stood with My Piccolo* recalls his Mason City upbringing and the surprises a country boy found in New York and other cities. *Eggs I Have Laid* portrays the author's pratfalls during a second career as a radio and television bandleader. *"But He Doesn't Know the Territory"* tells the vagaries of getting *The Music Man* written, produced, and past the critics. Meredith's wide interests, subdued egoism, and gift of gab make these books eminently readable, an important behind-the-scenes look at radio broadcasting and the music business during the swing era. Passages contrived in a light, even frivolous tone often reveal profound insights into human behavior.

**SELECTED WORKS:** Willson's books include *What Every Musician Should Know* (1938), *And There I Stood with My Piccolo* (1948, 1976), *Eggs I Have Laid* (1955), and *"But He Doesn't Know the Territory"* (1959). His two novels are *Who Did What to Fedalia?* (1952) and *The Music Man* (1962). Stage musicals for which he wrote book, music, and lyrics are *The Music Man* (1958) and *Here's Love* (1963); he wrote lyrics and music for *The Unsinkable Molly Brown* (1960).

**FURTHER READING:** Although Willson is cited often in reviews and surveys of musical theater, no book-length study or journal article dealing with the author or his work exists. Standard references include David Ewen's *Complete Book of the American Musical Theatre* (second ed. 1959) and *The Story of America's Musical Theatre* (1961); Gerald Bordman's *American Musical Theatre* (1978); Cecil Smith and Glenn Litton's *Musical Comedy in America* (1981); and Denny Martin Flinn's *Musical! A Grand Tour: The Rise, Glory, and Fall of an American Institution* (1997). A brief book with photos is *Meredith Willson* [and] *Jerry Herman* (1982) in the American Musicals series of Time Life Books. John S. Willson wrote a comprehensive obituary: "Meredith Willson, Composer of 'The Music Man' Is Dead at 82," appearing in the *New York Times* (June 17, 1984) 1:1, 24. Unpublished masters theses include Sharon S. Drane's "An Analysis and Production of *The Music Man*" (1980) and Erik Sterling Quam's "The Role of Mayor Shinn in *The Music Man*" (1997).

EDWARD MORIN            WAYNE STATE UNIVERSITY

# LANFORD (EUGENE) WILSON
April 13, 1937

**BIOGRAPHY:** Hailing from south central Missouri, Lanford Wilson was born in Lebanon, at the edge of the Mark Twain National Forest, to Violetta Careybelle (Tate) Wilson and Ralph Eugene Wilson. His upbringing in the Midwest proved to be a wellspring which he drew on again and again for inspiration in his art. Raised a Baptist in a small town, Wilson is nevertheless neither provincial in outlook nor regionally limited in appeal. His parents divorced when he was five, and he then lived with his mother in Springfield until he was fourteen, moving after that to a farm in Ozark, Missouri, when his mother married a dairy farmer. Playing Tom Wingfield in a high school production of Tennessee Williams's *The Glass Menagerie* and watching touring productions of *Brigadoon* and *Death of a Salesman* were rich influences which gave Wilson's early life direction and a dream. He majored in art at Southwest Missouri State for two quarters and became reunited for a year with his father in San Diego, where he attended San Diego State College while working at an aircraft factory.

Five years on his own in Chicago in his early twenties matured Wilson personally, allowed him to study play-writing in an extension class at the University of Chicago, and prepared him for professional transition from rural Midwest to off-off-Broadway experimental theater in New York City. Living in Greenwich Village and working odd jobs in a furniture store, a restaurant, and a hotel acquainted him with offbeat characters who later peopled his plays. Another critical influence during Wilson's formative years was his association with other young artists at the unusual, claustrophobic, yet congenial theater space at Caffe Cino, where he was riveted by a production of Eugene Ionesco's *The Lesson* and for which he wrote his earliest plays.

Wilson used an unidentified town in the Midwest for the setting of his 1965 play *This Is the Rill Speaking* and for the more substantial *The Rimers of Eldritch* (1966), his first full-length Midwestern play. Mark Busby, in his landmark monograph on Wilson, identifies *Rimers* as "an unsentimental *Our Town*" for its attack on the small-mindedness of small-town Midwestern life (*Lanford Wilson* 22). Wilson's other full-length plays of this period included *Balm in Gilead* (1965), *The Gingham Dog* (1968), *Lemon Sky* (1970), and *Serenading Louie* (1970), but their mixed reviews and his perceived lack of community post–Caffe Cino precipitated a writer's block.

In 1969 Wilson established the Circle Repertory Company, which gave him the "theater family" that he so craved and facilitated the production of two early and many later successes, notably *The Hot l Baltimore* (1973) and *The Mound Builders* (1976), both plays about the ambivalence of the past. *Hot l* also led Wilson to reassess and revise a previous harshly satiric view of the Midwest. *The Mound Builders*, the play that Wilson has identified as his "favorite," emphasizes the violent and vital

Lanford Wilson.
Photo © Nancy Crampton

importance of land in ways that would have surprised Frederick Jackson Turner (Busby 31). Three later plays focus on the fictitious Talley family of Lebanon, Missouri, Wilson's birthplace: *5th of July* (1978), *Talley's Folly* (1979), and *Talley and Son* (1985). Following the Talley cycle, Wilson set a slight one-act play in California, *Thymus Vulgaris* (1981), and an important full-length play in New Mexico, *Angels Fall* (1982); returned to several of his earlier plays to do revisions; and translated Anton Chekhov's *The Three Sisters*. More recent compelling plays include *Burn This* (1987), an intense love story about artistic growth and confronting an inner monster, perhaps Wilson's most on-the-edge work, and *Redwood Curtain* (1993), in which a young Asian American woman painfully seeks her Vietnam veteran father.

Having left the bustle of New York City for a more serene but no less productive life, Wilson lives by himself in Sag Harbor, New York, where tending his garden and restoring his large 1845 house are two logical pastimes for a "farmboy-become playwright who often writes about tilling the Midwestern soil and preserving the past" (Busby, *Lanford Wilson* 13). **SIGNIFICANCE:** Wilson's imagination has been firmly molded by his Midwestern heritage; "place" is a central concept in his work. As he himself writes in his recent one-act monologue *The Moonshot Tape*: "'How did living in a small town, essentially a rural area, prepare you for a career and living in a metropolitan area? Or not? When did you leave Missouri?' No. One. Ever. Leaves. Any. Place. Or. Any. One'" (*Antaeus* 66 [Spring 1991]: 491). The family is a second major theme, and nearly every Wilson play explores both the necessity and the impossibility of lasting family love. His characters may be eccentrics, but they have a compassionate morality, and Wilson's treatment of them is tolerant and even admiring. In them he endorses the traditional values of communication, edurance, compassion, humor, and hard work.

As Busby points out in his monograph, Wilson's desire for "a pastoral ideal shaped by human effort" connects him with other Midwestern writers such as F. Scott Fitzgerald (15). In his depictions of small-town American life, Wilson's plays are also akin to Sherwood Anderson's *Winesburg, Ohio*. Wilson's admiration for Tennessee Williams and their work together influenced Wilson's use, in *Lemon Sky*, of Williams's theme of problematic parent-child relationships. And, in images of the dying town on the frontier, Wilson's writing resembles Larry McMurtry's Western fiction.

Now into the fourth decade of his career, Wilson has been enormously prolific, having written forty-two produced plays, thirteen of them full-length. His many honors include the Pulitzer Prize for *Talley's Folly* (1980), an ABC-Yale Fellowship in motion picture writing (1968), two Outer Critics Circle Awards (1973 and 1980), two Obie Awards (1973 and 1975), the Drama Desk Vernon Rice Award (1967), two Guggenheim Fellowships (1970 and 1972), two Rockefeller grants (1967 and 1973), and an honorary doctor of letters from the University of Missouri (1981). **SELECTED WORKS:** Wilson's most significant drama includes *Balm in Gilead* (1965), *This Is the Rill Speaking* (1965), *The Rimers of Eldritch* (1966), *The Gingham Dog* (1968), *Lemon Sky* (1970), *Serenading Louie* (1970, 1976), *The Hot l Baltimore* (1973), *The Mound Builders* (1976), *5th of July*

(1978), *Talley's Folly* (1979), *Thymus Vulgaris* (1981), *Angels Fall* (1982), *The Three Sisters* (1984 translation of Chekhov's play), *Talley and Son* (1985), *Burn This* (1987), and *Redwood Curtain* (1993). Wilson has also written short stories, articles, reviews, and television screenplays. **FURTHER READING:** When one considers the recognition that Wilson has garnered and the sheer volume of his output, it is surprising that he has not been the subject of more serious and extensive scholarship. Only two book-length studies have been devoted exclusively to him, one by Gene A. Barnett (1987) in the Twayne Authors series and the other a monograph by Mark Busby (1987) in the Boise State University Western Writers series. Philip Middleton Williams published *A Comfortable House: Lanford Wilson, Marshall W. Mason and the Circle Repertory Theatre* in 1993. A year later Jackson R. Bryer edited a volume of ten original essays on Wilson's work under the title *Lanford Wilson: A Casebook*. A chronology of Wilson's life and an extensively annotated bibliography of primary and secondary works make Bryer's volume an essential study.

Jill B. Gidmark        University of Minnesota

## (Arthur) Yvor Winters
October 17, 1900–January 25, 1968
**BIOGRAPHY:** Chicago-born, the son of Harry and Faith (Ahnfeldt) Winters, Yvor Winters spent his youth in Oregon and California before enrolling at the University of Chicago in 1917. His studies were curtailed by tuberculosis, however, and he left for a sanitarium in Santa Fe, where he remained from 1918 to 1921. Winters never again spent any significant time east of the Rocky Mountains; he later founded the Poets of the Pacific School and even flaunted a rugged Western loneliness. Yet his brief Chicago stays limned his connection with Midwestern letters. In his no-nonsense critical tone and moral orientation, Winters all but identified himself with the region of his birth. His comprehensive oeuvre includes important work on John Berryman, T. S. Eliot, and particularly Hart Crane, whom he alternately championed and censured. Winters's alliance with Chicago-based *Poetry Magazine* launched his literary career, and his slim but polished lyric output secured his place among Midwestern poets.

Through the Poetry Club at the University of Chicago, Winters met HARRIET MONROE, editor of *Poetry*. She encouraged him, as did Alice Corbin Henderson, her assistant, whom he met in Santa Fe where she had also sought a cure. Stocking his personal library with *Poetry*, *Others*, and *The Little Review*, Winters at first wrote avant-garde verse. Three collections, composed in the sanitarium, in mining camps where he tutored and convalesced, and at the University of Colorado where he studied and taught between 1923 and 1927, bear the Imagist imprint of graphic presentation in few words. Even so, the earliest volume displays a penchant for rhyme and meter, two elements unusual to this mode. In 1926 he married writer Janet Lewis, his beacon over a tempestuous career. Winters received his doctorate in 1934 from Stanford, where he taught for forty years. He died in Palo Alto, of throat cancer, survived by his widow and two children. Janet Winters supervised preparation of the posthumous edition of his *Collected Poems* (1978).

**SIGNIFICANCE:** Winters penned few free-verse lines at Stanford. There he had embarked on a "systematic reading of English poetry from Skelton onward . . . and of American as well" (*Collected Poems*, 3rd ed. 16). That study convinced him of the restrictive nature and moral laxity of modern literature. Beginning with the provocatively titled *Primitivism and Decadence* (1937), Winters issued a series of savage critiques on contemporaries who valued obscurity.

Few critics were more reviled and respected. The host of artists who suffered his barbs almost invariably answered—unable to dismiss his eloquent testament to the necessity of linking logic with emotion.

Winters advocated what he himself labeled "moral" and "reactionary" aesthetics to oppose trends in ascendance for the past two centuries. He maintained that works resisting paraphrase, that rely on symbology concocted by the poet, and artists who depict men as mindless automatons violate that social ethos which literature ought to depend on and promote. On that basis he chastised Pound, Yeats, and Jeffers. Winters believed that moral writing combines reason and feeling in the crucible of technique. He sanctioned experiment only when circumscribed by convention.

Winters felt that literary decadence derived from distrust in reason. Modern literature he associated with outright decay. He believed modern artists suffered from "the fallacy of imitative form" ("Primitivism and Decadence" in *In Defense of Reason* 62): the belief that one can best express uncertainty through comparably ambiguous expression. Joyce, Whitman, Eliot, and Crane topped Winters's list of heretics. In the work of J. V. Cunningham, Edgar Bowers, and others touted in his *Poets of the Pacific* anthologies (1937, 1949), Winters saw hope.

Though his controversial criticism captured most attention, many established poets admired his sensitivity disclosed through formal mastery. Perhaps appreciation of him as a Midwestern writer ought to be grounded in his lyrics, which continually stave off chaos, turning that struggle into poetry: "Wisdom and wilderness are here at poise, / Ocean and forest are the mind's device, / But still I feel the presence of thy will: / The midnight trembles when I hear thy voice, / The noon's immobile when I meet thy eyes" (*Collected Poems* 170).

**SELECTED WORKS:** "The Testament of a Stone, Being Notes on the Mechanics of the Poetic Image" (1924; included in *Uncollected Essays and Reviews* 1973) derives its theories from Winters's poetic practice at that time. *In Defense of Reason* (1947) consists of four important early polemics: *Primitivism and Decadence: A Study of American Experimental Poetry* (1937); *Maule's Curse: Seven Studies in the History of American Obscurantism* (1938); *The Anatomy of Nonsense* (1943); and the essay "The Significance of *The Bridge* by Hart Crane, *or* What Are We to Think of Professor X" (1947). *On Modern Poets* (1959) contains the Crane essay and several pieces from *Anatomy*. It also expands on the concerns expressed in *Primitivism and Decadence*. *The Function of Criticism* (1957) and *Forms of Discovery: Critical and Historical Essays on the Forms of the Short Poem in English* (1967) exhibit his literary range by including perceptive essays on sixteenth- through nineteenth-century poetry. Francis Murphy has edited an impressive compilation of *Uncollected Essays and Reviews* (1973). Winters wrote one book-length monograph, *Edward Arlington Robinson* (1946, 1971), and edited three poetry anthologies. His experimental works, *The Immobile Wind*

(1921), *The Magpie's Shadow* (1922), *The Bare Hills* (1927), and several poems from *The Proof* (1930), are included in *The Early Poems of Yvor Winters 1920–28* (1966). These, his more traditional verses, and numerous translations appear in three increasingly inclusive editions of *Collected Poems* (1952, 1960, 1978); the last also contains his lone story, "The Brink of Darkness," a tale of resistance to a recondite evil. **FURTHER READING:** Richard J. Sexton's *The Complex of Yvor Winters' Criticism* (1973), Dick Davis's *Wisdom and Wilderness: The Achievement of Yvor Winters* (1983), and Terry Comito's *In Defense of Winters* (1986) treat Winters's criticism. Grosvenor Powell's *Language as Being in the Poetry of Yvor Winters* (1980) and Elizabeth Isaacs's *An Introduction to the Poetry of Yvor Winters* (1981) offer detailed studies of the poetry. Powell's *Yvor Winters: An Annotated Bibliography 1919–1982* (1983) displays great comprehensiveness. It cites, in addition to Winters's own works, responses and defenses that form a significant segment of his critical contribution. Winters's extensive interchange with Crane is documented by Thomas Parkinson in *Hart Crane and Yvor Winters: Their Literary Correspondence* (1978). Friends authoring retrospectives include David Levin, Robert Lowell, Donald Stanford, and Allen Tate. Students providing the same include Louise Bogan, Turner Cassity, Gerald Graff, Thom Gunn, and Judith Rascoe. By the terms of his will, Winters's letters could not be published in the twenty-five years following his death. Though that time has passed, no edition of the letters has been issued. His papers are located at Stanford, Princeton, and at the University of California at Los Angeles.

ETHAN LEWIS
SANGAMON STATE UNIVERSITY

## DOUGLAS WIXSON.
*See* appendix (1995)

## CHLOE ANTHONY WOFFORD.
*See* Toni Morrison

## LARRY WOIWODE
October 30, 1941
**BIOGRAPHY:** Larry Woiwode was born to Everett Carl and Audrey Leone (Johnston) in Carrington, North Dakota, and moved to Manito, Illinois, with his family at age ten. He

Larry Woiwode.
Photo © Nancy Crampton

attended the University of Illinois for five years, where he took classes in a variety of courses and left in 1964 with an associate's degree in rhetoric. Since that time he has been a freelance writer. After the success of his first two novels—*What I'm Going to Do, I Think* (1969), awarded the William Faulkner Foundation Award, and *Beyond the Bedroom Wall: A Family Album* (1975), nominated for the National Book Award and the National Book Critics Circle Award—he has held visiting professorships and writer-in-residence positions at major universities including the University of Wisconsin (1973–74) and the State University of New York at Binghamton (1983–85). He served as a judge for the National Book Awards in 1972, and he was awarded a doctor of letters degree from North Dakota State University in 1977. Woiwode spent his early career living in Manhattan, but he has returned with his family to live in the rural North Dakota of his boyhood.

**SIGNIFICANCE:** Woiwode's roots in North Dakota and Illinois are fundamental to much of his writing. The North Dakota and Illinois landscapes of *Beyond the Bedroom Wall* and the northern Michigan setting of *What I'm Going to Do, I Think* and *Indian Affairs* (1992) provide a natural background that often reflects the emotional state of the characters. In an essay in the journal *Renascence* (44.1), Woiwode explained why regional writers are often considered second-rate: "Whenever the academy labels a writer regional, it suggests that the writer isn't quite in the league with the big boys—equating regionalism with parochialism—and asserts that certain areas of the U.S. (or the world) are enshrined as right, preferable to others, and the remainder is regional" (3). While some of Woiwode's work, such as the novel *Poppa John* (1981), is set in that "right, preferable" place, New York City, the Midwestern boyhood home to which Woiwode has returned seems more essential in characters like Tim Neumiller of *Beyond the Bedroom Wall*. The novel begins with Tim dreaming of a street in Hyatt, North Dakota, a recurring dream of a place that consumes him with the power of its memory. Woiwode's Midwestern characters are often consumed with their place whether it be within their family or their region. Woiwode has said that in his fiction human beings are always more important than place, but one of the most important ways Woiwode has consistently defined those humans has been through their relationship to their place.

**SELECTED WORKS:** Woiwode's work includes novels, *What I'm Going to Do, I Think* (1969), *Beyond the Bedroom Wall: A Family Album* (1975), *Poppa John* (1981), *Born Brothers* (1988), *Indian Affairs* (1992); collections of short fiction, *The Neumiller Stories* (1989) and *Silent Passengers* (1993); nonfiction, *Acts* (1993); and poetry, *Even Tide* (1977). Interviews with Woiwode have appeared in *Contemporary Authors, New Revision Series* 16 and in *Renascence: Essays on Values in Literature* 44.1 (Fall 1991).

**FURTHER READING:** No full-length study of Woiwode has yet appeared. The *Dictionary of Literary Biography* contains an entry that discusses *Even Tide*, *What I'm Going to Do, I Think*, and *Beyond the Bedroom Wall: A Family Album*. Novelist John Gardner reviewed *Beyond the Bedroom Wall: A Family Album* in a cover story for the September 28, 1975, issue of the *New York Times Book Review*.

KEITH FYNAARDT          NORTHWESTERN COLLEGE

## TERRY WOOTEN

November 20, 1948

**BIOGRAPHY:** Terry Wooten, poet and bard

Terry Wooten.
Photo by Wendi Wooten.
Courtesy of Terry and Wendi Wooten

in the oral tradition, grew up in the northern Michigan town of Marion, son of Dale and Mona (Helmboldt) Wooten. After attending Western Michigan University, he furthered his education through travel and various jobs and in apprenticeship with northern Michigan bard Max Ellison. He married Wendi McLachlan in 1975; they have two children. In 1983 he founded the Stone Circle, an outdoor amphitheater at his home just north of Kewadin, Michigan, by Grand Traverse Bay. At this arrangement of eighty-eight boulders in concentric rings, hundreds gather around a fire every Friday and Saturday at dusk during the summer to hear poets, singers, and storytellers. Wooten also performs at schools, colleges, and civic organizations across Michigan and beyond, reciting his own poetry and that of poets from the Beowulf bard to the present.

**SIGNIFICANCE:** With more than eight hours of memorized literature, Wooten is a walking library, a latter-day bard recalling ancient storytelling traditions such as were found among Celtic, Germanic, and Native American tribes. Like Walt Whitman and CARL SAND-

BURG, earlier American poets of the common people, Wooten weaves folklore and landscape into personal narratives. His poem "Emergency Message" traces this lifework to an epiphany experienced as a hitchhiker stranded in Death Valley, California: "I made a silent pledge to myself / that if I made it / I would become a Michigan poet / and absorb the land, lakes, rivers / and rhythm of the folk / to the best of my ability" (*Jutting Out* n. pag.). This bioregional focus on people and place resulted in poems on diverse topics, such as radio broadcasts of Detroit Tigers baseball games ("Ode to Ernie Harwell"), shipwrecks on the Great Lakes ("Elegy for the Carl D. Bradley"), and an ancient Native American stone circle ("Beaver Island Archipelago"). Written in the Midwestern vernacular, his poems are meant to be spoken to, and understood by, ordinary people, not just the literati. By promoting the oral tradition in the Midwest, Wooten has introduced the world of poetry to thousands who might otherwise resist literature.

**SELECTED WORKS:** Wooten's first chapbook of poetry, *Got in an Argument over Harmony* (1978), traces his poetic genesis with verses from his teenage years and early twenties. *The 45th Parallel* (1983), a hand-bound limited edition, was followed by *Okeh* (1984), a culling of his first two books along with poems intended for teenage readers. *Words Wild with Bloom: An Oral History of Max Ellison* (1987) captures the conversational cadence and humor of Wooten's late mentor. *Boulders in Exile* (1989), *Jutting Out into the Water* (1991), and *The Abstracts of Romance and The Thrill of Being* (1998) portray life in northern Michigan, especially as influenced by the Great Lakes. *When the Bear Came Back* (1993), a selection of poems that appeal to children, features illustrations by Louan Lechler. His poems also appear in *The Stone Circle Anthology* (1984), *Contemporary Michigan Poetry: Poems from the Third Coast* (1987), and *The Stone Circle Anthology: Poems for Big Blue* (1995).

**FURTHER READING:** Articles about Wooten frequently appearing in Michigan periodicals tend to focus more on the Stone Circle than on his writing. In "Kewadin's Stone Circle: The Ancient Bridge Revisited," in *Michigan Explorer* (Fall 1994): 15–18, Therese Becker describes "the mystique that has developed around the Stone Circle," a reproduction of

"the ancient setting where the old oral tradition comes alive and builds bridges between strangers" (15). Similar evocations are found in Maggie Mendus's "Power of a Circle," in *Michigan Reading Journal* 27.3 (Spring 1994): 18–25; Nancy Jones Mann's "Sharing a Circle of Tradition," in *Traverse, The Magazine* (August 1987): 55–57; and Kathleen Prentice's "Stone Circle Draws Storytellers," in *Detroit Free Press* (August 9, 1985): 1E. In "To Sustain the Bioregion: Michigan Poets of Place," in *MidAmerica* 17 (1990): 10–33, William Barillas recognizes Wooten's contribution to a tradition also exemplified by THEODORE ROETHKE, JIM HARRISON, JUDITH MINTY, and DAN GERBER. The State of Michigan Library at Lansing holds an extensive collection of Wooten materials.

WILLIAM BARILLAS
UNIVERSITY OF WISCONSIN–LA CROSSE

# FRANK LLOYD WRIGHT
June 8, 1867–April 9, 1959
(Taliesin, Shining Brow)

**BIOGRAPHY:** Born Frank Lincoln Wright in Richland Center, Wisconsin, to William Cary Wright (1825–1904), variously a doctor, lawyer, preacher, and orator, and Anna Lloyd Jones (1842–1923), an immigrant from Wales, his middle name was silently changed by his mother sometime before his parents' divorce in 1885. Within a short time of his arrival in Chicago in 1887, Wright was working for the Adler and Sullivan firm where he learned to become "a good pencil" in Louis H. Sullivan's hand (*An Autobiography* 126).

Brendan Gill reports in *Many Masks: A Life of Frank Lloyd Wright* (1987) that Wright's marriage to Catherine Tobin produced six children, but the notoriety attendant upon his desertion of this family, added to publicity concerning subsequent affairs, contributed to a popular view of him as one unfit to design family homes (218). One of these romantic attachments was with Mamah Borthwick Cheney, who perished in a 1914 fire at Wright's newly built Taliesin in Spring Green, Wisconsin, together with her two children, who were visiting, and four of Wright's employees. Subsequently, Wright lived with, married, and eventually divorced Miriam Noel. Finally, Olgivanna Milanov, a native of Bosnia, settled in with her daughter, Svetlana, at Taliesin, newly rebuilt in 1925 after a third fire. Meryle Secrest's *Frank Lloyd Wright: A Biog-*

*raphy* (1992) indicates that although they wished to be married because Olgivanna was carrying their daughter, Iovanna, Miriam Noel refused a divorce until 1928 (284).

Wright and Olgivanna remained together until his death at the age of ninety-one, establishing the Taliesen Fellowship at Spring Green as an architectural apprenticeship and eventually shifting operations to Taliesin West, outside Scottsdale, Arizona. Wright was buried in the family cemetery at Spring Green, but in accordance with Olgivanna's deathbed wish his remains were disinterred, cremated in Madison, and commingled with hers in Arizona—an act thought "a desecration" and "a form of vandalism" (Secrest 14–18) by many of his former apprentices who understood Wright's abiding affection for the Wisconsin landscape.

**SIGNIFICANCE:** Wright wrote in the December 1928 issue of *Architectural Record* that he "would much rather build than write about building, but when I am not building I will write about building—or the significance of those buildings I have already built" (LXIV, 512). *An Autobiography* (1932), which Robert Sweeney in the introduction to his *Frank Lloyd Wright: An Annotated Bibliography* (1978) calls "a classic of American literature and one of the most durable works on architecture" (Sweeney xxxii), allowed Wright to expound his philosophy of democratic life and to show where his "organic" architecture fit in. In 1932 he also published the first version of *The Disappearing City* (1932), which contained his ideas on decentralization. In these two books Wright delineated a philosophy of building so the human spirit can flourish, connecting his views of "organic architecture" to perceived ideals of American democracy.

Wright was generally careful to incorporate his buildings into their environment, a peculiarly Midwestern theme. The buildings of the Taliesin complex at Spring Green, for example, were nestled into the gently sloping hills above the Wisconsin River. Secrest remarks on how Wright "particularly distinguished himself" from the Arts and Crafts movement "in the way he integrated his Prairie houses with the flat, unending horizons of the Midwest—hence the name—stressing the horizontal with his spreading roofs and bands of windows, and stretching out porches and pergolas into the surround-

ing gardens so that the house and its setting would merge and blur into a single harmonious whole" (153).

**SELECTED WORKS:** *An Autobiography* (1932) was partially rewritten for the 1943 edition, with some new material added. A posthumously published edition (1977) includes corrections and additions made by Wright. *The Disappearing City* (1932) advocated a decentralized, agrarian society. A revised edition, titled *When Democracy Builds* (1945), and a further revision under yet another title, *The Living City* (1958), including detailed plans for the concept of Broadacre City, indicate that Wright continued to refine this notion. His biography of Sullivan, *Genius and the Mobocracy* (1949), delineates his preference for genteel democracy.

Reiterations of some of Wright's views can be found in *The Natural House* (1954), which includes his writings on the Usonian houses he was designing to bring beauty to ordinary people, as well as his philosophy of materials, and in *A Testament* (1957), which includes his proposal for a mile-high tower to house one hundred thousand people on the Chicago lakefront—a project that flew in the face of his oft-expressed advocacy of decentralization.

**FURTHER READING:** Until Brendan Gill's *Many Masks: A Life of Frank Lloyd Wright* (1987), biographical accounts tended to hero-worship. According to Robert Sweeney's lengthy but enlightening introduction to his *Frank Lloyd Wright: An Annotated Bibliography* (1978), biographers have been hampered by "the closely held archives of the Wright Foundation" (xl). Gill has shown that Wright's *Autobiography* is principally a rhetorical work, modeled in part on LOUIS SULLIVAN's *Autobiography of an Idea* (1924); a useful guide to the book's complexities will be found in *An Index and Guide to "An Autobiography": The 1943 Edition by Frank Lloyd Wright,* compiled by Linn Ann Cowles (1976).

Wright's correspondence and personal papers have been published in several volumes (1982–89) under the editorship of Bruce Brooks Pfeiffer, who was Wright's archivist. Among critical studies of Wright and his ideas the following stand out: H. Allen Brooks's *The Prairie School: Frank Lloyd Wright and His Midwestern Contemporaries* (1972); Robert C. Twombly's *Frank Lloyd Wright: An Interpretive Biography* (1973); John Sergeant's *Frank Lloyd*

*Wright's Usonian Houses: The Case for Organic Architecture* (1976); Donald Hoffman's *Frank Lloyd Wright's Robie House* (1984); and Meryle Secrest's *Frank Lloyd Wright: A Biography* (1992). A volume published by the Columbia University School of Architecture, *Four Great Makers of Modern Architecture* (1963), contains two useful essays on Wright: "Broadacre City: Wright's Utopia Reconsidered," by George R. Collins, and "Wright and the Spirit of Democracy," by James Marston Fitch.

Not to be overlooked are the biographies and reminiscences of members of the family and the Taliesin Fellowship, notably John Lloyd Wright's *My Father Who Is on Earth* (1946); Olgivanna Wright's *Shining Brow* (1960) and *Frank Lloyd Wright: His Life, His Work, His Words* (1966); and Edgar Tafel's *Apprentice to Genius: Years with Frank Lloyd Wright* (1979).

Wright was widely considered the model for Howard Roark in Ayn Rand's novel *The Fountainhead* (1943), though both Rand and Wright scoffed at the idea (Gill 490). His exclusion from the 1933 Century of Progress Exhibition in Chicago was noted by *Time* in an article titled "Wrightites v. Chicago" (March 9, 1931): 63–64, but he made the cover of *Time* on January 17, 1938, and was featured in an article in that issue titled "Usonian Architect" (29–32). Despite the "socially visionary" theme of the 1939 New York World's Fair, Wright was not even invited to submit designs (Secrest 480).

Wright's manuscripts and drawings are held by the Frank Lloyd Wright Foundation in Scottsdale. A microfiche copy of these records has been deposited for the use of researchers at the Getty Center Archives for the History of Art and the Humanities in Santa Monica, California.

ROGER JIANG BRESNAHAN

MICHIGAN STATE UNIVERSITY

# HAROLD BELL WRIGHT
May 4, 1872–May 24, 1944

**BIOGRAPHY:** Born near Rome, New York, to William A. and Alma T. (Watson) Wright, Harold Bell Wright knew poverty early in his life because of his father's alcoholism. Wright reports in his autobiography, *To My Sons* (1934), that his father was a drunkard and wastrel. It was from his mother that he learned to love books and painting. Unfortunately, she died when he was ten. Her death had a profound impact on Wright's life. Because of the family's poverty, as a teenager he had to work at various jobs to help support the family. Wright's work kept him from getting a formal education; however, he was able to spend two years at the preparatory school of Hiram College, where he worked at the bookstore. From 1892 to 1897 he was a landscape painter who did sketches and watercolors near Lebanon and Branson, Missouri, having moved to the Midwest to recuperate from the chilling grip of pneumonia. Like the stranger in *The Shepherd of the Hills* (1907), Wright became a preacher, spending a dozen years pastoring churches in southern Missouri and Kansas. His ability to deliver a sermon composed of fables and tales proved valuable to him as a writer.

In 1902 when he was pastor at Pittsburg, Kansas, he completed his first book, *That Printer of Udell's*, the story of a young man, the son of a dissipated drunkard. The young man became a printer and devoted his life to service of God and others, a major theme in all of Wright's books. Because of the Christian moral of the first book and the others to follow, the publishers advertised his books in mass circulation magazines and in church papers of various religious denominations. Wright's stories of moral heroes triumphing over evil were very popular. His first book sold more than a half-million copies.

Because of the first book's success, in 1907 Wright published *The Shepherd of the Hills*, his most famous work. Its formula of a man finding true religion near nature while escaping the iniquity of the city appealed to fundamentalist readers; as a result, his second novel sold more than a million copies. From this point on Wright devoted himself to writing novels. In 1913 he moved from the Midwest to a cottage near Tucson, Arizona, where he continued to write until his death.

**SIGNIFICANCE:** Wright's early Midwestern Missouri experiences as a preacher, writer, and landscape painter provided him with the formula for his nineteen books. Always there is a young man who, with God's help, overcomes overwhelming odds to be successful. The protagonist possesses honesty, godliness, dependability, and determination, values of rural Midwestern people at the turn of the century. The feelings of all his novels' characters are represented in the thirteen chapter titles of *Their Yesterdays* (1912): "Dreams," "Occupation," "Knowledge," "Ignorance," "Religion," "Tradition," "Temptation," "Life," "Death," "Failure," "Success," "Love," and "Memories."

Because the novels are written from formula, the settings are generic, suggestive of any small American town. However, Wright's most famous novel, *The Shepherd of the Hills*, is set in the Midwest, in the southern part of Missouri. Although his novels were popular, making him in the 1920s the best-selling novelist in America, Wright never obtained a quality literary reputation. However, he is immortalized because of *The Shepherd of the Hills*, perennially enacted each summer in the Midwestern Ozark hills, near Branson.

**SELECTED WORKS:** Wright's major works include *That Printer of Udell's* (1903), *The Shepherd of the Hills* (1907), *The Calling of Dan Matthews* (1909), *The Uncrowned King* (1910), *The Winning of Barbara Worth* (1911), *Their Yesterdays* (1912), *The Eyes of the World* (1914), *When a Man's a Man* (1916), *The Re-Creation of Brian Kent* (1919), *Helen of the Old House* (1921), *The Mine with the Iron Door* (1923), *A Son of His Father* (1925), *God and the Groceryman* (1927), *Long Ago Told* (1929), *Exit* (1930), *The Devil's Highway* (1932), *Ma Cinderella* (1932), and *The Man Who Went Away* (1942). Wright's autobiography is entitled *To My Sons* (1934).

**FURTHER READING:** Lawrence V. Tagg's *Harold Bell Wright: Storyteller to America* (1986) provides a major biography. The University of Arizona holds some of Wright's papers and manuscripts.

LELAND MAY

NORTHWEST MISSOURI STATE UNIVERSITY

# JAMES WRIGHT

December 13, 1927–March 25, 1980

**BIOGRAPHY:** James Arlington Wright was born to Dudley and Jesse (Lyons) Wright and raised in Martins Ferry, Ohio, a mining and industrial town along the Ohio River in southeastern Ohio. After graduating from high school in 1946, Wright enlisted in the U.S. Army and served a tour of duty in Japan. Upon returning from the service, he entered Kenyon College in Gambier, Ohio, in 1948. Among his teachers there were John Crowe Ransom, Allen Tate, and Robert Penn Warren. Between 1952 and 1954, Wright married his first wife, Liberty Kardules; graduated

from Kenyon; received a Fulbright scholarship to the University of Vienna; witnessed the birth of his first son, Franz Paul; and began graduate study at the University of Washington, Seattle, where one of his professors was THEODORE ROETHKE. Wright's first book, *The Green Wall* (1957), was selected by W. H. Auden as the winner of the Yale Series of Younger Poets competition. Between 1957 and 1963, Wright taught at the University of Minnesota. During this time he met ROBERT BLY and CAROL BLY, beginning important friendships which would last for the rest of his life. Wright's second son, Marshall, was born in 1962, the same year Wright was divorced.

In 1966 Wright accepted a teaching position in the English Department at Hunter College in New York City. In 1967 Wright married Edith Anne Runk, and between 1968 and 1980, Wright traveled extensively and his translations and collections of poems appeared regularly, garnering numerous awards, including the Pulitzer Prize in 1972 for *Collected Poems* (1971). Wright died in New York City on March 25, 1980, from throat cancer. His last collection of poems, *This Journey*, was published posthumously in 1982.

**SIGNIFICANCE:** As a child growing up during the Depression in the scarred industrial landscapes of Ohio, Wright witnessed the poverty, struggles, and tragedies of the people of this region. Few poets have written about the marginalized and dispossessed as eloquently as Wright. Equally impressive is Wright's ability to bring the mystery and beauty of the natural world into his poems. This dynamic tension—between the beautiful and the ugly, between the natural and the industrial world—drives many of Wright's poems. One of Wright's major accomplishments is his ability to take the details of everyday life, details which might be considered unpoetic to some, and transform them into powerful lyrics. Wright's pastoral poems about rural Ohio and Minnesota are among his finest. In the lost boyhood paradise of Wright's beloved Ohio River Valley, the landscape to which he would return repeatedly in his poetry, love, compassion, and empathy are among his redemptive themes.

Wright's technical virtuosity remains impressive. Much has been written about his stylistic development throughout his career, especially that occurring between his first two volumes and his third, *The Branch Will Not Break* (1963). Wright's mastery of traditional forms, his experiments with free and open verse forms, "deep imagism," surrealism, and especially his experiments with the prose poem make his career one of the most interesting in contemporary American poetry. With Robert Bly and WILLIAM STAFFORD, Wright influenced a generation of writers, especially Midwestern writers, who learned from Wright how to see anew their regional landscapes and move from the particular to the general, from the local to the universal.

Wright's significance and importance as an American poet were quickly recognized by his hometown. Each year since 1981, the James Wright Poetry Festival has been held in Martins Ferry, appreciating, celebrating, and honoring the life and work of its hometown bard.

**SELECTED WORKS:** *Above the River: The Complete Poems* (1990), with an introduction by DONALD HALL, collects poems from Wright's major volumes, including *The Green Wall* (1957), *Saint Judas* (1959), *The Branch Will Not Break* (1963), *Shall We Gather at the River* (1968), *Two Citizens* (1973), *To a Blossoming Pear Tree* (1977), and *This Journey* (1982). *Above the River* also includes the sections entitled "Some Translations" and "New Poems," which appeared in Wright's *Collected Poems* (1971), as well as a section entitled "Selected Prose Pieces," Wright's prose poems collected in *The Shape of Light* (1986). *Collected Prose* (1983) gathers some of Wright's essays, reviews, interviews, and memoirs. An exchange of letters between Wright and poet and novelist Leslie Marmon Silko is collected in *The Delicacy and Strength of Lace* (1986). Wright's translations include *Twenty Poems of Georg Trakl* (with Robert Bly and JOHN KNOEPFLE, 1961); *Theodor Storm: The Rider on the White Horse* (1964); *Twenty Poems of Pablo Neruda* (with Robert Bly, 1968); *Hermann Hesse: Poems* (1968); *Neruda and Vallejo: Selected Poems* (with Robert Bly and John Knoepfle, 1971); and *Wandering: Notes and Sketches*, by Hermann Hesse (1972).

**FURTHER READING:** There is no full-length biography of James Wright as of this writing, but excellent biographical profiles of Wright can be found in the monograph *James*

**James Wright.**
Photo © Nancy Crampton

*Wright: An Introduction*, by William S. Saunders (1979); *James Wright: A Profile*, edited by Frank Graziano and Peter Stitt (1988); and Robert Bly's memoir *Remembering James Wright* (1991). David C. Dougherty's Twayne book *James Wright* (1987) is a good general introduction to Wright's life and work. Kevin Stein's critical study *James Wright: The Poetry of a Grown Man* (1989) is an excellent study of the growth of Wright's body of work. Andrew Elkins's *The Poetry of James Wright* (1991) is a valuable study of Wright's seven major collections of poetry. Also important and valuable are two collections of critical reviews and essays, Dave Smith's *The Pure Clear Word: Essays on the Poetry of James Wright* (1982) and Peter Stitt and Frank Graziano's *James Wright: The Heart of the Light* (1990). Excellent bibliographies of work by and about Wright appear in the works noted by Elkins, Smith, and Stein, as well as in Stitt and Graziano's *Heart of the Light*. James Wright's papers are held at the Wilson Library at the University of Minnesota.

THOM TAMMARO     MINNESOTA STATE UNIVERSITY

## RICHARD WRIGHT
September 4, 1908–November 28, 1960
BIOGRAPHY: Novelist, poet, playwright, journalist, and essayist, Richard Wright was born on a plantation near Natchez, Mississippi, and grew up in poverty and hunger in Mississippi, Tennessee, and Arkansas. When he was a small child, his father, Nathaniel Wright, deserted the family; subsequently, Wright received only a ninth-grade education because of frequent moves, the ill health of his mother, Ella (Wilson) Wright, and the necessity for him to be gainfully employed to support his mother and younger brother.

In 1927, after experiencing much job discrimination and white hostility as a young man working in Memphis, Wright achieved a long-time goal: to move to the North. In Chicago he held a variety of menial jobs while saving to send for his mother and brother but found racism pervasive in the North also. In Chicago he continued an ambitious program of self-education that he had begun with a borrowed library card in Memphis.

During the 1930s Wright joined the Chicago branch of the John Reed Club, serving as executive secretary, and the Communist Party, which he perceived as a tool for organizing and empowering oppressed minorities. During the Depression he worked for the Federal Writers' Project and the Federal Theatre Project, was active in a number of writers' groups, and was published in leftist periodicals.

After a decade in Chicago, Wright moved to New York to pursue a full-time literary career; his first book, *Uncle Tom's Children*, was published in 1938. In 1939 he married Dhima Rose Meadman, but the couple divorced in 1940. That year also saw the publication of *Native Son*, which made Wright's literary reputation and established him as the voice of protest for his generation of African Americans.

In 1941 Wright married Ellen Poplar; two daughters were born to them later that decade. By the mid-1940s Wright had broken with the Communist Party over issues of party discipline and artistic freedom. During the last two decades of his life, he wrote novels, stories, essays, poems, travel pieces, and lectures, traveled extensively in Africa, Asia, South America, and Europe, and mentored emerging writers such as CHESTER HIMES, James Baldwin, and GWENDOLYN BROOKS.

His relatively brief literary career was marked by many honors and accomplishments: a Guggenheim Fellowship in 1939, a 1941 Spingarn Medal from the NAACP, the phenomenal critical and commercial success of his first novel, *Native Son* (1940), and of the first volume of his autobiography, *Black Boy* (1945), the successful dramatization of *Native Son* on Broadway, and the translation of his books into French, Italian, German, Dutch, Swedish, and Czech.

In 1947 Wright, fed up with living in a racist America, moved his family to France and lived there for the rest of his life. He died in Paris of a heart attack following a battle with amoebic dysentery.

SIGNIFICANCE: Wright has been called the father of black American literature, an assessment implicit in Irving Howe's statement in "Black Boys and Native Sons" that when *Native Son* was published, American culture was changed forever (100). That novel and two others, *Lawd Today!* (1963) and *The Outsider* (1953), are set in Chicago, as is Wright's second autobiographical volume, *American Hunger* (1977). In her essay "Richard Wright in Chicago: Three Novels That Represent a Black Spokesman's Quest for Self-Identity," Patricia D'Itri writes that "Wright's characters are trapped in the interplay between polarities of black and white, the self and society, and the psychological dimensions of tension and relief, pride and defeat" (26). Thus, Wright's Chicago functions as an objective correlative for this state of psychological entrapment; ironically the city that early in his life represented a promised land of freedom from the terrors of Southern racism later came to be seen as yet another hostile environment that imprisoned black people in fear, ignorance, and alienation by more subtle and pervasive forms of racial oppression.

The first few lines of *American Hunger* describe Chicago as Wright saw it when he first arrived: "My first glimpse of the flat black stretches of Chicago depressed and dismayed me, mocked all my fantasies. Chicago seemed an unreal city whose mythical houses were built of slabs of black coal wreathed in palls of gray smoke, houses whose foundations were sinking slowly into the dank prairie" (1). Wright's description emphasizes not only the bleak ugliness of the city, dominated by the colors black and gray, but the insubstantiality of its structures, which, in turn, suggest the insubstantiality of the hopes and aspirations of its black inhabitants.

*Native Son* takes place in a snow-covered Chicago of rotting tenements and towering skyscrapers; these physical structures of the cityscape and the blinding blizzard that engulfs it reinforce Wright's naturalistic view that the individual is largely conditioned and controlled by his environment and is relatively powerless in the face of social and environmental forces.

Wright explains how these forces work in his well-known essay "How 'Bigger' Was Born" when he notes that "It was not that Chicago segregated Negroes more than the South, but that Chicago had more to offer, that Chicago's physical aspect—noisy, crowded, filled with the sense of power and fulfillment—did so much more to dazzle the mind with a taunting sense of possible achievement that the segregation it did impose brought forth from Bigger a reaction more obstreperous than in the South" (29).

The protagonists of all three of Wright's Chicago novels—Jake Jackson of *Lawd Today!*, Bigger Thomas of *Native Son*, and Cross Damon of *The Outsider*—experience this sense of entrapment by hunger, poverty, mind-numbing menial jobs, and dysfunctional family relationships, all functions of the rigid racial codes that divide the city and dictate where blacks may live and work. However, the plight of the protagonists of the first two novels, written in the 1930s, was represented naturalistically; the evolution in Wright's thinking over the course of his career was reflected in the existentialist thrust of *The Outsider*, written in the 1950s after Wright had discovered the works of the French existentialists Albert Camus, Jean-Paul Sartre, and Simone de Beauvoir a decade earlier.

**SELECTED WORKS:** Wright is the author of two collections of short stories, *Uncle Tom's Children* (1938) and *Eight Men*, published posthumously in 1961, and five novels: *Native Son* (1940), *The Outsider* (1953), *Savage Holiday* (1954), *The Long Dream* (1958), and *Lawd Today!*, written in 1936 and published posthumously in 1963. The 1966 Harper perennial classic edition of *Native Son* contains Wright's prefatory essay, "How 'Bigger' Was Born" (1–39).

His works of nonfiction include two volumes of autobiography, *Black Boy* (1945) and *American Hunger*, published posthumously in 1977. Wright also published *12 Million Black Voices* (1941), a folk history of black America; *Black Power* (1954), a study of the African Gold Coast; *The Color Curtain: A Report on the Bandung Conference* (1956); *Pagan Spain* (1957), an account of his travels through Spain and his reflections on that country's culture and politics; and *White Man, Listen!* (1957), a collection of lectures on race relations that Wright delivered in Europe from 1950 to 1956. In 1978 Wright's widow, Ellen, and Wright scholar Michel Fabre published the *Richard Wright Reader*.

**FURTHER READING:** From the decade following Wright's death through the end of the twentieth century there was a veritable explosion of Wright scholarship. Biographies include Constance Webb's *Richard Wright: A Biography* (1968); John A. Williams and Dorothy Sterling's *The Most Native of Sons: A Biography of Richard Wright* (1970); and Michel J. Fabre's *The Unfinished Quest of Richard Wright* (1973). Bibliographies include *Richard Wright: A Primary Bibliography*, edited by Charles T. Davis and Fabre (1982), and *A Richard Wright Bibliography: Fifty Years of Criticism and Commentary, 1933–1982*, compiled by Keneth Kinnamon (1988). Interviews are collected in *Conversations with Richard Wright*, edited by Kinnamon and Fabre (1993).

Critical studies include Lynn M. Weiss's *Gertude Stein and Richard Wright* (1998), Yoshinobu Hakutani's *Richard Wright and Racial Discourse* (1996), and Joyce A. Joyce's *Richard Wright's Art of Tragedy* (1982). Important essays are James Baldwin's "Everybody's Protest Novel" and "Many Thousands Gone," in *Notes of a Native Son* (1955): 13–22 and 23–42, which offer critiques of Wright's fictional representation of blacks; Irving Howe's "Black Boys and Native Sons," in *A World More Attractive* (1963): 98–110, presents a rebuttal.

Essays which focus on the way that place functions in Wright's fiction include Patricia D'Itri's "Richard Wright's Chicago: Three Novels That Represent a Black Spokesman's Quest for Self-Identity," in *Midwestern Miscellany* 4 (1976): 26–33; Houston A. Baker Jr.'s "Richard Wright and the Dynamics of Place in Afro-American Literature," in *New Essays on Native Son*, edited by Keneth Kinnamon

(1990): 85–116; Robert Butler's "Farrell's Ethnic Neighborhood and Wright's Urban Ghetto: Two Visions of Chicago's South Side," in *MELUS* 18 (Spring 1993): 103–11; Desmond Harding's "The Power of Place: Richard Wright's Native Son," in the *College Language Association Journal* 40 (March 1997): 367–79; and Yoshinobu Hakutani's "The City and Richard Wright's Quest for Freedom," in *The City in African-American Literature*, edited by Yoshinobu Hakutani and Robert Butler (1995): 50–63. In 1997 the Modern Language Association published *Approaches to Teaching Native Son*, edited by James A. Miller.

The Beinecke Library at Yale University holds a large collections of Wright's papers.

MARCIA NOE AND SCOTT DENT

THE UNIVERSITY OF TENNESSEE AT CHATTANOOGA

## RAY (ANTHONY) YOUNG BEAR
November 12, 1950
(Maqui-banash)

**BIOGRAPHY:** Ray Young Bear, poet, prose writer, and musician, is a full-blood Meskwaki, a tribe known in Euro-American history as the Fox, and a lifelong resident of the Meskwaki Settlement at Tama, Iowa. The name "Meskwaki," often spelled "Mesquakie," though "Meskwaki" is preferred by the tribe, translates as "People of the Red Earth." His parents were Leonard and Chloe (Old Bear) Young Bear and his paternal grandmother was Ada Kapayou Old Bear, whom Ray Young Bear credits as his major source of Meskwaki oral traditions and his most important literary influence. Young Bear began writing poetry at sixteen and from the outset earned the attention of scholars and critics at university-sponsored programs. He studied at Claremont College in California, Grinnell College in Iowa, Northern Iowa University, Iowa State University, and the University of Iowa. He has been a visiting faculty member at Eastern Washington University and the University of Iowa. An artist, singer, and performer as well as a writer, Young Bear and his wife, Stella, organized the Woodland Song and Dance Troupe of Arts Midwest, which has performed Meskwaki music and dance in North America and Europe.

Widely published in literary journals and anthologies of Native American writing, Young Bear published a book-length poem, *Waiting to Be Fed*, in 1975, with more collections

of his poetry in 1980 and 1990. His prose work *Black Eagle Child: The Facepaint Narratives,* which was written in a form regarded as fictional in English-language literature, was published in *Singular Lives: The Iowa Series in North American Autobiography* of the University of Iowa Press in 1992. In 1996 Young Bear published a second book in this narrative form, *Remnants of the First Earth*, which has been largely reviewed as a novel. Despite confusion in the literary establishment resulting from his adherence to Native American storytelling genres, he has been received critically as an immensely talented, innovative, and important writer of poetry and prose.

**SIGNIFICANCE:** Ray Young Bear's work fully engages and utilizes the Meskwaki collective consciousness and is infused with the oral traditions and ceremonial imagery that form the tribal consciousness and its strong sense of place in the Midwest. From the beginning of the eighteenth century until they were moved to a reservation in Kansas after the Black Hawk War in 1832, the Meskwakis were a political and cultural force in the western Great Lakes and upper Mississippi Valley, frustrating French attempts to build an empire of allied tribes in the region. After being moved to Kansas, some of their leaders became successful horse breeders and traders and were able to repurchase land in 1856 along the Iowa River, where a group of one hundred Meskwakis, led by Young Bear's great-great-grandfather, Maminwanike, established a settlement which the tribe now regards as home. Ray Young Bear has emerged as a powerful and authoritative voice in relating this Meskwaki cultural history to contemporary Midwestern and American life and in translating Meskwaki literary concepts into English works of literature.

Young Bear thinks, speaks, and writes in both English and Meskwaki and has mastered the literary forms of both traditions. He carefully practices his people's conservative tradition of presenting accounts of Meskwaki life which resist appropriation by anthropologists and folklorists. His work provides imaginative insights into the lives of the Meskwaki people and their special significance to the culture and history of the Midwest while it also speaks with rigorous integrity for and to Native Americans, careful not to transgress "certain codes and precepts" which have become "inherent parts of the storytelling regimen" of the Meskwakis, including the precept that words have inherent powers to create and illuminate, but also to destroy and inflict harm (*Black Eagle Child* 255–56). The code learned from Young Bear's grandmother requires that a storyteller never use words in destructive ways, whether through ignorance or intent.

**SELECTED WORKS:** Ray Young Bear's poetry has been extensively published in literary journals and anthologies of Native American literature. His first book publication, *Waiting to Be Fed* (1975), is an extended poem. In *Winter of the Salamander: The Keeper of Importance* (1980), Young Bear assumes the role of keeper and purveyor of the stories and ceremonies which define Meskwaki identity to tribal members and to others. *The Invisible Musician* (1990), another collection of poems, continues this voice but includes more works which emphasize Young Bear's role as the composer and singer of tribal songs. *Black Eagle Child: The Facepaint Narratives* (1992) demonstrates the Native American premise that individual lives are cosmically insignificant and attain their importance when examined and told in terms of tribal history and community relationships. Young Bear and his publisher term the book an autobiography, even though it treats tribal history and the lives of other people. *Remnants of the First Earth* (1996) continues this form of narrative.

**FURTHER READING:** Interviews with Ray Young Bear include Joseph Bruchac's "Connected to the Past: An Interview with Ray Young Bear," in *Survival This Way: Interviews with American Indian Poets* (1987), and David Moore and Michael Wilson's "Staying Afloat in a Chaotic World: A Conversation with Ray Young Bear," in *Callaloo* (Winter 1994): 205–13. Studies of his work include James Ruppert's "The Poetic Language of Ray Young Bear," in *Coyote Was Here: Essays on Contemporary Native American Literary and Political Mobilization* (1984); Gretchen M. Bataille's "Ray Young Bear: Tribal History and Personal Vision," in *Studies in American Indian Literatures* (Summer 1993): 17–20; and Robert Dale Parker's "To Be There, No Authority to Anything: Ontological Desire and Cultural and Poetic Authority in the Poetry of Ray A. Young Bear," in *Arizona Quarterly* (Winter 1994): 89–115. A recent

work dealing with his short fiction is Cheryl A. Roberts's "An Interview with Ray A Young Bear," in *Speaking of the Short Story: Interviews with Contemporary Writers* (1997).

DAVID L. NEWQUIST    NORTHERN STATE UNIVERSITY

## ZITKALA-ŠA (RED BIRD)

February 22, 1876–January 26, 1938
(Sitkala-Ša, Gertrude Bonnin, Gertrude Simmons)

**BIOGRAPHY:** Born to a Yankton Sioux (Nakota) mother named Tate I Yohin Win (Reaches for the Wind), whose English name was Ellen, and a white father, named Felker, who deserted his wife before Zitkala-Ša's birth, she was named Gertrude and given the surname of her mother's second husband, John Haysting Simmons. She was raised in South Dakota on the Yankton reservation as a traditional Nakota until at the age of eight, enthralled by stories of the wonders in the East, she importuned her mother to send her to a Quaker missionary school, White's Indian Manual Labor Institute at Wabash, Indiana. She divided her time between the Indian school and the Yankton reservation until she graduated at nineteen, after which she enrolled at Earlham College in Richmond, Indiana, where she began to excel in writing, oratory, drama, and the violin.

After teaching at Carlisle Indian Industrial School in Pennsylvania for two years, she studied violin at a music conservatory in Boston, at which time her literary talents gained recognition in national magazines and she published *Old Indian Legends* in 1901. She then took a job on the Standing Rock reservation, where she met and married Raymond Talesfase Bonnin, also a Nakota, on May 10, 1902, and had a son, Raymond Ohiya. The Bonnins worked on reservations in Utah, during which time Zitkala-Ša collaborated on an opera, *The Sun Dance* (1913), with William Hanson. In 1916 the Bonnins moved to Washington, D.C., where Bonnin was commissioned into the army and later became a law clerk. During this time Zitkala-Ša became active in the Society for the American Indians and was editor of *American Indian Magazine.* She published *American Indian Stories* in 1921 and devoted the rest of her life to lecturing and working on behalf of reform for American Indians. She died of cardiac dilatation and kidney disease in Washington, D.C., and is buried in the Arlington National Cemetery.

**SIGNIFICANCE:** Zitkala-Ša knew and understood profoundly both the Yankton and Euro-American cultures. Although the two cultural traditions contended for her allegiance, her published writings from the earliest to the most mature are demonstrations of a Native American aesthetic in which language, image, and experience comprise a coherent art form capable of dealing with matters of the spirit and its earthly and cosmic identity. Zitkala-Ša's writing identifies points of dissonance between Native American and Euro-American cultures: the indigenous people read nature through their regional landscape to inform their values, their language, and their attitudes as equal co-creatures with all of nature; the Euro-American culture reads "paper" which reproduces racial presumptions and judgments of a culture which believes itself superior and imposes a hierarchy of worth that degrades people and undermines nature. In her recording of Nakota oral stories, her collaboration on the opera *The Sun Dance,* and her political activist writing for Native American rights, Zitkala-Ša maintains a vision of conciliation without compromising the Native American origins of her literary work, a vision which holds the implicit hope that American democratic culture can deliver its promise of cultural equity and liberty to her people.

Her essays and stories portray the life and thought of the Yankton people along the Missouri River with an artistic imagery and lucidity that makes them much more than history or ethnography. The way specific features of landscape are made settings and figures in the oral literature is illustrated in her autobiographical sketch "The Great Spirit" in *American Indian Stories* (1921; originally published as *Old Indian Legends* [1901]), in which she recalls sitting on a rock embedded in a foothill of the Missouri River and is able to trace the legend of the rock "like a trail leading to the Indian Village" (102–103). The rock is the beginning point for her retelling of the Nakota version of the Stone Boy myth with its Missouri River Valley referents as well as for accounts which explain the simultaneous significance of rocks as natural occurrences and as important signifiers in sacred ceremonies. Zitkala-Ša's accounts are especially rich in recording how a profound respect was developed in children for their home environment and for members of the tribe, particularly the elderly, whose welfare was always paramount, but whose dignity was never to be compromised by an ostentatious or patronizing generosity. Zitkala-Ša records the ultimate practice of that democratic ethic of hospitality of the Midwest.

**SELECTED WORKS:** Zitkala-Ša's major works are *Old Indian Legends* (1901, reprinted 1985); *The Sun Dance* (1913), an opera with William F. Hanson, with performances by the original company in Vernal, Utah, and Brigham Young University, and as opera of the year by the New York Light Opera Guild (1937); and *American Indian Stories* (1921, reprinted 1985). A crusading work on which she collaborated under the name of Gertrude Simmons Bonnin with Charles H. Fabens and Matthew K. Sniffin is *Oklahoma's Poor Rich Indians: An Orgy of Graft and Exploitation of the Five Civilized Tribes—Legalized Robbery* (1924).

**FURTHER READING:** Much of the biographical material on Zitkala-Ša varies or is contradictory in details. Some interpretive studies of her work draw inferences from unverified and conflicting biographical details and venture far into conjecture. Studies drawn from general ethnographic sources establish a more credible significance for Zitkala-Ša's work. Biographical accounts include *Who's Who in the Nation's Capital,* edited by Stanley H. Williamson (1927); Marion Gridley, *American Indian Women* (1974); Frederick J. Dockstader, *Great North American Indians—Profiles in Life and Leadership* (1977); and *Notable American Women—1607–1950—A Biographical Dictionary,* edited by Edward T. James (1971). A study which establishes the historical and regional context for Zitkala-Ša is Janette K. Murray's "An Overview of Literature by Dakota/Lakota Authors," in *An Illustrated History of the Arts in South Dakota,* edited by Arthur Huseboe (1989). A number of recent studies reflect more scholarly attempts to establish Zitkala-Ša's significance in multicultural terms. These include Martha J. Cutter's "Zitkala-Ša's Autobiographical Writings: The Problems of a Canonical Search for Language and Identity," in *MELUS* (Spring 1994): 31–44; Dexter Fisher's "Zitkala-Ša: The Evolution of a Writer," in the *American Indian Quarterly* (August 1977): 229–38; "The Transformation of

Tradition: A Study of Zitkala-Ša and Mourning Dove, Two Transitional American Indian Writers," in *Critical Essays on American Indian Literature*, edited by Andrew Wiget (1985); Patricia Okker's "Native American Literature and the Canon: The Case of Zitkala-Ša," in *American Realism and the Canon* (1994); Mary Stout's "Zitkala-Ša: The Literature of Politics," in *Coyote Was Here: Essays in Contemporary Native American Literature*, edited by Bo Schöler (1984); Dorothea M. Susag's "Zitkala-Ša (Gertrude Simmons Bonnin): A Power(full) Literary Voice," in *Studies in American Indian Literature* (Winter 1993): 3–24; and William Willard's "Zitkala-Ša, A Woman Who Would Be Heard," in the *Wicazo Ša Review* (1985): 11–16. Three doctoral dissertations which focus on biography are listed on Zitkala-Ša: Laurie O'Dell Lisa's "The Life Story of Zitkala-Ša/Gertrude Simmons Bonnin: Writing and Creating A Public Image," Arizona State University (1996); Margaret A. Lukens's "The American Indian Story of Zitkala-Ša," in "Creating Cultural Spaces: The Pluralist Project of American Women Writers, 1843–1902 (Margaret Fuller, Harriet Jacobs, Sarah Winnemucca, and Zitkala-Ša)," University of Colorado (1992); and Deborah Welch's "American Indian Leader: The Story of Gertrude Bonnin," University of Wyoming (1985). A considerable body of Zitkala-Ša's correspondence from her work on Native American rights is stored in Record Group 75 of the National Archives, Washington, D.C., Central Files, 1907–39, Bureau of Indian Affairs. Letters from her are also included in the John Collier Papers and the Richard Henry Pratt Papers at Yale University; her personal correspondence with Carlos Montezuma is among his papers at the Wisconsin State Historical Society; and papers about the production of the opera *The Sun Dance* are among the William Hanson Papers at Brigham Young University.

DAVID L. NEWQUIST    NORTHERN STATE UNIVERSITY

## AMY JO ZOOK.

*See* Amy Jo Schoonover

# Appendix
Recipients of the MidAmerica Award

The older of two annual awards given by the membership of the Society for the Study of Midwestern Literature, the MidAmerica Award was named for the Society's annual publication, *MidAmerica: The Yearbook of the Society for the Study of Midwestern Literature*. Presented every year at the Society's annual conference since the award's inception in 1977, it is awarded to those, normally one person annually but occasionally two, who have made distinguished contributions to the study of Midwestern literature.

The award was initially established to honor those scholars and critics whose pioneering work led to the recognition of Midwestern literature as a distinct body of work within the rubric of American literature and ultimately to the founding of the Society, of which most of them became early members. In more recent years the award has been presented to scholars and critics who have built upon the work of these pioneers, have made considerable contributions of their own to the study of Midwestern literature, and in turn are directing the scholarship of those who will carry the study on into the future.

The first four scholars and critics to receive the award, beginning with the first recipient at the Seventh Annual Conference in 1977, were true pioneers in the study of the literary, cultural, and intellectual history of the region. The first to receive the award was John T. Flanagan (January 15, 1906–March 12, 1996), a native of St. Paul, Minnesota, and professor of English at the University of Illinois at Champaign–Urbana. Recipient of the BA, MA, and PhD from the University of Minnesota, including one of the first PhDs in American literature in the nation, and a pioneer in developing American literature courses and later Midwestern literature courses there and at the University of Illinois, he focused on Midwestern writers and writing in his work from the beginning, publishing *James Hall, Literary Pioneer of the Ohio Valley* in 1941 and an early and still important anthology of Midwestern writing, *America Is West*, in 1945. He also wrote *The American Way* (1953), *Profile of Vachel Lindsay* (1970), *Edgar Lee Masters: The Spoon River Poet and His Critics* (1974), and other works on Midwestern writers and writing, particularly of Minnesota, as well as Midwestern and American folklore.

The second award, in 1978, was to Russel B. Nye (February 17, 1913–September 2, 1993), University Distinguished Professor of English at Michigan State University. Born in Viola, Wisconsin, he received his AB from Oberlin College in 1934 and his MA and PhD from the University of Wisconsin in 1935 and 1939 respectively. At Wisconsin he studied American literature under Harry Hayden Clark. He came to Michigan State University in 1940, where he spent his professional career, leading many students to the study of American and Midwestern literature. A pioneer in American Studies and the study of popular culture, he won the Pulitzer Prize in 1944 for *George Bancroft, Brahmin Rebel*, and his broad, comprehensive studies of American culture, including *Civil Liberty and Slavery* (1948), *Midwestern Progressive Politics* (1951), *The Cultural Life of the New Nation* (1960), *The Unembarrassed Muse* (1970), and *Society and Culture in America* (1974), are major works that have pointed out the direction much Midwestern cultural study continues to take. He was a founding member of the Society for the Study of Midwestern Literature.

In 1979 the third award was presented to Walter Havighurst (November 28, 1901–February 3, 1994), Regents Professor of English at Miami University. He was born in Appleton, Wisconsin, in the Fox River Valley where, he liked to recall, French explorers once traveled. As a novelist, he drew upon his early experiences as a merchant seaman as well as on his own "midland America." His studies of the cultural and social history of the Midwest in *Wilderness for Sale* (1956), *Land of the Long Horizons* (1960), *The Heartland* (1962, 1974), and his remarkable Great Lakes studies continue to illuminate the transition of the region from Old West to modern Midwest.

The 1980 award was presented to Harlan Hatcher (September 9, 1898–February 25, 1998), professor of English and president emeritus of the University of Michigan, novelist, literary critic, cultural historian, and anthologist. Born in Ironton, Ohio, he served in the U.S. Army in World War I and then attended Ohio State University, from which he received the AB in 1922, the AM in 1923, and the PhD in 1927. His professional career was divided between Ohio State University, where he served as professor of English and dean and vice president between 1928 and 1951, and the University of Michigan, where he was president from 1951 to 1967. He served in the U.S. Navy in World War II.

His early study, *Creating the Modern American Novel* (1935, 1965) remains standard; he edited *The Ohio Guide* (1940) of the WPA Federal Writers Project, and he wrote three novels based on his youth in southern Ohio. His cultural and historical works *The Buckeye Country* (1940), *The Great Lakes* (1949), and *The Western Reserve: The Story of New Connecticut in Ohio* (1949, 1966) are major studies of the emergence of Ohio and the Great Lakes basin as central to the evolving Midwest.

In 1981 the nature of the award began to evolve from its earlier emphasis on those who contributed to the emergence of the study of what was becoming recognized as Midwestern literature to a growing emphasis upon the recognition of active members of the Society who have made significant contributions to the study of Midwestern literature. Significantly, the first award of the new series was to Bernard I. Duffey (October 18, 1917–February 22, 1994). A native of Cincinnati, he received his AB from Oberlin College and his MA and PhD from Ohio University. He taught at the University of Minnesota and Michigan State University before moving to Duke University in 1963, where he remained as professor of English. He was a founding member of the Society for the Study of Midwestern Literature and the author of *Poetry in America* (1978) and *A Poetry of Presence* (1986). His major contribution to the study of Midwestern literature, *The Chicago Renaissance in American Letters* (1954), remains a point of departure for the studies of the city, the region, and many of the Midwestern writers of this century. With Kenny J. Williams, he also edited *Chicago's Public Wits: A Chapter in the American Comic Spirit* (1983).

Clarence Andrews (b. October 24, 1912), a native of Waterloo, Iowa, professor emeritus of English at the University of Iowa and at Michigan Technical University, an early member of the Society, and a pioneer in the study of the literature of Iowa, received the award in 1982. He received all of his degrees from the University of Iowa, the BA in 1953, the MA in 1960, and the PhD in 1963. The founder of Midwest Heritage Publishing Company in 1979 and the publisher and editor of the company, he is also author of *A Literary History of Iowa* (1972), *Chicago in Story* (1982), and *Michigan in Literature* (1992) and editor of *Growing Up in Iowa* (1978), *Christmas in Iowa* (1979, 1984), and other critical editions.

In 1983 the award was presented to Walter B. Rideout (b. October 21, 1917), Harry Hayden Clark Professor Emeritus of English at the University of Wisconsin and an early member of the Society. A native of Lee, Maine, he received the AB degree from Colby College in 1938, the MA from Harvard University in 1939, and the PhD from Harvard in 1950. His relationship with the Midwest began almost simultaneously with his appointment to the faculty of Northwestern University in 1949 and his almost simultaneous discovery of SHERWOOD ANDERSON. Together with Howard

Mumford Jones, he edited *The Letters of Sherwood Anderson* (1953), a fundamental source for Anderson and Midwestern literature scholars. He also wrote *The Radical Novel in the United States, 1900–1954* (1956) and edited IGNATIUS DONNELLY's *Caesar's Column* (1960) and *Sherwood Anderson: A Collection of Critical Essays* (1974). He has published many essays on Midwestern writers, primarily on Sherwood Anderson, and has written introductions to Anderson's *Beyond Desire* (1961), *Poor White* (1966), *A Story Teller's Story* (1969), and *Letters to Bab* (1985), edited by William A. Sutton.

In 1984 the Society made a double award for the first time, to the Society's bibliographers, Donald S. Pady, then bibliographer and reference librarian at Iowa State University Library, and Robert Beasecker, archivist and reference librarian at Grand Valley State University Library, creators, developers, and editors of a unique and valuable research tool for the study of Midwestern literature, the "Annual Bibliography of Midwestern Literature, 1973–," which has appeared annually since 1975 in the Society's major publication *MidAmerica: The Yearbook of the Society for the Study of Midwestern Literature*. Initially, until 1978, under Pady's editorship and between 1979 and 1992 under the coeditorship of Pady and Beasecker, the bibliography has grown to include primary sources, original literary publications, and secondary sources, critical and biographical studies, as well as literary periodicals which appear during each designated year. The bibliography employs a staff of volunteer bibliographers, it defines its criteria for inclusion in each issue, and it employs state-of-the-art technology. Since 1993 it has been under Beasecker's editorship.

Donald Pady (b. August 17, 1937), a native of Kansas City, Missouri, received the BA from the University of Kansas in 1959, the MS from Emporia State University in 1962, and the MA from Iowa State University in 1977. His publications include bibliographic studies of numerous Midwestern authors, most notably of WILLIAM ALLEN WHITE. He served as librarian of the history of medicine and archivist at the Mayo Foundation, Rochester, Minnesota, until his recent retirement.

Robert Beasecker (b. February 3, 1946) is a native of Detroit, Michigan. He was awarded the AB from Hillsdale College in 1969 and the AMLS from the University of Michigan in 1970. His publications include numerous bibliographic studies of Michigan in the novel. Currently he is archivist and reference librarian at Grand Valley State University, Allendale, Michigan. His *Michigan in the Novel, 1816–1996* (1998) is an exemplary, definitive bibliographic study.

The 1985 award was presented to Arthur W. Shumaker (October 15, 1913–September 15, 2000), professor emeritus of English at DePauw University. Born in Indianapolis, he received his AB from DePauw in 1934, his AM from Indiana University in 1942, and, after military service in Europe in World War II, the PhD from the University of Iowa in 1958. A member of the Society from its beginning and a pioneer student of Indiana literature, he served on the committee that prepared *A Literary Map of Indiana* (1956, rev. 1974). His major study, *A History of Indiana Literature* (1962), not only began the study of the literature of that state but it has been a model for studies of the literature of other states. He published numerous essays on Indiana writers and contributed annually to the Society's programs. He was co-president of the Society in 1983, and he served on the editorial board of the *Dictionary of Midwestern Literature*.

In 1986 the Society again presented two awards to long-time members of the Society, regular contributors to its programs, former presidents of the Society, and distinguished contributors to the study of Midwestern literature. They are Kenny J. Williams, professor of English at Duke University, and Gene H. Dent (b. January 4, 1926), professor of English at Lakeland Community College. Kenny J. Williams is a scholar of Chicago literature, and Gene H. Dent is a writer-producer of videos.

Kenny J. Williams was born in Omaha, Nebraska, but grew up in Philadelphia and Chicago. She received the AB from Benedict College, the MA from DePaul University, and the MA and PhD from the University of Pennsylvania. As professor of English at Northeastern Illinois State University in Chicago, she developed an intense interest in the literature of the city, resulting in three major studies, *In the City of Men: Another Story of Chicago* (1974), *Prairie Voices: A Literary History of Chicago from the Frontier to 1893* (1980), and *A Storyteller and a City: Sherwood Anderson's Chicago* (1988). She also published *They Also*

*Spoke* (1970) and edited *Chicago's Public Wits: A Chapter in the American Comic Spirit* (1983) with Bernard Duffey. She was president of the Society in 1982.

Gene H. Dent, now professor emeritus, received his BA in 1951 and his MA in 1952 from Bowling Green State University after serving in the U.S. Marine Corps. A native of Mansfield, Ohio, he has produced a number of articles, essays, and works of fiction on Midwestern writers and writing, and his interest in television led to his writing and producing six videos for public television: *Sherwood Anderson: A Story Teller's Town* (1976), *Sherwood Anderson: Blue Ridge Country* (1979), *Louis Bromfield: Lo, the Rich Land* (1981), *Ernest Hemingway: Up in Michigan* (1984), *Sinclair Lewis: The Man from Main Street* (1987), and *Brand Whitlock: Forgotten Hero* (1993). All have been shown on national PBS television, and *The Man from Main Street* won the Ohio State Award for Excellence, the nation's oldest television award, as well as other awards. All were produced in conjunction with WBGU-TV of Bowling Green State University. He was president of the Society in 1979.

The 1987 award was presented to Ray Lewis White (b. August 11, 1941), distinguished professor of English at Illinois State University, whose name has become most prominent in the scholarship of the life and works of Sherwood Anderson. A native of Washington County, Virginia, and the recipient of the BA from Emory and Henry College in 1962 and the MA and PhD from the University of Arkansas in 1963 and 1971 respectively, as well as the LittD from Emory and Henry in 1990, White has published many essays on Midwestern writing, including those on SHERWOOD ANDERSON, ERNEST HEMINGWAY, BEN HECHT, WILLIAM H. GASS, ROSS LOCKRIDGE, JR., and others. His books on Anderson include editing *The Achievement of Sherwood Anderson* (1966), *Return to Winesburg* (1967), *Sherwood Anderson's Memoirs: A Critical Edition* (1969), *Sherwood Anderson/Gertrude Stein* (1972), *Sherwood Anderson: Early Writings* (1989), and *Sherwood Anderson's Secret Love Letters: For Eleanor—A Letter a Day* (1991). He wrote *Sherwood Anderson: A Reference Guide* (1977) and *Winesburg, Ohio: An Exploration* (1990) and edited a scholarly edition of *Winesburg, Ohio* (1997).

In 1988 the award was presented to Diana C. Haskell (b. June 9, 1935), Lloyd Lewis Curator of Midwestern manuscripts at the Newberry Library. Born in Northbrook, Illinois, she received her BA in 1956 and her MLS in 1958 from the University of Illinois, and she was a member of the First Archives–Library Institute on Historical Research Materials at the Ohio Historical Society in 1971. In various capacities at the Newberry Library since 1969, she has not only contributed substantially to the growth of the Midwestern literary manuscripts collection there, but she has been of inestimable value in their organization and in making them available to scholars. Between 1977 and 1990 she compiled the annual "Sherwood Anderson Checklist" in *The Winesburg Eagle* as well as other checklists and bibliographies, especially of the Newberry's holdings.

James C. Austin (November 27, 1923–March 7, 1990), professor emeritus of American Studies at Southern Illinois University at Edwardsville, received the award in 1989. Born in Kansas City, Missouri, he grew up in Cleveland and after U.S. Army service in World War II received the BA (1944), MA (1945), and PhD (1952) from Western Reserve University. Particularly interested in American humor, he was author of *Fields of the Atlantic Monthly* (1953), *Artemus Ward* (1964), the pioneering *Petroleum V. Nasby* (1965), and other books as well as many articles, essays, and chapters in books. A musician, he also wrote the librettos for four musical plays.

In 1990 the award was presented to Philip Gerber (b. December 4, 1923), professor of English at the State University of New York College at Brockport. Born in Aberdeen, South Dakota, he received the BA (1946), MA (1948), and PhD (1952), all from the University of Iowa, and he has taught and lectured at numerous universities here and abroad. His major scholarly interests are in THEODORE DREISER, Robert Frost, and WILLA CATHER. His books include four on Frost, and his major studies of Dreiser and Cather include *Theodore Dreiser* (1964), *Plots and Characters in the Fiction of Theodore Dreiser* (1977), *Theodore Dreiser Revisited* (1992), and *Willa Cather* (1975, 1980; translated into Japanese 1986). He has also edited *Bachelor Bess: The Homesteading Letters of Elizabeth Corey, 1909–1919* (1990). He has also published many articles and essays and is currently editing a series of Civil War letters.

The 1991 award was presented to Bernard F. Engel (b. November 25, 1921), professor emeritus of American thought and language at Michigan State University, a former president of the Society, and a leading scholar of Midwestern poetry. A native of Spokane, Washington, and U.S. Army veteran of World War II, he received the BA from the University of Oregon in 1946, the MA from the University of Chicago in 1949, and the PhD from the University of California at Berkeley in 1956. A former newspaperman, he is the author of twelve books including studies of native Midwesterners Marianne Moore and Richard Eberhart. His *Marianne Moore* (1964, rev. 1989) and *Richard Eberhart* (1977) are pioneering studies. He has published widely on Midwestern writers, especially on nineteenth-century Midwestern poets and poetry, on which he is completing a major study. He coedited, with Patricia W. Julius, *A New Voice for a New People: Midwestern Poetry, 1800–1910* (1985), and he was president of the Society in 1975.

In 1992 the award was presented to Frederick C. Stern (April 28, 1929–October 18, 1992), professor of English at the University of Illinois at Chicago. A native of Vienna, Austria, he came to New York as a youth and then moved on to Gary, Indiana. For fifteen years he was a steelworker at the Youngstown Sheet and Tube plant in East Chicago, while he received his BA and MA from the University of Chicago and his PhD from Purdue. His interest in Midwestern writing, especially poetry, and American social criticism has resulted in books on both. His works include *F. O. Matthiessen: Christian Socialist as Critic* (1981) and *The Revolutionary Poet in the United States: The Poetry of Thomas McGrath* (1988), as well as numerous essays on THOMAS MCGRATH, GWENDOLYN BROOKS, and others. He was an active member of the Society from its inception.

The award for 1993 was presented to Jane S. Bakerman (b. July 4, 1931), professor emerita of English at Indiana State University. A native of Gary, Indiana, she received the BA from Hanover College in 1953 and the MA from the University of Illinois in 1959, and she did further graduate study at Indiana University. The coeditor with Mary Jean DeMarr of *Adolescent Female Portraits in the American Novel: 1961–1981*, an annotated bibliography (1983), and *The Adolescent in the American Novel since 1960* (1986), she also edited *And Then There Were Nine . . . More Women of Mystery* (1985). She has published widely on Midwestern writers, especially mystery writers, and she specializes in the early identification of emerging women writers who promise to become significant, such as TONI MORRISON, JANE SMILEY, JANE HAMILTON, and others, including EDNA FERBER, VERA CASPARY, and JESSAMYN WEST, who have passed out of favor. The Jane S. Bakerman Award is presented annually by the Women's Caucus of the Popular Culture Association. She was copresident of the Society in 1983, and she served on the editorial board of the *Dictionary of Midwestern Literature*.

In 1994 two awards were made, to Edgar M. Branch (b. March 21, 1913), research professor emeritus and associate in American literature at Miami University, and John E. Hallwas (b. May 24, 1945), professor of English and university library archivist at Western Illinois University. Both are long-time members of the Society and widely published scholars, Branch specializing largely on the life and works of both MARK TWAIN and JAMES T. FARRELL and Hallwas on the literature and history of Illinois.

Branch, born in Chicago, Illinois, received the AB degree from Beloit College in 1934, the MA from the University of Chicago in 1938, and the PhD from the University of Iowa in 1941. He also studied at University College, London, and Brown University. His books on Mark Twain include the following editions: *Mark Twain's Letters in the Muscatine Journal* (1942), *The Literary Apprenticeship of Mark Twain* (1950, reprinted 1965, 1966), *Clemens of the Call* (1969), *Mark Twain's Early Tales and Sketches, 1851–65*, vol. 1 (1979) and vol. 2 (1981); *Mark Twain's Letters, 1853–1866*, vol. 1 (1988), *Roughing It* (1993), and three additional volumes of Mark Twain's early tales and sketches. A former member of the board of directors of the Mark Twain Project at Berkeley, California, he continues active in the project.

Branch's publications on James T. Farrell are also extensive, including *Bibliography of the Writings of James T. Farrell, 1921–1957* (1959), *James T. Farrell* (1963, reprinted 1967), *James T. Farrell* (1971), and *Studs Lonigan's Neighborhood* (1995). He is literary executor of the James T. Farrell estate. He has published many articles on Twain, Farrell, and others and has received numerous awards.

John T. Hallwas, born in Waukegan, Illinois, received his BA and MA from Western Illinois University in 1967 and 1968 respectively and the PhD from the University of Florida in 1972. He was founding editor of two journals, *Essays in Literature* (1973–79) and *Western Illinois Regional Studies* (1978–91), and has written three plays based on Illinois history, *The Conflict* (1982), *Four on the Frontier* (1983), and *The Paper Town* (1985). His works on Illinois literature and history include *The Poems of H.: The Lost Poet of Lincoln's Springfield* (1982), *Thomas Gregg: Early Illinois Journalist and Author* (1983), *Western Illinois Heritage* (1983), *Illinois Literature: The Nineteenth Century* (1986), *Spoon River Anthology: An Annotated Edition* (1992), *Cultures in Conflict: A Documentary History of the Mormon War in Illinois* (coauthor, 1995). He edited *The Vision of This Land: Studies of Vachel Lindsay, Edgar Lee Masters, and Carl Sandburg* (coeditor, 1976), *Studies in Illinois Poetry* (1989), and *Tales from Two Rivers*, 1–6 (coeditor, 1981–95). He edits Prairie State Books for the University of Illinois Press, and he has published many articles and essays on Illinois and other literature.

The award for 1995 was presented to Douglas Wixson (b. August 9, 1933), professor emeritus of English at the University of Missouri–Rolla, former fighter pilot in the U.S. Air Force, former research engineer, and leading scholar of Midwestern literary radicalism in the 1920s and 1930s. Born in Tulsa, Oklahoma, he received the BS in mechanical engineering from the Massachusetts Institute of Technology in 1955, the MS in mechanical/aerospace engineering from Stanford University in 1960, and the PhD in English from the University of North Carolina in 1971. He has lectured extensively in France as well as in the United States. His published works include editions with introductions of *The Weed King and Other Stories* by JACK CONROY (1985), *The Disinherited* by Jack Conroy (1991), and *The Lost Traveler* by Sanora Babb (1995). His study of Jack Conroy, literary radicalism, and the worker-writer movement in America, a major contribution to the study of Midwestern literature, is *Worker-Writer in America: Jack Conroy and the Tradition of Midwestern Literary Radicalism* (1994). He has also written a number of chapters and essays in books on Mid-

western literary topics as well as many articles and essays in periodicals, particularly on Jack Conroy and other Midwestern literary radicals of the 1920s and 1930s. As literary executor of the Jack Conroy estate, he helped establish the Jack Conroy collection and fellowship at the Newberry Library as well as the Jack Conroy collection at Moberly (Missouri) Area Community College in Conroy's hometown. He was the Mid-American Universities Association Honor Lecturer in 1988–1989, and he received the State of Missouri Thomas Jefferson Award for his work on Conroy.

The award for 1996 was presented to Scott Donaldson, Louise G. T. Cooley Professor Emeritus of American Literature at the College of William and Mary. Born in Minneapolis (November 17, 1928), he received his BA in English from Yale in 1951 and his MA in English and PhD in American Studies from the University of Minnesota in 1952 and 1966 respectively. Between 1956 and 1964 he worked on various Minnesota newspapers, and he has been a member of the English faculty at William and Mary since 1966. His works include *By Force of Will: The Life and Art of Ernest Hemingway* (1977), *Fool for Love: F. Scott Fitzgerald* (1983), *John Cheever: A Biography* (1988), and *Archibald MacLeish: An American Life* (1992). He has edited collections of essays on F. SCOTT FITZGERALD and ERNEST HEMINGWAY and has been the recipient of a number of grants and awards. He served in the U.S. Army from 1953 to 1956.

In 1997 the award was presented to Paul W. Miller (b. June 6, 1926), professor emeritus of English at Wittenberg University, Springfield, Ohio, where he taught from 1961 to 1991. A native of Canada, he graduated from Welland High School, Welland, Ontario, in 1943 and received the BA from McMaster University in 1947. In 1948 he received the MA from Brown University and the PhD from the University of Michigan in 1955. His training and early scholarship focused on English literature of the Renaissance and Shakespeare, but he soon acquired a deep interest in BRAND WHITLOCK and JAMES PURDY, publishing extensively on both, and more recently on ERNEST HEMINGWAY and SHERWOOD ANDERSON. He edited Brand Whitlock's previously unpublished novel *The Buckeyes: A Story of Politics and Abolitionism in an Ohio Town* (1977) and edited a new edition of Whitlock's *J. Hardin and Son* (1982). The recipient of a Fulbright Senior Research Grant to study Whitlock in Belgium and a Canadian Embassy Grant, he lectures widely on Midwestern literature and is a member of the editorial board of the *Dictionary of Midwestern Literature*. He was president of the Society in 1989.

The 1998 award was given to Larry Lockridge (b. July 1, 1942), professor of English at New York University. Born in Bloomington, Indiana, the son of Ross LOCKRIDGE JR., author of *Raintree County* (1948), he grew up in Bloomington, receiving his AB in English from Indiana University in 1964, the MA from Harvard University in 1968, and the PhD from Harvard in 1969. He has been the recipient of Guggenheim, Danforth, and Woodrow Wilson fellowships. His academic emphasis has been on English romanticism, particularly the life and work of Samuel Coleridge. His publications in that area include *Coleridge the Moralist* (1977), *Nineteenth Century Lives* (with John Maynard, 1989), and *The Ethics of Romanticism* (1989). In 1988 he began a biography of his father which was published as *Shade of the Raintree* (1994), a major literary biography that was nominated for the Pulitzer Prize that year. He also edited a new edition of *Raintree County*, which was published in 1994. Together the two publications have begun a retrospective examination of a novel that occupies a central role in the evolution of Midwestern literature in this century.

The award for 1999 was presented to Philip A. Greasley (b. December 30, 1945), associate professor of English and dean of University Extension at the University of Kentucky. Born in Chicago, he received the BA and MA in English from Northwestern University in 1967 and 1968 and the PhD, after interruption for army service, from Michigan State University in 1975. His interest in Midwestern literature has resulted in publications on GWENDOLYN BROOKS, SHERWOOD ANDERSON, CARL SANDBURG, GARRISON KEILLOR, and other Midwestern writers as well as studies in the Midwestern oral literary form, the Midwestern sense of place, and Midwestern poetry. In 1986 he was awarded the Society for the Study of Midwestern Literature's first annual Midwest Heritage Prize, established and funded by Gwendolyn Brooks. Chairman of the editorial board and general editor of the *Dictio-*

*nary of Midwestern Literature* since its inception in 1991, he has been largely responsible for its successful conclusion. He was president of the Society in 1987.

The MidAmerica Award for 2000 was presented at the 30th Annual Conference to Mary Ellen Caldwell, Associate Professor Emeritus of the University of North Dakota, and Mary Jean DeMarr, Professor Emerita of Indiana State University. Both scholars have been members of the Society since its inception. Mary Ellen Caldwell (b. Aug. 6, 1908) is a scholar of the literature of the Northern Plains, and Mary Jean DeMarr (b. Sept. 20, 1932) devotes much of her scholarly attention to Midwestern women writers as well as mystery fiction.

Mary Ellen Caldwell is a native of El Paso, Arkansas. She received the PhB in 1931 and the MA in 1933 from the University of Chicago, where she studied American literature under Percy N. Boynton. She taught English at the University of Arkansas, 1940–42, at the University of Toledo, 1946–48, and at the University of North Dakota from 1966 until her retirement in 1979. She still serves the University as a professor in the Extension Division.

At North Dakota she began her interest in Midwestern literature and particularly the literature of the Northern Plains. She developed a course in Great Plains literature and taught it for many years. She has reviewed and published many articles and reviews on Midwestern literature, particularly in the *North Dakota Quarterly*. She also serves on the Society's Bibliography Committee, which compiles the Annual Bibliography of Midwestern Literature published in *MidAmerica*. She is listed in *Who's Who of American Women* and other sources.

Mary Jean DeMarr is a native Midwesterner, born in Champaign, Illinois. She received her BA *cum laude* from Lawrence University in 1954 and her AM and PhD from the University of Illinois in 1957 and 1963, respectively. At Illinois she studied under John T. Flanagan, first recipient of the MidAmerica Award. She taught at Indiana State University from 1965 to her retirement in 1995. She has served as contributor, Deputy American Editor, and American Editor for the *Annual Bibliography of English Language and Literature* published by the Modern Humanities Research Association. She is a member of the *Dictionary of Midwestern Literature* Editorial Board and was President of the Society in 1985–86.

Among her publications are *The Adolescent and the American Novel since 1960* (1986), with Jane E. Bakerman; critical companions to Colleen McCullough (1996) and Barbara King-solver (1999); and numerous contributions to biographical and critical works. A regular contributor to *MidAmerica*, she has published essays on JANET AYER FAIRBANK, RUTH SUCKOW, MARI SANDOZ, and other Midwestern writers. She is listed in *Who's Who in America, Who's Who in the Midwest,* and other sources.

David D. Anderson
Michigan State University

## *The Society for the Study of Midwestern Literature*

The Society for the Study of Midwestern Literature, headquartered at Michigan State University, was founded in 1971 to provide opportunities to study the myth and reality of that region first acknowledged by Abraham Lincoln in his message to Congress, December 1, 1862; by Frederick Jackson Turner in his turn-of-the-century essay "The Middle West"; and by Sherwood Anderson, for whom it was in 1920 simply "the place between mountain and mountain. . . ."

SSML publishes several journals, sponsors sessions at numerous conferences, and holds an annual convention and poetry festival each May. For more information, contact Roger Bresnahan, Secretary-Treasurer (bresnaha@msu.edu).

# Contributors

PAULINE ADAMS is Associate Professor Emerita from Michigan State University. Her interest in Midwestern oeuvres continues into retirement.

STEVEN M. ALLEN is pursuing an MBA at the Sloan School of Management at the Massachusetts Institute of Technology.

DAVID D. ANDERSON is University Distinguished Professor Emeritus at Michigan State University. He is author of some thirty-five books and founder of the Society for the Study of Midwestern Literature.

PATRICIA ANDERSON graduated from Bowling Green State University, taught high school English in Ohio and Michigan, and, after receiving a Master of Science in Librarianship at Western Michigan University, was a librarian for the Lansing, Michigan, school system until her retirement.

MARILYN ATLAS is Associate Professor of English at Ohio University. She specializes in American literature, modernism, and women's studies.

LIAHNA BABENER is Dean of the College of Arts and Humanities and Professor of English at Central Washington University in Ellensburg, Washington. She specializes in film, popular culture, and regionalism, and is currently working on a book on Alfred Hitchcock.

WILLIAM BARILLAS is Assistant Professor of English at the University of Wisconsin–La Crosse. He has written extensively on environmental literature and Latino culture.

ROBERT BEASECKER is Special Collections Librarian and University Archivist at Grand Valley State University in Allendale, Michigan. His *Michigan in the Novel, 1816–1996: An Annotated Bibliography* was published in 1998 by Wayne State University Press, and he is currently working on its supplement.

KEVIN BEZNER has published three books of poetry, most recently *Particularities* from Volcanic Ash Books.

RUSS BODI is Adjunct Communications and Humanities Professor at Owens College in Toledo, Ohio. He has a primary interest in early modern literature but frequently writes about Midwestern authors and themes.

JAMES M. BOEHNLEIN is Director of Composition at the University of Dayton and is currently writing a book on advanced composition.

SUSAN BOURRIE is a doctoral candidate at Michigan State University and lectures in children's literature at Eastern Michigan University. Her research interests center upon vision, literacy, and learning.

ROGER J. JIANG BRESNAHAN is Professor of American Thought and Language at Michigan State University. He is Secretary-Treasurer of the Society for the Study of Midwestern Literature. He publishes in American Studies and also the literature and history of Southeast Asia.

BARBARA BURKHARDT of the University of Illinois will publish her book on Midwestern author and *New Yorker* editor William Maxwell in 2001. She received an honorary doctorate of humane letters from Lincoln College in February 2000 for this scholarship.

MARCUS CAFAGÑA is Assistant Professor of Creative Writing at Southwest Missouri State University and the author of two books of poetry: *The Broken World,* selected for the National Poetry Series, and the forthcoming *Roman Fever*. His poetry is widely published in major venues.

CHARLES R. CAMPBELL is Professor of Philosophy at Spring Arbor College, Spring Arbor, Michigan.

DAN CAMPION is Senior Test Editor at American College Testing Program in Iowa City, Iowa.

HAEJA CHUNG has written widely on Harriette Simpson Arnow. She is currently teaching Asian American Studies at Michigan State University.

WILL CLEMENS earned an MFA in 1997 and is a doctoral candidate in Literature and Creative Writing at the University of Cincinnati, where he specializes in U.S. fiction and poetry in traditional modes, 1950 to present.

DAVID N. CREMEAN is Instructor at Black Hills State University, Spearfish, South Dakota. His research centers on Cormac McCarthy and other literature of the West.

MATTHEW J. DARLING is Assistant Volleyball Coach at Marquette University, where he is pursuing a doctorate in American literature.

TODD F. DAVIS is Associate Professor of English at Goshen College in Goshen, Indiana. His research interests include the intersection of ethical criticism and postmodernity, as well as forms of ecocriticism.

LAWRENCE DAWSON is Professor Emeritus of English at Central Michigan University. His interests include modern British literature and Michigan history.

THOMAS DEAN is Program Assistant with the Honors Program at the University of Iowa; Adjunct Assistant Professor of Literature, Science, and the Arts at Iowa; and the Executive Director of the Iowa Place Education Initiative. His research interests include Midwestern regionalism, Native American Studies, late-nineteenth-century American literature, and environmental and community studies.

MARY JEAN DeMARR is Professor Emerita of English and Women's Studies at Indiana State University. Her research interests include popular literature, detective fiction, and enumerative bibliography.

SCOTT DENT graduated with an MA from The University of Tennessee at Chattanooga in 1999 and is now teaching at East Ridge High School in East Ridge, Tennessee.

TRACEY HOLMES DONESKY, JD 2000, University of Minnesota Law School, BA 1996, University of Kentucky, is serving as Law Clerk to the Honorable John R. Tunheim, United States District Court, Minnesota.

MARY BELLOR DUNNE finished her graduate degree from Boston University and works for the Antiquarian and Landmarks Society in Hartford, Connecticut. Her interests include twentieth-century American literature and architecture.

ROBERT DUNNE is Associate Professor of English at Central Connecticut State University. His research interests include Sherwood Anderson, nineteenth-century Irish immigrant writings, and nineteenth-century American literature and culture.

JOYCE DYER is Associate Professor of English and Director of Writing at Hiram College, Hiram, Ohio. She is the author of *"The Awakening": A Novel of Beginnings* and *In a Tangled*

*Wood: An Alzheimer's Journey,* and the editor of *Bloodroot: Reflections on Place by Appalachian Women Writers.*

**BERNARD ENGEL,** a World War II infantryman and journalist, is Emeritus Professor of American Thought and Language at Michigan State University. He has published thirteen books, including *Marianne Moore* (1964), and has served on the governing boards of the MLA, the NCTE, and the CCCC.

**KEITH FYNAARDT** is Assistant Professor of English at Northwestern College, Orange City, Iowa.

**MARSHALL BRUCE GENTRY** is Professor of English and English Department Chair at the University of Indianapolis. His research interests include Flannery O'Connor.

**PHILIP GERBER** is Professor of English at New York State University College, Brockport. He is a noted scholar on Theodore Dreiser's works, and a recipient of the Mid-America Award.

**JILL B. GIDMARK,** Morse-Alumni Distinguished Professor of Literature and Writing at the University of Minnesota, has published *Melville Sea Dictionary* and edited the forthcoming *Encyclopedia of American Literature of the Sea and Great Lakes.*

**CLARENCE A. GLASRUD** is Professor Emeritus of English at Minnesota State University at Moorhead, Minnesota. He has research interests centering on Minnesota and North Dakota authors.

**SCOTT S. GORDON** currently serves as Assistant Director of School Relations at Murray State University, Murray, Kentucky. He studied writing at the University of Kentucky and investigated potential *Dictionary of Midwestern Literature* formats.

**KENNETH B. GRANT** is Professor of English at the University of Wisconsin Baraboo/Sauk County. He is completing a biography of August Derleth.

**MARSHA O. GREASLEY** teaches in the Woodford County, Kentucky, schools and maintains a long-term interest in children's literature.

**PHILIP A. GREASLEY** is Associate Professor of English and Dean of University Extension at the University of Kentucky. He has served as General Editor of the *Dictionary of Midwestern Literature* and has published widely on Midwestern writers, the Chicago Renaissance, and modern poetics.

**KRISTA GREENBERG** is a graduate student in English and a scheduling assistant in the Office of Admissions at the University of Indianapolis. Her research interests include World War II, the Holocaust, and Beat Generation literature. She has worked at the Ernie Pyle State Historical Shrine in Dana, Indiana.

**DAN GUILLORY** is Chairman of the English Department of Millikin University, Decatur, Illinois. He is actively engaged in research on Vachel Lindsay and Abraham Lincoln.

**THEODORE HADDIN** is Emeritus Professor of English at the University of Alabama at Birmingham. His research interests include mid-nineteenth-century American literature and contemporary poetry. He is the author of two books of poetry, *The River and the Road* and *By a Doorway, in the Garden.*

**JOHN E. HALLWAS** is Professor of English and University Library Archivist at Western Illinois University. He specializes in the literature and history of Illinois.

**DONALD M. HASSLER** is Professor of English at Kent State University, Kent, Ohio. His research interests include modern science fiction and Erasmus Darwin.

**STEVEN F. HOPKINS** is a graduate student in the English Department at the University of Kentucky. With an emphasis in American literature, he is currently researching the changing portrayals of childhood and adolescence in the American Western.

**JAMES M. HUGHES** is Emeritus Professor of English, Wright State University, Dayton, Ohio. He serves on the Board of the Ohioana Library and teaches American drama, Walt

Whitman, Emily Dickinson, Henry James, and Gender Studies.

IMELDA HUNT is a practicing poet living in Toledo, Ohio.

BABETTE INGLEHART is Professor of English at Chicago State University. She is an Associate Editor of the forthcoming *Chicago Women 1770–1990: A Biographical Dictionary.*

MARY ELLEN JONES, Professor of English at Wittenberg University, is active in Native American scholarship. She is the author of a recent biography on John Jakes and a study of women on the American frontier.

KATHERINE JOSLIN is Professor of English and Director of American Studies at Western Michigan University. She has written *Edith Wharton,* co-edited *Wretched Exotic: Essays on Edith Wharton in Europe,* and published articles on Willa Cather, Kate Chopin, Charlotte Perkins Gilman, Percy Lubbock, and Theodore Dreiser. She is currently completing a book on Jane Addams.

JEFF JUSTIN has taught English at two western Michigan universities but is now working as a financial manager, including assignments in support of a Native American social-service agency and publishing enterprise. These contacts bring him full circle with his earlier interest in Indian sources.

THEODORE R. KENNEDY is Emeritus Professor of American Thought and Language at Michigan State University. He continues to be a strong advocate of the literature and culture of Indiana.

ROBERT L. KINDRICK is Professor of English and Vice President for Academic Affairs and Research at Wichita State University. He studied with Edward Dahlberg and has written on Dahlberg as well as medieval literature.

MARK KIPPERMAN is Professor of English at Northern Illinois University in DeKalb, Illinois. He writes on British romantic poetry.

SUSAN KOPPELMAN is a literary historian and the editor of nine books, including

*"Women in the Trees": U.S. Women's Stories about Battering and Resistance, 1839–1994; Between Mothers and Daughters;* and *Women's Friendships.* She lives in the desert outside Tucson, Arizona, where she continues her research and writing about U.S. women's short stories.

JEAN LAMING, of Clare, Michigan, teaches in Midland.

JAMES A. LEWIN is Assistant Professor of English at Shepherd College, Shepherdstown, West Virginia. He has written extensively on Nelson Algren.

ETHAN LEWIS is Assistant Professor of English at the University of Illinois at Springfield.

CLARENCE (BEN) LINDSAY is Associate Professor of English at the University of Toledo. His research interests include Sherwood Anderson, Joseph Conrad, Ernest Hemingway, and A. E. Housman.

LARRY LOCKRIDGE is Professor of English at New York University. He is the author of *Coleridge the Moralist; The Ethics of Romanticism;* and *Shade of the Raintree: The Life and Death of Ross Lockridge, Jr.* He is co-editor of *Nineteenth-Century Lives.*

LOREN LOGSDON, Professor of English at Eureka College, Eureka, Illinois, specializes in American literature and edits the *Eureka Literary Magazine.*

HERBERT WOODWARD MARTIN, Poet in Residence at the University of Dayton, is the author of six books of poetry and two opera libretti, as well as the editor of *In His Own Voice: The Uncollected Dramatic Works of Paul Laurence Dunbar.*

LELAND MAY is Professor Emeritus of English at Northwest Missouri State University. His research centers on Missouri authors.

WENDELL MAYO is Associate Professor of English and the Director of the Creative Writing Program at Bowling Green State University, Bowling Green, Ohio. He is the author of three short story collections and the recipient of numerous literary prizes.

SARA MCALPIN BVM, Professor of English at Clarke College in Dubuque, Iowa, teaches writing and literature and specializes in nineteenth- and twentieth-century American fiction.

ROBERT MCGOVERN, Professor Emeritus of English at Ashland University, Ashland, Ohio, is a practicing poet and co-editor of the Ashland Poetry Press.

NANCY MCKINNEY is a graduate student in English at Southern Illinois University at Carbondale. Her research interests include Vachel Lindsay and the early twentieth century.

WAYNE H. MEYER is an architectural librarian at Ball State University in Muncie, Indiana.

MARY JOAN MILLER is a retired teacher and librarian specializing in children's literature.

PAUL W. MILLER is Emeritus Professor of English at Wittenberg University. He pursues literary and professional interests in Renaissance poetry, Shakespeare, and Canadian and American literature, including Hemingway.

CLARA LEE R. MOODIE is Professor Emerita of English Language and Literature at Central Michigan University. She specializes in American literature of the 1920s and 1930s, with particular interest in Sinclair Lewis.

MARIA MOOTRY was Associate Professor of African American Studies and English at the University of Illinois at Springfield, where she specialized in African American literature and Gwendolyn Brooks. She passed away on May 29, 2000.

KENNETH R. MOREFIELD is Assistant Professor of English at Toccoa Falls College, Toccoa Falls, Georgia.

EDWARD MORIN wrote a dissertation on Archibald MacLeish's plays for his Ph.D. at Loyola University (Chicago), where he specialized in drama as literature. He has acted in many stage musicals, including a production of the *Music Man,* and is a practicing poet.

ROBERT NARVESON, Professor Emeritus of English at the University of Nebraska, continues his long-term interest in Nebraska writers.

ARNE NESET teaches American literature at Stavanger College in Norway and is active in the Nordic Association for American Studies.

DAVID L. NEWQUIST is Professor Emeritus from Northern State University, Aberdeen, South Dakota. He continues his writing and scholarship with special interest in Native American literature and regional culture. He serves as a publications editor for political and cultural groups and works with the field support staff of a U.S. senator.

MARCIA NOE is Professor of English at the University of Tennessee at Chattanooga. Much of her research is focused on the American playwright Susan Glaspell.

MARY DEJONG OBUCHOWSKI, Professor of English at Central Michigan University, specializes in American literature and modern poetry.

WILLIAM OSTREM is Assessment Specialist at the Educational Testing Service in Princeton, New Jersey. A poet and writer, he has published essays on Garrison Keillor, W. H. Auden, and Christopher Isherwood.

TOM L. PAGE, a native Kansan, is a poet interested in the poetry and prose of Kansas and the Midwest and the literature of Brazil and other Lusophone areas. Prior to retirement, he taught at the University of Florida, Wichita State University, and Longview Community College.

SANDRA PARKER is a practicing poet who teaches at Hiram College, Hiram, Ohio.

EUGENE H. PATTISON is Professor of English at Alma College, Alma, Michigan. He has done research on Annie Dillard, William Dean Howells, Robinson Jeffers, Booth Tarkington, and William Henry Venable, and has frequently taught courses in American realism.

DAVID J. PERUSEK is Adjunct Professor of Anthropology at Kent State. He is a native of Lorain, Ohio, and an alumnus of Kent State University and Michigan State University.

ROD PHILLIPS is a practicing poet and Visiting Assistant Professor at James Madison College, Michigan State University. His research interests include American literature and environmental history.

DAVID PICHASKE is Professor of English at Southwest State University. He is a prolific creative writer and literary critic.

WILLIAM J. POWERS is Professor Emeritus, Michigan Technological University.

THOMAS PRIBEK is Associate Professor of English at the University of Wisconsin–LaCrosse. He has published widely in American literature, with emphasis on the eighteenth and nineteenth centuries.

RON PRIMEAU is Professor of English at Central Michigan University and Director of the Master of Arts in Humanities Program. He is working on a book on Herbert Woodward Martin.

NEALE R. REINITZ is Professor Emeritus of English at Colorado College. He has done significant research on many Chicago writers.

MARCELLE SMITH RICE is currently an editor at the Raleigh, North Carolina, *News & Observer* and a lecturer at North Carolina State University. She is the author of the Twayne *Dawn Powell.*

ARLENE RODRIGUEZ is Assistant Professor of English and Honors Program Coordinator at Springfield Technical Community College in Springfield, Massachusetts. She is currently pursuing a doctorate at the University of Massachusetts Amherst. Her research focuses on Latino writers and theories of nationalism.

ROBIN KIDD ROENKER served as Assistant Editor for the *Dictionary of Midwestern Literature.* She is currently employed as a Promotion Assistant with Kentucky Educational Television.

JOHN ROHRKEMPER teaches at Elizabethtown College, Elizabethtown, Pennsylvania, and specializes in twentieth-century American literature and culture.

KAY KINSELLA ROUT, Professor of American Thought and Language at Michigan State University, does research focusing on African American Studies, American popular culture, and Anne Rice.

MARGARET (PEGGY) ROZGA, Professor of English at the University of Wisconsin–Waukesha, is interested in the work of contemporary Midwestern women writers. She is a practicing poet.

HERBERT K. RUSSELL is Director for College Relations at John A. Logan College in Carterville, Illinois. He is completing a biography of Edgar Lee Masters.

ELISABETH SANDBERG is Professor of English at Woodbury University, Burbank, California.

JAMES SEATON is Professor of English at Michigan State University. He writes on culture and criticism for such journals as *The American Scholar, The Hudson Review,* and the *Yale Journal of Law & Humanities.*

SANDRA SEATON, a playwright and Professor of English at Central Michigan University, teaches creative writing and African American literature.

ARTHUR W. SHUMAKER, Professor Emeritus at DePauw University, taught courses in English and American literature and published *A History of Indiana Literature.* He passed away on September 15, 2000.

PAUL SOMERS JR. is Professor of American Thought and Language at Michigan State University. He has published books and articles on American literature and American humor.

JEAN STRANDNESS is Associate Professor of English at North Dakota State University. She pursues research centering upon contemporary women writers and Native American writers.

JOHN SUTTON is a graduate student in English at New York University.

GUY SZUBERLA is Professor Emeritus of English at the University of Toledo. He is a past president of the Society for the Study of Midwestern Literature and has a strong interest in Chicago fiction.

THOM TAMMARO is Professor of Multidisciplinary Studies at Minnesota State University Moorhead. A practicing poet, he has co-edited *Imagining Home: Writing from the Midwest* and *Inheriting the Land: Contemporary Voices from the Midwest.*

ROBERT J. WARD is Professor Emeritus of English Language and Literature at the University of Northern Iowa, Cedar Rapids, Iowa.

PAMELA NEAL WARFORD is Associate Professor of American Studies and Director of the American Studies program, Georgetown College, Georgetown, Kentucky. She maintains a special interest in American Studies and popular culture.

KEVIN WALZER, of Cincinnati, Ohio, is an independent scholar specializing in contemporary American poetry and nonfiction.

PAMELA NEAL WARFORD is Associate Professor of American Studies and Director of the American Studies Program, Georgetown College, Georgetown, Kentucky. She researches early twentieth-century literature and culture as well as gender studies.

MICHAEL WENTWORTH is Professor of English and Director of the Master of Arts in Liberal Studies program at the University of North Carolina at Wilmington. He maintains a special interest in American Studies and popular culture.

KENNY J. WILLIAMS is Professor of English at Duke University and a noted scholar of Chicago literature. She has served on the Board of the National Endowment for the Humanities.

DOUGLAS WIXSON is Professor Emeritus of English at the University of Missouri at Rolla. A former fighter pilot, he specializes in Midwestern radical literature and is the author of an acclaimed biography of Jack Conroy.

JOSEPH J. WYDEVEN is Professor of English and Chair of the English Department at Bellevue University, Bellevue, Nebraska. His research centers on Wright Morris.

MELODY M. ZAJDEL is Associate Professor of English at Montana State University–Bozeman. She focuses on women and literature as well as feminist theory and is currently researching Montana women writers.

AMY JO ZOOK, a practicing poet living in Mechanicsburg, Ohio, is active in the Ohio Poets Society.

# Index

Italicized page numbers refer to illustrations.